The Kaleidoscope of Gender

Fifth Edition

SAGE was founded in 1965 by Sara Miller McCune to support the dissemination of usable knowledge by publishing innovative and high-quality research and teaching content. Today, we publish over 900 journals, including those of more than 400 learned societies, more than 800 new books per year, and a growing range of library products including archives, data, case studies, reports, and video. SAGE remains majority-owned by our founder, and after Sara's lifetime will become owned by a charitable trust that secures our continued independence.

Los Angeles | London | New Delhi | Singapore | Washington DC

The Kaleidoscope of Gender

Prisms, Patterns, and Possibilities

Fifth Edition

Joan Z. Spade

The College at Brockport, State University of New York

Catherine G. Valentine

Nazareth College

Los Angeles | London | New Delhi
Singapore | Washington DC

Los Angeles | London | New Delhi
Singapore | Washington DC

FOR INFORMATION:

SAGE Publications, Inc.
2455 Teller Road
Thousand Oaks, California 91320
E-mail: order@sagepub.com

SAGE Publications Ltd.
1 Oliver's Yard
55 City Road
London, EC1Y 1SP
United Kingdom

SAGE Publications India Pvt. Ltd.
B 1/I 1 Mohan Cooperative Industrial Area
Mathura Road, New Delhi 110 044
India

SAGE Publications Asia-Pacific Pte. Ltd.
3 Church Street
#10–04 Samsung Hub
Singapore 049483

Printed in the United States of America

Library of Congress Cataloging-in-Publication Data

Names: Spade, Joan Z., editor. | Valentine, Catherine G., editor.

Title: The kaleidoscope of gender : prisms, patterns, and possibilities /

Joan Z. Spade, The College at Brockport, State University of New York,

Catherine G. Valentine, Nazareth College.

Description: 5th edition. | Los Angeles : SAGE, [2017]

Identifiers: LCCN 2015040058 | ISBN 9781483379487 (pbk. : alk. paper)

Subjects: LCSH: Sex role. | Sex differences (Psychology) | Gender identity. |

Man-woman relationships. | Interpersonal relations.

Classification: LCC HQ1075 .K35 2017 | DDC 305.3–dc23 LC record available at http://lccn.loc.gov/2015040058

This book is printed on acid-free paper.

Acquisitions Editor: Jeff Lasser
Development Editor: Nathan Davidson
Editorial Assistant: Alex Croell
Production Editor: Veronica Stapleton Hooper
Copy Editor: Colleen B. Brennan
Typesetter: Hurix Systems Pvt. Ltd.
Proofreader: Penelope Sippel
Cover Designer: Rose Storey
Marketing Manager: Johanna Swenson

SUSTAINABLE FORESTRY INITIATIVE
Certified Chain of Custody
Promoting Sustainable Forestry
www.sfiprogram.org
SFI-01268

SFI label applies to text stock

16 17 18 19 20 10 9 8 7 6 5 4 3 2 1

CONTENTS

PREFACE

This fifth edition of *The Kaleidoscope of Gender: Prisms, Patterns, and Possibilities* provides an overview of the cutting-edge literature and theoretical frameworks in the sociology of gender and related fields for understanding the social construction of gender. Although not ignoring classical contributions to gender theory and research, this book focuses on where the field is moving and the changing paradigms and approaches to gender studies. *The Kaleidoscope of Gender* uses the metaphor of a kaleidoscope and three themes—prisms, patterns, and possibilities—to unify topic areas. It focuses on the prisms through which gender is shaped, the patterns gender takes, and the possibilities for social change through a deeper understanding of ourselves and our relationships with others, both locally and globally.

The book begins, in the first part, by looking at gender and other social prisms that define gendered experiences across the spectrum of daily lives. We conceptualize prisms as social categories of difference and inequality that shape the way gender is defined and practiced, including culture, race/ethnicity, social class, sexuality, age, and ability/disability. Different as individuals' lives might be, there are patterns to gendered experiences. The second part of the book follows this premise and examines these patterns across a multitude of arenas of daily life. From here, the last part of the book takes a proactive stance, exploring possibilities for change. Basic to the

view of gender as a social construction is the potential for social change. Students will learn that gender transformation has occurred and can occur and, consequently, that it is possible to alter the genderscape. Because prisms, patterns, and possibilities themselves intersect, the framework for this book is fluid, interweaving topics and emphasizing the complexity and ever-changing nature of gender.

We had multiple goals in mind as we first developed this book, and the fifth edition reaffirms these goals:

1. Creating a book of readings that is accessible, timely, and stimulating in a text whose structure and content incorporate a fluid framework, with gender presented as an emergent, evolving, complex pattern—not one fixed in traditional categories and topics

2. Selecting articles that creatively and clearly explicate what gender is and is not and what it means to say that gender is socially constructed by incorporating provocative illustrations and solid scientific evidence of the malleability of gender and the role of individuals, groups, and social institutions in the daily performance and transformation of gender practices and patterns

3. Including readings that untangle and clarify the intricate ways gender is embedded in, intersects with, and is defined by the prisms of culture/nation, race/ethnicity, class, sexuality, age, ability/disability, and other patterns of identities, groups, and institutions

4. Integrating articles with cross-cultural and global foci to illustrate that gender is a continuum of categories, patterns, and expressions whose relevance is contextual and continuously shifting, and that gender inequality is not a universal and natural social pattern but, rather, one of many systems of oppression

5. Assembling articles that offer students useful cognitive and emotional tools for making sense of the shifting and contradictory genderscape they inhabit, its personal relevance, its implications for relationships both locally and globally, and possibilities for change

These goals shaped the revisions in the fifth edition of *The Kaleidoscope of Gender*. New selections in this edition emphasize sex and gender diversity, including the experiences of transgender and intersex people. Global and intersectional analyses as well as new contemporary social movements for gender justice are incorporated throughout the book. We continue to explore the role of institutions in maintaining gender difference and inequality. Across the chapters, readings examine the individual, situational, and institutional bases for gendered patterns in relationships, behaviors, and beliefs. Additionally, many readings illustrate how multiple prisms of difference and inequality, such as race and social class, create an array of patterns of gender—distinct but sometimes similar to the idealized patterns in a culture.

As in the fourth edition, reading selections include theoretical and review articles; however, the emphasis continues to be on contemporary contributions to the field. A revised introduction to the book provides updated descriptions of the theories in the field, particularly theories based on a social-constructionist perspective. In addition, the introduction to the book develops the kaleidoscope metaphor as a tool for viewing gender and a guide for studying gender. Revised chapter introductions contextualize the literature in each part of the book, introduce the readings, and illustrate how they relate to analyses of gender. Introductions and questions for consideration precede each reading to help students focus on and grasp the key points of the selections. Additionally, each chapter

ends with questions for students to consider and topics for students to explore.

It is possible to use this book alone, as a supplement to a text, or in combination with other articles or monographs. It is designed for undergraduate audiences, and the readings are appropriate for a variety of courses focusing on the study of gender, such as sociology of gender, gender and social change, and women's studies. The book may be used in departments of sociology, anthropology, psychology, and women's studies.

We would like to thank those reviewers whose valuable suggestions and comments helped us develop the book throughout four editions, including the following.

Fifth edition reviewers:

Kathryn Feltey, University of Akron; Tennille Allen, Lewis University; Michelle Deming, University of South Carolina; Andrea Collins, University of St Mark & St John Plymouth; Kimberly Hoang, Boston College; Pamela Danker, Blackburn College; Amanda Miller, University of Indianapolis; Regina Davis-Sowers, Santa Clara University.

Fourth edition reviewers:

Nancy Ashton; Allison Alexy, Lafayette College; John Bartkowski, University of Texas at San Antonio; Beth Berila, St Cloud State University, Women's Studies Program; Ted Cohen, Ohio Wesleyan University; Francoise Cromer, Stony Brook University; Pamela J. Forman, University of Wisconsin–Eau Claire; Ann Fuehrer, Miami University; Katja Guenther, University of California, Riverside; William Hewitt, West Chester University of PA; Bianca Isaki, University of Hawai`i at Manoa; Kristin J. Jacobson, The Richard Stockton College of New Jersey; Brian Kassar, Montana State University; Julia Mason, Grand Valley State University; Janice McCabe, Florida State University; Kristen McHenry, University of Massachusetts Dartmouth; Elizabeth Markovits, Mount Holyoke College; Jennifer Pearson, Wichita State University; Sara Skiles-duToit, University of Texas, Arlington; Mary Nell Trautner, University of Buffalo, SUNY; Julianne Weinzimmer, Wright State University; and Lori Wiebold, Bradley University.

Third edition reviewers:

ChaeRan Freeze, Brandeis University; Patti Giuffre, Texas State University; Linda Grant, University of Georgia; Todd Migliaccio, California State University, Sacramento; J. Michael Ryan, University of Maryland, College Park; and Diane Kholos Wysocki, University of Nebraska at Kearney.

Second edition reviewers:

Patti Giuffre, Texas State University, San Marcos; Linda Grant, University of Georgia; Minjeong Kim, University at Albany, SUNY; Laura Kramer, Montclair State University; Heather Laube, University of Michigan, Flint; Todd Migliaccio, California State University, Sacramento; Kristen Myers, Northern Illinois University; Wendy Simonds, Georgia State University; Debbie Storrs, University of Idaho; and Elrol Waszkiewicz, Georgia State University.

Finally, we would like to thank students in our sociology of gender courses for challenging us to think about new ways to teach our courses and making us aware of arenas of gender that are not typically the focus of gender studies books.

CALLING ALL INSTRUCTORS!

It's easy to log on to SAGE's password-protected Instructor Teaching Site at http://study .sagepub.com/spade5e for complete and protected access to all text-specific Instructor Resources for *The Kaleidoscope of Gender: Prisms, Patterns, and Possibilities*, Fifth Edition. Simply provide your institutional information for verification and within 72 hours you'll be able to use your login information for any SAGE title! Password-protected **Instructor Resources** include the following:

- **Test banks** provide a diverse range of pre-written options as well as the opportunity to edit any question and/or insert your own personalized questions to effectively assess students' progress and understanding
- Chapter-specific *PowerPoint®* *slides* offer assistance with lecture and review preparation by highlighting essential content and features from the book.
- **Lecture Notes** summarize key concepts by chapter to ease preparation for lectures and class discussions.

INTRODUCTION

JOAN Z. SPADE AND CATHERINE G. VALENTINE

This book is an invitation to you, the reader, to enter the fascinating and challenging world of gender studies. Gender is briefly defined as the meanings, practices, and relations of femininities and masculinities that people create as we go about our daily lives in different social settings in the contemporary United States. Although we discuss gender throughout this book, it is a very complex term to understand and the reality of gender goes far beyond this simple definition. While a more detailed discussion of what gender is and how it is related to biological maleness and femaleness is provided in Chapter 1, we find the metaphor of a kaleidoscope useful in thinking about the complexity of the meaning of gender from a sociological viewpoint.

THE KALEIDOSCOPE OF GENDER

A real kaleidoscope is a tube containing an arrangement of mirrors or prisms that produces different images and patterns. When you look through the eyepiece of a kaleidoscope, light is typically reflected by the mirrors or prisms through cells containing objects such as glass pieces, seashells, and the like to create ever-changing patterns of design and color (Baker, 1999). In this book, we use the kaleidoscope metaphor to help us grasp the complex and dynamic meaning and practice of gender as it interacts with other social prisms—such as race, ethnicity, age, sexuality, and social class—to create complex patterns of identities and relationships. Three themes then emerge from the metaphor of the kaleidoscope: prisms, patterns, and possibilities.

Part I of the book focuses on prisms. A prism in a kaleidoscope is an arrangement of mirrors that refracts or disperses light into a spectrum of patterns (Baker, 1999). We use the term *social prism* to refer to socially constructed categories of difference and inequality through which our lives are reflected or shaped into patterns of daily experiences. In addition to gender, when we discuss social prisms, we consider other socially constructed categories such as race, ethnicity, age, physical ability/disability, social class, and sexuality. Culture is also conceptualized as a social prism in this book, as we examine how gender is shaped across groups and societies. The concept of social prisms helps us understand that gender is not a universal or static entity but, rather, is continuously created within the parameters of individual and group life. Looking at the interactions of the prism of gender with other social prisms helps us see the bigger picture—gender practices and meanings are a montage of intertwined social divisions and connections that both pull us apart and bring us together.

Part II of the book examines the patterns of gendered expressions and experiences created by the interaction of multiple prisms of difference and inequality. Patterns are regularized, prepackaged ways of thinking, feeling, and acting in society, and gendered patterns are present in almost all aspects of daily life. In the United States, examples of gendered patterns include the association of the color pink with girls and blue with boys (Paoletti, 2012). However, these patterns of gender are experienced and expressed in different ways depending on the other social prisms that shape our identities and life chances. Furthermore, these patterns are not static, as Paoletti illustrates. Before the 1900s, children were dressed similarly until around the age of 7, with boys just as likely as girls to wear pink— but both more likely to be dressed in white. In addition, dresses were once considered appropriate for both genders in Europe and America. It wasn't until decades later, in the 1980s, that color became rigidly gendered in children's clothing, in the pink-and-blue schema. You will find that gendered patterns restrict choices, even the colors we wear—often without our even recognizing it is happening.

Another example of a gendered pattern is the disproportionate numbers of female educators and male engineers (see Table 7.1 in this book). If you take a closer look at Table 7.1, you will note that architects and engineers are predominately White men and educational occupations are predominantly White women (Bureau of Labor Statistics, 2015a). The patterns of gender are a result of the complex interaction of multiple social prisms across time and space.

Part III of the book concerns possibilities for gender change. Just as the wonder of the kaleidoscope lies in the ever-evolving patterns it creates, gendered patterns are always in flux. Each life and the world we live in can be understood as a kaleidoscope of unfolding growth and continual change (Baker, 1999). This dynamic aspect of the kaleidoscope metaphor represents the opportunity we have, individually and collectively, to transform gendered patterns that are harmful to women and men. Although the theme of gender change is prominent throughout this book, it is addressed specifically in Chapter 10 and in the Epilogue.

One caveat must be presented before we take you through the kaleidoscope of gender. A metaphor is a figure of speech in which a word ordinarily used to refer to one thing is applied to better understand another thing. A metaphor should not be taken literally. It does not directly represent reality. We use the metaphor of the kaleidoscope as an analytical tool to aid us in grasping the complexity, ambiguity, and fluidity of gender. However, unlike the prisms in a real kaleidoscope, the meaning and experience of social prisms (e.g., gender, race, ethnicity, social class, sexuality, and culture) are socially constructed and change in response to patterns in the larger society. Thus, although the prisms of a real kaleidoscope are static, the prisms of the gender kaleidoscope are fluid and shaped by the patterns of society.

As you step into the world of gender studies, you'll need to develop a capacity to see what is hidden by the cultural blinders we all wear at least some of the time. This capacity to see into the complexities of human relationships and group life has been called sociological imagination or, to be hip, "sociological radar." It is a capacity that is finely honed by practice and training both inside and outside the classroom. A sociological perspective enables us to see through the cultural smokescreens that conceal the patterns, meanings, and dynamics of our relationships.

GENDER STEREOTYPES

The sociological perspective will help you think about gender in ways you might never have considered. It will, for example, help you debunk *gender stereotypes*, which are rigid, oversimplified, exaggerated beliefs about femininity and masculinity that misrepresent most women and men (Walters, 1999). To illustrate, let's analyze one gender stereotype that many people in American society believe—women talk more than men (Anderson & Leaper, 1998; Swaminathan, 2007; Wood, 1999).

Social scientific research is helpful in documenting whether women actually talk more than men, or whether this belief is just another gender stereotype. To arrive at a conclusion, social scientists study the interactions of men and women in an array of settings and count how often men speak compared with women. They almost always find that, on average, men talk more in mixed-gender groups (Brescoli, 2011; Wood, 1999). Researchers also find that men interrupt more and tend to ignore topics brought up by women (Anderson & Leaper, 1998; Wood, 1999). In and of themselves, these are important findings—the stereotype turns reality on its head.

So why does the stereotype continue to exist? First, we might ask how people believe something to be real—such as the stereotype that women talk more than men—when, in general, it isn't true. Part of the answer lies in the fact that culture, briefly defined as the way of life of a group of people, shapes what we experience as reality (see Chapter 3 for a more detailed discussion). As Allan Johnson (1997) aptly puts it, "Living in a culture is somewhat like participating in the magician's magic because all the while we think we're paying attention to what's 'really' happening, alternative realities unfold without even occurring to us" (p. 55). In other words, we don't usually reflect on our own culture; we are mystified by it without much awareness of its bewildering effect on us. The power of beliefs, including gender beliefs, is quite awesome. Gender stereotypes shape our perceptions, and these beliefs shape our reality.

A second question we need to ask about gender stereotypes is: What is their purpose? For example, do they set men against women and contribute to the persistence of a system of inequality that disadvantages women and advantages men? Certainly, the stereotype that many Americans hold of women as nonstop talkers is not a positive one. The stereotype does not assume that women are assertive, articulate, or captivating speakers. Instead, it tends to depict women's talk as trivial gossip or irritating nagging. In other words, the stereotype devalues women's talk while, at the same time, elevating men's talk as thoughtful and worthy of our attention. One of the consequences

of this stereotype is that both men and women take men's talk more seriously (Brescoli, 2011; Wood, 1999). This pattern is reflected in the fact that the voice of authority in many areas of American culture, such as television and politics, is almost always a male voice (Brescoli, 2011). The message communicated is clear—women are less important than men. In other words, gender stereotypes help legitimize status and power differences between men and women (Brescoli, 2011).

However, stereotypical images of men and women are not universal in their application, because they are complicated by the kaleidoscopic nature of people's lives. Prisms, or social categories, such as race/ethnicity, social class, and age, intersect with gender to produce stereotypes that differ in symbolic meaning and functioning. For example, the prisms of gender, race, and age interact for African American and Hispanic men, who are stereotyped as dangerous (as noted in Adia Harvey Wingfield's reading in Chapter 7). These variations in gender stereotypes act as controlling images that maintain complex systems of domination and subordination in which some individuals and groups are dehumanized and disadvantaged in relationship to others (see Bonnie Thornton Dill and Marla H. Kohlman's article and other readings in Chapter 2).

DEVELOPMENT OF THE CONCEPT OF GENDER

Just a few decades ago, social scientists described gender as two discrete categories called sex roles—masculine/men and feminine/women. These sex roles were conceptualized in a biological "essentialist" framework to be either an automatic response to innate personality characteristics and/or biological sex characteristics such as hormones and reproductive functions (Kimmel, 2004; Tavris, 1992) or a mix of biological imperatives and learning reinforced by social pressure to conform to one or the other sex role (Connell, 2010). For example, women were thought to be naturally more nurturing because of their capacity to bear children, and men were seen as prewired to take on leadership positions in major societal institutions such as family, politics, and business. This "sex roles" model of women and men was one-dimensional, relatively static, and ethnocentric, and it is *not* supported by biological, psychological, historical, sociological, or anthropological research.

The concept of gender developed as social scientists conducted research that questioned the simplicity and accuracy of the "sex roles" perspective. One example of this research is that social scientists have debunked the notion that biological sex characteristics cause differences in men's and women's behaviors (Tavris, 1992). Research on hormones illustrates this point. Testosterone, which women as well as men produce, does not cause aggression in men (see Robert M. Sapolsky's reading in Chapter 1), and the menstrual cycle does not cause women to be more "emotional" than men (Tavris, 1992; see L. Ayu Saraswati's reading in Chapter 6).

Another example is that social scientific research demonstrated that men and women are far more physically, cognitively, and emotionally alike than different. What were assumed to be natural differences and inequalities between women and men were clearly shown to be the consequence of the asymmetrical and unequal life experiences, resources, and power of women compared with men (Connell, 2010; Tavris, 1992). Consider the arena of athletics. It is a common and long-held belief that biological sex is related to physical ability and, in particular, that women are athletically inferior to men. These beliefs have been challenged by the outcomes of a recent series of legal interventions that opened the world of competitive sports to girls and women. Once legislation such as Title IX was implemented in 1972, the expectation that women could not be athletes began to change as girls and young women received the same training and support for athletic pursuits as did men. Not surprisingly, the gap in physical strength and skills between women and men decreased dramatically. Today, women athletes

regularly break records and perform physical feats thought impossible for women just a few decades ago.

Yet another example of how the "sex roles" model was discredited was the documentation of inequality as a human-created social system. Social scientists highlighted the social origins of patterns of gender inequality within the economy, family, religion, and other social institutions that benefit men as a group and maintain patriarchy as a social structure. To illustrate, in the 1970s, when researchers began studying gender inequality, they found that women made between 60 and 70 cents for every dollar men made. Things are not much better today. In 2014, the median salary for women was 82.5% of men's median salary (Bureau of Labor Statistics, 2015b).

The intellectual weaknesses of "sex roles" theory (Connell, 2010), buttressed by considerable contradictory evidence, led social scientists to more sophisticated theories and modes of studying gender that could address the complexities and malleability of sex (femaleness and maleness) and gender (femininities and masculinities). In short, social science documented the fact that we are made and make ourselves into gendered people through social interaction in everyday life (Connell, 2010). It is not natural or normal to be a feminine woman or a masculine man. Gender is a socially constructed system of social relations that can be understood only by studying the social processes by which gender is defined into existence and maintained or changed by human actions and interactions (Schwalbe, 2001). This theory of gender social construction will be discussed throughout the book.

One of the most important sources of evidence in support of the idea that gender is socially constructed is derived from cross-cultural and historical studies as described in the earlier discussion of the gendering of pink and blue. The variations and fluidity in the definitions and expressions of gender across cultures and over time illustrate that the American gender system is not universal. For example, people in some cultures have created more than two   genders (see Serena Nanda's reading in Chapter 1). Other cultures define men and women as similar, not different (see Christine Helliwell's reading in Chapter 3). Still others view gender as flowing and changing across the life span (Herdt, 1997).

As social scientists examined gender patterns through the prism of culture and throughout history, their research challenged the notion that masculinity and femininity are defined and experienced in the same way by all people. For example, the meaning and practice of femininity in orthodox, American religious subcultures is not the same as femininity outside those communities (Rose, 2001). The differences are expressed in a variety of ways, including women's clothing. Typically, orthodox religious women adhere to modesty rules in dress, covering their heads, arms, and legs.

Elaborating on the idea of multiple or plural masculinities and femininities, Australian sociologist Raewyn Connell coined the terms *hegemonic masculinity* and *emphasized femininity* to understand the relations between and among masculinities and femininities in patriarchal societies. Patriarchal societies are dominated by privileged men (e.g., upper-class White men), but they also typically benefit less privileged men in their relationships with women. According to Connell (1987), hegemonic masculinity is the idealized pattern of masculinity in patriarchal societies, while emphasized femininity is the vision of femininity held up as the model of womanhood in those societies. In Connell's definition, hegemonic masculinity is "the pattern of practice (i.e., things done, not just a set of role expectations or an identity) that allowed men's dominance over women to continue" (Connell & Messerschmidt, 2005, p. 832). Key features of hegemonic masculinity include the subordination of women, the exclusion and debasement of gay men, and the celebration of toughness and competitiveness (Connell, 2000). However, hegemony does not mean violence per se. It refers to "ascendancy achieved through culture, institutions, and persuasion" (Connell & Messerschmidt, 2005, p. 832). Emphasized femininity, in contrast, is about women's subordination, with its key features being sociability, compliance with men's sexual and ego desires, and acceptance of marriage and child care (Connell, 1987). Both hegemonic masculinity and emphasized femininity patterns are "embedded in specific social environments" and are, therefore, dynamic as opposed to fixed (Connell & Messerschmidt, 2005, p. 846).

According to Connell, hegemonic masculinity and emphasized femininity are not necessarily the most common gender patterns. They are, however, the versions of manhood and womanhood against which other patterns of masculinity and femininity are measured and found wanting (Connell & Messerschmidt, 2005; Kimmel, 2004). For example, hegemonic masculinity produces marginalized masculinities, which, according to Connell (2000), are characteristic of exploited groups such as racial and ethnic minorities. These marginalized forms of masculinity may share features with hegemonic masculinity, such as "toughness," but are socially debased (see Adia Harvey Wingfield's reading in Chapter 7).

In patriarchal societies, the culturally idealized form of femininity, emphasized femininity, is produced in relation to male dominance. Emphasized femininity insists on compliance, nurturance, and empathy as ideals of womanhood to which all women should subscribe (Connell, 1987). Connell does not use the term *hegemonic* to refer to emphasized femininity, because, she argues, emphasized femininity is always subordinated to masculinity. James Messerschmidt (2012) adds to our understanding of femininities by arguing that the construction of hegemonic masculinity requires some kind of "buy-in" from women and that, under certain circumstances and in certain contexts, there are women who create emphasized femininities. By doing so, they contribute to the perpetuation of coercive gender relations and identities. Think of circumstances and situations—such as within work, romantic, or family settings—when women are complicit in maintaining oppressive gender relations and identities. Why would some women participate in the production of masculinities and femininities that are oppressive? The reading by Karen D. Pyke and Denise L. Johnson in Chapter 2 is helpful in answering these questions, employing the term *hegemonic femininity* rather than *emphasized femininity*. They describe the lives of young, second-generation Asian women and their attempts to balance two cultural patterns of gender in which White femininity, they argue, is hegemonic, or the dominant form of femininity.

Another major source of gender complexity is the interaction of gender with other social categories of difference and inequality. Allan Johnson (2001) points out,

> Categories that define privilege exist all at once and in relation to one another. People never see me solely in terms of my race, for example, or my gender. Like everyone else's, my place in the social world is a package deal—white, male, heterosexual, middle-aged, married . . .—and that's the way it is all the time. . . . It makes no sense to talk about the effect of being in one of these categories—say, white—without also looking at the others and how they're related to it. (p. 53)

Seeing gender through multiple social prisms is critical, but it is not a simple task, as you will discover in the readings throughout this book. Social scientists commonly refer to this type of analysis as intersectionality, but other terms are used as well (see Chapter 2 for a discussion of this). We need to be aware of how other social prisms alter life experiences and chances. For example, although an upper-class African American woman is privileged by her social class category, she will face obstacles related to her race and gender. Or consider the situation of a middle-class White man who is gay; he might lose some of the privilege attached to his class and race because of his sexual orientation.

Finally, gender is now considered a social construct shaped at individual, interactional, and institutional levels. If we focus on only one of these levels, we provide only a partial explanation of how gender operates in our lives. This idea of gender being shaped at these three different levels is elaborated in Barbara J. Risman's article in Chapter 1 and throughout the book. Consider

these three different ways of approaching gender and how they interact or influence one another. At the *individual* level, sociologists study the social categories and stereotypes we use to identify ourselves and label others (see Chapter 4). At the *interactional* level, sociologists study gender as an ongoing activity carried out in interaction with other people, and how people vary their gender presentations as they move from situation to situation (see Carla A. Pfeffer's reading in Chapter 1). At the *institutional* level, sociologists study how "gender is present in the processes, practices, images and ideologies, and distributions of power in the various sectors of social life," such as religion, health care, language, and so forth (Acker, 1992, p. 567; see also Joan Acker's reading in Chapter 7).

THEORETICAL APPROACHES FOR UNDERSTANDING GENDER

Historically, conflict and functionalist theories explained gender at a macro level of analysis, with these theories having gone through many transformations since first proposed around the turn of the 20th century. Scholars at that time were trying to sort out massive changes in society resulting from the industrial and democratic revolutions. However, a range of theories—for example, feminist, postmodernist, and queer theories—provide more nuanced explanations of gender. Many of these more recent theories frame their understanding of gender in the lived experiences of individuals, what sociologists call microlevel theories, rather than focusing solely on a macrolevel analysis of society, wherein gender does not vary in form or function across groups or contexts.

Functionalism

Functionalism attempts to understand how all parts of a society (e.g., institutions such as family, education, economy, and the polity or state) fit together to form a smoothly running social system. According to this theoretical paradigm, parts of society tend to complement each other to create social stability (Durkheim, 1933). Translated into separate sex role relationships, Talcott Parsons and Robert Bales (1955), writing after World War II, saw distinct and separate gender roles in the heterosexual nuclear family as a functional adaptation to a modern, complex society. Women were thought to be more "functional" if they were socialized and aspired to raise children. And men were thought to be more "functional" if they were socialized and aspired to support their children and wives. However, as Michael Kimmel (2004) notes, this "sex-based division of labor is functionally anachronistic," and if there ever was any biological basis for specific tasks being assigned to men or women, it has been eroded (p. 55). The functionalist viewpoint has largely been discredited in sociology, although it persists as part of common culture in various discourses and ideologies, especially conservative religious and political thought.

Evolutionary Psychology and Neuroscience

Functionalist thinking is also replicated in the realms of neuroscience and evolutionary psychology. In brief, the former tries to explain gender inequality by searching for neurological differences in human females and males assumed to be caused by hormonally induced differences in the brain. The hypothesized behavioral outcomes, according to neuroscientists such as Simon Baron-Cohen (2003), are emotionally tuned in, verbal women in contrast to men who are inclined to superior performance in areas such as math and music (Bouton, 2010). The latter, evolutionary psychology, focuses on "sex differences" (e.g., high-risk-taking male behaviors) between human females and males that are hypothesized to have their origins in psychological adaptations to early human, intrasexual competition. Both approaches, which assume there are essential differences between males and females embedded in their bodies or psyches, have been roundly critiqued by researchers

(e.g., Fine, 2010; Fine, Jordan-Young, Kaiser, & Rippon, 2013) who uncovered a range of problems, including research design flaws, no significant differences between female and male subjects, overgeneralization of findings, and ethnocentrism. Feminist neuroscientists have carefully set out the serious, negative consequences of the tendency of evolutionary psychology and neuroscience to produce "untested stereotype-based speculation" that reinforces popular misconceptions about women and men (Fine, 2013). In a short essay titled "Plasticity, Plasticity, Plasticity… and the Rigid Problem of Sex," Cordelia Fine and colleagues (2013) discuss the ways in which behavioral neuroendocrinology "has been transformed by an increasingly large body of research demonstrating the power of an individual's behavior, the behavior of others, and aspects of the environment to influence behavior through reciprocal modulation of the endocrine system" (p. 551). Simply put, we are not hardwired. Our brains are "adaptively plastic," interacting and changing with individual life experiences and social contexts (p. 551).

Conflict Theories

Karl Marx and later conflict theorists, however, did not see social systems as functional or benign. Instead, Marx and his colleague Friedrich Engels described industrial societies as systems of oppression in which one group, the dominant social class, uses its control of economic resources to oppress the working class. The economic resources of those in control are obtained through profits gained from exploiting the labor of subordinate groups. Marx and Engels predicted that the tension between the "haves" and the "have-nots" would result in an underlying conflict between these two groups. Most early Marxist theories focused on class oppression; however, Engels (1942/1970) wrote an important essay on the oppression of women as the earliest example of oppression of one group by another. Marx and Engels inspired socialist feminists, discussed later in this introduction under "Feminist Theories."

Current theorists, while recognizing Marx and Engels's recognition of the exploitation of workers in capitalist economies, criticize early conflict theory for ignoring women's reproductive labor and unpaid work (Federici, 2012). They focus on the exploitation of women by global capitalism (see article by Bandana Purkayastha in Chapter 2). Conflict theories today call for social action relating to the oppression of women and other marginalized groups, particularly within this global framework.

Social Constructionist Theories

Social constructionist theories offer a strong antidote to biological essentialism and psychological reductionism in understanding the social worlds (e.g., institutions, ideologies, identities) constructed by people. This theory, as discussed earlier, emphasizes the social or collective processes by which people actively shape reality (e.g., ideas, inequalities, social movements) as we go about daily life in different contexts and situations. The underpinnings of social constructionist theory are in sociological thought (e.g., symbolic interactionism, dramaturgy, and ethnomethodology), as well as in anthropology, social psychology, and related disciplinary arenas.

Social constructionism has had a major impact on gender analysis, invigorating both gender research and theoretical approaches (e.g., discussions of doing gender theory, relational theory, and intersectional analysis). From a social constructionist viewpoint, we must learn and do gender (masculinities and femininities) in order for gender differences and inequalities to exist. We also build these differences and inequalities into the patterns of large social arrangements such as social institutions. Take education. Men predominate in higher education and school administration, while women are found at the elementary and preschool levels (Connell, 2010). Theories rooted in the fundamental principles of gender social construction follow.

"Doing Gender" Theory

Drawing on the work of symbolic interactionism, specifically dramaturgy (Goffman) and ethnomethodology (Garfinkel), Candace West and Don H. Zimmerman published an article in 1987 simply titled "Doing Gender." In this article, they challenged assumptions of the two previous decades of research that examined "sex differences" or "sex roles." They argued that gender is a *master identity*, which is a product of social interactions and "doing," not simply the acting out of a role on a social stage. They saw gender as a complicated process by which we categorize individuals into two sex categories based on what we assume to be their sex (male or female). Interaction in contemporary Western societies is based on "knowing the sex" of the individual we are interacting with. However, we have no way of actually knowing an individual's sex (genitalia or hormones); therefore, we infer sex categories based on outward characteristics such as hairstyle, clothing, etc. Because we infer sex categories of the individuals we meet, West and Zimmerman argue that we are likely to question those who break from expected gendered behaviors for the sex categories we assign to them. We are also accountable for our own gender-appropriate behavior. Interaction in most societies becomes particularly difficult if one's sex category or gender is ambiguous, as you will read in Betsy Lucal's article in Chapter 1.

Thus, this process of being accountable makes it important for individuals to display appropriate gendered behavior at all times in all situations. As such, "doing gender" becomes a salient part of social interactions and embedded in social institutions. As they note, "Insofar as a society is partitioned by 'essential' differences between women and men and placement in a sex category is both relevant and enforced, doing gender is unavoidable" (West & Zimmerman, 1987, p. 137).

Of course, they recognize that not everyone has the same resources (such as time, money, and/or expertise) to "do gender" and that gender accomplishment varies across social situations.

In considering the discussion of who talks more, "doing gender" might explain why men talk more in work groups, as they attempt to portray their gendered masculinity while women may be doing more gender-appropriate emotion work such as asking questions and filling in silences. As such, when men and women accomplish gender as expected for the sex categories they display and are assigned to by others, they are socially constructing gender.

This concept of "doing gender" is used in many articles included in this book, but the use of the concept is not always consistent with the way the authors originally presented it (West & Zimmerman, 2009). The article by Nikki Jones included in Chapter 2 is part of a 2009 symposium considering the original 1987 article and its implications, in which she examines the challenges of doing gender for young, poor Black girls. Doing gender is a concept that helped move the discussions of sex/gender to a different level where interactions (micro) and institutions (macro) can be studied simultaneously and gender becomes a more lived experience, rather than a "role."

Performative Theory

Judith Butler, a philosopher, conceptualizes gender as a performative act. Like West and Zimmerman, she emphasizes that gender is not a performance, or "a certain kind of enactment" (Butler, 2009, p. i). Instead, she argues that gender identities are understood and agreed on by self and others through bodily acts (e.g., walk and gestures) and speech acts. She argues that gender is always negotiated in a system of power that establishes norms within which it is reproduced or, when the norms are challenged, performances of gender are altered (Butler, 2009). As such, performative theory focuses on the intersubjective creation of gender in relationship to the larger social structure.

Postmodern Theories

Postmodernism focuses on the way knowledge about gender is constructed, not on explaining gender relationships themselves. To postmodernists, knowledge is never absolute—it is always situated in a social reality that is specific to a historical time period. Postmodernism is based on the idea that it is impossible for anyone to see the world without presuppositions. From a postmodernist perspective, then, gender is socially constructed through discourses, which are the "series of stories" we use to explain our world (Andersen, 2004). Postmodernists attempt to "deconstruct" the discourses or stories used to support a group's beliefs about gender (Andersen, 2004; Lorber, 2001). For example, Jane Flax argues that to fully understand gender in Western cultures, we must deconstruct the meanings in Western religious, scientific, and other discourses relative to "biology/sex/gender/nature" (cited in Lorber, 2001, p. 199). As you will come to understand from the readings in Chapters 1 and 3 (e.g., Nanda and Christine Helliwell), the association between sex and gender in Western scientific (e.g., theories and texts) and nonscientific (e.g., films, newspapers, media) discourses is not shared in other cultural contexts. Thus, for postmodernists, gender is a product of the discourses within particular social contexts that define and explain gender.

Queer Theories

Queer theories borrow from the original meaning of the word *queer* to refer to that which is "outside ordinary and narrow interpretations" (Plante, 2006, p. 62). Queer theorists are most concerned with understanding sexualities in terms of the idea that (sexual) identities are flexible, fluid, and changing, rather than fixed. In addition, queer theorists argue that identity and behavior must be separated. Thus, we cannot assume that people are what they do. From the vantage point of this theory, gender categories, much like sexual categories, are simplistic and problematic. Real people cannot be lumped together and understood in relationship to big cultural categories such as men and women, heterosexual and homosexual (Plante, 2006). Carla A. Pfeffer's reading in Chapter 1 sets out the premises and impact of queer theory on gender studies in considerable detail. She argues that the discipline of sociology is well positioned to examine the lives of queer social actors, and her work is an excellent example of the application of queer theory.

Relational Theory

The relational theory of gender was developed in response to the problems of the "sex roles" model and other limited views of gender (e.g., categoricalism, as critiqued by queer theory). Connell (2000) states that a gender relations approach opens up an understanding of "the different dimensions of gender, the relation between bodies and society, and the patterning of gender" (pp. 23–24). Specifically, from a relational viewpoint, (1) gender is a way of organizing social practice (e.g., child care and household labor) at the personal, interactional, and institutional levels of life; (2) gender is a social practice related to bodies and what bodies do but *cannot* be reduced to bodies or biology; and (3) masculinities and femininities can be understood as *gender projects* that produce the *gender order* of a society and interact with other social structures such as race and class (pp. 24–28).

Feminist Theories

Feminist theorists expanded on the ideas of theorists such as Marx and Engels, turning attention to the causes of women's oppression. There are many schools of feminist thought. Here, we briefly introduce you to those typically covered in overviews (see Chapter 10 for discussion of feminist theories such as women of color feminism). One group, socialist feminists, continued to emphasize the role of capitalism in interaction with a patriarchal family structure as the basis for the exploitation of women. These theorists argue that economic and power benefits accrue to men who dominate women in capitalist societies. Another group, radical feminists, argues that patriarchy—the domination of men over

women—is the fundamental form of oppression of women. Both socialist and radical feminists call for far-reaching changes in all institutional arrangements and cultural forms, including the dismantling of systems of oppression such as sexism, racism, and classism; replacing capitalism with socialism; developing more egalitarian family systems; and making other structural changes (e.g., Bart & Moran, 1993; Daly, 1978; Dworkin, 1987; MacKinnon, 1989).

Not all feminist theorists call for deep, structural, and cultural changes. Liberal feminists are inclined to work toward a more equitable form of democratic capitalism. They argue that policies such as Title IX and affirmative action laws opened up opportunities for women in education and increased the number of women professionals, such as physicians. These feminists strive to achieve gender equality by removing barriers to women's freedom of choice and equal participation in all realms of life, eradicating sexist stereotypes, and guaranteeing equal access and treatment for women in both public and private arenas (e.g., Reskin & Roos, 1990; Schwartz, 1994; Steinberg, 1982; Vannoy-Hiller & Philliber, 1989; Weitzman, 1985).

Although the liberal feminist stance may seem to be the most pragmatic form of feminism, many of the changes brought about by liberal varieties of feminism have "served the interests of only the most privileged women" (Motta, Fominaya, Eschle, & Cox, 2011, p. 5). Additionally, liberal feminist approaches that work with the state or attempt to gain formal equal rights within a fundamentally exploitive labor market fail to challenge the growth of neoliberal globalism and the worsening situation of many people in the face of unfettered markets, privatization, and imperialism (Motta et al., 2011; e.g., see discussion of the Great Recession in Chapter 5). In response to these kinds of issues and problems, 21st-century feminists are revisiting and reinventing feminist thinking and practice to create a "more emancipatory feminism" that can lead to "post-patriarchal, antineoliberal politics" (Motta et al., 2011, p. 2; see readings in Chapter 10).

Intersectional or Prismatic Theories

A major shortcoming with many of the theoretical perspectives just described is their failure to recognize how gender interacts with other social categories or prisms of difference and inequality within societies, including race/ethnicity, social class, sexuality, age, and ability/disability (see Chapter 2). A growing number of social scientists are responding to the problem of incorporating multiple social categories or social positions in their research by developing a new form of analysis, often described as intersectional analysis, which we also refer to as prismatic analysis in this book. Chapter 2 explores these theories of how gender interacts with other prisms of difference and inequality to create complex patterns. Without an appreciation of the interactions of socially constructed categories of difference and inequality, or what we call prisms, we end up with not only an incomplete but also an inaccurate explanation of gender.

As you read through the articles in this book, consider the basis for the authors' arguments in each reading. How do the authors apply the theories just described? What observations, data, or works of other social science researchers do these authors use to support their claims? Use a critical eye to examine the evidence as you reconsider the assumptions about gender that guide your life.

THE KALEIDOSCOPE OF GENDER: PRISMS, PATTERNS, AND POSSIBILITIES

Before beginning the readings that take us through the kaleidoscope of gender, let us briefly review the three themes that shape the book's structure: prisms, patterns, and possibilities.

Part I: Prisms

Understanding the prisms that shape our experiences provides an essential basis for the book. Chapter 1 explores the meanings of the pivotal prism—gender—and its relationship to biological sex and sexuality. Chapter 2 presents an array of prisms or socially constructed categories that interact with gender in many human societies, such as race/ethnicity, social class, sexuality, age, and ability/disability. Chapter 3 focuses on the prism of culture/nation, which alters the meaning and practice of gender in surprising ways.

Part II: Patterns

The prisms of the kaleidoscope create an array of patterned expressions and experiences of femininity and masculinity. Part II of this book examines some of these patterns. We look at how people learn, internalize, and "do" gender (Chapter 4); how gender is exploited by corporate capitalism (Chapter 5); how gender engages bodies, sexualities, and emotions (Chapter 6); how gendered patterns are reproduced and modified in work (Chapter 7); how gender is created and transformed in our intimate relationships (Chapter 8); and how conformity to patterns of gender is enforced and maintained (Chapter 9).

Part III: Possibilities

In much the same way as the colors and patterns of kaleidoscopic images flow, gendered patterns and meanings are inherently changeable. Chapter 10 examines the shifting sands of the genderscape and reminds us of the many possibilities for change. Finally, in the Epilogue, we examine changes we have seen and encourage you to envision future changes.

We use the metaphor of the gender kaleidoscope to discover what is going on under the surface of a society whose way of life we don't often penetrate in a nondefensive, disciplined, and deep fashion. In doing so, we will expose a reality that is astonishing in its complexity, ambiguity, and fluidity. With the kaleidoscope, you never know what's coming next. Come along with us as we begin the adventure of looking through the kaleidoscope of gender.

REFERENCES

Acker, J. (1992). From sex roles to gendered institutions. *Contemporary Sociology, 21*(5), 565–570.

Andersen, M. L. (2004). *Thinking about women: Sociological perspectives on sex and gender* (6th ed.). Boston: Allyn & Bacon.

Anderson, K. J., & Leaper, C. (1998). Meta-analysis of gender effects on conversational interruption: Who, what, when, where, and how. *Sex Roles, 39*(3–4), 225–252.

Baker, C. (1999). *Kaleidoscopes: Wonders of wonder.* Lafayette, CA: C&T.

Baron-Cohen, S. (2003). *The essential difference: The truth about the male and female brain.* New York: Basic Books.

Bart, P. B., & Moran, E. G. (Eds.). (1993). *Violence against women: The bloody footprints.* Newbury Park, CA: Sage.

Bouton, K. (2010, August 23). Peeling away theories on gender and the brain. *New York Times.* Retrieved from http://www.nytimes.com/2010/08/24/science/24scibks.html

Brescoli, V. (2011). Who takes the floor and why: Gender, power, and volubility in organizations. *Administrative Science Quarterly, 56*(4), 622–641.

Bureau of Labor Statistics. (2015a). Table A-2: 2014 Median weekly earnings of full-time wage and salary workers by detailed occupation, sex, race and Hispanic or Latino ethnicity and Non-Hispanic ethnicity. Annual Average 2014. Source: *Current Population Survey.* [Unpublished data – sent by request].

Bureau of Labor Statistics. (2015b). Table 39: Usual weekly earnings of employed full-time wage and salary workers by intermediate occupation and sex Annual Average 2014. Source: *Current Population Survey.* Retrieved from http://www.bls.gov/cps/cpsaat39.htm

Butler, J. (2009). Performativity, precarity, and sexual politics. *AIBR, 4*(3), i–xii.

Connell, R. W. (1987). *Gender and power: Society, the person and sexual politics.* Stanford, CA: University of Stanford Press.

Connell, R. W. (2000). *The men and the boys.* Berkeley: University of California Press.

Connell, R. W. (2010). Retrieved from www.raewynconnell.net/

Connell, R. W., & Messerschmidt, J. W. (2005). Hegemonic masculinity: Rethinking the concept. *Gender & Society, 19*(6), 829–859.

Daly, M. (1978). *Gyn/ecology, the metaethics of radical feminism.* Boston: Beacon Press.

Durkheim, E. (1933). *The division of labor in society.* Glencoe, IL: Free Press.

Dworkin, A. (1987). *Intercourse.* New York: Free Press.

Engels, F. (1970). *Origin of the family, private property, and the state.* New York: International Publishers. (Original work published in 1942)

Federici, S. (2012). *Revolution at point zero: Housework, reproduction, and feminist struggle.* Oakland, CA: PM Press.

Fine, C. (2010). *Delusions of gender: How our minds, society, and neurosexism create difference.* New York: Norton.

Fine, C. (2013). New insights into gendered brain wiring, or a perfect case study in neurosexism? *The Conversation.* Retrieved from http://theconversation.com/new-insights-into-gendered-brain-wiring-or-a-perfect-case-study-in-neurosexism-21083

Fine, C., Jordan-Young, R., Kaiser, A., & Rippon, G. (2013). Plasticity, plasticity, plasticity... and the rigid problem of sex. *Trends in cognitive sciences, 17*(11), 550–551.

Herdt, G. (1997). *Same sex, different cultures.* Boulder, CO: Westview Press.

Johnson, A. (1997). *The gender knot.* Philadelphia: Temple University Press.

Johnson, A. (2001). *Privilege, power, and difference.* Mountain View, CA: Mayfield.

Kimmel, M. S. (2004). *The gendered society* (2nd ed.). New York: Oxford University Press.

Lorber, J. (2001). *Gender inequality: Feminist theories and politics.* Los Angeles: Roxbury.

MacKinnon, C. A. (1989). *Toward a feminist theory of the state.* Cambridge, MA: Harvard University Press.

Messerschmidt, J. (2012). Engendering gendered knowledge: Assessing the academic appropriation of hegemonic masculinity. *Men and Masculinities, 15*(1), 56–76.

Motta, S., Fominaya, C. F., Eschle, C., & Cox, L. (2011). Feminism, women's movements and women in movement. *Interface, 3*(2), 1–32.

Paoletti, J. B. (2012). *Pink and blue: Telling the boys from the girls in America.* Bloomington: Indiana University Press.

Parsons, T., & Bales, R. F. (1955). *Family, socialization, and interaction process.* Glencoe, IL: Free Press.

Plante, R. F. (2006). *Sexualities in context: A social perspective.* Boulder, CO: Westview Press.

Reskin, B. F., & Roos, P. A. (1990). *Job queues, gender queues: Explaining women's inroads into male occupations*. Philadelphia: Temple University Press.

Rose, D. R. (2001). Gender and Judaism. In D. Vannoy (Ed.), *Gender mosaics: Social perspectives* (pp. 415–424). Los Angeles: Roxbury.

Schwalbe, M. (2001). *The sociologically examined life: Pieces of the conversation* (2nd ed.). Mountain View, CA: Mayfield.

Schwartz, P. (1994). *Love between equals: How peer marriage really works*. New York: Free Press.

Steinberg, R. J. (1982). *Wages and hours: Labor and reform in twentieth century America*. New Brunswick, NJ: Rutgers University Press.

Swaminathan, N. (2007, July 6). Gender jabber: Do women talk more than men? *Scientific American*. Retrieved from http://www.scientificamerican.com/article.cfm?id=women-talk-more-than-men&print=true

Tavris, C. (1992). *The mismeasure of woman*. New York: Simon & Schuster.

Vannoy-Hiller, D., & Philliber, W. W. (1989). *Equal partners: Successful women in marriage*. Newbury Park, CA: Sage.

Walters, S. D. (1999). Sex, text, and context: (In) between feminism and cultural studies. In M. M. Ferree, J. Lorber, & B. B. Hess (Eds.), *Revisioning gender* (pp. 193 257). Thousand Oaks, CA: Sage.

Weitzman, L. J. (1985). *The divorce revolution: The unexpected social and economic consequences for women and children in America*. New York: Free Press.

West, C., & Zimmerman, D. H. (1987). Doing gender. *Gender & Society, 1*(2), 125–151.

West, C., & Zimmerman, D. H. (2009). Accounting for doing gender. *Gender & Society, 23*(1), 112–122.

Wood, J. T. (1999). *Gendered lives: Communication, gender, and culture* (3rd ed.). Belmont, CA: Wadsworth.

PART I

PRISMS

1

THE PRISM OF GENDER

CATHERINE G. VALENTINE

In the metaphorical kaleidoscope of this book, gender is the pivotal prism. It is central to the intricate patterning of social life and encompasses power relations, the division of labor, symbolic forms, and emotional relations (Connell, 2000). The shape and texture of people's lives are affected in profound ways by the prism of gender as it operates in their social worlds. Indeed, our ways of thinking about and experiencing gender, and the related categories of sex and sexuality, originate in our society. As we noted in the introduction to this book, gender is very complex. In part, the complexity of the prism of gender in North American culture derives from the fact that it is characterized by a marked contradiction between people's beliefs about gender and real behavior. Our real behavior is far more flexible, adaptable, and malleable than our beliefs would have it. To put it another way, contrary to the stereotypes of masculinity and femininity, there are no gender certainties or absolutes. Real people behave in feminine, masculine, and nongendered ways as they respond to situational demands and contingencies (Glick & Fiske, 1999; Pfeffer, 2014; Tavris, 1992).

To help us think more clearly about the complexity of gender, two questions are addressed in this chapter: (1) How does Western culture condition us to think about gender, especially in relation to sex and sexuality? (2) How does social scientific research challenge Western beliefs about gender, sex, and sexuality?

WESTERN BELIEFS ABOUT GENDER, SEX, AND SEXUALITY

Most people in contemporary Western cultures, such as the United States, grow up learning that there are two and only two sexes, male and female; two and only two genders, feminine and masculine; and two and only two sexualities, heterosexual and homosexual (Bem, 1993; Lucal, 2008; Pfeffer, 2014; Wharton, 2005). We are taught that a real woman is female-bodied, feminine, and heterosexual; a real man is male-bodied, masculine, and heterosexual; and any deviation or variation is strange, unnatural, and potentially dangerous. Most people also learn that femininity and masculinity flow from biological sex characteristics (e.g., hormones, secondary sex characteristics, external and internal genitalia). We are taught that testosterone, a beard, big muscles, and a penis make a man, while estrogen, breasts, hairless legs, and a vagina make a woman. Many of us never question what we have learned about sex and gender, so we go through life assuming that gender is a relatively simple matter: A person who wears lipstick, high-heeled shoes, and a skirt is a feminine female, while a person who plays rugby, belches in public, and walks with a swagger is a masculine male (Lorber, 1994; Ridgeway & Correll, 2004).

The readings we have selected for this chapter reflect a growing body of social scientific research that challenges and alters the Western view of sex, gender, and sexuality. Overall, the readings are critical of the American tendency to explain virtually every human behavior in individual and biological terms. Americans overemphasize biology and underestimate the power of social facts to explain sex, sexuality, and gender (O'Brien, 1999). For instance, Americans tend to equate aggression with biological maleness and vulnerability with femaleness; natural facility in physics with masculinity and natural facility in child care with femininity; lace and ribbons with girlness and rough-and-tumble play with boyness (Glick & Fiske, 1999; Ridgeway & Correll, 2004). These notions of natural sex, gender, and sexuality difference, opposition, and inequality (i.e., a consistently higher valuation of masculinity than femininity) permeate our thinking, color our labeling of people and things in our environment, and affect our practical actions (Bem, 1993; Schilt & Westbrook, 2009; Wharton, 2005).

We refer to the American two-and-only-two sex/gender/sexuality system as the "pink and blue syndrome" (Schilt & Westbrook, 2009). This syndrome is deeply lodged in our minds and feelings and is reinforced through everyday talk, performance, and experience. It's everywhere. Any place, object, discourse, or practice can be gendered. Children's birthday cards come in pink and blue. Authors of popular books assert that men and women are from different planets. People love PMS and alpha-male jokes. In "The

Pink Dragon Is Female" (see Chapter 5), Adie Nelson's research reveals that even children's fantasy costumes are predictably gendered as masculine or feminine. The "pink and blue syndrome" is so embedded within our culture and, consequently, within individual patterns of thinking and feeling that most of us cannot remember when we learned gender stereotypes and expectations or came to think about sex, gender, and sexuality as natural, immutable, and fixed. It all seems so simple and natural. But is it?

What is gender? What is sex? What is sexuality? How are gender, sex, and sexuality related? Why do most people in our society believe in the "pink and blue syndrome"? Why do so many of us attribute one set of talents, temperaments, skills, and behaviors to women and another, opposing set to men? These are the kinds of questions social scientists have been asking and researching for well over 50 years. Thanks to the good work of an array of scientists, we now understand that gender, sex, and sexuality are not so simple. Social scientists have discovered that the gender landscape is complicated, shifting, and contradictory. Among the beliefs called into question by research are

- the notion that there are two and only two sexes, two and only two genders, and two and only two sexualities;
- the assumption that the two-and-only-two system is universal; and
- the belief that nature, rather than nurture, causes the "pink and blue syndrome."

USING OUR SOCIOLOGICAL RADAR

Before we look at how social scientists answer questions such as, "What is gender?" let's do a little research of our own. Try the following: Relax, turn on your sociological radar, and examine yourself and the people you know carefully. Do all the men you know fit the ideal of masculinity all the time, in all relationships, and in all situations? Do all the women in your life consistently behave in stereotypical feminine fashion? Do you always fit into one as opposed to the other culturally approved gender category? Or are most of the people you know capable of "doing" both masculinity and femininity, depending on the interactional context? If we allow ourselves to think and see outside the contemporary American cultural framework, we will observe that none of the people we know are aggressive all the time, nurturing all the time, sweet and submissive all the time, or strong and silent all the time. Thankfully, we are complex and creative. We stretch and grow and develop as we meet the challenges, constraints, and opportunities of different and new situations and life circumstances. Men can do mothering; women can "take care of business." Real people are not stereotypes.

Yet even in the face of real gender fluidity, variation, and complexity, the belief in sex/gender/sexuality dichotomy, opposition, and inequality continues to dominate almost every aspect of the social worlds we inhabit. For example, recent research shows that even though men's and women's roles have changed and blended, the tendency of Americans to categorize and stereotype people based on the simple male/female dichotomy persists (Glick & Fiske, 1999; Miller, Eagly, & Linn, 2014; Shields, Garner, Di Leone, & Hadley, 2006; Snyder, 2014). As Peter Glick and Susan Tufts Fiske (1999) put it, "We typically categorize people by sex effortlessly, even nonconsciously, with diverse and profound effects on social interactions" (p. 368). To reiterate, many Americans perceive humankind as divided into mutually exclusive, nonoverlapping groups: males/masculine/men and females/feminine/women (Bem, 1993; Lucal, 2008; Wharton, 2005). This perception is shored up by the belief that heterosexuality or sexual attraction between the two, and only two, sexes/genders is natural. *Heteronormativity* (see Chapter 6 for detailed discussion) is now the term commonly used by sociologists to refer to the "cultural, legal, and institutional practices" that maintain a binary and unequal system (Schilt & Westbrook, 2009, p. 441). The culturally created model of gender, as well as sex and sexuality, then, is

nonkaleidoscopic: no spontaneity, no ambiguity, no complexity, no diversity, no surprises, no elasticity, and no unfolding growth.

SOCIAL SCIENTIFIC UNDERSTANDINGS OF SEX, GENDER, AND SEXUALITY

Modern social science offers a rich and complex understanding of gender, sex, and sexuality. It opens the door to the diversity of human experience and rejects the tendency to reduce human behavior to simple, single-factor explanations. Research shows that the behavior of people, no matter who they are, depends on time and place, context and situation—not on fixed sex/gender/sexuality differences (Lorber, 1994; Tavris, 1992; Vespa, 2009). For example, just a few decades ago in the United States, cheerleading was a men's sport because it was considered too rigorous for women (Dowling, 2000), women were thought to lack the cognitive and emotional "stuff" to pilot flights into space, and medicine and law were viewed as too intellectually demanding for women. As Carol Tavris (1992) says, research demonstrates that perceived gender differences turn out to be a matter of "now you see them, now you don't" (p. 288).

If we expand our sociological examination of sex/gender/sexuality to include cross-cultural studies, the real-life fluidity of human experience comes fully alive (see Chapter 3 for a detailed discussion). In some cultures (e.g., the Aka hunter-gatherers), fathers as well as mothers suckle infants (Hewlett, 2001). In other cultures, such as the Agta Negritos, women as well as men are hunters (Estioko-Griffin & Griffin, 2001). Among the Tharus of India and Nepal, marriage is "woman-friendly" and women readily divorce husbands because each woman "enjoys a more dominant position and can find another husband more easily" (Verma, 2009, para. 14). As Serena Nanda discusses in depth in her reading in this chapter, extraordinary gender diversity was expressed in complex, more-than-two sex/gender/sexuality systems in many precontact Native American societies.

In addition, the complex nature of sex/gender/ sexuality is underscored by scholarship on multiple masculinities and femininities, as discussed in the introduction to this book. There is no single pattern of masculinity or femininity. Masculinities and femininities are constantly in flux (Coles, 2009). Recall that Raewyn Connell (2000), in her analysis of masculinities, argued that hegemonic masculinity produces complicit, marginalized, and subordinated masculinities. Similarly, there is no femininity, singular. Instead, the ideal and practice of femininity vary by class, race, sexuality, historical period, nation, and other social factors. Let's use sociological radar again and call on the work of social scientists to help us think more precisely and "objectively" about what gender, sex, and sexuality are. It has become somewhat commonplace to distinguish between gender and sex by viewing sex, femaleness and maleness, as a biological fact unaffected by culture and thus unchanging and unproblematic, while viewing gender as a cultural phenomenon, a means by which people are taught who they are (e.g., girl or boy), how to behave (e.g., ladylike or tough), and what their roles will be (e.g., mother or father) (Sørensen, 2000). However, this mode of distinguishing between sex and gender has come under criticism, largely because new studies have revealed the cultural dimensions of sex itself (Schilt, 2010). That is, the physical characteristics of sex cannot be separated from the cultural milieu in which they are labeled and given meaning. For example, Robert M. Sapolsky's chapter reading debunks the widely held myth that testosterone causes males to be more aggressive and domineering than females. He ends his article by stating firmly that "our behavioral biology is usually meaningless outside the context of the social factors and environment in which it occurs." In other words, the relationship between biology and behavior is reciprocal, both inseparable and intertwined (Yoder, 2003).

Sex, as it turns out, is not a clear-cut matter of DNA, chromosomes, external genitalia, and the like, factors that produce two and only two sexes—female and male. First, there is considerable biological variation. Sex is not fixed in two categories. Biologist Anne Fausto-Sterling (1993) suggests that sex is more like a continuum than a dichotomy. For example, all humans have estrogen, prolactin, and testosterone but in varying and changing levels (Abrams, 2002). Think about this: In American society, people tend to associate breasts and related phenomena, such as breast cancer and lactation, with women. However, men have breasts. Indeed, some men have bigger breasts than some women, some men lactate, and some men get breast cancer. Also, in our society, people associate facial hair with men. What's the real story? All women have facial hair, and some have more of it than do some men. Indeed, recent hormonal and genetic studies (e.g., Abrams, 2002; Beale, 2001) are revealing that, biologically, women and men, female and male bodies are far more similar than different.

Second, not only do femaleness and maleness share much in common, but variations in and complexities of sex development produce *intersex* people whose bodies do not fit either of the two traditionally understood sex categories (Fausto-Sterling, 2000; Fujimora, 2006). Until recently in the United States, intersex was kept a secret and treated as a medical emergency (Grabham, 2007). Now that activists and researchers are challenging the marginalization and medicalization of intersex people, we understand that intersex is not a rarity. Scientists estimate that up to 2% of live births are intersex. Among intersex births are babies born with both male and female characteristics and babies born with "larger-than-average" clitorises or "smaller-than-average" penises (Lucal, 2008). Joan H. Fujimora (2006) examined recent research on sex genes and concluded that "there is no single pathway through which sex is genetically determined" and we might consider sex variations, such as intersex, as resulting from "multiple developmental pathways that involve genetic, protein, hormonal, environmental, and other agents, actions, and interactions" (p. 71). Judith Lorber and Lisa Jean Moore (2007) argue that intersex people are akin to multiracial people. They point out that just as scientists have demonstrated through DNA testing that almost all of us are genetically interracial, similarly, "if many people were genetically sex-typed, we'd also find a variety of chromosomal, hormonal, and anatomical patterns unrecognized" in our rigid, two-sex system (p. 138). In their chapter reading, Georgiann Davis and Sharon Preves examine the harmful consequences of the medicalization of intersex in the United States. They also discuss in detail the emergence of the intersex rights movement both as a response to medically unnecessary "normalization" surgeries and as a challenge to the two-and-only-two sex/gender/sexuality system. Biology is a complicated business, and that should come as no surprise. The more we learn about biology, the more elusive and complex sex becomes. What seemed so obvious—two opposite sexes—turns out to be a gross oversimplification.

Then, what is gender? As discussed in the introduction to this book, gender is a human invention, a means by which people are sorted (in our society, into two gender categories), a basic aspect of how our society organizes itself and allocates resources (e.g., certain tasks assigned to people called women and other tasks to those termed men), and a fundamental ingredient in how individuals understand themselves and others ("I feel feminine"; "He's manly"; "You're androgynous").

One of the fascinating aspects of gender is the extent to which it is negotiable and dynamic. In effect, masculinity and femininity exist because people believe that women and men are distinct groups and, most important, because people "do gender," day in and day out. It is now common for gender scholars to refer to gender as a performance or a masquerade, emphasizing that it is through the ways we present ourselves in our daily encounters with others that gender is created and re-created. The chapter reading by Betsy Lucal illustrates vividly how gender is a matter of attribution and enactment.

We even do gender by ourselves, and sometimes quite self-consciously. Have you ever tried to make yourself look and act more masculine or feminine? What is involved in "putting on" femininity or masculinity? Consider *transvestism,* or cross-gender dressing. "Cross-dressers know that successfully being a man or a woman simply means convincing others that you are what you appear to be" (Kimmel, 2000, p. 104). Think about the emerging communities of *transgender* people who are "challenging, questioning, or changing gender from that assigned at birth to a chosen gender" (Lorber & Moore, 2007, p. 139). Although most people have deeply learned gender and view the gender category they inhabit as natural or normal, intersex and transgender activists attack the boundaries of "normal" by refusing to choose a traditional sex, gender, or sexual identity (Lorber & Moore, 2007). In so doing, cultural definitions of sex and gender are destabilized and expanded. Carla A. Pfeffer's chapter reading illustrates this process by exploring transgender identities and relationships, demonstrating how the experiences of "queer" social actors have the potential to shake the foundations of normative binaries of sex, gender, and sexuality.

You may be wondering why we have not used the term *role,* as in *gender role,* to describe "doing gender." The problem with the concept of roles is that many social roles, such as those of teacher, student, doctor, or nurse, are situation specific. However, gender, like race, is a status and identity that cuts across situations and institutional arenas. In other words, gender does not "appear and disappear from one situation to another" (Van Ausdale & Feagin, 2001, p. 32). In part, this is a consequence of the pressures that other people exert on us to "do gender" no matter the social location in which we find ourselves. Even if an individual would like to "give up gender," others will work hard to define and interact with that individual in gendered terms. If you were an accountant, you could "leave your professional role behind you" when you left the office and went shopping or vacationing. Gender is a different story. Could you leave gender at the office? What would that look like, and what would it take to make it happen?

So far, we have explored gender as a product of our interactions with others. It is something we do, not something we inherit. Gender is also built into the larger world we inhabit in the United States, including its institutions, images and symbols, organizations, and material objects. For example, jobs, wages, and hierarchies of dominance and subordination in workplaces are gendered. Even after decades of substantial increase in women's workforce participation, occupations continue to be allocated by gender (e.g., secretaries are overwhelmingly women; men dominate construction work) and a wage gap between men and women persists (Bose & Whaley, 2001; Steinberg, 2001; see also the introduction to this book and the introduction to Chapter 7). In addition, men are still more likely to be bosses and women to be bossed. The symbols and images that surround us and by which we communicate are another part of our society's gender story. Our language speaks of difference and opposition in phrases such as "the opposite sex" and in the absence of any words except awkward medical terms (e.g., hermaphrodite) or epithets (e.g., fag) to refer to sex/sexual/gender variants. In addition, the swirl of standardized gendered images in the media is almost overwhelming. Blatant gender stereotypes still dominate TV, film, magazines, and billboards (Lont, 2001). Gender is also articulated, reinforced, and transformed through material objects and locales (Sørensen, 2000). Shoes are gendered, body adornments are gendered, public restrooms are gendered, ships are gendered, wrapping paper is gendered, and deodorants are gendered. The list is endless. The point is that these locales and objects are transformed into a medium for gender to operate within (Sørensen, 2000). They make gender seem "real," and they give it material consequences (p. 82).

Just as culture spawns the binary and oppositional sex and gender template (Grabham, 2007), sexuality, too, is socially constructed (see discussion in Chapter 6). It is not "a natural occurrence derived from biological sex" (Schilt & Westbrook, 2009, p. 443). But in the United States, the imperative to do heterosexuality dominates and is bound to privilege and power. Kristen Schilt and Laurel Westbrook state that our gender system "must be conceived of as heterosexist, as power is allocated via positioning in the gender and sexual hierarchies" (p. 443). Masculinity and heterosexuality are privileged, while femininity and homosexuality are denigrated. Other sexualities (e.g., bisexuality and pansexuality) are relegated to the margins.

In short, social scientific research underscores the complexity of the prism of gender and demonstrates how gender/sex/sexuality are constructed at multiple, interacting levels of society. The first reading in this chapter, by Barbara J. Risman, is a detailed examination of the ways our gender structure is embedded in the individual, interactional, and institutional dimensions of our society, emphasizing that gender cannot be reduced to one level or dimension: individual, interactional, or institutional. We are literally and figuratively immersed in a gendered world—a world in which difference, opposition, and inequality are the culturally defined themes. And yet, that world is kaleidoscopic in nature. The lesson of the kaleidoscope is that "nothing in life is immune to change" (Baker, 1999, p. 29). Reality is in flux; you never know what's coming next. The metaphor of the kaleidoscope reminds us to keep seeking the shifting meanings as well as the recurring patterns of gender (Baker, 1999).

We live in an interesting time of kaleidoscopic change. Old patterns of sex/gender/sexuality difference and inequality keep reappearing, often in new guises, while new patterns of convergence, equality, and self-realization have emerged. Social science research is vital in helping us stay focused on understanding the prism of gender as changeable and helping us respond to its context—as a social dialogue about societal membership and conventions and "as the outcome of how individuals are made to understand their differences and similarities" (Sørensen, 2000, pp. 203–204). With that focus in mind, we can more clearly and critically explore our gendered society.

REFERENCES

Abrams, D. C. (2002, March–April). Father nature: The making of a modern dad. *Psychology Today,* pp. 38–42.

Baker, C. (1999). *Kaleidoscopes: Wonders of wonder.* Lafayette, CA: C&T.

Beale, B. (2001). The sexes: New insights into the X and Y chromosomes. *The Scientist, 15*(15), 18. Retrieved from http://www.the-scientist.com/?articles.view/articleNo/13499/title/The-Sexes—New-Insights-into-the-X-and-Y-Chromosomes/

Bem, S. L. (1993). *The lenses of gender.* New Haven, CT: Yale University Press.

Bose, C. E., & Whaley, R. B. (2001). Sex segregation in the U.S. labor force. In D. Vannoy (Ed.), *Gender mosaics* (pp. 228–239). Los Angeles: Roxbury.

Coles, T. (2009). Negotiating the field of masculinity: The production and reproduction of multiple dominant masculinities. *Men and Masculinities, 12*(1), 30–44.

Connell, R. W. (2000). *The men and the boys.* Berkeley: University of California Press.

Dowling, C. (2000). *The frailty myth.* New York: Random House.

Estioko-Griffin, A., & Griffin, P. B. (2001). Woman the hunter: The Agta. In C. Brettell & C. Sargent (Eds.), *Gender in cross-cultural perspective* (3rd ed., pp. 238–239). Upper Saddle River, NJ: Prentice Hall.

Fausto-Sterling, A. (1993, March–April). The five sexes: Why male and female are not enough. *The Sciences,* pp. 20–24.

Fausto-Sterling, A. (2000). *Sexing the body: Gender politics and the construction of sexuality.* New York: Basic Books.

Fujimora, J. H. (2006). Sex genes: A critical sociomaterial approach to the politics and molecular genetics of sex determination. *Signs, 32*(1), 49–81.

Glick, P., & Fiske, S. T. (1999). Gender, power dynamics, and social interaction. In M. Ferree, J. Lorber, & B. Hess (Eds.), *Revisioning gender* (pp. 365–398). Thousand Oaks, CA: Sage.

Grabham, E. (2007). Citizen bodies, intersex citizenship. *Sexualities, 10*(29), 28–29.

Hewlett, B. S. (2001). The cultural nexus of Aka father-infant bonding. In C. Brettell & C. Sargent (Eds.), *Gender in cross-cultural perspective* (3rd ed., pp. 45–46). Upper Saddle River, NJ: Prentice Hall.

Kimmel, M. S. (2000). *The gendered society.* New York: Oxford University Press.

Lont, C. M. (2001). The influence of the media on gender images. In D. Vannoy (Ed.), *Gender mosaics* (pp. 114–122). Los Angeles: Roxbury.

Lorber, J. (1994). *Paradoxes of gender.* New Haven, CT: Yale University Press.

Lorber, J., & Moore, L. J. (2007). *Gendered bodies.* Los Angeles: Roxbury.

Lucal, B. (2008). Building boxes and policing boundaries: (De)constructing intersexuality, transgender and bisexuality. *Sociology Compass, 2*(2), 519–536.

Miller, D. I., Eagly, A. H., & Linn. M. C. (2014, October 20). Women's representation in science predicts national gender-science stereotypes: Evidence from 66 nations. *Journal of Educational Psychology.* Advance online publication. Retrieved from http://dx.doi.org/10.1037/edu0000005

O'Brien, J. (1999). *Social prisms: Reflections on the everyday myths and paradoxes.* Thousand Oaks, CA: Pine Forge Press.

Pfeffer, C. (2014). "I don't like passing as a straight woman": Queer negotiations of identity and social group membership. *American Journal of Sociology, 120*(1), 1–44.

Ridgeway, C. L., & Correll, S. J. (2004). Unpacking the gender system: A theoretical perspective on gender beliefs and social relations. *Gender & Society, 18*(4), 510–531.

Schilt, K. (2010). *Just one of the guys? Transgender men and the persistence of gender inequality.* Chicago: University of Chicago Press.

Schilt, K., & Westbrook, L. (2009). Doing gender, doing heteronormativity: "Gender normals," transgender people, and the social maintenance of heterosexuality. *Gender & Society, 23*(4), 440–464.

Shields, S., Garner, D., Di Leone, B., & Hadley, A. (2006). Gender and emotion. In J. Stets & J. Turner (Eds.), *Handbook of the sociology of emotions* (pp. 63–83). New York: Springer.

Snyder, K. (2015). The abrasiveness trap: High-achieving men and women are described differently in reviews. *Fortune.* Retrieved from http://fortune.com/2014/08/26/performance-review-gender-bias/

Sørensen, M. L. S. (2000). *Gender archaeology.* Cambridge, UK: Polity Press.

Steinberg, R. J. (2001). How sex gets into your paycheck and how to get it out: The gender gap in pay and comparable worth. In D. Vannoy (Ed.), *Gender mosaics.* Los Angeles: Roxbury.

Tavris, C. (1992). *The mismeasure of woman.* New York: Simon & Schuster.

Van Ausdale, D., & Feagin, J. R. (2001). *The first R: How children learn race and racism.* Lanham, MD: Rowman & Littlefield.

Verma, S. C. (2009, October). Amazing Tharu women: Empowered and in control. *Intersections: Gender and Sexuality in Asia and the Pacific, 22.*

Retrieved from http://intersections.anu.edu.au/issue22/verma.htm

Vespa, J. (2009). Gender ideology construction: A life course and intersectional approach. *Gender & Society, 23*(3), 363–387.

Wharton, A. S. (2005). *The sociology of gender.* Malden, MA: Blackwell.

Yoder, J. D. (2003). *Women and gender: Transforming psychology.* Upper Saddle River, NJ: Prentice Hall.

Introduction to Reading 1

Barbara Risman is a sociologist who has made significant contributions to research and writing on gender in heterosexual American families. In this article, she argues that we need to conceptualize gender as a social structure so we can better analyze the ways gender is embedded in the individual, interactional, and institutional dimensions of social life. You will want to pay special attention to Table 1.1, in which Risman summarizes social processes that create gender in each dimension.

1. Why does Risman include the individual dimension of social life in her theory of gender as a social structure?

2. What are the benefits of a multidimensional structural model of gender?

3. Define the concept "trading power for patronage," and discuss at least two examples from your experience or observations of heterosexual relationships.

GENDER AS A SOCIAL STRUCTURE

THEORY WRESTLING WITH ACTIVISM

Barbara J. Risman

In this article, I briefly summarize my . . . argument that gender should be conceptualized as a social structure (Risman 1998) and extend it with an attempt to classify the mechanisms that help produce gendered outcomes within each dimension of the social structure.

GENDER AS SOCIAL STRUCTURE

With this theory of *gender as a social structure,* I offer a conceptual framework, a scheme to organize the confusing, almost limitless, ways in which gender has come to be defined in contemporary social science. Four distinct social scientific theoretical traditions have developed to explain gender. The first tradition focuses on how individual sex differences originate, whether biological (Udry 2000) or social in origin (Bem 1993). The second tradition . . . emerged as a reaction to the first and focuses on how the social structure (as opposed to biology or individual learning) creates gendered behavior. The third tradition, also a reaction to the individualist thinking of the first, emphasizes social interaction and accountability to others' expectations, with a focus on how "doing gender" creates and reproduces inequality (West and Zimmerman 1987). The sex-differences literature, the doing gender interactional analyses, and the structural perspectives have been portrayed as incompatible in my own early writings as well as in that of others (Epstein 1988; Ferree 1990; Kanter 1977; Risman 1987; Risman and Schwartz 1989). England and Browne (1992) argued persuasively that this incompatibility is an illusion: All structural theories must make assumptions about individuals, and individualist theories must make presumptions about external social control. While we do gender in every social interaction, it seems naive to ignore the gendered selves and cognitive schemas that children develop as they become cultural natives in a patriarchal world (Bem 1993). The more recent integrative approaches (Connell 2002; Ferree, Lorber, and Hess 1999; Lorber 1994; Risman 1998) treat gender as a socially constructed stratification system. This article fits squarely in the current integrative tradition.

Lorber (1994) argued that gender is an institution that is embedded in all the social processes of everyday life and social organizations. She further argued that gender difference is primarily a means to justify sexual stratification. Gender is so endemic because unless we see difference, we cannot justify inequality. I share this presumption that the creation of difference is the very foundation on which inequality rests.

I build on this notion of gender as an institution but find the institutional language distracting. The word "institution" is too commonly used to refer to particular aspects of society, for example, the family as an institution or corporations as institutions. My notion of gender structure meets the criteria offered by Martin (forthcoming). . . . While the language we use may differ, our goals are complementary, as we seek to situate gender as embedded not only in individuals but throughout social life (Patricia Martin, personal communication).

I prefer to define gender as a social structure because this brings gender to the same analytic plane as politics and economics, where the focus has long been on political and economic structures. While the language of structure suits my purposes, it is not ideal because despite ubiquitous usage in sociological discourse, no definition of the term "structure" is widely shared. Smelser (1988) suggested that all structuralists share the presumption that social structures exist outside individual desires or motives and that social structures at least partially explain human action. Beyond that, consensus dissipates. Blau (1977) focused solely on the constraint collective life imposes on the individual. Structure must be conceptualized, in his view, as a force opposing individual motivation. Structural concepts must be observable, external to the individual, and independent of individual motivation. This definition of "structure" imposes a clear dualism between structure and action, with structure as constraint and action as choice.

Constraint is, of course, an important function of structure, but to focus only on structure as constraint minimizes its importance. Not only are women and men coerced into differential social roles; they often choose their gendered paths. A social structural analysis must help us understand how and why actors choose one alternative over another. A structural theory of action (e.g., Burt 1982) suggests that actors compare themselves and their options to those in structurally similar positions. From this viewpoint, actors are purposive, rationally seeking to maximize their self-perceived well-being under social-structural constraints. As Burt

(1982) suggested, one can assume that actors choose the best alternatives without presuming they have either enough information to do it well or the options available to make choices that effectively serve their own interests. For example, married women may choose to do considerably more than their equitable share of child care rather than have their children do without whatever "good enough" parenting means to them if they see no likely alternative that the children's father will pick up the slack.

While actions are a function of interests, the ability to choose is patterned by the social structure. Burt (1982) suggested that norms develop when actors occupy similar network positions in the social structure and evaluate their own options vis-à-vis the alternatives of similarly situated others. From such comparisons, both norms and feelings of relative deprivation or advantage evolve. The social structure as the context of daily life creates action indirectly by shaping actors' perceptions of their interests and directly by constraining choice. Notice the phrase "similarly situated others" above. As long as women and men see themselves as different kinds of people, then women will be unlikely to compare their life options to those of men. Therein lies the power of gender. In a world where sexual anatomy is used to dichotomize human beings into types, the differentiation itself diffuses both claims to and expectations for gender equality. The social structure is not experienced as oppressive if men and women do not see themselves as similarly situated.

While structural perspectives have been applied to gender in the past (Epstein 1988; Kanter 1977), there has been a fundamental flaw in these applications. Generic structural theories applied to gender presume that if women and men were to experience identical structural conditions and role expectations, empirically observable gender differences would disappear. But this ignores not only internalized gender at the individual level . . . but the cultural inter-actional expectations that remain attached to women and men because of their gender category. A structural perspective on gender is accurate

only if we realize that gender itself is a structure deeply embedded in society.

Giddens's (1984) structuration theory adds considerably more depth to this analysis of gender as a social structure with his emphasis on the recursive relationship between social structure and individuals. That is, social structures shape individuals, but simultaneously, individuals shape the social structure. Giddens embraced the transformative power of human action. He insisted that any structural theory must be concerned with reflexivity and actors' interpretations of their own lives. Social structures not only act on people; people act on social structures. Indeed, social structures are created not by mysterious forces but by human action. When people act on structure, they do so for their own reasons. We must, therefore, be concerned with why actors choose their acts. Giddens insisted that concern with meaning must go beyond the verbal justification easily available from actors because so much of social life is routine and so taken for granted that actors will not articulate, or even consider, why they act.

This nonreflexive habituated action is what I refer to as the cultural component of the social structure: The taken for granted or cognitive image rules that belong to the situational context (not only or necessarily to the actor's personality). The cultural component of the social structure includes the interactional expectations that each of us meet in every social encounter. My aims are to bring women and men back into a structural theory where gender is the structure under analysis and to identify when behavior is habit (an enactment of taken for granted gendered cultural norms) and when we do gender consciously, with intent, rebellion, or even with irony. When are we doing gender and re-creating inequality without intent? And what happens to interactional dynamics and male-dominated institutions when we rebel? Can we refuse to do gender or is rebellion simply doing gender differently, forging alternative masculinities and femininities?

Connell (1987) applied Giddens's (1984) concern with social structure as both constraint and created by action in his treatise on gender and power (see particularly chapter 5). In his analysis, structure constrains action, yet "since human action involves free invention . . . and is reflexive, practice can be turned against what constrains it; so structure can deliberately be the object of practice" (Connell 1987, 95). Action may turn against structure but can never escape it.

A theory of gender as a social structure must integrate this notion of causality as recursive with attention to gender consequences at multiple levels of analysis. Gender is deeply embedded as a basis for stratification not just in our personalities, our cultural rules, or institutions but in all these, and in complicated ways. The gender structure differentiates opportunities and constraints based on sex category and thus has consequences on three dimensions: (1) at the individual level, for the development of gendered selves; (2) during interaction as men and women face different cultural expectations even when they fill the identical structural positions; and (3) in institutional domains where explicit regulations regarding resource distribution and material goods are gender specific.

Advantages to Gender Structure Theory

This schema advances our understanding of gender in several ways. First, this theoretical model imposes some order on the encyclopedic research findings that have developed to explain gender inequality. Thinking of each research question as one piece of a jigsaw puzzle, being able to identify how one set of findings coordinates with others even when the dependent variables or contexts of interest are distinct, furthers our ability to build a cumulative science. Gender as a social structure is enormously complex. Full attention to the web of interconnection between gendered selves, the cultural expectations that help explain interactional patterns, and institutional regulations allows each research tradition to explore the growth of their own trees while remaining cognizant of the forest.

A second contribution of this approach is that it leaves behind the modernist warfare version of

science, wherein theories are pitted against one another, with a winner and a loser in every contest. In the past, much energy . . . was devoted to testing which theory best explained gender inequality and by implication to discounting every alternative possibility.[1] Theory building that depends on theory slaying presumes parsimony is always desirable, as if this complicated world of ours were best described with simplistic mono-causal explanations. While parsimony and theory testing were the model for the twentieth-century science, a more postmodern science should attempt to find complicated and integrative theories (Collins 1998). The conceptualization of gender as a social structure is my contribution to complicating, but hopefully enriching, social theory about gender.

A third benefit to this multidimensional structural model is that it allows us to seriously investigate the direction and strength of causal relationships between gendered phenomena on each dimension. We can try to identify the site where change occurs and at which level of analysis the ability of agentic women and men seem able at this, historical moment, to effectively reject habitualized gender routines. For example, we can empirically investigate the relationship between gendered selves and doing gender without accepting simplistic unidirectional arguments for inequality presumed to be either about identities or cultural ideology. It is quite possible, indeed likely, that socialized femininity does help explain why we do gender, but doing gender to meet others' expectations, surely, over time, helps construct our gendered selves. Furthermore, gendered institutions depend on our willingness to do gender, and when we rebel, we can sometimes change the institutions themselves. I have used the language of dimensions interchangeably with the language of levels because when we think of gender as a social structure, we must move away from privileging any particular dimension as higher than another. How social change occurs is an empirical question, not an a priori theoretical assumption. It may be that individuals struggling to change their own identities (as in consciousness-raising groups of the early second-wave women's movement) eventually bring their new selves to social interaction and create new cultural expectations. For example, as women come to see themselves (or are socialized to see themselves) as sexual actors, the expectations that men must work to provide orgasms for their female partners becomes part of the cultural norm. But this is surely not the only way social change can happen. When social movement activists name as inequality what has heretofore been considered natural (e.g., women's segregation into low-paying jobs), they can create organizational changes such as career ladders between women's quasi-administrative jobs and actual management, opening up opportunities that otherwise would have remained closed, thus creating change on the institutional dimension. Girls raised in the next generation, who know opportunities exist in these workplaces, may have an altered sense of possibilities and therefore of themselves. We need, however, to also study change and equality when it occurs rather than only documenting inequality.

Perhaps the most important feature of this conceptual schema is its dynamism. No one dimension determines the other. Change is fluid and reverberates throughout the structure dynamically. Changes in individual identities and moral accountability may change interactional expectations, but the opposite is possible as well. Change cultural expectations, and individual identities are shaped differently. Institutional changes must result from individuals or group action, yet such change is difficult, as institutions exist across time and space. Once institutional changes occur, they reverberate at the level of cultural expectations and perhaps even on identities. And the cycle of change continues. No mechanistic predictions are possible because human beings sometimes reject the structure itself and, by doing so, change it.

Social Processes Located by Dimension in the Gender Structure

When we conceptualize gender as a social structure, we can begin to identify under what conditions and how gender inequality is being produced within each dimension. The "how" is important because without knowing the mechanisms, we cannot intervene. If indeed gender inequality in the division of household labor at this historical moment were primarily explained (and I do not suggest that it is) by gendered selves, then we would do well to consider the most effective socialization mechanisms to create fewer gender-schematic children and resocialization for adults. If, however, the gendered division of household labor is primarily constrained today by cultural expectations and moral accountability, it is those cultural images we must work to alter. But then again, if the reason many men do not equitably do their share of family labor is that men's jobs are organized so they cannot succeed at work and do their share at home, it is the contemporary American workplace that must change (Williams 2000). We may never find a universal theoretical explanation for the gendered division of household labor because universal social laws may be an illusion of twentieth-century empiricism. But in any given moment for any particular setting, the causal processes should be identifiable empirically. Gender complexity goes beyond historical specificity, as the particular causal processes that constrain men and women to do gender may be strong in one institutional setting (e.g., at home) and weaker in another (e.g., at work).

The forces that create gender traditionalism for men and women may vary across space as well as time. Conceptualizing gender as a social structure contributes to a more postmodern, contextually specific social science. We can use this schema to begin to organize thinking about the causal processes that are most likely to be effective on each dimension. When we are concerned with the means by which individuals come to have a preference to do gender, we should focus on how identities are constructed through early childhood development, explicit socialization, modeling, and adult experiences, paying close attention to the internalization of social mores. To the extent that women and men choose to do gender-typical behavior cross-situationally and over time, we must focus on such individual explanations. Indeed, much attention has already been given to gender socialization and the individualist presumptions for gender. The earliest and perhaps most commonly referred to explanations in popular culture depend on sex-role training, teaching boys and girls their culturally appropriate roles. But when trying to understand gender on the interactional/cultural dimension, the means by which status differences shape expectations and the ways in which in-group and out-group membership influences behavior need to be at the center of attention. Too little attention has been paid to how inequality is shaped by such cultural expectations during interaction. I return to this in the section below. On the institutional dimension, we look to law, organizational practices, and formal regulations that distinguish by sex category. Much progress has been made in the post–civil rights era with rewriting formal laws and organizational practices to ensure gender neutrality. Unfortunately, we have often found that despite changes in gender socialization and gender neutrality on the institutional dimension, gender stratification remains.

What I have attempted to do here is to offer a conceptual organizing scheme for the study of gender that can help us to understand gender in all its complexity and try to isolate the social processes that create gender in each dimension. Table 1.1 provides a schematic outline of this argument.[2]

Cultural Expectations During Interaction and the Stalled Revolution

In *Gender Vertigo* (Risman 1998), I suggested that at this moment in history, gender inequality between partners in American heterosexual couples could be attributed particularly to the interactional expectations at the cultural level: the differential expectations attached to being a mother and father, a husband and wife. Here, I extend this argument in two ways. First, I propose that the stalled gender revolution in other settings can similarly be traced to the interactional/cultural dimension of the social structure. Even when women and men with feminist identities work in organizations with formally gender-neutral rules, gender inequality is reproduced during everyday interaction. The cultural expectations attached to our sex category, simply being identified as a woman or man, has remained relatively impervious to the feminist forces that have problematized sexist socialization practices and legal discrimination. I discuss some of those processes that can help explain why social interaction continues to reproduce inequality, even in settings that seem ripe for social change.

Contemporary social psychological writings offer us a glimpse of possibilities for understanding how inequality is reconstituted in daily interaction. Ridgeway and her colleagues (Ridgeway 1991, 1997, 2001; Ridgeway and Correll 2000; Ridgeway and Smith-Lovin 1999) showed that

Table 1.1 Dimensions of Gender Structure, by Illustrative Social Processes[a]

	Dimensions of the Gender Structure		
	Individual Level	*Interactional Cultural Expectations*	*Institutional Domain*
Social Processes	Socialization Internalization Identity work Construction of selves	Status expectations Cognitive bias Othering Trading power for patronage Altercasting	Organizational practices Legal regulations Distribution of resources Ideology

[a]These are examples of social processes that may help explain the gender structure on each dimension. They are meant to be illustrative and not a complete list of all possible social processes or causal mechanisms.

the status expectations attached to gender and race categories are cross-situational. These expectations can be thought of as one of the engines that re-create inequality even in new settings where there is no other reason to expect male privilege to otherwise emerge. In a sexist and racist society, women and all persons of color are expected to have less to contribute to task performances than are white men, unless they have some other externally validated source of prestige. Status expectations create a cognitive bias toward privileging those of already high status. What produces status distinction, however, is culturally and historically variable. Thus, cognitive bias is one of the causal mechanisms that help to explain the reproduction of gender and race inequality in everyday life. It may also be an important explanation for the reproduction of class and heterosexist inequality in everyday life as well, but that is an empirical question.

Schwalbe and his colleagues (2000, 419) suggested that there are other "generic interactive processes through which inequalities are created and reproduced in everyday life." Some of these processes include othering, subordinate adaptation, boundary maintenance, and emotion management. Schwalbe and his colleagues suggested that subordinates' adaptation plays an essential role in their own disadvantage. Subordinate adaptation helps to explain women's strategy to adapt to the gender structure. Perhaps the most common adaptation of women to subordination is "trading power for patronage" (Schwalbe et al. 2000, 426). Women, as wives and daughters, often derive significant compensatory benefits from relationships with the men in their families. Stombler and Martin (1994) similarly showed how little sisters in a fraternity trade affiliation for secondary status. In yet another setting, elite country clubs, Sherwood (2004) showed how women accept subordinate status as "B" members of clubs, in exchange for men's approval, and how when a few wives challenge men's privilege, they are threatened with social ostracism, as are their husbands. Women often gain the economic benefits of patronage for themselves and their children in exchange for their subordinate status.

One can hardly analyze the cultural expectations and interactional processes that construct gender inequality without attention to the actions of members of the dominant group. We must pay close attention to what men do to preserve their power and privilege. Schwalbe and his colleagues (2000) suggested that one process involved is when superordinate groups effectively "other" those who they want to define as subordinate, creating devalued statuses and expectations for them. Men effectively do this in subversive ways through "politeness" norms, which construct women as "others" in need of special favors, such as protection. By opening doors and walking closer to the dirty street, men construct women as an "other" category, different and less than independent autonomous men. The cultural significance attached to male bodies signifies the capacity to dominate, to control, and to elicit deference, and such expectations are perhaps at the core of what it means for men to do gender (Michael Schwalbe, personal communication).

These are only some of the processes that might be identified for understanding how we create gender inequality based on embodied cultural expectations. None are determinative causal predictors, but instead, these are possible leads to reasonable and testable hypotheses about the production of gender. . . .

NOTES

1. See Scott (1997) for a critique of feminists who adopt a strategy where theories have to be simplified, compared, and defeated. She too suggested a model where feminists build on the complexity of each other's ideas.

2. I thank my colleague Donald Tomaskovic-Devey for suggesting the visual representation of these ideas as well as his usual advice on my ideas as they develop.

REFERENCES

Bem, Sandra. 1993. *The lenses of gender.* New Haven, CT: Yale University Press.

Blau, Peter. 1977. *Inequality and heterogeneity.* New York: Free Press.

Burt, Ronald S. 1982. *Toward a structural theory of action.* New York: Academic Press.

Collins, Patricia Hill. 1998. *Fighting words: Black women and the search for justice.* Minneapolis: University of Minnesota Press.

Connell, R. W. 1987. *Gender and power: Society, the person, and sexual politics.* Stanford, CA: Stanford University Press.

———. 2002. *Gender: Short introductions.* Malden, MA: Blackwell.

England, Paula, and Irene Browne. 1992. Internalization and constraint in women's subordination. *Current Perspectives in Social Theory* 12:97–123.

Epstein, Cynthia Fuchs. 1988. *Deceptive distinctions: Sex, gender, and the social order.* New Haven, CT: Yale University Press.

Ferree, Myra Marx. 1990. Beyond separate spheres: Feminism and family research. *Journal of Marriage and the Family* 53(4): 866–84.

Giddens, Anthony. 1984. *The constitution of society: Outline of the theory of structuration.* Berkeley: University of California Press.

Kanter, Rosabeth. 1977. *Men and women of the corporation.* New York: Basic Books.

Lorber, Judith. 1994. *Paradoxes of gender.* New Haven, CT: Yale University Press.

Martin, Patricia. Forthcoming. Gender as a social institution. In *Social Forces,* edited by Kristen A. Myers, Cynthia D. Anderson, and Barbara J. Risman, 1998. *Feminist foundations: Toward transforming society.* Thousand Oaks, CA: Sage.

Ridgeway, Cecilia L. 1991. The social construction of status value: Gender and other nominal characteristics. *Social Forces* 70(2): 367–86.

———. 1997. Interaction and the conservation of gender inequality: Considering employment. *American Sociological Review* 62(2): 218–35.

———. 2001. Gender, status, and leadership. *Journal of Social Issues* 57(4): 637–55.

Ridgeway, Cecilia L., and Shelley J. Correll. 2000. Limiting inequality through interaction: The end(s) of gender. *Contemporary Sociology* 29:110–20.

Ridgeway, Cecilia L., and Lynn Smith-Lovin. 1999. The gender system and interaction. *Annual Review of Sociology* 25:191–216.

Risman, Barbara J. 1983. Necessity and the invention of mothering. Ph.D. diss., University of Washington.

———. 1987. Intimate relationships from a micro-structural perspective: Mothering men. *Gender & Society* 1: 6–32.

———. 1998. *Gender vertigo: American families in transition.* New Haven, CT: Yale University Press.

Risman, Barbara J., and Pepper Schwartz. 1989. *Gender in intimate relationships.* Belmont, CA: Wadsworth.

Schwalbe, Michael, Sandra Godwin, Daphne Holden, Douglas Schrock, Shealy Thompson, and Michele Wolkomir. 2000. Generic processes in the reproduction of inequality: An interactionist analysis. *Social Forces* 79(2): 419–52.

Scott, Joan Wallach. 1997. Comment on Hawkesworth's "Confounding Gender." *Signs: Journal of Women in Culture and Society* 22(3): 697–702.

Sherwood, Jessica. 2004. Talk about country clubs: Ideology and the reproduction of privilege. Ph.D. diss., North Carolina State University.

Smelser, Neil J. 1988. Social structure. In *Handbook of sociology,* edited by Neil J. Smelser. Beverly Hills, CA: Sage.

Stombler, Mindy, and Patricia Yancey Martin. 1994. Bring women in, keeping women down: Fraternity "little sister" organizations. *Journal of Contemporary Ethnography* 23:150–84.

Udry, J. Richard. 2000. Biological limits of gender construction. *American Sociological Review* 65: 443–57.

West, Candace, and Don Zimmerman. 1987. Doing gender. *Gender & Society* 1:125–51.

Williams, Joan. 2000. *Unbending gender: Why family and work conflict and what to do about it.* New York: Oxford University Press.

Introduction to Reading 2

By analyzing the challenges she faces in the course of her daily experience of negotiating the boundaries of our gendered society, sociologist Betsy Lucal describes the rigidity of the American binary gender system and the consequences for people who do not fit. Since her physical appearance does not clearly define her as a woman, she must navigate a world in which some people interact with her as though she is a man. Through analysis of her own story, Lucal demonstrates how gender is something we do, rather than something we are.

1. Why does Lucal argue that we cannot escape "doing gender"?

2. How does Lucal negotiate "not fitting" into the American two-and-only-two gender structure?

3. Have you ever experienced a mismatch between your gender identity and the gender that others perceive you to be? If so, how did you feel and respond?

What It Means to Be Gendered Me

Betsy Lucal

I understood the concept of "doing gender" (West and Zimmerman 1987) long before I became a sociologist. I have been living with the consequences of inappropriate "gender display" (Goffman 1976; West and Zimmerman 1987) for as long as I can remember. My daily experiences are a testament to the rigidity of gender in our society, to the real implications of "two and only two" when it comes to sex and gender categories (Garfinkel 1967; Kessler and McKenna 1978). Each day, I experience the consequences that our gender system has for my identity and interactions. I am a woman who has been called "Sir" so many times that I no longer even hesitate to assume that it is being directed at me. I am a woman whose use of public rest rooms regularly causes reactions ranging from confused stares to confrontations over what a man is doing in the women's room. I regularly enact a variety of practices either to minimize the need for others to know my gender or to deal with their misattributions.

I am the embodiment of Lorber's (1994) ostensibly paradoxical assertion that the "gender bending" I engage in actually might serve to preserve and perpetuate gender categories. As a feminist who sees gender rebellion as a significant part of her contribution to the dismantling of sexism, I find this possibility disheartening.

In this article, I examine how my experiences both support and contradict Lorber's (1994) argument using my own experiences to illustrate and reflect on the social construction of gender. My analysis offers a discussion of the consequences of gender for people who do not follow the rules as well as an examination of the possible implications of the existence of people like me for the gender system itself. Ultimately, I show how life on the boundaries of gender affects me and how my life, and the lives of others who make similar decisions about their participation in the gender system, has the potential to subvert gender.

Because this article analyzes my experiences as a woman who often is mistaken for a man, my focus is on the social construction of gender for women. My assumption is that, given the gendered nature of the gendering process itself, men's experiences of this phenomenon might well be different from women's.

From Lucal, Betsy, "What It Means to Be Gendered Me." *Gender & Society, 13*(6), p. 781. Copyright © 1999. Sage Publications.

THE SOCIAL CONSTRUCTION OF GENDER

It is now widely accepted that gender is a social construction, that sex and gender are distinct, and that gender is something all of us "do." This conceptualization of gender can be traced to Garfinkel's (1967) ethnomethodological study of "Agnes."[1] In this analysis, Garfinkel examined the issues facing a male who wished to pass as, and eventually become, a woman. Unlike individuals who perform gender in culturally expected ways, Agnes could not take her gender for granted and always was in danger of failing to pass as a woman (Zimmerman 1992).

This approach was extended by Kessler and McKenna (1978) and codified in the classic "Doing Gender" by West and Zimmerman (1987). The social constructionist approach has been developed most notably by Lorber (1994, 1996). Similar theoretical strains have developed outside of sociology, such as work by Butler (1990) and Weston (1996). . . .

Given our cultural rules for identifying gender (i.e., that there are only two and that masculinity is assumed in the absence of evidence to the contrary), a person who does not do gender appropriately is placed not into a third category but rather into the one with which her or his gender display seems most closely to fit; that is, if a man appears to be a woman, then he will be categorized as "woman," not as something else. Even if a person does not want to do gender or would like to do a gender other than the two recognized by our society, other people will, in effect, do gender for that person by placing her or him in one and only one of the two available categories. We cannot escape doing gender or, more specifically, doing one of two genders. (There are exceptions in limited contexts such as people doing "drag" [Butler 1990; Lorber 1994].)

People who follow the norms of gender can take their genders for granted. Kessler and McKenna asserted, "Few people besides transsexuals think of their gender as anything other than 'naturally' obvious"; they believe that the risks of not being taken for the gender intended "are minimal for nontranssexuals" (1978, 126).

However, such an assertion overlooks the experiences of people such as those women Devor (1989) calls "gender blenders" and those people Lorber (1994) refers to as "gender benders." As West and Zimmerman (1987) pointed out, we all are held accountable for, and might be called on to account for, our genders.

People who, for whatever reasons, do not adhere to the rules, risk gender misattribution and any interactional consequences that might result from this misidentification. What are the consequences of misattribution for social interaction? When must misattribution be minimized? What will one do to minimize such mistakes? In this article, I explore these and related questions using my biography.

For me, the social processes and structures of gender mean that, in the context of our culture, my appearance will be read as masculine. Given the common conflation of sex and gender, I will be assumed to be a male. Because of the two-and-only-two genders rule, I will be classified, perhaps more often than not, as a man—not as an atypical woman, not as a genderless person. I must be one gender or the other; I cannot be neither, nor can I be both. This norm has a variety of mundane and serious consequences for my everyday existence. Like Myhre (1995), I have found that the choice not to participate in femininity is not one made frivolously.

My experiences as a woman who does not do femininity illustrate a paradox of our two-and-only-two gender system. Lorber argued that "bending gender rules and passing between genders does not erode but rather preserves gender boundaries" (1994, 21). Although people who engage in these behaviors and appearances do "demonstrate the social constructedness of sex, sexuality, and gender" (Lorber 1994, 96), they do not actually disrupt gender. Devor made a similar point: "When gender blending females refused to mark themselves by publicly displaying sufficient femininity to be recognized as women, they were in no way challenging patriarchal gender assumptions" (1989, 142). As the following discussion shows, I have found that my own experiences both support and challenge this argument. Before detailing these experiences, I explain my use of my self as data.

MY SELF AS DATA

This analysis is based on my experiences as a person whose appearance and gender/sex are not, in the eyes of many people, congruent. How did my experiences become my data? I began my research "unwittingly" (Krieger 1991). This article is a product of "opportunistic research" in that I am using my "unique biography, life experiences, and/or situational familiarity to understand and explain social life" (Riemer 1988, 121; see also Riemer 1977). It is an analysis of "unplanned personal experience," that is, experiences that were not part of a research project but instead are part of my daily encounters (Reinharz 1992).

This work also is, at least to some extent, an example of Richardson's (1994) notion of writing as a method of inquiry. As a sociologist who specializes in gender, the more I learned, the more I realized that my life could serve as a case study. As I examined my experiences, I found out things—about my experiences and about theory—that I did not know when I started (Richardson 1994).

It also is useful, I think, to consider my analysis an application of Mills's (1959) "sociological imagination." Mills (1959) and Berger (1963) wrote about the importance of seeing the general in the particular. This means that general social patterns can be discerned in the behaviors of particular individuals. In this article, I am examining portions of my biography, situated in U.S. society during the 1990s, to understand the "personal troubles" my gender produces in the context of a two-and-only-two gender system. I am not attempting to generalize my experiences; rather, I am trying to use them to examine and reflect on the processes and structure of gender in our society.

Because my analysis is based on my memories and perceptions of events, it is limited by my ability to recall events and by my interpretation of those events. However, I am not claiming that my experiences provide the truth about gender and how it works. I am claiming that the biography of a person who lives on the margins of our gender system can provide theoretical insights into the processes and social structure of gender. Therefore, after describing my experiences, I examine how they illustrate and extend, as well as contradict, other work on the social construction of gender.

GENDERED ME

Each day, I negotiate the boundaries of gender. Each day, I face the possibility that someone will attribute the "wrong" gender to me based on my physical appearance. I am six feet tall and large-boned. I have had short hair for most of my life. For the past several years, I have worn a crew cut or flat top. I do not shave or otherwise remove hair from my body (e.g., no eyebrow plucking). I do not wear dresses, skirts, high heels, or makeup. My only jewelry is a class ring, a "men's" watch (my wrists are too large for a "women's" watch), two small earrings (gold hoops, both in my left ear), and (occasionally) a necklace. I wear jeans or shorts, T-shirts, sweaters, polo/golf shirts, button-down collar shirts, and tennis shoes or boots. The jeans are "women's" (I do have hips) but do not look particularly "feminine." The rest of the outer garments are from men's departments. I prefer baggy clothes, so the fact that I have "womanly" breasts often is not obvious (I do not wear a bra).

Sometimes, I wear a baseball cap or some other type of hat. I also am white and relatively young (30 years old).[2] My gender display—what others interpret as my presented identity—regularly leads to the misattribution of my gender. An incongruity exists between my gender self-identity and the gender that others perceive. In my encounters with people I do not know, I sometimes conclude, based on our interactions, that they think I am a man. This does not mean that other people do not think I am a man, just that I have no way of knowing what they think without interacting with them.

Living With It

I have no illusions or delusions about my appearance. I know that my appearance is likely to be read as "masculine" (and male) and that how I see myself is socially irrelevant. Given our two-and-only-two gender structure, I must live with the consequences of my appearance. These consequences fall into two categories: issues of identity and issues of interaction.

My most common experience is being called "Sir" or being referred to by some other masculine linguistic marker (e.g., "he," "man"). This has happened for years, for as long as I can remember, when having encounters with people I do not know.[3] Once, in fact, the same worker at a fast-food restaurant called me "Ma'am" when she took my order and "Sir" when she gave it to me.

Using my credit cards sometimes is a challenge. Some clerks subtly indicate their disbelief, looking from the card to me and back at the card and checking my signature carefully. Others challenge my use of the card, asking whose it is or demanding identification. One cashier asked to see my driver's license and then asked me whether I was the son of the cardholder. Another clerk told me that my signature on the receipt "had better match" the one on the card. Presumably, this was her way of letting me know that she was not convinced it was my credit card.

My identity as a woman also is called into question when I try to use women-only spaces. Encounters in public rest rooms are an adventure. I have been told countless times that "This is the ladies' room." Other women say nothing to me, but their stares and conversations with others let me know what they think. I will hear them say, for example, "There was a man in there." I also get stares when I enter a locker room. However, it seems that women are less concerned about my presence, there, perhaps because, given that it is a space for changing clothes, showering, and so forth, they will be able to

make sure that I am really a woman. Dressing rooms in department stores also are problematic spaces. I remember shopping with my sister once and being offered a chair outside the room when I began to accompany her into the dressing room. Women who believe that I am a man do not want me in women-only spaces. For example, one woman would not enter the rest room until I came out, and others have told me that I am in the wrong place. They also might not want to encounter me while they are alone. For example, seeing me walking at night when they are alone might be scary.[4]

I, on the other hand, am not afraid to walk alone, day or night. I do not worry that I will be subjected to the public harassment that many women endure (Gardner 1995). I am not a clear target for a potential rapist. I rely on the fact that a potential attacker would not want to attack a big man by mistake. This is not to say that men never are attacked, just that they are not viewed, and often do not view themselves, as being vulnerable to attack.

Being perceived as a man has made me privy to male-male interactional styles of which most women are not aware. I found out, quite by accident, that many men greet, or acknowledge, people (mostly other men) who make eye contact with them with a single nod. For example, I found that when I walked down the halls of my brother's all-male dormitory making eye contact, men nodded their greetings at me. Oddly enough, these same men did not greet my brother.

I had to tell him about making eye contact and nodding as a greeting ritual. Apparently, in this case I was doing masculinity better than he was! I also believe that I am treated differently, for example, in auto parts stores (staffed almost exclusively by men in most cases) because of the assumption that I am a man. Workers there assume that I know what I need and that my questions are legitimate requests for information.

I suspect that I am treated more fairly than a feminine-appearing woman would be. I have not been able to test this proposition. However, Devor's participants did report "being treated more respectfully" (1989, 132) in such situations.

There is, however, a negative side to being assumed to be a man by other men. Once, a friend and I were driving in her car when a man failed to stop at an intersection and nearly crashed into us. As we drove away, I mouthed "stop sign" to him. When we both stopped our cars at the next intersection, he got out of his car and came up to the passenger side of the car, where I was sitting. He yelled obscenities at us and pounded and spit on the car window. Luckily, the windows were closed. I do not think he would have done that if he thought I was a woman. This was the first time I realized that one of the implications of being seen as a man was that I might be called on to defend myself from physical aggression from other men who felt challenged by me. This was a sobering and somewhat frightening thought.

Recently, I was verbally accosted by an older man who did not like where I had parked my car. As I walked down the street to work, he shouted that I should park at the university rather than on a side street nearby. I responded that it was a public street and that I could park there if I chose. He continued to yell, but the only thing I caught was the last part of what he said: "Your tires are going to get cut!" Based on my appearance that day—I was dressed casually and carrying a backpack, and I had my hat on backward—I believe he thought that I was a young male student rather than a female professor. I do not think he would have yelled at a person he thought to be a woman—and perhaps especially not a woman professor.

Given the presumption of heterosexuality that is part of our system of gender, my interactions with women who assume that I am a man also can be viewed from that perspective. For example, once my brother and I were shopping when we were "hit on" by two young women. The encounter ended before I realized what had happened. It was only when we walked away that I told him that I was pretty certain that they had thought both of us were men. A more common experience is realizing that when I am seen in public with one of my women friends, we are likely to be read as a heterosexual dyad. It is likely that if I were to walk through a shopping mall holding hands with a woman, no one would look twice, not because of their open-mindedness toward lesbian couples but rather because of their assumption that I was the male half of a straight couple. Recently, when walking through a mall with a friend and her infant, my observations of others' responses to us led me to believe that many of them assumed that we were a family on an outing, that is, that I was her partner and the father of the child.

Dealing With It

Although I now accept that being mistaken for a man will be a part of my life so long as I choose not to participate in femininity, there have been times when I consciously have tried to appear more feminine. I did this for a while when I was an undergraduate and again recently when I was on the academic job market. The first time, I let my hair grow nearly down to my shoulders and had it permed. I also grew long fingernails and wore nail polish. Much to my chagrin, even then one of my professors, who did not know my name, insistently referred to me in his kinship examples as "the son." Perhaps my first act on the way to my current stance was to point out to this man, politely and after class, that I was a woman.

More recently, I again let my hair grow out for several months, although I did not alter other aspects of my appearance. Once my hair was about two and a half inches long (from its original quarter inch), I realized, based on my encounters with strangers, that I had more or less passed back into the category of "woman." Then, when I returned to wearing a flat top, people again responded to me as if I were a man.

Because of my appearance, much of my negotiation of interactions with strangers involves attempts to anticipate their reactions to me. I need to assess whether they will be likely to assume that I am a man and whether that actually matters in the context of our encounters. Many times, my gender really is irrelevant, and it is just annoying to be misidentified. Other times, particularly when my appearance is coupled with something that identifies me by name (e.g., a check or credit card) without a photo, I might need to do something to ensure that my identity is not questioned. As a result of my experiences, I have developed some techniques to deal with gender misattribution.

In general, in unfamiliar public places, I avoid using the rest room because I know that it is a place where there is a high likelihood of misattribution and where misattribution is socially important. If I must use a public rest room, I try to make myself look as nonthreatening as possible. I do not wear a hat, and I try to rearrange my clothing to make my breasts more obvious. Here, I am trying to use my secondary sex characteristics to make my gender more obvious rather than the usual use of gender to make sex obvious. While in the rest room, I never make eye contact, and I get in and out as quickly as possible. Going in with a woman friend also is helpful; her presence legitimizes my own. People are less likely to think I am entering a space where I do not belong when I am with someone who looks like she does belong.[5]

To those women who verbally challenge my presence in the rest room, I reply, "I know," usually in an annoyed tone. When they stare or talk about me to the women they are with, I simply get out as quickly as possible. In general, I do not wait for someone I am with because there is too much chance of an unpleasant encounter.

I stopped trying on clothes before purchasing them a few years ago because my presence in the changing areas was met with stares and whispers. Exceptions are stores where the dressing rooms are completely private, where there are individual stalls rather than a room with stalls separated by curtains, or where business is slow and no one else is trying on clothes. If I am trying on a garment clearly intended for a woman, then I usually can do so without hassle. I guess the attendants assume that I must be a woman if I have, for example, a women's bathing suit in my hand. But usually, I think it is easier for me to try the clothes on at home and return them, if necessary, rather than risk creating a scene. Similarly, when I am with another woman who is trying on clothes, I just wait outside.

My strategy with credit cards and checks is to anticipate wariness on a clerk's part. When I sense that there is some doubt or when they challenge me, I say, "It's my card." I generally respond courteously to requests for photo ID, realizing that these might be routine checks because of concerns about increasingly widespread fraud. But for the clerk who asked for ID and still did not think it was my card, I had a stronger reaction. When she said that she was sorry for embarrassing me, I told her that I was not embarrassed but that she should be. I also am particularly careful to make sure that my signature is consistent with the back of the card. Faced with such situations, I feel somewhat nervous about signing my name—which, of course, makes me worry that my signature will look different from how it should.

Another strategy I have been experimenting with is wearing nail polish in the dark bright colors currently fashionable. I try to do this when I travel by plane. Given more stringent travel regulations, one always must present a photo ID. But my experiences have shown that my driver's license is not necessarily convincing. Nail polish might be. I also flash my polished nails when I enter airport rest rooms, hoping that they will provide a clue that I am indeed in the right place.

There are other cases in which the issues are less those of identity than of all the norms of interaction that, in our society, are gendered. My most common response to misattribution actually is to appear to ignore it, that is, to go on with the interaction as if nothing out of the ordinary has happened. Unless I feel that there is a good reason to establish my correct gender, I assume the identity others impose on me for the sake of smooth interaction. For example, if someone is selling me a movie ticket, then there is no reason to make sure that the person has accurately discerned my gender. Similarly, if it is clear that the person using "Sir" is talking to me, then I simply respond as appropriate. I accept the designation because it is irrelevant to the situation. It takes enough effort to be alert for misattributions and to decide which of them matter; responding to each one would take more energy than it is worth.

Sometimes, if our interaction involves conversation, my first verbal response is enough to let the other person know that I am actually a woman and not a man. My voice apparently is "feminine" enough to shift people's attributions to the other category. I know when this has happened by the apologies that usually accompany the mistake. I usually respond to the apologies by saying something like "No problem" and/or "It happens all the time." Sometimes, a misattributor will offer an account for the mistake, for example, saying that it was my hair or that they were not being very observant.

These experiences with gender and misattribution provide some theoretical insights into contemporary Western understandings of gender and into the social structure of gender in contemporary society. Although there are a number of ways in which my experiences confirm the work of others, there also are some ways in which my experiences suggest other interpretations and conclusions.

What Does It Mean?

Gender is pervasive in our society. I cannot choose not to participate in it. Even if I try not to do gender, other people will do it for me. That is, given our two-and-only-two rule, they must attribute one of two genders to me. Still, although I cannot choose not to participate in gender, I can choose not to participate in femininity (as I have), at least with respect to physical appearance. That is where the problems begin. Without the decorations of femininity, I do not look like a woman. That is, I do not look like what many people's commonsense understanding of gender tells them a woman looks like. How I see myself, even how I might wish others would see me, is socially irrelevant. It is the gender that I appear to be (my "perceived gender") that is most relevant to my social identity and interactions with others. The major consequence of this fact is that I must be continually aware of which gender I "give off" as well as which gender I "give" (Goffman 1959).

Because my gender self-identity is "not displayed obviously, immediately, and consistently" (Devor 1989, 58), I am somewhat of a failure in social terms with respect to gender. Causing people to be uncertain or wrong about one's gender is a violation of taken-for-granted rules that leads to embarrassment and discomfort; it means that something has gone wrong with the interaction (Garfinkel 1967; Kessler and McKenna 1978). This means that my non-response to misattribution is the more socially appropriate response; I am allowing others to maintain face (Goffman 1959, 1967). By not calling attention to their mistakes, I uphold their images of themselves as competent social actors. I also maintain my own image as competent by letting them assume that I am the gender I appear to them to be.

But I still have discreditable status; I carry a stigma (Goffman 1963). Because I have failed to participate appropriately in the creation of meaning with respect to gender (Devor 1989), I can be called on to account for my appearance. If discredited, I show myself to be an incompetent social actor. I am the one not following the rules, and I will pay the price for not providing people with the appropriate cues for placing me in the gender category to which I really belong.

I do think that it is, in many cases, safer to be read as a man than as some sort of deviant woman. "Man" is an acceptable category; it fits properly into people's gender worldview. Passing as a man often is "the path of least resistance" (Devor 1989; Johnson 1997). For example, in situations where gender does not matter, letting people take me as a man is easier than correcting them.

Conversely, as Butler noted, "We regularly punish those who fail to do their gender right" (1990, 140). Feinberg maintained, "Masculine girls and women face terrible condemnation and brutality—including sexual violence—for crossing the boundary of what is 'acceptable' female expression" (1996, 114). People are more likely to harass me when they perceive me to be a woman who looks like a man. For example, when a group of teenagers realized that I was not a man because one of their mothers identified me correctly, they began to make derogatory comments when I passed them. One asked, for example, "Does she have a penis?"

Because of the assumption that a "masculine" woman is a lesbian, there is the risk of homophobic reactions (Gardner 1995; Lucal 1997). Perhaps surprisingly, I find that I am much more likely to be taken for a man than for a lesbian, at least based on my interactions with people and their reactions to me. This might be because people are less likely to reveal that they have taken me for a lesbian because it is less relevant to an encounter or because they believe this would be unacceptable. But I think it is more likely a product of the strength of our two-and-only-two system. I give enough masculine cues that I am seen not as a deviant woman but rather as a man, at least in most cases. The problem seems not to be that people are uncertain about my gender, which might lead them to conclude that I was a lesbian once they realized I was a woman. Rather, I seem to fit easily into a gender category—just not the one with which I identify. In fact, because men represent the dominant gender in our society, being mistaken for a man can protect me from other types of gendered harassment. Because men can move around in public spaces safely (at least relative to women), a "masculine" woman also can enjoy this freedom (Devor 1989).

On the other hand, my use of particular spaces—those designated as for women only—may be challenged. Feinberg provided an intriguing analysis of the public rest room experience. She characterized women's reactions to a masculine person in a public rest room as "an example of genderphobia" (1996, 117), viewing such women as policing gender boundaries rather than believing that there really is a man in the women's rest room. She argued that women who truly believed that there was a man in their midst would react differently. Although this is an interesting perspective on her experiences, my experiences do not lead to the same conclusion.[6]

Enough people have said to me that "This is the ladies' room" or have said to their companions that "There was a man in there" that I take

their reactions at face value. Still, if the two-and-only-two gender system is to be maintained, participants must be involved in policing the categories and their attendant identities and spaces. Even if policing boundaries is not explicitly intended, boundary maintenance is the effect of such responses to people's gender displays.

Boundaries and margins are an important component of both my experiences of gender and our theoretical understanding of gendering processes. I am in effect both woman and not woman. As a woman who often is a social man but who also is a woman living in a patriarchal society, I am in a unique position to see and act.

I sometimes receive privileges usually limited to men, and I sometimes am oppressed by my status as a deviant woman. I am, in a sense, an outsider within (Collins 1991). Positioned on the boundaries of gender categories, I have developed a consciousness that I hope will prove transformative (Anzaldúa 1987). In fact, one of the reasons why I decided to continue my non-participation in femininity was that my sociological training suggested that this could be one of my contributions to the eventual dismantling of patriarchal gender constructs. It would be my way of making the personal political. I accepted being taken for a man as the price I would pay to help subvert patriarchy. I believed that all of the inconveniences I was enduring meant that I actually was doing something to bring down the gender structures that entangled all of us.

Then, I read Lorber's (1994) *Paradoxes of Gender* and found out, much to my dismay, that I might not actually be challenging gender after all. Because of the way in which doing gender works in our two-and-only-two system, gender displays are simply read as evidence of one of the two categories. Therefore, gender bending, blending, and passing between the categories do not question the categories themselves. If one's social gender and personal (true) gender do not correspond, then this is irrelevant unless someone notices the lack of congruence.

This reality brings me to a paradox of my experiences. First, not only do others assume that I am one gender or the other, but I also insist that I *really am* a member of one of the two gender categories. That is, I am female; I self-identify as a woman. I do not claim to be some other gender or to have no gender at all. I simply place myself in the wrong category according to stereotypes and cultural standards; the gender I present, or that some people perceive me to be presenting, is inconsistent with the gender with which I identify myself as well as with the gender I could be "proven" to be. Socially, I display the wrong gender; personally, I identify as the proper gender.

Second, although I ultimately would like to see the destruction of our current gender structure, I am not to the point of personally abandoning gender. Right now, I do not want people to see me as genderless as much as I want them to see me as a woman. That is, I would like to expand the category of "woman" to include people like me. I, too, am deeply embedded in our gender system, even though I do not play by many of its rules. For me, as for most people in our society, gender is a substantial part of my personal identity (Howard and Hollander 1997). Socially, the problem is that I do not present a gender display that is consistently read as feminine. In fact, I consciously do not participate in the trappings of femininity. However, I do identify myself as a woman, not as a man or as someone outside of the two-and-only-two categories.

Yet, I do believe, as Lorber (1994) does, that the purpose of gender, as it currently is constructed, is to oppress women. Lorber analyzed gender as a "process of creating distinguishable social statuses for the assignment of rights and responsibilities" that ends up putting women in a devalued and oppressed position (1994, 32). As Martin put it, "Bodies that clearly delineate gender status facilitate the maintenance of the gender hierarchy" (1998, 495).

For society, gender means difference (Lorber 1994). The erosion of the boundaries would problematize that structure. Therefore, for gender to operate as it currently does, the category "woman" is expanded to include people like me. The maintenance of the gender structure is dependent on the creation of a few categories that are mutually exclusive, the members of which are as different as possible (Lorber 1994). It is the clarity of the boundaries between the categories that allows gender to be used to assign rights and responsibilities as well as resources and rewards.

It is that part of gender—what it is used for—that is most problematic. Indeed, is it not *patriarchal*—or, even more specifically, *heteropatriarchal*—constructions of gender that are actually the problem? It is not the differences between men and women, or the categories themselves, so much as the meanings ascribed to the categories and, even more important, the hierarchical nature of gender under patriarchy that is the problem (Johnson 1997). Therefore, I am rebelling not against my femaleness or even my womanhood; instead, I am protesting contemporary constructions of femininity and, at least indirectly, masculinity under patriarchy. We do not, in fact, know what gender would look like if it were not constructed around heterosexuality in the context of patriarchy. Although it is possible that the end of patriarchy would mean the end of gender, it is at least conceivable that something like what we now call gender could exist in a postpatriarchal future. The two-and-only-two categorization might well disappear, there being no hierarchy for it to justify. But I do not think that we should make the assumption that gender and patriarchy are synonymous.

Theoretically, this analysis points to some similarities and differences between the work of Lorber (1994) and the works of Butler (1990), Goffman (1976, 1977), and West and Zimmerman (1987). Lorber (1994) conceptualized gender as social structure, whereas the others focused more on the interactive and processual nature of gender. Butler (1990) and Goffman (1976, 1977) view gender as a performance, and West and Zimmerman (1987) examined it as something all of us do. One result of this difference in approach is that in Lorber's (1994) work, gender comes across as something that we are caught in, something that, despite any attempts to the contrary, we cannot break out of. This conclusion is particularly apparent in Lorber's argument that gender rebellion, in the context of our two-and-only-two system, ends up supporting what it purports to subvert. Yet, my own experiences suggest an alternative possibility that is more in line with the view of gender offered by West and Zimmerman (1987): If gender is a product of interaction, and if it is produced in a particular context, then it can be changed if we change our performances. However, the effects of a performance linger, and gender ends up being institutionalized. It is institutionalized, in our society, in a way that perpetuates inequality, as Lorber's (1994) work shows. So, it seems that a combination of these two approaches is needed.

In fact, Lorber's (1994) work seems to suggest that effective gender rebellion requires a more blatant approach—bearded men in dresses, perhaps, or more active responses to misattribution. For example, if I corrected every person who called me "Sir," and if I insisted on my right to be addressed appropriately and granted access to women-only spaces, then perhaps I could start to break down gender norms. If I asserted my right to use public facilities without being harassed, and if I challenged each person who gave me "the look," then perhaps I would be contributing to the demise of gender as we know it. It seems that the key would be to provide visible evidence of the nonmutual exclusivity of the categories. Would *this* break down the patriarchal components of gender? Perhaps it would, but it also would be exhausting.

Perhaps there is another possibility. In a recent book, *The Gender Knot,* Johnson (1997) argued that when it comes to gender and patriarchy, most of us follow the paths of least resistance; we "go along to get along," allowing our actions to be shaped by the gender system. Collectively, our actions help patriarchy maintain and perpetuate a system of oppression and privilege. Thus, by withdrawing our support from this system by choosing paths of greater resistance, we can start to chip away at it. Many people participate in gender because they cannot imagine any alternatives. In my classroom, and in my interactions and encounters with strangers, my presence can make it difficult for people not to see that there *are* other paths. In other words, following from West and Zimmerman (1987), I can subvert gender by doing it differently.

For example, I think it is true that my existence does not have an effect on strangers who assume that I am a man and never learn otherwise. For them, I do uphold the two-and-only-two system. But there are other cases in which my existence can have an effect. For example, when people initially take me for a man but then find out that I actually am a woman, at least for that moment, the naturalness of gender may be called into question. In these cases, my presence can provoke a "category crisis" (Garber 1992, 16) because it challenges the sex/gender binary system.

The subversive potential of my gender might be strongest in my classrooms. When I teach about the sociology of gender, my students can see me as the embodiment of the social construction of gender. Not all of my students have transformative experiences as a result of taking a course with me; there is the chance that some of them see me as a "freak" or as an exception. Still, after listening to stories about my experiences with gender and reading literature on the subject, many students begin to see how and why gender is a social product. I can disentangle sex, gender, and sexuality in the contemporary United States for them. Students can begin to see the connection between biographical experiences and the structure of society. As one of my students noted, I clearly live the material I am teaching. If that helps me to get my point across, then perhaps I am subverting the binary gender system after all. Although my gendered presence and my way of doing gender might make others—and sometimes even me—uncomfortable, no one ever said that dismantling patriarchy was going to be easy.

Notes

1. Ethnomethodology has been described as "the study of commonsense practical reasoning" (Collins 1988, 274). It examines how people make sense of their everyday experiences. Ethnomethodology is particularly useful in studying gender because it helps to uncover the assumptions on which our understandings of sex and gender are based.

2. I obviously have left much out by not examining my gendered experiences in the context of race, age, class, sexuality, region, and so forth. Such a project clearly is more complex. As Weston pointed out, gender presentations are complicated by other statuses of their presenters: "What it takes to kick a person over into another gendered category can differ with race, class, religion, and time" (1996, 168). Furthermore, I am well aware that my whiteness allows me to assume that my experiences are simply a product of gender (see, e.g., hooks 1981; Lucal 1996; Spelman 1988; West and Fenstermaker 1995). For now, suffice it to say that it is my privileged position on some of these axes and my more disadvantaged position on others that combine to delineate my overall experience.

3. In fact, such experiences are not always limited to encounters with strangers. My grandmother, who does not see me often, twice has mistaken me for either my brother-in-law or some unknown man.

4. My experiences in rest rooms and other public spaces might be very different if I were, say, African American rather than white. Given the stereotypes of African American men, I think that white women would react very differently to encountering me (see, e.g., Staples [1986] 1993).

5. I also have noticed that there are certain types of rest rooms in which I will not be verbally challenged; the higher the social status of the place, the less likely I will be harassed. For example, when I go to the theater, I might get stared at, but my presence never has been challenged.

6. An anonymous reviewer offered one possible explanation for this. Women see women's rest rooms as their space; they feel safe, and even empowered, there. Instead of fearing men in such space, they might instead pose a threat to any man who might intrude. Their invulnerability in this situation is, of course, not physically based but rather socially constructed. I thank the reviewer for this suggestion.

References

Anzaldúa, G. 1987. *Borderlands/La Frontera.* San Francisco: Aunt Lute Books.

Berger, P. 1963. *Invitation to sociology.* New York: Anchor.

Butler, J. 1990. *Gender trouble.* New York: Routledge.

Collins, P. H. 1991. *Black feminist thought.* New York: Routledge.

Collins, R. 1988. *Theoretical sociology.* San Diego: Harcourt Brace Jovanovich.

Devor, H. 1989. *Gender blending: Confronting the limits of duality.* Bloomington: Indiana University Press.

Feinberg, L. 1996. *Transgender warriors.* Boston: Beacon.

Garber, M. 1992. *Vested interests: Cross-dressing and cultural anxiety.* New York: HarperPerennial.

Gardner, C. B. 1995. *Passing by: Gender and public harassment.* Berkeley: University of California.

Garfinkel, H. 1967. *Studies in ethnomethodology.* Englewood Cliffs, NJ: Prentice Hall.

Goffman, E. 1959. *The presentation of self in everyday life.* Garden City, NY: Doubleday.

———. 1963. *Stigma.* Englewood Cliffs, NJ: Prentice Hall.

———. 1967. *Interaction ritual.* New York: Anchor/Doubleday.

———. 1976. Gender display. *Studies in the Anthropology of Visual Communication* 3:69–77.

———. 1977. The arrangement between the sexes. *Theory and Society* 4:301–31.

hooks, b. 1981. *Ain't I a woman: Black women and feminism.* Boston: South End Press.

Howard, J. A., and J. Hollander. 1997. *Gendered situations, gendered selves.* Thousand Oaks, CA: Sage.

Johnson, A. G. 1997. *The gender knot: Unraveling our patriarchal legacy.* Philadelphia: Temple University Press.

Kessler, S. J., and W. McKenna. 1978. *Gender: An ethnomethodological approach.* New York: John Wiley.

Krieger, S. 1991. *Social science and the self.* New Brunswick, NJ: Rutgers University Press.

Lorber, J. 1994. *Paradoxes of gender.* New Haven, CT: Yale University Press.

———. 1996. Beyond the binaries: Depolarizing the categories of sex, sexuality, and gender. *Sociological Inquiry* 66:143–59.

Lucal, B. 1996. Oppression and privilege: Toward a relational conceptualization of race. *Teaching Sociology* 24:245–55.

———. 1997. "Hey, this is the ladies' room!": Gender misattribution and public harassment. *Perspectives on Social Problems* 9:43–57.

Martin, K. A. 1998. Becoming a gendered body: Practices of preschools. *American Sociological Review* 63:494–511.

Mills, C. W. 1959. *The sociological imagination.* London: Oxford University Press.

Myhre, J. R. M. 1995. One bad hair day too many, or the hairstory of an androgynous young feminist. In *Listen up: Voices from the next feminist generation,* edited by B. Findlen. Seattle, WA: Seal Press.

Reinharz, S. 1992. *Feminist methods in social research.* New York: Oxford University Press.

Richardson, L. 1994. Writing: A method of inquiry. In *Handbook of qualitative research,* edited by N. K. Denzin and Y. S. Lincoln. Thousand Oaks, CA: Sage.

Riemer, J. W. 1977. Varieties of opportunistic research. *Urban Life* 5:467–77.

———. 1988. Work and self. In *Personal sociology,* edited by P. C. Higgins and J. M. Johnson. New York: Praeger.

Spelman, E. V. 1988. *Inessential woman: Problems of exclusion in feminist thought.* Boston: Beacon.

Staples, B. 1993. Just walk on by. In *Experiencing race, class, and gender in the United States,* edited by V. Cyrus. Mountain View, CA: Mayfield. (Originally published 1986)

West, C., and S. Fenstermaker. 1995. Doing difference. *Gender & Society* 9:8–37.

West, C., and D. H. Zimmerman. 1987. Doing gender. *Gender & Society* 1:125–51.

Zimmerman, D. H. 1992. They were all doing gender, but they weren't all passing: Comment on Rogers. *Gender & Society* 6:192–98.

Introduction to Reading 3

Sociologists Georgiann Davis and Sharon Preves are at the cutting-edge of intersex theory and activism. In this reading, they bring their deep understanding together to explore what intersex is and how intersex advocacy emerged and developed in the United States. Intersex is a natural physical variation occurring in approximately 1 of every 2,000 births worldwide. The majority of intersex traits are not harmful. However, in the United States, intersex has been medicalized and intersex people have commonly been subjected to dangerous "normalization" surgeries and treatments in an effort on the part of medical providers to fit intersex bodies into the two-and-only-two sexes (female or male) binary. The intersex rights movement began in the late 1980s to challenge the medical establishment and has rapidly grown into a global movement. Davis and Preves detail the struggles of intersex advocates to challenge the ethics of normalization surgeries and, on a broader scale, to unsettle the sex binary itself.

1. How does the reality of intersex demonstrate the flaws of binary thinking about sex?

2. What is the terminology debate, and why is the language of intersex important?

3. What is the relationship between the intersex rights movement and other movements for gender and sexual equality?

REFLECTING ON INTERSEX

25 YEARS OF ACTIVISM, MOBILIZATION, AND CHANGE

Georgiann Davis and Sharon Preves

INTRODUCTION: THE SOCIAL CONSTRUCTION OF INTERSEX AS A MEDICAL PROBLEM

"A pregnancy test?" I, Georgiann Davis, was so confused. Before the medical scheduler would even agree to arrange the endocrinology consultation that my primary care provider had requested, she insisted that I needed a slew of lab work—eleven orders to be exact: progesterone, leutinizing hormone, prolactin, testosterone, free T4, vitamin D 1,25-dihydroxy, phosphorus, estradiol, glycohemoglobin, TSH ultra-sensitive, and serum qualitative pregnancy. I asked the medical scheduler again, but this time with obvious frustration: "Why a pregnancy test? That makes no sense. I can't get pregnant." Apologetically the medical scheduler explained that the endocrinologist required the results of my pregnancy test before even allowing her to schedule a consultation. While a pregnancy test might seem like a harmless and routine test for a medical provider to require of a thirty-four-year-old woman seeking an endocrinology consultation, I'm not your average woman. You might be thinking that I am trans,* but I'm not. I'm an intersex queer woman and a sociologist who studies intersex. I'm also the 2014–2015 president of the AIS-DSD Support Group, one of the largest intersex support groups in the world.[1] I was born with complete androgen insensitivity syndrome (CAIS), an intersex trait that was diagnosed in the mid-1990s. I later learned the mid-1990s was also the same point in history when the intersex rights movement was in its infancy in the United States. I have XY chromosomes and a vagina but no uterus. I had testes, but they were removed when I was a teenager. My parents agreed to this medically unnecessary surgery because my medical providers suggested that doing so would minimize my risk of cancer—a claim that is not empirically supported (Nakhal et al. 2013). Pregnancy is biologically impossible in my body, so the pregnancy test made no sense. I find my experiences with medical care, then and now, unnecessarily frustrating and humiliating, which leaves me asking, with a mentor, colleague, and friend, sociologist Sharon Preves, how much has intersex medical care, and the advocacy that seeks to critically examine and disrupt it, changed over the past twenty-five years, and how much has it stayed the same?[2]

Intersex is a natural physical variation occurring in approximately 1 of every 2,000 births worldwide. The term *intersex* represents the "I" in the acronym LGBTI and refers to the diversity in physical sex development that differs from typical female or male anatomy. The "LGB" in the acronym LGBTI refers to lesbian, gay, or bisexual sexual identities, and the "T" stands for transgender or transsexual (often abbreviated as "T*"), which relates specifically to one's sense of gender identity and gender expression as feminine or masculine in a way that is not congruent with their biological female or male sex at birth. The current medical model of surgically and hormonally "correcting" intersex variations emerged primarily from the work of Johns Hopkins University psychologist John Money in the mid-1950s.

Intersex terminology emerged in the late nineteenth century and was used not only when referring to hermaphrodites, the more popular pre-twentieth-century term for intersex people, but to homosexuals as well (Epstein 1990). Today, the term *hermaphrodite* is considered derogatory by many, although not all, people with intersex traits. The term *intersex*, and its derivatives, including intersex traits, intersex conditions, and the like, is still widely used and accepted by intersex people and their families. However, as we explain later, *intersex* was renamed a *disorder of sex development* throughout the medical community at the beginning of the twenty-first century, which has caused terminological tensions in the intersex community.

In contemporary Western societies, it is commonly understood that biological sex, which comprises chromosomes, hormones, gonads, external genitalia, and internal reproductive structures, is a simple two-category phenomenon that is naturally correlated with our gender identity. Men have penises, testes, and XY chromosomes while women have vaginas, ovaries, uteruses, and XX chromosomes. However, sex is anything but simple and one's biological sex isn't always correlated with their gender or sexual identity. For example, many people with CAIS, Georgiann included, are born with an outward female appearance, and most live their lives as women. They have vaginas, yet they also have undescended testes and XY chromosomes. Women with CAIS do not have a uterus. None of this, however, would be obvious without invasive exploratory surgeries or the power of medical technologies, such as imaging and chromosome testing, which reveal such complexities of biological sex. CAIS is only one example of an intersex trait. In fact, there are more than twenty different documented types of intersex traits. Hypospadias, for example, is an intersex trait in which the urethral opening of the penis is located along the base or shaft of the penis rather than at the tip. Some intersex traits result in externally ambiguous genitalia, but others, like CAIS or minor hypospadias, do not.

Hypospadias is quite common and has been increasing in frequency in recent decades, occurring in an estimated 1 of every 250 male births (Baskin 2012; Holmes 2011). Surgery to "correct" the position of the urethral opening to facilitate standing during urination is very common, as many medical providers view the ability to stand while urinating as central to masculine identity and social acceptance by one's peers. Note that many men with hypospadias do not identify as intersex and that historically men lived full lives with hypospadias prior to the invention of surgical "repair." Men with hypospadias often experience ongoing problems following hypospadias "repair" surgery, such as frequent urinary tract infections, narrowing of the urethral canal due to the buildup of scar tissue, and painful urination. Chronic complications resulting from surgeries to "correct" the position of the urethra are common—so common, in fact, that doctors coined the term *hypospadias cripple* to describe patients who experience ongoing and debilitating surgically induced complications (Craig et al. 2014).

Although the majority of intersex traits are not physiologically harmful, the birth of an intersex baby is often viewed as a medical emergency (see Davis and Murphy 2013; Preves 2003), a rather predictable response given that childbirth is medicalized throughout the Western world, especially in the United States where, more often than not, babies are born in hospitals under the care of medical doctors and nurses whose task is to ensure the safe delivery of a healthy baby. The issue here is that intersex traits rarely pose health concerns. Yet, because intersex bodies are viewed as unhealthy because they deviate from social expectations of what male and female bodies, especially genitalia, ought to look like, medical providers are quick to recommend and perform urgent surgical and hormonal "correction" (Davis and Murphy 2013; Preves 2003). Because childbirth occurs in a medical setting, the response to any "deviance" in a newborn's body is medical. Intersex "deviance" is medically "normalized" by surgical and hormonal interventions to create cosmetically typical female or male bodies.

Prior to the twentieth century, medical providers did not have the tools, for example surgical expertise and chromosomal testing, that they have now to "fix" intersex bodies. As Geertje Mak (2012) notes in a study of nineteenth-century hermaphrodite case histories, rather than attempt to biologically capture or prove an individual's sex, medical providers understood sex as embedded within the social, moral, and legal fabric of the individual's community through the type of occupation one held (or eventually held), the clothes one wore (or chose to wear when the individual was able to independently make such choices), and the social relationships one maintained. Sex was regarded as a social location and not a physical bodily phenomenon.

Medical advances of the twentieth century offered providers the tools to subject intersex people to "normalization" surgeries (Reis 2009; also see Warren 2014 for a discussion of an eighteenth-century surgery). These procedures are designed to "normalize" intersex bodies by erasing evidence of any sex difference that challenges a sex/gender binary. For instance, medical providers often recommend that people with CAIS undergo a gonadectomy, like Georgiann did, to remove their internal testes. Although providers justify these recommendations by claiming that removal of internal testes reduces the risk of testicular cancer, these claims are not empirically supported (Nakhal et al. 2013). Instead, as we and others have argued elsewhere, such "normalization" surgeries are not medically necessary but rather are recommended by medical practitioners in order to uphold a sex/gender binary that insists, for example, that women should not have testes (Davis 2015; Feder 2014; Holmes 2008; Karkazis 2008; Preves 2003; Reis 2009). This insistence on enforcing a sex/gender binary in the face of obvious and consistent sex/gender diversity is no doubt related to an overarching social system in which heterosexuality is deemed normative. If sexual identity were not a concern, diversity of sex development (in the case of intersex) or of gender identity (in the case of trans*) would be of far less concern to medical providers and others.

In the late 1980s and early 1990s, people with intersex traits began organizing to challenge the medically unnecessary interventions providers were performing on intersex babies and children to shoehorn intersex people into the male/female sex binary, planting the seeds of a global intersex rights movement (see Preves 2005). Such "social surgeries" were first conducted on intersex infants and children as early as the nineteenth century, if not before (see Warren 2014). Initially, as we describe in detail later, intersex activists engaged in confrontational mobilization strategies that involved public protests at medical conferences and media appearances where they shared their horrific experiences of medical trauma, notably stories about their diagnosis and the medically unnecessary and irreversible interventions they were subjected to as children. Today, intersex advocacy has shifted to a more collaborative model to promote social change; that is, a mobilization strategy where at least some intersex activists are collaborating with medical allies to bring about change in intersex medical care. This strategy of working within medicine to promote change occurs more frequently in the United States than in other countries, where it is more often than not contested as a viable strategy for changing intersex medical care.

Georgiann and Sharon have come together to write this piece as a critical reflection on intersex that explores the past, present, and potential future of U.S. intersex advocacy. We focus specifically on intersex advocacy in the United States because that is where our expertise resides. The questions we explore in this reflection are why and how did intersex advocacy come to be? In what ways is intersex advocacy different today than it was in the past? In what ways is it similar? And how might the visibility of intersex in mainstream youth media affect the lives of the next generation of intersex people?

THE RISE OF THE INTERSEX RIGHTS MOVEMENT: CHALLENGING THE MEDICAL TREATMENT OF INTERSEX, 1993–2003

Intersex is a relatively new area of sociocultural inquiry. Outside of medicine, relatively few people have studied intersex, in part due to the fact intersex people were rather invisible until the global intersex rights movement was formed toward the end of the twentieth century. One reason for this invisibility is that when providers told people that they were intersexed, and they often did not, they also typically informed them that their anatomical differences were extremely rare and that they were unlikely to ever meet another person with a similar anatomical trait. Providers commonly withheld the intersex diagnosis from their patients, lying to them to allegedly protect their gender identity development (i.e., how young children develop a sense of self as feminine or masculine). Medical providers encouraged their patients' parents to do the same, an experience Georgiann knows firsthand. When Georgiann was a teenager, she had surgery to remove what she was told by her providers and parents were precancerous, underdeveloped ovaries. In actuality, as mentioned earlier, providers removed her internal testes for a medically unnecessary reason: to ensure that a girl didn't have testes. Georgiann's testes were producing the majority of her body's sex hormones. By removing them, providers left her dependent on synthetic hormone replacement therapy for the rest of her life to replace what her testes were already producing naturally. These hormones are essential to prevent people from developing osteoporosis or other potentially debilitating physical ailments.

Intersex medicalization gained the attention of feminist scholars in the early 1990s. For example, in a 1993 article titled "The Five Sexes: Why Male and Female Are Not Enough," biologist Anne Fausto-Sterling refuted the widely accepted assumption that sex was a simple two-category phenomenon consisting only of "females" and "males." If we are going to categorize people into sex categories, Fausto-Sterling maintained in a tongue-to-cheek tone, then we must expand the sex binary to include true-hermaphrodites, male pseudo-hermaphrodites, and female pseudo-hermaphrodites. Social psychologist Suzanne Kessler (1998) further warned that the expansion of biological sex to five categories wouldn't suffice, for it rested on the assumption that people's sex could indeed be categorized. Rather than expand the available sex categories, Kessler argued for the recognition of the diversity of sex development. Later, in 2000, Fausto-Sterling accepted Kessler's critique in a piece she titled "The Five Sexes, Revisited."

By the early 2000s, Sharon was well on her way to documenting how intersex people were treated by medical providers and, more generally, how they live with their intersex traits. It was 1993 when Sharon was a first-year medical sociology doctoral student at the University of California, San Francisco, when she was assigned Fausto-Sterling's "Five Sexes" article in a Gender and Science seminar. She was simultaneously enrolled in a seminar on Medicine and the Family that semester for which she began a literature review to explore how parents made sex assignment and gender rearing decisions when their children were born intersex. What she found was a complete lack of discussion of this topic, or of intersex at all, in the sociology, social work, and psychology literature. When she extended her research to the medical literature, Sharon was shocked to find numerous reports of surgical sex assignment on seemingly healthy infants and children. These reports focused on the physical, rather than the psychosocial, outcomes of medical intervention, and many of them contained disturbing, grainy black and white photos of children's genitals or full naked bodies with their eyes blocked out (in an apparent attempt to protect their identities). Curiously, the majority of these publications didn't report long-term longitudinal follow-up with the patients about their gender and sexual identities or any quality-of-life measures; they were primarily limited to preadolescent reports. It was these alienating photographs coupled with a complete lack of quality-of-life outcomes that compelled Sharon to search further for the voices and stories behind these photos. She decided to document the experiences of intersex adults, including their long-term quality of life and psychosocial health. As a result of her systematic sociological analysis, Sharon produced a number of publications, including her book *Intersex and Identity: The Contested Self* (2003). This book provided the very first in-depth account of intersex experiences. It was in *Intersex and Identity* that we learned that contemporary intersex people felt isolated and stigmatized by medical providers—feelings that were minimized when these same people were able to connect with others who were intersex to offer peer support. We also learned that intersex people felt physically and emotionally harmed by the irreversible intersex "normalization" interventions of early surgery, ongoing examinations, and hormone treatments.

Although a handful of intersex people and their parents were connecting through support groups in the 1980s, the U.S. intersex community truly emerged in the early 1990s after Bo Laurent, using the pseudonym Cheryl Chase to protect her identity, founded the Intersex Society of North America (ISNA). Chase founded ISNA by publishing a letter to the editor of the journal *The Sciences* (Chase 1993). She wrote this letter in direct response to Fausto-Sterling's article "The Five Sexes." In her letter, Chase critiqued intersex medical sex assignment as destructive, raising concerns about the ethics and effectiveness of surgical procedures that impair sexual and psychological function. In the last line of her letter, Chase noted her affiliation with ISNA, an organization she fabricated in that very letter to increase her legitimacy. In her signature line, Chase listed a mailing address for ISNA at a San Francisco post office box. Much to her surprise, she soon began receiving mail from intersex people around the world and decided to form the Intersex Society of North America in earnest.

ISNA published the first issue of its newsletter, cleverly titled *Hermaphrodites with Attitude,* in the winter of 1994 (Intersex Society of North America 1994). By the time this first issue was published, ISNA had already established a mailing list that included recipients in fourteen of the United States and five countries. The political content of the publication, and the organization itself, worked to transform intersex, including the word *hermaphrodite,* from being a source of shame into a source of pride and empowerment. In other words, intersex activists were reclaiming intersex and hermaphrodite terminologies. The newsletter consisted primarily of personal stories, essays, poetry, and humor, providing formerly isolated individuals with the means to connect with others who had similar experiences. *Hermaphrodites with Attitude* was published from 1994 to 1999.

In addition to its newsletter, ISNA also provided support groups, a popular website, and annual retreats. Early on, ISNA's mission was divided between providing peer support to its members and its objective of medical reform. While other intersex organizations chose to address the mission of support as their primary focus, ISNA ultimately decided to pursue social change. The political action of ISNA members alienated them from some other intersex people and groups.

ISNA made deliberate appeals to queer activists, press outlets, and medical organizations, framing intersex as an issue of gender and sexuality. Lesbian, gay, bisexual, and transgender activist organizations, both in and outside of medicine, could easily relate to intersex grievances of stigma, shame, and alienation. At the same time, aligning intersex issues with sexual or gender minorities compromised intersex activists' ability to establish credibility with the non-LGBT medical mainstream, who viewed heterosexual normalcy as one of the primary objectives of intersex medical sex assignment.

In September 1996, former U.S. House Representative Patricia Schroeder's (D. Colorado) anti–female genital mutilation (FGM) bill became law. This law banned genital cutting on girls under the age of 18 in the United States except in cases where "health" demands its necessity, thus allowing for intersex "emergencies" to be exempt. Press coverage of this law included a front-page article in the *New York Times*. Chase and other members of ISNA were outraged by the law's complicit endorsement of intersex genital surgeries. They began to stage protests to draw attention not only to this law's loophole but to "intersex genital mutilation" (IGM) as well (Preves 2003, 2005).

In addition to lobbying members of Congress to extend the anti-FGM bill to include IGM, ISNA staged protests at medical conferences. ISNA's first major protest was at the 1996 American Academy of Pediatrics meeting in Boston. Members of ISNA joined with noted trans* activist Riki Anne Wilchins and members of Transsexual Menace for this event, collectively calling themselves "Hermaphrodites with Attitude" (HWA). They picketed the conference after intersex activists were denied floor time to address the doctors in attendance. ISNA representatives used the name HWA frequently during the 1990s when they engaged in protests (Preves 2003, 2005). This historic 1996 protest in Boston propelled the American Academy of Pediatrics to create a position statement on infant and childhood genital surgery (Committee on Genetics 2000). By 1997, the broader medical community began engaging in a debate about best practices for intersex infants and children, largely in response to the first reports of David Reimer's unsuccessful sex/gender reassignment, which served to discredit the validity of what is now known as the "optimum gender of rearing" (OGR) model (Money, Hampson, and Hampson 1957). The OGR model "held that *all* sexually ambiguous children should—indeed *must*—be made into unambiguous-looking boys or girls to ensure unambiguous gender identities" (Dreger and Herndon 2009:202).

David Reimer and his identical twin brother were born in 1965, as typical, non-intersex boys. During a circumcision accident at the age of eight months, David's penis was tragically burned off by electrocautery. His devastated parents worked with psychologist John Money, the primary clinician who developed the OGR model, to help their child live a healthy life. Dr. Money suggested bringing about optimal gender identity development through a surgical castration and social reassignment of David as female when he was twenty-two months old. For decades following his reassignment, the medical intervention on intersex children relied on the apparent successful outcome of this case until David spoke out against his sex reassignment in

1997 (Colapinto 1997, 2000). David had rejected the female-feminine gender that he had been assigned and had been living as a boy since the age of fourteen. He reported that the treatments that were intended to bring about a feminine gender identity were, in fact, a cause of great stigma, isolation, and shame. Despite being a very private person, he was motivated to speak out publicly after learning that other children were being subjected to the same treatments he received and that his case had been lauded as evidence of the success of sex reassignment in early childhood. Many intersex adults also decry their childhood medical sex assignment when they grow up to identify as a gender different than their surgical sex. Many of these intersex adults choose to physically transition their sex, as David Reimer did and many trans*-identified individuals do, so that their sex is congruent with their gender identity. The rate of intersex adults that are also trans* isn't well known. In Sharon's 2003 study, nearly 25% of her interviewees were living in a gender different from their medical sex assignment.

Medical debates about the efficacy of surgical and hormonal sex assignment of intersex children quickly followed the headlines of Reimer's male identity and the apparent failure of Dr. Money's optimal gender rearing model (Preves 2005). These debates were quite polarized and framed the issue at hand as whether to perform *immediate* or *delayed* medical treatment; that is, these discussions focused on *when* and not *whether* to intervene, and many physicians felt that they were being put on the defensive. In more recent years, some physicians have begun to advocate watchful waiting rather than emergency medical intervention in an appeal for additional and more systematic longitudinal research on intersex children and adults.

This debate came to a head in 2000 and was described as a crisis in medicine by physicians who had formerly considered this treatment to be in the best interest of intersex children and their families. The North American Task Force on Intersex was formed in 2000 with the intention of open and interdisciplinary collaboration and an aim to reach some consensus on best practices in intersex care. The membership of the task force included key players in the American Academy of Pediatrics and ISNA, as well as scholars and clinicians in many related fields (Preves 2005). While the task force was not long-lived, some of the conversations were, ultimately leading to the National Institutes of Health (NIH) issuing a program announcement in 2001 for funding dedicated to new and continued research on intersex. Well over a decade later, the NIH continues to dedicate resources to and requests for research on culturally competent care for intersex people and their families.

As ISNA sought credibility in medical circles by shedding its former confrontational "Hermaphrodites with Attitude" activism, it retooled itself to put forth an image more conducive to collaboration with medical providers. This included the publication of its new newsletter, *ISNA News,* in 2001, in place of its more radical *Hermaphrodites with Attitude* publication (Intersex Society of North America 2001). In addition to the newsletter's change in title, *ISNA News* moved away from the personal stories and humor that were commonplace in *Hermaphrodites with Attitude* to more professional and organizational concerns such as financial reports, profiles of board members, and continued coverage of medical conferences and research. This shift mirrors an overarching change within the intersex movement at the beginning of the twenty-first century when at least some intersex activists and doctors began working alongside one another for change rather than against each other as political adversaries. A mere four years after picketing outside of such conventions, Cheryl Chase began to be featured as an invited keynote speaker at prominent medical conventions (Preves 2005).

ISNA distanced itself even further from a narrative of personal medical trauma when Chase stepped down as the executive director and a non-intersex medical sociologist, Monica Casper, took the helm for one year, from 2003 to 2004. Chase stepped back in to serve as ISNA's executive director in 2004 until ISNA closed down in 2008. During her time at ISNA, Casper helped connect the intersex movement's concerns to other movements and communities, including women's health, disability rights, children's rights, sexual rights, and reproductive rights. She also helped expand ISNA's Medical Advisory Board, on which Sharon served from 2005 to 2008.

How Intersex Became a "Disorder of Sex Development": Terminological Tensions, 2004–2014

In October 2005, a few years before ISNA ceased operations, two medical providers convened a meeting in Chicago of fifty experts on intersex from around the world. This international group of experts consisted of medical specialists from various fields and two intersex activists, including Cheryl Chase. This meeting produced the very first consensus statement on the medical management of intersex conditions, which was published in various scholarly medical outlets (see Houk et al. 2006; Lee et al. 2006). According to meeting attendees, the consensus statement, which was a revision of the earlier American Academy of Pediatrics statement in 2000 (Committee on Genetics 2000), was necessary due to medical advances in intersex care and the recognition of the value of psychosocial support and patient advocacy to overall quality of life (Lee et al. 2006). This new statement made a number of recommendations, including avoiding unnecessary surgical intervention, especially cosmetic genital surgery. The authors also questioned the claim that early surgical intervention "relieves parental distress and improves attachment between the child and the parents" (Lee et al. 2006:491). Although this statement was promising, there was still no guarantee that medical professionals would follow its recommendations (and indeed, few have).

A second recommendation of the 2006 "Consensus Statement on Management of Intersex Disorders" was the call for an interdisciplinary team approach to treating individuals with intersex traits (Lee et al. 2006). This approach calls for various pediatric specialists, including endocrinology, surgery, psychiatry, and others, to collaborate when making medical recommendations and providing intersex medical care. While this team model seems like a step in the right direction away from Dr. John Money's OGR model that dominated much of the second half of the twentieth century, in *Contesting Intersex,* Georgiann questions the ability of this team model to account for the voices of intersex people and/or their parents (Davis 2015). Although the goal of this concentrated expertise is to provide a multidisciplinary approach to intersex medical care, it may work to intimidate intersex people and their parents through the illusion that every concern has been addressed by a diverse group of medical experts.

Perhaps the most controversial component of the consensus statement is the recommended shift away from intersex language and all uses of hermaphrodite terminology. The authors of the consensus statement claim that patients disapprove of such terms, and they also allege providers and parents find such language "confusing" (Lee et al. 2006:488). In place of intersex language and hermaphrodite terminology, the authors advocate for disorders of sex development (DSD) nomenclature. The introduction of DSD language created new conflict in the intersex community, which compelled Georgiann to bridge her personal and professional interests in intersex by conducting a sociological analysis of intersex in contemporary U.S. society during her doctoral studies at the University of Illinois at Chicago. As she first argued in a 2014 paper titled "The Power in a Name: Diagnostic Terminology and Diverse Experiences," many intersex people are adamantly against the DSD label due to the pathologization the word *disorder* implies (Davis 2014). A recent study that appeared in the *International Journal of Pediatric Endocrinology* shows that parents of intersex children also express dissatisfaction with DSD terminology (Lin-Su et al. 2015). However, there are intersex people, and their parents, who prefer DSD

terminology because of an internalized belief, problematic or not, that the word *disorder* is an accurate medical description of the intersex body, referring to a disruption in typical gestational development (Davis 2014, 2015). A minority of intersex people feel that individuals should use whatever term makes them feel most comfortable, be it *intersex* or *DSD* (Dreger and Herndon 2009). Indeed, as we have illustrated earlier in discussing the Intersex Society's use of the phrase "hermaphrodites with attitude," language can be an immensely powerful tool used deliberately to affect emotions and one's sense, or lack of, social control.

Having flexibility around terminology might be the most strategic approach, for it allows intersex people to benefit from all that each term provides (Davis 2015). For instance, when evoking DSD terminology, intersex people could benefit from insurance access to requested medical resources, government protection against discriminatory actions in the workplace, and more positive relationships with providers, parents, and society at large due to a societal norm of empathy for those with medical abnormalities. Although it certainly is the case that people with disabilities are subjected to discrimination (Green et al. 2005; Kumar et al. 2014), they are a legally protected class of citizens. Intersex people, on the other hand, are not legally protected in any capacity, but by medicalizing their difference, this could change.[3] There are, of course, serious problems with embracing DSD language. Intersex people who prefer DSD terminology express feelings of abnormality, and, more specifically, serious doubts about their gender authenticity (Davis 2015). For example, some women with CAIS wonder if they are "really" women given they were born with XY chromosomes and testes. Indeed, it is easy to see why accepting the label of being "disordered" could have negative consequences on one's sense of self. If, however, intersex people can be flexible with diagnostic terminology, acknowledging that there may even be power embedded in seemingly pejorative labels such as DSD (e.g., in seeking health insurance coverage for medically recommended hormone replacement therapy, protection from employment discrimination, and the like), they may be empowered to use such language to their advantage. This is precisely why Georgiann argues for flexibility around terminology in her book *Contesting Intersex: The Dubious Diagnosis* (2015). To effectively view and use diagnostic terminology in this flexible manner, one must be able to see medical diagnoses as a socially constructed phenomenon (see, e.g., Jutel 2011).

Other scholars across disciplines have offered different interpretations of the "disorders of sex development" terminology. Some have openly criticized it (see, e.g., Davidson 2009; Holmes 2009; Karkazis 2008; Reis 2009; Topp 2013). Historian Elizabeth Reis (2009) has, for example, offered "divergence of sex development" as an alternative to "disorders of sex development," and communication scholar Sarah Topp (2013) has supported "differences of sex development." Philosopher Ellen Feder (2009b) has argued that "the [nomenclature] change should be understood as normalizing in a positive sense" (134). She has also more directly stated that DSD "could be understood as progressive" (Feder 2009a:226). Sociologist Alyson Spurgas (2009) warns that "the DSD/intersex debate and its associated contest over treatment protocol has consequences for embodied (and thus sexed, gendered and desiring) individuals everywhere" (118). Sharon Preves suggests adopting the phrase "diversity of sex development" when using the DSD acronym.

Medical professionals, on the other hand, have widely embraced the disorders of sex development terminology, although a minority of providers have very recently started using the term *differences* rather than *disorders* of sex development, recommended by Topp (2013). Research demonstrates that providers may have embraced the DSD language because it allowed them to reclaim their medical authority and jurisdiction over intersex, which was in jeopardy as a result of the intersex activism of the 1990s and 2000s (Davis 2015). By referring to *intersex* as a DSD, providers escape criticism from

intersex activists and their allies who call for the end of intersex "normalization" surgeries—indeed, in a game of semantics, providers can now claim that they treat *disorders of sex development*, not *intersex*. In 2010, only four years after the consensus statement was published, several medical providers noted that DSD nomenclature had successfully replaced intersex language and hermaphrodite terminology (Aaronson and Aaronson 2010; Hughes 2010a, 2010b; Pasterski, Prentice, and Hughes 2010). But this was never Chase's goal when she participated in the 2005 Chicago "consensus meeting." Rather, by adopting DSD terminology, she had hoped that "disorders of sex development" language would replace only terminology that used or incorporated forms of the word *hermaphrodite*, such as *male pseudo-hermaphrodite*, not all uses of the term *intersex*. While Hughes and other providers frame this renaming as an all-encompassing and victimless victory, we must not forget that they are speaking from a medical perspective rather than from the perspective of those personally affected by intersex traits. This shift in diagnostic language has had major implications throughout the global intersex community, marking a shift in intersex advocacy from collective confrontation against the medical profession to contested collaboration with the medical community (Davis 2015).

This change in nomenclature spawned the death of ISNA and the birth of a new organization in 2008: Accord Alliance. Accord Alliance was also formed by Cheryl Chase in collaboration with other former ISNA leaders and allies. When she co-founded this new organization, Chase used her legal name, Bo Laurent, rather than her pseudonym and formally retired the activist pseudonym "Cheryl Chase." Whereas Accord Alliance embraces the disorders of sex development terminology, many other intersex organizations, activists, scholars, and even some clinicians do not. This debate over terminology is currently a very heated issue among people concerned with this topic. Today Accord Alliance continues to work alongside medical professionals to help educate and build bridges between parents with intersex children and medical providers who specialize in this field (www .accordalliance.org).

A second intersex organization that formed to fill ISNA's void is Advocates for Informed Choice (AIC), with its youth advocacy program Inter/Act (http://aiclegal.org/). AIC was formed in 2006 by legal advocate Anne Tamar-Mattis, the partner of Dr. Suegee Tamar-Mattis, a physician who happens to be intersex. AIC is first and foremost a legal advocacy organization fighting for the human rights of intersex children. AIC also sponsors several programs, including the Interface Project, which is an advocacy campaign curated by Jim Ambrose, a long-time intersex advocate who was involved with the ISNA in the 1990s. Ambrose's Interface Project features brief first person video accounts of people with intersex traits discussing their experiences and belief that "No Body Is Shameful." (These videos are reminiscent of the "It Gets Better" video campaign.) With representation from around the world, fourteen intersex people, including Georgiann, have contributed their voices via these brief autobiographical video accounts (www.interfaceproject.org).

Since ISNA's closure in 2008, the AIS-DSD Support Group has grown into one of the largest intersex support groups in the world, with membership now extending to those with intersex traits other than androgen insensitivity syndrome. Sherri Groveman Morris, an intersex woman, founded the AIS-DSD Support Group in 1995 so that women with androgen insensitivity syndrome wouldn't have to face their diagnosis alone. Organizational membership was initially only open to women with androgen insensitivity syndrome. The organization was, at the time it was formed, named the Androgen Insensitivity Syndrome Support Group-USA (AISSG-USA), after its sister intersex support group in the United Kingdom, AISSG-UK. In 2010, the then-named AISSG-USA started hosting a Continuing Medical Education (CME) event the day before its annual conference, during which medical experts on intersex would share their knowledge with interested parties, including medical residents, other physicians, and even some intersex activists. AISSG-USA became the AIS-DSD Support Group in the summer of 2011, when it launched its new website (www.aisdsd.org). This organizational name change made the group more inclusive by extending its membership to people with intersex traits besides AIS.

On January 1, 2014, Georgiann started a two-year term as president of the AIS-DSD Support Group. Since her presidency, Georgiann has worked with the AIS-DSD Support Group Board to continue to diversify the organization and has since witnessed several transformations. First, in late 2014, the AIS-DSD Support Group voted to open membership to anyone personally affected by intersex, regardless of gender identity or expression—that is, opening up group membership to men with intersex traits and to people with intersex traits who identify as genderqueer (those who reject conventional gender roles and expectations) or who reject gender labels altogether. This was a remarkable development as the organization previously had a strict women-only policy, with the exception of male parents of children with AIS. This change was inspired by a keynote address that Bo Laurent (the activist formerly known as Cheryl Chase) delivered at the 2012 AIS-DSD Support Group annual meeting that challenged the organization to include men born with intersex traits. This challenge became personal in 2013, when a teen member of the AIS-DSD Support Group decided to gender transition. Without changing the existing policy, this young man would not have been able to attend the annual meeting the following year. Many members considered it unethical and inappropriate to deny support to this young man and his family because he had gender transitioned, a sentiment that played a significant role in expanding organizational membership to include all intersex people, not just those who identify as women. Second, also in 2014, the AIS-DSD Support Group took a terminological stance and replaced "disorders of sex development" with "differences of sex development" language across their website and other publications. This change was made to prevent the problematic pathologization inherent within the "disorders of sex development" terminology. Third, in 2015, the AIS-DSD Support Group Board convened a Diversity Committee, which is committed to increasing the racial, ethnic, and socioeconomic diversity of its membership. Currently, the Diversity Committee is in the early stages of formulating concrete action plans.

Accord Alliance, AIC, and the AIS-DSD Support Group are just three of many intersex support and advocacy groups that exist around the world. We have chosen to focus on these three intersex advocacy organizations because they are among the most visible, especially in the United States. (With its online biographical video Interface Project, AIC also has international representation, and the AIS-DSD Support Group conference has attendees from outside the United States.) Although each of these organizations serves a unique purpose in the intersex rights movement, they share the goal of improving the lives of intersex people and their families. AIC and the AIS-DSD Support Group often collaborate with one another. For example, AIC and the AIS-DSD Support Group have overlapping leadership, and AIC has sponsored the AIS-DSD Support Group's youth program for the past few years. Each of these three organizations has experienced tremendous growth in recent years, in part due to the void created by ISNA's closure in 2008. Despite their collaboration and shared goals, they remain independent organizations with varying perceptions about the effectiveness of partnering with medical professionals to promote change in intersex medical care.

The Future of the Intersex Movement and Medical Care: 2015 and Beyond

Intersex individuals came together to form the U.S. intersex rights movement in the late 1980s and early 1990s. They mobilized in order to change intersex medical care that was based on John Money's "optimum gender of rearing" model. These activists represented the first generation of adults who had been subjected to intersex "normalization" surgeries and the secrecy and shame that surround such treatment. They demanded that medical providers stop performing "normalization" surgeries on intersex babies and young children. They also wanted providers to stop lying to intersex people about their diagnoses and encouraging parents to do the same. These activists wanted to raise public awareness about intersex through numerous venues including media appearances, talks at universities, and LGBT centers.

Although intersex babies and children are still subjected to "normalization" surgeries (see Davis 2015), it appears that now it is far less common for intersex people to be lied to about their diagnosis. Today, it seems that providers no longer instruct parents of intersex children to withhold an intersex diagnosis from their child. This is evidence of change because it likely minimizes at least some of the shame and secrecy tied to the lack of complete and honest diagnosis disclosure. However, many intersex people still struggle with their diagnosis, with some questioning their gender authenticity (Davis 2015).

The ethics of intersex "normalization" surgery, including medical liability for performing such interventions, is currently being determined in the courtroom. In 2013, Pamela and John Mark Crawford filed a lawsuit, in both federal and state courts, against the South Carolina Department of Social Services, the Greenville Hospital System, the Medical University of South Carolina, and specifically named individual employees on behalf of their adopted eight-year-old son, M.C., who was born with an intersex trait (Project Integrity 2013). Before the Crawfords adopted M.C., he was in the South Carolina foster care system, where medical providers, with the support of social service employees, performed surgery on him at the age of sixteen months to address his intersex trait. According to the lawsuit, the surgery removed "healthy genital tissue" with the result of feminizing his body, "potentially sterilizing him and greatly reducing if not eliminating his sexual function" (Project Integrity 2013). Despite undergoing this infant medical sex assignment to make him appear outwardly female, M.C. clearly and strongly identifies as male. While the federal portion of this lawsuit has been dismissed in court, the state suit against specific state entities and individuals is still in litigation.

Another significant recent development has been the unprecedented increase in the number of intersex people, and their parents, who are able to find and connect with each other, seek support, and organize to make up the second generation of intersex activists. This can almost exclusively be attributed to the expansion of various social media outlets, notably Facebook, Tumblr, and Twitter. For example, every active intersex social movement organization has a Facebook page that is easily located on the Internet. As another example, an intersex man created a Facebook page titled "The Commons" that allows intersex people, their parents, medical allies, and sociocultural scholars to connect with each other outside of a formal intersex social movement organization. While "The Commons" is a private Facebook group that one must be invited to join by its founder or one of its moderators, it is a virtual space for intersex people, and their allies from all around the world, to connect with each one another.

The third generation of intersex activists comprises youth born near or after 1990. These youth are coming of age at a time when there is growing societal acceptance of diverse gender and sexual identities, and also greater visibility of intersex in mainstream youth media. Many of these young people are connected through AIC's youth program titled Inter/Act, an advocacy and support program for intersex people between the ages of fourteen and twenty-five (http://interactyouth .org/). Members of Inter/Act, and its program coordinators, were heavily involved as consultants on the second (2014–2015) season of MTV's *Faking It*, a popular television show among youth. In the second season of the show, it was revealed that Lauren, one of the show's main characters, was intersex. This marked the first time that a major television program featured an intersex character. In addition, second-generation intersex activists who were, directly or indirectly, affiliated with Inter/Act, appeared in an immensely popular BuzzFeed video titled "What It's Like to Be Intersex" (BuzzFeed 2015). Within six weeks of its release on YouTube, in March 2015, this video had already amassed more than one million views. Just eight weeks later, at the time of this publication, the views number more than four million. It is likely that this visibility of intersex in mainstream youth media has profoundly impacted how younger intersex people see themselves and how their peers perceive and interact with them.

Since the formation of the U.S. intersex rights movement in the late 1980s and early 1990s, when Sharon was just beginning to shed light on the lives of intersex people and their struggles, there has been considerable change. Unfortunately, this progress has been limited primarily to the expansion of peer support and means of advocacy, notably the use of social media. Georgiann's recent work reveals that intersex people continue to be subjected to "normalization" surgeries, struggle to receive quality medical care, and experience stigma surrounding their bodily difference.

The intersex social movement is situated within the larger context of social change with regard to gender and sexual diversity. In the United States, for example, thirty-seven states legalized same-sex marriage within an eleven-year period (from 2004 to 2015), and in June 2015, the U.S. Supreme Court made same-sex marriage legal throughout the entire country. On the gender diversity front, trans* visibility and acceptance has increased in the 2010s. This social change was propelled in part by the wildly popular Netflix show *Orange Is the New Black* featuring a leading trans* character portrayed by a trans* actor (Laverne Cox). The show premiered in 2013 and Ms. Cox became a household name just a year later when she appeared on the cover of *Time Magazine* in a feature article titled "The Transgender Tipping Point" (Steinmetz 2014). In 2015, major media gave attention to other trans* celebrities, including

Caitlyn (formerly Bruce) Jenner's televised coming out on *20/20* and her appearance on the cover of *Vanity Fair* magazine.

The increasing visibility of gender and sexual diversity has been coupled with recent public attention to intersex issues. This has occurred not only through the MTV show *Faking It* but also through the global attention to intersex raised by the International Olympics Committee reinstating gender verification of female athletes in 2012 and Germany becoming the first country to allow an indeterminate gender on a newborn's birth certificate. The future of the intersex movement is likely to be more global than it has in the past, given the vast power of the Internet and social media to connect people throughout the world. Our hope is that the stigma intersex people face will be diminished for future generations as they come of age at a time when there is, for the first time ever, substantial intersex visibility in the mainstream media.

NOTES

1. AIS-DSD Support Group is the official name of this organization. *AIS* stands for androgen insensitivity syndrome, whereas *DSD* stands for differences (not disorders) of sex development. www.aisdsd.org.

2. We would like to thank the editors of this volume, Kay Valentine and Joan Spade, for the opportunity to write this article. Georgiann and Sharon represent two generations of scholars who have been working separately on intersex advocacy and (de)medicalization for many years. It is an honor and joy for us to come together to write this historical narrative.

3. While intersex is not a protected legal class, the Human Rights Commission of the City and County of San Francisco issued a human rights–based investigation into the medical "normalization" of intersex people in 2005 (Arana 2005). This investigation was largely compelled by the activism of Cheryl Chase and other members of ISNA.

REFERENCES

Aaronson, Ian A., and Alistair J. Aaronson. 2010. "How Should We Classify Intersex Disorders?" *Journal of Pediatric Urology* 6:443-46.

Arana, Marcus de María. 2005. *A Human Rights Investigation into the Medical "Normalization" of Intersex People: A Report of a Public Hearing by the Human Rights Commission of the City & County of San Francisco.* Retrieved from http://www.isna.org/files/SFHRC_Intersex_Report.pdf

Baskin, Laurence S., ed. 2012. *Hypospadias and Genital Development.* New York: Springer Science and Business Media.

BuzzFeed. 2015. "What It's Like to Be Intersex" [Video]. March 28. Retrieved from https://www.youtube.com/watch?v=cAUDKEI4QKI

Chase, Cheryl. 1993. "Letters from Readers." *The Sciences* (July/August):3.

Colapinto, John. 1997. "The True Story of John/Joan." *Rolling Stone,* December 11, pp. 54–73, 92–97.

_____. 2000. *As Nature Made Him: The Boy Who Was Raised as a Girl.* New York: HarperCollins.

Committee on Genetics: Section on Endocrinology and Section on Urology. 2000. "Evaluation of the Newborn with Developmental Anomalies of the External Genitalia." *Pediatrics* 106(1):138–42.

Craig, James R., Chad Wallis, William O. Brant, James M. Hotaling, and Jeremy B. Myers. 2014. "Management of Adults with Prior Failed Hypospadias Surgery." *Translational Andrology and Urology* 3(2):196–204.

Davidson, Robert J. 2009. "DSD Debates: Social Movement Organizations' Framing Disputes Surrounding the Term 'Disorders of Sex Development.'" *Liminalis—Journal for Sex/ Gender Emancipation and Resistance.* Retrieved from http://www.liminalis.de/2009_03/Aitikel_ Essay/Liminalis-2009-Davidson.pdf

Davis, Georgiann. 2014. "The Power in a Name: Diagnostic Terminology and Diverse Experiences. *Psychology & Sexuality* 5(1):15-27.

_____. 2015. *Contesting Intersex: The Dubious Diagnosis.* New York: New York University Press.

Davis, Georgiann, and Erin L. Murphy. 2013. "Intersex Bodies as States of Exception: An Empirical Explanation for Unnecessary Surgical Modification." *Feminist Formations* 25(2):129–52.

Dreger, Alice D., and April M, Herndon. 2009. "Progress and Politics in the Intersex Rights Movement: Feminist Theory in Action." *GLQ: A Journal of Lesbian and Gay Studies* 15(2):199–224.

Epstein, Julia. 1990. "Either/or–Neither/Both: Sexual Ambiguity and the Ideology of Gender." *Gender* 7(Spring):99–142.

Fausto-Sterling, Anne. 1993. "The Five Sexes: Why Male and Female Are Not Enough." *The Sciences* (March/April):20–25.

_____. 2000. "The Five Sexes, Revisited." *The Sciences* (July/August):18–23.

Feder, Ellen. 2009a. "Imperatives of Normality: From 'Intersex' to 'Disorders of Sex Development.'" *GLQ: A Journal of Lesbian and Gay Studies* 15(2):225–47.

_____. 2009b. "Normalizing Medicine: Between 'Intersexuals' and Individuals with 'Disorders' of Sex Development.'" *Health Care Analysis: Journal of Health Philosophy and Policy* 17(2):134–43.

_____. 2014. *Making Sense of Intersex: Changing Ethical Perspectives in Biomedicine.* Bloomington: Indiana University Press.

Green, Sara, Christine Davis, Elana Karshmer, Pete Marsh, and Benjamin Straight. 2005. "Living Stigma: The Impact of Labeling, Stereotyping, Separation, Status Loss, and Discrimination in the Lives of Individuals with Disabilities and Their Families." *Sociological Inquiry* 75(2):197–215.

Holmes, Lewis B. 2011. *Common Malformations.* New York: Oxford University Press.

Holmes, Morgan. 2008. *Intersex: A Perilous Difference.* Selinsgrove, PA: Susquehanna University Press.

_____, ed. 2009. *Critical Intersex.* Farnham, England: Ashgate.

Houk, Christopher P., Ieuan A. Hughes, S. Faisal Ahmed, Peter A. Lee, and Writing Committee for the International Intersex Consensus Conference Participants. 2006. "Summary of Consensus Statement on Intersex Disorders and Their Management." *Pediatrics* 118(2):753–57.

Hughes, Ieuan A. 2010a. "How Should We Classify Intersex Disorders?" *Journal of Pediatric Urology* 6:447–48.

_____. 2010b. "The Quiet Revolution: Disorders of Sex Development." *Best Practice & Research Clinical Endocrinology & Metabolism* 24(2):159–62.

Intersex Society of North America. 1994. *Hermaphrodites with Attitude* 1(1). Retrieved from http://www.isna.org/files/hwa/winter1995.pdf

_____. 2001. *ISNA News.* February. Retrieved from http://www.isna.org/files/hwa/feb2001.pdf

Jutel, Annemarie. 2011. *Putting a Name to It: Diagnosis in Contemporary Society.* Baltimore: Johns Hopkins University Press.

Karkazis, Katrina. 2008. *Fixing Sex: Intersex, Medical Authority, and Lived Experience.* Durham, NC: Duke University Press.

Kessler, Suzanne. 1998. *Lessons from the Intersexed.* New Brunswick, NJ: Rutgers University Press.

Kumar, Arun, Nivedita Kothiyal, Vanmala Hiranandani, and Deepa Sonpal. 2014. "Ableing Work, Disabling Workers?" *Development in Practice* 24(1):81–90.

Lee, Peter A., Christopher P. Houk, S. Faisal Ahmed, and Ieuan A. Hughes. 2006. "Consensus Statement on Management of Intersex Disorders." *Pediatrics* 118(2):488–500.

Lin-Su, Karen, Oksana Lekarev, Dix P. Poppas, and Maria G. Vogiatzi. 2015. "Congenital Adrenal Hyperplasia Patient Perception of 'Disorders of Sex Development' Nomenclature." *International Journal of Pediatric Endocrinology* 9:1–7.

Mak, Geertje. 2012. *Doubting Sex: Inscriptions, Bodies, and Selves in Nineteenth-Century Hermaphrodite Case Histories.* Manchester, England: Manchester University Press.

Money, John, Joan G. Hampson, and John L. Hampson. 1957. "Imprinting and the Establishment of Gender Role." *Archives of Neurology and Psychiatry* 77:333–36.

Nakhal, Rola S., Margaret Hall-Craggs, Alex Freeman, Alex Kirkham, Gerard S. Conway, Rupali Arora, Christopher R. J. Woodhouse, Dan N. Wood, and Sarah M. Creighton. 2013. "Evaluation of Retained Testes in Adolescent Girls and Women with Complete Androgen Insensitivity Syndrome." *Radiology* 268(1):153–60.

Pasterski, Vickie, P. Prentice, and Ieuan A. Hughes. 2010. "Impact of the Consensus Statement and the New DSD Classification System." *Best Practice & Research Clinical Endocrinology & Metabolism* 24:187–95.

Preves, Sharon E. 2003. *Intersex and Identity: The Contested Self.* New Brunswick, NJ: Rutgers University Press.

_____. 2005. "Out of the O.R. and into the Streets: Exploring the Impact of Intersex Media Activism." *Cardozo Journal of Law & Gender* 12(1):247–88. (Reprinted from *Research in Political Sociology.*)

Project Integrity. *Advocates for Informed Choice.* Retrieved from http://aiclegal.org/programs/project-integrity/

Reis, Elizabeth. 2009. *Bodies in Doubt: An American History of Intersex.* Baltimore: Johns Hopkins University Press.

Spurgas, Alyson K. 2009. "(Un)Queering Identity: The Biosocial Production of Intersex/DSD." Pp. 97–122 in *Critical Intersex,* edited by Morgan Holmes. Farnham, England: Ashgate.

Steinmetz, Katy. 2014. "The Transgender Tipping Point." *Time Magazine* May 29.

Topp, Sarah S. 2013. "Against the Quiet Revolution: The Rhetorical Construction of Intersex Individuals as Disordered." *Sexualities* 16(1-2):180–94.

Warren, Carol A.B. 2014. "Gender Reassignment Surgery in the 18th Century: A Case Study." *Sexualities* 17(7):872–84.

Introduction to Reading 4

Robert M. Sapolsky is professor of biology and neurology at Stanford University and a research associate with the Institute of Primate Research, National Museums of Kenya. He is the author of *The Trouble With Testosterone, Why Zebras Don't Get Ulcers,* and, most recently, *A Primate's Memoir.* Sapolsky has lived as a member of a baboon troop in Kenya, conducting cutting-edge research on these beautiful and complex primates. In this article, he uses his keen wit and scientific understanding to debunk the widely held myth that testosterone causes aggression in males.

1. Why do many Americans want to believe that biological factors, such as hormones, are the basis of gender differences and inequalities?

2. Sapolsky says that hormones have a "permissive effect." What does "permissive effect" mean in terms of the relationship between testosterone and aggression?

3. How does research on testosterone, male monkeys, and spotted hyenas help one grasp the role of social factors and environment in behavioral biology?

THE TROUBLE WITH TESTOSTERONE

Robert M. Sapolsky

Face it, we all do it. We all believe in certain stereotypes about certain minorities. The stereotypes are typically pejorative and usually false. But every now and then, they are true. I write apologetically as a member of a minority about which the stereotypes are indeed true. I am male. We males account for less than 50 percent of the population, yet we generate an incredibly disproportionate percentage of the violence. Whether it is something as primal as having an ax fight in an Amazonian clearing or as detached as using computer-guided aircraft to strafe a village, something as condemned as assaulting a cripple or as glorified as killing someone wearing the wrong uniform, if it is violent, males excel at it. Why should that be?

We all think we know the answer. A dozen millennia ago or so, an adventurous soul managed to lop off a surly bull's testicles and thus invented behavioral endocrinology. It is unclear from the historical records whether this individual received either a grant or tenure as a result of this experiment, but it certainly generated an influential finding—something or other comes out of the testes that helps to make males such aggressive pains in the ass.

That something or other is testosterone.[1] The hormone binds to specialized receptors in muscles and causes those cells to enlarge. It binds to similar receptors in laryngeal cells and gives rise to operatic basses. It causes other secondary sexual characteristics, makes for relatively unhealthy blood vessels, alters biochemical events in the liver too dizzying to even contemplate, has a profound impact, no doubt, on the workings of cells in big toes. And it seeps into the brain, where it binds to those same "androgen" receptors and influences behavior in a way highly relevant to understanding aggression.

What evidence links testosterone with aggression? Some pretty obvious stuff. Males tend to have higher testosterone levels in their circulation than do females (one wild exception to that will be discussed later) and to be more aggressive. Times of life when males are swimming in testosterone (for example, after reaching puberty) correspond to when aggression peaks. Among numerous species, testes are mothballed most of the year, kicking into action and pouring out testosterone only during a very circumscribed mating season—precisely the time when male–male aggression soars.

Impressive, but these are only correlative data, testosterone repeatedly being on the scene with no alibi when some aggression has occurred. The proof comes with the knife, the performance of what is euphemistically known as a "subtraction" experiment. Remove the source of testosterone in species after species and levels of aggression typically plummet. Reinstate normal testosterone levels afterward with injections of synthetic testosterone, and aggression returns.

To an endocrinologist, the subtraction and replacement paradigm represents pretty damning proof: this hormone is involved. "Normal testosterone levels appear to be a prerequisite for normative levels of aggressive behavior" is the sort of catchy, hummable phrase that the textbooks would use. That probably explains why you shouldn't mess with a bull moose during rutting season. But that's not why a lot of people want to understand this sliver of science. Does the action of this hormone tell us anything about individual differences in levels of aggression, anything about why some males, some human males, are exceptionally violent? Among an array of males—human or otherwise—are the highest testosterone levels found in the most aggressive individuals?

Generate some extreme differences and that is precisely what you see. Castrate some of the well-paid study subjects, inject others with enough testosterone to quadruple the normal human levels, and the high-testosterone males are overwhelmingly likely to be the more aggressive ones. However, that doesn't tell us much about the real world. Now do something more subtle by studying the normative variability in testosterone—in other words, don't manipulate anything, just see what everyone's natural levels are like—and high levels of testosterone and high levels of aggression still tend to go together. This would seem to seal the case—interindividual differences in levels of aggression among normal individuals are probably driven by differences in levels of testosterone. But this turns out to be wrong.

Okay, suppose you note a correlation between levels of aggression and levels of testosterone among these normal males. This could be because (a) testosterone elevates aggression; (b) aggression elevates testosterone secretion; (c) neither causes the other. There's a huge bias to assume option a, while b is the answer. Study after study has shown that when you examine testosterone levels when males are first placed together in the social group, testosterone levels predict nothing about who is going to be aggressive. The subsequent behavioral differences drive the hormonal changes, rather than the other way around.

Because of a strong bias among certain scientists, it has taken forever to convince them of this point. Behavioral endocrinologists study what behavior and hormones have to do with each other. How do you study behavior? You get yourself a notebook and a stopwatch and a pair of binoculars. How do you measure the hormones? You need a gazillion-dollar machine, you muck around with radiation and chemicals, wear a lab coat, maybe even goggles—the whole nine yards. Which toys would you rather get for Christmas? Which facet of science are you going to believe in more? Because the endocrine aspects of the business are more high-tech, more reductive, there is the bias to think that it is somehow more scientific, more powerful. This is a classic case of what is often called physics envy, the disease among scientists where the behavioral biologists fear their discipline lacks the rigor of physiology, the physiologists wish for the techniques of the biochemists, the biochemists covet the clarity of the answers revealed by the molecular biologists, all the way down until you get to the physicists, who confer only with God.[2] Hormones seem to many to be more real, more substantive, than the ephemera of behavior, so when a correlation occurs, it must be because hormones regulate behavior, not the other way around.

As I said, it takes a lot of work to cure people of that physics envy, and to see that interindividual differences in testosterone levels don't predict subsequent differences in aggressive behavior among individuals. Similarly, fluctuations in testosterone levels within one individual over time do not predict subsequent changes in the levels of aggression in that one individual—get a hiccup in testosterone secretion one afternoon and that's not when the guy goes postal.

Look at our confusing state: normal levels of testosterone are a prerequisite for normal levels of aggression, yet changing the amount of testosterone in someone's bloodstream within the normal range doesn't alter his subsequent levels of aggressive behavior. This is where, like clockwork, the students suddenly start coming to office hours in a panic, asking whether they missed something in their lecture notes.

Yes, it's going to be on the final, and it's one of the more subtle points in endocrinology—what is referred to as a hormone having a "permissive effect." Remove someone's testes and, as noted, the frequency of aggressive behavior is likely to plummet. Reinstate precastration levels of testosterone by injecting that hormone, and precastration levels of aggression typically return. Fair enough. Now this time, castrate an individual and restore testosterone levels to only 20 percent of normal and . . . amazingly, normal precastration levels of aggression come back. Castrate and now generate twice the testosterone levels from before castration—and the same

level of aggressive behavior returns. You need some testosterone around for normal aggressive behavior—zero levels after castration, and down it usually goes; quadruple it (the sort of range generated in weight lifters abusing anabolic steroids), and aggression typically increases. But anywhere from roughly 20 percent of normal to twice normal and it's all the same; the brain can't distinguish among this wide range of basically normal values.

We seem to have figured out a couple of things by now. First, knowing the differences in the levels of testosterone in the circulation of a bunch of males will not help you much in figuring out who is going to be aggressive. Second, the subtraction and reinstatement data seem to indicate that, nevertheless, in a broad sort of way, testosterone causes aggressive behavior. But that turns out not to be true either, and the implications of this are lost on most people the first thirty times you tell them about it. Which is why you'd better tell them about it thirty-one times, because it is the most important point of this piece.

Round up some male monkeys. Put them in a group together, and give them plenty of time to sort out where they stand with each other—affiliative friendships, grudges and dislikes. Give them enough time to form a dominance hierarchy, a linear ranking system of numbers 1 through 5. This is the hierarchical sort of system where number 3, for example, can pass his day throwing around his weight with numbers 4 and 5, ripping off their monkey chow, forcing them to relinquish the best spots to sit in, but, at the same time, remembering to deal with numbers 1 and 2 with shit-eating obsequiousness.

Hierarchy in place, it's time to do your experiment. Take that third-ranking monkey and give him some testosterone. None of this within-the-normal-range stuff. Inject a ton of it into him, way higher than what you normally see in a rhesus monkey; give him enough testosterone to grow antlers and a beard on every neuron in his brain. And, no surprise, when you then check the behavioral data, it turns out that he will probably be participating in more aggressive interactions than before. So even though small fluctuations in the levels of the hormone don't seem to matter much, testosterone still causes aggression. But that would be wrong. Check out number 3 more closely. Is he now raining aggressive terror on any and all in the group, frothing in an androgenic glaze of indiscriminate violence? Not at all. He's still judiciously kowtowing to numbers 1 and 2, but has simply become a total bastard to numbers 4 and 5. This is critical: testosterone isn't *causing* aggression, it's *exaggerating* the aggression that's already there.

Another example just to show we're serious. There's a part of your brain that probably has lots to do with aggression, a region called the amygdala.[3] Sitting right near it is the Grand Central Station of emotion-related activity in your brain, the hypothalamus. The amygdala communicates with the hypothalamus by way of a cable of neuronal connections called the stria terminalis. No more jargon, I promise. The amygdala has its influence on aggression via that pathway, with bursts of electrical excitation called action potentials that ripple down the stria terminalis, putting the hypothalamus in a pissy mood.

Once again, do your hormonal intervention; flood the area with testosterone. You can do that by injecting the hormone into the bloodstream, where it eventually makes its way to this part of the brain. Or you can be elegant and surgically microinject the stuff directly into this brain region. Six of one, half a dozen of the other. The key thing is what doesn't happen next. Does testosterone now cause there to be action potentials surging down the stria terminalis? Does it turn on that pathway? Not at all. If and only if the amygdala is sending an aggression-provoking volley of action potentials down the stria terminalis, testosterone increases the rate of such action potentials by shortening the resting time between them. It's not turning on the pathway, it's increasing the volume of signaling if it is already turned on. It's not causing aggression, it's exaggerating the preexisting pattern of it, exaggerating the response to environmental triggers of aggression.

This transcends issues of testosterone and aggression. In every generation, it is the duty of behavioral biologists to try to teach this critical point, one that seems a maddening cliché once you get it. You take that hoary old dichotomy between nature and nurture, between biological influences and environmental influences, between intrinsic factors and extrinsic ones, and, the vast majority of the time, regardless of which behavior you are thinking about and what underlying biology you are studying, the dichotomy is a sham. No biology. No environment. Just the interaction between the two.

Do you want to know how important environment and experience are in understanding testosterone and aggression? Look back at how the effects of castration were discussed earlier. There were statements like "Remove the source of testosterone in species after species and levels of aggression typically plummet." Not "Remove the source . . . and aggression always goes to zero." On the average it declines, but rarely to zero, and not at all in some individuals. And the more social experience an individual had being aggressive prior to castration, the more likely that behavior persists sans cojones. Social conditioning can more than make up for the hormone.

Another example, one from one of the stranger corners of the animal kingdom: If you want your assumptions about the nature of boy beasts and girl beasts challenged, check out the spotted hyena. These animals are fast becoming the darlings of endocrinologists, sociobiologists, gynecologists, and tabloid writers. Why? Because they have a wild sex-reversal system—females are more muscular and more aggressive than males and are socially dominant over them, rare traits in the mammalian world. And get this: females secrete more of certain testosterone-related hormones than the males do, producing the muscles, the aggression (and, as a reason for much of the gawking interest in these animals, wildly masculinized private parts that make it supremely difficult to tell the sex of a hyena). So this appears to be a strong vote for the causative powers of high androgen levels in aggression and social dominance. But that's not the whole answer. High up in the hills above the University of California at Berkeley is the world's largest colony of spotted hyenas, massive bone-crunching beasts who fight with each other for the chance to have their ears scratched by Laurence Frank, the zoologist who brought them over as infants from Kenya. Various scientists are studying their sex-reversal system. The female hyenas are bigger and more muscular than the males and have the same weirdo genitals and elevated androgen levels that their female cousins do back in the savannah. Everything is in place except . . . the social system is completely different from that in the wild. Despite being stoked on androgens, there is a very significant delay in the time it takes for the females to begin socially dominating the males—they're growing up without the established social system to learn from.

When people first grasp the extent to which biology has something to do with behavior, even subtle, complex, human behavior, there is often an initial evangelical enthusiasm of the convert, a massive placing of faith in the biological components of the story. And this enthusiasm is typically of a fairly reductive type—because of physics envy, because reductionism is so impressive, because it would be so nice if there were a single gene or hormone or neurotransmitter or part of the brain that was it, the cause, the explanation of everything. And the trouble with testosterone is that people tend to think this way in an arena that really matters.

This is no mere academic concern. We are a fine species with some potential. Yet we are racked by sickening amounts of violence. Unless we are hermits, we feel the threat of it, often as a daily shadow. And regardless of where we hide, should our leaders push the button, we will all be lost in a final global violence. But as we try to understand and wrestle with this feature of our sociality, it is critical to remember the limits of the biology. Testosterone is never going to tell us much about the suburban teenager who, in his after-school chess club, has developed a particularly aggressive style with his bishops. And it certainly isn't going to tell us much about the

teenager in some inner-city hellhole who has taken to mugging people. "Testosterone equals aggression" is inadequate for those who would offer a simple solution to the violent male—just decrease levels of those pesky steroids. And "testosterone equals aggression" is certainly inadequate for those who would offer a simple excuse: Boys will be boys and certain things in nature are inevitable. Violence is more complex than a single hormone. This is endocrinology for the bleeding heart liberal—our behavioral biology is usually meaningless outside the context of the social factors and environment in which it occurs.

NOTES

1. Testosterone is one of a family of related hormones, collectively known as "androgens" or "anabolic steroids." They all are secreted from the testes or are the result of a modification of testosterone, they all have a similar chemical structure, and they all do roughly similar things. Nonetheless, androgen mavens spend entire careers studying the important differences in the actions of different androgens. I am going to throw that subtlety to the wind and, for the sake of simplification that will horrify many, will refer throughout to all of these related hormones as "testosterone."

2. An example of physics envy in action. Recently, a zoologist friend had obtained blood samples from the carnivores that he studies and wanted some hormones in the sample assays in my lab. Although inexperienced with the technique, he offered to help in any way possible. I felt hesitant asking him to do anything tedious but, so long as he had offered, tentatively said, "Well, if you don't mind some unspeakable drudgery, you could number about a thousand assay vials." And this scientist, whose superb work has graced the most prestigious science journals in the world, cheerfully answered, "That's okay, how often do I get to do *real* science, working with test tubes?"

3. And no one has shown that differences in the size or shape of the amygdala, or differences in the numbers of neurons in it, can begin to predict differences in normal levels of aggression. Same punch line as with testosterone.

FURTHER READING

For a good general review of the subject, see E. Monaghan and S. Glickman, "Hormones and Aggressive Behavior," in J. Becker, M. Breedlove, and D. Crews, eds., *Behavioral Endocrinology* (Cambridge, Mass.: MIT Press, 1992), 261. This also has an overview of the hyena social system, as Glickman heads the study of the Berkeley hyenas.

For technical papers on the acquisition of the female dominance in hyenas, see S. Jenks, M. Weldele, L. Frank, and S. Glickman, "Acquisition of Matrilineal Rank in Captive Spotted Hyenas: Emergence of a Natural Social System in Peer-Reared Animals and Their Offspring," *Animal Behavior* 50 (1995): 893; and L. Frank, S. Glickman, and C. Zabel, "Ontogeny of Female Dominance in the Spotted Hyaena: Perspectives from Nature and Captivity," in P. Jewell and G. Maloiy, eds., "The Biology of Large African Mammals in Their Environment," *Symposium of the Zoological Society of London* 61 (1989): 127.

I have emphasized that while testosterone levels in the normal range do not have much to do with aggression, a massive elevation of exposure, as would be seen in anabolic steroid abusers, does usually increase aggression. For a recent study in which even elevating into that range (approximately five times the normal level) still had no effect on mood or behavior, see S. Bhasin, T. Storer, N. Berman, and colleagues, "The Effects of Supraphysiologic Doses of Testosterone on Muscle Size and Strength in Normal Men," *New England Journal of Medicine* 335 (1996): 1.

The study showing that raising testosterone levels in the middle-ranking monkey exaggerates preexisting patterns of aggression can be found in A. Dixson and J. Herbert, "Testosterone, Aggressive Behavior and Dominance Rank in Captive Adult Male Talapoin Monkeys *(Miopithecus talapoin)," Physiology and Behavior* 18 (1977): 539.

For the demonstration that testosterone shortens the resting period between action potentials in neurons, see K. Kendrick and R. Drewert, "Testosterone Reduces Refractory Period of Stria Terminalis Neurons in the Rat Brain," *Science* 204 (1979): 877.

Introduction to Reading 5

Carla A. Pfeffer's research is based on in-depth interviews with nontransgender (cis) women partners of transgender men from the United States, Canada, and Australia. The results of her data analysis are reported in detail in this reading. Pfeffer's findings demonstrate the powerful potential of the relationships and identities constructed by the people she interviewed to challenge the sex/gender/sexuality binaries that have been the foundation of binary thinking and acting in Western societies such as the United States. Pfeffer applies the idea of "recognition" to show how we "do" both gender and sexuality. Her study poses a direct challenge to the belief that sexual, as well as gender, identities are fixed and natural.

1. Why does Pfeffer refer to the people she interviewed as "queer social actors"?

2. Why does the author use the concept of "recognition" instead of "passing" in her analysis?

3. How do cis women and their trans partners work to (re)define their identities in ways that challenge linguistic and social categories?

4. What is queer theory, and how is it used in this reading?

"I Don't Like Passing as a Straight Woman"

Queer Negotiations of Identity and Social Group Membership

Carla A. Pfeffer

Despite broader social acknowledgment of gender and sexual diversity, . . . transgender individuals and their significant others remain relatively unrecognized in both mainstream and academic discourse and are often subsumed under the limited theoretical frame of social "passing" when they do appear. Building a sociological critique against overly simplified biological frameworks for understanding complex gender and sexual identities, I analyze in-depth interviews with nontransgender women partners of transgender men. The personal identifications and experiences of this group of "queer" social actors are proposed as sociopolitically distinguishable from those of other more commonly recognized sexual minority groups. Data reveal the interactive social processes that often determine "rightful" social inclusion and exclusion across gender and sexual identity categories as well as their capacities to generate and limit possibilities for social movements and political solidarity.

. . . The present study proposes cis women partners of trans men as queer social actors,[1] arguing that a more developed understanding of this understudied group may fruitfully extend sociological knowledge on contemporary sexual identity groups and communities.[2] The present work broadens the notion of "queer," as a politics established against identity, considering the ways in which "queer," as a relational subjectivity, usefully complicates our understanding of social identities and social group–based membership.

In this way, the present study is a move toward theorizing particular queer social actors, identities, social embodiments, and families as embedded within intersecting normative and regulatory social systems, structures, and institutions.

An exploration of the identities and experiences of cis women partners of trans men also provokes consideration of the complex management processes involved in negotiating both individual identity and social group–based memberships. A critical aspect of these social processes is being seen or not seen, recognized or not recognized, as a rightful member of particular social identity groups with which one identifies. For trans men and their cis women partners, these meaningful social recognition processes often include (sometimes unintentional or even undesired) social "passing" with regard to gender and sexual orientation.

A problematic aspect of many of the sociological studies employing this notion of "passing" is their tendency to reinforce the presumed essentiality of sex and gender binaries by assuming that some social actors hold authentic proprietary claims over particular social identity–group membership (e.g., only those categorized as "male" at birth can be "authentic" or "real" men), while others can stake only inauthentic or false claims. Indeed, it is only under such a framework that it makes sense that some individuals might be recognized as authentically (and therefore unremarkably) "belonging" as members, while others may only hope to "pass"

From Pfeffer, C. (2014). "I don't like passing as a straight woman": Queer negotiations of identity and social group membership. *American Journal of Sociology*, *120*(1), 1–44.

into relatively inauthentic membership as wannabes. Notions of "passing," therefore, tend to be predicated upon assumptions of essentialized and naturalized group difference.

. . . In this article, I draw upon Connell's (2009) notion of "recognition" (in lieu of "passing") to argue that social rights, privileges, and group membership connected to categories of sex, gender, and sexuality depend largely upon social interpellation. More specifically, I will demonstrate how gender and sexual identities are interactional accomplishments that often reveal more about the workings of normative social privilege than they reveal about the social actors whose gender and sexual identities are being (mis)recognized. This study considers queer social actors' often strategic and pragmatic management of these (mis)recognition processes to gain access to particular social and material benefits of social group membership, offering theoretical and empirical insights on identity negotiations, and moments of "trouble" in these negotiations, across contested and regulated social categories and groups more broadly. As such, this work provides insights that actively respond to Irvine's (1994, p. 245) still-relevant call to sociologists nearly two decades earlier: "Sociological theory must . . . [place] social categories such as sexuality and race in the foreground in the context of power and difference." Finally, this work proposes a sociological queer analytic framework that compels solidarity-based approaches to social movement organizing around identity-based rights.

TOWARD A SOCIOLOGY OF QUEER SOCIAL ACTORS AND IDENTITIES: EXTENDING THEORETICAL AND ANALYTICAL FRAMEWORKS

Emerging as a late 20th-century outgrowth of poststructuralist thought, a central analytic across much queer theory is its critique of notions of normativity, deviance, and stable/coherent identities. The interface between queer theory and sociology

has been slow to develop.[3] Michael Warner, one of the key figures in the development and popularization of academic queer theory, describes social science disciplines' reticence to adopt queer theoretical frames as paradoxical given that "the analysis of normativity . . . should have become central to such disciplines" (2012, p. 8). Epstein (1994, p. 197) writes that displacement of sexual minorities to the periphery rather than the center of social inquiry has had critical limiting effects on the discipline of sociology and that "the challenge that queer theory poses to sociological investigation is precisely in the strong claim that no facet of social life is fully comprehensible without an examination of how sexual meanings intersect with it."[4]

. . . Seidman (1994) argues that one of queer theory's central and most defining contributions is the way in which it challenges taken for granted assumptions about the existence of a relatively stable homosexual subject and identity. Queer theory and politics embraced (rather than attempted to reconcile) the messiness and fluidity of sexual acts, boundaries, and identities. Indeed, queer politics galvanized those who shared a burgeoning sense of disenfranchisement from (and reaction against) mainstream lesbian and gay politics of "normalization," generating expressly oppositional politics informed by postmodern and deconstructionist theorizing (Seidman 2001; Bernstein 2005).

Identities as Social Process: Sociological Queer Analysis

. . . As sociologists, rather than ignoring or sidelining critical social analyses of queer social subjects, we might query: What are some of the meaningful social and political processes that regulate queer social actors' membership within, or passage through, various identity and social-membership groups? How might sociologists contribute to a project that expands beyond the textual to consider the everyday lives of queer social actors?

Valocchi (2005, p. 766) offers one possible pathway for sociology, defining "sociological queer analysis" as that which blends "a queer sensibility about the performative nature of identity with sociological sensibility about how these performances are constrained, hierarchical, and rooted in social inequality."[5] As such, one of the primary goals of the present work is to develop an expressly sociological queer analysis that focuses upon fissures and moments of trouble in culture and identity, articulating the social process through which individuals come to embrace and resist subject identities as "queer" even as these identities are (mis)recognized by social others. The discipline of sociology is perhaps uniquely well positioned to seriously consider the daily lives of queer social actors and to begin to theorize the processes through which these lives and identities are constituted, (mis)recognized, resisted, and embraced. Namaste (1994) urges sociologists to consider the social constructedness of genders and sexualities and the ways in which some are normalized (or left unmarked, as nonqueer), as well as how all social actors negotiate various identities and subject positions (and limits to these identities and subject positions).

. . . Queer social actors, like everyone else, lead lives simultaneously produced through and against normative structures of sex, gender, and sexuality. These normative structuring forces of sex, gender, and sexuality operate primarily along presumably "natural," biological, and essentialized binaries of male/female, man/woman, and heterosexual/homosexual. The lives and experiences of cis women partners of trans men, however, call these normative structuring binaries into even greater question in their failure to adequately articulate and encapsulate these queer social actors' identities and social group memberships. The experiences of queer social actors, therefore, hold the potential to rattle the very foundations upon which normative binaries rest, highlighting the increasingly blurry intersections, tensions, and overlaps between sex, gender, and sexual orientation in the 21st century (Pfeffer 2012).

Theorizing Social "(Mis)recognition" Rather Than "Passing"

The incoherence of these normative binaries becomes clearer through focus on interactional processes by which social actors are granted insider/outsider social status. When individuals refer to someone "passing" as a man or "passing" as a woman, the social meaning making that is taking place lies at the thorny intersections of sex and gender categorization, expression, attribution, and identity (for further discussion of these and other concepts, language, and terminology related to transgender identity and experience, see Wentling et al. [2008]; Pfeffer [2010]). Studies of "passing," and the social accomplishments of sex and gender, have a long, revered, and contentious history in sociology, particularly among symbolic interactionists and ethnomethodologists (see Garfinkel 1967; Goffman 1976; Kessler and McKenna 1978; West and Zimmerman 1987; Denzin 1990; Rogers 1992; Zimmerman 1992). "Passing" carries the assumption that certain individuals somehow naturally embody particular identities to which others can stake only inauthentic membership claims. In a sense, some individuals are understood as rightful "owners" of membership to particular social identity groups—most notably, those groups holding disproportionate social power and authority (Harris 1993; Calavita 2000).

The concept of passing also relies on juxtaposed notions of conscious, intentional, deceptive "dupers" and presumably natural, authentic, deceived "dupes" (Serano 2007). Nevertheless, "passing" is often held as the gold standard of "successful" transsexualism—particularly by medical establishments; as such, "passing" is often conceptualized as emblematic of normativity or a desire to *be* normative (as reviewed by Connell [2009]). Analyses of "passing" in racial and class contexts (see Harris 1993; Calavita 2000; Kennedy 2002; Ong 2005), however, adopt a more nuanced lens that views "passing" as a potentially pragmatic (though fraught) interactional strategy for accessing and attaining regulated social, material, and legal resources, and consider the personal, interpersonal, and sociopolitical effects and consequences that the use of such strategies may involve.

While "passing" may grant reprieve from the social stigma and potential danger of ambiguous gender expression, as well as access to social and material resources granted only to particular group members, this access and these reprieves are often tenuous, context specific, and revocable. Trans men who most always "pass" in ordinary social situations may live in fear about the consequences of being involved in a serious accident during which the removal of clothing (or, in some cases, the accessing of identification records indicating legal sex or gender status) would seriously impair their ability to be unambiguously recognized in accordance with their gender identity. Employing a sociological queer analysis, the concept of "passing" may be further illuminated by focusing on those ordinarily granted "natural" and unquestioned status within particular identity categories. Elson (2004, p. 172), for example, presents a compelling exploration into cis women's experience of identity posthysterectomy and whether or not those who undergo this surgical procedure are still considered (and consider themselves) "women" or not—reaching the equivocal conclusion of yes, no, maybe. As such, Elson (2004) probes and destabilizes the supposedly "natural" and essential links between biology, gender identity, and social perceptions of which bodies rightfully constitute "woman."

Connell (2009) usefully troubles the notion of "passing" to consider how "recognition" may be a more precise conceptual framework for thinking about the juxtapositions between one's body, subjective identity, social group memberships, and social appraisals of all of these. Accordingly, we would do better to supplant our biologically essentialist notions of "passing" with a more sociological notion of "recognition." By doing so, we might come to consider and recognize that trans people's efforts to "pass" occur not when living in accordance with their subjective gender identities, but as they attempt to live within gender identities normatively corresponding to their sex assignment or sex categorization (West and Zimmerman 1987, p. 133).[6] In other words, many trans men do, indeed, "pass" for much of their lives—as girls or as women. They often report struggling, within bodies and social identities that do not feel like "home," until these efforts become

untenable and they take further steps to bring their bodies and social embodiments in line with their gender identity.

As this study will show, sexual identity is also a relationally formed construct, depending upon a constellation of dynamic, shifting, socially informed understandings that individuals hold about themselves and others. As Vidal-Ortiz (2002, p. 192) writes: "One interactional way in which gender and sexuality collide is as people interpret each others' attractions based on their gender presentations or expressions." Sexuality is about more than personal identities, autonomous desires, and sexual object choice alone. Rather, we "do sexuality"; our sexualities are interpellated every day, arising from social others' (mis)recognition of the ways in which we see and understand ourselves and our partners. I argue that we must further extend Connell's notion of "recognition" to attend not only to the ways in which we may come to see individuals in accordance with how they see themselves but also to the ways in which making any attribution of identity is part of the process of bringing identities into social being. In other words, by focusing on how we recognize and misrecognize others' self-identities, we come to better understand these identities not as individual and predetermined fixed entities, but as dynamic social processes. . . .

STUDY

Participant Recruitment and Sample

This work represents the largest and most comprehensive study conducted, to date, with cis women partners of trans men (for additional information about the size and growth of this emergent social group, see Pfeffer [2010]). Research participants were recruited using online and paper-flyer postings targeting the significant others, friends, families, and allies of trans men. Most study participants were recruited via Internet-facilitated social network ("snowball") sampling, the primary method of purposeful sampling when targeting sexual minorities and their partners (Patton 1990; Mustanski 2001; Shapiro 2004; Rosser et al. 2007). I also enlisted key informants across the United States and Canada to distribute materials to potential participants in their local regions.

I conducted interviews with 50 cis women partners of trans men for this study. Participants discussed their experiences in 61 individual relationships with trans men (several participants reported multiple relationships with trans men). Participants resided across 13 states in the United States, three Canadian provinces, and one Australian state, expanding existing work on sex and gender minorities that focuses almost exclusively on one or two states, with large urban centers, in the United States. This sample consists of participants from most of the U.S. geographic regions with the highest reported proportions of trans men (see Rosser et al. 2007), including two much underresearched regions with regard to studies of sex and gender minorities—the midwestern United States and Canada. The most frequent sexual orientation self-identification label, used by 50% of participants in this sample, was "queer." Participants' trans partners (according to participant reports) were also most likely to identify as "queer" (48%), with "heterosexual" as second most common (33%). When asked to describe how they would define or label their relationship(s) with their trans partner(s), study participants described their relationships as "queer" 65% of the time among those providing information for this question.

Despite aiming for racial and age diversity, only variation on age was successfully achieved. Interviewees' ages ranged from 18 to 51 years, with an average of 29 years, and, on average, cis women's trans partners were slightly younger. Participants largely self-identified as white. When considering the race/ethnicity of the trans partners of participants, the sample begins to reflect somewhat greater racial/ethnic variation, with 18% identified as "multiracial." Participants and their partners were highly educated (with 24% and 11%, respectively, holding postgraduate degrees) yet reported household incomes that were quite low among participants

providing these data. Trans men partners of participants were at various stages of sex or gender transition—with most being just a bit over two years into the process. Most were taking testosterone, a considerable minority had had "top" surgery, while a very slim minority had had "bottom" surgery of any kind. . . .

FINDINGS AND DISCUSSION: DOING GENDER AND SEXUALITY THROUGH (MIS)RECOGNITION PROCESS

Just as trans men have their own transition experiences to manage on multiple levels, so, too, do their cis women partners (see Nyamora 2004; Pfeffer 2008; Brown 2009; Joslin-Roher and Wheeler 2009; Ward 2010). Study participants relayed, in great detail, the various struggles they experienced as they sought to maintain, transform, understand, proclaim, and refute various personal and social identities in the context of their lives. The following sections present narrative data, using pseudonyms to protect participant confidentiality, illustrating the ways in which queer social actors negotiate intersecting and sometimes conflicting social identities, relationships, politics, and social groups. These narratives prompt consideration of the ways in which gender and sexual identity are interactive social accomplishments involving boundary negotiations and (mis)recognition processes that carry tangible personal and social consequences.

Language and Social "Reading"

"Queer" *as a distinct social identity category.*—Cis women partners of trans men frequently wondered aloud, when I asked them about their own shifting and contingent sexual identities in relation to their trans partners, "What does that make me?" Martha (25 years, Massachusetts) described the challenge of personally struggling with issues connected to identity in the context of her relationship with her trans partner:

I thought of myself as a dyke and then now I'm with someone who identifies as a man and I'm thinking—how do I identify now? I'm not a lesbian. . . . I'm not really perceived as queer by many other people right now. And it really messed with me for awhile—what am I? Who am I? Not that I didn't know who I was, but what identity should I give to people? A lot of times I'd try to adopt my identity as my own and it doesn't matter what other people think. But it's hard not to judge myself by other people's judgments.

Having difficulty figuring out how to self-identify was described often by participants in my sample as not only an internal struggle, but one that emerges from various social and cultural imperatives and in social interactions with others. . . .

Another participant, Linda (22 years, Sydney, Australia), explicitly rejected the social imperative to identify her relationship with her partner using particular identity labels: "All these people would go, 'Oh, what does that make you now?' And I would say, 'Happy and in love. That's all.' I didn't see why anything else has to matter." Current and former lesbian-identified respondents reported facing particular challenges in terms of identity and social/community membership and the attributions others made about their personal motivations, desires, and emotional health. As Polly (40 years, New York) noted: "If you're a lesbian, everybody works so hard to accept it. They accept it, then you fuck them up by being with a trans guy. And then they're like, 'Okay, next she's going to go to men.' That it's just this form of evolution . . . and you're just graduating in this progressive chain of eventually getting to the pinnacle of the 'real' man. I sort of feel like people see it as this progressive growth into being fully, Freudianly, 'correctly' socialized to heterosexuality." Cis women partners of trans men described facing persistent challenges in actively negotiating their own (and their partner's) shifting identities across a variety of personal, interpersonal, and social contexts. One of the ways in which this negotiation manifested for many participants was through language and determining how they would self-identify, with regard to sexuality, in the context of their unique relationships.

Just over half of the cis women participants in this study self-identified their sexual orientation as "queer" at the point of interview and about 65% described their relationship with their trans partner as "queer." According to these cis women's accounts, over 60% of their trans men partners were perceived as men in social spaces "always" or "almost always." When in public together, therefore, many cis women in this sample reported being frequently (mis)recognized as part of a heterosexual couple. Verbal evidence participants provided in their accounts of these social encounters included social others using the words "sir," "bro," "boyfriend," "husband," "dad," and "father," as well as pronouns such as "he" and "him" when referring to participants' trans partners, and use of words/pronouns such as "Miss," "Mrs.," "Ms.," "ma'am," "girl," "girlfriend," "wife," "mom," "mother," "she," and "her" when referring to the participants themselves. Several participants also described instances in which clerks "corrected" sex designators from "female/f" to "male/m" on their trans partner's paperwork or in computer records systems, remarking about how there must have been an "error in the system," upon seeing the man in front of them. This was an important example of the way in which being misrecognized (according to medical or legal systems, which serve as gatekeepers for sex marker designation changes on personal identification documents) and recognized (in accordance with one's gender identity) may go hand in hand, providing or preventing access to regulated social and material institutions (such as a marriage license).

Nonverbal indicators that trans partners were being socially "read" as men or that the couple was being "read" as heterosexual included the check being consistently handled to one's trans partner at restaurants and other service establishments, other men giving a head "nod" when passing one's trans partner on the street, being smiled at by older persons when holding hands with one's trans partner in public,[7] and not being scrutinized when in sex-segregated public spaces (such as restrooms). In these instances, (mis)recognition processes often conferred social advantage, privilege, and mainstream acceptance. Yet being (mis)recognized as heterosexual was described as personally and socially problematic by many participants—particularly insofar as they feared being (mis)recognized as "heteronormative" by social others. Participants described their understandings of heteronormativity as fulfilling stereotypically gendered "roles" in their relationships, endorsing majoritarian politics, and not being seen as queer or politically radical.[8]

Self-identifying as "queer," among study participants, was described as a fraught (though sometimes powerfully political) solution to the inadequacy of other currently existing language choices for expressing sexual identity in the context of one's relationship with a trans partner:

> Before my ex-partner . . . I had been sort of actively claiming that I wasn't straight . . . and I was very comfortable telling people that. But I also come from a small town and the options there were very much "gay," "lesbian," "bisexual" or "straight." I didn't feel that any of those fit me. So I started saying to my friends and to whoever else, "Well, I'm not straight." But that's as far as it went . . . I hadn't had any other partners that would actually complicate that at that point . . . But [once I met my trans ex partner], it just made sense for me to think about identifying as "queer" and that felt comfortable. (Sage, 21 years, Ontario)

Sage's narrative walks us through a process of queer identity consolidation. Sage considers sexual orientation self-identification labels in the context of her own life, coming to the conclusion that none of the existing labels accurately "fit." She first chooses a new identity category rooted in disidentification with an existing identity category ("not straight"). Later, a new relational context (partnering with a trans man) serves as the impetus for self-identifying in yet a new way—adopting an identity label ("queer") that was not part of the original range of self-identification choices of which she was aware or that were available to her. . . .

As this narrative illustrates, for some, choosing to self-identify as "queer" also serves as a conscious and intentional social indicator of a political stance that explicitly resists or rejects normativity in order to imagine a different or transformed social landscape. When asked what identifying as "queer" meant to her, Ani (21 years, Ohio) stated: "I needed a language for *not* being heteronormative." These experiences stand in stark contrast to calls for a "post-queer study of sexuality" (Green 2002, p. 537) in sociology or claims that the term "queer" exists primarily to symbolize a departure from sexual identity categories (Green 2002, 2007). Rather, these participants assert "queer" as one of the few (if not the only) sexual identity categories that does not overly constrain or threaten the relationships they have with their trans partners. Participants told me that self-identifying as "lesbian" in the social world carried the possibility of invalidating their trans partner's identity as a man.

It is possible to connect some of the identity and (mis)recognition struggles of these participants with those of bisexual-identified respondents from other sociological empirical work (Burrill 2001; Wolkomir 2009; Tabatabai and Linders 2011).[9] Specifically, women across each group described being (mis)recognized by social others in ways inconsonant with their own sexual self-identifications and in ways that often shifted based upon social assessments of their partner's gender identity in relation to their own. Empirical comparisons between this sample and earlier work on bisexual-identified cis women (Blumstein and Schwartz 1974, 1977, 1990; Richardson and Hart 1981; Ault 1996a, 1996b; Rust 2000) also attest to the fluidity and dynamic potential of sexual identifications. While many participants in my study reported moving from self-identifications as "lesbian" prior to a partner's transition (or partnering with a trans man) to self-identifications as "queer," women in these earlier studies often reported self-identification as lesbian when partnered with another woman and self-identification as heterosexual when partnered with a man, discussing the ways in which shifts in the sex of one's partner resulted in shifts of group membership, community, and sense of belonging. In other words, sexual identity was understood as largely situational and context/partner/community-dependent, rather than individual, inherent, or fixed and immutable.

One primary point of difference between these groups is that among the group of cis women partners of trans men I interviewed, identification as "bisexual" was reportedly an untenable choice for many as it could introduce identity and relationship insecurity through trans partners wondering whether participants were attracted to them as a man or as a woman. Further, very few of the participants in this study self-identified as "heterosexual" (n = 2), with most participants expressly rejecting such self-identification and discussing how much they valued their connection to (and membership within) LGBTQ communities.

"Queer" as an empty signifier.—Paradoxically, another dominant theme that emerged among participants who self-identified as "queer" was the sentiment that "queer" can become so all-encompassing, as a catchall identity, that it may be in peril of becoming an empty social category. Gamson (1995) describes this tendency as the "queer dilemma." While the lack of boundedness associated with "queer," as an identity, can make it particularly appealing to those for whom other categories feel overly restrictive or inappropriate, for others this very unboundedness can feel quite confining:

> I could say I'm queer but I also am not so sure I want to signal that identity either because I feel sometimes queerness is a little irresponsible because it's just so overused that it becomes sort of meaningless. I don't even know what people [are] trying to indicate to me when they say that. So I don't know if I feel comfortable saying it. . . . I think my sexual identity doesn't have a particular proclivity or erotic choice that has anything to do with a pre-existing terminology. . . . So I feel like in my life I slide myself into the term that worked mostly to make other people understand me—not necessarily because I feel like it really is

an adequate description of who I am. (Polly, 40 years, New York)

For Polly, therefore, "queer" serves as a social identity category in which she reluctantly places herself for the purposes of becoming socially intelligible to others rather than from a sense of its personal resonance. Polly's narrative thus highlights the critical importance and paradox of social recognition with regard to queer identities. Polly adopts a label that makes her socially recognizable and interpretable to social others. This label, however, fails to fully encapsulate or accurately describe the specificity of her particular partner choices and desires.

Amber (19 years, Ontario) offered another example of the limitations of "queer" as an identity signifier: "'Queer' is such a vague term. If you say you're queer then people will often just assume that, if you're a girl, then you're a lesbian. . . . But I date men so I don't want to . . . be just kind of lost in the queer umbrella. If you're going to look at me and want to know what box I go in, put me in the right one." For Amber, then, "queer" is a category that renders her attractions to cis men invisible. Rather than being overly all-encompassing, she finds it overly restrictive and exclusionary in the context of her own attractions and desires. Both Polly and Amber articulate such as "queer." Some of these struggles, once again, echo those of expressly bisexual-identified women who often report being (mis)recognized as heterosexual when partnered with men and as lesbian when partnered with a woman, rendering their bisexual self-identifications invisible (Burrill 2001; Wolkomir 2009; Tabatabai and Linders 2011).

Cis women and their trans partners must often work to (re)define their identities—as individuals and in relationship to one another—in ways that both challenge and extend existing linguistic and social categories. Furthermore, the rising visibility and media presence of partnerships between cis women and trans men, particularly via the medium of the Internet, contributes to the emergence of queer cultural communities through which language and support may be continuously developed, challenged, and shared (see Shapiro 2004). The Internet emergence of a new linguistic identity term, "queer-straight" (which two participants in this study used to describe their relationship with their trans partner), may be one way in which sociolinguistic innovation is developing out of existing frustrations over lack of specificity and meaning with "queer."

In addition to negotiating language and identity-classificatory systems, study participants reported marked and sometimes painful discrepancies between how they see and understand themselves and how they are seen and understood (or not) by others in their social communities and contexts. Two themes that frequently emerged for cis women partners of trans men were actually flip sides of the same "(mis)recognition coin"—being (mis)recognized (or "passing") as unremarkably straight in both queer and nonqueer social spaces and becoming invisibly queer (i.e., no longer being recognized as a rightful member of the queer community) within queer social spaces. Clearly, (mis)recognition—or being "seen" and "not seen"—by various communities is a powerful social process that critically informs, validates, and invalidates personal identities and group memberships. The following sections detail these flip sides of this same coin of social group (mis)recognition and membership processes as well as describe how the cis women in this study negotiated these processes.

Identity and Social Norm Resisting and Affiliating

"I don't want to be a housewife!"—Participants often spoke explicitly about not wanting to fall into relational patterns with their partner that might be interpreted as normative. Some cis women voiced this intention directly to their trans partner—as in the case of Emma (22 years, Ontario), who spoke of a conversation during which she reportedly told him: "I am a feminist and I don't want to be a housewife. . . . That's not who I am and that's not who you're

going to be in a relationship with." Some cis women and their trans partners shared in the desire to reject and resist normativity. According to Sage (21 years, Ontario): "It sort of is a little disturbing to both of us—as individuals and together—to think that we might fall into sort of a heterosexuality, a heteronormative pattern. Being queer, interacting as queer, presenting as queer, and being queer in the world is something that's really important to both of us." In a similar vein, Belinda (24 years, Ontario) explained: "We both say that it's a queer relationship. Neither of us are interested in passing as a straight couple or having people believe that we're a straight couple."

Recall that the majority of cis women's accounts include discussion of being (mis)recognized as heterosexual by social others. As such, these cis women's vocal and instrumental resistance to being socially (mis)recognized as anything but "queer" offers possibilities for destabilizing normativity insofar as it challenges social others' notions of what a "heterosexual couple" is like. Further, it reveals the ways in which participants position themselves explicitly against habituated, iterative enactments of normativity—which they explicitly counterpose to feminist and queer identities. Of course, their resistance may be limited given that opportunities to correct the social (mis)recognition of others do not always readily present themselves, may be unsuccessful, may be resisted by one's partner, or may be unsafe in certain social contexts. . . .

Axial coding of the data revealed that cis women participants more often judged themselves to more strongly reject or resist normative practices and politics than their trans partners, particularly when they self-identified as "queer." This finding might be expected when we consider that being recognized by others as male is often socially accomplished through relational enactments of normative or hegemonic masculinity (Connell 1987). In other words, trans men (like cis men) often gain social recognition of their gender identity as men when engaging in stereotypical social behaviors associated with "being a man" (see Connell 1987; Brown 2009; Pfeffer 2010; Ward 2010). While there was no difference in self-reports of enacting traditional versus nontraditional gender performances in relationships across age or sexual identity of participants, younger cis women (those under 35 years of age) more frequently worried that their relationships would be (mis)recognized as heterosexual than older cis women (those 35 years of age and older). These patterns likely reflect the influence of Third Wave feminist and queer politics in the lives of cis women under 35 years of age in this sample (see Pfeffer 2010).

"We're just another straight couple with an extra set of tits!"—Despite the fact that participants most frequently identified themselves (and their relationships) as "queer" and distanced themselves and their relationships from characterization as "heteronormative," a vocal minority made statements that could be interpreted as reflective of heteronormativity. These statements ranged from the seemingly blatant—such as that from Lily (26 years, Florida), which opens this section—to those couched in the feminist post-structuralist language of gender performativity (see Butler 1990, 1993). Axial coding of the data revealed that cis women ages 35 and older reported desires for heteronormativity more often than those younger than 35 years of age. Those cis women who reported that their trans partners were perceived socially as male "always" or "almost always" were most likely to report performing traditional enactments of gender in their relationships and to report that their trans partner embraced normativity. Cis women were also more likely to report performing traditional enactments of gender in their relationships when their partners transitioned over the course of the relationship and were trans identified when the relationship began (as opposed to those whose relationship began as lesbian or those who were with partners who had already completed most of their transition by the time the relationship began).

When Ellia (24 years, New Mexico) was asked how she would describe the type of relationship that she has with her partner, she responded: "We're just a straight couple. He's my fiancé, we're getting married, we're just a straight couple." While Ellia's description is laden with unremarkable, normative descriptors (e.g., "straight," "he," "fiancé," "married," "straight," "couple"), her invocation of the phrase, "We're *just* [my emphasis] a straight couple," twice, may be interpreted as awareness that, without defending the normativity of her partnership, her relationship may be quite unlikely to be understood by others as "just a straight couple." Margaret (29 years, Massachusetts) offered another perspective on distancing her family from counternormativity: "One of the first conversations we ever had was about kids, how many we wanted, and what the time frame was and we aligned completely. . . Sometimes, when you're *super* radical, you get to *not* be radical! And I want our kids to have one set of parents with one last name." Margaret's conceptualization is an interesting and provocative one—it suggests that privately held queer identities (which may be socially invisible or hidden, particularly in the context of family life) remain socially radical. Furthermore, it suggests that, based on this internally held queer identity, it is possible (and perhaps even acceptable) to access certain privileges and normative institutions that do not challenge or erode the "queerness" of these privately held queer identities. Margaret acknowledges and resists normative understandings of family as she casts herself in the part of "*super* radical" and relays the negotiations and deliberations in which she and her partner have engaged with regard to having and naming children. This vision of a possible future that Margaret envisions allows her to transform normative ("*not* radical") practices of having and naming children into a "*super* radical" enterprise of queer family building.

Cis women participants also articulated their experiences enacting what some may interpret as habituated and stereotypically gendered relational structures in ways they explicitly linked to conscious gender performativity and normative resistance (Pfeffer 2012). According to Rachel (27 years, Ohio): "I think he had this fantasy . . . which I don't think exists for anybody anymore.

But, in his head, part of becoming a man was becoming a *Leave It to Beaver* dad—like coming home and mom has dinner on the table and whatever else is happening. But it turns out he cleans house more than I do and he cooks more than I do. So I think, at this point, our relationship is undefinable by present terms; so I would just say, 'queer.' It's just different. It's different than anything available." Eliza (24 years, Nova Scotia) offered another example that paralleled Rachel's but also explicitly considered the importance of others' social perceptions of her relationship structure:

> We're both very sort of intrigued by 50s décor and roles and all that sort of stuff. . . . I will take on the role of housewife and, a lot of the time, it's this tongue-in-cheek sort of thing. He'll be like, "Get me a beer!" and I'll put on an apron and run off into the other room, "Here ya go, dear!" It's very sort of playful. Again, it's the performance of gender instead of *really* taking it all that seriously. But, at the same time . . . the kitchen is *my* kitchen and all this sort of stuff that's very gendered. . . . Sometimes I'm concerned that other people might not quite get it and that they might think that we're really espousing these very traditional roles. . . . I don't want to be the passive wife. . . . I'd much rather be the tough wife.

For these participants, performing normativity is a reportedly conscious dynamic that holds the potential to be simultaneously nostalgic, flexible, ironic, and difficult to define. Cis women and their trans men partners clearly engage in dynamic, relational processes that produce and validate enactments of gender in ways that may be simultaneously normative and counternormative, despite the commonly voiced concern to not be (mis)recognized as traditional or unremarkably heterosexual (for more on this, see Brown [2009]; Ward [2010]; Pfeffer [2010], [2012]).

A sociological queer analysis might also usefully trouble assertions that those in relationships with trans people must have relationships that are somehow more transgressive or counternormative than other types of relationships.

As Kessler and McKenna (2003) note, the prefix "trans" in "transgender" does not necessarily refer to the "transcendence" or "transformation" of gender or gender normativity, and to assume that it does is to minimize decades of sociological work testifying to the rigidity and recalcitrance of the socially structuring gender binary in our society. These assertions also fail to consider the ways in which identity choices are socially embedded, strategic, and constrained. From a queer sociological analytic perspective, we might approach questions about whether the relationships between cis women and trans men reflect a radical subversion of cultural normativity or merely mirror and repackage cultural normativity with some degree of critical suspicion. Such questions implicitly suggest that the onus of responsibility for radically reconfiguring gendered power relations ultimately lies with a numerical and marginalized social minority. Indeed, we might usefully redirect such questions toward whether or not relationships between cis women and cis men—the numerical majority in our culture—currently reflect radical subversion of cultural normativity. Doing so reminds us of the powerful structuring forces of inequality for all social actors and also points to potentially fruitful alliances between social actors working toward equality aims. Building these communities of political and social alliance and resistance was described as an area of particular struggle for the cis women in this study.

Community Belonging, Vanishing, and Outcasting

"A normal, boring couple" and *"I definitely don't miss being scared."*—Brown (2009) describes "sexual identity renegotiation" as a central challenge faced by cis women partners of trans men. When providing accounts of their experiences in social spaces, cis women sometimes discussed how being (mis)recognized as unremarkably heterosexual was a social phenomenon highly desired by one's trans partner, while their own feelings remained more

ambivalent or even conflicted. As Frieda (28 years, Ontario) discussed:

[My partner] definitely was into the whole idea of us passing as a straight couple, so nothing queer really fit into our everyday lives or relationship because his main priority was passing as a man and that I should look like a woman so we can pass as a straight couple and he can blend in. So he encouraged me to look more feminine and to have my hair long and things like that . . . [but] I wanted to shave my head and . . . pierce things and . . . do things that normal, boring, feminine, straight women didn't usually do and they didn't fit in with what he wanted . . . . I kind of felt guilty or selfish if I tried to dress the way that I wanted. . . . When we were going out together, I tried to look as feminine and as boring as I could so we could pass as a normal, boring couple.

Frieda's narrative speaks to the way in which her partner's accomplishment of recognition as a man depends, at least in part, on social others' recognition of her as normatively feminine. This makes sense if we consider that the accomplishment of social recognition as a "normal" man depends, centrally, upon being perceived by others as not a woman and not gay (Connell 1987). In other words, social recognition of Frieda's partner as a man is facilitated through social assumptions linking manhood and heteronormativity. This assumed connection to heteronormativity was both troubling and strange to many participants—particularly those for whom social recognition as lesbian and counternormative had become a critical aspect of their sense of self.

Polly (40 years, New York) discussed challenges connected to reinterpreting her own identity, the social perceptions of others, and social group memberships:

I think I'm still trying to sort out what it means *not* to be a lesbian. There is a nice *recognition* [author's emphasis] when you're walking down the street with your girlfriend and you're holding hands and see another lesbian and they see you as a lesbian and it's like you feel like you're all in the same club. So I miss that. . . . I just sort of feel like this level of boringness. I guess I have to say I definitely

got off on the transgression of having men look at me and then kissing my girlfriend. And now it's like I have men look at me and then I kiss him and it's like, "Big whoop." . . . It's just not the same charge. So I think I miss that. I miss some of that transgressive sort of fucking with people's heteronormative assumptions and now I'm just like basically following the script and it feels a little weird. It's not quite as fun. [I miss] the performativity of being gay. . . . Sometimes it's scary and you don't do it. So I definitely don't miss being scared.

For both Frieda and Polly, social experiences wherein they believed their partner was recognized by others as a man elided their own queer visibility, creating the paradoxical situation of gaining access to heteronormative social privilege while simultaneously losing access to (or recognition by) sexual minority communities with which they strongly identify/identified. Furthermore, both describe "passing" or being (mis)recognized as heterosexual as "boring," highlighting the power of visibly queer social identities to provoke and dynamically elicit sexually charged, emotional responses based upon their connection to transgressiveness. Polly's concluding remark, alluding to the danger associated with public expressions of intimacy that are recognized as lesbian, highlights a pragmatic aspect of being (mis)recognized as heterosexual: reduced threat of physical and sexual violence directed toward those who are more visibly queer.

Most cis women who reported being (mis) recognized as part of a heterosexual couple, by family, friends, or strangers, acknowledged the privilege that such (mis)recognition entails, while simultaneously expressing discomfort with this privilege and bemoaning the inevitable trade-off of losing social recognition as queer. Margaret (29 years, Massachusetts) stated: "I have mixed feelings about it Sometimes I really like passing. There's a real social benefit to it; it makes it a lot easier." Veronica (21 years, New York) told me: "It makes me feel safe in the world," but she also commented on the flip side: "It makes me feel really invisible and that's something he and I both deal with a lot. We don't like the invisibility factor. We're always looking for ways to be visible and to educate others. So maybe that's the only way because I don't really know how much we can walk down the street wearing shirts that say, 'We're not so straight!'" When Maya (30 years, California), who had just had a baby, was asked to discuss how she felt she and her partner are perceived by others, she responded: "It's annoying because we get such privilege everywhere we go. . . . My mother's like, 'Thank God!' And I provided her a grand-child, so I'm 'normal.' In some respects it's good and in other respects I wish *everyone* had that." Eliza (25 years, Nova Scotia), who is legally married to her trans partner, stated: "With family . . . there's a thing in the back of my head that wonders if it's so easy for them because now we're a 'straight couple.' It's almost less explain-ing for them to do in the future. Sometimes it's a mixed blessing." As Eliza reveals, family mem-bers' potential investments in processes of doing sexuality for their relatives further highlight sexuality as an interactive social accomplish-ment. These narratives also reveal a keenly developed consciousness of the way queer peo-ple experience the sometimes-marginalizing gaze of nonqueer people, poignantly highlight-ing the disjunctive between self-identification and social (mis)recognition.

"Another breeder couple invading."— Participants in this study also described the expe-rience of losing access to (and social recognition within) queer communities as they became "invisibly queer."[10] Margaret (29 years, Massa-chusetts) said: "When I see lesbian couples with a baby, I smile at them and have this moment of like, 'What a cute couple with a baby.' And [my partner] and I have this experience together because, at one point, he had been externally identified by others as a lesbian. So we have this moment of, 'Oh, another queer couple with a baby!' But [lesbian couples] . . . don't see that we're having this moment of camaraderie like, 'Yay, you did it, we're going to do it!' They see us as like, 'Oh, those straight people are looking at us.'" Maya (30 years, California) offered a similar story: "We can go anywhere and not have

people looking at us except when we're in [a gay neighborhood] and then it's like, 'Oh, another breeder couple invading.' And I just want to wear rainbow flags everywhere I go so I can prove that I belong in this community." Lilia (22 years, California) also articulated the not-uncommon experience of having her queer identity elided by others within the queer community: "My lesbian friends . . . [are] like, basically, 'Oh, so you turned straight.' . . . [But] I don't consider this a straight relationship since he's very queer. . . . I can see how it's straight in some context. But it's queer. His experiences of growing up as a woman [are] what makes it queer." In each of these narratives, participants describe experienc-ing the elision of their queerness—disappearing into the background of queer communities within which they often previously found community and recognition as queer. Many cis women participants described being (mis)recognized as heterosexual as not only personally invalidating but as alienating from queer communities of social support and belonging. Once again, these experiences echo those of bisexual-identified women who often report being ostracized from lesbian communities when partnered with men and from heterosexual communities when part-nered with women (Burrill 2001; Wolkomir 2009; Tabatabai and Linders 2011).

Cis women partners of trans men face chal-lenges of marginalization not only from social distancing, exclusion, and (mis)recognition by others within LGBTQ communities, but some-times as a result of their trans partner's wish to disassociate from these communities to reinforce their own social recognition as a man. Belinda (24 years, Ontario) spoke about losing her con-nection to the lesbian community when her part-ner disengaged from it:

It was tough for me as someone who had just kind of come out as a lesbian. I remember wanting to do lesbian things and go to lesbian bars and that kind of stuff. And I remember a switch in him where he was like, "No, I'm a straight guy." And I think that was hard because there was this community that I was trying to get involved with that suddenly didn't work with his identity. . . . I didn't really know that there was the option of him saying, "I'm queer." I just figured that's what happened when someone became trans—you were a lesbian and now you're straight.

Belinda articulates the limited (and often limiting) nature of social models of identity in the context of transition. Belinda was unaware that there were other ways (than "straight male") for trans men in relationships with cis women to identify and that these different identifications (if embraced by her partner) might generate alternate possibilities for her own identity and membership to social communities. Narratives like Belinda's also highlight how the accomplishment of social recognition as a man often necessitates social distancing from LGBTQ communities and spaces.

"The people that I dated would make me visibly queer."—When considering the personal and social identities and group memberships of cis women partners of trans men, it is also important to consider the often temporal-relational and contingent aspects of these ways of being and belonging in the world. Susan (23 years, Tennessee) articulated two distinct dilemmas she faced as a formerly lesbian-identified cis woman and as the former partner of a trans man: "I lost my community. . . . You lose the lesbian community and you really don't get anything else. . . . And the partners' [of trans men] community—you're only a valid member of that as long as you're in your relationship, which has nothing to do with *you* and everything to do with *him*." For Susan, carving out a space in the queer community along with other partners of trans men reflected both a contingent and tenuous subject position within such communities. Susan's experiences of being pushed out of lesbian community spaces upon partnering with a trans man was not uncommon. Rather than operating along explicit cut-and-dried practices of inclusion and exclusion, many cis women described more subtle social practices in which their rightful membership within lesbian community spaces was challenged or brought into question once they began

relationships with trans men or once a previously lesbian-identified partner began to move away from that identity and transitioned to living as a trans man.

Ani (21 years, Ohio) discussed another challenge in her relationship with a partner who socially identified as a "man" rather than as a "transgender man": "It's a lot easier to be able to [say]: 'Yes, I'm queer, I'm dating a *trans man*,' as opposed to, 'Yes, I'm queer, I'm dating a man.' People won't ask you to justify yourself in the same way. . . . Your sexuality clearly relies on your partner." Ani's partner's gender identity and recognition by social others as a man meant that her own queer identity was frequently made invisible—rendering her unremarkably heterosexual in the eyes of social others, including queer social others.

Nearly 30% of the participant sample self-identified, unprompted, as "femme"—meaning that the actual composition of femme-identifying or feminine-appearing cis women in the sample is likely higher than 30%. Nyamora (2004) and Brown (2009) both describe the ways in which cis femme-identified women partners of trans men frequently experience a grieving process in connection to the perceived loss of their queer femme visibility. Further, many of the participants in my study discussed how others' recognition of their queerness often relies upon their connection to a partner who embodies female masculinity in a visible and culturally intelligible way. For example, Teresa (24 years, Maine) told me:

I think as a femme. . . . I don't feel like I've ever been seen as queer when I've been by myself. I think so often in my history of dating people that the people that I dated would make me visibly queer. So it's really interesting when the person I'm dating makes me *invisible*. And so I don't gain any visibility as a lesbian or as someone who is queer when being out in public with [my trans partner] the way I would with past partners. So that's really, really hard. However, in a way it sort of feels almost liberating because now I and only I am responsible for my queer visibility. . . . I think that it's sexism, honestly, that femmes are seen as invisible beings when really we're radically queer in our own right and we're just never given that credit.

As Teresa articulates, femme-appearing/identifying cis women partnered with trans men, therefore, may face particular barriers with regard to being recognized as a member of the communities to which they belong and with which they identify (see also Nyamora 2004; Brown 2009; Joslin-Roher and Wheeler 2009; Ward 2010).[11]

These narratives reveal the extent to which queer visibility remains culturally synonymous with social perceptions of female masculinity and male femininity (Hutson 2010), often rendering those who embody cis femininity within queer communities invisible as queer. These narratives also echo earlier writings on lesbian butch and femme genders as socially intelligible identities around which communities materialized and organized (cf., Ponse 1978; Krieger 1983; Taylor and Whittier 1992; Kennedy and Davis 1993). Queer invisibility was of particular concern and consideration to many of the femme-identified cis women I interviewed. This articulated invisibility serves as a marked empirical contrast to theorizing around femme identity (e.g., Hollibaugh 1997; Munt 1998; Levitt, Gerrish, and Hiestand 2003), which marks it as politically transgressive (and even "transgender") in its own right. Such fissures between personal experience and political potential further highlight the need to examine the processes by which gender and sexual identities are produced through social interaction.

"You're not really gay" and "Take your pants off and show me."—Participants spoke about the ways in which queer femininities may not only be rendered invisible within queer and nonqueer cultural spaces, but how they may also be explicitly devalued within some queer communities relative to queer androgynies and queer masculinities (Kennedy and Davis 1993; Cogan 1999; Levitt et al. 2003). As Belinda (24 years, Ontario) told me:

> Basically within the lesbian community I was like completely made fun of. I used to have people make fun of me for carrying a purse and looking

"too girly" and, "Oh you're not really gay." Just those kinds of comments. So that was really hard for me when I was coming out because I just wanted to be taken seriously you know. . . . So my response to that [when I first came out] was to kind of change to become *less* feminine, change my body posturing and the way that I dress and cut off all my hair and that kind of stuff.

Narratives like Belinda's exemplified some queer cis women's experience of living in the liminal space of insider/outsider with regard to both queer and nonqueer communities.

Ward (2010) suggests that sidelining of the power and transgressive potential of femme identity among cis women partners of trans men may be an artifact of their primary social status within trans communities as allies and supporters of their partners—one of the forms of "gender labor" in which they engage. Some of the strategies self-identified femme participants described for rendering their queer identities more recognizable included adopting unique and unconventional hairstyles and hair colors, wearing rainbow jewelry and other LGBTQ pride symbols, dressing in vintage clothing, and obtaining visible tattoos and piercings, embodying counternormative embodiment practices with the intention of visually signifying their queer identities (see also Pitts 2000). Participants' narratives revealed the impact of being rendered invisible or an outsider not only in terms of one's own queer identity and relationship but also in determining the parameters of in-group/out-group social membership itself.

While some trans men and their cis women partners described being (mis)recognized as heterosexual and becoming invisible as queer within LGBTQ communities, other participants reported that their partners were (mis)recognized as trans men or as cis women, rather than cis men, more often in gay and lesbian social spaces than in mainstream or non-LGBTQ social spaces. The tensions between these (mis)recognition processes carried striking social consequences. One set of trends that emerged in participants' accounts involved (1) explicit exclusion of trans people and their partners from primarily gay and lesbian social spaces and (2) intimidating and even violent interactions aimed toward "finding out" the "real" sex of those who are trans as they interact within primarily gay and lesbian social spaces. Seventeen (34%) participants described instances of being told by leaders of gay and lesbian organizations (or hearing through the grapevine) that their or their partner's presence was no longer welcome since their partner's transition. Martha (25 years, Massachusetts) described making reservations at a lesbian bed and breakfast only to be told that she and her partner were no longer welcome upon the innkeeper's learning of her partner's transition. Lynne (35 years, California) described the exclusion of trans men from the yearly "dyke march" in her town.

June (21 years, Ontario), Kendra (21 years, Ohio), and Samantha (20 years, Michigan) each relayed harrowing and eerily similar experiences their trans partner had in gay and lesbian bars. According to June: "He went out to a . . . lesbian bar . . . and they wanted him to prove that he was actually male. So there was a lot of, 'Take your pants off and show me,' type of thing. They followed him into the bathroom and it was about an hour of harassment like that." Samantha told me: "He was going to the bathroom . . . and he was waiting for the stalls and . . . this old lesbian got up in [his] face and was like, 'Go use the other bathroom, we need this one more than you do. . . .' And she got really up in his face about it and he was like, 'I'm trans. I have to sit to pee.' And she was like, 'No you're not. . . .' She actually ripped his shirt off to see." In the context of a gay bar, Kendra relayed the following description:

> He almost got beat up that night . . . He went to the women's restroom because he wasn't fully male and he didn't want gay guys to find out that he didn't have a penis; so he chose to use the women's restroom that night. He was still fairly early into his transition and a guy followed him in there and watched him urinate and said, 'Take off that binder. I don't know why you want to be a guy. . . .' Later, the guy lunged across the dance floor at my partner and, luckily, one of our friends pushed him out of the way.

In each of these instances, trans men were held accountable for others' recognition of them as men—social processes that could have frightening and even dangerous consequences, even within communities that had formerly served as relatively safe havens from exclusion and discrimination.[12]

These narratives attest to the permeability and instability of membership and recognition within various identity-based communities. In a social context that continues to affirm fixed and naturalized binaries (male/female, man/woman, heterosexual/homosexual) despite increasing evidence documenting the fluidity and diversity of sex, gender, and sexual identifications, we find herein evidence for these identities as interactive social accomplishments. Perhaps even more important, we are urged to reconsider just who should be held accountable when it comes to recognizing the sex, gender, and sexual identities of others.

CONCLUSION: POSSIBILITIES FOR SOCIAL SOLIDARITY AND BROADER APPLICATION

In this study, I draw from Connell's (2009) notion of "recognition" to demonstrate the myriad ways in which we "do" not only gender, but sexuality as well, revealing sexual identities as interactional social accomplishments through which status, rights, and group membership may be stripped or conveyed. By challenging the essentialist notion that sexual identities are largely fixed and natural/biological, we are better poised to consider what is at stake when social actors recognize and misrecognize their peers' sexual self-identifications. The cis women I interviewed often vocally asserted their self-identification as queer. Yet in many instances, these cis women's accounts focused on being (mis)recognized by both queer and nonqueer social others as unremarkably heterosexual. Which of these accounts of their sexual identity is "true"? These findings prompt consideration of how the social effects of (mis)recognition processes (e.g., being able to access regulated social institutions and social membership within particular groups) are powerfully structuring—perhaps even largely determinant—of social group membership.

. . . . Extending Connell's (2009) "recognition" framework, this study highlights what is at stake in social (mis)recognition processes not only for queer social actors but also for everyone, as these processes reveal the ways in which access to regulated social groups and institutions is often mediated largely through interactional and perceptual social processes rather than static or essential aspects of individuals.

Namaste, writing about queerness and queer theory, states: "We cannot assert ourselves to be outside of heterosexuality, nor entirely inside, because each of these terms achieves its meaning in relation to the other. . . . We can think about the *how* of these boundaries . . . how they are created, regulated and contested" (1994, p. 224). This analysis offers further insight into that *how*—detailing the ways in which heterosexual, gay, lesbian, and queer identities and social identity group memberships overlap and are messily embraced, resisted, and (mis)recognized in the context of cis women's relationships with trans men. How might we make sense of the following narrative from a cis woman partner of a trans man that inspired the title for this article and was emblematic of many of the responses that I received? "I don't like passing as a straight woman. I would feel like I wasn't visible at times—and same with him, that he wasn't visible. . . . Both of our identities were very blurred; and that's a tough thing when so much of who we are is about other people perceiving us. . . . I like my queer identity and that's what I want people to see. So it was tough when I knew that wasn't being seen" (Martha, 25 years, Massachusetts). Much of the thrust of the mainstream lesbian and gay social movement over the past two decades has focused on protesting and bringing greater public awareness to discrimination against lesbians and gay men as well as their exclusion from various social institutions and privileges, such as legally recognized marriage.[13]

In calling for expanded rights and inclusion, mainstream lesbian and gay social movements have largely centered upon crafting a politics of sameness and respectability that stands in stark contrast to the oppositional politics of activist groups of the late 1960s through the early 1990s—such as the Gay Liberation Front, ACT UP, and Queer Nation (Duggan 2002; Ward 2008). Further, many of these more recent efforts depend largely upon appeals to the biological/ genetic etiology of sexual orientation and gender identity (e.g., Lady Gaga's aforementioned pop culture anthem, "Born This Way"). Couching demands for inclusion, equality, and freedom from discrimination within a framework of biological determinism consistently compels the following presumably rhetorical defense of these demands when they face social opposition: "In the context of historical and contemporary social discrimination and exclusion, why would anyone *choose* this?" Yet narratives and self-identifications like Martha's provide evidence against the counterfactual claim that no one would choose queerness if given such an option, just as they simultaneously recognize and explicitly value queer identities and queer cultures per se. They also reframe the issue of "choice" to consider that choosing to self-identify as queer is not synonymous with choosing social (mis)recognition, exclusion, and discrimination. In other words, many of the women I interviewed refused to be held accountable for other people's (mis)recognition of their or their partner's sex, gender, and sexual identities. . . .

Choosing queer self-identification and alliance as a form of normative resistance (see Pfeffer 2012) is not limited by the contours of one's own body in relation to those of one's partner(s). Normative social structures inscribe the parameters within which all social actors must live their daily lives. As such, all social actors desiring social change (perhaps especially those with normative privilege) are accountable for, and have a vested interest in, resisting and pushing against these parameters, as well as supporting others engaged in similar or parallel forms of resistance. Reframing and reorienting sociological analyses to the normative center, therefore, highlights the accountability and responsibility that those with relative privilege hold with regard to enacting social change, resisting stultifying normativity, and reconfiguring relationships of power. In doing so, we might further shift our inquiries to consider how and why anyone might develop and nurture their own and others' queer identities and relationships for the purposes of greater gender and sexual equality. . . .

NOTES

1. As Schilt and Westbrook, drawing from Serano (2007), note, "Cis is the Latin prefix for 'on the same side.' It complements trans, the prefix for 'across' or 'over' . . . to refer to individuals who have a match between the gender they were assigned at birth, their bodies, and their personal identity" (Schilt and Westbrook 2009, p. 461). Use of the phrase "cis women" throughout this manuscript is intended to mark the identities of women in my sample, just as the identities of men who are their partners are also marked. To not do so, as rightfully noted by an *AJS* reviewer, "reproduces the 'otherness' of trans by not marking the unmarked category."

2. The phrase "trans men" is used throughout for sake of consistency and simplicity. It should be noted, however, that gender identity labels and categories are often far from consistent or simple. The cis women in this sample identified their trans partners using various terms—transgender, transsexual, trans, female-to-male (ftm), man, boi, etc. The "trans men" referred to in this study are individuals who were assigned, by sex, as "female" at birth and whose gender identity does not directly correspond with this sex assignment or their sex categorization. Some trans men partners of the cis women I interviewed have pursued hormonal or surgical realignment surgeries to bring their bodies in closer alignment with their gender identities, while others have not. . . . For additional background information on the language, concepts, and terms related to transgender identity and experience, please see Wending et al. (2008) and Pfeffer (2010).

3. Epstein (1994) offers the provocative claim that much queer theory is rooted in and dependent upon sociological theoretical precedents, particularly across the areas of symbolic interactionism and labeling theory. These critiques are later echoed by Dunn (1977)

and Green (2007), who highlight the particular theoretical and empirical contributions of pragmatists, symbolic interactionists, and ethnomethodologists to the development of poststructuralist and queer theory produced by scholars such as Judith Butler. As Green (2007, pp. 26-27) writes: "With regard to gender and sexuality . . . sociology has been doing a kind of queer theory long before the first queer theorist set pen to paper."

4. As Sedgwick writes (1990, p.1) in a foundational text of queer, *Epistemology of the Closet:* "An understanding of virtually any aspect of modern Western culture must be, not merely incomplete, but damaged in its central substance to the degree that it does not incorporate a critical analysis of modern homo/heterosexual definition."

5. Judith Butler's (1990) theorization of "gender performativity" draws from Foucault's ([1976] 1990) theorizing around power, repression, and generativity. According to Butler (1990), being a "man" or a "woman" (or "male" or "female") is not a fixed, biological, or immutable human characteristic but, rather, is (re)produced through a system of power and social relations. While these operations of power may compel social relations that (re)produce the normative as ideal, and discipline deviations from normative ideals, these same repressive forces ultimately suggest and generate the potential for disobedience and alternate social relations—producing "gender trouble."

6. "Sex assignment" refers to the assignment of a person, at birth, to "male" or "female" based on bodily signifiers such as presence of a penis or vagina. "Sex categorization" refers to the everyday, iterative placement of a person into social categories such as "girl," "women." "boy," "man."

7. Some participants, who had been with the same partner prior to this transition, found this form of social exchange particularly salient as they noticed very different reactions from older persons when engaging in public hand-holding with the very same partner. Prior to transition, when their partner was reportedly "read" as female and the couple was "read" as lesbian, they recalled older individuals starting at them while not smiling, whispering, avoiding eye contact, and not returning smiles.

8. Participants themselves used the term "roles" (e.g., "1950s housewife role") to describe the enactments of traditional wife/husband, and mother/father family dynamics as they understood them.

9. See also Pfeffer (2012) for further discussion of the overlaps between this sample and those focusing on bisexual-identified cis women.

10. See Brown (2009) for a discussion of similar experiences among another sample of cis women partners of trans men.

11. It must also be noted that the gender presentation of trans men is of critical importance here in others' constructions of the couple's sexual identity. Women who told me that their trans partner was often perceived as a gay man by social others were often misrecognized as "friends" rather than romantic partners. Some women described instances of their partner being hit on by other men in their presence.

12. Of course it is important to consider that lesbian and gay communities, while often providing shelter from homophobia and heterosexism, still struggle with issues of inclusion and discrimination not only with regard to those who are trans or bisexual but with regard to racism, classism, ableism, and sizeism (to name just a few areas) as well.

13. For an overview of the public response to these efforts, see Stone (2012).

References

Ault, Amber. 1996a. "Ambiguous Identity in an Unambiguous Sex/Gender Structure: The Case of Bisexual Women." *Sociological Quarterly* 37(3):449–63.

_____. 1996b. "The Dilemma of Identity: Bi Women's Negotiations." In *Queer Theory/Sociology,* edited by Steven Seidman. London: Blackwell.

Bernstein, Mary. 2005. "Identity Politics." *Annual Review of Sociology* 31:47–74.

Blumstein, Phillip, and Pepper Schwartz. 1974. "Lesbianism and Bisexuality." Pp. 278–95 in *Sexual Deviance and Sexual Deviants*, edited by Erich Goode and Richard T. Troiden. New York: Morrow.

_____. 1977. "Bisexuality: Some Social Psychological Issues." *Journal of Social Issues* 33:30–45.

_____. 1990. "Intimate Relationships and the Creation of Sexuality." Pp. 307–20 in *Homosexuality/Heterosexuality: Concepts of Sexual Orientation*, edited by David P. McWhirter, Stephanie Sanders, and June Machover Reinisch. New York: Oxford University Press.

Brown, Nicola. 2009. "'I'm in Transition Too': Sexual Identity Renegotiation in Sexual-Minority Women's Relationships with Transsexual Men." *International Journal of Sexual Health* 21:61–77.

Burrill, Katkryn G. 2001. "Queering Bisexuality." *Journal of Bisexuality* 2(2/3):95–105.

Butler, Judith. 1990. *Gender Trouble: Feminism and the Subversion of Identity*. New York: Routledge.

_____. 1993. *Bodies That Matter: On the Discursive Limits of "Sex."* New York: Routledge.

Calavita, Kitty. 2000. "The Paradoxes of Race, Class, Identity, and 'Passing': Enforcing the Chinese Exclusion Acts, 1882–1910." *Law and Social Inquiry* 25:1–40.

Cogan, Jeannie C. 1999. "Lesbians Walk the Tightrope of Beauty: Thin Is In but Femme Is Out." Pp. 77–90 in *Lesbians, Levis, and Lipstick: The Meaning of Beauty in Our Lives*, edited by Jeannie C. Cogan and Joanie M. Erickson New York: Haworth.

Connell, R.W. 1987. *Gender and Power*. Sydney: Allen & Unwin.

Connell, Raewyn. 2009. "Accountable Conduct: 'Doing Gender' in Transsexual and Political Retrospect." *Gender and Society* 23:104–11.

Denzin, Norman K. 1990. "Harold and Agnes: A Feminist Narrative Undoing." *Sociological Theory* 8:198–216.

Duggan, Lisa. 2002. "The New Homonormativity: The Sexual Politics of Neoliberalism." In *Materializing Democracy: Towards a Revitalized Cultural Politics*, edited by Russ Castronovo and Dana D. Nelson. Durham, N.C.: Duke University Press.

Dunn, Robert G. 1997. "Self, Identity and Difference: Mead and the Poststructuralists." *Sociological Quarterly* 38:687–705.

Elson, Jean. 2004. *Am I Still a Woman? Hysterectomy and Gender Identity*. Philadelphia: Temple University Press.

Epstein, Steven. 1994. "A Queer Encounter: Sociology and the Study of Sexuality." *Sociological Theory* 12:188–102.

Foucault, Michel. (1976) 1990. *The History of Sexuality*. Vol. 1, *An Introduction*. New York: Vintage Books.

Gamson, Joshua. 1995. "Must Identity Movements Self-Destruct? A Queer Dilemma." *Social Problems* 42:390–407.

Garfinkel, Harold. 1967. *Studies in Ethnomethodology*. Englewood Cliffs, N.J.: Prentice Hall.

Goffman, Erving. 1976. "Gender Advertisements." *Studies in the Anthropology of Visual Communication* 3:69–154.

Green, Adam I. 2002. "Gay but Not Queer: Toward a Post-Queer Study of Sexuality." *Theory and Society* 31:521–45.

_____. 2007. "Queer Theory and Sociology: Locating the Subject and the Self in Sexuality Studies." *Sociological Theory* 25:26–45.

Harris, Cheryl I. 1993. "On Passing: Whiteness as Property." *Harvard Law Review* 106:1707–91.

Heritage, John. 1984. *Garfinkel and Ethnomethodology.* Cambridge: Polity Press.

Hollibaugh, Amber. 1997. "Gender Warriors: An Interview with Amber Hollibaugh." In *Femme: Feminists, Lesbians, Bad Girls*, edited by Laura Harris and Elizabeth Crocker. New York: Routledge.

Irvine, Janice M. 1994. "A Place in the Rainbow: Theorizing Lesbian and Gay Culture." *Sociological Theory* 12:232–48.

Joslin-Roher, Emily, and Darrell Wheeler. 2009. "Partners in Transition: The Transition Experience of Lesbian, Bisexual, and Queer Identified Partners of Transgender Men." *Journal of Gay and Lesbian Social Services* 21:30–48.

Kennedy, Elizabeth L., and Madeline Davis. 1993. *Boots of Leather, Slippers of Gold: The History of a Lesbian Community.* New York: Penguin.

Kennedy, Randall. 2002. *Interracial Intimacies: Sex, Marriage, Identity, and Adoption.* New York: Random House.

Kessler, Suzanne J., and Wendy McKenna. 1978. *Gender: An Ethnomethodological Approach.* New York: Wiley.

_____. 2003. "Who Put the 'Trans' in Transgender? Gender Theory and Everyday Life." In *Constructing Sexualities: Readings in Sexuality, Gender, and Culture,* edited by Suzanne LaFont. Upper Saddle River, N.J.: Prentice Hall.

Krieger, Susan. 1983, *The Mirror Dance: Identity in a Women's Community.* Philadelphia: Temple University Press.

Levitt, Heidi M., Elisabeth A. Gerrish, and Katherine R. Hiestand. 2003. "The Misunderstood Gender: A Model of Modern Femme Identity." *Sex Roles* 3:99–113.

Munt, Sally R., ed. 1988. *Butch/Femme: Inside Lesbian Gender.* London: Cassell.

Mustanski, Brian S. 2001. "Getting Wired: Exploiting the Internet for the Collection of Valid Sexuality Data." *Journal of Sex Research* 38:292–301.

Namaste, Kai. 1994. "The Politics of Inside/Out: Queer Theory, Poststructuralism, and a Sociological Approach to Sexuality." *Sociological Theory* 12:220–31.

Nyamora, Cory M. 2004. "Femme Lesbian Identity Development and the Impact of Partnering with Female-to-Male Transsexuals." Psy.D. dissertation, Alliant International University, California School of Professional Psychology.

Ong, Maria. 2005. "Body Projects of Young Women of Color in Physics: Intersections of Gender, Race and Science." *Social Problems* 52:593–617.

Patton, Michael Q. 1990. *Qualitative Evaluation and Research Methods.* Newbury Park, Calif.: Sage Publications.

Pfeffer, Carla A. 2008 "Bodies in Relation—Bodies in Transition: Lesbian Partners of Trans Men and Body Image." *Journal of Lesbian Studies* 12:325–45.

_____. 2010. "'Women's Work?' Women Partners of Transgender Men Doing Housework and Emotion Work." *Journal of Marriage and Family* 72:165–83.

_____. 2012. "Normative Resistance and Inventive Pragmatism: Negotiating Structure and Agency in Transgender Families." *Gender and Society* 26:574–602.

Ponse, Barbara 1978. *The Social Construction of Identity and Its Meanings within the Lesbian Subculture.* Westport, Conn.: Greenwood Press.

Richardson, Diane, and John Hart. 1981. "The Development and Maintenance of a Homosexual Identity." Pp. 73–92 in *The Theory and Practice of Homeosexuality,* edited by John Hart and Diane Richardson. London: Routledge & Kegan Paul.

Rogers, Mary. 1992. "They All Were Passing; Agnes, Garfinkel, and Company." *Gender and Society* 6:169–91.

Rosser, B., R. Simon, Michael J. Oakes, Walter O. Bockting, and Michael Miner. 2007. "Capturing the Social Demographics of Hidden Sexual Minorities: An Internet Study of the Transgender Population in the United States." *Sexuality Research and Social Policy: Journal of NSRC* 4:50–64.

Rust, Paula C. 2000. "Bisexuality: A Contemporary Paradox for Women." *Journal of Social Issues* 56(2): 205–21.

Schilt, Kristen, and Laurel Westbrook, 2009. "Doing Gender Heteronormativity: 'Gender Normals,' Transgender People, and the Social Maintenance of Heterosexuality." *Gender and Society* 23:440–64.

Sedgwick, Eve Kosofsky. 1990. *Epistemology of the Closet.* Berkeley and Los Angeles: University of California Press.

Seidman, Steven. 1994. "Queer-ing Sociology, Sociologizing Queer Theory: An Introduction." *Sociological Theory* 12:166–77.

_____. 2001. "From Identity to Queer Politics: Shifts in Normative Heterosexuality and the Meaning of Citizenship." *Citizenship Studies* 5:321–28.

Serano, Julia. 2007. *Whipping Girl: A Transsexual Woman on Sexism and the Scapegoating of Femininity.* Emeryville, Calif.: Seal Press.

Shapiro, Eve. 2004. "'Trans'cending Barriers: Transgender Organizing on the Internet." *Journal of Gay and Lesbian Social Services* 16:165–79.

Stone, Amy L. 2012. *Gay Rights at the Ballot Box.* Minneapolis: University of Minnesota Press.

Tabatabai, Ahoo, and Annulla Linders. 2011. "Vanishing Act: Non-Straight Identity Narratives of Women in Relationships with Women and Men." *Qualitative Sociology* 34:583–99.

Taylor, Verta, and Nancy E. Whittier. 1992. "Collective Identity in Social Movement Communities: Lesbian Feminist Mobilization." In *Frontiers in Social Movement Theory,* edited by Aldon D. Morris and Carol M. Mueller. New Haven, Conn.: Yale University Press.

Valocchi, Stephen. 2005. "Not Yet Queer Enough: The Lessons of Queer Theory for the Sociology of Gender and Sexuality." *Gender and Society* 19:750–70.

Vidal-Ortiz, Salvador. 2002. "Queering Sexuality and Doing Gender: Transgender Men's Identification with Gender and Sexuality." *Gender Sexualities* 6:181–233.

Ward, Jane. 2010. "Gender Labor: Transmen, Femmes, and Collective Work of Transgression." *Sexualities* 13:236–54.

Warner, Michael. 2012. "Queer and Then?" *Chronicle Review*, January 1, 1–14. http://chronicle. com/article/QueerThen-/130161/.

Wentling, Tre, Kristen Schilt, Elroi Windsor, and Betsy Lucal. 2008. "Teaching Trans-gender." *Teaching Sociology* 36:49–57.

West, Candace, and Don H. Zimmerman. 1987. "Doing Gender." *Gender and Society* 1:125–51.

Wolkomir, Michelle. 2009. "Making Heteronormative Reconciliations: The Story of Romantic Love, Sexuality, and Gender in Mixed-Orientation Marriages." *Gender and Society* 23:494–519.

Zimmerman, Don H. 1992. "They Were All Doing Gender, but They Weren't All-Passing: Comment on Rogers." *Gender and Society* 6:192–98.

Introduction to Reading 6

The anthropologist Serena Nanda is widely known for her ethnography of India's Hijaras, titled *Neither Man nor Woman*. The article included here is from her more recent book on multiple sex/gender systems around the world. Nanda's analysis of multiple genders among Native North Americans is rich and detailed. As you read this piece, consider the long-term consequences of the failure of European colonists and early anthropologists to get beyond their ethnocentric assumptions so they could understand and respect the gender diversity of North American Indian cultures.

1. Why does Serena Nanda use the term *gender variants* instead of *two-spirit* and *berdache*?

2. What was the relationship between sexual orientation and gender status among American Indians whose cultures included more than two sex/gender categories? How about hermaphroditism and gender status?

3. Why was there often an association between spiritual power and gender variance in Native American cultures?

Multiple Genders Among Native Americans

Serena Nanda

The early encounters between Europeans and Native Americans in the fifteenth through the seventeenth centuries brought together cultures with very different sex/gender systems. The Spanish explorers, coming from a Catholic society where sodomy was a heinous crime, were filled with contempt and outrage when they recorded the presence of men in Native North American societies who performed the work of women, dressed like women, and had sexual relations with men (Lang 1996; Roscoe 1995).

Europeans labeled these men *berdache*, a term originally meaning male prostitute. The term was both insulting and inaccurate, derived from the European view that these roles centered on the "unnatural" and sinful practice of sodomy as defined in their own societies. This European ethnocentrism also caused early observers to overlook the specialized and spiritual functions of many of these roles and the positive value attached to them in many Native American societies.

By the late-nineteenth and early-twentieth centuries, some anthropologists included accounts of Native American sex/gender diversity in their ethnographies, attempting to explain the contributions alternative sex/gender roles made to social structure or culture. These accounts, though less contemptuous than earlier ones, nevertheless largely retained the ethnocentric emphasis on berdache sexuality, defining it as a form of "institutionalized homosexuality." Influenced by functionalist theory, anthropologists viewed these sex/gender roles as functional because they provided a social niche for male individuals whose personality and sexual orientation did not match the definition of masculinity

in the anthropologists' societies, or because the roles provided a "way out" of the masculine or warrior role for "cowardly" or "failed" men (see Callender and Kochems 1983).

Increasingly, however, anthropological accounts paid more attention to the association of Native American sex/gender diversity with shamanism and spiritual powers; they also noted that mixed gender roles were often central and highly valued, rather than marginal and deviant within some Native American societies. Still, the identification of Native American sex/gender diversity with European concepts of homosexuality (erotic feelings for a person of the same sex), transvestism (cross-dressing), or hermaphroditism (the presence of both male and female sexual organs in an individual) continued to distort their indigenous meanings.

In Native American societies, the European homosexual/heterosexual dichotomy was not culturally relevant as a central or defining aspect of gender. While mixed sex/gender individuals in many Native American societies did engage in sexual relations and even married persons of the same sex, this was not central to their alternative gender role. Europeans also overemphasized the function of cross-dressing in these roles, labeling such individuals as *transvestites*; although mixed gender roles often did involve cross-dressing, this varied both within and among Native American societies. The label "hermaphrodite" was also inaccurate as a general category, although some societies did recognize biological intersexuality as the basis of sex/gender variation.

Given the great variation in Native North American societies, it is perhaps most useful to define their nonnormative sex/gender roles as referring to people who partly or completely adopted aspects of the culturally defined role of the other sex or gender and who were classified as neither woman nor man but as mixed, alternative genders; these roles did not involve a complete crossing over to an opposite sex/gender role (see Callender and Kochems 1983:443).

Both Native American sex/gender diversity and anthropological understandings of these roles have shifted in the past 30 years (Jacobs, Thomas, and Lang 1997: Introduction). Most current research rejects institutionalized homosexuality as an adequate explanation of Native American sex/gender diversity: It emphasizes occupation rather than sexuality as its central feature; considers multiple sex/gender roles as normal, indeed often integrated into and highly valued in Native American sex/gender systems (Albers 1989:134; Jacobs et al. 1997; Lang 1998); notes the variation in such roles across indigenous North (and South) America (Callender and Kochems 1983; Jacobs et al. 1997; Lang 1998; Roscoe 1998); and calls attention to the association of such roles with spiritual power (Roscoe 1996; Williams 1992).

Consistent with these new perspectives, the term "berdache" is somewhat out of fashion, though there is no unanimous agreement on what should replace it. One widely accepted suggestion is the term *two-spirit* (Jacobs et al. 1997; Lang 1998), a term coined in 1990 by urban Native American gays and lesbians. Two-spirit has the advantage of conveying the spiritual nature of gender variance in both traditional and contemporary Native American societies, although it emphasizes the Euro-American binary sex/gender construction of male and female/man and woman, which did not characterize all Native American groups.

DISTRIBUTION AND CHARACTERISTICS OF VARIANT SEX/GENDER ROLES

Multiple sex/gender systems were found in many, though not all, Native American societies. Variant male sex/gender roles are documented for 110 to 150 societies, occurring most frequently in the region extending from California to the Mississippi Valley and the upper-Great Lakes, the Plains and the Prairies, the Southwest, and to a lesser extent along the Northwest Coast. With few exceptions, gender variance is not historically documented for eastern North America, though it may have existed prior to the European invasion and disappeared before it could be recorded historically (Callender and Kochems 1983; Fulton and Anderson 1992).

There were many variations in Native American sex/gender diversity. Some cultures included three or four genders: men, women, male variants, and female variants (e.g., biological females who, by engaging in male activities, were reclassified as to gender). Gender variant roles also differed in the criteria by which they were defined; the degree of their integration into the society; the norms governing their behavior; the way the role was publicly acknowledged or sanctioned; how others were expected to behave toward gender variant persons; the degree to which a gender changer was expected to adopt the role of the opposite sex or was limited in doing so; the power, sacred or secular, that was attributed to them; and the path to recruitment.

In spite of this variety, however, there were also some widespread similarities: transvestism, cross-gender occupation, same-sex (but different gender) sexuality, a special process or ritual surrounding recruitment, special language and ritual roles, and associations with spiritual power.

TRANSVESTISM

Transvestism was often associated with gender variance but was not equally important in all societies. Male gender variants frequently adopted women's dress and hairstyles partially or completely, and female gender variants partially adopted the clothing of men; in some societies, however, transvestism was prohibited. The choice of clothing was sometimes an individual matter, and gender variants might mix their clothing and their accessories. For example, a female gender variant might wear a woman's dress but carry (male) weapons. Dress was also sometimes situationally determined: a male gender variant would have to wear men's clothing while engaging in warfare but might wear women's clothing at other times. Similarly, female gender variants might wear women's clothing when gathering (women's work) but male clothing when hunting (men's work) (Callender and Kochems 1983:447). Among the Navajo, a male gender variant, **nàdleeh**, would adopt almost all aspects of a woman's dress, work, language, and behavior; the Mohave male gender variant, called **alyha**, was at the extreme end of the cross-gender continuum in imitating female physiology as well as transvestism. The repression and ultimately the almost total decline of transvestism was a direct result of U.S. prohibitions against it.

OCCUPATION

The occupational aspects of Native American gender variance was central in most societies. Most frequently a boy's interest in the tools and activities of women and a girl's interest in the tools of male occupations signaled an individual's wish to undertake a gender variant role (Callender and Kochems 1983:447; Whitehead 1981). In hunting societies, for example, female gender variance was signaled by a girl rejecting the domestic activities associated with women and participating in playing and hunting with boys. In the Arctic and sub-Arctic this might be encouraged by a girl's parents if there were not enough boys to provide the family with food (Lang 1998). Male gender variants were frequently considered especially skilled and industrious in women's crafts and domestic work (though not in agriculture, where this was a man's task) (Roscoe 1991; 1996). Female gender crossers sometimes won the reputation of superior hunters and warriors.

The households of male gender variants were often more prosperous than others, sometimes because they were hired by whites. In their own societies the excellence of male gender variants' craftwork was sometimes ascribed

to a supernatural sanction for their gender transformation (Callender and Kochems 1983:448). Female gender variants opted out of motherhood, so they were not encumbered by caring for children, which may explain their success as hunters or warriors. In Borne societies, gender variants could engage in both men's and women's work, and this, too, accounted for their increased wealth. Another source of income was payment for the special social activities due to gender variants' intermediate gender status, such as acting as go-betweens in marriage. Through their diverse occupations, then, gender variants were often central rather than marginal in their societies.

The explanation of male gender variant roles as a niche for "failed" or cowardly men who wished to avoid warfare or other aspects of the masculine role is no longer widely accepted. To begin with, masculinity was not associated with warrior status in all Native American cultures. In some societies, male gender variants were warriors, and in many others, males who rejected the warrior role did not become gender variants. Sometimes male gender variants did not go to war because of cultural prohibitions against their using symbols of maleness, for example, the prohibition against their using the bow among the Illinois. Where male gender variants did not fight, they sometimes had other important roles in warfare, like treating the wounded, carrying supplies for the war party, or directing postbattle ceremonials (Callender and Kochems 1983:449). In a few societies male gender variants became outstanding warriors, such as Finds Them and Kills Them, a Crow Indian who performed daring feats of bravery while fighting with the U.S. Army against the Crow's traditional enemies, the Lakota Sioux (Roscoe 1998:23).

GENDER VARIANCE AND SEXUALITY

While generally sexuality was not central in defining gender status among Native Americans, in some Native American societies, same-sex sexual desire or practices were significant in the definition of gender variant roles (Callender and Kochems 1983:449). Some early reports noted specifically that male gender variants lived with and/or had sexual relations with women as well as with men; in other societies they were reported as having sexual relations only with men, and in still other societies, of having no sexual relationships at all (Lang 1998:189–95).

The bisexual orientation of some gender variant persons may have been a culturally accepted expression of their gender variance. It may have resulted from an individual's life experiences, such as the age at which he or she entered the gender variant role, and/or it may have been one aspect of the general freedom of sexual expression in many Native American societies. While male and female gender variants most frequently had sexual relations with, or married, persons of the same biological sex as themselves, these relationships were not considered homosexual in the contemporary Western understanding of that term. In a multiple gender system the partners would be of the same sex but different genders, and homogender, rather than homosexual, practices bore the brunt of negative cultural sanctions (as is true today, for example, in contemporary Indonesia). The sexual partners of gender variants were never considered gender variants themselves.

Among the Navajo there were four genders; man, woman, and two gender variants: the masculine female-bodied nàdleeh and the feminine male-bodied nàdleeh (Thomas 1997). A sexual relationship between a female-bodied nàdleeh and a woman or a sexual relationship between a male-bodied nàdleeh and a man were not stigmatized because these persons were of different genders, although they were of the same biological sex. A sexual relationship between two women, two men, two female-bodied nàdleeh, or two male-bodied nàdleeh, however, was considered homosexual, and even incestual, and was strongly disapproved of.

The relation of sexuality to variant sex/gender roles across North America suggests that sexual relations between gender variants and persons of the same biological sex were a result rather than a cause of gender variance. Sexual relationships between a man and a male gender variant were accepted in most Native American societies, though not in all, and appear to have been negatively sanctioned only when it interfered with child-producing heterosexual marriages. Gender variants' sexual relationships might be casual and wide-ranging (Europeans used the term "promiscuous"), or stable, and sometimes involved life-long marriages. In some societies, however, male gender variants were not permitted to engage in long-term relationships with men, either in or out of wedlock, and many male gender variants were reported as living alone.

A man might desire sexual relations with a (male) gender variant for different reasons: In some societies taboos on sexual relations with menstruating or pregnant women restricted opportunities for sexual intercourse; in other societies sexual relations with a gender variant person were exempt from punishment for extramarital affairs; in still other societies, for example among the Navajo, some gender variants were considered especially lucky, and a man might hope to have this luck transferred to himself though sexual relations (Lang 1998:349).

BIOLOGICAL SEX AND GENDER TRANSFORMATIONS

European observers often confused gender variants with **hermaphrodites** (biologically intersexed persons). Some Native American societies explicitly distinguished hermaphrodites from gender variants and treated them differently; others assigned gender variant persons and hermaphrodites to the same alternative gender status. In most Native American societies biological sex (or the intersexed condition of the hermaphrodite) was not the criterion for a gender variant role, nor were the individuals who occupied gender variant roles anatomically abnormal. The Navajo were an exception: They distinguished between the intersexed and the alternatively gendered but treated them similarly, though not exactly the same (Hill 1935; Thomas 1997).

Even as the traditional Navajo sex/gender system had biological sex as its starting point, the Navajo nàdleeh were also distinguished by gender-linked behaviors, such as body language, clothing, ceremonial roles, speech style, and occupation. Feminine, male-bodied nàdleeh might engage in women's activities such as cooking, weaving, household tasks, and making pottery. Masculine, female-bodied nàdleeh, unlike other female-bodied persons, avoided childbirth; today they are associated with male occupational roles such as construction or fire-fighting (although ordinary women also sometimes engage in these occupations). Traditionally, female-bodied nàdleeh had specific roles in Navajo ceremonials (Thomas 1997).

Thus, even where hermaphrodites occupied a special gender variant role, Native American gender variance was defined more by cultural than biological criteria. In the recorded case of a physical examination of a gender variant male, the previously mentioned Finds Them and Kills Them, his genitals were found to be completely normal (Roscoe 1998).

Native American gender variants were not generally conceptualized as hermaphrodites, but neither were they conceptualized as transsexuals (people who change from their original sex to the opposite sex). Gender transformations among gender variants were recognized as only a partial transformation, and the gender variant was not thought of as having become a person of the opposite sex/gender. Rather, gender variant roles were autonomous gender roles that combined the characteristics of men and women and had some unique features of their own. For example, among the Zuni a male gender variant was buried in women's dress but also in men's trousers on the men's side of the graveyard (Parsons, cited in Callender and Kochems 1983:454; Roscoe 1991:124, 145). Male gender variants were neither men—by virtue of their chosen occupations, dress, demeanor, and possibly sexuality—nor women, because of their anatomy and their inability to bear children. Only among the Mohave do we find the extreme imitation of women's physiological processes related to reproduction and the claims to have female sexual organs—both of which were ridiculed within Mohave society. Even here, however, where informants reported that female gender variants did not menstruate, this did not make them culturally men. Rather, it was the mixed quality of gender variant status that was culturally elaborated in Native North America and was the source of supernatural powers sometimes attributed to them.

SACRED POWER

The association between the spiritual power and gender variance occurred in most, if not all, Native American societies. Even where, as previously noted, recruitment to the role was occasioned by a child's interest in occupational activities of the opposite sex, supernatural sanction, frequently appearing in visions or dreams, was also involved, as among Prairie and Plains societies. These visions involved female supernatural figures, often the moon. Among the Omaha, the moon appeared in a dream holding a burden strap—a symbol of female work—in one hand, and a bow—a symbol of male work—in the other. When the male dreamer reached for the bow, the moon forced him to take the burden strap (Whitehead 1981). Among the Mohave, a child's choice of male or female implements heralding gender variant status was sometimes prefigured by a dream that was believed to come to an embryo in the womb (Devereux 1937).

In some but not all societies, sex/gender variants had sacred ritual roles and curing functions (Callender and Kochems 1983:453; Lang 1998). Where feminine qualities were associated with these roles, male gender variants might become spiritual leaders or healers, but where these roles were associated with masculine qualities they were not entered into by male gender variants. The Plains Indians, who emphasized a vision as a source of supernatural power, regarded male gender variants as holy persons, but California Indian societies did not. Moreover, in some Native American societies gender variants were specifically excluded from religious roles (Lang 1998:167). Nevertheless, sacred power was so widely associated with sex/gender diversity in Native North America that scholars generally agree that it is an important explanation of why such roles were so widespread.

In spite of cultural differences among Native American societies, some of their general characteristics are consistent with the positive value placed on sex/gender diversity and the widespread existence of multigender systems (Lang 1996). One cultural similarity is a cosmology (system of religious beliefs) in which transformation and ambiguity are recurring themes, applying to humans, animals, and objects in the natural environment. In many of these cultures, sex/gender ambiguity, lack of sexual differentiation, and sex/gender transformations are central in creation stories (Lang 1996:187). Native American cosmology may not be "the cause" of sex/gender diversity but it certainly (as in India) provides a hospitable context for it.

FEMALE GENDER VARIANTS

Female gender variants probably occurred more frequently among Native Americans than in other cultures, a point largely overlooked in the historic and ethnographic record (see Blackwood 1984; Jacobs et al. 1997; Lang 1998; Medicine 1983.)

Although the generally egalitarian social structures of many Native American societies provided a hospitable context for female gender variance, it occurred in perhaps only one-quarter to one-half of the societies with male variant roles (Callender and Kochems 1983:446; see also Lang 1998:262–265). This may be explained partly by the fact that in many Native American societies women could—and did—adopt aspects of the male gender role, such as engaging in warfare or hunting, and sometimes dressed in male clothing, without being reclassified into a different gender (Blackwood 1984; Lang 1998:261ff; Medicine 1983). . . .

While most often Native American women who crossed genders occupationally . . . were not reclassified into a gender variant role, several isolated cases of female gender transformations have been documented historically. One of these is Ququnak Patke, a "manlike woman" from the Kutenai (Schaeffer 1965). Ququnak Patke had married a white fur trader, and when she returned to her tribe, she claimed that her husband had transformed her into a man. She wore men's clothes, lived as a man, married a woman, and claimed supernatural sanction for her role change and her supernatural powers. Although whites often mistook her for a man in her various roles as warrior, explorer's guide, and trader, such transformations were not considered a possibility among the Kutenai, and many thought Ququnak Patke was mad. She died attempting to mediate a quarrel between two hostile Indian groups.

Because sexual relations between women in Native American societies were rarely historically documented, it is hard to know how far we can generalize about the relation of sexuality to female gender variance in precontact Native American cultures. The few descriptions (and those for males, as well) are mainly based on ethnographic accounts that relied on twentieth-century informants whose memories were already shaped by white hostility toward gender diversity and same-sex sexuality. Nevertheless, it seems clear that although Native American female gender variants clearly had sexual relationships with women, sexual object choice was not their defining characteristic. In some cases, they were described "as women who never marry"; this does not say anything definitive about their sexuality and it may be that the sexuality of female gender variants was more variable than that of men.

Contact with whites opened up opportunities for gender divergent individuals, males as well as females (see Roscoe 1998; 1991). Overall, however, as a result of Euro-American repression and the growing assimilation of Euro-American sex/gender ideologies, Native American female and male gender variant roles largely disappeared by the 1930s, as the reservation system was well under way. Yet, their echoes may remain, both in the anthropological interest in this subject and in the activism of contemporary two-spirit individuals.

REFERENCES

Albers, Patricia C. 1989. "From Illusion to Illumination: Anthropological Studies of American Indian Women." In *Gender and Anthropology: Critical Reviews for Research and Teaching*, edited by Sandra Morgan. Washington, DC: American Anthropological Association.

Blackwood, Evelyn. 1984. "Sexuality and Gender in Certain Native American Tribes: The Case of Cross-Gender Females." *Signs: Journal of Women in Culture and Society* 10: 1–42.

Callender, Charles, and Lee M. Kochems. 1983. "The North American Berdache." *Current Anthropology* 24 (4): 443–56 (Commentary, pp. 456–70).

Devereux, George. 1937. "Institutionalized Homosexuality of the Mohave Indians." *Human Biology* 9: 498–587.

Fulton, Robert, and Steven W. Anderson. 1992. "The American 'Man-Woman': Gender, Fulton, Robert, and Steven W. Anderson, 1992. *Current Anthropology* 33 (5): 603–10.

Hill, Willard W. 1935. "The Status of the Hermaphrodite and Transvestite in Navaho Culture." *American Anthropologist* 37: 273–79.

Jacobs, Sue-Ellen, Wesley Thomas, and Sabine Lang, eds. 1997. *Two-Spirit People: Native American Gender Identity, Sexuality and Spirituality*. Urbana and Chicago: University of Illinois Press.

Lang, Sabine. 1996. "There Is More than Just Men and Women: Gender Variance in North America." In *Gender Reversals and Gender Culture*, edited by Sabrina Petra Ramet, pp. 183–86. London and New York: Routledge.

_____. 1998. *Men as Women, Women as Men: Changing Gender in Native American Cultures*. Trans. from the German by John L. Vantine. Austin: University of Texas Press.

Medicine, Beatrice. 1983. "Warrior Women: Sex Role Alternatives for Plains Indian Women." In *The Hidden Half: Studies of Plains Indian Women*, edited by P. Albers and B. Medicine, pp. 267–80. Lanham Park, MD: University Press of America.

Roscoe, Will. 1991. *The Zuni Man-Woman*. Albuquerque: University of New Mexico Press.

_____. 1995. "Cultural Anesthesia and Lesbian and Gay Studies." *American Anthropologist* 97 (3): 448–52.

_____. 1996. "How to Become a Berdache: Toward a Unified Analysis of Gender Diversity." In *Third Sex, Third Gender: Beyond Sexual Dimorphism in Culture and History*, edited by Gilbert Herdt, pp. 329–72. New York: Zone (MIT).

_____. 1998. *Changing Ones: Third and Fourth Genders in Native North America*. London: Macmillan.

Schaeffer, Claude E. 1965. "The Kutenai Female Berdache: Courier, Guide, Prophetess, and Warrior." *Ethnohistory: The Bulletin of the Ohio Valley Historic Indian Conference* 12 (3): 173–236.

Thomas, Wesley. 1997. "Navajo Cultural Constructions of Gender and Sexuality." In *Two-Spirit People: Native American Gender Identity, Sexuality, and Spirituality*, edited by Sue-Ellen Jacobs, Wesley Thomas, and Sabine Lang, pp. 156–73. Urbana and Chicago: University of Illinois Press.

Whitehead, Harriet. 1981. "The Bow and the Burden Strap: A New Look at Institutionalized Homosexuality in Native North America." In *Sexual Meanings: The Cultural Construction of Gender and Sexuality*, edited by Sherry B. Ortner and Harriet Whitehead, pp. 80–115. Cambridge University Press.

Williams, Walter. 1992. *The Spirit and the Flesh: Sexual Diversity in American Indian Culture*. Boston: Beacon.

❦ Topics for Further Examination ❧

- Visit the websites of aisdsd.org and *www.interfaceproject.org to learn more about intersex and intersex activism*. In addition, you will find websites on male lactation and men breastfeeding to be helpful in expanding your understanding of biological overlap between males and females.
- Locate research on gender bending in the arts (e.g., performance art, literature, music videos). For example, visit Diane Torr's website (http://www.dianetorr.com).
- Google "doing gender" and explore the many websites that discuss the concept and its application.

2

The Interaction of Gender With Other Socially Constructed Prisms

Joan Z. Spade

After considering what gender is and isn't, we are going to complicate things a bit by looking at how other socially constructed categories of difference and inequality, such as race, ethnicity, social class, religion, age, ability/disability, culture/nation, and sexuality, shape gender. As is the case with prisms in a kaleidoscope, the interaction of gender with other social prisms creates complex patterns of identity and relationships for people across groups and situations. Because there are so many different social prisms that interact with gender in daily life, we can discuss only a few in this chapter; however, other social categories are explored throughout this book. The articles we have selected for this chapter illustrate three key arguments. First, gender is a complex and multifaceted array of experiences and meanings that cannot be understood without considering the social context within which they are situated. Second, variations in the meaning and display of gender are related to different levels of prestige, privilege, and power associated with membership in other socially constructed categories of difference and inequality. Third, gender intersects with other socially constructed categories of difference and inequality at all levels discussed in the introduction to this book—individual, interactional, and institutional.

Privilege

In our daily lives, there usually isn't enough time or opportunity to consider how the interaction of multiple social categories to which we belong affects beliefs, behaviors, and life chances. In particular, we are discouraged from critically examining our culture, as will be discussed in Chapter 3. People who occupy positions of privilege often do not notice how their privileged social positions influence them. In the United States, privilege is associated with white skin color, masculinity, wealth, heterosexuality, youth, able-bodiedness, and so on. It seems normal to those of us who occupy privileged positions and those we interact with that our positions of privilege be deferred to, allowing us to move more freely in society. Peggy McIntosh (1998) is a pioneer in examining these hidden and unearned benefits of privilege. She argues that there are implicit benefits of privilege and that persons with "unearned advantages" often do not understand how their privilege is a function of the disempowerment of others. For example, male privilege seems "normal" and White privilege seems "natural" to those who are male and/or White.

The struggle for women's rights in the United States also has seen the effects of privilege, with White women historically dominating this movement. The privilege of race and social class created a view of woman as a universal category, which essentially represented White women's interests. While many women of color stood up for women's rights, they did so in response to a universal definition of womanhood derived from White privilege (hooks, 1981). This pattern of White dominance is not a recent phenomenon and has been recognized within the African American community for some time, as discussed in the first reading in this chapter, by Bonnie Thornton Dill and Marla H. Kohlman. For example, in 1867, former slave Sojourner Truth responding to a White man who felt women were more delicate than men, described the exertion required of her work as a slave and asked, "Ain't I a woman?" (Guy-Scheftall, 1995). One hundred years later, women of color, including Audre Lorde (1982), bell hooks (1981), Angela Davis (1981), Gloria Anzaldúa (1987), and others, continued to speak out against White privilege within the women's movement. These women, recognizing that the issues facing women of color were not always the same as those of White women, carried on a battle to make African American women visible in the second wave of feminism. For example, while White

feminists were fighting for the right to abortion, African American women were fighting other laws and sterilization practices that denied them the right to control their own fertility and bear their own babies. Women of color, including Thornton Dill (with Kohlman, this chapter) and others, some of whom are listed in this chapter, continue to challenge the White-dominated definitions of gender and fight to include in the analysis of gender an understanding of the experience of domination and privilege of all women.

UNDERSTANDING THE INTERACTION OF GENDER WITH OTHER CATEGORIES OF DIFFERENCE AND INEQUALITY

Throughout this chapter, you will read about social scientists and social activists who attempt to understand the interactions between "interlocking oppressions." Social scientists develop theories, with their primary focus on explanation, whereas social activists explore the topic of interlocking oppressions from the perspective of initiating social change. Although the goals of explanation and social/political change are rarely separated in feminist research, they reflect different emphases that must be addressed (Collins, 1990; Walby, Armstrong, & Strid, 2012). As such, these two different agendas shape attempts to understand the interaction of gender with multiple social prisms of difference and inequality. Much of this research on intersectionality is written by women, with a focus on women, because it came out of conflicts and challenging issues within the women's movement. As you read through this chapter and book, it is important to remember that the socially defined gender categories in Western culture intersect with other prisms of difference and inequality. And, as Patricia Hill Collins (1998, 2001) has argued, consider how the meanings of gender and other categories of difference and inequality are embedded in the structure of social relations within and between nations (Bose, 2012).

The effort to include the perspectives and experiences of *all* women in understanding gender is complicated. Previous theories had to be expanded to include the interaction of gender with other social categories of difference and privilege. These efforts to refine or redefine the concept of intersectionality continue. Yet, as Kathy Davis (2008) argues, the ambiguity and open-endedness of the concept makes it successful as a feminist theory because it is more accessible and, thus, applied more meaningfully. To better understand the development of the concept of intersectionality, we group these efforts into three different approaches. The earliest approach is to treat each social category of difference and inequality as if it were separate and not overlapping. A second approach is to add up the different social categories that an individual belongs to and summarize the effects of the social categories of privilege and power. The third and newest approach attempts to understand the simultaneous interaction of gender with all other categories of difference and inequality. These three approaches are described in more detail in the following paragraphs because they help us understand the complexity of applying an intersectional approach.

Separate-and-Different Approach

Deborah King (1988) describes the earliest approach as the "race–sex analogy." She characterizes this approach as one in which oppressions related to race are compared with those related to gender, but each is seen as a separate influence. King quotes Elizabeth Cady Stanton, who in 1860 stated, "Prejudice against color, of which we hear so much, is no stronger than that against sex" (p. 43). This approach, the race–sex analogy, continued well into the late 20th century and can get in the way of a deeper understanding of the complexity of gender. For example, in the race–sex analogy, gender is assumed to have the same effect for African American and White women, while race is defined as the same experience for African American men and women. However, the reading

by Karen D. Pyke and Denise L. Johnson in this chapter, which explores Asian American women's definitions of "femininity," illustrates how we cannot assume that gender will mean the same thing to different women from the same society. Although these Vietnamese American and Korean American women were born and raised in the United States, they live with two different cultural definitions of femininity, an idea we will consider in more depth in the next chapter. Although they may try, the reality is that Asian American women cannot draw a line down their bodies separating gender from ethnicity and culture. As these women's words suggest, the effects of prisms of difference on daily experience are inextricably intertwined. For example, African American females cannot always be certain that the discrimination they face is due to race or gender, or both. As individuals, we are complex combinations of multiple social identities. Separating the effects of multiple social prisms theoretically does not always make sense and is almost impossible to do on an individual level.

Looking at these individual challenges, King (1988) argues that attempting to determine which "-ism" (e.g., sexism, racism, or classism) is most oppressive and most important to overcome does not address real-life situations. This approach pits the interests of each subordinated group against the others and asks individuals to choose one group identity over others. For example, must poor, African American women decide which group will best address their situations in society: groups fighting racial inequality, gender inequality, or class inequality? The situations of poor, African American women are more complex than this single-issue approach can address.

The race–sex analogy of treating one "-ism" at a time has been criticized because, although some needs and experiences of oppressed people are included, others are ignored. For instance, Collins (1990) describes the position of African American women as that of "outsiders within" the feminist movement and in relations with women in general. She and others have criticized the women's movement for leaving out of its agenda an awareness of the experiences and needs of African

American women (e.g., King, 1988). This focus on one "-ism" or another—the formation of social action groups around one category of difference and inequality—is called identity politics.

Additive Approach

The second approach used by theorists to understand how multiple social prisms interact at the level of individual life examines the effects of multiple social categories in an additive model. In this approach, the effects of race, ethnicity, class, and other social prisms are added together as static, equal parts of a whole (King, 1988). Returning to the earlier example of poor, African American women, the strategy is one of adding up the effects of racism, sexism, and classism to equal what is termed *triple jeopardy*. If that same woman was also a lesbian, her situation would be that of *quadruple jeopardy*, according to the additive model.

Although this approach takes into account multiple social identities in understanding oppression, King and others reject it as too simplistic. We cannot simply add up the complex inequalities across social categories of difference and inequality, because the weight of each social category varies based on individual situations. McIntosh (1998) argues that privileges associated with membership in particular social categories interact to create "interlocking oppressions" whose implications and meanings shift across time and situations. For example, for African American women in some situations, their gender will be more salient, while in other situations, their race will be more salient. The article by Nikki Jones in this chapter helps illustrate this fact. As Jones found, the behavior of a young woman she followed through life on the streets of San Francisco reflected both social and local expectations for multiple identities, including race, sex, class, and sexuality—to the point that her behavior was constantly changing.

Interaction Approach

The third approach to understanding the social and personal consequences of membership

in multiple socially constructed categories is called multiracial feminist theory. Various terms are used by multiracial feminist theorists to describe "interlocking oppressions," including *intersectional analysis* (Baca Zinn & Thornton Dill, 1996), *interrelated* (Weber, 2001), *simultaneous* (Collins, 1990; Weber, 2001), *multiplicative* or *multiple jeopardy* (King, 1988), *matrix of domination* (Collins, 1990), and *relational* (Baca Zinn, Hondagneu-Sotelo, & Messner, 2001; Baca Zinn & Thornton Dill, 1996). The first article in this chapter, by Thornton Dill and Kohlman, provides an overview of the meaning of intersectional analysis. For the purposes of this book, we describe this approach as consisting of "prismatic" or intersectional interactions, which occur when socially constructed categories of difference and inequality interact with other categories in individuals' lives. A brief discussion of some of these different models for explaining "interlocking oppressions" is useful in deepening our understanding of the complex interactions of membership in multiple social prisms.

King (1988) brings these interactions to light, discussing the concept of multiple jeopardy, in which she refers not only "to several, simultaneous oppressions, but to the multiplicative relationships among them as well" (p. 47). As a result, socially constructed categories of difference and inequality fold into individual identities, not in an additive way but in a way in which the total construction of an individual's identity incorporates the relationship of the identities to one another. King's model includes both multiple social identities and situational factors to understand individual differences. For example, being a submissive woman might matter more in certain religious groups where women have more restricted roles, while race or class may be less salient in that situation because the latter social prisms are likely to be similar across the religious group.

Maxine Baca Zinn, Pierrette Hondagneu-Sotelo, and Michael Messner (2001) emphasize that gender is relational. Focusing on gender as a process (Connell, 1987), they argue that "the meaning of *woman* is defined by the existence of women of different races and classes" (Baca Zinn et al., 2001, p. 174). As Pyke and Johnson's reading in this chapter illustrates, the fact that the Asian American women they interviewed were confused about whether to accept Asian standards of gender or American standards "normalizes" and makes White femininity dominant.

Collins (1990), on the other hand, conceptualizes oppressions as existing in a "matrix of domination" in which individuals not only experience but also resist multiple inequalities. Collins argues that domination and resistance can be found at three levels: personal, cultural, and institutional. Individuals with the most privilege and power—White, upper-class men—control dominant definitions of gender in this model. Collins discusses how "White skin privilege" has limited White feminists' understandings of gender oppression to their own experiences and created considerable tension in the women's movement. Tensions occur on all three levels—personal, within and between groups, and at the level of institutions such as the women's movement itself—all of which maintain power differentials. Furthermore, as she has since argued, these intersections of inequality are embedded in national identity systems of gendered social organizations (Collins, 1998, 2001).

As you can see, this third approach does not treat interlocking oppressions as strictly additive. The unequal power of groups created by systems of inequality affects interpersonal power in all relationships, both within and across gender categories. Thus, there is a clear political or activist orientation to intersectional analyses, which many scholars, including Thornton Dill and Kohlman, feel must be addressed (see also Walby et al., 2012). The articles in this chapter illustrate how multiple socially constructed prisms interact to shape both the identities and opportunities of individuals. They also show how interpersonal relationships are intricately tied to the larger structures of society or nations, as Collins (2001) argues, and how gender is maintained across groups in society.

These efforts to understand gender through the lens of multiple social prisms of difference

and inequality can be problematic. One concern is that gender could be reduced to what has been described as a continually changing quilt of life experiences (Baca Zinn et al., 2001; Connell, 1992). That is, if the third approach is taken to the extreme, gender is seen as a series of individual experiences and the approach can no longer be used as a tool for explaining patterns across groups, which is meaningless in generating social action. Thus, the current challenge for researchers and theorists is to forge an explanation of the interaction of gender with other socially constructed prisms that both recognizes and reflects the experiences of individuals, while at the same time highlighting the patterns that occur across groups of individuals.

The application of intersectional analyses continues to be riddled with debates over how it should be done. An article in this chapter by Bandana Purkayastha adds to this discussion by elaborating on the ways intersectionality can be applied in transnational or global spaces. This piece clearly points to the fact that intersectional analysis is a dynamic and lively addition to the study of gender difference and inequality.

Another current debate addresses the methods or the way we do research on intersectionality (Choo & Ferree, 2010). As you will see, much of the research applying intersectional analysis uses qualitative research. However, Leslie McCall (2005) carefully laid out an argument that considered why this was so. She argued that the methodology of intersectionality research is complicated by the need to define "categories" of difference and inequality. But when defining categories, such as gender or race, to individuals you are studying, you take away the meanings they bring to those categories and the way they experience them. McCall argues for using categories such as gender, race, and social class, even though they are imperfect, in quantitative research to study the complexity associated with examining multiple categories of difference and inequality.

Since we live in a world that includes many socially constructed categories of difference and inequality, understanding the ways social prisms come together is critical for understanding gender. How we visualize the effects of multiple social prisms depends on whether we seek social justice, theoretical understanding, or both. How can we use these experiences to better understand the lived lives of individuals and work to make those lives better, such as that of Kiara in the Jones article in this chapter? If multiple social categories are linked, then what are the mechanisms by which difference is created, supported, and changed? Are multiple identities multiplied, as King (1988) suggests; added, as others suggest; or combined into a matrix, as Collins (1990) suggests? Or, as Purkayastha suggests in this chapter, must we also consider nation in our analysis as we examine the interactions of gender with other categories of difference and inequality (see also Collins, 2001)? We raise these questions not to confuse you, but rather, to challenge you to try to understand the complexity of gender relations.

PRISMATIC INTERACTIONS

We return now to the metaphor of the kaleidoscope to help us sort out this question of how to deal with multiple social identities in explaining gender. Understanding the interaction of several socially constructed identities can be compared to the ray of light passing through the prisms of a kaleidoscope. Socially constructed categories serve as prisms that create life experiences. Just as the kaleidoscope produces a flowing and constantly changing array of patterns, we find individual life experiences to be unique and flowing. However, similar colors and patterns often reoccur in slightly different forms. Sometimes, when we look through a real kaleidoscope, we find a beautiful image in which blue is dominant. Although we may not be able to replicate the specific image, it would not be unusual for us to see another blue-dominant pattern. Gender differences emerge in a similar form—not as a single, fixed pattern but as a dominant, broad pattern that encompasses many unique but similar patterns. However, introducing the notion of category of gender adds questions relating to how these categories are defined. Are categories of gender based in individual identities, symbolic representations, or social structures (Choo & Ferree, 2010; Winker & Degele, 2011)?

The prism metaphor offers an avenue for systematically envisioning the complexity of gender relations. We would argue that to fully understand this interaction of social influences, one must focus on power. The distribution of privilege and oppression is a function of power relations (Baca Zinn et al., 2001). All the articles in this chapter examine differences defined by power relations, and power operates at every level of life, from the intimate and familial (see the reading by Pyke and Johnson in this chapter) to the global (see the reading by Purkayastha in this chapter). It is difficult to explain the combined effects of multiple social prisms without focusing on power. We argue that the power one accrues from a combination of socially constructed categories explains the patterns created by these categories. However, one cannot add up the effects from each category one belongs to, as in the additive approach described earlier. Instead, one must understand that, like the prisms in the kaleidoscope, the power of any single socially constructed identity is related to all other categories. The final patterns that appear are based on the combinations of power that shape the patterns. Individuals' life experiences, then, take unique forms as race, class, ethnicity, religion, age, ability/disability, body type, and other socially constructed characteristics are combined to create patterns that emerge across contexts and daily life experiences.

Consider your own social identities and the social categories to which you belong. How do they mold you at this time, and how did they, or might they, frame your experience of gender at other times and under different circumstances? Consider other social prisms such as age, ability/disability, religion, and national identity. If you were to build your own kaleidoscope of gender, what prisms would you include? What prisms interact with gender to shape your life? Do these prisms create privilege or disadvantage for you? Think about how these socially constructed categories combine to create your life experiences and how they are supported by the social structure in which you live. Keep your answers in mind as you read these articles to gain a better understanding of the role prisms play in shaping gender and affecting your life.

REFERENCES

Anzaldúa, G. (1987). *Borderlands/La Frontera: The new mestiza.* San Francisco: Aunt Lute Books.

Baca Zinn, M., Hondagneu-Sotelo, P., & Messner, M. A. (2001). Gender through the prism of difference. In M. L. Andersen & P. H. Collins (Eds.), *Race, class, and gender: An anthology* (4th ed., pp. 168–176). Belmont, CA: Wadsworth.

Baca Zinn, M., & Thornton Dill, B. (1996). Theorizing difference from multiracial feminism. *Feminist Studies, 22*(2), 321–327.

Bose, C. (2012). Intersectionality and global gender inequality. *Gender & Society, 26*(1), 67–72.

Choo, H. Y., & Ferree, M. M. (2010). Practicing intersectionality in sociological research: A critical analysis of inclusions, interactions, and institutions in the study of inequalities. *Sociological Theory, 28*(2), 129–149.

Collins, P. H. (1990). *Black feminist thought: Knowledge, consciousness, and the politics of empowerment.* New York: Routledge.

Collins, P. H. (1998). Intersections of race, class, gender, and nation: Some implications for Black family studies. *Journal of Comparative Family Studies, 29*(1), 27–36.

Collins, P. H. (2001). It's all in the family: Intersections of gender, race, and nation. *Hypatia, 13*(3), 62–82.

Connell, R. W. (1987). *Gender and power: Society, the person, and sexual politics.* Stanford, CA: Stanford University Press.

Connell, R. W. (1992). A very straight gay: Masculinity, homosexual experience, and the dynamics of gender. *American Sociological Review, 57,* 735–751.

Davis, A. Y. (1981). *Women, race, and class.* New York: Random House.

Davis, K. (2008). Intersectionality as buzzword: A sociology of science perspective on what makes a feminist theory successful. *Feminist Theory, 9*(1), 67–85.

Guy-Scheftall, B. (Ed.). (1995). *Words of fire: An anthology of African-American feminist thought.* New York: New Press.

hooks, b. (1981). *Ain't I a woman: Black women and feminism.* Boston: South End Press.

King, D. (1988). Multiple jeopardy: The context of a Black feminist ideology. *Signs, 14*(1), 42–72.

Lorde, A. (1982). *Zami: A new spelling of my name.* Trumansburg, NY: Crossing Press.

McCall, L. (2005). The complexity of intersectionality. *Signs, 30*(3), 1771–1800.

McIntosh, P. (1998). *White privilege and male privilege: Unpacking the invisible knapsack.* Wellesley, MA: Wellesley College Center for Research on Women.

Walby, S., Armstrong, J., and Strid, S. (2012). Intersectionality: Multiple inequalities in social theory. *Sociology, 46*(2), 224–240.

Weber, L. (2001). *Understanding race, class, gender, and sexuality: A conceptual framework.* Boston: McGraw-Hill.

Winker, G., & Degele, N. (2011). Intersectionality as multi-level analysis: Dealing with social inequality. *European Journal of Women's Studies, 18*(1), 51–66.

Introduction to Reading 7

Intersectional theory is not an easy concept to define for many of the reasons described in the introduction to this chapter. In this piece, Bonnie Thornton Dill and Marla H. Kohlman discuss some of the key issues relating to intersectional theory today. They look at the roots and history of intersectionality from the perspective of Black feminists and also review some debates about methodological issues surrounding intersectionality in terms of qualitative versus quantitative analyses. While their focus is also on social justice, we are not able to include that entire discussion in this excerpt, but we encourage you to be sensitive to issues of social justice and intersectionality that they weave throughout this piece, particularly in their conclusion to this reading. They end by contrasting "strong intersectionality" with "weak intersectionality," further illustrating the various ways this paradigm has been applied. This reading helps us understand the value of thinking deeply about differences and the need for intersectional analyses.

1. How have Blacks, particularly Black women, helped shape the development of intersectional analyses?

2. What are the problems of studying intersectionality using quantitative methodology, and what are the advantages of doing so?

3. Explain what the authors mean by the difference between "strong intersectionality" and "weak intersectionality."

INTERSECTIONALITY

A TRANSFORMATIVE PARADIGM IN FEMINIST THEORY AND SOCIAL JUSTICE

Bonnie Thornton Dill and Marla H. Kohlman

As a Black scholar writing about women's issues in the mid-1980s, Thornton Dill joined with several colleagues in calling for a feminist theoretical paradigm that would expose the disconnect between experience and theory in the often untold stories of women of color and those without economic privilege (Baca Zinn, Cannon, Dill, & Higginbotham, 1986). They understood that feminist theory was quite limited without the purposeful integration of the notion of difference, beginning with race, ethnicity, class, and culture. They also understood that the integration of race and class into the gendered discourses extant at that time would change the nature of feminist discourse in important and powerful ways.

More than two decades later, one of the first things students learn in women's studies classes is how to look at women's and men's lives through multiple lenses. The concept of *intersectionality* has been a key factor in this transition. This conceptual tool has become integral to both theory and research endeavors, as it emphasizes the interlocking effects of race, class, gender, and sexuality, highlighting the ways in which categories of identity and structures of inequality are mutually constituted and defy separation into discrete categories of analysis. Intersectionality provides a unique lens of study that does not question difference; rather, it assumes that differential experiences of common events are to be expected.

As scholars producing intersectional work began to apply their insights to institutional dynamics, they began to speak and write about the challenges and opportunities that exist within

From Thornton Dill, Bonnie, and Marla H. Kohlman. 2011. "Intersectionality: A Transformative Paradigm in Feminist Theory and Social Justice." Pp. 154–174 in *Handbook of Feminist Research,* 2nd ed., edited by Sharlene Hesse-Biber. Thousand Oaks, CA: Sage.

and through the academy and the labor market, and in law and public policy. Thus, intersectional scholarship is engaged in transforming both theory and practice across disciplinary divides, offering a wide range of methodological approaches to the study of multiple, complex social relations. In her widely cited 2005 article, "The Complexity of Intersectionality," sociologist Leslie McCall states that "intersectionality is the most important theoretical contribution that women's studies, in conjunction with related fields, has made so far" (p. 1771).

In this chapter, we map the developments in intersectional theorizing and institutional transformation in the past decade while also offering our views on the future of intersectionality for feminist theory and methodology.

ROOTS AND HISTORY

Intersectional scholarship emerged as an amalgamation of aspects of women's studies and race and ethnic studies. Its foundations are in the scholarly tradition that began in the 19th century with Black women such as Sojourner Truth, Maria Stewart, and Anna Julia Cooper and men like W. E. B. Du Bois—intellectuals who first articulated the unique challenges of Black women facing the multiple and simultaneous effects of race, gender, and class. What distinguished this early work on Black women was that it argued forcefully and passionately that the lives of African American women could not be understood through a unidimensional analysis focusing exclusively on either race or gender.

Intersectional scholarship, as we know it today, fused this knowledge from race and ethnic studies with aspects of women's studies and refined it in the debates and discourse that informed the civil and women's rights activism of the 1960s and 1970s. Before that time, women's studies emphasized the importance of gender and sexism while Black and Latino studies focused on race and racism as experienced within these respective communities. Each field

sought to interrogate historical patterns of subordination and domination, asserting that we live in a society that is organized around complex and layered sets of inequalities. . . .

Categories of race/ethnicity, class, and gender were defined as major markers and controllers of oppression in the earliest discussions of intersectionality, with limited attention given to other categories such as sexuality, nation, age, disability, and religion, which have been discussed in more recent years. One result of this historical trajectory is a perspective asserting that individuals and groups can simultaneously experience oppression and privilege. Mere recognition of this history is not sufficient to form a complete understanding of the extensive ranges of "structures and experiences produced by intersecting forms of race and gender"; neither does it ensure proper acknowledgment of the "interlocking inequalities, what Patricia Hill Collins calls the 'matrix of domination'" (Baca Zinn & Dill, 1996, p. 326).

Collins explains that "the matrix of domination is structured on several levels. People experience and resist oppression on three levels: the level of personal biography; the group or community level of cultural context created by race, class, and gender; and the systemic level of social institutions" (Collins, 1990, p. 227). Collins distinguishes her conceptualization of interlocking theories, or oppressions, from the traditional additive models of oppression found in much traditional feminist theory. . . .

By noting the ways in which men and women occupy variant positions of power and privilege across race, space, and time, intersectionality has refashioned several of the basic premises that have guided feminist theory as it evolved following the 1950s. Many have explicitly recognized that the prototypical model for feminist theory post-1950s was based on the lives of White women whose experiences as wives, daughters, and mothers were to be strictly differentiated from the experience of Black women as informed by historical precedent. "Judged by the evolving nineteenth century ideology of femininity, which emphasized women's roles as nurturing mothers and gentle companions and housekeepers for their husbands, Black women were practically anomalies" (Davis, 1981, p. 5). Indeed, "one cannot assume, as have many feminist theorists and activists, that all women have had the same experience of gender oppression—or that they will be on the same side of a struggle, not even when some women define that struggle as 'feminist' . . . [F]or peoples of color, having children and maintaining families have been an essential part of the struggle against racist oppression. [Thus, it is not surprising that] many women of color have rejected the white women's movement's view of the family as the center of 'women's oppression'" (Amott & Matthaei, 1991, pp. 16–17), which many find to be the decisive message of books regarded as pivotal foundations of the second wave of the feminist movement such as *The Feminine Mystique* by Betty Friedan or *Of Woman Born* by Adrienne Rich. We do not mean to imply, either, that all women of color would renounce the accounts offered in the pages of these books. We offer these textual examples as evidence that intersectional scholarship has been able to highlight the myriad ways in which the experiences of some White women and women of color differ in the nuances of the maintenance of family. More specifically, these differences are to be found within the inextricable lines of racial ethnicity and gender that were influential in the fomentation of a feminist consciousness for some women that was both distinct from and dependent upon the experiences of other women.

Indeed, the family has been for many women of color a sort of "haven in a heartless world" of racism that provides the needed support to fight against oppression of many types (Dill, 1979; hooks, 1984). Drawing on the work of a number of the pioneering Black feminist intersectional scholars, Landry (2000) argues in his book on Black middle-class women that this support enabled Black women to produce a new ideology of womanhood that permitted the formation of the modern dual-career and dual-earner family. This model of womanhood rejected the notion

that "outside work was detrimental to [Black women's roles] as wives and mothers" (Landry, 2000, p. 73). Indeed, Black women of the late 19th and early 20th centuries realized that "their membership in the paid labor force was critical to achieving true equality with men" (p. 74) in the larger U.S. society in a way that was not available to White women under the cult of true womanhood that constrained them to the exclusive domains of hearth and home. Women of color, having always been regarded as a source of labor in the United States, were never the beneficiaries of this ideology of protectionism and were not, therefore, hampered from developing an ideology that saw beyond the dictates of traditional feminist principles based in the experience of gender subordination perceived as endemic to all women (see, for example, Davis, 1972).

Winifred Breines (2006) provides an interesting reflection on the role and relationship of early intersectional thinking that promoted an understanding of mutually constituted structures of difference and inequality in feminist experiences. As she argues in *The Trouble Between Us: An Uneasy History of White and Black Women in the Feminist Movement,*

> In the development of the feminist movement, one of the most dramatic political shifts was from a desire to overcome difference to its promotion. Integration or interracialism as a goal migrated toward difference and an embrace of identity that precluded togetherness. This was a disturbing process but, in retrospect, probably inevitable. Postwar young people, especially whites, knew very little about racism and sexism. They had to separate to learn who they were in the race, class, and gender terms constructed by American society. . . . Just as identity politics divided the society that created such politics in the first place, they divided the movements. (Breines, 2006, p. 16)

Breines (2006) concludes her text on the differences that emerged between Black and White women in the feminist movement with words from several young feminists, one of whom contends that "unlike second wave feminism, which has operated from a monolithic center, multiplicity offers the power of existing insidiously and simultaneously everywhere. 'Women' as a primary identity category has ceased to be the entry point for much young activist work" (p. 196). Breines (2006) follows this with the admonition that young feminists have come to this knowledge having read the experiences of those who struggled before them: "They may not be aware of it, but the racial learning curve that began in the early 1960s continues among younger—and older—feminists in the twenty-first century" (p. 199). Similar to the project embarked upon by Breines, the research and writing of feminist scholars of color continues the tradition of theorizing the experience of women of color who have been ignored in the scholarship on both race and gender. These scholars have produced landmark studies based on lived experience at the intersections of race, gender, ethnicity, class, and sexuality.[1]

GROWTH AND DISSEMINATION: EMERGING INQUIRIES AND CONTROVERSIES

As an approach to creating knowledge that has its roots in analyses of the lived experiences of women of color—women whose scholarly and social justice work reveals how aspects of identity and social relations are shaped by the simultaneous operation of multiple systems of power—intersectional scholarship is interdisciplinary in nature and focuses on how structures of difference combine to create a feminist praxis that is new and distinct from the social, cultural, and artistic forms emphasized in traditional feminist paradigms that focus primarily upon contrasting the experiences of women in society to those of men. Intersectionality is intellectually transformative not only because it centers the experiences of people of color and locates its analysis within systems of ideological, political, institutional, and economic power as they are shaped by historical patterns of race, class, gender, sexuality, nation, ethnicity, and age but also

because it provides a platform for uniting different kinds of praxis in the pursuit of social justice: analysis, theorizing, education, advocacy, and policy development.

The people who engage with this work do so out of strong commitments to diversity, multiculturalism, and human rights, combined with a desire to create a more equitable society that recognizes, validates, and celebrates difference. The social justice agenda of this scholarship is crucial to its utility in fomenting theory and praxis specifically designed for analyzing inequalities of power and privilege, and, consequently, intersectionality is of interest to persons outside the academy who share concerns that underlie this scholarship. As Catharine MacKinnon contends, "What is important about intersectionality is what it is doing in our world, how it is traveling around the world and being used in defense of human rights, not just what it says" (MacKinnon, 2010).

The intellectual vibrancy within and around intersectional theory is yielding new frontiers of knowledge production that include, but are not limited to, scholarship on identity and the applicability of intersectionality to groups in other social locations or in multiple social locations simultaneously (Browne & Misra, 2003; Henderson & Tickamyer, 2009; Kohlman, 2010). Discussions about methodologies, language, and images most accurately convey the complexities of these interrelationships. For example, the development of the queer of color critique (Ferguson, 2003; Johnson & Henderson, 2005) as an intervention into sexuality studies establishes race and ethnicity as critical dimensions of queer studies, scholarship on globalization and international human rights moves intersectionality beyond the U.S. context (Davis, 2008; Knapp, 2005; Mohanty, 2003; Yuval-Davis, 2006), and work that continues explicitly to link theory and practice provides an analytical foundation for social justice and critical resistance. Within each of these topics, there are disagreements about approach and perspective, . . . and the debates and discussions contribute to the vibrancy of the topic and thus to advancing this scholarship and producing knowledge that illuminates the many factors that shape processes of experiencing multiple identities and social locations.

Because the contemporary growth of intersectionality as a theoretical approach is relatively recent and has developed in a number of different fields, future growth is largely defined by the trajectory of current debates and inquiries.

* * *

Methodological Concerns

Debates around methodologies center on the concern of remaining grounded in the questions, struggles, and experiences of particular communities that generate an intersectional perspective. At the same time, methodological debates about intersectionality often extend this approach to identify common themes and points of connection between specific social locations and broader social patterns. Stated somewhat differently: How do we benefit from comparisons and interrelationships without negating or undermining the complex and particular character of each group, system of oppression, or culture? Answers to this question are embedded in discussions about the language and metaphors that most effectively convey the concept of intersectionality as well as in debates about the use of qualitative and historical versus quantitative research methodologies.

Central to the discussion of language have been disputes about the adequacies and limitations of the term "intersectionality" and the metaphors associated with it. Scholars working with these ideas continue to seek ways to overcome an image that suggests that these dimensions of inequality, such as race, class, and gender, are separable and distinct and that it is only at certain points that they overlap or intersect with one another. This concern was specifically articulated by Deborah King in 1988 when she called for a model of analysis permitting recognition of the "multiple jeopardy" constituted by the interactive oppressions that circumscribe

the lives of Black women and defy separation into discrete categories of analysis. The modifier "multiple" refers not only to several simultaneous oppressions but to the multiplicative relationships among them as well (King, 1988, p. 47). It is now widely recognized that intersectionality is more than a car crash at the nexus of a set of separate roads (Crenshaw, 1989). Instead, it is well understood that these systems of power are mutually constituted (Weber, 2009) such that there is no point at which race is not simultaneously classed and gendered or gender is not simultaneously raced and classed. How to capture this complexity in a single term or image has been an ongoing conversation.

Recent work by Ivy Ken (2007) provides a useful overview of a number of the conceptual images in use: that is, the notion of "intersecting versus interlocking" inequalities, which has been expressed in metaphors such as crossing roads or a matrix or the importance of locating oppressions within "systems versus structures versus institutions." She then moves on to analyze the limitations of these analytical approaches and suggests aspects of intersectionality that remain unexplained. She further proposes an innovative and promising approach to thinking about these ideas using the processes of producing, using, experiencing, and digesting sugar as a metaphor for describing, discussing, and theorizing intersectionality (Ken, 2008). For example, she addresses the importance of context-specific relationships in understanding how race, class, and gender oppression is "produced, what people and institutions do with it once they have it in their hands, what it feels like to experience it, and how it then comes to shape us" (Ken, 2008, p. 154). Ken argues that the relationships among sources of oppression, like race, class, and gender, start with production—every aspect of race, class, and gender has been and is produced under particular social, historical, political, cultural, and economic conditions.

Given the intersectional argument that race, class, gender, and other axes of inequality are always intertwined, co-constructed, and simultaneous (Weber, 2009), questions and debates have arisen about how quantitative approaches that rely on the analysis of separate and distinct variables can account for such interactivity. Two issues frame this debate. The first is the idea that these axes of inequality are not simply characteristics of individuals to be used as variables, isolated from the particular histories, social relations, and institutional contexts that produced them (Amott & Matthaei, 1996; Stacey & Thorne, cited in Harnois, 2009). The second is the task of developing quantitative approaches that address and reveal the overlapping differences present in intersectional analyses in a way that will yield important, generalizable results.

The work of Leslie McCall (2001, 2005) with regard to race, class, and gender in different types of labor markets has been particularly important in efforts to rethink the use of quantitative tools so that they can reveal the differential ways race, class, and gender interact within different social contexts. Her *Signs* article (2005) has been an important tool in efforts to provide empirical evidence of the value of intersectional analysis in the quantitative social sciences. Specifically, McCall applies an intersectional approach to an examination of the impact of economic restructuring on wage inequalities (see also Hancock, 2008; Simien, 2007; Valentine, 2007). To do this, she studies the effect of multiple factors on different racial/ethnic, class, and gender groups and on the relationships both within and between those groups in different regional economies. What she finds is that the patterns are not the same: that a single economic environment may create advantages for some in a group and disadvantages for others in the same group relative to other groups, thus making some environments more appropriate for one set of social policies while a different set may be more appropriate for another. She states: "different contexts reveal different configurations of inequality [and] no single dimension of overall inequality can adequately describe the full structure of multiple, intersecting, and conflicting dimensions of inequality" (McCall, 2005, p. 1791).

Kohlman (2006, 2010) has utilized intersection theory to illustrate how the experiences of men and women who report having experienced sexual harassment in the U.S. labor market differ because of the interaction of several forces of oppression that influence behavior simultaneously. She employs quantitative methods to illustrate successfully that it is both possible and imperative to deconstruct commonly used additive models of analysis, which mask the intersectional effects shaping the experiences of those embedded within them. Catherine Harnois (2005, 2009), by applying multiracial feminist theory in the design of a quantitative analysis of women's paths to feminism, has both revealed and offered meaningful explanations for variations among women by race and ethnicity, differences within racial-ethnic categories that had not been thought to exist.

Because empirical findings from quantitative analyses dominate the social sciences, are seen as authoritative and generalizable, and often provide the documentation upon which social policy is built, quantitative research that demonstrates the importance of intersectionality offers the opportunity to expand the framework's applicability and impact. The danger, however, is that these axes of inequality may be read as a reductive analysis of the interaction of a set of individual characteristics, thus diluting the power and full meaning of the experiential theory these interactions have been constructed to illustrate. Quantitative methodologies, when read in conjunction with findings produced from the qualitative studies that continue to dominate research within the intersectional paradigm, provide analytic frames that complement, apply, and extend the impact and understanding of intersectionality.

It is also important to note that debates about methodology are not limited to a quantitative versus qualitative discussion, but, rather, embrace the idea that we must continue to explore and expand the approaches we use to address an even broader range of questions that can be generated by this scholarship. These should include applied and theoretical and interdisciplinary and transversal modes of inquiry, among others. Interdisciplinary research must embrace multiple methodological approaches to capture the complexities and nuances in the lives of individuals and the experiences of groups of people (see also Hancock, 2007). A key criterion is to avoid essentializing people's experiences by burying intragroup diversity within isolated analytical categories.

* * *

CONCLUSION

In 1979, Audre Lorde stood before an audience at a conference devoted to Simone de Beauvoir's book *The Second Sex* in New York City and spoke these words:

> Those of us who stand outside the circle of this society's definition of acceptable women; those of us who have been forged in the crucibles of difference—those of us who are poor, who are lesbians, who are Black, who are older—know that *survival is not an academic skill*. It is learning how to stand alone, unpopular and sometimes reviled, and how to make common cause with those others identified as outside the structures in order to define and seek a world in which we all can flourish. It is learning how to take our differences and make them strengths. (Lorde, 1984, p. 112)

More than three decades later, Lorde's clear mandate for social justice resonates at the very core of what intersectionality was, is, and must continue to be in order to serve the aims of those individuals who have found themselves to be situated in different social locations around the margins of feminist debates and inquiries. Just as Lorde called for feminists to turn difference into strengths, the theoretical paradigm of intersectionality has provided a voice and a vision to scholars seeking to make visible the interlocking structures of inequality to be found within the academic and everyday concerns that shape both our livelihoods and our experiences of the world.

Intersectionality has traveled a long distance, and, indeed, we recognize that it has taken many forms across academic disciplines and life histories. Intersectionality has now reached the point where it may be regarded as a member of the theoretical cannon taught in courses on law, social sciences, and the humanities. Intersectionality has, thus, increased in strength and, perhaps alternatively, suffered significant dilution in application as often happens when any theoretical tool is either misinterpreted or misapplied. As to the evidence of intersection theory's increasing strength, we know that intersectionality has been the practice of Black feminist scholars for generations; in that respect, this paradigm is not at all new. It has just been a long time coming into its own, and now, having been newly embraced as a powerful tool of social justice, social thought, and social activism by a larger population of feminist researchers, it has become more visible than ever before.

As to the evidence of its misapplication, we caution scholars to be mindful of what we consider to be "strong intersectionality" and "weak intersectionality." "Strong intersectionality" may be found in theoretical and methodological rubrics that seek to analyze institutions and identities *in relation to one another*. That is, "strong intersectionality" seeks to ascertain how phenomena are mutually constituted and interdependent, how we must understand one phenomenon in deference to understanding another. On the other hand, "weak intersectionality" explores differences without any true analysis. That is to say, "weak intersectionality" ignores the very mandate called for by Audre Lorde and seeks to explore no more than how we are different. "Weak intersectionality" eschews the difficult dialogue(s) of how our differences have come to be—or how our differences might become axes of strength, fortification, and a renewed vision of how our world has been—and continues, instead, to be socially constructed by a theory and methodology that seeks only occasionally to question difference, without arriving at a deep and abiding understanding of how our differences are continuing to evolve.

Part of the proliferation of "weak intersectionality" may be found in the interdisciplinary narratives advancing the argument that this paradigmatic tool operates in different ways in different institutional spaces. This argument is also reminiscent of the contention that intersectional theory has been individualized within separate fields of knowledge. We can only reply to such arguments by, first, acknowledging that intersectionality has developed disparately within different spheres of knowledge because of the way in which intersectional theorizing is applied across disciplinary fields. For example, some might encounter intersectionality as a concrete reality that hinders effective litigation under the law because whole people are literally required to split their identity(ies) in order to be properly recognized in a court of law. But when this same legal phenomenon is read and discussed in the social sciences or humanities, the scholars at issue might study it as a structural impediment or analytic frame that defies discrete analysis. That being said, this dilemma has the very real potential of diverting one's attention away from the theoretical imperative of intersectionality as a source of illumination and understanding to one that distorts and misrepresents lived experiences of the law, social norms, and social justice.

But we also recognize, as a second proposition, that intersectionality has developed differently across spheres of knowledge because of the differing experiences and privileges we enjoy as scholars and everyday citizens of the world. We noted previously, for example, that intersectionality has benefited tremendously from differing methodological applications and transnational discourses, even as we remain steadfast in our contention that this paradigm was born of the experiences of Black women in the United States that could not be properly understood using the unidimensional lens of race or of gender in academic and legal discourses.

Having established the foregoing premises of "strong intersectionality" and "weak intersectionality," we now see intersectional theorizing developing into a paradigm of analysis that defies separation into distinct fields of knowledge because of its explanatory power as a theoretical tool that does not require tweaking "to make it fit," so to speak. This is because the primacy of the basic core principles of intersectionality—that is, mutually constituted interdependence; interlocking oppressions and privileges; multiple experiences of race, gender, sexuality, and so forth—are now more widely recognized as such and scholars are more apt to hold one another to these basic rules of application, whatever methodology is employed. In fact, the debates occurring within intersectional scholarship today reflect the growth and maturation of this approach and provide the opportunity to begin, as Lynn Weber says, to "harvest lessons learned" (as cited in Dill & Zambrana, 2009, p. 287).

Among the lessons learned and knowledge produced is a broader and more in-depth understanding of the notion of race, racial formation, and racial projects. Another is a broader understanding of the concept of nation and of notions of citizenship both in the United States and globally. Concepts such as situated knowledge (Lorde), oppositional consciousness (Sandoval), and strategic essentialism (Hurtado) offer ways to theorize about difference and diversity. A third lesson is the knowledge that there is no single category (race, class, ethnicity, gender, nation, or sexuality) that can explain human experience without reference to other categories. Thus we have and will need to continue to develop more nuanced and complex understandings of identity and more fluid notions of gender, race, sexuality, and class. The work relies heavily on a more expanded sense of the concept of social construction and rests much of its analysis on the principle of the social construction of difference. Organista (2007) contests the dominant culture's imperialism and resistance to discussion of human differences within and across cultures and calls for a discussion of difference "beyond the kind of defensive and superficial hyperbole that leaves social oppression unchallenged" (p. 101). And, although the scholarship still struggles with the pull to establish either a hierarchy of difference or a list that includes all forms of social differentiation, both of which are antithetical to the specific objectives of intersectionality, a body of knowledge is being produced that provides a basis for understanding the various histories and organizations of these categories of inequality. This evolving body of knowledge is helping us better understand what differences render inequalities and how to resist reductionist impulses. As a theoretical paradigm,[2] intersectionality is unique in its versatility and ability to produce new knowledge. We remain optimistic about the future of intersectionality, particularly if this scholarship respects its crucial commitments to laying bare the roots of power and inequality, while continuing to pursue an activist agenda of social justice.

NOTES

1. This list is not meant to be exclusive or exhaustive but a reflection of the breadth of early intersectional scholarship: Patricia Hill Collins (1990), Kimberlé Crenshaw (1989), Gloria Anzaldúa (1987), Maxine Baca Zinn and Bonnie Dill (1996), Audre Lorde (1984), Angela Y. Davis (1981), Cherrie Moraga (1983), Chela Sandoval (1991), Chandra Talpade Mohanty (1988), and bell hooks (1984).

2. In 1998, Collins referred to intersectionality as an "emerging paradigm." In 2007, Hancock argues it has become a normative and empirical paradigm.

REFERENCES

Amott, T. L., & Matthaei, J. A. (1991). *Race, gender and work.* Boston: South End Press.

Amott, T. L., & Matthaei, J. A. (1996). *Race, gender and work* (New ed.). Boston: South End Press.

Anzaldúa, G. (1987). *La Frontera/Borderlands: The new Mestiza.* San Francisco: Aunt Lute Books.

Baca Zinn, M., Cannon, L. W., Dill, B. T., & Higginbotham, E. (1986). The costs of exclusionary practices in women's studies. *Signs: Journal of Women in Culture and Society, 11,* 290–303.

Baca Zinn, M., & Dill, B. T. (1996). Theorizing difference from multi-racial feminism. *Feminist Studies, 22*(2), 321–331.

Breines, W. (2006). *The trouble between us: An uneasy history of white and black women in the feminist movement.* New York: Oxford University Press.

Browne, I., & Misra, J. (2003). The intersection of gender and race in the labor market. *Annual Review of Sociology, 29,* 487–513.

Collins, P. H. (1990). *Black feminist thought: Knowledge, consciousness, and the politics of empowerment.* Boston: Unwin Hyman.

Crenshaw, K. (1989). Demarginalizing the intersection of race and sex: A black feminist of antidiscrimination doctrine, feminist theory, and antiracist politics. *University of Chicago Legal Forum,* 139–167.

Davis, A. Y. (1972). Reflections on the black woman's role in the community of slaves. *The Massachusetts Review, 13*(1/2), 81–100.

Davis, A. Y. (1981). *Women, race, and class.* New York: Random House.

Davis, K. (2008). Intersectionality as buzzword: A sociology of science perspective on what makes a feminist theory successful. *Feminist Theory, 9*(1), 67–85.

Dill, B. T. (1979). The dialectics of black womanhood. *Signs: Journal of Women in Culture and Society, 4*(3), 543–555.

Dill, B. T., & Zambrana, R. E. (2009). *Emerging intersections: Race, class, and gender in theory, policy, and practice.* New Brunswick, NJ: Rutgers University Press.

Ferguson, R. A. (2003). *Aberrations in black: Toward a queer of color critique.* Minneapolis: University of Minnesota Press.

Hancock, A. M. (2007). When multiplication doesn't equal quick addition: Examining intersectionality as a research paradigm. *Perspectives on Politics, 5*(1), 63–79.

Hancock, A. M. (2008). Intersectionality as a normative and empirical paradigm. *Politics & Gender, 3*(2), 248–254.

Harnois, C. E. (2005). Different paths to different feminisms? Bridging multiracial feminist theory and quantitative sociological gender research. *Gender & Society, 19*(6), 809–828.

Harnois, C. E. (2009). Imagining a "feminist revolution": Can multiracial feminism revolutionize quantitative social science research? In M. T. Berger & K. Guidroz (Eds.), *The intersectional approach: Transforming the academy through race, class, and gender* (pp. 157–172). Chapel Hill, NC: UNC Press.

hooks, b. (1984). *Feminist theory: From margin to center.* Cambridge, MA: South End Press.

Johnson, E. P., & Henderson, M. G. (Eds.). (2005). *Black queer studies: A critical anthology.* Durham, NC: Duke University Press.

Ken, I. (2007). Race-class-gender theory: An image(ry) problem. *Gender Issues, 24,* 1–20.

Ken, I. (2008). Beyond the intersection: A new culinary metaphor for race-class-gender studies. *Sociological Theory, 26*(2), 152–172.

King, D. (1988). Multiple jeopardy, multiple consciousness: The context of a black feminist ideology. *Signs: Journal of Women in Culture and Society, 14*(1), 42–72.

Knapp, G. A. (2005). Race, class, gender: Reclaiming baggage in fast-travelling theories. *European Journal of Women's Studies, 12*(3), 249–265.

Kohlman, M. H. (2006). Intersection theory: A more elucidating paradigm of quantitative analysis. *Race, Gender & Class, 13,* 42–59.

Kohlman, M. H. (2010). Race, rank and gender: The determinants of sexual harassment for men and women of color in the military. In V. Demos & M. Segal (Series Eds.), *Advances in Gender Research: Vol. 14. Interactions and intersections of gendered bodies at work, at home, and at play* (pp. 65–94). Boston: Elsevier.

Landry, B. (2000). *Black working wives: Pioneers of the American family revolution.* Berkeley: University of California Press.

Lorde, A. (1984). *Sister outsider.* Freedom, CA: Crossing Press.

MacKinnon, C. (2010, March 11). *Panelist remarks on "Rounding intersectionality: Critical foundations and contested trajectories."* Paper at the 4th Annual Critical Race Studies Symposium—Intersectionality: Challenging Theory, Reframing Politics, Transforming Movements, UCLA School of Law, Los Angeles, CA.

McCall, L. (2001). *Complex inequality: Gender, class, and race in the new economy.* New York: Routledge.

McCall, L. (2005). The complexity of intersectionality. *Signs: Journal of Women in Culture and Society, 30*(3), 1771–1800.

Mohanty, C. T. (1988). Under western eyes: Feminist scholarship and colonial discourses. *Feminist Review, 30,* 61–88.

Mohanty, C. T. (2003). *Feminism without borders.* Durham, NC: Duke University Press.

Moraga, C. (1983). *Loving in the war years.* Boston: South End Press.

Organista, C. K. (2007). *Solving Latino psychosocial and health problems: Theory, practice, and populations.* Hoboken, NJ: John Wiley & Sons, Inc.

Sandoval, C. (1991). U.S. third world feminism: The theory and method of oppositional consciousness in the postmodern world. *Genders, 10,* 1–24.

Simien, E. (2007). Doing intersectionality research: From conceptual issues to practical examples. *Politics and Gender, 3*(2), 264–271.

Valentine, G. (2007). Theorizing and researching intersectionality: A challenge for feminist geography. *Professional Geographer, 59,* 10–21.

Weber, L. (2009). *Understanding race, class, gender, and sexuality: An intersectional framework* (2nd ed.). New York: Oxford University Press.

Yuval-Davis, N. (2006). Intersectionality and feminist politics. *European Journal of Women's Studies, 13*(3), 193–210.

Introduction to Reading 8

In this piece, Nikki Jones points to the need to use an intersectional analysis when studying "doing gender." This piece was published as part of a symposium, 20 years after the original article on "doing gender" by Candace West and Donald Zimmerman. During those 20 years, many changes occurred in the approaches to studying gender, including development of the literature on intersectional analysis, as Bonnie Thornton Dill and Marla H. Kohlman described in the previous reading. In this article, Jones uses research from her study of Black girls and inner-city violence to provide an in-depth look at the need to combine intersectional analysis with the "doing gender" theoretical framework. Her argument emphasizes the importance of context as well. As you read through this article, consider why it is so important to use an intersectional approach when studying "doing gender."

1. What does this article mean by "categorical identity"?

2. What does intersectional analysis add to our understanding of "doing gender"?

3. Give an example of how Kiara was "doing gender," and explain how that used interactional analysis.

"I Was Aggressive for the Streets, Pretty for the Pictures"

Gender, Difference, and the Inner-City Girl

Nikki Jones

It is a late June afternoon and I am standing outside of a café on Fillmore Street in San Francisco. I am holding flyers for Kiara[1], a young woman I met a few hours earlier. Kiara is 22 years old with a light brown complexion and long, wavy hair that suggests a multiracial heritage. Her style of dress is 1980s-retro. She wears a purple lace glove with the finger cut off on her right hand, a short-sleeved jacket over a yellow and green Brazil fútbol jersey, and tight denim jeans that ride low, causing her belly to peek out sometimes between her jeans and her jersey. Two large star-shaped earrings dangle from her ears and a small white flower is tucked into her hair. She was born and raised in the Fillmore, a once-vibrant Black neighborhood that is now quickly gentrifying after decades of blight and neglect. I have conducted field research here since 2005 and just finished interviewing Kiara inside the café. Kiara's grandmother, like many older Black Fillmore residents, migrated from the South.

She owned the house in which she raised Kiara after Kiara's mother was killed by her father, who, Kiara tells me, was a big-time drug dealer in the neighborhood before he was sent to prison. Kiara remembers how her father's tough reputation influenced how others interacted with her in the neighborhood; even though she was a child she garnered a level of respect. She learned early on how to manage her interactions with others differently in different situations: "[as a child] I had the street element, and I was aggressive for the streets, pretty for the pictures."

Kiara is helping to collect signatures for an anti-redevelopment campaign in Hunter's Point-Bayview, a larger and even more distressed Black neighborhood in San Francisco. Kiara offers to give me a tour of the Fillmore and I follow along as she walks with clipboard in hand. Kiara's play on mainstream and local expectations of race, gender, class, sexuality, and power is on full display during her brief interactions with strangers.

From Jones, Nikki. 2009. "'I Was Aggressive for the Streets, Pretty for Pictures': Gender, Difference and the Inner-City Girl." *Gender & Society* 23(1): 89–93.

She confidently, assertively, even aggressively approaches men on the street to sign her petition and then draws on normative expectations of manhood and femininity to encourage them to add their names to the list: Babies and women are in danger, she tells them, letting the implication that real men would sign up to protect babies and women hang in the air. She switches from aggressive to demure just long enough to flirt with a man passing by on the street and then to defiant when she passes the police station on the corner. "They don't give a fuck!" she declares loudly. A few moments later we stop to observe the RIPs scratched into the concrete sidewalk of a neighborhood block "where a lot of the trouble happens." Kiara calls these scratches that mark the murders of young Black men "modern-day hieroglyphics." She gets silent and still, but just for a moment. She has work to do so she keeps on moving.

Twenty years after the publication of West and Zimmerman's "Doing Gender" (1987), critical and feminist scholars have the analytical tools to observe and represent Kiara's interactions on this city block in ways that illuminate how gender, race, and class are accomplished during situated interaction. An interactional analysis of Kiara's walk through the Fillmore reveals moments where the accomplishment of gender, race, or class emerges as most significant. Such an analysis is also likely to reveal moments when Kiara violates or manipulates the normative expectations associated with categorical identity, and the consequences of her doing so. Yet, as Patricia Hill Collins writes in her critical response to "Doing Difference" (1995), such an analysis, on its own, is not likely to reveal how the social contexts in which these interactions take place are shaped by the "messy" intersection of various systems of oppression (1995, 491–94). Kiara and other neighborhood residents describe these oppressive forces as "Redevelopment," referring to the urban redevelopment agency that many longtime Fillmore residents hold responsible for decades of neighborhood underdevelopment and exploitation. Another oppressive force that has shaped life for young people in the neighborhood—boys and girls—is the local police force, including the city's gang task force, which has grown stronger in the nation's never-ending War on Drugs.

If we focus only on interactional accomplishments of categorical identity we can miss the chance to illuminate the recursive relationship *between* Kiara's interactions with others, her identity (or identities), and these larger oppressive forces, which are shaped by various overlapping and intersecting -isms. To be fair, I do not think such an omission is a necessary or desired outcome of the theoretical frameworks of "doing gender" or "doing difference" (West and Fenstermaker 1995). However, the ubiquitous use (or misuse) of the respective frameworks can sometimes leave the impression that a scholar's most important objective is to "test" the respective theoretical approaches—spotting gender or difference here, there, and everywhere—not, instead, to use these frameworks to illuminate the complicated and sometimes contradictory ways in which situated interaction is linked to structural circumstances.

My recent ethnographic work on Black girls and inner-city violence does not set out to test either framework. My analysis is deeply and *simultaneously* informed by the interactional concerns of West, Zimmerman, and Fenstermaker *and* the theoretical and political concerns of Patricia Hill Collins, Howard Winant, and other critical race and feminist scholars. After the sometimes contentious but important debates on how to conceptualize intersecting identities and oppressions, I find that drawing on both approaches helps me to more accurately represent the lives of young women like Kiara. Drawing on both interactional analysis and Black feminist thought encourages us to situate Black women's and girl's experiences, *including their interactional experiences,* at the center of our empirical investigations. Such an integrative approach challenges us to develop better explanations for how interaction, identity, and various structural -isms are linked. Additionally, such an approach pushes social scientists to consider Black women and girls not simply as problems to be solved or explained (e.g., single mothers or "violent" girls) but rather draws attention to the dilemmas and contradictions that Black women and girls encounter and in some measure reconcile in their everyday lives. This is Black feminist interactional studies, perhaps.

At the same time that she is "doing gender" or "doing difference" with others, for example, Kiara is also deeply invested in a struggle for survival. "It's about being a survivor," she responds when I ask her how she developed the strong sense of independence that she revealed during our interview, "and we have to survive." This overarching concern for survival was also revealed during my field research amongst African American inner-city girls in Philadelphia (Jones 2004, 2008). In a recent article, for example, I describe how inner-city girls work the "code of the street" (Jones 2008), which is described by urban ethnographer and race scholar Elijah Anderson (1999) as a *system of accountability* that governs formal and informal interactions in distressed urban areas, especially interpersonal violence. At the heart of "the code" is a battle for respect and *manhood*. In *Black Sexual Politics* (2004), Patricia Hill Collins writes that as Black men embrace "the code," they embrace a hegemonic masculinity that is based on the *coupling* of strength with dominance—white men with wealth and power are able to demonstrate such masculinity through economic or military dominance (in addition to physical dominance). Poor Black men in distressed urban areas must rely primarily on physical domination, which makes them and others in their community more vulnerable to violent victimization.

African American inner-city girls may have no manhood to defend, yet the shared circumstances of inner-city life engender a shared concern for physical safety and survival. Over time, girls coming of age in distressed urban areas come to realize too how respect, reputation, and retaliation—the three R's at the heart of the code—organize their social worlds. Much like Kiara, the girls I met knew quite well the situations in which presenting oneself as "aggressive,"

"good," or "pretty" paid off. Listening to the stories of these girls, it is difficult to imagine them as held hostage to accountability. Instead, they strategically choose from a variety of gender, race, and class displays depending on the situation, the public identity they are invested in crafting, *and* in service of a survival project that has historically defined the lives of poor, Black women and girls in the United States—a project with especially high stakes in neighborhoods like the one in which Kiara has grown up.

These stories complicate our understandings of "doing gender" and "doing difference" in ways that take account the complexities of structure and its intersections with race, class and gender. . . .

NOTE

1. Kiara is a pseudonym.

REFERENCES

Anderson, E. 1999. *Code of the street: Decency, violence, and the moral life of the inner city*. New York: W.W. Norton Press.

Collins, Patricia Hill. 1995. Symposium: On West and Fenstermaker's "Doing difference." *Gender & Society* 9:491–94.

———. 2004. *Black sexual politics: African Americans, gender, and the new racism*. New York and London: Routledge.

Jones, N. 2004. "It's not where you live, it's how you live": How young women negotiate conflict and violence in the inner city. *Annals of the American Academy of Political and Social Science* 595:49–62.

———. 2008. Working "the code": On girls, gender, and inner-city violence. Special issue: Current approaches to understanding female offending. *Australia and New Zealand Journal of Criminology* 4:63–83.

West, Candace, and Sarah Fenstermaker. 1995. Doing difference. *Gender & Society* 9:8–37.

West, Candace, and D. H. Zimmerman. 1987. Doing gender. *Gender & Society* 1:125–51.

Introduction to Reading 9

In this article, Karen D. Pyke and Denise L. Johnson use both the social construction of gender and intersectional analysis to examine the experiences of second-generation Asian American women. They interviewed 100 daughters of Korean American (KA) and Vietnamese American (VA) immigrants to better understand how gender, ethnicity, and culture influenced the meaning respondents gave to their experiences. By living in two worlds, the Asian American women were acutely aware of the social construction of gender within culture, as they had to move between two cultural constructions of femininity. Thus, as in the previous reading by Nikki Jones, race and gender interact in ways that made the women conscious of their decision to "do gender" based on the women's strategic use of culturally defined, situational expectations for femininity.

1. Using this article as an example, explain what it means to "do gender."

2. Why don't these women just be "who they are" across situations?

3. How do these women's struggles between cultural definitions of femininity reinforce, and make dominant, White femininity?

ASIAN AMERICAN WOMEN AND RACIALIZED FEMININITIES

"DOING" GENDER ACROSS CULTURAL WORLDS

Karen D. Pyke and Denise L. Johnson

The study of gender in recent years has been largely guided by two orienting approaches: (1) a social constructionist emphasis on the day-to-day production or doing of gender (Coltrane 1989; West and Zimmerman 1987), and (2) attention to the interlocking systems of race, class, and gender (Espiritu 1997; Collins 2000). Despite the prominence of these approaches, little empirical work has been done that integrates the doing of gender with the study of race. A contributing factor is the more expansive incorporation of social constructionism in the study of gender than in race scholarship where biological markers are still given importance despite widespread acknowledgment that racial oppression is rooted in social arrangements and not biology (Glenn 1999). In addition, attempts to theoretically integrate the doing of gender, race, and class around the concept of "doing difference" (West and Fenstermaker 1995) tended to downplay historical macrostructures of power and domination and to privilege

From Karen D. Pyke, and Denise L. Johnson. 2003. "Asian American Women and Racialized Femininities: 'Doing' Gender Across Cultural Worlds." *Gender & Society* 17(1): 33–53. Copyright © 2003. Published by Sage Publications on behalf of Sociologists for Women in Society.

gender over race and class (Collins et al. 1995). Work is still needed that integrates systems of oppression in a social constructionist framework without granting primacy to any one form of inequality or ignoring larger structures of domination.

The integration of gender and race within a social constructionist approach directs attention to issues that have been overlooked. Little research has examined how racially and ethnically subordinated women, especially Asian American women, mediate cross-pressures in the production of femininity as they move between mainstream and ethnic arenas, such as family, work, and school, and whether distinct and even contradictory gender displays and strategies are enacted across different arenas. Many, if not most, individuals move in social worlds that do not require dramatic inversions of their gender performances, thereby enabling them to maintain stable and seemingly unified gender strategies. However, members of communities that are racially and ethnically marginalized and who regularly traverse interactional arenas with conflicting gender expectations might engage different gender performances depending on the local context in which they are interacting. Examining the ways that such individuals mediate conflicting expectations would address several unanswered questions. Do marginalized women shift their gender performances across mainstream and subcultural settings in response to different gender norms? If so, how do they experience and negotiate such transitions? What meaning do they assign to the different forms of femininities that they engage across settings? Do racially subordinated women experience their production of femininity as inferior to those forms engaged by privileged white women and glorified in the dominant culture?

We address these issues by examining how second-generation Asian American women experience and think about the shifting dynamics involved in the doing of femininity in Asian ethnic and mainstream cultural worlds. We look specifically at their assumptions about gender dynamics in the Eurocentric mainstream and Asian ethnic social settings, the way they think about their gendered selves, and their strategies in doing gender. Our analysis draws on and elaborates the theoretical literature concerning the construction of femininities across race, paying particular attention to how controlling images and ideologies shape the subjective experiences of women of color. This is the first study to our knowledge that examines how intersecting racial and gender hierarchies affect the everyday construction of gender among Asian American women.

CONSTRUCTING FEMININITIES

Current theorizing emphasizes gender as a socially constructed phenomenon rather than an innate and stable attribute (Lorber 1994; Lucal 1999; West and Zimmerman 1987). Informed by symbolic interactionism and ethnomethodology, gender is regarded as something people do in social interaction. Gender is manufactured out of the fabric of culture and social structure and has little, if any, causal relationship to biology (Kessler and McKenna 1978; Lorber 1994). Gender displays are "culturally established sets of behaviors, appearances, mannerisms, and other cues that we have learned to associate with members of a particular gender" (Lucal 1999, 784). These displays "cast particular pursuits as expressions of masculine and feminine 'natures'" (West and Zimmerman 1987, 126). The doing of gender involves its display as a seemingly innate component of an individual.

The social construction of gender provides a theoretical backdrop for notions of multiple masculinities put forth in the masculinities literature (Coltrane 1994; Connell 1987, 1995; Pyke 1996). We draw on this notion in conceptualizing a plurality of femininities in the social production of women. According to this work, gender is not a unitary process. Rather, it is splintered by overlapping layers of inequality into multiple forms of masculinities (and femininities) that are both internally and externally relational and hierarchical.

The concepts of hegemonic and subordinated masculinities are a major contribution of this literature. . . .

The concept of femininities has served mostly as a placeholder in the theory of masculinities where it remains undertheorized and unexamined. Connell (1987, 1995) has written extensively about hegemonic masculinity but offers only a fleeting discussion of the role of femininities. He suggested that the traits of femininity in a patriarchal society are tremendously diverse, with no one form emerging as hegemonic. Hegemonic masculinity is centered on men's global domination of women, and because there is no configuration of femininity organized around women's domination of men, Connell (1987, 183) suggested the notion of a hegemonic femininity is inappropriate. He further argued that women have few opportunities for institutionalized power relations over other women. However, this discounts how other axes of domination, such as race, class, sexuality, and age, mold a hegemonic femininity that is venerated and extolled in the dominant culture, and that emphasizes the superiority of some women over others, thereby privileging white upper-class women. To conceptualize forms of femininities that are subordinated as "problematic" and "abnormal," it is necessary to refer to an oppositional category of femininity that is dominant, ascendant, and "normal" (Glenn 1999, 10). We use the notion of hegemonic and subordinated femininities in framing our analysis.

Ideas of hegemonic and subordinated femininities resonate in the work of feminist scholars of color who emphasize the multiplicity of women's experiences. Much of this research has focused on racial and class variations in the material and (re)productive conditions of women's lives. More recently, scholarship that draws on cultural studies, race and ethnic studies, and women's studies centers the cultural as well as material processes by which gender and race are constructed, although this work has been mostly theoretical (Espiritu 1997; Collins 2000; St. Jean and Feagin 1998). Collins (2000) discussed "controlling images" that denigrate and objectify women of color and justify their racial and gender subordination. Controlling images are part of the process of "othering," whereby a dominant group defines into existence a subordinate group through the creation of categories and ideas that mark the group as inferior (Schwalbe et al. 2000, 422). Controlling images reaffirm whiteness as normal and privilege white women by casting them as superior.

White society uses the image of the Black matriarch to objectify Black women as overly aggressive, domineering, and unfeminine. This imagery serves to blame Black women for the emasculation of Black men, low marriage rates, and poverty and to control their social behavior by undermining their assertiveness (Collins 2000). While Black women are masculinized as aggressive and overpowering, Asian women are rendered hyperfeminine: passive, weak, quiet, excessively submissive, slavishly dutiful, sexually exotic, and available for white men (Espiritu 1997; Tajima 1989). This Lotus Blossom imagery obscures the internal variation of Asian American femininity and sexuality, making it difficult, for example, for others to "see" Asian lesbians and bisexuals (Lee 1996). Controlling images of Asian women also make them especially vulnerable to mistreatment from men who view them as easy targets. By casting Black women as not feminine enough and Asian women as too feminine, white forms of gender are racialized as normal and superior. In this way, white women are accorded racial privilege.

The dominant culture's dissemination of controlling imagery that derogates nonwhite forms of femininity (and masculinity) is part of a complex ideological system of "psychosocial dominance" (Baker 1983, 37) that imposes elite definitions of subordinates, denying them the power of self-identification. In this way, subordinates internalize "commonsense" notions of their inferiority to whites (Espiritu 1997; Collins 2000). Once internalized, controlling images provide the template by which subordinates make meaning of their everyday lives (Pyke 2000), develop a sense of self, form racial and gender identities, and organize social relations (Osajima 1993; Pyke and Dang 2003). For example, Chen (1998) found that Asian American women who joined predominately white sororities often did so to distance themselves from images of Asian femininity.

In contrast, those who joined Asian sororities were often surprised to find their ideas of Asian women as passive and childlike challenged by the assertive, independent women they met. By internalizing the racial and gendered myth making that circumscribes their social existence, subordinates do not pose a threat to the dominant order. As Audre Lorde (1984, 123) described, "the true focus of revolutionary change is never merely the oppressive situations which we seek to escape, but that piece of the oppressor which is planted deep within us."

Hegemonies are rarely without sites of resistance (Espiritu 2001; Gramsci 1971; Collins 2000). Espiritu (1997) described Asian American writers and filmmakers whose portraits of Asians defy the gender caricatures disseminated in the white-dominated society. However, such images are often forged around the contours of the one-dimensional stereotypes against which the struggle emerges. Thus, controlling images penetrate all aspects of the experience of subordinates, whether in a relationship of compliance or in one of resistance (Osajima 1993; Pyke and Dang [2003]).

The work concerning the effects of controlling images and the relational construction of subordinated and hegemonic femininities has mostly been theoretical. The little research that has examined how Asian American women do gender in the context of racialized images and ideologies that construct their gender as "naturally" inferior to white femininity provides only a brief look at these issues (Chen 1998; Lee 1996). Many of the Asian American women whom we study here do not construct their gender in one cultural field but are constantly moving between sites that are guided by ethnic immigrant cultural norms and those of the Eurocentric mainstream. A comparison of how

gender is enacted and understood across such sites brings the construction of racialized gender and the dynamics of hegemonic and subordinated femininities into bold relief. We examine how respondents employ cultural symbols, controlling images, and gender and racial ideologies in giving meanings to their experiences.

GENDER IN ETHNIC AND MAINSTREAM CULTURAL WORLDS

We study Korean and Vietnamese Americans, who form two of the largest Asian ethnic groups in southern California, the site of this research. We focus on the daughters of immigrants as they are more involved in both ethnic and mainstream cultures than are members of the first generation. . . . The second generation, who are still mostly children and young adults, must juggle the cross-pressures of ethnic and mainstream cultures without the groundwork that a long-standing ethnic enclave might provide. This is not easy. Disparities between ethnic and mainstream worlds can generate substantial conflict for children of immigrants, including conflict around issues of gender (Kibria 1993; Zhou and Bankston 1998).

Respondents dichotomized the interactional settings they occupy as ethnic, involving their immigrant family and other coethnics, and mainstream, involving non–Asian Americans in peer groups and at work and school. They grew up juggling different cultural expectations as they moved from home to school and often felt a pressure to behave differently when among Asian Americans and non–Asian Americans. Although there is no set of monolithic, stable norms in either setting, there are certain pressures, expectations, and structural arrangements that can affect different gender displays (Lee 1996). Definitions of gender and the constraints that patriarchy imposes on women's gender production can vary from culture to culture. The Confucian moral code, which accords male superiority, authority, and power over women in family and social relations, has influenced the patriarchal systems of Korea and Vietnam (Kibria 1993; Min 1998). Women are granted little decision-making power and are not accorded an individual identity apart from their family role, which emphasizes their service to male members. A woman who violates her role brings shame to herself and her family. Despite Western observers' tendency to regard Asian families as uniformly and rigidly patriarchal, variations exist (Ishii-Kuntz 2000). Women's resistance strategies, like the exchange of information in informal social groups, provide pockets of power (Kibria 1990). Women's growing educational and economic opportunities and the rise of women's rights groups in Korea and Vietnam challenge gender inequality (Palley 1994). Thus, actual gender dynamics are not in strict compliance with the prescribed moral code.

As they immigrate to the United States, Koreans and Vietnamese experience a shift in gender arrangements centering on men's loss of economic power and increased dependency on their wives' wages (Kibria 1993; Lim 1997; Min 1998). Immigrant women find their labor in demand by employers who regard them as a cheap labor source. With their employment, immigrant women experience more decision-making power, autonomy, and assistance with domestic chores from their husbands. However, such shifts are not total, and male dominance remains a common feature of family life (Kibria 1993; Min 1998). Furthermore, immigrant women tend to stay committed to the ethnic patriarchal structure as it provides resources for maintaining their parental authority and resisting the economic insecurities, racism, and cultural impositions of the new society (Kibria 1990, 1993; Lim 1997). The gender hierarchy is evident in parenting practices. Daughters are typically required to be home and performing household chores when not in school, while sons are given greater freedom.

Native-born American women, on the other hand, are perceived as having more equality, power, and independence than women in Asian societies, reflecting differences in gender attitudes. A recent study of Korean and American women found that 82 percent of Korean women agreed that "women should have only a family-oriented life, devoted to bringing up the children and looking after the husband," compared to 19 percent of U.S. women (Kim 1994). However, the fit between egalitarian gender attitudes and actual behavior in the United States is rather poor. Patriarchal arrangements that accord higher status to men at home and work are still the norm, with women experiencing lower job status and pay, greater responsibility for family work even when employed, and high rates of male violence. Indeed, the belief that gender equality is the norm in U.S. society obscures the day-to-day materiality of American patriarchy. Despite cultural differences in the ideological justification of patriarchy, gender inequality is the reality in both Asian and mainstream cultural worlds.

* * *

GENDER ACROSS CULTURAL TERRAINS: "I'M LIKE A CHAMELEON. I CHANGE MY PERSONALITY"

The 44 respondents who were aware of modifying their gender displays or being treated differently across cultural settings framed their accounts in terms of an oppressive ethnic world and an egalitarian mainstream. They reaffirmed the ideological constructions of the white-dominated society by casting ethnic and mainstream worlds as monolithic opposites, with internal variations largely ignored. Controlling images that denigrate Asian femininity and glorify white femininity were reiterated in many of the narratives. Women's behavior in ethnic realms was described as submissive and controlled, and that in white-dominated settings as freer and more self-expressive.

Some respondents suggested they made complete personality reversals as they moved across realms. They used the behavior of the mainstream as the standard by which they judged their behavior in ethnic settings. As Elizabeth (19, VA) said,

> I feel like when I'm amongst other Asians . . . I'm much more reserved and I hold back what I think. . . . But when I'm among other people like at school, I'm much more outspoken. I'll say whatever's on my mind. It's like a diametric character altogether. . . . I feel like when I'm with other Asians that I'm the *typical* passive [Asian] person and I feel like that's what's expected of me and if I do say something and if I'm the *normal* person that I am, I'd stick out like a sore thumb. So I just blend in with the situation. (emphasis added)

Elizabeth juxtaposes the "typical passive [Asian] person" and the "normal," outspoken person of the mainstream culture, whom she claims to be. In so doing, she reaffirms the stereotypical image of Asians as passive while glorifying Americanized behavior, such as verbal expressiveness, as "normal." This implies that Asian ethnic behavior is aberrant and inferior compared to white behavior, which is rendered normal. This juxtaposition was a recurring theme in these data (Pyke 2000). It contributed to respondents' attempts to distance themselves from racialized notions of the typical Asian woman who is hyperfeminine and submissive by claiming to possess those traits associated with white femininity, such as assertiveness, self-possession, confidence, and independence. Respondents often described a pressure to blend in and conform with the form of gender that they felt was expected in ethnic settings and that conflicted with the white standard of femininity. Thus, they often described such behavior with disgust and self-loathing. For example, Min-Jung (24, KA) said she feels "like an idiot" when talking with Korean adults:

> With Korean adults, I act more shy and more timid. I don't talk until spoken to and just act shy. I kind of speak in a higher tone of voice than I usually do. But then when I'm with white people and white adults, I joke around, I laugh, I talk, and I communicate about how I feel. And then my voice gets stronger. But then when I'm with Korean adults, my voice gets really high. . . . I just sound like an idiot and sometimes when I catch myself I'm like, "Why can't you just make conversation like you normally do?"

Many respondents distanced themselves from the compliant femininity associated with their Asianness by casting their behavior in ethnic realms as a mere act not reflective of their true nature. Repeatedly, they said they cannot be who they really are in ethnic settings and the enactment of an authentic self takes place only in mainstream settings. . . .

Wilma (21, VA) states, "Like some Asian guys expect me to be passive and let them decide on everything. Non-Asians don't expect anything from me. They just expect me *to be me*" (emphasis added). Gendered behavior engaged in Asian ethnic settings was largely described as performative, fake, and unnatural, while that in white-dominated settings was cast as a reflection of one's true self. The femininity of the white mainstream is glorified as authentic, natural, and normal, and Asian ethnic femininity is denigrated as coerced, contrived, and artificial. The "white is right" mantra is reiterated in this view of white femininity as the right way of doing gender.

The glorification of white femininity and controlling images of Asian women can lead Asian American women to believe that freedom and equity can be acquired only in the white-dominated world. For not only is white behavior glorified as superior and more authentic, but gender relations among whites are constructed as more egalitarian. . . .

Controlling images of Asian men as hypermasculine further feed presumptions that whites are more egalitarian. Asian males were often cast as uniformly domineering in these accounts. Racialized images and the construction of hegemonic (white) and subordinated (Asian) forms of gender set up a situation where Asian American women feel they must choose between white worlds of gender equity and Asian worlds of gender oppression. Such images encourage them to reject their ethnic culture and Asian men and embrace the white world and white men so as to enhance their power (Espiritu 1997). . . .

In these accounts, we can see the construction of ethnic and mainstream cultural worlds—and Asians and whites—as diametrically opposed. The perception that whites are more egalitarian than Asian-origin individuals and thus preferred partners in social interaction further reinforces anti-Asian racism and white superiority. The cultural dominance of whiteness is reaffirmed through the co-construction of race and gender in these narratives. The perception that the production of gender in the mainstream is more authentic and superior to that in Asian ethnic arenas further reinforces the racialized categories of gender that define white forms of femininity as ascendant. In the next section, we describe variations in gender performances within ethnic and mainstream settings that respondents typically overlooked or discounted as atypical.

GENDER VARIATIONS WITHIN CULTURAL WORLDS

Several respondents described variations in gender dynamics within mainstream and ethnic settings that challenge notions of Asian and American worlds as monolithic opposites. Some talked of mothers who make all the decisions or fathers who do the cooking. These accounts were framed as exceptions to Asian male dominance. For example, after Vietnamese women were described in a group interview as confined to domesticity, Ngâ (22, VA), who immigrated at 14 and spoke in Vietnamese-accented English, defined her family as gender egalitarian. She related,

> I guess I grow[sic] up in a *different* family. All my sisters don't have to cook, her husbands[sic] cooking all the time. Even my oldest sister. Even my mom—my dad is cooking. . . . My sisters and brothers are all very strong. (emphasis added)

Ngâ does not try to challenge stereotypical notions of Vietnamese families but rather reinforces such notions by suggesting that her family

is different. Similarly, Heidi (21, KA) said, "Our family was kind of *different* because . . . my dad cooks and cleans and does dishes. He cleans house" (emphasis added). Respondents often framed accounts of gender egalitarianism in their families by stating they do not belong to the typical Asian family, with "typical" understood to mean male dominated. This variation in gender dynamics within the ethnic community was largely unconsidered in these accounts.

Other respondents described how they enacted widely disparate forms of gender across sites within ethnic realms, suggesting that gender behavior is more variable than generally framed. Take, for example, the case of Gin (29, KA), a law student married to a Korean American from a more traditional family than her own. When she is with her husband's kin, Gin assumes the traditional obligations of a daughter-in-law and does all the cooking, cleaning, and serving. The role exhausts her and she resents having to perform it. When Gin and her husband return home, the gender hierarchy is reversed. . . .

Controlling images of Asian men as hyper-domineering in their relations with women obscures how they can be called on to compensate for the subservience exacted from their female partners in some settings. Although respondents typically offered such stories as evidence of the patriarchy of ethnic arenas, these examples reveal that ethnic worlds are far more variable than generally described. Viewing Asian ethnic worlds through a lens of racialized gender stereotypes renders such variation invisible or, when acknowledged, atypical.

Gender expectations in the white-dominated mainstream also varied, with respondents sometimes expected to assume a subservient stance as Asian women. These examples reveal that the mainstream is not a site of unwavering gender equality as often depicted in these accounts and made less so for Asian American women by racial images that construct them as compliant. Many respondents described encounters with non-Asians, usually whites, who expected them to be passive, quiet, and yielding. Several described non-Asian (mostly white) men who brought such expectations to their dating relationships. Indeed, the servile Lotus Blossom image bolsters white men's preference for Asian women (Espiritu 1997). As Thanh (22, VA) recounted,

> Like the white guy that I dated, he expected me to be the submissive one—the one that was dependent on the guy. Kind of like the "Asian persuasion," that's what he'd call it when he was dating me. And when he found out that I had a spirit, kind of a wild side to me, he didn't like it at all. Period. And when I spoke up—my opinions—he got kind of scared.

So racialized images can cause Asian American women to believe they will find greater gender equality with white men and can cause white men to believe they will find greater subservience with Asian women. This dynamic promotes Asian American women's availability to white men and makes them particularly vulnerable to mistreatment.

There were other sites in the mainstream, besides dating relationships, where Asian American women encountered racialized gender expectations. Several described white employers and coworkers who expected them to be more passive and deferential than other employees and were surprised when they spoke up and resisted unfair treatment. Some described similar assumptions among non-Asian teachers and professors. Diane (26, KA) related,

> At first one of my teachers told me it was okay if I didn't want to talk in front of the class. I think she thought I was quiet or shy because I'm Asian. . . . [Laughing.] I am very outspoken, but that semester I just kept my mouth shut. I figured she won't make me talk anyway, so why try. I kind of went along with her.

Diane's example illustrates how racialized expectations can exert a pressure to display stereotyped behavior in mainstream interactions. Such expectations can subtly coerce behavioral displays that confirm the stereotypes, suggesting a kind of self-fulfilling prophecy. Furthermore, as submissiveness and passivity are denigrated traits in the mainstream, and often judged to be indicators of incompetence, compliance with

such expectations can deny Asian American women personal opportunities and success. Not only is passivity unrewarded in the mainstream; it is also subordinated. The association of extreme passivity with Asian women serves to emphasize their otherness. Some respondents resist this subordination by enacting a more assertive femininity associated with whiteness. Lisa (18, KA) described being quiet with her relatives out of respect, but in mainstream scenes, she consciously resists the stereotype of Asian women as passive by adjusting her behavior. . . .

To act Asian by being reserved and quiet would be to "stand out in a negative way" and to be regarded as "not cool." It means one will be denigrated and cast aside. Katie (21, KA) consciously engages loud and gregarious behavior to prove she is not the typical Asian and to be welcomed by white friends. Whereas many respondents describe their behavior in mainstream settings as an authentic reflection of their personality, these examples suggest otherwise. Racial expectations exert pressure on these women's gender performances among whites. Some go to great lengths to defy racial assumptions and be accepted into white-dominated social groups by engaging a white standard of femininity. As they are forced to work against racial stereotypes, they must exert extra effort at being outspoken and socially gregarious. Contrary to the claim of respondents, gender production in the mainstream is also coerced and contrived. The failure of some respondents to recognize variations in gender behavior within mainstream and ethnic settings probably has much to do with the essentialization of gender and race. That is, as we discuss next, the racialization of gender renders variations in behavior within racial groups invisible.

The Racialization of Gender: Believing Is Seeing

In this section, we discuss how respondents differentiated femininity by race rather than shifting situational contexts, even when they were consciously aware of altering their own gender performance to conform with shifting expectations. Racialized gender was discursively constructed as natural and essential. Gender and race were essentialized as interrelated biological facts that determine social behavior.

Among our 100 respondents, there was a tendency to rely on binary categories of American (code for white) and Asian femininity in describing a wide range of topics, including gender identities, personality traits, and orientations toward domesticity or career. Racialized gender categories were deployed as an interpretive template in giving meaning to experiences and organizing a worldview. Internal variation was again ignored, downplayed, or regarded as exceptional. White femininity, which was glorified in accounts of gender behavior across cultural settings, was also accorded superiority in the more general discussions of gender.

Respondents' narratives were structured by assumptions about Asian women as submissive, quiet, and diffident and of American women as independent, self-assured, outspoken, and powerful. That is, specific behaviors and traits were racialized. As Ha (19, VA) explained, "sometimes I'm quiet and passive and shy. That's a Vietnamese part of me." Similarly, domesticity was linked with Asian femininity and domestic incompetence or disinterest, along with success in the work world, with American femininity. Several women framed their internal struggles between career and domesticity in racialized terms. Min-Jung said,

> I kind of think my Korean side wants to stay home and do the cooking and cleaning and take care of the kids whereas my American side would want to go out and make a difference and become a strong woman and become head of companies and stuff like that.

This racialized dichotomy was central to respondents' self-identities. Amy (21, VA) said, "I'm not Vietnamese in the way I act. I'm American because I'm not a good cook and I'm

not totally ladylike." In fact, one's ethnic identity could be challenged if one did not comply with notions of racialized gender. In a group interview, Kimberly (21, VA) described "joking around" with coethnic dates who asked if she cooked by responding that she did not. . . .

Similarly, coethnic friends tell Hien (21, VA), "You should be able to cook, you are Vietnamese, you are a girl." To be submissive and oriented toward family and domesticity marks Asian ethnicity. Conformity to stereotypes of Asian femininity serves to symbolically construct and affirm an Asian ethnic identity. Herein lies the pressure that some respondents feel to comply with racialized expectations in ethnic settings, as Lisa (18, KA) illustrates in explaining why she would feel uncomfortable speaking up in a class that has a lot of Asians:

> I think they would think that I'm not really Asian. Like I'm whitewashed . . . like I'm forgetting my race. I'm going against my roots and adapting to the American way. And I'm just neglecting my race.

American (white) women and Asian American women are constructed as diametric opposites. Although many respondents were aware that they contradicted racialized notions of gender in their day-to-day lives, they nonetheless view gender as an essential component of race. Variation is ignored or recategorized so that an Asian American woman who does not comply is no longer Asian. This was also evident among respondents who regard themselves as egalitarian or engage the behavioral traits associated with white femininity. There was the presumption that one cannot be Asian and have gender-egalitarian attitudes. Asian American women can engage those traits associated with ascendant femininity to enhance their status in the mainstream, but this requires a rejection of their racial/ethnic identity. This is evident by the use of words such as "American," "whitewashed," or "white"—but not Asian—to describe such women. Star (22, KA) explained, "I look Korean but I don't act Korean. I'm whitewashed.

[Interviewer asks, 'How do you mean you don't act Korean?'] I'm loud. I'm not quiet and reserved."

As a result, struggles about gender identity and women's work/family trajectories become superimposed over racial/ethnic identity. The question is not simply whether Asian American women like Min-Jung want to be outspoken and career oriented or quiet and family oriented but whether they want to be American (whitewashed) or Asian. Those who do not conform to racialized expectations risk challenges to their racial identity and charges that they are not really Asian, as occurs with Lisa when she interacts with her non-Asian peers. She said,

> They think I'm really different from other Asian girls because I'm so outgoing. They feel that Asian girls have to be the shy type who is very passive and sometimes I'm not like that so they think, "Lisa, are you Asian?"

These data illustrate how the line drawn in the struggle for gender equality is superimposed over the cultural and racial boundaries dividing whites and Asians. At play is the presumption that the only path to gender equality and assertive womanhood is via assimilation to the white mainstream. This assumption was shared by Asian American research assistants who referred to respondents' gender egalitarian viewpoints as evidence of assimilation. The assumption is that Asian American women can be advocates of gender equality or strong and assertive in their interactions only as a result of assimilation, evident by the display of traits associated with hegemonic femininity, and a rejection of their ethnic culture and identity. This construction obscures gender inequality in mainstream U.S. society and constructs that sphere as the only place where Asian American women can be free. Hence, the diversity of gender arrangements practiced among those of Asian origin, as well as the potential for social change within Asian cultures, is ignored. Indeed, there were no references in these accounts to the rise in recent years of women's movements in Korea and Vietnam.

Rather, Asian ethnic worlds are regarded as unchanging sites of male dominance and female submissiveness.

DISCUSSION AND SUMMARY

Our analysis reveals dynamics of internalized oppression and the reproduction of inequality that revolve around the relational construction of hegemonic and subordinated femininities. Respondents' descriptions of gender performances in ethnic settings were marked by self-disgust and referred to as a mere act not reflective of one's true gendered nature. In mainstream settings, on the other hand, respondents often felt a pressure to comply with caricatured notions of Asian femininity or, conversely, to distance one's self from derogatory images of Asian femininity to be accepted. In both cases, the subordination of Asian femininity is reproduced.

In general, respondents depicted women of Asian descent as uniformly engaged in subordinated femininity marked by submissiveness and white women as universally assertive and gender egalitarian. Race, rather than culture, situational dynamics, or individual personalities, emerged as the primary basis by which respondents gave meaning to variations in femininity. That is, despite their own situational variation in doing gender, they treat gender as a racialized feature of bodies rather than a sociocultural product. Specific gender displays, such as a submissive demeanor, are required to confirm an Asian identity. Several respondents face challenges to their ethnic identity when they behave in ways that do not conform with racialized images. Indeed, some claimed that because they are assertive or career oriented, they are not really Asian. That is, because they do not conform to the racialized stereotypes of Asian women but identify with a hegemonic femininity that is the white standard, they are different from other women of Asian origin. In this way, they manipulate the racialized categories of gender in attempting to craft identities that are empowering. However, this is accomplished by denying their ethnicity and connections to other Asian American women and through the adoption and replication of controlling images of Asian women.

Respondents who claim that they are not really Asian because they do not conform with essentialized notions of Asian femininity suggest similarities to transgendered individuals who feel that underneath, they really belong to the gender category that is opposite from the one to which they are assigned. The notion that deep down they are really white implies a kind of transracialized gender identity. In claiming that they are not innately Asian, they reaffirm racialized categories of gender just as transgendered individuals reaffirm the gender dichotomy (Kessler and McKenna 1978; Lorber 1994).

However, there are limitations to notions of a transracialized identity as racial barriers do not permit these women to socially pass into the white world, even though they might feel themselves to be more white than Asian. Due to such barriers, they use terms that are suggestive of a racial crossover, such as "whitewashed" or "American" rather than "white" in describing themselves. Such terms are frequently used among Asian Americans to describe those who are regarded as assimilated to the white world and no longer ethnic, further underscoring how racial categories are essentialized (Pyke and Dang 2003). Blocked from a white identity, these terms capture a marginalized space that is neither truly white nor Asian. As racial categories are dynamic, it remains to be seen whether these marginalized identities are the site for new identities marked by hybridity (Lowe 1991) or whether Asian Americans will eventually be incorporated into whiteness. This process may be hastened by outmarriage to whites and high rates of biracial Asian Americans who can more easily pass into the white world, thereby leading the way for other Asian Americans. While we cannot ascertain the direction of such changes, our data highlight the contradictions that strain the existing racial and gender order as it applies to second-generation Asian American women.

While respondents construct a world in which Asian American women can experience a kind of transracial gender identity, they do not consider the same possibility for women of other races. A white woman who is submissive does not become Asian. In fact, there was no reference in these accounts to submissive white women who are rendered invisible by racialized categories of gender. Instead, white women are constructed as monolithically self-confident, independent, assertive, and successful—characteristics of white hegemonic femininity. That these are the same ruling traits associated with hegemonic masculinity, albeit in a less exaggerated, feminine form, underscores the imitative structure of hegemonic femininity. That is, the supremacy of white femininity over Asian femininity mimics hegemonic masculinity. We are not arguing that hegemonic femininity and masculinity are equivalent structures. They are not. Whereas hegemonic masculinity is a superstructure of domination, hegemonic femininity is confined to power relations among women. However, the two structures are interrelated with hegemonic femininity constructed to serve hegemonic masculinity, from which it is granted legitimacy.

Our findings illustrate the powerful interplay of controlling images and hegemonic femininity in promoting internalized oppression. Respondents draw on racial images and assumptions in their narrative construction of Asian cultures as innately oppressive of women and fully resistant to change against which the white-dominated mainstream is framed as a paradigm of gender equality. This serves a proassimilation function by suggesting that Asian American women will find gender equality in exchange for rejecting their ethnicity and adopting white standards of gender. The construction of a hegemonic femininity not only (re)creates a hierarchy that privileges white women over Asian American women but also makes Asian American women available for white men. In this way, hegemonic femininity serves as a handmaiden to hegemonic masculinity.

By constructing ethnic culture as impervious to social change and as a site where resistance to gender oppression is impossible, our respondents accommodate and reinforce rather than resist the gender hierarchal arrangements of such locales. This can contribute to a self-fulfilling prophecy as Asian American women who hold gender egalitarian views feel compelled to retreat from interactions in ethnic settings, thus (re)creating Asian ethnic cultures as strongholds of patriarchy and reinforcing the maintenance of a rigid gender hierarchy as a primary mechanism by which ethnicity and ethnic identity are constructed. This marking of ethnic culture as a symbolic repository of patriarchy obscures variations in ethnic gender practices as well as the gender inequality in the mainstream. Thus, compliance with the dominant order is secured.

Our study attempts to bring a racialized examination of gender to a constructionist framework without decentering either race or gender. By examining the racialized meaning systems that inform the construction of gender, our findings illustrate how the resistance of gender oppression among our respondents draws ideologically on the denigration and rejection of ethnic Asian culture, thereby reinforcing white dominance. Conversely, we found that mechanisms used to construct ethnic identity in resistance to the pro-assimilation forces of the white-dominated mainstream rest on narrow definitions of Asian women that emphasize gender subordination. These findings underscore the crosscutting ways that gender and racial oppression operates such that strategies and ideologies focused on the resistance of one form of domination can reproduce another form. A social constructionist approach that examines the simultaneous production of gender and race within the matrix of oppression, and considers the relational construction of hegemonic and subordinated femininities, holds much promise in uncovering the micro-level structures and complicated features of oppression, including the processes by which oppression infiltrates the meanings individuals give to their experiences.

REFERENCES

Baker, Donald G. 1983. *Race, ethnicity and power.* Boston: Routledge Kegan Paul.

Chen, Edith Wen-Chu. 1998. The continuing significance of race: A case study of Asian American women in white, Asian American, and African American sororities. Ph.D. diss., University of California, Los Angeles.

Collins, Patricia Hill. 2000. *Black feminist thought.* New York: Routledge.

Collins, Patricia Hill, Lionel A. Maldonado, Dana Y. Takagi, Barrie Thorne, Lynn Weber, and Howard Winant. 1995. Symposium: On West and Fenstermaker's "Doing difference." *Gender & Society* 9:491–513.

Coltrane, Scott. 1989. Household labor and the routine production of gender. *Social Problems* 36:473–90.

———. 1994. Theorizing masculinities in contemporary social science. In *Theorizing masculinities,* edited by Harry Brod and Michael Kaufman. Thousand Oaks, CA: Sage.

Connell, R. W. 1987. *Gender and power.* Stanford, CA: Stanford University Press.

———. 1995. *Masculinities.* Los Angeles: University of California Press.

Espiritu, Yen L. 1997. *Asian American women and men.* Thousand Oaks, CA: Sage.

———. 2001. "We don't sleep around like white girls do": Family, culture, and gender in Filipina American life. *Signs: Journal of Women in Culture and Society* 26:415–40.

Glenn, Evelyn Nakano. 1999. The social construction and institutionalization of gender and race. In *Revisioning gender,* edited by Myra Marx Ferree, Judith Lorber, and Beth B. Hess. Thousand Oaks, CA: Sage.

Gramsci, Antonio. 1971. *Selections from the prison notebooks of Antonio Gramsci,* edited and translated by Quintin Hoare and Geoffrey Nowell Smith. New York: International.

Ishii-Kuntz, Masako. 2000. Diversity within Asian American families. In *Handbook of family diversity,* edited by David H. Demo, Katherine Allen, and Mark A. Fine. New York: Oxford University Press.

Kessler, Suzanne, and Wendy McKenna. 1978. *Gender: An ethnomethodological approach.* Chicago: University of Chicago Press.

Kibria, Nazli. 1990. Power, patriarchy, and gender conflict in the Vietnamese immigrant community. *Gender & Society* 4:9–24.

———. 1993. *Family tightrope: The changing lives of Vietnamese Americans.* Princeton, NJ: Princeton University Press.

Kim, Byong-suh. 1994. Value orientations and sex-gender role attitudes on the comparability of Koreans and Americans. In *Gender division of labor in Korea,* edited by Hyoung Cho and Pil-wha Chang. Seoul, Korea: Ewha Womans University Press.

Lee, Jee Yeun. 1996. Why Suzie Wong is not a lesbian: Asian and Asian American lesbian and bisexual women and femme/butch/gender identities. In *Queer studies,* edited by Brett Beemyn and Mickey Eliason. New York: New York University Press.

Lim, In-Sook. 1997. Korean immigrant women's challenge to gender inequality at home: The interplay of economic resources, gender, and family. *Gender & Society* 11:31–51.

Lorber, Judith. 1994. *Paradoxes of gender.* New Haven, CT: Yale University Press.

Lorde, Audre. 1984. *Sister outsider.* Trumansburg, NY: Crossing Press.

Lowe, Lisa. 1991. Heterogeneity, hybridity, multiplicity: Marking Asian American differences. *Diaspora* 1:24–44.

Lucal, Betsy. 1999. What it means to be gendered me: Life on the boundaries of a dichotomous gender system. *Gender & Society* 13:781–97.

Min, Pyong Gap. 1998. *Changes and conflicts.* Boston: Allyn & Bacon.

Osajima, Keith. 1993. The hidden injuries of race. In *Bearing dreams, shaping visions: Asian Pacific American perspectives,* edited by Linda Revilla, Gail Nomura, Shawn Wong, and Shirley Hune. Pullman: Washington State University Press.

Palley, Marian Lief. 1994. Feminism in a Confucian society: The women's movement in Korea. In *Women of Japan and Korea,* edited by Joyce Gelb and Marian Lief Palley. Philadelphia: Temple University Press.

Pyke, Karen. 1996. Class-based masculinities: The interdependence of gender, class, and interpersonal power. *Gender & Society* 10: 527–49.

———. 2000. "The normal American family" as an interpretive structure of family life among grown children of Korean and Vietnamese immigrants. *Journal of Marriage and the Family* 62:240–55.

Pyke, Karen, and Tran Dang. 2003. "FOB" and "whitewashed": Intra-ethnic identities and internalized oppression among second generation Asian Americans. *Qualitative Sociology* 26(2).

St. Jean, Yanick, and Joe R. Feagin. 1998. *Double burden: Black women and everyday racism.* Armonk, NY: M. E. Sharpe.

Schwalbe, Michael, Sandra Godwin, Daphne Holden, Douglas Schrock, Shealy Thompson, and Michele Wolkomir. 2000. Generic processes in the reproduction of inequality: An interactionist analysis. *Social Forces* 79:419–52.

Tajima, Renee E. 1989. Lotus blossoms don't bleed: Images of Asian women. In *Making waves,* edited by Asian Women United of California. Boston: Beacon.

West, Candace, and Sarah Fenstermaker. 1995. Doing difference. *Gender & Society* 9:8–37.

West, Candace, and Don H. Zimmerman. 1987. Doing gender. *Gender & Society* 1:125–51.

Zhou, Min, and Carl L. Bankston III. 1998. *Growing up American.* New York: Russell Sage.

Introduction to Reading 10

One of the most recent applications of intersectionality is in global/transnational research, as mentioned by Bonnie Thornton Dill and Marla H. Kohlman in the first reading in this chapter. In this article, Bandana Purkayastha develops the meaning of intersectionality using a transnational framework. As Nikki Jones and Karen D. Pyke and Denise L. Johnson did in their analyses, Purkayastha also considers race in this context. As you will see from this piece, scholars are still struggling with what intersectional analysis means in a changing world, but the process of doing so is exciting. This article gives good examples of how we could and should study the intersections of multiple identities while also considering a transglobal context.

1. What is meant by "transnational spaces"?

2. How does Purkayastha recommend doing an intersectional analysis in transnational spaces?

3. What does she mean by "axes of domination"? What other "axes" can you name in addition to race?

INTERSECTIONALITY IN A TRANSNATIONAL WORLD

Bandana Purkayastha

As a late entrant into the world of sociology, I read Patricia Hill Collins's *Black Feminist Thought: Knowledge, Consciousness, and the Politics of Empowerment* (1990) in a graduate seminar on gender. . . . Over the years, insights of many other scholars have helped me to understand intersectionality. As Hae Yeon Choo and Myra Marx Ferree (2010) have recently pointed out, these diverse works on intersectionality have highlighted the importance of "including the perspectives of multiply marginalized people, especially women of color; an analytic shift from addition of multiple independent strands of inequality toward a multiplication and thus transformation of their main effects into interactions; and a focus on seeing multiple institutions as overlapping in their co-determination of inequalities to produce complex configurations" (2010, 4). Nonetheless, I remain grateful to Professor Collins for moving the conversation on intersectionality, in the early 1990s, to a more visible level.

Professor Collins's work has remained dynamic, expanding far beyond the original idea of power relations organized through intersecting axes of race/class/gender (Collins 1990) to her recent articulation of the "intersecting power relations of race, class, gender, ethnicity, sexuality, age, ability, nation" (Collins 2010, 8). In this brief essay, I touch upon two related aspects of intersectionality that require additional clarification as we study social lives in the twenty-first century. My observations are focused on the ways in which we understand "race" even as our lives expand onto transnational—including virtual—social spaces. . . .

SOCIAL LIVES IN TRANSNATIONAL SPACES

Over the past decade, a rapidly growing literature has described how individuals and groups maintain connections across countries so that social lives are constructed, not only in single countries, but in transnational spaces. Transnational spaces are composed of tangible geographic spaces that exist across multiple nation-states *and* virtual spaces. With improvements in personal and media communication and travel technology, the ability to move money easily across the globe, and the marketing and ease of consuming "cultural" products—including fashions, cosmetics, music, foods, and art—have made it easier for many groups to create lives that extend far beyond the boundaries of single nation-states. We now know

From Purkayastha, Bandana. 2012. "Intersectionality in a Transnational World." *Gender & Society* 26(1): 55–66.

about first-generation immigrant "transnational villagers" who build lives in more than one country by traveling back and forth regularly, organizing family lives across countries, and remitting and investing money, as well as engaging in politics in "homelands" (e.g., Guevarra 2009; Hondagneu-Sotelo and Avila 1997; Levitt 2001; Purkayastha 2009). We also know about post-immigrant generations who actively maintain links with their parents' homelands (e.g., Purkayastha 2005); cyber migrants who work for Northern employers but are geographically based in the South (e.g., Abraham 2010); and participants in web-based communities, some of whom seek community, while others try on less-essentialist, choice-driven, multiple, fragmented, and hybrid identities on the web and thus dilute the consequences of gendering, racialization, class, and other social hierarchies to which they are subjected in their tangible lives (e.g., Diamandaki 2003; Ignacio 2006; Lee 2003; Mitra 1997; Mitra and Gajjala 2008; Narayan and Purkayastha 2011). Other scholars have analyzed web-based transnational linkages that enable geographically dispersed groups to form close-knit political networks (e.g., Earl 2006; Narayan, Purkayastha, and Banerji, forthcoming; Pudrovska and Ferree 2004). As a rapidly growing number of people are tied to transnational spaces—that is, they build lives that combine intersecting local, regional, national, and transnational spaces—single nation-states no longer wholly contain their lives.

At the same time, nation-states have responded in a variety of ways to control social lives in transnational spaces. For instance, the literature on immigration shows how nation-states are creating gendered categories of "overseas citizens" in order to attract remittances from migrants (e.g., Guevarra 2009) or to draw on the expertise or lobbying power of people settled in other countries (Purkayastha 2009). Equally important, nation-states have attempted to expand their ability to control people across transnational spaces; ideologies, interactions, and institutions that have sustained raced/

gendered/classed and other hierarchies *within nations,* have expanded in new ways across nations.[1] For most of the twentieth century, nation-states maintained separate apparatus for controlling groups within nations (e.g., police, prisons) from the apparatus used to dominate and control groups/states outside nations (e.g., the military, foreign intelligence agencies, facilities to house prisoners of wars). Now, these tools of control are increasingly blurred within nations; for instance, policies such as the PATRIOT Act and organizations such as Homeland Security have blurred the distinction between foreign surveillance and national surveillance in the United States. Security agreements *across* nations have created transnational security regions, where profiles developed in one powerful country are likely to be rapidly disseminated and acted on in other countries within the transnational security regime (Purkayastha 2009; Vertovec 2001). A *suspect* in a terrorism case in Scotland or Spain can, almost immediately, be arrested in Australia or the United States.[2] The profile of a "turbaned terrorist" or the suspicions against "Muslim-looking" people have generated contemporary racial profiles so that Sikh men—who wear turbans to comply with their religious tenets—and a range of people of Middle Eastern and South Asian origin are profiled as potential security threats. They are searched more stringently at airports, subject to extra questioning at national borders, subject to surveillance for communicating with people in "enemy countries," frequently visiting these countries, or sending money to "suspect" organizations through institutional arrangements as they travel through security regime (see Iwata and Purkayastha 2011; Purkayastha 2009). These new global security arrangements intersect with other processes for controlling racially marked populations within nations.

Overall, then, transnational spaces are composed of tangible and virtual social spaces that exist through and beyond single nation-states. Individuals, groups, corporations, and nation-states continue to expand their purview into such spaces.[3] At the same time, those who cannot access transnational spaces—for a variety of reasons, including the digital divide and stringent government control over travel and internet access—are marginalized in new ways within this expanded context. Contemporary discussions of marginalization and privilege have to take these new developments into account.

INTERSECTIONALITY IN TRANSNATIONAL SPACES

While her earlier work on Black feminist thought was focused on the United States, in her recent writings Professor Collins recognizes the expansion of social life beyond the nation-state (e.g., Collins 2010). She discusses the dispersion and consumption of cultural products, such as hip-hop, around the globe and the cultural familiarity this engenders among consumers, and the possibilities for "creat(ing) shifting patterns of face-to-face and mediated interactions . . . (as) new technologies create organizational opportunities for new sorts of political communities" (2010, 18). She discusses the ways in which people imagine local and far-flung political communities using new technologies, and the ways in which these multiple communities somewhat dilute concentrated power of the privileged. Despite this recognition of other worlds of experience, Professor Collins has not, as far as I am aware, discussed the structures of domination and control in transnational spaces. As a result, it is not clear how our current conceptualization of intersectionality—including the expanded version of race/class/gender/age/ability/sexuality/ethnicity/nation—might change if we incorporate social life in transnational space.

Professor Collins has offered a powerful critique of the "race-neutral" scholarship on gender, and her discussions of racism (and the ways this racism interacts with other axes of domination) led to the visibility of concepts such

as "controlling images" and "women of color." Her references to Black women and other people of color in the United States continue to serve as a reminder of their continuing marginalization and open up some space to include their experiences in developing theory. But she does not discuss the deviations from Euro-American organizations of racial hierarchies in different countries around the globe, which coexist with global-level Euro-American racialization processes. As a result, it is not always clear when and how we are to conceptualize "race" within the intersectionality matrix if we study transnational social lives.

I will begin with a simple example that focuses on women of color. A Ugandan Black immigrant and a Ugandan Indian immigrant—whose family lived for many generations in Uganda before being forcibly evicted by Idi Amin—are both racially marginalized, though in different ways, in the United States. While both share the effects of gendered/racialized migration policies that would prohibit or slow the process through which they might form families in the United States, their experiences differ in other ways. The Ugandan Black migrant is likely to experience the gamut of racisms experienced by African Americans, while the Indian Ugandan is likely to experience the racisms faced by Muslims and "Muslim-looking" people in the United States, and they may share other structural discriminations experienced by Asian Americans (Narayan and Purkayastha 2009). These similarities and differences are consistent with racist ideologies, interactions, and institutional arrangements in the United States. But if both return to their home country Uganda, they would encounter a different set of privileges and marginalization in this Black-majority country; the Black Ugandan migrant is advantaged here (though the other intersecting factors would together shape her exact social location). If both visit or temporarily live in India, the Indian-origin Uganda-born person may experience the privileges associated with the dominant group in the country. However, if she is a Muslim or a low-caste Hindu, she might experience a different set of social hierarchies. Similarly, Japanese-origin people from Brazil who returned to Japan, or Japanese-origin Americans who were forced to return to Japan, encountered different sets of social hierarchies. A broadly similar argument could be made about the relative position of Blacks and Indians under the different historical circumstances, for instance, during the apartheid regime and after apartheid in South Africa (see Govinden 2008).

There are variations of who is part of the privileged majority versus the marginalized minority *within* a country, and these hierarchies do not always fit the white-yellow/brown-Black hierarchy extant in Western Europe and North America. Thus concepts such as "women of color"—which act as an effective framework for indicating the social location of these women in Western Europe and North America, and continuing global hierarchies *between* countries in the global North and South—do not work as well if we wish to track the array of the axes of power and domination within countries *along with* existing global-level hierarchies. Yet considering these multiple levels is important if intersectionality is to retain its explanatory power in an increasingly transnational world where within-country *and* between-country structures shape people's experiences.

The possibility of forming community on virtual spaces and using the web to maintain meaningful connections with people in other countries also emphasizes the need to consider transnational spaces. A South African Black female immigrant in the United States who is able to maintain active connections with her friends, family, and political networks in her home country (via phone, email, and a variety of web-based media) may be able to minimize some of the toll of racism she experiences by making her South African relationships most salient in her life. The Indian-origin post-immigrant-generation American who regularly participates in a religio-social Hindu online community and visits India regularly is also able to position herself as a member of the majority group in India (and the Indian diaspora) even as

she experiences the deleterious effects of structural racism in the United States. In other words, people who can access transnational social spaces attempt to balance their lack of privilege in one country (their raced/classed/gendered/ability/sexual/age/nationality status in one nation-state) by actively seeking out privilege and power in another place and/or in virtual spaces.

While many of the axes Professor Collins identified—race, gender, class, sexuality, age, ability, and nation—remain relevant, they may not work in the same way as "women of color" constructs suggest. Being able to build transnational lives—the ability of groups to live within and beyond single nation-states—suggests that it is quite possible for groups to be part of *the racial majority and minority simultaneously* (Purkayastha 2010). Indeed, in places where caste and religious or ethnic hierarchies—with their own set of ideologies, interactions, and institutional structures—are more salient, we should consider the relative importance of these axes of domination within those countries (and the extent to which these structure transnational social lives) as we use intersectional frameworks.

I do not intend to suggest that we stop considering racial hierarchies. Along with variations in who makes up the racial majority or minority *within* different countries, hierarchies among nation-states continue to promote Western hierarchies of race and whiteness, yellowness, and Blackness across the world in ways that are broadly similar to the period of colonialism (see, e.g., Gilroy 1989; Kim 2008; Kim-Puri 2007; Nandy 2006; Sardar et al. 1993). Such racial hierarchies are maintained through ideologies, actions, and institutional arrangements associated with political and economic control. As Evelyn Nakano Glenn and her colleagues have documented, color-based hierarchies continue to structure people's lives in many countries around the globe, especially as "fairness as beauty" is marketed to places where the majority of the people are nonwhite (Glenn 2008).

Since Professor Collins's discussions focus on the United States and minority groups within the boundaries of this nation-state, the ideas about race she discusses are built upon the structures that are particularly relevant to the United States and Western Europe. While intersectionality remains an important framework, we need to encapsulate marginalization structures that are salient in other locales and the ways in which these hierarchies play out in transnational spaces.

* * *

LAST REMARKS

As a scholar who continues to use intersectionality as my primary theoretical framework, I can enumerate many ways in which the work of Professor Collins and others who have developed this framework have improved our ability to study social lives. The framework remains important, but we have to pay attention to and elucidate the complexities of using this framework beyond Euro-American societies. Understanding and attending to the complexities of transnationalism—composed of structures within, between, and across nation-states, and virtual spaces—alerts us to look for other axes of domination and the limits of using "women of color" concepts, as we use them now, to look across *and* within nation-states to understand the impact of transnationalism. My examples here were focused on those who can access transnational spaces. A focus on transnational intersectionality should alert us to the position of those who are unable to afford access to technology to build virtual communities, to participate in a medium because they are not proficient in English, which has become the dominant language in virtual spaces, or to build transnational social lives because of active government surveillance and control of their lives or because they are too poor and isolated to access transnational tangible and virtual spaces.

While I focused on "race" in this brief essay, the other axes of domination are likely to show some variations if we analyze multiple and simultaneous social locations to develop a better understanding of intersectionality.

The organization of power and processes of marginalization has continued to change in this century. We need to further elucidate the theoretical implications and methodologies for adequately capturing different mechanisms of domination and how these meld with the ones with which we are most familiar within Euro-American scholarship.

NOTES

1. The existence of global matrices of domination are not new phenomena—colonialism sustained the power and privilege of white Euro-America over Africa, Asia, and Latin America for centuries—but the contemporary organization of economic/social/political power, privilege, and marginalization reflect the development of transnational social spaces.

2. I deliberately picked Scotland and Spain because an Indian doctor in Australia was charged with complicity in the Glasgow bombings, while an American lawyer was charged with the Spanish bombings. Both were proven innocent (see Armaline, Glasberg, and Purkayastha 2011 for further details).

3. Individuals and groups need not participate in two or more countries (or virtual communities) equally. Indeed, their node of experience is often their country of residence. Other countries or virtual communities are often part of a larger field of experience, and the salience of these other spaces is likely to vary. My point here is that we need to seriously consider the node *and* the field, as these contribute to the experiences of privilege and marginalization that shape our lives in more complex ways than the model of intersectionality, based on single nations, suggests.

REFERENCES

Abraham, Margaret. 2010. Globalization, work and citizenship: The call centre industry in India. In *Contours of citizenship: Women, diversity and practices of citizenship*, edited by Margaret Abraham, Esther Ngan-ling Chow, Laura Maratou-Alipranti, and Evangelia Tastsoglou. Aldershot, UK: Ashgate.

Choo, Hae Yeon, and Myra Marx Ferree. 2010. Practicing intersectionality in sociological research: A critical analysis of inclusions, interactions, and institutions in the study of inequalities. *Sociological Theory* 28:129–49.

Collins, Patricia Hill. 1990. *Black feminist thought: Knowledge, consciousness, and the politics of empowerment.* Boston: Unwin Hyman.

Collins, Patricia Hill. 2010. The new politics of community. *American Sociological Review* 75: 7–30.

Diamandaki, K. 2003. Virtual ethnicity and digital diasporas: Identity construction in cyber-space. *Global Media Journal.* http://lass.calumet .purdue.edu/cca/gmj/sp03/graduatesp03/gmj-sp03grad-diamandaki.htm (accessed June 15, 2010).

Earl, Jennifer. 2006. Pursuing social change online: The use of four protest tactics on the Internet. *Social Science Computer Review* 24:362–77.

Gilroy, Paul. 1989. *There ain't no Black in the Union Jack.* Chicago: University of Chicago Press.

Glenn, Evelyn Nakano. 2008. *Shades of citizenship.* Stanford, CA: Stanford University Press.

Govinden, Devarakhsnam. 2008. *Sister outsiders: The representation of identity and difference in selected writings by South African Indian women.* Pretoria: University of South Africa Press.

Guevarra, Anna. 2009. *Marketing dreams, manufacturing heroes: The transnational labor brokering of Filipino workers.* New Brunswick, NJ: Rutgers University Press.

Hondagneu-Sotelo, Pierette, and Ernestine Avila. 1997. I'm here, but I'm there: The meanings of Latina transnational motherhood. *Gender & Society* 11:548–71.

Ignacio, Emily. 2006. *Building diaspora: Filipino community formation on the Internet.* New Brunswick, NJ: Rutgers University Press.

Iwata, Miho, and Bandana Purkayastha. 2011. Cultural human rights. In *Human rights in our own backyard: Social justice and resistance in the U.S.,* edited by William Armaline, Davita Glasberg, and Bandana Purkayastha. Philadelphia: University of Pennsylvania Press.

Kim, Nadia. 2008. *Imperial citizens: Koreans and race from Seoul to LA.* Stanford, CA: Stanford University Press.

Kim-Puri, H.-J. 2007. Conceptualizing gender/ sexuality/state/nation: An introduction. *Gender & Society* 19:137–59.

Lee, Rachel. 2003. *Asian America.net: Ethnicity, nationalism, and cyberspace.* New York: Routledge.

Levitt, Peggy. 2001. *The transnational villagers.* Berkeley: University of California Press.

Mitra, Ananda. 1997. Virtual commonality: Looking for India on the Internet. In *Virtual culture: Identity and communication in cybersociety,* edited by S. Jones. Thousand Oaks, CA: Sage.

Mitra, Rahul, and Radhika Gajjala. 2008. Queer blogging in Indian digital diasporas: A dialogic encounter. *Journal of Communication Inquiry,* originally published online July 16, 2008.

Nandy, Ashis. 2006. *The intimate enemy: Loss and recovery of self under colonialism.* New Delhi, India: Oxford University Press.

Narayan, Anjana, and Bandana Purkayastha. 2009. *Living our religions: South Asian Hindu and Muslim women narrate their experiences.* Stirling, VA: Kumarian Press.

Narayan, Anjana, and Bandana Purkayastha. 2011. Talking gender superiority in virtual spaces. *Journal of South Asian Diasporas* 3:53–69.

Narayan, Anjana, Bandana Purkayastha, and Sudipto Banerji. Forthcoming. Constructing virtual, transnational identities on the web: The case of Hindu student groups in the U.S. and UK. Special Issue on Virtual Ethnicities. *Journal of Intercultural Studies.*

Pudrovska, T., and M. M. Ferree. 2004. Global activism in "virtual space": The European women's lobby in the network of transnational women's NGOs on the web. *Social Politics: International Studies in Gender State and Society* 11:117–43.

Purkayastha, Bandana. 2005. *Negotiating ethnicity: Second-generation South Asian Americans traverse a transnational world.* New Brunswick, NJ: Rutgers University Press.

Purkayastha Bandana. 2009. Another word of experience? South Asian diasporic groups and the transnational context. *Journal of South Asian Diasporas* 1:85–99.

Purkayastha, Bandana. 2010. Interrogating intersectionality: Contemporary globalization and racialized gendering in the lives of highly educated South Asian Americans and their children. *Journal of Intercultural Studies* 31: 29–47.

Sardar, Ziauddin, Ashis Nandy, Merryl Wyn Davies, and Claude Alvares. 1993. *The blinded eye: 500 years of Christopher Columbus.* New York: Apex Press; Goa, India: The Other India Press.

Vertovec, Steven. 2001. Transnational challenges to the "new" multiculturalism. www.transcomm .ox.ac.uk/working papers.

❧ Topics for Further Examination ❧

- Using an academic database, look up the work of Patricia Hill Collins, Bonnie Thornton Dill, Maxine Baca Zinn, Raewyn Connell (formerly R. W. Connell), or others mentioned in the Introduction to Chapter 2 and the reading by Bonnie Thornton Dill and Marla H. Kohlman to find out what is currently being done on intersectionality. (Use parentheses around their names and ask for referred journals only.)
- Do a Web search using "feminist theory" and another category of difference and inequality (i.e., "feminist theory" and "race").
- Using the Web, locate information about the international women's movement.

3

Gender and the Prism of Culture

Catherine G. Valentine

Now that we have introduced you to the ways the contemporary U.S. gender system interacts with, and is modified by, a complex set of categories of difference and inequality, we turn to an exploration of the ways the prism of culture intersects with gender definitions and arrangements. Generations of researchers in the social sciences have opened our eyes to the array of "genderscapes" around the globe. When we look through our kaleidoscope at the interaction between the prisms of gender and culture, we see different patterns that blur, blend, and are cast into a variety of culturally gendered configurations (Baker, 1999).

What Is Culture?

Culture consists of the "implicit and explicit patterns of representations, actions, and artifacts" that are created and shared by people in their networks of interaction and social environments (DiMaggio & Markus, 2010, p. 348). The knowledge structures of human cultures provide predictability and meaning in human life, but they also vary significantly across history and place. Consider one simple example. We would not know what, how, when, where, and why to eat without cultural knowledge. Note, too, that the how/what/when/where/why of eating differs across cultures and over time. Additionally, in highly heterogeneous contemporary societies such as the United States, people shift between multiple, overlapping cultural configurations of norms, values, and the like (Patterson, 2014). The social scientific view of culture makes it clear that, without culture, human experience would have little, if any, shape or meaning (Schwalbe, 2005). That is, culture provides people with the assumptions and expectations on which their social interactions are built and in which their identities, behaviors, feelings, and thoughts are forged.

The term *cultural frame* is helpful for analyzing the socially created, unevenly shared schemas or knowledge structures by which people organize their social relations and coordinate behavior in the contexts in which they interact (Patterson, 2014; Ridgeway, 2009). Cultural frames rely on the human capacity to create categories, such as age-based categories (e.g., children and adults) and gender-based categories (e.g., women and men) (Patterson, 2014; Ridgeway, 2009). In the modern United States, the dominant gender frame is rooted in the Western history of oppositional binary thinking that molds people, in all their variety and complexity, into opposed categories: Black versus White; masculine versus feminine. This primary gender frame is reductionistic. It defines people as belonging to one of two, and only two, sex/gender/sexuality categories, as discussed in Chapter 1. This frame is the lens through which many, if not most, Americans perceive and label others and themselves. Central to the frame are sex/gender/sexuality stereotypes, the pink and blue syndrome presented in Chapter 1, of women and men as opposite types of people, and of men, in general, as having higher status and greater value than women (Ridgeway, 2009). The U.S. gender frame may seem fixed or absolute from the viewpoint of many Americans who have learned to perceive and interpret people in binary terms, but it is not. There is nothing universal or natural about oppositional binaries. As you move through the readings in this chapter, compare and contrast gender frames. For example, the articles by Christine Helliwell, Dredge Byung'chu Käng, and Maria Alexandra Lepowsky examine cultural worlds in which people's beliefs about sex, sexuality, and gender—and thus their representations, identities, and institutions—depart dramatically from American dualistic beliefs and patterns of interaction.

To repeat, cultures are created by people in the different social worlds in which they live, day-to-day and over time. Consequently, cultures can be strikingly different (DiMaggio & Markus, 2010, p. 349), as expressed in the extraordinary sex/gender/sexuality variation found within and across networks and groups. For example, in some cultures, people do not perceive or categorize humans as homosexual (vs. heterosexual), and yet young male members of such cultures regularly and ritually engage in same-sex "sexual encounters" (Herdt, 1997). The work of Gilbert Herdt (1997, 2011) covers several decades of life among the Sambia of New Guinea. Until quite recently, the Sambia were patriarchal and their way of life was characterized by warfare, male privilege, secret male cults, strong antagonisms between men and women, female pollution rituals, and male insemination rites (Miller, 1993). Believing that boys had to be made into men through the ingestion of semen, defined as a potent substance, initiation rituals involved an extended period in which older boys orally inseminated younger boys. Upon marriage, heterosexuality was enforced. Herdt is very careful to distinguish between sexual behavior and identity in his analysis of these rituals, although he notes that the same-sex rituals involved expressions of pleasure. We suggest that it is valuable to think through what might seem to be a vast cultural gulf between traditional Sambian gender/sex/sexuality beliefs and practices as compared to those in the United States. Are there contexts in the United States, both past and present, in which homoerotic encounters between "straight-identified" boys and men take place and are ritualized? Jane Ward (2015), a sociologist, studies the fluidity of sexuality in U.S. society. Her research shows that homoerotic encounters between heterosexual men are commonplace in the United States and, in some settings, these relations are ritualized. For example, hazing rites in college fraternities and the military often involve sexual contact. She points to the "elephant walk" in which fraternity pledges "strip naked and stand in a circle, with one thumb in their mouth and the other in the anus of the pledge in front of them" (p. 4). Instead of interpreting such behaviors in terms of gendered sexuality stereotypes, Ward, much as Herdt in his work on Sambian culture, proposes that we understand male heterosexuality as "a fluid set of desires," constrained by gender norms, not by biological imperatives. Not only do different groups of people produce different cultures, but the cultures they produce are dynamic. That is, people continually generate and alter culture, including gender systems, both as individuals and as members of particular networks and groups; as a result, all cultures undergo change as their members evaluate, resist, and challenge beliefs and practices (DiMaggio & Markus, 2010; Stone & McKee, 1999). To illustrate, in the United States today, transgender activists are pushing back against the boundaries and discipline of the gender binary, and the outcomes are encouraging as, for example, all-women's colleges are moving to accept trans women, gender-neutral bathrooms are becoming more common, and workplace rights for trans people are slowly being instituted. Similarly, intersex activists have organized to seek change in how biological sex is understood and how natural, intersex variations are regarded and treated (see Davis and Preves, Chapter 1).

The prisms of gender and culture are inextricably intertwined. That is, people construct specific gender beliefs and practices in relation to particular cultural traditions and societal conditions. Cultures are gendered in distinctive ways, and gender systems, in turn, shape both material and symbolic cultural products (see, e.g., Chapter 5). As you will discover, the cross-cultural analyses of gender presented in this chapter provide critical support for the social constructionist argument that gender is a situated, negotiated, contested, and changing set of practices and understandings.

Let's begin with observations about gender in different cultures that add to those discussed above. Do you know there are cultures in which individuals can move from one gender category to another without being stigmatized? If you traveled from country to country around the world, you would find cultures in which men are gentle, soft-spoken, and modest, and cultures in which women are viewed as strong and take on roles labeled masculine in the United States. Although you might hear news about extreme forms of oppression of women in some places in the world (e.g., bride burning or dowry death in parts of India), there are other places where women and men live in relative harmony and equality. Also, there are cultures in which the social prisms of difference and inequality that operate in the United States (e.g., social class, race, sexual orientation) are minimal, inconsequential, or nonexistent (see the chapter reading by Helliwell).

THE PROBLEM OF ETHNOCENTRISM IN CROSS-CULTURAL RESEARCH

If you find any of these observations unsettling or even shocking, then you have probably tapped into the problem of bias in cross-cultural studies. One of the great challenges of cross-cultural research is learning to transcend one's own cultural assumptions of what is normal or natural to be able to understand cultural differences. It takes practice, conscious commitment, and self-awareness to get outside one's own cultural frame. After all, seeing what our culture wants us to see is precisely what socialization is about (see Chapter 4). Not only do cultural blinders make it difficult for us to comprehend the fiction of the gender binary that characterizes cultural beliefs in the United States today, but they can make it even more challenging to grasp the profoundly different ways people in other cultures think about and organize human relations.

We tend to "see what we believe," which means we are likely to deny gender patterns that vary from our own cultural experience and/or to misinterpret patterns that are different from our own. For example, the Europeans who first explored and colonized Africa were horrified by the ways African forms of gender and sexuality diverged from their own. They had no framework in which to understand warrior women, such as Nzinga of the Ndongo kingdom of the Mbundu (Murray & Roscoe, 1998). Nzinga was king of her people, dressed as a man, and was surrounded by young men who dressed as women and were her "wives" (Murray & Roscoe, 1998). However, her behavior made sense in the context of her culture, one in which people defined gender as situational and symbolic, thus allowing for alternative genders (Murray & Roscoe, 1998). In his chapter reading, Dredge Byung'chu Käng analyzes the history of the emergence of five gender categories in Thailand, a culture in which gender-variant people have long been a part of the genderscape. The role of language in structuring and reflecting cultural frames, including gender schemas, is highlighted by Käng in his discussion of everyday Thai language which, unlike English, does not distinguish among sex, gender, and sexuality and does not collapse differences into two and only two categories. It is a challenge to resist the tendency toward ethnocentrism (i.e., the belief that the ideas and practices of one's own culture are the standard and that divergent cultures are substandard or inferior). However, the rewards for bracketing the ethnocentric attitude are extremely valuable because one is then able to understand how and why gender operates in cultures that are different from one's own experience and, thus, from one's cultural frame. Thanks to the wide-ranging research of sociologists and anthropologists, we are increasingly able to grasp the peculiarities of our gender system and understand more deeply lifeways, including genderscapes, in other places in the world.

The readings in this chapter will introduce you to some of the variety in gender beliefs and practices across cultures and illustrate three of the most important findings of cross-cultural research on gender: (1) There is no universal definition or experience of gender; indeed, gender is not constituted as oppositional and binary in all societies. (2) Gender inequality, specifically the dominance of men over women, is not the rule everywhere in the world. (3) Gender arrangements, whatever they may be, are socially constructed and, thus, ever evolving.

THERE IS NO UNIVERSAL DEFINITION OR EXPERIENCE OF GENDER

Although people in many contemporary cultures perceive at least some differences between women and men, and assign different tasks and responsibilities to people based on gender categories, these differences vary both from culture to culture and within cultures. There is no unified ideal or definition of masculinity or femininity across cultures. In some cultures, such as the Ju/'hoansi of Namibia and Botswana, women and men alike can become powerful and respected healers, whereas in others, such as the United States, powerful healing roles have been dominated by men (Bonvillain, 2001). Among the seminomadic, pastoral Tuareg of the Sahara and the Sahel, women have considerable economic independence as livestock owners, herders, gardeners, and leathersmiths, whereas in other cultural groups, such as the Taliban of Afghanistan, women are restricted to household labor and economic dependence on men (Rasmussen, 2001).

The readings in this chapter highlight some of the extraordinary cross-cultural differences in beliefs about men and women and in the tasks and rights assigned to them. They offer insights into how gender is shaped across cultures by a number of factors, including ideology, participation in economic production, and control over sexuality and reproduction. For example, in the chapter reading with the titillating title "It's Only a Penis," Christine Helliwell provides an account of the Gerai of Borneo, a cultural group in which rape does not exist. Helliwell argues that the Gerai belief in the biological sameness of women and men is a key to understanding their rape-free society. Her research offers an important report of how assumptions about human biology, in this case femaleness and maleness, are culturally shaped and have profound consequences for gender relations.

In addition, the two-sex (male or female), two-gender (feminine or masculine), and two-sexual-orientation (homosexual or heterosexual) system of Western, U.S. culture is not a universal mode of categorization and organization. As you know from reading Serena Nanda's article on gender variants in Native North America (Chapter 1), the two-spirit role was widespread and accepted in many American Indian tribes. Gilbert Herdt (1997; see discussion of Sambia, earlier), an expert on the anthropology of sexual orientation and gender, points out that the two-spirit role reached a high point in its cultural elaboration among the Mojave Indians, who "sanctioned both male (alyha) and female (hwame) two-spirit roles, each of which had its own distinctive social positions and worldviews" (p. 92).

GENDER INEQUALITY IS NOT THE RULE EVERYWHERE

Gender and power go together but not in only one way. The relationship of power to gender in human groups varies from radical male dominance to relative equality between women and men. At the extreme are intensely patriarchal societies in which women are dominated by men in multiple contexts and relationships. In traditional China, for example, sons were preferred, female infanticide was common, divorce could be initiated only by husbands, restrictions on girls and women were embodied in the mutilating practice of foot binding, and the suicide rate among young wives—who typically endured extreme isolation and hardship—was higher than in any other age and gender category (Bonvillain, 2001).

The United States has a complex history of gender relations in which White men as a group have had power over women as a group (and over men of color). This history was forged by European settlers who "seized and established property rights over land and resources and systematically removed Native Americans" through various strategies (e.g., cultural erasure through assimilation), including militarized genocide. (See reading by Andrea Smith in Chapter 10.) Evelyn Nakano Glenn (2015) uses the concept of "settler colonialism" to analyze how the European white settler undertaking involved the creation of racialized gender and gendered racial dualisms (p. 71). "White settler society understood extreme gender differentiation as a mark of civilization," and white settlers racialized certain groups as sub-human (e.g., Mexicans, Chinese, Native Americans as well as blacks). "Masculine whiteness . . . became central to settler identity," and it enshrined heteropatriarchal nuclear family arrangements as the model for other social arrangements, including the state (p. 60). For many decades, white men's power was overt and legal. For example, in the 19th century, husbands were legally empowered to beat their wives, women did not have voting rights, and women were legally excluded from many occupations (Nakano Glenn, 2015; Stone & McKee, 1999). Today, gender inequality takes more covert and subtle forms. For example, women earn less, on average, than do men of equal educational and occupational level; women are far more likely to be sexually objectified; and women are more likely to shoulder the burden of a double workday inside and outside the home (Coltrane & Adams, 2001; Chapters 7 and 8, this volume).

Understanding the relationship between power and gender requires us to use our sharpest sociological radar. To start, it is important to understand that power does not reside in individuals per se. For example, neither presidents nor bosses have power in a vacuum. They require the support of personnel and special resources such as media, weapons, and money. Power is a group phenomenon, and it exists only so long as a powerful group, its ruling principles, and its control over resources are sustained (Kimmel, 2000).

In addition, not all members of an empowered group have the same amount of power. In the United States and similar societies, male power benefits some men more than others. In fact, many individual men do not hold formal positions of power, and many do not feel powerful in their everyday lives (Johnson, 2001; Kimmel, 2000). Yet major institutions and organizations (e.g., government, big business, the military, the mass media) in the United States are gendered masculine, with controlling positions in those arenas dominated by men, but not just any men (Johnson, 2001). Controlling positions continue to be overwhelmingly held by White men who come from privileged backgrounds and whose lives appear to conform to a straight and narrow path (Johnson, 2001; Kimmel, 2000). As we learned in Chapter 2, the relationship of gender to power in a nation such as the United States is complicated by interactions among structures of domination and subordination such as race, social class, and sexual orientation. Not all societies are as highly and intricately stratified by gender, race, social class, and other social categories of privilege and power as is the United States. Many cultural groups organize relationships in ways that give most or all adults access to similar rights, prestige, decision-making authority, and autonomy in their households and communities. Traditional Agta, Ju/'hoansi, and Iroquois societies are good examples. In other cultural groups, such as the precontact Tlingit and Haida of the Canadian Pacific coastal region, relations among people were based on their position in economic and status hierarchies, yet egalitarian valuation of women and men prevailed (Bonvillain, 2001). In a widely reported new study (Migliano & Vinicius, 2015), anthropologists present their findings from research among the BaYaka from Congo and the Agta from the Philippines. Both are contemporary hunter-gatherer societies whose way of life is suggestive of how our human ancestors lived for most of human history. They are strikingly egalitarian. In fact, anthropologists such as Barry Hewlitt (2005), who has studied the Aka Pygmy people of central Africa, argue that they are fiercely egalitarian. Hierarchical structures are nonexistent. For example, among the Aka, while women hunt, men tend to babies and vice versa. Flexibility is the rule. Big egos are discouraged. Play is encouraged. Caring and fairness are the norm.

The point is that humans do not inevitably create inequalities out of perceived differences. Thus, even though there is generally some type of division of labor by gender across cultures today, differences in men's and women's work do not inexorably lead to patriarchal relations in which men monopolize high-status positions in important institutions and women are relegated to a restricted world of low-status activities and tasks. To help illustrate, Maria Alexandra Lepowsky's ethnography of Vanatinai social relations in the 1970s provides us with a model of a society in which the principles of personal autonomy and freedom of choice prevailed. The gender ideology of the Vanatinai was

egalitarian, and their belief in equality manifested itself in daily life. For example, women as well as men owned and inherited land and other valuables. Women chose their own marriage partners and lovers, and they divorced at will. Any individual on Vanatinai might try to become a leader by demonstrating superior knowledge and skill.

Gender inequality is not the rule everywhere. Male dominance, patriarchy, gender inequality—whatever term one uses—is not the inevitable state of human relations. Additionally, patriarchy itself is not unitary. Patriarchy does not assume a particular shape, and it does not mean that women have no control or influence in their communities. Even in the midst of patriarchy, women and men may create identities and relationships that allow for autonomy and independence. In her reading in this chapter, Charlotte Wrigley-Asante details the empowering benefits that young women migrant workers in Accra, Ghana, accrue from economic independence. Using trading as a resource, the young women are able to save and invest in housing and personal items. They are also able to supplement household budgets and, as a consequence, their status is enhanced, as is their ability to control intimate relations with men.

GENDER ARRANGEMENTS ARE EVER EVOLVING

The cross-cultural story of gender takes us back to the metaphor of the kaleidoscope. Life is an ongoing process of change from one pattern to another. We can never go back to "the way things were" at some earlier moment in time, nor can we predict exactly how the future will unfold. This is, of course, the story of gender around the world.

Two of the major sources of change in gender meanings and practices across cultures are culture contact and diffusion of beliefs and practices around the globe (Ritzer, 2004; Sørensen, 2000). Among the best documented accounts of such change have been those that demonstrate how Western gender systems were imposed on people whose gender beliefs and arrangements varied from Western assumptions and practices. For example, Native American multiple-gender systems were actively, and sometimes violently, discouraged by European colonists (Herdt, 1997; Nakano Glenn, 2015; see Nanda's reading in Chapter 1). Today, globalization—a complex process of worldwide diffusion of practices, images, and ideas (Ritzer, 2004)—raises the problem of the development of a world order, including a gender order, that may be increasingly dominated by Western cultural values and patterns (Held, McGrew, Goldblatt, & Perraton, 1999; see Chapter 10 for further discussion). Cenk Özbay, in his chapter reading, examines the emergence of exaggerated masculinity among rent boys in Istanbul. As part of his analysis, he offers insights into the process of diffusion as it plays out in the interpenetration of Western gay culture and the gender/sexuality frame of the rent boys and gay men of Istanbul.

Culture contact and diffusion via globalization are by no means the only source of changing gender arrangements (see Chapter 10 for detailed discussion of gender change). The forces of change are many and complicated, and they have resulted in a mix of tendencies toward rigid, hierarchical gender relations and toward gender flexibility and equality, depending on the specific cultural context and forces of change experienced by particular groups of people. In all this, there is one fact: People are not bound by any set of gender beliefs and practices. Culture change is inevitable, and so is change in the genderscape.

REFERENCES

Baker, C. (1999). *Kaleidoscopes: Wonders of wonder.* Lafayette, CA: C&T.

Bonvillain, N. (2001). *Women and men: Cultural constructs of gender* (3rd ed.). Upper Saddle River, NJ: Prentice Hall.

Coltrane, S., & Adams, M. (2001). Men, women, and housework. In D. Vannoy (Ed.), *Gender mosaics* (pp. 145–154). Los Angeles: Roxbury.

DiMaggio, P., & Markus, H. R. (2010). Culture and social psychology: Converging perspectives. *Social Psychology Quarterly, 73*(4), 347–352.

Held, D., McGrew, A., Goldblatt, D., & Perraton, J. (1999). *Global transformations.* Stanford, CA: Stanford University Press.

Herdt, G. (1997). *Same sex, different cultures.* Boulder, CO: Westview Press.

Herdt, G. (2011). Talking about sex: On the relationships between discourse, secrecy and sexual subjectivity in Melanesia. In D. Lipset & P. Roscoe (Eds.), *Echoes of the Tambaran: Masculinity, history and the subject in the work of Donald F. Tuzin* (pp. 259–273). Canberra: Australian National University Press.

Hewlitt, B. (2005, June 15). Are the men of the African Aka tribe the best fathers in the world? *The Guardian.* Retrieved from http://www.theguardian .com/society/2005/jun/15/childrensservices .familyandrelationships

Johnson, A. G. (2001). *Privilege, power, and difference.* Mountain View, CA: Mayfield.

Kimmel, M. (2000). *The gendered society.* New York: Oxford University Press.

Migliano, A., & Vinicius, L. (2015, May 18). Why our ancestors were more gender equal than us. *The Conversation.* Retrieved from http:// theconversation.com/why-our-ancestors-were-more-gender-equal-than-us-41902

Miller, B. D. (1993). Anthropology of sex and gender. In B. D. Miller (Ed.), *Sex and gender hierarchies* (pp. 3–31). Boston: Cambridge University Press.

Murray, S. O., & Roscoe, W. (1998). *Boy-wives and female-husbands: Studies of African homosexualities.* New York: St. Martin's Press.

Nakano Glenn, E. (2015). Settler colonialism as structure: A framework for comparative studies of U.S. race and gender formation. *Sociology of Race and Ethnicity, 1*(1), 54–74.

Patterson, O. (2014). Making sense of culture. *Annual Reviews of Sociology, 40*(1), 1–30.

Rasmussen, S. (2001). Pastoral nomadism and gender. In C. B. Brettell & C. F. Sargent (Eds.), *Gender in cross-cultural perspective* (pp. 280–293). Upper Saddle River, NJ: Prentice Hall.

Ridgeway, C. (2009). Framed before we know it: How gender shapes social relations. *Gender & Society, 23*(2), 145–160.

Ritzer, G. (2004). *The globalization of nothing.* Thousand Oaks, CA: Pine Forge Press.

Schwalbe, M. (2005). *The sociologically examined life.* New York: McGraw-Hill.

Sørensen, M. L. S. (2000). *Gender archeology.* Cambridge, UK: Polity Press.

Stone, L., & McKee, N. P. (1999). *Gender and culture in America.* Upper Saddle River, NJ: Prentice Hall.

Ward, J. (2015, February 2). It turns out that male sexuality is just as fluid as female sexuality. *The Conversation.* Retrieved from http://theconversation.com/it-turns-out-male-sexuality-is-just-as-fluid-as-female-sexuality-36189

Introduction to Reading 11

Anthropologist Christine Helliwell provides a challenging account of a cultural group, the Gerai of Indonesia, in which rape does not exist. She links the freedom from rape among the Gerai people to the relatively egalitarian nature of their gender relations. Helliwell's research questions many gender beliefs held by members of Western cultures today.

1. How are men's and women's sexual organs conceptualized among the Gerai, and what are the consequences for Gerai understandings of sexual intercourse?

2. Genitalia do not determine identity in Gerai. What does?

3. Why is Gerai culture rape-free, and are there lessons we can learn from the Gerai about how to diminish or even eliminate rape in the United States?

"It's Only a Penis"

RAPE, FEMINISM, AND DIFFERENCE

Christine Helliwell

In 1985 and 1986 I carried out anthropological fieldwork in the Dayak community of Gerai in Indonesian Borneo. One night in September 1985, a man of the village climbed through a window into the freestanding house where a widow lived with her elderly mother, younger (unmarried) sister, and young children. The widow awoke, in darkness, to feel the man inside her mosquito net, gripping her shoulder while he climbed under the blanket that covered her and her youngest child as they slept (her older children slept on mattresses nearby). He was whispering, "be quiet, be quiet!" She responded by sitting up in bed and pushing him violently, so that he stumbled backward, became entangled with her mosquito net, and then, finally free, moved across the floor toward the window. In the meantime, the woman climbed from her bed and pursued him, shouting his name several times as she did so.

His hurried exit through the window, with his clothes now in considerable disarray, was accompanied by a stream of abuse from the woman and by excited interrogations from wakened neighbors in adjoining houses.

I awoke the following morning to raucous laughter on the longhouse verandah outside my apartment where a group of elderly women gathered regularly to thresh, winnow, and pound rice. They were recounting this tale loudly, and with enormous enjoyment, to all in the immediate vicinity. As I came out of my door, one was engaged in mimicking the man climbing out the window, sarong falling down, genitals askew. Those others working or lounging near her on the verandah—both men and women—shrieked with laughter.

When told the story, I was shocked and appalled. An unknown man had tried to climb into the bed of a woman in the dead, dark of night? I knew what this was called: attempted rape. The woman had seen the man and recognized him (so had others in the village, wakened by her shouting). I knew what he deserved: the full weight of the law. My own fears about being a single woman alone in a strange place, sleeping in a dwelling that could not be secured at night, bubbled to the surface. My feminist sentiments poured out. "How can you laugh?" I asked my women friends; "this is a very bad thing that he has tried to do." But my outrage simply served to fuel the hilarity. "No, not bad," said one of the old women (a particular friend of mine), "simply stupid."

I felt vindicated in my response when, two hours later, the woman herself came onto the verandah to share betel nut and tobacco and to broadcast the story. Her anger was palpable, and she shouted for all to hear her determination to exact a compensation payment from the man. Thinking to obtain information about local women's responses to rape, I began to question her. Had she been frightened? I asked. Of course she had—Wouldn't I feel frightened if I awoke in the dark to find an unknown person inside my mosquito net? Wouldn't I be angry? Why then, I asked, hadn't she taken the opportunity, while he

was entangled in her mosquito net, to kick him hard or to hit him with one of the many wooden implements near at hand? She looked shocked. Why would she do that? she asked—after all, he hadn't hurt her. No, but he had wanted to, I replied. She looked at me with puzzlement. Not able to find a local word for rape in my vocabulary, I scrabbled to explain myself: "He was trying to have sex with you." I said, "although you didn't want to. He was trying to hurt you." She looked at me, more with pity than with puzzlement now, although both were mixed in her expression. "Tin [Christine], it's only a penis," she said. "How can a penis hurt anyone?"

Rape, Feminism, and Difference

A central feature of many feminist writings about rape in the past twenty years is their concern to eschew the view of rape as a natural function of male biology and to stress instead its bases in society and culture. It is curious, then, that so much of this work talks of rape in terms that suggest—either implicitly or explicitly—that it is a universal practice. To take only several examples: Pauline Bart and Patricia O'Brien tell us that "every female from nine months to ninety years is at risk" (1985, 1); Anna Clark argues that "all women know the paralyzing fear of walking down a dark street at night. . . . It seems to be a fact of life that the fear of rape imposes a curfew on our movements" (1987, 1); Catharine MacKinnon claims that "sexuality is central to women's definition and forced sex is central to sexuality," so "rape is indigenous, not exceptional, to women's social condition" (1989b, 172) and "all women live all the time under the shadow of the threat of sexual abuse" (1989a, 340); Lee Madigan and Nancy Gamble write of "the global terrorism of rape" (1991, 21–22); and Susan Brison asserts that "the fact that all women's lives are restricted by sexual violence is indisputable" (1993, 17). . . . This is particularly puzzling given that Peggy Reeves Sanday, for one, long ago demonstrated that while rape occurs widely throughout the world, it is by no means a human universal: some societies can indeed be classified as rape free (1981).

There are two general reasons for this universalization of rape among Western feminists. The first of these has to do with the understanding of the practice as horrific by most women in Western societies. In these settings, rape is seen as "a fate worse than, or tantamount to, death" (S. Marcus 1992, 387): a shattering of identity that, for instance, left one North American survivor feeling "not quite sure whether I had died and the world went on without me, or whether I was alive in a totally alien world" (Brison 1993, 10). . . .

A second, equally deep-seated reason for the feminist tendency to universalize rape stems from Western feminism's emphasis on difference between men and women and from its consequent linking of rape and difference. Two types of difference are involved here. The first of these is difference in social status and power; thus rape is linked quite explicitly, in contemporary feminist accounts, to patriarchal social forms. Indeed, this focus on rape as stemming from difference in social position is what distinguishes feminist from other kinds of accounts of rape (see Ellis 1989, 10). In this view, inequality between men and women is linked to men's desire to possess, subjugate, and control women, with rape constituting a central means by which the freedom of women is limited and their continued submission to men ensured. Since many feminists continue to believe that patriarchy is universal—or, at the very least, to feel deeply ambivalent on this point—there is a tendency among us to believe that rape, too, is universal.[1]

However, the view of women as everywhere oppressed by men has been extensively critiqued within the anthropological literature. A number of anthropologists have argued that in some societies, while men and women may perform different roles and occupy different spaces, they are nevertheless equal in value, status, and power.[2] . . .

But there is a second type of difference between men and women that also, albeit largely implicitly, underlies the assumption that rape is universal, and it is the linkage between this type of difference and the treatment of rape in feminist accounts with which I am largely concerned in this article. I refer to the assumption by most Western feminists writing on rape that men and women have different bodies and, more specifically, different genitalia: that they are, in other words differently sexed. Furthermore, it is taken for granted in most feminist accounts that these differences render the former biologically, or "naturally," capable of penetrating and therefore brutalizing the latter and render the latter "naturally" able to be brutalized. . . . Rape of women by men is thus assumed to be universal because the same "biological" bodily differences between men and women are believed to exist everywhere.

Unfortunately, the assumption that preexisting bodily difference between men and women underlies rape has blinded feminists writing on the subject to the ways the practice of rape itself creates and inscribes such difference. This seems particularly true in contemporary Western societies where the relationship between rape and bodily/genital dimorphism appears to be an extremely intimate one. Judith Butler (1990, 1993) has argued (following Foucault 1978) that the Western emphasis on sexual difference is a product of the heterosexualization of desire within Western societies over the past few centuries, which "requires and institutes the production of discrete and asymmetrical oppositions between 'feminine' and 'masculine' where these are understood as expressive attributes of 'male' and 'female'" (1990, 17).[3] The practice of rape in Western contexts can only properly be understood with reference to this heterosexual matrix, to the division of humankind into two distinct—and in many respects opposed—types of body (and hence types of person).[4] While it is certainly the case that rape is linked in contemporary Western societies to disparities of power and status between men and women, it is the particular discursive form that those disparities take—their elaboration in terms of the discourse of sex—that gives rape its particular meaning and power in these contexts.

Sharon Marcus has already argued convincingly that the act of rape "feminizes" women in

Western settings, so that "the entire female body comes to be symbolized by the vagina, itself conceived of as a delicate, perhaps inevitably damaged and pained inner space" (1992, 398). I would argue further that the practice of rape in these settings—both its possibility and its actualization—not only feminizes women but masculinizes men as well.[5] This masculinizing character of rape is very clear in, for instance, Sanday's ethnography of fraternity gang rape in North American universities (1990b) and, in particular, in material on rape among male prison inmates. In the eyes of these rapists the act of rape marks them as "real men" and marks their victims as not men, that is, as feminine.[6] In this iconography, the "masculine" body (along with the "masculine" psyche) is viewed as hard, penetrative, and aggressive, in contrast to the soft, vulnerable, and violable "feminine" sexuality and psyche. Rape both reproduces and marks the pronounced sexual polarity found in these societies.

Western understandings of gender difference have almost invariably started from the presumption of a presocial bodily difference between men and women ("male" and "female") that is then somehow acted on by society to produce gender. In particular, the possession of either male genitals or female genitals is understood by most Westerners to be not only the primary marker of gender identity but, indeed, the underlying cause of that identity. . . .

I seek to do two things in this article. First, in providing an account of a community in which rape does not occur, I aim to give the lie to the widespread assumption that rape is universal and thus to invite Western feminists to interrogate the basis of our own tendency to take its universality for granted.[7] The fundamental question is this: Why does a woman of Gerai see a penis as lacking the power to harm her, while I, a white Australian/New Zealand woman, am so ready to see it as having the capacity to defile, to humiliate, to subjugate and, ultimately, to destroy me?

Second, by exploring understandings of sex and gender in a community that stresses identity, rather than difference, between men and women

(including men's and women's bodies), I aim to demonstrate that Western beliefs in the "sexed" character of bodies are not "natural" in basis but, rather, are a component of specifically Western gendering and sexual regimes. And since the practice of rape in Western societies is profoundly linked to these beliefs, I will suggest that it is an inseparable part of such regimes. This is not to say that the practice of rape is always linked to the kind of heterosexual regime found in the West; even the most cursory glance at any list of societies in which the practice occurs indicates that this is not so.[8] But it is to point out that we will be able to understand rape only ever in a purely localized sense, in the context of the local discourses and practices that are both constitutive of and constituted by it. In drawing out the implications of the Gerai stress on identity between men and women for Gerai gender and sexual relations, I hope to point out some of the possible implications of the Western emphasis on gender difference for Western gender and sexual relations—including the practice of rape.

GENDER, SEX, AND PROCREATION IN GERAI

Gerai is a Dayak community of some seven hundred people in the Indonesian province of Kalimantan Barat (West Borneo).[9] In the twenty months I spent in the community, I heard of no cases of either sexual assault or attempted sexual assault (and since this is a community in which privacy as we understand it in the West is almost nonexistent—in which surveillance by neighbors is at a very high level [see Helliwell 1996]—I would certainly have heard of any such cases had they occurred). In addition, when I questioned men and women about sexual assault, responses ranged from puzzlement to outright incredulity to horror.

While relations between men and women in Gerai can be classified as relatively egalitarian in many respects, both men and women nevertheless say that men are "higher" than women (Helliwell 1995, 364). This greater status and authority does not, however, find expression in the practice of rape, as many feminist writings on the subject seem to suggest that it should. This is because the Gerai view of men as "higher" than women, although equated with certain kinds of increased potency vis-à-vis the world at large, does not translate into a conception of that potency as attached to and manifest through the penis—of men's genitals as able to brutalize women's genitals.

Shelly Errington has pointed out that a feature of many of the societies of insular Southeast Asia is a stress on sameness, even identity, between men and women (1990, 35, 39), in contrast to the Western stress on difference between the passive "feminine" object and the active, aggressive "masculine" subject.[10] Gerai understandings of gender fit Errington's model very well. In Gerai, men and women are not understood as fundamentally different types of persons: there is no sense of a dichotomized masculinity and femininity. Rather, men and women are seen to have the same kinds of capacities and proclivities, but with respect to some, men are seen as "more so" and with respect to others, women are seen as "more so." Men are said to be braver and more knowledgeable about local law (adat), while women are said to be more persistent and more enduring. All of these qualities are valued. Crucially, in terms of the central quality of nurturance (perhaps the most valued quality in Gerai), which is very strongly marked as feminine among Westerners, Gerai people see no difference between men and women. As one (female) member of the community put it to me: "We all must nurture because we all need."[11] The capacity both to nurture and to need, particularly as expressed through the cultivation of rice as a member of a rice group, is central to Gerai conceptions of personhood: rice is the source of life, and its (shared) production humanizes and socializes individuals (Helliwell, forthcoming). Women and men have identical claims to personhood based on their equal contributions to rice production (there is no notion that women are somehow diminished as persons even though they may be seen as less "high"). As in Strathern's account of Hagen (1988), the perceived mutuality of rice-field work in Gerai renders inoperable any notion of either men or women as autonomous individual subjects.

It is also important to note that while men's bravery is linked to a notion of their greater physical strength, it is not equated with aggression—aggression is not valued in most Gerai contexts.[12] As a Gerai man put it to me, the wise man is the one "who fights when he has to, and runs away when he can"; such avoidance of violence does not mark a man as lacking in bravery. . . . While it is recognized that a man will sometimes need to fight—and skill and courage in fighting are valued—aggression and hotheadedness are ridiculed as the hallmarks of a lazy and incompetent man. In fact, physical violence between adults is uncommon in Gerai, and all of the cases that I did witness or hear about were extremely mild.[13] Doubtless the absence of rape in the community is linked to this devaluing of aggression in general. However, unlike a range of other forms of violence (slapping, beating with a fist, beating with an implement, knifing, premeditated killing, etc.), rape is not named as an offense and accorded a set punishment under traditional Gerai law. In addition, unlike these other forms of violence, rape is something that people in the community find almost impossible to comprehend ("How would he be able to do such a thing?" one woman asked when I struggled to explain the concept of a man attempting to put his penis into her against her will). Clearly, then, more is involved in the absence of rape in Gerai than a simple absence of violence in general.

Central to all of the narratives that Gerai people tell about themselves and their community is the notion of a "comfortable life": the achievement of this kind of life marks the person and the household as being of value and constitutes the norm to which all Gerai people aspire. Significantly, the content of such a life is seen as identical for both men and women: it is marked by the production of bountiful rice harvests each year and the successful raising of a number of healthy children to maturity. The core values and aspirations of men and women are thus identical; of the many life histories that I collected while in the community—all of which are organized around this central image—it is virtually impossible to tell those of men from those of women. Two points are significant in this respect. First, a "comfortable life" is predicated on the notion of a partnership between a man and a woman (a conjugal pair). This is because while men and women are seen to have the same basic skills and capacities, men are seen to be "better" at certain kinds of work and women to be "better" at other kinds. Second, and closely related to this, the Gerai notion of men's and women's work does not constitute a rigid division of labor: both men and women say that theoretically women can perform all of the work routinely carried out by men, and men can perform all of the work routinely carried out by women. However, men are much better at men's work, and women are much better at women's work. Again, what we have here is a stress on identity between men and women at the expense of radical difference.

This stress on identity extends into Gerai bodily and sexual discourses. A number of people (both men and women) assured me that men sometimes menstruate; in addition, menstrual blood is not understood to be polluting, in contrast to how it is seen in many societies that stress more strongly the difference between men and women. While pregnancy and childbirth are spoken of as "women's work," many Gerai people claim that under certain circumstances men are also able to carry out this work—but, they say, women are "better" at it and so normally undertake it. In line with this claim, I collected a Gerai myth concerning a lazy woman who was reluctant to take on the work of pregnancy and childbirth. Her husband instead made for himself a lidded container out of bark, wood, and rattan ("like a betel nut container"), which he attached around his waist beneath his loincloth and in which he carried the growing fetus until it was ready to be born. On one occasion when I was watching a group of Gerai men cut up a boar, one, remembering an earlier conversation about the capacity of men to give birth, pointed to a

growth in the boar's body cavity and said with much disapproving shaking of the head: "Look at this. He wants to carry his child. He's stupid." In addition, several times I saw fathers push their nipples into the mouths of young children to quiet them; while none of these fathers claimed to be able to produce milk, people nevertheless claimed that some men in the community were able to lactate, a phenomenon also attested to in myth. Men and women are thought to produce the same genital fluid, and this is linked in complex ways to the capacity of both to menstruate. All of these examples demonstrate the community's stress on bodily identity between men and women.

Furthermore, in Gerai, men's and women's sexual organs are explicitly conceptualized as the same. This sexual identity became particularly clear when I asked several people who had been to school (and hence were used to putting pencil to paper) to draw men's and women's respective organs for me: in all cases, the basic structure and form of each were the same. One informant, endeavoring to convince me of this sameness, likened both to wooden and bark containers for holding valuables (these vary in size but have the same basic conical shape, narrower at the base and wider at the top). In all of these discussions, it was reiterated that the major difference between men's and women's organs is their location: inside the body (women) and outside the body (men).[14] In fact, when I pressed people on this point, they invariably explained that it makes no sense to distinguish between men's and women's genitalia themselves; rather, it is location that distinguishes between penis and vulva.[15]

Heterosexuality constitutes the normative sexual activity in the community and, indeed, I was unable to obtain any information about homosexual practices during my time there. In line with the stress on sameness, sexual intercourse between a man and a woman in Gerai is understood as an equal coming together of fluids, pleasures, and life forces. The same stress also underlies beliefs about conception. Gerai people believe that repeated acts of intercourse between the same two people are necessary for conception, since this "prepares" the womb for pregnancy. The fetus is deemed to be created through the mingling of equal quantities of fluids and forces from both partners. Again, what is seen as important here is not the fusion of two different types of bodies (male and female) as in Western understandings; rather, Gerai people say, it is the similarity of the two bodies that allows procreation to occur. As someone put it to me bluntly: "If they were not the same, how could the fluids blend? It's like coconut oil and water: they can't mix!"

What needs to be stressed here is that both sexual intercourse and conception are viewed as involving a mingling of similar bodily fluids, forces, and so on, rather than as the penetration of one body by another with a parallel propulsion of substances from one (male) body only into the other, very different (female) one. What Gerai accounts of both sexual intercourse and conception stress are tropes of identity, mingling, balance, and reciprocity. In this context it is worth noting that many Gerai people were puzzled by the idea of gender-specific "medicine" to prevent contraception—such as the injectable or oral contraceptives promoted by state-run health clinics in the area. Many believed that, because both partners play the same role in conception, it should not matter whether husband or wife received such medicine (and indeed, I knew of cases where husbands had taken oral contraceptives meant for their wives). This suggests that such contraceptive regimes also serve (like the practice of rape) to reinscribe sex difference between men and women (see also Tsing 1993, 104–20). . . .

While Gerai people stress sameness over difference between men and women, they do, nevertheless, see them as being different in one important respect: their life forces are, they say, oriented differently ("they face different ways," it was explained to me). This different orientation means that women are "better" at certain kinds of work and men are "better" at other kinds of work—particularly with respect to rice-field work. Gerai people conceive of the work of

clearing large trees for a new rice field as the definitive man's work and regard the work of selecting and storing the rice seed for the following year's planting—which is correlated in fundamental ways with the process of giving birth—as the definitive woman's work. Because women are perceived to lack appropriate skills with respect to the first, and men are perceived to lack appropriate skills with respect to the second, Gerai people say that to be viable a household must contain both adult males and adult females. And since a "comfortable life" is marked by success in production not only of rice but also of children, the truly viable household must contain at least one conjugal pair. The work of both husband and wife is seen as necessary for the adequate nurturance of the child and successful rearing to adulthood (both of which depend on the successful cultivation of rice). Two women or two men would not be able to produce adequately for a child since they would not be able to produce consistently successful rice harvests; while such a household might be able to select seed, clear a rice field, and so grow rice in some rudimentary fashion, its lack of expertise at one of these tasks would render it perennially poor and its children perennially unhealthy, Gerai people say. . . .

Gender difference in Gerai, then, is not predicated on the character of one's body, and especially of one's genitalia as in many Western contexts. Rather, it is understood as constituted in the differential capacity to perform certain kinds of work, a capacity assigned long before one's bodily being takes shape.[16] In this respect it is important to note that Gerai ontology rests on a belief in predestination, in things being as they should (see Helliwell 1995). In this understanding, any individual's *semongan* is linked in multifarious and unknowable ways to the cosmic order, to the "life" of the universe as a whole. Thus the new fetus is predestined to become someone "fitted" to carry out either men's work or women's work as part of the maintenance of a universal balance. Bodies with the appropriate characteristics—internal or external genitalia, presence or absence of breasts, and so on—then develop in line with this prior destiny. At first sight this may not seem enormously different from Western conceptions of gender, but the difference is in fact profound. While, for Westerners, genitalia, as significant of one's role in the procreative process, are absolutely fundamental in determining one's identity, in Gerai the work that one performs is seen as fundamental, and genitalia, along with other bodily characteristics, are relegated to a kind of secondary, derivative function.

Gerai understandings of gender were made quite clear through circumstances surrounding my own gender classification while in the community. Gerai people remained very uncertain about my gender for some time after I arrived in the community because (as they later told me) "I did not . . . walk like a woman, with arms held out from the body and hips slightly swaying; I was 'brave' trekking from village to village through the jungle on my own; I had bony kneecaps; I did not know how to tie a sarong in the appropriate way for women; I could not distinguish different varieties of rice from one another; I did not wear earrings; I had short hair; I was tall" (Helliwell 1993, 260). This was despite the fact that people in the community knew from my first few days with them both that I had breasts (this was obvious when the sarong that I wore clung to my body while I bathed in the river) and that I had a vulva rather than a penis and testicles (this was obvious from my trips to defecate or urinate in the small stream used for that purpose, when literally dozens of people would line the banks to observe whether I performed these functions differently from them). As someone said to me at a later point, "Yes, I saw that you had a vulva, but I thought that Western men might be different." My eventual, more definitive classification as a woman occurred [later]. . . . As I learned to distinguish types of rice and their uses, I became more and more of a woman (as I realized later), since this knowledge—including the magic that goes with it—is understood by Gerai people as foundational to femininity. . . .

Gerai people talk of two kinds of work as defining a woman: the selection and storage of

rice seed and the bearing of children.[17] But the first of these is viewed as prior, logically as well as chronologically. People are quite clear that in the womb either "someone who can cut down the large trees for a ricefield is made, or someone who can select and store rice." When I asked if it was not more important whether or not someone could bear a child, it was pointed out to me that many women do not bear children (there is a high rate of infertility in the community), but all women have the knowledge to select and store rice seed. In fact, at the level of the rice group the two activities of "growing" rice and "growing" children are inseparable: A rice group produces rice in order to raise healthy children, and it produces children so that they can in turn produce the rice that will sustain the group once their parents are old and frail (Helliwell, forthcoming). For this reason, any Gerai couple unable to give birth to a child of their own will adopt one, usually from a group related by kinship. The two activities of growing rice and growing children are constantly talked about together, and the same imagery is used to describe the development of a woman's pregnancy and the development of rice grains on the plant. . . .

Gerai, then, lacks the stress on bodily—and especially genital—dimorphism that most feminist accounts of rape assume. Indeed, the reproductive organs themselves are not seen as "sexed." In a sense it is problematic even to use the English categories *woman* and *man* when writing of this community, since these terms are saturated with assumptions concerning the priority of biological (read, bodily) difference. In the Gerai context, it would be more accurate to deal with the categories of, on the one hand, "those responsible for rice selection and storage" and, on the other, "those responsible for cutting down the large trees to make a ricefield." There is no discursive space in Gerai for the distinction between an active, aggressive, penetrating male sexual organ (and sexuality) and a passive, vulnerable, female one. Indeed, sexual intercourse in Gerai is understood by both men and women to stem from mutual "need" on the part of the two partners; without such need, people say, sexual intercourse cannot occur, because the requisite balance is lacking. . . . [T]he sexual act is understood as preeminently mutual in its character, including in its initiation. The idea of having sex with someone who does not need you to have sex with them—and so the idea of coercing someone into sex—is thus almost unthinkable to Gerai people. In addition, informants asserted that any such action would destroy the individual's spiritual balance and that of his or her rice group and bring calamity to the group as a whole.[18]

In this context, a Gerai man's astonished and horrified question "How can a penis be taken into a vagina if a woman doesn't want it?" has a meaning very different from that of the same statement uttered by a man in the West. In the West, notions of radical difference between men and women—incorporating representations of normative male sexuality as active and aggressive, normative female sexuality as passive and vulnerable, and human relationships (including acts of sexual intercourse) as occurring between independent, potentially hostile, agents—would render such a statement at best naive, at worst misogynist. In Gerai, however, the stress on identity between men and women and on the sexual act as predicated on mutuality validates such a statement as one of straightforward incomprehension (and it should be noted that I heard similar statements from women). In the Gerai context, the penis, or male genitalia in general, is not admired, feared, or envied. . . . In fact, Gerai people see men's sexual organs as more vulnerable than women's for the simple reason that they are outside the body, while women's are inside. This reflects Gerai understandings of "inside" as representing safety and belonging, while "outside" is a place of strangers and danger, and it is linked to the notion of men as braver than women.[19] In addition, Gerai people say, because the penis is "taken into" another body, it is theoretically at greater risk during the sexual act than the vagina. This contrasts, again, quite markedly with Western understandings, where women's sexual organs are constantly depicted as more vulnerable

during the sexual act—as liable to be hurt, despoiled, and so on (some men's anxieties about *vagina dentata* notwithstanding). In Gerai a penis is "only a penis": neither a marker of dimorphism between men and women in general nor, in its essence, any different from a vagina.

CONCLUSIONS

. . . With this background, I return now to the case with which I began this article—and, particularly, to the great differences between my response to this case and that of the Gerai woman concerned. On the basis of my own cultural assumptions concerning the differences—and particularly the different sexual characters—of men and women, I am inclined (as this case showed me) to read any attempt by a man to climb into a woman's bed in the night without her explicit consent as necessarily carrying the threat of sexual coercion and brutalization. The Gerai woman, in contrast, has no fear of coerced sexual intercourse when awakened in the dark by a man. She has no such fear because in the Gerai context . . . women's sexuality and bodies are no less aggressive and no more vulnerable than men's.

In fact, in the case in question, the intruding man did expect to have intercourse with the woman.[20] He claimed that the woman had already agreed to this through her acceptance of his initiatory gifts of soap.[21] The woman, however, while privately agreeing that she had accepted such gifts, claimed that no formal agreement had yet been reached. Her anger, then, did not stem from any belief that the man had attempted to sexually coerce her ("How would he be able to do such a thing?"). Because the term "to be quiet" is often used as a euphemism for sexual intercourse in Gerai, she saw the man's exhortation that she "be quiet" as simply an invitation to engage in sex with him, rather than the implicit threat that I read it to be.[22] Instead, her anger stemmed from her conviction that the correct protocols had not been followed, that the man ought to have spoken with her rather than taking her acceptance of the soap as an unequivocal expression of assent. She was, as she put it, letting him know that "you have sexual relations together when you talk together. Sexual relations cannot be quiet."[23]

Yet, this should not be taken to mean that the practice of rape is simply a product of discourse: that brutality toward women is restricted to societies containing particular, dimorphic representations of male and female sexuality and that we simply need to change the discourse in order to eradicate such practices.[24] Nor is it to suggest that a society in which rape is unthinkable is for that reason to be preferred to Western societies. To adopt such a position would be still to view the entire world through a sexualized Western lens.

In order to understand the practice of rape in countries like Australia and the United States, then—and so to work effectively for its eradication there—feminists in these countries must begin to relinquish some of our most ingrained presumptions concerning differences between men and women and, particularly, concerning men's genitalia and sexuality as inherently brutalizing and penetrative and women's genitalia and sexuality as inherently vulnerable and subject to brutalization. Instead, we must begin to explore the ways rape itself produces such experiences of masculinity and femininity and so inscribes sexual difference onto our bodies.

NOTES

1. Among "radical" feminists such as Andrea Dworkin and Catharine MacKinnon this belief reaches its most extreme version, in which all sexual intercourse between a man and a woman is viewed as akin to rape (Dworkin 1987; MacKinnon 1989a, 1989b).

2. Leacock 1978 and Bell 1983 are well-known examples. Sanday 1990a and Marcus 1992 are more recent examples, on Minangkabau and Turkish society, respectively.

3. See Laqueur 1990 for a historical account of this process.

4. On the equation of body and person within Western (especially feminist) thought, see Moore 1994.

5. See Plaza 1980: "[Rape] is very sexual in the sense that [it] is frequently a sexual activity, but especially in the sense that it opposes men and women: it is social sexing which is latent in rape. . . . Rape is sexual essentially because it rests on the very social difference between the sexes" (31).

6. The material on male prison inmates is particularly revealing in this respect. As an article by Stephen Donaldson, a former prisoner and the president of the U.S. advocacy group Stop Prisoner Rape, makes clear, "hooking up" with another prisoner is the best way for a prisoner to avoid sexual assaults, particularly gang rapes. Hooking up involves entering a sexual liaison with a senior partner ("jocker," "man," "pitcher," "daddy") in exchange for protection. In this arrangement, the rules are clear: the junior partner gives up his autonomy and comes under the authority of the senior partner; he is often expected by the senior partner to be as feminine in appearance and behavior as possible, including shaving his legs, growing long hair, using a feminine nickname, and performing work perceived as feminine (laundry, cell cleaning, giving backrubs, etc.) (Donaldson 1996, 17, 20). See also the extract from Jack Abbott's prison letters in Halperin 1993 (424–25).

7. While I am primarily concerned here with the feminist literature (believing that it contains by far the most useful and insightful work on rape), it needs to be noted that many other (nonfeminist) writers also believe rape to be universal. See, e.g., Ellis 1989; Palmer 1989.

8. For listings of "rape-prone" societies, see Minturn, Grosse, and Haider 1969; Sanday 1981.

9. I carried out anthropological fieldwork in Gerai from March 1985 to February 1986 and from June 1986 to January 1987. The fieldwork was funded by an Australian National University Ph.D. scholarship and carried out under the sponsorship of Lembaga Ilmu Pengetahuan Indonesia. At the time that I was conducting my research a number of phenomena were beginning to have an impact on the community—these had the potential to effect massive changes in the areas of life discussed in this article. These phenomena included the arrival of a Malaysian timber company in the Gerai region and the increasing frequency of visits by Malay, Bugis, Chinese, and Batak timber workers to the community; the arrival of two American fundamentalist Protestant missionary families to live and proselytize in the community; and the establishment of a Catholic primary school in Gerai, resulting

in a growing tendency among parents to send their children (both male and female) to attend Catholic secondary school in a large coastal town several days' journey away.

10. The Wana, as described by Jane Atkinson (1990), provide an excellent example of a society that emphasizes sameness. Emily Martin points out that the explicit Western opposition between the "natures" of men and women is assumed to occur even at the level of the cell, with biologists commonly speaking of the egg as passive and immobile and the sperm as active and aggressive even though recent research indicates that these descriptions are erroneous and that they have led biologists to misunderstand the fertilization process (1991). See also Lloyd 1984 for an excellent account of how (often latent) conceptions of men and women as having opposed characteristics are entrenched in the history of Western philosophical thought.

11. The nurture-need dynamic (that I elsewhere refer to as the "need-share dynamic") is central to Gerai sociality. Need for others is expressed through nurturing them; such expression is the primary mark of a "good" as opposed to a "bad" person. See Helliwell (forthcoming) for a detailed discussion.

12. In this respect, Gerai is very different from, e.g., Australia or the United States, where, as Michelle Rosaldo has pointed out, aggression is linked to success, and women's constitution as lacking aggression is thus an important element of their subordination (1980, 416; see also Myers 1988, 600).

13. See Helliwell 1996, 142–43, for an example of a "violent" altercation between husband and wife.

14. I have noted elsewhere that the inside-outside distinction is a central one within this culture (Helliwell 1996).

15. While the Gerai stress on the sameness of men's and women's sexual organs seems, on the face of it, to be very similar to the situation in Renaissance Europe as described by Laqueur 1990, it is profoundly different in at least one respect: in Gerai, women's organs are not seen as emasculated versions of men's—"female penises"—as they were in Renaissance Europe. This is clearly linked to the fact that, in Gerai, as we have already seen, *people* is not synonymous with *men*, and women are not relegated to positions of emasculation or abjection, as was the case in Renaissance Europe.

16. In this respect Gerai is similar to a number of other peoples in this region (e.g., Wana, Ilongot), for whom difference between men and women is also seen as primarily a matter of the different kinds of work that each performs.

17. In Gerai, pregnancy and birth are seen not as semimystical "natural" processes, as they are for many Westerners, but simply as forms of work, linked very closely to the work of rice production.

18. Sanday 1986 makes a similar point about the absence of rape among the Minangkabau. See Helliwell (forthcoming) for a discussion of the different kinds of bad fate that can afflict a group through the actions of its individual members.

19. In Gerai, as in nearby Minangkabau (Sanday 1986), vulnerability is respected and valued rather than despised.

20. The man left the community on the night that this event occurred and went to stay for several months at a nearby timber camp. Community consensus—including the view of the woman concerned—was that he left because he was ashamed and distressed, not only as a result of having been sexually rejected by someone with whom he thought he had established a relationship but also because his adulterous behavior had become public, and he wished to avoid an airing of the details in a community moot. Consequently, I was unable to speak to him about the case. However, I did speak to several of his close male kin (including his married son), who put his point of view to me.

21. The woman in this particular case was considerably younger than the man (in fact, a member of the next generation). In such cases of considerable age disparity between sexual partners, the older partner (whether male or female) is expected to pay a fine in the form of small gifts to the younger partner, both to initiate the liaison and to enable its continuance. Such a fine rectifies any spiritual imbalance that may result from the age imbalance and hence makes it safe for the relationship to proceed. Contrary to standard Western assumptions, older women appear to pay such fines to younger men as often as older men pay them to younger women (although it was very difficult to obtain reliable data on this question, since most such liaisons are adulterous and therefore highly secretive). While not significant in terms of value (women usually receive such things as soap and shampoo, while men receive tobacco or cigarettes), these gifts are crucial in their role of "rebalancing" the relationship. It would be entirely erroneous to subsume this practice under the rubric of "prostitution."

22. Because Gerai adults usually sleep surrounded by their children, and with other adults less than a meter or two away (although the latter are usually inside different mosquito nets), sexual intercourse is almost always carried out very quietly.

23. In claiming that "sexual relations cannot be quiet," the woman was playing on the expression "be quiet" (meaning to have sexual intercourse) to make the point that while adulterous sex may need to be even "quieter" than legitimate sex, it should not be so "quiet" as to preclude dialogue between the two partners. Implicit here is the notion that in the absence of such dialogue, sex will lack the requisite mutuality.

24. Foucault, e.g., once suggested (in a debate in French reprinted in *La Folie Encerclée* [see Plaza 1980]) that an effective way to deal with rape would be to decriminalize it in order to "desexualize" it. For feminist critiques of his suggestion, see Plaza 1980; de Lauretis 1987; Woodhull 1988.

REFERENCES

Atkinson, Jane Monnig. 1990. "How Gender Makes a Difference in Wana Society." In *Power and Difference: Gender in Island Southeast Asia,* ed. Jane Monnig Atkinson and Shelly Errington, 59–93. Stanford, Calif.: Stanford University Press.

Bart, Pauline B., and Patricia H. O'Brien. 1985. *Stopping Rape: Successful Survival Strategies.* New York: Pergamon.

Bell, Diane. 1983. *Daughters of the Dreaming.* Melbourne: McPhee Gribble.

Brison, Susan J. 1993. "Surviving Sexual Violence: A Philosophical Perspective." *Journal of Social Philosophy* 24(1): 5–22.

Butler, Judith. 1990. *Gender Trouble: Feminism and the Subversion of Identity.* New York and London: Routledge.

———. 1993. *Bodies That Matter: On the Discursive Limits of "Sex."* New York and London: Routledge.

Clark, Anna. 1987. *Women's Silence, Men's Violence: Sexual Assault in England, 1770–1845.* London and New York: Pandora.

de Lauretis, Teresa. 1987. "The Violence of Rhetoric: Considerations on Representation and Gender." In *Technologies of Gender: Essays on Theory, Film and Fiction,* 31–50. Bloomington and Indianapolis: Indiana University Press.

Donaldson, Stephen. 1996. "The Deal behind Bars." *Harper's* (August): 17–20.

Dworkin, Andrea. 1987. *Intercourse.* London: Secker & Warburg.

Ellis, Lee. 1989. *Theories of Rape: Inquiries into the Causes of Sexual Aggression.* New York: Hemisphere.

Errington, Shelly. 1990. "Recasting Sex, Gender, and Power: A Theoretical and Regional Overview." In *Power and Difference: Gender in Island Southeast Asia,* ed. Jane Monnig Atkinson and Shelly Errington, 1–58. Stanford, Calif.: Stanford University Press.

Foucault, Michel. 1978. *The History of Sexuality.* Vol. 1, *An Introduction.* Harmondsworth: Penguin.

Halperin, David M. 1993. "Is There a History of Sexuality?" In *The Lesbian and Gay Studies Reader,* ed. Henry Abelove, Michele Barale, and David M. Halperin, 416–31. New York and London: Routledge.

Helliwell, Christine 1993. "Women in Asia: Anthropology and the Study of Women." In *Asia's Culture Mosaic,* ed. Grant Evans, 260–86. Singapore: Prentice Hall.

———. 1995. "Autonomy as Natural Equality: Inequality in 'Egalitarian' Societies." *Journal of the Royal Anthropological Institute* 1(2): 359–75.

———. 1996. "Space and Sociality in a Dayak Longhouse." In *Things as They Are: New Directions in Phenomenological Anthropology,* ed. Michael Jackson, 128–48. Bloomington and Indianapolis: Indiana University Press.

———. Forthcoming. *"Never Stand Alone": A Study of Borneo Sociality.* Williamsburg: Borneo Research Council.

Laqueur, Thomas. 1990. *Making Sex: Body and Gender from the Greeks to Freud.* Cambridge, Mass., and London: Harvard University Press.

Leacock, Eleanor. 1978. "Women's Status in Egalitarian Society: Implications for Social Evolution." *Current Anthropology* 19(2): 247–75.

Lloyd, Genevieve. 1984. *The Man of Reason: "Male" and "Female" in Western Philosophy.* London: Methuen.

MacKinnon, Catharine A. 1989a. "Sexuality, Pornography, and Method: 'Pleasure under Patriarchy.'" *Ethics* 99: 314–46.

———. 1989b. *Toward a Feminist Theory of the State.* Cambridge, Mass., and London: Harvard University Press.

Madigan, Lee, and Nancy C. Gamble. 1991. *The Second Rape: Society's Continued Betrayal of the Victim.* New York: Lexington.

Marcus, Julie. 1992. *A World of Difference: Islam and Gender Hierarchy in Turkey.* Sydney: Allen & Unwin.

Marcus, Sharon. 1992. "Fighting Bodies, Fighting Words: A Theory and Politics of Rape Prevention." In *Feminists Theorize the Political,* ed. Judith Butler and Joan W. Scott, 385–403. New York and London: Routledge.

Martin, Emily 1991. "The Egg and the Sperm: How Science Has Constructed a Romance Based on Stereotypical Male-Female Roles." *Signs: Journal of Women in Culture and Society 16*(3): 485–501.

Minturn, Leigh, Martin Grosse, and Santoah Haider. 1969. "Cultural Patterning of Sexual Beliefs and Behaviour." *Ethnology 8*(3): 301–18.

Moore, Henrietta L. 1994. *A Passion for Difference: Essays in Anthropology and Gender.* Cambridge and Oxford: Polity.

Myers, Fred R. 1988. "The Logic and Meaning of Anger among Pintupi Aborigines." *Man 23*(4): 589–610.

Palmer, Craig. 1989. "Is Rape a Cultural Universal? A Re-Examination of the Ethnographic Data." *Ethnology 28*(1): 1–16.

Plaza, Monique. 1980. "Our Costs and Their Benefits." *m/f* 4: 28–39.

Rosaldo, Michelle Z. 1980. "The Use and Abuse of Anthropology: Reflections on Feminism and Cross-Cultural Understanding." *Signs 5*(3): 389–417.

Sanday, Peggy Reeves. 1981. "The Socio-Cultural Context of Rape: A Cross-Cultural Study." *Journal of Social Issues 37*(4): 5–27.

———. 1986. "Rape and the Silencing of the Feminine." In *Rape,* ed. Sylvana Tomaselli and Roy Porter, 84–101. Oxford: Blackwell.

———. 1990a. "Androcentric and Matrifocal Gender Representations in Minangkabau Ideology." In *Beyond the Second Sex: New Directions in the Anthropology of Gender,* ed. Peggy Reeves Sanday and Ruth Gallagher Goodenough, 141–68. Philadelphia: University of Pennsylvania Press.

———. 1990b. *Fraternity Gang Rape: Sex, Brotherhood, and Privilege on Campus.* New York and London: New York University Press.

Strathern, Marilyn. 1988. *The Gender of the Gift: Problems with Women and Problems with Society in Melanesia.* Berkeley: University of California Press.

Tsing, Anna Lowenhaupt. 1993. *In the Realm of the Diamond Queen: Marginality in an Out-of-the-Way Place.* Princeton, N.J.: Princeton University Press.

Woodhull, Winifred. 1988. "Sexuality, Power, and the Question of Rape." In *Feminism and Foucault: Reflections on Resistance,* ed. Irene Diamond and Lee Quinby, 167–76. Boston: Northeastern University Press.

Introduction to Reading 12

Dredge Byung'chu Käng is an anthropologist who conducted extensive fieldwork in Thailand between 2004 and 2011. His informants were *kathoey/gay* Thais as well as their family and friends. The traditional Thai gender/sexuality system consisted of three genders/sexes, including *kathoey*, a general term referring to all three-gender categories. However, the autocolonial, modern Thai state has promoted a Western heteronormative, two-and-only-two gender system and monogamous marriage. The efforts of the state have failed. Käng's research shows that a complex set of historical and contemporary forces have instead produced five key gender categories. Käng uses the term *genderscapes* to emphasize the possibilities for various genders, and he explores the multifaceted nature of the Thai *phet* system.

1. Why does Käng emphasize the public performance of gender and nonnormative gender presentation rather than sexuality?

2. Käng states that the categories of woman and man are not natural, nor do they require heterosexuality. How does this factor play out in the Thai genderscape?

3. What is the relationship between *kathoey* and *gay* in Thailand?

4. Discuss the conditions that may contribute to opportunities for female same-sex relationships in Thailand.

Conceptualizing Thai Genderscapes

Transformation and Continuity in the Thai Sex/Gender System

Dredge Byung'chu Käng

Historical Background and Theoretical Framework

Transformations in the Thai Sex/Gender System

Thailand is the only country in Southeast Asia that circumvented direct colonization. Without a colonial power, in either direct or indirect senses, Thailand is characterized by its semicolonial status (Jackson 2010). Yet, colonial history is important in understanding Thai gender/sexuality because the threat of foreign encroachment and subsequent nationalist modernization projects reformulated gender and produced unexpected consequences in gender relations. In part, Siam avoided external rule by proffering and employing autocolonial practices to demonstrate its *siwilai* (civilized) status (Winichakul 1994, 2000, 2010). While it would seem that these effects are more indirect since Thailand was never colonized, the consolidation of monarchical power and colonial impulse in the pursuit of *siwilai* actually heightened the ability of the state to recast cultural conventions. Arguably, autocolonial governmentality in Thailand was more direct and stronger a force of change than that imposed in its colonized neighbors by European rule. An intact absolute monarchy followed by a constitutional monarchy provided greater ability of the state to model and legislate gender norms than was possible in the colonies. For Thailand to remain free from Western domination, the population was subjected to new forms of rule (Connors 2007). . . .

The project of modernization contrasts the traditional Thai system of three sexes with a system that promotes standardization into two gender-normative sexes ideally engaged in monogamous marriage (Loos 2006). Semicolonialism imposed sexual dimorphism and heterosexual matrices that become refashioned in the Thai case of *siwilai*—but this state process of de-androgynizing local genders is a Foucauldian (1990) disciplinary mechanism that is productive of new kinds of thirds, which may or may not be ambiguous, since polarizing binary sex makes their transgressions more apparent. The early twentieth-century interventions, particularly those during the Field Marshal Plaek Phibunsongkhram era, were particularly virulent, legislating gender-specific hair, dress, and behavior (e.g., long hair and pantyhose for women, husbands kissing wives) that would be recognizable to Westerners (van Esterik 2000; Barmé 2002). These changes were not uniformly adopted, with urban elites being most influenced. Van Esterik (2000) notes how working-class women avoided and resisted Thai bureaucratic pressures to conform to ideals of Western femininity. Besides European encroachment and subsequent attempts at modernization, rapid pulses of gender and sexual transformation also followed other key historical, economic, and technological events such as the Vietnam/American War, AIDS, the Asian financial crisis,

From Käng, Dredge Byung'chu. 2014. "Conceptualizing Thai Genderscapes." In *Contemporary Socio-Cultural and Political Perspectives in Thailand*, edited by Pranee Liamputtong, pp. 409–429. New York: Springer.

and the availability of birth control, hormones, and sexual reassignment and cosmetic surgeries. Furthermore, cultural influence from the migration of Chinese immigrants has affected gender relations, particularly among the merchant class (Bao 2005).

A new era of development post-WWII increasingly drove capitalist modes of production and consumption in Thailand. These came to be inhabited under the skin and combined with new discourses around economic restructuring, consumerism, development, modern identity, and cosmopolitanism that produced a post-Fordist system of flexible gender identities that modified historical forms but whose contours vary by subject position and moral valence. Involvement with Vietnam as an American ally greatly expanded sex tourism in Thailand and helped develop Thailand's infrastructure and economy (Bishop and Robinson 1998; Jeffrey 2002). Ironically, the expansion of the middle class made possible by prostitution has increased stigma for sex workers among those eager to make novel class distinctions. More recently, the Asian financial crisis and the subsequent recovery have both produced anti-Western sentiment and greater political, economic, and cultural integration with other Southeast and East Asian nations.

Thai biopolitical intervention in the production of modern sex is thus the basis for the production of the current genderscapes. The autocolonial intervention rearticulates a newly localized sex/gender system. Discursive governmentality is the catalyst to create this shift, yet cannot fully account for the variation present. Its erasure of former gender conceptualizations and reconstruction of a system in line with modern Western sexual dimorphism remains incomplete. In fact, hybrid resistances, cosmopolitan engagements, and everyday practices exceed the limitations placed on sex forms. The microstructural adjustments in the performance of gender also provide a degree of fluidity that cannot be accounted for in taxonomic models of the Thai sex/gender system. Nevertheless, these mundane performances are enabled and constrained via socio-moral understandings of appearance. Here,

I turn to a theoretical elaboration of these additional processes.

Globalization and Localization of Gender Transformations

. . . I refer to genderscapes as a sex/gender system, a culturally elaborated mode of inhabiting reproductive differences in relation to subsistence, kinship, politics, and so forth (Rubin 1975). While I agree with Rubin (1984) that gender and sexuality should be separated analytically, they are emically intertwined and mutually constituted in Thailand and elsewhere. With the exception of masculine gay men, Thais typically do not distinguish gender and sexuality in their own lives. Sexuality is generally neither necessary nor sufficient to transform one's gender. Thus, following Jackson (2003) and Sinnott (2004), I conceptualize gender and sexuality within the purview of genderscapes as autonomous but related domains of a sex/gender order. Eroticism is corollary to but not necessarily derivative of gender, requiring relational rather than independent analysis.

Conceptualization as a -scape reveals greater possibilities for various genders. Modeling gender in a three-dimensional space rather than as a dualism opens up crosses, unities, mixes, alternatives, and liminalities beyond male-to-female and female-to-male transgenders. Incorporating time, the nodes of gender can shift and need not be fully formed to be recognized. I thus benefit from Herdt's conceptualization of third sexes, although I do not go as far as arguing that the ontology of third sexes requires a "stable social role, that can be inhabited—marking off a clear social status position, rights and duties, with indications for the transmission of corporeal and incorporeal property and rights" (Herdt 1996: 60). Instead, I embrace dynamism within the realm of habituated practice (Bourdieu 1990), as key nodes in the system help to anchor genderscapes. The performance or practice of gender allows for their ongoing rearticulation; yet the possibilities are always shaped through ritualization and regulatory discourses (Butler 2004; Morris 1995).

Currently, I argue for five major gender nodes, which exist in relation to one another based on anatomical differences, presentation of self, socioeconomic roles, desire for certain others, and so on. Each of these nodes has spin-offs or subdivisions, creating a large number of possible categories. However, they coalesce around five forms with significant ontological fixity in public everyday life. These are realized through the repetition of symbolic processes and everyday practices which make them appear to be real and part of the natural and hierarchical order of things (Bourdieu 1990). These processes include the presentation of a gendered self in daily life as well as the dissemination and reinstantiation of these practices via media representations. Face and appearance are key to Thai social norms and the regulation of behavior and propriety (Mulder 1997), especially gender performance and its formation (Barmé 2002). Surfaces (van Esterik 2000) and the gaze (Morris 1997) are technologies for the regulation of Thai gender and sexual relations. Appearances act as a mechanism to discipline idealized social forms, irrespective of interiority, through the fear of losing face. Within this public "regime of images" (Jackson 2004), private sexual practices are sequestered while gender presentation is brought to the fore. Therefore, public enactments of gender variance become highlighted for their difference at the same time sexuality can, and "should," remain unknown. In sum, the images one projects about the self are more important than identity in public interactions. Such exteriorities are not expected to access an essential truth. Furthermore, the Thai concept of *phet* frames sexuality as an extension of gender. Thus, my focus in constructing Thai genderscapes emphasizes the public performance of gender, and nonnormative gender presentation, rather than sexuality.

THAI GENDERSCAPES

Kathoey: a male-to-female transgender person, typically engaging in or desiring relationships with heterosexual men, irrespective of operative status

Gay: a male, masculine or feminine, who engages in or desires same-sex relationships with other males

Tom: a masculine woman who engages in or desires same-sex relationships with a woman

Dee: a feminine woman who engages in same-sex relationships with *tom*

Contemporary Thai Gender and Sexuality

. . . Every day Thai does not distinguish between sex, gender, and sexuality (*phet*). Jackson and Sullivan (1999: 5) suggest that "within Thai discourse, gay and *kathoey* are not distinguished as a sexuality and a gender, respectively. Rather, gay, *kathoey*, together with 'man' (*phu-chai*), 'woman' (*phu-ying*), and the lesbian identities *tom* and *dee*, are collectively labelled as different varieties of *phet*." Academics use specialized terms to differentiate sex, gender, sexuality, and other aspects of *phet*, but these are not commonly understood. Activists also have developed specialized terms. In the last decade, the development of HIV services for males who have sex with males and transgender women has also elaborated new specialized terms, often derived from international NGO, public health, and human rights discourses. In the general operations of *phet*, sex, gender, and sexuality are bound up in metaphorical packages which discourage dissonance between gender presentation and a presumably gendered desire rather than between sex and gender.

The multifaceted nature of *phet* has been conceptualized in two primary ways in the literature: a Westernization model and an indigenization model. In the former, modern Western understandings of gender/sexuality usurp and supplant Thai ones. In the latter, new sexual identities are ensconced within the Thai *phet* system. Morris (1994) contrasts the traditional three-sex system with a modern four-sexuality system. She argues that the Thai ternary of man, woman, and *kathoey* is increasingly being replaced by four modern Western sexualities based on the two binaries of male:female and homosexual:heterosexual, which create the four positions of female-hetero-sexual, female-homosexual, male-heterosexual, and male-homosexual. According to Morris (1994), these systems coexist but are incommensurable, and thus the "modern" system is replacing the "traditional" one. Similarly, van Esterik (2000: 218–219) states that "the influence of international gay culture including new media (magazines and videos) may be increasing the numbers of category labels, but is breaking down the diversity in the Thai gender system to stress identity based on object choice, heterosexual or homosexual."

In contrast, Jackson (2000) and Sinnott (2004) argue that Western sexual identities are indigenized through local conceptualizations of gender, thereby multiplying gender categories. Jackson (2003) uses the term "eroticized genders" and Sinnott (2004) uses the term "gendered sexualities." They emphasize that sexual desire is an extension of gender identification rather than separate domains of gender and sexual orientation. Based on the historical analysis of the Thai press and academic texts, Jackson (2000: 412) asserts that there are at least ten gender terms commonly used in contemporary Thai discourse. He charts how the three categories of (1) man, (2) *kathoey* (transgender), and (3) woman have proliferated into ten categories from the 1960s to the 1980s: (1a) man, (1b) *seua bai* (male bisexual); (2a1) *gay king*, (2a2) *gay queen*, (2b1) *kathoey*, (2b2) *kathoey plaeng phet* (transsexual), (2b3) *khon sorng phet* (hermaphrodite), (2c) *tom*; (3a) *dee* and (3b) woman, respectively. These terms refer to seven common *phet* categories: "man," *gay king*, *gay queen*, *kathoey*, *tom*, *dee*, and "woman" (414).

Yet, the categories of salience that I documented in everyday talk are those that are visibly distinguishable by outward appearance: man, effeminate *gay*, *kathoey*, *tom*, and woman. I want to note that the categories of woman and man are not natural, preexisting forms. Nor do they require heterosexuality. For instance, a woman can be a *dee* or a man can have a female, *kathoey*, or male partners while maintaining a gender-normative status. Additionally, the range

of acceptable demeanor, dress, and other gender markers is quite wide and has historically shifted. All Thai genders are modern formations that have undergone tremendous transformation over the last century. However, for lack of space, here I focus on individuals who would be considered gender variant and update the contemporary literature.

In Thai, *kathoey* is a general term encompassing all third-gender categories, theoretically referencing all nonnormative gender presentations and sexualities beyond heterosexual male and female. But in practice, *kathoey* seldom refers to female-bodied individuals, regardless of their gender expression. In cosmopolitan Bangkok, among the middle classes, *kathoey* only refers to male to female transgender persons, that is, transgender women (Jackson 2000; Sinnott 2004). *Gay* are typically offended when others refer to them as *kathoey*, although the term is used for in-group joking and accepted when outside Bangkok, as the locals are considered not to know better. People identified as *kathoey* may also be offended by the term as it can be used as a slur. There are numerous words that are considered more polite or respectful. Thus, if a person who is not *kathoey* is in the presence of one, she might use a term like *sao-praphet-sorng* (second category woman). Thai academics often refer to gender "fluidity," as identities follow a developmental trajectory and situational positioning. Witchayanee (2008) differentiates between "half and half" (those who have either breast implants or neo-vaginas but not both) and "fully transformed" transgender sex workers. Pramoj Na Ayuttaya (2008) identifies five types of *kathoey*: postoperative transgender, preoperative transgender, drag queen, penetrating girl (active in sexual intercourse), and those who live part time as transgender and part time as men.

In February 2010, the term *phu-ying-kham-phet* (transsexual woman) was introduced by Nok Yollada to differentiate a transsexual (who desires or has had gender surgery) from a transvestite. Around the same time, the Rainbow Sky

Association of Thailand, a sexual diversity NGO primarily funded to provide HIV prevention services, started using the term *sao-thi-ji* (transgender woman), borrowing from the English abbreviation "TG." However, most *kathoey* use the term among themselves or simply use *sao* (young woman). "Ladyboy" refers to *kathoey* who are cabaret performers, beauty pageant contestants, and bar-based sex workers. Some *kathoey* consider "ladyboy" distasteful as it upholds the stereotype that they are prostitutes and thus inherently indecent and criminal. *Kathoey* are also differentiated by their operative status. But, many *kathoey* consider it offensive to be asked whether they have had sexual reassignment or gender confirmation surgery because they feel their identity does not need to follow their genitalia. While there has been a proliferation of terms around male-to-female transgenderism, I suggest that they coalesce around one commonly understood gender form: *kathoey*.

For *kathoey*, transgenderism is made visible via sartorial practice, cosmetic use, bodily comportment, and language (Thai uses gendered particles that mark the speaker as male or female). Bisexual men, who are labeled based on sexual behavior rather than desire or gender presentation, are generally said to be gay, but ashamed (*ap-ai*) to identify themselves. There is no equivalent term for a bisexual woman. *Dee* and masculine *gay* express gender normativity. Thus, *dee* are only discernible when with their *tom* partners and masculine *gay* are said not to "show" (*sadaeng-ok*). Importantly, as public display of affection is considered impolite, nonnormative sexuality is generally not apparent while nonnormative gender presentation is. Sexuality is understood as private and thus not subject to social condemnation. However, for gender nonnormative individuals, sexuality is presumed as an extension of gender presentation. Thus, only effeminate *gay*, *kathoey*, and *tom* noticeably do not conform to gender norms; and among them, *kathoey* are the most stigmatized. Though, with the growing use of surgery and other medical technologies, *kathoey* visibility is decreasing, as they increasingly pass as women.

Gay are further characterized by age and effeminacy (*tut*, sissy or queen; *taeo*, sissy; *sao-sao*, girly; *i-aep*, a feminine person who presents masculinely in public). These terms are usually not labels of self-identity but are used as insults or for in-group joking. Use of the terms "*king*" and "*queen*" in relation to *gay* is now considered passé (although the terms have been taken up by lesbians in *lesking* and *lesqueen*), perhaps because gender presentation has become more independent of preferred sexual positioning (*baep*), and *baep* is often flexible depending on the partner. *Gay* rather matter-of-factly disclose their *baep* (*ruk*, penetrate; *rap*, receive; *bot*, versatile; *salap*, reciprocate or alternate) as Thais would their age. These are among the first questions one might be asked upon meeting a stranger in a gay venue or online. However, *baep* does not constitute a public identity.

Along the continuum of *kathoey-gay*, distinction making occurs at both ends (see also Jackson 1997). Masculine *gay* refer to effeminate *gay* as *tut*, *kathoey*, or *i-aep*, individuals who would be *kathoey* given the opportunity. Postoperative transsexuals differentiate themselves from those who have not had surgery. They say they have already become women and often assume they pass (even when they do not), confident in the alignment of their essentially female mind and body. At the same time, there is fluidity between *gay* and *kathoey* categories, both in identity and sartorial practice. *Kathoey-noi* (little *kathoey* or just a little transgendered), for instance, use makeup like women but dress in men's clothing. *Kathoey-noi* are not transgender; they are not *gay;* they are an in-between category. *Kathoey-noi* are not uncommon. They are generally young, around 16–26 and often said to be transitioning into a *kathoey* lifestyle. There are, however, adult males who fit into this pattern. Some *kathoey* become *gay* and vice versa, although the former conversion is more prevalent. As *kathoey-kathoey*, *gay-kathoey*, and effeminate *gay* pairings become more common, the disgust associated with similar-gender coupling is diminishing. New terms such as *sao-siap* (penetrating girl, referring to *kathoey* who are active in anal intercourse) and *tom-gay* (a *tom*, masculine female, in a relationship with another *tom*) describe variations that incorporate putatively discordant gender expression and sexual practice. These changes point to the breakdown of the heterogender sexual matrix (Peletz 2006), in which only sex between individuals of "opposite" genders is socially acceptable.

In English, we say "gay man," with "gay" sexuality (an adjective) modifying "man" (a noun). But in Thai, "*gay*" is already a noun so that one is either "*gay*" or "man." Thus, one can say "I am a *gay*" or "I am a man." However, these are not exclusive categories and there is a recognition that sexual desire does not have to follow gender identification. For example, one can say the two in sequence, as in *phom pen ke; phom pen maen* to emphasize that one is a masculine gay man. Bee, who is *gay*, once told me: *phom mai pen ke; phom pen maen* (literally "I am not gay; I am a man") to stress that he does not see himself as effeminate at all, since the term "*gay*" can invoke effeminacy, as in *ke map koen pay* (too *gay*). In the statement *mai pen ruk, mai pen rap; pen ke* (He is not top/penetrator or bottom/receiver; he is *gay*), the term is referencing sexual versatility. Thus, the term "*gay*" is polysemic in everyday use, contextually referencing effeminacy, masculinity, or sexual versatility. These examples show that while gender and sexuality are linked, they can be distinguished from one another. At the same time, they are conflated in everyday life.

Phet terms are not isomorphic with identities. Neologisms and variants do not necessarily constitute new forms; they can be situationally employed or used to label others and make fine distinctions. Masculine *gay* often refer to themselves as *maen-maen* (very manly, like a man), although this is more a descriptor of gender presentation than an identity. Similarly, the term *me-tho sek-chuan* (metrosexual), while defined in Thai Wikipedia and in many lifestyle magazines as a heterosexual man who appears gay based on his interest in fitness, fashion, and grooming, is typically used in speech to refer to someone who is *gay* or closeted. Indeed, this *phu-chai saiphan mai* (new breed of man) category was popularized by the film *Metrosexual* (2006, directed by Yongyoot Thongkongtoon), in which a group of women tries to prove to their friend that her fiancé, who is too perfect to be heterosexual, must be *gay*. The Thai title is *Kaeng chani kap i-aep* (Gang of Girls and the Closet Case). Metrosexuality is marked visibility by being too perfect a man to be straight, just as *kathoey* beauty contestants are often said to possess *owoe-bioti* (over beauty) in comparison to women. Many new gender expressions are derived from films, songs, and Internet sites, although their usage is typically short-lived and the terms do not constitute identities, though they may be variations upon them.

Female-bodied gender forms are highly visible but have less social presence in Thai society and media (Käng 2011). Like female same-sex sexuality in other parts of the world, it is limited by income differentials, safety concerns, and social proscriptions around propriety. Additionally, female same-sex relationships can also be less challenging to the sex/gender order. Many Thai women are able to circumvent the issue of respectability as being in a same-sex relationship can be morally less damaging than a heterosexual one (Sinnott 2004). In particular, one can avoid unwanted pregnancy and the contamination associated with the loss of virginity. This, however, is more applicable to young women and those from wealthier backgrounds. Compared to women in other regions of the world, Thai women also have relatively high employment and financial independence, allowing many of them to live independently of family and forestall marriage (Mills 1999; Muecke 1984). Thailand has the highest rate of single women in Asia and one of the lowest birthrates in the world. These factors perhaps provide more opportunity for female same-sex relationships than in other geographic areas.

Tom-dee (the terms are derived from the English "tomboy" and "lady") couples are ubiquitous and easily identifiable in mainstream commercial venues such as shopping malls (Wilson 2007). Suburban malls have stores targeted to *tom*, selling men's clothes in smaller sizes (in contrast to stores targeting *kathoey* that provide women's clothes in larger sizes). I suggest that *tom-dee* couples are actually more visible than gay men in Thai public space, where they become legible by learning their social codes. Female couples can be seen holding hands, one sporting short hair and men's clothes, the other with long hair and women's clothes. Sinnott (2004: 142) has referred to the public conspicuousness of these relationships in terms of "visual explicitness and verbal silence." The couples are discernible but unremarkable. Women are also highly active in Thai activism around sexual diversity, with organizations such as Anjaree (founded in 1986) among the most vocal advocates for sexuality rights. However, their work is often overshadowed by an infusion of international HIV prevention funding for *gay* and *kathoey* in the mid-2000s, which has been mobilized to promote the acceptance of sexual minorities and their human rights more broadly.

In *tom-dee* relationships, it is only the former who can be considered misgendered. *Toms* are masculine women. They are biological females attracted to women, but this attraction to women is an extension of their masculinity. Their gender does not match their sex, though their sexuality can be seen as an extension of their gender. *Dees* are their female partners. But, as gender normative or "ordinary women," *dee* identity becomes relevant in relation to *tom*. That is, *dee* are labeled as counterparts of *tom* rather than as another category of women, often being temporary members of the *tom-dee* community (Sinnott 2004). Thus, while *tom* represent a more or less stable *phet* identity in contemporary Thailand, *dee* have a more liminal position. They exist primarily in association with *tom* rather than as an independent category. *Dee* remain peripheral to the nodes of *tom* and woman in Thai genderscapes.

Dee inhabit a relational and situational identity (Sinnott 2007). Sexuality can be tied to temporal gender positions in the life cycle: what is appropriate in youth may not be so in adulthood. Engaging in sexual acts inappropriate for one's status can modify ascribed gender positions. Yet, being *dee* is considered relatively unproblematic. Many women, often married, have told me, without remorse or shame: "I was a *dee* before." From a Western perspective, *dee* is a lesbian sexual identity, women who desire or engage in sexual relations with other women. However, gender difference is more important to *tom-dee* couplings than sexual identity (Sinnott 2004). From the perspective of Thai *phet*, as a feminine woman attracted to the masculinity of another woman, their desire is homosexual but heterogender (Peletz 2006) and thus normatively paired.

In the alternate genders of *tom* and *kathoey*, blending of sex/gender attributes is a more typical feature than the disavowal of a biological sex and the recreation of a newly contrasting gendered persona. *Tom* maintain many characteristics of women (e.g., being good caretakers) as *kathoey* maintain many characteristics of men (e.g., being sexually assertive). Some *kathoey* are more like transsexuals in the classic sense of seeing themselves as an "opposite" sex, and this is essential to the new conceptualization of *phu-ying-kham-phet* (transsexual woman), literally a woman who has crossed sex. But, this is generally not the case for *tom* who see themselves as masculine women rather than as men. Sinnott (2004: 22) refers to *tom* "in the feminine form ('she,' 'her') to reflect the common understanding among Thais that *toms* are female, and although they are masculine, they are distinct from males."

Five Genders?

The proposal of *five phet* categories is reminiscent of Davies (2010) five genders among the Bugis of Sulawesi, Indonesia. Yet, the sex/gender system in Thailand does not follow the same pattern of crossings (i.e., female, female to male, male/female androgyny, male to female, and male). Nor are the spiritual aspects of *bissu* unity at play.[1] The five gender forms I propose are similar to the seven *phet* categories Jackson

(2000) states are commonly described in Thai literature. However, rather than representing the categories like a phylogenetic tree, which emphasizes the historical transformations of the categories, I propose a multidimensional -scape. On the one hand, this formation provides greater flexibility in the enactments of gender as they are practiced in everyday life at a point in time. On the other, a -scape model shows the layered relationships between nodes and can shift based on historical transformations, one's social positioning, or ideological perspective.

With the proposed five gender nodes, I have not included *dee*. As Sinnott (2004: 9) notes, "masculine women have long been evident in the Thai system of sex and gender, but the linguistic and social marking of feminine women who are partners of masculine women creates a new and precarious field of identity." Sinnott likens *dee* to the gender-normative partners of *kathoey*, who are simply categorized as men. As women who are feminine in dress, comportment, and speech, they are not marked as gender different. Most *dee* do not refer to themselves as *dee* but as "women." *Dee* is more frequently a label that *tom* use for their feminine partners. Ploy, a neighbor of mine who ran a noodle shop, talking to me about her brother's transition from *kathoey* to *gay,* stated matter-of-factly: "Well, I was a *dee* before I was with him," nodding her head in the direction of the unmarried father of their daughter. Many other women told me that they had been in relationships with women when younger, but typically did not refer to the relationship as *tom-dee.* Instead, the relationship was with another *phu-ying* (girl/ woman). The expectation among *tom* is that *dee* will eventually leave *tom* for a man. Similarly, a "real" man is anticipated to leave a *kathoey* for a "real" woman in order to have a family, or keep the *kathoey* as a mistress. A *dee* is thus generally considered *tham-mada* (ordinary or normal) but could shift positions within genderscapes, for example, if one emphasizes sexual object choice over gender presentation.

Additionally, I have not differentiated nodes for masculine and feminine *gay,* which can be thought of as two different categories based on different gender presentation, public visibility, and sense of self. Like *dee*, masculine *gay* are gender normative in presentation or often hypermasculine. However, unlike *dee*, *gay* have a strong sense of identity based on their sexual desires. Sinnott (2004: 29) suggests that "the category 'gay' has introduced a third possible kind of masculinity positioned between normative 'men' and *kathoeys*, in that gay men are masculine yet desire other masculine men as sexual partners. . . . [Masculine gay men] are not highly visible, in that they do not match the perception that gayness equals effeminacy— they simply fall off the radar for many Thais." Masculine *gay* break the rules of the hetero-gender matrix; they represent a singularity where the traditional three-sex system and the modern four-sexuality systems intersect in Thai genderscapes. Of course, feminine *gay* would provide a fourth male position. Yet, while only the feminine *gay* is visibly identifiable, both masculine and feminine *gay* have a sexual identity that is often an important component of self-concept and lifestyle. They also conceive of themselves as a community using shared social space and having a common identity and transnational ties with other gay communities around the world. The terms *king* and *queen* are rarely used and tend to reference sexual position more than an identity. Thus, while focusing on the appearance of gender-variant performance, which would exclude masculine *gay,* who are relatively invisible, I combine them here as a single node. Indeed, no genderscape nodes are homogenous or consistent. Yet, the gay node has a particularly two-faced characteristic. As Sinnott (2004: 30) notes, "an important difference between gay men and *dees* is that *dees* are only *dees* in relation to a *tom.* The masculine female gives the *dee* her identity, whereas gay men take pains to distinguish their community and identities from *kathoey* identity." *Gay, tom,* and *kathoey* are more like what Foucault (1990) might refer to as a "species" with discursive and ontological fixity. They all have elaborated subcultures with specific social spaces and organization.

At the same time, elaborating gender categories as nodes in the Thai genderscapes acknowledges the variation within each in relation to the others.

Social Position and Ideological Stance

Class, education, geography, and *phet* identification also affect how people conceptualize gender/sexuality categories. In Thailand, geographical regions and urban/rural distinctions are very important and highly associated with class differences. Central Thais, who are culturally and linguistically dominant, conceive of Northerners as "soft." The women are thought of as more gracile, polite, and lighter skinned. The men are similarly effeminized. Southern men, by contrast, are considered rough, hard, and dark. They are also portrayed as more patriarchal as a result of Islamic conversion or interaction. Northeasterners are often said not to be Thai and, instead, referred to as Lao, and therefore, less developed. For many Central Thais, Bangkok is the *only city*. All other areas are considered *tang-changwat* (provincial, upcountry) or, less politely, *ban-nok* (the boonies). While rural populations consume the same national media as produced in the capital, interpretations are filtered through their daily experience, which includes the out-migration of many young people, including the gender variant. There is also less access to the consumer products that allow for greater gender differentiation.

One of my best friends, Wan, who is a *kathoey* in her mid-30s from *Isan* (the Northeast region), often makes the statement: "I was the first *kathoey* in my village." This assertion struck me as strange because I imagined there must have been *kathoey* who preceded her since there is a history of *kathoey* in Thailand. I have traveled with her to her home village three times, and people have confirmed that she was the first *kathoey* that they can remember. Before, villagers were quite hostile to *kathoey*, until she and a few others showed themselves as *kathoey*, dressing and living as transgender women.[2] Now there are approximately ten adult *kathoey* in her village, one of whom was married to a man in 2009 in a day-long celebration attended by several hundred guests. Both sets of parents gave speeches about their happiness during the wedding. There are also several *kathoey* children. When I asked a mother of a 10-year-old boy about when the child started expressing herself as a girl, the mother replied: "Since birth. When she/he started talking, she/he used *kha*" (the female polite particle).[3] But, this increased acceptance has only occurred since around 2000. Wan only began living as a *kathoey* after the death of her father, who was a respected village leader. Others soon followed and transgenderism became a visible part of village life. Thus, Wan feels that the situation for *kathoey* is improving rapidly.

Wan believes that while there is a strong inclination toward being *kathoey*, one can choose to be *gay* instead. When we met with a 16-year-old at a temple fair who was cross-dressing, Wan immediately went to speak with her. "What are you?" she asked. "Are you like me or him [nodding toward me]?" She went on to ask whether her father accepted her cross-dressing, which the young *kathoey* affirmed. She then said: "You have to choose whether you will be like me or him. If you choose to be like me, life will be harder." Wan counseled the youth, acknowledging the fluidity between *kathoey* and *gay* as well as the different opportunities associated with these life trajectories.

Wan notes that the number of *gay* in her village is increasing, although their normative masculinity renders them relatively invisible and uncontroversial. Villagers simply refer to men and women; the distinction between the two is based on outward presentation. However, when someone is verbally identified as *gay*, the reaction is often: "I didn't know she/he was a woman." Such comments show that villagers perceive sexuality in terms of a gendered desire that should be an extension of their gender presentation. For most villagers, a *gay* is someone who appears like a man, but is actually a woman based on their *jit-jai* (mind/heart or inner being), their desire for male partners. One of Wan's friends, who used to be *kathoey* when living in the provinces but has since become *gay* after moving to Bangkok, overheard our discussion. He commented: "Before, things were bad for us, but now it is getting much better." The repetition of an improved situation for the "third gender" has become a refrain among Thais of all genders. But, the increased acceptability of gender variance is neither embraced nor uncontested (Jackson 1995, 1999b; Sinnott 2000).

In particular, moral stance can override other classificatory schemes, as was evident from a pile sort exercise I conducted to develop a conceptual map of Thai genders among a diverse group of Bangkok residents.[4] Respondents were asked to think aloud while making their taxonomic decisions. Individuals used a variety of factors in creating groups: anatomy, gender expression on a male-female continuum, romantic attraction, common/normal/natural status, and personal experience. I was not surprised when an early free list by a man in his 50s returned two items: man and woman. I was, however, taken aback when, after elaborating a wide number of gender categories, he created two piles: man and woman in one called "normal" and the rest in another called "abnormal" (*phit-pukati*). I had erroneously assumed that man and woman were counterparts and would remain in separate piles because I failed to account for the moral valence attached to *phet* categories.

Gender classification is not an amoral process. *Phet* are defined by factors which are variously invoked by different people, situationally dependent, and experientially based. Instead of seeing Morris's and Jackson's and Sinnott's interpretations as orthogonal, I suggest the three are complementary. Class, generation, rural/urban upbringing, moral stance, personal experience, and context mediate how the local repertoire of gender/sexuality is practiced, interpreted, and labeled in relation to differential exposure to market mechanisms, bureaucratic institutions, and cultural forms.

That is, social stances and life opportunities condition how Thais inhabit and interpret *phet*. Furthermore, I argue that gender forms are interpolated by the moral valence attached to their normativity. These concerns not only expand the terrain of gender/sexuality but also force a reconsideration of their topography. I suggest that *phet* should not be enumerated individually but conceptualized in nodes and clusters. That is, gender/sexuality categories are not fixed to four modern sexual positions. Nor are they proliferating with each new addition of a term. Rather, *phet*, which may or may not be publicly visible, cluster around several key nodes (man, woman, *kathoey*, *gay*, and *tom*), which are renewed through everyday experience. These forms shift over time, often proliferating in punctuated bursts that retreat into refined forms. Furthermore, as Thais use different criteria to assess *phet* (e.g., anatomy, sartorial presentation, desired partner, normality, personal experience), their classifications vary widely and the boundaries between groups overlap. For example, *phu-ying-kham-phet* (transsexual women) are variously grouped with men (based on anatomy at birth), women (based on postoperative anatomy, social presentation, or desired partner), or *kathoey* (based on their being transgender or "not normal"). The framework Thais use to think about these differences is conditioned by social experience. There are multiple stances and layers to the evaluation and categorization of gender/sexuality. Thus, I argue that the multidimensional nature of Thai *phet* are best conceptualized as a localized genderscape, a terrain of archetypes in which fields of power, morality, and experience shape its continually shifting boundaries over time.

DISCUSSION AND CONCLUSION

Conceptualizing Thai Genderscapes

I argue that the gender-inflected sexualities of Thailand were produced by the very forces of autocolonial governmentality, modernization, and globalization (including the institutionalization of sexual dimorphism, restructuring of kin relations, and the construction of tradition) that tried to erase them. While masculine *gay* represent a gender node where a "modern" sexuality intrudes into a system of multiple genders, *gay* is itself a product of modern *phet* formation that developed concomitantly with the West and in relation to *kathoey* and other local gender configurations. The addition of gay identity forms in Thailand cannot be described as a "rupture" as transgenderal homosexualities both continue unabated and modernize alongside new forms of homosexuality that, at least on the surface, appear modern and Western. That is, gay identity as Altman (2001) describes did not diffuse to Thailand from the West, but developed in parallel dialogue at approximately the same time (Jackson 1999a). While capitalist modes of consumption facilitate such new identities, the conditions are not the same, particularly in relation to a break in kinship relations.

. . . Thai genderscapes are a localized production of gender and sexual differences that negotiate the tensions between local and global gender/sexuality forms. As such, they are hybrid: indigenizing the global and recasting the local for international audiences. The disjuncture or tension arising from the differences of autochthonous and global forms produces local distinction, distinguishing Thailand from many of its Asian neighbors. Furthermore, regardless of whether a gender form is considered "traditionally" Thai or not, they are all constituted via historical transformations interacting within the forces of human, capital, technological, ideological, and other flows. Thai genderscapes are already completely hybrid and globalized. But, they maintain local character as gender/sexuality forms are, for the most part, indigenized through local conceptualizations of *phet*.

I have argued for the conceptualization of contemporary Thai gender and sexuality as genderscapes grounded in five major

gender/sexuality categories: *kathoey*, *tom*, *gay*, woman, and man. These categories are not the only ones that exist. Rather, they possess an ontological fixity which comes from their reproduction in the repetition of everyday performances and symbolic practices, which can shift norms over time. Moreover, key historical incidents produce punctuated expansions of possibilities, which may or may not shift the terrain of gender forms. Finally, the social position and ideological stance of an individual shapes how she/he inhabits and interprets *phet*, making genderscapes a perspectival endeavor.

NOTES

1. The *bissu* are transgender ritual specialists whose mixture of male and female characteristics identify and represent the undifferentiated nature of the universe. *Bissu* gender unity allows them to access spiritual powers unattainable by males or females. Peletz (2006) notes that this pattern exists throughout Southeast Asia. However, the situation in Thailand is more complex. Transgender and gay ritual specialists are currently increasing in popularity in both the North and Central regions, yet the lack of an historical record makes it unclear whether this is a resurgence of prior practices. Of course, transgender ritual specialists exist in other world areas, with the *hijras* of South Asia perhaps the most well-known case.

2. As in other parts of Asia, there is not an emphasis on "coming out" in Thailand. However, unlike Confucian Asian societies, there is less emphasis on hiding one's gender/sexual nonconformity. Effeminate *gay* will often state that people know about their sexual orientation, even if they have not been told, because they "show" themselves.

3. The third person singular pronoun in Thai is gender neutral.

4. Pile sorts are a cognitive mapping procedure to understand how community members think about and attach meaning to different items within a conceptual domain. I began the exercise with a free list to identify the *phet* respondents conceived of as most salient. Up to 22 terms were then sorted based on similarity. If there were more than three initial piles, I asked participants to subsequently sort into

three piles and then two piles as I wanted to see if the three-sex system would be reproduced and how genders in the third category, especially *kathoey,* would be categorized as males or females. There were 37 participants.

REFERENCES

Altman, D. (2001). *Global sex.* Chicago: University of Chicago Press.

Bao, J. (2005). *Marital acts: Gender, sexuality, and identity among the Chinese Thai Diaspora.* Honolulu: University of Hawaii Press.

Barmé, S. (2002). *Woman, man, Bangkok: Love, sex, and popular culture in Thailand.* Lanham: Rowman & Littlefield.

Bourdieu, P. (1990). *The logic of practice.* Stanford: Stanford University Press.

Butler, J. (2004). *Undoing gender.* New York: Routledge.

Connors, M. K. (2007). *Democracy and national identity in Thailand.* London: NIAS Press.

Foucault, M. (1990). *The history of sexuality:* Vol. 1. *An introduction.* New York: Vintage.

Herdt, G. (Ed.). (1996). *Third sex, third gender: Beyond sexual dimorphism in culture and history.* New York: Zone Books.

Jackson, P. (1997). *Kathoey >< gay >< man: The historical emergence of gay male identity in Thailand.* In L. Manderson & M. Jolly (Eds.), *Sites of desire, economies of pleasure: Sexualities in Asia and the Pacific* (pp. 166–190). Chicago: University of Chicago Press.

Jackson, P. (1999a). An American death in Bangkok: The murder of Darrell Berrigan and the hybrid origins of gay identity in 1960s Thailand. *GLQ: A Journal of Lesbian and Gay Studies, 5,* 361–411.

Jackson, P. (1999b). Tolerant but unaccepting: The myth of a Thai "gay paradise." In P. Jackson & N. Cook (Eds.), *Genders and sexualities in modern Thailand* (pp. 226–242). Bangkok: Silkworm Books.

Jackson, P. (2000). An explosion of Thai identities: Global queering and re-imagining queer theory. *Culture, Health & Sexuality, 40*(4), 405–424.

Jackson, P. (2003). Performative genders, perverse desires: A bio-history of Thailand's same-sex and transgender cultures. *Intersections: Gender, History and Culture in the Asian Context, 9.* Retrieved June 6, 2004, from http://intersections.anu.edu.au/issue9/jackson.html

Jackson, P. (2010). The ambiguities of semicolonial power in Thailand. In R. Harrison & P. Jackson (Eds.), *The ambiguous allure of the west: Traces of the colonial in Thailand* (pp. 37–56). Hong Kong: Hong Kong University Press.

Jackson, P. A., & Sullivan, G. (Eds.). (1999), *Lady boys, tom boys, rent boys: Male and female homosexualities in contemporary Thailand.* New York: Routledge.

Käng, D. B. (2011). Paradise lost and found in translation: Queer media loci in Bangkok. *GLQ: A Journal of Lesbian and Gay Studies, 17,* 169–191.

Käng, D. B. (2012). Kathoey "in trend": Emergent genderscapes, national anxieties, and the re-signification of male-bodied effeminacy in Thailand. *Asian Studies Review, 36,* 475–494.

Loos, T. (2006). *Subject Siam: Family, law, and colonial modernity in Thailand.* Ithaca: Cornell University Press.

Milk, M. B. (1999). *Thai women in the global labor force: Consuming desires, contested selves.* New Brunswick: Rutgers University Press.

Morris, R. (1994). Three sexes and four sexualities: Redressing the discourses of gender and sexuality in contemporary Thailand. *Positions: East Asian Cultures Critique, 2,* 215–243.

Morris. R. (1995). All made up: Performance theory and the new anthropology of sex and gender. *Annual Review of Anthropology, 24*(1), 567–592.

Morris, R. (1997). Educating desire: Thailand, transnationalism, and transgression. *Social Text, 15,* 53–79.

Muecke, M. (1984). Make money not babies: Changing status markers of Northern Thai women. *Asian Survey, 24,* 459–470.

Mulder, N. (1997). *Thai images: The culture of the public world.* Chiang Mai: Silkworm Books.

Peletz, M. (2006). Transgenderism and gender pluralism in Southeast Asia since early modern times. *Current Anthropology, 47*(2), 309–340.

Pramoj Na Ayuttaya, P. (2008, September 14). *The variety of kathoey in Thai society.* Unpublished paper presented at "*Kathoey* are not women and don't have to be as beautiful as a pageant contestant" seminar, Chiang Mai.

Rubin, G. (1975). The traffic in women: Notes on the political economy of sex. In R. R. Reiter (Ed.), *Toward an anthropology of women* (pp. 157–210). New York: Monthly Review Press.

Rubin, G. (1984). Thinking sex: Notes for a radical politics of sexuality. In C. S. Vance (Ed.), *Pleasure and danger: Exploring female sexuality* (pp. 267–319). Boston: Routledge & Kegan Paul.

Sinnott, M. (2000). The semiotics of transgendered sexual identity in the Thai print media: Imagery and discourse of the sexual other. *Culture, Health & Sexuality, 2*(4), 425–440.

Sinnott, M. (2004). *Toms and Dees: Transgender identity and female same-sex relationships in Thailand.* Honolulu: University of Hawaii Press.

Sinnott, M. (2007). Gender subjectivity. Dees and Toms in Thailand. In S. Wieringa, E. Blackwood, & A. Bhaiya (Eds.), *Women's sexualities and masculinities in a globalizing Asia* (pp. 119–138). New York: Palgrave Macmillan.

van Esterik, P. (2000). *Materializing Thailand.* Oxford: Berg.

Wilson, A. (2007). *The intimate economies of Bangkok: Tomboys, tycoons, and Avon ladies in the global city.* Berkeley: University of California Press.

Winichakul, T. (1994). *Siam mapped: A history of the geo-body of a nation.* Honolulu: University of Hawaii Press.

Winichakul, T. (2000). The quest for "siwilai": A geographical discourse of civilizational thinking in the late nineteenth- and early twentieth-century Siam. *Journal of Asian Studies, 59*(3), 528–549.

Winichakul, T. (2010). Coming to terms with the west: Intellectual strategies of bifurcation and post-westernism in Siam. In R. Harrison & P. Jackson (Eds.), *The ambiguous allure of the west: Traces of the colonial in Thailand* (pp. 135–151). Hong Kong: Hong Kong University Press.

Introduction to Reading 13

Sociologist Cenk Özbay used participant observation and interviews to understand the world of "rent boys" in contemporary Istanbul, Turkey. Özbay speaks Turkish and created a "careful ethnographic plan" to move with relative ease in the bars where he observed interactions among rent boys, gay men, and transvestites. Rent boys come from poor neighborhoods in the outlying areas of Istanbul, neighborhoods called *varoş*. Ranging in age from 16 to 25, rent boys are heterosexually identified and engage in compensated sex with gay men. The key concept in this reading is "exaggerated masculinity." Özbay examines the ways rent boys perform exaggerated masculinity as a strategy for dealing with their sexual interactions with gay men. Be sure to read the footnotes at the end of this article, because they provide valuable details about rent boys.

1. What are the tactics used by rent boys to maintain their masculine identities vis-à-vis gay men? How does *varoş* play a role in these tactics?

2. Discuss the risks faced by rent boys in their construction and maintenance of exaggerated masculinity.

3. What is global gay culture, and how does it shape the enactment of exaggerated masculinity by rent boys?

Nocturnal Queers

Rent Boys' Masculinity in Istanbul

Cenk Özbay

Recently, 'rent boys'[1] have become increasingly visible in the queer social spaces of Istanbul. Rent boys engage in different forms of compensated sex (Agustin, 2005) with other men. They construct their masculine identities through their clandestine homoerotic involvements. They invent and practice an embodied style that I call 'exaggerated masculinity'[2] in order to mark their manly stance and deal with the risks that same-sex sexual activities pose for the reproduction of their masculine selves. In this article, I examine how these heterosexually identified rent boys assemble and perform exaggerated masculinity in order to negotiate the tensions between their local socially excluded environments and a burgeoning western-style gay culture[3] while they conduct their 'risky' sexual interactions with other men.

Male prostitution takes place in different social settings around the world across a wide diversity of class, racial, cultural, and organizational arrangements (see, for example, Aggleton, 1999; Dorais, 2005; Fernández-Dávila et al., 2008; Hall, 2007; Jackson and Sullivan, 1999; McNamara, 1994; Minichiello et al., 2001; Mujtaba, 1997; Schifter, 1998; West, 1993). . . . By studying male prostitution we can gain insight into the social dynamics behind how dissident sexualities are experienced and interpreted in the margins of hegemonic masculinities. In this article, I aim to make a contribution to the gap in the field of compensated sex between men of different social classes who embody distinct masculinities in . . . non-western sexual geographies by using the Istanbul case in which a number of southern sexual cultures such as the Mediterranean, East European and Islamic meet and interface (Bereket and Adam, 2008; Tapinc, 1992). . . .

Rent boys come from lower-class neighborhoods in the outskirts of the Istanbul metropolitan region called *varoş*—a term . . . similar to the Brazilian 'favela' (Goldstein, 2003) and the French 'banlieue' (Wacquant, 2008). Rent boys (aged between 16 and 25) are mostly sons of the recently migrated large families that have coped with dislocation, poverty, and cultural exclusion. They speak Turkish with different regional accents, which show their symbolic marginalization and lack of cultural capital. Rent boys self-fashion their masculinity to produce a niche for themselves within a highly stratified, increasingly hegemonic gay culture in Istanbul. This self-fashioning via the embodied, stylized, continuously refined exaggerated masculinity operates through an 'outsider within' (Collins, 1986) position amongst self-identified gay men in Istanbul.

Varoş boys narrate a story . . . of their 'real' selves while they strive to become rent boys, which they claim is a temporary and transitory position. Exaggerated masculinity is a critical part of this construction in the context of male prostitution. *Varoş* boys transform themselves to achieve the rent boy identity through a discursive process, in which they reiterate the rules and characteristics of being a rent boy, and through a bodily process in which they learn and do exaggerated masculinity. . . .

From Özbay, Cenk. "Nocturnal Queers: Rent Boys' Masculinity in Istanbul." 2010. *Sexualities* 13(5), p. 645.

In . . . Istanbul . . . *varoş* is a highly marginal-ized social identity regarding the mainstream culture of the middle classes. When they attempt to enter the spaces of the western-style gay ven-ues in Istanbul, *varoş* boys are discriminated against and rejected in terms of their alterity to the . . . modern, urban, and liberal lifestyles that middle classes have long adopted.

'Rent boy' emerges in the liminal space between the *varoş* identity and the local reflec-tion of the global gay culture: A rent boy neither becomes gay nor stays as *varoş*. Rent boys animate a dynamic process of cultural hybrid-ization and theatrical displays of exaggerated masculinity as a response to double marginal-ization. While they strategically use their *varoş* backgrounds to underline their masculinity and consolidate their authenticity in order to attract gay men who are supposed to have a fantasy of having sex with heterosexual men, they con-comitantly take advantage of their encounters with middle-class gay men and empower them-selves in their *varoş* environments. In this sense, the agility of the identity of rent boy permits its subjects to be enriched and strength-ened in the symbolic hierarchies that they face in both *varoş* and gay cultures. Masculine embodiment and its deliberate and nuanced uses become crucial in rent boys' symbolic and material culture. . . .

VAROŞ AS CULTURE AND IDENTITY

After the 1980 military coup, neoliberal reforms in Turkey transformed both Istanbul's position within the country as well as its own socio-spatial organiza-tion. The population in Istanbul has multiplied almost four times and recently approached 12 mil-lion people. Urban segregation and social fragmen-tation escalated and reshaped Istanbul as a space of contestation in which previously silenced social groups including Islamists, Kurds, and queers claimed legitimacy and public visibility (Kandiyoti, 2002; Keyder, 1999, 2005).

Varoş was one of the names given by the middle-class . . . citizens of Istanbul . . . to the illegal squatter settlement neighborhoods around the city and to the migrant people who built houses and worked in the temporary jobs in the informal sector (White, 2004). . . . *Varoş* became synonymous with a regressive, 'pre-modern' subjectivity that is abject and disenfranchised.

In the 1990s, the term *varoş* started to designate urban poverty instead of backwardness and rurality while people living in *varoş* areas were increas-ingly identified as the 'threatening Other' (Demirtas and Sen, 2007; Erman, 2004). *Varoş* was con-structed as a space where fundamental Islamism, Kurdish separatism, illegality, criminality, and violence met. Through media representations, *varoş* was otherized in terms of culture, economy, ethnicity, and politics. . . . At the same time, inhab-itants of *varoş* reclaimed and appropriated the word as a way to identify their own cultural position distinctly from the Istanbulite. . . .

Rent boys are the children of *varoş*. They tactically constitute their identities as *varoş* to underline their differences from their gay clients not only in terms of sexuality but also in terms of class position. In this sense, being *varoş* refers to an embodied cultural difference as well as cer-tain gendered meanings regarding masculinity. Rent boys repetitively state that they are 'real' men because they are coming from *varoş*. In this way, *varoş* is naturalized and linked to an inher-ent masculinity that gay men do not (and cannot) have. In other words, *varoş* becomes a sign of an uncontaminated, natural, physical, and authentic masculinity, while gay stands for feminine val-ues and norms such as culture, refinement, and cleanness. In a symbolic order of masculinity, *varoş* boys turn to be 'naturally' and unchange-ably masculine while gay men's bodies represent a modern, inauthentic, and imperfect masculinity.

TACTICS OF MASCULINITY

In addition to the symbolic significance of *varoş* in creating a 'naturally' virile character, rent boys also employ tactics to maintain their mas-culine identities vis-à-vis gay men. The most important strategy is being 'top only.' Thus, rent boys claim that they engage sexually with other men only when they play thc top (active) role.[4] Protecting their bodies from penetration and becoming sexually available only as tops allow rent boys to reclaim their incontestably masculine identities. The gender of their sexual partner does not make a real difference either for their sexual repertoire or for their erotic subjectivities (for a similar situation among Brazilian male prostitutes, see Parker, 1998).

Another way that rent boys secure their masculinity is their heterosexualizing discourse. When they talk, rent boys position themselves in relation to an imagined girlfriend, fiancé, or long-term lover to-be-married with whom they have ongoing emotional and sexual affairs. When challenged, this discursive heterosexuality enables rent boys to prove their 'real' heterosexual identities. In order to distinguish themselves from gay men and to buttress their masculinity, rent boys also humiliate and denigrate gay men. It is important to note that rent boys' homophobia is, in most cases, a performative 'utterance' (Butler, 1993) to help maintain their masculine identities. It does not really prevent them from mingling, negotiating, and having sex with gay men in other situations.

Masculinity has always been a contested subject in the construction of queer sexualities in Turkey (Bereket and Adam, 2006; Hocaoglu, 2002; Özbay and Soydan, 2003; Tapinc, 1992; Yuzgun, 1986). However, rent boys' 'top only' positions and homophobic utterances are only one aspect of the exaggerated performances of masculinity. Different than the archetypical macho sexual pose of Latin America (Lancaster, 1994) rent boys do not brag about their sexual escapades with gay men. Instead, they have an evasive manner about their queer sexual practices. In addition to homophobia, the silence of rent boys about their homosexual involvements coincides with the tradition of the strict separation of intimate affairs from public sphere in some Muslim societies as Murray calls it 'the will not to know' (Murray, 1997). . . .

Within the framework of interpenetrating western gay culture and local constellations of gender and sexuality, masculinity matters for rent boys and gay men on another level: the appeal of passing and acting straight (Clarkson, 2006). Gay men in Istanbul have an increasing obsession with the 'straight-acting' and 'straight-looking' self-presentation, which demands a certain degree of heterosexual masculinity for erotic engagement. This fetishism for the 'more masculine' attributes and bodily gestures contributes to a hierarchy in which feminine qualities, as in effeminate men, are deemed inferior and unwanted, while masculine traits are presented as rare, desired, and superior. The negative attitude toward effeminacy and the desire for more masculine attributes contribute to an exaggerated masculinity to prevail as the 'most masculine,' and thus craved, in the gay culture in Istanbul. Rent boys take advantage of this erotic climate and relocate themselves in the eyes of their potential clients. Put in other words, rent boys convert their erotic and sexual positionalities into social and economic capital through their use of the encounter and desire between different masculinities.

THE INTERPLAY OF MULTIPLE MASCULINITIES

Since gender is conceptualized as a continual 'doing' rather than as a natural 'being' (Butler, 1999: 25; West and Zimmerman, 1987), gendered subjectivities are constituted through 'the repeated stylization of the body, a set of repeated acts within a highly rigid regulatory frame that congeal over time to produce the appearance of substance, of a natural sort of being' (Butler, 1999: 33). Gendered subjectivity comes into being via the constellation of bodily performances within the 'regulatory frame' of the heterosexual matrix. Rent boys subvert their regular and 'normal' heterosexual script with male prostitution while they simultaneously try to re-stabilize it by enacting exaggerated masculinity—a style that requires well-defined gendered performances before different audiences. The omnipresent sense of risk inaugurates the possibility for the exaggeratedly masculine identity to be questioned and imperiled. In this sense, the rent boy's masculinity is a[n] . . . insecure subject position that needs to be repetitively asserted and proven while it continuously introduces new risks to be contemplated by rent boys in order to achieve their heterosexual and masculine status.

In her seminal works, Raewyn Connell (1987, 1995) demonstrated that multiple masculinities coexist and interact in a society at any given time. The encounter and dialogue between a *varoş* boy and a middle-aged upper-class gay man might be seen as a manifestation of what Connell terms the relations between divergent masculinities. These relations ought to be seen through the prism of power. In this sense, the culturally exalted hegemonic masculinity brings complicity, subordination, intimidation, and exploitation into relations between different masculinities. The exclusion of same-sex desire is critical for the constitution of hegemonic masculinity (Connell, 2000: 83). As a model, an ideal, or a reference point, hegemonic masculinity—in relation to the heterosexual matrix—affects all other ways of being a man including its imitations (as in rent boys) as well as the resistant or alternative versions (as in queer masculinity).

In the eastern Mediterranean region, configurations of masculinities take shape between the westernizing influences of modernity and the history of Islamic culture and tradition (Bereket and Adam, 2008; Ghoussoub and Sinclair-Webb, 2000; Ouzgane, 2006). The case of rent boys in Istanbul is not an exception. . . .

Locating Rent Boys

Place: Taksim Square.

Time: Any evening, especially after 10 p.m.

The crowded Istiklal Street, which is a major promenade connected to . . . Taksim Square, is full of intermeshing people from all classes, ages, genders, ethnicities, religions, sexualities, and cultures representing Istanbul's social diversity. Among the carnivalesque crowd an attentive eye can notice some young men walking or leaning against walls, checking the passerby. It is obvious for these attentive eyes that these young men, who carefully prepared themselves for the peak hours, reciprocate with curious gazes that can speak the same language of the looker. Around midnight these young men suddenly disappear from the street. Now, it is . . . bar time.

After paying the entry fee (around $10) I enter Bientot, the most famous and much-frequented club of rent boys in Istanbul. Bientot is very close to the vivid Istiklal Street, near a well-known transgender dance club and the only gay bathhouse of the city. Bientot, like two other similar bars, is a 'limitative and disciplining' (Hammers, 2008) space in the sense that types of people (i.e., rent boys, transvestites, clients) are set, their roles are prescribed (i.e., who dances, who looks, who buys drinks), and interactions between visitors are stabilized (i.e., negotiations, flirting, cruising, kissing). . . . Gay men (whether clients of rent boys or not) told me that they do not 'have fun' in Bientot as they do in other gay bars and they come here just to see or talk to the *varoş* boys only in the predefined ways that are available to them.

Bientot is full of its . . . frequenters: Several single gay men from all ages, some mixed-friend groups, several transvestites, and more than 70 rent boys. In general, everyone seems to know each other. Everybody except rent boys drinks and rests on the walls surrounding the dance floor enjoying music (popular Turkish pop songs of the day) while most of the rent boys dance in a unique style without drinking unless a client is generous enough to buy them one. . . .

Here is a quotation from my field notes immediately after arriving home from Bientot:

> A shocking place . . . High volume of music, really bad ventilation, the smell of alcohol, the smell of sweat, the smell of cologne, the smoke from cigarettes . . . You can't escape from the piercing looks

into your eyes. These looks are masculine, you can tell, but they are also very inviting and flirtatious, which contradicts . . . the assertive masculinity. The dancing bodies are very close to each other. They are very straight looking like the ordinary boys at the street; but, on the other hand, the male-to-male intimacy of the dance destroys the desired heterosexual ambiance. It seems like they are straight boys in a gay club, dancing together passionately. . . .

PLAYING WITH FIRE: ELEMENTS OF RENT BOYS' STYLE

A weekly TV show filmed the gay bathhouse near Bientot with hidden cameras in early 2005. After recording each possible 'proof' of male prostitution (including negotiations for prices and actions) the programmers tried to talk with the manager of the bathhouse about the organization . . . while he kept refuting that he hired rent boys. During the interview the camera focuses on a young rent boy, half naked in his towel, arguing angrily with another one about the recruitment of new rent boys that they already knew. He said 'I told you don't bring everyone here from your neighborhood. Look at me. I only bring my brother. You may have a fight with one of them in the future and he can go and tell people, including your father, what you do here. You are playing with fire. I told you this before. Don't play with fire.'

. . . This warning against 'playing with fire' is neither unique to this rent boy nor restricted within the walls of the bathhouse. It offers a useful framework to better comprehend a rent boy's unceasing physical and social negotiations with other rent boys, gay men, and transvestites. Rent boy is a conditional and fragile identity. It surfaces between the contradictory discursive and sexual practices, which subvert the line between homo and heterosexuality. It is a contingent performance that links the *varoş* culture of Istanbul and the ostensibly global gay life-style. It is an interplay of competing working- and upper-middle class meanings and signifiers.

Through the incessant play of risk taking, a rent boy invests his heterosexuality as well as his social position and kinship networks which are likely to be harmed by an undesired disclosure, as the rent boy quoted earlier fears.

Here, I follow Agustin's (2005: 619) proposition to define and study prostitution, sex work, and compensated sex as a 'culture' to expose the previously under-researched links with systems of inequality and the production of social meaning. Wright (2005: 243) also highlights the 'percolation of queer theoretical concerns' and 'an array of cultural studies interventions' into the sociology of masculinities in order to pose new questions on masculine performances, cultural practices, and 'engenderment' processes that men undertake through the routes of non-hegemonic masculinities in diverse settings. Hence, I frame exaggerated masculinity as a product of the culture of rent boys in Istanbul. Rent boys learn, practice, and transform exaggerated masculinity through the mechanisms of social control and self-governance. The process of the construction and reconstruction of exaggerated masculinity is constantly under risk of disappointment and failure.

. . . Risk appears three-fold in animating exaggerated masculinity by rent boys. First and foremost, rent boys' involvement with male prostitution should not be revealed to their friends, family, and extended relatives. Otherwise, they cannot sustain their ordinary lives as young, decent, and respected members of their community. On the other hand, while the rent boy reproduces *varoş* culture as corroboration to his 'natural' masculinity, he should also play with and transmute it symbolically in order to have a subject position within gay culture instead of being abjected. So, the second risk is . . . a nuanced middle space between the two unwanted identities that a rent boy must navigate carefully: staying as an unmodified *varoş* or becoming (too) gay. While connecting closely with gay men, rent boys' third risk is about protecting their heterosexuality. Although rent boys have sex with gay men, they are not supposed to have a gay identity. In sum, a rent boy has to control meticulously and manage risk regarding his bodily acts, behaviors, and relations with other people in order not to be exposed while balancing between the discrepant meanings of *varoş* and gay positions. In this framework, I will now outline the elements of how rent boys sustain exaggerated masculinity through their risk-taking activities and their entanglements with different segments of the culture of male sex work in Istanbul.

The Body

The first point of risk that rent boys take into consideration focuses on their bodies. Almost all rent boys have athletic or skinny bodies. . . . They think that their gay clients like their bodies as skinny, fatless, and 'toned' and not over-muscular and 'hung.' They also believe that they look younger this way. . . . Hakan (aged 22) says, 'body is everything we have in this job, of course we need to take care of it.' Rent boys have a certain tension around their bodies in order to keep them in good condition, to seem young(er), and not to lose their virility through developing an over-muscled look.

Appearance

Another significant issue in the material culture of rent boys is about what they wear and how they look. Most rent boys wear denim jeans. They almost never wear shorts even when it is unbearably hot and humid in Istanbul. Burak (aged 18) states that 'real men never wear shorts, jeans are the best.' For their upper parts they commonly opt for white. 'White is better because it looks more attractive when you are tanned. Also, it shines in the dark bar and makes you more visible,' says Arda (aged 23). Black tops are also very popular for their taste because it is deemed to be more masculine and mature. They also wear some bright and lively colors like red and yellow to be seen in the bar. . . .

Rent boys do not wear earrings as Okan (aged 18) told me, 'Earrings would harm masculinity.' They are more tolerant toward wristbands, chains, and rings, but earrings are identified with gays and/or foreigners. . . . Rent boys in Istanbul insist on wearing sport shoes and sneakers even on snowy days. . . .

Perfume

Perfumes and colognes are significant manifestations of rent boys' risky relations with their gay clientele. It is always good for a rent boy to have the fragrance of a charming perfume because it increases his attractiveness when his client has to whisper into his ear in the noisy bar. Perfumes are very expensive for rent boys' budgets but sometimes they receive perfumes after satisfying a client with their sexual performance. . . . As Burak told me, 'if you smell [of] perfume, it shows that you recently got some work done.'

The risky point is . . . the gendered quality of the fragrance. The fragrance must smell masculine because otherwise it cannot contribute to the exaggerated masculinity of the rent boy. . . . On the other hand, a client who uses a very masculine perfume for himself endangers a rent boy's masculinity because it implies that the gay client was not a feminine man and he could turn active in sexual penetration. . . .

Most of the rent boys that I talked to said that they were against stealing or any other kind of criminal activity. On the other hand, they also revealed that they were not against asking for or even stealing perfumes from gays' houses after they have sex. Perfumes clearly are the exception for rent boys' moral stance against stealing. Hasan (aged 24) says 'when I see a nice perfume I ask for it. Honestly, if he does not want to give it to me I will try to take it anyway. I don't think this is stealing.' Hakan also noted that 'I am not interested in anything else, but if he has a nice perfume I will take it . . . He can buy another bottle easily and I will smell nice. Good deal.' Murat (aged 23) states that 'perfume is a connection between the Rich's life and mine. I can take it, I can use it and when I smell it I remember what I did and I enjoy about it. It makes my life more beautiful.'

Dance

Dance is another risky subject in the context of male prostitution in Istanbul. Rent boys have to dance in the bar in order to be seen by clients. The particular motions and gyrations of the boys' dancing give the impression that they are carrying out a predefined script of performing a task, but not reflecting pleasure by moving in a relaxed manner with the music and the rhythm. In other words, when rent boys dance, they perform another requirement of their work. Their dance is never visibly homoerotic although their bodies are pretty close and sometimes touch each other. It has its own sense of humor: If a rent boy puts himself at the back of another, the one in the front bounces in sudden panic—in an anxiety to save his back (his bottom). It manifests a rigid top-bottom code concerning the control and defense of your own back and a constant search to attack the others' backs.

If a rent boy oversteps the boundary of touching another's back or exhibits signs of pleasure, other rent boys explicitly disapprove the act and call him 'pervert,' *ergo*, humorous pleasure that comes from sodomizing others should be limited to activity with gays and not with other rent boys. In the bar, this is the main reason behind physical fights amongst rent boys. Thus, bodily humor is dangerous to play with, although avoiding it brings social exclusion because a rent boy ought to dance. He needs to 'show' in order to charm his audience. A motionless rent boy renders himself invisible, which seriously reduces his chances of finding a client. Anil (aged 20) says, 'dancing is the moment where we get the gays. We attract them when we dance. They love to watch us.'

Most importantly, a rent boy has to dance without looking feminine. Okan says, 'it is better not to do it [dance] if you do it like a girl.' Riza (aged 24) told me 'you should not shake your ass like a belly dancer. Arms and legs must be straight. Gaze is also important.' There are strict performative codes that most rent boys obey to protect the masculine image during the dance: The body should not be curved or shaken too much and it must repeat the same rough movements without flexibility. It must show strength. Shoulders and arms should be kept wide open, the waist should move only back and forth, imitating the sexual act of penetration. Dance is controlled and regulated by the surveillance of other rent boys. As long as they can perform it according to the unwritten rules of exaggerated masculinity, dance guarantees rent boys' masculine identities and makes them the center of attraction before potential clients.

Friends

As I recounted earlier . . . taking part in male prostitution or being seen while cruising is very risky. . . . Concealment paralyzes friendship mechanisms amongst rent boys. Most of the time, they come to the bars or other cruising places alone or at most in the company of one other rent boy, who is supposed to be trustworthy (mostly one's kin, for example a cousin). They usually know other rent boys personally and they have an intimate network of gossip and information exchange. They also spend time together chatting and dancing in the bars, but they always wind up alone while working or cruising. The solitude of rent boys might be seen as a tactic to increase their chance of negotiation for higher prices or as a part of the tradition of mendacity about what they do for how much. It actually protects them from unwanted rumors and from the dangers of unexpected disclosure. Can (aged 21) elaborates that 'I know some people in the bar, some other "rents" but I never see them out of the bar. Nobody knows that I am coming here in my neighborhood. I must be very careful. When my regular friends ask I tell them I will hang out with my cousins.' Mert (aged 24) adds, 'If you go out together he [a friend] can say that Mert let the guy fuck him, Mert turned bottom, etc. If he won't say it today, he will say it tomorrow. This is how it works. So, it is better to be alone instead of dealing with gossip and lies.'

Another point that poses a risk to the exaggerated masculinity is about emotions and sexual attraction between rent boys. In order to sustain fraternal heterosexuality, homoeroticism must be tamed and eliminated (Connell, 2000; Sedgwick, 1986). In male prostitution, who is feminine (gay) and who is masculine (rent boy) is rigidly defined. For rent boys, intimate relations are allowed only between these distinct gendered groups and not within them. Therefore, the possibility or manifestation of any kind of affect, eroticism, or sexuality between rent boys subverts their masculine positions as well as their 'natural' heterosexuality. Just like the uneasiness when they dance together, the risk of emotional and bodily intimacy as well as the ways it might be talked about create a certain tension and prevent rent boys from becoming further attached to each other.

Drinks and Drugs

. . . Drinking alcoholic beverages in the bar is a vital chance to look like an adult and demonstrate toughness. Soft drinks and soda are not preferred because they look juvenile and gentle. Beer is the drink that rent boys consume mostly because it is the cheapest and the most masculine beverage. . . . Beer is easy to drink while dancing, and more importantly, it does not make one drunk easily. Alcohol is a very risky issue just like drugs. Mixing different beverages, drinking tequila shots fast, or taking drugs can make a rent boy dizzy—sometimes almost unconscious. Emre (aged 25) notes 'gays try to make you drunk by buying you many drinks. They want to use you when you are drunk. If you are new here they can easily entrap you. You can have sex for no money, or worse things can happen.' These 'worse things' that Emre notes may lead to losing the masculine pose and roughness, which was carefully constructed. . . .

Transvestites

My framing of risk for rent boys' exaggerated masculinity includes their multifaceted relations with transvestite sex workers. Almost all the rent boys that I talked with have had sexual experiences with transvestites. A rent boy and a transvestite can become friends, sexual partners, and even lovers. The stories told about rent boys and transvestites range from scandals such as a drunken rent boy who was raped by a transvestite to some poignant love stories. Despite the fact that they are in two different sides of sex work, neither rent boys nor transvestites pay to have sex with each other. As Aykut (aged 25) says 'we are free for them, they are free for us. For all the rest, only money talks.'

While transvestites enjoy the young virility and 'real' masculinity of rent boys, the latter are happy to show how masculine and sexually active they are by having sex with the 'girls.' In most cases, a transvestite mentors an inexperienced rent boy and she teaches him how to have good sex. Although it seems a mutually satisfying relationship, these escapades with transvestites are indeed very risky for rent boys. Transvestites can easily ridicule a rent boy for not having a sufficiently large penis or for not achieving a fulfilling sexual performance. Emir (aged 20) said, 'I saw many guys like this. Everybody knows that they ejaculate really fast or it [the penis] is really small because one of the girls talked about it. They can still convince some clients, especially tourists, but it is more difficult to find a client for them.' Such a public display of physical or sexual insufficiency would permanently destroy a rent boy's sources of masculine respectability and reputation.

Safe Sex

The last component of what I conceptualize as risk for rent boys' construction of the exaggerated masculinity, is about 'sexual risk' (Fernández-Dávila et al., 2008) and bodily health. All the rent boys that I conducted interviews with had knowledge about STDs, HIV, condoms and how to use them. Nevertheless, my conversations with both rent boys and their clients testify that rent boys have a certain disinclination and resistance to concede their vulnerability and to use a condom during sexual intercourse.

They prefer to have *doğal* (natural) or *çiplak* (naked, without a condom) sex especially when the client asks for or pays more. Ilker (aged 19) told me 'I use it [a condom] sometimes. It does not really bother me. I prefer cleaner gays so it is not a big threat for me. I know many rents do it without condoms with tourists because they pay more. It is crazy because there is a higher chance for a foreigner to be sick.' Their negative attitude might originate from the practical difficulty to use condoms, or as more likely, the construction of their masculine self-identities rejects expressions of fear and protection while it promotes courage and adventure. Rent boys interpret the sexual encounter as an opportunity to challenge and prove their manhood; as Ozgur (aged 22) says, 'little boys might get scared of it, but for me, it is not the case. I know how to fuck a guy without a condom in a safe way. It is not necessary for me to put one on. I can protect myself.' Also, some clients opt for unprotected sex with younger rent boys whom they believe do not have a long sexual history and are thus 'cleaner'. On the other hand, Burak mentioned, 'Probably because I am younger they ask my age and how many times I did it [having sex]. Then, they say "it is OK with you, you are clean" and I don't put a condom on. That's what they want.' Therefore, rent boys' desire to demonstrate their courage and fearlessness operates along with some clients' demands for unprotected sex and produces a risky and dangerous encounter for both sides.

Concluding Remarks

In this article, I have explained how rent boys in Istanbul have developed cultural, bodily, symbolic, and material strategies both to challenge tacitly and to negotiate inventively with the social norms of hegemonic male sexuality (Plummer, 2005) and hegemonic masculinity (Connell, 1995). The 'top only' sexual positions whereby they make themselves sexually available, the protection of their bodies from penetration, and the distance they place between themselves and feminine connotations by the way they dance, smell, or dress, can be seen as attempts to save the penis-and-penetration-centered hegemonic virile sexuality. On the other hand, the enactment of exaggerated masculinity and the production of a story of authentic manhood via *varoş* culture are manifestations of their complicity in the hegemonic forms of masculinity in Istanbul despite their dissident sexual practices that contradict these narratives.

Is it acceptable for the embodiments of hegemonic masculinity, or its imitations, to operate alongside queer sex? Is it possible for one to reclaim his privileged heterosexual status while he engages in compensated sex with other men? Gary W. Dowsett and his colleagues note that the definitions and conceptualizations in which masculinities have been theorized are in need of reconsideration and recalibration since 'the prevailing formulation of masculinity represents a failure to engage with the creative meanings and embodied experiences evident in non-hegemonic sexual cultures, and with the effects these meanings and experiences may generate beyond their boundaries' (2008:124). In this sense, rent boys and their ambivalent sexual acts and identifications provide an excellent case for such inquiries regarding their involvement with the active meaning-making process of sexuality and masculinity. As a response to the possible inquiries and challenges toward their heterosexual and masculine self-identities, they use exaggerated masculinity in order to be able to continue their everyday lives as heterosexual members of their families and kinship networks. In other words, exaggerated masculinity repairs and masks the subverting effects of compensated sex for rent boys' heterosexuality and makes them closer to the hegemonic ideal of masculinity. They perform an assiduous self-governance through symbols and implicit meanings vis-à-vis different and contradictory class positions, gender identities, and sexual acts.

Rent boys constitute exaggerated masculinity relationally and strategically at the nexus of contradictory contexts of the local *varoş* culture and the impact of the global gay culture. Risk is central in understanding the mechanisms of exaggerated masculinity since it is a fragile, insecure, playful combination of various bodily acts, gestures, and symbols. . . .

NOTES

1. Rent boy (as in English) is the term my informants use for defining themselves. They say '*ben bir rent bovum*' (I am a rent boy) or just '*rentim*' (I am rent). Sometimes they prefer to say, '*parayla veya ücretli çikiyorum*' (I am going for money). I never encountered any other terms, either in the English versions or in Turkish translations, such as *erkek fahişe* (male prostitute), *seks işçisi* (sex worker) or *jigolo* (gigolo) used by my informants, their clients, or in the mass media. The subject of this article, rent boys, who are from the *varoş* segments of the city, is the only group of men who engage in compensated sex (receiving money or gifts) in the gay scene in Istanbul (Hocaoglu, 2002).

2. I prefer to describe the rent boys' stylized embodiment as 'exaggerated masculinity' in order to underline its theatrical, playful, performative, and decontexualizing characteristics. It is a constellation of learnt, imitated, calculated, and socially regulated displays of doing masculinity. There are other similar terms for such excessive masculine performances like hypermasculinity (Healey, 1996) or machismo (Gutmann, 1996) that are conceptualized in different webs of relations.

3. With the western-style gay culture, I basically mean the emergence of men who call themselves gay (as in English) or sometimes *gey* in Turkish (Bereket and Adam, 2006) because they engage in sexual, erotic, and emotional relations with other men. There are many components of this culture including enclosed spaces called gay bars or gay clubs, and access to foreign or local websites with gay content for various purposes such as online dating. Before the emergence of the modern gay identity in Turkey, there were various sorts of same-sex sexual relations going on under different identifications and social organizations (Tapinc, 1992; Yuzgun, 1986).

4. Rent boys claim that they are 'top only' in order to insist they do not let their clients penetrate their bodies, while they can insert their penises into their clients' bodies through oral and anal sex. Rent boys also claim that they never touch their client's penises and they never let their clients caress their bodies. In addition to the 'top only' rule, some of the rent boys I talked to stated that they never kiss their clients from their mouths and some told me that they do not 'make out' with clients and delimit their sexual activities with oral and anal penetration (Özbay, 2005).

REFERENCES

Aggleton P (ed.) (1999) *Men Who Sell Sex: International Perspectives on Male Prostitution and HIV/AIDS*. Philadelphia, PA: Temple University Press.

Agustin LM (2005) The cultural study of commercial sex. *Sexualities* 8(5): 618–631.

Bereket T and Adam BD (2006) The emergence of gay identities in Turkey. *Sexualities* 9(2): 131–151.

Bereket T and Adam BD (2008) Navigating Islam and same-sex liaisons among men in Turkey. *Journal of Homosexuality* 55(2): 204–222.

Butler J (1993) *Bodies That Matter: On the Discursive Limits of 'Sex'*. New York: Routledge.

Butler J (1999) *Gender Trouble: Feminism and the Subversion of Identity*. New York: Routledge.

Clarkson J (2006) 'Everyday Joe' versus 'pissy, bitchy, queens': Gay masculinity on StraightActing.com. *The Journal of Men's Studies* 14(2): 191–207.

Collins PH (1986) Learning from the outsider within. *Social Problems* 33(6): 14–32.

Connell RW (1987) *Gender and Power: Society, the Person and Sexual Politics*. Stanford, CA: Stanford University Press.

Connell RW (1995) *Masculinities*. Berkeley: University of California Press.

Connell RW (2000) *The Men and the Boys*. Berkeley: University of California Press.

Demirtas N and Sen S (2007) *Varoş* identity: The redefinition of low income settlements in Turkey. *Middle Eastern Studies* 43(1): 87–106.

Dorais M (2005) *Rent Boys: The World of Male Sex Workers*. Montreal: McGill-Queen's University Press.

Dowsett GW, Williams H, Ventuneac A, et al. (2008) Taking it like a man: Masculinity and barebacking online. *Sexualities* 11(1/2): 121–141.

Erman T (2004) Gecekondu Çalişmalarinda 'Öteki' Olarak Gecekondulu Kurgulari. *European Journal of Turkish Studies* 1. URL (accessed 15 June 2010): http://www.ejts.org/document85.html.

Ghoussoub M and Sinclair-Webb E (eds) (2000) *Imagined Masculinities: Male Identity and Culture in the Modern Middle East.* London: Saqi.

Goldstein DM (2003) *Laughter Out of Place: Race, Class, Violence, and Sexuality in a Rio Shantytown.* Berkeley: University of California Press.

Gutmann MC (1996) *The Meanings of Macho: Being a Man in Mexico City.* Berkeley: University of California Press.

Hall T (2007) Rent-boys, barflies, and kept men: Men involved in sex with men for compensation in Prague. *Sexualities* 10(4): 457–472.

Hammers CJ (2008) Making space for an agentic sexuality? The examination of a lesbian/queer bathhouse. *Sexualities* 11(5): 547–572.

Healey M (1996) *Gay Skins: Class, Masculinity, and Queer Appropriation.* London: Cassell.

Hocaoglu M (2002) *Escinsel Erkekler.* Istanbul: Metis.

Jackson P and Sullivan G (eds) (1999) *Lady Boys, Tom Boys, Rent Boys: Male and Female Homosexualities in Contemporary Thailand.* New York: Haworth.

Kandiyoti D (2002) Introduction: Reading the fragments. In: Kandiyoti D and Saktanber A (eds) *Fragments of Culture: The Everyday of Modern Turkey.* London: IB: Tauris, 1–21.

Keyder C (ed.) (1999) *Istanbul: Between the Global and the Local.* Boston. MA: Rowman & Littlefield Publishers.

Keyder C (2005) Globalization and social exclusion in Istanbul. *International Journal of Urban and Regional Research* 29(1): 124–134.

Lancaster R (1994) *Life is Hard: Machismo, Danger, and the Intimacy of Power in Nicaragua.* Berkeley: University of California Press.

McNamara RP (1994) *The Times Square Hustler: Male Prostitution in New York City.* New York: Praeger.

Minichiello V, Mariño R, Browne J, et al. (2001) Male sex workers in three Australian cities: Socio-demographic and sex work characteristics. *Journal of Homosexuality* 42(1): 29–51.

Mujtaba H (1997) The other side of midnight: Pakistani male prostitutes. In: Murray S and Roscoe W (eds) *Islamic Homosexualities: Culture, History, and Literature.* New York: New York University Press, 267–274.

Murray S (1997) The will not to know: Islamic accommodations of male homosexuality. In: Murray S and Roscoe W (eds) *Islamic Homosexualities: Culture, History, and Literature.* New York: New York University Press, 14–54.

Ouzgane L (ed.) (2006) *Islamic Masculinities.* London: Zed.

Özbay C (2005) Virilities for rent: Navigating masculinity, sexuality and class in Istanbul. Unpublished MA thesis, Bogazici University.

Özbay C and Soydan S (2003) *Escinsel Kadinlar.* Istanbul: Metis.

Parker R (1998) *Beneath the Equator: Cultures of Desire, Male Homosexuality, and Emerging Gay Communities in Brazil.* New York: Routledge.

Plummer K (2005) Male sexualities. In: Kimmel M, Hearn J and Connell RW (eds) *Handbook of Studies on Men and Masculinities.* Thousand Oaks, CA: Sage, 178–195.

Schifter J (1998) *Lila's House: Male Prostitution in Latin America.* New York: Haworth Press.

Sedgwick EK (1986) *Between Men: English Literature and Male Homosexual Desire.* New York: Columbia University Press.

Tapinc H (1992) Masculinity, femininity, and Turkish male homosexuality. In: Plummer K (ed.) *Modern Homosexualities: Fragments of Lesbian and Gay Experience.* London: Routledge, 39–50.

Wacquant L (2008) *Urban Outcasts: A Comparative Sociology of Advanced Marginality.* Cambridge: Polity.

West C and Zimmerman D (1987) Doing gender. *Gender & Society* 1(2): 125–151.

Wright L (2005) Introduction to 'queer' masculinities. *Men & Masculinities* 7(3): 243–247.

Yuzgun A (1986) *Escinsellik.* Istanbul: Huryuz.

Introduction to Reading 14

Charlotte Wrigley-Asante interviewed more than 100 young women migrant workers in the city of Accra, Ghana, in 2012 and 2013. The women were first-generation migrants from rural areas of Ghana who had been engaged in petty trading for at least 3 years. Each woman had moved independently to Accra, but used social networks, often older women, as initial support systems. Wrigley-Asante's research shows how these poor young women migrants used trading as a resource to define their own life choices and to pursue their own life goals and aspirations. Although the women work very long hours for small earnings, many were able to save and invest in housing and personal items. Their incomes also allowed them to supplement household budgets, raising their status in the eyes of rural, extended family members. Notably, many of the women migrants, married as well as single, were empowered by their economic independence to challenge patriarchal ideology. Their empowerment extended to control over sexual relations with their partners.

1. How do the findings of linkages between control over resources and women's status in this study complement the findings presented by Lepowsky in her chapter reading on gender equality on Vanatinai?

2. Why are the young women migrant workers willing to leave their extended families and villages behind to enter the world of petty trading in Accra?

3. What can we, in the United States, learn from the lives of the poor young women migrants in Ghana about gender relationships?

Accra Turns Lives Around

Female Migrant Traders and Their Empowerment Experiences in Accra, Ghana

Charlotte Wrigley-Asante

. . . This paper contributes to the expanding knowledge of feminist research in migration studies from the Ghanaian perspective by focusing on how young female internal migrants move from rural areas to urban centres to change their life circumstances. It argues that young female migrants should not only be looked at in the context of vulnerability, as many have done in Ghana, but within the context of empowerment, and as agents of change that could use trading as

pathways to improve their socio-economic lives and empower themselves. . . .

Contextualising Empowerment

This research has been largely influenced by the concept of empowerment drawn from Kabeer's (2001; 2010) conceptualisation of empowerment and Malhotra et al.'s (2002)

From Wrigley-Asante, Charlotte. 2014. "Accra Turns Lives Around: Female Migrant Traders and Their Empowerment Experiences in Accra, Ghana." *GENEROS—Multipdisciplinary Journal of Gender Studies* 3(2), 341.

multi-dimensional framework of analysing empowerment. Kabeer links empowerment with conditions of disempowerment and refers to the processes by which 'those who have been denied the ability to make choices acquire such ability' (Kabeer, 2010, p. 13). She further draws an association between poverty and disempowerment in the sense that the inability for an individual to meet one's basic needs often rules out the ability to exercise meaningful choices. Strategic life choices include where to live, whether and whom to marry, freedom of movement and association, among others (Kabeer, 2010, p. 14). For Kabeer, the ability for an individual to make choices can be thought of in terms of the resources, which is the precondition; agency, which is the process; and achievements, which is the outcome. Resources include material, human and social, which serve to enhance the ability to exercise choice. Agency refers to people's capacity to define their own life choices and to pursue their own goals. Resources and agency together constitute what Sen terms as capabilities, the potential that people have for living the lives they want, of achieving valued ways of 'being and doing' (Sen 1985 cited in Kabeer, 2001, p. 21).

Malhotra et al. (2002) also present a framework on women's empowerment that captures the commonly used dimensions or indicators of empowerment. Their framework is based on a nexus of some key overlapping terms such as *options, choice, control* and *power* which are most often included in defining empowerment and refers to women's abilities to make strategic decisions that affect their well-being (Kabeer, 2001; World Bank, 2004, 2010). Malhotra et al. (2002) view women's empowerment as a process which manifests at different dimensions, that is, economic, social, political, interpersonal/relational, psychological and legal dimensions of empowerment. At the individual level, economic empowerment includes women's access to credit, control over income, savings, contribution to family support and social empowerment includes skills acquisition, education, information and freedom of movement. Interpersonal and relational empowerment includes women's participation in decisions concerning their sexual relations, knowledge of family planning choices and freedom from violence. Political and legal empowerment includes women's collective action and knowledge of political and legal system and exercising the right to vote. Psychological empowerment includes women's self-development, self-esteem and psychological well-being.

This paper analyses how poor young female migrants have used trading as a resource to define their own life choices and to pursue their own life goals and aspirations. . . . The desire to achieve economic benefits and move out of poverty is a motivating factor for migrating. Through social networks and by engaging in economic activities (in this case trading), there are shifts from women's positions of disempowerment and limited life choices and toward achieving socio-economic, interpersonal/relational and psychological dimensions of empowerment. In this context, socio-economic empowerment means women earning income and controlling income earned, having choices in life, ability to support self and contributing to household needs. Interpersonal and relational empowerment means women's participation in decisions concerning their household needs including decisions on sexual relations; and psychological empowerment means a sense of self-esteem and self-confidence. The empirical analyses of these processes have been discussed in subsequent sections of the paper.

THE STUDY CONTEXT

In Ghana, the pattern of economic development has created three distinct geographic identities: the coastal zone dominated by Accra-Tema and Sekondi-Takoradi, a middle zone with Kumasi at its centre; and the northern savannah zone. The coastal zone of Ghana as the most industrialized and urbanized has been the focus of internal migration since the last century

(Agyei & Ofosu-Mensah, 2009, p. 20). The opening of the Takoradi deep-sea port and the Tema port in 1927 and 1962 respectively attracted many migrants to these areas. Similarly, the middle zone with its natural resource endowment such as extractive minerals, forest and agricultural products, became a dominant centre in the country and the focus of migration particularly from the savannah zone (ibid). Consequently, the pattern of north-south migration in the country has been influenced by the spatial differences in the level of development between the north and the south. Awumbila and Ardayfio-Schandorf (2008, p. 172) note that the British colonial policy promoted the north largely as a labour reserve for the south; thus, little investment and infrastructure were made in the north whilst conscious efforts were made to develop the forest and coastal belts of the south. As a result, there have been high rates of migration from the north to large towns and cocoa-growing areas of the south (ibid). Movement to towns has therefore been an important livelihood strategy as economic opportunities in these areas act as a pull factor attracting migrants particularly from the northern savannah zone (Awumbila & Ardayfio-Schandorf, 2008). People also move from rural to urban areas in search of social and cultural amenities such as good drinking water, electricity, medical care and entertainment (Awumbila & Ardayfio-Schandorf, 2008; Agyei & Ofosu-Mensah, 2009).

The city of Accra, the capital city of Ghana, located in the coastal zone has subsequently been the destination point for many migrants as a result of several factors such as infrastructural facilities, medical facilities, industries and closeness to port city Tema (ibid). Traditionally, it was young adult males who moved to seek employment in these areas. With time, migration has become more feminised with young females migrating independently, mostly to major urban cities without the company of their partners and relations (Awumbila & Ardayfio, 2008; Agyei & Ofosu-Mensah, 2009). Most of them have little or no education and often with no employable skills thus find themselves in the informal sector

economy as head porters, street vendors, traders and domestic workers (ibid).

RESEARCH METHODOLOGY AND THE SAMPLE

This study discusses the experiences of female migrant traders sampled from three geographical sites within the Accra Metropolitan Area (AMA): Kwame Nkrumah Circle, Tema Station and Kaneshie. These sites were selected based on the fact that they are well-known spots for the trading activities of female migrants. Both Kwame Nkrumah Circle and Tema Station accommodate very large fleets of vehicles that ply the routes within the city and to all other regions of the country. There are also markets adjacent to them and therefore attract a large number of traders and buyers from all parts of the city. Kaneshie is located outside the main city centre on a major highway. It also has a very large daily market which caters for traders from the Central and Western regions of the country. The area is also well-served with numerous shops and banks (Asiedu & Agyei-Mensah, 2008; p. 194). All three sites serve as terminals for local buses (trotros) and taxis that ply all routes in the city. They therefore provide attractive spaces for trading at the car parks.

Data for the study was collected in March-April 2012 and follow-ups done in August-September 2013. To address ethical issues, the women were briefed with respect to the nature of the study and their willingness to participate. Those who consented to be interviewed were selected and were assured of the anonymity of their responses. Since trading activities in Accra have grown to include people displaced from the formal sector, as a result of neoliberal policies and the presence of transnational traders (Overa, 2007; Darkwah, 2010), the purposive and snowballing methods were employed to sample a total of 117 young female migrants. This sample size was deemed appropriate to assess the proportion and percentages of data since the key objective of the study was to get a deeper understanding from the women's own narrations and accounts of their life experiences, their successes, benefits and challenges of their trading activities within the context of empowerment. It was therefore important to interact with the women involved and get first-hand information of the issue under study. With a key objective of analysing the effect of trading on rural migrants, the study targeted first generation migrants from rural areas and who have traded for at least three years. In-depth interviews using a semi-structured interview guide, as well as observation methods were employed in order to get a deeper understanding of the empowerment experiences of women. . . .

RESEARCH FINDINGS

Reasons for Migrating and Trading Activities

In Ghana, the main reason for internal migration is to look for work as asserted by Ackah and Medvedev (2010). The findings from this study corroborate this assertion. Indeed, the primary motive of the respondents for migrating to Accra was economic. Inability to secure jobs after completing their education, financial hardships and parents' inability to support children were factors that pushed these young females to the city. In effect, their desire to improve their socio-economic status was paramount as explained by these women:

> After completing Junior High School there was nothing to do. Life was very difficult for me. I barely survived. I had heard about Accra so I decided to come even though I really did not know anyone here. I came because I wanted a better life. (26-year-old woman)

> I had always wanted to travel outside my village because there's nothing to do there after school. It had been my dream to be in Accra because I always thought of it as a land of riches where people's destinies could be changed. So after school, I started contacting the few people I knew who were in Accra from my village and I came. (32-year-old woman)

These reasons for migrating recurred throughout the interviews. These also confirm the assertions that in contemporary times, women are migrating independently to fulfil their economic needs; thus, the traditional pattern of migration which is male-dominated and long distance in nature is becoming increasingly feminised (Awumbila & Ardayfio-Schandorf 2008; Agyei & Ofosu-Mensah, 2009). Strong social networks in the city appeared to be a motivating factor as it is a major source of initial support for these young women. Many mentioned that once they came to Accra, their first contact was often a close family friend, a relation or a member from their home communities. These relations assisted them by providing a 'temporary' place of abode, as they are expected to find their own apartment when they began an economic activity and started earning income. In effect, family relations and networks are the web within which the decision to migrate takes place as they are more likely to support migrants in their journeys, provide information, advice, economic and emotional needs (Awumbila et al., 2011, p. 56).

Once a temporary place of abode had been secured, women were immediately ushered into the trading business. Many started with consumable goods such as water, biscuits, fruits, which were considered as 'quick business' since they were highly patronized and monies recouped easily. Most often, goods were received on credit basis as women did not have any source of initial capital. For instance, a 27-year-old woman who had been trading for more than five years explained that she first came to Accra in a company of a friend from her village. Once they got to Accra, she was introduced to an elderly woman from their hometown who freely offered her goods to sell even though she didn't have any initial capital. But because she exhibited truthfulness in accounting properly for the goods sold, she won the trust of the woman and continued business with her until she saved enough profits to be on her own. The women, however, emphasised that untrustworthiness on the part of people in present times has made initial capital a necessary requirement. Thus, the relatively new entrants mentioned that they started with their own small capital which they carried along with them from their home communities. Whilst time for trading activities varied, it usually started very early in the morning. For some, trading started as early as 4:30 a.m. and ended at about 7:00 p.m. The number of days worked also varied but many worked from Monday to Saturday and rested on Sundays. However, some worked all seven days and these were usually those who had just started the business and desired to earn more. Another key observation was that the relatively older women (36–45 years) with much trading experience acted as older siblings and 'mothers' to the younger ones by providing advice, counselling and guidance. In the process, very strong social networks are built amongst them but these are mostly ethnic or region-based. Whatever its form, it provides a feeling of agency for women in the sense that an enabling environment is created for women to start the process of empowerment.

Pathways to Empowerment

Eighty-one (69.2 percent) women reported that their current status is better than before. Twenty-two (18.8 percent) women mentioned that their status had not changed much to their satisfaction and 14 (12 percent) women even felt that their lives were worse off. This implies that more than half of the women perceived themselves to be better off and that their lives had improved as compared to when they were in the rural areas. Among this group, however, women who were 36–45 years appeared to be relatively better off as reported by 31 (81.6 percent) [interviewees] than women in the other age groups. Moreover, those who had been trading for longer periods also seem to have relatively better status than the others.

One clear factor that seems to have brought significant changes in the lives of the women who felt their lives had improved was the economic activities that they engaged in. These activities had brought the traders the opportunity of earning personal incomes. Even though they

were reluctant to state how much they earned weekly or daily, many reported that there were *'good days and bad days'* with good days being days that very good sales and profit margins were made and bad days being days that little sales were done hence minimal profits. A few who stated how much they earned mentioned that they earned between Gh¢20 and Gh¢40[1] a day. Earning income appeared to be a major achievement for these women as many were in the position to make choices such as the ability to invest. Indeed, many reported having made some appreciable level of investment from personal incomes earned and these included savings. Whilst savings level varied, those who had just started their trading activities saved between GH¢1 and GH¢2[2] daily whilst those who had been in the business for more than two years saved at least GH¢3 to GH¢5[3] daily, with the majority saving GH¢5 daily. Savings in the past, according to the women, used to be more on an informal basis or through the 'susu'[4] system. With time, women are saving with more formal institutions as a result of the proliferation of micro finance institutions. As noted by Malhotra et al. (2002), ensuring good financial management, which includes cultivating the habit of savings, is one of the indicators of socio-economic empowerment. Other investments made by the majority who felt their lives were better included renting of own apartments, purchasing personal items such as clothes, shoes, cooking utensils, electrical equipments and in few cases other valuable assets such as jewellery and land as reported by these women:

> I have rented my own flat and everything I have in my room now was purchased with the money I earn from this trading. I have furniture, television, DVD player, rice cooker, pressing iron among others. I don't think I would have been able to buy all these had I continued to be in my village. (34-year-old single woman)

> I have bought all that I need as a woman, cooking utensils, blender, cloth, shoes and some jewellery. I have also purchased a land on which I intend to build so that my children do not struggle in future. (38-year-old single woman)

The savings and investments done by these women appeared to have given them a sense of hope for the future. For instance, a 43-year-old divorced woman who had been trading for over 15 years reported that apart from the personal items that she had acquired, she had built a two-bedroom house in her village for her aged mother. She had also purchased land in a peri-urban area of Accra and had plans to build for herself and her two children. She had subsequently advised her younger contemporaries to do likewise. She expressed pride that her 37-year-old contemporary had also purchased a piece of land in the same area. The investments these women have made thus seemed to give them a sense of satisfaction as they appeared proud of their achievements. This suggests that women's involvement in economic activities improves their confidence in their own capabilities, enhances their self esteem and improves their status (Nikoi, 1998; Mayoux, 2002). Even among those who thought their situation had not changed as reported by 22 (18.8 percent) women or even worsened as reported by 14 (12.0 percent) women, there appeared to be a sense of anxiety and ambitiousness to succeed in life. Many expressed hope that they will be able to fulfil their life aspirations. This was particularly so among some of the unmarried women who had spent less than two years in trading. They reported that they had purchased pieces of cloths and utensils, something they considered very important for a woman who is preparing towards marriage.

Contributions to Household Budget

Contributing to household budget as a result of increasing economic empowerment of women was also identified as a source of satisfaction for the women, particularly the married ones, because in traditional Ghanaian society, the husband is considered as the head of the home and has the responsibility of taking care of all household members (Oppong, 2005; Wrigley-Asante, 2012a). It has been argued that incomes earned by women often lead to an enhancement of their socio-economic status at the household level as a result of their contributions to household survival (Hashemi et al., 1996; Kabeer, 2010). According to the women, the income derived supplemented the family budget and this enabled them to feed, clothe and provide for their family needs regularly as explained by these women:

> These days life is tough, one can't depend solely on the man; that's why I work so that I can support my husband to take care of our children. I pay my children's school fees, send them to the hospital when sick, buy food and clothes for them and myself, so you see, had it not been this work, what would I have done. Because of that my husband cannot insult me. (30-year-old married woman)

> I have one child but have no husband. As a single mother, I cater for myself and my child and this is all from the work that I do. I pay my child's school fees, send him to the hospital when sick, buy food and clothes for him and myself; because of that my child's father really respects me because I don't beg him for money. You know, some women do that and they always quarrel with those men but I will not. So you see, I have to work hard. (28-year-old single woman)

These expressions from the women suggest that both married and single women contributed to the household budget. Whilst those who were single relied solely on their income to provide for their needs and that of their children, for the married women, incomes earned contributed substantially in supporting the sustenance of their households. It further suggests that when women's income improves, there's a multiplier effect on the children because women pass on the benefits to children, through increased spending on the household, education, health and nutrition. Moreover, it enhances women's status in the household (Mayoux, 2002; Wrigley-Asante, 2012a).

Interpersonal Relations and Decision Making

Women's control over resources including income earned is one of the major indicators of women's empowerment (Kabeer, 2010; Malhotra et al., 2002). Whilst only 4 women mentioned that their husbands or partners had a say in their incomes earned, the rest of the women including those whose situations had not changed or even worsened, controlled incomes earned themselves. Indeed, many women did not want their partners to have intimate knowledge of their businesses due to past experiences in relationships, lack of trust between partners and fear of husbands shirking their responsibilities. But the most important reason for women's control over income earned was their desire to exercise choices in life such as deciding to save or purchasing personal items as expressed by these women:

> I used to give my money to my former husband to keep. Later we divorced and he left and I never got that money back. So I have decided to control my own money no matter what and no matter how much my present partner loves me. I keep my own money so that I can save for my future and children. (37-year-old married woman)

> I control what I earn myself because I work tirelessly for it so I can decide to do whatever I want to do. I don't even discuss what I earn with my husband because once he gets to know, he will stop supporting me and the children. (40-year-old married woman)

Some studies have also shown that when rural women have enhanced control over their lives, they continue to conform to traditional ideas and gender relations and that men's positions as 'heads' are not explicitly brought into question (Erman et al., 2002; Wrigley-Asante, 2012a). Whilst a few married women appeared to conform to these traditional ideas and gender relations, the demeanour of most of the women gave an impression of not conforming totally. Rather, they appeared to challenge patriarchal ideology of male domination and female subordination due to the fact that women were economically engaged with little economic dependence on men. Indeed, the women considered themselves urbane and may not necessarily be tied to tradition and customs that prevailed in rural communities. The unmarried women who controlled and managed their incomes earned alone also did not seem to

conform to traditional ideas of men's control over resources as mooted by these women:

> Why should I let my husband control the money I earn after all this struggling? These days times are difficult so one has to be wise. If I let him control my money I cannot do what I want to do and even buy what I want to buy. (25-year-old single woman)

> I take care of myself and therefore have to control my own money. I don't trust anybody when it comes to money, so I have to keep my own money in order to buy anything I want. (26-year-old single woman)

With improvement in women's earnings and contributions to the household budget, women also did participate in decision-making at the household level particularly on what to eat, cook and children's education. The unmarried women seemed to take decisions on these issues alone but whilst a few of the married ones did take such decisions alone, the majority did that together with partners. But the fact that women took decisions in these areas, whether alone or in partnership, tends to confirm Oppong's assertion that the financial resources that urban women bring into the household play a significant factor in the decision-making role of women (Oppong, 2005). The decision-making role of women extended to issues of sexual relations with partners. Many unmarried women expressed full control over sexual relations with partners since they did not live with such partners and that *'in modern times, women could take decisions on anything including when to have sex'* as explained by a 23-year-old single woman. There however, were mixed responses about this issue among the married ones. Whilst some felt that their partners could not force them because of their economic independence, others thought that refusing a partner often suggested infidelity on the part of the woman as expressed by these women:

> He can't force me to agree to his will all the time. I refuse him sometimes, especially when I'm very tired. Sometimes he understands and agrees but I also have to give in sometimes otherwise he will

think that I am seeing someone else. (34-year-old married woman)

Because I work hard and bring money home, he cannot force me. If I'm tired, I'm tired and that's it. (29-year-old married woman)

If I explain to him that I'm tired, he agrees and understands. You know that marriage thrives on understanding and so we understand each other. (40-year-old married woman)

These mixed reactions suggest that whilst some women were conforming to traditional ideas and gender relations concerning sexual relations, others appeared to challenge patriarchal ideology of male domination and female subordination. Perhaps the most important aspect of the decision-making role of women was at the extended family level. Women seemed to have used their new-found earning opportunities to renegotiate their relations not only within marriages but also within their extended families. Women reported being respected by their elders in their family, their siblings and friends as a result of the financial support and regular remittances they provided for their extended families left behind. Consequently, they participated in key family decisions during festive occasions such as Christmas and cultural festivals when they visited home. A 26-year-old woman who has been trading for about five years for instance, reported that she took care of her mentally-retarded brother and this has won her admiration by her family members. Another 41-year-old woman who has been trading for over 15 years explained that because of her constant support of her family members she is called a 'queenmother' by all family members. This respect accorded them thus gives women a sense of social status and satisfaction as explained by these women:

You see, Accra has turned my life around and I believe many of my sisters here will testify that their lives have been turned around. Life has not been easy and it's still tough but I feel good when I go back home because of the respect accorded me. When there is a problem, my family calls me

to come back home and assist them to settle it. Some of my elderly aunties even call me 'maa' because I support them financially. I don't think I would have received that kind of respect had I continued to be in the village because some of my friends I left behind some 15 years ago are still wallowing in their poverty. I even give them money sometimes. (43-year-old divorced woman)

I am respected a lot when I go back home. As young as I am, they look up to me as their mother because I am the only person who has taken care of my father ever since he fell sick. Because of this, my uncle consults me for advice. I sit together with the elderly and take decisions at family gatherings. (36-year-old married woman)

At one time, some of my family members came to visit me in Accra. I took them to my apartment and they were surprised to see all the things that I have. They really have seen that Accra has been good for me and so they respect me a lot. (27-year-old single woman)

These expressions corroborate studies conducted in Asia that show that migrant girls from rural areas to urban areas who had previously not been able to assist their aging mothers were able to do so. Moreover, the respect received from family members and enhanced sense of self-worth and self-reliance has given them greater sense of freedom and autonomy (Attanapola, 2004; Espen & Brody, 2007).

Challenges and Future Aspirations

Trading activities by these migrant women were not all that rosy. They were characterised by numerous challenges that many informal sector workers experience such as lack of permanent working spaces and insurance schemes, health-related challenges such as tiredness, back pains and other musculoskeletal disorders (see for instance Wrigley-Asante, 2012b). But the most repeated challenge that the traders expressed was 'harassment' by city officials. Ejection, harassment and arrest have therefore characterised the official attitude and reactions towards such traders (Asiedu & Agyei-Mensali. 2008). In the event that goods were seized, one tends to fall on her savings or relied on friends and acquaintances for support. In effect, that individual tends to retrogress rather than progress. Even though all the traders mentioned that they faced these challenges, the most affected were those who felt their lives had not changed. Indeed, this category of traders complained bitterly about how these factors negatively impacted on their lives. The problem was further compounded by over-reliance of external family members. These women explained that in certain cases, monies meant for savings had to be given to family members in order not to be perceived as *'wicked'*. Further, in the event of ill-health, one had to spend profits made on hospital bills and medications rather than savings. These explanations imply that investments, in the form of financial and physical assets, were very significant to these women and they seemed to be measures of success for these women. Therefore not having substantial savings, relatively, connotes failure.

Interestingly, many of the respondents in this study, including those who had not yet seen significant changes in their lives, did not seem to have any regrets and fears but rather had hope that the challenges they encountered would be succumbed. Many were confident that they would be able to fulfil their life aspirations in spite of the challenges they faced as they had future plans of owning large supermarkets, operating commercial vehicles such as taxis, sending their children to the best of schools and having substantial amount of savings in the bank. Those who had not yet achieved some substantial investments had future plans of acquiring assets such as land. For the relatively younger ones, some desired to continue their education by enrolling in the polytechnics and/or learning a vocational skill such as hairdressing or sewing.

Concluding Discussions

In this study, the trading activities of women and income earned are critical material resources which serve to enhance the ability of women to exercise choice (Kabeer, 2010). Prior to their migration, many of them could be described as being in conditions of disempowerment in the sense that they had limited opportunities and choices in life. Migration thus became the channel for improving one's socio-economic status (Awumbila et al., 2011). The social networks of women play a significant role for women to realize their power and ability to improve on their status. Through these networks, trading activities are established, incomes are earned and these create conducive atmosphere and avenues for strategic life choices to be made. Even though not all these women were satisfied with their status in life, the majority of them seemed to be on the pathway to empowerment. These women were particularly those who have had longer years in trading and have gained the ability to purchase personal items and make investments such as savings and acquisition of land. Such women were also contributing substantially to their household needs including the needs of extended family relations. There is thus a sense of socio-economic empowerment amongst these women particularly those who perceived themselves to be relatively better off. The earnings of women, is a contributing factor for participating in decision-making at the household and wider family levels and through which substantial respect had been gained. In this way, women seemed to be achieving interpersonal and relational empowerment. The respect accorded them gave them a sense of social status and satisfaction. Many were also confident that they would fufil their life aspirations. Thus there is a sense of psychological empowerment which means a sense of self-esteem and self-confidence (Malhotra et al., 2002).

It has been argued that migration may be empowering for many migrants, but such empowerment cannot be deemed automatic and that a significant number of migrant women experience downward occupational mobility (Moreno-Fontes, 2008). Moreover, many of them who fall in the informal sector activities are not covered by labour legislation and other social security benefits (Mitullah, 2003;

Wrigley-Asante, 2012b). These assertions seem to be true and reflect in the lives of those who thought their status had not changed or even worsened due to the numerous challenges they encountered and their inability to make substantial investments. Therefore, whilst one cannot categorically state that all these women are empowered, one could nevertheless argue that the majority of them are in the pathway of empowerment. The analysis shows that women do not only portray greater extrinsic control over resources but also a growing intrinsic capability, greater self-confidence and an inner transformation of one's consciousness (Sen & Batliwala, 2000; Kabeer, 2010). As noted by Moser (1993), empowerment must show the capacity of women to increase their own self-reliance and internal strength. This is identified as the right to determine choices in life and to influence the direction of change, through the ability to gain control over material and non-material resources (Kabeer, 2001, 2010). In this study, women's ability to gain control over material resources, their strategic life choices, and their ability to influence the direction of change are all pathways towards achieving empowerment. In spite of their limited education, they appeared proud of themselves, and what they had achieved. As noted by Erman et al. (2002), the money these women earn appears to be the most important thing in their lives as it allows them to enjoy 'personal feelings of empowerment' despite the tendency to underestimate migrant women's financial status.

In conclusion, one could argue that these young female migrants must not only be looked at in the context of vulnerability but rather seen as agents of change and people who can change their life circumstances and that of their families. Therefore the necessary support that they need must be provided by all stakeholders such as government and non-governmental organisations, civil society, donor and bilateral organisations. The Ministry of Gender, Children and Social Protection in collaboration with women's advocacy groups and donor organisations could assist these women by providing vocational skills, business and entrepreneurial training programmes for them so that they can improve on their trading activities. These institutions should also encourage the women to enrol with the national social security system established for the informal sector. This could be done through an intervention programme to educate and sensitize these women to subscribe to the system. Moreover, the women should be sensitised to enrol with the national health insurance scheme so that they can fall on that when faced with health-related challenges. Finally, non-governmental organisations could support the relatively younger ones who desired to further their education and assist them to achieve their future aspirations.

NOTES

1. This is equivalent to US$7.5 – US$20 daily, based on exchange rate as of July 2012.
2. This is equivalent to US$0.5 – US$1 daily, based on exchange rate as of July 2012.
3. This is equivalent to US$1.5 – US$2.5 daily, based on exchange rate as of July 2012.
4. This is a long tradition of informal savings and credit association where groups of people come together to save and borrow in turns.

REFERENCES

Ackah, C. & Medvedev, D. (2010). *Internal migration in Ghana: determinants and welfare impacts.* (World Bank Policy Research Working Paper No. 5273). Washington, DC: World Bank Group. Retrieved from: https://openknowledge.worldbank.org/bitstream/handle/10986/3760/WPS5273.pdf?sequence=1

Agyei, J. & Ofosu-Mensah Ababio, E. (2009). Historical overview of internal migration in Ghana. In J. K. Anarfi & S. O. Kwankye (Eds.), *Independent Migration of Children in Ghana* (pp. 9–44). Legon, Ghana: Institute of Statistical Social and Economic Research.

Asiedu, A.B. & Agyei-Mensah, S. (2008). Traders on the run: the activities of street vendors in the

Accra Metropolitan Area, Ghana. *Norwegian Journal of Geography, 52*(3), 191–202. doi: 10.1080/00291950802335806

Attanapola, C. T. (2004). Changing gender roles and health impacts among female workers in export processing industries in Sri Lanka. *Social Science and Medicine, 58*(11), 2301–2312. doi: 10.1016/j.socscimed.2003.08.022

Awumbila, M., Alhassan, O., Badasu, D. M., Bosiakoh, T. A. & Dankyi, E. K. (2011). *Socio-cultural dimensions of migration in Ghana.* Technical Paper Series, No. 3. Accra: Centre for Migration Studies, University of Ghana.

Awumbila, M. & Ardayfio–Schandorf, E. (2008). Gendered poverty, migration and livelihood strategies of female porters in Accra, Ghana. *Norwegian Journal of Geography, 52*(3), 171–179. doi: 10.1080/00291950802335772

Darkwah, A. 2007. Work as duty and work as joy: understanding the role of work in the lives of Ghanaian female traders of global consumer items. In S. Harley (Ed.), *Women's Labor in the Global Economy: Speaking Multiple Voices* (pp. 206–220). New Brunswick, New Jersey and London: Rutgers University Press.

Erman, T., Kalaycioglu, S. & Rittersberger-Tilic, H. (2002). Money-earning activities and empowerment experiences of rural migrant women in the city: the case of Turkey. *Women's Studies International Forum, 25*(4), 395–410. doi: 10.1016/S0277-5395(02)00277-7

Esplen, E. & Brody, A. (2007). *Putting gender back in the picture: rethinking women's economic empowerment.* (BRIDGE report n°19). Brighton: Institute of Development Studies. Retrieved from: http://www.bridge.ids.ac.uk/reports/BB19_Economic_Empowerment.pdf

Hashemi, S.M., Schuler, S.R. & Riley, A.P. (1996). Rural credit programs and women's empowerment in Bangladesh. *World Development, 24*(4), 635–653. doi: 10.1016/0305–750X(95)00159–A

Kabeer, N. (2001). Resources, agency, achievements: reflections on the measurement of women's empowerment. In A. Sisask (Ed.), *Discussing Women's Empowerment—Theory and Practice* (pp. 17–57). Stockholm: Swedish International Development Agency. Retrieved from: http://www.sida.se/Publications/lmport/pdf/sv/Discussing-Womens-Empowerment—Theory-and-Practice.pdf

Kabeer, N. (2010). Gender equality and women's empowerment: a critical analysis of the third Millennium Development Goal. *Gender and Development, 13*(1), 13–24. doi: 10.1080/13552070512331332273

Malhotra, A., Schuler, S. R. & Boender, C. (2002). *Measuring women's empowerment as a variable in international development.* Background paper prepared for the World Bank workshop on poverty and gender. Washington, D.C.: International Center for Research on Women. Retrieved from: http://www.siyanda.org/static malhotra_empvariable.htm

Mayoux, L. (2002). *Women's empowerment or feminisation of debt: towards a new agenda in African micro finance.* London: One World Action. Retrieved from: http://www.eldis.org/static/DOCI 1355.htm

Mitullah, W. V. (2003). *Street vending in African cities: synthesis of empirical findings from Kenya, Cote d'Ivoire, Ghana, Zimbabwe, Uganda and South Africa.* Washington, DC: World Bank.

Moreno-Fontes, G. (2008, Sep. 24). *Migrant women worker: seizing opportunities, upholding rights.* International Labour Organization Newsoffice. Retrieved from: http://www.ilo.org/global/about-the-ilo/press-and-media-centre/insight/WCMS_098491/lang—en/index.htm

Moser, C. O. (1993). *Gender Planning and Development: Theory, Practice and Training.* London: Routledge.

Nikoi, G. (1998). *Gender and Development.* Accra, Ghana: University of Cape Coast, Publications Unit.

Oppong, C. (2005). *Conjugal resources, power, decision making and domestic labour: some historical and recent evidence of modernity from Ghanaian families.* Legon: Institute of African Studies, University of Ghana.

Overa, R. (2007). When men do women's work: structural adjustment, unemployment and changing gender relations in the informal economy of Accra, Ghana. *Journal of Modern African Studies, 45*(4), 539–563, doi: http://dx.doi.org/10.1017.S0022278X0700287X

Sen, G. & Batliwala (2000). Empowering women for reproductive rights. In H.B. Presser & G. Sen (Eds.), *Women's Empowerment and Demographic Processes* (pp. 15–36). New Delhi: Oxford University Press.

World Bank Group (2004). *What is empowerment?* Retrieved from: http://Inwebl8.worldbank.org/ESSD/sdvext.nsf/68ByDocName/WhatIs-Empowerment

Wrigley-Asante, C. (2012a). Out of the dark but not out of the cage: women's empowerment and gender relations in the Dangme West district of Ghana. *Gender, Place and Culture, 19*(3), 344–363. doi: 10.1080/0966369X.2011.572435

Wrigley-Asante, C. (2012b). Unraveling the health-related challenges of women in informal economy: accounts of women in cross border trading in Accra, Ghana. *GeoJournal*. First published online 3 February 2012, Springer, doi: 10.1007/s10708-012-9449-7

Introduction to Reading 15

Maria Alexandra Lepowsky is an anthropologist who lived among the Melanesian people of Vanatinai, a small, remote island near New Guinea, from 1977 to 1979, for 2 months in 1981, and again for 3 months in 1987. She chose Vanatinai, which literally means "motherland," because she wanted to do research in a place where "the status of women" is high. The egalitarianism of the Vanatinai challenges the Western belief in the universality of male dominance and female subordination.

1. What is the foundation of women's high status and gender equality among the people of Vanatinai?

2. What does gender equality mean on Vanatinai? Does it mean that women and men split everything fifty-fifty? Are men and women interchangeable?

3. What are the similarities and differences between the egalitarianism of the Gerai people (depicted in Christine Helliwell's article in this chapter) and that of the people of Vanatinai?

GENDER AND POWER

Maria Alexandra Lepowsky

Vanatinai customs are generally egalitarian in both philosophy and practice. Women and men have equivalent rights to and control of the means of production, the products of their own labor, and the products of others. Both sexes have access to the symbolic capital of prestige, most visibly through participation in ceremonial exchange and mortuary ritual. Ideologies of male superiority or right of authority over women are notably absent, and ideologies of gender equivalence are clearly articulated. Multiple levels of gender ideologies are largely, but not entirely, congruent. Ideologies in turn are largely congruent with practice and individual actions in expressing gender equivalence, complementarity, and overlap.

There are nevertheless significant differences in social influence and prestige among persons.

These are mutable, and they fluctuate over the lifetime of the individual. But Vanatinai social relations are egalitarian overall, and sexually egalitarian in particular, in that at each stage in the life cycle all persons, female and male, have equivalent autonomy and control over their own actions, opportunity to achieve both publicly and privately acknowledged influence and power over the actions of others, and access to valued goods, wealth, and prestige. The quality of generosity, highly valued in both sexes, is explicitly modeled after parental nurture. Women are not viewed as polluting or dangerous to themselves or others in their persons, bodily fluids, or sexuality.

Vanatinai sociality is organized around the principle of personal autonomy. There are no chiefs, and nobody has the right to tell another adult what to do. This philosophy also results in some extremely permissive childrearing and a strong degree of tolerance for the idiosyncrasies of other people's behavior. While working together, sharing, and generosity are admirable, they are strictly voluntary. The selfish and antisocial person might be ostracized, and others will not give to him or her. If kinfolk, in-laws, or neighbors disagree, even with a powerful and influential big man or big woman, they have the option, frequently taken, of moving to another hamlet where they have ties and can expect access to land for gardening and foraging. Land is communally held by matrilineages, but each person has multiple rights to request and be given space to make a garden on land held by others, such as the mother's father's matrilineage. Respect and tolerance for the will and idiosyncrasies of individuals is reinforced by fear of their potential knowledge of witchcraft or sorcery.

Anthropological discussions of women, men, and society over the last one hundred years have been framed largely in terms of "the status of women," presumably unvarying and shared by all women in all social situations. Male dominance and female subordination have thus until recently been perceived as easily identified and often as human universals. If women are indeed universally subordinate, this implies a universal primary cause: hence the search for a single underlying reason for male dominance and female subordination, either material or ideological.

More recent writings in feminist anthropology have stressed multiple and contested gender statuses and ideologies and the impacts of historical forces, variable and changing social contexts, and conflicting gender ideologies. Ambiguity and contradiction, both within and between levels of ideology and social practice, give both women and men room to assert their value and exercise power. Unlike in many cultures where men stress women's innate inferiority, gender relations on Vanatinai are not contested, or antagonistic: There are no male versus female ideologies which vary markedly or directly contradict each other. Vanatinai mythological motifs, beliefs about supernatural power, cultural ideals of the sexual division of labor and of the qualities inherent to men and women, and the customary freedoms and restrictions upon each sex at different points in the life course all provide ideological underpinnings of sexual equality.

Since the 1970s writings on the anthropology of women, in evaluating degrees of female power and influence, have frequently focused on the disparity between the "ideal" sex role pattern of a culture, often based on an ideology of male dominance, publicly proclaimed or enacted by men, and often by women as well, and the "real" one, manifested by the actual behavior of individuals. This approach seeks to uncover female social participation, overt or covert, official or unofficial, in key events and decisions and to learn how women negotiate their social positions. The focus on social and individual "action" or "practice" is prominent more generally in cultural anthropological theory of recent years. Feminist analyses of contradictions between gender ideologies of female inferiority and the realities of women's and men's daily lives— the actual balance of power in household and community—have helped to make this focus on the actual behavior of individuals a wider theoretical concern.[1]

In the Vanatinai case gender ideologies in their multiple levels and contexts emphasize the value of women and provide a mythological charter for the degree of personal autonomy and freedom of choice manifested in real women's lives. Gender ideologies are remarkably similar (though not completely, as I discuss below) as they are manifested situationally, in philosophical statements by women and men, in the ideal pattern of the sexual division of labor, in taboos and proscriptions, myth, cosmology, magic, ritual, the supernatural balance of power, and in the codifications of custom. Women are not characterized as weak or inferior. Women and men are valorized for the same qualities of strength, wisdom, and generosity. If possessed of these qualities an individual woman or man will act in ways which bring prestige not only to the actor but to the kin and residence groups to which she or he belongs.

Nevertheless, there is no single relationship between the sexes on Vanatinai. Power relations and relative influence vary with the individuals, sets of roles, situations, and historical moments involved. Gender ideologies embodied in myths, beliefs, prescriptions for role-appropriate behavior, and personal statements sometimes contradict each other or are contradicted by the behavior of individuals.

* * *

MATERIAL AND IDEOLOGICAL BASES OF EQUALITY

Does equality or inequality, including between men and women, result from material or ideological causes? We cannot say whether an idea preceded or followed specific economic and social circumstances. Does the idea give rise to the act, or does the act generate an ideology that justifies it or mystifies it?

If they are congruent, ideology and practice reinforce one another. And if multiple levels of ideology are in accord, social forms are more likely to remain unchallenged and fundamentally unchanged. Where levels of ideology, or ideology and practice, are at odds, the circumstances of social life are more likely to be challenged by those who seek a reordering of social privileges justified according to an alternative interpretation of ideology. When social life embodies these kinds of contradictions, the categories of people in power—aristocrats, the rich, men—spend a great deal of energy maintaining their power. They protect their material resources, subdue the disenfranchised with public or private violence, coercion, and repression, and try to control public and private expressions of ideologies of political and religious power.

On Vanatinai, where there is no ideology of male dominance, the material conditions for gender equality are present. Women—and their brothers—control the means of production. Women own land, and they inherit land, pigs, and valuables from their mothers, their mothers' brothers, and sometimes from their fathers equally with men. They have the ultimate decision-making power over the distribution of staple foods that belong jointly to their kinsmen and that their kinsmen or husbands have helped labor to grow. They are integrated into the prestige economy, the ritualized exchanges of ceremonial valuables. Ideological expressions, such as the common saying that the woman is the owner of the garden, or the well-known myth of the first exchange between two female beings, validate material conditions.

I do not believe it would be possible to have a gender egalitarian society, where prevailing expressions of gender ideology were egalitarian or valorized both sexes to the same degree, without material control by women of land, means of subsistence, or wealth equivalent to that of men. This control would encompass anything from foraging rights, skills, tools, and practical and sacred knowledge to access to high-paying, prestigious jobs and the knowledge and connections it takes to get them. Equal control of the means of production, then, is one necessary precondition of gender equality. Vanatinai women's major disadvantage is their lack of access to a key tool instrumental in gaining power and prestige, the spear. Control of the means of production is potentially greater in a matrilineal society.

* * *

GENDER IDEOLOGIES AND PRACTICE IN DAILY LIFE

In Melanesian societies the power of knowing is privately owned and transmitted, often through ties of kinship, to heirs or younger supporters. It comes not simply from acquiring skills or the experience and the wisdom of mature years but is fundamentally a spiritual power that derives from ancestors and other spirit forces.

In gender segregated societies, such as those that characterize most of Melanesia, this spiritual knowledge power is segregated as well into a male domain through male initiations or the institutions of men's houses or male religious cults. Most esoteric knowledge—and the power over others that derives from it—is available to Vanatinai women if they can find a kinsperson or someone else willing to teach it to them. There are neither exclusively male nor female collectivities on Vanatinai nor characteristically male versus female domains or patterns of sociality (cf. Strathern 1987:76).

Decisions taken collectively by Vanatinai women and men within one household, hamlet, or lineage are political ones that reverberate well beyond the local group, sometimes literally hundreds of miles beyond. A hundred years ago they included decisions of war and peace. Today they include the ritualized work of kinship, more particularly of the matrilineage, in mortuary ritual. Mortuary feasts, and the inter-island and inter-hamlet exchanges of ceremonial valuables that support them, memorialize the marriages that tied three matrilineages together, that of the deceased, the deceased's father, and the widowed spouse. Honoring these ties of alliance, contracted by individuals but supported by their kin, and threatened by the dissolution of death, is the major work of island politics. . . .

The small scale, fluidity (cf. Collier and Rosaldo 1981), and mobility of social life on Vanatinai, especially in combination with matriliny, are conducive of egalitarian social relations between men and women and old and young. They promote an ethic of respect for the individual, which must be integrated with the ethic of cooperation essential for survival in a subsistence economy. People must work out conflict through face-to-face negotiation, or existing social ties will be broken by migration, divorce, or death through sorcery or witchcraft.

Women on Vanatinai are physically mobile, traveling with their families to live with their own kin and then the kin of their spouse, making journeys in quest of valuables, and attending mortuary feasts. They are said to have traveled for these reasons even in precolonial times when the threat of attack was a constant danger. The generally greater physical mobility of men in human societies is a significant factor in sexual asymmetries of power, as it is men who generally negotiate and regulate relationships with outside groups (cf. Ardener 1975:6).

Vanatinai women's mobility is not restricted by ideology or by taboo, and women build their own far-ranging personal networks of social relationships. Links in these networks may be activated as needed by the woman to the benefit of her kin or hamlet group. Women are confined little by taboos or community pressures. They travel, choose their own marriage partners or lovers, divorce at will, or develop reputations as wealthy and generous individuals active in exchange.

BIG MEN, BIG WOMEN, AND CHIEFS

Vanatinai giagia, male and female, match Sahlins's (1989) classic description of the Melanesian big man, except that the role of gia is gender-blind. There has been renewed interest among anthropologists in recent years in the big man form of political authority.[2] The Vanatinai case of the female and male giagia offers an intriguing perspective. . . .

Any individual on Vanatinai, male or female, may try to become known as a gia by choosing to exert the extra effort to go beyond the minimum contributions to the mortuary feasts expected of every adult. He or she accumulates ceremonial valuables and other goods both in order to give them away in acts of public generosity and to honor obligations to exchange partners from the local area as well as distant islands. There may be more than one gia in a particular hamlet, or even household, or there may be none. A woman may have considerably more prestige and influence than her husband because of her reputation for acquiring and redistributing valuables. While there are more men than women who are extremely active in exchange, there are some women who are far more active than the majority of men.

Giagia of either sex are only leaders in temporary circumstances and if others wish to follow, as when they host a feast, lead an exchange expedition, or organize the planting of a communal yam garden. Decisions are made by consensus, and the giagia of both sexes influence others through their powers of persuasion, their reputations for ability, and their knowledge, both of beneficial magic and ritual and of sorcery or witchcraft. . . .

On Vanatinai power and influence over the actions of others are gained by achievement and demonstrated superior knowledge and skill, whether in the realm of gardening, exchange, healing, or sorcery. Those who accumulate a surplus of resources are expected to be generous and share with their neighbors or face the threat of the sorcery or witchcraft of the envious. Both women and men are free to build their careers through exchange. On the other hand both women and men are free not to strive toward renown as giagia but to work for their own families or simply to mind their own business. They can also achieve the respect of their peers, if they seek it at all, as loving parents, responsible and hardworking lineage mates and affines, good gardeners, hunters, or fishers, or skilled healers, carvers, or weavers.

Mead (1935) observes that societies vary in the degree to which "temperament types" or "approved social personalities" considered suitable for each sex or a particular age category differ from each other. On Vanatinai there is wide variation in temperament and behavior among islanders of the same sex and age. The large amount of overlap between the roles of men and women on Vanatinai leads to a great deal of role flexibility, allowing both individual men and women the freedom to specialize in the activities they personally enjoy, value, are good at performing, or feel like doing at a particular time. There is considerable freedom of choice in shaping individual lifestyles.

An ethic of personal autonomy, one not restricted to the powerful, is a key precondition of social equality. Every individual on Vanatinai from the smallest child to an aged man or woman possesses a large degree of autonomy. Idiosyncrasies of personality and character are generally tolerated and respected. When you ask why someone does or does not do something, your friends will say, emphatically and expressively, "We [inclusive we: you and I both] don't know," "It is something of theirs" [their way], or, "She doesn't want to."

Islanders say that it is not possible to know why a person behaves a certain way or what thoughts generate an action. Persisting in a demand to "know" publicly the thoughts of others is dangerous, threatening, and invasive. Vanatinai people share, in part, the perspectives identified with postmodern discussions of the limits of ethnographic representation: It is impossible to know another person's thoughts or feelings. If you try they are likely to deceive you to protect their own privacy or their own interests. Your knowing is unique to you. It is your private property that you transmit only at your own volition, as when you teach magical spells to a daughter or sister's son.[3]

The prevailing social sanction is also individualistic: the threat of somebody else's sorcery or witchcraft if you do not do what they want or if you arouse envy or jealousy. But Vanatinai cultural ideologies stress the strength of individual will in the face of the coercive pressures of custom, threat of sorcery, and demands to share.

This leads to a Melanesian paradox: The ethic of personal autonomy is in direct conflict to the ethic of giving and sharing so highly valued on Vanatinai, as in most Melanesian cultures. Nobody can make you share, short of stealing from you or killing you if you refuse them. You have to want to give: your nurture, your labor, your valuables, and your person. This is where persuasion comes in. It comes from the pressure of other people, the force of shame, and magical seduction made potent by supernatural agency. Vanatinai custom supplies a final, persuasive argument to resolve this paradox: By giving, you not only strengthen your lineage and build its good name, you make yourself richer and more powerful by placing others in your debt.

What can people in other parts of the world learn from the principles of sexual equality in Vanatinai custom and philosophy? Small scale facilitates Vanatinai people's emphasis on face-to-face negotiations of interpersonal conflicts without the delegation of political authority to a small group of middle-aged male elites. It also leaves room for an ethic of respect for the will of the individual regardless of age or sex. A culture that is egalitarian and nonhierarchical overall is more likely to have egalitarian relations between men and women.

Males and females on Vanatinai have equivalent autonomy at each life cycle stage. As adults they have similar opportunities to influence the actions of others. There is a large amount of overlap between the roles and activities of women and men, with women occupying public, prestige-generating roles. Women share control of the production and the distribution of valued goods, and they inherit property. Women as well as men participate in the exchange of valuables, they organize feasts, they officiate at important rituals such as those for yam planting or healing, they counsel their kinfolk, they speak out and are listened to in public meetings, they possess valuable magical knowledge, and they work side by side in most subsistence activities. Women's role as nurturing parent is highly valued and is the dominant metaphor for the generous men and women who gain renown and influence over others by accumulating and then giving away valuable goods.

But these same characteristics of respect for individual autonomy, role overlap, and public participation of women in key subsistence and prestige domains of social life are also possible in large-scale industrial and agricultural societies. The Vanatinai example suggests that sexual equality is facilitated by an overall ethic of respect for and equal treatment of all categories of individuals, the decentralization of political power, and inclusion of all categories of persons (for example, women and ethnic minorities) in public positions of authority and influence. It requires greater role overlap through increased integration of the workforce, increased control by women and minorities of valued goods—property, income, and educational credentials—and increased recognition of the social value of parental care. The example of Vanatinai shows that the subjugation of women by men is not a human universal, and it is not inevitable. Sex role patterns and gender ideologies are closely related to overall social systems of power and prestige. Where these systems stress personal autonomy and egalitarian social relations among all adults, minimizing the formal authority of one person over another, gender equality is possible.

NOTES

1. See, for example, Rogers (1975) and Collier and Rosaldo (1981) on ideal versus real gender relations. Ortner (1984) summarizes approaches to practice; cf. Bourdieu (1977).

2. The appropriateness of using the big man institution to define Melanesia versus a Polynesia characterized by chiefdoms, the relationship of big men to social equality, rank, and stratification, and the interactions of this form of leadership with colonialism and modernization are central issues in recent anthropological writings on big men (e.g., Brown 1987; Godelier 1986; Sahlins 1989; Strathern 1987; Thomas 1989; Lederman 1991). I discuss the implications of the Vanatinai case of the giagia at greater length in Lepowsky (1990).

3. See, for example, Clifford (1983); Clifford and Marcus (1986); and Marcus and Fischer (1986) on representations. In this book I have followed my own cultural premises and not those of Vanatinai by publicly attributing thoughts, motives, and feelings to others and by trying to find the shapes in a mass of chaotic and sometimes contradictory statements and actions. But my Vanatinai friends say, characteristically, that my writing is "something of mine"—my business.

REFERENCES

Ardener, Edwin. 1975. "Belief and the Problem of Women." In Shirley Ardener, ed., *Perceiving Women*. London: Malaby.

Bourdieu, Pierre. 1977. *Outline of a Theory of Practice*. T. R. Nice. Cambridge: Cambridge University Press.

Brown, Paula. 1987. "New Men and Big Men: Emerging Social Stratification in the Third World, A Case Study from the New Guinea Highlands." *Ethnology* 26:87–106.

Clifford, James. 1983. "On Ethnographic Authority." *Representations* 1:118–146.

Clifford, James, and George Marcus, eds. 1986. *Writing Culture: The Poetics and Politics of Ethnography*. Berkeley: University of California Press.

Collier, Jane, and Michelle Rosaldo. 1981. "Politics and Gender in Simple Societies." In Sherry Ortner and Harriet Whitehead, eds., *Sexual Meanings: The Cultural Construction of Gender and Sexuality*. Cambridge: Cambridge University Press.

Godelier, Maurice. 1986. *The Making of Great Men: Male Domination and Power Among the New Guinea Baruya*. Cambridge: Cambridge University Press.

Lederman, Rena. 1991. "'Interests' in Exchange: Increment, Equivalence, and the Limits of Bigmanship." In Maurice Godelier and Marilyn Strathern, eds., *Big Men and Great Men: Personifications of Power in Melanesia*. Cambridge: Cambridge University Press.

Lepowsky, Maria. 1990. "Big Men, Big Women, and Cultural Autonomy." *Ethnology* 29(10):35–50.

Marcus, George, and Michael Fischer, eds. 1986. *Anthropology as Cultural Critique: An Experimental Moment in the Human Sciences*. Chicago: University of Chicago Press.

Mead, Margaret. 1935. *Sex and the Temperament in Three Primitive Societies*. New York: William Morrow.

Ortner, Sherry. 1984. "Theory in Anthropology Since the Sixties." *Comparative Studies in Society and History* 26(1):126–166.

Rogers, Susan Carol. 1975. "Female Forms of Power and the Myth of Male Dominance: A Model of Female/Male Interaction in Peasant Society." *American Ethnologist* 2:727–756.

Sahlins, Marshall. 1989. "Comment: The Force of Ethnology: Origins and Significance of the Melanesia/Polynesia Division." *Current Anthropology* 30:36–37.

Strathern, Marilyn. 1987. "Introduction." In Marilyn Strathern, ed., *Dealing with Inequality: Analysing Gender Relations in Melanesia and Beyond*. Cambridge: Cambridge University Press.

Thomas, Nicholas. 1989. "The Force of Ethnology: Origins and Significance of the Melanesia/Polynesia Division." *Current Anthropology* 30:27–34.

❦ Topics for Further Examination ❧

- Locate and read scholarly research on the Hijras of India, the Fa'afafines of Samoa, and the Xanith of Oman.
- Look up scholarly studies that address the history of the egalitarian gender system of the Iroquois Confederacy.
- Challenge ethnocentric notions that women who practice Islam are antifeminist by reading investigative journalist and scholarly accounts of the rise of feminism among Muslim women in countries such as Indonesia, Pakistan, and Egypt.

PART II

PATTERNS

4

LEARNING AND DOING GENDER

JOAN Z. SPADE

We began this book by discussing the shaping of gender in Western and non-Western cultures. Part II expands on the idea of prisms by examining the *patterns* of gendered experiences that emerge from the practices of daily life and the interaction of gender with other socially constructed prisms. Patterns of individuals' lives are influenced by gender and other social prisms, just as multiple patterns are created by the refraction of light as it travels through a kaleidoscope containing prisms.

GENDERED PATTERNS

Social patterns are at the center of social scientists' work. Michael Schwalbe (1998), a sociologist, defines social patterns as "a regularity in the way the world works" (p. 101). For example, driving down the "right" side of the street is a regularity American people appreciate. You will read about different gendered patterns in Part II, many of which are regularities you will find problematic because they deny the individuality of women and men. Clearly, there are exceptions to social patterns; however, these exceptions are in the details, not in the regularity of social behavior itself (Schwalbe, 1998). Patterns in society are not simple and are even contradicted by other patterns. We have rigid gender expectations for things such as which colors are appropriate for children, teens, and even adults. At the same time, we practice resistance to these patterns and fluidity in the way gender is displayed in daily life. For example, an upper-class man might feel comfortable wearing a pink polo shirt to a golf tournament but not so comfortable putting a ruffled pink shirt on his 2-year-old son.

A deeper understanding of how and why particular social patterns and practices exist helps us interpret our own behavior and the world around us. Gender, as we discussed in Part I, is not a singular pattern of masculinity or femininity that carries from one situation to another. Instead, it is complex, multifaceted, and ever changing, depending on the social context, whom we are with, and where we are, as illustrated in the reading by Michela Musto in this chapter. Gender is also interpreted differently based on the community or group we associate with. That is, African American women are much less likely to adhere to idealized forms of gender or, as Karen D. Pyke and Denise L. Johnson labeled it in Chapter 2, hegemonic femininity—White, middle-class femininity. Our behavior in almost all situations is framed within our knowledge of idealized gender—hegemonic masculinity and emphasized femininity. Whether we resist or ridicule gender practices, we are almost always aware of them.

Keep the concepts of hegemonic masculinity and emphasized femininity in mind as we examine social patterns of gender. To illustrate this, let's return to the stereotype discussed in the introduction to this book—that women talk more than men. We know from research that the real social pattern in mixed-gender groups is that men talk more, interrupt more, and change the topic more often than do women (Anderson & Leaper, 1998; Brescoli, 2011; Wood, 1999). The stereotype, while trivializing women's talk and ignoring the dominance of men in mixed-gender groups, maintains the patterns of dominance and subordination associated with hegemonic masculinity and emphasized femininity, influencing women's as well as men's behaviors. Girls—particularly White, middle-class girls—are encouraged to use a pleasant voice and not talk too much. Later, as they grow older and join mixed-gender groups at work or in play, women's voices are often ignored and they are subordinated as they monitor what they say and how often they talk, checking to make sure they are not dominating the conversation. And since gender is relational, others learn that girls talk too much and should either shut up or speak in a "nice voice." Gender is an ever-present force in defining daily behavior and is used in marketing to entice us to "buy into" gender as we purchase all kinds of products (Chapter 5). By examining how these idealized versions of masculinity and femininity pattern daily practices, we can better understand the patterns and meanings of our behavior and the behaviors of others.

Gendered patterns of belief and behavior influence us throughout our lives, from birth until old age, in almost every activity in which we engage. Readings in Part II examine the process and consequences of learning to do gender (Chapters 4 and 5) and then describe gendered patterns in work (Chapter 7) and in daily intimate relationships (Chapter 8). We also explore how gendered patterns affect our bodies, sexualities, and emotions (Chapter 6), and how patterns of dominance, control, and violence enforce gender patterns (Chapter 9).

The patterns that emerge from the gender kaleidoscope are not unique experiences in individual lives; they are regularities that occur in many people's lives. They are not static patterns that remain the same across lifetimes or history, nor are they singular patterns with one and only one way of doing gender. Gendered patterns are many and fluid across time and space. If you don't pay attention, gendered patterns may seem as though they are individual choices. Institutions and groups enforce gendered patterns and practices in the home, workplace, and daily life, as described in the readings throughout Part II. These patterns overlap and reinforce gender differences and inequalities. For example, gender discrimination in wages and promotions affects families' decisions about parenting roles and relationships. Since most men still earn more than most women, the choices of families who wish to break away from idealized gender patterns and practices are limited by decisions surrounding household income. However, these patterns are complicated by intersections with race and social class, as you will see from the readings in Chapters 7 and 8.

LEARNING AND DOING GENDER

The readings in Chapter 4 examine the processes by which we acquire self-perceptions and behaviors and learn our culture's expectations for idealized patterns of masculinities and femininities. These readings emphasize that, regardless of our inability or unwillingness to attain idealized femininity and masculinity, almost everyone in a culture learns what idealized gender is and organizes their lives around those expectations, even if in resistance to them, as is the case of parents raising gender-variant children in the reading by Elizabeth P. Rahilly in this chapter. Of course, the genderscape is complex. While some people resist idealized gender and others try to ignore these signals, some communities develop alternatives to idealized gender, such as that in Irene Padavic and Jonniann Butterfield's article on lesbian co-parenting in Chapter 8.

SOCIALIZING CHILDREN

There are many explanations for why children gravitate toward idealized gender-appropriate behavior. The term sociologists use to describe how we learn gender is *gender socialization*, and sociologists approach it from a variety of different perspectives (Coltrane, 1998). Socialization is the process of teaching members of a society the values, expectations, and practices of the larger culture. Socialization takes place in all interactions and situations, with families and schools typically having primary responsibility for socializing infants and children in Western societies. Early attempts to explain gender socialization gave little attention to the response of individuals to agents of socialization, such as parents, peers, and teachers, and to the influence of mass media and a consumer culture. There was an underlying assumption in this early perspective that individuals were blank tablets (*tabulae rasae*) on which the cultural definitions of idealized gender and other appropriate behaviors were written. This perspective assumed that, as individuals developed, they took on a gender identity appropriate to their assigned biological sex category (Howard & Alamilla, 2001). Accepting the gender that is associated with your sex assignment is referred to as cisgender.

Social scientists now realize that individuals are not blank tablets, that sex categories are not easily determined (see reading by Georgiann Davis and Sharon Preves in Chapter 1), and that gender socialization is not just something that is "done" to us. Theorists now describe socialization into gender as a series of complex and dynamic processes. Individuals create, as well as respond to, social stimuli in their environments (Carlton-Ford & Houston, 2001; Howard & Alamilla, 2001). Moreover, socialization doesn't simply end after childhood. Socialization is a process that lasts across one's lifetime, from birth to death (Lutfey & Mortimer, 2003), and occurs continually with everyone we interact with—friends, peers, coworkers, and acquaintances—as well as the environment around us, including mass media, as discussed in Chapters 5 and 6. Furthermore, there is a fluidity to gender ideology, with changes occurring across the life course, across race–gender categories (Vespa, 2009), and even across social contexts. For example, beauty means something different for a young child, teenager, or older person. Throughout our lives, we assess cues around us and behave as situations dictate. All socialization is, of course, reinforced by social institutions, as Barbara J. Risman discussed in the first reading in this book, and which we will discuss later in this introduction. Thus, whether we want it or not, idealized gender is a key factor in determining what is appropriate throughout our lives—even though few of us actually attain an idealized form of gender.

The dominant pattern of gender expectations, the pink and blue schema described in the introduction to this book (Paoletti, 2012), begins at birth. Once external genital identification takes place, immediate expectations for masculine and feminine behavior follow. Exclamations of "He's going to be a great baseball (or football or soccer) player" and "She's so cute" are accompanied by gifts of little sleepers in pink or blue with gender-appropriate decorations. Try as we might, it is very difficult to find gender-neutral clothing for children (see Adie Nelson's article in Chapter 5). These expectations, and the way we treat young children, reinforce idealized gender constructions of dominance and subordination and illustrate how influential the role of marketing and consumer culture is in defining idealized gender.

It is not long then, before most children come to understand that they should be "boys" and "girls," and segregate themselves accordingly. These children learn their appropriate gender behavior (defined as cisgender in many studies). Family members are not alone in teaching children to behave as "good boys" or "good girls." Almost every person a child comes into contact with and virtually all aspects of a child's material world reinforce gender. In effect, children are taught that males and females are different and that they are expected to behave accordingly. In Chapter 5, you will read more about how capitalist societies reinforce and maintain gender difference and inequality for children and adults. Television, music, books, clothing, and toys differentiate and prescribe idealized gender behavior for girls and boys. For example, studies of children's books find some distinctive patterns that reinforce idealized forms of gender. As Janice McCabe, Emily Fairchild, Liz Grauerholz, Bernice A. Pescosolido, and Daniel Tope discuss in their reading in this chapter, boys outnumber girls in books (titles and main characters) published across the 20th century. Although books continue to depict traditional gender patterns, on the plus side, researchers find that girls and women are more likely to be portrayed in gender-atypical roles in many recent children's books (Gooden & Gooden, 2001).

Most children quickly understand the idealized gender-appropriate message directed toward them and try to behave accordingly. Although not all boys are dominant and not all girls are subordinate, studies in a variety of areas find that most White boys tend toward active and aggressive behaviors, while most White girls tend to be quieter and more focused on relationships. The patterning for African American boys is similar, and African American boys who do not act in gender-appropriate ways are seen as "soft" or feminine (Carter, 2005). These patterns for boys and girls have been documented in school and in play (e.g., Sadker & Sadker, 1994; Thorne, 1993).

It is important to note that the consequences for gender-appropriate behavior are not entirely positive. Gender-appropriate behavior is related to lower self-confidence and self-esteem for girls (e.g., Eder, 1995; Orenstein, 1994; Spade, 2001), whereas boys are taught to "mask" their feelings and compete with everyone for control, thus isolating themselves and ignoring their own feelings (e.g., Connell, 2000; Messner, 1992; Pollack, 2000).

SOCIAL INSTITUTIONS AND SOCIALIZATION

Many of our social institutions segregate children and adults by gender as well, thus creating gendered identities. All adults, not just parents, play a major role in teaching gender. Teachers also teach gender, and when they separate children into gender-segregated spaces in lunch lines or playground areas, they reinforce gender differences (Sadker & Sadker, 1994; Thorne, 1993). However, teachers are becoming more aware of their role in gendering children and, in some contexts, such as the swimming team described in the reading by Musto in this chapter, the importance of gender can be made irrelevant by focusing on the task at hand. Yet, as shown in Musto's reading, these lessons may not carry over to other contexts.

Schools, however, typically reinforce separate and unequal spheres for boys and girls (Orenstein, 1994; Sadker & Sadker, 1994; Thorne, 1993). Considerable research by the American Association of University Women (1992, 1998, 1999) documents how schools "shortchange" girls. Schools are social institutions that maintain patterns of power and dominance. Indeed, we teach dominance in schools in patterns of teacher–student interactions such as respecting the responses of boys while encouraging girls to be helpers in the classroom (Grant, 1985; Sadker & Sadker, 1994). A study using data collected from individuals during their high school years (2002, 2004, and 2006) showed that gender socialization in schools varies based on the race of the student. For example, math teachers tend to hold a biased perception of girls' abilities, particularly when comparing the abilities of White girls with those of White boys (Riegle-Crumb & Humphries, 2012). The reading by Maria Charles in this chapter describes how schools reinforce choices related to science, technology, engineering, and mathematics (STEM), eventually solidifying the gender segregation of STEM careers. Unfortunately, gender socialization and expectations continue well into the STEM careers, with some women scientists enforcing gender norms and expectations by distancing themselves from femininity and "typical feminine practices" as other women fight gender discrimination (Rhoton, 2011). Thus, according to Laura A. Rhoton, women scientists prefer to associate with females who act the role of "scientist" rather than with females who practice femininity, further reinforcing the perception of appropriate gender in science. And, unfortunately, this climate of gender difference and inequality persists in the workplace, as you will read about in the readings Chapter 7.

One very obvious example of institutions separating gender and socializing children differently is the Boy Scouts and Girl Scouts. These are two prominent social institutions organized to socialize children. A controversy occurred in 2012 as to whether to allow a transgendered boy who identified as a girl into the Girl Scouts, challenging formerly rigid gender categorizations used to group children. Despite the absurdity of trying to separate genders in a world with more gender fluidity, the Girl Scout and Boy Scout organizations still socialize children in gender-specific ways. Boy Scouts are more likely to offer science-based activities and less likely to offer art activities than are the Girl Scouts (Denny, 2011). While the Girl Scouts promote what Denny calls an image of the "up-to-date traditional woman" for young girls, with an emphasis on communal activities, Boy Scout badges are given for activities, with a general focus on ability and assertiveness (Denny, 2011). By creating these separate spaces with very different expectations for boys and girls, we are socializing our children in gender difference and inequality. Today, Boy Scouts and Girl Scouts, as well as other same-sex/gender organizations

such as same-sex/gender colleges and same-sex/gender teams, are struggling with changing their "rules" to be more flexible in their definitions of sex/gender and more accepting of transgendered people.

However, not all boys and men are allowed to be dominant across settings (Eder, 1995), and few girls come close to achieving idealized femininity. Ann Arnett Ferguson (2000) describes how schools discourage African American boys from claiming their Blackness and masculinity. Although White boys may be allowed to be "rambunctious" and disrespectful, African American boys are punished more severely than their White peers when they "act out," and there is less tolerance for African American boys who try to dominate. Girls also exist within a hierarchy of relationships (Eder, 1995). Girls from racial, ethnic, economically disadvantaged, or other subordinated groups must fight even harder to succeed under multiple systems of domination and inequality in schools. To illustrate this point, Julie Bettie (2002) compared the paths to success for upwardly mobile White and Mexican American high school girls and found some similarities in gender experiences at home and school, such as participation in sports, which facilitated mobility for both groups of girls. But, there were also differences in their experiences because race was always salient and was a barrier for the Mexican American girls. However, Bettie believes that achieving upward mobility may have been easier for these Mexican American girls than for their brothers because it is easier for girls to transgress gender boundaries. Their brothers, on the other hand, felt pressure to "engage in the rituals of proving masculinity" even though this behavior was rejected by those in control at school (p. 419).

Bettie's (2002) study emphasizes the fact that multiple social prisms of difference and inequality create an array of patterns, which would not be possible if gender socialization practices were singular or universal. Individuals' lives are constructed around many factors, including gender. Cultural values and expectations influence, and frequently contradict, the maintenance of hegemonic masculinity and emphasized femininity in

Western societies. Pyke and Johnson's reading in Chapter 2 and other readings throughout this book illustrate how the practice of gender is strongly influenced by culture. The process of gender socialization is rooted in the principle that girls/women and boys/men are not equal and that the socially constructed categories of difference and inequality (gender, race, ethnicity, class, religion, age, culture, etc.) are legitimate.

Sports, particularly organized sports, provide other examples of how institutionalized activities reinforce the gender identities children learn. Boys learn the meaning of competition and success, including the idea that winning is everything (e.g., Messner, 1992). Girls, on the other hand, are more often found on the edges of the playing field, or on the sides of the playground, watching the boys (Thorne, 1993). And, as you will read in Chapter 9, moms are typically relegated to the sidelines as well, while men coach. Even though girls are more involved in playing sports than in previous generations, Matthew B. Ezzell, in his reading in this chapter, describes a climate in which females are still expected to maintain some level of femininity during athletic competitions. Yet not all children play in the same ways. Marjorie Harness Goodwin (1990) finds that children from urban, lower-class, high-density neighborhoods—where households are closer together—are more likely to play in mixed-gender and mixed-age groups. In suburban, middle-class households, which are farther apart than urban households, parents are more likely to drive their children to sporting activities or houses to play with same-sex/gender, same-age peers. The consequences of social class and place of residence are that lower-class children are more comfortable with their sexuality as they enter preadolescence and are less likely to gender segregate in school (Goodwin, 1990).

Sports and play continue to segregate us and define gender throughout our lives. Although the formal rules for women's and men's rugby are the same, the reading by Ezzell in this chapter illustrates how adult women pressure themselves and other women to perform emphasized femininity, even when playing by the same game rules as do men. Although women are increasingly participating in traditionally "male" sports activities, the gendered nature of these sports still exists in the institutions supporting the activities (Buysse & Embser-Herbert, 2004), the game rules, and the minds of the participants, even in traditionally "male" sports such as basketball (Berlage, 2004), ice hockey (Theberge, 2000), and body building (Wesely, 2001). Socialization into gender does not stop at any particular age but occurs throughout our lifetimes and throughout our activities.

GENDER TRANSGRESSIONS

Change in social expectations comes slowly, but today there is more acceptance of individuals who do not accept or feel comfortable in the gender appropriate for their assigned sex, such as Bruce Jenner, the former Olympian and reality show star who feels more comfortable as a woman, Caitlyn. Rahilly addresses this issue in her piece in this chapter, which focuses on parents who are raising children who refuse to align their genders with expectations for behavior appropriate to their assigned sex. While all this attention to transgender might seem like a breakthrough for creating more flexibility in the hold gender has on our life choices, the acceptance of transgender may not be breaking down the gender binary. Instead, Eleanor Burkett (2015) asks in a *New York Times* editorial whether Bruce Jenner's coming out as a woman, Caitlyn, further reinforces the stereotypes and a gender binary. In fact, Jenner's public transgender event may be making those "tidy boxes" of boys/men and girls/women much more rigid as Bruce went from a man who was a star athlete to Caitlyn, a voluptuous woman laid out neatly and passively on the cover of *Vanity Fair*.

Although there is an increasing acceptance of transgendered people, beginning in the early 2000s, there still occurs what Laurel Westbrook and Kristen Schilt (2014) call "gender panics," when people's assumptions about biology-based gender ideology are disrupted. Using newspaper articles to determine how the press and public responded to such disruptions, they examined press reports of several events, including the move by New York City to allow individuals to change the sex listed on their birth certificates without requiring proof of genital reconstruction (a biological change that corresponded with their new sex identification). They also examined articles relating to competitive sports and workplace discrimination. They concluded that people were more likely to require biology-based criteria for gender if the activity was sex-segregated, particularly if the requirements protected females in female spaces from males or trans women who may still have some male biological sex characteristics. In sex-segregated competitive sports, however, identity-based definitions of gender were less likely to be accepted and, trans women who want to compete in women's competitions are more likely to have biological markers that indicate they are female, such as genital reconstruction and/or testosterone levels similar to females. However, in workplace discrimination, a space that is not sex-segregated, they found there is more acceptance of an identity-based definition of gender. These gender panics, as Westbrook and Schilt (2014) call them, are not new; rather, they are just becoming more apparent and a bit more complicated by the acceptance of identity-based markers of gender as opposed to biological markers.

Until recently, most persons who went through sex change operations were referred to as transsexuals. Yet, even with the appropriate biological markers, the transition from one gender to another was not necessarily easy. Renée Richards, who, in 1975 underwent sex reassignment surgery at the age of 40, was initially denied a spot in the U.S. Open Tennis Tournament in 1977 because she wasn't really a woman. That decision was reversed and she was allowed to compete in professional women's tennis. This change in terminology over time reflects an acknowledgment of the powerful force of social factors in determining our gender identities and moves away from the idea that gender is an essential part of our biological nature.

While most children learn to display idealized gender behaviors, at times we all step out of gender-appropriate zones in our daily lives. Girls and women are more likely to transgress and do masculine things than boys and men are to participate in feminine activities. C. Shawn McGuffey and B. Lindsay Rich (1999) find that girls who transgress into the "boys' zone" may eventually be respected by their male playmates if they are good at conventionally male activities, such as playing baseball. Boys, however, are harassed and teased when they try to participate in any activity associated with girls (McGuffey & Rich, 1999). By denying boys access to girls' activities, the dominance of masculinity is reinforced as when boys are ridiculed because they are not sufficiently dominant or because they "throw like a girl." Therefore, boys reinforce and maintain masculinity by goading one another to perform "manhood acts" (Schrock & Schwalbe, 2009), and we all end up devaluing feminine acts.

As you can see, learning gender is complicated. Clearly, gender is something that we "do" as much as learn, and in doing gender, we are responding to structured expectations from institutions in society as well as interpersonal cues from those we are interacting with. Throughout our lives, every time we enter a new social situation, we look around for cues and guides to determine how to behave in an appropriate manner. In some situations we might interpret gender cues as calling for a high degree of idealized gender difference and inequality, while in other situations the clues allow us to be more flexible. Thus, we create gender as well as respond to expectations for it. And we change gender when we resist it!

DOING MASCULINITY AND FEMININITY THROUGHOUT OUR LIVES

Most men have learned to "do" the behaviors that maintain hegemonic masculinity, while at the same time suppressing feelings and behaviors that might make them seem feminine (Connell, 1987). As a result, being a "man" or a "woman" requires an awareness of and responses to the other gender. Our cues and behaviors change whether we are responding to someone we identify as being of the same gender or of a different gender. That is, masculinities or femininities are enacted based on how those we are interacting with are displaying femininities or masculinities (Connell & Messerschmidt, 2005).

As argued, hegemonic masculinity is maintained in a hierarchy in which only a few men achieve close-to-idealized masculinity, with everyone else subordinated to them—women, poor White men, men of color, gay men, and men from devalued ethnic and religious groups. Furthermore, this domination is not always one-on-one but, rather, can be institutionalized in the structure of the situation. As you read the articles in this chapter, you will see that gender is not something we learn once, in one setting. Instead, we learn to do gender over time in virtually everything we undertake. And, although we do gender throughout our lives, we rarely achieve idealized gender; yet, by doing gender, we continue to maintain a system of gender difference and inequality. Also, remember that learning to "do" gender is complicated by the other prisms that interact in our lives. Recall the lessons from Chapter 2 and remember that gender does not stand alone but, rather, is reflected in other social identities.

It is not easy to separate the learning and doing of gender from other patterns. As you read selections in other chapters in Part II of this book, you will see the influence of social processes and institutions on how we learn and do gender across all aspects of our lives. Before you start to read, ask yourself how you learned gender and how well you do it. Not succeeding at doing gender is normal. That is, if we all felt comfortable with ourselves, no one would be striving for idealized forms of gender—hegemonic masculinity or emphasized femininity. Imagine a world in which we all feel comfortable just the way we are! As you read through the rest of this book, ask yourself why that world doesn't exist.

REFERENCES

American Association of University Women. (1992). *How schools shortchange girls.* Washington, DC: Author.

American Association of University Women. (1998). *Gender gaps: Where schools still fail our children.* Washington, DC: Author.

American Association of University Women. (1999). *Voices of a generation: Teenage girls on sex, school, and self.* Washington, DC: Author.

Anderson, K. J., & Leaper, C. (1998). Meta-analysis of gender effects on conversational interruption: Who, what, when, where, and how. *Sex Roles, 39*(3–4), 225–252.

Berlage, G. I. (2004). Marketing and the publicity images of women's professional basketball players from 1997 to 2001. In J. Z. Spade & C. G. Valentine (Eds.), *The kaleidoscope of gender: Prisms, patterns, and possibilities* (pp. 377–386). Belmont, CA: Wadsworth.

Bettie, J. (2002). Exceptions to the rule: Upwardly mobile White and Mexican American high school girls. *Gender & Society, 16*(3), 403–422.

Brescoli, V. (2011). Who takes the floor and why: Gender, power, and volubility in organizations. *Administrative Science Quarterly, 56*(4), 622–641.

Burkett, E. (2015, June 6). "What makes a woman?" *The New York Times.* Retrieved from http://www .nytimes.com/2015/06/07/opinion/sunday/what-makes-a-woman.html?emc=edit_th_20150607& nl=todaysheadlines&nlid=44913438

Buysse, J. M., & Embser-Herbert, M. S. (2004). Constructions of gender in sport: An analysis of intercollegiate media guide cover photographs. *Gender & Society, 18*(1), 66–81.

Carlton-Ford, S., & Houston, P. V. (2001). Children's experience of gender: Habitus and field. In D. Vannoy (Ed.), *Gender mosaics: Societal perspectives* (pp. 65–74). Los Angeles: Roxbury.

Carter, P. L. (2005). *Keepin' it real: School success beyond Black and White.* New York: Oxford University Press.

Coltrane, S. (1998). *Gender and families.* Thousand Oaks, CA: Pine Forge Press.

Connell, R. W. (1987). *Gender and power: Society, the person, and sexual politics.* Stanford, CA: Stanford University Press.

Connell, R. W. (2000). *The men and the boys.* Berkeley: University of California Press.

Connell, R. W., & Messerschmidt, J. W. (2005). Hegemonic masculinity: Rethinking the concept. *Gender & Society, 19*(6), 829–859.

Denny, K. E. (2011). Gender in context, content, and approach: Comparing gender messages in Girl Scout and Boy Scout handbooks. *Gender & Society, 25*(1), 27–47.

Eder, D. (1995). *School talk: Gender and adolescent culture.* New Brunswick, NJ: Rutgers University Press.

Ferguson, A. A. (2000). *Bad boys: Public schools in the making of Black masculinity.* Ann Arbor: University of Michigan Press.

Gooden, A. M., & Gooden, M. A. (2001). Gender representation in notable children's picture books: 1995–1999. *Sex Roles, 45*(1–2), 89–101.

Goodwin, M. H. (1990). *He-said-she-said: Talk as social organization among Black children.* Bloomington: Indiana University Press.

Grant, L. (1985). Race-gender status, system attachment, and children's socialization in desegregated classrooms. In L. C. Wilkinson & C. Bagley Marret (Eds.), *Gender influences in classroom interaction* (pp. 57–77). New York: Academic Press.

Howard, J. A., & Alamilla, R. M. (2001). Gender and identity. In D. Vannoy (Ed.), *Gender mosaics: Societal perspectives* (pp. 54–64). Los Angeles: Roxbury.

Lutfey, K., & Mortimer, J. C. (2003). Development and socialization through the adult life course. In J. Delamater (Ed.), *Handbook of social psychology* (pp. 183–204). New York: Kluwer/Plenum.

McGuffey, C. S., & Rich, B. L. (1999). Playing in the gender transgression zone. *Gender & Society, 13*(5), 608–627.

Messner, M. A. (1992). *Power at play: Sports and masculinity.* Boston: Beacon Press.

Orenstein, P. (1994). *School girls: Young women, self-esteem, and the confidence gap.* New York: Anchor Books.

Paoletti, J. B. (2012). *Pink and blue: Telling the boys from the girls in America.* Bloomington: Indiana University Press.

Pollack, W. S. (2000). *Real boys' voices.* New York: Random House.

Rhoton, L. A. (2011). Distancing as a gendered barrier: Understanding women scientists' gender practices. *Gender & Society, 25*(6), 696–716.

Riegle-Crumb, C., & Humphries, M. (2012). Exploring bias in math teachers' perceptions of students' ability by gender and race/ethnicity. *Gender & Society, 26*(2), 290–322.

Sadker, D., & Sadker, M. (1994). *Failing at fairness: How our schools cheat girls.* New York: Simon & Schuster.

Schrock, D., & Schwalbe, M. (2009). Men, masculinity, and manhood acts. *Annual Review of Sociology, 35,* 277–295.

Schwalbe, M. (1998). *The sociologically examined life: Pieces of the conversation.* Mountain View, CA: Mayfield.

Spade, J. Z. (2001). Gender and education in the United States. In D. Vannoy (Ed.), *Gender mosaics: Societal perspectives* (pp. 85–93). Los Angeles: Roxbury.

Theberge, N. (2000). *Higher goals: Women's ice hockey and the politics of gender.* Albany: State University of New York Press.

Thorne, B. (1993). *Gender play: Girls and boys in school.* New Brunswick, NJ: Rutgers University Press.

Vespa, J. (2009). Gender ideology construction: A life course and intersectional approach. *Gender & Society, 23*(3), 363–387.

Wesely, J. K. (2001). Negotiating gender: Bodybuilding and the natural/unnatural continuum. *Sociology of Sport Journal, 18,* 162–180.

Westbrook, L., & Schilt, K. (2014). Doing gender, determining gender: Transgender people, gender panics, and the maintenance of the sex/gender/sexuality system. *Gender & Society, 28*(1), 32-57.

Wood, J. T. (1999). *Gendered lives: Communication, gender, and culture* (3rd ed.). Belmont, CA: Wadsworth.

Introduction to Reading 16

Parents play a major role in socializing young children into appropriate genders, the genders that match the sexes assigned to them at birth. Males become boys and females become girls, by learning to present themselves in appropriate ways such that others recognize their gender. An individual whose gender and sex align is referred to as cisgender. However, not every child wants to be socialized into their "appropriate" gender. Elizabeth P. Rahilly addresses this issue, focusing on parents who are raising children who refuse to align their genders with expectations for behavior appropriate to their assigned sex. She conducted interviews with 24 parents of 16 gender-variant children. These parents are predominantly White, middle class, and well educated. In this reading she describes the strategies parents developed to deal with their children's gender variance, with most of their attention focused on the people their children interacted with. She recruited these parents at a support conference for parents of gender-variant children and also from an Internet blog that one of the parents in her study authored. This research provides an interesting glimpse at parenting against the norm.

1. How did the parents respond to their children's desire to be gender variant?

2. What role did outsiders play in the way parents managed the gender variance of their children?

3. In accepting the gender variance of their children, are these parents still upholding the "truth regime" of a gender binary?

The Gender Binary Meets the Gender-Variant Child:

Parents' Negotiations With Childhood Gender Variance

Elizabeth P. Rahilly

Tristan's just everything, he's not limited, and I think part of it is that gender thing, there's no boxes for him . . . I just want to keep it that way, I don't want the world to crush him.

—Shella[1]

Transgender identity has long been significant in sociocultural analyses of gender (Bornstein 1995; Halberstam 2005). Gender variance exposes the limits of the gender binary and the overly deterministic role it ascribes to assigned sex, in turn signaling possibilities for social change against dominant ideologies and practices. Pursuant to West and Zimmerman's (1987) canonical distinctions between sex, sex category, and gender, several empirical studies have addressed trans persons' experiences to illuminate the logics of the gender binary, both when it prevails and when it is troubled (Connell 2010; Gagne and Tewksbury 1998; Jenness and Fenstermaker 2014; Schilt and Westbrook 2009). As crucial as these studies are to a sociology of

From Rahilly, Elizabeth P. 2015. "The gender binary meets the gender-variant child." *Gender & Society* 29(3): 338–61.

gender, their principal substrate for analysis has been *adult* experiences and perspectives. Save Tey Meadow's research (2011, 2013), childhood gender variance is largely absent from the empirical repertoire. Only recently has the prospect of raising children as categorically "gender-variant" or "transgender"[2] surfaced on the cultural landscape.

Over the last decade, preadolescent gender-variant children have garnered widespread visibility, beyond the walls of the "medicopsychological" clinic, where much of the research on, and management of, childhood gender variance traditionally has occurred (Bryant 2006). These children's behaviors consistently and significantly stray from the expectations of their assigned sex—from the clothes, toys, and play groups they prefer to their repeated articulations about their sense of self (e.g., "I'm your son, not your daughter!"). This visibility is due in no small part to the parents who raise these children and reject traditional reparative interventions (e.g., Green 1987; Zucker 2008). An increasing number of mental health practitioners reject reparative approaches as well (Ehrensaft 2011; Lev 2004).

This article draws on interview data with 24 parents of gender-variant children, who represent 16 childhood cases altogether and are part of a larger longitudinal project on parents of gender-variant and transgender children. I examine three practices—"gender hedging," "gender literacy," and "playing along"—to illuminate the ways in which these parents come to an awareness of the gender binary as a limited cultural ideology, or a "truth regime" (Foucault 2000), and in turn devise various practical and discursive strategies to navigate that regime and accommodate their children's nonconformity. These parents widen the options their children have, not only regarding interests and activities, as conventional "gender-neutral" parenting would advocate, but also with regard to a potentially transgender sense of self. They also adhere to essentialist understandings of gender identity and expression, in ways that expand, rather than limit, the range of gendered possibilities. Altogether, these families are inventing a new mode of social response to a problem that would, in previous decades, be the province of psychotherapeutic intervention and exposing new challenges to the gender binary during early childhood development.

PARENTING AND GENDER: THE GENDER "TRUTH REGIME"

Following her work on "transgender families," Pfeffer (2012) called for more concerted research into "the increasingly diverse family forms of the twenty-first century," whose members expose new strategies for negotiating and resisting gender norms (Pfeffer 2012, 596). Meadow's (2011, 2013) ethnography offered some of the first insights into a new generation of parents who are raising transgender children. Meadow found that parents drew on traditional explanatory tropes—including biomedical, psychiatric, and spiritual—to explain their child's gender-variant "self" to others, thereby "assimilat[ing] their children's atypical identities into familiar knowledge and belief systems" (Meadow 2011, 728). Meadow argues that these traditional frameworks bear as much potential for embracing non-normative genders as they do for constricting them. I build on this budding sociological terrain, turning my focus to specific methods and strategies parents develop in everyday interactions to navigate the gender binary, starting with their initial reckonings with the gender binary as faulty cultural ideology.

Of course, parents' potential to challenge the gender binary is not new. Attendant with ideological aspects of second-wave feminism, many scholars have been interested in parenting practices that resist stereotyping male and female children, often referred to as "gender-neutral" or "feminist" parenting (Bem 1983; Pogrebin 1980; Risman and Meyers 1997; Statham 1986). Both Kane (2006) and Martin (2005), however, have noted the limited legacy of such parenting ideals, which they attribute to negative cultural associations between childhood gender nonconformity and adult homosexuality, fostering parents' maintenance of compulsory heterosexuality and hegemonic masculinity. More recently, Kane (2012) revealed a range of tendencies among contemporary parents, from those who presume stereotypical gender behaviors in their children to those who consciously seek to widen their children's social options. Nonetheless, Kane observed that almost all parents succumb to the "gender trap," or social expectations that limit parents' best intentions against the binary (Kane 2012, 3). Even the most progressively minded parents in Kane's sample still felt accountable to a modicum of gender normativity in public, especially with their sons. And few, if any of them, seemed cognizant of the prospect of a transgender child. Indeed, one of the parents in Kane's sample—who chased down a store clerk when the clerk assumed her boys would not use glitter in a crafts project—easily dismissed the notion that her three-year-old son would grow up to be a "girl": "So I said, 'Eli, you'll never be a girl, but if you want that Barbie pool you can have it'" (Kane 2012, 150). As traditionally conceived, gender-progressive parenting encouraged boys and girls to be whatever they wanted to be, regardless of stereotypes—but they were ever and always (cisgender[3]) boys and girls, respectively.[4]

In this article, the "gender binary" refers to a dominant cultural presumption about sex and gender: namely, that there is an expected "congruent" relationship between one's sexed body and their gender identity and expression—that is, babies assigned "male" grow up to be "boys" and babies assigned "female" grow up to be "girls," and without many options in between. I use "male" and "female" to refer to the sexual anatomy that is coded at birth, and "boy" and "girl" to refer to the gender identities that are presumed of bodies assigned as such. Many parents no longer expect stereotypically "masculine" and "feminine" behaviors from their children—and often laud a child for stepping outside these in certain respects (e.g., boys who exhibit sensitivity, girls who prefer sports to Barbies). However, the presumption that a child's assigned sex will predict and circumscribe their gendered sensibilities and identities ("boy" or "girl") still holds force in our culture. The first question that is asked after a child is born is the first of many iterations of this belief system, around which myriad institutions and practices are arranged. . . .

I employ the concept of "truth regime" to analyze the practical, discursive, and intellectual strategies these parents engage in to navigate the gender binary and legitimize childhood gender-variant subjectivities. The power of the gender truth regime lies in its erasure of childhood transgender possibilities; children assigned male who present as "girls" and children assigned female who present as "boys"[5] are culturally unintelligible. And the parents who permit such possibilities are implicated negatively by others, including neighbors, doctors, teachers, and extended family, who might question the apparent "mismatch" (especially if they were aware of the assigned sex). I draw on the concept of "truth regime" to examine these parents' newfound negotiations with, and increasing resistance to, the gender binary in the face of its regulatory effects, particularly during everyday discursive interactions.

The "truth regime" framework intersects with the "doing gender" approach. The dictates of the gender truth regime powerfully inform interactional practices, to which parents at first feel accountable. However, parents' growing awareness of the falsehoods of the gender binary enables "redoing gender" (West and Zimmerman 2009), or "doing gender differently" (Dalton and Fenstermaker 2002), through which alternative gender practices become possible. Rather than "undoing gender" altogether, parents still attribute gendered meaning to their children's preferences—they are atypically masculine or feminine, but masculine and feminine nonetheless. I use the term "truth regime" to emphasize the discursive and ideological foundations of the gender binary that parents work to resist, through which changes to the system of normative gender accountability might transpire.

As I demonstrate, parents' strategies emerge *in response* to children's demands and preferences, and not necessarily due to a "gender-neutral" agenda of their own. This child-directed dynamic speaks to more general "bidirectional" or "reciprocal influence" theories of childhood socialization (Coltrane and Adams 1997; Peterson and Rollins 1987), in which both parents and children are seen as active agents in the progress.

* * *

CHALLENGING THE GENDER TRUTH REGIME

By the time they enter parenthood, many adults have internalized a dominant cultural ideology that presumes a deterministic relationship between sex and gender; "males" are boys and "females" are girls. But the parents in this study confront the limits of these "certainties" in the face of their children's persistent gender-variant preferences and expressions. In this section, I describe three major practices that surfaced in parents' narratives: "gender hedging," "gender literacy," and "playing along." Through these practices, parents come to an awareness of the gender binary as a restrictive truth regime, and work to carve out more inclusive understandings of, and practices around, gender nonconformity, despite a world that is largely ignorant of childhood transgender possibilities.

Gender Hedging: "Walking the Fine Line" of the Gender Binary

When referring to the early stages of their parenting careers, before they grew cognizant of the prospect of a "gender-variant" or "transgender" child, almost all parents described engaging in a kind of boundary work with their children's "atypical" behaviors, especially as the child approached school age. I refer to this work as "gender hedging," or parents' creative efforts to curb their child's nonconformity and stay within gender-normative constraints. A parent purchases pink socks for their "son," for example, but not a skirt. I introduce gender hedging as parents' first strategic negotiations with the gender truth regime, as it marks a crucial phase in their developing consciousness about this dominant belief system: gender proves as much a set of cultural dictates to which parents feel beholden as it does a given "truth" about their child's sex, which offers little reference for their child's persistent preferences and behaviors. While gender hedging largely upholds the gender truth regime, as parents work to fashion an overall front of normativity (e.g., no dresses at the store), it also permits small concessions to a child's gender-variant interests (e.g., a pink shirt is okay), and stirs parents' questioning about how much of these they should regulate and restrain, if at all.

When I asked parents to orient me to their child's gender nonconformity, they listed a variety of activities their child engaged in, often starting around the age of two, that were the stereotypical stock of the "other sex's" interests and preferences, including toys, clothing, types of play, and friend groups.[6] Tim, for example, adored playing dress-up in an Ariel mermaid costume (which Beth purchased for him after he repeatedly begged for it at the store), which came complete with jewelry and high heels. However, the outfit proved "too much" for Beth and Barry to accept, and lines were drawn regarding the extent to which Tim could wear it: The dress was allowed, but not the accessories, and only indoors. Tim also wanted to carry a purse in public. Beth offered him a "substitute"; she gave him a small boutique shopping bag with handles instead of a woman's handbag, so as to be less conspicuous. Beth described such efforts as a "daily tightrope walk" and "a fine line that [they] walk."

Katy also remembered trying to accommodate her child's preferences for girly clothes in public: "He started wearing some feminine stuff, [at the store] I'd pick out, okay, it's not pink but it's got Hello Kitty on it, that'll be okay, you know." Theresa recalled her efforts to "soft pedal" around Lisa's girliness in one emblematic move: when Lisa started kindergarten, Theresa made an interactive chart with popsicle sticks designating the kinds of daily attire Lisa could wear to school. On some days, Lisa could wear more feminine clothes (skorts—half shorts, half skirt); on others, she had to wear boy clothes (pants). Now, Theresa cringes at the thought of it, but at the time, she felt she had to "enforce a balance . . . not to go all the way into girly-girly land." . . .

Parents, in both male and female cases, also expressed fear about their child's risk of bullying and exclusion, which largely compelled their early efforts to keep the nonconformity at bay and indoors.

Notably, Kane (2006, 2012) described similar kinds of "boundary maintenance" among the parents she studied, who allowed gender-atypical play indoors but ensured gender-normative presentations in public, especially with male children. However, the parents in this study eventually allowed children assigned male access to proverbial "icons of femininity" (Kane 2006), including frilly skirts and dresses outside of the house, and long hair. With children assigned female, parents obliged more and more clothing from the boys' department and short haircuts. Moreover, these parents mentioned what their children *said* (i.e., "I'm your son, not your daughter!" or "I feel more like a girl than a boy") as much as what they *did or liked*, and the significance attributed to these verbal declarations cannot be underestimated. These parents would argue that their child's repeated self-identifications are what set them apart from other children who "just" prefer occasional gender-atypical activities (and whose parents permit this).[7]

Interestingly enough, in a quarter of the cases, parents confessed to cloaking their regulation of certain behaviors in excuses that did not have to do with gender: Molly told Gil that his clothing preferences were too "sloppy," versus too masculine for a little girl, which she now recognizes was her "ulterior motive." Beth gave Tim's favorite dress-up heels to the dog so she didn't have to tell him they didn't want him wearing them. Theresa routinely framed pants as more comfortable for playtime with peers, versus more appropriate for boys. Parents' rhetorical moves to hide the true motives of their gender hedging are perhaps the most intriguing element of the practice: While parents felt bound to conform, they sought to avoid teaching that conformity explicitly to their children.

Parents' strategic work in gender hedging makes them increasingly frustrated with the regulatory forces of the gender truth regime, which presumes certain behaviors and dispositions relative to particular sex categories but which do not align with those of their children, time and again. In attempting to comply with the regime and not "bother other people"—including, fundamentally, protecting their children from negative attention—parents devise a variety of crafty maneuvers to satisfy their child's preferences while staying just within binary limits, but these continue to belie what their children really want. As Carl relayed, "We saw him when he was being pushed into, because of our own ignorance, a gender that wasn't his to accept . . . he would push back and [say], 'I'm not doing that.'" These tiresome negotiations ultimately catalyze their search for insights online, where they encounter a body of trans-affirming discourses that radically shift their perceptions about gender.

Gender Literacy: Talking Back to the Gender Binary

Parents' encounters on the Internet usher in a new stage of consciousness about childhood gender nonconformity, which challenges their attempts to curb it and breeds a new set of strategies. These strategies manifest in the form of explicit dialogues and discourse, with their children and with others, about more expansive (trans)gender possibilities than the gender truth regime allows. Through their online searches, parents find a flurry of talk among other parents, professionals, advocates, blogs, listservs, and advocacy organizations about gender-variant and transgender children. In these virtual forums—which often lead to live support groups and conferences with other parents—gender variance is affirmed as a natural, normal part of human diversity. Longstanding cultural beliefs rooted in the gender binary are the problem, as represented in the following excerpt from one prominent advocacy organization: "When a child is born, a quick glance between the legs determines the gender label that the child will carry for life. But . . . a binary concept still fails to capture [that] . . . biological gender occurs across a continuum of possibilities" (Gender Spectrum, n.d.). This discursive community also asserts that gender and sexuality are "separate, distinct parts of our overall identity" and that "gender expression should not be viewed as an indication of sexual orientation" (Gender Spectrum, n.d.). This distinction reverberated, often passionately, in my interviews. Tellingly, a striking majority of parents also volunteered awareness that their child could be both "trans and gay" as adults (the two adolescents in the sample, for example, transgender boys, identified as "gay" and "bi" at the time of our interviews). Parents' affirmation of their children's nonconformity as a matter of *gender*, and not (homo)sexuality, surfaced as a key component of the newfound transgender-aware principles they espoused.

During our interviews, it became apparent that parents sought to reiterate these discourses within their homes. Parents frequently recounted conversations with their children in which they aimed to pass on a more inclusive, less binary understanding of gender. I refer to these efforts as "gender literacy," which I adapt from France Winndance Twine's (2010) work on "racial literacy." . . .

One aspect of gender literacy entails parents' efforts to equip their children with a simple vocabulary for explaining their nonconformity to peers. Laurie said, "We would have to coach him on the kinds of responses to have to other kids . . . [he says] he's a boy who likes feminine things." Similarly, Heather claimed, "We kind of say together . . . You're always gonna be a girl in your heart."' Both Molly and Lynne said that prior to their children's transitions they used the phrase "boy with a girl's body." Katy actually tried defining "transgender," "gender-variant," and "inter-sex" for Liam, because she thought

these might resonate with how he feels. While Katy worried that these terms were too complicated for Liam, they signify her enduring attempts to provide a language in her home that normalizes gender variance. In contrast, Becca and Sara preferred using labels their children derived themselves. Becca, who adopted her child's coinage "boygir," exemplified this philosophy: "One of the things I've really had to struggle with . . . is the labeling . . . We're just trying to put our own experiences around it . . . [but] I want him to define himself." Here, Becca testifies not only to the child-directed nature of this process (parents defer to their children's self-conceptions) but to the intellectual work she does to deconstruct conventional "truths" about sex and gender, including their categorical referents, that she has internalized.

Another facet of this strategy is parents' warning their children about prejudice toward gender nonconformity, similar to the "preparation for bias" that racial socialization scholars have observed among parents and children of color (Hughes et al. 2006). Ally, for example, believes that she has to be candid with Ray about potential harassment from peers: "I think that was how I explained it to him early on was, there are some people . . . who are gonna be really mean, 'cause they don't understand that . . . boys can wear girly clothes, play with girly toys." Tracy compared the importance of these lessons to dialoguing about racism: "I still think that we have to talk openly about what society is gonna expect because I think, just like with racism . . . ignoring race and pretending it doesn't exist is . . . not helpful to children."

Parents also strive to articulate trans-inclusive understandings of bodies and gender. Sam, for example, recalled making the following "edits" for Jamie when the topic of bodies appeared in a children's book: "I'd say, 'Nearly all girls' bodies are like this and nearly all boys' bodies are like that' . . . I [told him] that there are some people whose bodies don't match up with the genital parts that you traditionally associate." Tracy said that when her children use public restrooms, she will ask them which bathroom someone would use who does not identify as man or woman, "just to kind of plant the seed [that] it doesn't have to be one or the other." Moreover, in half of the preadolescent cases, parents indicated that they made their children aware, in the simplest terms possible, that there are "drugs," "medication," and/or "surgeries" that can help with body change in the future, when such questions surfaced (Liam, for example, expressed interest in having breasts "like his Mommy's"). These are striking examples of parents' attempts to actively affirm transgender and transsexual subjectivities during early childhood, versus regurgitating the body logics of the gender truth regime (i.e., "You can't have breasts like your Mommy's, you're a boy").

Parents engage their gender-normative children in gender literacy as well. For example, when their younger son, Eddy, asked them if Liam identifies as a boy or girl, Katy and Brian responded, "Well, sometimes Liam doesn't know, and sometimes Liam feels like a girl, and sometimes Liam feels like a boy, and that's okay . . . how do you feel on the inside?" As a testament to the gender-progressive potential of these strategies, Eddy wore a skirt to school over his shorts so that he could tell his friends, "Boys can wear skirts [too]." Clarise described her youngest child, who is six, as the one who "gets it" the best: "[She] gets that there's all kinds of varieties of gender . . . because it's always been that way for her." The gender literacy in which parents engage *all* of their children is indicative of how the presumptions of the gender truth regime are being radically resisted and retold in these families.

Parents practice gender literacy in more public institutions, too, including their children's schools. Parents work with teachers and administrators to coordinate gender-inclusiveness training, as well as to draft school policies that specifically protect "gender identity and/or expression." Carl joined an organization that teaches LGBT awareness to religious bodies in his community: "I wouldn't [have] done it if it weren't for Mark . . . I don't want him growing up in an environment that doesn't accept him."

Several parents also launched online blogs detailing their experiences. Alicia reflected, "[Parents are] starting to move into an advocacy role, so they're wanting to include the general public in these discussions . . . parents are looking to have a voice." . . .

"Playing Along" (or Not): "Head Games" With the Gender Binary

While parents enact multiple forms of "gender literacy" to challenge the gender truth regime, they also feel that not every instance is appropriate for, or receptive to, such explicit deconstructionist efforts. This proved particularly true for interactions with strangers, who often attribute the wrong gender to a child (for example, at the grocery store, someone refers to a gender-variant male child as a "beautiful little girl"). . . . During such interactional routines, parents confront the power effects of the gender truth regime and must manage others' normative assumptions about sex and gender vis-á-vis their gender-variant children. Becca described these encounters as a "head game": "Up until this point, I have a little boy, and I know what's going on with my little boy, but [then] . . . suddenly, it's like I have to think of this as like having a little girl, which is its own . . . head game." . . . Parents advised that "playing along," as it was often described to me, was the most appropriate strategy with people whom they were unlikely to see again, when candid lessons about gender variance felt inapt: "In the interest of just keeping . . . the social construct together, I went with it, and I was just, like, whatever, I'm not in a space to educate" (Becca). Moreover, most children ask their parents *not* to correct strangers in these instances (such early requests are often regarded as indicative of a transgender identity later on). While "playing along" may not rupture the "social construct" for parents' interlocutors—and I seek to emphasize parents' heightened awareness that the construct exists—this strategy permits gender-variant expressions in public in a way that the norms of a child's assigned sex would disallow. Parents' decisions to honor their children's requests and "play along" with strangers thus affords their children safety and privacy that more explicit kinds of "gender literacy" might make uncomfortable. Indeed, many parents adopt the perspective that what their child has "between their legs" is nobody's business and irrelevant to their preferred gender presentation. Theresa reflected on these early negotiations: "She did start saying, 'Don't tell anybody I'm a boy'. . . . I realize now that I was very anxious to take care of [other people], how do I help people to understand. . . . What I'm really trying to figure out [is] how to protect her privacy and still run interference." In short, playing along and not saying anything, versus effectively revealing their child's assigned sex to strangers, proved an important discursive practice in its own right to accommodate their children's most comfortable self-expressions, particularly for gender-variant children who had not claimed a binary identity.

When it comes to people parents see more frequently, "playing along" feels less viable. Beth claimed, "I felt the need to explain it to acquaintances and friends . . . you see the parents every day at drop-off . . . so I did feel the need to say, 'He prefers girl stuff.'" Here, Beth seeks to mediate between her child's apparent nonconformity (the boy who likes the girly toys and dress-up at school) and others' potential scrutiny, in turn signaling her own allowances of these preferences. Parents' discursive interventions in more familiar contexts, versus staying silent, work to carve out space for gender nonconformity where it might be otherwise inhibited. Disclosure is also important when parents fear their child's safety and well-being is at stake. Theresa, for instance, advised the host parent of a girls-only slumber party that her daughter was transgender, just in case her status was revealed by a potential "wild card" from her old school. Parents' use of terms like "playing along," "head game," and "wild card" are duly reflective of the strategic awareness they have developed to navigate the gender truth regime in everyday life, protecting and accommodating their children in the most appropriate ways they see fit with different audiences.

In contrast to the logics of the gender truth regime, parents adopt new ideologies that imagine a wider "spectrum" of (trans)gender possibilities, which are not moored to two, static sex categories. Shella reflected, "It's amazing to watch somebody really be strong in who they are to try and tackle something huge, because okay, you're born with a penis, okay, you're a boy, boom, done—*NO, not necessarily.*" Ally reiterated this perspective: "You wanna call somebody with a penis 'male'? Yeah, talk to the hyenas."[8] Alongside this de-linking of sex and gender, parents discussed more fluid, nonbinary identities, which Ally mused about as "a whole 'nother space that doesn't have to be just girl, just boy." Katy also mentioned a desire to "[go] beyond the binary" and advocate for the "boy in the skirt." This kind of intellectual work is particularly important for parents whose children had not articulated a binary identity (boy or girl), but were more fluid or switched their expressions day-to-day.

As parents reject traditional binary beliefs for a more spectrum-oriented perspective, they also embrace the idea that we are "born" with our gender, that it is an innate, "immutable" part of us. Several of the mothers in my study—self-proclaimed feminists who came of age during the 1970s—advised that having a gender-variant child has made them rethink the constructionist beliefs they adopted during second-wave feminism. Laurie typified this attitude:

> Having grown up with this sort of . . . feminist attitude . . . I grew up in the '70s, the free-to-be-you-and-me generation . . . and I always thought that we could choose our gender expression, and I didn't realize until I had a kid that gender expression or gender identity is just this immutable part of you, like the color of your skin, or any other fixed part of you.

Similarly, Brian asserted that gender variance stems "from the first duplication of those cells . . . this is how they're made." Joe raised the possibility of genetic or hormonal factors: "It's got to be either in vitro [utero] or hormonal . . . or maybe there's some gene . . . there seems to be a gene that causes everything else." For these parents, only an innate hard-wiring during fetal development, or a "core biology," could explain a child's gender (variance) that resisted all cues to normative socialization. Evidently, these parents reconceive of gender in ways that harness both essentialist and constructionist frameworks. They reject the conventional sex-based assumptions of the gender truth regime, which they now see as hardly representative of the various ways masculinity and femininity manifest in the human population. Simultaneously, they embrace gender variance as a matter of "natural" human variation, often literally at the genomic or cellular level. In imagining "beyond the binary," these parents do not abandon the essentialist underpinnings of normative gender ideology.

* * *

NOTES

1. All names are pseudonyms.
2. "Gender-variant" serves as an umbrella term for all the children represented in this study, whose behaviors are considered significantly more masculine or more feminine relative to their assigned sex. When referring to individual cases, I use "transgender" to refer to a child who had a "cross-gender" identity (i.e., transgender girls who were assigned male at birth and transgender boys who were assigned female). For children who did not identify with one specific gender, I refer to their assigned sex to signal their gender variance (i.e., "gender-variant male") and use the pronouns parents used at the time of the interviews.
3. I use "cisgender" to mean not transgender, or identifying with the gender presumed at birth.
4. In contrast, Jane Ward (2011) advocates "cultivating children's gender-queerness."
5. "Tomboys," of course, complicate this simple symmetry, as "masculine" girls are often given more latitude than "feminine" boys. However, parents of transgender boys in this sample advised that their children's persistent desires to be addressed as "boys" (including requesting boys' haircuts and male pronouns) made the "tomboy" category feel

nonviable early into grade school, signaling the potential limits of this category for significant female masculinity.
6. The children represented here come from a variety of family contexts that would impact the availability of gender-atypical items (i.e., older/younger siblings, only children). However, these children often expressed their preferences through objects found at the store.
7. I do not give these observations to suggest objective distinctions between these children and their potentially more normative counterparts. Rather, I aim to highlight specific actions and interpretations these parents cited for coming to conceive of, and embrace, their child as categorically gender-variant or transgender.
8. The female spotted hyena has an enlarged clitoris that becomes erect, which scientists name a "pseudo-penis."

REFERENCES

Bern, Sandra. 1983. Gender schema theory and its implications for child development. *Signs* 8: 598–616.

Bornstein, Kate. 1995. *Gender outlaw.* New York: Routledge.

Bryant, Karl. 2006. Making gender identity disorder of childhood. *Sexuality Research and Social Policy* 3:23–39.

Charmaz, Kathy. 2006. *Constructing grounded theory.* Thousand Oaks, CA: Sage.

Coltrane, Scott, and Michelle Adams. 1997. Children and gender. In *Contemporary parenting*, edited by Terry Arendell. Thousand Oaks, CA: Sage.

Connell, Catherine. 2010. Doing, undoing, or redoing gender? Learning from the workplace experiences of transpeople. *Gender & Society* 24:31–55.

Dalton, Susan, and Sarah Fenstermaker. 2002. "Doing gender" differently. In *Doing gender, doing difference.* New York: Routledge.

Ehrensaft, Diane. 2011. *Gender born, gender made.* New York: Experiment, LLC.

Foucault, Michel. 2000. Truth and power. In *Essential works of Foucault 1954-1984,* Vol. 3, edited by Paul Rabinow. New York: The New Press.

Gagne, Patricia, and Richard Tewksbury. 1998. Conformity pressures and gender resistance among transgendered individuals. *Social Problems* 45:81–102.

Gender Spectrum. n.d. Understanding gender, https://www.genderspectrum.org/ understanding-gender.

Green, Richard. 1987. *The sissy boy syndrome and the development of homosexuality*. New Haven, CT: Yale University Press.

Halberstam, Judith. 2005. *In a queer time and place*. New York: New York University Press.

Hughes, Diane, James Rodriguez, Emilie P. Smith, Deborah J. Johnson, Howard C. Stevenson, and Paul Spicer. 2006. Parents' ethnic-racial socialization practices. *Developmental Psychology* 42:747–70.

Jenness, Valerie, and Sarah Fenstermaker. 2014. Agnes goes to prison. *Gender & Society* 28:5–31.

Kane, Emily. 2006. "No way my boys are going to be like that!" *Gender & Society* 20:149–76.

Kane, Emily. 2012. *The gender trap*. New York: New York University Press.

Lev, Arlene Istar. 2004. *Transgender emergence*. New York: Berkley Books.

Martin, Karin. 2005. William wants a doll. Can he have one? *Gender & Society* 19:456–79.

Meadow, Tey. 2011. "Deep down where the music plays." *Sexualities* 14:725–47.

Meadow, Tey. 2013. Studying each other. *Journal of Contemporary Ethnography* 42:466–81.

Peterson, Gary, and Boyd Rollins. 1987. Parent-child socialization. *In Handbook of marriage and the family*, edited by Marvin B. Sussman and Suzanne K. Steinmetz. New York: Plenum.

Pfeffer, Carla. 2012. Normative resistance and inventive pragmatism. *Gender & Society* 19:456–79.

Pogrebin, Letty Cottin. 1980. *Growing up free*. New York: McGraw-Hill.

Risman, Barbara J., and Kristen Myers. 1997. As the twig is bent. *Qualitative Sociology* 20: 229–52.

Introduction to Reading 17

This reading by Michela Musto is about gender socialization, how males and females learn to be boys and girls, emphasizing the role of adult authority figures other than parents in this process. In this reading, Musto describes peer influence on gender socialization, but she also describes something we have been emphasizing throughout this book—the influence of context on the way we display gender. Over the course of one season, she observed children in the Shark swimming group, the fastest swimmers in their age bracket. She watched these children disregard gender during swim practice but continue to practice gender "borderwork" during free time, albeit in a modified form. Her research helps us understand how gender is not an essential or inborn characteristic of people but rather something that is reinforced in the structural and contextual settings in which we enact gender.

1. What makes the children in the Shark group less likely to do gender than children in the other swimming groups with the same coach?

2. Think about ways you can use this reading to argue that gender is not an inborn, biological trait of children.

3. Imagine other settings in which children are less likely to engage in gender "borderwork." What characteristics of these settings are important in undoing gender?

Athletes in the Pool, Girls and Boys on Deck

The Contextual Construction of Gender in Coed Youth Swimming

Michela Musto

Although it is only eight o'clock in the morning, the swimming pool at the Sun Valley Aquatics Center is bustling with activity.[1] It is a warm, sunny day in southern California, and 300 kids are participating in a Sun Valley Swim Team (SVST) swim meet. Girls and boys as young as five years old rummage through their swim bags, grabbing goggles and swim caps as they walk toward the starting blocks. Between races, swimmers slather their arms with waterproof sunblock, laugh with their friends, and offer each other bites of half-eaten bagels. To my right, three 11-year-old boys, Alex, Kevin, and Andrew, are sitting in a semicircle, scrutinizing a "heat sheet" that lists the names of other boys and girls they are racing against in their upcoming events.[2] Alex notices he is the only boy in his race, sparking the following conversation:

Alex: They're all girls! That's sad.

Kevin: That must suck.

Andrew: I know her [points to a name on the paper]. You're the only male! Have fun! You have the second-fastest time—she's first, you're second.

Alex: What's her time?

Andrew: [Sophia's] really fast. She was in Sharks.

Andrew flips the page, and the boys continue looking at their other events.

Throughout their conversation, Alex, Kevin, and Andrew draw upon multiple and contradictory meanings of gender. Although they agree that it "sucks" to be the "only male" in an "all girls' event," the boys then discuss Sophia's athleticism in a relatively unremarkable manner. Instead of teasing Alex for being slower than a girl, Andrew nonchalantly informs Alex that Sophia is "really fast," something neither Alex nor Kevin contests. How was it possible for gender to simultaneously be of minimal and significant interest to the swimmers?

Because gender is a social structure that is embedded within individual, interactional, and institutional relations, social change toward gender equality is uneven across the gender order (Connell 1987, 2009; Lorber 1994; Martin 2004; Risman 2004). The salience of gender varies across contexts, allowing some contexts to support more equitable patterns of gender relations than others (Britton 2000; Connell 1987; Deutsch 2007; Schippers 2002; Thorne 1993). Within a context, both structural mechanisms and hegemonic beliefs play an important role in determining whether individuals draw on and affirm group boundaries between the genders—what Thorne (1993) calls "borderwork" (see also Messner 2000; Morgan and Martin 2006; Ridgeway 2009; Ridgeway and Correll 2004). Although scholars have theorized that alternative patterns of gender relations may shape social relations when gender is less sailent

From Musto, Michela. 2014. "Athletes in the pool, girls and boys on deck: The contextual construction of gender in coed youth swimming." *Gender & Society* 28(3): 359–80.

(Britton 2000; Connell 1987; Deutsch 2007; Ridgeway 2009; Schippers 2007), few empirical studies have followed a group of individuals across different contexts to understand how gender relations and meanings may change. As the dialogue among the boys on the swim team suggest, because individuals negotiate different systems of accountability as they move from one setting to the next, gender can take on multiple meanings as a result of contextually specific, group-based interactions.

In what follows, I analyze nine months of participant observation research and 15 semi-structured interviews conducted with 8- to 10-year-old swimmers at SVST. . . .

THE VARIABLE SALIENCE OF GENDER ACROSS CONTEXTS

Existing scholarship has identified specific structural mechanisms, such as formal and informal policies and practices, within an array of institutions that help explain how gender becomes a salient organizing principle in interactions (Messner 2000; Thorne 1993). In schools, the formal age separation and large number of students encourage boys and girls to engage in borderwork (Thorne 1993). At the same time, teachers can implement rules and seating charts that allow children to interact in "relaxed and non-gender-marked ways" (Thorne 1993, 64; see also Moore 2001). Similarly, bureaucratic policies reduce the amount of discrimination women experience within office workplaces (Morgan and Martin 2006; Ridgeway and Correll 2000). Yet the organization of many out-of-office business settings—such as having different tees for men and women on golf courses—continues to hold women professionals accountable to normative conceptualizations of gender (Morgan and Martin 2006).

In addition to structural mechanisms, hegemonic cultural beliefs also impact the salience of gender within interactions (Ridgeway and Correll 2000, 2004; Ridgeway 2009, 2011).

Although the "default expectation" (Ridgeway and Correll 2004, 513) may be to treat individuals in accordance with hegemonic beliefs, these beliefs can be less salient within interactions depending on a context's gender composition, gender-typing, and institutional frame (Ridgeway and Correll 2004; Ridgeway 2009, 2011). However, even when structural mechanisms allow for less oppressive gender relations within some contexts, individuals often "implicitly fall back on cultural beliefs about gender" in new and unscripted settings (Ridgeway 2009, 156), thus reinscribing hegemonic patterns of gender relations.

Although individuals are often framed by hegemonic patterns of gender relations within interactions, interactions can also be framed by less oppressive patterns of gender relations and meanings (Deutsch 2007; Hollander 2013; Ridgeway 2009; Ridgeway and Correll 2000, 2004; Schippers 2007). However, the processes that allow individuals to enact alternative patterns of gender relations remain undertheorized within existing scholarship (for exceptions, see Finley 2010; Hollander 2013; Schippers 2002; Wilkins 2008). As sociologists have argued, there is not always a direct relationship between the cultural order and the meanings individuals associate with cultural representations (Connell 1987; Eliasoph and Lichterman 2003; Fine 1979; Swidler 1986). Instead, hegemonic meanings are negotiated and contested within group-based interactions (Eliasoph and Lichterman 2003). When applied to gender theory, the meanings people associate with gender may vary, perhaps dramatically, across contexts depending on whether gender is a salient organizing principle within group-based relations. Furthermore, if a context allows for nonhegemonic patterns of gender relations, perhaps aspects of the more egalitarian patterns of social relations can transfer across contexts (Hollander 2013).

Competitive youth swimming is an ideal setting to examine how gender boundaries and meanings are constructed and negotiated within everyday life (McGuffey and Rich 1999; Messner 2000). Within the United States, sport has historically played a visible role in naturalizing hierarchical, categorical, and essentialist differences between the genders (Kimmel 1996; Lorber 1994; Messner 2011). Because the institutional "center" of sport often affirms hegemonic masculinity (Messner 2002), girls' and boys' interactions within athletic contexts often help strengthen hierarchical and categorical group boundaries between the genders, thus maintaining the power, prestige, and resources boys have over girls (McGuffey and Rich 1999; Messner 2000; Thorne 1993). Yet at the same time, research finds that girls' and women's athleticism is becoming normalized (Ezzell 2009; Heywood and Dworkin 2003; Messner 2011), potentially calling into question hegemonic gender meanings pertaining to athleticism (Kane 1995; Messner 2002). Since it may be easier for individuals to enact alternative patterns of gender relations within contexts that are considered feminine (Finley 2010), the enactment of alternative patterns of gender relations may be especially apparent within competitive youth swimming, a sport that has historically been considered acceptable for white, middle-class girls to participate in (Bier 2011; Cahn 1994).

In this article, I follow a group of 8- to 10-year-old swimmers across different contexts at swim practices, asking: Do the meanings swimmers associate with gender vary as a result of their contextually specific, group-based interactions? If so, what are the conditions that allow swimmers to associate alternative cultural meanings with gender? To answer these questions, I outline the "gender geography" of swimmers' gender relations within two main contexts, arguing that when gender was less salient and children could "see" athletic similarity between the genders, children interacted in ways that undermined hegemonic beliefs about gender. Yet when the salience of gender was high and structural mechanisms encouraged kids to engage in borderwork, swimmers affirmed beliefs in essentialist and categorical—but nonhierarchical—differences between the genders. By paying attention to structural mechanisms and the variable salience of gender, we can thus see whether

and how children associate different meanings with gender across contexts. Furthermore, because the swimmers enacted nonhierarchical gender relations in both contexts, this article contributes to gender theory by introducing the concept of "spillover," theorizing that aspects of less oppressive gender relations may transfer across contexts.

* * *

THE "GENDER GEOGRAPHY" OF SUN VALLEY SWIM TEAM

On my first day of research with SVST, Coach Elizabeth started Sharks swim practice with a team meeting. The day before, she explained, she had to "excuse" the athletes from practice early for misbehaving—something she had not done to a group of swimmers in more than three years. While solemnly addressing the swimmers, Elizabeth reminded the athletes that they were the fastest swimmers in their age category; she thus expected more from them than if they were in the Dolphins or Piranhas groups. Elizabeth told the swimmers that while they were at swim practices, "There is a time to listen and a time for fun." When it was "time to listen," Elizabeth stressed that the swimmers should pay attention, remain focused, and follow her instructions. By doing so, they would achieve their goals of becoming faster swimmers.

As Elizabeth's speech suggests, there were two main contexts that organized swimmers' relations at the pool: focused athletic contexts in which swimmers were expected to follow their coach's instructions, and unfocused free time in which swimmers had fun with their friends. . . . [T]he variable salience of gender at the pool played an important role in shaping the different meanings swimmers associated with gender within and across these contexts. As a result of the structural mechanisms instituted by Coach Elizabeth during focused aspects of practice, gender was less salient in this context, and the swimmers interacted in nonantagonistic ways. While doing so, the swimmers regularly witnessed athletic parity between the genders and associated alternative, nonhegemonic meanings pertaining to athleticism. Because the gender meanings changed across contexts at the pool, however, gender was highly salient during the swimmers' free time. Structural mechanisms instead encouraged the kids to engage in borderwork in this context. Because swimmers tended to interact in antagonistic ways in their free time, similarities between the genders were less visible, ultimately encouraging the swimmers to associate gender with categoricalism and essentialism.

Racing "for Times": Focused Aspects of Practice

The most focused aspects of Sharks swim practices occurred when athletes raced "for times." While racing "for times," athletes swam a distance, such as 50 or 100 yards, as fast as they could—like they did during formal competitions. Afterwards, the athletes calculated how fast they swam the interval and reported their times to Coach Elizabeth. In interviews, athletes described racing "for times" as having "to sprint and go as fast as you can" while trying "to get the same time [as] in the [swim] meet." Zoe, a nine-year-old Asian girl, told me that during these workouts, she compares herself to Olympians like Michael Phelps and Natalie Coughlin, reminding herself, "If you were one of them, you wouldn't be able to stop, so just try to push through it and work hard and think of something else besides how hard it is." As Zoe's strategy suggests, racing "for times" was not a time to goof around. Instead, in this context, swimmers were expected to work hard, swim fast, and push themselves when tired.

During these workouts, Elizabeth often organized swimmers into groups according to their athletic ability. While assigning the swimmers to lanes, Elizabeth either instructed the fastest athletes to share a lane or assigned several fast swimmers to each lane. To motivate the athletes,

Elizabeth often encouraged the swimmers to race the swimmers next to them, catch the swimmers in front of them, and compare times with other swimmers in their lanes. Because the girls and boys had relatively equal athletic abilities, racing for times was a context where swimmers of both genders regularly trained and raced together. . . .

[D]uring focused aspects of practice, Coach Elizabeth organized lanes based on athletes' fastest times, not gender. While following Elizabeth's instructions to race other swimmers, Nick and Jon compared themselves to Sophia—a girl. After hearing Lesley's time on the first 200-yard Individual Medley, Elizabeth instructed Lesley to swim with faster swimmers—both were boys. Instances where the girls and boys compared times and raced each other occurred regularly in this context.

As previous scholarship has argued, gender is often highly salient when kids engage in mixed-gender competitions—especially within athletic contexts (McGuffey and Rich 1999; Messner 2000; Moore 2001; Thorne 1993). While racing "for times," Sophia could have teased Nick and Jon for losing to "a girl," or Jon could have told Lesley that "girls suck" at swimming. However, when coaches or athletes directly compared girls' and boys' performances during SVST practices, I never heard athletes use these comparisons as an opportunity to evoke antagonistic interactions. Instead, similar to how teachers can encourage boys and girls to interact in relaxed, nonantagonistic ways by dividing students by reading abilities instead of gender (Thorne 1993), the informal policies instituted by Coach Elizabeth minimized the salience of gender within this context. The swimmers were instructed to complete tasks with specific goals (Moore 2001; Ridgeway 2011), allowing the girls and boys to interact in ways that did not affirm group boundaries between the genders.

"It's Just, Like, the Same Thing": Alternative Meanings of Gender

Because gender was less salient during focused aspects of Sharks swim practices, the swimmers interacted in ways that allowed them to associate alternative meanings with gender. This became clear when the athletes discussed instances they raced against swimmers of the other gender. Without nervously giggling or averting his eyes, Jon talked about getting "killed" by Sophia when they swam breaststroke. Cody leaned back and shrugged as he told me, "It doesn't matter . . . It's just, like, the same thing" if he loses to a girl or a boy. When asked who he races during practices, Nick spontaneously compared his times to Sophia's:

> When Brady (11, white) was in the group I always raced against him. Now that he's gone the only one left is Sophia. Which, 200 IMs, no question, she's gonna win because my breaststroke sucks. Butterfly . . . I'll usually [win]—well, most of the time. Backstroke, it's a 50-50 game, and freestyle, 50-50. Breaststroke, no doubt she's in front.

Without a hint of defensiveness about losing to a girl, Nick made detailed comparisons between himself and Sophia. Even in butterfly, his fastest stroke, Nick recognized that he wins only "most of the time." Although boys often have much at stake in maintaining hierarchical and categorical differences between the genders (McGuffey and Rich 1999; Thorne 1993), at SVST the boys instead associated alternative meanings with gender while talking about racing "for times," where athleticism was not associated with hierarchy or difference.

The girls also talked about racing "for times" in ways that suggested they were not inferior or fundamentally different athletes because of their gender. Chelsea, a 10-year-old Asian girl, told me that boys are "not always faster [in swimming], sometimes they can be slower." Similarly, Anna, a 10-year-old white girl, discussed a race she lost to Elijah, a 10-year-old white boy. Instead of justifying defeat by saying that boys are always faster than girls, Anna identified a specific reason why she lost. She explained that when she dove into the water, "I [dove] to the side. It was not a good dive." Even Wendy, a nine-year-old white girl—one of the slowest athletes in the group—told me that because Sophia

is as fast as Nick, there was "not really" a difference between the girls' and boys' swimming abilities.

There are two reasons Sharks swim practices were an ideal context for swimmers to enact nonhegemonic patterns of gender relations pertaining to athleticism. First, the Sharks swimmers were the fastest group of "ten and under" swimmers on the team, and highly committed to athletics. Many of the Sharks swimmers told me they attended practice to "get better times" or to "get better" at swimming. Several of the boys and girls expressed a desire to swim in the Olympics one day, and Grace, a 10-year-old white girl, even chose to attend swim practice instead of her best friend's birthday party. Because of the athletes' commitment, the majority of swimmers willingly followed Elizabeth's instructions—even if it meant sharing lanes with swimmers of the other gender. Swimmers in the other "10 and under" groups on the team, however, did not always follow their coaches' instructions as readily. I occasionally noticed girls and boys in the Dolphins and Piranhas groups make faces and shriek when instructed to share lanes with swimmers of the other gender—something Sharks swimmers never did while racing "for times." As a result of the Sharks swimmers' commitment to athleticism, acting in accordance with the structural mechanisms instituted by Elizabeth likely mattered more than it did to other "10 and under" athletes.

Additionally, while following Elizabeth's instructions to share lanes and race one another, the swimmers compared times, a relatively transparent measure of ability. If the athletes were playing a team sport like basketball or soccer, where athleticism is assessed through less quantifiable skills, such as dribbling or blocking ability, it may have been easier for the boys to marginalize or masculinize the girls' abilities (McGuffey and Rich 1999; Thorne 1993). Indeed, during interviews, several of the girls and boys discussed instances during recess and physical education classes when boys invoked hierarchical and categorical notions of gender while playing team sports, such as when they refused to play with girls or became upset after losing to girls. During Sharks swim practices, however, the swimmers were frequently provided with specific, quantifiable instances of girls beating boys and boys beating girls. Through these time-based comparisons, it became clear that the girls' and boys' abilities overlapped (Kane 1995). As a result, within a context where swimmers willingly interacted in ways that illuminated similarities between the genders, girls and boys associated nonhegemonic meanings with gender.

Having Fun with Friends: Unsupervised Free Time

The least focused aspects of swimming occurred during the swimmers' free time. Sharks swimmers were never completely unsupervised on the pool deck, but there were times—such as before swim practices or between races at swim meets—when SVST coaches were busy coaching other swimmers. As opposed to focused aspects of practice, which were "hard" and "tiring," unsupervised free time was a chance for the kids to have fun with their friends. David, a 10-year-old Latino boy, explained that before and after swim practice, he and his friends had "lots of fun together." Grace told me, "It's always fun to come here and see [my friends]," and Chelsea similarly said that she had "fun" while "hanging out" with her friends before practices.

The unsupervised aspect of the swimmers' free time played an important role in shaping kids' social interactions with their friends. At the pool, I did not observe patterns of age and racial separation that other scholars have observed among children in schools and summer camps (Lewis 2003; Moore 2001; Perry 2002). In interviews, furthermore, most of the swimmers had a difficult time naming their closest friends on the team, explaining that they were close friends with "everyone" and had "a lot of good friends [on the team]." Despite the ostensive unity among the swimmers, none of the swimmers

reported being friends with kids of the other gender. For example, Nick, a multiracial nine-year-old, named every male swimmer and male coach he could think of when describing his "good friends." . . .

Nick's "good friends" range from boys in the Sharks group to one of the men who worked at the pool's café. Like other swimmers in the Sharks group, moreover, Nick developed friendships across racial and age categories. Although the requirements for being Nick's friend are not particularly stringent—you simply needed to "chat a lot" or give him a discount on food—the only girl he mentions is his sister, who can be "very annoying." This is striking because Nick's parents were good friends with the parents of Chelsea, a girl in the Sharks group. On several different occasions, Nick talked about going fishing with Chelsea's family and having her family over for barbecues. Once, he even told me he dreamed about raiding her family's food pantry. Based on Nick's criteria, Chelsea should count as a friend. However, when I asked Nick if he ever "hangs out" with Chelsea, he simply responded, "No." When asked to elaborate, he explained, "I don't hang out with girls."

As Nick's comments suggest, gender was a highly salient category that structured kids' friendships during their free time. Among swimmers in the Sharks group, this gender separation was marked with extensive physical separation. After changing into their swim suits in sex-segregated locker rooms, the girls would set their swim bags near the right end of the bleachers that lined the length of the pool. The boys would walk past the girls, often without even glancing in their direction, to the far end of the benches, placing their bags almost 50 meters from the girls' space.

There were three reasons why gender became a highly salient organizing principle within the kids' group-based relations during unsupervised free time. First, as opposed to when Coach Elizabeth instructed the girls and boys to share lanes and compare times, in unsupervised aspects of practices, no policies encouraged the boys and girls to interact. Because the swimmers' unsupervised free time was not formally scripted, the kids relied on gender as a highly salient criterion when developing friendships (Ridgeway 2011). Furthermore, similar to how formal gender segregation on soccer teams and golf courses can increase the salience of gender within interactions (Messner 2000; Morgan and Martin 2006), the policy of physically separating the swimmers into gender-segregated locker rooms before and after practice formally marked the boys and girls as different when they entered and exited the pool deck. And finally, the crowded nature of the pool deck may have contributed to the salience of gender in this context (Thorne 1993). Because there were often between 50 and 100 kids on the pool deck during SVST practices, there were plenty of witnesses who could tease kids for having "crushes" on kids of the other gender, making it risky for the girls and boys to socialize with each other. Thus, in the swimmers' free time, rather than developing friendships based on similar interests or athletic ability, the lack of rules, the threat of heterosexual teasing, and gender-segregated locker rooms helped create a context where gender was highly salient.

"Boys Are Always Wild" and "Girls Are Very Nice and Sweet": Hegemonic Meanings of Gender

Given the high salience of gender boundaries during swimmers' unsupervised free time, the girls' and boys' interactions often strengthened gender-based group boundaries during unsupervised aspects of practice (McGuffey and Rich 1999; Messner 2000; Thorne 1993). Once, before practice, Nick shouted his last name while jumping toward Katie. While mimicking his motion, Katie shouted, "Weirdo!" back at him. Several times, I watched Nick, Brady, and Sophia dump cold water on one another's heads after practice. After a swimming fundraiser, Katie, Jon, and Cody spent 10 minutes hitting and splashing one another with foam swimming "noodles" in the pool. Toward the end of a swim meet, several boys filled their swim caps with water and tried splashing Lesley and Grace. After wrestling the swim caps out of the boys' hands, Grace came over to me and told me that Elijah gave her "cooties."

Although the swimmers tended to interact in antagonistic ways during their free time, borderwork at the pool did not seem to be based on beliefs in male supremacy. Unlike existing research has suggested (McGuffey and Rich 1999; Messner 2000; Thorne 1993), boys did not provoke antagonistic relations more frequently than girls, nor did the boys control more space on the pool deck. Furthermore, the girls never tried to avoid confrontations with the boys, and instead seemed confident in their ability to interact as equals. Once, for example, I was talking with Katie when Amy, an 11-year-old Asian girl, walked over to us. Elijah and Jon were standing several feet away, wearing swimming flippers on their hands. Katie warned Amy that the boys would "smack you with that fin" if Amy got too close. Amy, however, rolled her eyes and told Katie, "I'm not scared." She then punched Katie's arm a couple of times, demonstrating how she would fight if provoked. If the swimmers had believed that boys on the pool deck were stronger than the girls, Amy may have been more cautious about fighting Jon and Elijah. Instead, she confidently proclaimed that she was "not scared" and demonstrated how she would punch them.

Other girls in the Sharks group also seemed confident in their ability to engage in borderwork as equals with the boys. Once, much to the girls' excitement, Katie "pantsed" Elijah at a swim meet.[3] Another time, after Nick dumped what he described as "ice cold" water on Sophia's head, she got "revenge" by pouring red Gatorade on him. If Katie or Sophia had believed the boys were stronger or more powerful than the girls, they may have been afraid to instigate such interactions. Fear of the boys' reactions, however, did not stop Katie from "pantsing" Elijah, or Sophia from dumping a red, sticky drink on Nick's head. Although hegemonic cultural beliefs about gender often become activated when gender is a salient aspect of social interactions (Ridgeway 2011), the swimmers' antagonistic interactions in this context did not appear to be based upon a sense of male supremacy. Instead, they were transformative in the sense that they allowed the girls to occupy space and express agency when interacting as equals with the boys. However, because these interactions continued to affirm categorical and essentialist differences between the genders, they simultaneously undermined and reproduced aspects of hegemonic gender relations.

Furthermore, all the swimmers talked about sharing close physical space with kids of the other gender in ways that were markedly different from how they talked about racing one another. When talking about racing "for times," the swimmers willingly recognized and discussed the overlap between girls' and boys' abilities. However, on a social level, the meanings kids associated with gender were firmly grounded in categorical differences. Perhaps because of the risk of heterosexual teasing (Thorne 1993), boys and girls told me that spending time with athletes of the other gender was "not fun," "awkward," "annoying," "awful," "super uncomfortable," "gross," "kinda weird," and "really bad and really messed up." Furthermore, many of the kids articulated essentialist understandings of gender within these narratives, explaining that "boys are always wild," "girls are very nice and sweet," "girls are more limber," and "boys are more competitive." Notably, however, the swimmers did not include assumptions about male supremacy within these explanations. Instead, as suggested by their patterns of borderwork, the swimmers associated categorical and essentialist—but nonhierarchical—meanings with gender.

As an observer who spent an equal amount of time with the girls and boys, it was puzzling to hear girls and boys make categorical and essentialist distinctions between the genders. If girls were always "more limber" than boys, then how could the swimmers account for the boy from the Sharks group who frequently did the splits before swim practice? If "girls are very nice and sweet," then how could they explain the times when the girls screamed at and hit one another? Although it was easy for me to think of exceptions to the kids' generalizations, whenever I asked kids about these exceptions, my questions were met with shrugs and surprise.

Despite being quite knowledgeable about one another's swimming abilities, the girls and boys were relatively unaware of the other group's social experiences. Because the swimmers tended to provoke antagonistic interactions with one another, similarities between the genders were obscured. Unlike focused aspects of practice, structural mechanisms did not illuminate the similarities between the girls and boys (Kane 1995). In this less scripted context, the kids instead drew upon and enacted aspects of hegemonic patterns of gender relations (Morgan and Martin 2006; Ridgeway 2009, 2011). The swimmers, however, did not default to enacting all aspects of hegemonic gender relations. The swimmers' group-based interactions led the swimmers to associate gender with categorical and essentialist meanings, but the assumption that boys are superior to girls was notably absent from swimmers' interactions during unsupervised free time.

DISCUSSION AND CONCLUSION

Gender is a social structure embedded within individual, interactional, and institutional relations (Connell 2009; Lorber 1994; Martin 2004; Messner 2000; Risman 2004). At the institutional level, femininities and masculinities are ranked in societal-wide, historically based hierarchies that are created and re-created through laws, policies, practices, collective representations, symbols, and hegemonic meanings of gender (Connell 1987; Lorber 1994), but the impact of structural mechanisms and hegemonic cultural beliefs within interactions varies based on the context (Britton 2000; Connell 1987; Deutsch 2007; Messner 2000; Morgan and Martin 2006; Ridgeway 2009, 2011; Ridgeway and Correll 2004; Thorne 1993).

My research contributes to existing literature by exploring how gender meanings and relations change across contexts. By following the same group of individuals across different contexts, I found that the meanings kids associated with a social category such as "gender" did not always align with hegemonic beliefs. Instead, the swimmers' understandings of gender were filtered through group-based interactions and thus varied dramatically depending on the context (Fine 1979; Eliasoph and Lichterman 2003; Swidler 1986).

NOTES

1. The swim team name and names of all participants are pseudonyms.

2. SVST coaches occasionally organized intra-squad swim meets, where boys and girls of all ages race against one another in heats arranged from slowest to fastest.

3. Because the kids often wore pants and T-shirts over their swimsuits during their free time, summers occasionally tried to pull down other swimmers' pants, revealing their swimsuits in the process.

REFERENCES

Anderson, Eric. 2008. "I used to think women were weak": Orthodox masculinity, gender segregation, and sport. *Sociological Forum* 23:257–80.

Bier, Lisa. 2011. *Fighting the current: The rise of American women's swimming: 1870–1926.* Jefferson, NC: McFarland.

Britton, Dana M. 2000. The epistemology of the gendered organization. *Gender & Society* 14:418–34.

Cahn, Susan K. 1994. *Coming on strong: Gender and sexuality in twentieth-century women's sport.* Cambridge, MA: Harvard University Press.

Connell, Raewyn. 1987. *Gender and power: Society, the person and sexual politics.* Stanford, CA: Stanford University Press.

Connell, Raewyn. 2009. *Short introductions: Gender.* Maiden, MA: Polity Press.

Deutsch, Francine M. 2007. Undoing gender. *Gender & Society* 21:106–27.

Eliasoph, Nina, and Paul Lichterman. 2003. Culture in interaction. *American Journal of Sociology* 108:735–94.

Ezzell, Matthew B. 2009. "Barbie dolls" on the pitch: Identity work, defensive othering, and inequality in women's rugby. *Social Problems* 56:111–31.

Fine, Gary Alan. 1979. Small groups and culture creation: The idioculture of little league baseball teams. *American Sociological Review* 44: 733–45.

Heywood, Leslie, and Shari L. Dworkin. 2003. *Built to win: The female athlete as cultural icon.* Minneapolis: University of Minnesota Press.

Kane, Mary Jo. 1995. Resistance/transformation of the oppositional binary: Exposing sport as a continuum. *Journal of Sport and Social Issues* 19:191–218.

Kimmel, Michael S. 1996. *Manhood in America.* New York: Free Press.

Lewis, Amanda. 2003. *Race in the schoolyard: Negotiating the color line in classrooms and communities.* New Brunswick, NJ: Rutgers University Press.

Lorber, Judith. 1994. *Paradoxes of gender.* New Haven: Yale University Press.

Martin, Patricia Yancey. 2004. Gender as social institution. *Social Forces* 82:1249–73.

McGuffey, C. Shawn, and B. Lindsay Rich. 1999. Playing in the gender transgression zone: Race, class, and hegemonic masculinity in middle childhood, *Gender & Society* 13:608–27.

Messner, Michael A. 1992. *Power at play: Sports and the problem of masculinity.* Boston: Beacon Press.

Messner, Michael A. 2000. Barbie girls versus sea monsters: Children constructing gender. *Gender & Society* 14:765–84.

Messner, Michael A. 2002. *Taking the field: Men, women and sports.* Minneapolis: University of Minnesota Press.

Messner, Michael A. 2009. *It's all for the kids: Gender, families, and youth sports.* Berkeley: University of California Press.

Messner, Michael A. 2011. Gender ideologies, youth sports, and the production of soft essentialism. *Sociology of Sport Journal* 28:151–70.

Moore, Valerie Ann. 2001. "Doing" racialized and gendered age to organize peer relations: Observing kids in summer camp. *Gender & Society* 15:835–58.

Morgan, Laurie A. and Karin A. Martin. 2006. Taking women professionals out of the office: The case of women in sales. *Gender & Society* 20:108–28.

Ridgeway, Cecilia L. 2009. Framed before we know it: How gender shapes social relations. *Gender & Society* 23:145–60.

Ridgeway, Cecilia L. 2011. *Framed by gender: How gender inequality persists in the modern world.* Oxford, UK: Oxford University Press.

Ridgeway, Cecilia L., and Shelley J. Correll. 2000. Limiting inequality through interaction: The end(s) of gender. *Contemporary Sociology* 29:110–20.

Ridgeway, Cecilia L., and Shelley J. Correll. 2004. Unpacking the gender system: A theoretical perspective on gender beliefs and social relations. *Gender & Society* 18:510–31.

Risman, Barbara J. 2004. Gender as a social structure: Theory wrestling with activism. *Gender & Society* 18:429–50.

Schippers, Mimi. 2002. *Rockin' out of the box: Gender maneuvering in alternative hard rock.* New Brunswick, NJ: Rutgers University Press.

Schippers, Mimi. 2007. Recovering the feminine other: Masculinity, femininity, and gender hegemony. *Theory and Society* 36:85–102.

Swidler, Ann. 1986. Culture in action: Symbols and strategies. *American Sociological Review* 51:273–86.

Thorne, Barrie. 1993. *Gender play: Girls and boys in school.* New Brunswick, NJ: Rutgers University Press.

Wilkins, Amy. 2008. *Wannabes, goths, and Christians: The boundaries of sex, style and status.* Chicago: University of Chicago Press.

Introduction to Reading 18

In this piece, Janice McCabe, Emily Fairchild, Liz Grauerholz, Bernice A. Pescosolido, and Daniel Tope conducted a quantitative analysis of Little Golden Books (1942–1993), Caldecott award winners (1938–2000), and *Children's Catalog* (1900–2000). This sample covers a wide range of children's books through the 20th century. Little Golden Books are relatively inexpensive and available widely, including in grocery stores; the Caldecott award is given annually by the Association for Library Service to Children for "the most distinguished picture book for children" (books receiving honorable mention were also included in the sample); and *Children's Catalog* is an extensive listing of all books for children. The authors coded gender information from titles and main characters—including animals if they were the subject of the story—for 5,618 books. Their findings of the distribution of female and male characters in children's books throughout the 20th century might surprise you.

1. Were males or females more likely to be included in the titles of books and as main characters?

2. In which type of book were the differences in gender representation more extreme?

3. Why does it matter that both sexes are not equally represented in the books studied?

—— Gender in Twentieth-Century Children's Books ——

Patterns of Disparity in Titles and Central Characters

Janice McCabe, Emily Fairchild, Liz Grauerholz, Bernice A. Pescosolido, and Daniel Tope

Research on gender representation in children's literature has revealed persistent patterns of gender inequality, despite some signs of improvement since Weitzman et al.'s (1972) classic study more than 35 years ago. Recent studies continue to show a relative absence of women and girls in titles and as central characters (e.g., Clark, Lennon, and Morris 1993; Hamilton et al. 2006), findings that mirror those from other sources of children's media, including cartoons and coloring books (e.g., Fitzpatrick and McPherson 2010; Klein and Shiffman 2009). Theoretically, this absence reflects a "symbolic annihilation" because it denies existence to women and girls by ignoring or underrepresenting them in cultural products (Tuchman 1978). As such, children's books reinforce, legitimate, and reproduce a patriarchal gender system.

Because children's literature provides valuable insights into popular culture, children's worlds, stratification, and socialization, gender representation in children's literature has been researched extensively. Yet most studies provide snapshots of a small set of books during a particular time period while making sweeping claims about change (or lack thereof) and generalizing to all other books. . . . While examining particular books during limited time periods may reveal important insights about these periods and books, we know little about representation of males and females in the broad range of books available to children throughout the twentieth century. . . .

Children's Understandings of Gender: Schemas, Reader Response, and Symbolic Annihilation

No medium has been more extensively studied than children's literature. This is no doubt due, in part, to the cultural importance of children's books as a powerful means through which children learn their cultural heritage (Bettelheim 1977). Children's books provide messages about right and wrong, the beautiful and the hideous, what is attainable and what is out of bounds—in sum, a society's ideals and directions. Simply put, children's books are a celebration, reaffirmation, and dominant blueprint of shared cultural values, meanings, and expectations.

Childhood is central to the development of gender identity and schemas. By preschool, children have learned to categorize themselves and others into one of two gender identity categories, and parents, teachers, and peers behave toward children based on these categories. The development of a gender identity and understandings of the expectations associated with it continue throughout childhood. Along with parents, teachers, and peers, books contribute to how children understand what is expected of women and men and shape how they think of their place in the social structure: Through stories, "children learn to constitute them selves [*sic*] as bipolar males or females with the appropriate patterns of power and desire" (Davies 2003, 49). Books are one piece of

McCabe, Janice, Emily Fairchild, Liz Grauerholz, Bernice A. Pescosolido, and Daniel Tope. 2011. "Gender in Twentieth-Century Children's Books: Patterns of Disparity in Titles and Central Characters." *Gender & Society* 25(2): 197–226.

a socialization and identity formation process that is colored by children's prior understandings of gender, or gender schemas. Because schemas are broad cognitive structures that organize and guide perception, they are often reinforced and difficult to change. It takes consistent effort to combat dominant cultural messages (Bem 1983), including those sent by the majority of books.

The extensive body of research (often referred to as "reader response") examining the role of the reader in constructing meanings of literature (e.g., Applebee 1978; Cullingford 1998) comes to a similar conclusion. We interpret stories through the filter of our prior knowledge about other stories and everyday experiences; in other words, schemas shape our interpretations. Reading egalitarian books to children over a sustained period of time shapes children's gender attitudes and beliefs (e.g., Barclay 1974; Trepanier-Street and Romatowski 1999). However, one book is unlikely to drastically change a child's gender schema.

The effects of gender schemas can be seen in children's preferences for male characters. Boys and, to a lesser extent, girls prefer stories about boys and men (e.g., Bleakley, Westerberg, and Hopkins 1988; Connor and Serbin 1978). This research suggests that children see girls and women as less important and interesting. Even seeming exceptions to the pattern of male preference support the underlying premise: When boys identify with a girl as a central character, they redefine her as a secondary character (Segel 1986) and they identify male secondary characters as central characters when retelling stories (Davies 2003). Patterns of gender representation in children's books, therefore, work with children's existing schemas and beliefs about their own gender identity. A consistently unequal pattern of males and females in children's books thus contributes to and reinforces children's gender schemas and identities.

While representation in the media conveys social existence, exclusion (or underrepresentation) signifies nonexistence or "symbolic annihilation" (Tuchman 1978). Not showing a particular group or showing them less frequently than their proportion in the population conveys that the group is not socially valued. This phenomenon has been documented in a range of outlets—from television (Tuchman 1978) to introductory sociology textbooks (Ferree and Hall 1990) to animated cartoons (Klein and Shiffman 2009). Yet, research on "symbolic annihilation" has neglected children's books and failed to tie representations to broader historical changes.

HISTORICAL CHANGE: GENDER THROUGHOUT THE TWENTIETH CENTURY

Inequitable gender representations may have diminished over time in the United States, corresponding with women gaining rights throughout the century (e.g., voting and reproductive rights) and entrance into the public sphere via the workplace, politics, and media. However, it seems more likely that there will be periods of greater disparity and periods of greater parity, corresponding with upsurges in feminist activism and backlash against progressive gender reforms. For instance, Cancian and Ross (1981) identified a curvilinear pattern in newspapers' and magazines' coverage of women, finding that coverage peaked during the first wave of feminist activism (1908–1920) and dipped until the second wave was well underway in 1970, when it began to rise again.

Thus, we have reason to believe that representations during midcentury—after the 19th Amendment gave women the right to vote but before the second-wave women's movement—may differ from other parts of the century. Historians have identified the 1930s as a time of backlash against the changes in gender expectations and sexual freedom of the 1920s (Cott 1987; Scharf 1980). While resistance to these changes existed in the first two decades of the century (Kimmel 1987), the tide shifted with the Great Depression. Women were scorned for taking "male jobs" (Evans 1997; Scharf 1980), the increase in the number of women in the professions "came to a halt" (Scharf 1980, 85), and the media asked "Is Feminism Dead?" in 1935 (Scharf 1980, 110). Even when women's employment skyrocketed during WWII, traditional notions of gender persisted through the valuation of the "domestic ideology" (Evans 1997; Friedan 1963; Rupp and Taylor 1987) and women were "criticized for failing to raise their sons properly" (Evans 1997, 234). This gender traditionalism and antifeminism persisted into the 1960s, although feminist challenges to gender expectations began to swell again with President Kennedy's Commission on the Status of Women, the Equal Pay Act, the publication of *The Feminine Mystique*, and the founding of the National Organization for Women (NOW) (Rupp and Taylor 1987). The cumulative effects of these events were apparent in the 1970s as feminism rapidly expanded in a second wave of activism (Cancian and Ross 1981; Evans 1997). Although there was some resistance to feminism during the 1980s (Evans 1997; Faludi 1991), this latter part of the century saw a more consistent presence of activism; by the mid-1990s, feminist solidarity was growing among younger women (Evans 1997) identified as feminism's "third wave."

Based on these patterns of feminist activism and backlash, we expect representation of women and girls to be closer to parity during activist periods (1900–1929 and 1970–2000) and more absent during greater gender traditionalism (1930–1969). We link the theoretical concept of symbolic annihilation to gender representation throughout the century.

* * *

Findings

Twentieth-Century Representations

We first provide general yearly trends of the percentage of books featuring males and females in titles, as well as among central characters. Here, the unit of analysis is year rather than book. With all book series combined,

there are 101 cases (representing 5,618 books across 101 years).

Because we are interested primarily in (dis)parity between representations of male and female characters, we focus on the *presence* of males or females. However, it is noteworthy that male or female characters are not present in many titles: 55 to 57 percent of Caldecott award winners and *Children's Catalog*; 43 percent in Little Golden Books. There were also some instances in which it was not possible to determine whether a character was male or female: 4 percent of Goldens, 8 percent of Caldecotts, and 19 percent of *Catalogs* had at least one such character.

[There are] three interesting patterns in representations. First, there is a clear disparity across all measures: Males are represented more frequently than females in titles and as central characters. For instance, on average, 36.5 percent of books each year include a male in the title compared to 17.5 percent that include a female. By no measure are females present more frequently than males. In fact, the mode for males in titles is 33, meaning that the most common distribution is that one-third of the books published that year include a male in the title, whereas the mode for females is 0, meaning that the most common distribution is that no book titles include females. Similarly, the mode for male central characters (overall) is 50, but 0 for females. . . . For instance, 13 years had no male animal characters while 24 years had no female animals. Examining each variable's range shows that males are present in up to 100 percent of the books, but females never exceed 75 percent. More striking, no more than 33 percent of books published in a year contain central characters who are adult women or female animals, whereas adult men and male animals appear in up to 100 percent.

Second, [there are] important variations by type of character. The greatest parity exists for child central characters; the greatest disparity exists for animal characters. Boys appear as central characters in 26.4 percent of books and girls in 19 percent, but male animals are central characters in 23.2 percent of books while female animals are in only 7.5 percent. The data show one instance of a higher range of books including female characters than male: that for children, where up to 75 percent of books in a year contain girl central characters while a maximum of 50 percent contain boys. It should be noted, however, that only one year has 75 percent girls and that most years have higher ranges for boys than for girls.

Third, there are differences across book series, but—as with variations by type of character—these differences are by degree, not direction. Regardless of book series, males are always represented more often than females in titles and as central characters; however, the *extent* of the disparities differs. Golden Books tend to have the most unbalanced representations; Goldens have the highest mean and mode of males in the titles of any of the book types and the highest mean value of male central characters, followed by Caldecotts and the *Catalog*. The greatest disparity—animal characters—and the smallest—child characters—are also consistent across book types.

. . . All of the male to female comparisons . . . are statistically significant; in other words, for each variable in each book series, males are present in significantly more books than are females. When all books are combined, we find 1,857 (out of 5,618) books where males appear in the titles, compared to 966 books with females; a ratio of 1.9:1. For central characters, 3,418 books featured any male and 2,098 featured any female (1.6:1). Once again, the greatest disparity is for animal characters (2.6:1) and the least for child characters (1.3:1). . . .

A closer look at the types of characters with the greatest disparity reveals that only one Caldecott winner has a female animal as a central character without any male central characters. The 1985 Honor book *Have You Seen My Duckling?* . . . follows Mother Duck asking other pond animals this question as she searches for a missing duckling. One other Caldecott has a female animal without a male animal also in a central role; however, in *Officer Buckle and Gloria*, the female dog is present alongside a male police officer. Although female animal characters do exist, books with male animals, such as *Barkley* . . . and *The Poky Little Puppy* . . . were more than two-and-a-half times more common across the century than those with female animals.

The greatest disparity in titles and overall characters occurs among the Little Golden Books and Caldecott award winners and the least disparity in the *Catalog* books. . . . Regardless of type of character (i.e., child or adult, human or animal), books in the *Catalog* are significantly more equal than the Goldens. . . .

Trends by Historical Period

Data presented thus far provide a general picture of disparity in children's books. However, we expect historical and social factors to affect representation. . . . Books published during the 1930s–1960s are more likely than earlier or later decades to feature males in the titles and, with one exception (1900s), as central characters. Books in early and later years are more likely to feature females, such as Harriet and Mirette while midcentury books, like *The Poky Little Puppy* feature more males. In rare cases, there are actually more females than males in both the early and later parts of the twentieth century. . . . The most equitable category is child central characters. In contrast, animal characters are the least equitable. Although the most recently published books come quite close to parity for human characters (ratios of 0.9:1 [children] to 1.2:1 [adults] for the 1990s), a significant disparity remains for animals (1.9:1). All of [our analyses] show a nonlinear pattern, with greatest inequality midcentury.

* * *

Discussion

Gender is a social creation; cultural representation, including that in children's literature, is a key source in reproducing and legitimating gender systems and gender inequality. The messages conveyed through representation of males and females in books contribute to children's ideas of what it means to be a boy, girl, man, or woman. The disparities we find point to the symbolic annihilation of women and girls, and particularly female animals, in twentieth-century children's literature, suggesting to children that these characters are less important than their male counterparts.

We provide a comprehensive picture of children's books and demonstrate disparities on multiple measures. Still, there may be reason to believe that our findings are conservative regarding the unequal representation children actually experience. This is due in part to how gender schemas and developing gender ideologies are compounded. Reader response research suggests that as children read books with male characters, their preferences for male characters are reinforced, and they will continue reaching for books that feature boys, men, and male animals. Children's exposure, moreover, is likely narrower than the range of books we studied.

Adults also play important roles as they select books for their own children and make purchasing decisions for schools and libraries. Because boys prefer male central characters while girls' preferences are less strong, textbooks in the 1980s advised: "the ratio of 'boy books' should be about two to one in the classroom library collection" (Segel 1986, 180). Given this advice, disparities in actual libraries and classrooms could be even larger than what we found. Although feminist stories have circulated since at least the 1970s, "neither feminist versions of old stories nor new feminist stories are readily available in bookshops and libraries, and schools show almost no sign of this development" (Davies 2003, 49). Therefore, combating the patterns we found with "feminist stories" requires parents' conscious efforts. While some parents do this, most do not. A study of parents' reasons for selecting books finds most choices are based on parents' personal childhood favorites—indicating the continued impact of books from generations ago—and rarely on concern for

stereotypes, particularly gender stereotypes (Peterson and Lach 1990).

Our historical lens allowed us to see change over time, but not consistent improvement. Rather, our findings support what other studies of media have shown: that coverage of social groups corresponds to changes in access to political influence (Burstein 1979; Cancian and Ross 1981). We found that the period of greatest disparity between males and females in children's books was the 1930s–1960s—precisely the period following the first-wave women's movement. Historians have noted, "No question, feminism came under heavy scrutiny—and fire—by the end of the 1920s" (Cott 1987, 271), coinciding with the beginning of this midcentury period. And, "'women's lib' was on everyone's lips" by 1970 (Evans 1997, 287), coinciding with the end of this period. Certainly, shifts in gender politics affect representation. . . .

Why is there a persistence of inequality among animal characters? There is some indication that publishers, under pressure to publish books that are more balanced regarding gender, used animal characters in an attempt to avoid the problem of gender representation. . . . As one book editor in Turow's (1978) study of children's book publishing remarked about the predominant use of animal central characters: "It's easier. You don't have to determine if it's a girl or boy—right? That's such a problem today. And if it's a girl, God forbid you put her in a pink dress" (p. 89). However, our findings show that most animal characters are sexed and that inequality among animals is greater—not less—than that among humans. The tendency of readers to interpret even gender-neutral animal characters as male exaggerates the pattern of female underrepresentation. For example, mothers (even those scoring high on the Sex Role Egalitarianism Questionnaire) frequently label gender-neutral animal characters as male when reading or discussing books with their children (DeLoache, Cassidy, and Carpenter 1987) and children assign gender to gender-neutral animal characters (Arthur and White 1996). Together with research on reader interpretations, our findings regarding imbalanced representations among animal characters suggest that these characters could be particularly powerful, and potentially overlooked, conduits for gendered messages. The persistent pattern of disparity among animal characters may reveal a subtle kind of symbolic annihilation of women disguised through animal imagery—a strategy noted by others (Adams 2004; Grauerholz 2007; Irvine 2007).

Although children's books have provided a steady stream of characters privileging boys and men over girls and women, examining representation across the long range illuminates areas where such messages are being challenged. Clearly, children's book publishing has been responsive to social change, and girls are more likely to see characters and books about individuals like themselves today than midcentury. Feminist activism during the 1970s specifically targeted children's books. For example, the publication of Weitzman et al.'s (1972) study appears to have influenced the publishing industry in important ways. Weitzman received funding from the NOW Legal Defense and Education Fund to reproduce children's book illustrations for a slide show to parents, educators, and publishers. This presentation made its way around the world in an effort to promote social change (Tobias 1997). Some argue that Weitzman et al.'s study profoundly shaped the children's book industry as a "rallying point for feminist activism," including the creation of "nonsexist" book lists and feminist publishing companies and the "raising of consciousness among more conventional publishers, award committees, authors, parents, and teachers" (Clark, Kulkin, and Clancy 1999, 71). The linear change we found since 1970 for most measures suggests this second-wave push for gender equity in children's books may have had a lasting impact.

Nonetheless, disparities remain in recent years, and our findings suggest ways that children's books are less amenable to change, especially in the case of animals. Although we do not know the complete impact of unequal representation on children, these data, in conjunction with previous research on the development and maintenance of gender schemas and gender identities, reinforce the importance of continued attention to symbolic annihilation in children's books. While children do not always interpret messages in books in ways adults intend (see, e.g., Davies 2003), the messages from the disparities we find are reinforced by similar—or even more unequal—ones among characters in G-rated films (Smith et al. 2010), cartoons (Klein and Shiffman 2009), video games (Downs and Smith 2010), and even coloring books (Fitzpatrick and McPherson 2010). This widespread pattern of underrepresentation of females may contribute to a sense of unimportance among girls and privilege among boys. Gender is a structure deeply embedded in our society, including in children's literature. This research highlights patterns that give us hope for the success of feminist attention to issues of disparity and remind us that continued disparities have important effects on our understandings of gender and ourselves.

REFERENCES

Adams, Carol. 2004. *The sexual politics of meat*. New York: Continuum.

Applebee, Arthur. 1978. *The child's concept of a story*. Chicago: University of Chicago Press.

Arthur, April G., and Hedy White. 1996. Children's assignment of gender to animal characters in pictures. *Journal of Genetic Psychology* 157:297–301.

Barclay, Lisa K. 1974. The emergence of vocational expectations in preschool children. *Journal of Vocational Behavior* 4:1–14.

Bem, Sandra Lipsitz. 1983. Gender schema theory and its implications for child development: Raising gender-aschematic children in a gender-schematic society. *Signs* 8:598–616.

Bettelheim, Bruno. 1977. *Uses of enchantment*. New York: Vintage.

Bleakley, Mary Ellen, Virginia Westerberg, and Kenneth D. Hopkins. 1988. The effect of character sex on story interest and comprehension in children. *American Education Research Journal* 25:145–55.

Burstein, Paul. 1979. Public opinion, demonstrations, and the passage of anti-discrimination legislation. *Public Opinion Quarterly* 43:157–72.

Cancian, Francesca M., and Bonnie L. Ross. 1981. Mass media and the women's movement: 1900–1977. *Journal of Applied Behavioral Science* 17:9–26.

Clark, Roger, Heidi Kulkin, and Liam Clancy. 1999. The liberal bias in feminist social science research on children's books. In *Girls, boys, books, toys: Gender in children's literature and culture*, edited by B. L. Clark and M. R. Higonnet. Baltimore: Johns Hopkins University Press.

Clark, Roger, Rachel Lennon, and Leanna Morris. 1993. Of Caldecotts and Kings: Gendered images in recent American children's books by black and non-black illustrators. *Gender & Society* 7:227–45.

Connor, Jane Marantz, and Lisa A. Serbin. 1978. Children's responses to stories with male and female characters. *Sex Roles* 4:637–45.

Cott, Nancy F. 1987. *The grounding of modern feminism*. New Haven, CT: Yale University Press.

Cullingford, Cedric. 1998. *Children's literature and its effects: The formative years*. London: Continuum.

Davies, Bronwyn. 2003. *Frogs and snails and feminist tales: Preschool children and gender*. Rev. ed. Cresskill, NY: Hampton Press.

DeLoache, Judy S., Deborah J. Cassidy, and C. Jan Carpenter. 1987. The three bears are all boys: Mothers' gender labeling of neutral picture book characters. *Sex Roles* 17:163–78.

Downs, Edward, and Stacy L. Smith. 2010. Keeping abreast of hypersexuality: A video game character content analysis. *Sex Roles* 62:721–33.

Evans, Sara. M. 1997. *Born for liberty: A history of women in America*. New York: Free Press.

Faludi, Susan. 1991. *Backlash: The undeclared war against American women*. New York: Doubleday.

Ferree, Myra Marx, and Elaine J. Hall. 1990. Visual images of American society: Gender and race in introductory sociology textbooks. *Gender & Society* 4:500–33.

Fitzpatrick, Maureen L., and Barbara J. McPherson. 2010. Coloring within the lines: Gender stereotypes in contemporary coloring books. *Sex Roles* 62:127–37.

Friedan, Betty. 1963. *The feminine mystique*. New York: W. W. Norton.

Grauerholz, Liz. 2007. Cute enough to eat: The transformation of animals into meat for human consumption in commercialized images. *Humanity & Society* 31:334–54.

Hamilton, Mykol C., David Anderson, Michelle Broaddus, and Kate Young. 2006. Gender stereotyping and under-representation of female characters in 200 popular children's picture books: A twenty-first century update. *Sex Roles* 55:757–65.

Irvine, Leslie. 2007. Introduction: Social justice and the animal question. *Humanity & Society* 31: 299–304.

Kimmel, Michael. 1987. Men's responses to feminism at the turn of the century. *Gender & Society* 1:261–83.

Klein, Hugh, and Kenneth S. Shiffman. 2009. Underrepresentation and symbolic annihilation of socially disenfranchised groups ("out groups") in animated cartoons. *Howard Journal of Communications* 20:55–72.

Peterson, Sharyl Bender, and Mary Alyce Lach. 1990. Gender stereotypes in children's books: Their prevalence and impact on cognitive and affective development. *Gender & Education* 2:185–97.

Rupp, Leila J., and Verta Taylor. 1987. *Survival in the doldrums: The American women's rights movement, 1945 to the 1960s*. New York: Oxford University Press.

Scharf, Lois. 1980. *To work and to wed: Female employment, feminism, and the Great Depression*. Westport, CT: Greenwood Press.

Segel, Elizabeth. 1986. "As the twig is bent . . .": Gender and childhood reading. In *Gender and reading: Essays on readers, texts, and contexts*, edited by E. A. Flynn and P. P. Schweickart. Baltimore: Johns Hopkins University Press.

Smith, Stacy L., Katherine M. Pieper, Amy Granados, and Marc Choueiti. 2010. Assessing gender-related portrayals in top-grossing G-rated films. *Sex Roles* 62:774–86.

Tobias, Shelia. 1997. *Faces of feminism: An activist's reflections on the women's movement*. Boulder, CO: Westview.

Trepanier-Street, Clary A., and Kimberly Wright Romatowski. 1999. The influence of children's literature on gender role perceptions: A reexamination. *Early Childhood Education Journal* 26:155–59.

Tuchman, Gaye. 1978. The symbolic annihilation of women by the mass media. In *Hearth and home: Images of women in the mass media*, edited by G. Tuchman, A. K. Daniels, and J. Benét. New York: Oxford University Press.

Turow, Joseph. 1978. *Getting books to children: An exploration of publisher-market relations.* Chicago: American Library Association.

Weitzman, Lenore, Deborah Eifler, Elizabeth Hokada, and Catherine Ross. 1972. Sex-role socialization in picture books for preschool children. *American Journal of Sociology* 77:1125–150.

Introduction to Reading 19

Many people erroneously believe that the reason women do not pursue careers in STEM (science, technology, engineering, and mathematics) fields is because of innate differences between females and males. This article takes a different direction in trying to understand why these fields are so sex segregated. Maria Charles pursues cultural, economic, social, and institutional explanations for sex segregation in these areas. She compares gender across culture to give a deeper explanation for why there are fewer women than men in STEM careers in the United States.

1. Are interests in STEM subjects in school innate? Why or why not?

2. As you read this article, consider three arguments you could make for why more women do not pursue STEM careers in the United States.

3. What does Charles mean when she says "believing in difference can actually produce difference"? How does this fit with a socialization explanation?

What Gender Is Science?

Maria Charles

Gender equality crops up in surprising places. This is nowhere more evident than in science, technology, engineering, and mathematics (STEM) fields. The United States should be a world leader in the integration of prestigious male-dominated occupations and fields of study. After all, laws prohibiting discrimination on the basis of sex have been in place for more than half a century, and the idea that men and women should have equal rights and opportunities is practically uncontested (at least in public) in the U.S. today.

This egalitarian legal and cultural context has coincided with a longstanding shortage of STEM workers that has spurred countless initiatives by government agencies, activists, and industry to attract women into these fields. But far from leading the world, American universities and firms lag considerably behind those in many other countries with respect to women among STEM students and workers. Moreover, the countries where women are best represented in these fields aren't those typically viewed as modern or "gender-progressive." Far from it.

Sex segregation describes the uneven distributions of women and men across occupations, industries, or fields of study. While other types of gender inequality have declined dramatically since the 1960s (for example, in legal rights, labor force participation rates, and educational attainment), some forms of sex segregation are remarkably resilient in the industrial world.

In labor markets, one well-known cause of sex segregation is discrimination, which can occur openly and directly or through more subtle, systemic processes. Not so long ago, American employers' job advertisements and recruitment efforts were targeted explicitly toward either men or women depending on the job. Although these gender-specific ads were prohibited under Title VII of the 1964 Civil Rights Act, less blatant forms of discrimination persist. Even if employers base hiring and promotion solely on performance-based criteria, their taken-for-granted beliefs about average gender differences may bias their judgments of qualification and performance. (See Chapter 7 for a fuller discussion of sex segregation and discrimination in the labor force.)

Discrimination isn't the whole story. It's well-established that girls and young women often avoid mathematically intensive fields in favor of pursuits regarded as more human-centered. Analyses of gender-differentiated choices are controversial among scholars because this line of inquiry seems to divert attention away from structural and cultural causes of inequalities in pay and status. Acknowledging gender-differentiated educational and career preferences, though, doesn't "blame the victim" unless preferences and choices are considered in isolation from the social contexts in which they emerge. A sociological analysis of sex segregation considers how the economic, social, and cultural environments influence preferences, choices, and outcomes. Among other things, we may ask what types of social context are associated with larger or smaller gender differences in aspirations. Viewed through this lens, preferences become much more than just individuals' intrinsic qualities.

An excellent way to assess contextual effects is by investigating how career aspirations and patterns of sex segregation vary across countries. Recent studies show international differences in the gender composition of STEM fields, in beliefs about the masculinity of STEM, and in girls' and women's reported affinity for STEM-related activities. These differences follow unexpected patterns.

STEM AROUND THE WORLD

Many might assume women in more economically and culturally modern societies enjoy greater equality on all measures, since countries generally "evolve" in an egalitarian direction as they modernize. This isn't the case for scientific and technical fields, though.

Statistics on male and female college graduates and their fields of study are available from the United Nations Educational, Scientific, and Cultural Organization (UNESCO) for 84 countries covering the period between 2005 and 2008. Sixty-five of those countries have educational systems large enough to offer a full range of majors and programs (at least 10,000 graduates per year).

One way of ranking countries on the sex segregation of science education is to compare the (female-to-male) gender ratio among science graduates to the gender ratio among graduates in all other fields. By this measure, the rich and highly industrialized U.S. falls in about the middle of the distribution (in close proximity to Ecuador, Mongolia, Germany, and Ireland—a heterogeneous group on most conventional measures of "women's status"). Female representation in science programs is weakest in the Netherlands and strongest in Iran, Uzbekistan, Azerbaijan, Saudi Arabia, and Oman, where science is disproportionately female. Although the Netherlands has long been considered a gender-traditional society in the European context, most people would still be intrigued to learn that women's representation among science graduates is nearly 50 percentage points lower there than in many Muslim countries. . . . The most gender-integrated science programs are found in Malaysia, where women's 57-percent share of science degree recipients precisely matches their share of all college and university graduates.

"Science" is a big, heterogeneous category, and life science, physical science, mathematics, and computing are fields with very different gender compositions. For example, women made up 60 percent of American biology graduates, but only about 19 percent of computing graduates, in 2008, according to the National Center for Educational Statistics.

But even when fields are defined more precisely, countries differ in some unexpected ways. A case in point is computer science in Malaysia and the U.S. While American computer scientists are depicted as male hackers and geeks, computer science in Malaysia is deemed well-suited for women because it's seen as theoretical (not physical) and it takes place almost exclusively in offices (thought to be woman-friendly spaces). In interviews with sociologist Vivian Lagesen, female computer science students in Malaysia reported taking up computing because they like computers and because they and their parents think the field has good job prospects. The students also referenced government efforts to promote economic development by training workers, both male and female, for the expanding information technology field. About half of Malaysian computer science degrees go to women.

Engineering is the most strongly and consistently male-typed field of study worldwide, but its gender composition still varies widely across countries. Female representation is generally weaker in advanced industrial societies than in developing ones. In our 2009 article in the *American Journal of Sociology*, Karen Bradley and I found this pattern using international data from the mid-1990s; it was confirmed by more recent statistics assembled by UNESCO. Between 2005 and 2008, countries with the most male-dominated engineering programs include the world's leading industrial democracies (Japan, Switzerland, Germany, and the U.S.) along with some of the same oil-rich Middle Eastern countries in which women are so well-represented among science graduates (Saudi Arabia, Jordan, and the United Arab Emirates). Although women do not reach the 50-percent mark in any country, they come very close in Indonesia, where 48 percent of engineering graduates are female (compared to a 49-percent share of all Indonesian college and university graduates). Women comprise about a third of recent engineering graduates in a diverse group of countries including Mongolia, Greece, Serbia, Panama, Denmark, Bulgaria, and Malaysia.

While engineering is uniformly male-typed in the West, Lagesen's interviews suggest Malaysians draw gender distinctions among engineering *subfields*. One female student reported, ". . . In chemical engineering, most of the time you work in labs. . . . So I think it's quite suitable for females also. But for civil engineering . . . we have to go to the site and check out the constructions."

GIRL GEEKS IN AMERICA

Women's relatively weak presence in STEM fields in the U.S. is partly attributable to some economic, institutional, and cultural features that are common to affluent Western democracies. One such feature is a great diversity of educational and occupational pathways. As school systems grew and democratized in the industrial West, educators, policymakers, and nongovernmental activists sought to accommodate women's purportedly "human-centered" nature by developing educational programs that were seen to align functionally and culturally with female domestic and social roles. Among other things, this involved expansion of liberal arts programs and development of vocationally oriented programs in home economics, nursing, and early-childhood education. Subsequent efforts to incorporate women, *as women,* into higher education have contributed to expansion in humanities programs, and, more recently, the creation of new fields like women's studies and human development. These initiatives have been supported by a rapid expansion of service-sector jobs in these societies.

In countries with developing and transitional economies, though, policies have been driven more by concerns about advancing economic development than by interests in accommodating women's presumed affinities. Acute shortages of educated workers prompted early efforts by governments and development agencies to increase the supply of STEM workers. These efforts often commenced during these fields' initial growth periods—arguably before they had acquired strong masculine images in the local context.

Another reason for stronger sex segregation of STEM in affluent countries may be that more people (girls and women in particular) can afford to indulge tastes for less lucrative care and social service work in these contexts. Because personal economic security and national development are such central concerns to young people and their parents in developing societies, there is less latitude and support for the realization of gender-specific preferences.

Again, the argument that women's preferences and choices are partly responsible for sex segregation doesn't require that preferences are innate. Career aspirations are influenced by beliefs about ourselves (What am I good at and what will I enjoy doing?), beliefs about others (What will they think of me and how will they respond to my choices?), and beliefs about the purpose of educational and occupational activities (How do I decide what field to pursue?). And these beliefs are part of our cultural heritage. Sex segregation is an especially resilient form of inequality because people so ardently believe in, enact, and celebrate cultural stereotypes about gender difference.

Believing Stereotypes

Relationship counselor John Gray has produced a wildly successful series of self-help products in which he depicts men and women as so fundamentally different that they might as well come from different planets. While the vast majority of Americans today believe women should have equal social and legal rights, they also believe men and women are very different, and they believe innate differences cause them to *freely choose* distinctly masculine or feminine life paths. For instance, women and men are expected to choose careers that allow them to utilize their hard-wired interests in working with people and things, respectively.

Believing in difference can actually produce difference. Recent sociological research provides strong evidence that cultural stereotypes about gender difference shape individuals' beliefs about their own competencies ("self-assessments") and influence behavior in stereotype-consistent directions. Ubiquitous cultural depictions of STEM as intrinsically male reduce girls' interest in technical fields by defining related tasks as beyond most women's competency and as generally unenjoyable for them. STEM avoidance is a likely outcome.

Shelley Correll's social psychological experiment demonstrates the self-fulfilling effects of gender beliefs on self-assessments and career preferences. Correll administered questions purported to test "contrast sensitivity" to undergraduates. Although the test had no objectively right or wrong answers, all participants were given identical personal "scores" of approximately 60 percent correct. Before the test, subjects were exposed to one of two beliefs: that men on average do better, or that men and women perform equally well. In the first group, male students rated their performance more highly than did female students, and male students were more likely to report aspiring to work in a job that requires contrast sensitivity. No gender differences were observed among subjects in the second group. Correll's findings suggest that *beliefs about difference* can produce gender gaps in mathematical self-confidence even in the absence of actual differences in ability or performance. If these beliefs lead girls to avoid math courses, a stereotype-confirming performance deficit may emerge. . . .

Enacting Stereotypes

Whatever one believes about innate gender difference, it's difficult to deny that men and women often behave differently and make different choices. Partly, this reflects inculcation of gender-typed preferences and abilities during early childhood. This "gender socialization" occurs through direct observation of same-sex role models, through repeated positive or negative sanctioning of gender-conforming or nonconforming behavior, and through assimilation of diffuse cultural messages about what males and females like and are good at. During much of the 20th century, math was one thing that girls have purportedly not liked or been good at. Even Barbie said so. Feminists and educators have long voiced concerns about the potentially damaging effects of such messages on the minds of impressionable young girls.

But even girls who don't believe STEM activities are inherently masculine realize others do. It's likely to influence their everyday interactions and may affect their life choices. For example, some may seek to affirm their femininity by avoiding math and science classes or by avowing a dislike for related activities. Sociologists who study the operation of gender in social interactions have argued that people expect to be judged according to prevailing standards of masculinity or femininity. This expectation often leads them to engage in behavior that reproduces the gender order. This "doing gender" framework goes beyond socialization because it doesn't require that gender-conforming dispositions are internalized at an early age, just that people know others will likely hold them accountable to conventional beliefs about hard-wired gender differences.

The male-labeling of math and science in the industrial West means that girls and women may expect to incur social sanctions for pursuing these fields. Effects can be cumulative: taking fewer math classes will negatively affect achievement in math and attitudes toward math, creating a powerful positive feedback system.

Celebrating Stereotypes

Aspirations are also influenced by general societal beliefs about the nature and purpose of educational and occupational pursuits. Modern education does more than bestow knowledge; it's seen as a vehicle for individual self-expression and self-realization. Parents and educators exhort young people, perhaps girls in particular, to "follow their passions" and realize their "true selves." Because gender is such a central axis of individual identity, American girls who aim to "study what they love" are unlikely to consider male-labeled science, engineering, or technical fields, despite the material security provided by such degrees.

Although the so-called "postmaterialist" values of individualism and self-expression are spreading globally, they are most prominent in affluent late-modern societies. Curricular and career choices become more than practical economic decisions in these contexts; they also represent acts of identity construction and self-affirmation. Modern systems of higher education make the incursion of gender stereotypes even easier, by allowing wide latitude in course choices.

The ideological discordance between female gender identities and STEM pursuits may even generate attitudinal aversion among girls. Preferences can evolve to align with the gender composition of fields, rather than vice versa. Consistent with these arguments is new evidence showing that career-related aspirations are more gender-differentiated in advanced industrial than in developing and transitional societies. . . . [T]he gender gap in eighth-graders' affinity for math, confidence in math abilities, and interest in a math-related career is significantly smaller in less affluent countries than in rich ("postmaterialist") ones. Clearly, there is more going on than intrinsic male and female preferences.

QUESTIONING STEM'S MASCULINITY

Playing on stereotypes of science as the domain of socially awkward male geniuses, CBS's hit comedy "The Big Bang Theory" stars four nerdy male physicists and one sexy but academically challenged waitress. (Female physicists, when they do show up, are mostly caricatured as gender deviants: sexually unattractive and lacking basic competence in human interaction.) This depiction resonates with popular Western understandings of scientific and technical pursuits as intrinsically masculine.

But representations of scientific and technical fields as *by nature* masculine aren't well-supported by international data. They're also difficult to reconcile with historical evidence pointing to long-term historical shifts in the gender-labeling of some STEM fields. In *The Science Education of American Girls*, Kim Tolley reports that it was *girls* who were overrepresented among students of physics, astronomy, chemistry, and natural science in 19th-century American schools. Middle-class boys dominated the higher-status classical humanities programs thought to require top rational powers and required for university admission. Science education was regarded as excellent preparation for motherhood, social work, and teaching. Sociologist Katharine Donato tells a similar story about the dawn of American computer programming. Considered functionally analogous to clerical work, it was performed mostly by college-educated women with science or math backgrounds. This changed starting in the 1950s, when the occupation became attractive to men as a growing, intellectually demanding, and potentially lucrative field. The sex segregation of American STEM fields—especially engineering, computer science, and the physical sciences—has shown remarkable stability since about 1980.

The gender (and racial) composition of fields is strongly influenced by the economic and social circumstances that prevail at the time of their initial emergence or expansion. But subsequent transformative events, such as acute labor shortages, changing work conditions, and educational restructuring can effect significant shifts in fields' demographic profiles. Tolley, for example, links men's growing dominance of science education in the late 19th and early 20th century to changing university admissions requirements, the rapid growth and professionalization of science and technology occupations, and recurrent ideological backlashes against female employment.

A field's designation as either "male" or "female" is often naturalized through cultural accounts that reference selected gender-conforming aspects of the work. Just as sex segregation across engineering subfields is attributed to physical location in Malaysia (inside work for women, outside work for men), American women's overrepresentation among typists and sewers has been attributed to these occupations' "feminine" task profiles, specifically their requirements for manual dexterity and attention to detail. While the same skills might be construed as essential to the work of surgeons and electricians, explanations for men's dominance of these fields are easily generated with reference to other job requirements that are culturally masculine (technical and spatial skills, for example). Difference-based explanations for sex segregation are readily available because most jobs require diverse skills and aptitudes, some equated with masculinity, some with femininity.

LOOKING FORWARD

What then might be done to increase women's presence in STEM fields? One plausible strategy involves changes to the structure of secondary education. Some evidence suggests more girls and women complete degrees in math and science in educational systems where curricular choice is restricted or delayed; *all* students might take mathematics and science throughout their high-school years or the school might use performance-based tracking and course placement. Although such policies are at odds with Western ideals of individual choice and self-expression, they may weaken penetration of gender stereotypes during the impressionable adolescent years.

Of course, the most obvious means of achieving greater integration of STEM is to avoid reinforcing stereotypes about what girls and boys like and what they are good at. Cultural shifts of this sort occur only gradually, but some change can be seen on the horizon. The rise of "geek chic" may be one sign. Aiming to liberate teen-aged girls from the girls-can't-do-math and male-math-nerd stereotypes, television star and self-proclaimed math geek Danica McKellar has written three how-to math books, most recently *Hot X: Algebra Exposed*, presenting math as both feminine and fun. Even Barbie has been updated. In contrast to her math-fearing Teen Talk sister of the early 1990s, the new Computer Engineer Barbie, released in December 2010, comes decked out in a tight t-shirt printed in binary code and equipped with a smart phone and a pink laptop. Of course, one potential pitfall of this math-is-feminine strategy is that it risks swapping one set of stereotypes for another.

So, what gender is science? In short, it depends. When occupations or fields are segregated by sex, most people suspect it reflects fields' inherently masculine or feminine task content. But this presumption is belied by substantial cross-national variability in the gender composition of fields, STEM in particular. Moreover, this variability follows surprising patterns. Whereas most people would expect to find many more female engineers in the U.S. and Sweden than in Colombia and Bulgaria, new data suggest that precisely the opposite is true.

Ironically, the freedom of choice that's so celebrated in affluent Western democracies seems to help construct and give agency to stereotypically gendered "selves." Self-segregation of careers may occur because some believe they're naturally good at gender-conforming activities (attempting to build on their strengths), because they believe that certain fields will be seen as appropriate for people like them ("doing" gender), or because they believe they'll enjoy gender-conforming fields more than gender-nonconforming ones (realizing their "true selves"). It's just that, by encouraging individual self-expression in post-materialist societies, we may also effectively promote the development and expression of culturally gendered selves.

Recommended Resources

Shelley J. Correll, "Constraints into Preferences: Gender, Status, and Emerging Career Aspirations." *American Sociological Review* (2004), 69:93–113. Presents evidence from experiments on how beliefs about gender influence our own competence and constrain career aspirations.

Paula England, "The Gender Revolution: Uneven and Stalled." *Gender & Society* (2010), 24:149–66. Offers reasons for the persistence of some forms of gender inequality in the United States.

Wendy Faulkner, "Dualisms, Hierarchies and Gender in Engineering." *Social Studies of Science* (2000), 30:759–92. Explores the cultural linkage of masculinity and technology within the engineering profession.

Sarah Fenstermaker and Candace West (eds.), *Doing Gender, Doing Difference: Inequality, Power, and Institutional Change* (Routledge, 2002). Explores how and why people reproduce gender (and race and class) stereotypes in everyday interactions.

Cecilia L. Ridgeway, *Framed by Gender: How Gender Inequality Persists in the Modern World* (Oxford University Press, 2011). Describes how cultural gender beliefs bias behavior and cognition in gendered directions and how this influence may vary by context.

Yu Xie and Kimberlee A. Shauman, *Women in Science: Career Processes and Outcomes* (Harvard University Press, 2003). Uses data from middle school to mid-career to study the forces that lead fewer American women than men into science and engineering fields.

Introduction to Reading 20

This reading provides an in-depth and theoretical analysis of ways we "do" gender in everyday activities, thus supporting the gender structure of our collective lives. Matthew B. Ezzell spent 13 months as a participant observer studying a women's rugby team at a large, public university in the southeastern United States. He identified himself as a "white, (pro)feminist man" who recognized his position of privilege in our society. This created both problems and advantages as he carried out his research. The women on this team were very open while, at the same time, testing their performance of emphasized femininity on him—a member of the White, male audience, the target of their displays of gender. Notice the various strategies the women used to enforce appropriate gendered performances for themselves and other players on their team.

1. What is the advantage to these women of "defensive othering"?

2. How does the context described in this article that supports traditional forms of gender differ from the context in the pool in the Musto article?

3. As you read through this article, think about the ways we do gender. Try to come up with other situations in which women may participate in "identifying with the dominants" and thus reinforce traditional patterns of gender.

"Barbie Dolls" on the Pitch

Identity Work, Defensive Othering, and Inequality in Women's Rugby

Matthew B. Ezzell

Identities are the "meanings one attributes to oneself as an object" (Burke and Tully 1977:883). Michael L. Schwalbe and Douglas Mason-Schrock (1996) expound on this understanding by focusing on identity claims as "indexes of the self" (p. 115). By this, they mean that identities are not meanings in and of themselves, but signs that individuals and groups use to *evoke* meanings in the form of responses from others. Identities, then, are signifiers of the self. They are not fixed, as if they were personality traits, but mutable consequences of reflection and interaction (Blumer 1969; McCall and Simmons 1978; Strauss 1959). Accordingly, individuals and groups can *work on* their identities. Identity work is "anything people do, individually or collectively, to give meaning to themselves or others" (Schwalbe and Mason-Schrock 1996:115).

Race, class, and gender, as Candace West and Don H. Zimmerman (1987) and West and Sarah

Fenstermaker (1995) have argued, are interlocking systems of oppression; moreover, they are the social arrangements from which we derive our core identities. This view implies that identity creation and affirmation are parts of the process whereby inequality is reproduced. The study of identity work, thus, has the potential to yield insight into the processes that uphold large-scale inequalities. Conversely, we can learn about social change by studying the dynamics of identity change (see, e.g., Stryker, Owens, and White 2000).

What happens when, as part of their identity work, members of subordinated groups act in ways that challenge dominants' expectations for their groups, yet seek approval from dominants? How do they manage this potential dilemma? I examine these questions through an ethnographic analysis of collegiate female athletes, addressing how they resist and reproduce inequality through interaction. Specifically, I analyze how a group of female rugby players, responding to subordinated status and the stigma that arose from their transgression of conventional gendered norms, managed their identities as women, as athletes, and, for most of them, as heterosexuals. Some of their strategies fall into the category of "defensive othering." This occurs when subordinates "[accept] the legitimacy of a devalued identity imposed by the dominant group, but then [say], in effect, 'There are indeed Others to whom this applies, but it does not apply to me'" (Schwalbe et al. 2000:425). Michael Schwalbe and associates include defensive othering as one of the generic processes in the reproduction of inequality. They note:

> To call these processes "generic" does not imply that they are unaffected by context. It means, rather, that they occur in multiple contexts wherein social actors face similar or analogous problems. The precise form a process takes in any given setting is a matter for empirical determination. (p. 421)

This paper offers such an empirical analysis within a specific context. I expand on the work of Schwalbe and associates by adding two subcategories of defensive othering, offering insights into how inequality is reproduced through face-to-face interaction. In particular, I analyze how the players (a) *identified with dominants* (identifying with the values associated with dominant group members)[1] and (b) engaged in what I call *normative identification* (identifying with the normative values prescribed by dominants for subordinated group members). Also, I discuss how the players deflected stigma through a boundary maintenance process I call *propping up dominants* (reinforcing the idea that dominant group members are, and should be, dominant).

In brief, I offer a situated analysis of the processes of identity management in a sexist and homophobic context. The female "ruggers" at the heart of this study were successful athletes throughout high school, but they did not make it onto varsity collegiate teams in their high school sports. Rugby provided an attractive alternative. A nationally competitive, yet nonvarsity sport at their university, rugby is unique among women's sports in having the same rules and equipment as the men's game. The sport offered identity resources for the women, as athletes, because of its hypermasculine structure and style of play. These same aspects of the game, however, exposed the players, as women, to sexist and homophobic stigma from outsiders. In response to the conditions under which they interacted, the players worked to create a seemingly contradictory (collective) identity that was simultaneously tough, fit, feminine, and heterosexual. It is an identity I call *heterosexy-fit*.[2]

The players' construction and accomplishment of this identity challenged the notion that women are passive and incompetent at a male-defined activity (sports), but also unintentionally reinforced ideas and practices that contribute to women's subordination. In this sense, the identity work of the women at the heart of this study is similar to the "apologetic" model of resistance (when women "apologize" for their gendered transgressions by emphasizing other conventional aspects of gender presentation and performance) found among female athletes (see Broad

2001; Felshin 1974; Griffin 1992, 1998; Messner 2002; and Sabo 1993). Apologetics have also been found among women in other traditionally male-defined and -centered institutions. . . .

I argue that the heterosexy-fit identity of the female ruggers in the current study represents an updated version of "emphasized femininity" (Connell 1987) that combines toughness, assertiveness, and hard-body athleticism along with more conventional feminine qualities.[3] This expands on the "contemporary emphasized femininity" found among female cheerleaders (Adams and Bettis 2003; Grindstaff and West 2006), athletes in a sport in which performed femininity is part of the sport itself. Further, my findings stand in sharp contrast to research on other women's rugby teams, which has largely focused on the sport as a site of transgressive (Chase 2006; Howe 2003; Wheatley 1994) and "unapologetic" queer (Broad 2001) resistance. Throughout the paper, I will highlight the features of the specific context in which my participants interacted that shaped their identity work in ways to mark them as unique within the world of women's rugby.

Finally, this is a case study of a single rugby team, and it is not my intention to generalize my findings to the population of female rugby players, particularly given the uniqueness of this team within the larger rugby culture. Instead, I use the data from this case to cull the strategies of identity work that members of any subordinated group may use when they challenge prescribed norms for their group but still seek the approval of dominants.

* * *

SPORT AND DEFENSIVE OTHERING

Historically, one coping strategy for subordinated group members working within systems of oppression and privilege is the imitation of dominants (Miller 1976). Because these systems are dominated by, identified with, and centered on members of the oppressor class (Johnson 2006), this involves taking on and/or supporting the norms, values, and behaviors of that class (see Gramsci 1971). At times, members of subordinated groups may engage in defensive othering—reinforcing the power of stigmatizing labels by arguing that the label is true for other members of their social category, but not for themselves. . . .

Members of subordinated groups may use defensive othering to specifically deflect resistance to their participation in dominant-identified institutions. One such institution for women in Western societies is sport (Bolin and Granskog 2003; Burstyn 1999; Heywood and Dworkin 2003; Lenskyj 1986; Lorber 1994; Messner 1990). Women's participation in sport challenges the essentialist equation of femininity with physical weakness and passivity. Historically, the institution has been a core site for boys' and men's socialization into and performance of hegemonic masculinity (Connell 1987; Messner 2002). Not surprisingly, female athletes' participation has been met with resistance by many men and some women. Pat Griffin (1992) notes that women who were caught *watching* male athletes competing in the early Greek Olympics were put to death. Men justified women's exclusion from and restriction within sport (and other core institutions) based on medical and paternalistic arguments about protecting women's health and reproductive functions. Over time, the rhetorics evolved, taking on a heterosexist frame. Men positioned athletic women as dangerous and masculinized lesbians. This was done, Griffin notes, as a means of social control to keep women in the roles of wife and mother. It also worked to reinscribe a belief in "natural" differences between men and women that legitimate gender inequalities. . . .

Female athletes have responded to sexist and heterosexist stigma in a variety of ways. Griffin highlights strategies female athletes use to confront the stigma—for example, education campaigns, lesbian/queer visibility, and heterosexual/homosexual solidarity—and strategies they use to reproduce or accommodate the stigma—for example, silence, denial, and attacks on lesbians in sport. An additional strategy of accommodation is apology, when female athletes "compensate" for their sport participation by emphasizing traditional notions of white, middle-class femininity and heterosexuality (see Broad 2001; Felshin 1974; Griffin 1992, 1998; Messner 2002; Sabo 1993). Apologetics are institutionalized in athletic practices like cheerleading (see Adams and Bettis 2003; Grindstaff and West 2006), in which female participants are encouraged or required to wear short skirts, don makeup, and smile while performing athletic and acrobatic movements that require stamina and technical skill. As Laura Grindstaff and Emily West (2006) argue, this represents a contemporary version of emphasized femininity that combines athleticism with a (hetero)sexualized performance of normative femininity (see also Heywood and Dworkin 2003). As the current study demonstrates, in addition to being performed through gender display, apologetics can be enacted through defensive othering: Those other female athletes may be "mannish lesbians," but not me.

Research on female athletes in a range of sports reveals resistance to conventional gendered and sexual norms and expectations alongside the adoption of apologetics. This represents the athletes' active and tense negotiations of masculinity and femininity, resistance, and reproduction (see, notably, Cahn 1994; Griffin 1998). Yet researchers have found a different process in studies of women's rugby. P. David Howe (2003), Elizabeth E. Wheatley (1994), and Laura Frances Chase (2006) found the sport, a traditionally male-defined and -identified practice, to be a site of transgressive resistance for female athletes. They argued that their participants challenged sport's status as a "male domain" (Howe 2003:242), created a vision of "sport in general (and of rugby, specifically) that provides an alternative to male-centered, -defined, -controlled, and -practiced sport" (Wheatley 1994:207), and resisted "dominant discourses of normative femininity" (Chase 2006:232). Additionally, K. L. Broad (2001) found her participants to adopt a queer "unapologetic" resistance comprised of "transgressing

gender, destabilizing the heterosexual/homosexual binary, and 'in your face' confrontations of stigma" (p. 182). Rugby, it would seem, offers fertile ground for resistance.

I found, however, a more complicated engagement with strategies of resistance and reproduction on the Comp U Women's Rugby Football Club. In the following sections, I show how the Comp U ruggers, subordinated by men as women and as female athletes, engaged in defensive othering by identifying with dominants *and* disidentifying with women outside of their team. The players *identified with dominants* by positioning themselves as closer to men and men's style of play within the institution of sport relative to nonathletic women generally and to female athletes outside of rugby specifically. They engaged in *normative identification* by positioning themselves as closer to conventional notions of femininity and heterosexuality than other female ruggers. Finally, the players *propped up dominants* by reasserting the superiority of men as athletes and as the standard for athletic play. These strategies emerged when the players ran head-on into stereotypes about female athletes—particularly female rugby players—both on and off campus.

IDENTIFYING WITH DOMINANTS

Given the historical association between (white, middle class) women and physical weakness and passivity, many women have interpreted their sport practice as an act of resistance (see, e.g., Heywood and Dworkin 2003). The female ruggers at Comp U, however, did not do this. Even as their success on the pitch (the rugby playing field) shattered the belief that all women are passive, the players used their athleticism to suggest that only *they*, and not women *as a class*, were tough and aggressive. Further, they used their status as ruggers to position themselves above women in general, whom they dismissed as weak. In doing so the players identified with dominants, claiming a heightened status relative to other members of their subordinated group (women) through closer identification with the behavior and traits associated with members of the dominant class (men).

To contest the image of themselves, as women, as being weak, the female ruggers distinguished themselves from women in (white) sororities. Frequently, the Comp U players referred to these women as "sorostitutes." This term—combining "sorority" and "prostitute"—implied promiscuity on the part of sorority women. Yet, the Comp U players commonly engaged in bantering, joking, and bragging about drunken sexual escapades. They did not believe, moreover, that the women in sororities literally sold sex acts. In fact, it was the ruggers themselves who held an eroticized mud wrestling fundraiser annually, selling access to the sexual display of their bodies as the most lucrative fundraiser of the year. Why, then, did the Comp U ruggers sexually libel women in sororities?

The players' reasons for setting up "sorostitutes" as a foil became clearer when they created a t-shirt listing the "Top Ten Reasons to Play on the Comp U Women's Rugby Football Club." One reason was: "You just laugh when people ask what sorority you're in." I asked Frankie, a vet player, what this meant and she explained that (white) "sorority girls in general are stereotyped to be, you know, like, pansy girly-girls, makeup all the time, and that kind of stuff." Yet most, if not all, of the Comp U players wore makeup (for some, even during games) and were invested in the same conventionally feminine appearance that sorority women projected. Moreover, women on the rugby team spoke glowingly about how rugby offered the same benefits for which sororities are often celebrated (see Robbins 2004): a sense of community and belonging, social outlets in the forms of parties and dances, and social networks that could offer payoffs in the future. Also, both groups were predominantly white and middle to upper middle class. These similarities with nonathletic ("girly-girl") sorority women potentially threatened the Comp U players' identities as tough and aggressive. In response, they asserted that despite similarities in their gender presentation, they were

different from—and superior to—women in sororities because they were not "pansies" (weak). The Comp U players, then, claimed a closer association to the dominant (masculine) persona.

* * *

The players put forward the identity of "rugger," and its attendant toughness, as an expression of their true athletic self. They did this by creating a life narrative in which their previous sport participation, though extensive and positive, was lacking. In this way, they projected a consistent self in the face of not making it onto collegiate varsity teams in their previous sports. As they spoke, the players cast themselves as too competitive for the less (physically) demanding sports they had played in high school. Many noted that they were "always angry" as children, were "too aggressive" for other sports, or "always wanted to hit people.". . .

When I asked in interviews about what made a good rugby player, the women responded: "an aggressive personality," "an anger management problem to work out," "someone really intense," "a competitive personality," "it's just in their genes," or someone "with that little bit of craziness in 'em." The players thus justified their claim to the rugger identity by naturalizing aggression and competition: This is who I am. Female rugby players, in this account, are not just different from other female athletes; they are *better*. Carter, one of the coaches, echoed these sentiments in an interview: "You get girls who play soccer and play basketball and you get them to come out here and stand on the sidelines and watch this and you tell me how many of them will raise their hands and say they want to try it: Not very many."

Were the players tough? By many measures of successful rugby play (see Schacht 1996), they were. They valorized hard tackles and played through pain and injury, sometimes incurring permanent damage to their bodies. They policed dirty play by opponents with targeted hits and other forms of retribution that sometimes left opposing players unconscious or sent them to the hospital. And, they taunted their defeated opponents. Tammie, who refused treatment for torn shoulder ligaments for over a year in order to continue playing, famously tackled a player who had been "talking trash" during the game, then stood over her and yelled, "Get up, bitch; I'm not done with you yet!" Words like "bitch" are used in traditionally male sports to denigrate boys and men who show a lack of aggression or masculinity (Messner 2002). Some women attempt to claim the word as a sign of toughness, or to undermine its stigmatizing power by "choosing" it (see Miya-Jervis and Zeisler 2007). By using this word to subordinate her opponent, however, Tammie adopted and reinforced this sexist theme of the larger institution of sport and positioned the Comp U team, and Comp U players, as masculine (tough) in relation to their feminine (weak) opponents. . . .

NORMATIVE IDENTIFICATION

Marilyn Frye (1983) notes that the socially constructed lines dividing dominant and subordinated groups are vigilantly policed, often by members of both groups. When members of subordinated groups cross these lines, they may experience backlash and social sanction. She notes that homophobia is used as a policing resource to maintain sex inequality. Faced with such threats, women (or members of other subordinated groups) may engage in *normative identification*, aligning themselves with the norms and values prescribed by dominants for a subordinated group.

To the extent that the Comp U players made successful claims to an essential toughness in comparison to women in general as well as other female athletes, they created a dilemma for themselves. Historically, athletic women have been stereotyped as masculine lesbians (Blinde and Taub 1992; Griffin 1992). The very things that made rugby attractive as a resource for the players' identity work—its pervasive physicality and its similarity to the men's game—made the Comp U players vulnerable to such labeling.

The players were keenly aware of this. When I asked them about the dominant view of female ruggers, they said, in matter-of-fact or angry tones: "scary, butch lesbians," "she-males," "he-shes," "lesbian man-beasts," and "butch, big—definitely gay." Many players reported experiencing intense resistance from their parents. One player told me that when she told her mother she was playing rugby, her mother responded, "Isn't that a dyke sport?" They also ran into social sanction from friends. Peg, a fourth-year player known on the team for her aggressive play, told me that when one of her male friends heard her talking about playing rugby he said, "Peg, if you turn out to be a lesbian, I'll kill you." He was "joking," but Peg received the message of his sanction loud and clear. Comp U players did not say that these stereotypes were false or try to strip them of their stigmatizing power. They asserted only that the stereotypes did not apply to *them*.

Comp U players positioned themselves as the exception to the rule by emphasizing their conformity to traditional notions of white, middle class, heterosexual femininity—what Griffin (1992) calls "promoting a heterosexy image" (p. 252)—in their style of dress and appearance on and off the pitch. They thus engaged in normative identification. The players essentialized their femininity and heterosexuality, claiming them as natural expressions of their selves. Additionally, they privileged their smaller physical size—in comparison to female rugby players on other teams—as a mark of their hard work and dedication to the sport, treating their bodies as social projects—objects that are shaped, scrutinized, and negotiated (see Bourdieu 1984; Brumberg 1997; Foucault 1977). They saw themselves as both *essentially* different (heterosexual and feminine) from other female ruggers, as well as relationally superior athletes as a result of their *accomplished* fitness.

Essential Femininity and Heterosexuality

Conventional femininity carries with it compulsory heterosexuality (Frye 1983; Griffin 1992; Rich 1994). One way for women to engage in normative identification as an attempt to please the dominant group (or at least not alienate them) while breaking other gendered norms is to make an appeal to their own "natural" femininity and heterosexuality. More than simply "apologizing" for the transgression by emphasizing other conventional gendered norms, this strategy involves claiming those norms as an essential aspect of the self. The women on the Comp U rugby team, coming up against expressed and internalized sanctions for their tough and aggressive (unfeminine) rugby play, did exactly this.

During interactions at practices and games, the players negotiated and policed acceptable gender and sexual performances for each other and for the team as a whole. For example, at a game early in the season, Doris, a newbie, saw an opposing player whose biological sex she could not clearly identify. She asked Carter, one of the coaches, if there were any coed teams:

> He answered, "No, there are no coed teams. In women's rugby, you'll see a lot of *interesting*-looking women, but they *are* always women." Maeve, a vet player, said "They're all *technically* women." Doris laughed.

* * *

. . . Such comments positioned the Comp U team as the exception and, as the comments came from veteran players, modeled acceptable gender performances for the newbies. A few of the Comp U players self-identified as lesbian or bisexual and two of the players were openly dating one another, but the team, as a collectivity, presented itself as heterosexual.

* * *

[A]s noted earlier, naturalized aggression was the most common account I heard from players when I asked how they came to play rugby. This account worked to validate the athletes' claim to the identity of tough rugby player; but, it also came close to outsiders' beliefs that all lesbians are aggressive, hence all female rugby players are lesbians. Susie dealt with this problem by essentializing the feminine gender performance of *this* team: "we just tend to be effeminate people."

Comp U players often claimed that they were special because, in addition to being tough, they were also heterosexual *and* feminine—closer to normative expectations of (white, middle class) women than other female ruggers. Importantly, the overwhelmingly white status of the team enabled their use of this strategy. Black women are typically stereotyped as more "masculine" than white women (Collins 2004; Kaplan 1987), and may not have been able to draw on this strategy in the same ways. Thus, the players used their racial identities, here and elsewhere, as a buffer in their identity work.

Time and again, in practices and in interviews, players touted the "diversity" on the team and noted how welcoming the club was to anyone who was serious about the sport. Seeing the team as "open" may have been important for the players because it suggested that they were good people. Despite their claims of inclusivity, though, the players were disproportionately "feminine" in appearance, white, and heterosexual. This had not always been the case.

The third- and fourth-year players remembered a time when the team was less heterosexual and feminine identified and fractured along lines of sexuality (the racial makeup of the team, though, had consistently been white dominated). According to Susie: "there was a big division on the team between the straight girls and the lesbians on the team . . . I mean, they wouldn't stay in the same rooms in the hotels and stuff. It was a big issue."

* * *

[T]here was a conscious decision to move away from a lesbian, or lesbian-*perceived*, collective identity (and lesbian-identified players) in order to attract and please rugby men. Vet players socialized the newbies to adopt this account. When I asked Tina, a newbie, what she had heard about the previous tension, she said, "somebody told me one time the whole reason was because the team used to be composed of all angst-ridden, butch, man-hating lesbians."

Two players, both respected and valued athletes on the team who fit the privileged heterosexy-fit presentation of self, began openly dating during my research. Importantly, they did not self-identify as lesbians. Hannah, one of the women, explained to me, "I'm *not* a lesbian, but I'm dating Wendy . . . That's our major thing. We're like, why do you need the label?"[4] Still, after they went public with their relationship, Frankie, who was Christian identified, told them they were "going to hell." Her intervention was not well-received by the team. Joanne, a respected fourth-year player, said, "That was tough for a while. People were really angry with Frankie because of that. We don't want that."

* * *

The Comp U female ruggers were invested in a collective heterosexual identity. They were not, however, intolerant homophobes allergic to any sign of lesbianism. The problem was the homophobic context that compelled them to publicly distance themselves from the stigma and stereotypes attached to their sport. . . .

Why would the heterosexual-identified players give so much weight to the male players' response? Female athletes—and female rugby players in particular—are stereotyped as butch lesbians, so the heterosexual-identified players said they feared that most men would not be attracted to them. Male rugby players, in this context, became even more important as potential dating partners. Frankie put it simply: "I think that a girl rugby player is intimidating for a lot of guys, *except* for the guy rugby players." The women, then, tried to recruit players who would be deemed attractive to heterosexual men. Eden, a second-year player, said, "It's just like, we've kind of, over the years, weeded them [physically larger, lesbian-identified players] out and kind of replaced them with girls that are more like us and athletic and everything." This highlights the importance of recruitment as a resource for the team's collective identity.

The players' belief in an already reduced dating pool was compounded by the fact that female students were the majority at Comp U. The players reported that "the ratio" created fierce competition for men as dating partners. Mo, a second-year player, told me that a popular men's magazine had described the women at Comp U as "goddesses." Given the players' ages and the undergraduate culture of romance (see Holland and Eisenhart 1990), it makes sense that dating was important to them. Because outsiders stereotype female rugby players as masculine lesbians, and "goddesses" were their competition for dates, it is not surprising that they emphasized feminine and heterosexual signifiers on and off the pitch. Surprising or not, their use of defensive othering relied on and reinforced heteronormative ideals of body presentation and performance.

Accomplishing Fitness

In another example of defensive othering through normative identification, the players positioned themselves as better than other female ruggers because of their smaller physical size and greater commitment to fitness, qualities closer to normative understandings of "femininity." To claim these qualities, players used a contradictory mix of essentialist and social constructionist rhetoric. . . . As described above, the players on the Comp U women's rugby team made use of an essentialist rhetoric in which they were simultaneously tough, feminine, and heterosexual. Yet, they also used a rhetoric of accomplishment that treated the body as a project—an interpreted, governed, and fashioned social object.

Throughout my observations, players repeatedly told me how physically different—that is, smaller and more "fit"—*their* members were compared to other women's rugby teams. The players granted toughness, seemingly by default, to all female ruggers through their assertions of a naturalized aggression as the foundation of rugby play. But being "fit"—a body presentation that often necessitates the middle class privileges of gym memberships, flexible schedules, and access to sports teams and equipment—was an accomplishment reached through hard work. The players' idea of fitness (strong, yet smaller and thin) located them closer to conventional understandings of white, middle class femininity (and, thus, heterosexuality) and reaffirmed their claims of difference from nonathletic (unfit) women in general. . . .

Being "fit" and not "fat" was something for which this team was known. In fact, as many players and both coaches told me with pride, Comp U players were called "The Barbie Dolls" within the national rugby community. Male players from opposing teams applauded the Comp U women during warm-ups before games, calling out: "Let's hear it for the hottest rugby team in the South!" And, male business associates of one of the coaches, after seeing images of the team, remarked: "There's no way those girls play rugby!" Told that the "girls" did just that, the men said, "Tell your girls that the boys from New Jersey say hello."

Players reinforced team norms for body size through their informal interactions. In the middle of the fall semester of 2002, the vet players on the Comp U team held an initiation for the newbies, attended by both the men's and the women's teams. As part of the evening's events, the vets required the newbies to dress up as characters and perform skits. . . .

Not being "fit"—being larger than the "size-zero bod[ies]" on the Comp U team—was regarded with derision and contempt.

In these ways the players used a rhetoric of accomplishment, in addition to their appeals to an essential toughness and heterosexuality, to position themselves as superior to other female ruggers, other female athletes, and nonathletic women—an updated version of emphasized femininity I call heterosexy-fit. . . .

This heterosexy-fit identity emerged out of the contradictions between "tough" and "feminine," the seemingly incompatible identities to which the players made simultaneous claim. It was enabled by the team's whiteness and middle class privileges, and it was a rewarding identity in a variety of ways. Constructing it relied, however, on the devaluation of other female athletes and women in general. The defensive othering of the women ruggers thus helped to maintain women's status as others within the dominant gender order.

PROPPING UP DOMINANTS

In addition to defensive othering, maintaining boundaries between dominant and subordinate groups is an essential component of the reproduction of inequality (Schwalbe et al. 2000). Boundary maintenance allows members of dominant groups to hoard resources, and is thus not usually in the interest of subordinates. But, because the Comp U players saw the rugby men as comprising a small and threatened dating pool, they had an investment in protecting their access to these men. Their identity work as tough athletes challenged the conventional equation of women with physical weakness and passivity, thus pushing them closer to the status of men. This could have been interpreted as unattractive by rugby men, and the Comp U female ruggers worried that it did. To position themselves above other women by virtue of their toughness, but still below men, the players maintained the boundary between men and women by propping up dominants—(re)asserting the superiority of dominant group members. The female players, in short, put men forward as essentially superior athletes.

As mentioned earlier, the female ruggers at Comp U were proud of the fact that they played by the same rules as the men. However, they did not want to play *against* or *with* the men. Tammie said:

> I'm not this kind of person that thinks, "Oh, girls should be able to play with the boys if they want to." No. Like, I would never step on that field and play full-contact rugby with the boys. They're so much stronger than me I would get killed, you know? . . . 'Cause I mean, yeah, there is that level of difference there and nobody can do anything about it . . . I'm just happy I can play exactly what they play, just on my level.

To the women, the men were the more valued rugby players, and the women sought higher status by approaching, but not surpassing, the men's style of play as the standard. The men's valued status was evident when I asked Tammie why she liked playing by the same rules as the men: "I think it's a big deal because I think men's rugby teams really respect you for it." Joanne said, "Men's games are a lot more fast-paced. I mean, obviously, we're not ever gonna be able to sprint quite as fast." She, like Tammie, reinforced the idea of men's natural athletic prowess.

Not wanting to be tackled by an opponent who is physically larger and stronger is understandable. And male athletes, on average, may be faster than female athletes.[5] But reinforcing the men's superiority in these ways worked as a form of boundary maintenance that lessened the potential threat the women posed to the men, thus increasing the female players' desirability. Yes, the women were tough athletes on the pitch, but they were tough *with other women*, not with men. In addition to maintaining the boundary between women and men, this strategy reasserted the women's specialness by distancing them from other female athletes who believe that women can do anything that men do. Jana derisively described such players as "super unathletic" (unfit) and "definite feminists," in contrast to the "fit" and apolitical ruggers on the Comp U team. . . .

Carter put it simply: "There's a big gap between [men's and women's] playing ability.". . .

I asked both coaches what accounted for the differences they had noted between the men's and women's games and styles of play. They highlighted a mix of nature and nurture. They said there were inherent differences between men's and women's physical abilities and "drives," but they acknowledged that social conditioning also played a role. Their message to the players, however, was clear: Real ruggers are men and the women's game is derivative and, thus, second class.

. . . Men's and women's bodies fall along a continuum of human differences; however, there are average differences between them.

The most valued sports, in terms of media coverage and funding, are typically organized through rules, strategies, and norms that privilege men's bodies (Messner 2002). This does not mean that men are inherently better athletes. It only means that what is valued in sport reflects the premium put on size, strength, and masculine behavior.

By propping up dominants, Comp U's female players (with help from their coaches) strengthened their claim to a heterosexy-fit identity that did not threaten men or male dominance. They positioned themselves and their sport as exceptional in that they (and it) were tough and aggressive, while they were also feminine, heterosexual, and sexy. They "knew their place" (below men), and thus could be desirable to men.

CONCLUSION

The female rugby players at Comp U were successful athletes in high school, but found themselves unable to compete in their chosen sports at the varsity level at Comp U. So they turned to rugby, an intensely physical yet nonvarsity sport, as an alternative. They stepped onto the pitch and met with success, only to find themselves stigmatized by outsiders as "butch lesbians." Instead of resisting and rejecting the power of such stigma, as others have found female rugby players to do, the Comp U players turned to defensive othering, casting themselves as the exception to the stereotype, and thereby unintentionally reinforcing the dominant heterosexist ideology. In doing so, they created a unique identity as heterosexy-fit—simultaneously tough, heterosexual, and conventionally attractive.

The women's presentation of the heterosexy-fit identity helped them respond to sexist and homophobic stigma and backlash to women's participation in sport. They wanted to be seen as tough and serious athletes without sacrificing their sexual appeal to men. To some extent they succeeded. For example, the heterosexy-fit identity insulated them from outsiders' negative beliefs; granted them higher status relative to other women, other athletic women generally, and other female ruggers in particular; and, promoted an individual and collective presentation of self they personally valued and saw as desirable to rugby men. The women did not create the conditions of inequality under which they acted, nor did they create the devalued identities imposed on them. Understandably, they managed their identities in ways that promoted a sense of self-worth and affirmation. However, their solution to the identity dilemmas they faced reinforced the stigmatizing power of the devalued identities they sought to deflect. . . .

NOTES

1. Miller (1976) discusses the tendency for some subordinated group members to imitate dominants in various forms. The process I highlight here is an example of that.

2. Although the players did not use the term heterosexy-fit, it reflects the constellation of meanings they sought to attach to themselves. This identity is similar to the identity constructed and performed by the moderate weightlifters that Shari Dworkin (2001) studied who "actively pressed beyond thinness ideals but also feared masculinization and what might be considered a loss of heterosexual attractiveness" (p. 346).

3. I am indebted to the comments of an anonymous reviewer for emphasizing this point.

4. Some might argue that such a statement is a challenge to essentialist understandings of sexual identity, one that calls into question the heterosexual/homosexual binary. While such an analysis makes sense, my data do not suggest any degree of intentionality on Hannah's part toward such an end, and internalized homophobia within the homophobic context of the team may be a more appropriate reading. In interviews and in team interaction, the players conflated "lesbian" with "feminist," "man-hating," and "butch."

5. As Lorber (1993) notes, these average differences in strength and speed may largely be due to gender socialization and conditioning. For example, in the first twenty years of women's marathon competition, they "reduced their finish times by more than one-and-one-half hours" (p. 570).

REFERENCES

Adams, Natalie and Pamela Bettis. 2003. "Commanding the Room in Short Skirts: Cheering as the Embodiment of Ideal Girlhood." *Gender & Society* 17(1):73–91.

Blinde, Elaine M. and Diane E. Taub. 1992. "Women Athletes as Falsely Accused Deviants: Managing the Lesbian Stigma." *Sociological Quarterly* 33:521–33.

Blumer, Herbert. 1969. *Symbolic Interactionism: Perspective and Method*. Berkeley: University of California Press.

Bolin, Anne and Jane Granskog. 2003. *Athletic Intruders: Ethnographic Research on Women, Culture, and Exercise*. Albany: State University of New York Press.

Bourdieu, Pierre. 1984. *Distinction: A Social Critique of the Judgment of Taste*. London, UK: Routledge.

Broad, K. L. 2001. "The Gendered Unapologetic: Queer Resistance in Women's Sport." *Sociology of Sport* 18:181–204.

Brumberg, Joan Jacobs. 1997. *The Body Project: An Intimate History of American Girls*. New York: Vintage Books.

Burke, Peter J. and Judy C. Tully. 1977. "The Measurement of Role Identity." *Social Forces* 55:881–97.

Burstyn, Varda. 1999. *The Rites of Men: Manhood, Politics, and the Culture of Sport*. Toronto: University of Toronto Press.

Cahn, Susan K. 1994. *Coming on Strong: Gender and Sexuality in Twentieth-Century Women's Sports*. Cambridge, MA: Harvard University Press.

Chase, Laura Frances. 2006. "(Un)Disciplined Bodies: A Foucauldian Analysis of Women's Rugby." *Sociology of Sport Journal* 23:229–47.

Collins, Patricia Hill. 2004. *Black Sexual Politics: African Americans, Gender, and the New Racism*. New York: Routledge.

Connell, R. W. 1987. *Gender and Power*. Stanford, CA: Stanford University Press.

Dworkin, S. L. 2001. "Holding Back: Negotiating a Glass Ceiling on Women's Muscular Strength." *Sociological Perspectives* 44:333–50.

Felshin, Jan. 1974. "The Triple Option . . . for Women in Sport." *Quest* 21:36–40.

Foucault, Michel. 1977. *Discipline and Punish*. London, UK: Allen Lane.

Frye, Marilyn. 1983. *The Politics of Reality: Essays in Feminist Theory*. New York: The Crossing Press.

Gramsci, Antonio. 1971. *Selections from the Prison Notebooks*. New York: International Publishers.

Griffin, Pat. 1992. "Changing the Game: Homophobia, Sexism, and Lesbians in Sport." *Quest* 44: 251–65.

———. 1998. *Strong Women, Deep Closets: Lesbians and Homophobia in Sport*. Champaign, IL: Human Kinetics.

Grindstaff, Laura and Emily West. 2006. "Cheerleading and the Gendered Politics of Sport." *Social Problems* 53:500–18.

Heywood, Leslie and Shari L. Dworkin. 2003. *Built to Win: The Female Athlete as Cultural Icon*. Minneapolis: University of Minnesota Press.

Holland, Dorothy C. and Margaret A. Eisenhart. 1990. *Educated in Romance: Women, Achievement, and College Culture*. Chicago: University of Chicago Press.

Howe, P. David. 2003. "Kicking Stereotypes into Touch: An Ethnographic Account of Women's Rugby." Pp. 227–46 in *Athletic Intruders: Ethnographic Research on Women, Culture, and Exercise*, edited by A. Bolin and J. Granskog. Albany: State University of New York Press.

Johnson, Allan. G. 2006. *Privilege, Power, and Difference*. 2d ed. Boston: McGraw-Hill.

Kaplan, Elaine Bell. 1987. "'I Don't Do No Windows': Competition between the Domestic Worker and the Housewife." Pp. 92–105 in *Competition: A Feminist Taboo?*, edited by V. Miner and H. E. Longino. New York: The Feminist Press.

Lenskyj, Helen. 1986. *Out of Bounds: Women, Sport, and Sexuality*. Toronto, Canada: Women's Press.

Lorber, Judith. 1993. "Believing Is Seeing: Biology as Ideology." *Gender and Society* 7:568–81.

———. 1994. *Paradoxes of Gender*. New Haven, CT: Yale University Press.

McCall, George and J. L. Simmons. 1978. *Identities and Interaction*. 2d ed. New York: Free Press.

Messner, Michael A. 1990. "Men Studying Masculinity: Some Epistemological Questions in Sport Sociology." *Sociology of Sport Journal* 7:136–53.

———. 2002. *Taking the Field: Women, Men, and Sports*. Minneapolis: University of Minnesota Press.

Miller, Jean Baker. 1976. *Toward a New Psychology of Women*. Boston: Beacon Press.

Miya-Jervis, Lisa and Andi Zeisler, eds. 2007. "About Bitch." *Bitch: Feminist Response to Pop Culture*. Retrieved June 14, 2007 (www.bitchmagazine. org/about.shtml).

Rich, Adrienne. 1994. *Blood, Bread, and Poetry: Selected Prose (1979–1985)*. Reissue ed. New York: W. W. Norton & Company, Inc.

Robbins, Alexandra. 2004. *Pledged: The Secret Life of Sororities*. New York: Hyperion.

Sabo, Don. 1993. "Psychosocial Impacts of Athletic Participation on American Women: Facts and Fables." Pp. 374–87 in *Sport in Contemporary Society, an Anthology*, edited by D. S. Eitzen. New York: St. Martin's Press.

Schacht, Steven. P. 1996. "Misogyny on and off the 'Pitch.'" *Gender and Society* 10:550–65.

Schwalbe, Michael and Douglas Mason-Schrock. 1996. "Identity Work as Group Process." Pp. 115–49 in *Advances in Group Processes* (vol. 13), edited by B. Markovsky, M. Lovaglia and R. Simon. Greenwich, CT: JAI Press.

Schwalbe, Michael, Sandra Godwin, Daphne Holden, Douglas Schrock, Shealy Thompson, and Michele Wolkomir. 2000. "Generic Processes in the Reproduction of Inequality: An Interactionist Analysis." *Social Forces* 79:419–52.

Strauss, Anselm L. 1959. *Mirrors and Masks: The Search for Identity*. Glencoe, IL: Free Press.

Stryker, Sheldon, Timothy J. Owens, and Robert W. White. 2000. *Self, Identity, and Social Movements*. Minneapolis: University of Minnesota Press.

West, Candace and Sarah Fenstermaker. 1995. "Doing Difference." *Gender & Society* 9:8–37.

West, Candace and Don H. Zimmerman. 1987. "Doing Gender." *Gender & Society* 1:125–51.

Wheatley, Elizabeth E. 1994. "Subcultural Subversions: Comparing Discourses on Sexuality in Men's and Women's Rugby Songs." Pp. 193–211 in *Women, Sport, and Culture*, edited by S. Birrell & C. L. Cole. Champaign, IL: HumanKinetics.

❧ Topics for Further Examination ❧

- Go to the main websites for Girl Scouts (http://www.girlscouts.org) and Boy Scouts (http://www.boyscouts.org) and compare the two organizations. Are their programs similar or different? What similarities and differences do you observe in the websites themselves? What gender-related changes have they made recently?
- Go to the U.S. Department of Education website (http://www.ed.gov) and search for differences in men and women in higher education. Look for tables that list majors or graduation rates by sex.
- Do a search for the Women's National Rugby Foundation to learn more about the sport and its history in the United States. Also look up another, typically male sport that females now play, such as "women's" basketball or ice hockey. What makes them a "women's" sport?

5

BUYING AND SELLING GENDER

CATHERINE G. VALENTINE

In the video *Adventures in the Gender Trade* (Marenco, 1993), Kate Bornstein, a transgender performance artist and activist, looks into the camera and says, "Once you buy gender, you'll buy anything to keep it." Her observation goes to the heart of deep connections between economic processes and institutionalized patterns of gender difference, opposition, and inequality in contemporary society. Readings in this chapter examine the ways modern marketplace forces such as commercialization, commodification, and consumerism exploit and construct gender. However, before we explore the buying and selling of gender, we want to review briefly the major elements of contemporary American economic life—elements that embody corporate capitalism—which form the framework for the packaging and delivery of gender to consumers.

DEFINING CORPORATE CAPITALISM

Corporate capitalism (also termed commodity capitalism, consumer capitalism, or neoliberal capitalism) is an economic system in which large national and transnational corporations are the dominant forces. The basic goal of corporate capitalism is the same as it was when social scientists such as Karl Marx studied early capitalist economies: converting money into more money (Johnson, 2001). Corporate capitalists invest money in the production of all sorts of goods and services for the purpose of selling at a profit. Capitalism, as Todd Gitlin (2001) observes, requires a consumerist, market-driven way of life.

In today's society, corporate capitalism affects virtually every aspect of life—most Americans work for a corporate employer, whether a fast-food chain or bank, and virtually everyone buys the products and services of capitalist production (Johnson, 2001; Ritzer, 1999). Those goods and services include things we must have to live (e.g., food and shelter) and, most important for contemporary capitalism's survival and growth, things we have learned to want or desire (e.g., microwave ovens, televisions, cruises, fitness fashions, cosmetic surgery), even though we do not need them to live (Ritzer, 1999).

The United States can be fairly characterized as a nation of consumers—people who buy and use a dizzying array of objects and services conceived, designed, and sold to us by corporations. George Ritzer (1999), a leading analyst of consumerism, observes that consumption plays such a big role in the lives of contemporary Americans that it has, in many respects, come to define our society. In fact, as Ritzer notes, Americans spend most of their available resources on consumer goods and services. Corporate, consumer capitalism depends on luring people into what he calls the "cathedrals of consumption"—such as book superstores, shopping malls, theme parks, fast-food restaurants, and casinos—where we will spend money to buy an array of goods and services.

Our consumption-driven economy counts on customers whose spending habits are relatively unrestrained and who view shopping as pleasurable. Indeed, Americans spend much more today than they did just 40 years ago (Ritzer, 1999). Most of our available resources go to purchasing and consuming "stuff." Americans consume more of everything and more varieties of things than do people in other nations. We are also more likely to go into debt than Americans of earlier generations and people in other nations today. Some social scientists (e.g., Schor, 1998, p. 204) use the term *hyperconsumption* to describe what seems to be a growing American passion for and obsession with consumption.

Ritzer (2011) also argues that the Great Recession, beginning in 2007, was preceded by "the greatest consumer-driven expansion" in U.S. history and resulted in "perhaps the greatest economic setbacks," including high unemployment and foreclosure rates. He and others such as Robert Manning (2011) and Juliet Schor (2010) are persuaded that hyperconsumption and our "business-as-usual" economy (Schor, 2010) are unsustainable, if not outright dysfunctional, and they predict that as these economic patterns move to other economies, such as those in Asia (Ritzer, 2011), we will witness economic setbacks in those nations similar to the Great Recession in the United States. In addition, scholars of the ethics of consumption (e.g., Adams & Raisborough, 2008; Lewis & Potter, 2010; Shaw & Newhold, 2002) ask if "sustainable consumption" is, in fact, possible and what it would look like given the reality of fast-diminishing resources and rapidly increasing consumption worldwide.

MARKETING GENDER

Gender is a fundamental element of the modern machinery of marketing. It is an obvious resource from which the creators and distributors of goods and services can draw ideas, images, and messages. The imagery of consumer culture thrives on gender difference and asymmetry. For example, consumer emblems of hyperfemininity and hypermasculinity, such as Barbie and GI Joe, stand in stark physical contrast to each other (Schiebinger, 2000). This is not happenstance. Barbie and GI Joe intentionally reinforce belief in the idea of essential differences between women and men. The exaggerated, gendered appearances of Barbie and GI Joe can be purchased by adult consumers who have the financial resources to pay for new cosmetic surgeries, such as breast and calf implants, that literally inscribe beliefs about physical differences between women and men into their flesh (Sullivan, 2001).

As Suzanna Dunata Walters (2001) observes, turning difference into "an object of barter is perhaps the quintessentially American experience" (p. 289). Indeed, virtually every product and service, including the most functional, can be designed and consumed as masculine or feminine (e.g., deodorants, bicycles, greeting cards, wallpaper, cars, and hairstyles). In a recent study of gender differences in prices charged for personal care products and services (i.e., women pay more), Megan Duesterhaus, Liz Grauerholz, Rebecca Weichsel, and Nicholas A. Guittar (2011) underscore the fact that "marketers have successfully convinced women and men that the gendered products they sell [e.g., body lotions and deodorants] are in fact different . . . and consumers have 'bought into' this essentialist-based marketing" (p. 187).

Gender-coding of products and services is a common strategy employed by capitalist organizations to sell their wares. It is also integral to the processes by which gender is constructed, because it frames and structures gender practices. As contemporary anthropologists argue, material culture (e.g., weaponry, musical instruments, cloth and clothing, residential buildings) are a significant "medium through which people come to know and understand themselves" and others (Tilley, 2011, p. 348).

To illustrate how consumer culture participates in the construction of gender through one material form, let's look at the gender coding of clothing. Gender archeologist Marie Louise Stig Sørensen (2000) observes that clothing is an ideal medium for the expression of a culture's gender beliefs because it is an extension of the body and an important element in identity and communication. No wonder corporate capitalists have cashed in on the business of fabricating gender through dress (Sørensen, 2000). Sørensen notes that simple observation of the clothing habits of people reveals a powerful pattern of "dressing gender" (p. 124). Throughout life, she argues, the gender coding of colors, patterns, decorations, fabrics, fastenings, trimmings, and other aspects of dress create and maintain differences between boys and girls and men and women. Even when clothing designers and manufacturers create what appear to be "unisex" fashions (e.g., tuxedos for women), they incorporate just enough gendered elements (e.g., lacy trim or a revealing neckline) to ensure that the culturally created gender categories—feminine and masculine—are not completely erased. Consider the lengths to which the fashion industry has gone to create dress that conveys a "serious yet feminine" business appearance for the increasing number of women in management and executive levels of the corporate world (Kimle & Damhorst, 1997). Contemplate the ferocity of the taboo against boys and men wearing skirts and dresses. Breaking the taboo (except on a few occasions, such as Halloween) typically results in negative sanctions. The reading in this chapter by Adie Nelson examines the extent to which even fantasy dress for children ends up conforming to gender stereotypes.

Gender-coded clothing is one example of corporate exploitation of gender to sell all kinds of goods and services, including gender itself. Have we arrived at a moment in history when identities, including gender identity, are largely shaped within the dynamics of consumerism? Will we, as Bornstein observed, buy anything to keep up gender appearances? The readings in this chapter help us answer these questions. They illuminate some of the key ways capitalist, consumer culture makes use of cultural definitions and stereotypes of gender to produce and sell goods and services.

In our "consumers' republic" (Cohen, 2003), the mass media (e.g., television and magazines) play a central role in delivering potential consumers to advertisers whose job it is to persuade us to buy particular products and services (Kilbourne, 1999; Ritzer, 1999). The advertising industry devotes itself to creating and keeping consumers in the marketplace, and it is very good at what it does. Today's advertisers use sophisticated strategies for hooking consumers. The strategies work because they link our deepest emotions and most beloved ideals to products and services by persuading us that identity and self-worth can be fashioned out of the things we buy (Featherstone, 1991; Zukin, 2004). Advertisers transform gender into a commodity and convince consumers that we can transform ourselves into more masculine men and more feminine women by buying particular products and services. Men are lured into buying cars that will make them feel like hypermasculine machines, and women are sold a wondrous array of cosmetic products and procedures that are supposed to turn them into drop-dead beauties.

Jacqueline Urla and Alan Swedlund (1995) explore the story that Barbie, a well-advertised and wildly popular toy turned icon, tells about femininity in consumer culture. They note that although Barbie's long, thin body and big breasts are remarkably unnatural, she stands as an ideal that has played itself out in the real body trends of *Playboy* magazine centerfolds and Miss America contestants. The authors provide evidence that between 1959 and 1978, the average weight and hip size for women centerfolds and beauty contestants decreased steadily. A follow-up study for 1979 to 1988 found the acceleration of this trend with "approximately 69 percent of Playboy centerfolds and 60 percent of Miss America contestants weighing in at 15 percent or more below their expected age and height category" (p. 298). One lesson we might glean from this story is that a toy (Barbie) and real women (centerfolds and beauty contestants) are converging in a culture in which the bonds of beauty norms are narrowing and tightening their grip on both products and persons (Sullivan, 2001; see also Erin Hatton and Mary Nell Trautner's reading in Chapter 6). To further illustrate the influence of representations of gender in advertising, Kyle Green and Madison Van Oort's chapter reading takes a close look at the slick ways in which 2010 Super Bowl commercials used American men's fears about their physical bodies and their relationship to middle-class success ideals by urging them to take charge of their bodies and their manhood by buying manly products. This article highlights the exploitation of negative self-feelings in male consumers by corporate advertisers to persuade men that buying and using particular products will make them more masculine. Any analysis of the marketing of femininity and masculinity has to take into account the ways the gendering of products and services is tightly linked to prisms of difference and inequality such as sexuality, race, age, and ability/disability. Consumer culture thrives, for example, on heterosexuality, whiteness, and youthfulness. Automobile advertisers market cars made for heterosexual romance and marriage. Liquor ads feature men and women in love (Kilbourne, 1999). Recent research on race and gender imagery in the most popular advertising medium, television, confirms the continuing dominance of images of White, affluent young adults. "Virtually all forms of television marketing perpetuate images of White

hegemonic masculinity and White feminine romantic fulfillment" (Coltrane & Messineo, 2000, p. 386). In spite of what is called niche marketing or marketing to special audiences such as Latinos, gay men, and older Americans, commercial television imagery continues to rely on stereotypes of race, gender, age, and the like (Coltrane & Messineo, 2000). Stereotypes sell.

Two readings in this chapter address intersections of prisms of difference and inequality in consumer culture. The first, by Kimberly Hoang, is an intriguing analysis of women sex workers in Ho Chi Minh City, Vietnam, who sell impressions of themselves as dark-skinned, poor women to Western businessmen and budget travelers who not only want to purchase sex and intimacy but also want to see themselves as helping poor, Third World women. The workers Hoang studied "racialized their bodies" by using skin darkeners and wearing either simple clothing or ethnic, Orientalizing dresses to cater to the racialized, sexualized, and gendered stereotypes of Western men. The second reading, by Toni Calasanti and Neal King, offers detailed insight into the mass-marketing of "successful aging" products, services, and activities to older men in the United States. They highlight the fact that marketing that targets older people plays on the stigma of aging in American culture and, specifically, on the often desperate attempts of aging men to hang on to youthful manliness.

CAN YOU BUY IN WITHOUT SELLING OUT?

The tension between creativity, resistance, and rebellion on the one hand, and the lure and power of commercialization on the other is a focus of much research on consumerism and consumer culture (Quart, 2003; Schor, 2004). Can we produce and consume the gendered products and services of corporate capitalism without wanting and trying to be just like Barbie or Madonna, the Marlboro Man or Brad Pitt? Does corporate, commercial culture consume everything and everyone in its path, including the creators of countercultural forms?

The latter question is important. Consider the fact that "grunge," which began as anti-establishment fashion, became a national trend when companies such as Diesel and Urban Outfitters co-opted and commercialized it (O'Brien, 1999). Then contemplate how commercial culture has cleverly exploited the women's movement by associating serious social issues and problems with trivial or dangerous products. "New Freedom" is a maxi pad. "ERA" is a laundry detergent. Commercial culture is quite successful in enticing artists of all sorts to "sell out." For example, Madonna began her career as a rebel who dared to display a rounded belly. But, over time, she has been "normalized," as reflected in the transformation of her body to better fit celebrity appearance norms (Bordo, 1997).

The culture of the commodity is also successful in mainstreaming the unconventional by turning nonconformity into obedience that answers to Madison Avenue (Harris, 2000). Analysts of the commodification of gayness have been especially sensitive to the potential problems posed by advertising's recent creation of a largely fictional identity of gay as "wealthy White man" with a lifestyle defined by hip fashion (Walters, 2001). What will happen if lesbian and gay male styles are increasingly drawn into mass-mediated, consumer culture? Will those modes of rebellion against the dominance of heterosexism lose their political clout? Will they become mere "symbolic forms of resistance, ineffectual strategies of rebellion" (Harris, 2000, p. xxiii)?

The commodification of modes of rebellion and activist politics is serious business in our corporate, consumer culture, and marketers have been successful in manipulating our feelings of compassion and our sense of justice by persuading many Americans that they can "make a difference" by buying products and services. One of the best examples of this phenomenon is explored in the chapter reading by Gayle Sulik. She focuses on the commodification of the breast cancer movement by the pink ribbon industry and carefully sets out the negative consequences, which include, for example, the sale of products from which little or no money goes to breast cancer research and the sale of products whose manufacturers are linked to the production of toxic substances implicated in breast cancer.

The Global Reach of American Gender Images and Ideals

The global reach of American culture is yet another concern of consumer culture researchers. Transnational corporations are selling American popular culture and consumerism as a way of life in countries around the world (Kilbourne, 1999; Ritzer, 1999). People across the globe are now regularly exposed to American images, icons, and ideals. For example, *Baywatch,* with its array of perfect (albeit cosmetically enhanced) male and female bodies, was seen by more people in the world than any other television show during the years it aired (Kilbourne, 1999). American popular music and film celebrities dominate the world scene. Everyone knows Marilyn Monroe and James Dean, Tom Cruise and Julia Roberts.

You might ask, and quite legitimately, so what? The answer to that question is not a simple one, in part because cultural import–export relations are intricate. As Gitlin (2001) observes, "the cultural gates . . . swing both ways. For example, American rhythm and blues influenced Jamaican ska, which evolved into reggae, which in turn was imported to the United States via Britain" (p. 188). However, researchers have been able to document some troubling consequences of the global advantage of American commercial, consumer culture for the lifeways of people outside the United States. Thus, social scientists (e.g., Collins, 2009; Connell, 1999; Herdt, 1997) are tracing how American categories of sexual orientation are altering the modes of organization and perception of same-gender relations in some non-Western societies that have traditionally been more fluid and tolerant of sexual diversity than the United States or have constructed different, non-Western performances of gay masculinity.

Scientists are also documenting the impact of American mass media images of femininity and masculinity on consumers in far corners of the world. The island country of Fiji is one such place. Researchers have discovered that as the young women of Fiji consume American television on a regular basis, eating disorders such as anorexia nervosa are being recorded for the first time. The ultra-thin images of girls and women that populate U.S. TV shows and ads have become the measuring stick of femininity in a culture in which an ample, full body was previously the norm for women and men (Goode, 1999). The troubling consequences of the globalization of American consumer culture do not end with these examples. Consider the potential negative impact of idealized images of whiteness in a world in which most people are brown. (See reading by L. Ayu Saraswati in Chapter 6.) Or how about the impact of America's negative images of older women and men on the people of cultures in which the elderly are revered?

Although corporate, capitalist economies provide many people with all the creature comforts they need and more, as well as making consumption entertaining and more accessible, there is a price to pay (Ritzer, 1999). This chapter explores one troubling aspect of corporate, consumer culture—the commodification and commercialization of gender.

A few final questions emerge from our analysis of patterns of gender in relationship to consumer capitalism. How can the individual develop an identity and self-worth *not* contingent on and defined by a whirlwind of products and services? How do we avoid devolving into caricatures of stereotyped images of femininity and masculinity whose needs and desires can be met only by gendered commodities? Is Bornstein correct when she states, "Once you buy gender, you'll buy anything to keep it"? Or can we create and preserve alternative ways of life, even those that undermine the oppression of dominant images and representations?

References

Adams, M., & Raisborough, J. (2008). What can sociology say about fair trade? Class, reflexivity and ethical consumption. *Sociology, 42,* 1165–1182.

Bordo, S. (1997). Material girl: The effacements of postmodern culture. In R. Lancaster & M. di Leonardo (Eds.), *The gender/sexuality reader* (pp. 335–358). New York: Routledge.

Cohen, L. (2003). *A consumers' republic: The politics of mass consumption in postwar America.* New York: Vintage Books.

Collins, D. (2009). We're there and queer: Homonormative mobility and lived experience among gay expatriates in Manila. *Gender & Society, 23*(4), 465–493.

Coltrane, S., & Messineo, M. (2000). The perpetuation of subtle prejudice: Race and gender imagery in 1990s television advertising. *Sex Roles, 42,* 363–389.

Connell, R. W. (1999). Making gendered people: Bodies, identities, sexualities. In M. Ferree, J. Lorber, & B. Hess (Eds.), *Revisioning gender* (pp. 449–471). Thousand Oaks, CA: Sage.

Duesterhaus, M., Grauerholz, L., Weichsel, R., & Guittar, N. A. (2011). The cost of doing femininity: Gendered disparities in pricing of personal care products and services. *Gender Issues, 28*(4), 175–191.

Featherstone, M. (1991). The body in consumer culture. In M. Featherstone, M. Hepworth, & B. S. Turner (Eds.), *The body: Social process and cultural theory* (pp. 170 196). London: Sage.

Gitlin, T. (2001). *Media unlimited: How the torrent of images and sounds overwhelms our lives.* New York: Henry Holt.

Goode, E. (1999, May 20). Study finds TV alters Fiji girls' view of body. *The New York Times,* p. A17.

Harris, D. (2000). *Cute, quaint, hungry and romantic: The aesthetics of consumerism.* Cambridge, MA: Da Capo Press.

Herdt, G. (1997). *Same sex, different cultures.* Boulder, CO: Westview Press.

Johnson, A. (2001). *Privilege, power, and difference.* Mountain View, CA: Mayfield.

Kilbourne, J. (1999). *Can't buy my love.* New York: Simon & Schuster.

Kimle, P. A., & Damhorst, M. L. (1997). A grounded theory model of the ideal business image for women. *Symbolic Interaction, 20*(1), 45–68.

Lewis, T., & Potter, E. (Eds.). (2010). *Ethical consumption: A critical introduction.* Abingdon, UK: Routledge.

Manning, R. D. (2011). Crisis in consumption OR American capitalism: A sociological perspective on the consumer-led recession. *Consumers, Commodities & Consumption, 13*(1). Retrieved from http://csrn.camden.rutgers.edu/newsletters/13-1/manning.htm

Marenco, S. (with Bornstein, K.). (1993). *Adventures in the gender trade: A case for diversity* [Motion picture]. New York: Filmakers Library.

O'Brien, J. (1999). *Social prisms*. Thousand Oaks, CA: Pine Forge Press.

Quart, A. (2003). *Branded: The buying and selling of teenagers*. New York: Basic Books.

Ritzer, G. (1999). *Enchanting a disenchanted world*. Thousand Oaks, CA: Pine Forge Press.

Ritzer, G. (2011). The dinosaurs of consumption. *Consumers, Commodities & Consumption, 13*(1). Retrieved from http://csrn.camden.rutgers.edu/newsletters/13-1/ritzer.htm

Schiebinger, L. (2000). Introduction. In L. Schiebinger (Ed.), *Feminism and the body* (pp. 1–21). New York: Oxford University Press.

Schor, J. (1998). *The overspent American*. New York: Basic Books.

Schor, J. (2004). *Born to buy*. New York: Scribner.

Schor, J. (2010). *Welcome to Plenitude* [Blog]. Retrieved from http://www.julietschor.org/2010/05/welcome-to-plenitude/

Shaw, D., & Newholm, T. (2002). Voluntary simplicity and the ethics of consumption. *Psychology and Marketing, 19,* 167–185.

Sørensen, M. L. S. (2000). *Gender archaeology*. Cambridge, UK: Polity Press.

Sullivan, D. A. (2001). *Cosmetic surgery: The cutting edge of commercial medicine in America*. New Brunswick, NJ: Rutgers University Press.

Tilley, C. (2011). Materializing identities: An introduction. *Journal of Material Culture, 16,* 347–357.

Urla, J., & Swedlund, A. C. (1995). The anthropometry of Barbie: Unsettling ideals of the feminine body in popular culture. In J. Terry & J. Urla (Eds.), *Deviant bodies: Critical perspectives on difference in science and popular culture* (pp. 277–313). Bloomington: Indiana University Press.

Walters, S. D. (2001). *All the rage: The story of gay visibility in America*. Chicago: University of Chicago Press.

Zukin, S. (2004). *Point of purchase: How shopping changed American culture*. New York: Routledge.

Introduction to Reading 21

Adie Nelson's article offers a marvelously detailed analysis of one way the modern marketplace reinforces gender stereotypes—the gender coding of children's Halloween costumes. Nelson describes the research process she employed to label costumes as masculine, feminine, or neutral. She provides extensive information about how manufacturers and advertisers use gender markers to steer buyers, in this case parents, toward "gender-appropriate" costume choices for their children. Overall, Nelson's research indicates that gender-neutral costumes, whether ready-to-wear or sewing patterns, are a tiny minority of all the costumes on the market.

1. Many perceive Halloween costumes as encouraging children to engage in fantasy play. How does Nelson's research call this notion into question?

2. Describe some of the key strategies employed by manufacturers to "gender" children's costumes. What strategies do manufacturers use to "gender" adults' costumes? To answer the latter question, look at adult costumes online or in costume shops in malls.

3. How do Halloween costumes help reproduce an active-masculine/passive-feminine dichotomy?

THE PINK DRAGON IS FEMALE

HALLOWEEN COSTUMES AND GENDER MARKERS

Adie Nelson

The celebration of Halloween has become, in contemporary times, a socially orchestrated secular event that brings buyers and sellers into the marketplace for the sale and purchase of treats, ornaments, decorations, and fanciful costumes. Within this setting, the wearing of fancy dress costumes has such a prominent role that it is common, especially within large cities, for major department stores and large, specialty toy stores to begin displaying their selection of Halloween costumes by mid-August if not earlier. It is also evident that the range of masks and costumes available has broadened greatly beyond those identified by McNeill (1970), and that both children and adults may now select from a wide assortment of ready-made costumes depicting, among other things, animals, objects, superheroes, villains, and celebrities. In addition, major suppliers of commercially available sewing patterns, such as Simplicity and McCall's, now routinely include an assortment of Halloween costumes in their fall catalogues. Within such catalogues, a variety of costumes designed for infants, toddlers, children, adults, and, not infrequently, pampered dogs are featured.

On the surface, the selection and purchase of Halloween costumes for use by children may simply appear to facilitate their participation in the world of fantasy play. At least in theory, asking children what they wish to wear or what they would like to be for Halloween may be seen to encourage them to use their imagination and to engage in the role-taking stage that Mead (1934) identified as play. Yet, it is clear that the commercial marketplace plays a major role in giving expression to children's imagination in their Halloween costuming. Moreover, although it might be facilely assumed that the occasion of Halloween provides a cultural "time out" in which women and men as well as girls and boys have tacit permission to transcend the gendered rules that mark the donning of apparel in everyday life, the androgyny of Halloween costumes may be more apparent than real. If, as our folk wisdom proclaims, "clothes make the man" (or woman), it would be presumptuous to suppose that commercially available children's Halloween costumes and sewing patterns do not reflect both the gendered nature of dress (Eicher & Roach-Higgins, 1992) and the symbolic world of heroes, villains, and fools (Klapp, 1962, 1964). Indeed, the donning of Halloween costumes may demonstrate a "gender display" (Goffman, 1966, p. 250) that is dependent on decisions made by brokering agents to the extent that it is the aftermath of a series of decisions made by commercial firms that market ready-made costumes and sewing patterns that, in turn, are purchased, rented, or sewn by parents or others. . . .

Building on Barnes and Eicher's (1992, p. 1) observation that "dress is one of the most significant markers of gender identity," an examination of children's Halloween costumes provides a unique opportunity to explore the extent to which gender markers are also evident within the fantasy costumes available for

From Nelson, Adie. 2000. "The Pink Dragon Is Female: Halloween Costumes and Gender Markers." *Psychology of Women Quarterly*, 24.

Halloween. To the best of my knowledge, no previous research has attempted to analyze these costumes or to examine the ways in which the imaginary vistas explored in children's fantasy dress reproduce and reiterate more conventional messages about gender.

In undertaking this research, my expectations were based on certain assumptions about the perspectives of merchandisers of Halloween costumes for children. It was expected that commercially available costumes and costume patterns would reiterate and reinforce traditional gender stereotypes. Attempting to adopt the marketing perspective of merchandisers, it was anticipated that the target audience would be parents concerned with creating memorable childhood experiences for their children, envisioning them dressed up as archetypal fantasy characters. In the case of sewing patterns, it was expected that the target audience would be primarily mothers who possessed what manufacturers might imagine to be the sewing skills of the traditional homemaker. However, these assumptions about merchandisers are not the subject of the present inquiry. Rather, the present study offers an examination of the potential contribution of marketing to the maintenance of gender stereotypes. In this article, the focus is on the costumes available in the marketplace; elsewhere I examine the interactions between children and their parents in the selection, modification, and wearing of Halloween costumes (Nelson, 1999).

METHOD

The present research was based on a content analysis of 469 unique children's Halloween ready-made costumes and sewing patterns examined from August 1996 to November 1997 at craft stores, department stores, specialty toy stores, costume rental stores, and fabric stores containing catalogues of sewing patterns. Within retail stores, racks of children's Halloween costumes typically appeared in August and remained in evidence, albeit in dwindling

numbers, until early November each year. In department stores, a subsection of the area generally devoted to toys featured such garments; in craft stores and/or toy stores, children's Halloween costumes were typically positioned on long racks in the center of a section devoted to the commercial paraphernalia now associated with the celebration of Halloween (e.g., cardboard witches, "Spook trees," plastic pumpkin containers). Costumes were not segregated by gender within the stores (i.e., there were no separate aisles or sections for boys' and girls' costumes); however, children's costumes were typically positioned separately from those designed for adults. . . .

All costumes were initially coded as (a) masculine, (b) feminine, or (c) neutral depending on whether boys, girls, or both were featured as the models on the packaging that accompanied a ready-to-wear costume or were used to illustrate the completed costume on the cover of a sewing pattern. . . . The pictures accompanying costumes may act as safekeeping devices, which discourage parents from buying "wrong"-sexed costumes. The process of labeling costumes as masculine, feminine, or neutral was facilitated by the fact that these public pictures (Goffman, 1979) commonly employed recognizable genderisms. For example, a full-body costume of a box of crayons could be identified as feminine by the long curled hair of the model and the black patent leather pumps with ribbons she wore. In like fashion, a photograph depicting the finished version of a sewing pattern for a teapot featured the puckish styling of the model in a variant of what Goffman (1979, p. 45) termed "the bashful knee bend" and augmented this subtle cue by having the model wear white pantyhose and Mary-Jane shoes with rosettes at the base of the toes. Although the sex of the model could have been rendered invisible, such feminine gender markers as pointy-toed footwear, party shoes of white and black patent leather, frilly socks, makeup and nail polish, jewelry, and elaborately curled (and typically long and blonde) hair adorned with bows/barrettes/hairbands facilitated this initial stage of costume placement. By and large, female models used to illustrate Halloween costumes conformed to the ideal image of the "Little Miss" beauty pageant winner; they were almost overwhelmingly White, slim, delicate-boned blondes who did not wear glasses. Although male child models were also overwhelmingly White, they were more heterogeneous in height and weight and were more likely to wear glasses or to smile out from the photograph in a bucktooth grin. At the same time, however, masculine gender markers were apparent. Male models were almost uniformly shod in either well-worn running shoes or sturdy-looking brogues, while their hair showed little variation from the traditional little-boy cut of short back and sides.

The use of gender-specific common and proper nouns to designate costumes (e.g., Medieval Maiden, Majorette, Prairie Girl) or gender-associated adjectives that formed part of the costume title (e.g., Tiny Tikes Beauty, Pretty Witch, Beautiful Babe, Pretty Pumpkin Pie) also served to identify feminine costumes. Similarly, the use of the terms "boy," "man," or "male" in the advertised name of the costume (e.g., Pirate Boy, Native American Boy, Dragon Boy) or the noted inclusion of advertising copy that announced "Cool dudes costumes are for boys in sizes" was used to identify masculine costumes. Costumes designated as neutral were those in which both boys and girls were featured in the illustration or photograph that accompanied the costume or sewing pattern or in which it was impossible to detect the sex of the wearer. By and large, illustrations for gender-neutral ads featured boys and girls identically clad and depicted as a twinned couple or, alternatively, showed a single child wearing a full-length animal costume complete with head and "paws," which, in the style of spats, effectively covered the shoes of the model. In addition, gender-neutral costumes were identified by an absence of gender-specific nouns and stereotypically gendered colors.

Following this initial division into three categories, the contents of each were further coded into a modified version of Klapp's (1964) schema of heroes, villains, and fools. In his work, Klapp suggested that this schema represents three dimensions of human behavior. That is, heroes are praised and set up as role models, whereas villains and fools are negative models, with the former representing evil to be feared and/or hated and the latter representing figures of absurdity inviting ridicule. However, although Klapp's categories were based on people in real life, I applied them to the realm of make-believe. For the purposes of this study, the labels refer to types of personas that engender or invite the following emotional responses, in a light-hearted way from audiences: Heroes invite feelings of awe, admiration, and respect, whereas villains elicit feelings of fear and loathing, and fools evoke feelings of laughter and perceptions of cuteness. All of the feelings, however, are mock emotions based on feelings of amusement, which make my categories quite distinct from Klapp's. For example, although heroes invite awe, we do not truly expect somebody dressed as a hero to be held in awe. . . .

For the purposes of this secondary classification of costumes, the category of hero was broadened to include traditional male or female heroes (e.g., Cowboy, Robin Hood, Cinderella, Cleopatra), superheroes possessing supernatural powers (e.g., Superman, Robocop, Xena, the Warrior Princess) as well as characters with high occupational status (e.g., Emergency Room Doctor, Judge) and characters who are exemplars of prosocial conformity to traditional masculine and feminine roles (e.g., Team USA Cheerleader, Puritan Lady, Pioneer Boy). The category of villain was broadly defined to include symbolic representations of death (e.g., the Grim Reaper, Death, The Devil, Ghost), monsters (e.g., Wolfman, Frankenstein, The Mummy), and antiheroes (e.g., Convict, Pirate, The Wicked Witch of the West, Catwoman). Fool was a hybrid category, distinguished by costumes whose ostensible function was to amuse rather than to alarm. Within this category, two subcategories were distinguished. The first subcategory, figures of mirth, referred to costumes of clowns, court jesters, and harlequins. The second, nonhuman/inanimate objects, was composed of costumes representing foodstuffs (e.g., Peapod, Pepperoni Pizza, Chocolate Chip Cookie), animals and insects, and inanimate objects (e.g., Alarm Clock, Bar of Soap, Flower Pot). Where a costume appeared to straddle two categories, an attempt was made to assign it to a category based on the dominant emphasis of its pictorial representation. For example, a costume labeled Black Widow Spider could be classified as either an insect or a villain. If the accompanying illustration featured a broadly smiling child in a costume depicting a fuzzy body and multiple appendages, it was classified as an insect and included in the category of nonhuman/inanimate objects; if the costume featured an individual clad in a black gown, long black wig, ghoulish makeup, and a sinister mien, the costume was classified as a villain. Contents were subsequently reanalyzed in terms of their constituent parts and compared across masculine and feminine categories. In all cases, costumes were coded into the two coding schemes on the basis of a detailed written description of each costume. . . .

RESULTS

The initial placement of the 469 children's Halloween costumes into masculine, feminine, or neutral categories yielded 195 masculine costumes, 233 feminine costumes, and 41 gender-neutral costumes. The scarcity of gender-neutral costumes was notable; costumes that featured both boys and girls in their ads or in which the gender of the anticipated wearer remained (deliberately or inadvertently) ambiguous accounted for only 8.7% of those examined. Gender-neutral costumes were more common in sewing patterns than in ready-to-wear costumes and were most common in costumes designed for newborns and very young infants. In this context, gender-neutral infant costumes largely featured a winsome assortment of baby animals (e.g., Li'l Bunny, Beanie the Pig) or foodstuffs

(e.g., Littlest Peapod). By and large, few costumes for older children were presented as gender-neutral; the notable exceptions were costumes for scarecrows and emergency room doctors (with male/female models clad identically in olive-green "scrubs"), ready-made plastic costumes for Lost World/Jurassic Park hunters, a single costume labeled Halfman/Halfwoman, and novel sewing patterns depicting such inanimate objects as a sugar cube, laundry hamper, or treasure chest.

Beginning most obviously with costumes designed for toddlers, gender dichotomization was promoted by gender-distinctive marketing devices employed by the manufacturers of both commercially made costumes and sewing patterns. In relation to sewing patterns for children's Halloween costumes, structurally identical costumes featured alterations through the addition or deletion of decorative trim (e.g., a skirt on a costume for an elephant) or the use of specific colors or costume names, which served to distinguish masculine from feminine costumes. For example, although the number and specific pattern pieces required to construct a particular pattern would not vary, View A featured a girl-modeled Egg or Tomato, whereas View B presented a boy-modeled Baseball or Pincushion. Structurally identical costumes modeled by both boys and girls would be distinguished through the use of distinct colors or patterns of material. Thus, for the peanut M&M costumes, the illustration featured girls clad in red or green and boys clad in blue, brown, or yellow. Similarly, female clowns wore costumes of soft pastel colors and dainty polka dots, but male clowns were garbed in bold primary colors and in material featuring large polka dots or stripes. Illustrations for ready-to-wear costumes were also likely to signal the sex of the intended wearer through the advertising copy: models for feminine costumes, for example, had long curled hair, were made up, and wore patent leather shoes. Only in such costumes as Wrinkly Old Woman, Grandma Hag, Killer Granny, and Nun did identifiably male children model female apparel. . . .

[A]lthough hero costumes constituted a large percentage of both masculine and feminine costumes, masculine costumes contained a higher percentage of villain costumes, and feminine costumes included substantially more fool costumes, particularly those of nonhuman/inanimate objects. It may be imagined that the greater total number of feminine costumes would provide young girls with a broader range of costumes to select from than exists for young boys, but in fact the obverse is true. . . . [W]hen finer distinctions were made within the three generic categories, hero costumes for girls were clustered in a narrow range of roles that, although distinguished by specific names, were functionally equivalent in the image they portray. It would seem that, for girls, glory is concentrated in the narrow realm of beauty queens, princesses, brides, or other exemplars of traditionally passive femininity. The ornate, typically pink, ball-gowned costume of the princess (with or without a synthetic jeweled tiara) was notable, whether the specific costume was labeled Colonial Belle, the Pumpkin Princess, Angel Beauty, Blushing Bride, Georgia Peach, Pretty Mermaid, or Beauty Contest Winner. In contrast, although hero costumes for boys emphasized the warrior theme of masculinity (Doyle, 1989; Rotundo, 1993), with costumes depicting characters associated with battling historical, contemporary, or supernatural Goliaths (e.g., Bronco Rider, Dick Tracy, Sir Lancelot, Hercules, Servo Samurai, Robin the Boy Wonder), these costumes were less singular in the visual images they portrayed and were more likely to depict characters who possessed supernatural powers or skills.

Masculine costumes were also more likely than feminine costumes to depict a wide range of villainous characters (e.g., Captain Hook, Rasputin, Slash), monsters (e.g., Frankenstein, The Wolfman), and, in particular, agents or symbols of death (e.g., Dracula, Executioner, Devil Boy, Grim Reaper). Moreover, costumes for male villains were more likely than those of female villains to be elaborate constructions that were visually repellant; to feature an assortment

of scars, mutations, abrasions, and suggested amputations; and to present a wide array of ingenious, macabre, or disturbing visual images. For example, the male-modeled, ready-to-wear Mad Scientist's Experiment costume consisted of a full-body costume of a monkey replete with a half-head mask featuring a gaping incision from which rubber brains dangled. Similarly, costumes for such characters as Jack the Ripper, Serial Killer, Freddy Krueger, or The Midnight Stalker were adorned with the suggestion of bloodstains and embellished with such paraphernalia as plastic knives or slip-on claws.

In marked contrast, the costumes of female villains alternated between relatively simple costumes of witches in pointy hats and capes modeled by young girls, costumes of the few female arch villains drawn from the pages of comic books, and, for older girls, costumes that were variants of the garb donned by the popular TV character Elvira, Mistress of the Dark (i.e., costumes that consisted of a long black wig and a long flowing black gown cut in an empire-style, which, when decorated with gold brocade or other trim at the top of the ribcage, served to create the suggestion of a bosom). The names of costumes for the female villains appeared to emphasize the erotic side of their villainy (e.g., Enchantra, Midnite Madness, Sexy Devil, Bewitched) or to neutralize the malignancy of the character by employing adjectives that emphasized their winsome rather than wicked qualities (e.g., Cute Cuddly Bewitched, Little Skull Girl, Pretty Little Witch).

Within the category of fools, feminine costumes were more likely than masculine costumes to depict nonhuman/inanimate objects (33.1% of feminine costumes vs. 17.4% of masculine costumes). Feminine costumes were more likely than masculine costumes to feature a wide variety of small animals and insects (e.g., Pretty Butterfly, Baby Cricket, Dalmatian Puppy), as well as flowers, foodstuffs (BLT Sandwich, Ice Cream Cone, Lollipop), and dainty, fragile objects such as Tea Pot. For example, a costume for Vase of Flowers was illustrated with a picture of a young girl wearing a cardboard cylinder from her ribcage to her knees on which flowers were painted, while a profusion of pink, white, and yellow flowers emerged from the top of the vase to form a collar of blossoms around her face. Similarly, a costume for Pea Pod featured a young girl wearing a green cylinder to which four green balloons were attached; on the top of her head, the model wore a hat bedecked with green leaves and tendrils in a corkscrew shape. When costumed as animals, boys were likely to be shown modeling larger, more aggressive animals (e.g., Velociraptor, Lion, T-Rex); masculine costumes were unlikely to be marketed with adjectives emphasizing their adorable, "li'l," cute, or cuddly qualities. In general, boys were rarely cast as objects, but when they were, they were overwhelmingly shown as items associated with masculine expertise. For example, a costume for Computer was modeled by a boy whose face was encased in the computer monitor and who wore, around his midtorso, a keyboard held up by suspenders. Another masculine costume depicted a young boy wearing a costume for Paint Can; the lid of the can was crafted in the style of a chef's hat, and across the cylindrical can worn from midchest to midknee was written "Brand X Paint" and, in smaller letters, "Sea Blue." Although rarely depicted as edibles or consumable products, three masculine costumes featured young boys as, variously, Root Beer Mug, Pepperoni Pizza, and Grandma's Pickle Jar.

DISCUSSION

Although the term "fantasy" implies a "play of the mind" or a "queer illusion" (Barnhart, 1967, p. 714), the marketing illustrations for children's Halloween costumes suggest a flight of imagination that remains largely anchored in traditional gender roles, images, and symbols. Indeed, the noninclusive language commonly found in the names of many children's Halloween costumes reverberates throughout many other dimensions of the gendered social life depicted in this fantastical world. For example, the importance of participation in the paid-work

world and financial success for men and of physical attractiveness and marriage for women is reinforced through costume names that reference masculine costumes by occupational roles or titles but describe feminine costumes via appearance and/or relationships (e.g., "Policeman" vs. "Beautiful Bride"). Although no adjectives are deemed necessary to describe Policeman, the linguistic prompt contained in Beautiful Bride serves to remind observers that the major achievements for females are getting married and looking lovely. In addition to costume titles that employ such sex-linked common nouns as Flapper, Bobby Soxer, Ballerina, and Pirate Wench, sex-marked suffixes such as the -*ess* (e.g., Pretty Waitress, Stewardess, Gypsy Princess, Sorceress) and -*ette* (e.g., Majorette) also set apart male and female fantasy character costumes. Costumes for suffragettes or female-modeled police officers, astronauts, and fire fighters were conspicuous only by their absence.

Gender stereotyping in children's Halloween costumes also reiterates an active-masculine/ passive-feminine dichotomization. The ornamental passivity of Beauty Queen stands in stark contrast to the reification of the masculine action figure, whether he is heroic or villainous. In relation to hero figures, the dearth of female superhero costumes in the sample would seem to reflect the comparative absence of such characters in comic books. Although male superheroes have sprung up almost "faster than a speeding bullet" since the 1933 introduction of *Superman,* the comic book life span of women superheroes has typically been abbreviated, "rarely lasting for more than three appearances" (Robbins, 1996, p. 2). Moreover, the applicability of the term "superhero" to describe these female characters seems at least somewhat dubious. Often their role has been that of the male hero's girlfriend or sidekick "whose purpose was to be rescued by the hero" (Robbins, 1996, p. 3).

In 1941 the creation of *Wonder Woman* (initially known as Amazon Princess Diana) represented a purposeful attempt by her creator, psychologist William Marston, to provide female readers with a same-sex superhero. . . . Nevertheless, over half a decade later, women comic book superheroes remain rare and, when they do appear, are likely to be voluptuous and scantily clad. If, as Robbins (1996, p. 166) argued, the overwhelmingly male comic book audience "expect, in fact demand that any new superheroines exist only as pinup material for their entertainment," it would seem that comic books and their televised versions are unlikely to galvanize the provision of flat-chested female superhero Halloween costumes for prepubescent females in the immediate future.

The relative paucity of feminine villains would also seem to reinforce an active/passive dichotomization on the basis of gender. Although costumes depict male villains as engaged in the commission of a wide assortment of antisocial acts, those for female villains appear more nebulous and are concentrated within the realm of erotic transgressions. Moreover, the depiction of a female villain as a sexual temptress or erotic queen suggests a type of "active passivity" (Salamon, 1983), whereby the act of commission is restricted to wielding her physical attractiveness over (presumably) weak-willed men. The veritable absence of feminine agents or symbols of death may reflect not only the stereotype of women (and girls) as life-giving and nurturing, but also the attendant assumption that femininity and lethal aggressiveness are mutually exclusive.

Building on the Sapir–Whorf hypothesis that the language we speak predisposes us to make particular interpretations of reality (Sapir, 1949; Whorf, 1956) and the assertion that language provides the basis for developing the gender schema identified by Bem (1983), the impact of language and other symbolic representations must be considered consequential. The symbolic representations of gender contained within Halloween costumes may, along with specific costume titles, refurbish stereotypical notions of what women/girls and men/boys are capable of doing even within the realm of their imaginations. Nelson and Robinson (1995) noted that deprecatory terms in the English language often ally women with animals. Whether praised as a "chick," "fox," or "Mother Bear" or condemned

as a "bitch," "sow," or an "old nag," the imagery is animal reductionist. They also noted that language likens women to food items (e.g., sugar, tomato, cupcake), with the attendant suggestion that they look "good enough to eat" and are "toothsome morsels." Complementing this, the present study suggests that feminine Halloween costumes also employ images that reduce females to commodities intended for amusement, consumption, and sustenance. A cherry pie, after all, has only a short shelf life before turning stale and unappealing. Although a computer may become obsolete, the image it conveys is that of rationality, of a repository of wisdom, and of scientifically minded wizardry.

In general, the relative absence of gender-neutral costumes is intriguing. Although it must remain speculative, it may be that the manufacturers of ready-to-wear and sewing pattern costumes subscribe to traditional ideas about gender and/or believe that costumes that depart from these ideas are unlikely to find widespread acceptance. Employing a supply–demand logic, it may be that marketing analysis of costume sales confirms their suspicions. Nevertheless, although commercial practices may reflect consumer preferences for gender-specific products rather than biases on the part of merchandisers themselves, packaging that clearly depicts boys or girls—but not both—effectively promotes gendered definitions of products beyond anything that might be culturally inherent in them. This study suggests that gender-aschematic Halloween costumes for children compose only a minority of both ready-to-wear costumes and sewing patterns. It is notable that, when male children were presented modeling female garments, the depicted character was effectively desexed by age (e.g., a wizened, hag-like "grandmother") or by calling (e.g., a nun).

The data for this study speak only to the gender practices of merchandisers marketing costumes and sewing patterns to parents who themselves may be responding to their children's wishes. Beyond this, the findings do not identify precisely whose tastes are represented when these costumes are purchased. It is always possible that, despite the gendered nature of

Halloween costumes presented in the illustrations and advertising copy used to market them, parents and children themselves may engage in creative redefinitions of the boundary markers surrounding gender. A child or parent may express and act on a preference for dressing a male in a pink, ready-to-wear butterfly costume or a female as Fred Flintstone and, in so doing, actively defy the symbolic boundaries that gender the Halloween costume. Alternatively, as a strategy of symbolic negotiation, those parents who sew may creatively experiment with recognizable gender markers, deciding, for example, to construct a pink dragon costume for their daughter or a brown butterfly costume for their son. Such amalgams of gender-discordant images may, on the surface, allow both male and female children to experience a broader range of fantastical roles and images. However, like Persian carpets, deliberately flawed to forestall divine wrath, such unorthodox Halloween costumes, in their structure and design, may nevertheless incorporate fibers of traditional gendered images.

References

Barnes, R., & Eicher, J. B. (1992). *Dress and gender: Making and meaning in cultural contexts.* New York: Berg.

Barnhart, C. L. (1967). *The world book dictionary: A–K.* Chicago: Field Enterprises Educational Corporation.

Bem, S. L. (1983). Gender schema theory and its implications for child development: Raising gender-aschematic children in a gender-schematic society. *Signs: Journal of Women in Culture and Society, 8,* 598–616.

Doyle, J. A. (1989). *The male experience.* Dubuque, IA: Wm. C. Brown.

Eicher, J. B., & Roach-Higgins, M. E. (1992). Definition and classification of dress: Implications for analysis of gender roles. In R. Barnes & J. B. Eicher (Eds.), *Dress and gender: Making and meaning in cultural contexts* (pp. 8–28). New York: Berg.

Goffman, E. (1966). Gender display. *Philosophical Transactions of the Royal Society of London, 279,* 250.

Goffman, E. (1979). *Gender advertisements.* London: Macmillan.

Klapp, O. (1962). *Heroes, villains and fools.* Englewood Cliffs, NJ: Prentice-Hall.

Klapp, O. (1964). *Symbolic leaders.* Chicago: Aldine.

McNeill, F. M. (1970). *Hallowe'en: Its origins, rites and ceremonies in the Scottish tradition.* Edinburgh: Albyn Press.

Mead, G. H. (1934). *Mind, self and society.* Chicago: University of Chicago Press.

Nelson, E. D. (1999). *Dressing for Halloween, doing gender.* Unpublished manuscript.

Nelson, E. D., & Robinson, B. W. (1995). *Gigolos & Madame's bountiful: Illusions of gender, power and intimacy.* Toronto: University of Toronto Press.

Robbins, T. (1996). *The great women superheroes.* Northampton, MA: Kitchen Sink Press.

Rotundo, E. A. (1993). *American manhood: Transformations in masculinity from the revolution to the modern era.* New York: Basic Books.

Salamon, E. (1983). *The kept women: Mistresses of the '80s.* London: Orbis.

Sapir, E. (1949). *Selected writings of Edward Sapir on language, culture and personality.* Berkeley: University of California Press.

Whorf, B. L. (1956). The relation of habitual thought and behavior to language. In J. B. Carroll (Ed.), *Language, thought, and reality* (pp. 134–159). Cambridge, MA: Technology Press of MIT.

Introduction to Reading 22

Kimberly Hoang, a sociologist and Vietnamese American woman, conducted 22 months of participant observation and ethnography in a variety of roles (e.g., hostess and bartender) in a variety of settings (e.g., bars, cafés, malls, streets) in which sex workers and their clients met in Ho Chi Minh City (HCMC), Vietnam, between 2006 and 2007 and 2009 and 2010. When she began her project she discovered that the women sex workers she studied, all over the age of 18, were not only aware of the conditions of their work but also willing participants in sex work because it offered financial opportunities for themselves and their families that could not be matched by doing factory work or service-sector work. In this article, Hoang focuses on two sex work arenas, one catering to Western budget travelers and the other to Western businessmen. She highlights the complexities of client–worker relationships, in particular the ways sex workers sell impressions of themselves as dark-skinned, poor women to Western men who embrace fantasies of helping poor women living in the third world.

1. Why/how does Hoang challenge the widespread view in Western nations that sex workers in countries such as Vietnam are kidnapped, sold, or forced into sex work?

2. Discuss the ways buying and selling gender, race, and class are incorporated into the sex worker–client relationship in Hoang's study.

3. How do you feel about the ways sex workers "dupe" clients and, in turn, clients play into the "game" as described in this article?

PERFORMING THIRD WORLD POVERTY

RACIALIZED FEMININITIES IN SEX WORK

Kimberly Hoang

Over the last two decades, the issue of human trafficking has captivated governments, NGOs, researchers, and activists around the world. Images of women in handcuffs and chains circulate through print, television, and online news outlets, perpetuating a view of trafficked women as victims of Third World poverty who are kidnapped, sold, or forced into sex work. As governments, corporations, religious organizations, and celebrities devote millions of dollars to save trafficked women, they neglect to conduct systematic research on the ground to assess this problem.

This article advances the scholarship on sex trafficking by providing a different lens through which to examine the sex industry. Rather than viewing women as victims of global poverty who are kidnapped, forced, or duped into the sex industry, I follow the work of Brennan (2004), Mahdavi (2011), and Parreñas (2011) to analyze the complex social structures that shape the *range of choices* available to women in their relationships with clients, club owners, and brokers. I show how sex workers in Ho Chi Minh City [HCMC], Vietnam, capitalized on media images and NGO narratives that portray sex workers as victims to advance their lives. By *performing Third World poverty*, sex workers who freely entered the sex industry portrayed themselves as victims to procure large remittances from their male clients.

Hoang, Kimberly.

In this article, I raise two primary questions. First, how do sex workers capitalize on global economic restructuring to improve not only their lives but also the lives of their extended families? Second, how do male clients make sense of and respond to sex workers' performances of Third World poverty? To answer these questions, I turn to my ethnographic research in HCMC's sex industry conducted over a total of 22 months in two phases between 2006–2007 and 2009–2010 as well as in-depth interviews with 71 sex workers and 55 clients in two niche markets that catered to Western budget travelers/tourists and Western businessmen who were part of a transnational circuit.[1] I show that just as organizations in the developed world pull on the heartstrings of their donors in the "fight" to end human trafficking, sex workers capitalize on globally circulating narratives to dupe male clients for money and visas by engaging in strategic and racialized performances of third world poverty. This article also looks at how male clients respond, react to, and make meaning out of sex workers' performances as they open their wallets to "save" women from a lifetime of poverty or entrapment in sex work. As such, this article also fills a gap in the literature by paying attention to both sides of client and sex-worker relationships.

Global Sex Work

In recent years, sex work abolitionists examined the lives of women forced into the sex trade (Bales and Soodalter 2009; Bolkovac and Lynn 2011; Mukherjee 2010). Their work fueled a worldwide explosion of representations of Third World women as victims routinely bought and sold to fulfill male sexual desires. These efforts sensationalized poor Third World women as victims while making heroes of those who studied them and worked to save them. These efforts also prompted serious policy changes regarding the sex industry.

Sex work abolitionists sensationalize this "multibillion dollar industry" and the "millions of women" kidnapped and forced into sex work without engaging in systematic, in-depth research of the women involved.

In addition, abolitionists assert that in order to end human trafficking, we need to eliminate the demand side of the equation. These researchers depict male sex patrons as predators who brutalize poor Third World women. However, very few studies engage in any kind of systematic research on the men who patronize these establishments. As I have shown elsewhere (Hoang 2011), male patrons of sex work vary a great deal in their behaviors, motivations, and desires. These men are involved in complex, and sometimes intimate, relationships with sex workers, that involve much more than one-time direct sex-for-money exchanges as sex workers engage in a variety of emotional labors that involve a complex intermingling of money and intimacy (Bernstein 2007; Hoang 2010).

A parallel body of research emerged in recent years from sociologists and anthropologists who conducted in-depth ethnographies inside the bars and brothels where sex workers work. These researchers engaged in systematic research, spending a significant amount of time building rapport with sex workers (Brennan 2005), working alongside them (Parreñas 2011; Zheng 2009), and providing complex analyses of the *choices* women made as they entered into sex work. These studies show that, contrary to popular belief, women often knowingly and willingly entered into complex arrangements with brokers, club owners, and entertainment establishments in what Parreñas (2011) refers to as a process of *indentured mobility*.

This article builds on these studies by illustrating how sex workers in HCMC, Vietnam, *perform Third World poverty* to procure large sums of money from Western male clients and how they strategically darkened their skin to embody what I term *racialized femininities*. This article not only points to women's *range* of choices in entering sex work but also highlights how workers strategically capitalize on global economic restructuring to enhance their socioeconomic trajectories. More importantly, I illustrate two sides of the client-worker relationship.

SEX TRAFFICKING: DUPED VICTIMS OR HUSTLERS?

In 2006, when I first began preliminary research for this project, I went to Vietnam equipped with information on local NGOs who "helped" the women I thought I would find. I visited a small but growing number of organizations looking to save victims of sex trafficking. However, I was shocked to find that few of the sex workers I met had been duped or sold into the sex trade. Many workers migrated to HCMC from villages to work in factories or the service sector before entering into sex work. During a tour of a local NGO, I was surprised to find that the organization had set up a private business exporting garments made by local sex workers to be sold abroad with "fair trade" stickers and pamphlets with images of women in handcuffs or trapped behind barbed wire fences.

Naively, I approached the workers and asked them how they ended up in this small clothing factory. At first, the women were quiet and refused to acknowledge my presence. After a long moment of awkward silence, Ai-Nhi, a 19-year-old worker, said to me, "I got caught on the street and had to spend several months in the rehabilitation center. This organization came to get me, so I am here now, but I would rather be in the bars." Dumbfounded, I asked her why she would rather be there and she responded:

> I used to work in a factory making $70 US a month. I did that for many years but I was not making enough money to send to my family, so I quit and went to work on the streets . . . One day, I got caught and was sent into the center, and then this woman told me that I could get out early if I went with this organization that would teach me how to sew clothes. I agreed so that I could get out of the center . . . I am here now doing the same thing I was trying to escape. . . . They say they want to help us, but they are only helping themselves. I get paid $30 million VND [$200 US] a month to work here . . . [but] I know that they sell these clothes for a lot more money abroad. . . .

When I asked the women if they were happier in this shop sewing clothes than engaging in sex work, Ha, a 23-year-old worker, told me that she could make a lot more money in the bars where she also had more control over her time. She told me to go to the backpackers' area (*khu tay ba lo*) where I would meet several women who went right back into the bars after leaving the rehabilitation center. She wrote down the name of a bar in that area and told me to talk to the women working there. This was my first introduction to sex work in the backpackers' area, where I would eventually meet several women and their clients who were Western men traveling on a budget.

PERFORMING THIRD WORLD POVERTY

Racialized Bodies

In 2006, both budget travelers and transnational businessmen spent time in the backpackers' area of HCMC. However, by 2009, the area was run down by transient tourists looking to explore Vietnam as cheaply as possible and Western businessmen had carved out a distinct niche in the sex industry. In the backpackers' area, clients could walk into bars where women would immediately greet them, serve them drinks, wipe their faces with wet towels, and provide them with shoulder massages. Men would receive all of these services just by ordering a $2 US beer. The women in this bar engaged in a variety of practices to make their bodies desirable to their male clients. For example, all of the workers darkened their skin with bronzers and skin creams. When I asked the workers why they did so, Xuong, a 26-year-old worker, said to me:

> The men here like darker skin and women who just came up from the village. Girls who just come up from the villages get the most clients because they look fresh. Men like women with dark skin. They will always touch you and say, 'Wow, your skin is so dark and soft.'

Altering their skin color was the most notable strategy these women adopted to racialize their bodies to look like poor women in a Third World country. Those who were darker often received more attention, particularly from white men traveling on a budget.

Sex workers in the backpackers' area also wore very plain clothing consisting of jean skirts or shorts and a plain tank top because they wanted to convey to their clients that they were poor workers. One afternoon while helping Thu, a 22-year-old worker, pack for a trip home, I rummaged through her clothes and noticed that she had a lot of beautiful dresses. When I asked her why she never wore them to work, she explained:

> I have two sets of clothes—one for work and one for the village. I don't wear nice clothes to work because I don't want the men to think that I have money. If they think that I have money, they will not give me any money. I have to make sure that I look like a poor village girl.

Thu was not the only one who strategically dressed down in the bars. All of the sex workers did the same because it allowed them to convey an image that they were poor workers who could not even afford food, let alone nice things. They saved their nicer clothing for their visits to the village because these displays of wealth at home de-stigmatized their work in the bars.

Sex workers who catered to Western businessmen also played into their clients' racialized desires by strategically darkening their skin. However, rather than wearing simple clothing, these workers wore low-cut versions of the traditional Vietnamese *Ao dai*. Women who catered to Western businessmen dressed in ethnic dresses that made them look exotic while allowing workers to appear more expensive than the women in the poor backpackers' area. Lilly, the owner of the bar I studied in this district, reminded her workers on a daily basis that the clients in her bar were respectable businessmen, not cheap backpackers. The women who catered to this higher-paying clientele should therefore dress accordingly. She commissioned a tailor to come to her shop to measure all of her workers and sew their uniforms. Each dress was cut a little differently so that each woman would have a unique look. However, all of the dresses were made of the same faux silk Chinese fabric that closed in around the neck but had

an opening that exposed women's cleavage and slits along the skirt to expose the workers' full thigh and bottom.

By darkening their skin and dressing in either plain clothing or exotic, Orientalizing garments, sex workers racialized their bodies to make themselves desirable to their clients. Their outward appearance was crucial to attracting men into the bars. However, workers also had to engage in a variety of emotional and bodily labors (Hoang 2010) to maintain ties with their clients and procure small and large sums of money from them. The next section examines how women enacted *Third World poverty* in ways that extended beyond simple self-presentation in order to attract long-term remittances from their clients.

PERFORMANCES OF POVERTY

Regardless of whether women catered to Western men traveling on a budget or Western businessmen, all of the women engaged in various performances of gender (West and Zimmerman 1987) through their embodied practices and through relational work (Zelizer 2005) with their clients. I learned of women's strategies to *perform Third World poverty* through the English lessons that I provided them in the afternoons. I visited *Naughty Girls*, the bar in the backpackers' area, at 2:00 pm, three to four days a week for four months between 2009–2010 to provide the women with free English lessons. Many of the women were excited about the opportunity to work with someone who would help them translate fabricated stories without judging them for lying or duping their clients. During these days, I helped women translate a series of emails, text messages, and key phrases that they wanted to have in their back pockets. They asked me to help them translate phrases like "My motorbike broke down. I have to walk to work. Can you help me buy new motorbike?" and "My father very sick and no one in my family help so I have to work. I am from An Giang village. You go to village before?"

During these lessons, I often asked the women why they lied to their clients and why they were careful not to display too much wealth in front of them. Xuan, a 19-year-old worker, said to me:

> A lot of the men here think that Vietnam is still a poor country. They want to hear that your family is poor and that you have no options so you came here to work. If you make them feel sorry for you as a poor Vietnamese village girl, they will give you a lot more money. We lie to them because it works ... We tell them that Vietnam is changing and growing so fast and that the price of food and gas has gone up and people from poor rural areas cannot afford to live off of the rice fields anymore.

The act of creating fictive stories about their "rural lives" enabled many women to procure large sums of money from clients through remittances. Xuan's strategic move allowed her to capitalize on Vietnam's changing position in the global economy and the widening inequalities between local rich and local poor. The women I studied were certainly much more financially secure than their family members who worked in the rice fields, textile or manufacturing industries, or even as service workers in HCMC. In an informal interview with Vy, a 22-year-old worker, she said to me:

> Western men in America hear about girls who are sold and forced to sell their bodies, but no one here is forced to do anything. I come to the bar to work and if I want to have sex with a client, I have sex with him. If I don't, then I won't. No one forces me to do anything I don't want to do. People come here trying to give us condoms or save us, but how can they help me when I make more than them?

In that same conversation Chau, a 23-year-old worker interjected and said:

> There are some men who come to Vietnam often and they know what bar life is like ... There are other men who are new to Vietnam—it is their first trip. Sometimes after sex, I will cry in the room and tell them how hard my life is and how mean the bar owner is. I will tell him that I want to get out and that I need $5000 US to pay for my debt to get out. So they help us.

Sex workers like Vy and Chau were aware of images that circulated across the globe of Asian sex workers as victims forced into a trade that involved horrific forms of violence. Their lives did not match these representations, but they capitalized on the images to procure large sums of money from their clients. Several men willingly provided the $5000 US the workers requested or some portion of that amount to "save" them from their life as a bargirl. In this way, sex workers also helped men feel like superior Western men from strong nations who were engaged in charity projects by helping poor women desperately looking to change their lives in a developing nation.

In their quest to see an authentic Vietnam, from a local's perspective, male clients often asked women if they would take them on tours of their villages and hometowns. Sex workers whose families were based in the city sometimes relied on their connections in the bar to take clients on tours of the Mekong Delta to visit with fake families. For example, in a conversation that I had with Thuy-Linh, she said:

> I am going to Kien Giang tomorrow with one of the guys here because he wants to see my village, but most of my family lives in Saigon now. We moved here about 10 years ago ... I am taking him to stay with Vi's family so that he will think that I am really poor and maybe give me money to rebuild the house or help my family out.

Several clients expressed a desire to visit villages where they could walk through rice fields, ride bicycles, and bargain for produce in street markets. Therefore, the women in the bars organized tours to visit fake families in nearby villages. In my conversations with the workers about these tours, I was struck by their awareness of their clients' desire to see Vietnam as a developing Third World country. They organized tours that would portray an "authentic" Vietnam removed from signs of global change, modernization, and capitalism. More often than not, sex workers were happy to play into their clients' desires because doing so enabled them to ask for larger sums of money.

In conversations with the clients upon their return from visiting the Mekong Delta, many expressed a sense of deep sadness for the conditions of poverty that the women portrayed to them. For example, after spending three days with Nhi's family in their village, John, a man in his late 50s to early 60s, said to me:

> There are so many things that we in the West take for granted. Roofs over our heads, hot water, shoes . . . When I was with Nhi, I had to shower with buckets of cold water. It was so disgusting because I was brushing my teeth and I didn't realize that the bucket had a bunch of maggots in there. I felt these tiny worms swimming around in my mouth and I had to spit it out. I asked them how much it would cost to put in a proper shower and they said $500 US, so I gave it to them. They were such gracious hosts to me that I wanted to give something back.

While workers certainly employed strategies to embody Third World poverty, they also engaged in performances that highlighted their poverty in relation to the economic situations of their clients. John sympathized with Nhi's life and her conditions of poverty, and he genuinely wanted to help provide her family with a new faucet. Regardless of whether they were to women's true families, these visits to the village allowed workers to capitalize on their client's genuine concern, compassion, and empathy. Men provided women with money to help them escape poverty and transition from a basic standard of living to a comfortable standard of living.

By allowing men to believe that they were fulfilling the provider role, workers performed a femininity that was linked to financial dependence. Clients displayed a class-based masculinity in relation to these women. Several of the men I spoke with expressed a desire to have a traditional marriage where men were the economic providers and women took care of the home. However, because they could not maintain these roles in the US, many hoped to develop these relationships across transnational spaces in less-developed nations. In a long conversation with Jason, a man in his mid-60s from Montana, he told me:

> Men like me probably make women like you very uncomfortable. We come here and get hooked to younger women . . . I grew up at a time in America when women stayed home and took care of the family while men worked. My wife and I were happily married for many years. When she died two years ago, my world fell apart. I didn't know how to cook, or clean, or take care of myself. I was depressed. I needed a wife . . . [or] someone to take care of me. In Asia . . . some women still hold on to those traditional values, and I can afford to take care of a woman on my retirement fund.

It was clear in Jason's mind that while he could not be an economic provider for a woman in the US, he could successfully assert his masculinity across transnational borders because of Vietnam's status as a Third World country. The act of creating fictive stories about their "rural lives" enabled many women to procure large sums of money from clients like Jason through remittances. These scripts enabled men to act as the economic provider and in effect preserve a sense of masculinity lost back at home.

CLIENTS' SCRIPTED PERFORMANCES

Not all men were as easily duped for their money. By 2009, stories had circulated among male clients of workers lying to them for their money. I sat in the bars listening day after day as men warned each other of the various ways that they might be tricked. However, I was surprised to find that several of the men I spoke with actually preferred to be unaware of workers' desires to consume luxury goods like nicer clothing, expensive cellular phones, and electronics because those items symbolized access to global capital, mobility, status, and most importantly, dignity in their work. For example, Edward, a 38-year-old man from the US said to me:

> We're not as naive as you think we are. We know better. But here is the thing. When you walk into a bar, everyone plays a role. The girls pretend to act excited to see us and flirt with us. We flirt back. They tell us about their poor families and we give them

money here and there to help them. We may never know their real stories, but that is not the point. The point is that they make us feel like strong men who can provide for them and they get paid for it.

Some clients developed long-term relationships or friendships with a few workers; those relationships also involved a certain level of duplicity. Howard, a 39-year-old expatriate from Sweden, told me about his experience with duplicitous games:

I have known this one worker for three years now and I still do not know very much about her. I feel comfortable there. It is predictable. I go in and have the same conversation with her every night. Someone could write a short story about this because it is the same script every single night. I come in and tell her I missed her, that I think she looks beautiful. She tells me about her family and money problems and I pretend to care. Sometimes we have sex, and that is it.

Relationships between clients and sex workers were bound by a set of predictable scripts that allowed clients to feel comfortable. As Howard described, when he walked into a bar, he also engaged in an emotional performance by telling a woman he saw on a regular basis that he missed her, thought she was beautiful, and was concerned about her financial situation.

These games became particularly apparent when new clients came in with friends who were regulars. Often, I listened in as men coached each other on what were appropriate and inappropriate behaviors within the bar. For example, one night while I was working in *Secrets*, a bar that catered to Western expatriates, I listened as Kevin, a regular client, explained the workings of the bar to his friend, Joseph. Kevin said:

The girls in this bar are really nice. They are very low-key. You can talk and flirt with them with no pressure. If you like them, *you* ask them to meet you afterwards for about $100 US. It is a game. They play it and you play it.

Indeed, clients paid for a service from sex workers who worked as bartenders and hostesses.

However, the clients also performed their own scripts in relation to the workers. They informed each other of the unspoken set of norms that guided interactions between workers and clients in the bar. Male clients did not always believe that the workers were truthful, but that was beside the point, because both men and women played a particular role inside the bars. Regardless of their truth, scripted interactions enabled men to maintain a comfortable and predictable relationship with workers based on a fantasy that they were heroic saviors helping women in need.

Conclusion

The issue of human trafficking has become a topic of great interest around the world. Celebrities like Demi Moore, Lucy Liu, and Ricky Martin and fashion designers such as Calvin Klein, Donna Karan, and Diane von Furstenberg have committed resources to raise awareness around the issue of sex trafficking. Presidents George W. Bush and Barack Obama both agree that the US should commit resources to save women from the horrors of forced sexual labors internationally. Through in-depth ethnography, this article explores beneath the surface of this issue to examine the lives of men and women deeply embedded in the sex industry. None of the women I describe in this article were kidnapped, forced, or duped into sex work. Rather, they made conscious choices to sell sex because they saw factory work and service work as more exploitative forms of labor.

This is not to say that trafficking does not occur, or that women are not subject to forms of *indentured mobility* (Parreñas 2011). Rather, I suggest that the story involves greater complexity than the representations of NGOs might suggest. Indeed, women capitalize on images of victimized women and on Vietnam's rapid economic restructuring by *performing Third World poverty* to get money from their clients. Some clients played into these stories because it allowed them to preserve a sense of masculinity lost back at home. While nearly all of the men that I met in 2006 believed the sex workers' lies, by 2009, enough men had been duped that stories of women procuring large sums of money by lying began to circulate among Western clients. Even with this knowledge, clients and sex workers both engaged in scripted practices and discourses related to Third World poverty and women's victimhood. These scripts not only allowed "men to be men," as Nhi put it, but to enable men to be Western men from developed nations by maintaining a fantasy that they are helping poor women living in the Third World. Beyond images of barbed wire and handcuffs are actual men and women engaged in complex relationships. As governments and activists intervene in women's lives, aid efforts must move beyond the sex industry and into other locations such as factories to address the multiple and interconnected sources of women's "exploitation."

NOTE

1. I have used pseudonyms for all individuals and bars in this paper to protect the anonymity of my research participants.

REFERENCES

Bales, Kevin and Ron Soodalter. 2009. *The Slave Next Door: Human Trafficking and Slavery in New America Today*. Berkeley: University of California Press.

Bernstein, Elizabeth. 2007. *Temporarily Yours: Intimacy, Authenticity, and the Commerce of Sex*. Chicago: University of Chicago Press.

Bolkovac, Kathryn and Cari Lynn. 2011. *The Whistle-blower: Sex Trafficking, Military Contractors, and One Woman's Fight for Justice*. New York: Palgrave Macmillan.

Brennan, Denise. 2004. *What's Love Got to Do with It? Transnational Desires and Sex Tourism in the Dominican Republic*. Durham: Duke University Press.

———. 2005. "Methodological Challenges in Research with Trafficked Persons: Tales from the Field." *International Migration* 43:35–54.

Hoang, Kimberly. 2010. "Economies of Emotion, Familiarity, Fantasy and Desire: Emotional Labor in Ho Chi Minh City's Sex Industry." *Sexualities* 13:255–272.

———. 2011. "'She's Not a Low Class Dirty Girl': Sex Work in Ho Chi Minh City, Vietnam." *Journal of Contemporary Ethnography* 40: 367–396.

Mahdavi, Pardis. 2011. *Gridlock: Labor, Migration, and Human Trafficking in Dubai*. Palo Alto: Stanford University Press.

Parreñas, Rhacel. 2011. *Illicit Flirtations*. Palo Alto: Stanford University Press.

West, Candace and Don Zimmerman. 1987. "Doing Gender." *Gender and Society* 1:125–151.

Zelizer, Viviana. 2005. *The Purchase of Intimacy*. Princeton: Princeton University Press.

Zheng, Tiantian. 2009. *Red lights: The lives of sex workers in postsocialist China*. Chicago: University of Chicago Press.

Introduction to Reading 23

This reading is a good example of the application of intersectional analysis, employing categories of gender, age, and social class. The authors studied a mass-marketed program of "successful aging" that targets old men in an effort to persuade them to spend their money on products and activities that will supposedly make them look and feel youthfully and heterosexually virile and successful. Toni Calasanti and Neal King analyze the ageism of "successful aging" consumer campaigns and their implications for old men's "physical health, unequal access to wealth, heterosexual dominance, and fears of impotence" (from abstract).

1. How does ageism permeate "successful aging" consumer campaigns?

2. Why is it important to examine age relations and their intersections with other inequalities?

3. Discuss the "dirty"/"impotent" double bind and its link to the rise of "successful aging" consumer programs.

FIRMING THE FLOPPY PENIS

AGE, CLASS, AND GENDER RELATIONS IN THE LIVES OF OLD MEN

Toni Calasanti and Neal King

The rise of a consumer market that targets old people and their desire to remain young brings into sharp relief the problems that old age poses to manhood. This article proposes an expansion of research approaches to the lives of old men so that they may enrich our understandings of masculinities at a time when scientific breakthroughs and high-priced regimens sell visions of manhood renewed. We begin with a brief review of the (relative lack of) research on old men, continue with a look at the mass marketing of "successful aging," and conclude with an overview of the potential rewards that sustained scholarship on the old, and a theorizing of age relations as a dimension of inequality, can offer the studies of men and masculinities.

(YOUNG) MEN'S STUDIES

Studies of old men are common in the gerontological literature, but those that theorize masculinity remain rare. As in many academic endeavors, men's experiences have formed the basis for much research, but this androcentric foundation goes largely unexplored because manhood has served as invisible norm rather than as explicit focus of theory. Men's lives have formed the standard for scholarship on retirement, for example, to such an extent that even the *Retirement History Study,* a longitudinal study conducted by the Social Security Administration, excluded married women as primary respondents (Calasanti 1993). In recent years, feminist gerontologists have urged that scholars examine not only women but gender relations as well, and a handful of scholars such as Woodward (1999), Cruikshank (2003), and Davidson (2001) have done so. Despite the proliferation of feminist theorizing, however, most mainstream gerontological studies of women still ignore gender (Hooyman 1999), and research on men lags further. Few studies examine old men *as men* or attend to masculinity as a research topic.

At the same time, profeminist studies of masculinity have studied neither old men nor the age relations that subordinate them. Ageism, often inadvertent, permeates this research, stemming from failures to study the lives of old men, to base questions on old men's accounts of their lives, or to theorize age the way we have theorized relations of gender, race, and class. Mentions of age inequality arise as afterthoughts, usually at the ends of lists of oppressions, but they remain unexamined. As a result, our understanding and concepts of manhood fall short because they assume, as standards of normalcy, men of middle age or younger. Aging scholars' inattention to old *men*, combined with men's studies' lack of concern with *old* men, not only renders old men virtually invisible but also reproduces our own present and future oppression. This article examines a range of popular representations of old men in the context of research about their lives to outline some ways in which the vital work on men and masculinity might benefit by taking age relations into account as a form of inequality that intersects with gender, race, sexuality, and class.

Denial of Aging

Our ageism—both our exclusion of the old and our ignorance of age relations as an inequality affecting us all—surfaces not only in our choices of what (not) to study but also in how we theorize men and masculinities. Listening to the old and theorizing the inequality that subordinates them require that we begin with elementary observations. People treat signs of old age as stigma and avoid notice of them in both personal and professional lives. For instance, we often write or say "older" rather than "old," usually in our attempts to avoid negative labels. But rather than accept this stigma attached to the old and help people to pass as younger than that, we should ask what seems so wrong with that stage of life. In a more aggregate version of this ageism, one theorizes old age as social construction and then suggests that people do not automatically become old at a particular age. One continues to treat "old age" as demeaning and merely seeks to eradicate recognition of it by granting reprieves from inclusion in the group. As well intended as such a theoretical move may be, it exacts a high price. It maintains the stigma rather than examining or removing it. As Andrews

(1999) observed, all life cycle stages are social constructions, but "there is not much serious discussion about eliminating infancy, adolescence, or adulthood from the developmental landscape. It is only old age which comes under the scalpel" (302). Emphasis on the socially constructed status of this age category does nothing to eliminate its real-world consequences.

Old age has material dimensions, the consequences of actors both social and biological: bodies *do* age, even if at variable rates, just as groups categorize and apportion resources accordingly. Emphasizing their subjective nature makes age categories no less real. Bodies matter; and the old are not, in fact, just like the middle-aged but only older. They are different, even though cultures and people within them define the differences in divergent ways. We need to consider the social construction of old age in conjunction with the aging of bodies (which, in a vexing irony, we understand only through social constructions).

Successful Aging

A more refined form of ageism attempts to portray old age in a positive light but retains the use of middle age as an implicit standard of goodness and health, in contrast to which the old remain deviant. One may see this ageism in the popular notion that men should "age successfully." From this "anti-aging" perspective, some of the changes that occur with age might seem acceptable—gray hair and even, on occasion, wrinkles—but other age-related changes do not, such as losses of libido, income, or mobility. Aging successfully requires that the old maintain the activities popular among the middle-aged. Successful aging, in effect, requires well-funded resistance to culturally designated markers of old age, including relaxation. Within this paradigm, those signs of seniority remain thoroughly stigmatized.

To be sure, a research focus on men who have aged "successfully" flows from good intentions. Study of successful agers helps us negate stereotypes of the old as "useless," unhappy, and the like. Nevertheless, a theory of the age relations underlying this movement must recognize their interrelations with class, sexual, and racial inequalities. The relevant standards for health and happy lifestyles have been based on leisure activities accessible only to the more well-to-do and middle-aged: tennis, traveling, sipping wine in front of sunsets, and strolls on the beaches of tony resorts that appear in the advertising campaigns for such lifestyles.

The dictate to age successfully by remaining active is both ageist and ignorant of the lives of the working classes. Spurred by the new anti-aging industry, the promotional images of the "active elder" are bound by gender, race, class, and sexuality. The sort of consumption and lifestyles implicated in ads for posh retirement communities with their depiction of "'imagineered' landscapes of consumptions marked by 'compulsively tidy lawns' and populated by 'tanned golfers'" (McHugh 2000, 110) assumes a sort of "active" lifestyle available only to a select group: men whose race and class make them most likely to be able to afford it, and their spouses.

Regimens of successful aging also encourage consumers to define any old person in terms of "what she or he is no longer: a mature productive adult" (McHugh 2000, 104). One strives to remain active to show that one is not really old. In this sense, successful aging means not aging and not being old because our constructions of old age contain no positive content. Signs of old age continue to operate as stigma, even in this currently popular model with its many academic adherents. The successful aging movement disapproves implicitly of much about the lives of the old, pressuring those whose bodies are changing to work hard to preserve their "youth" so that they will not be seen as old. As a result, the old and their bodies have become subject to a kind of disciplinary *activity*. This emphasis on productive activity means that those who are chronically impaired, or who prefer to be contemplative, become "problem" old people, far too comfortable just being "old" (Holstein 1999; Katz 2000).

This underlying bias concerning successful aging and "agelessness" is analogous to what many white feminists have had to learn about race relations, or indeed many men have had to learn about gender relations. Many whites began with the notion that nonwhites were doing fine as long as they acted like whites (just as women in many workplaces were deemed OK to the extent that they acted like men). That actual diversity would benefit our society was news to many, its recognition hard-won by activists of color who championed an awareness of the structuring effects of race relations. Only when we can acknowledge and validate these constructed differences do we join the fights against racism and sexism. The same is true of age relations and the old. We must see the old as legitimately different from the middle-aged, separated by a systematic inequality—built on some set of biological factors—that affects all of our lives. To theorize this complex and ever-changing construction is to understand age relations.

The experience of ageism itself varies by gender and other social inequalities (just as the experience of manhood varies by age and the like). Others have already pointed to the double standard of aging whereby women are seen to be old sooner than men (Calasanti and Slevin 2001). But the experience of ageism varies among different social hierarchies. Women with the appropriate class background, for instance, can afford to use various technologies to "hide" signs of aging bodies (such as gray hair and wrinkles) that will postpone their experiences of ageism. Some women of color, such as African Americans, accept more readily the superficial bodily signs of aging that might bother middle-class white women. Within their communities, signs of aging may confer a status not affirmed in the wider culture (Slevin and Wingrove 1998). By failing to reflect on our own ageism and its sources, we have left age relations and its intersections with such other inequalities unquestioned and misunderstood. We have given lip service to age relations by placing it on a list of oppressions, but we have only begun to theorize them. And so we have left unexplored one of the most important systems shaping manhood.

Examining age relations and its intersections with other inequalities will allow us to address ageism in its deepest form and address the structural inequities that deny power to subgroups of the old. It involves breaking the ethical hold that successful, active aging has on our views of aging. Just as feminists have argued for women's emancipation from stigmatizing pressure to avoid the paths that they might like to take, so too must the old be free to choose ways to be old that suit them without having to feel like slackards or sick people. Old age should include acceptance of inactivity as well as activity, contemplation as well as exertion, and sexual assertiveness as well as a well-earned break. Old people will have achieved greater equality with the young when they feel free not to try to be young, when they need not be "exceptional," and when they can be frail, or flabby, or have "age spots" without feeling ugly. *Old* will have positive content and not be defined mainly by disease, mortality, or the absence of economic value.

Old Men in Popular Culture

The study of masculinity benefits from a look at mass-produced images of old men, because they suggest much about the changing definitions of their problems and the solutions offered. Viewed in context of the experiences of diverse old men as well as the structural constraints on various groups, these popular images illustrate the pressures to be masculine and ways in which men respond to accomplish old manhood. On one hand, the goal of consumer images is to convince others to buy products that will help them better their lives. What is instructive about such images is what they reveal about how people—in this case, aging men—should go about improving their lives (i.e., what it is that they should strive for). On the other hand, images of powerful older men—such as CEOs and politicians—periodically appear in the news media, demonstrating what old men should be striving for in the consumer ads: money, power,

and the like. We use mass-produced images of old men, then, to explore the ways that men and masculinities intersect with other systems of inequality—including age relations—to influence various experiences of manhood.

Current Images: New Manhood in Old Age

The recent demographic shift toward an aged population has inspired consumer marketers to address the old with promises of "positive" or successful aging. A massive ad campaign sells anti-aging—the belief that one should deny or defy the signs and even the fact of aging, and treat the looks and recreation of middle-aged as the appropriate standards for beauty, health, and all-around success. As Katz (2001–2002) recently put it, "The ideals of positive aging and anti-ageism have come to be used to promote a widespread anti-aging culture, one that translates their radical appeal into commercial capital" (27). These ads present a paradox for old men, whom ads depict as masculine but unable by virtue of infirmity and retirement to achieve the hegemonic ideals rooted in the lives of the young. Thus, old masculinity is always wanting, ever in need of strenuous affirmation. Even when blessed with the privileges of money and whiteness, old men lack two of hegemonic masculinity's fundamentals: hard-charging careers and robust physical strength. The most current ads promise successful aging with interesting implications for these forms of male privilege.

"Playing Hard"

The first image in this "new masculinity" shows men "playing hard," which differs from previous ads in important ways. It emphasizes activities modeled after the experiences of middle-aged, white, middle-class men. Men pursue leisure but not in terms of grandparenting, reading, or other familial and relaxing pastimes. Instead, they propel themselves into hard play as consumers of expensive sports and travel. Having maintained achievement orientations during their paid-work years, they now intensify their involvement in the expanding consumerist realm, trading production or administration for activity-based consumption. They compete not against other men for salaries and promotions but against their own and nature's incursions into their health as they defy old age to hobble them.

Katz (2001–2002) noted that many ads portray the "older person as an independent, healthy, flexi-retired 'citizen'; who bridges middle age and old age without suffering the time-related constraints of either. In this model . . . 'retirement is not old age'" (29). For instance, McHugh observed that the marketing of sunbelt retirement communities includes the admonition to seniors to busy themselves in the consumption of leisure, to "rush about as if their very lives depended upon it" (McHugh 2000, 112). Similarly, Aetna advertisements selling retirement financial planning show pictures of retired men in exotic places, engaging in such activities as surfing or communing with penguins. Captions offer such invitations as

> Who decided that at the age of 65 it was time to hit the brakes, start acting your age, and smile sweetly as the world spins by? . . . [W]hen you turn 65, the concept of retirement will be the only thing that's old and tired. (*Newsweek* January 5, 1998, 9)

This active consumer image reinforces a construction of old age that benefits elite men in two ways. First, it favors the young in that the old men pictured do nothing that would entitle them to pay. Instead, they purchase expensive forms of leisure. Readers can infer that old men neither need money nor deserve it. Retired, their roles center around spending their money (implicitly transferring it to the younger generations who do need and deserve it). Such ads affirm younger men's right to a cushion from competition with senior men for salaried positions, power, and status. Second, this active consumer image favors the monied classes by avoiding any mention of old men's financial struggles or (varied) dependence on the state. Indeed, age relations work to heighten economic inequalities, such that the greatest differences in income and wealth appear among the old (Calasanti and Slevin 2001). This

polarization of income and wealth creates a demographic situation in which only the most privileged men—white, middle-class or better, and physically similar to middle-aged men—can engage in the recreation marketed.

There, we see an additional benefit to the young of such images of men—the emphasis on the physical abilities that the young are more likely to have. Featherstone and Hepworth (1995) noted that the consumer images of "positive aging" found in publications for those of retirement age or planning retirement ultimately have "serious shortcomings" because they do not counter the ageist meanings that adhere to "other" images of the old, that is, "decay and dependency." In other words, we look more kindly on those old persons engaged in "an extended plateau of active middle age typified in the imagery of positive aging as a period of youthfulness and active consumer lifestyles" (46). In this sense, the new, "positive," and consumer-based view of the old is one steeped in middle-aged, middle-class views and resources. The wide variety of retirement and other magazines—and, more recently, a large and expanding number of Web sites—convey the idea that the body can be "serviced and repaired, and . . . cultivate the hope that the period of active life can be extended and controlled" through the use of a wide range of advertised products (44). This image does not recognize or impute value to those more often viewed to be physically dependent, for example. As a result, those men who are able to achieve this masculine version of "successful aging" appear acceptable within this paradigm, but this new form of acceptance does not mitigate the ways in which we view the old. It denies the physical realities of aging and is thus doomed to failure. Not only are the majority of old men left out of this image of new masculinity for old men, but also the depiction is in itself illusory and transitory. Note the gender inequality in these depictions of aging denied through consumption. Most women participate in the lifestyles of the well-to-do as parts of married couples, dependent on men. Old men may lose status relative to younger men but still maintain privilege in relation to old women.

However hollow such promises of expensive recreation might be for most men, the study of men's physical aggression and self-care suggests that illusions drive many indeed and that men will often sacrifice health and even their lives to accomplish this exaggerated sense of physical superiority to women and resistance to the forces of nature. Researchers of health, violence, and manhood have already documented the harms that men do to themselves. Whether disenfranchised men of color in neighborhoods of concentrated poverty (Franklin 1987; Lee 2000; Staples 1995), athletes desperate to perform as champions (Dworkin and Messner 1999; Klein 1995; White, Young, and McTeer 1995), or ordinary men expressing rage through violence (Harris 2000) and refusing to consult physicians when ill (Courtenay 2000), all manner of men undercut themselves and endanger their lives in the pursuit of their ideals. Harris (2000, 782), for instance, referred to the violence as part of the "doing" of manhood, in line with the sociological theory of gender as accomplishment (Fenstermaker and West 2002). Injury in the pursuit of masculinity extends to social networks, which men more often than women neglect to the point of near isolation and desolation (Courtenay 2000). For those not killed outright, the accumulated damage results in debilitating injury and chronic disease leading to depression (Charmaz 1995; McTeer, White and Young 1995), fatal heart disease (Helgeson 1995), and high rates of suicide born of lonely despair (Stack 2000). The effect of all of this on old manhood is tremendous, with men experiencing higher death rates than women at every age except after age ninety-five (Federal Interagency Forum on Aging-Related Statistics 2000), at which point few men remain alive.

More important to this discussion, however, than the results of such self-abuse on old age are the effects of age relations on this doing of manhood. To be sure, criminal combat and bone-crunching sports decline with age (much earlier in life, actually) such that old men commit few assaults and play little rugby. The increasing fragility of their bodies leads to relatively sedate lifestyles. Nevertheless, the recent anti-aging boom sells the implicit notion that relaxation equals death or at least defeat

and that, once he retires, only high-priced recreation keeps a man a man. Age and gender ideals to which any man can be held accountable shift from careerism to consumption, from sport to milder recreation, but maintain notions of performance all the while.

The theoretical gain here lies in recognizing the historical (and very recent) shift to old manhood as a social problem solved through the consumption of market goods. Men throughout history and across the globe appear always to feel defensive about manhood, in danger of losing or being stripped of it (Solomon-Godeau 1995). This theme takes different forms in different periods, however, and in our own appears as the notion that old men lose their hardness if they relax but can buy it back from leisure companies and medical experts.

"Staying Hard"

Given the importance of heterosexuality to hegemonic masculinity, we should consider the ways in which age and gender interact with sexuality, so often equated for men with "the erect phall[us]" (Marsiglio and Greer 1994, 126). Although graceful acceptance by men of their declining sexual desire had previously served as a hallmark of proper aging (Marshall and Katz 2002), current depictions of old men's masculinity focus on virility as expressed in a (hetero) sexuality enabled by medical products. "Staying hard" goes hand-in-hand with playing hard in the construction of age-appropriate gender ideals in this consumer economy.

Examples of the link among continued sexual functioning, manhood, and resistance to aging, in a context of individual responsibility and control, appear throughout the anti-aging industry, which has been growing as a part of our popular culture through the proliferation of Web sites, direct-mail brochures, journal and magazine advertisements, blurbs in academic newsletters, appearances on talk shows and infomercials, self-help paperbacks, and pricey seminars designed to empower the weakening old. For instance, a few passages from *Newsweek* (Cowley 1996) on the movement toward the use of human growth hormone (HGH) and testosterone draw connections among virility, aging, masculinity, individual control, and consumerism.

> Five years ago, on the eve of his 50th birthday, Ron Fortner realized that time was catching up with him. . . . His belly was soft, his energy and libido were lagging and his coronary arteries were ominously clogged up. After his advancing heart disease forced him into a quintuple bypass operation, Fortner decided he wasn't ready to get old. He . . . embarked on a hormone-based regimen designed to restore his youthful vigor. . . . [H]e started injecting himself with human growth hormone. . . . He claims the results were "almost instantaneous." First came a general sense of wellbeing. Then within weeks, his skin grew more supple, his hair more lustrous and his upper body leaner and more chiseled. . . . Awash in all these juices, he says he discovered new reserves of patience and energy, and became a sexual iron man. "My wife would like a word with you," he kids his guru during on-air interviews, "and that word is stop." (Cowley 1996, 68, 70)

Significantly, a yearlong supply of HGH in 1996 ran between $10,000 and $15,000, making it most accessible to elite men.

Another "success story" from the article concerns

> Robert, a 56-year-old consultant who wore a scrotal patch [for testosterone] for two and a half years. . . . Since raising his testosterone level from the bottom to the top of the normal range, Robert has seen his beard thicken, his body odor worsen and his libido explode. "Whether it's mental or physical, you start feeling older when you can't do physical things like you could," he says. "Sexually, I'm more comfortable because I know I'm dependable." His only complaint is that he's always covered with little rings of glue that won't come off without a heavy-duty astringent. (Cowley 1996, 71–72)

Finally, the story concludes by noting that

> as the population of aging males grows, the virility preservation movement is sure to grow with it. "Basically, it's a marketing issue," says epidemiologist John McKinley, director of the New

England Research Institute. . . . "The pharmaceutical industry is going to ride this curve all the way to the bank." (Cowley 1996, 75)

Scientific discourse and practice equate, especially for men, sex with "not aging," and propose technology to retain and restore sexual "functionality" (Katz and Marshall 2003). Indeed, as anti-aging guru Dr. Karlis Ullis, author of *Age Right* and *Super T* (for testosterone), proclaims on his Web site, "Good, ethical sex is the best anti-aging medicine we have" (2003). The appearance of such chemical interventions as sildenafil (Viagra) and the widespread advertising campaigns to promote them have also helped to reconstruct old manhood. A recent ad shows an old, white, finely dressed couple dancing a tango, with the man above and the woman leaning back over his leg. The strenuous dance combines with the caption to convey his virility: "Viagra: Let the dance begin" (*Good Housekeeping* April 1999, 79). Here is a man who likes to be on top and has the (newly enhanced) strength to prove it. Still another ad affirms the role of phallic sex in marital bliss. The bold letters next to a black man with visibly graying hair state, "With Viagra, she and I have a lot of catching up to do." And, at the bottom: "Love life again" (*Black Enterprise*, March 2000, 24–25).

Such ideals of virility appear in age-defying ads for active leisure—such as one for Martex towels, which features the caption, "Never, ever throw in the towel." Below this line, three old men stand, towels around their waists, in front of three surfboards that stand erect, stuck in the beach sand. Beneath, one reads that the towels are "for body and soul" (*Oprah*, April 2001, 118). An Aetna financial planning ad shows an old white man paddling in the surf, his erect board standing upward between his legs. The caption reads, "A Rocking Chair Is a Piece of Furniture. Not a State of Mind" (*Newsweek*, October 27, 1997, 15). In the ideal world of these ads, age is a state of mind, one to be conquered through public displays of a phallic, physical prowess. One accomplishes old manhood, then, by at least appearing to try to live up to some of the ideals pictured in these magazines. The resulting widespread doing of old manhood as consumption of the right products and maintenance of the right activities serves in turn to render natural the ideals toward which men strive.

Masculinity and sexual functioning have long been linked to aging in our popular culture, but the nature of this relationship has shifted as age relations have transformed and come under medical authority. Contemporary drug marketers build on an ancient quest but market it in new ways.

By the 1960s, therapists blamed psychological factors for male impotence and suggested that "to cease having sex would hasten aging itself" (Katz and Marshall 2003, 7). They later redefined male impotence as a physiological event—"erectile dysfunction"—to be addressed through such technologies as penile injections and sildenafil (Viagra)—and declared intercourse vital to successful aging (Marshall and Katz 2002; Potts 2000). More recently, advertisers have catered to a popular notion of "male menopause"—an umbrella label for the consequences of the fears of loss that expectations of high performance, in the context of women's rising status, can engender (Featherstone and Hepworth 1985). Marketers have built their depictions of old manhood on these links among sex, success, and masculinity. Sexual functioning now serves as a vehicle for reconstructions of manhood as "ageless," symbolizing the continued physical vigor and attractiveness derived from the experiences of younger men. To the extent that men can demonstrate their virility, they can still be men and stave off old age and the loss of status that accrues to that label.

To be sure, this shift in advertising imagery toward the phallic can work to the benefit of old men, convincing people to take them seriously as men full of potency as well as consumer power. To stop our analysis there, however, leaves unquestioned the ageism on which these assertions rest, the fact that we root these ideals of activity and virility in the experiences of the younger men. The ads avoid sexuality based on attributes other than hard penises and

experiences other than heterosexual intercourse, and these are hegemonic sexual symbols of the young. The little research available suggests that orgasm and intercourse recede in importance for some old men, who turn to oral sex and other expressions of love (Wiley and Bortz 1996). But these phallic ads value men only to the extent that they act like younger, heterosexual (and wealthy) men. Their emphases on both playing and staying hard reveal some of the ways in which gender and other inequalities shape old age. Old men are disadvantaged in relation to younger men, no matter how elite they may be.

The renewed emphasis on sexual intercourse among old men also reinforces the gender inequalities embedded in phallic depictions of bodies and sexuality. Historically, women's bodies and sexualities have been of only peripheral interest in part because they did not fit the "scientific" models based on men's physiologies. For example, rejuvenators were uncomfortable touting sex gland surgery for women (one variation promoted grafting the ovaries of chimpanzees to those of female patients) partly because they knew that they could not restore fertility in women. Thus, when they did speak of women, they tended to focus instead on the "mental" fertility that might result. Part of the problem was that women's "losses" in terms of sexuality (i.e., menopause) occurred much earlier in life. Those women were often "young," which confounded the equation of "loss of sexuality" with "old" (Hirshbein 2000).

People continue to define old women's sexuality in relation to old men's, assessing it in terms of penile-vaginal penetration. An old woman, in such popular imagery, remains passive and dependent on her man's continued erection for any pleasure of her own. Research on old women's accounts of their experiences, however, makes clear that these models represent little of what they want from their sex lives. These popular definitions also ignore that many old women have no partners at all. Even if old women "accept" and try to live up to the burden of being sexual and "not old" in male-defined terms, there are not enough old men for them to be partnered (and our age-based norms do not allow them to date younger men).

Finally, the ageism implicit in the demand to emulate the young is self-defeating and ignores the reality that even with technology and unlimited resources, bodies still change. Ultimately, individuals cannot control this; it is a "battle" one cannot win.

THEORIZING AGE, CLASS, AND GENDER RELATIONS

The rewards for the inclusion of a marginalized group into research extend beyond the satisfaction of listening to oft-ignored voices. The study of old manhood stands to enrich our theories of masculinity as social problem, as disciplinary consumer object, as the accomplishment of heterosexuality, and as the "crisis"-torn struggle to achieve or resist the hegemonic ideals spread through our popular culture.

Studying age relations can render insights into ways that we theorize gender. For instance, Judith Kegan Gardiner (2002) suggested that we clarify gender relations by making an analogy to age relations. This would help reconstruct thinking about gender in our popular culture, she argued, because many people already recognize *continuity* in age categories while they still see gender as dichotomous. People already see themselves as *performing* age-appropriate behavior ("acting their ages") while continuing to take for granted the doing of gender (Fenstermaker and West 2002). And popular culture more fully recognizes enduring group *conflicts* (over divisions of resources) between generations than between sexes. Gardiner (2002) suggested that a fuller theorizing of age relations has much to offer the study of men, that scholars may move beyond their polarization of biological and social construction, and that our popular culture may more fully appreciate the power struggles that govern gender relations.

We recommend just this view—of age and gender, race and class, and other dimensions of inequality—as accomplished by social as well as biological actors; as accountable to ever-changing ideals of age- and sex-appropriate behavior; as constructed in the context of a popular culture shaped by consumer marketing and technological change; and as imposing disciplinary regimens in the names of good health, empowerment, beauty, and success.

Taken together, the mass media reviewed above posit ideals of old manhood to which most if not all men find themselves held accountable. To the men fortunate enough to have been wealthy or well paid for their careerism, corporations (often with the support of those gerontologists who implicitly treat old age as a social problem) sell regimens through which those old men may live full lives, working, playing, and staying hard. If careerism kept the attention of these men from their families and leisure lives, constricting their social networks and degrading their physical health, then this high-priced old age serves as a promised payoff. Once retired, those few wealthy enough to do it can enjoy a reward: high-energy time with a spouse and some friends, enjoyment of tourism, surfing, and sex. Men sacrificed much, even their lives, in their pursuits of hegemonic masculine status. Those who survive face a rougher time with old age as a result: few sources of social support and bodies weakened by self-abuse. Thus, the accomplishment of manhood comes to require some response to the invitation to strain toward middle-age activities. Some men reach with all of their strength for the lifestyle ideals broadcast so loudly, whereas many give up for lack of means to compete, and still others deliberately resist. In a cruel irony, the ideals move all the further out of reach of the men who pursued them with such costly vigor in younger years and damaged their health beyond repair. The final push for hegemonic masculinity involves spending money and enjoying health that many old men do not have to pursue the recreation and phallic sex that the ads tell them they need.

Certainly, the study of old men offers striking views of a popular struggle over heterosexuality (although the study of old gay men will surely be as transforming, the near total lack of research on them prevents us from speculating how). Widely held views of old men's sexuality suggest dominance over women as a form of virility. But, as bodies change, outright predation recedes as an issue and impotency moves to the center of concern. A popular (consumer) culture that figures old manhood in terms of *loss* hardly departs from any trend in images of masculinity. Men have always felt that they were losing their manhood, their pride, and their virility, whether because their penises actually softened or because women gained status and so frightened them. But the study of this transition—from the feelings of invincibility that drive the destructiveness of youth to the growing expectation of vulnerability—throws old masculinity into a valuable relief. For instance, theories that center on violence and predation capture little of the realities of old men's lives, just as scholarly emphasis on coercion and harassment of women excludes most of the experiences of old women. For old women, the more important sexual theme may be that of being *cast aside* (Calasanti and Slevin 2001, 195). For old men, *impotence* in its most general sense, leading to many responses ranging from suicidal depression to more graceful acceptance, may be a more productive theme. It serves as both positive and negative ideal in a classic double-bind: old men should, so as not to intrude on the rights of younger men, retreat from the paid labor market; but they should also, so as to age successfully, never stop consuming opportunities to be active. They should, so as not to be "dirty," stop becoming erect; but they should also, so as to age successfully, never lose that erection. Old men fear impotence to the point that many suffer it who otherwise would not. Anxieties drain them at just the moment when expectations of aggressive consumption, of proving themselves younger than they are, reach their heights.

The notion that men accomplish age just as they do gender has much to offer, with its sensitivity to relations of inequality, its moment-to-moment accountability to unreachable but hegemonic ideals, and the perpetually changing nature of such accomplishments. Never have erections been so easily discussed in public, and never has this "dirty"/"impotent" double bind been tighter, than since the rise of this consumer regimen. Nor have old men, before now, lived

under such pressure to remain active further into their lengthening life spans. The ideals of manhood that tempted so many to cripple themselves in younger years now loom large enough to shame those who cannot play tennis or waltz the ballrooms of fancy resorts. The study of manhood should take careful notice of the ways in which men do old manhood under such tight constraints. The popular images that we have reviewed provide ideals of old manhood, but they do not necessarily describe the lives of very many old men. Given how little we know of the ways in which old men respond to such ideals, the research task before us seems clear.

CONCLUSION

Scholars tend to ignore age relations in part because of our own ageism. Most are not yet old, and even if we are, we often deny it (Minichiello, Browne, and Kendig 2000). Most people know little about the old because we seldom talk to them. Family and occupational segregation by age leave the old outside the purview of the work that most young people do.

Resulting in part from such segregation, the study of men, although no more than any other social science and humanist scholarship, has focused on the work, problems, sexuality, and consumption patterns of the young. This neglect of the old results in theories of masculinity that underplay the lengths to which men go to play and stay hard, the long-term effects of their strenuous accomplishment of manhood, and the variety of ways in which men remain masculine once their appetites for self-destruction begin to wane. Research on the old can reveal much about the desperate struggle for hegemonic masculinity and the varied ways in which men begin to redefine manhood. At the same time, it also uncovers the young and middle-aged biases that inhere in typical notions of masculinity that tend to center on accomplishments and power in the productive sphere, for instance. Few researchers have considered the reality of masculinities not directly tied to the fact of or potential for paid labor.

To leave age relations unexplored reinforces the inequality that subordinates the old, an inequality that we unwittingly reproduce for ourselves. Unlike other forms of oppression, in which the privileged rarely become the oppressed, we will all face ageism if we live long enough. As feminists, scientists, and people growing old, we can better develop our sense of interlocking inequalities and the ways in which they shape us, young and old. Our theories and concepts have too often assumed rather than theorized these age relations. The study of men and masculinity and the scholarship on age relations are just beginning to inform each other.

REFERENCES

Andrews, M. 1999. The seductiveness of agelessness. *Ageing and Society 19*(3): 301–18.

Calasanti, T. M. 1993. Bringing in diversity: Toward an inclusive theory of retirement. *Journal of Aging Studies 7*(2): 133–50.

Calasanti, T. M., and K. F. Slevin. 2001. *Gender, social inequalities, and aging.* Walnut Creek, CA: Alta Mira.

Charmaz, K. 1995. Identity dilemmas of chronically ill men. In *Men's health and illness: Gender, power, and the body,* edited by D. Sabo and D. F. Gordon, 266–91. Thousand Oaks, CA: Sage.

Courtenay, W. H. 2000. Behavioral factors associated with disease, injury, and death among men: Evidence and implications for prevention. *Journal of Men's Studies 9*(1): 81–142.

Cowley, Geoffrey. 1996. Attention: Aging men. *Newsweek,* September 16, 68–75.

Cruikshank, M. 2003. *Learning to be old: Gender, culture, and aging.* Lanham, MD: Rowman & Littlefield.

Davidson, K. 2001. Later life widowhood, selfishness, and new partnership choices: A gendered perspective. *Ageing and Society* 21: 297–317.

Dworkin, S. L., and M. A. Messner. 1999. Just do . . . what? Sport, bodies, gender. In *Revisioning gender,* edited by M. M. Ferree, J. Lorber, and B. B. Hess, 341–61. Thousand Oaks. CA: Sage.

Featherstone, M., and M. Hepworth. 1985. The male menopause: Lifestyle and sexuality. *Maturitas* 7: 235–46.

———. 1995. Images of positive aging: A case study of *Retirement Choice* magazine. In *Images of aging: Cultural representations of later life,* edited by M. Featherstone and A. Wernick, 29–47. London: Routledge.

Federal Interagency Forum on Aging-Related Statistics. 2000. *Older Americans 2000: Key indicators of well-being.* http://www.agingstats.gov.

Fenstermaker, S., and C. West, eds. 2002. *Doing gender, doing difference: Inequality, power, and institutional change.* New York: Routledge.

Franklin, C. 1987. Surviving the institutional decimation of black males: Causes, consequences, and intervention. In *The making of masculinities: The new men's studies,* edited by H. Brod, 155–69. Winchester, MA: Allen and Unwin.

Gardiner, J. K. 2002. Theorizing age and gender: Bly's boys, feminism, and maturity masculinity. In *Masculinity studies & feminist theory: New directions,* edited by J. K. Gardiner, 90–118. New York: University of Columbia Press.

Harris, A. P. 2000. Gender, violence, and criminal justice. *Stanford Law Review* 52: 777–807.

Helgeson, V. S. 1995. Masculinity, men's roles, and coronary heart disease. In *Men's health and illness: Gender, power, and the body,* edited by D. Sabo and D. F. Gordon, 68–104. Thousand Oaks, CA: Sage.

Hirshbein, L. D. 2000. The glandular solution: Sex, masculinity and aging in the 1920s. *Journal of the History of Sexuality 9*(3): 27–304.

Holstein, Martha. 1999. Women and productive aging: Troubling implications. In *Critical gerontology: Perspectives from political and moral economy,* edited by Meredith Minkler and Carroll L. Estes, 359–73. Amityville, NY: Baywood.

Hooyman, N. R. 1999. Research on older women: Where is feminism? *The Gerontologist* 39: 115–18.

Katz, S. 2000. Busy bodies: Activity, aging, and the management of everyday life. *Journal of Aging Studies 14*(2): 135–52.

———. 2001–2002. Growing older without aging? Positive aging, anti-ageism, and anti-aging. *Generations 25*(4): 27–32.

Katz, S., and B. Marshall. 2003. New sex for old: Lifestyle, consumerism, and the ethics of aging well. *Journal of Aging Studies 17*(1): 3–16.

Klein, A. M. 1995. Life's too short to die small: Steroid use among male bodybuilders. In *Men's health and illness: Gender, power, and the body,* edited by D. Sabo and D. F. Gordon, 105–21. Thousand Oaks, CA: Sage.

Lee, M. R. 2000. Concentrated poverty, race, and homicide. *Sociological Quarterly 41*(2): 189–206.

Marshall, B., and S. Katz. 2002. Forever functional: Sexual fitness and the ageing male body. *Body & Society 8*(4): 43–70.

Marsiglio, William, and Richard A. Greer. 1994. A gender analysis of older men's sexuality. In *Older men's lives,* edited by Edward H. Thompson, Jr., 122–40. Thousand Oaks, CA: Sage.

McHugh, K. 2000. The "ageless self"? Emplacement of identities in sun belt retirement communities. *Journal of Aging Studies 14*(1): 103–15.

Minichiello, V., J. Browne, and H. Kendig. 2000. Perceptions and consequences of ageism: Views of older people. *Ageing and Society 20*(3): 253–78.

Potts, A. 2000, The essence of the "hard on": Hegemonic masculinity and the cultural construction of "erectile dysfunction." *Men and Masculinities 3*(1): 85–103.

Slevin, K. F., and C. R. Wingrove. 1998. *From stumbling blocks to stepping stones: The life experiences of fifty professional African American women.* New York: New York University Press.

Solomon-Godeau, A. 1995. Male trouble. In *Constructing masculinities,* edited by M. Berger, B. Wallis, and S. Watson, 69–76. New York: Routledge.

Stack, S. 2000. Suicide: A 15-year review of the sociological literature. *Suicide & Life-Threatening Behavior 30*(2): 145–76.

Staples, R. 1995. Health among Afro-American males. In *Men's health and illness: Gender, power, and the body,* edited by D. Sabo and D. F. Gordon, 121–38. Thousand Oaks, CA: Sage.

Ullis, Karlis. 2003. *Agingprevent.com.* http://www.agingprevent.com/flash/index.html.

White, P. G., K. Young, and W. G. McTeer. 1995. Sport, masculinity, and the injured body. In *Men's health and illness: Gender, power, and the body,* edited by D. Sabo and D. F. Gordon, 158–82. Thousand Oaks, CA: Sage.

Wiley, D., and W. M. Bortz. 1996. Sexuality and aging—usual and successful. *Journal of Gerontology 51A*(3): M142–M146.

Woodward, K., ed. 1999. *Figuring age: Women, bodies, generations.* Bloomington: Indiana University Press.

Introduction to Reading 24

Gayle Sulik is a medical sociologist and one of the most sought-after experts in breast cancer and women's health. Her ground-breaking analysis of the culture and cult of breast cancer is titled *Pink Ribbon Blues: How Breast Cancer Culture Undermines Women's Health*. In this reading, Sulik describes the commodification of the breast cancer movement by the pink ribbon industry. Pink ribbon culture has reduced breast cancer to "pink visibility and symbolic gestures," in particular buying pink-ribbon branded products. The consequences of the growth of a pink-ribbon marketplace are largely negative (e.g., fear-mongering).

1. What is the "she-ro" storyline, and how does it function as a controlling image?

2. How have pink-ribbon campaigns used objectifying techniques, and why is that a problem?

3. Where do profits from pink-ribbon merchandise go?

4. Discuss the false information about breast cancer that is spread in pink-ribbon culture.

#RETHINKPINK

MOVING BEYOND BREAST CANCER AWARENESS

Gayle Sulik

BREAST CANCER ADVOCACY: A BRIEF HISTORY

Long before breast cancer and the pink ribbon took hold in common vernacular, the breast itself had been imbued with history and meaning (Yalom 1997). In eighteenth-century Europe, the breast was the touchstone of bourgeois family values and women's roles as mothers. The nineteenth-century Victorians cast the breast as shameful, not to be seen. And the medical environment, steeped in these attitudes, positioned the docile female[1] patient and her body at the mercy of patriarchal medicine (Bartky 1988; Ehrenreich and English 1989). Medical drawings of the Halsted Radical Mastectomy—standard treatment for breast cancer from 1895 to the mid-1970s, performed mostly by male physicians—filled medical books.

The invasive surgery removed the entire breast, chest muscles, and lymph nodes up to the collarbone. The procedure elevated Halsted's status to "father of modern surgery" and canonized a "more is better" approach to treatment[2] (Lerner 2001; Mukherjee 2010). The first half of the twentieth century brought the breast back from the textbooks and into the visual field, especially in the arts (Yalom 1997). By the second half of the century, the breast became a marker of female power and health, as medicine and advertising shaped perceptions of how a breast can, and should, look. Breast cancer confronts this history—a legacy in which women have tried to claim ownership of their bodies and

medical decisions while supporting other women and, in some cases, questioning the authority of medicine (Morgen 2002; Ruzek 1978; Spanier 2010; Sulik and Eich-Krohm 2008). This context is crucial for understanding the current breast cancer landscape.

Into the 1960s, high mortality rates, social mores, and fear that breast cancer was a death sentence still made public discourse about the disease taboo (Lerner 2001). Inaccessible medical language, invasive procedures, and authoritative doctor-patient interactions further silenced women and thwarted support (Leopold 1999). Women worked against this background to expand information and support, foster a patient-centered approach, and advocate for social justice in health care. Breast cancer advocates developed support groups such as Reach to Recovery (adopted by the American Cancer Society in 1969), which was started in 1952 by two women who had been treated with the Halsted Radical Mastectomy. Women founded their own organizations (e.g., the National Women's Health Network in 1975; the Susan G. Komen Breast Cancer Foundation in 1982; the first national breast cancer network, the National Alliance of Breast Cancer Organizations in 1986). Activists gained involvement with federal agencies such as the National Cancer Institute to give voice to patients, influence medical practice, and help shape the direction of research (see Batt 1994; Boehmer 2000; Kasper and Ferguson 2000; Lerner 2001; Ley 2009; Sulik 2011a).

By the time the American Cancer Society launched what would become National Breast

From Sulik, Gayle. 2014. #Rethinkpink. Moving beyond breast cancer awareness. *Gender & Society, 28*(5), 655–678.

Cancer Awareness Month in 1985, incidence rates were high: 1 in 8, up from 1 in 11 in 1975 (American Cancer Society 2008). Breast cancer had achieved the status of an epidemic. The week-long awareness event (with funding from chemical-turned-pharmaceutical company Zeneca, now AstraZeneca) became a year-long series of activities culminating in October. The regular timeline helped to make women's health in relation to breast cancer a national priority and turned the focus of advocacy almost exclusively toward screening mammograms vis-à-vis "awareness."

By the early 1990s, the increased presence and visibility of resources, changes in public policy, increased funding for research, and heightened media exposure elevated breast cancer's social status. *Dr. Susan Love's Breast Book* (Love 2005), called the "bible" for newly diagnosed women, set the stage for a new level of patient empowerment. Love helped to form the National Breast Cancer Coalition, a network of hundreds of organizations oriented to advocacy and public policy. Evelyn Lauder of Estée Lauder Companies and *Self* magazine teamed up to introduce the pink ribbon as the official symbol of breast cancer awareness in 1992. Businesses jumped on the pink bandwagon, and many charities welcomed it. By this time, there were already controversies over the benefits of mammograms, concerns over conflicts of interest, rising competition in pharmacology, and infighting among thought leaders and scientists. Yet cause promotion and the desire to do *something* for breast cancer held the public's attention.

During those 30 years, the breast cancer movement helped to make breast cancer a national priority, raise awareness and funds, galvanize social support, and impact the direction of research. Women were on the forefront of information sharing, activism, and patient empowerment. Treatments improved incrementally, and breast cancer mortality rates declined overall. By these indicators, the breast cancer movement was a success. But by the early 1990s, the focus of the mainstream movement started to shift, as did the general perception, that the way to solve the breast cancer problem was, quite simply, to buy and display pink (Belkin 1996; King 2006; Leopold 2014; Sulik 2011a).

Shifting representations of breast cancer in mass media paint a clear picture. A 1993 cover of *The New York Times* Magazine featured artist Matuschka (1993) wearing a headscarf and baring her mastectomy scar (Ferraro 1993). The cover caption "You Can't Look Away Anymore" referred to the successes of the breast cancer movement and to the photograph "Beauty out of Damage," a self-portrait that speaks to body image, the brutality of treatment, and the desire for truth. Matuschka, diagnosed with breast cancer in 1991, said in an interview, "One should speak and show the truth. If we keep quiet about what cancer does to women's bodies . . . we['re] doing a disservice to womankind" (Ferraro 1993). The message was short-lived, at least in public portrayals. The covers of *Time* magazine on February 18, 2002, and October 15, 2007, presented an idealized vision of breast cancer and the beautiful, young nude women who should cup their breasts in fear of it, and did not represent the median age of women diagnosed with breast cancer, which is age 61 (Howlader et al. 2013). The white women on these covers appear to be in their twenties. What's more, there is no other disease imagery that reveals women's bodies to the degree that breast cancer does, one of the common themes in pink ribbon culture.

BREAST CANCER BRAND: GENDER, CULTURE, AND CONSUMPTION

When Evelyn Lauder of Estée Lauder Companies and *Self* magazine introduced the pink ribbon as the official symbol for breast cancer awareness in 1992, there was already a ribbon dedicated to breast cancer. Charlotte Haley, a 65-year-old activist with several family members diagnosed with breast cancer, folded peach ribbons and attached cards saying "Only 5 percent [of the National Cancer Institute budget] goes for . . . prevention. Help us wake up our legislators, and America, by wearing this ribbon." Haley's ribbon got attention. Lauder and *Self* "wanted to use it for what would be their second annual awareness campaign. Haley declined because she didn't want the ribbon to become commercialized. Simple solution: Change the color (Fernandez 1998).

Pink, the quintessential color of femininity, represents everything breast cancer is not. The color pink capitalizes on traditional femininity and normative assumptions about women's beauty, sexuality, emotionality, nurturance, and morality. By associating with traditional femininity, breast cancer may be cast as nonthreatening, blameless, and even virtuous (Katz Rothman 2006; Klawiter 2004; Skinner 2012). Pink ribbon culture relies on imagery of pretty, happy, optimistic survivors who wear their survivorship with pride, elegance, sensuality, and the perfect blend of cosmetic enhancements (Sulik and Deane 2008).

The "Look Good, Feel Better" program sponsored by the American Cancer Society (with support from the cosmetics industry) holds beauty workshops for women in treatment, along with free cosmetics. The "HOPE is Beautiful" caption from one of the program's print advertisements replaces the letter "O" in hope with a woman's puckered, pink lips. We see only part of her soft, pale face. The ad continues:

. . . AND SO IS EVERY WOMAN BEING TREATED FOR CANCER. LOOK GOOD . . . FEEL BETTER® CAN HELP WOMEN *FACE* THE CHALLENGE OF A LIFETIME [emphasis added].

The alliteration of "face" in word and image further stresses the importance of outward appearances. Many women love this program and feel better after getting a makeover. This is not surprising. Makeup is strongly associated with assumptions about health, heterosexuality, credibility, and women's efforts to resist invisibility (Clarke and Griffin 2008; Dellinger and Williams 1997; Franzoi 2001). Marketing beauty ideology to further a narrowly defined aspect of cancer survivorship has implications beyond dealing with treatment-related side effects. By prioritizing the return from illness to normalized femininity (Lorber and Moore 2002), there is little space in cancer survivorship (and pink ribbon culture in particular) for suffering, pain, disfigurement, or any other perceived threats to socially expected norms (Klawiter 2004; Lorde 1980).

Like Susan Sontag's (2001) concern that patients suffering from a particular disease are somehow characterized as having a kind of exceptional humanity, the "culture of survivorship" surrounding breast cancer carries a survivor identity steeped in femininity, optimism, and personal empowerment (Ehrenreich 2001; Goldenberg 2010; King 2006; Sulik 2011a, 2013e). No figure brings these elements together better than the "she-ro," the protagonist of the epic breast cancer story. She exists in many iterations: in magazines, advertisements, news stories, and awareness events. She is a superwoman who courageously, passionately, and aggressively battles disease. She faces tremendous difficulties. With style and optimism, she learns from her experience, is transformed, and shares lessons learned. She is the triumphant survivor who fights breast cancer and wins (Sulik 2011a).

Cancer Vixen is the breast cancer story of Marisa Acocella Marchetto, published first as a six-page cartoon spread in *Glamour* magazine and later as a book (Marchetto 2009). This graphic memoir is a stylized glimpse into the cartoonist's alter ego as she faces breast cancer diagnosis and treatment. The narrative evokes key elements of the She-ro type: inspiration, emotional drama ending in triumph, personal transformation, and a vivacious style that thrives on feminine accessories (Sulik 2013f). Cancer Vixen is a bold, stylish, sexually attractive woman who stands victorious above the battleground of her colorful and transformative breast cancer saga.

Cancer Vixen does what she-roes do best: tell stories of courage, hope, and inspiration. She rides an emotional roller coaster with tidbits of life sprinkled between the highs and lows. The image of Cancer Vixen post-diagnosis, as the "Electrolux of the universe sucks [her] into a black hole" (Marchetto 2009) suggests a feeling of being out of control, a melodramatic portrayal of cancer's capacity to wreak havoc in her life as she wonders what will happen physically, emotionally, and existentially. Cancer Vixen's strong, sexy exterior relies on fashion therapy, as she puts on "Brave" lipstick and wears new designer shoes to each chemotherapy session. With feisty resolve, the Vixen proclaims: "Cancer, I am gonna kick your butt. And, I'm gonna do it in killer five-inch heels" (Marchetto 2009). She-roic stories emphasize how breast cancer helps women salvage relationships, establish friendships, rethink priorities, gain self-confidence, and find happiness.

The she-ro storyline functions as a controlling narrative accompanied by a controlling image that encourages the diagnosed to smile and look good, and marginalizes those who do not, or cannot, live the ideal. A woman with incurable breast cancer said, "I can't just mark time and get through knowing the hardest parts will soon be over. I know the hardest parts are yet to come" (Adams 2013). Unlike the she-ro, this woman's reality is heavy. Her personal will, no matter how optimistic or feisty, will not lead to a happy ending, and she does not think of cancer as a meaningful learning experience. She is just a person living, for now, with a terminal disease.

With traditional femininity and a cancer-fighting aesthetic at its core, pink ribbon culture helped to reframe the concept of awareness from something functional and evidence-based to something "symbolic," from a consciousness-raising symbol to a logo for the breast cancer brand—a collection of images and associations used to encourage people to "choose" the breast cancer brand over competing causes.

Breast cancer had already become the "darling of corporate America" by 1996, embracing the ribbon as a safe symbol for corporate investment (Belkin 1996; King 2006). By 2000, Lauder's pink ribbon initiative illuminated 26 landmarks in 22 countries in pink lights to raise awareness in a new and dramatic way. Even awareness month itself transmuted into a commercial adaptation with upbeat messages and pink swag.

Commonly referred to as "Pinktober," the blockbuster month of October boasts celebrity and style, from the Hard Rock Cafe to the National Football League's pink cleats, to the hot pink frosting on the cupcakes at my local grocery store. The new breast cancer awareness is about pink visibility and symbolic gestures, while encouraging consumers to treat themselves to a vast selection of pink products, services, and "cancertainment." In the name of empowerment, a carefree pink ribbon lifestyle may include having the courage to take off your shirt and run topless through Westin Hotels and Resorts. Or you can get "tied to the cause" with celebrities like Mary J. Blige (PR Newswire 2003). A four-page ad in *Self* magazine (2004) for the $30 "The Cure Card" entitles shoppers to discounts at participating stores (for a limited time) and gives a percentage of proceeds to two charities (amount not disclosed). The message that pink consumption is the best way to solve breast cancer is coupled with an aesthetic that focuses on "doing good for a good cause with status and style." Meanwhile, the industry thrives.

Federal breast cancer research costs about $1 billion per year; breast cancer drug sales totaled $12.7 billion in 2010; predictive breast cancer diagnostic and drug technologies are estimated to reach $24 billion by 2016; the digital mammography market is set to reach $1.3 billion by 2017; approximately 1,400 breast cancer nonprofits raise $2.5–3.25 billion per year; and the profits from all those pink ribbon products: unknown. Companies are not required to disclose their profits from pink ribbon merchandise. New York is the only state in the nation to have a "best practices" guideline for "official" cause-marketing promotions, but there are no sanctions for failure to comply. Some companies advertise with a breast cancer-related motif to give the impression of donating to the cause without ever doing so. In addition, few nonprofit organizations involved in product-related fundraising have published financial accounts beyond the basic Form 990 required by the Internal Revenue Service. Many consumers look to organizations like Charity Navigator to learn whether a charity is reputable, but such groups have limited criteria (mostly financial, all self-reported) to determine their ratings.

Trends in Breast Cancer Campaigns

As a culture of breast cancer survivorship grew into a massive pink ribbon marketplace, branding efforts fueled the reproduction of the culture. In addition to beauty, idealized femininity, and the effervescence of the she-roic survivor, several trends are predominant. Fear-mongering (to sustain the urgency and vitality of the breast cancer cause) is coupled with trivialization, infantilization, and sexual objectification (to keep the culture entertaining, digestible, and, therefore, profitable). To lend legitimacy to the stated goal of awareness, scientific factoids frequently accompany breast cancer events, advertisements, product placements, and educational materials. Too often, these informational sound bites are inaccurate, out of context, lack scientific substantiation, or mislead audiences in other ways.

Fear-mongering: The use of fear to *influence the opinions and actions of others toward some specific end.* The feared object or subject is sometimes exaggerated. An ad for BMW reads, "1 in 8 women will be diagnosed with breast cancer. Will it be someone close to you?" Women are ten times more likely to die from heart disease, or lung and digestive cancers than they are to die from breast cancer. Yet widespread statistics seem to indicate that breast cancer is almost inevitable. The probability of getting breast cancer increases with age. The National Cancer Institute (2012) reports that only one in 233 women will be diagnosed with breast cancer from birth to age 39. That ratio changes to one in 29 between the ages of 60 and 69. By the time a woman would die of old age, about one in eight who avoided equally serious life-threatening events while they were younger would likely be diagnosed with breast cancer. So, if you live to be 80 years old, and nothing else kills you first, you have a 12.5 percent chance of being diagnosed with breast cancer. That's still a lot of cases, but it doesn't mean that if we count off by eight, one person in each of our groups will get breast cancer.

Trivialization: To downplay, minimize, and understate. Pink confetti. Pink balloon animals. Ribbon-shaped fake tattoos. People on an escalator wearing boob costumes (yes, literally). A Facebook game in which women post the status of their underwear for breast cancer awareness. "Extreme Truth or Dare," culminating in a YouTube personality's live jump from an airplane, while wearing a Power Ranger costume, to raise funds for the "Susan G. Kormen [*sic*—original press release] breast cancer organization." These kinds of awareness symbols/games/stunts have a light quality that keeps the breast cancer brand palatable for mass consumption and may, at times, raise money for a charity. But they do not promote mindfulness, consciousness, or useful information about breast cancer. Putting energy into trivializing activities diverts focus from other, more meaningful actions.

Infantilization: To treat or condescend to, as if still a young child. In her classic essay, "Welcome to Cancerland," Barbara Ehrenreich (2001) wondered why adult women diagnosed with breast cancer received gifts of teddy bears and other child-like items—as if femininity were incompatible with adulthood. "Men diagnosed with prostate cancer," she wrote, "[do] not receive gifts of Matchbox cars."

The 2014 Kohl's Cash® for the Cure campaign featured a candy-striped elephant with a pink ribbon tattoo on its cheek (Sulik 2014). Is this a Walt Disney character or does it have something to do with breast cancer? The campaign (for a limited time) offered a "$10 Pink Kohl's Cash" coupon for every $50 spent, increasing in value with each $50 purchase. Consumers who spent $250 would receive $50 in Pink Kohl's Cash. Kohl's Cash wasn't really cash, but a price reduction on a future purchase (if made within a specified time period). Kohl's then donated $1 to Susan G. Komen® for each valid coupon redeemed, up to $1 million. To reach the donation goal, which Kohl's did, consumers had to spend at least $5 million. To help customers spend their Cash, Kohl's leveraged the color pink, and its association with breast cancer, to sell a range of products: Go "pink chic" to debut your spring style; "Paint the town pink" with rosy shades to add the perfect dose of color [lipstick as medicine] to any outfit.

Kohl's is clear that it wants consumers to spend more time shopping than thinking about breast cancer: "While you're shopping, be sure to *stop by our Pink Elephant page*" [emphasis added]. A quick awareness visit to the campaign page makes all that shopping seem worthwhile. But in addition to spending money at Kohl's, the department store encourages consumers to advertise the campaign (for free) using the hashtag #TALKPINK, a mechanism for grouping messages in micro-blogging sites like Twitter. The website then features the #TALKPINK Twitter feed, streaming with upbeat messages aimed at "starting" a conversation about breast cancer because breast cancer is "the (pink) elephant in the room."

Breast cancer is the most visible of disease-related causes and the only disease for which national landmarks get lighted in pink. But apparently, 30 years after the dawning of the age of awareness, there is now a need to "start" a conversation about breast cancer. I have argued that there is a need to change the conversation on breast cancer; get real about breast cancer; acknowledge misinformation, trivialization, and commercialization; demand transparency and accountability. But the Kohl's campaign is not about that. Cause-marketing programs are housed in companies' marketing departments, geared toward profit, employee loyalty, and public relations (Sulik 2013a, 2014). The Kohl's campaign is about buying and displaying pink, while a childish elephant diverts attention from the seriousness of a disease and turns it into an entertaining shopping spree.

Objectification: Portraying people as objects (to be looked at, ogled, or touched), commodities to be purchased, used, discarded, or replaced, or any way that dehumanizes a person.

Sexual objectification: The practice of regarding or treating another person merely as an instrument (object) for one's sexual gratification. A porn site donates a penny to charity for every thirty "boob-themed videos" watched; a Las Vegas restaurant promises to "Save 2nd Base" and provide an open bar to guests in pink bathing suits; campaigns like "Save the Ta-tas" and "Feel Your Boobies" use slang and provocative

imagery to raise funds and visibility. Such techniques also demean women and have negative outcomes that go well beyond the scope of this article (Sulik 2011b, 2012b).

The objectifying techniques used in breast cancer campaigns are common. They use women's bodies as objects, such as a body-painting project that uses nude breast cancer survivors as canvases; hone in on the breasts, like the American Cancer Society's chest-level-only "Making Strides" video; use objects in place of breasts, be they ribbons, bowling balls, or hooters; depict breasts as things to be groped, especially popular in campaigns targeting young women and promoting Breast Self-Exam; show women as objects of the male gaze, a technique used in the "Don't your breasts deserve more attention from you than they get from random guys?" awareness postcard; objectify breasts with language, as in a college poll in which students voted for their favorite Think Pink advertisement: hooters, jugs, knockers, melons, mosquito bites, mountains, headlights, rack, twins—I don't know which slang term won. Sexy breast cancer campaigns are an extension of the broader social context that already sexually objectifies women. They just do it in the name of awareness and fundraising.

Misinformation: False or inaccurate information that is spread unintentionally. If cancer prevention is to be fully integrated into health promotion strategies, it is necessary to target the multiple levels of health literacy so that individuals may make optimal decisions about their health based on evidence-based information (Sulik, Cameron, and Chamberlain 2012). Yet, in the desire to simplify information and awareness messages, important details may be distorted, misused, or left without context. Misinformation abounds in pink ribbon culture, with Breast Self-Exam/Awareness, screening mammography, and genetic testing topping the list.

"Do boob checks regularly" because they "may save your life." The National Cancer Institute and World Health Organization confirm that Breast Self-Exam (BSE) does not find breast cancers early or reduce mortality, and the U.S.

Preventive Services Task Force recommends against teaching the exercise. Yet some groups (especially sexy campaigns targeting younger women and men) still focus on BSE in their education/awareness campaigns. I still see shower cards explaining the proper technique for checking your breasts, and in 2012 Google+ Hangouts featured an hour-long live tutorial demonstrating the technique. Some groups, knowing BSE has been discredited, now recommend a newly repackaged version of the practice called Breast Self-Awareness (BSA). Loosely defined as "knowing what is normal for you," BSA is usually bundled with advice about knowing your breast cancer risk, getting mammograms at a specific age, and making healthy lifestyle choices—not bad directives in general terms (though mammography is controversial as a population screening tool). But the life-saving promise of checking one's breasts is scientifically unsubstantiated. In addition, framing BSA or BSE as a way to reduce one's risk of dying from breast cancer makes people responsible for self-surveillance, setting up illness as a consequence of personal negligence.

After *Good Morning America*'s Amy Robach announced that her on-air mammogram got her a breast cancer diagnosis, the correspondent's "I got lucky by catching it early" so "every woman should get a mammogram" message spread like wildfire. Sandwiched between a personal story of "denial, panic, and bravery" and the ongoing mammogram wars, the plain truths about breast cancer—namely, biology and large bodies of evidence—kept getting lost (Sulik 2013b). Breast cancer is not a single disease that consistently behaves in the same way, progressing from early to late to lethal, and cancer stage (0, 1, 2, 3, 4) is not a point in a definite progression but a snapshot of some of cancer's characteristics. Eight randomized controlled trials have found mammography screening to be associated with a 0 to 15 percent reduction in breast cancer mortality (Sulik and Spanier 2014).

The longest-running study, recently reported from Canada, followed women for 25 years and found that screening mammography added no benefit to routine clinical exam and health care.

It did, however, lead to 22 percent overdiagnosis and overtreatment (identification and treatment of cancers that would never cause symptoms in a person's lifetime). Mammograms do not prevent cancer or guarantee that cancers will be found early or at all. Cancer biology, which cannot be determined on a mammogram, indicates whether a type of breast cancer is indolent, lethal, or in between. Even the American Cancer Society, which still heavily promotes screening beginning at age 40, acknowledges that mammography has overpromised and underdelivered.

In an op-ed piece in the *The New York Times,* actress Angelina Jolie announced that, after learning she had inherited a mutation on one of the so-called breast cancer genes, she decided to have a preventive double mastectomy to reduce her risk of developing breast cancer (a 65 percent lifetime risk compared to 12.5 percent for an average-risk woman). She planned to have her ovaries removed to reduce her lifetime risk of ovarian cancer, which was 39 percent by age 80. Angelina Jolie was only 37 years old.

The significance of preventive measures for high-risk people notwithstanding, risk is a valuable commodity (Sulik 2013c, 2013d). In conjunction with Angelina Jolie's public revelation, Kristi Funk, her doctor at the Pink Lotus center, wrote in her blog: "Like Angelina, I urge women who feel they *might* have reason to be at *risk* for a BRCA gene mutation, *perhaps* because of a strong family history of cancer, to seek medical advice and to *take control* of their futures [emphasis added]" (Funk 2013). The uncertain language ("might," "risk," "perhaps"), coupled with "take control" of one's future, is a common fear-hope formula. It is not surprising that doctors had a record number of inquiries about genetic testing in the weeks that followed Jolie's public disclosure. In addition, the stock for Myriad Genetics—the company that, at the time, owned the patents on the breast cancer genes,[3] had twice the usual trading volume the day of Jolie's announcement.

Despite the heightened concern and fear-mongering that accompanied the "Jolie effect," most women do not fit high-risk profiles. Only about one-quarter of 1 percent (0.025 percent) of U.S. women have variants on the breast cancer genes known to increase risk. In addition, only 5–10 percent of breast cancer cases and 10–15 percent of ovarian cancer cases involve mutations on the BRCA genes. Seventy percent of those diagnosed with breast cancer have none of the known risk factors other than being a woman and aging. The Jolie case opens the door for thinking about what is at stake for people who are at increased cancer risk, but it is crucial to remember that Angelina Jolie is in a unique, privileged position. She gets the best care, top surgeons, support, and everything that comes with power and wealth. For the rest, tough medical decisions come with other costs.

Resistance and Countermovements

Pink ribbon celebrations continue to maintain public focus on the feel-good aspects of the breast cancer cause along with wishful thinking about a future without the disease. Still, more people are starting to look behind the pink curtain. Lea Pool's Canadian documentary *Pink Ribbons, Inc.* explored breast cancer as a dream cause (Pool 2012). Based on a book of the same title by Samantha King (2006), the film considers the larger context of breast cancer, current approaches to research and health care, and what it means to challenge the corporations, organizations, and breast cancer charities that stand in the way of progress. The film provides a useful starting point for thinking about the system behind the pink ribbon. Likewise, disease wars and controversies involving breast cancer charities and corporations alike have opened the public's eyes to mounting dissent surrounding what had long been an untouchable social cause.

One of the recent eye-opening controversies involved Susan G. Komen for the Cure (now, Susan G. Komen). After Komen changed its granting policies in 2012 in a way that would preclude one group, Planned Parenthood, from applying for funds, many were outraged for what appeared to be a political decision (Baralt and Weitz 2012; Sulik 2012a, 2012b). Hackers

gained access to Komen's website and at 12:30 a.m. on February 2, 2012, altered the copy to read "Help us run over poor women on our way to the bank." The hack was short-lived, but its impact was lasting. Hashtags like #RETHINK PINK and #OCCUPYTHECURE lit up social media sites. Komen reversed the decision in three days. Komen leadership did not explain how the organization would safeguard programming from partisan politics, nor did they respond to concerns about the pink ribbon industry. There were changes in staff and the board of directors, and a stated desire to involve affiliates in decision making. It remains to be seen whether these actions will lead to meaningful change. What is clear is that the largest and most visible breast cancer charity is under scrutiny in a way that it had not been in the past. Damage to Komen's reputation has already resulted in a 22 percent decline in public support (Sulik 2011a).

Breast Cancer Action (BCAction) is an advocacy group that, for decades, has been calling for transparency and accountability in pink ribbon promotions. In 2002, the group started the Think Before You Pink® campaign, which encourages consumers to ask critical questions about cause marketing. BCAction coined the term "pinkwasher" to describe any company involved in pink ribbon promotions while producing, manufacturing, or distributing products linked to the disease. Over the course of the campaign, BCAction highlighted some of the most egregious pinkwashing examples: cosmetics with known carcinogens and reproductive toxins; dairy products with synthetic hormones; fragrances such as Komen's *Promise Me* perfume (containing chemicals with negative health effects as well as those that have not been evaluated for human safety).

The "Revlon Cares" program is a breast cancer awareness campaign that says, "Your lips can save lives: Use them to talk with the women you love about cancer. Talking creates awareness. Awareness brings about early detection. Early detection saves lives." But the fine print should read "Just don't talk about what's in our lipstick!" Last year, Breast Cancer Fund, a group focused on environmental links to breast cancer, took action against Revlon for this clear example of pinkwashing. After reviewing Revlon's products, they found formaldehyde-releasing chemicals, parabens, and carbon black (linked to cancer); endocrine disrupters (linked to breast cancer and thyroid disorders); and *p*-phenylenediamine (a respiratory toxicant). Pinkwashing highlights one of the many conflicts of interest that may be involved in cause marketing and corporate partnerships (Sulik 2011a).

The visibility, popularity, and considerable monies going to breast cancer create an uneven field when it comes to other diseases and health conditions. A controversial campaign by UK-based Pancreatic Cancer Action (2014) featured a young woman with pancreatic cancer saying that she wished she'd had breast cancer. The campaign sparked outrage among those who said it was misleading to imply that breast cancer is a more desirable form of disease. The CEO said, "We're all campaigning for the same cause—to improve everyone's chances of beating cancer. We just had to shout that little bit louder to get heard." Pancreatic cancer has the highest mortality of the 22 most common cancers in the UK but receives the least amount of research funding. In the United States, the 5-year survival rate for pancreatic cancer is only 6 percent, compared to 89 percent for breast cancer overall. The lack of attention and research across the board is concerning. I've heard similar sentiment from people with brain, ovarian, lung, metastatic breast, and other cancers. Yet the White House only ever gets lit up in pink.

Questions such as these and alternative representations of breast cancer are gaining entrée to public discourse. Five months after Jen and Angelo Merendino got married in 2008 they entered the world of cancer. After chemotherapy, double mastectomy, radiation, and reconstructive surgery, the couple celebrated their first anniversary with news that Jen was "cancer free." Two years later the cancer recurred, spreading to her liver and bones. When the cancer metastasized, many people fell out of their life. They didn't know what to say or do, so

they stepped back. Realizing that most people had no idea what they were going through, Angelo, a photographer, tried to capture it with his camera. He shared the pictures on his website and Facebook page, saying, "My photographs show this daily life. They humanize the face of cancer, on the face of my wife." The collection came together as a photo-documentary, *The Battle We Didn't Choose: My Wife's Fight with Breast Cancer* (Merendino 2010).

Jen's life, captured on film, gave people a chance to see aspects of cancer that are often hidden behind normalizing gestures, or a strong, courageous front. Watching the progression of Jen's illness through these photographs gave viewers a chance to bear witness to Jen's suffering, to the authenticity of her experience, to an essence of the human condition. It filled many of us with deep sadness and a sense of dread. Many had personally seen the face of cancer before, up close. Too many times we witnessed its cruelty and the equally dire effects of its treatment. None of this was easy. Neither was learning of Jen's death on December 22, 2011. She left a community of people, both virtual and real, in grief.

The landscape of breast cancer advocacy has always involved more than the breast cancer movement alone. There is a system underlying the pink ribbon that involves many dimensions: survivors, social movements and countermovements, family, community, gender, politics, consumption, mass media, biomedicine, and the health care system itself. Sometimes it's hard to see the system because it's hidden beneath so much "awareness."

The system surrounding breast cancer fuels pink ribbon culture, communicates it, publicizes it, profits from it, and, in some cases, resists it. The system is being exposed both from within and outside of the breast cancer movement. Peggy Orenstein's nine-page exposé in *The New York Times Magazine,* "Our Feel-Good War on Breast Cancer," is an indicator of change (Orenstein 2013). But shifting the breast cancer paradigm requires people to look deeper, learn more, share, resist, act, and support those organizing for change. The first step is to notice. Then, ask questions.

If you want to move *beyond awareness,* please visit my website (GayleSulik.com) to find links to my "Pink Ribbon Blues" blog (www.pinkribbonblues.org) and the Breast Cancer Consortium (www.breastcancerconsortium.net), an international network I started in 2012 to promote collaborative efforts aimed at increasing the public's understanding of the societal factors affecting breast cancer and using that knowledge to improve the system.

Join the movement. Change the paradigm.

NOTES

1. The term "female" is intentionally used here to denote the biological underpinnings associated with woman as body.

2. We are now realizing that less may be more when it comes to medical interventions (Bleyer and Welch 2012; Love 2005; Moynihan and Cassels 2005).

3. Gene patents were finally deemed unconstitutional by the Supreme Court in June 2013.

REFERENCES

Adams, Lisa Bonchek. 2013. A particular kind of hope. *Lisa Bonchek Adams* (blog), September 23, http://lisabadams.com/2013/09/23/particular-kind-hope/.

Baralt, Lori, and Tracy Weitz. 2012. The Komen-Planned Parenthood controversy: Bringing the politics of breast cancer advocacy to the forefront. *Women's Health Issues* 22:509-12.

Bartky, Sandra Lee. 1988. Foucault, femininity, and the modernization of patriarchal power. In *Feminism and Foucault: Reflections on resistance*, edited by Irene Diamond and Lee Quinby. Boston: Northeastern University Press.

Batt, Sharon. 1994. *Patient no more: The politics of breast cancer.* Charlottetown, P.E.I., Canada: Gynergy Books.

Belkin, Lisa. 1996. How breast cancer became this year's hot charity. *The New York Times Magazine,* December 22.

Bleyer, Arehie, and H. Gilbert Welch. 2012. Effects of three decades of screening mammography on breast-cancer incidence. *New England Journal of Medicine* 367:1998-2005.

Boehmer, Ulrike. 2000. *The personal and the political: Women's activism in response to the breast cancer and AIDS epidemic.* New York: State University of New York Press.

Clarke, Laura Hurd, and Meredith Griffin. 2008. Visible and invisible ageing: Beauty work as a response to ageism. *Ageing and Society* 28: 653-74.

Dellinger, Kirsten, and C. Christine Williams. 1997. Makeup at work: Negotiating appearance rules in the workplace. *Gender & Society* 11:151-77.

Ehrenreich, Barbara. 2001. Welcome to cancerland: A mammogram leads to a cult of pink kitsch. *Harper's Magazine,* November.

Ehrenreich, Barbara, and Deirdre English. 1989. *For her own good: 150 years of the experts' advice to women.* New York: Anchor Books.

Fernandez, Sandy. 1998. Pretty in pink. *MAMM magazine,* June/July.

Ferraro, Susan. 1993. You can't look away anymore. *The New York Times Magazine,* August 15.

Franzoi, Stephen. 2001. Is female body esteem shaped by benevolent sexism? *Sex Roles* 44:177-88.

Funk, Kristi. 2013. A patient's journey: Angelina Jolie. *Pink Lotus Breast Center* (blog). http://pinklotusbreastcenter.com/breast-cancer-101/2013/05/a-patients-journey-angelina-jolie.

Goldenberg, Maya. 2010. Working for the cure: Challenging pink ribbon activism. In *Configuring health consumers: Health work and the imperative of personal responsibility,* edited by Roma Harris, Nadine Wathen, and Sally Wyatt. Amsterdam: Palgrave Macmillan.

Howlader, N., A. M. Noone, M. Krapcho, J. Garshell, N. Neyman, S. F. Altekruse, C. L. Kosary, M. Yu, J. Ruhl, Z. Tatalovich, H. Clio, A. Mariotto, D. R. Lewis, H. S. Chen, E. J. Feuer, and K. A. Cronin, eds. 2013. *SEER cancer statistics review, 1975-2010.* Bethesda, MD: National Cancer Institute, April, http://seer.cancer.gov/csr/1975_2010. Based on November 2012 SEER data submission.

Kasper, Anne, and Susan Ferguson, eds. 2000. *Breast cancer: Society shapes an epidemic.* New York: Palgrave.

Katz Rothman, Barbara. 2006. Genetic technology and women. In *Women, gender, and technology,* edited by Mary Frank Fox, Deborah G. Johnson, and Sue V. Rosser. Urbana: University of Illinois Press.

King, Samandia. 2006. *Pink ribbons, inc.: Breast cancer and the politics of philanthropy.* Minneapolis: University of Minnesota Press.

Klawiter, Maren. 2004. Breast cancer in two regimes: The impact of social movements on illness experience. *Sociology of Health & Illness* 26: 845-74.

Leopold, Ellen. 1999. *A darker ribbon: Breast cancer, women, and their doctors in the twentieth century.* Boston: Beacon Press.

Leopold, Ellen. 2014. *My soul is among lions: Pages from the breast cancer archives.* Charleston, SC: Valley Green Press.

Lerner, Barron. 2001. *The cancer wars: Hope, fear, and the pursuit of a cure in twentieth-century America.* New York: Oxford University Press.

Ley, Barbara. 2009. *From pink to green: Disease prevention and the environmental breast cancer movement.* New Brunswick, NJ: Rutgers University Press.

Lorber, Judith, and Lisa Jean Moore. 2002. *Gender and the social construction of illness.* New York: Altamira.

Lorde, Audre. 1980. *The cancer journals.* San Francisco: Spinster, Aunt Lute.

Love, Susan. 2005. *Dr. Susan Love's breast book.* New York: Addison-Wesley.

Marchetto, Marisa Acocella. 2009. *Cancer Vixen: A true story.* New York: Knopf Doubleday.

Matuschka. 1993. Why I did it. *Glamour,* November.

Merendino, Angelo. 2010. *The battle we didn't choose: My wife's fight with breast cancer.* http://mywifesfightwithbreastcancer.com.

Morgen, Sandra. 2002. *Into our own hands: The women's health movement in the United States, 1969-1990.* New Brunswick, NJ: Rutgers University Press.

Moynihan, Ray, and Alan Cassels. 2005. *Selling sickness: How the world's biggest pharmaceutical companies are turning us all into patients.* New York: Nation Books.

Mukherjee, Siddhartha. 2010. *The emperor of all maladies: A biography of cancer.* New York: Simon & Schuster.

National Cancer Institute. 2012. National Cancer Institute fact sheet: Breast cancer risk in American women, http://www.cancer.gov/cancertopics/factsheet/detection/probability-breast-cancer.

Orenstein, Peggy. 2013. Our feel-good war on breast cancer. *The New York Times Magazine,* April 25.

Pancreatic Cancer Action. 2014. Latest official statement from Ali Stunt at Pancreatic Cancer Action, http://pancreaticcanceraction.org/community/blog/latest-official-statement-ali-stunt-pancreatic-cancer-action.

Pool, Léa. 2011. *Pink ribbons, inc.* Saint Laurent, QC: National Film Board of Canada, 2012 DVD.

PR Newswire. 2003. Ford and Lilly Pulitzer "tie up" to fight breast cancer, May 8, http://www.prnewswire.com/news-releases/ford-and-lilly-pulitzer-tie-up-to-fight-breast-cancer-55580127.html.

Ruzek, Sheryl Burt. 1978. *The women's health movement: Feminist alternatives to medical control.* New York: Praeger.

Self. 2004. The Cure Card. December.

Skinner, Daniel. 2012. The gendering of cancer survivorship. *Health, Culture and Society* 3:64-76.

Sontag, Susan. 2001. *Illness as metaphor and AIDS and its metaphors.* New York: Picador.

Spanier, Bonnie. 2010. Science and politics of breast cancer activism: The power of feminist science coupled with evidence-based medicine. In *Ethik-Geschlecht-Medizin: Koerpergeschichten in politischer Reflexion. Internationale Frauen- und Genderforschung in Niedersachsen. Teilband 6 (Ethics-gender-medicine: Narrations of the body in political reflection. International Women's and Gender Studies in Lower Saxony, volume 6,* edited by Ernst Waltraud. Berlin/ Muenster/ Wien/Zuerich/London: LIT.

Sulik, Gayle. 2011a. *Pink ribbon blues. How breast cancer culture undermines women's health.* New York: Oxford University Press.

Sulik, Gayle. 2011b. Boobies, for fun & profit. Oxford University Press (blog), April 28, http://blog.oup.com/2011/04/boobies.

Sulik, Gayle. 2012a. Is Susan G. Komen cleaning house? *Ms.* (blog), August 9, http://msmagazine.com/blog/2012/08/09/is-susan-g-komen-cleaning-house.

Sulik, Gayle. 2012b. Bringing on the pink. *Philadelphia Inquirer,* October 31.

Sulik, Gayle. 2012c. Do sexy breast cancer campaigns demean women? *Psychology Today* (blog), November 21, http://www.psychologytoday.com/blog/pink-ribbon-blues/201211/do-sexy-breast-cancer-campaigns-demean-women.

Sulik, Gayle. 2013a. Cause marketing is not philanthropy. *Psychology Today* (blog), October 27, http://www.psychologytoday.com/blog/

pink-ribbon-blues/201310/cause-marketing-is-not-philanthropy.

Sulik, Gayle. 2013b. The mammogram myth, alive and well on *Good Morning America*. *Psychology Today* (blog), November 14, http://www.psychologytoday.com/blog/pink-ribbon-blues/201311/the-mammogram-myth-alive-and-well-good-morning-america.

Sulik, Gayle. 2013c. Angelina Jolie and the one percent. *Scientific American* (blog), May 20, http://blogs.scientificamerican.com/guest-blog/2013/05/20/angelina-jolie-and-the-one-percent.

Sulik, Gayle. 2013d. Why Jolie's cancer test costs so much. *CNN*, May 24.

Sulik, Gayle. 2013e. What cancer survivorship means. *Virtual Mentor. American Medical Association Journal of Ethics* 15:697-703.

Sulik, Gayle. 2013f. The she-ro. *Psychology Today* (blog), September 29, http://www.psychologytoday.com/blog/pink-ribbon-blues/201309/the-she-ro.

Sulik, Gayle. 2014. The cause marketing dilemma. *Psychology Today* (biog), April 24, http://www.psychologytoday.com/blog/pink-ribbon-blues/201404/the-cause-marketing-dilemma.

Sulik, Gayle, Carrie Cameron, and Richard Chamberlain. 2012. The future of the cancer prevention education workforce: Why health literacy, advocacy, and stakeholder collaborations matter. *Journal of Cancer Education* 27:165-72.

Sulik, Gayle, and Amber Deane. 2008. Coping in pink: Representations of breast cancer support and survivorship in women's magazines. Paper presented at Annual Meeting, American Sociological Association, Boston.

Sulik, Gayle, and Astrid Eich-Krohm. 2008. No longer a patient: The social construction of the medical consumer. In *Advances in medical sociology, volume 10: Patients, consumers and civil society,* edited by Susan Chambré and Melinda Goldner. Bingley, UK: Emerald Group.

Sulik, Gayle, and Bonnie Spanier. 2014. Time to debunk the mammography myth. *CNN*, March 18.

Time. 2002. The new thinking on breast cancer, February 18.

Time. 2007. Why breast cancer is spreading around the world, October 15.

Yalom, Marilyn. 1997. *A history of the breast.* Toronto, Ontario, Canada: Ballantine.

Introduction to Reading 25

Kyle Green and Madison Van Oort study the representations of gender within advertising with a special focus on men and advertising. Their research adds to the literature on the ways in which advertising disseminates dominant definitions of masculinity in the United States. In this study, they do a careful analysis of the 2010 Super Bowl commercials and show how advertisers engaged men's fears about their physical bodies and their relationship to success to urge them to take charge of their bodies and their manhood by buying specific products.

1. What is the "crisis of masculinity" trope and how was it used by advertisers in the 2010 Super Bowl commercials?

2. How did Dockers use "failed bodies" as a sign of middle-class failure and loss of patriarchal status?

3. How does homophobia play a role in the commercials examined by the authors?

"We Wear No Pants"

Selling the Crisis of Masculinity in the 2010 Super Bowl Commercials

Kyle Green and Madison Van Oort

Our interest in the representation of gender within advertising, and specifically men and advertising, follows a long lineage of social and feminist scholars who have called for greater attention to the role that institutions of consumer culture play in the construction of masculine identities (e.g., Patterson and Elliott 2002; Schroeder and Zwick 2004). In particular, we build on the work of Michael A. Messner and Jeffrey Montez de Oca (2005), who trace the different narratives of masculinity in Super Bowl beer commercials and *Sports Illustrated* print advertisements from 2002 and 2003. Messner and Montez de Oca analyze the then newfound emergence of the lovable happy loser trope of masculinity in advertising, which depicted scrawny, nerdy men who fail to get the girl but who can still have a good laugh and a cold brew with their buds. For instance, one commercial in their analysis shows two men getting caught spying on a women's yoga class, as well as a man getting punched in the face by a woman after delivering an unintentionally offensive pickup line. Messner and Montez de Oca claim that this happy loser is "caught between the excesses of a hypermasculinity that is often discredited and caricatured in popular culture and the increasing empowerment of women, people of color, and homosexuals [and is] simultaneously undercut by the postindustrial economy" (2005, 1905). But how does this character hold up eight years later?

While the lovable loser trope continues to hold sway in popular TV shows like *King of Queens* or "bromance" movies like *Knocked Up* and *Forty-Year-Old Virgin*, the 2009 and 2010 Super Bowl commercials show a shift in how that trope is deployed. In 2009, men are both physically and emotionally vulnerable, but supposedly okay in the end. Distinct from the men in Messner and Montez de Oca's (2005) commercials, these men are not losers only in their inability to attract women, who are notably absent as sexual objects here, but also in relation to more general expectations of normative masculinity concerning physical prowess and economic security. The 2010 commercials, in contrast, express a profound aggression in reaction to the supposed failure of attempts to properly perform masculinity. The loser, instead of appearing endearing or laughable, is illustrated as a delusional dope—pitiful, stupid, and downright disgusting. No longer lovable despite his flaws, the male loser becomes in 2010 a frighteningly pathetic victim of collective delusions.

Our goal for this article is to examine the narrative of the crisis of masculinity in the 2010 Super Bowl commercials. We begin with a review of literature on advertising, gender, and the body. Next, we discuss a few commercials from 2009, highlighting the distinct ways in which elements of the crisis narrative begin to emerge through humorous injuries and nostalgia for childhood joys. We then engage in detailed analysis of three key commercials from 2010, in attempts to illuminate their strikingly overt

From Green, Kyle, and Van Oort, Madison. 2013. "We wear no pants." Selling the crisis of masculinity in the 2010 Super Bowl commercials. *Signs, 38*(3), 695–719.

attempt at mass marketing a crisis of masculinity. While advertising does not generally undergo such drastic shifts, instead moving along with slow-changing social norms, we find a surprising distance between the discourse Messner and Montez de Oca examine in 2003 and what we observe in 2010.

THE DISCURSIVE STRUCTURE OF ADVERTISING

In studying commercials we seek to explore the meaning attached to the products being sold and how advertising not only caters to but produces a particular group of consumers. Advertising has served as a key site for the dissemination of dominant discourses on masculinity [1] As Michel Foucault explains, discourse can be understood as "practices that systematically form the objects of which they speak" (1972, 49). We focus on how discourse guides the meanings of certain images—like the portrayal of the lovable (male) loser. This approach does not treat advertising agencies as the sole-creators of discourses on gender. Rather, they play a key role in filtering and disseminating discourse, and in doing so, they aid in stabilizing and building upon existing public sentiment. As Raymond Williams writes, "It must not be assumed that magicians—in this case, advertising agents—disbelieve their own magic. They may have limited professional cynicism about it, from knowing how some of the tricks are done. But fundamentally they are involved, with the rest of the society, in the confusion to which magical gestures are a response" ([1980] 2005, 193).

When looking at the crisis of the masculinity theme within the 2010 Super Bowl commercials, we do not argue that the crisis of masculinity exists as an objective fact of the social world that is merely reflected in advertising. In fact, we generally agree with Rosalind Gill, Karen Henwood, and Carl McLean (2005), who criticize crisis-inspired analyses for reifying the crisis of masculinity by grouping together a number of social forces not necessarily related. Judith

Halberstam similarly excoriates men's studies scholars for not "taking apart the patriarchal bonds between white maleness and privilege; they are much more concerned to detail the fragilities of male socialization, the pains of manhood, and the fear of female empowerment" (1998, 19). Drawing from these critiques, we by no means give full credence to the idea of the crisis, any more than we argue that the crisis of masculinity is simply the construction of a puppet-master media. Rather, we treat the crisis of masculinity, especially as it comes together in the Super Bowl, as a prominent discursive construction that is a powerful force in commonsense understandings of masculinity.

In popular culture, sport has long been viewed as a bastion of masculinity and a site for the transmission and reproduction of what it means to be a man (Messner 1992; Burstyn 1999; Connell 2000), which makes sporting events singularly attractive to advertisers seeking the elusive young male demographic. For instance, the symbiotic relationship between beer, sports, and hegemonic masculinity has reached such heights that Lawrence A. Wenner and Steven Jackson (2009) described it as "a holy trinity" (25). Football, and the Super Bowl especially, serves as a particularly popular site for advertisements targeting men. We therefore treat the emergence of a discourse within Super Bowl advertisements as a seal of approval—a moment where the discourse ascends to the realm of other dominant discourses about what it means to be a man.

CRAFTING THE CRISIS OF MASCULINITY AS A CONSUMABLE TROPE

Advertising, as a function of discourse, shapes what is knowable about social life and gender relations (Jhally 1987, 135). A large body of scholarship critiques the way advertisements depict women as passive subjects, needy girlfriends, or sexual objects to be consumed or won over by active men.[2] Women are active only to the extent that they must constantly monitor their bodies and work to make them more attractive. Even when women appear to defy gender roles, through drinking, smoking, or wearing masculine clothing, they are shown as merely imitating rather than challenging dominant masculinity (Barthel 1989). Thus, advertising largely reinforces sexist depictions of women.

Since the 1980s, however, advertisers have paid increasing attention to men as consumers of identity-related products (Patterson and Elliott 2002; Schroeder and Zwick 2004). In particular, there has been an exponential growth in advertising that seeks to build upon insecurities by encouraging men to view their own bodies as inadequate and in need of consumer-based improvements (Atkinson 2008). Advertisers have shaped masculinities to embrace styles and pleasures that were previously viewed as socially undesirable (Nixon 1996); beyond the "holy trinity," products like body wash, weight loss supplements, deodorant, and clothing are now being mass-marketed to male consumers. Whether this is an inversion of the male gaze (Patterson and Elliott 2002) or an expansion of it (Schroeder and Zwick 2004), it is clear that John Berger's famous observation that "men act and women appear. Men look at women. Women watch themselves being looked at" (1972, 45) no longer rings as true.

Susan Bordo's tour de force examination of the male body, *The Male Body: A New Look at Men in Public and in Private* (1999), chronicles the increasing visibility of and societal pressures on men. To be a man is to be hard in body and emotion, never showing pain, emotion, suffering, or physical weakness. The increased presence of nearly naked male models in advertising and the proliferation of men's "health" magazines ensure that eating disorders affect more than just women (Bordo 1999, 218). However, unlike the all-but-naked women that have become ubiquitous in television and print, the pressure is not for men to invoke sex through vulnerability. Rather, with men, dignity and strength remain: "the bodies are a kind of natural armor" (Bordo 1999, 30). The men of advertising are not objects ready to be simply enjoyed; their muscular exoskeleton and aggressive posture ensure that the audience does

not forget that even in their current state of undress, the potential to dominate remains.

The current rendition of the crisis shares elements with the men's movements that arose during the 1980s—another time of insecurity that was more directly linked to the success of the feminist movement (Patterson and Elliott 2002, 235). Although not a uniform collective, with various subfactions like men's rights, mythopoetic, and profeminist men's movements, the cohesive element was a stated desire to repair the damage that had been done to men and their masculinity within the United States. The participants, often affluent, white males, attempted to restore the power, control, and independence once afforded to them by mainstream society by returning to a "lost era when men were men" (Kimmell and Kaufman 1995, 18). And again advertisers were quick to capitalize, presenting images in leisure magazines of hypermasculine men with bulging muscles (Connell 1987; Rutherford 1988). Of course, the idea of a crisis of masculinity in the United States is not a new concept now, nor was it a new concept in the 1980s.[3] It would be a fallacy to suggest that advertisers had never recognized the potential to shape, and cater to, particular masculinities by emphasizing a return to traditional power dynamics.[4]

In this study, we therefore seek to add to existing literature on gender and advertising by conducting a close, critical reading of the 2010 Super Bowl commercials. What does the marketing of masculinity look like in this contemporary moment? Which discursive tropes remain unchanged, and which new elements are being brought to the fore? What might these media strategies mean for gender relations in the United States? We illustrate the drama and the sensationalism advertisers use in these commercials to narrate a renewed crisis of masculinity, with a fierce emphasis on the importance of the physical body.

METHODS

For this project, we watched every Super Bowl commercial presented from 2008 to 2010. We paid particular attention to the company, type of product, characters portrayed (in terms of race, class, and gender), dominant messages and themes, and discursive strategies employed (i.e., violence or humor) in the commercials. In analyzing our commercials we draw inspiration from semiotic analysis, and in particular from Judith Williamson's now classic semiotic study *Decoding Advertisements* (1978). Semiotics approaches focus on understanding signs, which are, in most simple terms, objects or images imbued with social meaning. Semiotic analysis allows us to pay attention to the ways in which layers of meaning become mapped and remapped onto the mundane, and as such, we see ourselves as archeologists of meaning, peeling back the layers of signs. These archeological formations are always changing, albeit slowly, while other images and meanings stick together for longer periods of time. . . .

It follows that our sampling is theoretical and purposive rather than representative in nature, since we seek to analyze a significant discursive theme and its semiotic workings. We analyze three paradigmatic commercials from 2010 and two from 2009, chosen because they all strongly suggest a broad crisis of masculinity of some kind. Traces of similar themes may be found in Super Bowl commercials from other years, but our viewing of commercials from a wide range of years, combined with other existing research on Super Bowl advertisements, suggests that the prominence of the crisis of masculinity trope in 2010 is indeed highly notable.

We do not argue that our semiotic-based reading of the commercials is absolute, nor do we suggest it is the only correct one. No semiotic analysis can achieve this level of objectivity, as different viewers will bring differing histories and orientations to the project of interpretation. We approach the commercials as two individuals trained to be sociologists, each with an interest in gender and its intersections with other social categories. We agree with visual studies scholars Jonathan E. Schroeder and Janet L. Borgerson that "for describing complex, sexually infused representations, symbols and signs offer a more comprehensive method than discrete content analysis" (1998, 163). What semiotics lacks in scientific objectivity, it makes up for in its

in-depth focus on meaning and context, drawing on a variety of theoretical traditions, including Marxism, literary theory, and psychoanalysis (Rose 2001). We additionally turn to queer theory to more fully understand the role of sexuality in our sample. We hope that through a rich analysis of these Super Bowl commercials, we can demonstrate their significance and stimulate further conversation about contemporary constructions of gender and sexuality in the United States.

2009: Don't Worry, the Men Are Fine

In the few years prior to 2010, the commercials were marked by a dominant humorous theme: men get hurt in an extremely violent manner but rise at the end to claim that they are okay. Margaret C. Duncan and Alan Aycock (2009) previously examined this theme's emergence in the 2008 Super Bowl commercials, and below we highlight a similar case from 2009, Pepsi Max's "I'm Good." These commercials begin to hint at men's lack and insecurity: Men everywhere are being challenged, here even being physically injured. In 2008 and 2009, after suffering a direct and painful affront, they reassure the audience that they are okay (although the damage is such that survival, much less escape from injury, is difficult to believe). Our second example, Universal Studios' "Universal Heroes," criticizes the monotony of the corporate ladder, telling men to seek temporary escape, with their families, to a land of physical play. The messages here remain somewhat restrained, and only in 2010 will the men of the ads explicitly acknowledge their collective displacement in the American gendered imaginary.

Pepsi Max's "I'm Good" (2009)

Pepsi Max offers a commercial with variations on a simple plot: three male friends are hanging out, one gets hurt (either because of his own stupidity or that of his friend), but he ultimately claims he is okay. The commercial starts with three men in a suburban garage, full of tools and complete with a stuffed fish adorning the back wall. Two hefty men stand on one side of the garage talking, while their friend on the other side saws a long piece of wood. The wood suddenly flies out from behind the saw, shoots across the garage, and hits a man in the back. A close-up shot shows the plaid shirted, messy-haired victim raise his hand and say, "I'm good!" Queer theory is helpful here in describing how hegemonic masculinity relies on displacing men's penetrability onto others, especially women and homosexuals (Thomas 2002). Throughout the commercial, the men repeatedly get blasted from behind, often with phallic objects like the piece of wood or a golf club, which likely signify threats that heterosexual men face to their masculinity on a daily basis.

The theme repeats in various traditionally guys'-club locations—the golf course, the bowling alley, the limo during a guys' night out—until finally we return to the first bastion of masculinity, manual labor. A white man stands on a ladder with an electrical cord hanging from his mouth. "Ready, go!" yells a friend, as a man on the ground flips a switch. The man on the ladder is subsequently shot backward, yelling frantically until he hits his backside on a trailer with a loud thump. "I'm good," the man assures his friends as smoke billows out with each word. The narrator explains, "Men can take anything. Except the taste of diet cola. Until now! Pepsi Max. The first diet cola for men." The audience is presented with the soda can, which shrivels from an imaginary male fist crunching it into submission. The screen returns to the latest injured man, holding the cola can in front of him, soot streaked along his face. "Yeah," the man says to his friend who holds the can to his head. "Feels good."

The Pepsi Max commercial presents a familiar narrative of the funny, lovable loser, much like those sketched out in earlier years (Messner and Montez de Oca 2005). The audience sees men fail repeatedly after engaging in foolish activity. The taste of diet cola, something long associated with women and dieting, is something that will not satisfy men. Yet the images in the commercial do not show men being dissatisfied but physically attacked from behind, therefore linking men's feminine behavior or metrosexuality (here synonymous with drinking a diet drink) with the more devastating effects of homosexual assault. Semiotically speaking, diet cola is usually part of a sign for femininity, either of women or queer men. Pepsi Max must first alter the figure typically associated with diet cola by focusing the commercial on men. To keep the men from being read as feminine, which they dangerously approach in being assaulted from behind, they must also show men being okay, drinking Pepsi Max and displaying power by crushing the can.

But even as they are threatened, men can always revert to the safe space of regular (not diet) cola, wherein safety connotes something that is soothing (as the cool can comforts the injured man) in its very ability to be dominated (as the can is crunched). These images likewise signify the safe space of patriarchal domination, in which men can seek comfort in women while still being able to dominate them. This precise combination allows men to find safety in an apparently unsafe world. As men struggle to maintain their masculinity in other arenas, as the injured men humorously depict, Pepsi Max offers a place to seek comfort without admission of any pain. In fact, they assure us they are okay. And like Messner's lovable losers, the men suffer, or deny suffering, *with* their buddies. However, unlike the case of the lovable losers, their assurance that they are okay seems forced, an act of denial rather than true satisfaction. Of course, this denial is the source of the comedic value of the commercial, as it unveils how men are expected to hide their pain. Since the men here do not yet explicitly suffer from a crisis, as we will see in 2010, there is no explicit call to action.

Universal Studios' "Universal Heroes" (2009)

While Pepsi Max shows, but denies, male vulnerability, the Universal Studios' 2009 Super Bowl ad links vulnerability more directly to men's dissatisfaction with the corporate world.

In this commercial a young, pudgy boy wanders a busy city street dressed as a superhero. The ad sets up a heavy-handed opposition between play and the business world—the colorful child wandering against the ride of faceless, nondescript businesspeople dressed in drab gray and black who walk briskly in the other direction. In his makeshift costume, he engages in fantasy in the few urban spaces not oriented toward business, leaping from a bench in an empty park and running down a dark alley. We soon learn that he represents a powerful businessman's inner child. A grown man stares out of his office window, brow drawn, lips clenched. The two stare at each other with eerily similar blue eyes, but the man looks forlorn. The man embodies the capitalist success story, yet something is clearly lacking, and the child reminds him of a time when dreaming about being a hero was fun. After the businessman answers the call of his inner child, we see him enjoying the thrills of a roller coaster ride with his wife and daughter. And the bright colors, here clearly invoking the excitement and vitality of a youthful outlook, are once more present for the adult man. Universal Studios is a place where men can once again discover their inner superhero, whether flexing like the Hulk or arm-wrestling Popeye.

Like the Pepsi Max commercial, Universal Studios portrays men as having lost something they need to reclaim. Similar to what we will observe in 2010, there is a disconnect between social pressures and the unhappiness that results from trying to meet those expectations. However, the commercial calls not for a return to power and seriousness but for a temporary escape to a liminal space where childhood joys can be recaptured (and where the family is brought along on the ride). The man regrets something about his success but is not running scared. What he lacks are the simple joys one can experience outside of the quest for power. The semiotic meaning of the successful businessman and that of the playful child, normally mutually exclusive, are here linked through the body as both man and child flex their biceps in the classic bodybuilder pose. The theme park is not simply a place where men become children; it is also a place to enforce a corporeal brand of masculinity by testing their strength against superheroes as their children watch. The 2010 Super Bowl commercials build on this orientation toward the body, offering a much sharper narrative of individualism and crisis.

2010: THE YEAR OF MEN

The Super Bowl, of course, has always been about men. The commercials, long filled with objects of desire (like beer and attractive women), have made little room for anything else. In 2010, though, men do not relish in their masculinity but instead scramble to salvage it. Numerous blogs and media outlets also caught on to the strong gender messages: feminist gossip blog *Jezebel* said the commercials sung the "woes of bros" (Smith 2010), *Slate* thought the misogyny was "rawer and angrier than usual" (Stevenson 2010), and the *Washington Post* pondered the "perpetual fear of emasculation" (Shales 2010).

The nuances of the crisis crystallize when situated within a broader socio-political context. Dominant masculinity in the United States is intertwined with nationalism and patriotism (Connell 2000), and in turn the 2010 Super Bowl commercials cannot be analyzed without taking into consideration the lingering economic recession. Beginning in 2008, the most recent economic crisis in the United States has shaken individual lives, knocking millions out of their jobs and onto the streets. Numerous studies emerged in 2009 and 2010 claiming that the downturn more strongly hit men, with more women in the service sector holding onto their jobs, going so far as to dub the recession the "mancession" (Thompson 2009). Psychological studies pointed to increasing depression among men, stemming from their anxiety about maintaining their breadwinning role (Daily Mail Reporter 2009; Dunlop and Mletzko 2011). However, we now know that a veritable recovery is taking over the supposed mancession, with women more slowly regaining employment (Kochar 2011). The mancession concept likewise obscures the extent to which men of color have long faced higher unemployment levels than whites (Lui et al. 2006; Cawthorne 2009), allowing us to reiterate the extent to which the crisis of masculinity as we see it in these Super Bowl commercials is a crisis of almost exclusively white middle-class masculinity.

In such a moment of perceived crisis, popular media could either place a newfound value on minority masculinities (see Halberstam's 2005 analysis of British masculinity, the unstable economic climate, and *The Full Monty*) or it could continue to use humor as a tool for attempting to uphold a masculinity now in peril. Part of the reason the 2010 Super Bowl commercials followed the latter path may also have something to do with an unmistakable right-wing backlash, most notably through the rise of the Tea Party movement. Not surprisingly, in addition to the commercials we analyze below, the 2010 Super Bowl included a pro-life advertisement from conservative football player Tim Tebow, while denying commercial airtime to a gay online dating service (CBS News 2010; Plocher 2010).

Perhaps unsurprisingly, nostalgia served an important role in comforting the aging male population through humor while reminding them of better times. For instance, a cell phone company remade the "Super Bowl Shuffle" rap, which was originally performed in 1985 by that year's Super Bowl champions, the Chicago Bears. Only this time, instead of rapping about being smooth or protecting their neighborhoods, the aging men, once revered for their strength, power, and unmatched ferocity, joke about their failing bodies. One player raps: "I still could play, if my groin didn't feel like paper maché. But it does. Ain't gettin any better." Even as older viewers laugh, their physical failure is brought to their attention. The younger generation is provided a warning of their bodies' impending failure, setting the stage for calls for more active and immediate action to reinforce their dominance.

The following three 2010 Super Bowl commercials serve as exemplars of the crisis, highlighting the theme of the diminishing power of men and men's bodies in contemporary society.

The significant differences in the commercials lie in how this crisis is explained. The first commercial, Dockers' "Wear No Pants," makes implied assumptions about class and body power. Next, Career Builders' "Casual Fridays" more explicitly lays blame on contemporary economic structures and cultures of flexibility and informality. Finally, Dodge Charger's "Man's Last Stand" overtly points to a combination of economic, cultural, and familial relations in disempowering middle-class men. It is in this last instance that the men most aggressively blame women for their unbearable pains.

Dockers' "I Wear No Pants" (2010)

A stout, pantless, middle-aged white man marches across the savanna. "I wear no pants!" he sings. Another pudgy man proudly sings along from another spot in the grass. "I wear, I wear, I wear no pants!" Finally, the group coalesces. The pack of fifteen pantless men march and shout, alone in the prairie. They are oblivious to their location, or the fact that birds ominously soar above their heads, cawing in warning. "Calling all men," an authoritarian narrator interrupts as the shot sweeps to a faceless, statuesque man standing in front of a brick wall. "It's time to wear the pants."

A closer reading of this commercial reveals the importance of men's bodies and their relationship to success. The failed men have soft, unkempt bodies. And while nature has long been seen as something for male domination, here the men roam aimlessly, as if they are animals themselves. The discursive implication is clear: The pantless men symbolize the professional class of men suffering from a shared delusion. They celebrate without shame, enjoying the open air in untucked dress shirts and underwear, an image usually used in movies to depict women following sex. These bodies signify failure on various levels: Their middle-class status offers them no protection from the more primitive dangers of the natural world; their lack of pants implies their inability to head their families; and finally, the homosocial men quite literally dance on the border of homosexuality.

Most broadly, the failed bodies act as a sign of middle-class failure, leaving the men unable to dominate their surroundings or maintain their ideal muscular physique. The juxtaposition of the failing group of middle-class men with the clearly working-class single figure at the end—who is muscular, wearing a T-shirt and jeans, and safely bounded by the man-made brick wall—might initially be read as a desire to return to working-class status. However, we argue that the working-class man is less a sign of the working class itself than a sign of a particular masculine lifestyle. Men can still make money *and* wear Dockers, for as Williamson writes: "Products are thus set up as being able to *buy* things *you* cannot buy. This puts them in a position of replacing you. They do things you can't do, for you" (1978, 38). Thus middle-class men can still retain their capitalist gains without sacrificing the patriarchal power of wearing the pants. So while this commercial implies a waning of power for middle-class men, it calls on men to renew their power precisely through the capitalist system that failed them.

Finally, the failing bodies in the Dockers' commercials are used as a caution against homosexuality. As the men are oblivious to the dangers of wandering the field, their painlessness presents an even more imminent danger in their unprotected derrieres. Advertisements commonly focus on female rear ends, as women and queer men have long been associated with penetrability (Thomas 2002). In this commercial, Dockers transfers that semiotic meaning onto common men, which comes into full view with the shot of fifteen saggy male butts in close contact with each other, signifying the growing acceptance of homosexuality and its outed presence in daily life.

This shot, of course, juxtaposes the solitary idyllic figure at the end, who rotates like a car on display, signifying straight masculinity. More important, though, the model figure never rotates in a complete 360-degree turn; never is his butt—the ultimate signifier of vulnerability, penetrability, and homosexuality—revealed. In 2009, the men in Pepsi Max were assaulted from behind but were ultimately okay. In 2010, though, Dockers instead creates crisis by unequivocally associating men

with penetrability and queerness, only to juxtapose them with the sign of "real" manhood, an impenetrable man in Dockers. Contrary to the portrayal of lovable losers and mythopoetic men, who sought solace in male friendship, Dockers tells men to be wary of homosocial behavior; only individualism can ensure total protection from homosexuality. While previous research indicates that mass media has in some ways become more queer friendly by showing more queer or potentially queer images (Schroeder and Zwick 2004; Tsai 2010), the Dockers commercial aggressively responds, signifying that successful masculinity is not only white, strong, and middle class but also unequivocally straight.

CareerBuilder's "Casual Fridays" (2010)

CareerBuilder, an Internet-based job search company, provides another humorous presentation of the erosion of traditional values in "Casual Fridays." The commercial opens with Terry, a rather ordinary-looking white man in a blue polo shirt, drinking a cup of coffee. His shoulders slump, his goatee shows signs of gray, and his body is beginning to sag. In the background we see a typical office, except the employees are wearing only their underwear. As the main character begins to explain his plight, his tone conveying defeat, "when I first started here . . .," an old man in his underwear pushes a mail cart up to his desk and stops to sort the mail. The main character shields his eyes and explains, "I was like, casual Friday, awesome." From this opening scene we learn that the man is embarrassed by those who have embraced comfort and no longer make an effort to hide their failing, out-of-shape bodies. The commercial successfully invokes a sense of body horror so often seen in advertisements geared toward women, in which average bodies are repulsive and shameful. The lovable loser, we see, is not so lovable in old age but is in fact a cause of disgust.

In another scene, our narrator is greeted by a scrawny man who suavely rests his elbow on the water cooler. Terry bends down to grab his water but avoids grabbing the white cup, which is placed suspiciously close to the other man's white briefs, succeeding in what Williamson identifies as "connecting an object to a person" (1978, 22). The color of the cup and underwear perfectly match, and our narrator decides the risk is too great, for he might mistake the man's crotch for the cup and fall into a possibly queer space. Here, for the first time, we see the coworkers poking fun at the main character for being a prude and not letting his rigid hetero-sexual guard down. Our viewer response is guided by the reaction of the main character, who, instead of being swept along in the fun, is embarrassed and revolted.

The scene shifts to the conference room, where the boss announces, "we've decided to make casual Fridays . . . all week." Everyone in the office, save Terry, cheers and jumps. Two men sandwich Terry's head between their crotches while they stand to high-five, and our narrator again shows physical repulsion at his close proximity to another man's penis. A queer reading of this commercial might point out the joy of the men slamming crotches together, but the underlining point remains Terry's disgust at such behavior. CareerBuilder cashes in on a con-servative backlash, as Terry longs for a return to normative, conservative, and hetero spaces.

"Of course, if it's mandatory, it can't be casual," notes the narrator, now standing alone with his coffee cup. The water cooler coworker begins to walk by, stops, and leans in: "Nice pants, Terry." Terry looks down at his pants and up again at the audience in despair. The tension has reached its climax, as the coworker points out that Terry no longer belongs. "Wearing the pants"—and, in particular, nice pants—comes to stand for everything Terry holds onto: manners, formality, tradition, and control (over his body, his space, and his sexuality). A voice-over states: "Expose yourself to something better. Career-Builder. Start building."

As in "I Wear No Pants," the scantily clad men here are semiotically associated with a new mas-culinity and vulnerability. The underlining message is about a return to "real" masculinity, as Terry, alone in his pants, symbolizes classic hege-monic masculinity, old-time homophobia, and heterosexuality. In one telling scene, the main character is confronted with a fat woman in pearls who rushes past him, flesh and necklace bounc-ing, into the meeting room. He rolls his eyes as he makes a "go ahead" motion with his hand. He appears as disappointed in this woman's body as in the failing male bodies entering his space. The stripped figure thus generally signifies the failure of the strong, male physique, of his presumed heterosexuality (as in the water cooler scene), and of his ability or desire to act on his heterosexual urges (as with the woman in pearls). At the same time, though, CareerBuilder also equates the semiotic meaning of the near-nude men with what is wrong with corporate America. Instead of job insecurity, increasing hours, and declining wages, corporate disappointment is now linked with the changing social order. Universal Studios' "Universal Heroes" (2009) hinted at corporate dissatisfaction but told men simply to take a break, go to an amusement park, arm-wrestle with Popeye. In 2010 a more serious call is made: Put the pants back on, or at least find—or "start building"—a place where wearing the pants is respected.

Dodge Charger's "Man's Last Stand" (2010)

Dodge offered the most explicit example of men's call to action in 2010. Here, instead of suffering from the delusions of Dockers' femi-nized field frolickers, the men individually reclaim what they think is rightfully theirs. The commercial presents head shots of diverse men, all disheveled, standing in traditionally feminine locations: the bedroom, the kitchen, the living room. Each man remains motionless while a narrator laments the daily struggles that men endure in modern life. The narrator, Michael C. Hall, also plays the doctor and serial killer in the TV series *Dexter*. As in Williamson's famous analysis of Catherine Deneuve and Chanel No. 5 (1978), the ad displays an assumption that the product and the celebrity are the same, when in fact the product gains its meaning precisely through the celebrity. In "Man's Last Stand," the Dodge Charger becomes synonymous with aggression through Michael C. Hall (as Dexter)'s voice. While the men in the commercial steer clear of murder, the semiotic association communicated in Hall's narration is obvious, highlighting the dangerously misogynistic tones of the advertisement.

The commercial begins with a shot of an attractive white man lying in bed, eyes open. The man looks straight into the camera and remains motionless as the narrator says, monotonously: "I will walk the dog at 6:30 a.m. I will eat some fruit as part of my breakfast. I will shave. I will clean the sink after I shave." Here, even the most basic domestic responsibilities, cleaning up after oneself, are presented as unreasonable burdens and affronts to masculinity. In general, fruit implies a pressure to be concerned with one's health and appearance, but here fruit further signifies both the feminine—delicate and unreasonable—and the threat to heteronormativity, as fruit is a classic sign for homosexuality.

The body here again signifies middle-class masculinity, but in a slightly different way than in the Dockers or CareerBuilder commercials. In those instances, the flabby, fleshy bodies are torn down in favor of a hard masculinity. This Dodge Charger commercial warns that, perhaps in response to the rising metrosexual image of recent years, too much concern with the body likewise throws men too far into femininity and queerness. These messages about appearance, when taken in tandem with the Dockers and CareerBuilder ads, illustrate somewhat contradictory tensions surrounding the male body. The body, as signifier for patriarchal, heteronormative power, must exude hardness, but not hyperawareness of itself (see also Bordo 1999).

The commercial continues, showing two other equally phlegmatic men while the narrator recites the daily drudgeries of conforming to the demands of work and women: "I will be at work at 8 a.m. . . . I will be civil to your mother." The final scene shows a fit man in a suit standing in front of a fireplace. "I will carry your *lip balm,*" the narrator enunciates with indignation. By now, all the audience can see are his furrowed brow and piercing eyes, a symbol Erving Goffman (1979) links to male aggression and power. "And because I do this . . ."

An engine revs, and the view of the camera switches from being on the men to being from their fantasy viewpoint, inside the car. "I will drive the car I want to drive." As in the Dockers commercial, the ideal man is never fully revealed; his humanity, his emotions, can never be fully accessible. The car speeds away into the distance. "Charger. Man's last stand."

In this commercial, the sports car is a sign of status and escape, a phallic remedy to castration anxiety; men charge their way out of domestic life, running over everything in their path. The relationship between men and car advertising has been well documented (Barthel 1989), but in "Man's Last Stand" Dodge offers a narrative that differs in its level of bitterness and its astonishingly explicit call for escape (rather than getting the girl). The subtitle of the commercial on the Dodge Charger's website is clear: "You've sacrificed a lot, but surely there is a limit to your chivalry. Drive the car you want to drive." While the message presents a call to arms, the conclusion of this commercial is ultimately a sad one; the only solution to men's rage is individual consumption. The men are not shown coming together in resistance, and significantly, the war cry is not *men's* last stand, but *man's* last stand.

The relationship between the narrative message and the images is key to understanding the semiotic sleight of hand that attacks women. The linking between the narrative audio and the images should make a clear symbolic connection between the modern men and domesticity—"I will clean the sink after I shave"—but the anger in the narrator's voice undermines that semiotic connection; men aren't *really* meant to perform these frivolities. When the commercial turns in its conclusion to frantic anger as the engine revs, Dodge breaks the connection between men and femininity, relinking the men with traditional manhood and Dodge Charger. What's more, this semiotic move also points to modern women, who want men to perform a bigger share of housework, as the source of men's anger: "Surely, there is a limit to your chivalry."

While "Man's Last Stand" stands out in its inclusion of women as a source of suffering, it is not the only commercial to emphasize this variable. For instance, Flo TV's "Spineless" commercial . . . serves as a suitable, although less intense, companion. Like the bodies of the men in the Dodge commercial, Jason's body is stationary, lacking any focus of attention. His lone moment of interest, when he sees a football game being shown on a television mounted on the wall, is only temporary as his girlfriend drags him over to an escalator. In this case, instead of escaping to a fast car, the solution is a mobile, handheld television, so that no matter what personal affront he faces, he retains his individual escape to a world of proper masculinity—live sports. Also, similar to the Dockers commercial, a change of clothing is imbued with meaning as Jason is urged to "change out of that skirt."

CONSUMERISM, ANXIETY, AND THE BODY

In this article we argue that an explicit discourse of a crisis of masculinity emerges with the 2010 Super Bowl commercials.[5] By providing in-depth analysis of the commercials, we are able to explicate a number of central themes involved in this crisis, including discontent over the loss of traditional patriarchal status and heteronormative family values, diminishing confidence in failing bodies, and uncertainty over the economy. In 2009, we only see hints of a crisis. Pepsi Max men have their sexuality threatened symbolically, as they are physically assaulted from behind, but ultimately they are okay. Universal Studios shows a man feeling a sharper disconnect between his current position and the fun, but still masculine, freedom of childhood. In this scenario men are reinserted into the family structure, but the goal is joy. The collective call to action in 2010, however, is more obvious: men, we are shown, have been tricked into submissive roles, ultimately wearing away at the once well-established heteronormative patriarchy.

. . . While we provide in-depth discursive analysis of the commercials in the 2009 and 2010 Super Bowl, we are unable to know the extent to which the magic of the advertising succeeds in bedazzling the consumer. Millions of people tune in precisely to view the commercials, becoming active consumers who vote on the best and worst ads of the year. Do the men watching the game heed the call to "wear the pants" or take their "last stand"? Or has their attention already shifted back to their chips and salsa before the final call to arms? To what extent does humor influence the interpretation of these ads? How do women, queer people, or men of color watching these commercials interpret, embody, or resist these messages? How do the images we analyze take on different currencies in contexts outside the United States? Although we feel that these commercials in themselves bear examination, future research should examine reactions to this widely consumed advertising event. . . .

NOTES

1. "Discourse" is a term that is often used but less frequently understood. This is in part due to the varied usage of the term by different methodological and theoretical approaches. We understand discourse analysis as a study of power that explicates how knowledge and ways of seeing the world are organized. See Mills (1997) for an excellent introduction to the term and its varied use.

2. See Goffman (1979), Barthel (1989), Stern (1993), Bordo (1999), and Shields (2002).

3. Muscular Christianity and the founding of the Boy Scouts serve as two examples of attempts to save white masculinity in the late nineteenth and early twentieth century. See Kimmel (1996), Putney (2001), and Denny (2011).

4. The historical reach of the marketing of the crisis of masculinity is demonstrated in Kenon Breazeale's examination of how *Esquire* grew by packaging and selling misogyny during the Depression era (1994). Leisure became "a buzzword among Roosevelt braintrusters who hoped that commodifying the free time attendant on a reduced work week would lead to more consumer spending," but *Esquire* simultaneously had to underline women as objects of desire whose attempts to prepare dinner could not match male *Esquire* readers' sophisticated and refined (but certainly not feminine) palates (3). In that case, however, the male body was not emphasized as a key element of masculinity.

5. Following Foucault, we do not see history as a steady, linear march. As Sara Mills explains, for

Foucault "there is not a seamless narrative which we can decipher underlying history, nor is there any continuity at all. He argues for seeing history as shifting and lurching" (1997, 23). We see this Super Bowl as a moment of discursive rupture.

REFERENCES

Atkinson, Michael. 2008. "Exploring Male Femininity in the 'Crisis': Men and Cosmetic Surgery." *Body and Society* 14(1):67–87.

Barthel, Diane. 1989. *Putting on Appearances: Gender and Advertising*. Philadelphia: Temple University Press.

Berger, John. 1972. *Ways of Seeing: Based on the BBC Television Series*. London: British Broadcasting Corporation.

Bordo, Susan. 1999. *The Male Body: A New Look at Men in Public and in Private*. New York: Farrar, Straus & Giroux.

Breazeale, Kenon. 1994. "In Spite of Women: *Esquire* Magazine and the Construction of the Male Consumer." *Signs: Journal of Women in Culture and Society* 20(1):1–22.

Burstyn, Varda. 1999. *The Rites of Men: Men, Manhood, Politics, and the Culture of Sport*. Toronto: University of Toronto Press.

Career Builder. 2010. "Casual Friday." YouTube video, 0:30, posted February 7 by "2010SuperBowlIXLIV." https://www.youtube.com/watch?v=XjlAPEHm4Xs.

Cawthorne, Alexandra. 2009. "Weathering the Storm: Black Men in the Recession." Report, Center for American Progress, Washington, DC. http://www.americanprogress.org/issues/2009/04/pdf/black_men_recession.pdf.

CBS News. 2010. "Gay Dating Ad Sacked before Super Bowl." February 1. http://www.cbsnews.com/stories/2010/01/29/national/main6154905.shtml.

Connell, R W. 1987. *Gender and Power: Society, the Person and Sexual Politics*. Cambridge: Polity.

———. 2000. *The Men and the Boys*. Berkeley: University of California Press.

Daily Mail Reporter. 2009. "Recession Depression: Men Are Twice as Likely to Suffer Stress in Silence." *Daily Mail Online*, May 11. http://www.dailymail.co.uk/health/article-1180366/Men-struggle-recession-depression-twice-likely-suffer-stress-silence.html.

Denny, Kathleen E. 2011. "Gender in Context, Content, and Approach: Comparing Gender Messages in Girl Scout and Boy Scout Handbooks." *Gender and Society* 25(1):27–47.

Dockers. 2010. "I Wear No Pants." YouTube video, 0:30, posted February 7 by "2010SuperBowlIXLIV." http://www.youtube.com/watch?v=nys0i_FRjTI.

Dodge Charger 2010. "Man's Last Stand." http://www.youtube.com/watch?v=hPmYxLUoZVc.

Duncan, Margaret C., and Alan Aycock. 2009. "'I Laughed until I Hurt': Negative Humor in Super Bowl Ads." In *Sport, Beer, and Gender: Promotional Culture and Contemporary Social Life*, ed. Lawrence A. Wenner and Steven J. Jackson, 243–59. New York: Peter Lang.

Dunlop, Boadie W., and Tanja Mletzko. 2011. "Will Current Socioeconomic Trends Produce a Depressing Future for Men?" *British Journal of Psychiatry* 198(3):167–68.

Flo TV. 2010. "Spineless." http://www.youtube.com/watch?v=5Mr31JemdOs.

Foucault, Michel. 1972. *The Archaeology of Knowledge*. Trans. A. M. Sheridan Smith. New York: Pantheon.

Gill, Rosalind, Karen Henwood, and Carl McLean. 2005. "Body Projects and the Regulation of Normative Masculinity." *Body and Society* 11(2):37–62.

Goffman, Erving. 1979. *Gender Advertisements*. New York: Harper & Row.

Halberstam, Judith. 1998. *Female Masculinity*. Durham, NC: Duke University Press.

———. 2005. *In a Queer Time and Place: Transgender Bodies, Subcultural Lives*. New York: New York University Press.

Jhally, Sut. 1987. The *Codes of Advertising: Fetishism and the Political Economy of Meaning in the Consumer Society*. New York: Routledge.

Kimmel, Michael S. 1996. *Manhood, in America: A Cultural History*. New York: Free Press.

Kimmel, Michael S., and Michael Kaufman. 1995. "Weekend Warriors: The New Men's Movement." In *The Politics of Manhood: Profeminist Men Respond to the Mythopoetic Men's Movement (and the Mythopoetic Leaders Answer)*, ed. Michael S. Kimmel, 15–43. Philadelphia: Temple University Press.

Lui, Meizhu, Bárbara Robles, Betsy Leondar-Wright, Rose Brewer, and Rebecca Adamson, with United for a Fair Economy, 2006. *The Color of Wealth: The Story Behind the U.S. Racial Wealth Divide*. New York: New Press.

Messner, Michael A. 1992. *Power at Play: Sports and the Problem of Masculinity*. Boston: Beacon.

Messner, Michael A., and Jeffrey Montez de Oca. 2005. "The Male Consumer as Loser: Beer and Liquor Ads in Mega Sports Media Events." *Signs* 30(3):1879–1909.

Nixon, Sean. 1996. *Hard Looks: Masculinities, Spectatorship, and Contemporary Consumption.* New York: St. Martin's.

Patterson, Maurice, and Richard Elliott. 2002. "Negotiating Masculinities: Advertising and the Inversion of the Male Gaze." *Consumption, Markets, and Culture* 5(3):231–46.

Pepsi Max. 2009. "I'm Good." YouTube video, 0:33, posted February 1 by "reggicp08v2." http://www.youtube.com/watch?v5=qUZaSf7T7ig&playnext=l&list=PLBD661EDEC86735DC.

Plocher, Carolyn. 2010. "*USA Today* Still Stomping on Tebow Ad." *NewsBusters .org*, February 16.

Putney, Gilford. 2001. *Muscular Christianity: Manhood and Sports in Protestant America, 1880-1920.* Cambridge, MA: Harvard University Press.

Rose, Gillian. 2001. *Visual Methodologies: An Introduction to the Interpretation of Visual Materials.* London: Sage.

Rutherford, Jonathan. 1988. "Who's That Man?" *In Male Order: Unwrapping Masculinity,* ed. Rowena Chapman and Jonathan Rutherford, 21–67. London: Lawrence & Wishart.

Schroeder, Jonathan E., and Janet L. Borgerson. 1998. "Marketing Images of Gender: A Visual Analysis." *Consumption, Markets, and Culture* 2(2):161–201.

Schroeder, Jonathan E., and Detlev Zwick. 2004. "Mirrors of Masculinity: Representation and Identity in Advertising Images." *Consumption, Markets and Culture* 7(1):21–52.

Shales, Tom. 2010. "Once Again, Letterman's 'Late Show' Promo Is Spot On." *Washington Post,* February 8. http://www.washingtonpost.com/wp-dyn/content/article/2010/02/07/AR2010020703677.html?wprss=rss_print/style.

Shields, Vickie Rutledge. 2002. *Measuring Up: How Advertising Affects Self-Image.* With Dawn Heinecken. Philadelphia: University of Pennsylvania Press.

Smith, Hortense. 2010. "The Woes of Bros: Super Bowl Ads Scar Pathetic Men—and the Women Who Ruined Them." *Jezebel,* February 7. http://jezebel.com/5466296/woes-of-bros-super-bowl-ads-star-pathetic-men—and-the-women-who-ruined-them/gallery/?skyline=true&s=i.

Stern, Barbara B. 1993. "Feminist Literary Criticism and the Deconstruction of Ads: A Postmodern View of Advertising and Consumer Responses." *Journal of Consumer Research* 19(4):556–66.

Thomas, Calvin. 2002. "Reenfleshing the Bright Boys; or, How Male Bodies Matter to Feminist Theory." In *Masculinity Studies and Feminist Theory: New Directions,* ed. Judith Kegan Gardiner, 60–89. New York: Columbia University Press.

Tsai, Wan-Hsui Sunny. 2010. "Assimilating the Queers: Representations of Lesbians, Gay Men, Bisexual, and Transgender People in Mainstream Advertising." *Advertising and Society Review* 11(1). http://muse.jhu.edu/journals/*advertising_and_society_review*/v011/11.1.tsai.html.

Universal Studios. 2009. "Universal Heroes." YouTube video, 0:41, posted February 3 by "SuperBowlBestAds." http://www.youtube.com/watch?v=X2dIt_ykaK4.

Wenner, Lawrence A., and Steven Jackson. 2009. "Sport, Beer, and Gender in Promotional Culture: On the Dynamics of a Holy Trinity." In *Sport, Beer, and Gender in Promotional Culture and Contemporary Social Life,* 1–34. New York: Peter Lang.

Williams, Raymond. (1980) 2005. "Advertising: The Magic System." In *Culture and Materialism: Selected Essays,* 170–95. New York: Verso.

Williamson, Judith. 1978. *Decoding Advertisements: Ideology and Meaning in Advertising.* London: Boyars.

❦ Topics for Further Examination ❧

- Find articles and websites that offer critiques of gender stereotypes in the mass media, popular culture, and consumer culture. For intriguing insights into sexism in "art," visit www.guerrillagirls.com.
- Google automobile ads. Compare and contrast the gendered "marketing" strategies within and across manufacturers. Select other products and compare, contrast, and critique.
- Check out song lyrics by artists who criticize hegemonic masculinity and emphasize femininity. For example, Google Pink's lyrics for the tune titled "Stupid Girls."

6

TRACING GENDER'S MARK ON BODIES, SEXUALITIES, AND EMOTIONS

CATHERINE G. VALENTINE

This chapter explores the ways gender patterns are woven into three of the most intimate aspects of the self: body, sexuality, and emotion. The readings we have selected make the general sociological argument that there is no body, sexuality, or emotional experience independent of culture. That is, all cultures sculpt bodies, shape sexualities, and produce emotions. One of the most powerful ways a gendered society creates and maintains gender difference and inequality is through its "direct grip" on these intimate domains of our lives (Schiebinger, 2000, p. 2). Gender ideals and norms require work to be done in, and on, the body to make it appropriately feminine or masculine. The same ideals and norms regulate sexual desire and expression, and require different emotional skills and behaviors of women and men.

At first glance, it may seem odd to think about body, sexuality, and emotion as cultural and gendered products. But consider the following questions: Do you diet, lift weights, dehair your legs or face, or use makeup? In public places, do you feel more comfortable sitting with legs splayed or legs crossed at the ankles? Are you conscious of how you feel and move your body through city streets when you are alone at night? How you answer these questions offers insight into the types of gendered body work you do. Now think about the gendering of sexuality in the United States. The mark of gender on sexual desire and expression is clear and deep, tied to gendered body ideals and norms. Whose breasts are eroticized and why? Are women who have many sexual partners viewed in the same way as men who have many sexual partners? Why are many heterosexually identified men afraid of being perceived as homosexual? Why do women shoulder the major responsibility for contraceptive control? Like sexuality, emotions are embodied modes of being. And like sexuality and body, emotions are socially regulated and constructed. They are also deeply gendered.

Consider these questions: Do you associate emotionality with women or men? Is an angry woman taken as seriously as an angry man? Why do we expect women's body language (e.g., their touch and other gestures) to be more affectionate and gentle than men's? What is your reaction to this word pair—tough woman/soft man? The readings in this chapter explore the complex and contradictory ways bodies, sexualities, and emotions are brought into line with society's gender scheme. Two themes unite the readings. First, they demonstrate how the marking of bodily appearance, sexual desire and behavior, and emotional expression as masculine or feminine reinforces Western, U.S. culture's insistence on an oppositional gender binary pattern. Second, the readings show how patterns of gender inequality become etched into bodies, sexualities, and emotions.

Gendered Bodies

All societies require body work of their members (Black & Sharma, 2004; Lorber & Moore, 2007). But not all societies insist on the molding of men's and women's bodies into visibly oppositional and asymmetrical types—for example, strong male bodies and fragile female bodies. Only societies constructed around the belief and practice of gender dualism and hierarchy require the enactment of gender inequality in body work. To illustrate, consider the fact that the height ideal and norm for heterosexual couples in the United States consists of a man who is taller and more robust than his mate (Gieske, 2000). This is not a universal cultural imperative. As Sabine Gieske states, the tall man/short woman pattern was unimportant in 18th-century Europe. In fact, the ideal was created in the Victorian era under the influence of physicians and educators who defined men as naturally bigger and stronger than women. The expectation that men be taller than their female partners persists today, even though the average height gap between men and women is closing (Schiebinger, 2000). The differential

height norm is so strong that many contemporary Americans react to the pairing of a short man and a tall woman with shock and even disapproval (Schiebinger, 2000).

How are bodies made feminine and masculine as defined by U.S. culture? It takes work, and lots of it. Well into the 20th century, American gender ideology led men and women alike to perceive women as frail in body and mind. Boys and men were strongly exhorted to develop size, muscle power, physical skills, and the "courage" to beat each other on the playing field and the battlefield, while girls and women were deeply socialized into a world of distorted body image, dangerous dieting, and physical incompetence (Dowling, 2000). Throwing, running, and hitting "like a girl" was a common cultural theme that we now understand to be a consequence of the cultural taboo against girls developing athletic stature and skills. As Collette Dowling (2000) notes, "There is no inherent biological reason for girls not to throw as far, as fast, or as hard as boys do" (p. 64). But there is a cultural reason: the embodiment of the belief in gender difference and inequality. We literally translate the "man is strong, woman is weak" dictum into our bodies. This dictum is so powerful that many people will practice distressed and unhealthy body routines and regimens to try to emulate the images of perfect male and female bodies. The mere threat of seeming masculine or mannish has kept a lot of girls and women from developing their own strength, and the specter of seeming effeminate or sissy has propelled many boys and men into worlds in which their bodies are both weapons and targets of violence (Dowling, 2000; Messner, 1990).

The power of masculinity requirements in the United States to compel some men to risk serious injury and even death has crystallized around the revelation that football players, at every level of the sport, regularly suffer brain injuries from repeat concussions and sub-concussive trauma (amanda, 2012). Research on football and other violent sports (e.g., rugby) shows that men and boys police one another's gender performance on the playing field, enforcing a "pain principle" that is perverse (Sabo, 1994; Vaccaro, Schrock, & McCabe, 2011). But perhaps there is no better example of an institution that molds men's bodies into weapons and targets than the military. The chapter reading by Orna Sasson-Levy examines masculinity requirements in the Israeli military and focuses on the harsh, even violent, individualized bodily and emotional practices that transform Israeli men into combat soldiers who will serve the interests of the state, as well as reinforcing a strong link between hegemonic masculinity and Israeli militarism. The practices examined by Sasson-Levy are typical of militaries globally, including the United States.

However, men's bodies in the United States and similar nations are not held to equally severe ideals and expectations of body work as are women's bodies. Gender inequality is etched into women's flesh in more debilitating ways.

American cultural definitions of femininity equate attractiveness with a youthful, slim, fit body that, in its most ideal form, has no visible "flaws"—no hair, pores, discolorations, perspiration marks, body odors, or trace of real bodily functions. In fact, for many women, the body they inhabit must be constantly monitored and managed—dehaired, deodorized, denied food—so that it doesn't offend. At the extreme, girls and women turn their own bodies into fetish objects to which they devote extraordinary amounts of time and money. What are the models of feminine bodily perfection against which girls and women measure themselves and are evaluated by others? The images and representations are all around us in magazine ads, TV commercials and programs, music videos, and toy stores.

Although much media and scholarly attention has been paid to topics such as anorexia and "fear of fat" among thin women, Janna Fikkan and Esther Rothblum (2011) bring together wide-ranging data on what may be a far more troubling issue, "the disproportionate degree of bias experienced by fat women" in the United States (p. 576). Fikkan and Rothblum use the term *fat* because it is descriptive while, as they point out, the term *overweight* implies "unfavorable comparison" to a socially constructed

standard and, similarly, the term *obese* is problematic, created by medical practitioners through a biased medical–economic lens (p. 576; see also Kwan, 2010, p. 147). They emphasize two aspects of the oppression of women by impossible ideals of thinness: (1) "The ever thinner cultural ideal means that practically every woman will feel badly about her body," and (2) "because of the pervasiveness and gendered nature of weight-based stigma, a majority of women stand to *suffer significant discrimination*" because they do not and cannot conform to a near-impossible bodily ideal intended to enforce gender inequality (Fikkan & Rothblum, 2011, p. 590). "Weight bias" against women has far-reaching and significant harmful consequences in almost every aspect of women's lives—including, for example, discrimination in hiring, wages, and promotion in the workplace, barriers to good health care; and degrading representation in the mass media (pp. 578–585).

In sharp contrast, the evidence is clear that men pay few if any penalties in any realm of life (e.g., employment and romantic relationships) for being robust and large-bodied (Fikkan & Rothblum, 2011). Samantha Kwan's (2010) study of fat women and men reinforces the findings of Fikkan and Rothblum. As she states, the men in her research sample experienced "very little body consciousness" and rarely spoke of concerns about body management (Kwan, 2010, p. 153). For example, they viewed dining out in pleasurable terms and had no qualms about eating with gusto. Just think of ads for man-sized meals and foods and consider the fact that a comparable "feminine" concept (e.g., woman-sized meal) is either unimaginable or would have the opposite meaning.

Kwan's (2010) study provides us with a useful framework for understanding what scholars such as Joan Chrisler (2011) argue is the threat, even hatred, of women's bodies in patriarchies. Kwan theorizes that a "Western cultural body-hierarchy" has created what she calls body privilege, "an invisible package of unearned assets that thin or normal-sized individuals can take for granted" in everyday life (p. 147).

This body-hierarchy is complicated and mediated by prisms such as race and sexual orientation. It appears from as-yet-limited research that lesbians and African American women are more likely to experience greater body satisfaction and protection (via family and community support) from the oppressive ideal of thinness compared with White, heterosexual women (Fikkan & Rothblum, 2011; Kwan, 2010).

The embodiment of women's subordination in gender-stratified societies takes some extreme forms. For example, in highly restrictive patriarchies, women's bodies may be systematically deformed, decimated, and restricted. Foot binding in traditional China is one of the most dramatic examples of an intentionally crippling gender practice. Although foot binding may seem to have no parallels in Western societies, sociologist Fatema Mernissi (2002) challenges the ethnocentric tendency to dismiss practices such as foot binding in China—and the veiling of women in some nations today—as alien or primitive. She does so by revealing the symbolic violence hammered directly on the Western female body by fashion codes and cosmetic industries that place Western women in a state of constant anxiety and insecurity. Mernissi's work suggests the usefulness of comparing practices such as foot binding in China to cosmetic surgery, extreme dieting, and body sculpting among contemporary Western girls and women. Consider the following questions: What do these seemingly different forms of body work have in common? Do they serve similar functions? How do they replicate gender inequality?

The story of the gendering of bodies in the United States and other countries is not only about oppositional and asymmetrical masculinity and femininity. Prisms of difference and inequality come into play. Social class, race, and gender intersect in Erynn Masi de Casanova's chapter reading. She looks at the ways in which women domestic workers felt degraded as "classed, gendered, and sometimes racialized bodies" in her study of embodied dimensions of domestic work in Ecuador's largest city (p. 309). Casanova shows how unequal relations between employers and workers are played out through the degradation of paid domestic workers' bodies. If we focus on the intersections of race and gender in the United States, specifically, the power of appearance norms to engage women's bodies is striking. Consider the following:. What's the answer to the question, "Mirror, mirror on the wall, who's the fairest of them all?" (Gillespie, 1998). You know what it is. The beauty standard is White, blonde, and blue-eyed. It is not Asian American, African American, Latin American, or Native American. In other words, there is a hierarchy of physical attractiveness, and the Marilyn Monroes and Madonnas of the world are at the top. Yes, there are African and Asian American models and celebrities. But they almost always conform to White appearance norms. When they don't, they tend to be exoticized as the "Other." Just consider the fact that eyelid surgery, nasal implants, and nasal tip refinement procedures are the most common cosmetic surgery procedures undergone by Asian American patients, largely women (Kaw, 1998). The facial features that Asian American women seek to alter, including small, narrow eyes and a flat nose, are those that define them as racially different from White norms (Kaw, 1998). Racial and gender ideologies come together to reinforce an ethnocentric and racist beauty standard that devalues the "given" features of racial and ethnic minority women. The medical system has cashed in on it by promoting a beauty standard that requires the surgical alteration of features that don't fit the ideal.

GENDERED SEXUALITIES

Like the body, sexuality is shaped by culture. The sexualization process in a gendered society such as the United States is tightly bound to cultural ideas of masculinity and femininity. In dominant Western culture, a real man and a real woman are assumed to be opposite human types, as expressed in the notion of the "opposite sex." In addition, both are assumed to be heterosexual as captured in the notion that "opposites attract." Conformity to this gendered sexual dichotomy is strictly enforced.

The term *compulsory heterosexuality* refers to the dominance of heterosexual values and the fact that the meanings and practices of nonhetero(sexuality) as well as hetero(sexuality) are shaped by the dominant heterosexual script. For example, "real sex" is generally conceived of as penile–vaginal intercourse. This "coital imperative" limits the control individuals have in determining what counts as sexual activity and frames women's sexuality as passive/receptive and men's as active/penetrative (Gavey, McPhillips, & Doherty, 2001; Katz & Tirone, 2009). That is, the coital imperative defines sex as something men "do" to women privileging men's sexual needs above women's, limiting possibilities for men and women to have truly reciprocal, safe sexual relations. Importantly, the Western obsession with the homosexual/heterosexual identity distinction is relatively new. Created in the 19th century, it became a mechanism by which masculinity and femininity could be further polarized and policed (Connell, 1999). Gay masculinity and lesbian femininity came to be defined as abnormal and threatening to the "natural gender order." Consequently, in the United States, the fear of being thought of as homosexual has had a powerful impact on presentation of self. Men and boys routinely police each other's behavior and mete out punishment for any suggestion of "effeminacy" (Connell, 1999; Pascoe, 2005; Plante, 2006), while women and girls who engage in masculinized activities such as military service and elite sports risk being labeled lesbians.

Contemporary Western gender and sexuality beliefs have spawned stereotypes of lesbians as "manly" women and gay men as "effeminate." The reality is otherwise. For example, research shows that many gay men and lesbians are gender conformists in their expression of sexuality (Kimmel, 2000). Gay men's sexual behavior patterns tend to be masculine—oriented toward pleasure, orgasm, experimentation, and many partners—while lesbian sexuality is feminine in a Western sense, emphasizing sexual intimacy within romantic relationships. However, this account of nonheterosexuality is incomplete. Recent research suggests that compared with heterosexuals, nonheterosexuals have more opportunities to reflect on and experiment with ways of being sexual. Although the meanings attached to sexuality in society at large shape their erotic encounters, they are also freer to challenge the dominant sexual scripts (Weeks, Heaphy, & Donovan, 2001).

The imposition of gender difference and inequality on sexuality in societies such as the United States is also reflected in the sexual double standard. The double standard, which emphasizes and normalizes male pleasure and female restraint, is a widespread product and practice of patriarchy. Although Western sexual attitudes and behaviors have moved away from a strict double standard, the sexual lives of women remain more constrained than those of men. For example, girls and women are still under the control of the good-girl/bad-girl dichotomy, a cultural distinction that serves to pit women against each other and to produce sexual relations between women and men that can be confusing and dissatisfying. Men grow up with expectations to embrace a sexual script by which they gain status from sexual experience (Kimmel, 2000). Women grow up with expectations that being sexually active compromises their value—but, at the same time, that they must be flirtatious and sexy. Doesn't this seem confusing? Imagine the relationship misunderstandings and disappointments that can emerge out of the meeting of these "opposite-sex" sexual scripts.

In their chapter reading, Erin Hatton and Mary Nell Trautner offer persuasive evidence that the sexual double standard persists and has intensified in new negative ways for girls and women. They studied more than 40 years of covers of *Rolling Stone* magazine and found that although sexualized images of both men and women have increased, women are more frequently sexualized than men and, most significantly, women are "increasingly likely to be 'hypersexualized,'" but men are not (p. 303). Hatton and Trautner conclude that the dramatic increase in hypersexualized representations of women signifies a dangerous trend toward a narrowing of culturally acceptable ways to do femininity, including the diminishment of other aspects of "emphasized femininity" such as sociability and nurturance (p. 338).

The prisms of difference and inequality alter the experience and expression of gendered sexuality in significant ways in the United States. For example, Trautner (2005) found that social class differences are scripted and represented as sexual differences in exotic dance clubs catering to clientele who come from either the middle class or the working class. Dancers in working-class clubs are more likely to perform stereotypes of bad-girl sexuality, while those who dance in middle-class clubs enact good-girl sexuality. Rebecca Plante (2006), an expert on the sociology of sexuality, analyzes the intersection of race and sexuality in the United States and argues that African Americans "do not enter the discourse and debate about sexualities from the same place where white, middle-class people enter" (p. 231). Black sexuality was historically stereotyped as perverted and predatory, a theme that continues today in pornographic and other representations of African Americans. In a recent study of Black women who work in the pornography industry, Mireille Miller-Young (2010) confirms Plante's observations about the interactions among gender, race, and sexuality. Miller-Young found that Black women are "devalued as hyperaccessible and superdisposable in an industry that simultaneously invests in and ghettoizes fantasies about black sexuality" (p. 219).

The chapter reading by Breanne Fahs is very helpful in summarizing and sorting out the contradictions that overwhelm women's (and men's) experience of sexuality in the contemporary United States, where living between celebrations of sexual liberation and progress is often cancelled out by alarming rates of sexual violence, body shaming, and other forms of sexual repression. She argues for a more inclusive and critical feminist sex-positive movement that integrates *freedom from* oppressive sexual mandates and requirements for women alongside *freedom to* enjoy and express sexuality in consenting relationships. She states that "women need to be able to deny access to their bodies, say no to sex as they choose, and engage in sexual expression free of oppressive homophobic, sexist, and racist intrusions" (p. 364).

GENDERED EMOTIONS

Masculinity and femininity are defined as emotionally opposed in Western culture (Bendelow & Williams, 1998). This opposition expresses itself in both obvious and subtle ways. The obvious opposition is that the emotions that can be expressed—for example, anger and love—and how they are expressed are tied to gender. Boys and men must appear "hard" by hiding or shutting down feelings of vulnerability, such as fear, while girls and women are encouraged to be "soft"—that is, emotionally in touch, vulnerable, and expressive. Consider the impact of learning and enacting different, even oppositional, emotional scripts and feeling rules on intimate relationships. If men are not supposed to be vulnerable, then how can they forge satisfying affectionate bonds with women and other men? Additionally, men who embrace the gender–emotion stereotype of hard masculinity may pay a price in well-being by concealing their own pain, either physical or psychological (Real, 2001; Shields, Garner, Di Leone, & Hadley, 2006; Vaccaro et al., 2011). Also, it is important to recognize the negative consequences of gendered emotionality for girls and women. Although girls and women receive cultural encouragement to be "in touch with" themselves and others emotionally, this has strong associations with weakness and irrationality. Thus, Stephanie Shields and colleagues (2006) observe that the strong cultural association between emotionality and femininity has emphasized "the comparatively ineffectual nature of women's emotion" (p. 63). When women express emotion according to cultural rules, they run the risk of being labeled hypersensitive, temperamental, and irrational. The stereotype of the emotionally erratic and unstable woman has been widely used in efforts to undermine the advancement of women in politics, higher education, the professions, business, and other realms of public life. You know how it goes: "We can't risk having a moody, irritable, irrational woman at the helm."

How do the prisms of difference and inequality interact with gendered emotions in the United States? Looking through a number of prisms simultaneously, we can see that the dominant definition of hard, stiff-upper-lip masculinity is White, heterosexual, and European (Seidler, 1998). Hegemonic masculinity assigns rationality and reason to privileged adult men. All other people, including women, minorities, and children, are assumed to be more susceptible to negative influence by their bodies and emotions and, as a consequence, less capable of mature, reasoned decision making (Seidler, 1998).

In her chapter reading, L. Ayu Saraswati analyzes yet another way in which gendered emotions intersect with other inequalities. Saraswati argues that some emotions are instruments of conformity that compel women to conform to restrictive appearance ideals and norms. In her research on Indonesian women's decisions to use skin whiteners, Saraswati found that the emotion of *malu* or shame, a gendered emotion, played a central role in pressuring women to cover their skin with whiteners. On the surface, it may seem that Saraswati's research has little meaning for women in the United States, but, just scratch the surface, and the relevance will become clear. Skin whiteners are widely available in the United States and have a long history of use by women of color. As Saraswati emphasizes, the use of skin whiteners by women is linked to the maintenance of gender, racial, and global hierarchies of race, color, and nation. We'd like to conclude this chapter introduction by asking you to think about individual and collective strategies to reject conformity to patterns of gendered body work, sexual expression, and emotionality that demean, disempower, and prove dangerous to women and men. What would body work, emotional life, and sexual desire and experience be like if they were not embedded in and shaped by structures of inequality? How would personal growth, self-expression, and communication

with others change if we were not under the sway of compulsory attractiveness, compulsory heterosexuality, the sexual double standard, and gendered emotional requirements? How would your life change? What can we do, as individuals and collectively, to resist and reject the pressure to bring our bodies, sexual experience, and emotional life in line with oppressive and dangerous ideals and norms?

References

amanda. (2012, November 15). Football and brain damage, or how American masculinity ravages men's bodies [Web log post]. Retrieved from http://thesocietypages.org/sociologylens/2012/11/15/football-and-brain-damage-or-how-american-masculinity-ravages-mens-bodies/

Bendelow, G., & Williams, S. J. (1998). Introduction: Emotions in social life. In G. Bendelow & S. Bendelow (Eds.), *Emotions in social life* (pp. xv–xxx). London: Routledge.

Black, P., & Sharma, U. (2004). Men are real, women are "made up." In J. Spade & C. Valentine (Eds.), *The kaleidoscope of gender* (pp. 286–296). Belmont, CA: Wadsworth.

Chrisler, J. C. (2011). Leaks, lumps, and lines: Stigma and women's bodies. *Psychology of Women Quarterly, 35*(2), 202–214.

Connell, R. W. (1999). Making gendered people. In M. Feree, J. Lorber, & B. Hess (Eds.), *Revisioning gender* (pp. 449–471). Thousand Oaks, CA: Sage.

Dowling, C. (2000). *The frailty myth*. New York: Random House.

Fikkan, J. L., & Rothblum, E. D. (2011). Is fat a feminist issue? Exploring the gendered nature of weight bias. *Sex Roles, 66,* 575–592.

Gavey, N., McPhillips, K., & Doherty, M. (2001). "If it's not on it's not on"—or is it? Discursive constraints on women's condom use. *Gender & Society, 15*(6), 917–934.

Gieske, S. (2000). The ideal couple: A question of size? In L. Schiebinger (Ed.), *Feminism and the body* (pp. 375–394). New York: Oxford University Press.

Gillespie, M. A. (1998). Mirror mirror. In R. Weitz (Ed.), *The politics of women's bodies* (pp. 184–188). New York: Oxford University Press.

Katz, J., & Tirone, V. (2009). Women's sexual compliance with male dating partners: Associations with investment in ideal womanhood and romantic well-being. *Sex Roles, 60,* 347–356.

Kaw, E. (1998). Medicalization of racial features: Asian-American women and cosmetic surgery. In R. Weitz (Ed.), *The politics of women's bodies* (pp. 167–183). New York: Oxford University Press.

Kimmel, M. (2000). *The gendered society.* New York: Oxford University Press.

Kwan, S. (2010). Navigating public spaces: Gender, race, and body privilege in everyday life. *Feminist Formations, 22*(2), 144–166.

Lorber, J., & Moore, L. J. (2007). *Gendered bodies: Feminist perspectives.* Los Angeles: Roxbury.

Mernissi, F. (2002). *Scheherazade goes west.* New York: Washington Square Press.

Messner, M. (1990). When bodies are weapons: masculinity and violence in sport. *International Review for Sociology of Sport, 25,* 203–218.

Miller-Young, M. (2010). Putting hypersexuality to work: Black women and illicit eroticism in pornography. *Sexualities, 13*(2), 219–235.

Pascoe, C. J. (2005). "Dude, you're a fag": Adolescent masculinity and fag discourse. *Sexualities, 8*(3), 329–346.

Plante, R. (2006). *Sexualities in context.* Boulder, CO: Westview Press.

Real, T. (2001). Men's hidden depression. In T. Cohen (Ed.), *Men and masculinity* (pp. 361–368). Belmont, CA: Wadsworth.

Sabo, D. (1994). Pigskin, patriarchy, and pain. In M. Messner & D. Sabo (Eds.) *Sex, violence and power in sports: Rethinking masculinity.* Berkeley, CA: Crossing Press.

Schiebinger, L. (2000). Introduction. In L. Schiebinger (Ed.), *Feminism and the body* (pp. 1–21). New York: Oxford University Press.

Seidler, V. J. (1998). Masculinity, violence and emotional life. In G. Bendelow & S. Williams (Eds.), *Emotions in social life* (pp. 193–210). London: Routledge.

Shields, S., Garner, D., Di Leone, B., & Hadley, A. (2006). Gender and emotion. In J. Stets & J. Turner (Eds.), *Handbook of the sociology of emotions* (pp. 63–83). New York: Springer.

Trautner, M. N. (2005). Doing gender, doing class: The performance of sexuality in exotic dance clubs. *Gender & Society, 19*(6), 771–778.

Vaccaro, C. A., Schrock, D. P., & McCabe, J. M. (2011). Managing emotional manhood: Fighting and fostering fear in mixed marital arts. *Social Psychology Quarterly, 74*(4), 414–437.

Weeks, J., Heaphy, B., & Donovan, C. (2001). *Same sex intimacies: Families of choice and other life experiments.* New York: Routledge.

Introduction to Reading 26

Erynn Masi de Casanova's study of women domestic workers in Guayaquil, Ecuador, examines the embodied dimensions of domestic work and demonstrates how unequal relations between domestic workers and their employers are played out in and on the bodies of women workers through health, food, and appearance. She asks: What can domestic work done by women reveal about the social categorization of bodies? To answer that question, Casanova interviewed fourteen domestic workers, all women, and three employers. She adopted the vantage point of the workers in order to understand their accounts of issues such as the physical demands of their work and the toll it takes on their bodies. Their bodies, Casanova found, are marked as poor and undesirable in relationship to their employers' bodies.

1. What are the racial dynamics of the creation of embodied differences between women domestic workers and their employers?

2. How does embodied inequality manifest itself in dress and physical appearance?

3. How does the author employ both "body as resource" and "body as symbol" theoretical frameworks in the analysis of her data?

EMBODIED INEQUALITY

THE EXPERIENCE OF DOMESTIC WORK IN URBAN ECUADOR

Erynn Masi de Casanova

I was cooking and I felt like I was suffocating. I wanted to lie down, because I felt sick . . . I took [spread out] some newspapers and lay on the kitchen floor. I felt like I was dying, that I couldn't get air . . . And the employer gets home and the other employee tells her, "The *empleada* [domestic worker] is sick." "Oh, no," she says, "what's my daughter going to eat now, who will cook for her?"

Cristina, domestic worker, age 40

Cristina has spent much of her life cooking and cleaning in private homes in Guayaquil, Ecuador. Her anecdote highlights domestic work's physical demands, and employers' privileging of their corporeal needs over those of their employees. Based on interviews with domestic workers and employers, I argue that bodies matter for how domestic employees experience their work (apart from often discussed issues of sexual harassment or abuse). Domestic workers' accounts emphasized physical labor and the embodied inequality between employer and employee. Domestic work assumes particular forms in coastal Ecuador, where workers and employers often have similar racial backgrounds, and middle-class people see their position as increasingly precarious under a left-leaning political regime.

What can domestic work reveal about social categorizations of bodies? Domestic employment entails a unique physical proximity of bodies from different class groups, a boundary-threatening situation that must be managed by workers and employers. In this private sphere, bodies can reproduce or challenge class inequality. Although "domestic work constitutes bodily subjectivity in a particular way" (Bahnisch 2000, 59, referencing Gatens 1996, 69), research tends not to place the social meanings of workers' bodies at the center of the analysis. Ecuador, with its long history of paid domestic work and rigid class system (Miles 1998; Roberts 2012)—in which even lower-middle-class families have traditionally employed domestics—is the ideal site for exploring class/work/body. Like many low-prestige jobs, domestic work draws on and propagates social constructions of poor people's bodies as deviant and worthless.

Necessary research on working bodies "progress[es] only by adopting the vantage point of the embodied worker and listening to their accounts of workplace experience 'from the inside'" (Wolkowitz 2006, 183). I take domestic workers' accounts of issues concerning health, food, and appearance/clothing as a starting point, asking: How do bodies matter in domestic work? How does this employment arrangement relate to broader ideas about differently classed bodies in Ecuador?

THEORETICAL PERSPECTIVES

Two complementary theoretical and empirical approaches apply to working bodies. The first,

From Casanova, Erynn Masi de. (2013). Embodied inequality: The experience of domestic work in Urban Ecuador. *Gender & Society, 27*(4), 561–585.

rooted in Marxian theory, views the body as a limited resource, damaged and deformed in exploitative production processes. Marx described factory work's destructive effects on workers' bodies and psyches ([1844] 1978, 74) as the collateral damage of capitalist expansion. Indeed, Labor power, the power of the body, is central to the reproduction and accumulation of capital (Bahnisch 2000, 64). In today's service economies, the "human body continues to be deeply involved in every aspect of paid work" (Wolkowitz 2006, 55). The "body as resource" perspective is often used to describe the types of physical labor identified with men.

The second approach, drawing on Bourdieu's (1990) concept of *habitus* and symbolic interactionism (e.g., Goffman 1959), views the body as symbol. The symbolic body does not communicate unequivocal messages, comprehended similarly by everyone we encounter.[1] However, habitus is observed and interpreted by others according to the "dominant symbolic" (Skeggs 2004a, 87), even if we are unconscious of how social structures produce particular behaviors and (bodily) dispositions. For Bourdieu, habitus "causes an individual agent's practices, without either explicit reason or signifying intent, to be . . . 'sensible' and 'reasonable' to members of the same society" (1977, 79). Bodily aspects of habitus make sense to those able to recognize and classify them.

Dress, appearance, and movement communicate bodies' positions in hierarchies of race, class, gender, and occupation. Embodied habitus is "a statement of social entitlement" (Skeggs 2004b, 22), reproducing class inequalities in, on, and through bodies and becoming a source of conflict or approbation in interactions between people of different classes. Workplaces can be agents of socialization, building or reinforcing habitus, especially when workers begin at young ages, as in domestic employment. Expanding on Bourdieu, Wolkowitz (2006) elaborated the idea of *occupational habitus* related to people's work identities. Domestic work is one setting for the construction of occupational habitus.

The "body as symbol" perspective often focuses empirically on gendered appearance.

Research shows how workplaces value certain forms of gender performance (Freeman 2000; Hall, Hockey, and Robinson 2007; McDowell 1997; Nencel 2008; Salzinger 2003). Yet there is scant research on embodied work outside of organizations, except for sex work. Building on the "body as resource" approach, research shows how emotions, signaled through physical cues, are harnessed in gender-segregated service occupations (Hochschild 1983; Kang 2010). Yet Wolkowitz laments the "relative invisibility of the corporeal in the employment-oriented literature on emotion" (2006, 79), and the sociology of the body is just beginning to examine the large portion of an employed person's life that is spent at work.

The term body *work* (Kang 2010; Shilling [1993] 2003) synthesizes the material and symbolic aspects of bodies. Here, drawing on Gimlin, I consider body work: "(iii) the management of embodied emotional experience and display, and (iv) the production or modification of bodies through work" (2007, 353). Consistent with a "body as symbol" frame, employers expect domestic workers to present a certain appearance. As in "body as resource" theories, domestic workers' bodies are produced and transformed through the work.

I propose a more holistic micro-level approach, "embodied inequality." A theoretical framework of embodied inequality bridges the "body as resource" and "body as symbol" approaches and their conceptual offshoots, "body work" and "occupational habitus." In this case, domestic workers' bodies are used as tools, and suffer the physical consequences, yet they must also have an appearance acceptable to their employers and indicative of their socioeconomic position. Unlike academic narratives that privilege only the material or the symbolic, the workers' accounts combine these perspectives for a broader view of embodied inequality.

Paid Domestic Work

. . . This article investigates embodied aspects of domestic work in a thus far unexplored site, urban coastal Ecuador. Taking my cue from workers' interview accounts, I set the body at the center of my inquiry. "Zooming in" on the body, we see how crucial embodiment is to women's understanding and experience of this type of work. Domestic workers described how class relations become embodied and personalized when acted out between individuals in the private sphere. Distinctions between employers' and employees' bodies are not simply symptoms of larger inequalities, played out in rote ways; the very distinctions themselves are created through sometimes hurtful everyday interactions. Although bodily aspects of habitus build up over time so that people are not always conscious of the reasons for their actions (Bourdieu 1977), the domestic workers interviewed point to specific moments when they felt degraded as classed, gendered, and sometimes racialized bodies. We can better understand domestic workers' experience of their work by listening to how they talk about their working bodies.

THE LOCAL CONTEXT

. . . The female labor market in Ecuador is bifurcated, with a limited set of "good" jobs available to college-educated women, and a set of less desirable jobs, or informal self-employment, to less educated women (Casanova 2011). Women see domestic work as the least appealing employment option because of low pay and potential exploitation by unregulated employers; many prefer other informal work (e.g., selling goods) (Casanova 2011, 164–65).

Guayaquil, Ecuador's largest city, has approximately 2.4 million people living inside the city limits (M.I. Municipalidad de Guayaquil 2012) and a metro area population of around 3 million. Many of Guayaquil's residents live in poverty (87 percent in the early 2000s [Floro and Messier 2006, 234]), and middle-class families commonly employ domestic workers. Employment arrangements vary, from elite families employing entire live-in staffs to lower-middle-class households having someone work a few hours per week. Many families' only claim to middle-class status is the presence of a domestic worker

in their household. Long an informal, under the table, contract-free type of employment, domestic work is now the object of increased government scrutiny and public consciousness raising by worker organizations, giving workers and employers the sense that the sands are shifting.

The timing of this study was ideal, as the left-leaning government of President Rafael Correa began enforcing labor laws protecting domestic workers—though not systematically or continuously—in 2009. Domestic workers' issues were frequently featured in news media, and workers' organizations ramped up advocacy and outreach to leverage state support and improve working conditions. It had always been difficult for domestic workers to negotiate living wages and bearable workloads because of the unequal positions of employer and employee and the lack of regulation; public attention around domestics' legal rights in this period made such discussions even more uncomfortable. In 2010, when I began fieldwork, the Ministry of Labor was conducting house-by-house inspections in wealthy neighborhoods to determine the presence of domestic workers in the home and whether they were receiving the government-mandated minimum wage and benefits (e.g., Social Security). Inspections have since ended, though the middle and upper classes still feel threatened by the populist, socialist-identified rhetoric of the current administration. Employers hearing of the inspectors' presence in their neighborhood often "erased" a domestic worker's body by giving her the day off, hiding her in another part of the house, or presenting her as a cousin visiting from the countryside.

The complex racial dynamics of contemporary Ecuador, with most citizens identifying as *mestizo* (of mixed indigenous and European ancestry) and sizable indigenous and Afro-Ecuadorian minorities, are discussed in many studies (Casanova 2004; de la Torre and Striffler 2008; Rahier 1998; Roberts 2012). Throughout Latin America, the high degree of social and economic inequality is often literally written on the body (Bank Muñoz 2008; Casanova 2011; Edmonds 2010; Roberts 2012). Nonwhite appearance and darker skin are generally associated with low class status, and domestic workers are stereotyped as having these characteristics. In Guayaquil, few people self-identify as indigenous or wear traditional dress. Coastal *mestizos/as* have much less contact with their indigenous compatriots than do *mestizos* in the Andean region [sierra]; and the paternalistic *mestizo*-indigenous relations seen in the *sierra* are largely absent on the coast. Thus, it is rare to find indigenous domestic workers in guayaquileños' homes. In fact, in 13 years of conducting research in Guayaquil, I have never encountered a woman who self-identified (or was identified by others) as indigenous laboring in a private home. Guayas province, where Guayaquil is located, has the country's largest concentration of self-identified Afro-Ecuadorians (INEC 2012). While it is more common to find Afro-Ecuadorian women among Guayaquil's domestic workers, there is widespread discrimination against Blacks. My sense from speaking informally with Employers is that they prefer *mestizo* domestic workers; I have also observed more *mestizo* than Black workers in middle-class homes.

Thus, unlike locales where employers and employees are separated by caste (Ray and Qayum 2009) or race (Gill 1990, 1994; Rollins 1985), in Guayaquil it is common for domestic employment arrangements to link women whose official racial classification would be *mestizo*. As in the Philippines (Arnado 2003), this employment relationship is not usually a cross-racial one, meaning that class differences—especially embodied ones—can be more fruitfully explored, as they are not conflated with racial differences. However, identifications of race and class in Ecuador are somewhat fluid and mutually constituting: *mestizos* with higher class status are perceived (and see themselves) as whiter than poorer *mestizos,* regardless of phenotype. Whereas popular conceptions of race in the U.S. rest on ideas about immutable biological differences, in Andean societies, including Ecuador, race is "experienced as alterable, through changes in body and comportment . . . [rather than] genetically determined" (Roberts 2012, 120). People who are *mestizo/a* can

become white(r) by complying with middle-class norms of bodily self-presentation, education, and employment—by successfully embodying middle-class habitus. Thus, the "fabrication" of race is not "theoretical" or a priori, but rather, race is enacted and . . . reenacted through a wider range of characteristics than physical appearance as transmuted through genes (Roberts 2012, 114). This racial mutability makes creating embodied differences a priority for employers, who want to visually distinguish themselves from "the help." Compounding the racial uncertainty and jockeying for whiteness is the precarious status of the middle class. In my recent ethnographic research, middle-class people's generally low salaries and their (mostly overblown) sense that they are targeted by government policies that favor the poor have surfaced as important to this group's self-identification. Thus, it is unsurprising to see lines drawn in the sand in the home-as-workplace to remind domestic workers of their (racialized) class position. The most obvious means for marking the bodies of employees is the uniform. The more frequent use of uniforms in Latin America (compared to the United States) underlines the different and perhaps more acute embodied experience of these workers.[2] Strategies of corporeal distance, degradation, and differentiation are best seen as ways of shoring up tenuous claims to privileged statuses such as whiteness, decency [*decencia*], and middle-classness in one local race/class gender context.

Meanwhile, the daily life of domestic workers—as described by participants and as I have observed—remains much the same as in decades past. Most families eat their largest meal at midday, which (in households that can afford it) includes a first course of soup, followed by a protein with rice and vegetables. Cooking can be laborious, often requiring tedious and physically demanding tasks such as grating green plantains by hand or peeling and straining fruits for juice. Rather than using sponge or string mops, domestic workers are usually asked to clean floors with wet rags draped over brooms or long sticks. Most middle-class homes have washing machines; however, employers sometimes require special clothing (like children's school uniforms) to be washed by hand, usually at stone sinks with washboard-like ridges. Even in homes with automatic dryers, clothing is usually hung outside to dry, which is more physically taxing. Other considerations include the dust that accumulates in this urban environment (even in closed-in structures) and the caustic contents of common cleaning products (domestic workers tend not to bring their own products or request specific products). Most live-out domestic workers have long workdays and live in areas distant from public transportation, making for long commutes.

Methods

This article draws on interviews with fourteen current and former domestic workers (all women) and three employers (two women and one man) conducted in Guayaquil, Ecuador, from June through August 2010.[3] Because of the volatility of the domestic labor market, seven of the worker-interviewees were unemployed, though all self-identified as domestic workers and expressed interest in returning to work in private homes (two of these women had been recently hired and were negotiating start dates with new employers). Interviewees ranged in age from 28 to 62. Some had spent most of their working lives in domestic employment, often from adolescence. I asked women about each of their domestic work experiences, beginning with their first and ending with the most recent or current job.[4] Despite the stereotype of domestic workers as rural-to-urban migrants, eight of the fourteen workers interviewed were born in or near Guayaquil. Although I did not ask about racial self-identification, three of the women would likely be identified as Black by most Guayaquileans, and two others appear to have some African ancestry but may not be considered Black. All the women but one were mothers, and most were not legally married. . . .

Findings

Physical Labor in Domestic Work (Body as Resource)

Nearly every worker interviewed stressed the physical demands of housework and child care: "the production or modification of bodies through work" (Gimlin 2007, 353). Cecilia, middle-aged and unemployed, complained that "physical exhaustion" set in over time:

> In the first month, we're wonderful, but in two or three months we're feeling a physical exhaustion (*agotamiento físico*) that leads to us feeling more and more tired, and we end up getting an illness . . . related to the tiredness, the stress . . . and then the employer begins to complain . . ."What's going on with you? You started off working hard but now you don't clean here, you don't clean over here"—but she doesn't recognize that I am human, too.

Most of the domestic workers interviewed began work at a young age, some at 10 or 12. The toll on the body over time, and the difficulty of getting hired and danger of being fired as an older worker because of perceived or actual physical limitations, were common concerns.

Some domestic tasks are more physically demanding than others. Longtime domestic Patty recounted:

> I have been doing laundry for 22 years, and my hands began to swell up on me . . . there was a horrible pain that grabbed me in my [lower] back . . . and my whole hands were full of fungus, and they bled every time I washed [by hand], they were so irritated . . . it was a rash . . . from the detergent, the soap . . . and the bleach.

After spending a day washing clothes for her employers, Patty would return home and wash her own family's clothes. She consulted a doctor, who recommended she stop hand-washing clothes: "If you keep washing, you are going to die," because the exposure to bleach could cause cancer. Despite the tremendous pain, Patty "went on for some time more for [her] children," whom she helped support. She said, "I was not the same person you see today"—strong, energetic, with a physically commanding presence—because of her overwork. Despite the fact that she no longer washes clothes for a living, I could see the effects of this toil on her hands. For Patty, one of the most troubling aspects of domestic work is that "physically a person gets worn out, deteriorates, doesn't care for herself."

As with much manual labor, domestic work's detrimental physical effects are not well compensated.[5] In interviews, workers listed negative physical consequences: back pain, exposure to hazardous chemicals without protective masks or gloves, and injuries. Former worker Ximena recounted cleaning marble stairs during the final weeks of her pregnancy, when she slipped and fell. The pain she felt afterward, she soon realized, was the beginning of labor. (Perhaps Ximena was fortunate to be working, as two other domestic workers reported being fired when employers learned of their pregnancies.) Patty affirmed, "The work in the home is hard . . . and one arrives home dead, pulverized." Since asking for time off is often not an option, several workers noted that they would simply quit a job when they needed rest, taking a month or two off before returning to work, usually for a new employer.

Workers used embodied metaphors to describe their toil. Belén, employed in one of Guayaquil's wealthiest neighborhoods, referred to her job as earning money "with the sweat of your brow," and Cristina claimed to have "given up even my lungs" to the work; these powerful embodied images signify the bodily sacrifice of domestic work. Such statements recall a tradition of "body as resource" theories inspired by Marx, who saw the body destroyed by the capitalist mode of production. These bodies are modified negatively, and (re)produced as lower-class bodies, through physically demanding tasks. Although their occupational habitus involves executing physically difficult work, the women identify its negative consequences on their bodies.

Employers' Bodies as More Valuable (Body as Symbol)

Workers often discussed distinctions made by employers between employers' and workers' bodies as related to health and health care, food, and clothing. These accounts recall the "body as symbol" perspective: Bodies are seen as carrying different amounts of social worth. Health issues also relate to the physicality of the work and the body as an exhaustible resource. Workers' bodies are so devalued by differential treatment that Cecilia asserted, "The family dog is treated better than the household worker."

Nearly all the workers described myriad health problems, some leaving them temporarily unable to work. Ailments may stem from a variety of causes, including physically demanding work, poor women's precarious health status, and lack of health care access. As former domestic Ana Maria put it, "A [domestic] worker has little time to go to the doctor." Rather than seeing a doctor, she said domestic workers "go to the pharmacy[6] to self-medicate," or consult neighbors and friends. Because most of these women depend on subsidized health services or low-cost clinics, a doctor visit can involve waiting an entire day (or more) to be seen.[7] Paola, a full-time student and former domestic worker, discussed employers' inflexibility with regard to workers' schedules: "We don't have any right to get sick." Paola and other interviewees connected health disparities to class inequality: "We are also human, just like them [employers], except the difference is that they have money, and we don't." When employers get sick, they visit the doctor and take time off from work to recuperate; when domestic employees get sick, they are often unable to do either. When Fátima asked her last employer to help pay for her prescription, she was berated by his adult son, and felt that skin color and class prejudice were at play: "They let me know that because a person is ugly, [and] Black . . . and they [the employers] are white, they can give you a kick in the rear. . . . But why, if we are all human and have feelings?" She compared this employer to a previous one, who, when she fell ill, took her to an expensive private hospital and paid the bill. Workers see the body as a resource they can use, and see the employers' denial of their health needs as a material and symbolic devaluation of their bodies.

Food was another site for drawing lines between upper- and lower-class bodies. Based on my interviews and observations, deep-rooted practices, such as having domestic workers eat separately and offering them different (or less) food, are still common in urban Ecuador. Several women complained that employers denied them food during the work-day. Fátima said, "They didn't even give me a piece of warm bread." Others recounted having to eat reheated leftovers when there was plenty of fresh food available, or watching employers throw out food the worker had requested. Domestic workers, said Cecilia, often do not get "decent food."

More offensive to Belén was being forced to use dishes that were just for the help: "From the teacups to the spoons, everything . . . all the utensils were different from theirs." This humiliating experience made her feel insignificant. The symbolism of objects that touch only a worker's body, but never an employer's body, communicates a powerful message of inferiority to the worker. Another worker recalled having to eat outdoors while the employer's family ate inside; typically, domestic workers eat in the kitchen or an adjoining room. Legitimating the study of food as a social and cultural object, Bourdieu ([1984] 2007) focused on divergent eating habits based on class-based tastes, yet here different eating practices are based not on taste but on the exclusion of lower-class bodies from nourishment and desirable foods. By refusing to share eating utensils and eating space with domestic workers, employers shore up embodied class boundaries and prevent even indirect bodily contact.[8] In describing "good" employers, workers often pointed to eating the same food, or eating together at the table, as evidence of kindness. Alternatively, we could see this egalitarian gesture as a distraction from the inherent economic inequality in the employment situation.[9] Given

the incorporation of food-related routines into domestic workers' occupational habitus, it is likely that many workers, unlike those interviewed, do not resist or complain about these practices.

Cristina recalled taking her young daughter to work, so she could "see what I do." Her daughter asked, "*Mami,* why do you make such delicious food here?" Cristina replied, "At home we don't have the same money as they do here." Her daughter complimented Cristina's cooking, saying she wished she could cook such rich foods at home. Cristina responded, "*M'ija* [My daughter], that is why I am working here, because sometime we want to eat well too."

Employers I spoke with connected food and bodies in ways that reaffirmed or obscured class boundaries. Clara, a 30-something woman, claimed to have fired a previous employee in part because of her messy cooking style, saying the food "had a bad flavor [because] her hands were dirty, and her whole appearance was . . . messy." With their current worker, Clara and her husband Alfredo emphasized, they all ate together.

They looked down on those who made domestic workers eat separately, since "we are the same, human beings." The new employee's ability to present a neat appearance made her presence at the dinner table palatable to her employers.

Interviewees also discussed embodied inequality in dress and physical appearance. Domestic workers admitted that there were clothes or other items that they enjoyed or aspired to purchase. As Cristina put it, "Although I don't have money, I like to go to stores, to look and to fantasize." Fátima referred to the popular Ecuadorian saying, "They treat you according to how you look [*a uno como lo ven, lo tratan*]." She used this social practice of judging appearance (Casanova 2011, Chapter 4), which connotes a particular—often racialized—class status, as a justification for always wanting to look good in public. With such statements, workers like Fátima reaffirmed the symbolic importance of physical appearance for women of all class backgrounds. Her employers took notice, and when she requested their help in buying her prescription medicine, they criticized her for having money to do her hair and nails and buy perfume but not to provide for her health, implying that lower-class bodies did not deserve to be made attractive. Her attempt to make a claim on middle-class bodily habitus was thus delegitimized.

Workers often criticized employers' "vanity" or "fashion," referring to the value placed on presenting a socially acceptable middle-class appearance. Elsa had recently left her job over issues of back pay and vacation time. Elsa's employers claimed they couldn't pay her the salary she was owed, yet Elsa noted that any time the mother and daughter were invited to "half a party [*medio reunión*]," they would rush out to get their hair or nails done. Other workers said money that could have been used to pay domestic workers (whose presence in the home is a key symbol of middle-class status) was spent on what they perceived as superficial, temporary, bodily markers of class. Irma, an experienced domestic worker, was overwhelmed by the quantity of clothing, makeup, and accessories in her employer's home, confiding, "I'd go crazy with so much clothing, it's amazing . . . there were suitcases full of purses, full of every kind of makeup." It is harder for low-income women, including domestic workers, to access and "properly" use these symbolic props for middle-class respectability.

Female employers sometimes loan clothing to workers, or give them used clothing. Some workers viewed this as a benefit of their job. At Christmas, Patty's former employer gave her money to buy clothes, and loaned her clothes to attend social events in her rural hometown.[10] Yet she maintained the class line distinguishing worker from employer: Patty was told never to wear her employer's borrowed clothing "in the [employer's] neighborhood," only out of town, and she complied. Marina, a worker whose daughter had also worked in private homes, told me that she accepted used clothes from her former employer because she did not want to waste them; she distributed them among family and friends. Not all workers appreciate

hand-me-down clothing. Marina's daughter Francisca frowned on those "who give you the blouse they don't want any more . . . No, that's not a good employer. A good employer says, 'Come on and I'll buy you a new blouse.'" Cast-off clothing, especially if worn or ill-fitting, marks the lower-class body (Adair 2001), whereas new clothing adds value to the worker's appearance.[11]

The Uniform as Embodiment of Inequality

In popular culture portrayals, it is easy to pick out the domestic worker in a privileged space: She's the one wearing the maid uniform. Uniforms are sold in Guayaquil's department stores and grocery stores, where uniformed domestic workers can be spotted pushing employers' shopping carts or tending to their children. These garments tend to be loose-fitting housecoats, or resemble medical scrubs: The stereotypical, black-and-white version is rare. Uniforms are different enough from everyday street clothing to visually distinguish women as domestics at a glance. Many employers pay for or provide uniforms for their employers, whereas others (to the chagrin of workers) take the cost out of the employee's pay.

I asked both workers and employers[12] about uniforms. The employers interviewed did not require uniforms, describing them as unnecessary and old-fashioned. They mentioned wanting the worker to feel comfortable, especially when caring for young children. Employer Clara, who wore a uniform in her job as a hotel manager, said she had denied her domestic worker's request for a uniform. Perhaps because of her own embodied experience of wearing a uniform as a professional, she saw uniforms not as indicative of low social status, but the opposite: "I personally see the uniform as a differentiation of social strata, so here you see people wearing uniforms who are . . . from a higher socioeconomic level." For Clara, the uniform symbolized middle-class, professional, rather than low, status; it was part of her occupational habitus as a college-educated manager.

Of the workers who expressed opinions about uniforms, seven viewed them negatively and one positively.[13] Plain-spoken Paola, who had to wear a uniform a few times at a previous job, declared it "a humiliation" and "a piece of trash [*una porqueria*]." When a domestic worker goes out in public with her employer, Paola said, "a person can distinguish who is the employee and who is the boss." This is especially relevant when both the employer and employee are *mestiza*. Patty, who had never worn a uniform, described domestic workers' uniforms as "sad dresses." She said that simply because a woman was a domestic she shouldn't have to be "all scruffy . . . with ugly sandals." (In Guayaquil, "ugly" sandals or flip-flops signal lower-class status—middle-class habitus generally reserves flip-flops for beachwear or housewear.) The point of such a display, Patty said, was for an employer to demonstrate that "that person is his/her employee." When the lady of the house goes shopping with her daughter, no one mistakes the daughter for a domestic worker, Patty remarked. Domestic workers generally felt that when they wore uniforms in public, people thought, "Look, there's an *empleada*, a nanny." The uniform clarifies and amplifies the message of the symbolic body.

Francisca, otherwise calm and soft-spoken as we chatted, spoke excitedly when the talk turned to uniforms: "It's like they [uniforms] make you feel like a [derogatory term for maid], like you're less than." While working for a downtown family, she had to wear a uniform only when she went shopping. When asked how she felt, she replied, "Ooooh, like the lowest, because, imagine, in the middle of downtown and dressed like that . . . I felt really very bad [*me senti recontra que mal*]." Francisca eventually told her employer that she didn't like going shopping, and, surprisingly, the employer did not push back. Francisca forfeited an opportunity to escape the confines of the home because of the embarrassment the uniform entailed.

While workers expressed concerns about public perceptions, they also discussed how these stigmatizing clothes looked and felt on the body. Several bemoaned the poor quality of the uniforms required by employers. Francisca described feeling physically uncomfortable in the uniform, which was "like, too hot, different, [when] one is used to wearing her own little clothes." Paola said vehemently:

Aside from everything else, it's a poorly made uniform. . . . If it were a uniform, a little pantsuit with a little T-shirt, great, fine. Or, why can't I wear pants and a T-shirt like they do in offices? . . . But instead they have to buy the worst . . . fabric because that's how they've treated us, like the lowest of the low [*la última rueda del coche*].

More egregious than bad fabric was bad fit. Patricia complained about having to use worn-out uniforms left behind by previous employees. Women's bodies are all different: "One is fat and the other is thin . . . there should be a uniform that fits one's body." When Belén protested the poor fit of her uniform, her employer replied, "I bought it for your body." Belén disagreed, telling me, "I look like a potato sack with no potatoes, because it fits me so big, and I don't like that." So she wore it around the house, but changed into her own clothes to go out, because the uniform "fit me so ugly." Ugliness is thus associated with both domestic work and lower-class status.

Several workers described households as having just one uniform, to be used by whoever was working in the home. References to a one-size-fits-all, used uniform evoke the image of a garment hanging on a hook in the kitchen, waiting for a domestic worker to literally put on or to embody the role of the help. The uniform stays on the hook and the individual worker (with her unique size, shape, and preferences) changes. This represents the ultimate de-individualization of the worker, in which anybody can be stuffed into or swim around in a generic uniform not chosen for her needs, but to symbolize a social/occupational role. Irma, who generally liked uniforms and whom I often saw wearing medical scrubs-type garments, decided to get her own well-fitting uniforms in order to avoid those provided by employers, which she described as "mistreated" and "badly washed."

Some interviewees interpreted the employer's choice of ill-fitting (usually too large) and unattractive uniforms not just as a demarcation of workers' low status but as an effort to desexualize their bodies, to prevent them from being viewed or targeted sexually by male employers. Patricia commented, "The important thing is that it fits you big, because they don't like it small," yet for workers, such a large garment felt like "a nightgown." When Cristina was searching for words to describe the physical encumbrance posed by overly large uniforms, I interjected:

Erynn: You have to be able to move to do things . . .

Cristina: Yes, of course, right? So sometimes they give you a long dress, but I say, what's the reason for the long dress? . . . They must be thinking that you're going to steal their husband or something, right?

Cumbersome clothes limit the ability to use the body as a resource, but also have a symbolic dimension: Cristina viewed these modesty requirements as a way of managing the sexual threat posed by the presence of an unrelated female in the home of a married couple. Paola was explicitly instructed by a female employer to "be careful around the son and the husband," and to "wear a bigger pair of shorts, so that you couldn't see my . . ." While we might applaud the employer for wanting to protect her, it is worth noting that she put the onus on Paola to discourage harassment, rather than expecting her male relatives to behave appropriately. Paola agreed with the employer's suggestion, saying "it was obvious" that she should dress more modestly. Domestic workers thus adjust their appearance as employers require, whether or not they internalize stereotypes that characterize them as hypersexual.

CONCLUSION: EMBODIED INEQUALITY

The questions driving this research were (1) How do bodies matter in domestic work? and

(2) How does this employment arrangement relate to broader social ideas about bodies of different class status? In the accounts presented here, workers described their embodied employment experience in ways that fit both "body as resource" and "body as symbol" theoretical frameworks, pointing to the usefulness of a more comprehensive, holistic approach to embodied inequality.

Bodies matter in all jobs: Even the most cerebral, intellectual tasks are performed by humans who have/are bodies. In discussing their work, domestic workers emphasized the physicality of the tasks and the deleterious effects on their bodies. They described their work as exhausting, accelerating the deterioration of their bodies, and potentially dangerous. These accounts conceive of the body as a limited resource women draw on to do their work, which can be used up or damaged in the process.

Bodies also matter in terms of the symbolic distinctions drawn between "good," middle-class/elite bodies and "bad," lower-class/deviant bodies—between employers' and workers' bodies. Workers face clear boundaries between themselves and employers in relation to health, food consumption, and appearance. Even employers who buck tradition by pursuing more egalitarian relations (e.g., dining with their workers) are aware of the differential values typically placed on differently classed bodies. The uniform, an iconic symbol of domestic service throughout the Americas, was viewed by most of the workers and, interestingly, by the young employers I interviewed, as a superfluous relic of a more oppressive class order. Yet, 70 percent of the domestic workers interviewed had been asked by employers to wear uniforms, so the practice is still alive. Most workers hated being made to wear ill-fitting, cheaply-made uniforms, and several described feeling embarrassed for other women they saw visibly marked as domestics in public spaces. Many who referred to the physical challenges of domestic work also drew on the idea of the body as a malleable symbol of status in describing the embodied aspects of their relations to employers. . . .

These accounts highlight "the management of embodied emotional experience and display" (Gimlin 2007, 353) seen in domestic workers' acquiescence to the bodily regimes of employers in a context of limited employment alternatives. The successful embodiment of modesty (in dress and manner) required by employers is one example of the ways that domestic workers manage their bodies and emotions. Workers' stories of the physical damage and health hazards of the job exemplify "the production or modification of bodies through work" (Gimlin 2007, 353). Bodies are often changed for the worse by engaging in domestic work, and lower-class women's bodies are reproduced as "less than" or "the lowest of the low," to use the workers' terms.

This empirical study can help further theoretical understandings of bodies, work, and class in Latin America and beyond, following the lead of the domestic workers as folk theorists who combine the "body as resource" and "body as symbol" perspectives in a comprehensive view of embodied inequality. Examining one case in depth demonstrates how class-based occupational habitus is created or resisted in employment situations, especially those that begin early in life, like domestic work. Domestics in Guayaquil come from lower-class (sometimes rural) backgrounds, and their bodies are marked as poor and undesirable prior to entering the workforce—in a sense, the lower-class body is already a sort of uniform. Workers become further accustomed to the material and symbolic devaluation of their bodies as they are fed inferior food with separate dishes in separate areas of the home, not permitted to attend to their health problems (some of which emerge from the repetitive physical damage of domestic labor), and denied the objects associated with an acceptable or attractive middle-class feminine appearance. Workers exercise the most resistance in the area of appearance, subverting employers' dress codes, or compensating for the symbolic degradation of their bodies at work by investing in a feminine appearance outside of work. In a local context characterized by racial and class anxiety, and (perceived or actual) political challenges to middle-class status by Ecuador's left-leaning government, employers are invested in holding the line that separates them from employees, and employees are acutely aware of this.

NOTES

1. Aside from its symbolic aspects, habitus can be a source of identification and meaning-making for individuals.

2. In her study of domestic work in contemporary South Africa, King identifies the uniform as a "symbolic representation of the regulation of their [workers'] constructed role" (King 2007, 36), For uniforms' role in society, see Joseph (1986).

3. These interviews are part of an ongoing multimethod study of domestic work in Guayaquil, including informal interviews, participant observation with a domestic worker organization, archival research, and analysis of help wanted ads. I met the domestic worker-interviewees through fieldwork at the organization, and employer interviewees were referred by personal contacts.

4. All workers interviewed were connected to the domestic worker advocacy organization where I conducted ethnographic fieldwork. This may bias my sample: Interviewees may be more committed to domestic workers' rights or more politically oriented than other domestic workers.

5. The legal monthly minimum wage in Ecuador, to which domestic workers were legally entitled at the time of the interviews, was $240 (plus benefits: Social Security, overtime, vacation, etc.). Most domestic workers in Guayaquil were paid around $200 per month, with unpaid overtime and no benefits.

6. In Ecuador (as in many developing countries), most drugs are available in pharmacies without a prescription.

7. See Auyero's (2011) excellent ethnography of "poor people's waiting" in government benefits offices in Argentina. Sutton's interviews with domestic workers in Argentina also highlighted long waits to see doctors as a reason that women "neglected signs of illness in their bodies' (Sutton 2010, 56). One domestic worker Sutton interviewed said, "I know I cannot get sick" (ibid.).

8. Historian Shailaja Paik notes the similar embodied exclusion of Datit people in India, particularly in educational settings (personal communication).

9. Thanks to Tamara Mose Brown for highlighting this point (personal communication).

10. Patty offered clothes lending as an example of how a "good employer" behaves.

11. Rollins argues that gifts from employer to domestic, not expected to be reciprocated and often used or worn, highlight employees' inferior status, symbolically defining them as "needy" and "dependent" (1985, 192–94).

12. The employers I interviewed were working professionals in their 30s, just starting their families. Thus, their opinions on uniforms may differ from older or wealthier employers.

13. This worker favored uniforms, yet was critical of the quality and appearance of those typically offered by employers, and thus preferred to buy or make her own (at her expense).

REFERENCES

Adair, Vivyan C. 2001. Branded with infamy: Inscriptions of poverty and class in the United States. *Signs* 27:451–71.

Auyero, Javier. 2011. Patients of the state: An ethnographic account of poor people's waiting. *Latin American Research Review* 46:5–29.

Bahnisch, Marc. 2000. Embodied work, divided labour: Subjectivity and the scientific management of the body in Frederick W. Taylor's 1907 "Lecture on Management." *Body & Society* 6:51–68.

Bank Muñoz, Carolina. 2008. *Transnational tortillas: Race, gender, and shop-floor politics in Mexico and the United States.* Ithaca, NY: Cornell University Press.

Bourdieu, Pierre. 1977. *Outline of a theory of practice.* Cambridge, UK: Cambridge University Press.

Bourdieu, Pierre. 1990. *The logic of practice.* Cambridge, UK: Polity.

Bourdieu, Pierre. (1984) 2007. *Distinction: A social critique of the judgment of taste* (R. Nice, trans.). Cambridge, MA: Harvard University Press.

Casanova, Erynn Masi de. 2011. *Making up the difference: Women, beauty, and direct selling in Ecuador.* Austin: University of Texas Press.

De la Torre, Carlos, and Steve Striffler, eds. 2008. *The Ecuador reader: History, culture, politics.* Durham, NC: Duke University Press.

Edmonds, Alexander, 2010. *Pretty modern: Beauty, sex, and plastic surgery in Brazil.* Durham, NC: Duke University Press.

Ehrenreich, Barbara, and Arlie R. Hochschild, eds. 2004. *Global woman: Nannies, maids, and sex workers in the new economy.* New York: Henry Holt.

Estrada, Daniela. 2009. Strides and setbacks for domestic and rural workers. *Inter Press Service.* http://www.ipsnews.net/2009/09/latin-america-strides-and-setbacks-for-domestic-and-rural-workers.

Floro, María, and John Messier, 2006. Tendencias y patrones de crédito entre hogares urbanos pobres en Ecuador. In *La Persistencia de la desigualdad: Género, trabajo y pobreza en América Latina,* edited by Gioconda Herrera. Quito, Ecuador: FLASCO.

Freeman, Carla. 2000. *High tech and high heels in the global economy. Women, work, and pink-collar identities in the Caribbean.* Durham, NC: Duke University Press.

Gatens, Moira. 1996. *Imaginary bodies: Ethics, power, and corporeality.* London: Routledge.

Gill, Lesley. 1990. Painted faces: Conflict and ambiguity in domestic servant employer relations in La Paz, 1930–1988. *Latin American Research Review* 25:119–36.

Gill, Lesley. 1994. *Precarious dependencies: Gender, class and domestic service in Bolivia.* New York: Columbia University Press.

Gimlin, Debra. 2007. What is "body work"? A review of the literature. *Sociology Compass* 1:353–70.

Goffman, Erving. 1959. *The presentation of self in everyday life.* Garden City. NY: Doubleday.

Hall, A., J. Hockey, and V. Robinson. 2007. Occupational cultures and the embodiment of masculinity: Hairdressing, estate agency and firefighting. *Gender, Work, and Organization* 14:534–51.

Hochschild, Arlie R. 1983. *The managed heart: The commercialization of human feeling.* Berkeley: University of California Press.

INEC (Instituto Nacional de Estadística y Censos). 2012. http://www.inec.gob.ec.

Joseph, Nathan. 1986. *Uniforms and nonuniforms: Communication through clothing.* New York: Greenwood.

Kang, Miliann. 2010. *The managed hand: Race, gender; and the body in beauty service work.* Berkeley: University of California Press.

King, Alison Jill. 2007. *Domestic service in post-apartheid South Africa: Deference and disdain.* Burlington, VT: Ashgate.

Marx, Karl. (1844) 1978. Economic and philosophic manuscripts of 1844. In *The Marx-Engels reader,* 2nd edition, edited by Robert C. Tucker: New York: Norton.

McDowell, Linda. 1997. Capital culture: Gender at work in the city. Oxford: Blackwell.

M.I. Municipalidad de Guayaquil. 2010. http://www.guayaquil.gob.ec.

Miles, Ann. 1998. Women's bodies, women's selves: Illness narratives and the "Andean" body. *Body & Society* 4:1–19.

Nencel, Lorraine. 2008. "Que viva la minifalda!": Secretaries, miniskirts and daily practices of sexuality in the public sector in Lima. *Gender, Work, and Organization* 17:69–90.

Rahier, Jean Muteba. 1998. Blackness, the "racial"/spatial order, migrations, and Miss Ecuador 1995–1995. *American Anthropologist* 100: 421–30.

Ray, Raka, and Seemin Qayum. 2009. *Cultures of servitude: Modernity, domesticity, and class in India.* Stanford, CA: Stanford University Press.

Roberts, Elizabeth F.S. 2012. *God's laboratory. Assisted reproduction in the Andes.* Berkeley: University of California Press.

Rollins, Judith. 1985. *Between women: Domestics and their employers.* Philadelphia, PA: Temple University Press.

Salzinger, Leslie. 2003. *Genders in production: Making workers in Mexico's global factories.* Berkeley: University of California Press.

Shilling, Curt. (1993) 2003. *The body and social theory,* 2nd edition. London: Sage.

Skeggs, Beverly. 2004a. Exchange, value, and affect: Bourdieu and the "self." *The Sociological Review* 52:75–95.

Skeggs, Beverly. 2004b. Context and background. Pierre Bourdieu's analysis of class, gender, and sexuality. *The Sociological Review* 52: 19–33.

Sutton, Barbara. 2010. *Bodies in crisis: Culture, violence, and women's resistance in neoliberal Argentina.* New Brunswick, NJ: Rutgers University Press.

Introduction to Reading 27

Orna Sasson-Levy, a sociologist at Bar-Ilan University in Israel, is a specialist in gender and ethnic aspects of the military and militarism. She is the author of *Identities in Uniform: Masculinities and Femininities in the Israeli Military* (2006, Jerusalem: Magnes Press). In this article, she offers extensive analysis of the transformative bodily and emotional practices that have become key to framing male combat service in Israel as an individualistic enterprise in which the soldier perceives his military activities as "masculine self-actualization." Sasson-Levy argues that young men in Israel are willing to kill and be killed not only for the good of the collective but also in the name of individualized hegemonic masculinity. The author's exploration of links between sexist views and nationalist views in Israel has resulted in both praise and condemnation.

1. How does the soldier's body provide the "material infrastructure" of the connection between military service and the state?

2. Discuss the role of self-control and thrill as sources of the soldier's "status of exclusivity and its justification."

3. How does gendering of the soldier's body act as a control mechanism that encourages young men to go to war and risk their lives?

INDIVIDUAL BODIES, COLLECTIVE STATE INTERESTS

THE CASE OF ISRAELI COMBAT SOLDIERS

Orna Sasson-Levy

This article seeks to advance a new understanding of the ways in which hegemonic institutions are embodied and reproduced through the construction of extreme masculinities. In particular, I focus on the management of the body and emotions among Israeli combat soldiers as an interface between state and military constructions and individual experience.

Until recently, most writing on the military and gender focused on the problematic of women's military service, while taking men's service for granted. However, Kovitz suggests that research should "shift from problematizing women's service to problematizing that of men" (Kovitz 2003, 1). For Kovitz, the main question is why men agree to go to war and not why women are excluded from it. More specifically, she asks how democratic societies, whose liberal values would seem to contradict the coercive values found in the military, succeed in persuading men that they want to enlist in the army and participate in warfare.

The primary question this article raises, then, concerns how states convince young men to go to war. This is not a new question, and it has been answered before in different ways. First and foremost, states generate nationalist feelings in their subjects by constructing collective identities based on (real or invented) traditions and a common origin, and develop militarized patterns of socialization that prepare their youth to join the military forces (Furman 1999). At the same time, they produce (or maintain) a perception of

existential threat, which can be very real or utterly constructed. In both cases, men enlist into the army in response to the call of the state.

The state's call to sign up for military service is supplemented by a promise for equal citizenship. In the West, military service and war have been integral to the definition of citizenship (Janowitz 1994; Tilly 1996). Thus, minority groups sought to perform military service to demonstrate their political loyalty and worthiness as citizens and to enhance their civic standing (Burk 1995; Gill 1997).

These appeals to men to risk their lives for the good of the collective are always gendered. Militaries have been identified as masculine institutions not only because they are populated with men but also because they constitute a major arena for the construction of masculine identities and play a primary role in shaping images of masculinity in society at large (Barrett 1996; Connell 1995; Morgan 1994). Nagel (1998) shows that terms like *honor, cowardice, bravery, heroism, duty,* and *adventure* are hard to distinguish as either nationalistic or masculine. Thus, despite far-reaching political, social, and technological changes, the warrior is still a key symbol of masculinity (Morgan 1994, 165), and militaries are often described as "the last bastion of masculinity" (Addelston and Stirratt 1996). The chance to "become a man" is therefore another important enticement into military life.

Another reason for mobilization is economic: When the military in many Western states shifted from mandatory conscription to all-volunteer forces, it was often those in dire economic situations who enlisted. In the United States, for example, military service is perceived as a path for social mobility, and most soldiers sign up for economic reasons (Enloe 1980 ; Moskos 1993, 86). And, finally, in some countries, though not as many as in the past, men enlist because of coercive state laws requiring mandatory conscription, which is the case in Israel.

Most of these reasons for enlistment are related to the formation of the modern nation state and are thus relevant to Israel as well. However, with the impact of globalization, the configuration of the modern nation-state is rapidly changing (Comaroff 1996), and the link between citizen and state is taking on a new character, a consequence of which is changing mobilization rates. In Israel, the impact of globalization has been a gradual shift from a collective orientation toward a more individualistic one (Horowitz and Lissak 1989; Ram 1999).[1] The roots of this social shift are usually traced to the end of the 1970s, with Israel's signing of a peace accord with Egypt, the growth of the capitalist free market, and the influence of globalizing developments that accelerated processes of privatization. These processes stimulated the decline of communal public spiritedness and the rise of an individualistic orientation that emphasizes self-fulfillment and human and civic rights (Shafir and Peled 1998).

One might expect that the decline of Israeli collectivism would result in the devaluing of the militaristic ethos in general and the status of the warrior in particular. Moreover, the current armed conflict is not perceived as posing an existential threat to Israel's security and does not demand total mobilization. In such a situation of a protracted "low-intensity" conflict, the state may well encounter difficulties in maintaining the dominance of a republican discourse, which exalts the self-sacrifice of the masculine combat soldier.

However, in spite of social and ideological changes, Israel's Jewish community perceives the military as the emblem of pure patriotism and

as one of the major symbols of the collective (Kimmerling 1993). In this militaristic culture, the (Jewish) combat soldier has achieved the status of hegemonic masculinity and is identified with good citizenship.

There seems to be a gap, then, between the individualistic trends and the tenacity of the status of the combat soldier. How can we explain the persistence of the warrior's hegemonic status, despite the changes in the relationship between the individual and the collective, the citizen and the nation-state? In this ambivalent social context, how can the state create and maintain "armed masculinity" (Snyder 1999) as a normative social ideal? My aim in this article is to propose other, more subtle ways through which men are lured into fighting at a time when the link between the individual and the state is being transformed.

In the past few years, there has been a growing interest in militarized masculine bodies (Armitage 2003). The research in this field explores how the masculine civilian body is adapted to military use and demonstrates how, with the inculcation of military principles, the body is classified, transformed, and reshaped to meet military and state goals (Ben-Ari 1998; Higate 2003; Peniston-Bird 2003). I suggest that we should look at the connection between these transformative body techniques and the motivation or persuasion question posed by Kovitz (2003), to analyze how specific constructions of militarized bodies lure men into fighting and thus serve the interests of the state. Based on in-depth interviews with combat soldiers, I argue that the construction of the Israeli combat soldier involves two seemingly opposing themes: on one hand, self-control, and on the other, thrill (in Hebrew, *rigush*). While the theme of self-control is characterized by introversion, self-restraint, and self-repression, the theme of thrill accentuates the outward expression of wild, unrestrained feelings, stemming from life-endangering events, adventurous activities, and unique opportunities the military offers for intimacy among men. These interdependent themes accentuate a growing sense of agency and self-actualization, thus allowing, and even promoting, their interpretation through an individualistic frame. The individualistic framing of bodily and emotional practices enables an ambivalent and nonpolitical interpretation of military actions, as it disguises the coercive nature of military service and obscures the collective state interests that are served by the individual male body.

THEORETICAL OVERVIEW: GENDERED BODY AND EMOTION MANAGEMENT

Social theories have shifted in the past two decades from emphasizing the cognitive dimension of identity construction to exploring the embodiment of identities (Shilling 1993, 3). The growing interest in the sociology of the body derives both from feminist thought, which highlighted women's bodies as the major political site of patriarchal domination (Bordo 1993), and from Foucault's (1975, 1978, 1980) writings, which enabled research on the "history of the body" and provided the outline for it.

Foucault's innovation lies in analyzing the body as produced by and existing in the discourses and social institutions that govern it. For Foucault (1975), the body is an object of power and a direct locus of social control. His ultimate example of the external construction of the body is the soldier, who, by the late eighteenth century, had "become something that can be made; out of formless clay, an inept body, the machine required can be constructed" (p. 135). The soldier's docile body serves to exemplify the link between daily practices on one hand and the large-scale organization of power on the other (Dreyfus and Rabinow 1982).

While Foucault's writings portrayed the body as a surface to be written on, other sociologists argue that one does not have to accept naturalistic or sociobiological views to acknowledge the body's materiality and corporeality, which always limit its range of possibilities. Frank, for example, proposes to analyze the body as constituted in the intersection of an equilateral triangle, the points of which are institutions, discourses,

and corporeality (Frank 1991, 48–49). Similarly, Shilling (1993, 12) conceptualizes the body as "an unfinished biological and social phenomena, which is transformed, within certain limits, as a result of its entry into and participation in society." Foucault himself, in his later writings, attributed more agency to the individual, suggesting that a theory of domination must start with the body dominating itself (Foucault 1978). Social analysis has thus expanded from studying the body as an object of social control and discipline "in order to legitimate different regimes of domination" (Bordo 1993; Foucault 1980) to perceiving the body as participating in its own shaping, as it creates meaning and performs social action (Davis 1997).

As a signifier of social identity, the body participates in the constitution of social inequalities. This is clear when we look at men's and women's bodies. Connell (1987) argued that by neglecting biological similarities and exaggerating biological differences, gendered practices create corporeal differences between men and women where none existed previously. These differences are then used to justify and legitimize the original hierarchal social categories.

Frank (1991) points to two types of bodies that can characterize the combat soldier: the disciplined body (pp. 54–61) and the dominating body (pp. 69–79). When the disciplined body, which "makes itself predictable through its regimentation" (p. 55), directs practices of discipline and control upon others, this body turns into the second type, the dominating body, which is, according to Frank, exclusively male. A prime example of the dominating body can be found in *Male Fantasies,* Theweleit's (1987–1989) rich description and analysis of masculinities constructed in the German Freikorps, an army unit that was formed at the end of World War I (soldiers in this unit later served in the SA and SS). For the German fascist, Theweleit argues, there existed only two types of bodies; the first was the erect, steel-hard, "organized machine" body of the German master. This controlled and emotionally bereft male warrior ideal reacts with revulsion and fear to the second body, the flaccid and fluid female body of the negative Other, lurking inside the male body.

As is obvious from this analysis, bodies and embodiment cannot be discussed in isolation from emotions, which are experienced through the body and shape the way we experience it (Csordas 1993). Similarly to the body, emotions "are treated as material things" (Lutz and White 1986, 407), as a universal aspect of human experience that is least subjected to social construction (Abu-Lughod and Lutz 1990, 1). However, the historical and cultural variability of emotions suggests that "subjective experiences and emotional beliefs are both socially acquired and socially structured" (Thoits 1989, 319; Rosaldo 1984). Emotions can thus be understood as *discursive practices,* which are "created in, rather than shaped by, speech" (Abu-Lughod and Lutz 1990, 10, 12).

As socially constructed *ideological practices,* emotions are always "involved in negotiation over the meaning of events, over rights and morality, over control of resources" (Lutz 1988, 5). Power relations determine what must, can, or cannot be said about the self and emotions; what is believed to be true or false about them; and what can only be said about them by certain individuals and not others. These "feeling rules" (Hochschild 1983) are always gendered; since women are believed to be "more emotional than men," any discourse on emotion is also a discourse on gender (Lutz 1988, 69). The masculine imperative for emotional self-control, which is especially pertinent to combat soldiers, confers men with prestige and locates them in a superior position to women. Emotional norms are thus produced by dominant institutional arrangements and function to sustain them (Thoits 1989, 328). This is particularly accurate when one examines "extreme" gender identities that are constituted by and for the state, identities such as warrior masculinity.

Combat Masculinity and the State

Military service, and especially warfare, is one of the primary means by which Western states established their power within societies (Giddens 1985; Tilly 1985). The link between war and state building is expressed in the republican

ethos, which defines the subject's citizenship according to his (but not her) contribution to the state. In militaristic societies, the most significant contribution to the state is participating in the armed forces. This connection between military service and the state is based upon the glorification of militarized masculinity, with the soldier's body providing its material infrastructure.

Following the transition to voluntary professional armies in Western nation-states, the military lost some of its power to shape the meaning of citizenship. In Israel, however, the link between citizenship, military service, and masculinity carries a special meaning (Kimmerling 1993). War and routine conflict management have played a central role in shaping Israel's Jewish community of citizens, a community in which civic virtue is often constructed in terms of military virtue (Helman 1997). In this social context, the Jewish combat soldier has achieved the status of hegemonic masculinity,[2] which has become synonymous with good citizenship (Lomsky-Feder and Ben Ari 1999; Sasson-Levy 2003a). Although combat soldiers make up only 20 percent of the total complement (Cohen 1997, 86), the ideal of warrior masculinity is consensual, transcending ethnic, religious, and class boundaries (though not national ones).

War and military service are represented as enabling the male subject to "become a man" (Morgan 1994; Mosse 1996; Peniston-Bird 2003). Although the military should not be seen as constructing a single embodied masculinity (Barrett 1996; Enloe 1988; Higate 2003; Morgan 1994; Theweleit 1987–1989), theoretical literature on the combat soldier's identity tends to emphasize the single aspect of physical and emotional self-control (Arkin and Dubrofsky 1978; Ben-Ari 1998). War provides the opportunity to nurture the individual's ability to endure pain and even mutilation and to control emotion. Any sign of weakness, vulnerability, or even sensitivity can be interpreted in the military as a sign of homosexuality and, hence, of "failed masculinity" (Petersen 1998, 53).

The Israeli militarized body is fashioned according to a utopian collectivist and gendered ideology, emphasizing the "chosen body" of the healthy, strong, and active Jewish male (Weiss 2002). This "perfect" body, which in reality was the lot of only a select few, was seen as an ideal type, and comparisons with it generated a hierarchy of bodies, defining the boundaries of the collective and its internal stratification (see also Peniston-Bird 2003). The combat soldier—who possesses the perfect body—proves his masculinity through emotional self-control that is attained to cope with stress, anxiety, chaos, and confusion, all of which characterize the battlefield (Ben-Ari 1998, 42–46). As the schema of the battle is also a schema for achieving and reaffirming Jewish Israeli manhood (Ben-Ari 1998, 112), controlling one's emotions is perceived as successfully passing the test of masculinity.

My argument is that alongside the discourse of self-control and discipline, an additional discourse of thrill and excitement enacts and shapes the body and emotions of the warrior in different ways. The discourse of thrill is of critical importance, as it is emphasized by soldiers as a major force in mobilizing their motivation and willingness to go to war. Thrill plays an important role both in the discourse the army uses to lure men into soldiering and in the narratives of soldiers themselves. It appears, then, that even within the military cultural arena, which has been presented as the epitome of hegemonic top-down construction, there are signs of agency, where soldiers actively seek bodily and emotional experiences with which to constitute and assert themselves.

METHOD

This article is based on interviews with twenty male combat soldiers within one year of their release from army service: one artillery man, three infantry soldiers, three parachutists, four from the engineering corps, three from reconnaissance units, one from the navy, four from the armored forces, and one former combat intelligence officer.

Body practices and emotional management were not the main focus of the interviews. However, these issues were raised by the soldiers so often that I was forced to recognize their centrality in the military experience of the combat soldier. In comparison, noncombat soldiers whom I also interviewed (see Sasson-Levy 2003b) did not talk about body practices in the interviews at all.

It is important to note right from the start that there is no unified and universal version of "Israeli combat masculinity." The masculine model of the pilot, for example, is quite different from that of men in the armored forces, the navy, or the infantry brigades. Moreover, there are even differences between one infantry brigade and another. For instance, the masculinity of the paratroopers' unit in Israel emphasizes rationality, self-control, and self-discipline, while the men of the Golani infantry brigade accentuate resistance to discipline and rebelliousness along with physical capabilities and courage. These different masculine identities indicate that the act of fighting itself does not require one specific gendered ideology and that there is nothing "natural" or essential about the warrior's identity that derives from the act of fighting itself. Due to space limitations, this article cannot show the different nuances of armed masculinity in Israel and can only delineate its general contours.

BODILY AND EMOTIONAL SELF-CONTROL

Soldiering the Body

According to military belief, "masculinity is determined primarily by a healthy body, not a healthy mind" (Arkin and Dobrofsky 1978, 156). Having a masculine body that is healthy, strong, and sturdy is a prerequisite to becoming a combat soldier. However, having the right body is insufficient; one must also be willing to shape and discipline it so that it meets military objectives. Therefore, the tests for combat units (held a few months before enlistment) examine both the physical abilities of adolescent boys and their willingness to stretch these capacities to the limits. Yonatan, who served in the prestigious air force rescue unit, explained, "In basic training, you receive all your credit through physical activity alone. The minute you're physically inactive [if you're injured], you're a leper, you're a leech, you're a parasite, and you're good for nothing."[3]

In other interviews, soldiers repeatedly emphasized the theme of self-control over their bodies. To be more precise, the men did not talk about self-control as much as they described their struggles to achieve control over their bodies. Eldad, a tank commander, explained,

> During long marches, the strain would push people into screaming at each other, really cursing one another; their legs would hurt and they'd feel that this is the end, that they'd reached their limit, and then they would see that they could stretch that limit a little further. This exercise teaches them that the limit is not where they thought it was but always a little further.

Basic training is devoted to forging and strengthening the male body, to taking it to new extremes. At the same time, it inscribes on the body the signs of one's specific combat role. Through the specific body management of each unit, the soldiers shape a new military identity. Simple daily activities such as walking, eating, and sitting assume a new form and meaning. Guy, an infantry soldier in an elite unit, vividly described the unique bodily dimensions of each unit, even during supposedly "passive" activities such as platoon talks:

> We would see the other platoons, sitting relaxed and talking to their commanders. But in my unit, we would have to sit absolutely straight, our gun upright and hands stretched straight in front of the body. The talk could last forty-five minutes, or an hour, but if a fly zooms by your eyes and you take your hand off your rifle to shoo the fly away, you pay. You start running, and running, and running.

Guy's description of his unit's specific style demonstrates how military thinking and culture are transmitted through the body and imprinted on it (Foucault 1975). His quote alludes to the central role of the body in military punishment. As one of the main mechanisms for discipline, punishment is often inflicted directly on the body, through recurring "stretcher hikes," carrying heavy loads, crawling on thorns, doing dozens of push-ups or hundreds of sit-ups, and more. Physical punishment inscribes on the soldier's body the fear of military discipline and the dread of authority, until he internalizes military principles and they become a part of who he is. Thus, formal homogenization processes, such as uniforms and haircuts, are accompanied by violent mechanisms that aim at creating a standardized combatant male body.

Foucault (1975, 138) argued that "the military apparatus explores and studies the soldier's body in order to break it down and rearrange it according to its needs." Indeed, at the end of basic training, if the soldier completes it "in one piece" (and not all do), he has a body capable of things it was not capable of before; he has built the "body of a soldier." Dudi, an officer in the combat engineering corps, said,

> I never understood how it works, but after you're in the army for about a year, all these problems vanish. I don't know why, but I guess the body adjusts somehow. As a commander, I would carry things much heavier than during basic training, and I would say to myself that this is it, you just get used to it. I guess that just as the soles of your feet are getting rough, the skin on your back also gets rough at a certain stage.

The thick skin that Dudi develops "should not be understood metaphorically" (Theweleit 1987–1989, 144). The physical transformation bears institutional implications: as the soldier ceases to experience his body's pain or hunger as his own (Frank 1991, 56), soldiering becomes easier and more tolerable. Now, the soldier can better meet the needs of the state.

Bodily Masculinity Rites

The transformation of a body into a "soldier's body" has an unmistakable gendered meaning. Through the soldiering "body project"

(Connell 1995, 50), men's bodies become visibly different from those of women. In this sense, the soldier's embodiment plays a central role in the social construction of polarized gender identities and hierarchal gender regimes (Connell 1987). While intense physical strain prepares soldiers for combat conditions, it also serves as a selection mechanism and a rite of passage into Israeli hegemonic masculinity.

Service in the Israeli military is seen as the primary rite of passage that initiates adolescent boys into full membership in the masculine Zionist civil religion (Aronoff 1999; Ben-Ari 2000; Levy-Schreiber and Mazali 1993). Reuven's description of crucial moments during basic training indicates that the body is the main arena for these militarized rites of passage:

> The procedure is you get into the shooting position; you have to remain firm so that nothing moves you. We would get into shooting position, stand in line, and the officer . . . the bastard . . . he would come and kick us in the knees, the chest, the muscles of the legs, and we're supposed to stand firm, not to move, the muscles all tight . . . all your strength is invested in holding the weapon so that when he kicks you again it won't move you and won't make you shoot off-target.
>
> If I moved . . . did you notice my eye's reflex action? If that would have happened to me then it would have been a sign that I was frightened and that would have meant I was finished. He would have grabbed me by the shoulders and kneed me in the gut. He would beat me to a pulp.

Recall Spencer's (1965, 103) description of rites of passage through public circumcision by the Samburu: "Each youth, placed on view before his male relatives and prospective in-laws, must remain motionless and silent during the cutting. Even an involuntary twitch would be interpreted as a sign of fear." The similarities between the two descriptions of rites of passage—one in an African culture, the other in a seemingly modern western culture—are self-evident. In the same way, parachuting in the Israeli army is viewed as "a test which allows those who pass it to join an exclusive club, to be initiated into an

elite group" (Aran 1974, 150). Soldiers who go through military hardships intuitively understand that those who withstand them will achieve elite status. As hardship becomes the mark of masculinity, soldiers not only expect to suffer in basic training but are also proud of it and reiterate this in the interviews, as if to validate their hegemonic status (see also Gill 1997). Moreover, most combat soldiers complete basic training with various physical afflictions, some of which will never disappear. Military casualties are often the most dramatic claim to centrality in Israeli society (Aronoff 1999, 42). Therefore, the soldiers are proud of their wounds and scars, which serve as evidence of their willingness to sacrifice their bodies for the good of the collective.

The combat body project not only creates hierarchal gender differences, however, but also stratifies male bodies. The "chosen body" (Weiss 2002) of the combat soldier depends on the existence of the wrong body, the body that fails to become a combat soldier. The literature often specifies female or homosexual bodies as representative of the "wrong" military body. However, the soldiers I talked to did not compare themselves to women or homosexuals but mostly to other male heterosexual soldiers who had failed to endure the physical training—that is, the fat soldier, the lazy soldier, the "crybaby," or the soldier who is too small. As Robert Connell (1995, 75) notes, masculinity is a relational identity that is often constructed in relation to other masculinities. Michael Kimmel quotes the playwright David Mamet, saying, "Women have, in men's minds, such a low place on the social ladder . . . that it's useless to define yourself in terms of a woman. What man needs is men's approval" (Kimmel 1996, 7).

This self-comparison among men is, for Connell (1995), the reason behind most acts of violence. Most episodes of major violence are transactions among men, used as a means of drawing boundaries and making exclusions (Connell 1995, 83). Violence can become a way of claiming or asserting masculinity in struggles between groups. This is obvious in the attitudes of combat soldiers to those of their peers who do not meet the hegemonic model of masculinity.

Among those who fail the tests, the fat soldier is especially prone to abuse. The overweight soldier represents the opposite of "everything military." Omer, the tank driver, told the following story, which demonstrates the moral threat embodied in the fat soldier's body:

> We wouldn't let soldiers weep during punishments. We had this fat soldier, Danny. He would cry as a matter of principle, whether or not it was difficult. I remember that fatso starting to put on a show as if he was throwing up. I told him, "Hey, watch it, I'm warning you. Shut up," I told him, "You're crying like a little girl."

Danny, the antihero of this story, is doubly wrong—he is fat and cries. The other soldiers are angry with him because they see him as a spoiled, childish liar—all the characteristics that represent for them the opposite of manhood—but also because they worry that his behavior will reflect negatively on them. "It projects on all of us," Omer said. "We wanted to be seen as good guys, the best team." Those who have the wrong body present a threat to the masculinity of the whole group, a threat to social solidarity, and therefore, they constitute a legitimate target for ostracism, ridicule, and abuse. Thus, militarized initiation rites may produce group bonding, solidarity, and coherence (Winslow 1999), but they also create and maintain hierarchical differences among men.

Emotional Control

The perception of emotional control as a signifier of masculinity and hence of higher status (Lutz 1988) is not unique to the Israeli context. Emotional control has been associated with masculinity in Western culture from the early writings of the Greek philosophers through Kant, Descartes, and Hegel (Lloyd 1986; Ortner 1974). In their writings, men's emotional self-control (in other words, the emphasis on reason) signifies superiority (Seidler 1989) and is used to arrange and justify gendered hierarchies. Militarized masculinities seem particularly "obsessed" with emotional control. The Israeli combat soldier refers to emotional control or composure (in Hebrew, *kor ruach*—literally, "coolness of spirit"; Ben-Ari 1998, 45) as a personal and professional masculine achievement, an ideal that should be adopted by all soldiers. Kor ruach, which refers to the ability to act with confidence, poise, and composure under trying circumstances (Ben-Ari 1998, 45), is perceived as a key element of effective performance in day-to-day situations and especially in times of crisis. Alon, a tank commander, said, "Eventually, I became a better commander, more professional, and more understanding. I mean, I became better at commanding with composure: they shoot at us and I remain composed, a soldier tries to commit suicide and I remain composed." Alon describes a process by which he gradually achieves composure. This is important because he equates composure with successfully performing as an officer and considers it a criterion for evaluating competence. Similarly to Alon, other soldiers I talked to also did not perceive emotional self-control as a given masculine characteristic. Rather, they described it as an attribute that one learns, acquires, and perfects as one develops into a more professional soldier (and by extension, "more of a man"). Rami, a combat medic, described how the military creates this composure during the medics' course. Note how he links emotional composure to hypermasculinity:

> [In the medics course,] you come in, play with the dog, it wags its tail and all that, and a minute later, you see him in pieces like in a butcher's shop. It's this kind of act, which says, "I'm macho. I'm not afraid of blood." They want to get you to a certain threshold, so they show you pictures of horrible things. Victims of accidents, smashed limbs, smashed people. They show this to you so that you get accustomed to all this kind of stuff.

While the military applauds emotional self-control and develops mechanisms for teaching and even enforcing it, it would not be accurate to say that the army forbids all emotional expression. Rather, there seems to be an unwritten social and spatial "emotional mapping," similar to Hochschild's (1983, 18) "emotional rules," that dictates which emotions are allowed, when, where, and for what audience. Soldiers are encouraged, for example, to feel motivation and ambition; they can express happiness and pride on the day they complete basic training or more advanced courses; they are allowed to feel homesick (but only to a limited degree); and they are expected to feel desire for women. Most of all, they are supposed to feel affection and camaraderie toward other soldiers in the unit, an emotion that the army creates and exploits (and to which I will return later).

However, the demand for emotional self-control is often loaded with internal contradictions and paradoxical effects. First, acquiring emotional self-control facilitates the soldier's "automatic docility" (Foucault 1975), as it ensures that the soldier will not rebel or be paralyzed by fear in combat. By guaranteeing a high level of obedience and passivity, the imperative of emotional self-discipline provides a solid base for the constitution of the conformist citizen. However, paradoxically, the docility of the "good citizen" is experienced by the soldier as increased self-control and heightened masculinity. Thus, compulsory military service contributes to the disciplining of the citizen and reproduces the association between rational and restrained masculinity (Seidler 1989) and the interests of the state.

The second paradox relates to the fact that although power and control are perceived as central to the definition of *combat masculinity,* in reality, the combat soldier has only a limited degree of autonomy. To become a combat soldier, one must surrender one's autonomy and obey one's commanders for the major part of everyday life. Amos, a paratrooper, expressed this paradox when he explained how he survived basic training: "You simply have to say O.K., you, the army, can do whatever you want with me. I . . . in the end, I will make it. Even if I'm the last one, I will get there and succeed." When Amos says, "You can do whatever you want with

me," we learn that the power and control of the combat soldier are paradoxically achieved by surrendering control over the self. Moreover, giving up autonomy is not a passive project. On the contrary, the soldier needs to mobilize all his willpower to get through his seemingly endless training and to gain control over his body and emotions. Obedience is associated here with strenuous effort, hard physical work, and a strong will. Stiehm observed that "patriarchy promises power and benefits to the young men who ultimately prove themselves. But is that proof one of talent, of merit or of morality? No. It is, in fact, proof of submission. It is evidence of obedience. It is a demonstration of compliance and of willingness to risk and sometimes sacrifice" (Stiehm 1989, 227). As a reward for their strenuous efforts to attain physical and emotional self-control, soldiers are given the opportunity to experience physical and emotional thrill, which is regarded as an exclusive experience of combat soldiers.

THRILL

While most of the literature focuses on the theme of self-control, a second, and apparently contradictory, theme of thrill (in Hebrew, *rigush*—or "rush" in American slang) appeared time and again in the soldiers' narratives. Rigush implies intense feelings, both emotional and physical, that derive from extraordinary experiences that are perceived as inaccessible in everyday life. While militarized masculinity demands emotional control, military life nonetheless provides unique opportunities for experiencing the extraordinarily deep feeling of rigush.

The major source of rigush is the risk to one's life involved in being a combat soldier. Israeli culture imparts the heroic notion of self-sacrifice to Israeli males from early childhood. Even at this age, children are exposed to themes of persecution, heroism, and war, which recur throughout the year. Aronoff, for instance, claims that the memorialization of the dead soldier is so central in Israeli culture that it has evolved into a "national cult of the dead" (Aronoff 1999, 43). Although the ethos of self-sacrifice has been modified in the past twenty years (Zerubavel 1995), it still constitutes a major part of the combat soldiers' narratives. Dudi, a platoon commander in the combat engineering corps, explained,

> Do I think the army makes a man out of the boy? Look, it all depends on where you serve. The army turns a child into a man only if he serves in a combat unit. There you have to deal with issues of life and death, you get a sense of proportion concerning what life is all about, and you understand what is real in life. But I don't think the army makes men out of everybody. If you were in the units where I served, or in the infantry, or even in the armored corps or artillery [then it does], but the rest of the units I can't guarantee it.

For Dudi, masculinity is directly associated with confronting issues of life and death and is achieved through facing the biggest test of all: the willingness to sacrifice one's life for one's country. Self-sacrifice is the sign of the hero, he who has the courage to rise above his basic instinct for life and fight for the good of his imagined community. Serving as a combat soldier provides one of the very few chances in life to receive recognition for heroism, which is a source of honor and thrill in itself. Endangering one's life is seen by soldiers as the ultimate actualization of both masculinity and nationality, and thus, it serves as a criterion in social and military stratification systems (E. Levy 1998; Lomsky-Feder 1998; Weiss 2002). Soldiers perceive life-threatening events as rewards in and of themselves, a source of gratifying rigush. This is what Alon, the tank commander, said about it:

> When we were in Lebanon, they shot at me lots of times. It gives you a feeling of gratification. To my mom, it sounded dumb, but I felt gratified. Because when they shoot at you, you feel the best in the world. Whether you returned fire or not, it doesn't matter. The minute they shoot at you, you already

feel satisfaction. Why? Because your life was at risk. . . . It's a special feeling, reserved only for combat soldiers.

The Lebanon war (1982–2000) was perceived by many Israelis as a war of choice rather than a war of self-defense, and it was therefore a bone of contention in Israeli society, a cause for demonstrations and political strife. Alon and his friends, however, interpreted their combat experience in Lebanon as an adventurous and thrilling way to actualize their masculinity and seldom talked about the political meanings and ramifications of their service.

Somewhat different voices were heard when the soldiers talked about serving in the occupied territories, where they were primarily fighting against civilians. There, the soldiers were more aware of the political meanings of their military service and expressed moral doubts. Yet only a tiny minority of soldiers refused to serve in the territories, an act which had the potential to modify the link between masculinity and self-sacrifice in Israel (Helman 1997).

Only three of the combat soldiers whom I interviewed spoke out explicitly against the collective ethos of risking one's life. Eli, from the Nachal infantry brigade, said,

> Look, most of the soldiers that were killed were from *Giva'ati* [another infantry brigade]. In my brigade, people didn't like getting killed. We liked the good life, we liked doing things wisely. If you ask people honestly if they want to fight, without the pretence of the other guys, they'll say no.

Yoram, a soldier in the prestigious bomb squad unit, reached the same conclusion but only during a long trip abroad after his release from the army. Apparently, his long stay outside of Israel enabled his estrangement, lending a new perspective to his role as combat soldier:

> When I was in South America, I became very, very antimilitaristic. I had thoughts I never had before. . . . I asked myself: Do I really want to die for my country? Am I really prepared to die for my country? No way. What kind of twisted thinking is

that? I've only got one life, what good will it do if I . . . what good will it do me?

Yoram and Eli represent an alternative perspective. They do not see life-endangering events as exciting and prestigious goals in their own right. By disclaiming the ethos of self-sacrifice, they abrogate the connection between masculinity and risking one's life. However, they reflect the opinions of only a small minority of combat soldiers; furthermore, they continue to serve as combat soldiers when called to reserve duty.[4]

A second source of militarized thrill lies in having control over weapons and technology. Sally Hacker (1989) has pointed out that basic pleasure is gained from the ability to operate complicated technological instruments. This widespread masculine fascination with technology (Morgan 1994, 173) seems to increase when it involves weaponry, which is linked to control, hierarchy, prestige, and power over others.

Rami, a combat medic in the armored corps, described an officer giving the command to open fire:

> You see the armored regiment commander waging a war with his words. . . . It's a crazy male act, wacko machoism. He utters these few phrases, and then he lets them go, as if letting go of their reins, or as if he's lifting the gate at the horse race, and you see forty tanks fire at once. . . . You cannot but be impressed.

Rami associates the enjoyment of warfare technologies with domination and hypermasculinity. Note the sexual undercurrent in his choice of metaphor of "letting go of the horses at the race." Hacker (1989) has pointed out illuminating parallels between technology and eroticism: both inscribe feelings on the body through kinesthetic experience, the pleasure in both is shaped by domination and control, and both are defined predominantly by men and are stratified by gender. When the soldiers express the "near orgasmic excitement of nighttime explosions" (Morgan 1994, 173), technologies of destruction become erotic in and of themselves (Hacker 1989, 46–55). Indeed,

describing weapons in terms of sexual metaphors is by now utterly clichéd, but soldiers do it often, especially when talking about the actual act of shooting. Eli, an infantry soldier who was earlier quoted expressing his rejection of the ethos of sacrifice and military values, admitted that he enjoys shooting:

> Why do I like shooting? I don't know, I can't even explain to myself what I love about it. But it's both something physical, and something you can see. It's real, it moves. And there are very close and immediate measures of success. And maybe it's also the feeling, of, ha. . . [sexual] relief.

This "peculiar masculine eroticism of technology" (Hacker 1989, 46) was reiterated by many soldiers when referring to rifles, tanks, or hand grenades, again turning a blind eye to the violent and destructive effects of the technologies of war.

A third source of excitement was the unique feeling of youthful adventure that characterizes combat life. "If you like action, you'll love [military] service in the territories," said Guy.[5] In a similar way, Alon only saw "fun" in the occupied city of Hebron, where forty-two thousand Palestinians are bullied and intimidated by five hundred extremist rightwing Jewish settlers:

> In Hebron, we would go wherever we felt like. We'd raise hell. They'd throw stones, shoot at you, and throw things at you. What a mess. It's just paradise for those who like this kind of thing. It was the most action you could get.

Ofer, an officer from the engineering corps, said explicitly, "I love action. Action itself. Once, I didn't sleep for three days because I couldn't bear the thought that something would happen and I wouldn't be there."

The excitement of dangerous situations is felt in the body itself, in the tone of the muscles, the heartbeat, and the bloodstream. Parachuting, for example, which involves both exhilaration and fear, "brings men into a state of trance, a sort of ecstasy" (Aran 1974, 125, 131). This is a unique emotional "perk" that the military offers to combat soldiers. They feel that they are "alive," their bodies, emotions, and senses all exposed and active. "I was willing to die for the thrill," said a soldier in an interview with a daily newspaper (Alon 1998, 22).

> True, in bungee jumping or car racing, one can also experience an emotional and physiological rush associated with achieving and proving hypermasculinity. But the differences between bungee jumping and combat are not trivial. First, combat is more dangerous as it is connected to real risks to one's life, and second, one does not enter it out of choice—it is always linked to the interests of the state. Its significance, then, is always beyond the individual.

The last source of excitement, albeit an unspoken one, is military homosociality (Sedgwick 1985). Military service provides rare legitimacy for physical and emotional intimacy among men, including homoerotic sensations, without the stigma of homosexuality. Yoram, from the bomb squad, explained,

> It was in the army that all the barriers about physical contact between men came down. In the army, there is always touching. You walk together, shower together, you touch, you live, everything together. I think most people in the army touch each other. I really can't explain it. Maybe it's because it's so tough in the army, so you slap each other and it helps; it feels good.

The soldiers' narratives on men's bonding in the military reveal the contradictions inherent within combat masculinity. While hegemonic masculinity does not allow for emotional expressiveness, it does create specific areas in which physical and emotional intimacy among men is allowed and even encouraged. This intimacy, known as "camaraderie in arms," is a significant motif in Israel's heroic epics and is conveyed to Israeli youth long before they enlist into the army. Camaraderie in arms is described in Israeli culture (through popular songs, canonical prose and poetry, and Memorial Day rituals, for instance) as a lifelong relationship that flourishes despite social or political differences. Research

among eighteen-year-old boys found that they rank camaraderie in arms as one of the main motivating factors for enlisting to combat units (E. Levy 1998, 263). The perception of camaraderie as a significant reward for military service (Lieblich 1989) is reflected in the words of Oren Abman, an infantry lieutenant colonel, who was quoted in the newspaper as saying, "The amazing intimacy that is created among men after combat, the affection they express for each other, it may sound strange to you, but it doesn't exist even in sex" (Becker 2000). Abman creates a hierarchy whereby the bond between warriors is superior to any relationship with a woman. Ofer, from the engineering corps, added,

> [It's] freezing cold, everybody is hugging and huddling under the covers with each other. No problem. These are the fun parts of the army that you remember later, and you miss them. It's all so natural, there's nothing sexual in these relationships. Even today, I don't hug everyone I bump into on the street, but if he's an army buddy, then yes, I'll hug him.
>
> The fraternity I told you about—hugging an army buddy but not another guy—it couldn't happen with women.

Ofer proclaims an exclusive link between male intimacy and combat life, but he hastens to reject any homoerotic interpretation of this relationship, thus reinforcing the centrality of heterosexuality in the construction of hegemonic masculinity. Apparently, the social license for male intimacy is only awarded to combat soldiers (and football players), probably because they have already proven their masculinity beyond any doubt (Chapkis 1988). Noncombat soldiers, on the other hand, often talk with envy about warriors' camaraderie, which they missed out on by not serving in combat units.

By marking the uniqueness of the combat soldier, camaraderie in arms creates an exclusive, imagined community of warriors, a community that embodies "the essence of Israeliness" (Helman 1997). This masculine community is based on inner unity and homogeneity and connects the individual with the state. At the same time, the mutual commitment among men serves to draw hierarchal boundaries between those who are entitled to belong to dominant groups and those who will never be able to, namely, women, Palestinian citizens of Israel, and lower-class noncombat soldiers.

DISCUSSION: THE INDIVIDUAL BODY AND THE COLLECTIVE STATE

As we have seen, the management of the Israeli combat soldier's body and emotions merges two seemingly contradictory themes: self-control and thrill. This combination creates someone who ostensibly has the agency to take charge of his destiny—a man who can control his body and emotions—and dares to take risks and enjoys them. Thus, the combination of self-control and thrill accentuates values of autonomy and self-actualization, which call for an individualistic frame of interpretation.

The individualization of military practices leads soldiers to interpret their military experience in ambivalent and nonpolitical terms. For example, in the interviews, soldiers often framed their growing obedience to military discipline as increasing physical and emotional self-control, which created a strong sense of agency and empowerment. As we saw in the soldiers' quotations, life-endangering events were perceived as unique and rewarding opportunities for self-actualization. The strict surveillance typical of military life was interpreted as their own choice and sometimes even as a privilege, a sign of the intensity of their specific combative "trials of manhood" (Ben-Ari 1998). The authoritarian principles and practices of the military are thus disguised as belonging to, and even as promoting, an individualistic discourse.

The individualization of the soldier's body can be seen as an expression of the effects of globalization on Israeli society. One primary effect of globalization in the cultural sphere is the permeation of consumerist values, which present self-fulfillment as a prime social virtue

(Ram 1999; Shafir and Peled 1998). In a consumerist society, with its focus on the individual, cultivation of the masculine body is seen, for the first time in Israeli history, as no less legitimate than the cultivation of the feminine body. Military bodily transformation, which involves strenuous efforts, can be framed in this context as a personal choice that brings prestige. Thus, the soldier's identity is not that of the Spartan, who is willing to sacrifice himself for the good of the collective. Rather, it can be seen as an individual effort to improve oneself, a masculine personal achievement of self-actualization.

When military combat service is framed in an individualistic discourse, it turns out to have a dual, ambivalent nature. This duality in the perception of the military blurs the boundaries between choice and compulsion, and the coercive nature of military service becomes obscured. This dual nature of military experience enables mandatory conscription to be perceived as voluntary and fulfilling (Y. Levy 1993). In fact, only volunteers can serve in the most prestigious, dangerous, and secretive units. Thus, voluntarism becomes a status symbol in itself. At the same time, voluntarism conceals the military disciplining of Israel's body of citizens.

Likewise, the "individual" nexus of self-control and thrill masks the price entailed by combat masculinity and conceals its repressive nature. Current research has pointed at some of the mental and physical injuries suffered by combat soldiers, but since I interviewed only soldiers who served their full terms of three years as combat soldiers, I could not expose the more brutal damages of combat military service, such as physical and emotional disability. Most soldiers who encounter serious emotional difficulties do not stay in combat courses, and at times, they are exempt from service altogether. Thus, the voices of the soldiers who did not conform to the norm are missing, as are the voices of the mentally impaired or those suffering posttraumatic symptoms. It is these injured and distressed soldiers who pay the high price for the image of the ideal of combat masculinity in Israel.

Furthermore, as noted earlier, when soldiers perceive their militaristic activities as masculine self-actualization, they can ignore their moral and political consequences. The individualistic interpretation of military endeavors enables the soldier to overlook the evils that are often carried out in the name of combat masculinity. Thus, the individualistic framing allows for the perpetuation of Israel's militant aggressive policies, in particular the nearly forty-year-long occupation of the West Bank and (until recently) the Gaza Strip.

Therefore, the individualized body and emotion management of the combat soldier serves the symbolic and pragmatic interests of the state, as it reinforces and reproduces the cooperation between hegemonic masculinity and Israeli militarism: Young men are still willing to kill and be killed for the good of their country but now in the name of individualized dominant masculinity. It is the individual body that functions as the instrument of the militaristic state. The gendering of the soldier's body turns out to be a control mechanism that encourages young men to go to war and risk their lives.

Individualism here is harnessed for the good of the collective and is hence an instrument that creates, in a roundabout way, collectivism and obedience to the state. The soldier's autonomy and individualism are a kind of illusion, a façade, because as the body of the soldier is transformed, he becomes part of the state. His body is the material superstructure that links the (male) individual to the state.

I claim that the combat soldier is "marked" as an idealized figure that others cannot emulate. Levy-Schreiber and Ben-Ari (2000), for example, follow Connell (1987, 85) in claiming that through military body practices, state power becomes naturalized, as if it belongs to the order of nature. I argue to the contrary: Through military body practices, the soldier's power becomes unique and visible; the body belongs to the order of nation, signifying the link between manhood and nationhood. Through specific gendered body practices, and their relation with the nation-state, particular male bodies become more significant than others (Petersen 1998, 42). When the body

of the adolescent boy turns into the muscular and brave body of the combat soldier, this transformation marks him with an air of heroism and masculinity, the signs of devotion and contribution to the state. His uniform, posture, walk, muscle tone, facial expression, and manner of speech, all signal both self-control and anticipation of the rare thrill of combat. This body provides the combat soldier with a physical presence that many Israelis claim they can identify even from afar. The soldier's body becomes a focus for public identification, a source of national pride, and a locus of sympathy and support. The signs of the nation are inscribed on the body, and the soldier's body becomes the symbol of the nation. This national symbol provides a common, consensual symbol around which a Jewish Israeli imagined community gathers—a symbol that is both masculine and militarized. Nationality, that unseen, imagined quality, receives a public visual expression in the body of the soldier. Thus, the body of the combat soldier is signified by the mark of the nation and serves as a signifier of the gendered nation-state.

NOTES

1. Others modify this statement, arguing that the collective ethos has been replaced by two contesting ideologies that crystallized as the major alternatives for future development. The first ideology is a neo-Zionist ethnonationalism (Ram 1999; Shafir and Peled 1998), which characterizes the lower classes and the religious groups. This ideology elevates the exclusionary Jewish collectivity and its motherland, rather than the Israeli state, as a political community defined by common citizenship (Ram 1999, 333–35). The second, competing ideology is a liberal-individual-oriented post-Zionist one (Ram 1999; Shafir and Peled 1998). Held by the secular, mostly Ashkenazi middle class and the Israeli Palestinians, this sensibility values individual rights more highly than collective glory. In sharp contrast to neo-Zionism, it is less national, considering the collectivity as a tool for the welfare of the individual (Ram 1999, 333).

2. Evidence of the soldier's dominant status is found in various studies that indicate that young men

(and most women) rank the combat soldier at the top of social and military hierarchies (E. Levy 1998; Sasson-Levy 2000). Applications for various prestigious combat units exceed available places by a ratio of eight to one (Cohen 1997, 107). Combat soldiers receive higher salaries during military service and enjoy a range of privileges after their release. For example, they are entitled to academic scholarships and grants that are not available to noncombat soldiers. In the economic and political realms, Israeli ex-colonels still enjoy immense power, as is clear from their growing presence in Israeli governments. In the cultural sphere, the consensual esteem for the combat soldier is reflected in the many commercials that use his image to sell anything from cell phones and medical insurance to laundry detergent and cream cheese. Noncombat soldiers, on the other hand, do not feature in commercials and are rarely represented in the media at all (E. Levy 1998).

3. All names have been changed to protect the soldiers' privacy.

4. Real resistance, however, is not to be found among combat soldiers. Young Israeli men who resist the warrior ethos either make a special effort not to serve in combat roles or refuse to serve in the army altogether, for ideological or personal reasons. In refusing to serve, they express dissension over the essence of the warrior ethos and rejection of the militarized nature of hegemonic Jewish Israeli masculinity. The majority, however, still strongly support compulsory military service in general and the warrior ethos in particular (Ben-Ari 1999; Cohen 1997 and Lomsky-Feder).

5. All the soldiers interviewed used the English word action in their Hebrew speech.

REFERENCES

Abu-Lughod, L., and C. A. Lutz. 1990. Introduction: Emotion, discourse, and the politics of everyday life. In *Language and the politics of emotion,* edited by C. A. Lutz and L. Abu-Lughod, 1–23. Cambridge, UK: Cambridge University Press.

Addelston, J., and M. Stirratt. 1996. The last bastion of masculinity. In *Masculinities in organizations,* edited by C. Cheng, 54–76. Thousand Oaks, CA: Sage.

Alon, M. 1998. Perhaps the I.D.F. prefers its heroes dead? [Hebrew] *Yediot Aharonot,* November 27.

Aran, G. 1974. Parachuting. *American Journal of Sociology* 80(1): 124–53.

Arkin, W., and L. R. Dubrofsky. 1978. Military socialization and masculinity. *Journal of Social Issues* 34(1): 151–69.

Armitage, J. 2003. Militarized bodies: An introduction. *Body and Society* 9(4): 1–12.

Aronoff, M. 1999. Wars as catalysts of political and cultural change. In *The military and militarism in Israeli society,* edited by E. Lomsky-Feder and E. Ben-Ari, 37–57. Albany: State University of New York Press.

Barrett, F. 1996. The organizational construction of hegemonic masculinity: The case of the U.S. navy. *Gender, Work and Organization* 3(3): 129–42.

Becker, A. 2000. The last ones on the ridge [Hebrew]. *Ha'aretz weekend supplement,* June 16, pp. 76–80.

Ben-Ari, E. 1998. *Mastering soldiers.* New York: Berghan.

Bordo, S. 1993. *Unbearable weight.* Berkeley: University of California Press.

Burk, J. 1995. Citizenship status and military service: The quest for inclusion by minorities and conscientious objectors. *Armed Forces and Society* 21(4): 503–29.

Chapkis, W. 1988. Sexuality and militarism. In *Women and the military system,* edited by E. Isaksson, 106–13. New York: St. Martin's.

Cohen, S. 1997. Towards a new portrait of the (new) Israeli soldier. *Israeli Affairs* 3(3/4): 77–117.

Comaroff, J. L. 1996. Ethnicity, nationalism, and the politics of difference in an age of revolution. In *The politics of difference: Ethnic premises in a world of power,* edited by E. N. Wilmsen and P. McAllister. Chicago: University of Chicago Press.

Connell, R. W. 1987. *Gender and power: Society, the person and sexual politics.* Stanford, CA: Stanford University Press.

———. 1995. *Masculinities.* Berkeley: University of California Press.

Csordas, J. T. 1993. Somatic modes of attention. *Cultural Anthropology* 8(2): 135–56.

Davis, K. 1997. Embodying theory: Beyond modernist and postmodernist reading of the body. In *Embodied practices: Feminist perspectives on the body,* edited by K. Davis, 1–23. London: Sage.

Dreyfus, H., and P. Rabinow. 1982. *Michel Foucault: Beyond structuralism and hermeneutics.* Sussex, UK: Harvester.

Enloe, C. 1980. *Ethnic soldiers: State security in divided society.* Athens: University of Georgia Press.

———. 1988. *Does khaki become you?* London: Pandora.

Foucault, M. 1975. *Discipline and punishment: The birth of the prison.* New York: Vintage.

———. 1978. *The history of sexuality.* New York: Vintage.

———. 1980. *Power/knowledge.* New York: Pantheon.

Frank, A. W. 1991. For sociology of the body: An analytical review. In *The body,* edited by M. Featherstone, M. Hepworth, and B. S. Turner, 36–102. London: Sage.

Furman, M. 1999. Army and war: Collective narratives of early childhood in contemporary Israel. In *The military and militarism in Israeli society,* edited by E. Lomski-Feder and E. Ben-Ari, 141–69. New York: State University of New York Press.

Giddens, A. 1985. *The nation-state and violence.* Berkeley: University of California Press.

Gill, L. 1997. Creating citizens, making men: The military and masculinity in Bolivia. *Cultural Anthropology* 12(4): 527–50.

Hacker, S. 1989. *Pleasure, power and technology: Some tales of gender, engineering and the cooperative workplace.* Boston, MA: Unwin Hyman.

Helman, S. 1997. Militarism and the construction of community. *Journal of Political and Military Sociology* 25:305–32.

Higate, P. 2003. *Military masculinities: Identity and the state.* Westport, CT: Praeger.

Hochschild, A. 1983. *The managed heart: The commercialization of human feeling.* Berkeley: University of California Press.

Horowitz, D., and M. Lissak. 1989. *Troubles in utopia: The overburdened polity of Israel.* Albany: State University of New York Press.

Janowitz, M. 1994. Military institutions and citizenship in Western societies. In *Citizenship,* edited by B. Turner and P. Hamilton. London: Routledge.

Kimmel, M. 1996. *Manhood in America.* New York: Free Press.

Kimmerling, B. 1993. Patterns of militarism in Israel. *European Journal of Sociology* 34:196–223.

Kovitz, M. 2003. The roots of military masculinity. In *Military masculinities: Identities and state,* edited by P. Higate, 1–14. Westport, CT: Praeger.

Levy, E. 1998. Heroes and helpmates: Militarism, gender and national belonging in Israel. PhD diss., University of California, Irvine.

Levy, Y. 1993. The role of the military sphere in constructing the social-political order in Israel [Hebrew]. PhD diss., Tel Aviv University.

Levy-Schreiber, E., and E. Ben-Ari. 2000. Body building, character building and nation-building: Gender and military service in Israel. *Studies in Contemporary Judaism* 16:171–90.

Lieblich, A. 1989. *Transition to adulthood during military service: The Israeli case.* Albany: State University of New York Press.

Lloyd, G. 1986. Selfhood, war and masculinity. In *Feminist challenges: Social and political theory,* edited by C. Pateman and E. Gross, 63–76. Boston: Northeastern University Press.

Lomsky-Feder, E. 1998. *As if there was no war: The perception of war in the life stories of Israeli men* [Hebrew]. Jerusalem: Magnes.

Lomsky-Feder, E., and E. Ben-Ari, eds. 1999. *The military and militarism in Israeli society.* Albany: State University of New York Press.

Lutz, C. 1988. *Unnatural emotions.* Chicago: Chicago University Press.

Lutz, C., and G. White. 1986. The anthropology of emotions. *Annual Review of Anthropology* 15:405–36.

Mazali, R. 1993. Military service as initiation rite. *Challenge* IV(4): 36–37.

Morgan, D. H. J. 1994. Theatre of war: Combat, the military and masculinities. In *Theorizing masculinities,* edited by H. Brod and M. Kaufman, 165–83. London: Sage.

Moskos, C. 1993. From citizens' army to social laboratory. *Wilson Quarterly* 17:83–94.

Mosse, G. L. 1996. *The image of man: The creation of modern masculinity.* Oxford, UK: Oxford University Press.

Nagel, J. 1998. Masculinity and nationalism: Gender and sexuality in the making of nations. *Ethnic and Racial Studies* 21(2): 242–70.

Ortner, S. 1974. Is female to male as nature is to culture? In *Women culture and society,* edited by M. Rosaldo and L. Lamphere. Stanford, CA: Stanford University Press.

Peniston-Bird, C. 2003. Classifying the body in the Second World War: British men in and out of uniform. *Body & Society* 9(4): 31–48.

Petersen, A. 1998. *Unmasking the masculine: "Men" and "identity" in a sceptical age.* London: Sage.

Ram, U. 1999. The state and the nation: Contemporary challenges to Zionism in Israel. *Constellations* 6(3): 325–39.

Rosaldo, M. 1984. Toward an anthropology of self and feeling. In *Cultural theory essays on mind, self and emotion,* edited by R. Shweder and R. Le Vine, 137–57. Cambridge, UK: Cambridge University Press.

Sasson-Levy, O. 2000. Constructions of gender identities within the Israeli army. PhD diss., Hebrew University, Jerusalem.

———. 2003a. Feminism and military gender practices: Israeli women soldiers in "masculine" roles. *The Sociological Inquiry* 73(3): 440–65.

———. 2003b. Military, masculinity and citizenship: Tensions and contradictions in the experience of blue-collar soldiers. *Identities: Global Studies in Culture and Power* 10(3): 319–45.

Sedgwick, E. K. 1985. *Between men—English literature and male homosocial desire.* New York: Columbia University Press.

Seidler, V. 1989. *Rediscovering masculinity.* London: Routledge.

Shafir, G., and Y. Peled. 1998. Citizenship and stratification in an ethnic democracy. *Ethnic and Racial Studies* 21(3): 408–28.

Shilling, C. 1993. *The body and social theory.* London: Sage.

Snyder, C. R. 1999. *Citizen-soldier and manly warriors: Military service and gender in the civic republic tradition.* Lanham, MD: Rowman & Littlefield.

Spencer, P. 1965. *The Samburu: A study of gerontocracy in a nomadic tribe.* Berkeley: University of California Press.

Stiehm, J. H. 1989. *Arms and the enlisted woman.* Philadelphia: Temple University Press.

Theweleit, K. 1987–1989. *Male fantasies.* Minneapolis: University of Minnesota Press.

Thoits, P. 1989. The sociology of emotions. *Annual Review of Sociology* 15:317–42.

Tilly, C. 1985. War making and state making as organized crime. In *Bringing the state back in,* edited by P. Evans, D. Rueschemeyer, and T. Skocpol, 169–91. Cambridge, UK: Cambridge University Press.

———. 1996. The emergence of citizenship in France and elsewhere. *International Review of Social History* 40(3): 223–36.

Weiss, M. 2002. *The chosen body: The politics of the body in Israeli society.* Stanford, CA: Stanford University Press.

Winslow, D. 1999. Rites of passage and group bonding in the Canadian airborne. *Armed Forces and Society* 25(3): 429–57.

Zerubavel, Y. 1995. *Recovered roots: Collective memory and the making of Israeli national tradition.* Chicago: University of Chicago Press.

Introduction to Reading 28

In this reading, Erin Hatton and Mary Nell Trautner employ a longitudinal content analysis of images of women and men on the covers of more than four decades of *Rolling Stone* magazine. Their central finding is that images of women, not men, have become dramatically "hypersexualized." The authors argue that this finding points to a dangerous trend—a shrinking repertoire of culturally acceptable ways of "doing femininity" and, thus, the continuing subordination of women to men.

1. In the realm of popular media images, how does hypersexualization differ from sexualization, and why is the difference important in understanding gender inequality?

2. According to research, what are the negative consequences on real women and girls of hypersexualized images of women?

3. Why did the authors choose to title this reading "Equal Opportunity Objectification"?

4. What is the value of conducting longitudinal research of the type reported on in this reading?

EQUAL OPPORTUNITY OBJECTIFICATION?

THE SEXUALIZATION OF MEN AND WOMEN ON THE COVER OF *ROLLING STONE*

Erin Hatton and Mary Nell Trautner

INTRODUCTION

In recent years, a number of scholars and journalists have argued that American culture has become "sexualized" (APA Task Force 2007; Attwood 2009; Olfman 2009) or even "pornified" (Paul 2005; see also Dines 2010; McRobbie 2004; Paasonen et al. 2007). This widely examined phenomenon has been given a plethora of names, including "the rise of raunch culture" (Levy 2005), "striptease culture" (McNair 2002), "porno chic" (McRobbie 2004; Rush and La Nauze 2006), "rape culture" (Ezzell 2009), the "mainstreaming of prostitution" (Farley 2009), and the "amazing expanding pornosphere" (McNair 2002). "Increasingly *all* representations of women," Gill (2007:81) argues, "are being refracted through sexually objectifying imagery" (emphasis in original). It is not only women who are sexualized in the popular media, scholars argue; men are sexualized as well (Bordo 1999; Pope et al. 2000; Rohlinger 2002). "The erotic male," Rohlinger (2002:70) contends, "is increasingly becoming *the* depiction that dominates mainstream conceptions of masculinity" (emphasis in original).

Researchers find evidence for the increased sexualization of women and men in a spate of cultural artifacts, including the mainstream popularity of adult film actress Jenna Jameson and her memoir, *How to Make Love Like a Porn Star* (e.g., Dines 2010; Levy 2005; Paul 2005); the "skyrocketing" number of undressed men in advertisements (Pope et al. 2000:56); the

prevalence of pole-dancing exercise classes for women (e.g., Farley 2009; Levy 2005); the "blatant sexual fetishization—even idolatry—of the male organ" in TV and movies (Bordo 1999:30); and the success of "Girls Gone Wild," the "reality" television program and website that feature young women being urged to take off their clothes by off-screen cameramen in exchange for a T-shirt with the show's logo (e.g., Dines 2010, Farley 2009; Levy 2005; Paul 2005).

Yet analyzing only sexualized cultural artifacts—and there are certainly many to choose from—does not provide conclusive evidence that American culture has become "pornified." Indeed, it is easy to dismiss such charges unless we know whether sexualized representations of women and men have become more common—or more intensely sexualized—over time. Moreover, although the existence of sexualized images of men might suggest that, today, the popular media is something of an "equal opportunity objectifier" as some observers suggest (e.g., Frette 2009; Taylor and Sharkey 2003), the simple presence of images of sexualized men does not signal equality in media representations of women and men.

In a longitudinal content analysis of more than four decades of *Rolling Stone* magazine covers (1967–2009), we begin to answer such questions. Using a unique analytical framework that allows us to measure both the frequency and intensity of sexualization, we find that representations of women and men have indeed become

From Hatton, Erin and Mary Nell Trautner. 2011. "Equal Opportunity Objectification? The Sexualization of Men and Women on the Cover of *Rolling Stone*." *Sexuality & Culture* 15: 256–278.

more sexualized over time, though women continue to be more frequently sexualized than men. Yet our most striking finding is the change in *how* women but not men—are sexualized. Women are increasingly likely to be "hypersexualized," while men are not. In our analysis, hypersexualization is the combination of a multitude of sexualized attributes—body position, extent of nudity, textual cues, and more—the cumulative effect of which is to narrow the possible interpretations of the image to just, as de Beauvoir (1949) wrote, "the sex." Our findings thus not only document changes in the sexualization of men and women in popular culture over time, they also point to a narrowing of the culturally acceptable ways for "doing" femininity (West and Fenstermaker 1995; West and Zimmerman 1987) as presented in popular media.

These findings are important because research has shown that sexualized images may legitimize or exacerbate violence against women and girls, sexual harassment, and anti-women attitudes among men (Farley 2009; Kalof 1999; Lanis and Covell 1955; Machia and Lamb 2009; MacKay and Covell 1997; Malamuth and Check 1981; Malamuth et al. 2000; Milburn et al. 2000; Ohbuchi et al. 1994; Ward 2002; Ward et al. 2005), increase rates of body dissatisfaction and/or eating disorders among men, women, and girls (Abramson and Valene 1991; Aubrey and Taylor 2009; Aubrey et al. 2009; Groesz et al. 2002; Hargreaves and Tiggemann 2004; Harrison 2000; Hofschire and Greenberg 2001; Holmstrom 2004; Lucas et al. 1991; Pope et al. 2000; Stice et al. 1994; Tiggeman and Slater 2001; Turner et al. 1997), increase teen sexual activity (Brown et al. 2005; Pardun et al. 2005; Villani 2001), and decrease women and men's sexual satisfaction (American Psychological Association 2007; Roberts and Gettman 2004; Weaver et al. 1984; Zillmann and Bryant 1988).

Before turning to our findings, we consider research on the sexualization of women and men within the broader literature on gender and the media. We then discuss our data and methods, outlining our analytical framework that measures both the incidence and extent of sexualization. We conclude with a discussion of the implications of our findings.

SEXUALIZATION, GENDER, AND THE MEDIA

In *Gender Advertisements,* Erving Goffman (1979) sought to uncover the covert ways that popular media constructs masculinity and femininity. In a detailed analysis of more than 500 advertisements, Goffman contrasted women's lowered heads with men's straight-on gazes, men's strong grasps versus women's light touches, women's over-the-top emotional displays with men's reserved semblances, and more. The relationship between men and women, Goffman argued, was portrayed as a parent-child relationship, one characterized by male power and female subordination . . .

Missing from Goffman's analysis, however, was an examination of the sexualization of women (and men) in these images.

Many contemporary studies of gender and sexualization in popular culture take as their starting point Goffman's analysis . . . (e.g., Binns 2006; Johnson 2007; Kang 1997; Krassas et al. 2001, 2003; Lindner 2004; Rohlinger 2002; Umiker-Sebeok 1996). This is somewhat perplexing given that Goffman specifically excluded questions related to sexualization and objectification in his study. But these researchers have attempted to redress this mismatch by adding variables intended to capture sexualization. For example, in an examination of advertisements in women's magazines in 1979 and 1991, Kang (1997) added two new variables to Goffman's coding categories: body display (degree of nudity) and independence (self-assertiveness). Using this expanded empirical framework, Kang finds that while some aspects of gender stereotyping—such as men shown as taller than women—had virtually disappeared by 1991, body displays of women had increased. Interpreting this combination of increases and decreases in gender stereotyping as a kind of balancing scale, Kang concludes that little changed in advertisements' portrayal of women over the 11-year time span. "Twelve years after the Goffman study," Kang writes, "magazine advertisements are still showing the same stereotyped images of women" (988–989). But a closer look at Kang's data, in fact, reveals substantial changes: nude or partially nude images of women increased nearly 30% from 1979 to 1991.

Lindner (2004) further developed Kang's analytical framework in a study of women in advertisements in *Time* and *Vogue* from 1955 to 2002. In addition to Goffman's and Kang's coding schemes, Lindner used three other variables: movement (the ability to move fast and far), location (domestic versus public), and objectification (whether the major function of the model is to "be looked at"). Using these measures, Lindner finds that both magazines rely on gender stereotypes but in different ways, particularly in terms of sexualization. "Stereotyping in *Time* occurs without the use of sexualized images of women," Lindner concludes, "whereas in *Vogue*, these sexualized images are the primary way of portraying women in positions of inferiority and low social power" (419–420). Although her data reveal a clear difference between the two magazines, they do not indicate any change in the sexualization of women over time. . . .

Krassas et al. (2003) also built on Goffman's framework in a study of sexualized representations of women and men in two men's magazines, *Maxim* and *Stuff*, in 2001. In addition to Goffman's categories, the authors added measures of nudity (breast/chest and buttock exposure) and objectification (some concealment of face combined with some level of body exposure). Using these variables, the authors find that—in 2001 at least—women were much more likely than men to have exposed breasts and buttocks, and were three times more likely to be sexually objectified.

These studies have made important steps in empirically examining sexualized representations of women and men in popular media. But they tell only part of the story. For example,

Krassas et al. (2003) analyze images of both men and women, but only at a single point in time. Kang (1997) and Lindner (2004) examine change over time, but look only at images of women. This raises the question of whether men too have been increasingly sexualized in popular culture, as some have suggested (e.g., Bordo 1999; Pope et al. 2000; Rohlinger 2002; Thompson 2000). Additionally, Kang (1997) and Lindner (2004) datasets may not be sufficient to adequately measure change over time. Kang's analysis is based on only 2 years of data (1979 and 1991), and Lindner's analysis is based on just twelve issues of each magazine across five decades.

Furthermore, although each of the studies described uses additional variables in order to measure sexualization, in our assessment they do not yet capture the full range of sexualized attributes. They do not include variables for genital accentuation (but see Krassas et al. 2001), open mouths and/or tongue exposure, sex acts or simulations (but see Reichert and Carpenter 2004; Reichert et al. 1999; Soley and Kurzbard 1986), and sexual referents in the textual description of the images (but see Johnson 2007; Soley and Kurzbard 1986). And, perhaps more importantly, all studies of sexualization measure only the presence or absence of aspects of sexualization in isolation. As a consequence, while they document the incidence of sexualized attributes, they do not measure whether the image as a whole—the woman rather than just her breasts—has become more frequently or more intensely sexualized over time. In the following section, we outline our empirical framework that builds on these studies to provide a more comprehensive measure of sexualization.

DATA AND METHODS

We examine the covers of *Rolling Stone* for two key reasons. First and foremost, *Rolling Stone* is a well-known popular culture magazine in the U.S. Although in the early years the magazine focused almost exclusively on music and music culture, by the 1970s its covers regularly featured an array of pop culture icons not limited to the music world. Today the magazine is well known for its coverage of politics, film, television, current events and, of course, popular music. Its covers generally feature a wide range of celebrities, including comedians, actors, musicians, models, politicians, record producers, military analysts, civil rights activists, journalists, film directors, athletes, and more. As a result, representations of men and women on the cover of *Rolling Stone* resemble popular cultural images broadly, particularly more so than lifestyle magazines which are often explicitly about sex, relationships, or sexuality. Our second reason for choosing *Rolling Stone* is its longevity. Launched in 1967, *Rolling Stone* has published more than one thousand covers across its lifespan. This extensive dataset offers an ideal window into changes in the sexualization of women and men in popular culture over time.

Dataset

There are 1,046 covers of *Rolling Stone,* starting with its first issue in November of 1967 through the end of 2009 (including those issues that featured multiple covers). We downloaded all covers from the *Rolling Stone* website in January 2010. We then cross-checked the cover images and their dates with two books that chronicled the history of *Rolling Stone* (Gatten 1993; *Rolling Stone* 2006), as well as with another website which had compiled all of its covers (Kabouter 2010).

Of the full set of 1,046 covers, we excluded 115 from our analysis for a number of reasons: They did not portray people (e.g., just text or cartoon characters), they showed crowds with no discernible image to code, or they featured collages of covers that had previously been published. Of the remaining 931 covers, 651 featured only men and 205 featured only women (either alone or in groups). In those covers that showed groups of either men or women, we coded the central figure in the image (usually this was literally the person at the center of the image, but at times it was the dominant person in terms of

his/her size or action). Another 75 covers featured women and men together. In those cases, the central man and woman were each coded separately. We thus analyzed a total of 1,006 cover images (726 images of men and 280 images of women) across 42 years of *Rolling Stone* magazine.

Coding Scheme

We conceptualize representations of women and men as falling along a continuum of sexualization: images may be not at all sexualized, slightly sexualized, clearly sexualized, or highly sexualized. To capture these differences, we developed a 23-point additive scale consisting of 11 separate variables, the sum of which indicates the degree to which an image is sexualized. We briefly describe each of the variables below, and Table 6.1 shows the frequency distribution for each.

Clothing/Nudity (0–5 points)

A number of studies have found style of clothing and extent of nudity to be important markers of sexualization (e.g., Johnson 2007; Kang 1997; Krassas et al. 2003; Lambiase and Reichert 2006; Nitz et al. 2007; Paek and Nelson 2007; Reichert 2003; Reichert and Carpenter 2004; Reichert et al. 1999; Soley and Kurzbard 1986; Soley and Reid 1988). We developed a six-point scale for this variable, ranging from unrevealing clothing (0 points) to completely naked (5 points). Those images that featured models wearing slightly revealing clothing, such as women wearing shirts with modestly low necklines or exposed arms and shoulders, scored a "1" on this measure. Images that scored a "2" in this category featured models wearing clothing that was somewhat revealing; this included exposed midriffs on both women and men. Images that scored a "3" featured models wearing highly revealing and/or skin-tight clothing. Images that scored "4" in this category featured models wearing swimsuits and lingerie, that is, apparel that is not generally considered

Table 6.1 Frequency Distribution of Coding Categories for Men (M) and Women (W)

	Coded as "0"		Coded as "1"		Coded as "2"	
	M	W	M	W	M	W
Clothing/nudity	n = 554 (77%)	n = 78 (28%)	n = 70 (10%)	n = 44 (16%)	n = 56 (8%)	n = 20 (7%)
Touch	n = 496 (69%)	n = 141 (50%)	n = 206 (28%)	n = 93 (33%)	n = 20 (3%)	n = 39 (14%)
Pose	n = 659 (91%)	n = 149 (53%)	n = 50 (7%)	n = 99 (35%)	n = 15 (2%)	n = 34 (12%)
Mouth	n = 595 (82%)	n = 154 (55%)	n = 116 (16%)	n = 105 (37%)	n = 13 (2%)	n = 23 (8%)
Breasts	n = 653 (90%)	n = 154 (55%)	n = 54 (7%)	n = 59 (21%)	n = 17 (2%)	n = 69 (24%)
Genitals	n = 666 (92%)	n = 213 (76%)	n = 48 (7%)	n = 42 (15%)	n = 10 (1%)	n = 27 (10%)
Buttocks	n = 718 (99%)	n = 254 (90%)	n = 3 (< 1%)	n = 16 (6%)	n = 3 (<1%)	n = 12 (4%)
Text	n = 652 (90%)	n = 177 (63%)	n = 52 (7%)	n = 79 (28%)	n = 20 (3%)	n = 26 (9%)
Head vs. body shot	n = 258 (36%)	n = 40 (14%)	n = 466 (64%)	n = 242 (86%)	—	—
Sex act	n = 720 (99%)	n = 277 (98%)	n = 4 (1%)	n = 5 (2%)	—	—
Sexual role play	n = 719 (99%)	n = 259 (92%)	n = 5 (1%)	n = 23 (8%)	—	—

	Coded as "3"		Coded as "4"		Coded as "5"	
	M	W	M	W	M	W
Clothing/nudity	n = 30 (4%)	n = 38 (13%)	n = 7 (1%)	n = 76 (27%)	n = 7 (1%)	n = 26 (9%)
Touch	n = 2 (< 1%)	n = 9 (3%)	—	—	—	—
Pose	—	—	—	—	—	—
Mouth	—	—	—	—	—	—
Breasts	—	—	—	—	—	—
Genitals	—	—	—	—	—	—
Buttocks	—	—	—	—	—	—
Text	—	—	—	—	—	—
Head vs. body shot	—	—	—	—	—	—
Sex act	—	—	—	—	—	—
Sexual role play	—	—	—	—	—	—

"clothing" at all. Images that scored a "5" in this category featured models wearing nothing at all (or only minimal clothing, such as socks and shoes but nothing else).

Touch (0–3 points)

A number of researchers have examined the use of "touch" to suggest sexualization in media images (e.g., Reichert and Carpenter 2004; Reichert et al. 1999; Soley and Kurzbard 1986). We analyzed the nature of "touch" for each cover image on a 0–3 scale. Our measure included all forms of touch, including self-touch, touching others, and being touched. Cover models who were neither touching nor being touched scored "0" on this measure. "Casual touching," for example, a model clasping his hands together or resting her arm on someone else's shoulder, scored a "1." Those images that scored a "2" exhibited some kind of provocative touching. These included, for example, Cameron Diaz lifting her shirt and resting her hand on her bare stomach just under her breast (August 22, 1996). The highest score in this category—3 points— was given to those covers that featured explicitly sexual touching (by oneself or someone else). These included, for example, David Spade pinching a woman's nipple (September 16, 1999) and Janet Jackson's breasts being cupped by disembodied male hands (September 16, 1993).

Pose (0–2 points)

Extending Goffman's (1979) analysis of body posture to studies of sexualization, researchers have analyzed an image's pose as a key element of its sexualization (e.g., Johnson 2007; Krassas et al. 2003; Lambiase and Reichert 2006). We created three codes to capture sexualized body postures. Images in which the cover model was not posed in any way related to sexual activity— standing upright, for example—scored "0" in this category. Images scored "1" for a variety of poses that were suggestive or inviting of sexual activity, including lifting one's arms overhead and any kind of leaning or sitting. Images that scored a "2" on this measure were overtly posed

for sexual activity; this included lying down or, for women, sitting with their legs spread wide open.

Mouth (0–2 points)

Goffman (1979) found that women were often shown in advertisements to be covering their mouths or sucking on their finger as part of what he called "licensed withdrawal"—a lack of presence and, therefore, power. Although a number of studies have analyzed images in terms of their licensed withdrawal (e.g., Binns 2006; Kang 1997; Lindner 2004), we are not aware of any study that has examined a model's mouth as an element of his or her sexualization. In our study of *Rolling Stone* covers, however, we found mouths to be an important characteristic of sexualization and we developed three scores to measure it. The lowest score (0 points) was for mouths that did not suggest any kind of sexual activity, including closed lips, broad toothy smiles, and active singing, talking, or yelling. One point was given to mouths that were somewhat suggestive of sex; this included images in which the model's lips were parted slightly but not smiling. Images that scored a "2" featured models whose mouths were explicitly suggestive of sexual activity: This included models whose mouths were wide open but passive (not actively singing or yelling but, perhaps, posed for penetration), whose tongue was showing, or who had something (such as a finger) in his or her mouth.

Breasts/Chest; Genitals; Buttocks (0–2 points each)

A small number of studies have examined whether a focal point of the image is the model's breasts/chest, genitals, and/or buttocks (e.g., Krassas et al. 2001, 2003; Rohlinger 2002). We used these as three separate variables, scoring each of them on a 0–2 scale. Those images in which these body parts were either not visible or not a focal point scored a "0" for each of the three variables. If one or more of these body parts were somewhat emphasized—if, for example, a women's breasts were a centerpiece of the image but still mostly concealed by clothing—the image received a "1" in the appropriate category. If one of these body parts was a major focus of the image—if a model's pants were unbuttoned and pulled down, for example—the image received a "2" for that variable.

Text (0–2 points)

Relatively few studies analyze an image's text as part of its sexualization (but see Johnson 2007; Soley and Kurzbard 1986). In our examination of *Rolling Stone* cover images, however, we found the text describing an image to be an important element of its sexualization. We coded only the text on the magazine cover that was directly related to the cover image. Most of these "coverlines" were not related to sex or sexuality and scored "0" on this measure. Text that contained some sexual innuendo, such as "Kid Rock Gets Lucky" (October 10, 2007), scored "1" in this category, and coverlines that made explicit references to sex or sexuality, such as "Asia Argento: She Puts the Sex in XXX" (September 5, 2002), scored "2."

Head vs. Body Shot (0–1 point)

A number of studies in this field distinguish between those images which are primarily headshots, featuring only the model's head and perhaps shoulders, and those which feature substantially more of their body (e.g., Baumann 2008; Goffman 1979; Lambiase and Reichert 2006; Johnson 2007; Schwarz and Kurz 1989). On our scale of sexualization, headshots scored "0" and body shots scored "1."

Sex Act (0–1 point)

Perhaps because relatively few popular media images depict models engaging in (or simulating) sex acts, only a few studies measure this variable (e.g., Reichert and Carpenter 2004; Reichert et al. 1999; Soley and Kurzbard 1986). In our analysis of *Rolling Stone* magazine covers, however, a small but hard to ignore number of such images prompted the creation of this new

variable. Images in which the cover model was engaged in a sex act (e.g., kissing or embracing someone while lying naked in bed) or simulating a sex act (e.g., affecting fellatio or masturbation) scored "1" in this category.

Sexual Role Play (0–1 point)

Finally, although we found no studies that measured symbols of sexual role playing—such as infantilization (e.g., child-like clothes) or bondage/domination (e.g., leather bustier, leather straps, dog collars, studded bracelets)—in our analysis the infrequent yet conspicuous presence of such symbols led to the creation of this variable. Cover images that suggested sexual role playing scored "1" in this category.

Analytic Strategy

We coded the covers of *Rolling Stone* in several passes. The authors first worked together to establish coding rules for all variables, jointly coding three randomly selected years of covers. The second author then coded the remaining cover images, working closely with the first author to resolve any questions that arose. . . .

After coding was complete, the images' scores on the 23-point scale of sexualization clustered into three distinct groups: nonsexualized images (which scored 0–4 points), sexualized images (5–9 points), and hypersexualized images (10 or more points). We tested for reliability between coders for these three categories as well. In our 10% random sample of covers, there was near-perfect agreement between authors' categorization of images as nonsexualized, sexualized, and hypersexualized: Kappa was found to be .972 ($p < .001$).

Dividing the images into these three categories—nonsexualized, sexualized, and hypersexualized—captures important differences between them. Consider, for example, the two images presented in Figure 6.1. Both covers feature people who are naked and in a kneeling position, yet the impact of the images is quite different. The band members of Blind

Figure 6.1   Sexualization vs. hypersexualization

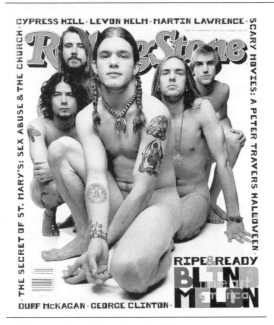

Blind Melon (band) November 11, 1993

Laetitia Casta (model) August 20, 1998

Melon are clearly sexualized—they are naked and the text asserts that they are "ripe and ready"—but they are not hypersexualized. They are not posed to engage in sexual activity; they do not touch themselves or each other; they are not arching their backs to emphasize their chests, genitals, or buttocks (in fact, their backs are rather slumped); and they gaze somberly into the camera, with their mouths closed. In fact, their nudity and textual description seem at odds with their otherwise nonsexualized characteristics.

In contrast, the cover image of Laetitia Casta is *hypersexualized*. Like the members of Blind Melon, she is both naked and kneeling, but her back is arched to emphasize her breasts and buttocks. Rather than posing on an unremarkable white background, Casta is kneeling on a bed of pink rose petals. Her body faces away from the camera, but her head is tilted back and is turned so that her eyes can meet the viewer's gaze. Her lips are slightly parted. Her arm is raised over her

head and touches her hair, which falls down her back. Her skin glistens, as though it has just been oiled. Casta, the text tells us, is the star of *Rolling Stone*'s "hot list."

The difference between these two images is clear, yet measuring nudity alone would not capture it. Our scale of sexualization does. By our measure, the Blind Melon cover scored 9 points, placing it at the top of the sexualized category. The Casta image, by contrast, scored 15 points, placing it well into the hypersexualized category. A gestalt-level analysis confirms this difference; in this paper we offer the tools to measure it. In the following sections, we detail our findings and discuss their implications.

FINDINGS

Before looking at questions of intensity, we first examine changes in the frequency of sexualized images over time. In order to do so, we combine sexualized and hypersexualized images into one category and compare them to nonsexualized images. The data show that sexualized representations of women have increased significantly (χ^2 = 6.8, p < .01), and sexualized representations of men have also increased, but not significantly (χ^2 = .99). . . .

These findings speak clearly to debates about the sexualization of men in popular media. While sexualized images of men have increased, men are still dramatically less likely to be sexualized than women. This difference is further highlighted by looking at the numerical frequency of such images: In the 2000s, there were 28 sexualized images of men (17% of male images) but 57 sexualized images of women (83% of female images), and there were 136 nonsexualized images of men (83% of male images) but only 12 nonsexualized images of women (17% of female images). Perhaps even more telling is the difference between men and women at the low end of the scale. In the 2000s, there were 35 images of men which scored a "0" on our scale and another 39 images which scored just 1 point, indicating that these images displayed no (or almost no) sexualized attributes. Together they accounted for 45% of all images of men in the 2000s. By contrast, there was not a single image of a woman in the 2000s that scored 0 points, and only 2 images of women scored 1 point on the scale, accounting for less than 3% of images of women in the 2000s.

Intensity of Sexualization

The difference in the sexualization of men and women is even more striking when we examine the intensity of their sexualization. In our analysis, we find a broad range in the degree of sexualization—some images are only somewhat sexualized while others are so intensely sexualized that we have labeled them "hypersexualized." In order to capture such differences, we split the sexualized category into two groups: those that were simply sexualized (such as the Blind Melon image described above) and those that were hypersexualized (such as the Casta image).

Looking first at images of men, we see that the vast majority of them—some 83% of men in the 2000s—fall in the nonsexualized category. This represents a noteworthy, though comparatively small, decrease from the 1960s when 89% of men were not sexualized. Many nonsexualized images of men are close-up headshots (36% across all years): They do not show the man's body nor do they indicate any level of nudity with bare shoulders or chest. Typically the man's mouth is closed and he is looking directly into the camera, though at times he might be smiling or looking to one side. The text in such images usually does not carry any sexual innuendo. On more than four decades of *Rolling Stone*'s covers, 162 images of men—or 22%—scored a zero on our scale, displaying no sexualized attributes.

Other images of men in the nonsexualized category are slightly more sexualized. One example of this is a 1997 image of actor Brad Pitt (April 3). On our scale, this image scored 4 points, placing it at the top of the nonsexualized category. The cover shows Pitt's face and part of his torso (1 point). He is wearing a plush white bathrobe (1 point), which is open to reveal part of his chest (1 point). He looks directly into the camera through tousled hair, his lips are very slightly parted (1 point). The text reads, "Leader of the Pack: Brad Pitt Talks Tough."

Although the majority of men on the cover of *Rolling Stone* are not sexualized, a sizable minority fall into the sexualized (but not hypersexualized) category. In the 1960s, 10.5% of men were sexualized, and in the 1970s their proportion increased slightly to 12%. In the 1980s, sexualized representations of men dropped to just 5%, but in the 1990s sexualized images of men increased to 13.3%. Their numbers continued to increase somewhat, so that in the 2000s 14.6% of images of men were sexualized.

A 2006 cover featuring singer Justin Timberlake (September 21) offers an example of this category of sexualized men. On our scale, Timberlake's image scored 8 points—double that of the Brad Pitt cover described above—and falls squarely within the sexualized category.

The image shows Timberlake's body from the thighs up (1 point). He is wearing a white T-shirt and jeans; he is looking directly into the camera and smiling broadly. Timberlake is carrying a guitar over one shoulder as if he were off to a gig, but his white T-shirt is soaking wet (3 points), clinging to his body and revealing his chest (2 points). The text reads, "Justin Timberlake: Wet Dream, The New King of Sex Gets Loose" (2 points).

Although sexualized images of men such as this one have become more common over time, *Rolling Stone* rarely features hypersexualized images of men. In the 1960s, there were no such images and, in the 1970s, there was just one hypersexualized image of a man, representing 1% of male images in that decade. In the 1980s, 2% of men were hypersexualized and, in the 1990s, 3% were. But in the 2000s, hypersexualized images of men dropped again to just over 2%.

The most prominent example of this category is a 2009 cover featuring pop singer Adam Lambert (June 25) (see Fig. 6.2). On our scale, the image scored 13 points, the highest score among men on the cover of *Rolling Stone*. The cover shows Lambert's body from the thighs up (1 point). He is lying on a bed (2 points) with his arms lifted overhead, conveying a sense of sexual passivity or vulnerability. One of his hands touches his hair (2 points). His eyes, which are lined with make-up, gaze into the camera, and his lips are slightly parted (1 point). Lambert is wearing tight black jeans and an unbuttoned black shirt (3 points), revealing part of his chest (1 point). His legs are spread and a bright green snake crawls up his leg, its head remarkably near his genitals (2 points). The text reads, "The Liberation of Adam Lambert: Wild Idol" (1 point). Given that Lambert is openly gay, perhaps it is not surprising that he is the most intensely sexualized man on the cover of *Rolling Stone,* since popular media portrayals of gay men often overemphasize their sexuality (Gross 2001; Nardi and Bolton 1998). But what *is* perhaps surprising about this image is its comparison to the highest scoring image of women, described below.

Figure 6.2 Hypersexualized man

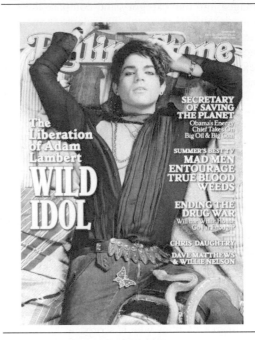

Adam Lambert (singer) June 25, 2009

Turning to images of women, we see different trends not only in the frequency but also in the intensity of their sexualization. Overall, nonsexualized representations of women have decreased since the start of *Rolling Stone.* In the 1960s, 56% of women on the magazine's cover were nonsexualized. In the 1970s, nonsexualized images of women increased slightly to 58% and then, in the 1980s, dropped to 49%. In the 1990s, nonsexualized images of women took a sharp downturn, falling to 22%. In the 2000s, just 17% of women were nonsexualized.

A 2009 cover featuring country singer Taylor Swift (March 15) offers an example of this nonsexualized category. On our scale, Swift's image scored 3 points, placing it in the nonsexualized category even though it contains minor elements of sexualization, much like the Brad Pitt cover described above. The image shows Swift's upper body (1 point). She is wearing a white halter top that reveals her shoulders and arms (1 point), though her body is largely covered by her long blonde hair. Swift stares directly into the camera; her lips are closed. She is holding a guitar as though she is just about to play it, her fingers poised over the guitar strings. The text reads, "Taylor Swift: Secrets of a Good Girl" (1 point).

Just as nonsexualized images of women such as this one have become less common, in recent years sexualized (but not hypersexualized) images of women have also become less prevalent, though to a much lesser extent. In the 1960s, 33% of women on the cover of *Rolling Stone* were sexualized. This rate increased somewhat over the next several decades, taking an upturn in the 1990s to 42%. In the 2000s, however, sexualized (but not hypersexualized) images of women decreased by nearly half to 22%. But, as we will see in a moment, an even greater increase in hypersexualized images of women more than made up the difference.

A 2008 portrait of pop star Britney Spears (December 11) is an example of this sexualized category. On our scale, this image scored 6 points, placing it near the bottom of the category's range. The cover shows Spears' body from the hips up (1 point). She is looking away from the camera and smiling widely, as though she were laughing heartily. Her tousled blonde hair falls below her shoulders. She is wearing low-slung jeans and a gray T-shirt, which is rolled up to reveal much of her stomach (3 points). One hand holds her cheek (1 point), conveying a sense of youthful enthusiasm, and her other hand rests in her jeans' belt loop, pulling down her pants slightly (1 point) to reveal a glimpse of a tattoo below. The text reads, "Yes She Can! Britney Returns."

Although sexualized images of women such as this one have become less common in recent years, hypersexualized images of women have increased significantly since the start of *Rolling Stone* magazine. In the 1960s, there was just one hypersexualized image of a woman, representing 11% of images of women at the time. In the 1970s, 6% of women on the magazine's cover were hypersexualized and, in the 1980s, that number more than doubled to 13%. Hypersexualized images of women increased even more in

the 1990s and 2000s, reaching 36% and 61% in each decade, respectively. As these data show, in the 2000s women were three and a half times more likely to be hypersexualized than nonsexualized, and nearly five times more likely to be sexualized to any degree (sexualized or hypersexualized) than nonsexualized. . . .

In our analysis, it might seem that the hypersexualized category encompasses a wide range of sexualized images because its scale (10–23) is wider than the other categories. Yet even with such a wide range, the images in this category leave little room for interpretation as being about anything other than sex. To demonstrate this, it is instructive to look at two images of hypersexualized women, one at each end of the category's range (see Fig. 6.3). An example of the lower end of this category is a 2009 image of Blake Lively and Leighton Meester (April 2), two leads of the television show "Gossip Girl." On our scale, this image scored 12 points, one point less than the Adam Lambert cover, the top scorer among men. The image shows the upper bodies of both women (1 point), though Lively's portrait dominates the cover. She is wearing a very low-cut black tank top (3 points) that reveals much of her breasts (2 points). Meester leans in toward Lively; her face is touching Lively's hair (1 point), suggesting that beyond the image their bodies are also pressed together. The focal point of the image is a dripping, double-scoop ice cream cone, a phallus-like object which Lively holds up for both women to lick (1 point). Their mouths are wide open and their protruding tongues (2 points) are covered in ice cream. The text reads, "The Nasty Thrill of 'Gossip Girl'" (2 points).

Compare this image to one at the top end of the hypersexualized category: a 2002 cover featuring pop singer Christina Aguilera (November 14). This image scored 20 points, earning the highest score in our dataset. The picture shows nearly all of Aguilera's body (1 point). She is naked (5 points), except for black fishnet stockings on her lower legs and black motorcycle boots (1 point). She is lying on a bed (2 points), which is covered with a rippling red satin sheet.

Figure 6.3 Hypersexualized women

Blake Lively and Leighton Meester (actors) April 2, 2009

Christina Aguilera (singer) November 14, 2002

Her head is tilted downwards, but she is looking into the camera. Her lips are parted (1 point), and her long hair is spread out around her shoulders. Aguilera's left hand holds a guitar, but only decoratively, not giving any indication that it is an instrument she might play. The guitar's neck is strategically placed so that it covers her left nipple. Her right hand clasps her other breast, not to cover it but to push it up provocatively. Her breasts are otherwise uncovered (2 points). Aguilera's body is contorted so that not only are her breasts exposed, but her buttocks (2 points) and, to a lesser degree, her genitals (1 point) are accentuated. The text reads, "Christina Aguilera: Inside the Dirty Mind of a Pop Princess" (2 points).

The new predominance of hypersexualized images of women such as these is illustrated further by examining the numerical frequency of such images. In the 2000s, there were 12 non-sexualized images of women, 15 sexualized images, and 42 hypersexualized images.[1] By

contrast, there were 136 nonsexualized images of men, 24 sexualized images, and only 4 hyper-sexualized images of men in the 2000s. That there are more sexualized images of men than women should not be too surprising. Images of men have long dominated the cover of *Rolling Stone*. (Recall that our dataset is comprised of 726 images of men compared to 280 images of women.) What is surprising, however, is the asymmetry in nonsexualized and hypersexual-ized representations of men and women. In the 2000s, there were more than 10 times the number of hypersexualized images of women than men, and there were more than 11 times the number of nonsexualized images of men than women.

DISCUSSION AND CONCLUSION

In *The Male Body: A New Look at Men in Public and in Private,* Susan Bordo (1999) describes the different implications for men and women when they are sexualized in the same way. As evidence, she analyzes advertisements in which women and men are shown with their pants around their ankles. Bordo (1999:28) argues that women in such images seem "stripped or exposed," even more than if their pants were off altogether, because they resemble rape or murder victims shown in movies and television. By contrast, Bordo observes, men shown with their pants around their ankles convey "much the same confident, slightly challenging machismo" as they would otherwise.

If similarly sexualized images can suggest victimization for women but confidence for men, consider the implications when women are sexualized at the same rate as men are *not* sexualized, as they were on the covers of *Rolling Stone* in the 2000s. And the vast majority of those sexualized images of women—some 74%—were hypersexualized, meaning that they did not exhibit only one or two signals of sex, but a multitude of them. Often women in these images were shown naked (or nearly so); they were shown with their legs spread wide open or lying down on a bed—in both cases sexually accessible; they were shown pushing up their breasts or pulling down their pants; they were described as having "dirty minds" or giving "nasty thrills"; and, in some cases, they were even shown to be simulating fellatio or other sex acts.

Some researchers argue against using the phrase "sexual objectification" to describe such images because they often depict women as active, confident, and/or sexually desirous (e.g., Bordo 1999; Gill 2003, 2008, 2009). We argue, however, that the intensity of their sexualization suggests that "sexual object" may indeed be the only appropriate label. The accumulation of sexualized attributes in these images leaves little room for observers to interpret them in any way other than as instruments of sexual pleasure and visual possession for a heterosexual male audience. Such images do not show women as sexually agentic musicians and actors; rather, they show female actors and musicians as ready and available for sex.

Yet some scholars have criticized such statements as overly homogenizing because they

render invisible differences in this process of sexualization (e.g., Gill 2009).[2] In our view, however, the very problem is one of homogenization. We argue that the dramatic increase in hypersexualized images of women—along with the corresponding decline in nonsexualized images of them—indicates a decisive narrowing or homogenization of media representations of women. In *Female Chauvinist Pigs: Women and the Rise of Raunch Culture,* journalist Ariel Levy (2005:5) describes this trend: "A tawdry, tarty, cartoonlike version of female sexuality has become so ubiquitous, it no longer seems particular. What we once regarded as a *kind* of sexual expression," Levy writes, "we now view *as* sexuality" (emphases in original). In this article we offer empirical evidence for this claim.

Of concern is that this narrowing down of media representations of women to what Levy calls a single "cartoonlike version of female sexuality"—or what we might call "hypersexualized femininity"—suggests a corresponding narrowing of culturally acceptable ways to "do" femininity (West and Fenstermaker 1995; West and Zimmerman 1987). This is not to say that there are no culturally available alternatives for women and girls as they make decisions about how to look and behave, but it does suggest that there may increasingly be fewer competing cultural scripts for ways of doing femininity. Thus, at least in popular media outlets such as *Rolling Stone,* it seems that just one aspect of femininity—sexuality, and *hypersexuality* at that—has overshadowed other aspects of "emphasized femininity" (Connell 1987), such as nurturance, fragility, and sociability. Although such characteristics are themselves problematic, the ascendancy of only one version of femininity (and, at the same time, one version of female sexuality) seems particularly troubling. . . .

NOTES

1. Some might attribute the increase in the hypersexualization of women on the cover of *Rolling Stone* to a change in management: In 2002, *Rolling*

Stone hired a new managing editor, Ed Needham, who was the former editor of *FHM*—the rather notorious "lad mag" that regularly features scantily-clad women on its covers. A closer look at our data, however, reveals a strong increase in the hypersexualization of women on the cover of *Rolling Stone* since the 1980s. Moreover, the proportion of hypersexualized images of women actually peaked at 78% in 1999, well before Needham's tenure. Hypersexualized images of women reached their second highest point (75%) in 2002, the first year of Needham's appointment, and then again in 2006, after Needham's 2-year stint at the magazine had ended.

2. Although a number of researchers have found that nonwhites are often sexualized in print media (Collins 1990; Hansen and Hansen 2000; West 2009), our analyses show no discernible difference in the frequency or intensity of sexualization of whites and nonwhites. Overall, 12% of women and 12% of men on the cover of *Rolling Stone* were nonwhite. They were nonsexualized, sexualized, and hypersexualized at about the same rate as their white counterparts.

REFERENCES

Abramson, E., & Valene, P. (1991). Media use, dietary restraint, bulimia, and attitudes toward obesity: A preliminary study. *British Review of Bulimia and Anorexia Nervosa, 5,* 73–76.

American Psychological Association (APA) Task Force. (2007). *Report of the APA task force on the sexualization of girls.* Washington, DC: American Psychological Association. Retrieved 10 March 2010 from http://www.apa.org/pi/women/programs/girls/report-full.pdf.

Attwood, F. (2009). *Mainstreaming sex: The sexualization of western culture.* London: I.B. Tauris.

Aubrey, J., Stevens, J., Henson, K., Hopper, M., & Smith, S. (2009). A picture is worth twenty words (about the self): Testing the priming influence of visual sexual objectification on women's self-objectification. *Communication Research Reports, 26,* 271–284.

Aubrey, J. S., & Taylor, L. (2009). The role of lad magazines in priming men's chronic and temporary appearance-related schemata: An investigation of longitudinal and experimental findings. *Human Communication Research, 35,* 28–58.

Baumann, S. (2008). The moral underpinnings of beauty: A meaning-based explanation for light and dark complexions in advertising. *Poetics, 36,* 2–23.

Binns, R. K. (2006). "On the cover of a *Rolling Stone*": A content analysis of gender representation in popular culture between 1967–2004. M.A. Thesis, Wichita State University, Wichita, KS.

Bordo, S. (1999). *The male body: A new look at men in public and in private.* New York: Farrar, Straus, and Giroux.

Brown, J., Halpern, C. T., & L'Engle, K. L. (2005). Mass media as a sexual super peer for early maturing girls. *Journal of Adolescent Health, 36,* 420–427.

Brown, J., L'Engle, K. L., Pardun, C., Guo, G., Kenneavy, K., & Jackson, C. (2006). Sexy media matter: Exposure to sexual content in music, movies, and magazines predicts black and white adolescents' sexual behavior. *Pediatrics, 117,* 1018–1027.

Collins, P. H. (1990). *Black feminist thought: Knowledge, consciousness, and the politics of empowerment.* New York: Routledge.

Connell, R. W. (1987). *Gender & power: Society, the person, and sexual politics.* Palo Alto, CA: Stanford University Press.

de Beauvoir, S. (1949, 1972). *The second sex.* New York: Penguin.

Dines, G. (2010). *Pornland: How porn has hijacked our sexuality.* Boston, MA: Beacon Press.

Ezzell, M. (2009). Pornography, lad mags, video games, and boys: Reviving the canary in the cultural coal mine. In S. Olfman (Ed.), *The sexualization of childhood.* Westport, CT: Praeger.

Farley, M. (2009). Prostitution and the sexualization of children. In S. Olfman (Ed.), *The sexualization of childhood.* Westport, CT: Praeger.

Frette, J. (2009). Men are altered and objectified too: Ryan Reynolds graces the cover of *Entertainment Weekly.* Retrieved 20 December 2010 http://www.examiner.com/women-s-issues-in-national/men-are-altered-and-objectified-too-ryan-reyn olds-graces-the-cover-of-entertainment-weekly.

Gatten, J. (1993). *The* Rolling Stone *index: Twenty-five years of popular culture, 1967–1991.* Ann Arbor, MI: Popular Culture, Ink.

Gill, R. (2003). From sexual objectification to sexual subjectification: The resexualisation of women's bodies in the media. *Feminist Media Studies, 3,* 100–106.

Gill, R. (2007). *Gender and the media.* Cambridge, UK: Polity Press.

Gill, R. (2008). Empowerment/sexism: Figuring female sexual agency in contemporary advertising. *Feminism & Psychology, 18,* 35–60.

Gill, R. (2009). Beyond the "sexualization of culture" thesis: An intersectional analysis of "sixpacks," "midriffs" and "hot lesbians" in advertising. *Sexualities, 12,* 137–160.

Goffman, E. (1979). *Gender advertisements.* Cambridge, MA: Harvard University Press.

Groesz, L., Levine, M., & Mumen, S. (2002). The effect of experimental presentation of thin media images on body satisfaction: A meta-analytic review. *International Journal of Eating Disorders, 31,* 1–16.

Gross, L. (2001). *Up from invisibility: Lesbians, gay men, and the media in America.* New York: Columbia University Press.

Hansen, C., & Hansen, R. (2000). Music and music videos. In D. Zillmann & P. Vorderer (Eds.), *Media entertainment: The psychology of its appeal.* Mahwah, NJ: Erlbaum.

Hargreaves, D., & Tiggemann, M. (2004). Idealized media images and adolescent body image: "Comparing" boys and girls. *Body Image, 1,* 351–361.

Harrison, K. (2000). The body electric: Thin-ideal media and eating disorders in adolescents. *Journal of Communication, 50,* 119–143.

Hofschire, L., & Greenberg, B. (2001). Media's impact on adolescents' body dissatisfaction. In J. Brown & J. R. Steele (Eds.), *Sexual teens, sexual media.* Mahwah, NJ: Erlbaum.

Holmstrom, A. (2004). The effects of the media on body image: A meta-analysis. *Journal of Broadcasting & Electronic Media, 48,* 196–217.

Johnson, S. (2007). Promoting easy sex without genuine intimacy: *Maxim* and *Cosmopolitan* cover lines and cover images. In M.-L. Galician & D. L. Merskin (Eds.), *Critical thinking about sex, love, romance in the mass media: Media literacy applications.* Mahwah, NJ: Erlbaum.

Kabouter. (2010). *Rolling Stone* magazine cover gallery. Retrieved 1 April 2010. http://rateyourmusic.com/list/kabouter/rolling_stone_magazine_cover- gallery.

Kalof, L. (1999). The effects of gender and music video imagery on sexual attitudes. *Journal of Social Psychology, 139,* 378–385.

Kang, M.-E. (1997). The portrayal of women's images in magazine advertisements: Goffman's gender analysis revisited. *Sex Roles, 37,* 979–996.

Krassas, N., Blauwkamp, J., & Wesselink, P. (2001). Boxing Helena and corseting Eunice: Sexual rhetoric in *Cosmopolitan* and *Playboy* magazines. *Sex Roles, 44,* 751–771.

Krassas, N., Blauwkamp, J., & Wesselink, P. (2003). "Master your johnson": Sexual rhetoric in *Maxim* and *Stuff* magazines. *Sexuality and Culture, 7,* 98–119.

Lambiase, J., & Reichert, T. (2006). Sex and the marketing of contemporary consumer magazines: How men's magazines sexualized their covers to compete with *Maxim.* In T. Reichert & J. Lambiase (Eds.), *Sex in consumer culture: The erotic content of media, marketing.* Mahwah, NJ: Erlbaum.

Lanis, K., & Covell, K. (1995). Images of women in advertisements: Effects on attitudes related to sexual aggression. *Sex Roles, 32,* 639–649.

Levy, A. (2005). *Female chauvinist pigs: Women and the rise of raunch culture.* New York: Free Press.

Lindner, K. (2004). Images of women in general interest and fashion magazine advertisements from 1955 to 2002. *Sex Roles, 51,* 409–421.

Lucas, A., Beard, C. M., O'Fallon, W. M., & Kurland, L. (1991). 50-year trends in the incidence of anorexia nervosa in Rochester, Minn.: A population-based study. *American Journal of Psychiatry, 148,* 917–922.

Machia, M., & Lamb, S. (2009). Sexualized innocence: Effects of magazine ads portraying adult women as sexy little girls. *Journal of Media Psychology, 21,* 15–24.

MacKay, N., & Covell, K. (1997). The impact of women in advertisements on attitudes toward women. *Sex Roles, 36,* 573–583.

Malamuth, N., Addison, T., & Koss, M. (2000). Pornography and sexual aggression: Are there reliable effects and can we understand them? *Annual Review of Sex Research, 11,* 26–91.

Malamuth, N., & Check, J. (1981). The effects of mass media exposure on acceptance of violence against women: A field experiment. *Journal of Research in Personality, 15,* 436–446.

McNair, B. (2002). *Striptease culture: Sex, media and the democratization of desire.* London, New York: Routledge.

McRobbie, A. (2004). The rise and rise of porn chic. *Times Higher Education Supplement.* Retrieved 1 June 2010. http://timeshigher-education.co.uk/story.asp?sectioncode=26&storycode=182087.

Milburn, M., Mather, R., & Conrad, S. (2000). The effects of viewing R-rated movie scenes that objectify women on perceptions of date rape. *Sex Roles, 43,* 645–664.

Nardi, P., & Bolton, R. (1998). Gay bashing: Violence and aggression against gay men and lesbians. In P. M. Nardi & B. E. Schneider (Eds.), *Social perspectives in lesbian, gay studies: A reader.* London: Routledge.

Nitz, M., Reichert, T., Aune, A. S., & Velde, A. V. (2007). All the news that's fit to see? The sexualization of television news journalists as a promotional strategy. In T. Reichert (Ed.), *Investigating the use of sex in media promotion, advertising.* Binghamton, NY: Best Business Books.

Ohbuchi, K.-I., Ikeda, T., & Takeuchi, G. (1994). Effects of violent pornography upon viewers' rape myth beliefs: A study of Japanese males. *Psychology, Crime, and the Law, 1,* 71–81.

Olfman, S. (Ed.). (2009). *The sexualization of childhood.* Westport, CT: Praeger.

Paasonen, S., Nikunen, K., & Saarenmaa, L. (Eds.). (2007). *Pornification: Sex and sexuality in media culture.* Oxford: Berg.

Paek, H.-J., & Nelson, M. (2007). A cross-cultural and cross-media comparison of female nudity in advertising. In T. Reichert (Ed.), *Investigating the use of sex in media promotion, advertising.* Binghamton, NY: Best Business Books.

Pardun, C., L'Engle, K. L., & Brown, J. (2005). Linking exposure to outcomes: Early adolescents' consumption of sexual content in six media. *Mass Communication and Society, 8,* 75–91.

Paul, P. (2005). *Pornified: How pornography is transforming our lives, our relationships, and families.* New York: Times Books.

Pope, H. Jr., Phillips, K., & Olivardia, R. (2000). *The Adonis complex: The secret crisis of male body obsession.* New York: Free Press.

Reichert, T. (2003). *The erotic history of advertising.* Amherst, NY: Prometheus.

Reichert, T., & Carpenter, C. (2004). An update on sex in magazine advertising: 1983 to 2003. *Journalism & Mass Communications Quarterly, 81,* 823–837.

Reichert, T., Lambiase, J., Morgan, S., Carstarphen, M., & Zavoina, S. (1999). Cheesecake and beefcake: No matter how you slice it, sexual explicitness in advertising continues to increase. *Journalism & Mass Communication Quarterly, 76,* 7–20.

Roberts, T.-A., & Gettman, J. (2004). Mere exposure: Gender differences in the negative effects of priming a state of self-objectification. *Sex Roles, 51,* 17–27.

Rohlinger, D. (2002). Eroticizing men: Cultural influences on advertising and male objectification. *Sex Roles, 46,* 61–74.

Rolling Stone. (2006). *1,000 covers: A history of the most influential magazine in pop culture.* New York: Abrams.

Rush, E., & La Nauze, A. (2006). *Corporate paedophilia: Sexualisation of children in Australia.* Canberra: The Australia Institute.

Schwarz, N., & Kurz, E. (1989). What's in a picture? The impact of face-ism on trait attribution. *European Journal of Social Psychology, 19,* 311–316.

Soley, L., & Kurzbard. G. (1986). Sex in advertising: A comparison of 1964 and 1984 magazine advertisements. *Journal of Advertising, 15,* 46–64.

Soley, L., & Reid, L. (1988). Taking it off: Are models in magazine ads wearing less? *Journalism Quarterly, 65,* 960–966.

Stice, E., Schupak-Neuberg, E., Shaw, H., & Stein, R. (1994). Relation of media exposure to eating disorder symptomatology: An examination of mediating mechanisms. *Journal of Abnormal Psychology, 103,* 836–840.

Taylor, E., & Sharkey, L. (2003). Em & Lo's sex myths: Women's bodies are sexier. *The Guardian* (22 March). Retrieved 20 December 2010. http://www.guardian.co.uk/lifeandstyle/2003/mar/22/weekend.emmataylor.

Thompson, M. (2000). Gender in magazine advertising: Skin sells best. *Clothing and Textiles Research Journal, 18,* 178–181.

Tiggeman, M., & Slater, A. (2001). A test of objectification theory in former dancers and non-dancers. *Psychology of Women Quarterly, 2,* 57–64.

Turner, S., Hamilton, H., Jacobs, M., Angood, L., & Dwyer, D. H. (1997). The influence of fashion magazines on the body image satisfaction of college women: An exploratory analysis. *Adolescence, 32,* 603–614.

Umiker-Sebeok, J. (1996). Power and construction of gendered spaces. *International Review of Sociology, 6,* 389–404.

Villani, S. (2001). Impact of media on children and adolescents: A 10-year review of the research. *Journal of the American Academy of Child and Adolescent Psychiatry, 40,* 392–401.

Ward, L. M. (2002). Does television exposure affect emerging adults' attitudes and assumptions about sexual relationships? Correlational and experimental confirmation. *Journal of Youth & Adolescence, 31,* 1–15.

Ward, L., Monique, E., & Hansbrough, E. W. (2005). Contributions of music video exposure to black adolescents' gender and sexual schemas. *Journal of Adolescent Research, 20,* 143–166.

Weaver, J., Masland, J., & Zillmann, D. (1984). Effect of erotica on young men's aesthetic perception of their female sexual partners. *Perceptual and Motor Skills, 58,* 929–930.

West, C. (2009). Still on the auction block: The sexploitation of black adolescent girls in rape music and hip-hop culture. In S. Olfman (Ed.), *The sexualization of childhood.* Westport, CT: Praeger.

West, C., & Fenstermaker, S. (1995). Doing difference. *Gender & Society, 9,* 8–37.

West, C., & Zimmerman, D. (1987). Doing gender. *Gender & Society, 1,* 125–151.

Zillmann, D., & Bryant, J. (1988). Pornography's impact on sexual satisfaction. *Journal of Applied Social Psychology, 18,* 438–453.

Introduction to Reading 29

Breanne Fahs explores the tensions between *freedom to* and *freedom from* in the feminist sex-positive movement. Sex-positive feminists argue that women's freedom must include sexual freedom to explore and enjoy sex within consenting relationships. The focus of the sex-positive movement, Fahs argues, has been "positive liberty" or women's *freedom to* expand sexual expression and embrace sexual diversity. This focus ignores "negative liberty," defined as women's freedom from oppressive sexual mandates and requirements. Fahs makes a strong argument that the sex-positive movement must integrate *freedom from* as it relates to *freedom to* in order to create a feminist movement that is cohesive and powerful. Thus, women must have freedom from oppressive heterosexist and racist constraints over their sexuality as well as positive liberty. Fahs examines seven examples of contemporary dilemmas (e.g., rape and sexual coercion; same-sex eroticism) women face in their sexual lives demonstrating the ways in which *freedom from* can be incorporated into the feminist sex-positive movement.

1. How does Fahs employ anarchist theories of liberation and freedom to advance her argument that the sex-positive movement must include negative liberty in its theory and activism?

2. Why did sex-positive feminism come to focus on *freedom to* rather than *freedom from*?

3. What role has radical feminism played in forwarding the importance of negative liberty in the movement for women's sexual freedom?

4. Discuss the three goals that Fahs sees as essential to a new vision for sex positivity.

"Freedom to" and "Freedom from"

A New Vision for Sex-Positive Politics

Breanne Fahs

Introduction

Walking through the exhibit hall at the Society for the Scientific Study of Sexuality conference recently, the displays featured a vast array of new possibilities for sexual expression: dildos shaped like tongues, edgy books and journals on bisexuality and polyamory, videos for helping heterosexual women gain comfort with penetrating their (receptive) boyfriends and husbands, and even a pamphlet for an "autoerotic asphyxiation support club." Clearly, the sex-positive movement—inclusive of those who argue against all restrictions on sexuality aside from issues of safety and consent—has made significant advances in how scholars, feminists, practitioners, and the public think about, feel about, and "do" sexuality. For example, women's access to feminist sex toy shops, pornography, blogs, and representations of queer sexuality have increased dramatically in the past several decades (Loe, 1999; Queen, 1997a; Queen, 1997b). Despite the relentless attacks from conservatives in the U.S., people today generally have more expansive options for how they express "normal" sexuality, and they can do so more openly and with more formal and social support. Sex-positive feminists have, in many ways, turned upside-down the notion of the once highly-dichotomous public/private, virgin/whore, and deviant/normal. The sex-positive movement has helped to decriminalize sex work (Jenness, 1993), expand representations in pornography (McElroy, 1995), teach people how

to embrace sexuality as normal and healthy (Queen, 1997a; Queen, 1997b), explore "sexual enhancement" devices (Reece et al., 2004), advocate comprehensive sex education (Irvine, 2002; Spencer et al., 2008; Peterson, 2010), and challenge overly simplistic notions of "good" and "bad" sex (Rubin, 1993). From Annie Sprinkle showing her cervix as a "Public Cervix Announcement" (Shrage, 2002), to Carol Queen (1997a) arguing against "whore stigma," to Gayle Rubin (1993) fighting tirelessly against a fixed (and faulty) construction of sex offending, sex positivity has laid the groundwork to depathologize sexuality, particularly for women, sexual minorities, people of color, and sex workers.

Still, the whole scene—clearly intent on a "progress narrative" of sexuality—gives me a strong sense of unease, as many contradictions still overwhelm women's sexual lives. Along with these newfound modes of pleasure-seeking and knowledge-making, women struggle within a plethora of urgent contemporary challenges: alarming rates of sexual violence (Luce, 2010), body shame (Salk and Engeln-Maddox, 2012), eating disorders (Calogero and Pina, 2011), pressure to orgasm (Farvid and Braun, 2006; Fahs, 2011a), distance from their bodily experiences (Martin, 2001), disempowerment with childbirth (Martin, 2001; Lyerly, 2006), masochistic sexual fantasies (Bivona and Critelli 2009), and a host of other sexual and political crises. When asked why they orgasm, women cite their partner's pleasure as more important than their own

From Fahs, Breanne. 2014. "Freedom to" and "Freedom from": A new vision for sex-positive politics. *Sexualities, 17*(3): 267–290.

(Nicolson and Burr, 2003) and they increasingly associate sexual freedom with consumerism, fashion, and commodities (Hakim, 2010). Women internalize normative pressures to hate their pubic hair and body hair (Riddell et al., 2010; Fahs, 2011b; Bercaw-Pratt, 2012) and hide their menstrual cycles from others (Bobel, 2006; Mandziuk, 2010). Across demographic categories, women suffer immensely from feeling disempowered to speak, explore, and embrace the kinds of sexual lives they most want.

This paper takes this vast contradictory moment—that is, living between celebrations of progress and alarmingly regressive notions of women's sexual "empowerment"—to explore the problems of (uncritical) sex positivity in this post-sexual-revolution age. Drawing from anarchist theories from the past two centuries—particularly the notion that true liberation and freedom must include *both* the freedom *to* do what we want to do AND the freedom *from* oppressive structures and demands—I argue that the sex-positive movement must advance its politics to include a more serious consideration of the freedom from repressive structures (or "negative liberty"). More specifically, by outlining several ways that the *freedom from* and the *freedom to* are currently in conversation in discourses of women's sexuality, I argue that the integration of these two halves could lead to a subtler and more complete understanding of contemporary sexual politics, particularly around tensions that arose during the infamous "sex wars" of the 1980s, thus helping to build a more cohesive and powerful feminist movement as a whole.

ANARCHISM AND SEXUALITY

. . . While anarchy and political theory may not seem like an intuitive bedfellow for feminists who study sex, the political and social bases of anarchy have much to teach feminists interested in bodies and sexualities as sites of social (in) justice. Anarchists have long espoused important divisions between those interested in individualist

versus social anarchism. On the one hand, individualist anarchism, what Isaiah Berlin (1969) termed "negative liberty," argued for freedom from the state and corporate apparatuses. On the other hand, social anarchism advocated for both negative liberty (freedom from the state) and positive liberty (freedom to do what we want to do). . . .

Anarcha-feminists were among the first who refused to conceptualize love, relationships, and domesticity as separate from state politics, calling for an end to "sex slavery" (de Cleyre, 1914), jealousy (Goldman, 1998), oppression through motherhood, marriage, and love (Goldman, 1917; Marso, 2003), and control of love and relationships (Haaland, 1993; Molyneux, 2001). In the 1960s, rifling on the work of anarchists, radical feminists—many of whom came from Marxist backgrounds that prioritized the elimination of class inequalities and the importance of structural equalities—fought for the *freedom to* as much as the *freedom from,* simultaneously advancing ideas about women *gaining* access to certain previously impenetrable spheres (e.g., all-male faculty clubs, all-male jobs) and *blocking access* to others (e.g., all-women consciousness-raising groups, all-women classrooms, all-women music festivals). (While *freedom to* and *freedom from* rarely serve as precise opposites, the ability to willfully *separate* has been considered more a "freedom from" than a "freedom to.") Though radical feminists rarely referred directly to anarchism as their inspiration, these same ideological concepts (negative and positive liberty) informed the center of their political claims about the pathological implications of patriarchy. Radical feminist circles explored the varying modes of power imbalances between men and women (and, later, between women) and attended to distinctions between "power over" (domination and oppression), "power to" (freedom to do and act), and "power with" (collective power to do and act) (Allen, 2008). Far from the oversimplified notion of a singular, rebellious anarchy, they argued for a multifaceted approach to understanding the workings of power, the state, and social relationships. . . .

Even though anarchist theories of rebellion from the state form an intuitive companion to claims for sexual "freedom," sexuality and anarchy have not typically joined forces (with Greenway, 1997; Passet, 2003; and Heckert and Cleminson, 2011 as notable exceptions). Nevertheless, the two share an important set of common goals, particularly around the *freedom from* oppressive structures, mandates, statutes, and interventions. As Gustav Landauer wrote, "The state is not something which can be destroyed by a revolution, but is a condition, a certain relationship between human beings, a mode of human behavior; we destroy it by contracting other relationships, by behaving differently" (Heckert, 2010). Sexuality, then, allows us to "relate differently" and "behave differently," to reimagine our relationships to sex, love, friendship, and kinship (Heckert, 2011), to forego the boredom and monotony capitalism engenders (CrimethInc, 2012). If we understand sexuality as a tool of creativity, as a force that reconsiders power, equality, and freedom, it becomes a perfect companion for anarchist sensibilities. Sexuality as *process* rather than *outcome* (as desire rather than merely orgasm, as exchange rather than merely physical release) links up with the political sentiments of anarchy by suggesting that interaction between people—ideally devoid of power imbalances—matters far more than goal-oriented drives toward an *end*. Thus, drawing upon these claims, I argue that merging the *freedom from* and the *freedom to* with sexuality may result in a powerful overhaul of fragmented segments of social and political life: the personal and political, the corporeal and the cognitive, the "sex-positive" and the "radical feminist."

SEX POSITIVES AND THE 'FREEDOM TO'

Though sex-positive feminists as currently constituted would likely not categorize themselves exclusively as fighting for the *freedom to,* the vast majority of their work has centered on the expansion of sexual rights, freedoms, and modes of expression (Queen, 1997a; Queen, 1997b). The movement emerged in response to highly repressive discourses of sexuality, particularly those that they perceived as embracing a state-centered, conservative ideology of "good sex"—as heterosexual, married, monogamous, procreative, non-commercial, in pairs, in a relationship, same generation, in private, no pornography, bodies only, and vanilla—and "bad sex"—as homosexual, unmarried, promiscuous, non-procreative, commercial, alone or in groups, casual, cross-generational, in public, pornography, with manufactured objects, and sadomasochistic (Rubin, 1993). Though the sex wars of the 1980s—where feminists battled about pornography in particular—suggest that sex positivity arose in response to the supposedly pro-censorship notions from radical feminists (though that, too, is highly controversial), in fact sex positivity more clearly rebelled against conservatism, evangelical culture, homophobia, and religious dogma (Duggan and Hunter, 1995). . . .

Sex positives fought fiercely for the *freedom to* have diverse, multiple, expansive, and agentic sexual expression; that is, to dislodge histories of repression, sex positives argued that women (and men) should freely embrace new modes of experiencing and expressing their sexuality. Often taking a sort of libertarian perspective on sexual freedom, some wings of the sex-positive movement value lack of government intervention into sex as their top priority (Weeks, 2002) while other aspects of the sex-positive movement more clearly value education and expansion of sexual knowledge (Irvine, 2002). Sex positives share a concern with external limitations placed on sexual expression and with the moralizing judgments placed upon diverse sexualities. For example, Carol Queen defined sex positivity as a community of people who "don't denigrate, medicalize, or demonize any form of sexual expression except that which is not consensual" (Queen, 1997a, p. 128).

One of the key battlegrounds for sex positives—sex education—has also been (arguably) its most successful terrain. Sex positives fought against abstinence-only sex education in favor of comprehensive sex education that would support not only *more* knowledge about STIs and birth control, but also more expansive ideas about queer sexuality, pleasure, alternative families, and options for abortion (Irvine, 2002). Further, as an offshoot of the push toward *more* sex education, feminist-owned sex toy shops began to open (and thrive) throughout the country (e.g., Good Vibes in San Francisco, Smitten Kitten in Minneapolis, Early to Bed in Chicago, Aphrodite's Toy Box in Atlanta, and several others). These stores state that they promoted safe, fun, non-sexist ways to enjoy sex toys, pornography, and erotica, and have worked hard to navigate the tricky terrain of selling commercial products while nurturing an inclusive, community-based, potentially activist space (Loe, 1999; Attwood, 2005). The conflicts between supposedly promoting sex education while also embracing commercial gains presents tricky territory for feminist critics.

As another key victory for sex-positive feminists, they have fought for heightened awareness about, and advocacy for, queer sexualities. This has included the expansion of trans rights (NCTE, 2003; Currah et al., 2006), more legal and social rights for lesbians and gay men (Bevacqua, 2004; Sycamore, 2004), and acceptance for bisexuality within the queer movement (Garber, 1995). Sex positives have rejected anti-gay-marriage statutes even while exploring marriage as fundamentally flawed (Sycamore, 2004), encouraged better social services for queer youth (McCabe and Rubinson, 2008; Orechia, 2008), and worked to understand sexuality as fluid, flexible, and not beholden to dogmatic and religious doctrines (Diamond, 2009). In doing so, they have embraced a diversity of bodies, expressions, and identities and have critically examined the all-too-narrow construction of the "sexual body" as white, heterosexual, young, female, and passive. Instead, sex positives have moved to recognize the sexualities of those on the "fringe": fat bodies (Johnson and Taylor, 2008), older bodies (Chrisler and Ghiz, 1993), people of color (Landrine and Russo,

2010; Moore, 2012), gender queer (Branlandingham, 2011), and "alternative" bodies (Hughes, 2009). These *freedom to* victories have certainly helped the feminist movement link up with other movements for social and political justice, particularly as sex positives reject claims of "deviance" for any particular group (Showden, 2012).

RADICAL FEMINISTS AND THE 'FREEDOM FROM'

At the same time that sex positives argued to decriminalize, expand, and embrace sexuality—often constructing pornography as positive, educational, and antirepressive—radical feminists countered these claims by looking at the *freedom from* (MacKinnon, 1989). While radical feminists have often been seen as the *opposite* of, or contrary to, the beliefs of sex positivity, I argue that radical feminists have merely wanted *more* recognition of "negative liberty," or the *freedom from* oppressive structures that most women confront on a daily basis. (Not all sex positives have totally neglected the *freedom from,* but rather, have *deprioritized* the *freedom from* in comparison to other goals and priorities.) Advocating caution about the unconditional access to women that is built into the sex-positive framework, radical feminists essentially said that, without women's *freedom from* patriarchal oppression, women lacked freedom at all. Real sexual freedom, radical feminists claimed, must include the *freedom from* the social mandates to have sex (particularly the enforcement of sex with men) and *freedom from* treatment as sexual objects.

Looking collectively at the work of Teresa de Lauretis (1988), Marilyn Frye (1997), Adrienne Rich (1980), Audre Lorde (2007), Andrea Dworkin (1997), and Catharine MacKinnon (1989), they all share the belief that men's access to women is a *taken-for-granted* assumption often exercised on women's bodies and sexualities. Indeed, all powerful groups demand unlimited access to less powerful groups, while less powerful groups rarely have access to more powerful groups. As Marilyn Frye (1997) said, "Total power is unconditional access; total powerlessness is being unconditionally accessible. The creation and manipulation of power is constituted of the manipulation and control of access" (411). For example, the poor rarely have access to the rich (particularly if demanded by the poor), while the rich almost always have access to the poor (e.g., buying drugs or sex in poor neighborhoods and returning to their "safe" communities). Affluent whites often live in gated communities, in part to deny access to people of color, while middle-class whites live in segregated suburban cul-de-sacs. Men notoriously operate in spheres of power that exclude women (e.g., country clubs, golf circles, "good ol' boys" hiring practices, and so on). At its core, radical feminism argues against the patriarchal assumption that men have the right to access women (and the patriarchal notion that women must internalize this mandate).

Lesbian separatism, particularly *political* lesbian separatism not based specifically or primarily on sexual desire for women (Atkinson, 1974; Densmore, 1973), represents a rebellion against this mandated access. By revealing the assumptions of access embedded within sexuality— namely that men can always access the bodies of women for their sexual "needs"—lesbian separatists make a clear case for the *freedom from.* All-women spaces that excluded men did not merely allow women to physically separate from men, but also to rebel against the constant surveillance of the male gaze and men's *assumptions of access* (Fahs, 2011a). These separatists understood that the "free love" of the 1970s, far from a celebratory moment of progress for women, merely allowed men's sexual access to *more* women and largely ignored women's experiences with "brutalization, rape, submission [and] someone having power over them" (Dunbar, 1969, 56). They also (rightly) noted that women's assertion of their *freedom from* interacting with men provokes dangerous resistances, anger, and hostilities.

Moving forward to the 1980s, scholars like Dworkin (1997) and MacKinnon (1989) made similar claims about sexual access when they argued for the *freedom from* messages and images embedded in pornography that portrayed women as "hot wet fuck tubes" (Dworkin, 1991). Further, they called out the power-imbalanced practices of sexual intercourse and theorized about the dangers of women tolerating their own oppression (e.g., not reporting rape). By calling out sexuality as a site of dangerous power imbalances between men and women, their version of *freedom from* became particularly threatening within and outside of feminist circles. Recall that both MacKinnon and Dworkin received death threats and had to retain security personnel for even *suggesting* that women can and should assert their *freedom from* pornography and power-imbalanced sex (MacKinnon and Dworkin, 1998). Taken together, these examples reveal that the *freedom from* provokes greater threat from men and the culture at large, with increasingly hostile backlashes against those who assert their right to negative liberty. To suggest that women *deny access to men* undercuts core cultural assumptions about gender politics and patriarchal power.

CYCLES OF LIBERATION

Looking at these histories together, a clear pattern emerges: Rarely does the feminist movement (or the queer movement, or sexuality studies) adequately address the dialectic between the *freedom from* and the *freedom to.* I am particularly concerned about the degree to which sex positivity neglects the *freedom from,* particularly when the rhetoric of sex positivity often inadvertently allows for the unconditional access to women that many of their projects, goals, and narratives rely upon. That said, I also worry about the ways that negative liberty (ironically) could create new norms that require women to label their (heterosexual, pornographic, masochistic, etc.) desires as necessarily patriarchal (e.g., Showden, 2012 has suggested that sex positivity must become a "politics of *maybe*" rather than a "politics of *yes*"). The relative crisis of women's "sexual freedom"—along with the hazards of *solving* this problem—becomes increasingly clear when examining contemporary dilemmas and quandaries women face in their sexual lives. In the following seven examples, I outline the ways that the *freedom from* has fallen more and more out of focus, even as the *freedom to* achieves small victories.

ORGASM

In my previous work (Fahs, 2011a), I looked at what I consider to be the most dangerous aspect of defining sexual freedom: It is subject to continued appropriations and distortions, and it requires continual reinvention. Sexual freedom has no fixed definition and is not static. Rather, because freedoms are easily co-opted, all definitions of freedom (sexual or otherwise) are transient and transitory, require constant re-evaluation and reassessment, and present an ongoing set of new challenges to each cohort and generation. In the articulation of freedom, co-optation is not only possible, but *probable,* particularly when addressing issues of women's sexuality. As a key example, consider a brief history of women's orgasms. During the sexual revolution, women fought hard for the right to have the clitoris recognized as a site of legitimate pleasure. Until the late 1960s, it was assumed (largely due to the influence of psychoanalysis) that vaginal orgasm represented "maturity" and clitoral orgasm represented "immaturity" (studies by medical doctors—as recent as 2011—still argue this! See Costa and Brody, 2011; and Brody and Weiss, 2011); still more, women were expected to prioritize phallic male pleasure over anything clitoral, often resulting in harsh pressures for women to vaginally orgasm. As Ti-Grace Atkinson (1974) said, "Why *should* women learn to vaginal orgasm? Because that's what men want. How about a facial tic? What's the difference?" (7). During the sexual revolution, the convergence of the queer movement, the

women's movement, and the sexual revolution led to a concerted interest in dethroning the vaginal orgasm in favor of the clitoral orgasm (Gerhard, 2000). If women valued and recognized the power of the clitoris, some argued, they could embrace sex with other women, orgasm more easily and efficiently, and enjoy the same sexual pleasures men had always enjoyed (Koedt, 1973).

This celebration of progress on the orgasm front—notably something radical feminists expressed some concerns about even then—had a short-lived period of revolutionary potential. At the tail end of the sexual revolution, radical feminists like Dana Densmore (1973) and Roxanne Dunbar (1969) began to worry that all of this focus on women's clitoral orgasms could lead to an "orgasm frenzy" where women would feel *mandated* to orgasm and men would use clitoral orgasms as yet another tool to oppress women. Dunbar believed that sexual liberation became equated with "the 'freedom' to 'make it' with anyone anytime" (49), while Sheila Jeffreys (1990) claimed retrospectively that "sexual liberation" from the 1960s and 1970s merely substituted one form of oppression for another. Indeed, over the next twenty years, clitoral orgasms evolved from a much-fought-for occurrence to a social mandate between (heterosexual) sex partners. Fast-forward to today and we find some startling data: over half of women have faked orgasms, often regularly (Wiederman, 1997), and women describe faking orgasms for reasons that still ensure male dominance and power: they want to support the egos of their (male) partners; they want to end the encounter (primarily intercourse), often because they feel exhausted; and they imagine that orgasms make them "normal" (Fahs, 2011a; Roberts et al., 1995). This suggests that, though orgasm once served a symbolic role as a tool of liberation (a new *freedom to* personal desire), orgasm eventually reverted to being another tool of patriarchy as orgasm became a marker of male prowess. Given the high rates of faking orgasm (Fahs, 2011a; Roberts et al., 1995) now seen among women, many women may now need the *freedom from* orgasm as a *mandate;* further, the mandate exists not primarily to please women themselves, but to please their (male) partners.

SEXUAL SATISFACTION

As an offshoot of the "orgasm problem," recent research on sexual satisfaction has pointed to some disturbing trends. While popular culture (particularly movies, music, and magazines) generally advocates women's *freedom to* have sexual pleasure and satisfaction, little attention is paid to how women themselves *construct* satisfaction or how women's sexual satisfaction still showcases men's overwhelming sexual power. What does a "satisfied woman" say about her sexual experiences? Studies consistently suggest correlations between sexual satisfaction and intimacy, close relationships (Pinney et al., 1987; Sprecher et al., 1995), emotional closeness (Trompeter et al., 2012), reciprocal feelings of love, and versatile sexual techniques (Haavio-Mannila and Kontula, 1997). These findings underlie the relational dimensions of women's sexual satisfaction (and undermine pop culture's "bodice ripping" stereotypes). In this regard, women may have the *freedom to* sexual pleasure as long as it remains in the stereotyped confines of marriage and romantic love. This may represent a sign of progress, or it may signify the trappings of traditional femininity. Similarly, studies also show that sexually satisfied women typically have better body image (Meltzer and McNulty, 2010), lower rates of eating disorders, lower self-objectification tendencies (Frederickson and Robert, 1997; Calogero and Thompson, 2009), thereby suggesting other modest victories for the association between sexual expression and personal empowerment even while raising questions about women's interpretation of "satisfaction."

When looking more closely at data about women's sexual satisfaction, particularly measures of "deservingness" and "entitlement," women fall far short of full equality with men with regard to seeking pleasure, though differing definitions and assessments of satisfaction make these gender findings increasingly complicated (McClelland, 2010; McClelland, 2011). For example, the same relational dimensions that may help women equate sexual satisfaction with emotional closeness also demand that they prioritize their partner's (especially men's) pleasure over their own. When asked why they want to orgasm, women say that their partners' pleasure matters more than their own and that their partners' pleasure is a conditional factor that determines their own pleasure (Nicholson and Burr, 2003), calling into question *whose* pleasure women value when assessing their own satisfaction. Compared to men, women also more often equate sex with submissiveness, and when they do so, this leads to lower rates of sexual arousal, autonomy, and enjoyment (Sanchez et al., 2006). Further, compared to men, women also describe orgasm as a far less important component of their sexual satisfaction (Kimes, 2002).

Additionally, sexual satisfaction is certainly not static or equally distributed *between* all women, as different demographic groups report vastly different sexual satisfaction. Strong correlations between sexual satisfaction, sexual activity, and social identities have been found, as lower status women (e.g., women of color, less-educated women, working-class women) reported having more *frequent* but less satisfying sex, particularly compared to white, upper-class (typically higher status) women (Fahs and Swank, 2011). That is, women without as much social and political power still have sex, but they have to endure less satisfying sex on a much more regular basis than women with more power. This suggests, most specifically, that lower status women more often lack the *freedom from* unwanted sex or unsatisfying sex even while they have the apparent *freedom to* have frequent sexual activity. Compared to higher status women, lower status women do not have the same social permissions to deny others access to their bodies, and they do not feel as entitled to refuse sex when not satisfied.

TREATMENT FOR SEXUAL DYSFUNCTION

Medicalization has also served as a tool for ensuring women's lack of *freedom from* sex, as women who abstain from sex, refuse sex, or construct themselves as "asexual" or celibate have been labeled as fundamentally dysfunctional by the medical community. For example, to turn a social problem into something supposedly derived from women's inadequacies, a recent study characterized a staggering 43.1% of women as "sexually dysfunctional," even though far fewer women reported subjective distress about such sexual "problems" (Shifren, 2008). When the medical community decides that women have dysfunction if they do not conform to some medically defined prescription of the "normal," they do not account for women's own narratives about their sexual experiences. Rarely do studies account for partner abilities, contextual factors in women's lives, or women's personal narratives about their "dysfunction." As it stands now, women can receive a psychiatric diagnosis of sexual dysfunction (according to the DSM-IV) if they refuse penetration, fail to orgasm, have "inadequate" lubrication or swelling response, refuse to have sex with partners, and feel aversion toward sexuality in general. (These diagnoses are labeled Hypoactive Sexual Desire Disorder, Sexual Aversion Disorder, Female Sexual Arousal Disorder.) Such diagnoses normalize heterosexuality and penetrative intercourse as the pinnacle of "healthy sex" while setting clear and monolithic standards for sexual normality.

As a more precise example of the dangerous power of medicalization, consider the (especially egregious) recent treatments developed by the medical community to cure vaginal pain disorders like vaginismus. One recent treatment advises doctors to inject Botox into three sites of the vagina in order to allow women to "tolerate" penetrative intercourse (Ghazizadeh and Nikzad, 2004). Another common treatment advises doctors to insert vaginal dilators into women's vaginas in order to stretch out their vaginal opening to allow for penile penetration (Crowley et al., 2009; Grazziotin, 2008; Raina et al., 2007).

These treatments ensure that women's vaginas can effectively ingest a penis, thereby constructing "normal" vaginas and "normal" sex as penile-vaginal intercourse. Normal sex becomes that which meets men's sexual needs even if it induces pain in women. Even if women can orgasm through manual or oral stimulation, even if women report sexual violence and abuse histories, and even with reliable statistics that consistently point to penile-vaginal intercourse as an unreliable facilitator of women's orgasms (Hite, 1976), these treatments are considered standard and routine for sexual pain disorders. Women do not have the *freedom from* penile-vaginal intercourse, even if it causes them physical or psychological discomfort and pain. If sociocultural scripts mandate that a "normal" woman has "normal" sex, the medical community will ensure that she complies.

RAPE AND SEXUAL COERCION

In an age so often characterized as "empowering" for women—and with so much rhetoric devoted to women's supposed choices about their bodies and sexualities—the occurrence of rape and sexual coercion of women serve as a sobering reminder of patriarchy's widespread influence. In addition to the staggering rates of reported sexual violence both within the U.S. (Elwood et al., 2011) and globally (Koss et al., 1994), women also deal (sometimes on a daily basis) with their lack of *freedom from* sexual harassment, street harassment, pornography, objectification, and coercion. Women typically minimize coercive encounters they have had, often to avoid the stigma and label of "rape victim" (Bondurant, 2001; Kahn et al., 2003). They also protect boyfriends, husbands, family members, and dating partners as "not rapists" by denying or minimizing the coercion that these men enact (Fahs, 2011a), often while endorsing "rape myth" beliefs that women deserve rape or brought it on themselves (Haywood & Swank, 2008). While women may have the *freedom to* experiment with their sexuality in new ways, such experimentation often goes hand-in-hand with coercion, abuses of power, pressure, and lopsided power dynamics.

Women's lack of *freedom from* coercion and harassment also extends into their relationship with space itself. Women construct "outside" as unsafe and "inside" as safe, refuse to walk alone at night (Valentine, 1989), and imagine their (benevolent) boyfriends, husbands, brothers, male acquaintances, and male friends as "protectors," even when these men most often perpetrate sexual violence (Fahs, 2011a). Women's relative lack of freedom to occupy public space, travel alone, protect themselves from violence, or ensure non-coercive sexual exchanges represents a major component of women's sexual consciousness, even if they have not experienced violent rape or clear-cut coercion. The literature on "sexual extortion"—where women engage in sexual acts to avoid domestic violence—also speaks to this continuum between rape and not rape (DeMaris, 1997). Their lack of *freedom from* violence is, for many women, an everyday occurrence that harms their well-being and blocks access to institutions that men use as sources of their power (e.g., better paying jobs, education, public space).

Body Hair as 'Personal Choice'

As a reminder of the invisibility of power, women also imagine that they have far more personal freedom when "choosing" how to groom and present their bodies to the outside world and to friends, partners, and families. As a prime example, women, particularly younger women, generally endorse the idea that removing body hair (particularly underarm, leg, and pubic hair) is a "personal choice" that they simply "choose" to do. That said, when women refuse to remove their body hair, they often face intense negative consequences: homophobia, harassment, objectification, partner disapproval, family disapproval, coworker disapproval, threats of job loss, anger and stares from strangers, and internal feelings of discomfort and disgust (Fahs, 2011b).

Women who do not remove body hair are labeled by others as "dirty" or "gross" (Toerien and Wilkinson, 2004), and are seen as less sexually attractive, intelligent, happy, and positive compared to hairless women (Basow and Braman, 1998). Women who do not shave their body hair were also judged as less friendly, moral, or relaxed, and as *more* aggressive, unsociable, and dominant compared to women who removed their body hair (Basow and Willis, 2001). While older age, feminist identity, and lesbian identity predicted less negative attitudes toward body hair (Toerien et al., 2005), few women receive full protection from the cultural negativity surrounding women's body hair.

These findings reveal that women overwhelmingly lack the *freedom from* regulating their bodies through depilation. With increasingly vicious rhetoric directed toward their "natural" body hair as inherently dirty, disgusting, and unclean, women spend great energy and time fighting against these stereotypes in an effort to have acceptable bodies, particularly for already stigmatized groups like women of color and working-class women (Fahs, 2011b; Fahs and Delgado, 2011). With trends indicating that increasing numbers of women in the U.S. remove pubic hair, the hairlessness norms seem only to expand, particularly in the last decade (Herbenick et al., 2010). Women may have the *freedom to* groom their pubic hair into triangles, landing strips, or Vajazzled ornaments (thanks to the growth of corporate techniques of hair maintenance, see Bryce, 2012), but they cannot go *au natural* or not shave their bodies without serious social punishments (Toerien et al., 2005).

Same-sex Eroticism

For several decades, the queer movement has fought to expand legal and social rights for same-sex couples, increase representation of same-sex eroticism, and garner cultural acceptance of LGBT identities as normative and non-"deviant" (Clendinen and Nagourney, 2001; Swank, 2011). In particular, women have more *freedoms to* express their sexual interests in other women and to explore same-sex eroticism more openly, with blatant hostile homophobia diminishing some in the last decades (Loftus, 2001). That said, these supposed "freedoms" have also been appropriated by the patriarchal lens and converted into actions that women undertake to gain acceptance and approval in certain settings: bars, fraternity parties, clubs, bars, and so on (Yost and McCarthy, 2012). Women "making out" and "hooking up" with other women in these settings constitutes an increasingly normative practice, as long as men *watch* women doing this behavior and as long as the women fit stereotypical standards of "sexiness" for male viewers. Following the trends of *Girls Gone Wild,* increasing numbers of women report *pressure* to kiss and have sex with other women in front of men, either by "hooking up" at bars, engaging in threesomes (male partner initiated, only involving multiple women and one man), or allowing men to watch women kiss in public (Fahs, 2009; Yost & McCarthy, 2012).

Such pressures exist regardless of women's sexual identity, as queer women report pressures to "hook up" in front of men just as heterosexual women say their boyfriends and male friends ask them to "pretend" to enjoy same-sex eroticism for their viewing benefit (Fahs, 2009). Women increasingly describe these pressures toward "bisexuality" as compulsory (Fahs, 2009), as 33% of college women had engaged in this behavior, while 69% of college students had observed this behavior (Yost and McCarthy, 2012). Thus, large segments of women lack the relative *freedom from* mandated same-sex eroticism that is performed *in front of* men and for the sake of men's pleasure. The rebellious, transformative qualities of same-sex eroticism have also been distorted to serve the interests of men (and patriarchy) by ensuring that men are physically and psychologically present during these encounters. No wonder, then, that such "performative bisexuality" (Fahs, 2009) has *not,* for the women engaging in these acts, consistently translated into shifts in political consciousness like increased identification with bisexuality, more

support for gay marriage laws, and more LGBT activism (Fahs, 2009; Fahs, 2011a).

SEXUAL FANTASY

As a final example—and likely the one most directly contrasting with sex positivity—women lack the *freedom from* a sexuality that corresponds with mainstream (pornographic?) fantasies. They also lack the freedom from internalized heterosexist beliefs that distorts their imagination about what constitutes exciting sex. Even when women enjoy pornography without internalizing pornographic fantasies *as real,* they still grapple with increasingly narrow definitions of "the sexual." When examining women's sexual fantasies, an incredible amount of internalized passivity, lack of agency, and desire for domination appears (Bivona and Critelli, 2009; Fahs, 2011a). In particular, women report fantasies of men dominating them as their most common sexual fantasies, even when their best lived sexual experiences do not include such content. When women described their most pleasurable sexual encounters, these descriptions did not include dominance and power narratives, yet when women described their sexual fantasies, themes of power, coercion, dominance, and passivity appeared (Fahs, 2011a). In addition to fantasy, women described pressures from their partners to engage in (increasingly rough) anal sex (Stulhofer and Ajduković, 2011), threesomes (Fahs, 2009), forceful encounters (Koss et al., 1994), role playing, and dominance (Bivona and Critelli, 2009), indicating that many women negotiate these themes not only in their minds, but also in their partnered practices.

While women have certainly made advances in their *freedoms to* expand sexual expression and ideas about sexuality, they now face their relative lack of *freedom from* such dynamics both in their imaginations and in their body practices. Pornographic fantasies have entered mainstream consciousness in many ways: body and hair grooming (Fahs, 2011b), new procedures like anal bleaching, increasing desires for "designer vaginas" and labiaplasty surgeries (Braun and Tiefer, 2010), the much-read and discussed *Fifty Shades of Gray* (at the time of writing it held the number one spot on the *New York Times* bestseller list), and pressures for women to conform to men's desires for three-somes, painful anal sex (Stulhofer and Ajduković, 2011), and rougher sex in general. (Indeed, the only recent study about women's experiences with anal sex [Stulhofer and Ajduković, 2011] asks in the title, "Should we take [anal pain] seriously?") Sexual fantasy cannot be dismissed as mere frivolity, as rape fantasies have become increasingly common (Bivona & Critelli, 2009), and men's treatment of women often closely reflects the messages and themes they absorb from pornography (Jensen, 2007).

New Visions for Sex Positivity

The tensions between *freedom to* and *freedom from* in women's sexuality constitute a central dialectic in the study of, and experience of, women's sexuality (Vance, 1984). In order to move toward the ever-elusive "sexual liberation," women need to be able to deny access to their bodies, say no to sex as they choose, and engage in sexual expression free of oppressive homophobic, sexist, and racist intrusions. Women should have, when they choose, the *freedom from* unwanted, mediated versions of their sexuality (e.g., Facebook, Internet intrusions, "sexting"), hetero-sexist constructions of "normal sex," and sexist assumptions about what satisfies and pleases them. If women cannot have *freedom from* these things without social penalty, they therefore lack a key ingredient to their own empowerment.

Those who avoid sex, choose asexuality, embrace celibacy (either temporary or permanent), or otherwise feel disinclined toward sex (perhaps due to personal choice, histories of sexual violence, health issues, hormonal fluctuations, irritation or emotional distance with a partner, and so on) should be considered healthy and *normal* individuals who are making healthy and normal choices. Recent studies have begun to look at "sexual assertiveness," sexual autonomy, and the importance of women's right to refuse sex (Morokoff et al., 1997; Sanchez et al., 2005). The assumption that women must have consistency in their sexual expression, desire, and behavior does not fit with the way sexuality ebbs and flows and responds to circumstances in their lives. Sexual freedom means both the *freedom to* enjoy sexuality, and *freedom from* having to "enjoy" it, just as reproductive freedom means the *freedom to* have children when desired *and* the *freedom from* unwanted pregnancies.

As a new vision for sex positivity, I argue that we need three broadly defined goals, each of which contributes to a larger vision that prioritizes a complex, multi-faceted sexual freedom that fuses the political goals of both sex positives and radical feminists: first, *more* critical consciousness about any vision of sexual liberation. Definitive and universal claims about freedom and choice for all women must be met with caution or even downright suspicion. For example, while sex toys can represent a positive aspect of women's lives—they allow for more efficient masturbation for some, exploration for others, and fun and quirkiness for still others—these toys still exist within a capitalistic framework. While sex toys can be empowering, pleasurable, fun, and exciting, they also equate liberated sexuality with *purchasing power,* buying things, and (perhaps) distancing women from their bodies (not to mention that the labor politics around making such toys, where women's labor in developing countries is often exploited in the name of First World pleasure). These debates also overlap with notions of "sexual citizenship" and the ways capitalism shapes not only sexual rights but also desire itself (see Evans, 2002). Also, when women masturbate with sex toys, they learn *not* to touch their vaginas in the same way. When couples "spice things up" with accessories, they often avoid the harder conversations about their goals, desires, and relationship needs. Further, sex toy packaging and marketing fall into the all-too-common associations between acquiring objects and achieving personal happiness (not to mention that sex toy companies often use poor quality plastics and exploit their workers, another decidedly "unsexy" side to the industry). In short, the relentless insistence upon a critical consciousness regarding sexual liberation (and claims of what is "sexually liberating") is a *requirement* if we want to illuminate the complexities of women's sexual freedom.

Second, *more* attention should be paid to how sexual access functions in the lives of lower status people (particularly women). Those with lower socially-inscribed statuses—women, people of color, queer people, working-class and poor people, less educated people (etc.)—are often expected, in numerous areas in their lives, to provide *access* to higher status people. Their bodies are expected to provide certain kinds of labor that serve the interests of high status people (e.g., physical, sexual, emotional labor) (Barton, 2006). Thus, it is especially important that lower-status people not equate sexual liberation with sexual access. These groups should not equate sexual empowerment with providing sexual access to others; rather, their sexual empowerment might derive from the *freedom from* such access to their bodies and (eroticized) labor.

Third, *more* attention must be devoted to the insidious aspects of disempowerment. There is no single definition of "liberated sex." Rather, sexual empowerment is a constantly moving target that requires continual critique, revision, self-reflexiveness, and (re)assessment of our own practices, cultural norms, ideologies, and visions for the self. Even my own vision of better incorporating the *freedom from* into ideas of sexual empowerment carries with it many dangerous trappings that must be cautiously navigated (e.g., not creating new norms and hierarchies of "good" and "bad" sex; forgetting about the "politics of maybe"). Because our culture so often pathologizes "non-normative" sexual behavior, many individuals spend much time and energy defending their sexual choices, behaviors, and lifestyles against conservative, religious, politically regressive individuals and institutions. While this work is much needed and often politically effective, particularly in our

current political climate, these defenses *cannot* preclude a *critical assessment* of how our sexual choices still often reflect and perpetuate sexist, classist, racist, and homophobic ideals. We must release our attachment to certain forms of negative liberty that defend us against critical "intruders." In other words, when we insist upon radically examining, critiquing, and unpacking our own sexual lives—even at the cost of unsettling and dislodging the barricades that defend us against intrusions and judgments from the radical right—we move ever closer to a fully realized notion of sexual liberation, sexual empowerment, and sexual equality for all.

REFERENCES

Allen A (2008) Feminist perspectives on power. *Stanford Encyclopedia of Philosophy,* URL (accessed 10 April 2012): http://plato.stanford.edu/entries/feminist-power/

Atkinson T-G (1974) *Amazon Odyssey: The First Collection of Writings by the Political Pioneer of the Women's Movement.* New York: Links Books.

Barton BC (2006) *Stripped: Inside the Lives of Exotic Dancers.* New York: New York University Press.

Bercaw-Pratt JL (2012) The incidence, attitudes, and practices of the removal of pubic hair as a body modification. Journal of *Pediatric & Adolescent Gynecology* 25(1): 12–14.

Berlin I (1969) *Four Essays on Liberty.* New York: Oxford University Press.

Bevacqua M (2004) Feminist theory and the question of lesbian and gay marriage. *Feminism & Psychology* 14(1): 36–40.

Bivona J and Critelli J (2009) The nature of women's rape fantasies: An analysis of prevalence, frequency, and contents. *Journal of Sex Research* 46(1): 35–45.

Bobel C (2006) "Our revolution has style": Contemporary menstrual product activists "doing feminism" in the third wave. *Sex Roles* 54(5): 331–345.

Bondurant B (2001) University women's acknowledgment of rape: Individual, situational, and social factors. *Violence Against Women* 7(3): 294–314.

Branlandingam B (2011) Hot piece of hipster: Summer genderqueer hair. *The Queer Fat Femme Guide* to Life, URL (accessed 7 March 2012): http://queerfatfemme.com/2011/05/29/hot-piece-of-hipster-summer-genderqueer-hair/

Braun V and Tiefer L (2010) The "designer vagina" and the pathologisation of female genital diversity: Interventions for change. Radical Psychology 8(1), http://www.radicalpsychology.org/v018-1/brauntiefer.html

Brody S and Weiss P (2011) Simultaneous penile-vaginal intercourse orgasm is associated with satisfaction (sexual, life, partnership, and mental health). The Journal of Sexual Medicine 8(3): 734–741.

Bryce (2012) I got vajazzled (and had a camera crew). The Luxury Spot URL (accessed 2 April 2012): http://www.theluxuryspot.com/features/i-got-vajazzled-and-had-a-camera-crew/

Calogero RM and Thompson JK (2009) Potential implications of the objectification of women's bodies for women's sexual satisfaction. Body Image 6 (2): 145–148.

Calogero RM and Pina A (2011) Body guilt: Preliminary evidence for a further subjective experience of self-objectification. Psychology of Women Quarterly 35(3): 428–440.

Chryslers JC and Ghiz L (1993) Body images of older women. Women & Therapy 14(1–2): 67–75.

Clendinen D and Nagourney A (2001) Out for Good: The Struggle to Build a Gay Rights Movement in America. New York: Simon & Schuster.

Costa MR and Brody S (2011) Sexual satisfaction, relationship satisfaction, and health are associated with greater frequency of penile-vaginal intercourse. Archives of Sexual Behavior 41(1): 9–10.

CrimethInc Ex-Workers Collective (2012) Your politics are boring as fuck. CrimethInc, URL (accessed 25 March 2012): http://www.crimethinc.com/texts/selected/asfuck.php

Crowley T, Goldmeier D and Hiller J (2009) Diagnosing and managing vaginismus. BMJ 339: 2284.

Currah P, Juang RM and Minter S (2006) Transgender Rights. Minneapolis: University of Minnesota Press.

De Cleyre V (1914) Sex slavery. Selected Works of Voltairine de Cleyre. New York: Mother Earth Publishing Association, pp. 342–358.

De Lauretis T (1988) Sexual indifference and lesbian representation. Theatre Journal 40(2): 155–177.

DeMaris A (1997) Elevated sexual activity in violent marriages: Hypersexuality or sexual extortion? Journal of Sex Research 34: 361–373.

Densmore D (1973) Independence from the sexual revolution. In: Koedt A, Levine E and Rapone A (eds) Radical Feminism. New York: Quadrangle Books, pp. 107–118.

Diamond LM (2009) Sexual Fluidity: Understanding Women's Love and Desire. Cambridge: Harvard University Press.

Duggan L and Hunter ND (1995) Sex Wars: Sexual Dissent and Political Culture. New York: Routledge.

Dunbar R (1969) Sexual liberation: More of the same thing. No More Fun and Games 3: 49–56.

Dworkin A (1997) Intercourse. New York: Simon & Schuster.

Dworkin A (1991) Woman hating. New York: Plume.

Elwood LS, Smith DW, Resnick HS, Gudmundsdottir B, Amstadter A, Hanson RF, Saunders BE and Kilpatrick DG (2011) Predictors of rape: Findings from the National Survey of Adolescents. Journal of Traumatic Stress 24(2): 166–173.

Evans DT (2002) Sexual Citizenship: The Material Construction of Sexualities. New York: Routledge.

Fahs B (2011a) Performing Sex: The Making and Unmaking of Women's Erotic Lives. Albany, NY: SUNY Press.

Fahs B (2011b) Dreaded "Otherness": Heteronormative patrolling in women's body hair rebellions. Gender & Society 25(4): 451–472.

Fahs B (2009) Compulsory bisexuality? The challenges of modern sexual fluidity. Journal of Bisexuality 9(3): 431–149.

Fahs B and Delgado DA (2011) The specter of excess: Race, class, and gender in women's body hair narratives. In: Bobel C and Kwan S (eds) Embodied Resistance: Breaking the Rules, Challenging the Norms. Nashville: Vanderbilt University Press, pp. 13–25.

Fahs B and Swank E (2011) Social identities as predictors of women's sexual satisfaction and sexual activity. Archives of Sexual Behavior 40(5): 903–914.

Farvid P and Braun V (2006) "Most of us guys are raring to go anytime, anyplace, anywhere": Male and female sexuality in Cleo and Cosmo. Sex Roles 55(5): 295–310.

Frederickson BL and Roberts T-A (1997) Objectification theory: An explanation for women's lived experience and mental health risks. *Psychology of Women Quarterly* 21: 173–206.

Frye M (1997) Some reflections on separatism and power. In: Meyers DT (ed.) *Feminist Social Thought: A Reader.* New York: Routledge, pp. 406–414.

Garber MB (1995) *Vice Versa: Bisexuality and the Eroticism of Everyday Life.* New York: Simon & Schuster.

Gerhard J (2000) Revisiting "The myth of the vaginal orgasm": The female orgasm in American sexual thought and second wave feminism. *Feminist Studies* 26(2): 449–476.

Ghazizadeh S and Nikzad M (2004) Botulinum toxin in the treatment of refractory vaginismus. *Obstetrics & Gynecology* 104(5): 922–925.

Goldman E (1917) Marriage and love. In: Goldman E (ed.) *Anarchism and Other Essays,* 2nd ed. New York: Dover Publications, pp. 227–239.

Goldman E (1998) Jealousy: Causes and a possible cure. In: Shulman AK (ed.) *Red Emma speaks: An Emma Goldman reader.* Amherst, NY: Humanity Books, pp. 214–221.

Grazziotin A (2008) Dyspareunia and vaginismus: Review of the literature and treatment. *Current Sexual Health Reports* 5(1): 43–50.

Greenway J (1997) Twenty-first century sex. In: Purkis J and Bowen J (eds) *Twenty-first century anarchism: Unorthodox ideas for a new millennium.* London: Continuum Books, pp. 170–180.

Haaland B (1993) *Emma Goldman: Sexuality the Impurity of the State.* Montreal: Black Rose Books.

Haavio-Mannila E and Kontula O (1997) Correlates of increased sexual satisfaction. *Archives of Sexual Behavior* 26(4): 399–419.

Hakim C (2010) Erotic capital. *European Sociological Review* 26(5): 499–518.

Haywood H and Swank E (2008) Rape myths among Appalachian college students. *Violence and Victims* 23: 373–389.

Heckert J (2010) Love without borders? Intimacy, identity, and the state of compulsory monogamy. In: Barker M and Langdridge D (eds) *Understanding Non-Monogamies.* New York: Routledge, pp. 255–265.

Heckert J (2011) Fantasies of an anarchist sex educator. In: Heckert J and Cleminson R (eds) *Anarchism & Sexuality: Ethics, Relationships,*

and Power. London/New York: Routledge, pp. 154–180.

Heckert J and Cleminson R (2011) Ethics, relationships, and power: An introduction. In: Heckert J and Cleminson R (eds) *Anarchism & Sexuality: Ethics, Relationships, Power.* London: Routledge, pp. 1–22.

Herbenick D, Schick V, Reece M, Sanders S and Fortenberry JD (2010) Pubic hair removal among women in the United States: Prevalence, methods, and characteristics. *The Journal of Sexual Medicine* 7(10): 3322–3330.

Hite S (1976) *The Hite Report: A Nationwide Study of Female Sexuality.* New York: Macmillan.

Hughes B (2009) Wounded/monstrous/abject: A critique of the disabled body in the sociological imaginary. *Disability & Society* 24(4): 399–410.

Irvine JM (2002) *Talk About Sex: The Battles Over Sex Education in the United States.* Berkeley: University of California Press.

Jeffreys S (1990) *Anticlimax: A Feminist Perspective on the Sexual Revolution.* New York: New York University Press.

Jenness V (1993) *Making It Work: The Prostitute's Rights Movement in Perspective.* New York: Aldine de Gruyter.

Jensen R (2007) *Getting Off: Pornography and the End of Masculinity.* Cambridge: South End Press.

Johnston J and Taylor J (2008) Feminist consumerism and fat activists: A comparative study of grassroots activism and the Dove real beauty campaign. *Signs* 33(4): 941–966.

Kahn AS, Jackson J, Kully C, Badger K and Halvorsen J (2003) Calling it rape: Differences in experiences of women who do or do not label their sexual assault as rape. *Psychology of Women Quarterly* 27(3): 233–242.

Kimes LA (2002) "Was it good for you too?" An exploration of sexual satisfaction. PhD dissertation, University of Kansas.

Koedt A (1973) The myth of the vaginal orgasm. In: Koedt A, Levine E and Rapone A (eds) *Radical Feminism.* New York: Quadrangle Books, pp. 199–207.

Koss MP, Heise L and Russo NF (1994) The global health burden of rape. *Psychology of Women Quarterly* 18(4): 509–537.

Landrine H and Russo NF (2010) *Handbook of Diversity in Feminist Psychology.* New York: Springer.

Loftus J (2001) America's liberalization in attitudes toward homosexuals. *American Sociological Review* 66: 762–782.

Loe M (1999) Dildos in our toolbox: The production of sexuality at a pro-sex feminist sex toy store. *Berkeley Journal of Sociology* 43: 97–136.

Lorde A (2007) *Sister Outsider: Essays and Speeches.* Berkeley: Crossing Press.

Luce H (2010) Sexual assault of women. *American Family Physician* 81(4): 489–495.

Lyerly AD (2006) Shame, gender, birth. *Hypatia* 21: 101–118.

MacKinnon CA (1989) *Toward a Feminist Theory of State.* Cambridge: Harvard University Press.

MacKinnon CA and Dworkin A (1998) *In Harm's Way: The Pornography Civil Rights Hearings.* Cambridge: Harvard University Press.

Mandziuk RM (2010) "Ending women's greatest hygienic mistake": Modernity and the mortification of menstruation in Kotex advertising, 1921–1926. *Women's Studies Quarterly* 38(2): 42–62.

Marso LJ (2003) A feminist search for love: Emma Goldman on the politics of marriage, love, sexuality, and the feminine. *Feminist Theory* 4(3): 305–320.

Martin E (2001) *The Woman in the Body: A Cultural Analysis of Reproduction.* Boston: Beacon Press.

McCabe PC and Rubinson F (2008) Committing to social justice: The behavioral intention of school psychology and education trainees to advocate for lesbian, gay, bisexual, and transgendered youth. *School Psychology Review* 37(4): 469–486.

McClelland SI (2010) Intimate justice: A critical analysis of sexual satisfaction. *Social and Personality Psychology Compass* 4(9): 663–680.

McClelland SI (2011) Who is the "self" in self-reports of sexual satisfaction? Research and policy implications. *Sexuality Research and Social Policy* 8(4): 304–320.

McElroy W (1995) *XXX: A Woman's Right to Pornography.* New York: St. Martin's Press.

Meltzer AL and McNulty JK (2010) Body image and marital satisfaction: Evidence for the mediating role of sexual frequency and sexual satisfaction. *Journal of Family Psychology* 24(2): 156–64.

Molyneux M (2001) *Women's Movements in International Perspective: Latin America and Beyond.* New York: Palgrave Macmillan.

Moore MR (2012) Intersectionality and the study of black, sexual minority women. *Gender & Society* 26(1): 33–39.

Morokoff PJ, Quina K, Harlow LL, Whitmire L, Grimley DM, Gibson PR and Burkholder GJ (1997) Sexual Assertiveness Scale (SAS) for women: Development and validation. *Journal of Personality and Social Psychology* 73(4): 790–804.

National Center for Transgender Equality (2011) About trans equality. NCTE, URL (accessed 5 April 2012): http://transequality.org/About/about.html

Nicolson P and Burr J (2003) What is "normal" about women's (hetero)sexual desire and orgasm?: A report of an in-depth interview study. *Social Science & Medicine* 57(9): 1735–1745.

Orecchia AC (2008) Working with lesbian, gay, bisexual, transgender, and questioning youth: Role and function of the community counselor. *Graduate Journal of Counseling Psychology* 1(1): 66–77.

Passet JE (2003) *Sex Radicals and the Quest for Women's Equality.* Urbana, IL: University of Illinois Press.

Peterson ZD (2010) What is sexual empowerment? A multidimensional and process-oriented approach to adolescent girls' sexual empowerment. *Sex Roles* 62(5–6): 307–313.

Pinney EM, Gerrard M and Denney NW (1987) The Pinney Sexual Satisfaction inventory. *The Journal of Sex Research* 23(2): 233–251.

Queen C (1997a) Sex radical politics, sex-positive feminist thought, and whore stigma. In: Nagle J (ed.) *Whores and Other Feminists.* New York: Routledge, pp. 125–135.

Queen C (1997b) *Real, Live, Nude Girl: Chronicles of Sex-Positive Culture.* San Francisco: Cleis Press.

Raina R, Pahlajani G, Khan S, Gupta S, Agarwal A and Zippe CD (2007) Female sexual dysfunction: Classification, pathophysiology, and management. *Fertility & Sterility* 88(5): 1273–1284.

Reece M, Herbenick DM and Sherwood-Puzello C (2004) Sexual health promotion and adult retail stores. *Journal of Sex Research* 41(2): 173–180.

Rich A (1980) Compulsory heterosexuality and lesbian existence. *Signs* 5(4): 631–660.

Riddell L, Varto H and Hodgson ZG (2010) Smooth talking: The phenomenon of pubic hair removal in women. *Canadian Journal of Human Sexuality* 19(3): 121–130.

Roberts C, Kippax S, Waldby C and Crawford J (1995) Faking it: The story of "Ohh!." *Women's Studies International Forum* 18(5–6): 523–532.

Rubin G (1993) Thinking sex: Notes for a radical theory of the politics of sexuality. In: Barale MA, Abelove H and Halperin DM (eds) *The Lesbian and Gay Studies Reader.* New York: Routledge, pp. 3–44.

Salk RH and Engeln-Maddox R (2012) Fat talk among college women is both contagious and harmful. *Sex Roles* 66(9–10): 636–645.

Sanchez D, Crocker J and Boike KR (2005) Doing gender in the bedroom: investing in gender norms and the sexual experience. *Personality and Social Psychology Bulletin* 31(10): 1445–1455.

Sanchez D, Kiefer AK. and Ybarra O (2006) Sexual submissiveness in women: Costs for sexual autonomy and arousal. *Personality and Social Psychology Bulletin* 32(4): 512–524.

Shifren JL, Monz BU, Russo PA, Segreti A and Johannes CB (2008) Sexual problems and distress in United States women: Prevalence and correlates. *Obstetrics and Gynecology* 112(5): 970–978.

Showden C (2012) Theorising maybe: A feminist/queer theory convergence. *Feminist Theory* 13(1): 3–25.

Shrage L (2002) From reproductive rights to reproductive Barbie: Post-porn modernism and abortion. *Feminist Studies* 28(1): 61–93.

Spencer G, Maxwell C and Aggleton P (2008) What does "empowerment" mean in school-based sex and relationships education? *Sex Education* 8(3): 345–356.

Sprecher S, Barbee A and Schwartz P (1995) "Was it good for you, too?" Gender differences in first sexual intercourse experiences. *The Journal of Sex Research* 32(1): 3–15.

Stulhofer A and Ajduković D (2011) Should we take anodyspareunia seriously? A descriptive analysis of pain during receptive anal intercourse in young heterosexual women. *Journal of Sex & Marital Therapy* 37(5): 346–358.

Swank E and Fahs B (2011) Pathways to political activism among Americans who have same-sex sexual contact. *Sexuality Research and Social Policy* 8(2): 126–138.

Sycamore MB (2004) *That's Revolting: Queer Strategies for Resisting Assimilation.* Berkeley: Soft Skull Press.

Toerien M and Wilkinson S (2004) Exploring the depilation norm: A qualitative questionnaire study of women's body hair removal. *Qualitative Research in Psychology* 1(1): 69–92.

Toerien M, Wilkinson S and Choi PY (2005) Body hair removal: The "mundane" production of normative femininity. *Sex Roles* 52(5–6): 399–406.

Trompeter SE, Bettencourt R and Barrett-Connor E (2012) Sexual activity and satisfaction in healthy community-dwelling older women. *The American Journal of Medicine* 125(1): 37–43.

Valentine G (1989) The geography of women's fear. *Area (London 1969)* 21(4): 385–390.

Vance C (1984) *Pleasure and Danger: Exploring Female Sexuality.* New York: Routledge & Kegan Paul.

Wiederman MW (1997) Pretending orgasm during sexual intercourse: Correlates in a sample of young adult women. *Journal of Sex & Marital Therapy* 23(2): 131–139.

Yost MR and McCarthy L (2012) Girls gone wild? Heterosexual women's same-sex encounters at college parties. *Psychology of Women Quarterly* 36(1): 7–24.

Introduction to Reading 30

L. Ayu Saraswati offers a deep analysis of the meaning of skin-whitening practices among Indonesian women of Indian, Malay, Chinese, European, and Arab backgrounds. For this study, she conducted interviews with 46 women living in two cities, Jakarta and Balikpapan, and from the interviews she developed the proposition that Indonesian women are motivated to use skin whiteners, not by a strong desire to look attractive, but by the desire to avoid shame and embarrassment. Thus, Saraswati argues, the practice of skin whitening is an embodied expression of the "gendered management of affect." Central to this reading is *malu,* an Indonesian term that is similar to shame. However *malu* also signals vulnerability, worry, shyness, and propriety. Importantly, *malu* is a moral and gendered emotion. Saraswati's research demonstrates how women manage feelings of *malu,* or shame, about their skin color by using skin whiteners, and, in so doing, gender, racial, and global hierarchies are reinforced.

1. How do race and nation play a major role in shaping the meaning of skin color among Indonesian women?

2. How does putting on skin-whitening cream result in a "never-ending cycle of *malu*"? Do you think that the use of cosmetics by women in the United States might have a similar outcome?

3. Discuss the links among "being good," "feeling good," "looking good," and "having good" skin color as presented in this reading.

"Malu": Coloring Shame and Shaming the Color of Beauty in Transnational Indonesia

L. Ayu Saraswati

In Indonesia, the fourth most populous nation in the world, skin-whitening products are ranked highest among all revenue generating products in the cosmetics industry.[1] Unilever Indonesia spent IDR 97 billion ($10.4 million) in 2003 advertising just one of its skin-whitening creams.[2] This sum is larger than the estimated IDR 72 billion spent on advertising anti-dandruff shampoo—the top product in the hair care industry.[3] Indonesia is not anomalous in this regard: Transnational corporations such as Unilever, L'Oreal, and Shiseido have aggressively marketed their skin-whitening creams throughout Asia, Africa, Europe, and the United States.[4] Skin-whitening products are available in Indonesia, the Philippines,[5] Vietnam, Singapore, Malaysia, Japan, China, Korea, Hong Kong, Taiwan, India, Saudi Arabia, Brazil, Peru, Bolivia, Venezuela, Mexico, Malawi, Ivory Coast, the Gambia, Tanzania, Senegal, Mali, Togo, Ghana, Canada, and the United States. Even in countries where they have been banned due to medical or political reasons—South Africa, Zimbabwe, Nigeria, and Kenya, for example—skin-whitening products continue to be circulated underground.[6]

Many skin-whitening products have been deemed medically dangerous[7] because they contain illegal ingredients such as mercury or hydroquinone beyond the allowable 2 percent limit.[8] Mercury can cause black spots, skin irritation, and in high dosages can cause brain and kidney damage, fetal problems, lung failure, and cancer;

From Saraswati, L. Ayu. (2012). "Malu": Coloring shame and shaming the color of beauty in transnational Indonesia. *Feminist Studies, 38*(1), 113–140.

hydroquinone is known to cause skin irritation, nephropathy (kidney disease), leukemia, hepato-cellular adenoma (liver cell adenoma), and ochronosis (adverse pigmentation). And yet, despite warnings that the chemicals in these products may cause harm, women—the target market and primary consumers of these products—continue to use them.

Why are these products so popular even when they are known to be harmful? I am not the first to pose this question. Existing studies on the popularity of skin-lightening creams tend to focus on the political and racial meanings of these products within the context of colonialism and/or transnationalism. . . .

Other studies focus on media representations of skin-lightening creams and, less frequently, reference biological or psychological perspectives. Nancy Etcoff suggests that a preference for lighter-skinned women may reveal the working of a "fecundity detector" whereby possible mates detect women's fecundity by looking at their skin color believing that young ovulating women have lighter skin.[9] She is not oblivious, of course, to the fact that women's skin-whitening practices are also related to racism.[10]

I propose to offer a different approach. Although I shall also situate whitening practices within a transnational context and query their political and racial meanings, I have turned to the users themselves to ask why they use whitening creams and how they understand their meanings. What would we learn if we relied on women's representation of *themselves* as they make sense of skin-whitening practices? In 2015 I pursued this question through in-depth interviews of forty-six Indonesian women; they ranged across many occupations, and their median age was twenty-nine years.[11] This article draws on my analysis of these interviews. Indonesia is a particularly interesting site to carry out such an exploration, with its highly variegated demography: the country claims over three hundred ethnic groups. The two cities where I conducted my interviews, Jakarta and Balikpapan, are the most transnational in their populations: My interviewees included women with Indian, Malay,

Chinese, European, and Arab backgrounds.[12] Although the focus of this article is on women living in Indonesia, this article also attends to the ways in which women's experiences of living and traveling abroad have helped shape how they felt (and managed their feelings) about their skin color. Fifteen out of the forty-six women had lived or traveled abroad, and three of them had lived in North America.[13] All of the women interviewed came from lower, middle, and upper-middle classes—the demographic groups that are most targeted in the marketing of whitening creams.

The interviews led me to a fascinating proposition: that it was the urge to avoid shame and embarrassment rather than an active desire to be attractive that shaped women's decisions to practice (or not practice) skin-whitening routines. I argue that women's practice of skin whitening is a manifestation of "gendered management of affect"—"affect" here drawing from Theresa Brennan's definition of the term as a "physiological shift accompanying a judgment."[14] This gendered management of affect is also important in the maintenance of gender, racial, and global hierarchies. I came to this proposition after noting that the women in my study typically articulated their responses through various "affective vocabularies."[15] One example of affective vocabulary that was often mentioned during the interviews is *malu*. Malu is an Indonesian term that registers not only as a mostly negative affect equivalent to "shame" but also as a positive affect.[16] For the anthropologist Clifford Geertz, malu, or its Balinese equivalent *lek,* can be understood as "a diffuse, usually mild, though in certain situations virtually paralyzing, nervousness before the prospect (and the fact) of social interaction, a chronic, mostly low grade worry that one will not be able to bring it off with the required finesse."[17] In this sense, malu signals one's "vulnerability to interaction."[18] Similarly, social anthropologist Johan Lindquist, drawing from the works of linguist Cliff Goddard and anthropologist Michael Peletz, points out that malu can be translated as "shame, embarrassment, shyness, or restraint and propriety"[19] and is culturally understood as a "moral affect" that is considered "necessary to constrain the individuated self from dangerous and asocial act of impulse, lust, and violence."[20] Lindquist further argues, "it is the experience of malu, or of being identified as someone who should be malu, which becomes an organizing principle for social action and the management of appearances."[21] Hence, malu is an important affective term that works beyond the level of the individual and, as Lindquist points out, has the capacity to structure social encounters and feelings and to link the individual to his or her larger transnational social structures. As such, malu can be regarded both as a negative and a productive affect, a "constraint" or a "stimulus,"[22] rather than having only negative connotations as is often the case in the Western world.[23]

Moreover, malu, as I will tease out throughout this article, is a gendered affect. Men, as Elizabeth F. Collins and Ernaldi Bahar argue, tend to "react aggressively" when managing their feelings of malu.[24] The religious-based violence toward non-heterosexuals that occurred in the late 1990s and early 2000s in Indonesia, for example, can be understood as the behavior of religious men exercising their feelings of malu, according to Tom Boellstorff.[25] Women, however, tend to be "withdrawn or avoidant" when experiencing feelings of malu.[26] This article demonstrates how women tend to manage their feelings of malu about their skin color by becoming withdrawn and avoiding uninvited attention, as well as by performing skin-whitening practices.

In writing about malu or "feelings," there were times when the rich literature of malu proved insufficient to address some of the difficulties I encountered. In such instances, I turned to feminist literature on affect and particularly on shame. For example, many of the women interviewed narrated stories that highlighted specific experiences of being discriminated against because of their skin color, but when I followed up by asking how they felt about being ignored for not having lighter skin or not being considered "beautiful," many simply said "fine" (biasa

saja) in a tone that suggested it did not matter to them. Comments such as "maybe they were just lucky" or "but we were indeed physically different from them, so [we] just accepted our fate" were also common. Feminist geographer Liz Bondi, who has written that some feelings are "unexpressed and inexpressible,"[27] was helpful here. Feminist philosopher Teresa Brennan provides another, but equally helpful explanation for this phenomenon:

> "Feeling" refers to the sensations that register these stimuli and thence to the senses, but feelings includes something more than sensory information insofar as they suppose a unified interpretation of that information. . . . I define feelings as sensations that have found the right match in words.[28]

Applying Brennan's insight to make sense of the interviewees' comments leads me to suggest that although these women might have felt "sensations," they might not have found the "right match in words" to name them. Particularly because many women are taught to sugarcoat their feelings,[29] they might be at a loss for adequate words to articulate negative emotions.

Additionally, I identify a problem related to the mutability, fluidity, and flexibility of feelings. For example, the same affective vocabulary may mean different things in different times and cultures;[30] indeed, the feelings themselves may change.[31] This means that during the interviews the women might no longer harbor any particular feelings about those moments in the past; they had learned to "accept their fate" and felt "fine." Not being attentive to the fluidity and flexibility of feelings, scholars may fall into the trap of writing about feelings as "fetishized" objects of inquiry detached from their historical context.[32] This article therefore situates malu within a specific context. Hence, rather than simply drawing from theories of affect that are produced and circulated in the United States to analyze women's representation of skin whitening in Indonesia, this article employs malu, an Indonesian term, and places it in conversation with feminist theories of affect and cultural studies of emotions produced elsewhere to make an intervention in the fields of feminist theories of affect and Indonesian theories of malu.

Also, with the disparities between "affective vocabularies" and actual emotions, it became necessary to look for the underlying emotions implicit in the interviewees' statements by paying attention to their body language and tone of voice and by employing the malu perspective to decode the interviews. To understand what I mean by employing a malu perspective, an analogy with a "gender" perspective is helpful. Stories that women tell might not be in and of themselves "gendered," let alone "feminist," stories; yet by employing a gender perspective to decode their stories, it is possible to make gender visible in their stories. Similarly, the interviewees might not necessarily have told stories of malu as such; however, by employing malu as a theoretical-emotional lens to decode the stories, the ways in which malu has been deployed in these women's lives become visible.

In what follows, I provide evidence that the "gendered management of affect" plays a significant role in perpetuating gender, racial, and global hierarchies and in shaping women's decision to practice skin-whitening routines. . . .

MALU IN A TRANSNATIONAL CONTEXT

What causes a person to feel malu to begin with? Writing from a Western perspective, psychologist Rom Harré argues that embarrassment ("the major affective instrument of conformity"[33]) happens when "[o]ne has become the focus of (an apparently excessive) attention from others whose opinion one values with respect to what one has said or done, or how one appears" and that that person "has become aware that others have taken the sayings, doings or appearances in question to be abnormal."[34] Focusing on the specific context of Southeast Asia, Michelle Rosaldo argues that shame involves "the sanction of tradition, the acknowledgment of authority, the fear of mockery . . . the anxiety associated with inadequate or morally unacceptable

performance" and "embracing notions of timidity, embarrassment, awe, obedience, and respect."[35] Particularly relevant to the women interviewed in this study is the fear of mockery as a driving force for them to lighten their skin.

This is best explained by using an example from the interviews: Alya, a middle-class Javanese woman who was born in 1973 in Jakarta and was working in Balikpapan at the time of the interview, shared her childhood experiences of being called *dakko-chan* (from a Japanese term for dark-skinned African dolls). This clearly caused her to feel malu.

> My relatives would twist my name so it had the word "Negro" in it. At school, I was called *dakko-chan* [laughing]. So I was happy when there was someone else in the classroom who was darker than me. That means I wouldn't be the target of their jokes.

There are various layers at work here. First, when she laughed, she turned her head away from me as if wanting to hide. This turning away action is body language that suggests that a person is feeling malu. Even if the assumption that she feels malu can be applied only at the time of the interview, and not necessarily to the past, it is telling that she expressed how happy she was (exposing the implicit feeling of unhappiness at being subjected to the comments) whenever there were darker-skinned people in the classroom because they drew unwanted attention away from her. She recognized that it was her dark skin color that invited the attention. Moreover, these seemingly harmless jokes further expose the racial and color hierarchy in transnational Indonesia within which "Negro" and Japanese *dakko-chan* dolls were represented as "abnormal," and therefore a cause for malu. Interestingly, these racialized concepts that originated in other national locations were the ones producing these Indonesian women's feelings of malu about themselves and their skin color.

The history of racial formation in Indonesia is deeply transnational. Prior to European colonialism, as early as the late ninth century, Aryan

Indian domination of high culture and the ruling class had already imprinted its light-skinned beauty standard upon Java, as is evidenced in the oldest surviving Indonesian literatures.[36] In the nineteenth and through the early twentieth century when Dutch colonialism peaked in colonial Indonesia, preference for light skin color was strengthened through specific gendered racial projects. A comment made in 1925 suggested that if men could afford it, they preferred to keep their wives at home because they "like[d] pretty hands and a pretty complexion."[37] At schools, students and teachers highly valued white and fair-skinned European students.[38] When Japan took over as the new colonial power in Indonesia (1942–1945), they propagated a new Asian beauty ideal; although "Asian" was constructed as the preferred race, white remained the preferred color, while dark skin was configured as an abject form of femininity. In postcolonial Indonesia, particularly since the late 1960s, US popular culture has become one of the strongest influences against which an Indonesian white beauty ideal is articulated. This transnational history of racial formation provides a rich context for understanding how women feel and manage malu as it relates to constructions of gender, skin color, and race in transnational Indonesia.

Based on my interviews, dark-skinned people in today's Indonesia are perceived as "scary," "criminal,"[39] "smelly," "dirty," and "weird-looking." When asked about their perceptions of dark-skinned Indonesians and Africans in Indonesia, almost all of the women interviewed articulated how dark-skinned people are deemed undesirable. . . .

Although dark-skinned people of whatever nationality are often considered undesirable, the opposite is not necessarily the case with light skin color. Not all white skin color is considered desirable in the same way. In the Indonesian context, desiring white skin does not translate to desiring the skin color of those of European descent. This becomes clear in how the interviewed women answered the question, "what is your ideal skin color?" They would often say that they disliked the skin color of *bule* (a slang term used to refer to white foreigners), as well as Chinese white skin color, and that they preferred Indonesian or Japanese white skin color:

> Ami (age 34): "I like Japanese [women's] skin color . . . Japanese [skin] is not pale. Their look is more elegant than the Chinese. I just don't like Chinese white skin."

> Dian (age 29): "I don't like white like bule. . . . Japanese women are so beautiful and so white, they are yellowish. I like Sundanese [western Javanese] white; [it is] transparent."

. . . What is most striking is that in specifying a particular skin color, the women use race, nation, and ethnicity to signify the skin color they prefer. The *quality* of white skin is signified by nationality and race. The whiteness of a particular skin color often becomes undesirable because of the race or nation that signifies it. This is most evident in the case of the Chinese. The long history of discrimination against Chinese people in Indonesia seems to resurface when these women discuss the ideal skin color: Chinese skin color is not preferred. . . . I argue that because it is race and nation that give meaning to skin color, this construction disrupts the otherwise neat racial hierarchy of white at the top and black at the bottom. This allows us to understand that in the Indonesian context, lighter skin color is *not* always better because skin color, rather than being a signifier of race, is signified by both race and nation. Lighter could only be better insofar as the race and nation that signify it is the preferred race and nation. Although there is little discernible difference between Japanese and Chinese skin color, a person may prefer Japanese white skin above Chinese white skin, for example, because of perceptions about race and nation. Interestingly, the presence of people from other countries such as Japan, China, or the United States in Indonesia has helped these women articulate the specific skin color that they prefer. Their construction of an ideal skin color is inevitably linked to national identities; it is typically constructed against people from other nations.

Although it is obvious that they do not desire the skin color of those of European descent, these women are aware that such people are considered superior and receive preferential treatment in Indonesia. This perception of whites as superior may be traced back to the Dutch colonial period.

. . . The interviewees recognized white foreigners as receiving better treatment than Indonesians allowed for the possibility of reading the women's whitening practices as reflecting their desire to be treated well and not necessarily their desire for whiteness as such.

In the interviews, all of the women shared some story to indicate how white foreigners in Indonesia are considered "better" and receive better treatment. Here are just a couple of examples. Both comments came from women married to "non-Indonesian" white-skinned men:

Andarini (age 33): Why do they always think that [my daughters] are beautiful because of their father? Don't they think the mother is also beautiful? [laughing]. They want to know why my children are so beautiful; and they never say that their mother is beautiful. They always think that there is something else. When they see my husband, they say, "No wonder."

Widhi (age 41): They always ask me where the father came from. . . . Sometimes people even thought I was their nanny [laughing].

These expressions expose the underlying assumptions that Indonesian women were considered less valuable compared to their white-skinned husbands whose "good genes" were perceived to have made their children beautiful.

As Benedict Anderson has noted, one of the residues of colonial racism is that white Americans and Europeans receive preferential treatment in Indonesia.

Indonesia has a long history of transnational circulation of people coming from India, China, Arab countries, the United States, and Europe that continues to the present day. Based on 2004 data, foreign (and not necessarily white) workers in Indonesia number about 20,000 (6,000 top

executives, 11,600 professionals, 1,200 supervisors, 500 technicians, and the rest were "other").[40] More than half of these workers live in Jakarta; only 400 workers live in East Kalimantan (mostly in Balikpapan). Foreign workers are given many privileges in order to encourage them to feel at home and spend their dollars in Indonesia. Examples from the interviews include being seated at different lunch tables (marked as "staff only") with more menu choices compared to Indonesians, getting their requests met faster compared to Indonesian employees, or being given more expensive airline tickets so that they could fly on time when a flight was canceled while Indonesians only got their money back. Here is an example from Ira (age 40):

When I was staying in B. hotel [in Indonesia] and my relatives came, they were not allowed to swim. They [the staff] came right away and said that it was for members only. But when my bule friend came with her kid [and they were] swimming there, no one asked anything. They weren't members nor staying in the hotel. But they let them (swim). . . . But when my relatives came with their kids, they said "members only." I even asked, "Can I pay you, can we pay you?" "Oh no, it's members only" [they said]. So it seemed that we were dirty, while bule were not.

This example reflects the notion of Indonesia as a good host welcoming white foreigners even over and above its own citizens, to the point of refusing Indonesians and thus making them feel "dirty" and less worthy.

Interestingly, in cases where the interviewed women had moved to another country and had fewer encounters with other Indonesian women who, by way of embarrassing comments, would make them feel bad about their skin color, they felt less pressured to conform to the light-skinned norm. Ira, Andarini, and Amanda, all of whom currently reside in North America, admitted that they are less concerned about whitening practices when they are in the United States. Alya, Lily, Nia, and Lidya, who have lived abroad, in France, England, and the Netherlands, also claimed that they began to value their "tanned" skin once they left Indonesia. The examples in this section suggest that the transnational emulation of people plays a role in producing certain feelings about specific skin colors and helps maintain hierarchies of gender, race, and color in a transnational context.

COLORING MALU

This article argues that malu is deployed as an affective instrument of conformity, particularly in regard to compelling a person to conform to color, race, national, and gender norms. Interestingly, the majority of women in Indonesia do not have light skin, at least not like the light skin that is on view in whitening advertisements. A light-skin norm does not really exist if by "norm" one supposes that everyone's skin is light and one person's dark skin therefore stands out. Rather, the light-skin norm works by way of comparison: Women are compared to others or to themselves in the past. This is why the presence of others who have darker skin, such as in Alva's case, would change one's position within the skin-color hierarchy.

In the interviews, I often heard the women say that they began using skin-whitening creams after comments were addressed to them about their dark skin color. For example, Nina, who was born in 1977 in Kediri and who worked at a fitness center in Balikpapan at the time of the interview, admitted that in a previous job, her office mates often said to her:

> "Goodness (Aduh), you have the darkest skin." Although I would tell them "I don't care," inside I felt like saying how dare you say that. But then I always thought about how I could look not too dark. . . . So every time there was going to be a big meeting, I'd make sure that I whitened my skin, at least my hand, legs, and face, so that I would feel ahem ahem [making a sound of clearing her throat while smiling].

Here, the "big meeting" became a public space where an "audience" important in the production of shame[41] gathered. It is also a point of social contact that exposes her "vulnerability to interaction,"[42] or to feel malu. In this case, her use of skin-whitening cream could be read as her desire to not stand out, or to conform, because to stand out would invite (undesirable) attention from other office mates. The attention was deemed undesirable because it would embarrass rather than flatter her. Interestingly, her application of skin-whitening cream was intended to avert rather than as commonly narrated in whitening ads, to invite the gaze of others. The assumption is that to be noticed for having dark skin is to be exposed to the possibility of embarrassing comments. This desire not to attract the gaze of others echoes Frantz Fanon's famous depiction of the colonial subject's plea: "I strive for anonymity, for invisibility. Look, I will accept the lot, as long as no one notices me!"[43]

Nina chose to use lightening cream so that others would think well of her. Another interviewee, Ajeng (age 31), admitted that she used whitening cream so that other people would not comment that her skin was jorok (dirty). Women pay attention to these comments because they are "signs" that tell them whether or not they are accepted by their group. . . .

More importantly, because light skin color is not a "norm" in Indonesia but made into an imaginary ideal, comments and practices of whitening routines are crucial in perpetuating a light-skinned norm. . . .

The very act of dropping remarks about each other's skin color normalizes light skin as desirable; it is an example of the constant "surveillance"[44] that women carried out. Women get rewarded by receiving pleasing comments such as "you look beautiful: your skin looks lighter" and get punished by receiving embarrassing comments such as "your skin looks darker; you should . . ." (and one may fill in the blank with various tips that women offer each other).

Offering comments about others' skin color also suggests that malu in the Indonesian context is "collectively shared."[45] One's identity is linked to others' behaviors. Not surprisingly, mothers discipline their daughters, as women-friends discipline each other, as a form of caring about the other, or acting in "solidarity"[46] and preventing the other from feeling malu—by reminding each other, they could all avoid feeling malu.

Out of forty-six interviewees, only eight claimed that they had never tried any skin-whitening product. These eight women, however, admitted that they had seen other women use it and were pressed to try it but never did. However, when asked what they did everyday to care for their skin, almost all admitted that there were some things they did or avoided doing became they did not want their skin to get darker. These various acts, from putting on skin-whitening cream or staying out of the sun, to choosing particular colors and outfits that would make their skin appear lighter, further perpetuate light skin as the "imaginary" norm.

The interviews reveal that skin color mattered for these women because it is one of the sources of their self-confidence. The interviewees reacted with a loss of self-esteem to comments that exposed their "abnormality."[47] In this sense, there was a specifically gendered affect produced. Some of the more common expressions during the interviews were:

Ina (age 32): "When I had to meet with many people and my skin was dark, I didn't feel confident."

Vanti (age 34): "Generally women feel more confident when their skin is white."

Wati (age 30): "Because I was born dark-brown (*sawo matang*), I didn't have any self confidence. So I whiten my skin to be more confident."

These kinds of statements came up over and over again in the interviews, suggesting the extent to which women's self-confidence is closely linked to their skin color. An interviewee, Ira, an Indonesian American 40-year-old stay-at-home mom, born in West Sumatra and currently living in the United States, admitted that she knew from a very young age that she was ugly and undesirable because of her dark skin color. She said:

Sometimes people would tell me, "You don't have any sex appeal. Your skin is too dark." Even guys said things like, "Why are you so black?" So they didn't think that they would hurt you, you know. They just blurted it out in front of you, so I got used to it. Even my family, relatives, they would say, "Oh, how come you're so black, so ugly? You're a girl!" . . . I married a bule but not necessarily because they're not Indonesians [and therefore considered better]. But it's the other way around. Indonesian men didn't really think I was beautiful so I had no chance with Indonesian men.

It was these comments about how ugly she was because her skin was dark, so often made to her that she got "used to" hearing them, that made her accept her place in society. She admitted that, contrary to the common assumption that women married bule men because they were of higher status, she came to believe that she *had* to marry a bule man because Indonesian men perceived her as ugly. There are a couple of points here that are noteworthy. First, although she ended up being the one who moved to the United States, it was the presence of white foreign men in Indonesia that provided her with a solution to being perceived as undesirable by Indonesians: She learned that many of these white foreign men chose dark-skinned Indonesian women as their romantic partners. Second, and importantly, most Indonesian men do not actually always marry light-skinned Indonesian women—there are more women in Indonesia with medium tanned skin than light skin. Yet, it was her "feeling" that played a key role here: the comments about her dark skin made her feel malu and hence that she would never be able to attract an Indonesian man. Thus, her marriage to a European American is a result of her *feelings* about her skin color.

In teasing out the gendering of malu based on skin color that impacts a person's self-esteem, it is useful to take a step back and look at how women in general are positioned differently from men. Gendered socialization, as psychologists Tamara Ferguson and Heidi Eyre point out, provides an environment in which women are more likely than men to feel guilt and shame.[48] . . .

There is much evidence in the interviews that women were socialized differently from men. First, from their babyhood, girls, more so than boys, received comments on their skin color and how the "right" color would make them "pretty." Second, men, unlike women, were not asked (by other people in their lives or by popular culture) to put on different kinds of make-up[49] to cover up their otherwise "deficient" selves.[50] Whitening cream advertisements circulating in Indonesia mostly target women. The recent fad of whitening lotion for men is nonetheless marketed in gendered terms—L'Oreal, for example, launched a whitening cream for men called "White Active," highlighting the masculine aspect of men as active beings. Moreover, the interviewees consistently revealed that men are not subjected to the same light-skinned beauty standard as women. Men can have dark skin color because, as the interviewees suggested, dark skinned men are actually perceived as more masculine. Third, fathers, unlike mothers, were not asked to "shame" their daughters about their looks. An interviewee, Titi (age 47), bluntly noted, the most significant person who made her feel bad about herself was her mother. Mothers are responsible for teaching their children about malu and for the moral standard of the family. [51] Taking care of their looks may not be important for men because they are not threatened by other men's beauty—unlike women, who can feel threatened by the beauty of other women because their husbands might take an additional wife or leave their spouse for a more beautiful woman. Representations of second wives as more beautiful are popular in Indonesia and certainly promote such fear.

If light-skinned beauty is desired to keep one's husband, are lesbians then immune from this light-skinned beauty norm? Although I interviewed only two women who identified themselves as lesbians, too few to draw any conclusions, it is interesting that both these women indicated that light-skinned women are also considered more desirable than dark-skinned women in the lesbian communities that they belonged to.

COVERING MALU

The desire to conform, to avoid embarrassing comments, or to feel more self-confident are all adequate reasons for using whitening creams; however, I wish to add yet another perspective on malu to further the understanding of these practices. That is that the feeling of malu underpins the very act of covering one's skin with whitening cream. Various scholars have pointed out that the English word "shame" comes from "the Goth word *Scham,* which refers to covering the face,"[52] or from the 'Indo-Germanic root *kam/kem* meaning "to cover.'"[53] In addition to "cover," other scholars mention other expressions for feelings of malu, such as to "hide from that other" or to "turn away from the other's gaze."[54] . . .

When interviewees heard embarrassing comments about their dark skin color, they took note of how the skin is an important site upon which their feelings (good or bad) hinge. Managing the skin becomes necessary for the management of affect. The logic here is that if a woman *feels* "good" about her skin color, she will feel more confident in uncovering her skin. Accordingly, when she feels "bad" or ashamed about her skin color, she "resolve[s] the experience of shame"[55] by "hiding" or "covering" her skin to resolve the feeling of malu. In a few cases, women admitted that they would rather stay home than go out when their skin was dark because, in Yasmin's (age 27) words, "I was embarrassed (malu)." Her staying home can be understood as "hiding," or in Collins and Baliar's term, "withdrawing" herself, which is a gendered manifestation of malu. Moreover, malu is understood as an emotion "that describes the failures to live up to the ideals of the nation,"[56] or, in this case, the beauty ideal. Yasmin's feeling of malu can therefore be read as her recognizing how she failed to live up to the light-skinned beauty ideal. She resolved feeling malu by avoiding contacts with others.

In many other cases, however, malu is resolved in covering oneself. . . .

The need to cover oneself often manifests itself in the (psychological) covering of the skin with "whitening" cream that is perceived to have the capacity to free a person from feeling malu. I am extending here a notion that cultural studies scholar Elspeth Probyn articulates: "most experiences of shame make you want to disappear, to hide away and to cover yourself."[57] Yolanda's (age 38) succinct response when asked why she would use whitening cream indicated this: "so that when I look in the mirror I am not ashamed (malu) of myself." Here, the shame of the self is articulated by the very action of covering the skin with whitening cream. What I am hinting at is this: just as popular culture often represents women taking a shower after a rape scene to signify the desire to cleanse the body and psyche, women putting skin-lightening cream on their bodies can be read as a psychological covering of their malu about their skin color. As such, whitening practices can be read as manifesting women's managing of that experience of malu.

But why, when these women feel malu, is it the skin that is being covered?

. . . Skin is a site where the self is "exposed" to others. It is both the public and private nature—at times what literally "borders" the private self from others—of the skin that allows the skin to be one of the sites through which others can "read" us, and hence upon which our feelings can be (dis)articulated. I am invoking here both Harré's notion of the "body," taking it to mean specifically the skin as a "legible" surface from which the moral judgment can be read,[58] and Fanon's notion of "epidermalization of inferiority."[59] Because the skin is (constructed to be) telling of who the person is and is a site where one's "inferiority" or one's "shame" materializes, there is a need to "manage" it to reflect what the person wants it to tell others. I am intrigued here by how skin functions similarly to shame in that it "resides on the borderline between self and other."

Certainly, not all parts of the skin are seen by others. That is why, to recall an example mentioned earlier, Nina would whiten "at least" her face, legs, and hands prior to an important meeting. Another interviewee, Pingkan (age 25), explained that the face is most important for her because "usually people notice the face first, not other parts." . . .

Hence, it is the capacity of the skin to expose the self to others and the ways in which others may respond to that exposed skin that make the skin an important site to be "managed." But, taking it further while drawing from Harré and Fanon, I argue that the interviewees' emphasis on face and other visible parts of the skin indicate how the skin, because of its embodiment of private and public self, functions as a site upon which moral judgments are based. Because the skin is exposed for others to see, it grants others permission to judge people based on how "good" their skin (and therefore the person inhabiting that skin) is. . . .

As a marketing executive of a whitening-cream company, who agreed to talk to me on condition of anonymity, explained: "a woman proves to her family and society that she is responsible enough to take care of herself and therefore can be trusted to care for her family by using whitening cream." General expressions of negative feelings, such as "I don't feel good" (*nggak enak*), to illustrate how the interviewees felt when not using these whitening creams, were quite common. Although the line separating "*feeling* good" from a feeling of "*being* good" is not always sharply delineated, what is unmistakable is the equating of "being good," "feeling good," "looking good," and "having good" skin color.

Interestingly, putting on whitening cream turns out to put women in a never-ending cycle of malu: women usually end up feeling more malu for using whitening creams. This is evident from the interviews: when asked the first time around if they had ever tried whitening their skin, many women said they had not. However, as I asked differently phrased questions throughout the interviews, the same women began to tell me which whitening brand they used. Riana (age 24), a waitress in one of Balikpapan's cafes, did not want to be interviewed at first because she said she never used whitening cream and hence had nothing to say, After she changed her mind, she asked me, "I told you that I didn't use whitening cream when you asked me about it the other day. How did you know I used it?" I did not, in fact, know if she had used whitening cream; but I was certain that even if she hadn't, she would still have many things to share with me. Nonetheless, what so many of the interviewees suggested is that the whitening practice itself needs to be covered up, because it is considered in and of itself to be a shameful practice. Herlina, a recent high school graduate who worked at a mall in Balikpapan, commented on her friends:

> They use it but they won't admit it. . . . Maybe they were afraid that they would be mocked for turning white all of a sudden.

Her comment further exposed the feeling of malu that underpins the whitening practice. As Ferguson and Eyre point out, people tend to hide and manage their shame privately because these experiences are painful for them.[60]

However, as women cover their skin with whitening cream, possibly as a psychological "covering" of malu, it leaves larger institutional structures of racism/colorism and (hetero)sexism unarticulated. Instead of feeling the need to "fix" these structures, women displace their feelings onto their skin and therefore feel the need to fix their skin to manage their feelings.

CONCLUSION

This article uses the optic of malu to expose how people and objects that circulate transnationally to and from Indonesia have helped structure the feeling of malu among Indonesian women, as well as to show that the gendered management of affect is key to understanding women's decision to practice skin-whitening routines. This management of affect in turn maintains racial, color, gender, and global hierarchies.

NOTES

1. In Asia alone the market for skin-whitening products is estimated at thirteen billion euros. See http://www.cosmeticsdesign-europe.com/Products-Markets/In-Cosmetics-Asia-focuses-on-skin-lightening-trend (accessed August 25, 2009).

2. Jason W. Clay, *Exploring the Links between International Business and Poverty Reduction: A Case Study of Unilever in Indonesia* (London: Oxfam, 2005), 95.

3. From 2007 data, http://www.asiamedia.ucla.edu/article.asp?parentid=70144 (accessed August 25, 2009).

4. Evelyn Nakano Glenn, "Yearning for Lightness: Transnational Circuits in the Marketing and Consumption of Skin Lighteners," *Gender and Society* 22, no. 3 (June 2008): 281–302.

5. Joanne Rondilla, "Filipinos and the Color Complex: Ideal Asian Beauty," in *Shades of Difference: Why Skin Color Matters,* ed. Evelyn Nakano Glenn (Stanford, CA: Stanford University Press, 2009), 63.

6. Evelyn Nakano Glenn, "Consuming Lightness: Segmented Markets and Global Capital in the Skin-Whitening Trade," in *Shades of Difference,* 171.

7. Not all whitening products are dangerous. Whitening products come in different forms: creams, pills, body and facial soaps, "papaya" soaps, moisturizers, facial cleansers, deodorants, sunblocks, lamb placenta, prescribed drugs, and injections. Most of the interviewees used whitening soaps, lotions, and moisturizers, which they applied twice daily—Pond's and Citra were the two most popular brands among the interviewees. These creams, according to the dermatologist whom I interviewed, are usually not effcient because they contain 2% or less of hydroquinone—to be effcient, creams must contain at least 5% hydroquinone. To buy products with a higher level of hydroquinone, women have to go to dermatologists, beauty salons, or underground markets.

8. This limit is set by the BPOM (Badan Pengawas Obat dan Makanan)—the Indonesian equivalent to the US Food and Drug Administration.

9. Nancy Etcoff, *Survival of the Prettiest: The Science of Beauty* (New York: Doubleday, 1999), 105–106.

10. Ibid., 106.

11. I used snowball and random methods. I chose Jakarta because it is the most developed, most populated, and most transnational city in Indonesia. I also

included Balikpapan—a city on the island of Kalimantan—to avoid a "Java-centric" research. Balikpapan has the highest number of foreign workers in Kalimantan.

12. Although the women I interviewed lived in Jakarta and Balikpapan, they came from various cities on the island of Java (Bandung, Brebes, Cianjur, Gombong, Indra-mayu, Jakarta, Kediri, Pekalongan, Purwodadi, Semarang, Sidoarjo, Solo, Sukanagalih, Surabaya), Kalimantan (Balikpapan, Banjarmasin, Pulau Bulu, Tarakan), Sumatra (Medan, Padang, Palembang), Bali, and various other islands from the eastern part of Indonesia (Maluku, Sumba, Ternate); and one was born in Portugal. Their occupations were: engineers, domestic workers, homemakers, sales associates, herb beverage (*jamu*) sellers, owners of small convenience stores, researchers, live-in nannies, preschool teachers, bookstore attendants, gas-station attendants, waitresses, students, foreign language teachers, entrepreneurs, and event organizers. A few occupied managerial level positions at transnational corporations while others were unemployed high school graduates. One of the women was illiterate; several had not graduated from elementary school; many were high school graduates; some had completed four years of college education and even attained master's degrees. Most of the women were heterosexual and two women identified themselves as lesbian. Almost everyone was able-bodied, except for one woman who was partially blind. At the time of the interviews, the women were in their twenties (24 people), thirties (18 people), forties (1 person), fifties (2 people) and eighties (1 person).

13. I put these women's narratives in conversation with each other, rather than grouping them based on the city where they lived. I did so to demonstrate the similarities and linkages of these women's stories, to show that skin-whitening practices are found across various geographical locations among women in Indonesia, and to show how their feelings toward their skin color changed once they moved abroad. As such, I do not essentialize them—I noted and recognized their differences when appropriate.

14. Teresa Brennan, *The Transmission of Affect* (Ithaca, NY: Cornell University Press, 2004), 5. For other definitions of affect see Brian Massumi, *Parables for the Virtual: Movement, Affect, Sensation* (Durham, NC: Duke University Press, 2002); and Patricia Clough and Jean Hayley, eds., *The Affective Turn: Theorizing the Social* (Durham, NC: Duke University Press, 2007).

15. Thomas Hunter, "Indo as Other: Identity, Anxiety and Ambiguity in 'Salah Asoehan,'" *in Clearing a Space: Postcolonial Readings of Modern Indonesian Literature,* ed. Keith Foulcher and Tony Day (Leiden, Holland: KITLV, 2002), 125.

16. See Eve Sedgwick and Adam Frank, *Shame and Its Sisters: A Silvan Tomkins Reader* (Durham, NC: Duke University Press, 1995) on the transformative aspect of shame.

17. Clifford Geertz, *Interpretation of Cultures* (New York: Basic Books, 1973), 402.

18. Ward Keeler, "Shame and Stage Fright in Java," *Ethnos* 11, no. 3 (1983): 158.

19. Johan Lindquist, "Veils and Ecstasy: Negotiating Shame in the Indonesian Borderlands," *Ethnos* 69, no. 4 (2004): 487–508.

20. Michelle Rosaldo, "The Shame of Headhunters and the Autonomy of Self," *Ethnos* 2, no. 3 (1983): 136.

21. Lindquist, "Veils and Ecstasy," 488.

22. Rosaldo, "The Shame of Headhunters," 139.

23. Elizabeth Fuller Collins and Ernaldi Bahar, "To Know Shame: *Malu* and Its Uses in Malay Societies," *Crossroads: An Interdisciplinary Journal of Southeast Asian Studies* 14, no. 1 (2000): 39.

24. Collins and Bahar, "To Know Shame," 48.

25. Tom Boellstorff, A Coincidence of Desires: Anthropology, Queer Studies, Indonesia (Durham, NC: Duke University Press, 2007).

26. Collins and Bahar, "To Know Shame," 48.

27. Liz Bondi, "The Place of Emotions," in *Emotional Geographies,* ed. Liz Bondi, Joyce Davidson, and Mick Smith (Aldershot, UK: Ashgate, 2005), 237.

28. Brennan, *The Transmission of Affect,* 5.

29. Mario *Jacoby, Shame and the Origins of Self-Esteem: A Jungian Approach,* trans. Douglas Whitcher (New York: Routledge, 2001), 56.

30. Rom Harré and Grant Gillett, *The Discursive Minds* (Thousand Oaks, CA: Sage, 1994), 160.

31. Bondi, "The Place of Emotions," 237.

32. Sara Ahmed, *The Cultural Politics of Emotion* (Edinburgh: Edinburgh University Press, 2004), 32.

33. Ibid.

34. See L. Ayu Saraswati Prasetyaningsih, *Seeing Beauty, Sensing Race in Transnational Indonesia* (Honolulu: University of Hawai'i Press, Forthcoming).

35. See L. Ayu Saraswati Prasetyaningsih, *Seeing Beauty, Sensing Race in Transnational Indonesia* (Honolulu: University of Hawai'i Press, Forthcoming).

36. Elsbeth Locher-Scholten, *Women and the Colonial State: Essays on Gender and Modernity in the Netherlands Indies 1900–1942* (Amsterdam: Amsterdam University Press, 2000), 50.

37. Paul van der Veur, "Race and Color in Colonial Society: Biographical Sketches by a Eurasian Woman Concerning Pre-World War II Indonesia," *Indonesia* 8 (October 1969): 71.

38. Saraswati, *Seeing Beauty.*

39. In Indonesia, criminals are most often represented as lower class. See James Siegel, *A New Criminal Type in Jakarta: Counter-Revolution Today* (Durham, NC: Duke University Press, 1998).

40. Benedict Anderson, *Mythology and the Tolerance of the Javanese* (Ithaca, NY: Cornell University Southeast Asia Program Publications, 1988), 2.

41. Most of these workers came from Japan (3,500), South Korea (1,900), the United States, Australia, England, India, Canada, Malaysia, and China (about 1,500 each). (http://www.nakertrans .go.id/pusdatinnaker/tka/TKA_WNegara%202004. htm, http://www.nakertrans.go.id/pusdatinnaker/tka/ TKA_Jab2004.htm, and http://www.nakertrans.go.id/ pusdatinnaker/tka/TKA_Jab%202004.htm.) This number does not include families accompanying the workers, tourists, students, unemployed, and other undocumented workers and foreigners in Indonesia.

42. Gabriele Taylor, *Pride, Shame, and Guilt: Emotions of Self-Assessment* (Oxford: Clarendon, 1985), 53.

43. Keeler, "Shame and Stage Fright," 158.

44. Frantz Fanon, *Black Skin, White Masks,* trans. Charles Markmann (New York: Grove Press, 1967), 116.

45. Ibid., 84.

46. Collins and Bahar, "To Know Shame," 41.

47. To understand how malu is linked to "social harmony and group solidarity," see ibid., 42.

48. In the US context, Sandra Bartky, citing John Rawls, pointed out "shame is an emotion felt upon the loss of self-esteem." See Sandra Bartky, *Femininity and Domination* (New York: Routledge, 1990), 87.

49. Tamara Ferguson and Heidi Eyre, "Engendering Gender Differences in Shame and Guilt: Stereotypes, Socialization, and Situational Pressures," in *Gender and Emotion: Social Psychological Perspectives,* ed. Agneta H. Fischer (Cambridge: Cambridge University Press, 2000), 256.

50. In South Korea men have begun to use whitening cream.

51. Bartky, *Femininity and Domination,* 40.

52. Collins and Bahar, "To Know Shame," 49–50.

53. Probyn, *Blush,* 131.

54. Jacoby, *Shame and the Origins,* 1.

55. Sara Ahmed, "The Politics of Bad Feeling," *Australian Critical Race and Whiteness Studies Association Journal* 1 (2005): 75; and Janice Lindsay-Hartz, Joseph de Rivera, and Michael Mascolo, "Differentiating Guilt and Shame and Their Effects on Motivation," in *Self-Conscious Emotions: The Psychology of Shame, Guilt, Embarrassment, and Pride,* ed. June Tangney and Kurt Fisher (New York: Guilford Press, 1995), 295.

56. Lindsay-Hartz et al., "Differentiating Guilt," 298.

57. Johan Lindquist, *The Anxieties of Mobility: Migration and Tourism in the Indonesian Borderlands* (Honolulu: University of Hawai'i Press, 2009, 14.

58. Probyn, *Blush,* 39.

59. Rom Harré, *Physical Being: A Theory for a Corporeal Psychology* (Oxford: Blackwell, 1991), 142.

60. Fanon, *Black Skin,* 13.

❦ Topics for Further Examination ❧

- Look up research and reliable websites on patterns of eating disorders and cosmetic surgery procedures among women and men in the United States today. Discuss the gender and racial politics of procedures such as skin bleaching, brachioplasty, and labiaplasty.
- There is a complex relationship between hooking-up culture on college campuses and the sexual double standard. To explore this relationship, read online articles by sociologists who have studied hooking up.
- Compare and contrast the messages about gendered emotions in ads, articles, columns, and other features in popular women's and men's magazines.

7

GENDER AT WORK

JOAN Z. SPADE

Throughout this book, we emphasize the social construction of gender, a dominant prism in people's lives. This chapter explores some of the ways the social and economic structures within capitalist societies create gendered opportunities and experiences at work, and how work and gender affect life choices, particularly as they relate to family and parenting. The gendered patterns of work that emerge in capitalist systems are complex, like those of a kaleidoscope. These patterns reflect the interaction of gender with other social prisms such as race, sexuality, and social class. Furthermore, gendered patterns at work are intertwined with patterns from other social institutions such as education and family. Readings in this chapter support points made throughout the book. First, women's presence, interests, orientations, and needs tend to be diminished or marginalized within occupational spheres. Second, one can use several of the concepts we have been studying to understand the relationships of men and women at work, including hegemonic masculinity, "doing gender," the commodification of gender, and the idea of separate spaces for men and women.

In this chapter, we explore the construction and maintenance of gender within both paid and unpaid work in the United States, including one article that considers gender in the global workplace. We begin with a discussion of work and gender inequality. The history of gender discrimination in the paid labor market is a long one (Reskin & Padavic, 1999), with considerable social science research that documents gendered practices in workplace organizations. The first reading, by Joan Acker, discusses what she calls "inequality regimes," or the ways work organizations create and maintain inequality across the intersections of gender, race, and social class. In this piece, she looks beneath the surface to almost invisible institutional practices that maintain unequal opportunities within organizations (see also Acker, 1999). The second reading in this chapter, by Christine L. Williams, Chandra Muller, and Kristine Kilanski, applies Acker's paradigm to examine the characteristics of gendered organizations that women geoscientists face in the global oil and gas industry.

Consider the various ways the workforce in the United States is gendered. Think about different jobs (e.g., nurse, engineer, teacher, mechanic, domestic worker) and ask yourself if you consider them to be "male" or "female" jobs. Now take a look at Table 7.1, which lists job categories used by the

Bureau of Labor Statistics (2015a). You will note that jobs tend to be gender typed; that is, men and women are segregated into particular jobs. The consequences for men and women workers of this continuing occupational gender segregation are significant in the maintenance of gendered identities. Included in Table 7.1 are jobs predominantly held by men (management, architecture and engineering, and construction) and those predominantly held by women (education, health care support, and office and administrative support).

Gender segregation of jobs is linked with pay inequity in the labor force. In 2014, all full-time women workers earned, on average, 82.5% of what all men earned, or median weekly earnings of $719 compared with $871 for men (Bureau of Labor Statistics, 2015b). As you look through Table 7.1, locate those jobs that are the highest paid and determine whether they employ more men or more women. Also, compare women's to men's salaries across occupational categories. Clearly, a "gender wage gap" is evident in Table 7.1. Even in those job categories predominantly filled by women, men earn more than women. For example, going beyond the data in Table 7.1 and looking specifically at elementary and middle school teachers—a traditionally female job in which women outnumber men 4.11 to 1—the 2014 median weekly earnings for men, regardless of race or ethnicity, is $1,096 compared with $956 for women (a $140/week or $7,280/year average difference; Bureau of Labor Statistics, 2015b). The article by Adia Harvey Wingfield in this chapter discusses the "glass escalator" effect, where men in predominately female jobs earn more and get promoted more easily. But, as she discusses in her article, the glass escalator effect does not have a similar impact for African American men, as shown in Table 7.1. However, there is no glass escalator effect for women in traditionally male jobs. For example, looking at the specific occupation of lawyer, men still outnumbered women 1.94 to 1 in 2011 and also out-earned women $1,915 to $1,590 (a $325/week or $16,900/year difference on average; Bureau of Labor Statistics, 2015b);

or civil engineers, where men outnumber women 4.96 to 1 and earn $1,406 per week to women's $1,275 per week median wages (a $131/week or $6,812/year difference on average; Bureau of Labor Statistics, 2015b); or physicians and surgeons, where men outnumber women 1.67 to 1 and earn $2002 per week median wages to women's $1246 per week (a $756/week or $39,312/year difference on average; Bureau of Labor Statistics, 2015b). These four specific job categories are contained within the larger selected occupational categories in Table 7.1 and provide further understanding of the differences you see there (the Bureau of Labor Statistics only calculates median weekly incomes within specific occupations when there are more than 50,000 persons in that category; therefore, we were limited in the detailed job categories available to us).

The pattern you see does not deny that *some* women are CEOs of corporations, and today we see women workers everywhere, including on construction crews (the article by Amy M. Denissen and Abigail C. Saguy in Chapter 9 describes what it is like for women working in the construction trades). However, although a few women crack what is often called "the glass ceiling," getting into the top executive or hypermasculine jobs is not easy for women and minority group members. The glass ceiling refers to the point at which women and others, including racial minorities, reach a position in their organizations beyond which they cannot continue on an upward trajectory (Purcell, MacArthur, & Samblanet, 2010; see also the articles by Acker, Harvey Wingfield, and Williams, Muller, and Kilanski in this chapter). Informal networks generally maintain the impermeability of glass ceilings, with executive women often isolated and left out of "old boys' networks," finding themselves "outsiders on the inside" (Davies-Netzley, 1998, p. 347). Similar internal mechanisms within union and trade-related organizations also keep women and minority group members out, because "knowing" someone often helps one get a job in the higher paid, blue-collar occupations.

Table 7.1 2014 Median Weekly Salary and Percentages of Men and Women in Selected Occupational Categories by Gender and Race/Ethnic Group[1]

Median Weekly Wages

Occupational Category	Total Number Employed in Category (16 years and older) (all numbers in this table are in thousands)	White Females	% in Category	White Males	% in Category	Black Females	% in Category	Black Males	% in Category	Hispanic[2] Females	% in Category	Hispanic[2] Males	% in Category
All occupations	$791 / 106,526	$734	33.9%	$897	45.1%	$611	6.4%	$680	5.8%	$548	6.3%	$616	10.1%
Management, professional, and related occupations													
Management occupations	$1,295 / 11,881	$1,132	34.1%	$1,472	50.6%	$991	4.1%	$1,099	3.5%	$874	4.1%	$1,102	5.4%
Business and financial operations occupations	$1,107 / 5,681	$987	44.1%	$1,337	35.7%	$866	6.7%	$966	3.0%	$832	5.0%	$1,003	3.6%
Computer and mathematical occupations	$1,368 / 3,879	$1,158	16.6%	$1,412	52.2%	$895	3.1%	$1,148	5.5%	$1,001	1.5%	$1,216	5.2%
Architecture and engineering occupations	$1,377 / 2,527	$1,153	10.9%	$1,415	69.1%	$917[3]	1.2%	$1,233	4.2%	$992[3]	1.2%	$1,266	7.0%
Life, physical, and social science occupations	$1,168 / 1,124	$1,058	32.1%	$1,245	44.9%	$742[3]	2.9%	$1,079[3]	4.3%	$997[3]	3.0%	$1,091	5.2%
Community and social services occupations	$858 / 2,005	$847	45.9%	$962	27.7%	$746	13.2%	$754	5.8%	$799	7.9%	$830	5.2%
Legal occupations	$1,271 / 1,313	$1,004	45.1%	$1,751	40.7%	$972	5.6%	$1,666[3]	1.8%	$861	5.3%	$1,530[3]	2.4%

(Continued)

Table 7.1 (Continued)

Occupational Category	Total Number Employed in Category (all numbers in this table are in thousands)	Median Weekly Wages												
			White Females	% in Category	White Males	% in Category	Black Females	% in Category	Black Males	% in Category	Hispanic[2] Females	% in Category	Hispanic[2] Males	% in Category
Education, training, and library occupations	6,595	$953	$909	61.1%	$1,159	22.5%	$824	8.3%	$948	2.7%	$808	7.2%	$1,066	2.2%
Arts, design, entertainment, sports, and media occupations	1,573	$956	$863	34.1%	$1,045	48.9%	$954	3.4%	$899	3.8%	$687	3.8%	$1,015	6.8%
Health care practitioner and technical occupations	6,438	$1,033	$997	56.1%	$1,281	19.4%	$809	10.4%	$981	2.3%	$875	5.9%	$1,049	2.4%
Service occupations														
Health care support occupations	2,368	$498	$496	55.0%	$590	7.5%	$478	24.6%	$497	6.4%	$488	15.5%	$504	2.0%
Protective service occupations	2,740	$833	$660	12.0%	$940	62.2%	$566	6.3%	$732	13.6%	$578	2.7%	$821	12.0%
Food preparation and serving related occupations	4,017	$439	$418	35.1%	$467	38.6%	$418	7.4%	$413	7.3%	$393	11.0%	$441	18.9%
Building and grounds cleaning and maintenance occupations	3,568	$480	$410	24.4%	$523	42.9%	$412	7.0%	$473	9.2%	$387	14.2%	$458	24.5%
Personal care and service occupations	2,326	$487	$454	49.0%	$605	18.2%	$469	13.0%	$562	4.7%	$441	12.5%	$577	4.6%

Sales and office occupations

	Earnings	Number	$	%	$	%	$	%	$	%	$	%	$	%
Sales and related occupations	$705	9,626	$584	34.8%	$887	47.3%	$482	5.5%	$607	4.9%	$463	7.2%	$660	7.1%
Office and administrative support occupations	$651	13,776	$637	56.8%	$718	21.2%	$619	10.2%	$595	4.1%	$588	10.4%	$594	5.4%
Natural resources, construction, and maintenance occupations														
Farming, fishing, and forestry occupations	$429	776	$377	16.9%	$459	71.4%	$373[3]	1.7%	$474[3]	5.3%	$363	11.1%	$408	39.2%[2]
Construction and extraction	$756	5,756	$701	1.8%	$766	86.0%	$630[3]	0.2%	$633	6.8%	$485[3]	0.6%	$600	33.2%
Installation, maintenance, and repair occupations	$821	4,231	$744	2.7%	$833	83.1%	$524[3]	0.5%	$727	7.9%	$538[3]	0.6%	$682	15.7%
Production, transportation, and material moving occupations														
Production occupations	$646	7,481	$499	18.2%	$730	59.8%	$499	4.4%	$648	8.2%	$425	6.5%	$599	15.7%
Transportation and material moving occupations	$637	6,845	$525	9.7%	$684	65.6%	$472	2.8%	$614	15.0%	$397	3.4%	$580	19.8%

[1] Data for this table were taken from the Current Population Survey, Table A2: Usual Weekly Earnings of Employed Full-Time Wage and Salary Workers by Intermediate Occupation, Sex, Race, and Hispanic or Latino Ethnicity and Non-Hispanic Ethnicity, Annual Average 2014 (Bureau of Labor Statistics, 2015a).

[2] Categories of race and ethnicity are overlapping in this table, as Hispanic is a non-exclusive category. Therefore, an individual can identify as both Hispanic and White or Black. This overlap is particularly apparent for the category "farming, fishing, and forestry occupations."

[3] These estimates do not meet the Bureau of Labor Statistics standard for statistical reliability (50,000 cases); therefore, they must be used cautiously.

Gender, Race, and Social Class at Work

When we incorporate the prisms of race/ethnicity, and social class with gender, segregation in the workforce and pay inequality become more complex, as illustrated in the Harvey Wingfield article in this chapter. Another look at Table 7.1 indicates that individuals who identify as Hispanic or Latino and African American earn less than White, non-Hispanic men and women, although minority men earn more than White women in some occupational categories. In addition, Hispanic and African American women and men are much less likely to be found in the job categories with higher salaries than their percentages in the labor force would suggest. The continuing discrimination against African Americans, Hispanics, and other ethnic minority groups (as indicated in Table 7.1) shows patterns similar to the discrimination against women, both in the segregation of certain job categories and in the wage gap that exists within these same job categories. These processes operate to keep African American, Hispanic, and other marginalized groups "contained" within a limited number of occupational categories in the labor force.

The inequities of the workplace carry over into retirement (Calasanti & Slevin, 2001). Women and other marginalized groups are at a disadvantage when they retire, because their salaries are lower during their paid work years. Toni M. Calasanti and Kathleen F. Slevin find considerable inequalities in retirement income, which indicate that the inequalities in the labor force have a long-term effect for women and racial/ethnic minorities. They argue that only a small group of the workforce—privileged White men—are able to enjoy their "golden years," and the reasons for this situation are monetary.

Efforts to change inequality in the workplace by combating wage and job discrimination through legislation have included both gender and race. In 1963, Congress passed the Equal Pay Act, prohibiting employment discrimination by sex but not by race. Men and women in the same job, with similar credentials and seniority, could no longer receive different salaries. Although this legislation was an important step, Kim M. Blankenship (1993) cites two weaknesses in it. First, by focusing solely on pay equity, this legislation did not address gender segregation or gender discrimination in the workplace. Thus, it was illegal to discriminate by paying a woman less than a man who held the same job, but gender segregation of the workforce and differential pay across jobs was legal. As Blankenship notes, this legislation saved "men's jobs from women" (p. 220) because employers could continue to segregate their labor force into jobs that were held by men and those held by women and then pay the jobs held by men at a higher rate. Second, this legislation did little to help minority women, as a considerable majority of employed women of color were in occupations such as domestic workers in private households or employees of hotels/motels or restaurants that were not covered by the act (Blankenship, 1993).

In 1964, Congress passed Title VII of the Civil Rights Act. Congress drafted this legislation to address racial discrimination in the labor force. This act prohibited discrimination in "hiring, firing, compensation, classification, promotion, and other conditions of employment on the basis of race, sex, color, religion, or national origin" (Blankenship, 1993, p. 204). Sex-based discrimination was not originally part of this legislation but was added at the last minute, an addition that some argue was to ensure the bill would not pass Congress. However, the Civil Rights Act did pass Congress and women were protected along with the other groups. Unfortunately, the enforcement of gender discrimination legislation was much less enthusiastic than that for race discrimination (Blankenship, 1993).

Blankenship (1993) argues that the end result of these two pieces of legislation to overcome gender and race discrimination was to "protect white men's interests and power in the family" (p. 221), with little concern about practices that kept women and men of color out of higher paying jobs. Sadly, these attempts seem to have had little impact on race and gender discrimination

(Sturm & Guinier, 1996). In this chapter, articles by Acker, and Williams, Muller, and Kilanski describe the more subtle ways wage discrimination can take place in higher paying occupations. Take another look at Table 7.1 and think about the ways the different allocations of jobs and wages affect women's and men's lives across race and social class—their ability to be partners in relationships and their ability to provide for themselves and their families.

As you think about the differences that remain in wage inequality, consider what still needs to be accomplished. Pay equity may seem like a simple task to accomplish. After all, now we have laws that should be enforced. However, the process by which most companies determine salaries is quite complex. They rank individual job categories based on the degree of skill needed to complete job-related tasks. Ronnie Steinberg (1990), a sociologist who has studied comparable worth of jobs for almost 40 years, portrays a three-part process for determining wages for individual jobs. First, jobs are evaluated based on certain job characteristics, such as "skill, effort, responsibility, and working conditions" (p. 457). Second, job complexity is determined by applying a "value to different levels of job complexity" (p. 457). Finally, the values determined in the second step help set wage rates for the job. However, care work and other types of work typically performed by women are undervalued in this wage-setting process (England, 2005; Steinberg, 1990).

On the surface, this system of determining salaries seems consistent and "compatible with meritocratic values," where each person receives pay based on the value of what he or she actually does on the job (Steinberg, 1987, p. 467). What is recognized as "skill," however, is a matter of debate and is typically decided by organizational leaders who are predominately White, upper-class men. The gender and racial bias in the system of determining skills is shocking. Steinberg (1990, p. 456) gives an example from the State of Washington in 1972 in which two job categories, legal secretary and heavy equipment operator, were evaluated as "equivalent in job complexity," but the heavy equipment operator was paid $400 more per month than the legal secretary. Although it appears that all wages are determined in the same way based on the types of tasks they do at work, Steinberg (1987, 1990, 1992) and others (including Acker in this chapter) argue that the processes used to set salaries are highly politicized and biased.

GENDER DISCRIMINATION AT WORK

One way of interpreting why these gendered differences continue in the workforce is to examine workplaces as gendered institutions, as discussed in the introduction to this book. Acker, and Williams, Muller, and Kilanski—in the first two readings in this chapter—and other researchers examine work as a gendered institution (Acker, 1999, 2012). For example, Patricia Y. Martin (1996) studied managerial styles and evaluations of men and women in two different organizations: universities and a multinational corporation. She found that when promotions were at stake, male managers mobilized hegemonic masculinity to benefit themselves, thus excluding women. Understanding the processes and patterns by which hegemonic masculinity is considered "normal" within organizations is one avenue to understanding how organizations work to maintain sex segregation and pay inequity. These "inequality regimes" disadvantage all but a few, and, as Acker notes in this chapter, things are not likely to get better.

Gender discrimination at work is much more than an outcome of cultural or socialization differences in women's and men's behaviors in the workplace. Corporations have vested interests in exploiting gender labor. The exploitation of labor is a key element in the global as well as the U.S. economy, particularly as companies seek to reduce labor costs. Women in particular are likely targets for large, multinational corporations. In developing nations, companies exploit poor women's desires for freedom for themselves and responsibility to their families. The reading by Steven C. McKay illustrates these points as he describes local factories in the Philippines owned and managed by three multi-national corporations based in three different countries and three different cultures. The gendered assumptions, policies, and practices these corporations bring to their factories in the Philippines reflect the cultures of their home countries and illustrate the various ways "inequality regimes" are created in the workplace. As you read McKay's description of how corporations structure their employees' work experiences, ask yourself how other structures and patterns within the workplace reinforce gender difference and inequality in men's and women's identities, relationships, and opportunities.

Looking at some of the top-wage jobs in the United States, Williams, Muller, and Kilanski in this chapter describe some of the subtle and not-so-subtle mechanisms of discrimination for geoscientists in the global gas and oil industry. The "inequality regimes" surrounding career trajectories and compensation patterns make meritocracy a myth and discourage women from trying because it is clear that they are on an uneven playing field. As you read the articles in this chapter, consider those mechanisms and others where gender segregates workplaces and keeps women from advancing into particular jobs.

The Effect of Work on Our Lives

The work we do shapes our identities, affecting our expectations for ourselves and others (Kohn, Slomczynski, & Schoenbach, 1986) and our emotions. It is not just paid work that affects our orientations toward self and others (Spade, 1991) but also work done in the home. In Western societies, work also defines leisure, with leisure related to modernization and the definition of work being "done at specific times, at workplaces, and under work-specific authority" (Roberts, 1999, p. 2). Although the separation of leisure from work is much more likely to be found in developed societies, work is not always detached from leisure, as evidenced by the professionals who carry home a briefcase at the end of the day or the beepers that summon individuals to call their workplaces (see the reading by Carla Shows and Naomi Gerstel in Chapter 8).

Care Work

Care work is one gendered pattern that restricts women's leisure more so than men's (England, 2005). Women's leisure is often less an escape from work and more a transition to another form of work—domestic work. In an international study using time budgets collected from almost 47,000 people in 10 industrialized countries, Michael Bittman and Judy Wajcman (2000) found that men and women have a similar amount of free time; however, women's free time tends to be more fragmented by demands of housework and caregiving. Another study using time budgets found that women spent 30.9 hours on average performing various different family care tasks such as cooking, cleaning, repairs, yard work, and shopping, while men spent 15.9 hours per week performing such tasks (Robinson & Godbey, 1997, p. 101). Women also reported more stress in the Bittman and Wajcman (2000) study, which the authors attributed to the fact that "fragmented leisure, snatched between work and self-care activities, is less relaxing than unbroken leisure" (p. 185).

Domestic work, while almost invisible and generally devalued, cannot be left out of a discussion of work and leisure (Gerstel, 2000). Care work is devalued—particularly unpaid care work, which rests largely on women's shoulders. Gerstel and others refer to the contribution of women to care work as "the third shift." As a result, domestic labor and caregiving, being unpaid, are done by people least valued in the paid market. The undervaluation of care work carries over to the paid market as well. Look again at Table 7.1 and identify those job categories that encompass care work, such as health support workers and personal care and service workers. Now compare salaries and percentages of men and women in these caregiving jobs. As you start to consider these issues, ask why we undervalue care work—the unpaid care work in the home as well as care work in the workplace? Why are men encouraged not to participate in care work, and why are women the default caregivers? How is it that the work of the home is undervalued, and how is this pattern related to the workplace and the amount of leisure time available to men and women?

Work, Family, and Parenting

Unfortunately things have changed very little since the Bittman and Wajcman (2000) study, as Amy S. Wharton reports in her review of changes in the distribution of domestic labor in this chapter. Wharton calls it a "stalled revolution," as the changes that did occur hit a plateau in the late 1990s. Women's progress slowed in the workforce as well. Wharton sees the problems associated with this uneven workload as related to the institutions of work, family, and gender. With care work perceived as a "feminine" activity, it is not surprising that women's lives are more likely to be focused around, or expected to be focused around, care work activities, whereas the image of the ideal worker is an employee who is totally devoted to his or her job with no other responsibilities that might interfere with those work responsibilities. Thus, work, family, and parenting become gendered institutions, reinforcing each other in maintaining a gender binary of separate spheres for women and men. Brooke Conroy Bass, in her reading in this chapter, discusses how women in egalitarian couples modify expectations for their careers and work plans based upon perceived parenting responsibilities well before children are born to the couple. Although couples may have egalitarian views of their relationships, parenting complicates those plans. Women and men alike buy into a traditional caregiving pattern, while at the same time reproducing inequalities in the labor market. Caregiving and parenting have been

transformed, yet both men and women still must respond to the constraints on their time as they balance what they want in their lives with idealized visions of careers and parenthood. Of course, such decisions are made irrelevant by the needs of families in which both parents work in lower earning jobs.

We can illustrate only a few patterns of work in this chapter. The rest you can explore on your own as you take the examples from the readings and apply them to your own life. When you read through the articles in this chapter, consider the consequences of maintaining gendered patterns at work for yourself and your future. While you are at it, consider why these patterns still exist and what these patterns of inequality look like in your life.

References

Acker, J. (1999). Gender and organizations. In J. S. Chafetz (Ed.), *The handbook of the sociology of gender* (pp. 171–194). New York: Kluwer Academic/Plenum.

Acker, J. (2012). Gender and organizations and intersectionality: Problems and possibilities. *Equality, Diversity and Inclusion: An International Journal, 31*(3), 214–224.

Bittman, M., & Wajcman, J. (2000). The rush hour: The character of leisure time and gender equity. *Social Forces, 79*(1), 165–189.

Blankenship, K. M. (1993). Bringing gender and race in: U.S. employment discrimination policy. *Gender & Society, 7*(2), 204–226.

Bureau of Labor Statistics. (2015a). Table A-2: 2014 Median weekly earnings of full-time wage and salary workers by detailed occupation, sex, race and Hispanic or Latino ethnicity and Non-Hispanic ethnicity. Annual Average 2014. Source: *Current Population Survey* [Unpublished data—sent by request].

Bureau of Labor Statistics. (2015b). Table 39: Usual weekly earnings of employed full-time wage and salary workers by intermediate occupation and sex. Annual Average 2014. Source: *Current Population Survey.* Retrieved June 21, 2015, from http://www.bls.gov/cps/cpsaat39.htm

Calasanti, T. M., & Slevin, K. F. (2001). *Gender, social inequalities, and aging.* Walnut Creek, CA: AltaMira Press.

Davies-Netzley, S. A. (1998). Women above the glass ceiling: Perceptions on corporate mobility and strategies for success. *Gender & Society, 12*(3), 339–355.

England, P. (2005). Emerging theories of care work. *Annual Review of Sociology, 31*(1), 381–399.

Gerstel, N. (2000). The third shift: Gender and care work outside the home. *Qualitative Sociology, 23*(4), 467–483.

Kohn, M. L., Slomczynski, K. M., & Schoenbach, C. (1986). Social stratification and the transmission of values in the family: A cross-national assessment. *Sociological Forum, 1,* 73–102.

Martin, P. Y. (1996). Gendering and evaluating dynamics: Men, masculinities, and managements. In D. Collinson & J. Hearn (Eds.), *Men as managers, managers as men* (pp. 186–209). Thousand Oaks, CA: Sage.

Purcell, D., MacArthur, K. R., & Samblanet, S. (2010). Gender and the glass ceiling at work. *Sociology Compass, 4*(9), 705–717.

Reskin, B. F., & Padavic, I. (1999). Sex, race, and ethnic inequality in United States workplaces. In J. S. Chafetz (Ed.), *Handbook of the sociology of gender* (pp. 343–374). New York: Kluwer Academic/Plenum.

Roberts, K. (1999). *Leisure in contemporary society.* Oxon, UK: CABI.

Robinson, J. P., & Godbey, G. (1997). *Time for life: The surprising ways Americans use their time.* University Park: Pennsylvania State University Press.

Spade, J. Z. (1991). Occupational structure and men's and women's parental values. *Journal of Family Issues, 12*(3), 343–360.

Steinberg, R. J. (1987). Radical changes in a liberal world: The mixed success of comparable worth. *Gender & Society, 1*(4), 446–475.

Steinberg, R. J. (1990). Social construction of skill: Gender, power, and comparable worth. *Work and Occupations, 17*(4), 449–482.

Steinberg, R. J. (1992). Gendered instructions: Cultural lag and gender bias in the Hay System of job evaluation. *Work and Occupations, 19*(4), 387–423.

Sturm, S., & Guinier, L. (1996). Race-based remedies: Rethinking the process of classification and evaluation: The future of affirmative action. *California Law Review, 84*(4):953–1036.

Introduction to Reading 31

Joan Acker draws from her vast research on gender, class, work, and organizations to describe the structure of organizations that maintain gender, class, and race disparities in wages as well as power in organizations. She also explores why inequalities in organizational structures and practices are not likely to change. She describes "inequality regimes," or practices and policies embedded in the organization itself, and shows how they work to create and maintain inequality across gender, race, and class. In this article, Acker provides detailed examples of how organizations maintain the gender inequalities in wages described in Table 7.1 and also why individuals seem powerless to overcome these gender inequalities.

1. Using your own life, think about whether you can identify any "inequality regimes" in the organizations you have worked in.

2. How does her description of inequality regimes explain the data in Table 7.1?

3. What would have to change to reduce "inequality regimes" in the workplace? How might this threaten masculinity?

--------- **INEQUALITY REGIMES** ---------

GENDER, CLASS, AND RACE IN ORGANIZATIONS

Joan Acker

All organizations have inequality regimes, defined as loosely interrelated practices, processes, actions, and meanings that result in and maintain class, gender, and racial inequalities within particular organizations. The ubiquity of inequality is obvious: Managers, executives, leaders, and department heads have much more power and higher pay than secretaries, production workers, students, or even professors. Even organizations that have explicit egalitarian goals develop inequality regimes over time, as considerable research on egalitarian feminist organizations has shown (Ferree and Martin 1995; Scott 2000).

I define inequality in organizations as systematic disparities between participants in power and control over goals, resources, and outcomes; workplace decisions such as how to organize work; opportunities for promotion and interesting work; security in employment and benefits; pay and other monetary rewards; respect; and pleasures in work and work relations. Organizations vary in the degree to which these disparities are present and in how severe they are. Equality rarely exists in control over goals and resources, while pay and other monetary rewards are usually unequal. Other disparities may be less evident, or a high degree of equality might exist in particular areas, such as employment security and benefits.

Inequality regimes are highly various in other ways; they also tend to be fluid and changing.

These regimes are linked to inequality in the surrounding society, its politics, history, and culture. Particular practices and interpretations develop in different organizations and subunits. One example is from my study of Swedish banks in the late 1980s (Acker 1994). My Swedish colleague and I looked at gender and work processes in six local bank branches. We were investigating the degree to which the branches had adopted a reorganization plan and a more equitable distribution of work tasks and decision-making responsibilities that had been agreed to by both management and the union. We found differences on some dimensions of inequality. One office had almost all women employees and few status and power differences. Most tasks were rotated or shared, and the supervision by the male manager was seen by all working in the branch as supportive and benign. The other offices had clear gender segregation, with men handling the lucrative business accounts and women handling the everyday, private customers. In these offices, very little power and decision making were shared, although there were differences in the degrees to which the employees saw their workplaces as undemocratic. The one branch office that was most successful in redistributing tasks and decision making was the one with women employees and a preexisting participatory ethos.

* * *

WHAT VARIES? THE COMPONENTS OF INEQUALITY REGIMES

Shape and Degree of Inequality

The steepness of hierarchy is one dimension of variation in the shape and degree of inequality. The steepest hierarchies are found in traditional bureaucracies in contrast to the idealized flat organizations with team structures, in which most, or at least some, responsibilities and decision-making authority are distributed among participants. Between these polar types are organizations with varying degrees of hierarchy and shared decision making. Hierarchies are usually gendered and racialized, especially at the top. Top hierarchical class positions are almost always occupied by white men in the United States and European countries. This is particularly true in large and influential organizations. The image of the successful organization and the image of the successful leader share many of the same characteristics, such as strength, aggressiveness, and competitiveness. Some research shows that flat team structures provide professional women more equality and opportunity than hierarchical bureaucracies, but only if the women function like men. One study of engineers in Norway (Kvande and Rasmussen 1994) found that women in a small, collegial engineering firm gained recognition and advancement more easily than in an engineering department in a big bureaucracy. However, the women in the small firm were expected to put in the same long hours as their male colleagues and to put their work first, before family responsibilities. Masculine-stereotyped patterns of on-the-job behavior in team-organized work may mean that women must make adaptations to expectations that interfere with family responsibilities and with which they are uncomfortable. In a study of high-level professional women in a computer development firm, Joanne Martin and Debra Meyerson (1998) found that the women saw the culture of their work group as highly masculine, aggressive, competitive, and self-promoting. The women had invented ways to cope with this work culture, but they felt that they were partly outsiders who did not belong.

Other research (Barker 1993) suggests that team-organized work may not reduce gender inequality. Racial inequality may also be maintained as teams are introduced in the workplace (Vallas 2003). While the organization of teams is often accompanied by drastic reductions of supervisors' roles, the power of higher managerial levels is usually not changed: Class inequalities are only slightly reduced (Morgen, Acker, and Weigt n.d.).

The degree and pattern of segregation by race and gender is another aspect of inequality that varies considerably between organizations. Gender and race segregation of jobs is complex because segregation is hierarchical across jobs at different class levels of an organization, across jobs at the same level, and within jobs (Charles and Grusky 2004). Occupations should be distinguished from jobs: An occupation is a type of work; a job is a particular cluster of tasks in a particular work organization. For example, emergency room nurse is an occupation; an emergency room nurse at San Francisco General Hospital is a job. More statistical data are available about occupations than about jobs, although "job" is the relevant unit for examining segregation in organizations. We know that within the broad level of professional and managerial occupations, there is less gender segregation than 30 years ago, as I have already noted. Desegregation has not progressed so far in other occupations. However, research indicates that "sex segregation at the job level is more extensive than sex segregation at the level of occupations" (Wharton 2005, 97). In addition, even when women and men "are members of the same occupation, they are likely to work in different jobs and firms" (Wharton 2005, 97). Racial segregation also persists, is also complex, and varies by gender.

Jobs and occupations may be internally segregated by both gender and race: What appears to be a reduction in segregation may only be its reconfiguration. Reconfiguration and differentiation have occurred as women have entered previously male-dominated occupations. For example, women doctors are likely to specialize in pediatrics, not surgery, which is still largely a male domain. I found a particularly striking example of the internal gender segregation of a job category in my research on Swedish banks (Acker 1991). Swedish banks all had a single job classification for beginning bank workers: They were called "aspiranter," or those aspiring to a career in banking. This job classification had one description; it was used in banking industry statistics to indicate that this was one job that was not gender segregated. However, in bank branches, young women aspiranters had different tasks than young men. Men's tasks were varied and brought them into contact with different aspects of the business. Men were groomed for managerial jobs. The women worked as tellers or answered telephone inquiries. They had contact only with their immediate supervisors and coworkers in the branch. They were not being groomed for promotion. This was one job with two realities based on gender.

The size of wage differences in organizations also varies. Wage differences often vary with the height of the hierarchy: It is the CEOs of the largest corporations whose salaries far outstrip those of everyone else. In the United States in 2003, the average CEO earned 185 times the earnings of the average worker; the average earnings of CEOs of big corporations were more than 300 times the earnings of the average worker (Mishel, Bernstein, and Boushey 2003). White men tend to earn more than any other gender/race category, although even for white men, the wages of the bottom 60 percent are stagnant. Within most service-sector organizations, both white women and women of color are at the bottom of the wage hierarchy.

The severity of power differences varies. Power differences are fundamental to class, of course, and are linked to hierarchy. Labor unions and professional associations can act to reduce power differences across class hierarchies. However, these organizations have historically been dominated by white men with the consequence that white women and people of color have not

had increases in organizational power equal to those of white men. Gender and race are important in determining power differences within organizational class levels. For example, managers are not always equal. In some organizations, women managers work quietly to do the organizational housekeeping, to keep things running, while men managers rise to heroic heights to solve spectacular problems (Ely and Meyerson 2000). In other organizations, women and men manage in the same ways (Wajcman 1998). Women managers and professionals often face gendered contradictions when they attempt to use organizational power in actions similar to those of men. Women enacting power violate conventions of relative subordination to men, risking the label of "witches" or "bitches."

Organizing Processes That Produce Inequality

Organizations vary in the practices and processes that are used to achieve their goals; these practices and processes also produce class, gender, and racial inequalities. Considerable research exists exploring how class or gender inequalities are produced, both formally and informally, as work processes are carried out (Acker 1989, 1990; Burawoy 1979; Cockburn 1985; Willis 1977). Some research also examines the processes that result in continuing racial inequalities. These practices are often guided by textual materials supplied by consultants or developed by managers influenced by information and/or demands from outside the organization. To understand exactly how inequalities are reproduced, it is necessary to examine the details of these textually informed practices.

Organizing the general requirements of work. The general requirements of work in organizations vary among organizations and among organizational levels. In general, work is organized on the image of a white man who is totally dedicated to the work and who has no responsibilities for children or family demands other than earning a living. Eight hours of continuous work away from the living space, arrival on time, total attention to the work, and long hours if requested are all expectations that incorporate the image of the unencumbered worker. Flexibility to bend these expectations is more available to high-level managers, predominantly men, than to lower-level managers (Jacobs and Gerson 2004). Some professionals, such as college professors, seem to have considerable flexibility, although they also work long hours. Lower-level jobs have, on the whole, little flexibility. Some work is organized as part-time, which may help women to combine work and family obligations, but in the United States, such work usually has no benefits such as health care and often has lower pay than full-time work (Mishel, Bernstein, and Boushey 2003). Because women have more obligations outside of work than do men, this gendered organization of work is important in maintaining gender inequality in organizations and, thus, the unequal distribution of women and men in organizational class hierarchies. Thus, gender, race, and class inequalities are simultaneously created in the fundamental construction of the working day and of work obligations.

Organizing class hierarchies. Techniques also vary for organizing class hierarchies inside work organizations. Bureaucratic, textual techniques for ordering positions and people are constructed to reproduce existing class, gender, and racial inequalities (Acker 1989). I have been unable to find much research on these techniques, but I do have my own observations of such techniques in one large job classification system from my study of comparable worth (Acker 1989). Job classification systems describe job tasks and responsibilities and rank jobs hierarchically. Jobs are then assigned to wage categories with jobs of similar rank in the same wage category. Our study found that the bulk of sex-typed women's jobs, which were in the clerical/secretarial area and included thousands of women workers, were described less clearly and with less specificity than the bulk of sex-typed men's jobs, which were spread over a wide range of areas and levels in the organization. The women's jobs were grouped into four

large categories at the bottom of the ranking, assigned to the lowest wage ranges; the men's jobs were in many more categories extending over a much wider range of wage levels. Our new evaluation of the clerical/secretarial categories showed that many different jobs with different tasks and responsibilities, some highly skilled and responsible, had been lumped together. The result was, we argued, an unjustified gender wage gap: Although women's wages were in general lower than those of men, women's skilled jobs were paid much less than men's skilled jobs, reducing even further the average pay for women when compared with the average pay for men. Another component in the reproduction of hierarchy was revealed in discussions with representatives of Hay Associates, the large consulting firm that provided the job evaluation system we used in the comparable worth study. These representatives would not let the job evaluation committees alter the system to compare the responsibilities of managers' jobs with the responsibilities of the jobs of their secretarial assistants. Often, we observed, managers were credited with responsibility for tasks done by their assistants. The assistants did not get credit for these tasks in the job evaluation system, and this contributed to their relatively low wages. But if managers' and assistants' jobs could never be compared, no adjustments for inequities could ever be made. The hierarchy was inviolate in this system.

In the past 30 years, many organizations have removed some layers of middle management and relocated some decision making to lower organizational levels. These changes have been described as getting rid of the inefficiencies of old bureaucracies, reducing hierarchy and inequality, and empowering lower-level employees. This happened in two of the organizations I have studied—Swedish banks in the late 1980s (Acker 1991), discussed above, and the Oregon Department of Adult and Family Services, responsible for administration of Temporary Assistance to Needy Families and welfare reform (Morgen, Acker, and Weigt n.d.). In both cases, the decision-making responsibilities of frontline workers were greatly increased, and their jobs became more demanding and more interesting. In the welfare agency, ordinary workers had increased participation in decisions about their local operations. But the larger hierarchy did not change in either case. The frontline employees were still on the bottom; they had more responsibility, but not higher salaries. And they had no increased control over their job security. In both cases, the workers liked the changes in the content of their jobs, but the hierarchy was still inviolate.

In sum, class hierarchies in organizations, with their embedded gender and racial patterns, are constantly created and renewed through organizing practices. Gender and sometimes race, in the form of restricted opportunities and particular expectations for behavior, are reproduced as different degrees of organizational class hierarchy and are also reproduced in everyday interactions and bureaucratic decision making.

Recruitment and hiring. Recruitment and hiring is a process of finding the worker most suited for a particular position. From the perspectives of employers, the gender and race of existing job-holders at least partially define who is suitable, although prospective coworkers may also do such defining (Enarson 1984). Images of appropriate gendered and racialized bodies influence perceptions and hiring. White bodies are often preferred, as a great deal of research shows (Royster 2003). Female bodies are appropriate for some jobs; male bodies for other jobs.

A distinction should be made between the gendered organization of work and the gender and racial characteristics of the ideal worker. Although work is organized on the model of the unencumbered (white) man, and both women and men are expected to perform according to this model, men are not necessarily the ideal workers for all jobs. The ideal worker for many jobs is a woman, particularly a woman who, employers believe, is compliant, who will accept orders and low wages (Salzinger 2003). This is often a woman of color; immigrant women are sometimes even more desirable (Hossfeld 1994).

Hiring through social networks is one of the ways in which gender and racial inequalities are maintained in organizations. Affirmative action programs altered hiring practices in many organizations, requiring open advertising for positions and selection based on gender- and race-neutral criteria of competence, rather than selection based on an old boy (white) network.

These changes in hiring practices contributed to the increasing proportions of white women and people of color in a variety of occupations. However, criteria of competence do not automatically translate into gender- and race-neutral selection decisions. "Competence" involves judgment: The race and gender of both the applicant and the decision makers can affect that judgment, resulting in decisions that white males are the more competent, more suited to the job than are others. Thus, gender and race as a basis for hiring or a basis for exclusion have not been eliminated in many organizations, as continuing patterns of segregation attest.

Wage setting and supervisory practices. Wage setting and supervision are class practices. They determine the division of surplus between workers and management and control the work process and workers. Gender and race affect assumptions about skill, responsibility, and a fair wage for jobs and workers, helping to produce wage differences (Figart, Mutari, and Power 2002).

Wage setting is often a bureaucratic organizational process, integrated into the processes of creating hierarchy, as I described above. Many different wage-setting systems exist, many of them producing gender and race differences in pay. Differential gender-based evaluations may be embedded in even the most egalitarian-appearing systems. For example, in my study of Swedish banks in the 1980s, a pay gap between women and men was increasing within job categories in spite of gender equality in wage agreements between the union and employers (Acker 1991). Our research revealed that the gap was increasing because the wage agreement allowed a small proportion of negotiated increases to be allocated by local managers to reward particularly high-performing workers. These small increments went primarily to men; over time, the increases produced a growing gender gap. In interviews we learned that male employees were more visible to male managers than were female employees. I suspected that the male managers also felt that a fair wage for men was actually higher than a fair wage for women. I drew two implications from these findings: first, that individualized wage-setting produces inequality, and second, that to understand wage inequality it is necessary to delve into the details of wage-setting systems.

Supervisory practices also vary across organizations. Supervisory relations may be affected by the gender and race of both supervisor and subordinate, in some cases preserving or reproducing gender or race inequalities. For example, above I described how women and men in the same aspiranter job classification in Swedish banks were assigned to different duties by their supervisors. Supervisors probably shape their behaviors with subordinates in terms of race and gender in many other work situations, influencing in subtle ways the existing patterns of inequality. Much of this can be observed in the informal interactions of workplaces.

Informal interactions while "doing the work." A large literature exists on the reproduction of gender in interactions in organizations (Reskin 1998; Ridgeway 1997). The production of racial inequalities in workplace interactions has not been studied so frequently (Vallas 2003), while the reproduction of class relations in the daily life of organizations has been studied in the labor process tradition, as I noted above. The informal interactions and practices in which class, race, and gender inequalities are created in mutually reinforcing processes have not so often been documented, although class processes are usually implicit in studies of gendered or racialized inequalities.

As women and men go about their everyday work, they routinely use gender-, race-, and class-based assumptions about those with whom they interact, as I briefly noted above in regard to wage setting. Body differences provide clues to the appropriate assumptions, followed by appropriate behaviors. What is appropriate varies, of course, in relation to the situation, the organizational culture and history, and the standpoints of the people judging appropriateness. For example, managers may expect a certain class deference or respect for authority that varies with the race and gender of the subordinate; subordinates may assume that their positions require deference and respect but also find these demands demeaning or oppressive. Jennifer Pierce (1995), in a study of two law firms, showed how both gendered and racialized interactions shaped the organizations' class relations: Women paralegals were put in the role of supportive, mothering aides, while men paralegals were cast as junior partners in the firms' business. African American employees, primarily women in secretarial positions, were acutely aware of the ways in which they were routinely categorized and subordinated in interactions with both paralegals and attorneys. The interaction practices that re-create gender and racial inequalities are often subtle and unspoken, thus difficult to document. White men may devalue and exclude white women and people of color by not listening to them in meetings, by not inviting them to join a group going out for a drink after work, by not seeking their opinions on workplace problems. Other practices, such as sexual harassment, are open and obvious to the victim, but not so obvious to others. In some organizations, such as those in the travel and hospitality industry, assumptions about good job performance may be sexualized: Women employees may be expected to behave and dress as sexually attractive women, particularly with male customers (Adkins 1995).

The Visibility of Inequalities

Visibility of inequality, defined as the degree of awareness of inequalities, varies in different organizations. Lack of awareness may be intentional or unintentional. Managers may intentionally hide some forms of inequality, as in the Swedish banks I studied (Acker 1991). Bank workers said that they had been told not to discuss their wages with their coworkers. Most seem to have complied, partly because they had strong feelings that their pay was part of their identity, reflecting their essential worth. Some said they would rather talk about the details of their sex lives than talk about their pay.

Visibility varies with the position of the beholder: "One privilege of the privileged is not to see their privilege." Men tend not to see their gender privilege; whites tend not to see their race privilege; ruling class members tend not to see their class privilege (McIntosh 1995). People in dominant groups generally see inequality as existing somewhere else, not where they are. However, patterns of invisibility/visibility in organizations vary with the basis for the inequality. Gender and gender inequality tend to disappear in organizations or are seen as something that is beside the point of the organization. Researchers examining gender inequality have sometimes experienced this disappearance as they have discussed with managers and workers the ways that organizing practices are gendered (Ely and Meyerson 2000; Korvajärvi 2003). Other research suggests that practices that generate gender inequality are sometimes so fleeting or so minor that they are difficult to see.

Class also tends to be invisible. It is hidden by talk of management, leadership, or supervision among managers and those who write and teach about organizations from a management perspective. Workers in lower-level, nonmanagement positions may be very conscious of inequalities, although they might not identify these inequities as related to class. Race is usually evident, visible, but segregated, denied, and avoided. In two of my organization studies, we have asked questions about race issues in the workplace (Morgen, Acker, and Weigt n.d.). In both of these studies, white workers on the whole could see no problems with race or racism, while workers of color had very different views. The one exception was in an office with a very diverse workforce, located in an area with many minority residents and high poverty rates. Here, jobs were segregated by race, tensions were high, and both white and Black workers were well aware of racial incidents. Another basis of inequality, sexuality, is almost always invisible to the majority who

are heterosexual. Heterosexuality is simply assumed, not questioned.

The Legitimacy of Inequalities

The legitimacy of inequalities also varies between organizations. Some organizations, such as cooperatives, professional organizations, or voluntary organizations with democratic goals, may find inequality illegitimate and try to minimize it. In other organizations, such as rigid bureaucracies, inequalities are highly legitimate. Legitimacy of inequality also varies with political and economic conditions. For example, in the United States in the 1960s and 1970s, the civil rights and the women's movements challenged the legitimacy of racial and gender inequalities, sometimes also challenging class inequality. These challenges spurred legislation and social programs to reduce inequality, stimulating a decline in the legitimacy of inequality in many aspects of U.S. life, including work organizations. Organizations became vulnerable to lawsuits for discrimination and took defensive measures that included changes in hiring procedures and education about the illegitimacy of inequality. Inequality remained legitimate in many ways, but that entrenched legitimacy was shaken, I believe, during this period.

Both differences and similarities exist among class, race, and gender processes and among the ways in which they are legitimized. Class is fundamentally about economic inequality. Both gender and race are also defined by inequalities of various kinds, but I believe that gender and racial differences could still conceivably exist without inequality. This is, of course, a debatable question. Class is highly legitimate in U.S. organizations, as class practices, such as paying wages and maintaining supervisory oversight, are basic to organizing work in capitalist economies. Class may be seen as legitimate because it is seen as inevitable at the present time. This has not always been the case for all people in the United States; there have been periods, such as during the depression of the 1930s and during the social movements of the 1960s, when large numbers of people questioned the legitimacy of class subordination.

Gender and race inequality are less legitimate than class. Antidiscrimination and civil rights laws limiting certain gender and race discriminatory practices have existed since the 1950s. Organizations claim to be following those laws in hiring, promotion, and pay. Many organizations have diversity initiatives to attract workforces that reflect their customer publics. No such laws or voluntary measures exist to question the basic legitimacy of class practices, although measures such as the Fair Labor Standards Act could be interpreted as mitigating the most severe damages from those practices. In spite of antidiscrimination and affirmative action laws, gender and race inequalities continue in work organizations. These inequalities are often legitimated through arguments that naturalize the inequality (Glenn 2002). For example, some employers still see women as more suited to child care and less suited to demanding careers than men. Beliefs in biological differences between genders and between racial/ethnic groups, in racial inferiority, and in the superiority of certain masculine traits all legitimate inequality. Belief in market competition and the natural superiority of those who succeed in the contest also naturalizes inequality.

Gender and race processes are more legitimate when embedded in legitimate class processes. For example, the low pay and low status of clerical work is historically and currently produced as both a class and a gender inequality. Most people take this for granted as just part of the way in which work is organized. Legitimacy, along with visibility, may vary with the situation of the observer: Some clerical workers do not see the status and pay of their jobs as fair, while their bosses would find such an assessment bizarre. The advantaged often think their advantage is richly deserved. They see visible inequalities as perfectly legitimate.

High visibility and low legitimacy of inequalities may enhance the possibilities for change. Social movements may contribute to both high visibility and low legitimacy while agitating for change toward greater equality, as I argued above. Labor unions may also be more successful when visibility is high and legitimacy of inequalities is low.

Control and Compliance

Organizational controls are, in the first instance, class controls, directed at maintaining the power of managers, ensuring that employees act to further the organization's goals, and getting workers to accept the system of inequality. Gendered and racialized assumptions and expectations are embedded in the form and content of controls and in the ways in which they are implemented. Controls are made possible by hierarchical organizational power, but they also draw on power derived from hierarchical gender and race relations. They are diverse and complex, and they impede changes in inequality regimes.

Mechanisms for exerting control and achieving compliance with inequality vary. Organization theorists have identified many types of control, including direct controls, unobtrusive or indirect controls, and internalized controls. Direct controls include bureaucratic rules and various punishments for breaking the rules. Rewards are also direct controls. Wages, because they are essential for survival in completely monetized economies, are a powerful form of control (Perrow 2002). Coercion and physical and verbal violence are also direct controls often used in organizations (Hearn and Parkin 2001). Unobtrusive and indirect controls include control through technologies, such as monitoring telephone calls or time spent online or restricting information flows. Selective recruitment of relatively powerless workers can be a form of control (Acker and Van Houten 1974). Recruitment of illegal immigrants who are vulnerable to discovery and deportation and recruitment of women of color who have few employment opportunities and thus will accept low wages are examples of this kind of control, which preserves inequality.

Internalized controls include belief in the legitimacy of bureaucratic structures and rules as well as belief in the legitimacy of male and white privilege. Organizing relations, such as those between a manager and subordinates, may be legitimate, taken for granted as the way things naturally and normally are. Similarly, a belief that there is no point in challenging the fundamental gender, race, and class nature of things is a form of control. These are internalized, often invisible controls. Pleasure in the work is another internalized control, as are fear and self-interest. Interests can be categorized as economic, status, and identity interests, all of which may be produced as organizing takes place. Identities, constituted through gendered and racialized images and experiences, are mutually reproduced along with differences in status and economic advantage. Those with the most powerful and affluent combination of interests are apt to be able to control others with the aim of preserving these interests. But their self-interest becomes a control on their own behavior.

GLOBALIZATION, RESTRUCTURING, AND CHANGE IN INEQUALITY REGIMES

Organizational restructuring of the past 30 years has contributed to increasing variation in inequality regimes. Restructuring, new technology, and the globalization of production contribute to rising competitive pressures in private-sector organizations and budget woes in public-sector organizations, making challenges to inequality regimes less likely to be undertaken than during the 1960s to the 1980s. The following are some of the ways in which variations in U.S. inequality regimes seem to have increased. These are speculations because, in my view, there is not yet sufficient evidence as to how general or how lasting these changes might be.

The shape and degree of inequality seem to have become more varied. Old, traditional bureaucracies with career ladders still exist.

Relatively new organizations, such as Wal-Mart, also have such hierarchical structures. At the same time, in many organizations, certain inequalities are externalized in new segmented organizing forms as both production and services are carried out in other, low-wage countries, often in organizations that are in a formal, legal sense separate organizations. If these production units are seen as part of the core organizations, earnings inequalities are increasing rapidly in many different organizations. But wage inequalities are also increasing within core U.S.-based sectors of organizations.

White working- and middle-class men, as well as white women and all people of color, have been affected by restructuring, downsizing, and the export of jobs to low-wage countries. White men's advantage seems threatened by these changes, but at least one study shows that white men find new employment after layoffs and downsizing more rapidly than people in other gender/race categories and that they find better jobs (Spalter-Roth and Deitch 1999). And a substantial wage gap still exists between women and men. Moreover, white men still dominate local and global organizations. In other words, inequality regimes still seem to place white men in advantaged positions in spite of the erosion of advantages for middle- and lower-level men workers.

Inequalities of power within organizations, particularly in the United States, also seem to be increasing with the present dominance of global corporations and their free market ideology, the decline in the size and influence of labor unions, and the increase in job insecurity as downsizing and reorganization continue. The increase in contingent and temporary workers who have less participation in decisions and less security than regular workers also increases power inequality. Unions still exercise some power, but they exist in only a very small minority of private-sector organizations and a somewhat larger minority of public-sector unions.

Organizing processes that create and re-create inequalities may have become more subtle, but in some cases, they have become more difficult to challenge. For example, the unencumbered male worker as the model for the organization of daily work and the model of the excellent employee seems to have been strengthened. Professionals and managers, in particular, work long hours and often are evaluated on their "face time" at work and their willingness to put work and the organization before family and friends (Hochschild 1997; Jacobs and Gerson 2004). New technology makes it possible to do some jobs anywhere and to be in touch with colleagues and managers at all hours of day and night. Other workers lower in organizational hierarchies are expected to work as the employer demands, overtime or at odd hours. Such often excessive or unpredictable demands are easier to meet for those without daily family responsibilities. Other gendered aspects of organizing processes may be less obvious than before sex and racial discrimination emerged as legal issues. For example, employers can no longer legally exclude young women on the grounds that they may have babies and leave the job, nor can they openly exclude consideration of people of color. But informal exclusion and unspoken denigration are still widespread and still difficult to document and to confront.

The visibility of inequality to those in positions of power does not seem to have changed. However, the legitimacy of inequality in the eyes of those with money and power does seem to have changed: Inequality is more legitimate. In a culture that glorifies individual material success and applauds extreme competitive behavior in pursuit of success, inequality becomes a sign of success for those who win.

Controls that ensure compliance with inequality regimes have also become more effective and perhaps more various. With threats of downsizing and off-shoring, decreasing availability of well-paying jobs for clerical, service, and manual workers, and undermining of union strength and welfare state supports, protections against the loss of a living wage are eroded and employees become more vulnerable to the control of the wage system itself. That is, fear of loss of livelihood controls those who might challenge inequality.

CONCLUSION

* * *

Greater equality inside organizations is difficult to achieve during a period, such as the early years of the twenty-first century, in which employers are pushing for more inequality in pay, medical care, and retirement benefits and are using various tactics, such as downsizing and outsourcing, to reduce labor costs. Another major impediment to change within inequality regimes is the absence of broad social movements outside organizations agitating for such changes. In spite of all these difficulties, efforts at reducing inequality continue. Government regulatory agencies, the Equal Employment Opportunity Commission in particular, are still enforcing antidiscrimination laws that prohibit discrimination against specific individuals (see www.eeoc.gov/eeoc/statistics/). Resolutions of complaints through the courts may mandate some organizational policy changes, but these seem to be minimal. Campaigns to alter some inequality regimes are under way.

REFERENCES

Acker, Joan. 1989. *Doing comparable worth: Gender, class and pay equity.* Philadelphia: Temple University Press.

———. 1990. Hierarchies, jobs, and bodies: A theory of gendered organizations. *Gender & Society* 4:139–58.

———. 1991. Thinking about wages: The gendered wage gap in Swedish banks. *Gender & Society* 5:390–407.

———. 1994. The gender regime of Swedish banks. *Scandinavian Journal of Management* 10:117–30.

Acker, Joan, and Donald Van Houten. 1974. Differential recruitment and control: The sex structuring of organizations. *Administrative Science Quarterly* 19:152–63.

Adkins, Lisa. 1995. *Gendered work.* Buckingham, UK: Open University Press.

Barker, James R. 1993. Tightening the iron cage: Concertive control in self-managing teams. *Administrative Science Quarterly* 38:408–37.

Burawoy, Michael. 1979. *Manufacturing consent.* Chicago: University of Chicago Press.

Charles, Maria, and David B. Grusky. 2004. *Occupational ghettos: The worldwide segregation of women and men.* Stanford, CA: Stanford University Press.

Cockburn, Cynthia. 1985. *Machinery of dominance.* London: Pluto.

Ely, Robin J., and Debra E. Meyerson. 2000. Advancing gender equity in organizations: The challenge and importance of maintaining a gender narrative. *Organization* 7:589–608.

Enarson, Elaine. 1984. *Woods-working women: Sexual integration in the U.S. Forest Service.* Tuscaloosa: University of Alabama Press.

Ferree, Myra Max, and Patricia Yancey Martin, eds. 1995. *Feminist organizations.* Philadelphia: Temple University Press.

Figart, D. M., E. Mutari, and M. Power. 2002. *Living wages, equal wages.* London: Routledge.

Glenn, Evelyn Nakano. 2002. *Unequal freedom: How race and gender shaped American citizenship and labor.* Cambridge, MA: Harvard University Press.

Hearn, Jeff, and Wendy Parkin. 2001. *Gender, sexuality and violence in organizations.* London: Sage.

Hochschild, Arlie Russell. 1997. *The time bind: When work becomes home & home becomes work.* New York: Metropolitan Books.

Hossfeld, Karen J. 1994. Hiring immigrant women: Silicon Valley's "simple formula." In *Women of color in U.S. society,* edited by M. B. Zinn and B. T. Dill. Philadelphia: Temple University Press.

Jacobs, Jerry A., and Kathleen Gerson, 2004. *The time divide: Work, family, and gender inequality.* Cambridge, MA: Harvard University Press.

Korvajärvi, Päivi. 2003. "Doing gender"—Theoretical and methodological considerations. In *Where have all the structures gone? Doing gender in organizations, examples from Finland, Norway and Sweden,* edited by E. Gunnarsson, S. Andersson, A. V. Rosell, A. Lehto, and M. Salminen-Karlsson. Stockholm, Sweden: Center for Women's Studies, Stockholm University.

Kvande, Elin, and Bente Rasmussen. 1994. Men in male-dominated organizations and their encounter with women intruders. *Scandinavian Journal of Management* 10:163–74.

Martin, Joanne, and Debra Meyerson. 1998. Women and power: Conformity, resistance, and disorganized coaction. In *Power and influence in organizations,* edited by R. Kramer and M. Neale. Thousand Oaks. CA: Sage.

McIntosh, Peggy. 1995. White privilege and male privilege: A personal account of coming to see correspondences through work in women's studies. In *Race, class, and gender: An anthology,* 2nd ed., edited by M. L. Andersen and P. H. Collins. Belmont, CA: Wadsworth.

Mishel, L., J. Bernstein, and H. Boushey. 2003. *The state of working America 2002/2003.* Ithaca, NY: Cornell University Press.

Morgen, S., J. Acker, and J. Weigt. n.d. *Neo-Liberalism on the ground: Practising welfare reform.*

Perrow, Charles. 2002. *Organizing America.* Princeton, NJ: Princeton University Press.

Pierce, Jennifer L. 1995. *Gender trials: Emotional lives in contemporary law firms.* Berkeley: University of California Press.

Reskin, Barbara. 1998. *The realities of affirmative action in employment.* Washington, DC: American Sociological Association.

Ridgeway, Cecilia. 1997. Interaction and the conservation of gender inequality. *American Sociological Review* 62:218–35.

Royster, Dierdre A. 2003. *Race and the invisible hand: How white networks exclude Black men from blue-collar jobs.* Berkeley: University of California Press.

Salzinger, Leslie. 2003. *Genders in production: Making workers in Mexico's global factories.* Berkeley: University of California Press.

Scott, Ellen. 2000. Everyone against racism: Agency and the production of meaning in the anti racism practices of two feminist organizations. *Theory and Society* 29:785–819.

Spalter-Roth, Roberta, and Cynthia Deitch. 1999. I don't feel right-sized; I feel out-of-work sized. *Work and Occupations* 26:446–82.

Vallas, Steven P. 2003. Why teamwork fails: Obstacles to workplace change in four manufacturing plants. *American Sociological Review* 68:223–50.

Wajcman, Judy. 1998. *Managing like a man.* Cambridge, UK: Polity.

Wharton, Amy S. 2005. *The sociology of gender.* Oxford, UK: Blackwell.

Willis, Paul. 1977. *Learning to labor.* Farmborough, UK: Saxon House.

Introduction to Reading 32

In this article, Christine L. Williams, Chandra Muller, and Kristine Kilanski use Joan Acker's theory (from the previous reading) to examine the work experiences of women geoscientists in oil and gas companies. The 30 women they interviewed are highly educated (22 had master's degrees, and 8 had PhDs), ranged in age from 30 to 52 (average age 38), and worked in 14 different companies, including large global corporations such as Exxon Mobil, BP, and Shell. They used snowball sampling to locate the women they interviewed by asking women at professional meetings they attended to refer them to other women who held similar jobs. Through this process, they were also able to include three women who had left the industry. In-depth interviews with these women ranged from 1 to 2 hours. They also did observations at three professional meetings and interviewed three men supervisors. Their findings give us an inside look at the job experiences of women in STEM (science, technology, engineering, and mathematics; see also the article by Maria Charles in Chapter 4) and help us understand why women leave these fields.

1. Do men and women "do gender" in these professional fields, thus maintaining a system of inequality?

2. How does the "looser" style of "new management" practices in these powerful global corporations advantage or disadvantage women?

3. Using the findings from this study, explain why women engineers earn less than men.

GENDERED ORGANIZATIONS IN THE

NEW ECONOMY

Christine L. Williams, Chandra Muller, and Kristine Kilanski

After making spectacular strides toward gender equality in the twentieth century, women's progress in the workplace shows definite signs of slowing (England 2010). Although women have entered occupations previously closed to them, many jobs remain as gender segregated today as they were in 1950. At both the top and the bottom of the employment pyramid, women continue to lag behind men in terms of pay and authority, despite closing gender gaps in educational attainment and workplace seniority. What accounts for these persistent gender disparities?

To explain gender inequality at work, many sociologists draw on Joan Acker's (1990) theory of gendered organizations. Acker argued that gender inequality is tenacious because it is built into the structure of work organizations.

From Williams, Christine, Chandra Muller, and Kristine Kilanski. 2012. "Gendered Organizations in the New Economy." *Gender & Society 26*(4): 549–573.

Even the very definition of a "job" contains an implicit preference for male workers (Acker 1990). Employers prefer to hire people with few distractions outside of work who can loyally devote themselves to the organization. This preference excludes many women, given the likelihood that they hold primary care responsibilities for family members. Consequently, for many employers the "ideal worker" is a man (see also Williams 2001).

Acker (1990) further identified five processes that reproduce gender in organizations: the division of labor, cultural symbols, workplace interactions, individual identities, and organizational logic. The latter process—organizational logic—was at the center of Acker's original critique of gendered organizations (Acker 1990) and is the focus of this article. The concept of organizational logic draws attention to how hierarchies are rationalized and legitimized in organizations. It encompasses the logical systems of work rules, job descriptions, pay scales, and job evaluations that govern bureaucratic organizations. Acker describes organizational logic as the taken-for-granted policies and principles that managers use to exercise legitimate control over the workplace. Workers comply because they view these policies and principles as "natural" or normal business practices.

While others had previously identified organizational logic as key to the reproduction of class inequality, Acker's breakthrough identified it as a source of gender inequality as well, even though it appears gender neutral on the surface. . . .

For example, organizations supposedly use logical principles to develop job descriptions and determine pay rates. But Acker argues that managers often draw on gender stereotypes when undertaking these tasks, privileging qualities associated with men and masculinity that then become reified in organizational hierarchies. Through organizational logic, therefore, gender discourses are embedded in organizations, and gender inequality at work results.

A great deal of research supports Acker's theoretical claims (for a review, see Britton and Logan 2008). But in the decades since the article was published, the social organization of work has changed considerably. Starting in the 1970s, organizations began to experience downsizing, restructuring, computerization, and globalization (DiMaggio 2001; Kalleberg 2000; Vallas 2011). Referred to as "work transformation," this general and vast process of change is affecting the structure of work in the United States and around the world. Whereas in the past, many workers looked forward to a lifetime of loyal service to a single employer, workers in the so-called new economy expect to change employers frequently in search of better opportunities and in response to lay-offs, mergers, and downsizing. Organizational logic is changing, too. Under the former system, workers carried out narrow and specific tasks identified by their job descriptions and were evaluated and compensated by managers who controlled the labor process. Today, as corporations shed layers of management, work is increasingly organized into teams composed of workers with diverse skills who work with considerable discretion on time-bounded projects and are judged on results and outcomes, often by peers. Furthermore, in the new economy, standardized career "ladders"—with clearly demarcated rungs that lead to higher-paying and more responsible positions—are being eliminated or replaced by career maps, or "I-deals," which are individualized programs of career development. Networking has become a principal means through which workers identify opportunities for advancement both inside and outside their firms (Babcock and Laschever 2003; DiMaggio 2001; Osnowitz 2010; Powell 2001; Rousseau 2005; Vallas 2011).[1]

In this study, we seek to extend Acker's (1990) analysis and critique of gendered organizations by investigating how gender is embedded in the organizational logic of the new economy. Acker's theory explains how gender is embedded in traditional organizations that value and reward worker loyalty and that are characterized by standardized job descriptions, career ladders, and manager-controlled evaluations—features that do not characterize jobs in the new economy.

We investigate how organizational logic is gendered when work is precarious, teams instead of managers control the labor process, career maps replace career ladders, and future opportunities are identified primarily through networking.

GEOSCIENTISTS IN THE OIL AND GAS INDUSTRY

To investigate gendered organizations in the new economy, we draw upon our research on women geoscientists in the oil and gas industry. Women geoscientists have increased their numbers radically in recent decades, currently constituting about 45 percent of graduates with master's degrees in geology, the entry-level credential in the field (AGI 2011). Also, according to anecdotal data, women geoscientists are entering professional careers in industry in almost equal numbers as men. Despite these encouraging advances, there is a strong perception that women stall out in mid-career and eventually leave their jobs at the major companies (AAPG 2009). This pattern is not uncommon among women scientists in general (Preston 2004). The glass ceiling is firmly in place in the oil and gas industry, with very few women represented at the executive levels and on boards of directors (*Catalyst* 2011).

The oil and gas industry is an ideal setting to study gendered organizations in the new economy for several reasons. First, it is arguably the most powerful, global, essential, and lucrative industry in the world. In 2007, the largest oil and gas companies made roughly two trillion dollars (U.S.) in combined revenue and 150 billion dollars in profit (Pirog 2008). Despite its critical importance, few sociologists have examined the gender dynamics in this industry (see Miller 2004 for an exception). Second, the industry has a high demand for so-called knowledge workers (scientists and engineers), which is a defining feature of the new economy; one solution to the perceived shortage of these workers has been to increase the numbers of women in these fields (National Academy of Sciences 2010). Third,

and most importantly for our analysis, the industry has been in the forefront of implementing the new organizational logic (McKee, Mauthner, and Maclean 2000). Throughout the 80s and 90s, the industry experienced numerous mergers, leading to reorganization and downsizing that exacerbated the vulnerability of its workforce. Consistent with the general process of work transformation, the major corporations have altered the career structure for their professional workforce by institutionalizing career maps and teamwork. The expectation of frequent career moves has enhanced the importance of networking for professional success. These innovations make the oil and gas industry a paradigmatic case for investigating gendered organizations in the twenty-first century.

* * *

FINDINGS

Organizational changes associated with the new economy are reflected in the careers of geoscientists in the oil and gas industry. Gone is the expectation of a lifelong career spent in loyal service to a single employer. Oil and gas companies frequently expand and contract their workforce in response to economic cycles and mergers (Yergin 1993). . . . Job insecurity is described by [one] respondent as both a constant and a "very scary" feature of the oil and gas industry.

The constant threat of layoffs no doubt causes high levels of stress and performance pressures for geoscientists. But how is performance measured? In periods of downsizing and merging, how do individuals survive the periodic cuts and even succeed in the industry?

Given the work geoscientists are hired to do, it would seem that whoever finds the most oil and gas would receive the most rewards. Indeed, after a respondent drilled a successful well, headhunters tried to lure her away from her current company, offering incentives such as stock options. But corporations have good reason to be wary of using this particular metric of productivity, since it may incentivize geologists to overstate their claims, a risky and costly prospect for companies. To protect themselves from this lone wolf phenomenon and insure greater reliability, companies instituted the team structure. This geologist, who experienced both individual- and team-based work, explains the economic stakes:

> When I first started in the mid-80s, I was working an exploration play in northern Louisiana, and the engineer who was going to drill a well for me was based in Corpus Christi. I never met him. I would do my maps and put them in the mail because we didn't have electronic submission. We might have a few conference calls before we drilled a million dollar well. That was when it cost $50,000 a day to drill a well. Now a well in the Gulf of Mexico is a million dollars a day. And so, [changing to the team structure] was part of that. You had to be able to get people face-to-face. There was too much on the line from a risk standpoint, and from a financial standpoint.

In the experience of this geologist, teams produce more reliable results than do individuals working alone. With more people involved, she believes that companies get better advice on where to drill and also where not to drill, lessening their economic risks.

Teams are now a standard organizational form for scientists working in industry (Connelly and Middleton 1996). The Bureau of Labor Statistics (2009) identifies the ability to work on teams as an important feature of geoscientists' careers. The women we talked to worked on teams ranging in size from five to 20. Some teams were interdisciplinary, while others were composed of members with a single specialty, all of whom were investigating a particular "play" or geographical area for potential drilling. Individuals' team assignments typically last from three to five years, and many require relocation to a different city, oil field, and/or country. Each team is headed by a supervisor, typically a professional peer working alongside the rest of the team. Supervisors also move around to different teams

every few years. The result is a work organization in perpetual flux, with teams forming and disbanding, and team members and supervisors constantly circulating around the country and, indeed, all over the globe.

Even though work is team based and essentially collaborative, careers are still individual. Raises, promotions, and opportunities are allocated to individuals, not to teams (although team members can receive additional bonuses if their collective results contribute to a company's profits). Out of this particular context, oil and gas companies replaced career ladders and standardized job descriptions with career maps—individualized programs for career development. A career map establishes goals and sets expectations that are then used to monitor a worker's productivity and evaluate his or her performance. The supervisor plays a central role in crafting workers' career maps and making sure that they have the tools to achieve their goals. As the primary channel to management, the supervisor identifies high performers on the team, recommends raises and bonuses, and determines the quality of future placements. Thus, individual workers must gain the support of their supervisors in order to further their careers in the industry.

A second major pathway to success in the oil and gas industry is through networking. In many of the large corporations, professionals are assigned mentors for their first three to five years, but by mid-career, we were told, they are basically left on their own to find support and encouragement as well as opportunities for career growth. Networking is viewed by respondents as the principal means to this end. Networks can be internal or external, formal or informal. Through these networks professionals gain exposure for lateral moves (after layoffs) and for leadership opportunities.

The new organizational logic appears gender neutral on the surface. Some have argued that because the new system of teams, career maps, and networking is less rigid than the older system of standardized career ladders and job descriptions, it may be more compatible with women's careers (e.g., Hewlett 2007). In fact, the transition to the new economy has taken place at the same time that major corporations have embraced gender and racial/ethnic diversity (Eisenstein 2009). The giant oil and gas companies tout their efforts to recruit women and minority men. Both Chevron and BP, for example, feature women scientists in recent publicity campaigns. Nevertheless, as we explain in the remainder of this article, these new forms may explain persistent patterns of gender inequality. . . .

Teamwork

In some recent studies, the team structure has been found to attenuate gender inequality in organizations (Kalev 2009; Plankey Videla 2006; Reskin 2002; Smith-Doerr 2004). However, we found that women may be disadvantaged on male-dominated teams. By the very nature of teamwork, the individual's contribution to the final product is obscured. Yet because careers are still individual, members of the team must engage in self-promotion to receive credit and rewards for their personal effort. Our study suggests that women encounter difficulties when promoting their accomplishments and gaining the credibility of their supervisors and other team members. This finding is consistent with experimental studies showing that, in general, women are given disproportionately less credit than men for the success they achieve when they work on teams in male-dominated environments (Heilman and Haynes 2005).

Because female workers are not given the benefit of the doubt in assessments of their work efforts by others, it is especially important that they are willing and able to tout their contributions to team accomplishments. Many of the women we interviewed are conscious of the importance of self-promotion, though they are not always secure in their ability to do it effectively. One geoscientist shared her misgivings about her own presentation skills, as well as her hunch that presentation skills may be

more important than scientific ability to get ahead in industry:

> I don't know especially if you have to be as good, or if you have to be just as loud and belligerent as the other people. You definitely/the personality here is, to prove your point, you have to bang the table sometimes. I think women are more reluctant to do that. It's not me to do that.

This woman attributes her reluctance to "bang the table" to her personality, which she suggests is a reflection of an essential gender difference. But the following quote, from the only woman geoscientist in her entire division, indicates that women may be regarded negatively when they promote themselves:

> It's kind of interesting that I feel that I have to fight more to keep promoting what my expertise is. And it keeps getting kind of pushed back. The other people with less expertise in structural geology, they seem to get a little more recognition. Now, they've been working for the company for years. But still, I'm the one that has the expertise in that area. I just don't know how to do it. You don't want to be the one that yells and screams all the time. It's a delicate balance to keep promoting yourself.

Virtually everyone we interviewed talked about the fine line, or "delicate balance," between being assertive and being a "bitch." This perennial dilemma faced by women in the workplace is exacerbated in a team structure that requires workers to engage in assertive self-promotion in order to achieve recognition.

One woman reflected on her experience speaking at a partner meeting, at which she was the only woman, and youngest person, in attendance:

> I had to stand up and tell why I thought the well location should be somewhere and I could absolutely tell that no one was taking me seriously. They didn't care what I had to say—it was very obvious. Part of that I'm sure is being young, part of it was being the first time I had to stand up and tell them that. Because now, after eleven years, I can stand up and I can talk [laughs], but you have

to get to that point. You have to know your stuff. I know that I have to cross every "t" and dot every "i," because if I don't, someone is going to pick it apart. There will be some man in the audience that wants to heckle you because he can—and I know that.

As this observation suggests, the difficulties that women encounter with self-promotion may be compounded by age. The following quote also indicates that younger women may face additional hurdles when attempting to bring attention to their accomplishments:

I think automatically that anything I say is questioned. My supervisor, in my first go-round through the performance, told me I had to speak up—I have to believe what I'm saying, and I can't let them railroad me . . . which, I think he feels is more of an age thing. You get some credibility with age. I'm sure some people think you get more credibility being a guy. [I've got] kind of the short stick on both of those.

Her supervisor admonished her for not being assertive enough. But she perceived that, even when she did speak up, her views were constantly challenged because she was the only woman and the youngest member of the team.

At the professional meetings we attended, we observed that age is often treated as a status group in the industry. For example, when executives discussed "diversity" goals at their companies, they included age as well as gender and race/ethnicity. Layoffs that occurred in the 1980s and late 1990s were reported to have contributed to a large age gap among industry geoscientists (with a virtual absence of workers aged 35–45). Some of the geoscientists that we interviewed believed the age gap contributed to tension within teams. Young geoscientists do not always receive the recognition they seek from the older generation nearing retirement.

However, youth tends to operate differently based on gender and race. Youth can convey certain advantages to men, who may become the protégés of senior men (Roper 1994). In contrast, young women struggle to get noticed in positive

ways. Some young women described feeling sexualized by men in their work teams. Others told us that they succeeded only because they fell into the "daughter" role with senior male mentors. Both roles are constraining in the quest for professional credibility. As Ollilainen and Calasanti (2007) have argued, family metaphors can disadvantage women who work on teams by encouraging a gendered division of labor and compelling women to engage in uncompensated emotional labor. Furthermore, in white male-dominated teams, metaphorical family roles may be available only to white women (Bell and Nkomo 2001).

Minority women may be disadvantaged compared to white men and women in additional ways, according to one Asian American woman we interviewed:

It's all sorts of behaviors and soft skills that they look at for leadership potential. And a lot of the Asian people don't do well in those because we're culturally expected to be modest and we're culturally expected to not stand out. It's OK for us to be introverted or quiet. You actually get respected for being quiet, a man of few words. But at [my oil and gas company], that is not how you get success.

This statement suggests that self-promotion may have different meanings for racial/ethnic minority men and women. Furthermore, other research suggests that those who engage in it may be viewed negatively by white colleagues and supervisors (Harvey Wingfield 2010).

Interestingly, we observed that women who worked in gender-balanced teams (absent in some companies) felt like they received greater recognition and respect for their contributions. If correct, this observation would confirm theories of tokenism that predict less bias in numerically balanced work groups (Kanter 1977). But how do teams achieve this numerical balance? Supervisors play a key role in determining the composition of the work group. However, as we suggest in the next section, supervisor's discretionary power is not necessarily exercised in the interest of gender equality.

In sum, in order to achieve recognition and rewards for their contributions, individuals working on teams must be willing and able to stand out from the group and advertise their accomplishments. Our findings suggest that this apparently gender neutral requirement can discriminate against women. As other researchers have found (Babcock and Laschever 2003; Bowles, Babcock, and Lai 2007; Broadbridge 2004), self-promotion can have negative meanings and consequences for women in male-dominated environments. When work is organized on the teamwork model, gender inequality is the likely result.

Career Maps

In many companies, career maps have replaced standardized career ladders for highly valued professionals. The purpose of a career map is to chart an individualized course of professional development that incorporates both the company's needs and the personal aspirations of the worker. Sometimes called "I-deals" (Rousseau 2005), these idiosyncratic arrangements often include employees' plans for reduced or flexible hours (e.g., to accommodate family needs) in addition to their career ambitions. Career maps are normally negotiated with supervisors, and they evolve over time.

Respondents were mostly positive about career maps because of the perception that they allow workers to manage their own careers. This was preferable to having, in the words of one geologist, "big brother" determine their futures with a one-size-fits-all set of career expectations (see also Hewlett 2007). However, in practice, the geoscientists we interviewed experienced several problems with career maps, stemming from the perceived ineptitude or gender bias of their supervisors. First, difficulties can arise if the criteria drawn are too vague or subjective. A woman with a PhD in geophysics explained that some workers, and especially new employees, struggled to figure out their job responsibilities. Supervisors sometimes assigned work without explaining the steps necessary or directing new employees to the resources needed to complete their assigned tasks. In fact, it wasn't until right before she left the industry that [one] particular woman felt she understood the "work flow." . . .

Without standardized job descriptions, workers can experience confusion about their job duties. Developing excellent communication skills becomes mandatory in this new context. One geologist attributed her success in the industry to the fact that she has "effectively communicated my career plan to the right people." She said, "Not everyone is so fortunate. . . . I do know of some people who haven't had as much influence on where they have gone. But when I've spoken with them, I really feel like they have not effectively communicated what they wanted to do." From her perspective, it is up to individual workers—not the corporation—to ensure that careers stay on the right track.

A second problem with career maps is that decisions about raises, promotions, and other rewards based on this system can appear arbitrary. This woman shared her confusion and frustration that her husband—who had started his job around the same time she did—had been promoted "a lot faster" than she had:

> And I've seen that, just on the side, watching. . . . I'm like, "OK, what are you doing differently that I need to do to get this going?" He said, "Nothing. I haven't done anything." He is a quiet guy by nature. So he didn't know why he was getting promoted himself. And I thought that was very interesting.

The lack of common job descriptions and career ladders contributes to uncertainty about why some individuals receive recognition and others do not. Because career maps are tailored to the individual—and because most companies prohibit employees from sharing salary information—it is difficult for workers to compare their career progress with others.[2]

Third, geoscientists perceive problems with career maps when supervisors do not actively advocate for them. A 35-year-old geologist working at a major described the importance of supervisors in obtaining good project assignments. . . .

This worker was grateful when a supervisor several levels above her recommended her for a job opening. Even though she didn't end up receiving that job, she felt "fortunate" to have been considered. She wondered aloud, "How do I get that to happen again?"

When opportunities are experienced as a windfall, workers are unsure how to advance themselves. At the same time, workers felt pressured to take any opportunities presented by a supervisor. Turning down more than one assignment was believed to foreclose them from receiving any in the future.

Without a supportive supervisor, careers can flounder. One geologist found herself in a precarious position when her supervisor left the company and another group subsumed her team. The manager of this group was an engineer rather than a geologist, which this respondent saw as a disadvantage. Not only did the person in charge of assigning and judging her work not understand it, he was already responsible for the careers of a large number of people. Without a supervisor advocating for her, this geologist said she felt "unnerved" and stressed out because she didn't know what her next assignment or career move would be.

While all of these issues with supervisors' discretion over career maps can impact both men and women equally, women may be especially disadvantaged if their supervisors harbor gender biases. As we know from previous research, supervisors who harbor biases against women (or in favor of men) can easily derail women's careers, even in the sciences (DiTomaso et al. 2007). Virtually every woman we interviewed encountered an individual supervisor at some point in her career who stymied her advancement. One geoscientist felt her career at a mid-size company was progressing well until she was assigned a new supervisor. The new supervisor would accept her work only if she had it pre-approved by a male employee on her team. . . .

Gender bias is also expressed in supervisors' decisions about whom to hire into their teams. Studies suggest that managers favor people who are like themselves, a process known as "homosocial reproduction" (Elliott and Smith 2004; Kanter 1977). Gender differences emerge because women are rarely in a position to make personnel decisions. Even when women are in a supervisory position, their hiring decisions may be scrutinized. One female supervisor hired a woman to her team. When asked if it was controversial to pick a woman, she said that she "got that comment" but was able to defend herself because she had offered the job to a man first. She said, "I wasn't out looking for a female. It turns out we got a female in the group. In this particular case, she is the best fit." Thus, she was put on the defensive for a practice that is common among male supervisors. When gender bias appears to favor women, it is noticed and controversial (a topic we return to in the next section).

Part of developing a career map involves planning for maternity leave and flexible schedules, including part-time. Supervisors often have a great deal of control over these arrangements. One woman said the human resources (HR) department at the major company where she worked "purposefully wrote the rules [regarding flex time] kind of in a gray zone," leaving them open to the interpretation of supervisors. Smaller companies, which often lack formal HR departments, may give supervisors even more discretion than the larger companies do. However, a number of women working at majors gave examples of how supervisory discretion could impact workers' knowledge and ability to take advantage of flexible working options. . . .

This situation captures a paradox at the heart of career maps. On the one hand, they enable greater flexibility in career development, which some argue is in women's best interests (Hewlett 2007). As this geologist attests, "everybody" is unlikely to "want the same thing." On the other hand, if designing a career map that accommodates motherhood depends on having a sympathetic supervisor, potential gender bias is built into the organization. The lack of a "consistent, accepted solution" is frustrating and anxiety producing. . . .

Those we interviewed who had experience working in European offices experienced standardized maternity leave policies that were part of their host country's social welfare system. However, those who worked for European companies in the U.S. faced similarly limited options as those working in U.S. companies, with only supervisor-approved accommodations for maternity leave and part-time schedules available to them.

Because this study was motivated in part to understand women's attrition from the industry, we asked respondents their opinions about why women leave. Many speculated that it was because women tend to "opt out" of the labor force to bear and raise children, which they considered a deeply personal choice. Interestingly, few could cite specific examples. And the three women we talked to who left the industry did not regard children or family as their primary reason for leaving. Nevertheless, we contend that the institution of career maps, which grants supervisors the ability to negotiate family accommodations on a case-by-case basis, may leave mothers without viable and meaningful alternatives. Furthermore, in an industry characterized by constant mergers and downsizing, we suspect that some women may use the framework of "opting out" as a face-saving way to explain a decision to leave prior to an impending layoff. Unfortunately, this framing reinforces the stereotype that women naturally prioritize family over careers and absolves organizations of the responsibility for structuring the workplace in more equitable ways.

In sum, career maps give supervisors a great deal of discretion over individuals' career development. In the absence of accountability or an effective affirmative action program, supervisory discretion can be a breeding ground for gender bias (Reskin and McBrier 2000). Given the difficulty of comparing career progression in this context, patterns of gender and racial disparities may be obscured. Nevertheless, the logic of career maps encourages workers to blame themselves, not the organization, when their careers are stymied.

Networking

Virtually everyone we talked to said that networks are fundamental to achieving professional success. In an industry where layoffs are common and anticipated, workers must rely on their formal and informal networks to survive periodic cuts and to identify new opportunities. Yet, as we know from numerous research studies, networks are highly gendered and racialized (Burt 1998; Loscocco et al. 2009; McGuire 2002; Smith 2007). A geophysicist who worked for several large companies and who now owns her own consulting business explained that many people, and women especially, "work hard as opposed to work smart." Networking, rather than simply doing one's job well, was, she believed, the key to success in the industry. She reflected on the importance of this knowledge to boosting one's career: "If I had known then what I know now, I would be CEO of a company."

In the male-dominated oil and gas industry, not surprisingly, the most powerful networks are almost exclusively male. Often these are organized around golf or hunting (Morgan and Martin 2006). The women we interviewed provided classic accounts of exclusion from these groups.

> The men at upper management were quite comfortable making seat-of-the-pants decisions with each other, and they trusted each other. They had lunch together, they played golf together, they trusted each other. If somebody is going to make a seat-of-the-pants decision, the other guy's going to say "fine." A woman comes in and tries to make a seat-of-the-pants decision, same process, same gut kind of thing, you're not going to be trusted, you're not going to be believed.

Some women perceive that men's networks, sustained through company-sponsored sports and hunting/fishing trips, are not considered networks at all, even though in these spaces men are likely to develop strong relationships of mutual trust (see also DiTomaso et al. 2007). In one egregious case, a woman described how female strippers were positioned at each putting green at an annual company-sponsored golf tournament. While some women have no interest in attending these networking events, others try to fit in because of their critical importance to success in the industry. One independent producer told us that although she doesn't play golf, she makes it a point to "ride in the cart." Another woman tried to join her male colleagues' fantasy football league. Although they were resistant to letting a woman join, she was finally allowed when one man agreed to be her partner (to the others' chagrin).

In response to this exclusion, and in acknowledgment of the importance of networking for career development, some corporations have formed official women's networks. However, these networks have dubious status in corporations and joining may not be in women's best interest. For instance, DiTomaso and colleagues argue that "special mentoring programs for women set up by companies may be a disadvantage for those who use them" (DiTomaso et al. 2007, 198). The women we interviewed concurred, viewing women's corporate-sponsored networks as neither powerful nor especially useful. . . .

One problem [mentioned] was that the company brought together all women from the company, rather than just geoscientists. While she saw value in allowing women to network from across the company, she thought the other women came from "a little bit of a different perspective." Moreover, this type of networking is unlikely to result in future opportunities for a geologist.

At some companies, the women's network is not limited to women, the rationale being that in the interests of "equal opportunity," women should not receive "special treatment." Consequently, when women's groups are formed, they rarely address issues concerning discrimination or inequality. Topics like work-family balance are sometimes addressed, but in a way that does not challenge the structure or policies of the organization. For example, a few years after joining the major at which she works, one respondent and her colleagues started an online "family support network" in order to provide employees with children a chance to connect and give them a place to ask questions and receive advice. This "grass-roots network" received immense support from top managers and has since become institutionalized. . . .

Importantly, this network requires no resources from the employer, nor does it

challenge the company's limited support for new parents. Yet the existence of the network makes the company appear to be doing something to promote gender equity.

Furthermore, while some women appreciate this focus on work-family balance, others find it alienating because they do not have children, and feel oppressed by the assumption that they do. For example, one woman spoke of receiving an invitation to a "women in science" session at a local seismic conference. She explained that she was originally excited to hear the experiences of "wicked smart" women scientists talking about how to thrive in a male-dominated environment. Instead she was disappointed that the group focus would be on motherhood. She added, "I don't tend to seek out female-dominated groups because you inadvertently end up sitting next to someone talking about their kids—which is fine. I can hear about your kids for a while. But I don't want to have kids."

On the other hand, some convey more than a hint of cynicism about corporate-sponsored events that highlight the accomplishments of senior women. One woman expressed frustration that corporate diversity events seemed to feature the same senior women retelling their success stories. She explained, "Marilyn is [the company's] poster child. But for every Marilyn there are fifteen women who are not getting what Marilyn gets"—referring to the same opportunities, exposure, and access to powerful networks.

Given the perceived limitations of official women's networks, some women turn to informal networks instead. Unfortunately, these also occupy a highly dubious space in the corporate world. They may be perceived as mere outlets for complaining, venting, or "bitching." A woman who organized a weekend retreat for a group of senior executive women was criticized by detractors for arranging a "ladies' boondoggle," an accusation she felt was "outrageous" because men do equivalent outings all the time.

Not surprisingly, some women are reluctant to disclose their interest in forming or joining a women's group. One woman talked about returning from an AAPG [American Association of Petroleum Geologists] event with the idea of starting a women's mentoring group to mimic those in the larger companies. She and a small group of women had started to organize, but had decided it was in their best interest to keep their intentions secret. This woman expressed palpable fear that if found out, the women involved would suffer negative repercussions since company policy strictly forbids any discussion of salary or contracts among employees. These women knew they were taking a chance by organizing a women's group, so they were planning to hold their meeting 200 miles away in order to avoid detection.

Networking has always been important for professional development. In the new economy, strong networks are needed not only to thrive but to survive periodic downsizing and layoffs. The heightened importance of networking places women geoscientists in a paradoxical position: They are often excluded from powerful men's networks, yet women's formal networks, when they exist, are not powerful and may actually have negative consequences for women's career development. Women's informal networks may be forced to operate under the radar. Because of the centrality of networking, the resulting gender inequality is thus embedded in the organizational logic of the new economy.

CONCLUSION

The traditional career model, in which a worker spends his or her entire career with one employer, in some, cases climbing a defined career ladder, is on the decline (Vallas 2011). Workers today expect to switch jobs and employers frequently throughout their careers. While some moves are in response to better opportunities, in many cases they are the result of corporate practices, common to some industries, that make workers vulnerable to job loss.

The new career model, created by corporations to reduce their economic risk and responsibility for workers, has several defining features. Under this new model, employees are evaluated based on individualized standards developed in conjunction with their direct supervisors, rather than by a standardized assessment tool. Although workers are evaluated on an individual basis, work is typically performed by self-managed teams. As it is difficult to determine individuals' level of effort, supervisors have a great deal of discretionary power in rewarding employees for a job well done (i.e., giving employees good team placements). The proliferation of career maps may obscure inequality in the pace of career progress. Given the level of job insecurity, the ability to maintain large networks to identify job opportunities inside and outside of the organization becomes critically important for successful careers.

We examined the careers of geoscientists in the oil and gas industry—an industry at the forefront of implementing these organizational changes—to explore the gendered consequences of these job features. Our research suggests that teams, career maps, and networking reflect gendered organizational logics. To excel at teamwork, individuals must be able to engage in self-promotion, which can be difficult for women in male-dominated environments—even though they are the ones who may need to do it the most. In contexts where supervisors have discretion over careers, gender bias can play a significant role in the allocation of rewards. And networking is gendered in ways that disadvantage women.

These features of work organization are not new, and, in fact, previous research has shown that all three of these elements can be problematic for women (Bowles, Babcock, and Lai 2007; Broadbridge 2004; Burt 1998; Loscocco et al. 2009; McGuire 2002; Ollilainen and Calasanti 2007). This article's contribution has been to connect them to work transformation. Previously, gender inequality has been institutionalized (in part) through the mechanisms of career ladders, job descriptions, and formal evaluations (Acker 1990). In the new economy, these elements of organizational logic have been replaced by teams, career maps, and networking. These have become principal mechanisms through which gender inequality is reproduced in the new economy. . . .

Our findings suggest that addressing workplace gender inequality in the twenty-first century will require focused attention on transforming these job features, or altering their consequences for women. For example standard options for organizing career maps should be made available to workers. In the interest of gender equity, workers should be informed of the I-deals and salaries of their peers. In addition, supervisors should be made accountable to diversity goals, and incentivized to encourage workers to use company flexibility options. While companies should encourage networking activities, all corporate-sponsored events must include women and minority men, and informal male-only social events must somehow be made culturally taboo. These are the sorts of changes that we believe will enhance the careers of women scientists in the new economy.

When Joan Acker (1990) first articulated the organizational logic underlying gendered organizations, she was operating under the assumptions of the traditional career model. Those assumptions no longer apply in many organizations. Organizations are still gendered, but the mechanisms for reproducing gender disparities are different than those in the traditional career path. By exploring women's experiences of work in the new economy, we add an essential but previously missing dimension to the critique of work transformation. By paying close attention to the new organizational logic, we hope that effective policies can be devised to enhance gender equality in the twenty-first century workplace.

Notes

1. These descriptions of "old" and "new" forms of work organizations refer to trends that in actual practice can overlap considerably, so they should be treated as "ideal types" in the Weberian sense.

2. The proliferation of career maps may also make it difficult for human resource departments to detect patterns (and potential disparities) in men's and women's career development.

References

AAPG (American Association of Petroleum Geologists). 2009. Results from the American Association of Petroleum Geologists (AAPG) Professional Women in the Earth Sciences (PROWESS) Survey. American Association of Petroleum Geologists. June 7, 2011, http://www.aapg.org/committees/prowess/AAPG_Jun3.final.pdf.

Acker, Joan. 1990. Hierarchies, jobs, bodies: A theory of gendered organizations. *Gender & Society* 4:139–58.

AGI (American Geological Institute). 2011. Currents 30–35: Minorities, temporary residents, and gender parity in the geosciences. June 27, 2011, http://www.agiweb.org/workforce/webinar-videos/video_currents30–35.html.

Babcock, L., and S. Laschever. 2003. *Women don't ask: Negotiation and the gender divide.* Princeton, NJ: Princeton University Press.

Bell, E. E., and S. Nkomo. 2001. *Our separate ways: Black and white women and the struggle for professional identity.* Boston: Harvard Business School Press.

Bowles, H. R., Babcock, L., and L Lai. 2007. Social incentives for gender differences in the propensity to initiate negotiations: Sometimes it does hurt to ask. *Organizational Behavior and Human Decision Processes* 103:84–103.

Britton, D., and L. Logan. 2008. Gendered organizations: Progress and prospects. *Sociology Compass* 2:107–21.

Broadbridge, A. 2004. It's not what you know, it's who you know. *Journal of Management Development* 23:551–62.

Bureau of Labor Statistics. 2009. Geoscientists and hydrologists. December 13, 2011, http://www.bls.gov/oco/ocos312.htm.

Burt, Ronald S. 1998. The gender of social capital. *Rationality and Society* 10:5–46.

Catalyst. 2011. Women in U.S. mining, quarrying, and oil and gas extraction. September 12, 2011, http://www.catalyst.org/publication/503/women-in-us-mining-quarrying-and-oil-gas-extraction.

Connelly, J. D., and J. C. Middleton. 1996. Personal and professional skills for engineers: One industry's perspective. *Engineering Science and Education Journal* 5:139–42.

DiMaggio, Paul. 2001. *The twenty-first century firm.* Princeton, NJ: Princeton University press.

DiTomaso, N., C. Post, R. Smith, G. Farris, and R. Cordero. 2007. The effects of structural position on allocation and evaluation decisions for scientists and engineers in industrial R&D. *Administrative Science Quarterly* 52:175–207.

Elliott, J., and R. Smith. 2004. Race, gender, and workplace power. *American Sociological Review* 69:365–86.

England, Paula. 2010. The gender revolution: Uneven and stalled. *Gender & Society* 24:149–66.

Harvey Wingfield, Adia. 2010. Are some emotions marked "whites only"? Racialized feeling rules in professional workplaces. *Social Problems* 57:251–68.

Heilman, M.E., and M.C. Haynes. 2005. No credit where credit is due: Attributional rationalization of women's success in male-female teams. *Journal of Applied Psychology* 90:905–16.

Hewlett, Sylvia A. 2007. *Off-ramps and on-ramps: Keeping talented women on the road to success.* Boston, MA: Harvard Business School Publishing.

Kalev, Alexandra. 2009. Cracking the glass cages? Restructuring and ascriptive inequality at work. *American Journal of Sociology* 114:1591–1643.

Kalleberg, Arne. 2000. Nonstandard employment relations. *Annual Review of Sociology* 26:341–65.

Kanter, Rosabeth Moss. 1977. *Men and women of the corporation.* New York: Basic.

Loscocco, K., S. M. Monnat, G. Moore, and K. B. Lauber. 2009. Enterprising women: A comparison of women's and men's small business networks. *Gender & Society* 23:388–411.

McGuire, G. M. 2002. Gender, race, and the shadow structure: A study of informal networks and inequality in a work organization. *Gender & Society* 16:303–22.

McKee, L., N. Mauthner, and C. Maclean. 2000. Family friendly policies and practices in the oil and gas industry: Employer's perspectives. *Work, Employment and Society* 14:557–71.

Miller, Gloria E. 2004. Frontier masculinity in the oil industry: The experience of women engineers. *Gender; Work and Organization* 11:47–73.

Morgan, L., and K. Martin. 2006. Taking women professionals out of the office: The case of women in sales. *Gender & Society* 20:108–28.

National Academy of Sciences. 2010. *Rising above the gathering storm, revisited: Rapidly approaching category 5.* Washington, DC: National Academies Press.

Ollilainen, M., and T. Calasanti. 2007. Metaphors at work: Maintaining the salience of gender in self-managing teams. *Gender & Society* 21:5–27.

Osnowitz, Debra. 2010. *Freelancing expertise: Contract professionals in the new economy.* Ithaca, NY: ILR Press.

Pirog, Robert. 2008. *Oil industry profit review 2007.* Washington, DC: Congressional Research Service. September 1, 2011, assets.opencrs.com/rpts/RL34437_20080404.pdf.

Plankey Videla, Nancy. 2006. Gendered contradictions: Managers and women workers in self-managed teams. *Research in the Sociology of Work* 16:85–116.

Powell, Walter W. 2001. The capitalist firm in the 21st century: Emerging patterns in western enterprise. In *The twenty-first century firm,* edited by Paul DiMaggio. Princeton, NJ: Princeton University Press.

Preston, Anne E. 2004. *Leaving science. Occupational exit from science careers.* New York: Russell Sage Foundation.

Reskin, Barbara. 2002. Rethinking employment discrimination and its remedies. In *The new economic sociology: Developments in an emerging field,* edited by M. F. Guillen, R. Collins, P. England, and M. Meyer. New York: Russell Sage.

Reskin, B., and D. McBrier. 2000. Why not ascription? Organizations' employment of male and female managers. *American Sociological Review* 65:210–33.

Roper, Michael. 1994. *Masculinity and the British organization man since 1945.* Oxford: Oxford University Press.

Rousseau, Denise. 2005. *I-deals: Idiosyncratic deals employees bargain for themselves.* Armonk, NY: M. E. Sharpe.

Smith, Sandra. 2007. *Lone pursuit: Distrust and defensive individualism among the Black poor.* New York: Russell Sage.

Smith-Doerr, Laurel. 2004. *Women's work: Gender equality versus hierarchy in the life sciences.* Boulder, CO: Lynne Rienner.

Vallas, Steven. 2011. *Work: A critique.* Boston: Polity Books.

Williams, Joan. 2001. *Unbending gender: Why family and work conflict and what to do about it.* New York: Oxford University Press.

Yergin, Daniel. 1993. *The prize: The epic quest for oil, money, and power.* New York: Free Press.

Introduction to Reading 33

Sociologists and others use the term *glass ceiling* to describe the barriers to promotion and advancement that women face in the world of work. At the same time, however, it is argued that men have a glass escalator, particularly men employed in what are traditionally women's jobs. In this article, Adia Harvey Wingfield describes the glass escalator and gives an overview of the research on men in traditionally female occupations. While men make up 8% of all nurses, the percentage of nurses who are Black men is unknown. Therefore, this study helps us understand the intersections of race and gender and how the experiences of Black men differ from those of White men in previous studies. Harvey Wingfield's study gives insight into the various ways race and gender intersect to discriminate against Black men in the workplace.

1. How are the experiences of the Black men she studied different from the results of previous studies of White men on the glass escalator?

2. Do Black male nurses do masculinity differently than White male nurses? Why or why not?

3. What forms of discrimination are described in this article? What would you recommend to eradicate such discrimination?

RACIALIZING THE GLASS ESCALATOR

RECONSIDERING MEN'S EXPERIENCES WITH WOMEN'S WORK

Adia Harvey Wingfield

Sociologists who study work have long noted that jobs are sex segregated and that this segregation creates different occupational experiences for men and women (Charles and Grusky 2004). Jobs predominantly filled by women often require "feminine" traits such as nurturing, caring, and empathy, a fact that means men confront perceptions that they are unsuited for the requirements of these jobs. Rather than having an adverse effect on their occupational experiences, however, these assumptions facilitate men's entry into better paying, higher status positions, creating what Williams (1995) labels a "glass escalator" effect.

The glass escalator model has been an influential paradigm in understanding the experiences of men who do women's work. Researchers have identified this process among men nurses, social workers, paralegals, and librarians and have cited its pervasiveness as evidence of men's consistent advantage in the workplace, such that even in jobs where men are numerical minorities

Harvey Wingfield, Adia. 2009. "Racializing the Glass Escalator: Reconsidering Men's Experiences With Women's Work." *Gender & Society* 23(1): 5–26. Published by Sage Publications on behalf of Sociologists for Women in Society.

they are likely to enjoy higher wages and faster promotions (Floge and Merrill 1986; Heikes 1991; Pierce 1995; Williams 1989, 1995). Most of these studies implicitly assume a racial homogenization of men workers in women's professions, but this supposition is problematic for several reasons. For one, minority men are not only present but are actually overrepresented in certain areas of reproductive work that have historically been dominated by white women (Duffy 2007). Thus, research that focuses primarily on white men in women's professions ignores a key segment of men who perform this type of labor. Second, and perhaps more important, conclusions based on the experiences of white men tend to overlook the ways that intersections of race and gender create different experiences for different men. While extensive work has documented the fact that white men in women's professions encounter a glass escalator effect that aids their occupational mobility (for an exception, see Snyder and Green 2008), few studies, if any, have considered how this effect is a function not only of gendered advantage but of racial privilege as well.

In this article, I examine the implications of race–gender intersections for minority men employed in a female-dominated, feminized occupation, specifically focusing on Black men in nursing. Their experiences doing "women's work" demonstrate that the glass escalator is a racialized as well as gendered concept.

THEORETICAL FRAMEWORK

In her classic study *Men and Women of the Corporation,* Kanter (1977) offers a groundbreaking analysis of group interactions. Focusing on high-ranking women executives who work mostly with men, Kanter argues that those in the extreme numerical minority are tokens who are socially isolated, highly visible, and adversely stereotyped. Tokens have difficulty forming relationships with colleagues and often are excluded from social networks that provide mobility. Because of their low numbers, they are

also highly visible as people who are different from the majority, even though they often feel invisible when they are ignored or overlooked in social settings. Tokens are also stereotyped by those in the majority group and frequently face pressure to behave in ways that challenge and undermine these stereotypes. Ultimately, Kanter argues that it is harder for them to blend into the organization and to work effectively and productively, and that they face serious barriers to upward mobility.

Kanter's (1977) arguments have been analyzed and retested in various settings and among many populations. Many studies, particularly of women in male-dominated corporate settings, have supported her findings. Other work has reversed these conclusions, examining the extent to which her conclusions hold when men were the tokens and women the majority group. These studies fundamentally challenged the gender neutrality of the token, finding that men in the minority fare much better than do similarly situated women. In particular, this research suggests that factors such as heightened visibility and polarization do not necessarily disadvantage men who are in the minority. While women tokens find that their visibility hinders their ability to blend in and work productively, men tokens find that their conspicuousness can lead to greater opportunities for leadership and choice assignments (Floge and Merrill 1986; Heikes 1991). Studies in this vein are important because they emphasize organizations—and occupations—as gendered institutions that subsequently create dissimilar experiences for men and women tokens (see Acker 1990).

In her groundbreaking study of men employed in various women's professions, Williams (1995) further develops this analysis of how power relationships shape the ways men tokens experience work in women's professions. Specifically, she introduces the concept of the glass escalator to explain men's experiences as tokens in these areas. Like Floge and Merrill (1986) and Heikes (1991), Williams finds that men tokens do not experience the isolation, visibility, blocked access to social networks, and stereotypes in the same ways that women tokens do. In contrast, Williams argues that even though they are in the minority, processes are in place that actually facilitate their opportunity and advancement. Even in culturally feminized occupations, then, men's advantage is built into the very structure and everyday interactions of these jobs so that men find themselves actually struggling to remain in place. For these men, "despite their intentions, they face invisible pressures to move up in their professions. Like being on a moving escalator, they have to work to stay in place" (Williams 1995, 87).

The glass escalator term thus refers to the "subtle mechanisms in place that enhance [men's] positions in [women's] professions" (Williams 1995, 108). These mechanisms include certain behaviors, attitudes, and beliefs men bring to these professions as well as the types of interactions that often occur between these men and their colleagues, supervisors, and customers. Consequently, even in occupations composed mostly of women, gendered perceptions about men's roles, abilities, and skills privilege them and facilitate their advancement. The glass escalator serves as a conduit that channels men in women's professions into the uppermost levels of the occupational hierarchy. Ultimately, the glass escalator effect suggests that men retain consistent occupational advantages over women, even when women are numerically in the majority (Budig 2002; Williams 1995).

Though this process has now been fairly well established in the literature, there are reasons to question its generalizability to all men. In an early critique of the supposed general neutrality of the token, Zimmer (1988) notes that much research on race comes to precisely the opposite of Kanter's conclusions, finding that as the numbers of minority group members increase (e.g., as they become less likely to be "tokens"), so too do tensions between the majority and minority groups. . . . Reinforcing, while at the same time tempering, the findings of research on men in female-dominated occupations, Zimmer (1988, 71) argues that relationships between tokens and the majority depend on understanding

the underlying power relationships between these groups and "the status and power differentials between them." Hence, just as men who are tokens fare better than women, it also follows that the experiences of Blacks and whites as tokens should differ in ways that reflect their positions in hierarchies of status and power. . . .

Relationships With Colleagues and Supervisors

One key aspect of riding the glass escalator involves the warm, collegial welcome men workers often receive from their women colleagues. Often, this reaction is a response to the fact that professions dominated by women are frequently low in salary and status and that greater numbers of men help improve prestige and pay (Heikes 1991). Though some women workers resent the apparent ease with which men enter and advance in women's professions, the generally warm welcome men receive stands in stark contrast to the cold reception, difficulties with mentorship, and blocked access to social networks that women often encounter when they do men's work (Roth 2006; Williams 1992). In addition, unlike women in men's professions, men who do women's work frequently have supervisors of the same sex. Men workers can thus enjoy a gendered bond with their supervisor in the context of a collegial work environment. These factors often converge, facilitating men's access to higher-status positions and producing the glass escalator effect.

The congenial relationship with colleagues and gendered bonds with supervisors are crucial to riding the glass escalator. Women colleagues often take a primary role in casting these men into leadership or supervisory positions. In their study of men and women tokens in a hospital setting, Floge and Merrill (1986) cite cases where women nurses promoted men colleagues to the position of charge nurse, even when the job had already been assigned to a woman. In addition to these close ties with women colleagues, men are also able to capitalize on gendered bonds with (mostly men) supervisors in ways that engender upward mobility. Many men supervisors informally socialize with men workers in women's jobs and are thus able to trade on their personal friendships for upward mobility. Williams (1995) describes a case where a nurse with mediocre performance reviews received a promotion to a more prestigious specialty area because of his friendship with the (male) doctor in charge. According to the literature, building strong relationships with colleagues and supervisors often happens relatively easily for men in women's professions and pays off in their occupational advancement.

For Black men in nursing, however, gendered racism may limit the extent to which they establish bonds with their colleagues and supervisors. The concept of gendered racism suggests that racial stereotypes, images, and beliefs are grounded in gendered ideals (Collins 1990, 2004; Espiritu 2000; Essed 1991; Harvey Wingfield 2007). Gendered racist stereotypes of Black men in particular emphasize the dangerous, threatening attributes associated with Black men and Black masculinity, framing Black men as threats to white women, prone to criminal behavior, and especially violent. Collins (2004) argues that these stereotypes serve to legitimize Black men's treatment in the criminal justice system through methods such as racial profiling and incarceration, but they may also hinder Black men's attempts to enter and advance in various occupational fields.

For Black men nurses, gendered racist images may have particular consequences for their relationships with women colleagues, who may view Black men nurses through the lens of controlling images and gendered racist stereotypes that emphasize the danger they pose to women. This may take on a heightened significance for white women nurses, given stereotypes that suggest that Black men are especially predisposed to raping white women. Rather than experiencing the congenial bonds with colleagues that white men nurses describe, Black men nurses may find themselves facing a much cooler reception from their women coworkers.

Gendered racism may also play into the encounters Black men nurses have with supervisors. In cases where supervisors are white men, Black men nurses may still find that higher-ups treat them in ways that reflect prevailing stereotypes about threatening Black masculinity. Supervisors may feel uneasy about forming close relationships with Black men or may encourage their separation from white women nurses. In addition, broader, less gender-specific racial stereotypes could also shape the experiences Black men nurses have with white men bosses. Whites often perceive Blacks, regardless of gender, as less intelligent, hardworking, ethical, and moral than other racial groups (Feagin 2006). Black men nurses may find that in addition to being influenced by gendered racist stereotypes, supervisors also view them as less capable and qualified for promotion, thus negating or minimizing the glass escalator effect.

Suitability for Nursing and Higher-Status Work

The perception that men are not really suited to do women's work also contributes to the glass escalator effect. In encounters with patients, doctors, and other staff, men nurses frequently confront others who do not expect to see them doing "a woman's job." Sometimes this perception means that patients mistake men nurses for doctors; ultimately, the sense that men do not really belong in nursing contributes to a push "*out* of the most feminine-identified areas and *up* to those regarded as more legitimate for men" (Williams 1995, 104). The sense that men are better suited for more masculine jobs means that men workers are often assumed to be more able and skilled than their women counterparts. As Williams writes (1995, 106), "Masculinity is often associated with competence and mastery," and this implicit definition stays with men even when they work in feminized fields. Thus, part of the perception that men do not belong in these jobs is rooted in the sense that, as men, they are more capable and accomplished than women and thus belong in jobs that reflect this.

Consequently, men nurses are mistaken for doctors and are granted more authority and responsibility than their women counterparts, reflecting the idea that, as men, they are inherently more competent (Heikes 1991; Williams 1995).

Black men nurses, however, may not face the presumptions of expertise or the resulting assumption that they belong in higher-status jobs. Black professionals, both men and women, are often assumed to be less capable and less qualified than their white counterparts. In some cases, these negative stereotypes hold even when Black workers outperform white colleagues (Feagin and Sikes 1994). The belief that Blacks are inherently less competent than whites means that, despite advanced education, training, and skill, Black professionals often confront the lingering perception that they are better suited for lower-level service work (Feagin and Sikes 1994). Black men in fact often fare better than white women in blue-collar jobs such as policing and corrections work (Britton 1995), and this may be, in part, because they are viewed as more appropriately suited for these types of positions. . . .

As minority women address issues of both race and gender to negotiate a sense of belonging in masculine settings (Ong 2005), minority men may also face a comparable challenge in feminized fields. They may have to address the unspoken racialization implicit in the assumption that masculinity equals competence. Simultaneously, they may find that the racial stereotype that Blackness equals lower qualifications, standards, and competence clouds the sense that men are inherently more capable and adept in any field, including the feminized ones.

Establishing Distance From Femininity

An additional mechanism of the glass escalator involves establishing distance from women and the femininity associated with their occupations. Because men nurses are employed in a culturally feminized occupation, they develop strategies to disassociate themselves from the femininity associated with their work and retain some of the privilege associated with masculinity. Thus, when men nurses gravitate toward hospital emergency wards rather than obstetrics or pediatrics, or emphasize that they are only in nursing to get into hospital administration, they distance themselves from the femininity of their profession and thereby preserve their status as men despite the fact that they do "women's work." Perhaps more important, these strategies also place men in a prime position to experience the glass escalator effect, as they situate themselves to move upward into higher-status areas in the field.

Creating distance from femininity also helps these men achieve aspects of hegemonic masculinity, which Connell (1989) describes as the predominant and most valued form of masculinity at a given time. Contemporary hegemonic masculine ideals emphasize toughness, strength, aggressiveness, heterosexuality, and, perhaps most important, a clear sense of femininity as different from and subordinate to masculinity (Kimmel 2001; Williams 1995). Thus, when men distance themselves from the feminized aspects of their jobs, they uphold the idea that masculinity and femininity are distinct, separate, and mutually exclusive. When these men seek masculinity by aiming for the better paying or most technological fields, they not only position themselves to move upward into the more acceptable arenas but also reinforce the greater social value placed on masculinity. Establishing distance from femininity therefore allows men to retain the privileges and status of masculinity while simultaneously enabling them to ride the glass escalator.

For Black men, the desire to reject femininity may be compounded by racial inequality. Theorists have argued that as institutional racism blocks access to traditional markers of masculinity such as occupational status and economic stability, Black men may repudiate femininity as a way of accessing the masculinity—and its attendant status—that is denied through other routes (hooks 2004; Neal 2005). Rejecting femininity is a key strategy men use to assert masculinity, and it remains available to Black men even when other means of achieving masculinity are unattainable. Black men nurses may be more likely to distance themselves from their women colleagues and to reject the femininity associated with nursing, particularly if they feel that they experience racial discrimination that renders occupational advancement inaccessible. Yet if they encounter strained relationships with women colleagues and men supervisors because of gendered racism or racialized stereotypes, the efforts to distance themselves from femininity still may not result in the glass escalator effect.

On the other hand, some theorists suggest that minority men may challenge racism by rejecting hegemonic masculine ideals. . . . The results of these studies suggest that Black men nurses may embrace the femininity associated with nursing if it offers a way to combat racism. In these cases, Black men nurses may turn to pediatrics as a way of demonstrating sensitivity and therefore combating stereotypes of Black masculinity, or they may proudly identify as nurses to challenge perceptions that Black men are unsuited for professional, white-collar positions.

Taken together, all of this research suggests that Black men may not enjoy the advantages experienced by their white men colleagues, who ride a glass escalator to success. In this article, I focus on the experiences of Black men nurses to argue that the glass escalator is a racialized as well as a gendered concept that does not offer Black men the same privileges as their white men counterparts. . . .

Findings

Reception From Colleagues and Supervisors

When women welcome men into "their" professions, they often push men into leadership roles that ease their advancement into upper-level positions. Thus, a positive reaction from colleagues is critical to riding the glass escalator. Unlike white men nurses, however, Black men do not describe encountering a warm reception from women colleagues (Heikes 1991). Instead, the men I interviewed find that they often have unpleasant interactions with women coworkers

who treat them rather coldly and attempt to keep them at bay. Chris is a 51-year-old oncology nurse who describes one white nurse's attempt to isolate him from other white women nurses as he attempted to get his instructions for that day's shift:

> She turned and ushered me to the door, and said for me to wait out here, a nurse will come out and give you your report. I stared at her hand on my arm, and then at her, and said, "Why? Where do you go to get your reports?" She said, "I get them in there." I said, "Right. Unhand me." I went right back in there, sat down, and started writing down my reports.

Kenny, a 47-year-old nurse with 23 years of nursing experience, describes a similarly and particularly painful experience he had in a previous job where he was the only Black person on staff:

> [The staff] had nothing to do with me, and they didn't even want me to sit at the same area where they were charting in to take a break. They wanted me to sit somewhere else. . . . They wouldn't even sit at a table with me! When I came and sat down, everybody got up and left.

These experiences with colleagues are starkly different from those described by white men in professions dominated by women (see Pierce 1995; Williams 1989). Though the men in these studies sometimes chose to segregate themselves, women never systematically excluded them. Though I have no way of knowing why the women nurses in Chris's and Kenny's workplaces physically segregated themselves, the pervasiveness of gendered racist images that emphasize white women's vulnerability to dangerous Black men may play an important role. For these nurses, their masculinity is not a guarantee that they will be welcomed, much less pushed into leadership roles. As Ryan, a 37-year-old intensive care nurse says, "[Black men] have to go further to prove ourselves. This involves proving our capabilities, *proving to colleagues that you can lead,* be on the forefront" (emphasis added). The warm welcome and subsequent opportunities for leadership cannot be taken for granted. In contrast, these men describe great challenges in forming congenial relationships with coworkers who, they believe, do not truly want them there.

In addition, these men often describe tense, if not blatantly discriminatory, relationships with supervisors. While Williams (1995) suggests that men supervisors can be allies for men in women's professions by facilitating promotions and upward mobility, Black men nurses describe incidents of being overlooked by supervisors when it comes time for promotions. Ryan, who has worked at his current job for 11 years, believes that these barriers block upward mobility within the profession:

> The hardest part is dealing with people who don't understand minority nurses. People with their biases, who don't identify you as ripe for promotion. I know the policy and procedure, I'm familiar with past history. So you can't tell me I can't move forward if others did. [How did you deal with this?] By knowing the chain of command, who my supervisors were. Things were subtle. I just had to be better. I got this mostly from other nurses and supervisors. I was paid to deal with patients, so I could deal with [racism] from them. I'm not paid to deal with this from colleagues.

Kenny offers a similar example. Employed as an orthopedic nurse in a predominantly white environment, he describes great difficulty getting promoted, which he primarily attributes to racial biases:

> It's almost like you have to, um, take your ideas and give them to somebody else and then let them present them for you and you get no credit for it. I've applied for several promotions there and, you know, I didn't get them. . . . When you look around to the, um, the percentage of African Americans who are actually in executive leadership is almost zero percent. Because it's less than one percent of the total population of people that are in leadership, and it's almost like they'll go outside of the system just to try to find a Caucasian to fill a position. Not that I'm not qualified, because I've been master's prepared for 12 years and I'm working on my doctorate.

According to Ryan and Kenny, supervisors' racial biases mean limited opportunities for promotion and upward mobility. This interpretation is consistent with research that suggests that even with stellar performance and solid work histories, Black workers may receive mediocre evaluations from white supervisors that limit their advancement (Feagin 2006; Feagin and Sikes 1994). For Black men nurses, their race may signal to supervisors that they are unworthy of promotion and thus create a different experience with the glass escalator.

Strong relationships with colleagues and supervisors are a key mechanism of the glass escalator effect. For Black men nurses, however, these relationships are experienced differently from those described by their white men colleagues. Black men nurses do not speak of warm and congenial relationships with women nurses or see these relationships as facilitating a move into leadership roles. Nor do they suggest that they share gendered bonds with men supervisors that serve to ease their mobility into higher-status administrative jobs. In contrast, they sense that racial bias makes it difficult to develop ties with coworkers and makes superiors unwilling to promote them. Black men nurses thus experience this aspect of the glass escalator differently from their white men colleagues. They find that relationships with colleagues and supervisors stifle, rather than facilitate, their upward mobility.

Perceptions of Suitability

Like their white counterparts, Black men nurses also experience challenges from clients who are unaccustomed to seeing men in fields typically dominated by women. As with white men nurses, Black men encounter this in surprised or quizzical reactions from patients who seem to expect to be treated by white women nurses. . . .

Yet while patients rarely expect to be treated by men nurses of any race, white men encounter statements and behaviors that suggest patients expect them to be doctors, supervisors, or other higher-status, more masculine positions (Williams 1989, 1995). In part, this expectation accelerates their ride on the glass escalator, helping to push them into the positions for which they are seen as more appropriately suited.

(White) men, by virtue of their masculinity, are assumed to be more competent and capable and thus better situated in (nonfeminized) jobs that are perceived to require greater skill and proficiency. Black men, in contrast, rarely encounter patients (or colleagues and supervisors) who immediately expect that they are doctors or administrators. Instead, many respondents find that even after displaying their credentials, sharing their nursing experience, and, in one case, dispensing care, they are still mistaken for janitors or service workers. Ray's experience is typical:

> I've even given patients their medicines, explained their care to them, and then they'll say to me, "Well, can you send the nurse in?"

Chris describes a somewhat similar encounter of being misidentified by a white woman patient:

> I come [to work] in my white uniform, that's what I wear—being a Black man, I know they won't look at me the same, so I dress the part—I said good evening, my name's Chris, and I'm going to be your nurse. She says to me, "Are you from housekeeping?." . . I've had other cases. I've walked in and had a lady look at me and ask if I'm the janitor. . . .

These negative stereotypes can affect Black men nurses' efforts to treat patients as well. The men I interviewed find that masculinity does not automatically endow them with an aura of competency. In fact, they often describe interactions with white women patients that suggest that their race minimizes whatever assumptions of capability might accompany being men. They describe several cases in which white women patients completely refused treatment. Ray says,

> With older white women, it's tricky sometimes because they will come right out and tell you they don't want you to treat them, or can they see someone else.

Ray frames this as an issue specifically with older white women, though other nurses in the sample described similar issues with white women of all ages. Cyril, a 40-year-old nurse with 17 years of nursing experience, describes a slightly different twist on this story:

> I had a white lady that I had to give a shot, and she was fine with it and I was fine with it. But her husband, when she told him, he said to me, I don't have any problem with you as a Black man, but I don't want you giving her a shot.

While white men nurses report some apprehension about treating women patients, in all likelihood this experience is compounded for Black men (Williams 1989). Historically, interactions between Black men and white women have been fraught with complexity and tension, as Black men have been represented in the cultural imagination as potential rapists and threats to white women's security and safety—and, implicitly, as a threat to white patriarchal stability (Davis 1981; Giddings 1984). In Cyril's case, it may be particularly significant that the Black man is charged with giving a shot and therefore literally penetrating the white wife's body, a fact that may heighten the husband's desire to shield his wife from this interaction. White men nurses may describe hesitation or awkwardness that accompanies treating women patients, but their experiences are not shaped by a pervasive racial imagery that suggests that they are potential threats to their women patients' safety.

This dynamic, described primarily among white women patients and their families, presents a picture of how Black men's interactions with clients are shaped in specifically raced and gendered ways that suggest they are less rather than more capable. These interactions do not send the message that Black men, because they are men, are too competent for nursing and really belong in higher-status jobs. Instead, these men face patients who mistake them for lower-status service workers and encounter white women patients (and their husbands) who simply refuse treatment or are visibly uncomfortable with the prospect. These interactions do not situate Black men nurses in a prime position for upward mobility. Rather, they suggest that the experience of Black men nurses with this particular mechanism of the glass escalator is the manifestation of the expectation that they should be in lower-status positions more appropriate to their race and gender.

Refusal to Reject Femininity

Finally, Black men nurses have a different experience with establishing distance from women and the feminized aspects of their work. Most research shows that as men nurses employ strategies that distance them from femininity (e.g., by emphasizing nursing as a route to higher-status, more masculine jobs), they place themselves in a position for upward mobility and the glass escalator effect (Williams 1992). For Black men nurses, however, this process looks different. Instead of distancing themselves from the femininity associated with nursing, Black men actually embrace some of the more feminized attributes linked to nursing. In particular, they emphasize how much they value and enjoy the way their jobs allow them to be caring and nurturing. Rather than conceptualizing caring as anathema or feminine (and therefore undesirable), Black men nurses speak openly of caring as something positive and enjoyable.

This is consistent with the context of nursing that defines caring as integral to the profession. As nurses, Black men in this line of work experience professional socialization that emphasizes and values caring, and this is reflected in their statements about their work. Significantly, however, rather than repudiating this feminized component of their jobs, they embrace it. Tobias, a 44-year-old oncology nurse with 25 years of experience, asserts,

> The best part about nursing is helping other people, the flexibility of work hours, and the commitment to vulnerable populations, people who are ill.

Simon, a 36-year-old oncology nurse, also talks about the joy he gets from caring for others. He contrasts his experiences to those of white men nurses he knows who prefer specialties that involve less patient care:

> They were going to work with the insurance industries, they were going to work in the ER where it's a touch and go, you're a number literally. I don't get to know your name, I don't get to know that you have four grandkids, I don't get to know that you really want to get out of the hospital by next week because the following week is your birthday, your 80th birthday and it's so important for you. I don't get to know that your cat's name is Sprinkles, and you're concerned about who's feeding the cat now, and if they remembered to turn the TV on during the day so that the cat can watch *The Price Is Right*. They don't get into all that kind of stuff. OK, I actually need to remember the name of your cat so that tomorrow morning when I come, I can ask you about Sprinkles and that will make a world of difference. I'll see light coming to your eyes and the medicines will actually work because your perspective is different.

Like Tobias, Simon speaks with a marked lack of self-consciousness about the joys of adding a personal touch and connecting that personal care to a patient's improvement. For him, caring is important, necessary, and valued, even though others might consider it a feminine trait.

For many of these nurses, willingness to embrace caring is also shaped by issues of race and racism. In their position as nurses, concern for others is connected to fighting the effects of racial inequality. Specifically, caring motivates them to use their role as nurses to address racial health disparities, especially those that disproportionately affect Black men. Chris describes his efforts to minimize health issues among Black men:

> With Black male patients, I have their history, and if they're 50 or over I ask about the prostate exam and a colonoscopy. Prostate and colorectal death is so high that that's my personal crusade.

Ryan also speaks to the importance of using his position to address racial imbalances:

> I really take advantage of the opportunities to give back to communities, especially to change the disparities in the African American community. I'm more than just a nurse. As a faculty member at a major university, I have to do community hours, services. Doing health fairs, in-services on research, this makes an impact in some disparities in the African American community. [People in the community] may not have the opportunity to do this otherwise.

As Lamont (2000) indicates in her discussion of the "caring self," concern for others helps Chris and Ryan to use their knowledge and position as nurses to combat racial inequalities in health. Though caring is generally considered a "feminine" attribute, in this context it is connected to challenging racial health disparities. Unlike their white men colleagues, these nurses accept and even embrace certain aspects of femininity rather than rejecting them. They thus reveal yet another aspect of the glass escalator process that differs for Black men. As Black men nurses embrace this "feminine" trait and the avenues it provides for challenging racial inequalities, they may become more comfortable in nursing and embrace the opportunities it offers.

CONCLUSIONS

Existing research on the glass escalator cannot explain these men's experiences. As men who do women's work, they should be channeled into positions as charge nurses or nursing administrators and should find themselves virtually pushed into the upper ranks of the nursing profession. But without exception, this is not the experience these Black men nurses describe. Instead of benefiting from the basic mechanisms of the glass escalator, they face tense relationships with colleagues, supervisors' biases in achieving promotion, patient stereotypes that

inhibit caregiving, and a sense of comfort with some of the feminized aspects of their jobs. These "glass barriers" suggest that the glass escalator is a racialized concept as well as a gendered one. The main contribution of this study is the finding that race and gender intersect to determine which men will ride the glass escalator. The proposition that men who do women's work encounter undue opportunities and advantages appears to be unequivocally true only if the men in question are white.

REFERENCES

Acker, Joan. 1990. Hierarchies, jobs, bodies: A theory of gendered organizations. *Gender & Society* 4:139–58.

Britton, Dana. 1995. *At work in the iron cage.* New York: New York University Press.

Budig, Michelle. 2002. Male advantage and the gender composition of jobs: Who rides the glass escalator? *Social Forces* 49(2): 258–77.

Charles, Maria, and David Grusky. 2004. *Occupational ghettos: The worldwide segregation of women and men.* Palo Alto, CA: Stanford University Press.

Collins, Patricia Hill. 1990. *Black feminist thought.* New York: Routledge.

———. 2004. *Black sexual politics.* New York: Routledge.

Connell, R. W. 1989. *Gender and power.* Sydney, Australia: Allen and Unwin.

Davis, Angela. 1981. *Women, race, and class.* New York: Vintage.

Duffy, Mignon. 2007. Doing the dirty work: Gender, race, and reproductive labor in historical perspective. *Gender & Society* 21:313–36.

Espiritu, Yen Le. 2000. *Asian American women and men: Labor, laws, and love.* Walnut Creek, CA: AltaMira.

Essed, Philomena. 1991. *Understanding everyday racism.* New York: Russell Sage.

Feagin, Joe. 2006. *Systemic racism.* New York: Routledge.

Feagin, Joe, and Melvin Sikes. 1994. *Living with racism.* Boston: Beacon Hill Press.

Floge, Liliane, and Deborah M. Merrill. 1986. Tokenism reconsidered: Male nurses and female physicians in a hospital setting. *Social Forces* 64:925–47.

Giddings, Paula. 1984. *When and where I enter: The impact of Black women on race and sex in America.* New York: HarperCollins.

Harvey Wingfield, Adia. 2007. The modern mammy and the angry Black man: African American professionals' experiences with gendered racism in the workplace. *Race, Gender, and Class* 14(2): 196–212.

Heikes, E. Joel. 1991. When men are the minority: The case of men in nursing. *Sociological Quarterly* 32:389–401.

hooks, bell. 2004. *We real cool.* New York: Routledge.

Kanter, Rosabeth Moss. 1977. *Men and women of the corporation.* New York: Basic Books.

Kimmel, Michael. 2001. Masculinity as homophobia. In *Men and masculinity,* edited by Theodore F. Cohen. Belmont, CA: Wadsworth.

Lamont, Michelle. 2000. *The dignity of working men.* New York: Russell Sage.

Neal, Mark Anthony. 2005. *New Black man.* New York: Routledge.

Ong, Maria. 2005. Body projects of young women of color in physics: Intersections of race, gender, and science. *Social Problems* 52(4): 593–617.

Pierce, Jennifer. 1995. *Gender trials: Emotional lives in contemporary law firms.* Berkeley: University of California Press.

Roth, Louise. 2006. *Selling women short: Gender and money on Wall Street.* Princeton, NJ: Princeton University Press.

Snyder, Karrie Ann, and Adam Isaiah Green. 2008. Revisiting the glass escalator: The case of gender segregation in a female dominated occupation. *Social Problems* 55(2): 271–99.

Williams, Christine. 1989. *Gender differences at work: Women and men in non-traditional occupations.* Berkeley: University of California Press.

———. 1992. The glass escalator: Hidden advantages for men in the "female" professions. *Social Problems* 39(3): 253–67.

———. 1995. *Still a man's world: Men who do women's work.* Berkeley: University of California Press.

Zimmer, Lynn. 1988. Tokenism and women in the workplace: The limits of gender neutral theory. *Social Problems* 35(1): 64–77.

Introduction to Reading 34

The globalization of the economy brings many interesting twists as cultures of the multicultural companies spread to the countries they relocate to. Steven C. McKay's article provides an interesting examination of the workplace policies and practices of three high-tech companies in the Philippines. These factories are owned by three different multinational companies from America, Europe, and Japan. Each multinational corporation brings its own culture, along with gendered assumptions to its factory in the Philippines. While the basic needs of workers for decent wages, reasonable hours, and safe working conditions are the same around the world, these companies used gendered assumptions to attract and maintain their workforce, not always to the benefit of the women and men working for them.

1. Which of the three factories has the most female-friendly practices?

2. What workplace practices and gender-based assumptions about work disadvantage women in these factories?

3. Why was it so difficult for women to be promoted from "operators" of machines to technical positions?

HARD DRIVES AND GLASS CEILINGS

GENDER STRATIFICATION IN HIGH-TECH PRODUCTION

Steven C. McKay

Rapid industrialization and foreign direct investment in developing countries since the 1960s touched off what has become a three-decades-old debate about the impact of technology and "the global assembly line" on women and the division of labor (see Mills 2003). Recent trends in globalization, technological change, and flexible work reorganization have reawakened the debate (Acker 2004; Kelkar and Nathan 2002). In the electronics industry, where women have dominated production work, technological upgrading has been held up as a potential avenue for increased women's employment, empowerment, and socioeconomic mobility (Kuruvilla 1996; Yun 1995). Yet others argue that globalization and more flexible work organization may only intensify the exploitation of women workers and exacerbate occupational gender segmentation (Fox 2002; Joekes and Weston 1994).

While many recent studies document global restructuring, they—like earlier studies of women workers—tend to frame their analysis in terms of whether employment in advanced electronics represents either empowerment or exploitation. Thus, Chhachhi (1999) poses but cannot possibly answer the question of whether women electronic workers in India represent "dormant volcanoes," with a new, structural potential to explode, or "fresh green vegetables," that remain naïve, docile, and dominated by global capital.

However, focusing on either empowerment or exploitation becomes an analytical cul-de-sac, particularly given the wide variations in how firms organize high-tech production, how workers struggle over and make sense of their own employment, and the gendered meanings that emerge from these intersecting processes within a specific sociopolitical context. In this article, I concentrate on the myriad ways gender and inequality are constituted—even within a single industry and in a single national context— analyzing at multiple levels the links between gender ascription and the division of labor (Mills 2003). At the workplace level, I focus on management's structuring of the shop floor and key sources of variation that influence how advanced technologies and flexible work are organized, stratified, and gendered (Salzinger 2003). Equally important, I also examine the extra-organizational contexts—particularly the role of the state and persistent gender ideologies—that shape firm-level decision making as well as workers' assessments and action. Finally, to better assess the meaning of flexible production for women workers, I analyze high-tech work in terms of its impact on a range of issues concerning the gender division of labor. Specifically, I focus on the degree to which the three firms' gender and flexibility strategies address women's more "practical" everyday responsibilities and individual survival needs within the existing gendered division of labor versus their impact on the more "strategic" gender interest of women in "extending the conditions for choices to be made *about* the gender division of labor" (Chhachhi and Pittin 1998, 71, emphasis added; Molyneux 1985). In this sense, I hope to gauge to what

From McKay, S. C. "Hard Drives and Glass Ceilings: Gender Stratification in High-Tech Production." *Gender & Society 20:* 207–235. Published by Sage Publications on behalf of Sociologists for Women in Society.

extent changes in the organization of high-tech work directly challenge deeper gender inequality or "the structural roots of unequal access to resources and control" (Chow and Lyter 2002, 41). . . .

Data and analysis are based on 11 months of interview and observation-based field research conducted in the Philippines in 1999 and follow-up research conducted during several weeks in 2003. Following interviews with human resource managers or staff at 20 firms, I selected three cases, representing the three dominant types of electronics products produced in the Philippines—disk drives, discrete semiconductors, and integrated chips—and the diverse nationalities of the home corporation.

* * *

The State, the Electronics Industry, and Gender

The Philippines has been a site of low-cost electronics assembly since the early 1970s, in large part because it offers—and the Philippine state has helped guarantee—an investment context favored by foreign high-tech manufacturers: political and economic stability; inexpensive, educated, and disciplined labor; good infrastructure; few operational restrictions; and investment/tax incentives tailored to the electronics industry (Austria 1999; Ernst 2002). State-led labor control has gone hand in hand with foreign investment policies at least since the early 1970s, when then-president Ferdinand Marcos launched an export-oriented industrialization program while also declaring martial law, rewriting the labor code, banning all strikes in export manufacturing, and cracking down on militant labor (Bello, Kinley, and Elinson 1982). The debt crisis of the 1980s only increased the Philippines's dependence on foreign investment, as structural adjustment packages attached to International Monetary Fund loans forced the Philippines to further open its economy and compete directly with other developing countries—particularly

Malaysia, Thailand, and Indonesia—for mobile investment capital (Bello et al. 2004). By the 1990s, the Philippines had fully embraced a neoliberal economic growth model, centered on courting foreign investment through reregulating employment and production conditions, especially in its booming export-processing zones (World Bank 1997). . . .

As it has since the 1970s, the electronics industry continues to hire primarily women for factory operator positions largely because women can be paid less and are viewed as more patient, docile, and detail oriented (Chant and McIlwaine 1995). Management's desire to develop such a "cheapened" labor force is directly connected to the intensity of the labor process: production workers still make up 82 percent of the electronics workforce. Overall, 74 percent of the electronics industry workers are women and 78 percent younger than 30. But the workforce is increasingly well educated: More than 60 percent of the workers are high school graduates, and 37 percent have college degrees (Bureau of Labor Relations 1999).

Although women have made strides through their electronics employment, they still face a host of challenges, particularly given prevailing gender ideologies and complex gender relations in the Philippines. Women in the Philippines are sometimes viewed as having relatively more power than women in other Asian countries since women in the Philippines traditionally control domestic budgets and make most household decisions (Eviota 1992). And the preference for women in two key industries, electronics and garments, has contributed to overall employment and wage gains made by women in recent decades. While women's labor force participation rates have remained stable since 1975 at about 47 percent, women make up nearly 70 percent of the export industry workforce, women's unemployment rate (9.9 percent) is slightly below the men's rate (10.3 percent), and the wage differential between women and men, at 87 percent, is one of the lowest for a developing country (National Statistical Coordination Board 2001; Seguino 2000).

Despite these gains, employers' preference for female labor both taps into and reproduces gender ideologies and gendered labor market segmentation that systematically undervalues the labor of young educated women (Chant and McIlwaine 1995). As Parrenas (2001) points out, although women dominate the workforces of the two largest foreign exchange earning sectors—overseas contract labor and electronics—women are nevertheless constructed through Philippine families, churches, and the state as "secondary earners," whose proper roles of "mother," "daughter," and/or caregiver tie them primarily to the home, particularly after marriage (Eviota 1992). Thus, although many women have secured formal waged work through electronics assembly jobs, they nevertheless still confront a rigid gender division of labor, gendered labor control strategies, and gendered associations with technology. These issues, which only intensify as firms upgrade production technologies, will be discussed in each of the cases below.

Storage Ltd.

Storage Ltd., a subsidiary of a leading Japanese hard disk drive producer, demonstrates that while new flexibilities do lead to different labor practices than those documented in earlier studies of transnational assembly, such restructuring may also sharpen gendered labor control regimes. The firm's $124 million plant, operational since 1996, assembles and tests high-end hard disk drives for computer servers, requiring expensive semi-automated machinery, sophisticated quality control systems, and enormous startup costs. To meet these demands, Storage Ltd. has chosen a labor process and control regime that diverge somewhat from past practices in electronics and other export industries. For example, the firm does not subcontract out its labor-intensive assembly nor rely on temporary workers to boost its external flexibility (Standing 1999). Instead, to meet quality standards and enhance internal flexibility, the firm develops multi-skilled workers, trained to operate from one to three machines or workstations. Such training can take up to

three months and considerable firm investment, so the firm tries hard to keep turnover down, making all employees permanent after six months and providing some positive incentives. For example, although base pay is only minimum wage, the company does pay more for overtime, pushing take-home pay up to 300 pesos per day (about US$6) or 50 percent more than the legal minimum. The company also provides transportation, free uniforms, subsidized meals, emergency medical insurance, and 12 days of sick and vacation leave a year—benefits relatively high by local standards.

Yet in other ways, the demanding character of disk drive production coupled with cut-throat cost competition has led the firm to develop more sophisticated forms of gendered labor control focused on stability, cost saving, and "disciplinary management." First, the actual production process remains quite labor intensive: The plant employs more than 9,000 workers, 87 percent of whom are shop floor operators, who churn out more than 1.5 million disk drives per month. To maintain such high productivity, the firm uses both high-tech strategies and more traditional direct control. On the technical side, the firm relies on a computerized assembly line that automatically gathers data for statistical process control, providing managers and customers with real-time productivity and quality data down to the individual workstation. On the social side, there is strict enforcement of company rules. As one human resources staff member admitted, "For most operators, they have no control. They are treated like robots; told what to do, when, where and how. Every movement is controlled. . . . They are told where to go, when to eat. And everything is timed, even going to the bathroom." While officially, there are three 8-hour shifts, in practice, there are only two 12-hour shifts with 4 hours of daily forced overtime. The work week is six and often seven days a week. The long hours clearly take a toll on workers. Irma, a production operator noted, "The overtime is just too much. I only sleep five hours a day. I get home (from the night shift) at nine a.m., I'm asleep by ten. Then, I get up again at three or four p.m. just so I can do my laundry and clean up before I go in again."

In addition to such in-plant intensity, the firm utilizes and helps construct gender stereotypes to dampen its labor costs and extend its labor control far beyond the factory. The process begins in hiring. The company selectively recruits rural women, assuming—to some degree correctly—that they have fewer labor market options and will thus be cheaper, more dependent on the firm, and willing to put up with the demanding labor process. The profile of the company's 9,000 workers is remarkably uniform: 88 percent are women; 83 percent between 16 and 22, with an average age of 21; and 97 percent single. Fifty-one percent have some college or vocational training, and the rest are high school graduates. The reasons given for this rigid hiring profile follow and reinforce the gender stereotypes and "public narratives" about the nature of women's work that have become the norm in export factories around the world (Mills 2003). Managers say they prefer women because the work requires "patience, dexterity, and attention to detail," while men are viewed as lazy, sloppy, impatient, and generally *magulo* or disruptive. The company also wants intelligent, English-speaking workers, but ones without high job, pay, or promotion expectations. For this reason, management again prefers women—stereotyped as loyal but not ambitious—and does not hire anyone at the operator level with more than two years of college. This gendered hiring and job allocation essentially cuts women operators off from promotions to the more lucrative technical jobs, since these positions require a three-year technical or four-year college degree. Women operators can thus aspire only to a horizontal move to office clerk or to a climb up a short job ladder to line leader or quality control inspector. Technicians and engineers in the plant are almost all men.

Finally, Storage Ltd. also tries to localize its labor control, tapping into gender subordination at the family and community level. For example, when screening potential workers, recruiters ask extensively about an applicant's family and her role in the household. While seemingly innocent, the line of questioning aims to judge an applicant's level of dependence and reflects another of the firm's gendered strategies: to hire oldest daughters. Since the eldest are usually responsible for aiding parents and younger siblings, they are considered less likely to quit. The firm also maintains a Background Investigation Unit to scrutinize both workers and their families and make links with village-level officials to head off potential unionizing efforts. Before workers are made permanent following six months' probationary employment, the Background Investigation Unit conducts a home visit to interview workers' parents, inspect their residence, and contact the lowest-level officials. Primary targets for investigations are those reported to have gotten married since being hired and who may be hiding families back home.

The firm's sophisticated labor control strategies have important implications for both women's practical needs and strategic gender interests. In a practical sense, employment at Storage Ltd. does benefit women workers by providing permanent work paying above-minimum wages in a high-status industry. Ironically, because the firm can legally and explicitly target women with little experience and few labor market options, it has created a workforce that is grateful for its jobs despite the demanding working conditions, yet one with little collective or individual bargaining power to directly confront the hierarchical divisions of labor. Although workers complained of the overtime and lack of rest days, they also referred to the work as "clean" and "light," particularly in contrast to the physically demanding and low-status agricultural- or informal-sector work in their rural hometowns. For many, the job also gave them their first experience of living away from parents, increased status, control over income, and a means to fulfill independently their basic survival needs. As one operator noted, "This is my first job and I'm satisfied with the pay and benefits. . . . Working for 12 hours is not so bad. The work's pretty light . . . my parents treat me better now that I already have my own job." . . .

Integrated Production

Integrated Production, a subsidiary of an American semiconductor firm producing advanced integrated circuits, shows a different gendered strategy to promote labor stability, as well as the possible—but unrealized—potential of high-tech flexible production for women. Production at the firm's $200 million plant opened in late 1996 is less standardized, less labor intensive, and more automated than at Storage Ltd. At the core of the labor process are engineers and technicians, who make up more than 20 percent of the workforce and are crucial for ramping up production, programming in flexibility, and keeping the lines running. Due to the high level of automation, only 55 percent of the 1,373 permanent employees are production workers. These operators play only a minor role in flexible production: They work under strict supervision and are told to simply check the computer readouts from the quality control programs and report any problems to engineers.

Yet the automated machinery is extremely expensive and critical to production, so Integrated Production, like the other firms in the study, wants to minimize turnover or production disruption and thus provides training and employs only permanent workers. However, unlike Storage Ltd., Integrated Production combines its "hard" engineering-intensive labor process with a "soft" strategic labor relations approach—modeled after a Silicon Valley variant of the American human resources model—that stresses positive incentives, loyalty, and "empowerment" through ritual participation (Katz and Darbishire 2000). First, although take-home pay is actually less than at the other two firms, production operators are monthly-paid salaried employees, considered a notch up in status from daily-paid laborers. In addition, workers receive other benefits such as stock options, education reimbursement, and a free computer after two years. The firm also provides an assortment of morale-boosting activities, such as outings, sports fests, and pizza parties. The employee relations manager boasted, "It is really like an American company [in America]—there's really toilet paper in the bathroom, really free coffee all the time." Finally, the company "empowers" individual workers through an employee suggestion program and open intercompany communication. Yet the firm also studiously avoids—and actively disrupts—any collective worker action through anti-union trainings and surveillance.

The organization of work and labor relations is also gendered, in ways both similar to and different from that at Storage Ltd. Overall, the firm has one of the most balanced gender ratios of the companies visited: 38 percent men and only 63 percent women. But when broken down by position, the gender segregation typical of the industry becomes clearer: All nine directors and 90 percent of the engineers and technicians are men, while 85 percent of shop-floor workers are women. As we will see below, this strict gender division of labor makes upward mobility for current women operators into new technical positions extremely difficult.

Nevertheless, gender strategies differ. First, unlike Storage Ltd., the firm is less concerned with trying to maximize women's multiple labor market vulnerabilities by recruiting only from rural areas and screening out experienced or married workers. The human resources manager complained that local rural residents are poorly educated. . . . Rather, the firm puts a premium on educated workers, requiring a minimum of two years of college or technical training and preferring college graduates. Its emphasis on education has led to a frontline workforce dominated by women yet demographically distinct from other plants: Only 60 percent of workers are younger than 24 years of age, and only 70 percent are single. Operators are more likely from urban areas, 95 percent have finished at least two-year technical degrees, and a large portion are college graduates.

However, the firm's gendered strategy to hire educated women but to maintain a strict gender division of labor has also created problems. In part because these women are well educated, they also have higher career aspirations, more labor market options, and more individual bargaining power. Thus, the firm must rely more on positive rather than negative incentives to reduce turnover. In fact, some women took jobs in production in the hopes that they could eventually move up in the company. . . . In terms of internal promotion, the technical job ladder has far better prospects for earning and security but requires increasingly specific qualifications and is thus generally blocked to nontechnically trained (if formally educated) operators. . . . The mismatch between women's high education and blocked mobility has led to a turnover rate of more than 9 percent, the highest among the three companies. . . .

As the plant moves toward full automation, the new technical operators, who are slated to replace other shop-floor workers, will still handle basic production but also take on responsibilities of current technicians, performing all minor maintenance and repairs. These enhanced operator positions would then have a direct promotional ladder leading to full technicians and possibly engineers—an avenue previously closed to operators. If women operators were to gain access to these jobs, their increased skills and mobility could provide more decision-making power over the division of labor and help break down gendered notions associated with technology and technical positions that have helped keep women out of technical work.

Unfortunately, such potential remains unrealized. First, the firm requires these new technical operators to have at least two years' training from an accredited electronics training school. In fact, managers, operating under gendered assumptions about women's technical (in)capacities, do not fill these new positions by training current operators. Rather, the firm recruits directly from engineering or technical schools, where almost all the trainees, and thus all the new technical operators, are men.

In other ways, technological upgrading may already be shifting management's gendered notions about electronics assembly, effectively masculinizing the work and the workforce. The human resources manager explained that, in the early days, women dominated semiconductor assembly in the Philippines because "everyone followed the dictum that women work better with small things." But with the increase in the number of technicians and technical operators, he noted, "Guys are beginning to gain ground."

Specifically, men have been gaining ground by masculinizing the new machines and processes. For example, the manager noted that the new automated machines are not as "gender specific" as old machines and that production has become "less dependent on the fine skills of women. . . . The machines have large screens instead of microscopes, so [operators] don't need 20/20 vision or the patience to sit at a scope." Thus, there is a regendering process as managers and skilled male workers try to capture a new technology or area of production and revalue previously feminized assembly labor. The human resources manager went on to explain why women do not make "ideal workers": "Women get sick, they need maternity leave, have monthly periods." Men, on the other hand, were seen as "stronger" and able to work longer shifts. Here, the manager referred to the 12-hour day as an important reason for the shifting gender balance. According to the manager, "with the long shifts, we need more stamina and not agility. . . . Guys are strong and can work for 24 hours. With the right pay, they will do anything." Thus, the demands of an essentially still-standardized labor process become regendered: from the stereotyped call for feminized patience into a new demand for masculine stamina. In such cases, where the gendering of technology is widening the divide between male technical workers and female shop-floor operators, women operators facing mass layoffs and blocked paths to promotion ladders may find that upgrading serves neither their practical survival needs nor their strategic gender interests.

Discrete Manufacturing

Discrete Manufacturing, a branch of a leading European electronics multinational that produces discrete semiconductors, refutes arguments that electronics work is necessarily exploitative of women workers, particularly if workers act collectively. Yet the introduction of new technologies may threaten the hard-fought gains won through unionization. The $110 million plant, opened in 1994, employs nearly 3,500 permanent employees, 85 percent of whom are factory workers and almost half of whom transferred from an older assembly plant. Relocation allowed management to reorganize production with more automated equipment, new line layouts, increased multiskilling, and the introduction of teamwork. But the firm was constrained from taking full advantage of an otherwise greenfield investment since workers at Discrete Manufacturing are unionized and have been able to check management's ability to introduce flexibility in the same manner as at the other two firms.

Discrete Manufacturing also differs in how its gendered employment practices have played out over time. Ironically, Discrete Manufacturing—like other foreign electronics firms—originally recruited women with only high school educations because it too sought "cheap assembly hands" for its labor-intensive plant. However, workers at the older plant successfully unionized during the height of the Philippine labor movement's organizing surge in the turbulent 1980s. When production and the workforce shifted to the new plant, management initially hired a human resources director to bust the union. But when the union successfully resisted these attempts, the firm shifted to a more cooperative stance. This crucial development helped women workers, who traditionally have little bargaining power, to collectively shape an agenda for fulfilling both their practical needs and, to some extent, their strategic gender interests.

The most immediate areas in which unionization has made a difference are in pay and benefits. Although new workers' base pay is similar to that at other firms, experienced production workers earn nearly three and a half times the starting rate. The high pay is a big reason so many women have stayed with the company.

Thus, while the firm's overall gender balance is similar to other electronics firms—75 percent of the factory workers are women—the workforce is quite a bit older. Among factory workers, 77 percent are 26 years old or older, with an average age of 29, and less than 1 percent are younger than 20. In part a reflection of their older age, 35 percent of operators are married. Interestingly, 72 percent of married women had spouses who were unemployed, meaning that a large percentage of women workers, 26 percent, were sole breadwinners for their families. It is also interesting to note that the older women remain largely unmarried. While managers joked that there are "a lot of *sultera* [old maids] in this company," this pattern may also reflect women's ability to delay marriage, since earning a decent wage has allowed them some measure of independence (Chant and McIlwaine 1995; Wolf 1992).

The breadth of benefits—which are negotiated rather than simply defined by management—also reflects workers' own priorities as both workers and women. First, all union members enjoy general provisions such as seniority-based pay, family health insurance, and protection against layoffs and subcontracting. Second, workers have negotiated gender-sensitive benefits not found in most other companies. For example, maternity leave and childbirth subsidies take into account the kind of delivery (caesarian, normal, or miscarriage). Since women in the Philippines are usually responsible for attending to sick family members or emergencies, workers have negotiated benefits such as bereavement assistance and a total of 26 days of leave a year. Women are also often responsible for family finances, so they have bargained for an array of low-interest loans and subsidies for housing, education, and emergencies to finance expenses.

With the unionized status and negotiated benefits, many workers recognize their jobs as some of the best in the industry and are committed to staying with the firm. Carmen, a production operator, stated, "The work is hard. . . . Two machines I have to watch over and I'm standing the whole shift," but, "I'm not planning to look for anything else. I figure I'll be here at Discrete Manufacturing for the next 10 years. There's a CBA [collective bargaining agreement]. My projection . . . is that it's really lifetime employment." Indeed, the average tenure of the 24 operators interviewed was 4.75 years, and the overall yearly turnover rate was between just 3 and 5 percent. That these women remain in the workforce and consider themselves "lifetime" employees is again in contrast to other studies that have focused on the temporary nature of women's factory work.

But despite wide gains by the union, workers now face a dual challenge: technological upgrading and a restive management trying to reassert its command over the labor process. Like Integrated Production, Discrete Manufacturing is also experimenting with a new, fully automated assembly line run by new technical operators. And also like Integrated Production, the technical operator positions have the potential for increasing upward mobility. Previously, when new equipment was introduced, the union had been able to negotiate technical training for its frontline workers, ensuring gradual upgrading of skills. Initially, when the new technical operator positions were developed, union officers tried to get these positions filled by senior workers, who are primarily women. However, management has taken this opportunity of more radical redesign to enhance its control over workers. Invoking their claim to "management prerogative" over production issues, managers have refused to promote existing operators into the technical operator positions. Thus, the firm, like Integrated Production, is not filling these positions with its women employees but with new "fresh graduates" of four-year engineering or two-year electronics training programs, who all happen to be men. Thus, it is clear that while women workers have made many gains through their employment and collective bargaining, the industry is also changing in ways that may not bode well for the future.

* * *

CONCLUSIONS: REALIZING PRACTICAL AND STRATEGIC GENDER INTERESTS

The three case studies demonstrate that the impact of high-tech employment and technological upgrading on women workers varies: It is impossible to speak of exploitation or empowerment. But how then to assess the variation and what it might mean for the gendering of high-tech production in the future? To conclude, it will be useful to return to the issue of practical needs versus strategic gender interests.

Focusing first on the practical material needs of women, the cases confirm what other studies have also pointed out: that multinational electronics firms tend to pay higher wages and provide higher job security and better working conditions than local factories or the informal sector (Elson 1999; Mills 2003). In this sense, work in the electronics sector does seem to help meet women's daily needs and improve their lives. Workers themselves often have positive assessments of their jobs, as waged work helps increase their mobility, independence, and control over income. Equally important for interviewees has been the higher status that their "clean" and "modern" employment in the electronics industry provides. As others have argued, these gains from formal-sector jobs are significant and may help women workers renegotiate power and gender relations within their families, particularly regarding child care and household spending decisions (Chant and McIlwaine 1995). Nevertheless, these "practical" gains are made within existing gender divisions of labor—both in the firms and in wider Philippine society—which still slot women into lower-level, secondary positions (Eviota 1992; Parrenas 2001). Workers' positive views of seemingly punishing factory work are also relative to the limited options these women face in the informal economy or service sector due to the persistence of gender-stratified labor markets. Thus, while women workers do benefit from their factory jobs, such labor is embedded in and subjected to persistent gender ideologies that employers have long used to feminize and cheapen assembly work. Therefore, work in the electronics sector, in and of itself, is unlikely to lead to a transformation of traditional gender divisions of labor.

The dialectics of gendered work organization are most extreme in the case of Storage Ltd. While the firm may serve its women employees' survival needs by hiring them, it also has by far the most exploitative gendered labor control strategy. By consciously leveraging wider gender inequalities in the labor market, the firm creates a kind of asymmetrical agency, which allows a sense of individual worker autonomy and empowerment yet only within the confines of existing organizational and gender hierarchies that help (re)produce rather than challenge management's authority in production and broader gendered social relations.

Nevertheless, the variation across the three firms in terms of individual versus collective bargaining power suggests that the most potent vehicle for maximizing the benefits of industrial work is through collective organization (Elson 1999; Hutchinson and Brown 2001). At Discrete Manufacturing, a group of initially marginal women workers—selected along stereotypical lines for their cheapness and docility—have in fact increased their income security, class mobility, and autonomy by negotiating a gender-income sensitive contract that addresses worker-defined needs. This is similar to Fernandez's (2001) findings that although technological upgrading can lead to greater wage inequality, an active union can at least help mitigate the most polarizing gender and racial effects. Unfortunately, the conditions at Discrete Manufacturing are not widely shared: Despite similar structural conditions of permanent employment across most of the industry, fewer than 10 percent of electronics firms in the Philippines are unionized.

But more important, even impressive collective bargaining agreements such as the one at Discrete Manufacturing do not directly address strategic gender interests, as they focus primarily on improving wages and benefits and not on challenging the gender division of labor. Thus,

the development in the industry that has the most potential for transforming workplace gender hierarchies and expanding women's choices about the gender division of labor is the emergence of the technical operator. As shown most vividly at Integrated Production—but also at Discrete Manufacturing—the new technical operator positions fuse the jobs, responsibilities, and promotional ladders of production workers (traditionally women) and technicians (traditionally men). These positions, which are likely to dominate high-end production facilities not only in the Philippines but across the global industry could allow current women operators to breach both the glass ceiling for women that has predominated in high-tech production work and the gendered associations with technology that have helped reproduce and sustain it. Yet despite the real potential that technological upgrading holds for realizing strategic gender interests, management at both firms chose to extend—rather than challenge—traditional associations between masculinity and technology, demonstrating the power and durability of gendered ideologies and frameworks.

Thus, while the gendering of work is always an ongoing, contested, and negotiated process, the ongoing trope of productive femininity, low unionization rates, and the complicity of the Philippine government means that there are few checks on management's power to implement and gender the new technology in ways it sees fit. And given the polarizing character of high-tech production and the current trends in the global industry toward automation, downsizing, and the masculinization of production, women electronics workers may witness—but have little access to—more skilled high-tech manufacturing jobs that the industry is finally producing.

REFERENCES

Acker, Joan. 2004. Gender, capitalism and globalization. *Critical Sociology* 30(1): 17–41.

Austria, Myrna S. 1999. *Assessing the competitiveness of the Philippine IT industry.* PIDS discussion paper. Makati: Philippine Institute for Development Studies.

Bello, Walden, David Kinley, and Elaine Elinson. 1982. *Development debacle: The World Bank in the Philippines.* San Francisco: Institute for Food and Development Policy.

Bureau of Labor Relations. 1999. *Labor management schemes and workers' benefits in the electronics industry.* Unpublished draft. Manila, Philippines: Bureau of Labor Relations.

Chant, Sylvia, and Cathy McIlwaine. 1995. *Women of a lesser cost: Female labor, foreign exchange and Philippine development.* London: Pluto.

Chhachhi, Amrita. 1999. *Gender, flexibility, skill and industrial restructuring: The electronics industry in India.* Working paper series no. 296. The Hague, the Netherlands: Institute of Social Studies.

Chhachhi, A., and R. Pittin. 1998. Multiple identities, multiple strategies: Confronting state, capital and patriarchy. In *Labor worldwide in the era of globalization,* edited by P. Waterman and R. Munck. London: Macmillan.

Chow, E. N., and D. M. Lyter. 2002. Studying development with gender perspectives: From mainstream theories to alternative frameworks. In *Transforming gender and development in East Asia,* edited by E. N. Chow. New York: Routledge.

Elson, Diane. 1999. Labor markets as gendered institutions: Equality, efficiency and empowerment issues. *World Development* 27(3): 611–27.

Ernst, Dieter. 2002. *Digital information systems and global flagship networks: How mobile is knowledge in the global network economy?* East West Center working papers, economics series no. 48. Honolulu, HI: East West Center.

Eviota, Elizabeth U. 1992. *The political economy of gender: Women and the sexual division of labor in the Philippines.* London: Zed Books.

Fernandez, Roberto. 2001. Skill-biased technological change and wage inequality: Evidence from a plant retooling. *American Journal of Sociology,* 107(2): 273–320.

Fox, J. 2002. Women's work and resistance in the global economy. In *Labor and capital in the age of globalization,* edited by B. Berberoglu. Lanham, MD: Rowan and Littlefield.

Hutchinson, Jane, and Andrew Brown, eds. 2001. *Organizing labour in globalizing Asia.* London: Routledge.

Joekes, Susan, and Ann Weston. 1994. *Women and the new trade agenda.* New York: UNIFEM.

Katz, Harry C., and Owen Darbishire. 2000. *Converging divergences.* Ithaca, NY: Cornell University Press.

Kelkar, G., and D. Nathan. 2002. Gender relations and technological change in Asia. *Current Sociology* 50(3): 427–41.

Kuruvilla, Sarosh. 1996. Linkages between industrialization strategies and industrial relations/human resource policies: Singapore, Malaysia, the Philippines and India. *Industrial & Labor Relations Review* 49(4): 635–58.

Mills, Mary Beth. 2003. Gender and inequality in the global labor force. *Annual Review of Anthropology* 32:41–62.

Molyneux, Maxine. 1985. Mobilization without emancipation? Women's interests, the state and revolution in Nicaragua. *Feminist Studies* 11:225–54.

National Statistical Coordination Board. 2001. *Various years. Statistics on men and women in the Philippines.* Government of the Philippines. Available from http://www.nscb.gov.ph/stats/wmfact.htrm.

Parrenas, R. S. 2001. *Breaking the code: Women, migration, and the 1987 family code of the Republic of the Philippines.* Paper presented at the Workshop on Globalization and the Asian "Migrant" Family, National University of Singapore, April 16.

Salzinger, Leslie. 2003. *Gender in production: Making workers in Mexico's global factories.* Berkeley: University of California Press.

Seguino, Stephanie. 2000. Accounting for gender in Asian economic growth. *Feminist Economics* 6(3): 27–58.

Standing, Guy. 1999. Global feminization through flexible labor: A theme revisited. *World Development* 27(3): 583–602.

Wolf, Diane L. 1992. *Factory daughters: Gender, household dynamics, and rural industrialization in Java.* Berkeley: University of California Press.

World Bank. 1997. *Philippines: Managing global integration.* Vol. 2, report no. 17024-PH. Poverty Reduction & Economic Management Sector, East Asia and the Pacific Office. Washington, DC: World Bank.

Yun, Hing Ai. 1995. Automation and new work patterns: Cases from Singapore's electronics industry. *Work, Employment & Society* 9(2): 309–27.

Introduction to Reading 35

In her presidential address to the Pacific Sociological Association, Amy S. Wharton provides an overview of changes in the institutions of work, family, and gender. She frames this address within the 50 years since the passage of the Civil Rights Act. In this piece, she describes the changes that have been made and the patterns that remain problematic. Using her own research on academic institutions, Wharton helps to explain why the social institutions of work, family, and gender are so resistant to change.

1. What was the intent of the Civil Rights Act? In what ways did it succeed? In what ways did it fail?

2. What does she mean by the "stalled revolution"?

3. What is meant by "egalitarian essentialism," and will it usher in further change in equity in institutions?

(Un)Changing Institutions

Work, Family, and Gender in the New Economy

Amy S. Wharton

As sociologists, we are all students of change. In fact, at the most abstract level, change is central to sociological thinking and practice. The study of social life at all levels involves close attention to the reciprocal and interdependent relations between social reproduction and transformation, or between continuity and disruption. Both forces are simultaneously present in the social world—whether at the societal level, the organizational level, in social interaction, or within individuals. In the larger society, change and the forces that produce it receive much more attention than continuity or stability, and this is perhaps not that surprising. However, our agenda in sociology is to capture both the ongoing reproduction of social life and its moments of disturbance or disorder. An interest in exploring those relations as they are expressed in the interconnected realms of work, gender, and family motivates this address.

The timing is right for this discussion. The year 2014 marks the 50th anniversary of the War on Poverty, which was launched by President Lyndon Johnson in his 1964 State of the Union Address. One of the most significant pieces of legislation passed that year was the Civil Rights Act. For those like myself who study workplace inequality, this law's most critical element is the fact that it outlawed discrimination by race, color, religion, national origin, and sex in employment. . . .

From Wharton, Amy S. 2015. (Un)Changing Institutions: Work, Family, and Gender in the New Economy. *Sociological Perspectives* 59(1).

In his book *Inventing Equal Opportunity,* Frank Dobbin (2009:22) notes that the Civil Rights Act was a "broad brush" attempt to forbid discrimination and promote equal opportunity, but it left open exactly what this meant and how it was to be done. Dobbin's argument is germane to this address in a number of important respects. First, the story of civil rights legislation is relevant for underscoring the important role of organizations, particularly work organizations, as a critically important arena where large-scale societal changes are played out. Second, the history of civil rights as told by Dobbin also underscores the messiness of organizational change and the factors that thwart or make it possible for change to occur. Among these factors is the process whereby legislation or other initiatives move from the realm of language to the realm of implementation and practice.

Finally, this history calls attention to the multifaceted and changing societal definitions of gender equality. The civil rights era made equal opportunity central to the meaning of this concept (Burstein, Bricher, and Einwohner 1995), and this emphasis remained predominant over decades of change in women's and men's lives. For example, almost 30 years after the passage of the 1964 Civil Rights Act, President George H. W. Bush signed the Civil Rights Act of 1991 to strengthen laws prohibiting sex discrimination in the workplace, but he vetoed family and medical leave bills (Burstein and Wierzbicki 2000). Today, equal opportunity is viewed as a necessary but not sufficient condition for gender equality, while work-family issues and new narratives about equality and choice have become more central.

To examine these ideas, I begin at the societal level, reviewing progress toward and away from gender equality. Next, I turn to the topic of organizational change. Societal changes are played out in the workplace, but organizations have their own change dynamics. These dynamics are important in understanding why and how organizational change fails. Finally, I use an example drawn from my own research on the academic workplace to examine leaders' gender narratives during a time of organizational change.

SOCIETAL CHANGES IN GENDER, WORK, AND FAMILY

The last half-century or more has been a time of fundamental change in gender, work, and family (Goldin 2006). In North America, Western Europe, and indeed throughout the globe, women's participation in the paid labor force rose steadily during the latter half of the twentieth century (Heymann and Earle 2009). In the United States, the increase in women's labor force participation occurred across all educational levels and among almost all racial and ethnic groups. During this time, women made inroads into jobs traditionally dominated by men and they made progress closing the gender earning gap. This pattern was fueled (and reinforced) by women's increasing levels of educational attainment—from primary school to college and to professional and graduate programs (Buchmann and DiPrete 2006). With respect to caregiving and household work, trends suggest a similar pattern of relatively continuous change over the past several decades and across a wide geographic area. Women spend fewer hours working at home, while more men spend more (Geist and Cohen 2011).

Gender attitudes have changed as well. Survey data show relatively consistent movement toward more liberal gender attitudes in the United States between the mid-1970s and 1990s (Cotter, Hermsen, and Vanneman 2011). Majorities of both women and men came to agree that a mother's employment was not damaging to her children, that women's role was not simply to care for the home, and that men did not necessarily make better politicians. North America, Europe, and other developed economies show similar patterns. In fact, attachment to women's and men's "traditional roles" has weakened among both women and men across the globe (Pew Research Global Attitudes Project 2010).

That progress toward gender equality in one area is connected to progress in another is not surprising. Thus, rather than a series of distinct changes, many note a pattern of convergence toward greater gender equality. One form of convergence is cross-national. For example, Claudia Geist and Philip N. Cohen (2011) found that in the last few decades, the amount of housework shouldered by women declined faster in more traditional countries than in those that were less traditional. This created a cross-national convergence of sorts as countries moved at different rates as they converged toward the same outcome: greater equality in the domestic division of labor. Economist Claudia Goldin (2014) conceives of convergence in a slightly different way, referring to "the converging roles of men and women," which she views as among the most important advances in society and the economy in the last century. As evidence for this, she points to the shrinking gap between women and men in labor force participation, hours of paid and unpaid work, labor force experience, occupational attainment, and education.

Uneven Gender Change and the Stalled Revolution

The evidence for twentieth century change (and convergence) in gender, work, and family is thus powerful and compelling. Increasingly, too, is the evidence that progress toward gender equality has gone through a period of deceleration or "stalling," as David A. Cotter, Joan M. Hermsen, and Reeve Vanneman (2004) referred to it in their report for the Russell Sage Foundation (see also England 2010). However, while there is some evidence of a global slowdown in progress toward gender equality, the United States is distinctive in certain respects (Lee 2014).

Cotter et al. (2004) show that the slowdown in the United States occurred across a number of domains. For example, U.S. women's rates of labor force participation leveled off in the late 1990s and have declined from their peak in 1999. This leveling off appears to have occurred across all categories of education, presence of children, and marital status (Lee 2014). With respect to the gender wage gap, the pattern is roughly similar. The wage gap narrowed steadily through the 1970s and 1980s, but progress slowed in the 1990s and early 2000s (Blau and Kahn 2007). During the 10-year period between 2004 and 2013, the gender wage gap barely changed, declining by only 1.7 percent (Institute for Women's Policy Research 2014).

Sociological research has revealed other, more nuanced looks at the stalled progress toward gender equality. In their study of occupational sex and race segregation from the 1960s to the present, Kevin Stainback and Donald Tomaskovic-Devey (2012) find that desegregation slowed considerably after political pressure by the civil rights and (later) the women's movement eased. Similarly, U.S. women's entrance into management positions increased steadily in the second half of the twentieth century, only to slow in the 1990s (P. N. Cohen, Huffman, and Knauer 2009). Although most women do not hold management positions—especially higher level positions—this slowdown has broader relevance. Several studies have shown that the demographic mix of managers shapes many aspects of the work environment, including the behaviors of managers themselves. The percentage of women in management jobs in an organization is positively related to the percentage of women in non-management jobs, and it affects the percentage of new jobs in an organization that are filled by women relative to men (L. E. Cohen and Broschak 2013).

Women in almost all industrialized countries earn a higher proportion of college degrees than men (Buchmann and DiPrete 2006; Charles and Bradley 2009). In the United States, the proportion of degrees received by women surpassed men in the early 1980s, and the gender gap has been growing steadily ever since, as men's college graduation rates decline. Despite their advantage in college graduation rates, other aspects of education show a more complicated picture with respect to movement toward gender parity or equality. In particular, the increase in women's share of college degrees in industrialized countries has been accompanied by a robust pattern of gender segregation by field of study (Charles and Bradley 2009). Paula England (2010) found a similar type of pattern when she looked at trends in doctoral degree attainment. Women's share of doctoral degrees went up fairly steadily over the last several decades (since the 1970s), but there has not been much change in the relative femaleness of different fields. Fields of study that were more female relative to others in the 1970s remain more female than others; fields of study that were less female than others 40 years ago remain less female than others today (England 2010).

Compared with data on employment and education, the evidence with respect to gender attitudes is more equivocal, especially with respect to recent trends. Cotter et al. (2011) show that support for more egalitarian views leveled off somewhat in the mid-1990s, and this leveling occurred among both women and men, of all ethnicities (except Asians) and across all levels of income and education. They found a small "rebound" in more egalitarian attitudes since 2000, but note "a growing but decelerating social liberalism among recent generations" (Cotter et al. 2011:282). However, in more recent analyses, these authors suggest that this rebound has been more robust, as indicated by steady increases since 2006 in popular support for gender equality and women's labor force participation (Cotter, Hermsen, and Vanneman 2014).

The Rise of Egalitarian Essentialism

Although many forces have contributed to the "stalled revolution," the role of cultural factors has received particular attention. Central to these arguments is the claim that a new frame or narrative about gender has gained prominence in politics and popular culture. Sociologists refer to this cultural frame as "egalitarian essentialism" (Cotter et al. 2011:261; see also Charles and Grusky 2004). This frame is distinct from traditional notions of "separate spheres," a dominant perspective in the first half of the twentieth century.

It is also distinct from feminist egalitarianism, a frame that emerged from and helped to fuel the feminist movements of the 1960s and 1970s. Egalitarian essentialism is a hybrid, containing an endorsement of the principle of gender equality, while defining equality as the right of individual women to choose what is best for them.

This emphasis on choice aligns with other efforts to describe new "post-feminist" standpoints. The most prominent is "choice feminism," a position described as being "concerned with increasing the number of choices open to women and with decreasing judgments about the choices individual women make" (Kirkpatrick 2010:241). When combined with a belief in essential gender differences, an emphasis on the value of individual choice tends to reinforce the status quo. Maria Charles and Karen Bradley (2009) show how this cultural frame has helped to perpetuate gender segregation in higher education, especially in industrial societies where beliefs in individual self-expression and choice are deeply entrenched. In addition to reinforcing the status quo, these narratives have been critiqued for their political implications. Choice feminism, in particular, has been described as an attempt to represent feminism as non-threatening and "seem appealing to the broadest constituency possible" (Ferguson 2010:248).

In sum, recent history reminds us that that social reproduction and social transformation are inextricably linked. The steady and mostly broad-based progress toward gender equality that marked the last half of the twentieth century has been disrupted or slowed. However, change and stability are relative concepts, and there is room for debate about whether and to what degree gender inequality has increased in recent years. Whether egalitarian essentialism, choice feminism, or similar cultural logics have contributed to this pattern is also in need of further study. Nevertheless, these gender narratives remain alive and well in popular debates about professional women "opting out" of the workforce and have become deeply embedded in work-family debates more generally (Kirkpatrick 2010; Stephens and Levine 2011).

Societal forces, including cultural logics and ideologies, also penetrate organizations, where they are expressed in the perspectives and practices of workers and employers. Organizations have their own change dynamics, however, which shape how cultural narratives are deployed.

Organizational Change and Changing Organizations

Organizational change receives a tremendous amount of attention from researchers. Perhaps one reason for this is that so much of what we understand to be true about organizations emphasizes their immobility or immovability. Rules, routines, and hierarchy are defining features of bureaucratic organizations and help to explain the tremendous inertia (and dysfunction) that is often associated with them (Perrow 1986). Organizations also act to prevent or deflect change. For example, loose coupling is a means by which organizations can create a firewall between outside demands and their normal operations and ways of doing business. Organizations portray themselves to outside constituencies in ways that signal movement, while leaving existing practices and routines untouched (Meyer and Rowan 1977).

The case of work-family policies provides a good example of this process. Many organizations have adopted formal work-family policies around flexibility, parental leaves, and so forth, but implementation often lags (Williams, Blair-Loy, and Berdahl 2013). The policies themselves face resistance or indifference among key organizational gatekeepers, such as managers or supervisors. Meanwhile, workers who may want to use these policies avoid doing so, as they recognize that their employer's commitment is more symbolic than real (Blair-Loy and Wharton 2002; Jacobs and Gerson 2004). The gendered culture of work and its ideal worker norms persist despite even well-intentioned efforts to make work accommodating to parents.

Organizations can face pressures to change from the outside, yet the external environment is more often a source of organizational continuity rather than disruption. Imitation is a major principle of human *and* organizational action (March 1996). Whether seeking solutions to immediate problems, or attempting to chart aspirations for the future, organizations (as well individuals) look not only to their own past performance but also to the past performance of relevant others (March 1996). Imitation contributes to the diffusion of ideas, knowledge, policies, or practice. It not only helps to increase predictability and continuity but also constrains large-scale change and transformation. Thus, when considering some of the basic principles that drive organizations, continuity often wins.

The continuity-change tradeoff is not always resolved in favor of continuity, however. Organizations do change and sometimes change in the direction of greater gender equality. When we look sociologically at these cases, however, the prime movers are often "behind our backs"— unexpected, unanticipated, and difficult to explain. In their study of work on offshore oil rigs, Robin J. Ely and Debra E. Meyerson (2010) identified an unforeseen effect of organizational efforts to enhance safety and performance. Expressions of hegemonic masculinity most often associated with dangerous, predominately male, jobs were significantly reduced. New workplace practices around safety ushered in new kinds of masculine identities and behaviors. In this way, the organization inadvertently "disrupt[ed] the gender status quo through practices that encourage[d] men to let go of conventional masculine scripts" (Ely and Meyerson 2010:28).

In contrast to unplanned or inadvertent transformation, organizations sometimes intentionally seek change. Yet, these experiences sometimes end up validating the most change averse among us. This is because a planned organizational change often goes badly awry (Hannan, Polos, and Carroll 2003). Organizational actors may miscalculate the risks and rewards of change; leaders underestimate how long a change will take and its costs, both monetary and in human terms. Furthermore, as sociologists, we are only too familiar with the unintended consequences of changes, whether planned or unplanned, and sometimes the failure of what seem like self-evident fixes.

Cautionary tales abound. Research by Alexandra Kalev, Frank Dobbin, and Erin Kelly (2006), for example, shows that one of the most ubiquitous approaches to increasing diversity in the workplace—diversity training—has been among the least effective in increasing the racial and gender diversity of managers in U.S. firms. Emilio J. Castilla and Stephen Benard's (2010) study of merit-based reward systems finds that these practices, which are enthusiastically embraced as a means to insure that pay is based on performance—not gender, race, or other considerations—may not be doing what many hoped. Instead, Castilla and Benard have uncovered what they call "the paradox of meritocracy." Organizations that emphasize meritocracy can (under some conditions) unintentionally create conditions that lead to more bias, not less, in the evaluative process.

Another example of well-intentioned organizational change that produces unintended negative consequences derives from the work-family literature. In their 20-nation, cross-national study of the effects of family-friendly policies on women's wages, Hadas Mandel and Moshe Semyonov (2005) found that these policies were associated with a larger gender earning gap, not a more egalitarian earning distribution. The reasons for this are complex, but these researchers suggest that it can be partly attributed to the fact that mothers more so than fathers are likely to take advantage of policies that facilitate work-family integration. This leaves mothers (and women in general) subject to discrimination by employers who penalize them for their work interruptions (such as long maternity leave).

This is not an argument against change efforts or work-family policies but rather another reminder that organizational changes—in the form of practices aimed at reducing inequality and discrimination or to increase work-family flexibility—are much more complicated than they seem. The mechanisms that facilitate change, like those that undermine it, operate at more than one level and sometimes work at cross purposes. For example, formalization is encouraged as a way to reduce bias and discrimination (such as the case of pay for performance or other mechanisms), yet while this may help mitigate the effects of cognitive bias, formalization can introduce biases of its own. Well-intentioned and planned organizational change can be resisted, deflected, or transformed in ways that undermine rather than facilitate desired outcomes.

CONTINUITY AND CHANGE IN THE ACADEMIC WORKPLACE

The academic workplace is a useful site for examining the dueling forces of continuity and change and understanding the role that gender narratives play in these dynamics. While bureaucratic organizations of all types may resist change, academic institutions are perceived as especially resistant (Lane 2007; Lucas 2000). Yet, as we have seen, higher education has not been immune from the broader set of forces reshaping gender, work, and family over the last several decades. One particular way these forces have affected the academic workplace is through federally funded initiatives designed to increase the gender diversity of the faculty. Much of this interest derives from concerns about the future of STEM disciplines (i.e., science, technology, engineering, and math) in the academy and the barriers faced by women and underrepresented minorities in these fields (Committee on Women in Science and Engineering 2006).

In 2001, the National Science Foundation created its ADVANCE Program to address these issues. The goals of ADVANCE are to increase the representation of women in academic science and engineering careers, develop ways to promote gender equity in STEM, and increase the diversity of the STEM workforce. This program has not been modest about its investments or intentions. Since 2001, ADVANCE has spent over 130 million dollars to support ADVANCE projects at over 100 colleges and universities and some non-profit (National Science Foundation 2014). The most visible and well-funded ADVANCE award is its Institutional Transformation award. Averaging about 3.5 million dollars, these institutional grants are intended to transform universities in ways that make academe and STEM in particular more accommodating to women and other underrepresented groups.

ADVANCE-funded institutions have pursued many strategies to accomplish this goal (Bilimoria and Liang 2012; Bystydzienski and Bird 2006; Laursen and Rocque 2009). In general, ADVANCE initiatives fall into three broad categories, including those focused on policy reform and creation, departmental or institutional climate, and training of faculty and administrators (Stewart, Malley, and LaVaque-Manty 2007). This investment in institutional change has been fueled by and helped foster an outpouring of sociological research on gender, work, and family in the academe, both within and outside of STEM. This research has included studies of work-family issues in the academy (e.g., Fox, Fonseca, and Bao 2011; King 2008; Mason and Goulden 2004; Misra, Lundquist, and Templer 2012), as well as research on gender inequality in academic life (e.g., Bird 2011; Ecklund, Lincoln, and Tansey 2012; Jacobs and Winslow 2004; Misra et al. 2011; Roos and Gatta 2009; Winslow 2010). Climate, especially departmental climate, has also received significant attention in ADVANCE institutions, and climate studies have become useful diagnostic tools for universities trying to understand the experiences of women and other underrepresented groups (Callister 2006; Maranto and Griffin 2011; Settles et al. 2006).

Leadership and Organizational Change

These studies have helped to explain women's underrepresentation in STEM fields and the barriers that remain to be overcome. Less attention, however, has been paid to the organizational change process itself and particularly the forces that derail or deflect change efforts.

My own research examines this issue with a focus on departmental leaders.

Leaders are vitally important to the change process. Frank Dobbin and Alexandra Kalev (2007:280) argue that "In the corporate world, as in academia, programs that establish clear leadership and responsibility for change have produced the greatest gains in diversity." Similarly, Sara I. McClelland and Kathryn J. Holland (2014:3) suggest that leaders' sense of accountability and personal responsibility for diversity initiatives are critical to the success of these efforts. Michael Schwalbe et al. (2000:435) highlight leaders' role in "regulating discourse" through formal or informal mechanisms. By filtering and framing information, leaders shape perceptions of their subordinates (Dragoni 2005). Leaders' beliefs about gender may be especially powerful, given the role of these beliefs in reproducing gender inequality (Ridgeway 2011).

Leadership in academe is multi-layered, but for faculty, the departmental leader is most critical. That institutional transformation in academe requires attention to departmental processes is widely acknowledged, making departmental practices, policies, routines, relationships, and dynamics important topics. Chairs influence all these aspects of departmental life (Bilimoria et al. 2006). In this way, they also shape faculty's satisfaction with their careers, colleagues, and work environment (Bensimon, Ward, and Sanders 2000). Chairs seem to have a particularly important influence on women's work lives in the academy (Settles et al. 2006). Recognition of their role has made departmental leaders a key audience for various types of training opportunities, and climate surveys typically ask faculty about their perceptions of their chair and other leaders. Ironically, however, while we know much about faculty perceptions, chairs' own beliefs are less well understood.

In 2010, I was part of a four-person research team at an ADVANCE institution that set out to investigate departmental leaders' perspectives on their own roles and responsibilities with respect to diversity and organizational change. During the course of this project, graduate student Mychel Estevez and I became attuned to the ways that chairs framed issues of gender and gender inequality, especially as these topics were invoked in the context of the university's broader efforts at improving gender equity and increasing women's representation in STEM fields (see Wharton and Estevez 2014, for a full discussion of this research). Some data from this project, in addition to more recently published research by other scholars, have revealed how leaders' narratives about gender, work, and family can slow or undermine change efforts. Leaders may deflect responsibility for change by emphasizing the choices of others, particularly female faculty, and many fail to act out of a belief that gender change is inevitable and progressive.

* * *

Choice and Change

Choice is personally empowering, connoting independence, freedom, and autonomy. It has many positive consequences for those who have choices or believe themselves to have them (Savani, Stephens, and Markus 2011; Stephens and Levine 2011). This is especially true in American society and, as we have seen, in academe, where the ability to control the conditions of one's work is highly valued. Although having the ability to choose is personally beneficial, it is socially disadvantageous. Experimental research shows that exposure to a choice perspective weakens support for policies designed to advance collectivities or society as a whole (Savani et al. 2011). As Nicole M. Stephens and Cynthia S. Levine (2011:1235) note, Americans' strong embrace of a choice framework helps explain why they "readily dismiss gender barriers as a vestige of the past in the face of evidence to the contrary." Choice fortifies notions of personal responsibility and thereby assigns blame to others for their disadvantages while minimizing the role of external forces or constraints.

Marieke van den Brink and Yvonne Benschop (2012:89) argue that change in the academy is slow because practices and beliefs that perpetuate inequality "may hinder, alter, or transform equality measures." This summarizes the story

told here, as good faith and intentional efforts to make change are deflected, rearticulated, and transformed. Leaders perceive work-family issues through the lens of choice, treating these matters as the responsibility of the individual (women) faculty members, and not the institution. This belief in choice also shapes chairs' perceptions of gender inequality more generally. They do not necessarily believe that gender inequality has been eliminated, yet are reluctant to view problems as structural or systemic. The need for change is depoliticized and viewed as inevitable, incremental, and "naturally" occurring over time through generational replacement. Most important, by assigning responsibility for change to others, chairs' willingness, capacity, and resolve to act are substantially weakened.

CONCLUSION

The passage of the Civil Rights Act and the pursuit of equal opportunity it endorsed were about improving the chances for women and other underrepresented groups to compete in an essentially unchanged workplace. Paul Burstein and colleagues (Bricher 1997; Burstein et al. 1995; Burstein and Wierzbicki 2000) note that what they call the "work-family accommodation" frame was more far reaching politically. This frame contained an implicit critique of the organization of work and drew attention to its impact on women's and men's family responsibilities and commitments. This broader vision of gender equality has yet to gain popular support or a foothold in the political arena. The resurgence of a choice framework—in the form of egalitarian essentialism or choice feminism—has likely played a role in depoliticizing the work-family agenda and undermining the case for change. It has also served as a reminder that narratives about gender are a central ingredient in the broader system of practices that reproduce inequality.

The strong forces of change in the gender system that occurred during the twentieth century were set into motion by numerous forces—including by conscious, political efforts to reduce gender inequality. These changes were not inevitable, nor can they be assumed to be permanent and ongoing. This makes it all the more important that we return our attention to the ways of change. These include the recognition that the forces of continuity and change are simultaneously present in society and the organizations that comprise it, that beliefs and practices that maintain continuity or the status quo restrain and circumvent those that promote equality practices and beliefs, and that many forces tip the balance in favor of continuity.

It is impossible to predict the twists and turns that are in our future. The past decade may look like a small blip 20 years out or may in fact represent a major turning point of some kind. Most of us here are not waiting to see how things turn out or believe (naively) that evolution or generational replacement will by itself pave a way toward greater gender equality. Instead, we seek change—to transform the workplace, to eliminate discrimination and reduce inequality, and to restart the stalled gender revolution. Fulfilling these goals requires us to look carefully at the ways in which inequality practices and beliefs may be undermining our efforts.

References

Bensimon, Estela M., Kelly Ward, and Karla Sanders. 2000. *The Department Chair's Role in Developing New Faculty into Teachers and Scholars.* Bolton, MA: Anker.

Bilimoria, Diana and Xiangfen Liang. 2012. *Gender Equity in Science and Engineering: Advancing Change in Higher Education.* New York: Routledge.

Bilimoria, Diana, Susan R. Perry, Xiangfen Liang, Eleanor P. Stoller, Patricia Higgins, and Cyrus Taylor. 2006. "How Do Female and Male Faculty Members Construct Job Satisfaction? The Role of Perceived Institutional Leadership and Mentoring and Their Mediating Processes." *Journal of Technology Transfer* 31:355–65.

Bird, Sharon. 2011. "Unsettling the Universities' Incongruous, Gendered Bureaucratic Structures: A Case Study Approach." *Gender, Work & Organization* 18:202–30.

Blair-Loy, Mary and Amy S. Wharton. 2002. "Employees' Use of Work-Family Policies and the Workplace Social Context." *Social Forces* 80: 813–845.

Blau, Francine D. and Lawrence M. Kahn. 2007. "The Gender Pay Gap: Have Women Gone as Far as They Can?" *Academy of Management Perspectives* 21:7–23.

Buchmann, Claudia and Thomas A. DiPrete. 2006, "The Growing Female Advantage in College Completion: The Role of Family Background and Academic Achievement." *American Sociological Review* 71:515–41.

Burstein, Paul and Marie Bricher. 1997. "Problem Definition and Public Policy: Congressional Committees Confront Work, Family, and Gender, 1945–1990." *Social Forces* 75:135–69.

Burstein, Paul, Marie Bricher, and Rachel L. Einwohner. 1995. "Policy Alternatives and Political Change: Work, Family, and Gender on the Congressional Agenda, 1945–1990." *American Sociological Review* 60:67–83.

Burstein, Paul and Susan Wierzbicki. 2000. "Public Opinion and Congressional Action on Work, Family, and Gender, 1945–1990." Pp. 31–66 in *Work & Family: Research Informing Policy,* edited by Toby L. Parcel and Daniel B. Cornfield. Thousand Oaks, CA: Sage Publications.

Bystydzienski, Jill and Sharon R. Bird, eds. 2006. *Removing Barriers: Women in Academic Science, Engineering, Technology and Mathematics Careers.* Bloomington, IN: Indiana University Press.

Callister, Ronda R. 2006. "The Impact of Gender and Department Climate on Job Satisfaction and Intentions to Quit for Faculty in Science and Engineering Fields." *Journal of Technology Transfer* 31:367–75.

Castilla, Emilio J. and Stephen Benard. 2010. "The Paradox of Meritocracy in Organizations." *Administrative Science Quarterly* 55:543–76.

Charles, Maria and Karen Bradley. 2009. "Indulging Our Gendered Selves: Sex Segregation by Field of Study in 44 Countries." *American Journal of Sociology* 114:924–76.

Charles, Maria and David B. Grusky. 2004. *Occupational Ghettoes: The Worldwide Segregation of Women and Men.* Stanford, CA: Stanford University Press.

Cohen, Lisa E. and Joseph P. Broschak. 2013. "Whose Jobs Are These? The Impact of the Proportion of Female Managers on the Number of New Management Jobs Filled by Women." *Administrative Science Quarterly* 58:509–41.

Cohen, Philip N., Matt L. Huffman, and Stefanie Knauer. 2009. "Stalled Progress? Gender Segregation and Wage Inequality among Managers, 1980–2000." *Work and Occupations* 36:318–42.

Committee on Women in Science and Engineering. 2006. *To Recruit and Advance: Women Students and Faculty in Science and Engineering.* Washington, DC: National Academy Press.

Cotter, David A., Joan M. Hermsen, and Reeve Vanneman. 2004. *Gender Inequality at Work.* A volume in the series, The American People: Census 2000. New York: Russell Sage Foundation and Population Reference Bureau.

Cotter, David A., Joan M. Hermsen, and Reeve Vanneman. 2011. "The End of the Gender Revolution? Gender Role Attitudes from 1977 to 2008." *American Journal of Sociology* 117:259–89.

Cotter, David A., Joan M. Hermsen, and Reeve Vanneman. 2014. "Back on Track? Stall and Rebound for Gender Equality 1977–2012." Retrieved November 3, 2014 (http://thesocietypages.org/ccf/2014/08/05/gender-revolution-rebound-symposium/).

Dobbin, Frank. 2009. *Inventing Equal Opportunity.* Princeton, NJ: Princeton University Press.

Dobbin, Frank and Alexandra Kalev. 2007. "The Architecture of Inclusion: Evidence from Corporate Diversity Programs." *Harvard Journal of Law & Gender* 30:279–301.

Dragoni, Lisa. 2005. "Understanding the Emergence of State Goal Orientation in Organizational Work Groups: The Role of Leadership and Multilevel Climate Perceptions." *Journal of Applied Psychology* 90:1084–95.

Ecklund, Elaine Howard, Anne E. Lincoln, and Cassandra Tansey. 2012. "Gender Segregation in Elite Academic Science." *Gender & Society* 26:693–717.

Ely, Robin J. and Debra E. Meyerson. 2010. "An Organizational Approach to Undoing Gender: The Case of Offshore Oil Platforms." *Research in Organizational Behavior* 30:3–34.

England, Paula. 2010. "The Gender Revolution: Uneven and Stalled." *Gender & Society* 24:149–66.

Ferguson, Michaele L. 2010. "Choice Feminism and the Fear of Politics." *Perspectives on Politics* 8:247–70.

Fox, Mary Frank, Carolyn Fonseca, and Jinghui Bao. 2011. "Work and Family Conflict in Academic Science: Patterns and Predictors among Women and Men in Research Universities." *Social Studies of Science* 41:715–35.

Geist, Claudia and Philip N. Cohen. 2011. "Headed toward Equality? Housework Change in Comparative Perspective." *Journal of Marriage and Family* 73:832–44.

Goldin, Claudia. 2006. "The Quiet Revolution That Transformed Women's Employment, Education, and Family." *AEA Papers and Proceedings* 96 (May): 1–21.

Goldin, Claudia. 2014. "A Grand Gender Convergence: Its Last Chapter." *American Economic Review* 104:1091–119.

Hannan, Michael T., Laszlo Polos, and Glenn R. Carroll. 2003. "The Fog of Change: Opacity and Asperity in Organizations." *Administrative Science Quarterly* 48:399–432.

Heymann, Jody and Alison Earle. 2009. *Raising the Global Floor: Dismantling the Myth That We Can't Afford Good Working Conditions for Everyone.* Stanford, CA: Stanford University Press.

Institute for Women's Policy Research. 2014. "The Gender Wage Gap 2013: Differences by Race and Ethnicity, No Growth in Real Wages for Women." Fact Sheet. Retrieved December 15, 2014 (http:// www.iwpr.org/publications/pubs/the-gender-wage-gap-2013-differences-by-race-and-ethnicity-no-growth-in-real-wages-for-women).

Jacobs, Jerry A. and Kathleen Gerson. 2004. *The Time Divide: Work, Family, and Gender Inequality.* Cambridge, MA: Harvard University Press.

Jacobs, Jerry A. and Sarah Winslow. 2004. "Understanding the Academic Life Course, Time Pressures, and Gender Inequality." *Community, Work & Family* 7:143–61.

Kalev, Alexandra, Frank Dobbin, and Erin Kelly. 2006. "Best Practices or Best Guesses? Assessing the Efficacy of Corporate Affirmative Action and Diversity Policies." *American Sociological Review* 71:589–617.

King, Eden B. 2008. "The Effect of Bias on the Advancement of Working Mothers: Disentangling Legitimate Concerns from Inaccurate Stereotypes as Predictors of Advancement in Academe." *Human Relations* 61:1677–711.

Kirkpatrick, Jennet. 2010. "Introduction: Selling Out? Solidarity and Choice in the American Feminist Movement." *Perspectives on Politics* 8:241–45.

Lane, India F. 2007. "Change in Higher Education: Understanding and Responding to Individual and Organizational Resistance." Retrieved December 5, 2014 (http://www.ccas.net/files/ADVANCE/Lane_Change%20in%20higher%20ed.pdf).

Laursen, Sandra and Bill Rocque. 2009. "Faculty Development for Institutional Change: Lessons from an ADVANCE Project." *Change: The Magazine of Higher Learning,* March-April 2009. Retrieved December 5, 2014 (http://www

.changemag.org/archives/back%20issues/mnrch-april%202009/full-advance-project.html).

Lee, Jin Y. 2014. "The Plateau in U.S. Women's Labor Force Participation: A Cohort Analysis." *Industrial Relations* 53:46–71.

Lucas, Ann F., ed. 2000. *Leading Academic Change: Essential Roles for Department Chairs.* San Francisco, CA: Jossey-Bass.

Mandel, Hadas and Moshe Semyonov. 2005. "Family Policies, Wage Structures, and Gender Gaps: Sources of Earnings Inequality in 20 Countries." *American Sociological Review* 70:949–67.

Maranto, Cheryl and Andrea E. C. Griffin. 2011. "The Antecedents of a 'Chilly Climate' for Women Faculty in Higher Education." *Human Relations* 64:139–59.

March, James G. 1996. "Continuity and Change in Theories of Organizational Action." *Administrative Science Quarterly* 41:278–87.

Mason, Mary A. and Marc Goulden. 2004. "Marriage and Baby Blues: Redefining Gender Equity in the Academy." *The Annals of the American Academy of Political and Social Science* 596:86–103.

McClelland, Sara I. and Kathryn J. Holland. 2014. "You, Me, or Her: Leaders' Perceptions of Responsibility for Increasing Gender Diversity in STEM Departments." *Psychology of Women Quarterly,* doi: 10.1177/0361684314537997, first published on June 5, 2014.

Meyer, John W. and Brian Rowan. 1977. "Institutionalized Organizations: Formal Structure as Myth and Ceremony." *American Journal of Sociology* 83:340–63.

Misra, Joya, Jennifer H. Lundquist, Elissa Holmes, and Stephanie Agiomavritis. 2011. "The Ivory Ceiling of Service Work." *Academe* 97:22–26.

Misra, Joya, Jennifer H. Lundquist, and Abby Templer. 2012. "Gender, Work Time, and Care Responsibilities among Faculty." *Sociological Forum* 27:300–23.

National Science Foundation. 2014. ADVANCE at a Glance. Retrieved November 3, 2014 (http://www.nsf.gov/crssprgm/advance/).

Perrow, Charles. 1986. *Complex Organizations: A Critical Essay.* New York: McGraw-Hill.

Pew Research Global Attitudes Project. 2010. Gender Equality Universally Embraced, but Inequalities Acknowledged. Retrieved November 3, 2014 (http://www.pewglobal.org/2010/07/01/gender-equality/).

Ridgeway, Cecilia L. 2011. *Framed by Gender: How Gender Inequality Persists in the Modern World.* New York: Oxford University Press.

Roos, Patricia A. and Mary L. Gatta. 2009. "Gender (In)Equity in the Academy: Subtle Mechanisms and the Production of Inequality." *Research in Social Stratification and Mobility* 27:177–200.

Savani, Krishna, Nicole M. Stephens, and Hazel R. Markus. 2011. "The Unanticipated Interpersonal and Societal Consequences of Choice: Victim Blaming and Reduced Support for the Public Good." *Psychological Science* 22:795–802.

Schwalbe, Michael, Sandra Godwin, Daphne Holden, Douglas Schrock, Shealy Thompson, and Michele Wolkomir. 2000. "Generic Processes in the Reproduction of Inequality: An Interactionist Analysis." *Social Forces* 79:419–52.

Settles, Isis H., Lilia M. Cortina, Janet Malley, and Abigail J. Stewart. 2006. "The Climate for Women in Academic Science: The Good, the Bad, and the Changeable." *Psychology of Women Quarterly* 30:47–58.

Stainback, Kevin and Donald Tomaskovic-Devey. 2012. *Documenting Desegregation: Racial and Gender Segregation in Private-Sector Employment since the Civil Rights Act.* New York: Russell Sage Foundation.

Stephens, Nicole M. and Cynthia S. Levine. 2011. "Opting Out or Denying Discrimination? How the Framework of Free Choice in American Society Influences Perceptions of Gender Inequality." *Psychological Science* 22:1231–236.

Stewart, Abigail, Janet E. Malley, and Danielle LaVaque-Manty (eds.). 2007. *Transforming Science and Engineering: Advancing Academic Women.* Ann Arbor, MI: University of Michigan Press.

Van den Brink, Marieke and Yvonne Benschop. 2012. "Slaying the Seven-Headed Dragon: The Quest for Gender Change in Academia." *Gender, Work & Organization* 19:71–92.

Wharton, Amy S. and Mychel Estevez. 2014. "Department Chairs' Perspectives on Work, Family, and Gender Pathways for Transformation." *Advances in Gender Research* 19:131–50.

Williams, Joan C., Mary Blair-Loy, and Jennifer L. Berdahl. 2013. "Cultural Schemas, Social Class, and the Flexibility Stigma." *Journal of Social Issues* 69:209–34.

Winslow, Sarah. 2010. "Gender Inequality and Time Allocations among Academic Faculty." *Gender & Society* 24:769–93.

Introduction to Reading 36

In this reading Brooke Conroy Bass addresses the oft-given theory that women simply are not as interested in work and careers as men are. In her research she addresses this issue looking at the future plans for work and family of early-career heterosexual couples. She used snowball sampling (craigslist, referrals, etc.) to locate 30 couples (between 25 and 34 years old) in the San Francisco area. Individuals were interviewed separately, and interviews averaged about 2 hours in length. Subjects completed a survey before the interviews, through which she identified their views about equity in relationships. All individuals were "relatively egalitarian in their gender ideologies." All of the couples were childless, although over half said they planned to have children "in the near future." Most of the couples (73%) were married, with the remaining either engaged or cohabitating. She approached the interviews without mentioning gender or focusing on parenting; however, you will see that the women in her study focused on the topics without prompting. This is a valuable glance at how gender is involved in career and work decisions.

1. Since this is predominantly a middle- to upper-middle-class sample, consider how social class would intersect with gender in the decision making of individuals from other social classes.

2. How does gender work for the men and women sampled in this study? Does it provide as many conditions and constraints as other institutions, such as work organizations, discussed in the readings by Acker and Wharton in this chapter?

3. Think about how you and your friends make/made your work and career plans. Are they gendered in the same ways that are described in this reading?

PREPARING FOR PARENTHOOD

GENDER, ASPIRATIONS, AND THE REPRODUCTION OF LABOR MARKET INEQUALITY

Brooke Conroy Bass

Over the last several decades, there has been considerable interest among sociologists to explain the role of parenthood in shaping the labor market experiences of mothers and fathers. This is because new parenthood remains a critical juncture in which women's and men's career trajectories often diverge substantially, with women tending to scale back and men tending to ramp up their involvement in paid labor (Cohen and Bianchi 1999; Grunow, Schultz, and Blossfeld 2012; LaRossa and LaRossa 1981; Sanchez and Thomson 1997).

From Bass, Brooke Conroy. 2015. "Preparing for Parenthood: Gender, Aspirations, and the Reproduction of Labor Market Inequality." *Gender & Society 29*(3): 362–385.

Labor market involvement is closely linked to the gender gap in pay, which, on average, is also larger among parents (Waldfogel 1998).

Qualitative attempts by sociologists to explain the influence of parenthood expectations and constraints on individual career choice have relied almost exclusively on the accounts of new parents (Cowan and Cowan 1992; Stone 2007; Walzer 1996; Webber and Williams 2008). Yet scholarship that empirically addresses the career choices women and men make during the critical period that precedes parenthood, when many young adults are forming committed partnerships and forging their paths in the workplace, is scant. This article aims to fill this gap by exploring the role of cultural assumptions about gender, parenthood, and family care work in shaping the imagined work paths of middle- and upper-class young adults who are engaged or married but who do not yet have children. Since this is a stage when career and family paths are particularly salient and pliable, it is important to ask how anticipations of parenthood influence the decisions that childless individuals make in the workplace. For example, do future plans to have children differentially affect the career aspirations and choices of women and men?

I draw on data from in-depth interviews with 60 college-educated childless young adults (30 heterosexual couples) living in the San Francisco Bay Area to show how gender shapes the mental, emotional, and behavioral aspects of early career choice.

THE FORMATION OF CAREER ASPIRATIONS

Survey data consistently show that while the majority of contemporary couples maintain egalitarian labor arrangements before having children, many tend to shift to more traditional arrangements upon the birth of their first child (Grunow, Schultz, and Blossfeld 2012; LaRossa and LaRossa 1981; Sanchez and Thomson 1997). This finding remains even among gender egalitarians (Grunow, Schultz, and Blossfeld 2012).

In one particularly compelling in-depth study on the topic, Stone (2007) interviewed 54 high-achieving mothers who had "opted out" of the paid labor force. She, as well as others doing research in the field (Hays 1996; Webber and Williams 2008), found that mothers are pulled toward their family lives by the cultural ideology of intensive mothering. Simultaneously, mothers in Stone's sample describe being pushed out of their careers by unrealistic workplace policies and bosses who made balancing "ideal worker norms" (Williams 2000) with childrearing demands nearly impossible.

While structural forces like these undoubtedly influence the reproduction of labor market inequality that results from new parenthood, it is also possible that some of what drives couples' decisions at new parenthood begins well in advance of the birth of a child. In other words, couples may make what they deem as rational choices at the time of a child's birth based on each partner's relative earnings, occupational satisfaction, and tenure, all of which may be impacted by processes occurring before parenthood. This article takes a step toward building our understanding of these processes by asking whether anticipations of parenthood shape aspirations in gender differentiated ways.

The literature on aspirations shows that gendered career choices begin very early in the life course, well in advance of family formation. Female high school and college students tend to be less likely to enter more lucrative male-typed majors and jobs (Jacobs 1995; Lips 2007; Machung 1989); and the gap between college-educated women's and men's reported likelihood of entering a career in the fields of math or science widens as they age (Lips 2004). College-age women are also less likely to believe they will be in positions of power in the paid labor force (Lips 2000).

Social psychologists have provided some of the best evidence of the causal mechanisms that may be at play, linking self-assessments to aspirations early in the life course. Correll (2004) finds that women tend to assess themselves lower in performance of culturally defined male-typed tasks (e.g., math- and science-oriented tasks) because of the lower status accorded to women in society, making them less likely to enter careers in these fields. Other research on the topic suggests the potential for gender stereotypes and environmental messages to similarly dissuade women from entering male-dominated domains by priming them with ideas about their potential fit in such positions (Cheryan et al. 2009).

It is clear, then, that career aspirations and the social forces that shape them are both gendered and consequential. But what bearing, if any, do family aspirations and expectations have on individuals' work lives? Some social scientific evidence suggests that aspirations for family life, and for a certain work-family structure, in particular, may also play a key role in shaping individual career aspirations. For instance, using in-depth interviews with college students, Machung (1989) found that women's career-related aspirations are curbed early on by a preference for work-family balance and by privileging men's careers over their own.

This finding is contrasted in the literature, however, by those who find that young adults' family expectations have little impact on early labor market aspirations. For instance, Gerson (1985, 20) argues that youth aspirations often diverged from women's later work-family orientations because "early plans can ultimately turn out to be uninviting or even impossible, encouraging or perhaps requiring individual change." Damaske (2011) interviewed 80 women about their early workforce participation expectations and found that the vast majority of middle- and upper-class women, the group most directly comparable to those in my (and Machung's) study sample, expected to work continuously throughout their adult lives, suggesting that intermittent work in anticipation of child care needs may not affect those with the most access to human capital. Thus, it is unclear whether (and how) family aspirations and expectations are linked to early workplace choices.

One burgeoning area of sociological work that offers insight, however, explores college-age young adults' work-family structure preferences. In a recent study on the work-family structure expectations of unmarried women and men, Gerson (2010) finds that, while the vast majority of young adults report a strong desire for an egalitarian relationship (their "Plan A" work-family structure), many believe it will be an impossibility because of highly rigid, institutionalized work structures. In turn, they form gendered "Plan B" preferences, with men opting for a type of neotraditional family structure and women opting for a self-reliant model. A recent experimental study by Pedulla and Thébaud (2013) largely corroborated Gerson's (2010) qualitative findings.

While these studies offer unique insight into the potential disconnect between young adult work-family ideals and outcomes, their empirical focus remains on single young adults for whom the option of falling back on self-reliance is likely not accompanied by thoughts of separation from a partner to whom they've committed, as it would imply for coupled young adults. Coupled young adults may also have shifted aspirations and preferences in response to the gendered expectations that accompany marriage (Davis and Greenstein 2009; Risman 1998). Vespa argues that "changes in gender ideology are more likely a consequence, or by-product, of exposure to new social situations and roles that are embedded with gendered expectations" (2009, 365), such as the role of wife-husband or mother-father. Given the implicit link between gender ideology and work-family aspirations, the transition to marriage and its culturally assumed association with parenthood is likely one such social situation that shapes aspirations. Yet the extent and effects of parenthood expectations on childless *coupled* young adults is unclear.

Thus, myriad unanswered questions remain about the complex process of navigating conflicting ideals and interests in the face of constraint as individuals move through the life course, from singlehood toward coupled parenthood. This article takes a step toward filling this gap by asking how, if at all, coupled young adults without children interpret gendered parenthood expectations and work-family conflict at a critical juncture in their labor force trajectory.

* * *

THE ROLE OF GENDER IN PREPARING FOR PARENTHOOD

I argue that one vehicle through which labor inequality is perpetuated is through anticipations of parenthood. I identify three processes through which this cultural mechanism influences coupled women and men without children . . .

1. The Mental Work of Anticipating Parenthood

Among the individuals that I interviewed, gender played a critical role in determining the mental work associated with anticipating parenthood, particularly as it intersected with respondents' imagined labor trajectories. I use the term *mental work* to describe the active thinking and feeling work that takes place in anticipation of family needs. The concept was first introduced to gender and family scholarship by Walzer (1996) in her discussion of new parenthood, but similar concepts have also been developed in research on household labor (DeVault 1991; Hochschild 1989). . . .

The gendering of mental work evident in my sample is best illustrated when quantified. After asking respondents to describe their current work situation, and prior to explicitly asking about their considerations of parenthood, I asked each the following question: "Where do you see your work life going in the next five to ten years?" While the topic of children had rarely been discussed at this point in the interview, this question alone elicited a bevy of gendered responses. Indeed, in response to this focal question, approximately 77 percent of women in my sample mentioned parenthood or child care in their description of their imagined work paths without interviewer probing; this is in stark contrast to the 10 percent of men who mentioned it. Men, for the most part, viewed their future careers through an unmuddled career-focused lens while women viewed it through the lens of future motherhood.

For example, Tamar[1] (age 30, married) had recently begun a public sector job evaluating the effects of environmental programs, which she enjoyed. When asked about the direction of her work life in the next five to ten years, she cited uncertainty, saying, "I don't know when we're gonna have kids. We're thinking about it. So I'm not sure how that would work in with the career path and all that." In response to the same question, Cindy (age 32, married) immediately said, "Well, we do wanna have kids soon . . ." before continuing on to describe the various employment paths she was considering, making clear that the idea of motherhood complicated her envisioned work path.

Erin (age 32, engaged) told me that having kids "is kind of like in the back of my mind," as she discussed whether she wanted to stay in her current job or look for something she found more fulfilling. Sandy (age 25, married), who was working as a restaurant manager, anticipated the conflict that motherhood might present to her career when she told me, "I'd love to just stay where I'm at. I feel like I finally found a place where I fit, where it feels right, feels good. And everything's lined up. But I also want to be a mom."

Marcella (age 28, married), an office manager at a law firm, was interviewing candidates for open positions. In response to my focal question, she replied that while she routinely asked potential job candidates the same exact question, "I can't answer it for myself." She continued on, describing the back and forth dialogue she has with herself and her "girlfriends" about the matter: "It's hard for me to, like, keep it in perspective. . . . In five or ten years, maybe I'll just be a mom. Maybe I'll be working part-time. Maybe I'll take maternity leave and return back to work." Like Marcella, many women respondents' discussions of their future labor trajectories were intertwined with ideas about parenthood and uncertainty about how new motherhood might affect their involvement in the paid labor force.

Men's considerations of parenthood were largely absent from their discussions of career aspirations. When I explicitly asked whether theirs or their partners' work lives might change upon new parenthood, their answers seemed to convey that they had not considered the topic, at least not seriously, before. For instance, Donald (age 27, married), a sales manager at an IT firm, replied, "Oh, that's a good question. Um . . . I don't know." Nathan (age 30, married), a computer programmer, offered a similar response: "That's a good question . . . I dunno. I think that's it's hard. It's an interesting question. . . . I don't know if we've put a ton of thought into exactly how that process would work or not." While Nathan implies that he and his partner *together* have not considered the topic, my interview with his partner, Marcella (quoted above), tells a different story.

When asked to comment on how his or his wife's work might change upon parenthood, Caleb (age 32, married) told me he had not thought much about the topic, but instead worried about other aspects of his life in imagining parenthood:

> I honestly haven't thought about it that much. I guess the one thing that, like, scares me about having a kid and that I *have* thought about a lot is, like, I have to make sure that I have my own time. That I can go play sports or go and be with friends and it's okay. Like, I have some specified amount of time each week that's my time without the kid, and [my wife] will take care of it. And vice versa, of course. But I worry about that much more than almost anything else, I'd just hate losing my life for the kid.

Others contrasted their personality types with that of their wives, who they frequently dubbed "the planners." For instance, Bobby (age 29, married) told me, "I'm more of a procrastinator. I worry about things as they become more urgent

or close to the deadline. So until we have kids, it's not a big concern of mine."

Some women were attuned to the fact that their partners were not giving the idea of parenthood and work-life balance as much consideration as they were. But like their partners, they offered individual-level personality differences as the reason for these differences. For example, when I asked Denise (age 27, married) whether her partner similarly thought about the issues of balancing work with children, she replied:

> No, he hasn't. He hasn't really. He's always open to discussion, and he would never shy away from it. It's just he doesn't initiate those types of discussions because we're not there yet, so he doesn't think about it. He's not sure where a year from now is because we're not there yet. And that's different for me because I'm constantly trying to maybe change what I'm doing now to get ready for a year from now. I'm always looking ahead. And he doesn't.

I suspect that the personality differences described by Denise may actually be the product of a long-established system of domesticity in the United States (Williams 2000) rather than innate gender differences in planning preferences and abilities. One pertinent detail that lends support to this argument is that, as a whole, men in my sample had little trouble discussing their future career plans, indicating that they do plan for the future when it comes to their careers. For instance, David (age 31, married), a finance executive, told me that he would likely be pursuing a more entrepreneurial path, saying, "I need to feel like I'm sort of central and important in my work. The best way to do that is just to do it myself; you know, do whatever I wanna do myself as opposed to signing onto somebody else's payroll." Another man (age 27, engaged) working in tech told me that he hoped for a new position that was a bit more "interesting" and personally satisfying. Reid (age 34, engaged), a senior executive at a health care company, also planned to "go more entrepreneurial" in the near future since "in a couple years I'll get tired of [my current role]. It won't challenge me anymore.

I'll need something new." He described the appeal of this path, saying, "I think it would be cool to build something that you can call your own. Also, at that level you can probably do more." At the time of our interview, however, his fiancée (age 26) was looking for a new job in sales, which she felt was a more "family friendly" position than her current office administrative job.

Other men described looking for more seniority in their 5- to 10-year trajectories. Steven (age 29, married), a financial analyst, told me that he was hoping to attain more education to move into "more senior-level jobs," like a director position. Rex (age 29, engaged), who was working as an engineer, said he hoped to work his way into either a more senior role or an entrepreneurial role so that he could have more autonomy:

> I could do really well in an unstructured kind of thing where it's up to me to get work done when I need to and not when I don't need to. So I like the idea of that . . . when you run your own company you choose who you're going to work with or not work with and you sort of call the shots at the end of the day.

Here, I have extended the concept of mental work (Walzer 1996) to the life stage that precedes parenthood and demonstrated the gender-differentiated ways in which men and women perform (or don't) mental work when anticipating parenthood. Young women's imagined work paths are often obfuscated by anticipations of parenthood, while their male counterparts tend to imagine full-time uninhibited investment in more satisfying and senior-level positions.

2. The Emotional Consequences of Mental Work

For many women, mental work was not confined to surface-level thought. Instead, it was accompanied by feelings of worry and anxiety. Because men were unlikely to engage in mental work, they were also free from its emotional consequences. One woman (age 26, married) told me it was "challenging to think about" how

her work life might change upon becoming new parents: "I think it's stressful to think about the change of what I'm gonna do. I think [my current place of employment] definitely would allow me to work part-time, but it's more the money aspect." In response to thinking about how her work life could also accommodate new parenthood, one woman (age 26, engaged) told me matter-of-factly, "It freaks me out!" Hannah (age 27, married), a guidance counselor, described it as "stressful to think about."

Many women experienced stress around trying to blend their current aspirations with their timeline for motherhood, feeling they had to plan everything at just the right time in order to achieve both work and family goals. For instance, Allie (age 29, married) was excelling in her career in the IT industry and hoped to attain her MBA to further her career. However, she felt anxiety around the idea of completing the requisite application materials well in advance of parenthood. . . .

Not a single man in my sample who was considering additional education or career changes mentioned anxiety around coordinating career moves with future parenthood.

Denise (age 27, married), a physician's assistant, described how the topic of paid work and child care preoccupied her thoughts. She had spoken with her mother and girlfriends about what kinds of labor strategies she was considering in the future and illustrates here the emotional struggle of anticipating parenthood in conjunction with gendered expectations of parenthood, which she views as a struggle unique to women:

> I feel like just, as a woman, it's really hard because if I choose to work full-time, someone's gonna think negatively on me that I'm not investing at home. But if I'm a stay-at-home, is that necessarily, like, a cop-out? Because I know sometimes opinions go that way. Or if I work part-time, well, then I'm not fully invested in either, so am I really doing anyone a favor by working part-time and being a part-time home role? I'm always talking about it, and ultimately whatever we decide it's gonna be based on what we need for the family.

Denise continued to describe the prominent place the topic occupied in her thoughts lately: "I do talk about it quite a bit. But it's just kind of to talk out loud and process some of my thoughts. Like, 'What do I think about this? What's my attitude toward it? How am I gonna be portrayed?' Because to some extent, that's important to me too."

3. The Interplay Between Gender, Imagined Work Paths, and the Reproduction of Labor Market Inequality

Despite that respondents had almost never discussed the topic of how their work lives might change upon parenthood with their partners, many were making critical choices based on gendered parenthood expectations. In this section, I show how the anticipated work-family conflict that often accompanies parenthood looms large in the minds of women, influencing their aspirations and career choices. Men, on the other hand, were less likely to be burdened by these anticipations, either mentally or behaviorally.

An Assumed Reordering of Preferences. Cultural expectations about motherhood assume that women should invest extensive amounts of emotion into childrearing (Hays 1996). Even though they were not yet parents, women in my sample seemed attuned to this expectation that their personalities or preferences might (or should) change upon parenthood. For example, one woman (age 27, engaged) was considering going back to school to obtain her PhD, but hesitated to commit to an academic path with children as a near possibility, saying, "With raising a child, who knows how my priorities are gonna change?"

Lacy (age 26, married), a certified public accountant, also longed to go back to school and change careers, but told me, "I would go back to school to do a career change. I actually am really interested in animal science. That's my thing. So I would go back for that, but I think it really depends on kids." Lacy worried specifically that her interests might change after having children. . . .

According to Lacy, her husband was not constrained by fatherhood expectations. When asked about his likelihood of attaining more education, she told me, "I wouldn't be surprised if Zach does an executive MBA at night. He is still very interested in doing an MBA." Another respondent (age 34, married), who remained undecided about her work plans, told me, "It all depends on when it [kids] actually happens. Because I've seen people say, 'Oh, I'm gonna go back to work.' And then they get there and they take the whole year off. And then they start to shift everything around just because of that intense experience."

One man (age 27, married) alluded to the culturally assumed reordering of preferences expectation placed on women, but not men, in a rare instance when the couple *had* openly discussed (nontraditional) gender strategies with others: "I don't see her staying at home with kids. But I mean, the thing people tell us is, like, 'Oh, as soon as you have children, that's going to change. She's going to want to stay at home.'" His comments exemplify the external pressure for women to experience a shift in life priorities and preferences upon the birth of a baby.

Anticipating Being the Central Caregiver. Like the gendering of expected changes in *preferences,* expectations of caretaking *responsibilities* were also gendered. One woman (age 27, engaged) struggled to decide which of many possible career paths to pursue, saying that when she has her first child, "I just don't even know what kind of responsibilities I'm gonna have." Frances (age 32, married), a community college counselor, wanted to attain an advanced degree, but worried about how she could balance her educational and professional goals with family caretaking responsibilities:

I feel like I almost have to plan my life around that [future parenthood] a little bit and when that happens. Going to school and being pregnant makes me wonder, "How will that work out?" And then also, everybody says you're exhausted for your first couple of years. I don't do exhausted well.

Frances's husband, on the other hand, planned to go back to school to complete his bachelor's degree and receive several certifications for his work in contracting, but did not mention parenthood responsibilities as barriers to his goals.

Another particularly compelling example comes from the case of Jessica and Steven, a married couple. Jessica (age 30) was a dental hygienist, but felt unsatisfied in her current position and the prospects it offered. Her husband, Steven, was a financial analyst at a large corporate firm. When I asked where she thought her career would go in five to ten years, Jessica told me:

> I've thought a lot about that, actually. Because I feel like I want to diversify and not just work in an office, but maybe go into teaching—maybe getting my master's and pursuing public health or something related to the dental field. I'm not really sure what my timeframe would be, though. Because we, actually, we're thinking about having kids soon. Starting to try within the next year. And I think that would be difficult for me to pursue a master's and have kids at the same time. I'd probably have kids, wait 'til they get a little older, and then go back to school.

Jessica's response is strikingly different from her husband's (age 29) despite that both wanted to pursue a graduate degree in the near future:

> Oh, man, 5, 10 years from now. I guess the career path that I see is that I'd like to go back to school to get my MBA and then kinda use that to launch into more senior-level jobs. I think I have . . . the job that I have right now kinda gives me a good background and good, I guess, foundation to have more senior-level jobs. So five years down the line I'd hope to be in a director-level position, having had an MBA and more experience.

Deferring educational opportunity was not the only way in which women's career trajectories became limited when anticipating family responsibilities. Others shied away from pursuing different work or leadership positions. Betsy (age 30, married), a program director for a midsized nonprofit organization, referenced her concerns about blending work and family when discussing her career trajectory, worrying that her original career goals might not be compatible with motherhood:

> I go back and forth a lot. For a very long time, I had it in my head that I wanted to be an executive director. Mostly because I wanted to be in charge of everything. But I've been reconsidering that. . . . You know, I think it's a challenge to balance my schedule as it is, but it's a lot more of a load when we have kids. I definitely want to keep working and I'm almost 99, 98 percent positive that includes continuing to work full-time through having kids. But you know . . . there's also, like, this outside chance that, you know, maybe I'll end up consulting for a few years and ending up at this place [being an executive director] later on.

Betsy's 31-year-old husband seemed attuned to her worry and similarly linked it to anticipatory sacrifices in her present career, saying, "I think when she's feeling like she would wanna be a stay-at-home mom for a period of time, it's because she's seeing how she doesn't think she could do all of this [work] plus motherhood at the same time." He, on the other hand, did not mention worrying about this balancing act.

Erin (age 32, engaged), an environmental policy analyst, told me that she was not entirely satisfied in her current position, which left her feeling unchallenged, but she was nevertheless planning to remain in that position rather than seeking something more fulfilling:

> It's very low-pressure. A few of the women there have told me, "Oh, it's a great place to have kids." I don't know that it has that great of benefits 'cause I feel like nowhere really does anymore unless you happen to work at some tech start-up or something. . . . But it could be a good reason to hold on to the job if everything else is okay.

In addition to constraining women's preferences for advancement, anticipations of parenthood also led to gendered industry and job choices, offering insight into one cultural mechanism reproducing occupational sex segregation.

For instance, Paula (age 26) and her husband were both nearing graduation from law school at the time of their interviews. In discussing their career choices, however, Paula's was to enter the field of dependency, a public sector of legal practice, while her husband's was to enter the more lucrative private practice, free from the expectations and worry described by Paula here:

> It's so difficult, because the beginning years of your career are really intense and so it's hard for me to know how that would play out in terms of being able to take time off or even just maternity leave for children. I think that has been something that has a little bit driven my career track, because dependency tends to be much more independent. You can kind of take as many cases as you want. You're essentially your own boss depending on where you work. . . . It tends to have a lot more women and so it's a little bit more friendly towards work, life, and family balance. . . . That has been a driving factor to stay in public practice because I don't see how you can have a family and stay in private practice. I mean, it's possible, but it just makes it a lot harder. So I think that in my head, I've been planning my transition into dependency sort of around that timing as well.

Another woman (age 27, married) told me that she had fully planned on becoming a physician her whole life, saying, "I was just curious about things. I kind of have that natural drive so I thought that would be a good fit." After meeting her husband in college, however, she began to imagine the family life that they would build together and worried that a doctor's schedule and responsibilities would not be able to accommodate the demands of motherhood. She eventually shifted her career goals to become a physician's assistant, which she believed would allow her to be "flexible later, when we do have a family."

Men's Breadwinner Expectations and Ramping Up. While men were much less likely to alter their career aspirations in anticipation of parenthood, some did; however, these men were similarly affected by traditional breadwinner expectations (Williams 2000). For instance, Charles (age 27, married), husband of Denise, had recently started a contract position in city planning. He told me that he needed to have a "more stable job, for sure" by the time they had kids and that "the pay needs to increase quite a bit in the next five to ten years." Toby (age 31, engaged), a sales associate at a large corporation, said, "Yeah . . . I've put quite a bit of pressure on myself to make sure that I'm earning enough so that when we do get to that point [of having kids], that Tinsley can make whatever decision she wants to around her work." His response highlights not only that the decision to work or stay at home is framed in a rhetoric of "her choice" as other scholars have also found (Stone 2007; Webber and Williams 2008; Williams 2000) but also that his use of the term "pressure" indicates the ties that the system of domesticity has on *his* day-to-day emotions and career choices. Zach (age 31, married), who worked as a business executive and whose wife had recently shifted her career (and salary) in search of a more "mom-friendly company," told me:

> I'm kind of at a manager level right now. I'd like to get to director and VP in the next five to ten years. I'm very focused on being successful. It's something that's very important to me. . . . It's something that, if I wanna make my life really good, I wanna make sure my career's really good. Because then I'm a better husband, a better everything, right? It's something that's been ingrained in me as something that's very important.

In the aggregate, these individual-level career choices, which occur early on in couples' relationships, make it more likely that the career outcomes of newly married men and women will diverge even more substantially in the years leading up to parenthood. Zach's wife (age 26) picked up on this divergence in her own marriage and told me, "At some point it's [her career] not gonna matter. Not because I don't know what I'm doing, but because he works at a place where they definitely compensate." She continued on, describing exactly how their diverging salaries might ultimately affect the labor strategy they adopt upon parenthood, saying, "As he and

I become more disparate in how much we make, I think that [choice] will become less of an issue because his salary is gonna ultimately completely eclipse mine at some point."

CONCLUSIONS

Through an analysis of in-depth interviews with 60 childless young adults, I show that anticipations of parenthood are gendered. Irrespective of their age, marital status, and background, women in my sample tended to be more likely to think and worry about combining work with family in the future. Moreover, I find that women tended to downshift certain educational or professional opportunities in conjunction with anticipating parenthood. This occurred when they worried that their preferences and family responsibilities might shift upon the birth of a child, something that men were not affected by. Thus, the study contributes to the extant literature by demonstrating the impact of children on women's work lives before children are actually born.

Additionally, the study builds in the voices of men, which are more often than not absent from the literature on parenthood and career choices (for notable exceptions, see Cowan and Cowan 1992; Gerson 2010; Walzer 1996). Doing so makes clear that parenthood is less influential in men's minds and present-day career choices than it is for women. This article also contributes to current theoretical understandings of how gendered career aspirations emerge and shift through the life course by showing that it is not only gender status and stereotypes that push women into lower-rewarded educational and professional paths, as previous research has found (Cheryan et al. 2009; Correll 2004; Lips 2000, 2007), but also anticipation of motherhood and family responsibilities that constrains preferences even before individuals actually enter into parenthood.

The study diverges in important ways from earlier scholarship as well. For instance, I have argued here that at least some, if not all, of the reasons that young women are more likely to

think about, worry about, and plan for future parenthood is because of socially constructed gender expectations surrounding parenthood. It is possible, however, that some of the gendered behavior described here could also be attributed to interactional dynamics within the couple. In other words, women worry and prepare for parenthood because their partners do not (see Walzer 1996, 223–24). Given that my respondents had not yet had children and almost none had explicitly talked to their partners about their work-family lives upon parenthood, couple-level dynamics appear to be a smaller factor in my study. . . .

It is important to note that seven of the 30 couples in my sample diverged substantially from the patterns reported earlier, offering preliminary insight into the conditions surrounding the process described here. One of these couples was counter-conventional by fully anticipating that the husband would assume the primary caretaker role upon parenthood. This couple had similarly begun the process of recalibrating their present career aspirations in accordance with this expectation, with her ramping up and him moving into a more flexible work arrangement. The other six couples were also unique in two distinct ways, indicating two potential conditions under which these patterns occur. Among the three couples that were uncertain about their likelihood of becoming parents, not a single one followed the patterns described here. We can speculate, then, that formed parenthood aspirations are a condition under which gendered anticipations of parenthood are likely to occur. Another condition is couples' financial resources. While all could be, at minimum, considered middle-class, those at the very bottom end of the household income distribution did not follow the patterns described here. They cited less uncertainty, saying instead that each partner needed to maximize his or her income in order to survive financially.

One limitation to the study is that it is focused on mostly class-privileged heterosexual couples. This precludes me from speaking to how this process might work among a group of couples with lower levels of human and economic capital or couples in same-sex partnerships. Further, because of the small-scale nature of this and any in-depth study based on a nonprobability sample, the findings cannot be interpreted as generalizable to the broader population. The sample size also precludes me from analyzing how factors like age, length of time together, and marital status affect the process. My analysis suggests gender expectations associated with marriage and parenthood supersede variation in these characteristics, perhaps because respondents are all in a similar life stage, facing similar anticipations, constraints, and expectations; however, further research should be conducted in order to address these lingering questions. . . .

NOTE

1. Respondents' names and some identifying characteristics have been changed to protect confidentiality.

REFERENCES

Bockerman, Petri, and Pekka Ilmakunnas. 2009. Job disamenities, job satisfaction, quit intentions, and actual separations: Putting the pieces together. *Industrial Relations* 48:73–96.

Cheryan, Sapna, Victoria C. Plaut, Paul G. Davies, and Claude M. Steele. 2009. Ambient belonging: How stereotypical cues impact gender participation in computer science. *Journal of Personality and Social Psychology* 97:1045–60.

Cohen, Philip, and Suzanne M. Bianchi. 1999. Marriage, children, and women's employment: What do we know? *Monthly Labor Review* 122:22–31.

Correll, Shelley. 2004. Constraints into preferences: Gender, status, and emerging career aspirations. *American Sociological Review* 69:93–113.

Cowan, Carolyn Pape, and Philip A. Cowan. 1992. *When partners become parents: The big life change for couples.* New York: Basic Books.

Damaske, Sarah. 2011. A "major career woman"? How women develop early expectations about work. *Gender & Society* 25:409–30.

Davis, Shannon N., and Theodore N. Greenstein. 2009. Gender ideology: Components, predictors, and consequences. *Annual Review of Sociology* 35:87–105.

De Vault, Marjorie L. 1991. *Feeding the family: The social organization of caring as gendered work.* Chicago: University of Chicago Press.

Gerson, Kathleen. 1985. *Hard choices: How women decide about work, career, and motherhood.* Los Angeles: University of California Press.

Gerson, Kathleen. 2010. *The unfinished revolution: How a new generation is reshaping family, work, and gender in America.* New York: Oxford University Press.

Grunow, Daniela, Florian Schultz, and Hans-Peter Blossfeld. 2012. What determines change in the division of housework over the course of marriage? *International Sociology* 27:289–307.

Hays, Sharon. 1996. *The cultural contradictions of motherhood.* New Haven, CT: Yale University Press.

Hochschild, Arlie. 1989. *The second shift.* New York: Penguin Group.

Jacobs, Jerry. 1995. Gender and academic specialties: Trends among recipients of college degrees in the 1980s. *Sociology of Education* 68:81–98.

LaRossa, Ralph, and Maureen Mulligan LaRossa. 1981. *Transition to parenthood: How infants change families.* Beverly Hills, CA: Sage.

Lips, Hilary M. 2000. College students' visions of power and possibility as moderated by gender. *Psychology of Women Quarterly* 24:39–43.

Lips, Hilary M. 2004. The gender gap in possible selves: Divergence of academic self-views among high school and university students. *Sex Roles* 50:357–71.

Lips, Hilary M. 2007. Gender and possible selves. *New Directions for Adult and Continuing Education* 114:51–59.

Machung, Anne. 1989. Talking career, thinking job: Gender differences in career and family expectations of Berkeley seniors. *Feminist Studies* 15:35–58.

Pedulla, David S., and Sarah Thébaud. 2013. *Can we finish the revolution? Gender, work-family ideals, and institutional constraint.* Paper presented at the American Sociological Association Annual Meeting, New York.

Risman, Barbara J. 1998. *Gender vertigo: American families in transition.* New Haven, CT: Yale University Press.

Sanchez, Laura, and Elizabeth Thomson. 1997. Becoming mothers and fathers: Parenthood, gender, and the division of labor. *Gender & Society* 11:747–72.

Stone, Pamela. 2007. *Opting out? Why women really quit careers and head home.* Berkeley: University of California Press.

Vespa, Jonathon. 2009. Gender ideology construction: A life course and intersectional approach. *Gender & Society* 23:363–87.

Waldfogel, Jane. 1998. Understanding the "family gap" in pay for women with children. *Journal of Economic Perspectives* 12:137–56.

Walzer, Susan. 1996. Thinking about the baby: Gender and divisions of infant care. *Social Problems* 43:219–34.

Webber, Gretchen, and Christine Williams. 2008. Mothers in "good" and "bad" part-time jobs: Different probelms, same results. *Gender & Society* 22:752–77.

Williams, Joan. 2000. *Unbending gender: Why family and work conflict and what to do about it.* New York: Oxford University Press.

❧ Topics for Further Examination ❧

- Look up the most recent research on women and work done by the Institute for Women's Policy Research (http://www.iwpr.org) and the current activism under way at 9 to 5 National Association of Working Women (http://www.9t05.0rg/). Check out workplace policies related to the topics discussed in this chapter, for example, family-work leaves and practices related to workplace discrimination.

- Using the Web, find a list of the top executives in a sample of the largest firms in this country and calculate a gender ratio of women to men. (Hint: Fortune 500 is one such list.)

- Find information on workplace discrimination policies in your state or country. Search the Web to find workplace discrimination policies in another country to compare with those where you live.

8

GENDER IN INTIMATE RELATIONSHIPS

JOAN Z. SPADE

Although social institutions and organized activities such as work, religion, education, and leisure provide frameworks for our lives, it is the relationships within these activities that hold our lives together. What surprises many people is that these everyday relationships are patterned. We don't mean "the daily routine" kind of patterns; we are referring to gendered patterns across individuals and relationships. For example, sociologists consider "the family" to be more than just a personal relationship; they view it as a social institution, with relatively fixed roles and responsibilities that meet some basic needs in society such as caring for dependent members and providing emotional support for its members. As you read through this chapter, you will come to realize how social norms influence all gendered relationships, including intimate relationships. This introduction and the readings in this chapter illustrate two key points. First, gendered intimate relationships always evolve, often in response to social changes unrelated to the relationships themselves. Second, gender is embedded in an idealized version of intimacy—the traditional, heterosexual family. As you probably already know, the traditional family is not the reality in the United States and most parts of the world today, as illustrated in readings in Chapters 1 and 3.

Before going on about these details of intimacy, let's stop for a moment and look at relationships in general. The word *relationship* takes on many different meanings in our lives. We can have a relationship with the server at our favorite restaurant because he or she is usually there when we dine out. We have relationships with our friends; some we may have known most of our lives, whereas others we have met more recently. And we have relationships with our family and with people who are like family. Some of these relationships surround us with love, economic support, intimacy, and/or almost constant engagement. All these relationships are shaped by gender. You have already read about relationships at work in Chapter 7; in this chapter, you will learn about how gender shapes more intimate relationships—from friendships to partnering to parenting.

GENDERED RELATIONSHIPS

Consider the impact of gender on our relationships. We can have many friends, with whom we share affection. In the past, researchers often argued that friendships varied by gender in predictable and somewhat stereotypical ways. That is, they described women's friendships as more intimate, or focused on sharing feelings and private matters, while describing men's friendships as more instrumental or focused around doing things, such as golfing or fishing (Walker, 1994). Some time ago, Francesca M. Cancian (1990) argued that men were more instrumental or task oriented in their love relationships, whereas women expected emotional ties. For example, in Cancian's study, when one man was asked how he expressed his love to his wife, he told the interviewer that he washed her car. A recent study (Felmlee, Sweet, & Sinclair, 2012) focused on same-gender and cross-gender friendships and found that both had somewhat similar norms, which is an encouraging sign in terms of a breakdown in the gender binary. However, women were more upset than men when friends broke trust and intimacy, for example, when their friends failed to be there for them and stand up for them if they were being attacked. And, men and women both judged a woman who betrayed them more severely than a man (Felmlee et al., 2012).

While these studies are revealing, it is important to remember that other social prisms influence the gendering of our relationships, putting social constraints and expectations on even our most intimate times. For example, Karen Walker (1994) found that while both men and women hold stereotypical views of gendered behavior in friendships, actual friendship patterns were more complex and related to the social class of the individual. Even though working-class men recognized what was gender-appropriate behavior for friendships, they tended to describe their friendships in ways that would be defined as more stereotypically female (disclosure and emotional intimacy), while professional women tended to describe more masculine friendship patterns with other women. These exceptions to stereotypical views of gendered friendships, however, are also

patterned; that is, they appear to vary by social class and reflect the constraints of work lives. Readings in this chapter contribute to our understanding of how prisms of class and race influence gendered patterns in relationships.

GENDER AND CHANGING HOUSEHOLDS

One of the strongest gendered influences on relationships is the expectation that only men and women will fall in love and marry. As we have emphasized throughout this book, American culture assumes idealized intimate relationships to be heterosexual, accompanied by appropriate gendered behaviors and, of course, based in nuclear families. As gender changes, we should expect relationships to change as well. It may surprise you as you read Ellen Lamont's reading on courtship to find that, even as college-educated women have become more egalitarian and independent, they still expect traditional courtship rituals such as having the man ask for and pay for a date or to propose marriage.

Despite the fact that the idealized version of love and marriage is expected to last forever, it often does not. In another reading in this chapter, Christin L. Munsch looks at how changing gender patterns in the workforce are related to the incidence of infidelity for men and women. In this excerpt from a quantitative study of more than 2,700 individuals, she looks at the effect of spouses' incomes relative to each other and finds a relationship to infidelity, a condition that is not related to happily ever after!

You will notice that we did not include the word *family* in the title of this chapter. We did this because the stereotypical vision of family—mom, dad, two kids, and a dog, all living in a house behind a white picket fence—is only a small percentage of households today and never was the predominant form of family relationships.

As we explore relationships in this chapter, it is important to begin by examining how households actually are patterned. In Table 8.1, we list the various household configurations and the percentage in each category by race and ethnicity in the United States today. These data may surprise you. Relationships in the United States are changing, as indicated by the diversity noted in Table 8.1. Only 49.0% of all Americans age 15 or older were married and living with a spouse in 2014 with just over half of individuals over 15 in the United States living in another situation (U.S. Census Bureau, 2015a). These percentages differ for racial and ethnic groups. For example, 29.2% of Black people are married with a spouse present, compared to 52.0% of White people (see Table 8.1). As you look at other relationship statuses on Table 8.1, you will see that clearly, race and ethnicity, and, although not included in this table, social class, influence the patterns of intimate relationships of men and women.

The increase in single and nonfamily households reflects both a trend toward postponing marriage and a longer life expectancy. A White boy born in 2010 is projected to live to 76.5 years, and a White girl, 81.3 years (U.S. Census Bureau, 2015c). These life expectancies are shaped by social factors such as race and social class as well as gender. For example, the projected life expectancy for a Black boy born in 2010 is 70.2 years and for a Black girl, 77.2 years (U.S. Census Bureau, 2015c).

Table 8.1   Marital Status of People 15 Years and Over in the United States, 2014

| | *Percentage* | | | | |
	All races	*White Non-Hispanic*	*Black*	*Hispanic[1]*	*Asian*
Married Spouse Present	49.0	52.0	29.9	42.2	57.9
Married Spouse Absent	1.4	1.2	2.0	2.6	3.0
Widowed	5.7	5.8	5.8	3.2	3.9
Divorced	10.0	10.4	10.8	8.0	4.5
Separated	2.1	1.9	4.1	3.6	1.0
Never Married	31.7	28.8	47.3	40.5	29.8

Percentages for Men Only

	All Races	*White Non-Hispanic*	*Black*	*Hispanic*	*Asian*
Married Spouse Present	50.6	53.1	33.8	41.3	57.2
Married Spouse Absent	1.5	1.2	2.2	3.0	3.0
Widowed	2.5	2.6	2.6	1.4	1.3
Divorced	8.8	9.2	9.1	6.6	2.9
Separated	1.8	1.6	3.4	2.7	0.7
Never Married	34.9	32.2	48.9	45.1	34.9

Percentages for Women Only

	All races	*White Non-Hispanic*	*Black*	*Hispanic*	*Asian*
Married Spouse Present	47.6	50.8	25.7	43.0	58.5
Married Spouse Absent	1.3	1.1	1.9	2.1	2.9
Widowed	8.6	8.9	8.6	5.0	6.1
Divorced	11.3	11.5	12.2	9.4	6.0
Separated	2.4	2.1	4.7	4.5	1.3
Never Married	28.7	25.5	46.0	35.9	25.2

Source: U.S. Census Bureau (2015a).

[1] Note: Hispanic is an overlapping category. All other racial groups are individuals who filled out their Census form indicating that racial group only and not people who indicated more than one race/ethnicity.

Increased life expectancy means we have more "time"; therefore, postponing first marriage makes sense. The median age at first marriage has risen for both men and women. In 1980, the median age at first marriage for women was 22 and for men 24.7; however, by 2014 the estimated median age at first marriage increased to 27.0 for women and 29.3 for men (U.S. Census Bureau, 2015d). Also, because we live longer, we may be less inclined to stay in a bad relationship, since it could last for a very long time. The distributions in Table 8.1 are influenced by multiple "prisms" beyond race and ethnicity in the patterning of relationships across groups in the United States.

The "Idealized" Family

The growing diversity of household and family configurations in the United States has reshaped and challenged the rigid gender roles that pattern the ways we enter, confirm, maintain, and envision long-term intimate relationships. Not surprisingly, the rigid gender roles associated with that mythical little home behind the white picket fence, with mom staying at home to care for children and dad heading off to work, is not the reality for households in the United States. Instead, as noted earlier, we have many different household patterns, with some households headed by a single person, same-sex households, and others unrelated by blood or family bonds living together. Some new household patterns include more single-person households. Others, such as grandparents raising grandchildren or single parents (typically mothers) raising children alone, often arise out of divorce and/or poverty. Whatever the reasons, the idealized, traditional family with its traditional gendered relationships never really was the norm (Coontz, 2000) and certainly is not the norm in American households today.

To illustrate how rare that idealized family is, only 24.1% of all married partner family groups with children under 18 years of age had a stay-at-home mother and less than 1% (0.98% or 211,000 married-couple family groups) had stay-at-home fathers in the United States in 2013 (U.S. Census Bureau, 2015b). When looking only at mothers who are married with spouses present and children under the age of 3, 42% work full-time in the labor force (Bureau of Labor Statistics, 2015). Considering these numbers, it is easy to see that only a small percentage of households fit the "Ozzie and Harriet" model for traditional families in the United States, with mom at home taking care of the children while dad is off at work. Like gender, "the family" is a culturally constructed concept that often bears little resemblance to reality. Simply put, the idealized, traditional family with separate and distinct gender roles does not exist in most people's lives.

Historically, families changed considerably in terms of how they are formed and how they function. While enduring relationships typically involve affection, economic support, and concern for others, marriage vows of commitment are constructed around love in the United States today. In previous generations, most marriage vows promised commitment and love "until death do us part."

However, marriages in the 1800s, even when rooted in love, often were based on economic realities. These 19th-century marriages were likely to evolve into fixed roles for men and women linked to the economy of the time, roles that reinforced gender difference but not necessarily gender inequality. For example, farm families developed patterns that included different, but not always unequal, roles for men and women, with both earning money from different tasks on the farm (Smith, 1987). In the latter half of the 19th century and into the early 1900s, families—particularly immigrant families—worked together to earn enough for survival. Women often worked in the home, doing laundry and/or taking in boarders, and many children worked in the factories (Bose, 2001; Smith, 1987).

What changed, and how did the current idealized roles of men and women within the stereotypical traditional family come to be? Martha May (1982) argues that the father as primary wage earner was a product of early industrialization in the United States. She notes that unions introduced the idea of a family wage in the 1830s to try to give men enough income so their wives and children were not forced to work. In the early 1900s, Henry Ford expanded this idea and developed a plan to pay his male workers $5.00 per day if their wives did not work for money (May, 1982). The Ford Motor Company then hired sociologists to go into workers' homes to make sure that the wives were not working for pay either outside or inside the home (i.e., taking boarders or doing laundry) before paying this family wage to male workers (May, 1982). In fact, very few men actually were paid the higher $5.00 per day wage (May, 1982). You might ask, why was Ford Motor Company so interested in supporting the family with an adequate wage? At that time, factories faced high turnover because work on these first assembly lines was demanding, paid very little, and the job was much more rigid and unpleasant than the farm work that most workers were accustomed to. Ford enacted this policy to reduce this turnover and lessen the threat of unionization. Thus, one reason behind the social construction of the "ideal family" was capitalist motivation to tie men to their jobs for increased profits, not the choices of individual men wanting to control their families (May, 1982).

Workplace policies are very important in ushering in changes in work, family, and gender. Erin M. Rehel describes three different family leave policies, one in the United States, one in Canada, and the third in the Canadian province of Quebec. New fathers who worked for the same company responded to these different policies, which influenced the length of the parenting leave they took. Those who took the most generous parental leaves, in Quebec, ended up being more attached to their new baby and much more respectful of the work involved in parenting.

These historical and structural changes in the family affect our interpersonal relationships both inside and outside of marriage. For example, Amy S. Wharton in Chapter 7 describes the (un)changing institutions of work, family, and gender, including some changes over the past 50 years and also what she calls a "stalled revolution" that began in the late 1990s.

SAME-SEX/GENDER COUPLES

A change that is hidden in Table 8.1 is the growing number of same-sex/gender couples. Beginning with the 2000 Census, the category "unmarried partner" was added to the questionnaire, allowing an estimated count of same-sex/gender couples. In 2010, the Census Bureau estimated that 0.6% of households described themselves as partners of same-sex/ gender (Lofquist, Lugaila, O'Connell, & Feliz, 2012). In 2013, the Census Bureau estimated there to be 726,600 same-sex couples in the United States, 34.6% of whom described their relationship as married (Census Bureau, 2015e). A more recent report by the Census Bureau (Lewis, Bates, & Streeter, 2015) warns that there are still inconsistencies in how individuals respond to two measures on the American Housing Survey identifying same-sex couples, one asking about the relationship with the second adult in the household (including same-sex and opposite-sex married and unmarried partners) and the other asking about the sex of the other adult in the household. Although these estimates are better than in the past, they still must be treated cautiously.

It is important to note that the identification of same-sex/gender relationships is complicated by the use of terms to define these relationships, all of which are imprecise—*sex, gender,* and *sexuality.* Each of these terms refers to a false dichotomy (Lucal, 2008; also see the introduction to Chapter 1), with the expectation that there are two and only two categories in each. However, social relationships and individuals are much more complicated than male/female, man/woman, and heterosexual/homosexual. As Paula C. R. Rust (2000) notes, *same-sex* may be appropriate in some instances and *same-gender* in others as we describe one social context versus another. For example, *same-sex* may be appropriate for describing sexual interactions between men in prisons. Many male prisoners in the United States define themselves as heterosexual and maintain that identity in sexual relationships with other incarcerated men by having sexual interactions in which they are the penetrators, thus feminizing their male partners. Given the inadequacy of these categories to describe the complexity of sex, gender, and sexual identities and the shifting terminology used to do so, we use *same-sex/ gender* in our text throughout this book. However, we honor authors' use of their terminology in readings selected for this book.

The legal parameters for same-sex/gender couples are rapidly changing, beginning when Massachusetts was the first state to allow same-sex/gender marriages in 2004. Other states in the United States followed, but the big change came in June, 2015, when the Supreme Court ruled that same-sex marriage is a right under the U.S. Constitution, thus making it legal in all states in the United States. This followed changes in the Netherlands, Norway, and Canada, who were among the first nations to allow same-sex/gender marriages, with gender-neutral marriage laws that transcend the problematic terms *same-sex* and *opposite-sex* and instead extend marriage rights to any two adults. However, many other countries legally recognize same-sex/gender couples, giving them some of the rights of married couples. At the same time, some countries still prohibit same-sex/gender marriages.

Same-sex/gender couples create families and, in doing so, redefine gender, parenthood, and family, as Irene Padavic and Jonniann Butterfield describe in their reading in this chapter. Padavic and Butterfield help us understand the constraints on parenting children within lesbian families as the reactions of others constrain their mothering behaviors. Indeed, parenting relationships, while continuously changing, are clearly socially constructed, and expectations for motherhood and fatherhood have strong impacts on gendered behavior across societies (Christopher, 2012; Gregory & Milner, 2011).

FEMINIZATION AND JUVENILIZATION OF POVERTY

Another reality of today's families that differs from the idealized, traditional family is the number of children living in poverty, with only a broken picket fence, if that. In 2012, the official poverty level for a family of four was $23,492. According to the Children's Defense Fund (2014), over 16 million children lived below that income level in the United States in 2012, with over 40% of those children living at less than half the poverty level in extreme poverty. The youngest children are the most vulnerable, with one in four children under the age of 5 living in poverty in 2012 (Children's Defense Fund, 2014). This change in household composition challenges idealized gendered relationships expected in families but also relates to social class inequalities tied to gender. The increase in the number of households headed by poor women raising children has been called the feminization or juvenilization of poverty (Bianchi, 1999; McLanahan & Kelly, 1999). Diana Pearce coined the term *the feminization of poverty* in 1978 (Bianchi, 1999, p. 308), at a time when the number of poor, women-headed families rapidly increased. The rate of women's poverty relative to men's fluctuates over time and is 50% to 60% higher than for men (Bianchi, 1999, p. 311), a reflection of the inequality in wages for men and women discussed in Chapter 7. These rates also reflect racial and ethnic inequalities, with children of color disproportionately represented among the poor. In 2012, the poverty rate for Black children was 39.6%, American Indian/Native Alaskan children 36.8%, and Hispanic children 33.7%. Approximately 1 in 5 Black children were living in extreme poverty in 2012, considerably higher than the rate for White, non-Hispanic children at about 1 in 18. (Children's Defense Fund, 2014).

The juvenilization of poverty refers to an increase in the poverty rates for children that began in the early 1980s, whether in single- or two-parent families (Bianchi, 1999). Unfortunately, the juvenilization of poverty continues to increase. From 2000 to 2010, the rate of child poverty increased 36% (Children's Defense Fund, 2014). The feminization and juvenilization of poverty are serious problems, and both are gender as well as race and social class issues.

GOVERNMENT POLICIES AND FAMILY RELATIONSHIPS

Governmental policies play a role in shaping families in the form of tax laws, health and safety rules, and other legislation. These policies have real gender implications as well as implications for parenting in a modern world. A multitude of policies frame parents' decisions to have children, structure how much time parents have with their children, and shape how children are expected to act in societies, with varying impact across social class (Williams, 2010; see also Wharton and Conroy Bass in Chapter 7 and Rehel in this chapter). Early in the 20th century in the United States, health and safety laws increased the age of employment for factory workers (Bose, 2001); these laws are still in effect in terms of dictating what age a child can begin to work for pay. These laws related to the creation of adolescence, with the expectation that children would remain in school throughout high school. Another act of legislation, the dependent deduction on tax returns, was first intended to encourage families to have more children at a time when politicians worried about the declining birth rate in the U.S. At the same time and for the same reason, Canada instituted a policy, the Canada Child Tax Benefit, in which caregivers are given a payment each month for every child under the age of 18. The government makes this payment directly to the caregiver. This law was based on the assumption that, in a two-parent family, the mother assumes responsibility for the children; however, payment may go to the father if a written note is submitted by the mother to indicate that he is the primary caregiver. While only a nominal sum, it was distributed across social classes as an incentive to bear and raise children. In 2007, Canada also instituted the Universal Child Care Benefit, which provides $160 per month for child care for each child under age 6 and $60 for children ages 6 through 17 (Government of Canada, 2015).

Work-family policies vary across nations, as Rehel illustrates in this chapter, and can enforce or challenge gendered assumptions about roles at work and home. Joan C. Williams (2010) describes U.S. policies as "family-hostile." Policies and laws affect all relationships because they often idealize the woman's role in two-parent families, reinforcing hegemonic masculinity and emphasizing femininity, while ignoring other choices and life situations, such as same-sex/gender couples. The impact of policies and practices on relationships in poor families is also considerable, making it difficult to "do" idealized gender because living, in and of itself, is challenging.

CHANGING RELATIONSHIPS

Marital and parenting relationships have changed considerably over time, as has the way sociologists study the family (Ferree, 2010). In addition to government regulations, the feminization of the workforce has affected men's and women's roles in marriages (Blackwelder, 1997). The fact that most families now have two workers has changed relationships in the home, as discussed in the reading by Munsch in this chapter. Kathleen Gerson (2002) described how young people imagine their commitments to marriage and family, balancing that against the autonomy they believe is necessary to succeed in the world of work. This is not an unrealistic assessment, as described in the Conroy Bass reading in Chapter 7. Carla Shows and Naomi Gerstel in their reading in this chapter study emergency medical technicians and physicians to examine how men's work lives impact their relationships with their children and spouses. They describe how the structure of work, embedded in a social class hierarchy, has a strong influence on the possibilities for fathering behaviors and the subsequent parenting relationships with one's spouse. The constraints of social class may surprise you as you read about how work affects fathering and as you compare the options these fathers have with those in place for fathers in Quebec, as discussed in Rehel's article in this chapter. Race is another prism that influences families and parenting and should also be considered as it relates to social class and gender differences in salaries, discussed in Chapter 7.

Gender difference and inequality continue to permeate and frame ever-evolving relationships even though fathers are more involved in household labor, particularly caring for children (Bianchi, Robinson, & Milkie, 2006; see also Wharton in Chapter 7). However, although there may be more equal distribution of household labor today, mothers continue to feel the pressure of caring for children and the household (Bianchi et al., 2006). Thus, the idealized, traditional gendered responsibility for women in the United States to care for children and the household remains, even though most women work outside the home. Jerry A. Jacobs and Kathleen Gerson (2001) argue that the changes in family composition and gender relations have created situations in which members of families, particularly women and most particularly single women, are overworked, with little free time left for themselves or their families. They describe the situation as particularly acute for those couples whose work weeks are 100 hours or more and who tend to be highly educated men and women with prestigious jobs. Shows and Gerstel and other readings in this chapter help us understand how patterns at work can influence patterns at home and lead to conflict between commitments to work and those to family discussed in the previous chapter.

The readings in this chapter provide a fuller understanding of how our most intimate relationships are socially constructed around gender. As friends, lovers, parents, and siblings, we are defined in many ways by our gender. Compare, for instance, the dilemmas young people face in Conroy Bass's reading in the previous chapter with the realities of the couples in the selections by Lamont, Rehel, Shows and Gerstel, Padavic and Butterfield, and Munsch, all in this chapter. Ask yourself what choices you have made or wish to make as you consider how gender influences what you expect in your intimate relationships. It is important to keep in mind that many social factors, including institutional rules and policies as well as social class position, influence the decisions people make in terms of hours worked outside and inside the home (Craig, 2011; Hook, 2010).

REFERENCES

Bianchi, S. M. (1999). Feminization and juvenilization of poverty: Trends, relative risks, causes, and consequences. *Annual Review of Sociology, 25,* 307–333.

Bianchi, S. M., Robinson, J. P., & Milkie, M. A. (2006). *Changing rhythms of American family life.* New York: Russell Sage Foundation.

Blackwelder, J. K. (1997). *Now hiring: The feminization of work in the United States, 1900–1995.* College Station: Texas A&M University Press.

Bose, C. E. (2001). *Women in 1900: Gateway to the political economy of the 20th century.* Philadelphia: Temple University Press.

Bureau of Labor Statistics. (2015). Economic News Release. Table 6: Employment status of mothers with own children under 3 years old by single year of age of youngest child and marital status, 2010–2011 annual averages. Retrieved from http://www.bls.gov/news.release/famee.t06.htm

Cancian, F. M. (1990). The feminization of love. In C. Carlson (Ed.), *Perspectives on the family: History, class and feminism* (pp. 171–185). Belmont, CA: Wadsworth.

Children's Defense Fund. (2014). Child poverty. In *The state of America's children 2014* (pp. 21–23). Washington, DC: Author. Retrieved from http://www.childrensdefense.org/library/state-of-americas-children/documents/2014-SOAC_child-poverty.pdf

Christopher, K. (2012). Extensive mothering: Employed mothers' constructions of the good mother. *Gender & Society, 26*(1), 73–96.

Coontz, S. (2000). *The way we never were: American families and the nostalgia trap.* New York: Basic Books.

Craig, L. (2011). How mothers and fathers share childcare: A cross-national time-use comparison. *American Sociological Review, 76*(6), 834–861.

Felmlee, D., Sweet, E., & Sinclair, H. C. (2012). Gender rules: Same- and cross-gender friendship norms. *Sex Roles, 66,* 518–529.

Ferree, M. M. (2010). Filling the glass: Gender perspectives on families. *Journal of Marriage and Family, 72*(3), 420–439.

Gerson, K. (2002). Moral dilemmas, moral strategies, and the transformation of gender: Lessons from two generations of work and family change. *Gender & Society, 16*(1), 8–28.

Government of Canada. (2015). *Families and children.* Service Canada, Government of Canada website: http://www.servicecanada.gc.ca/eng/audiences/families/

Gregory, A., & Milner, S. (2011). What is "new" about fatherhood: The social construction of fatherhood in France and the UK. *Men and Masculinities, 14*(5), 588–606.

Hook, J. L. (2010). Gender inequality in the welfare state: Sex segregation in housework, 1965–2003. *American Journal of Sociology, 115*(5), 1480–1523.

Jacobs, J. A., & Gerson, K. (2001). Overworked individuals or overworked families? Explaining trends in work, leisure, and family time. *Work and Occupations, 28*(1), 40–63.

Lewis, J. M., Bates, N., and Streeter, M. (2015). *Measuring same-sex couples: The what and who of misreporting on relationship and sex* (SEHSD Working Paper 2015–12). U. S. Census Bureau.

Lofquist, D., Lugaila, T., O'Connell, M., & Feliz, S. (2012, April). Table 3: Household type by race and Hispanic origin. In *Households and Families: 2010* (p. 8). Washington, DC: U.S. Census Bureau. Retrieved from http://www.census.gov/prod/cen2010/briefs/c2010br-14.pdf

Lucal, B. (2008). Building boxes and policing boundaries: (De)constructing intersexuality, transgender, and bisexuality. *Sociology Compass, 2*(2), 519–536.

May, M. (1982). The historical problem of the family wage: The Ford Motor Company and the five dollar day. *Feminist Studies, 8*(2), 399–424.

McLanahan, S. S., & Kelly, E. L. (1999). The feminization of poverty: Past and future. In J. S. Chafetz (Ed.), *Handbook of the sociology of gender* (pp. 127–145). New York: Kluwer Academic/Plenum.

Rust, P. C. R. (2000). *Bisexuality in the United States: A social science reader.* New York: Columbia University Press.

Smith, D. (1987). Women's inequality and the family. In N. Gerstel & H. E. Gross (Eds.), *Families and work* (pp. 23–54). Philadelphia: Temple University Press.

U.S. Census Bureau. (2015a). *America's families and living arrangements: 2014* Table A-1. Marital status of people 15 years or older by age, sex, personal earnings, race and Hispanic origin: 2014. Retrieved from https://www.census.gov/hhes/families/data/cps2014A.html

U.S. Census Bureau. (2015b). *America's families and living arrangements: 2014: Family groups.* Table FG8. Married couple family groups with children under 15 by stay-at-home status of both spouses: 2014. Retrieved from https://www.census.gov/hhes/families/data/cps2014FG.html

U.S. Census Bureau. (2015c). *Births, deaths, marriages, and divorces: Life expectancy.* Table 104. Expectation of life at birth, 1960 to 2008, and projections, 2010 to 2020. Retrieved from http://www.census.gov/compendia/statab/cats/births_deaths_marriages_divorces/life_expectancy.html

U.S. Census Bureau. (2015d). Table MS-2. Estimated median age at first marriage, by sex: 1890 to present. *Current Population Survey.* Retrieved from http://www.census.gov/hhes/families/data/marital.html 8/21/15

U.S. Census Bureau. (2015e). Table 3. Same-Sex Couple Households: 2013. *American Community Survey.*

Walker, K. (1994). Men, women, and friendship: What they say and what they do. *Gender & Society, 8*(2), 246–265.

Williams, J. C. (2010). The odd disconnect: Our family-hostile public policy. In K. Christensen & B. Schneider (Eds.), *Workplace flexibility: Realigning 20th-century jobs for a 21st century workforce* (pp. 23–54). Ithaca, NY: ILR Press.

Introduction to Reading 37

The world of gender is constantly changing. Women and men are increasingly looking for egalitarian relationships in their lives. However, as noted in this research by Ellen Lamont, women are still looking for traditional gendered patterns in serious relationships. This reading provides some interesting insights in terms of how women reconcile these two opposing behaviors; that is, how does one manage an egalitarian relationship while, at the same time, expecting one's date to pick up the tab for dinner and open the car door? She reports results of interviews with 38 women between the ages of 25 and 40 in the San Francisco area. The interviews with these middle- to upper-middle-class women lasted about 3 hours and should provide some insights into contradictions in our own attitudes and behaviors.

1. How did the respondents in this sample reconcile the discrepancies between what they expect from men in serious dating relationships and their desire for equality?

2. Why did the women's behaviors and acceptance of traditional gender norms change over the course of getting to know someone in a dating relationship?

3. Do you think the social class of these women might affect some of the results reported here? If so, how might findings be different for women lower or higher in social class?

--------------------- NEGOTIATING COURTSHIP ---------------------

RECONCILING EGALITARIAN IDEALS WITH TRADITIONAL GENDER NORMS

Ellen Lamont

Courtship conventions delineate distinct gendered behaviors for men and women based on the model of an active, breadwinning male and a passive, dependent female (Bailey 1988; Cate and Lloyd 1992). These norms situate men as the initiators in relationships. Men are responsible for asking women out, paying for dates, determining when the relationship will shift from casual to committed, and proposing marriage, while women are limited to reacting to men's overtures (Bogle 2008; England, Shafer, and Fogarty 2008; Laner and Ventrone 2000; Sassler and Miller 2011). Yet, as women have increased their access to earned income, there has been a rising ideological and behavioral commitment to egalitarian relationships (Bianchi, Robinson, and Milkie 2006; Gerson 2010). College-educated women expect to pursue lucrative and rewarding careers and form peer relationships that provide room for independence and self-development (Coontz 2005; Hamilton and Armstrong 2009). In spite of these destabilizing shifts, traditional gender ideologies remain remarkably resilient, as courtship conventions symbolizing men's dominant, breadwinning status stubbornly persist (Eaton and Rose 2011). These competing sets of behavioral rules create a "moral dilemma" (Gerson 2002) for women as they seek to negotiate romantic relationships in what has been referred to as an "uneven" gender revolution (England 2010), with women's employment opportunities changing more rapidly than gendered patterns in the home. This study looks at how a sample of highly educated women navigate this contradiction, examining how their

From Lamont, Ellen. 2014. "Negotiating Courtship: Reconciling Egalitarian Ideals With Traditional Gender Norms." *Gender & Society 28*(2): 189–211.

economic resources and their expressed support for egalitarian relationships intersect with persisting gender norms to shape their contemporary courtship behaviors and attitudes.

Since the courtship period may influence couples' expectations regarding gendered behaviors during marriage (Humble, Zvonkovic, and Walker 2008; Laner and Ventrone 2000), it is important to understand how courtship conventions may impede women's equal status in romantic relationships and where openings for change, and greater equality, may be occurring. While some scholars have speculated that the intransigence of these norms may not be critical to achieving equality (Graf and Schwartz 2011), others posit that they contribute to the power imbalance between men and women (England 2010; Sassier and Miller 2011). Given that the focus of recent research on middle-class women's relationships has been on the college years (Bogle 2008; England, Shafer, and Fogarty 2008; Hamilton and Armstrong 2009), little is known about how women are negotiating conventional scripts in the changing social landscape as they exit college and begin the process of forming long-term partnerships. By looking at how college-educated women navigate courtship and the narratives they use to make sense of their behaviors, this study reveals the contradictory processes of social change among middle-class women.

SYMBOLIC GENDERING AND THE CHANGING CONTEXT OF COURTSHIP

Gender scholars have pointed to the ways that gendered meanings continue to influence social relationships, even as the material dimensions that support inequality erode (England 2010; Ridgeway 2011; Tichenor 2005). Ridgeway asserts that gender remains a primary frame that men and women use to define who they are, how they will behave, and how they expect others to behave. Individuals draw on cultural knowledge, or "shared," "common" knowledge that "everybody knows," to coordinate their behavior

and facilitate social cohesion (Ridgeway 2011, 35). This knowledge reflects cultural stereotypes about how men and women behave as a result of their sex category and emphasizes the perceived differences between the two groups. As Ridgeway shows, most adults continue to believe that men and women are innately different with either complementary or conflicting needs and desires, especially in heterosexual romantic relationships where sex differences are highlighted. In particular, many studies reveal the existence and pervasiveness of beliefs about men's and women's relative levels of assertiveness versus responsiveness and interest in casual sex versus a committed relationship (Hamilton and Armstrong 2009; Ridgeway 2011). These perceived differences are especially salient during courtship, when people tend to fall back on scripts to ease uncertainty and reassure themselves and others that they conform to normative sexual standards (Eaton and Rose 2011).

Scripts that become culturally hegemonic tend to enshrine the behavior of white, middle-class heterosexuals, who remain the dominant social group (Bailey 1988; Ridgeway 2011). As a result, research on dating and courtship shows remarkable stability and agreement between men and women in support of the traditional, and highly gendered, courtship script (Eaton and Rose 2011; Laner and Ventrone 2000). This script demonstrates men's status as active economic providers and women as more passive dependents, dictating that men initiate, plan, and pay for first dates while women limit themselves to reactive behavior, such as accepting physical contact and being walked to the door (Laner and Ventrone 2000). Relationship progression, including decisions about exclusivity and engagement, also favors the man's desired timetable, with women less empowered to openly seek their desired outcomes (Bogle 2008; England, Shafer, and Fogarty 2008; Sassler and Miller 2011). According to the prevailing narrative, women are looking for commitment, while men are trying to avoid it (Bogle 2008), but women's lack of power to define the terms of courtship holds true even when women do not desire commitment. Hamilton and Armstrong (2009) thus show that women are often coerced into a commitment they do not desire. Alternatively, women who act "too forward" are often passed over for future dates (Bogle 2008) or face relationship destabilization (Sassler and Miller 2011). Even college students who describe themselves as egalitarian engage in these inegalitarian dating patterns, as beliefs about men's assertiveness and women's responsiveness continue to function "unconsciously" (Laner and Ventrone 1998, 475). Drawing on Goffman's (1976) argument that individuals symbolically enact cultural beliefs about men and women through "gender displays," I use the term "symbolic gendering" to refer to the cultural practices associated with courtship. These practices are used to represent what are assumed to be essential, biological differences between women and men, making them appear inevitable while obscuring how they privilege men (Bourdieu 1998).

Yet changes in U.S. women's educational and employment opportunities challenge conventional beliefs about gender difference. As women's wages become increasingly important to attaining middle-class status, romantic relationships based on women's financial dependence appear increasingly less desirable to both men and women (Gerson 2010). Middle-class parents prepare their daughters for professional careers (Lareau 2003), and, with women's college graduation rates now exceeding men's, these women are far more likely to expect career trajectories that mirror those of their male counterparts (Damaske 2011). Among highly educated women, successes in the workplace have undermined the use of gendered self-descriptions, with women more likely to think of themselves as agentic than in the 1960s (Twenge 2001).

The changes have prompted new approaches to relationships. College-educated women expect to pursue career opportunities in young adulthood while delaying marriage until their late twenties or early thirties (Hamilton and Armstrong 2009). The hook-up culture on college campuses allows young adults to engage in sexual encounters outside the context of a relationship, which are often viewed as too time consuming by women hoping to succeed at school and in careers (Hamilton and Armstrong 2009). When relationships *are* formed, women thus expect room for independence and self-development (Cancian 1987; Coontz 2005). The majority of young women seek a relationship in which both partners share work and home responsibilities, while many say they would rather forgo a relationship than be in an unequal one (Gerson 2010). Although women continue to do the majority of housework and child care, men have increased their contributions, while women have decreased theirs (Bianchi, Robinson, and Milkie 2006), and there is some evidence that indicates that this shift is at least partly due to women's increased earnings relative to men's (Bianchi et al. 2000).

As women form stronger attachments to paid labor, conflicts between a commitment to self-development and personal relationships (Hamilton and Armstrong 2009) create a "moral dilemma" with no clear socially sanctioned solutions (Gerson 2002). This dilemma provides an opportunity to challenge conventional gender norms, which no longer represent an obvious, or necessarily viable, pathway. This tension between convention and change can be found in the contrasting findings on hooking up and dating, which highlight the constraints on women's ability to negotiate their desired ends (Bogle 2008; Hamilton and Armstrong 2009), and the literature on relationships, which points to women's efforts to reject inequality in the home and find value in their personal achievements (Graf and Schwartz 2011). These cultural messages are especially likely to clash for college-educated women, who face pressures both to achieve autonomy and to defer to men. In this study, I ask: How does women's commitment to self-development and economic independence intersect with traditional gender norms to shape their courtship narratives and behaviors? To explain how middle-class women negotiate these conflicting norms, I argue that women have disassociated the two scripts, drawing on cultural narratives of choice, individualism, and essentialism to assert that the symbolic gendering in courtship is unrelated to the equality they seek in their married lives as high-achieving professionals. In this manner, however, women inadvertently perpetuate ideologies of gender difference, a basis of inequality in both the household and the workplace.

* * *

FINDINGS

The majority of the women expressed a preference for conventional courtship behaviors and expected men to ask and pay for the first date, confirm the exclusivity of the relationship, and propose marriage. Drawing on the interview data, I illustrate how women justified their support for these conventions in spite of their desire for egalitarian relationships. . . .

Narratives of Gender Difference

Women referred to popular, essentialist beliefs about men's need to be the assertive, dominant partner to explain why they preferred men to ask for dates. Over a third indicated that they did not ask men on dates because it was in man's nature to like "the thrill of the chase" or it was the man's "role" to do the pursuing. Jenna, 26, a research assistant, said, "It's just partly biological. In animals, the guy always flashes. The male bird always flashes his colors—his feathers or something—to go after what he wants." By locating behavioral differences in biology, women framed these behaviors as natural, inevitable, and legitimate and so did not challenge them (Bourdieu 1998). And because they assumed that men need to be the dominant partners, they argued that women who took that away from men would be considered unappealing partners. Caroline, 31, a marketing director, said, "I feel like men need to feel like they are in control and, if you ask them out, you end up

looking desperate and it's a turn-off to them." Anna, 40, a high school teacher, said, "I know that with a man they like to take charge." Although Anna admitted that she, too, really liked to be in control, saying that she liked to ask men out, she attributed this to her personality, rather than to her nature. As a result, women believed they must adjust their behavior to men's natural, unchanging desires.

Only two women made essentialist arguments about women's needs. Instead, like Anna, women discussed their own preferences in terms of their personalities. Indeed, almost one third of the women explained that their unwillingness to ask for a date was due to their personality. Olivia, 26, a lawyer, said she didn't like to approach men "more because I'm shy than out of traditional gender roles or anything like that." Breanna, 36, an internal auditor, said, "I would never approach a guy. I think one is, I'm shy. Two is I've never felt like 'Oh, I'm gorgeous,' so it would be fear of rejection." As Ridgeway (2011) argues, people are more likely to explain the behaviors of others using stereotypes than their own, making gendered self-reports more progressive. Yet, while these women didn't explicitly discuss gendered expectations as a factor, they still attributed to themselves a level of acceptable passivity. Women did not view this passivity as a hindrance to getting dates, a position not possible for men. None of the women acknowledged that men, too, might be shy and afraid of rejection, and none of these women admitted to shyness in their professional lives, indicating that their courtship narratives are potentially unconsciously gendered.

Women's passivity provided assurance of men's interest and protected them from rejection. Amelia, 33, an environmental consultant, said, "I think it's just because I'm old-fashioned that way. I want to know the guy is interested in me." Only 10 of the 38 women had ever asked a man out, and half of them described their actions in less than empowering terms. Their experiences reinforced the cultural stereotype that if a man is actually interested, he *will* pursue, and that women are better off waiting for the man to take the lead. Abby, 33, a postdoctoral fellow, said, "I tended to be the one to approach guys, but those were usually the ones that didn't like me." Heather, 27, an operations technician, said that she had stopped contacting men on an online dating site:

> When I have, they're not interested. There was this one time I saw this guy was looking at my profile two or three times. He was kind of a dick. He was like, "Yeah. Sometimes I just click on people's profiles. It doesn't mean I want to date them." It's funny. The times I've contacted people, I've never ended up meeting them.

Women experienced men's negative reactions as sanctions for transgressing appropriate gendered behavior. Because people know what is expected of their gender and can anticipate these sanctions (Rudman and Fairchild 2004), many women focused on making their interest clear in ways other than suggesting a date. While only a handful of women reported asking a man out on a first date, half reported at least one partnership in which she had pursued a man. Ariana, 30, a doctor, described aggressively pursuing a man she was interested in dating: "I called him and told him to come to a party and that I would make it worth his while. I told him to sit next to me, and took his arm and put it around me. I said, 'Finally, I have all of your attention.' He said, 'You sure do' and kissed me. Then he asked me out." Caroline said, "I approached him at a bar and flirted with him and then invited him [and his friends] to go to a strip club with me and my friends. While we were there, I sat on his lap. . . . But I let him call me the next day. He did and he asked me out on our first date." In this manner, women were able to test the boundaries of appropriate gender behavior without completely challenging them. . . .

Ensuring Men's Commitment

The ubiquity of the hook-up culture on college campuses continued to influence women's understandings of men even after they exited college and entered adulthood. While they may have felt ambivalent about long-term commitment during college (Bogle 2008; Hamilton and Armstrong 2009), as adults in their late twenties and early thirties most of the women were looking for a partner interested in the possibility of marriage. Because many of the women viewed men as still commitment phobic or more interested in casual sex than a relationship, a belief that was reinforced by popular narratives of men's "nature" (Geller 2001), they used an adherence to courtship norms to confirm men's genuine interest in them. Thus, women used the formal date, with its attendant rituals, to distinguish men who were interested in the possibility of a relationship from men who were just looking for a casual sexual encounter.

Since women frequently cited "chivalry" as a sign that the man was respectful, caring, and interested in more than sex, many wanted the man to ask for, plan, and pay for the first few dates. Olivia said, "I tend to like a formal date, like asking me out on a date. Like, 'Would you like to go to dinner?' It just seems like a more clear idea of what's going on. And I also think I like the chivalry of the formal date invitation as opposed to 'Let's just see what happens, maybe we'll hook up.'" Ariana also alluded to chivalry, saying,

> I mean, usually the first time they go out with me I'll offer to pay. I'm like, "Oh, let me split it with you," you know? And it's really honestly a test. I don't want them to say, "Okay." I want them to say, "No, I'll get it," you know? But I usually offer to split it. And then if we go out, like, four times, by the fourth time I'll be like, okay, this is my turn now. Like I want to make sure the guy offers to pay, the guy opens my door, the guy, you know, doesn't just walk ahead of me. Things like that. And that's become more important to me, how gentlemanly they are. I've talked to guys about it before. If you like a chick and you want to impress her, you do everything you can. [If a guy doesn't pay] they just probably don't like you that much.

More than two thirds of the women said that all their first dates were paid for by men. Just like

Ariana, many of the women referenced payment of the first date as a test. If the man took them up on their offer to pay or split the check, it was a sign that he wasn't someone they wanted to date, assuming he wasn't "out to impress" and must not be sufficiently interested in them. Only a handful of the women indicated that men's payment was a way to confirm breadwinning ability, perhaps because men who weren't able to take on this responsibility in the long run were screened out before the date even took place, as the majority of the women dated men with similar career opportunities. Instead, men's payment for the first date appears to have taken on new meanings as women have gained their own breadwinning abilities.

These dating conventions became less important to women over the course of their relationships. Most of the women reported, for example, that, once they started dating a man regularly, payment for dates frequently alternated between the two of them. The conventions acquired significance again, however, during moments that were highly scripted and where assumptions about men's commitment to the relationship became salient. Therefore, women expected men to confirm the exclusivity of the relationship and propose marriage as a signal that let women know they were committed to the relationship, as there was a consistently stated belief that men were reluctant to commit. As a result, women initiated fewer than a fifth of the conversations on the exclusivity of the relationship. Consistent with previous findings on gender performance (Sassler and Miller 2011), when women did bring up the exclusivity of the relationship, they tended to do so in an indirect manner, asking questions such as "Where is this relationship going?" or "What are we?" This approach provided women with the ability to initiate the conversation topic, protecting them from a more direct rejection of their desired ends, but gave men the power to confirm or deny an exclusive commitment.

In addition, because many of the women believed that men who were interested in commitment were rare because of essentialist beliefs that men are naturally promiscuous, when men initiated conversations about exclusivity, women sometimes ended up committing to a relationship before they were ready (Hamilton and Armstrong 2009). Nicole, 28, a marketing manager, described how the man she had been dating gave her an ultimatum after he found out she was also having sex with other men: "He said that he wanted me to be his girlfriend and that I couldn't see other people." She agreed because his insistence on commitment "made me see how much he cared about me." Because of the cultural belief that women always want commitment, they worried that their attempts to secure exclusivity could be construed as desperation. In contrast, because of the cultural belief that men avoid commitment, men who did commit were viewed as especially devoted. As a result, women frequently ended up prioritizing men's desires.

Women were even more reluctant to propose marriage. Men proposed in each of the 22 cases analyzed in this study; in addition, all the unmarried women expected men to do the proposing. Again, women discussed men's initiation of the proposal as a sign of commitment to her and to the marriage. Caroline said, "I wanted him to do it since he was really the one who had been slower to be there emotionally. I wanted him to be the one to drive it." Jane, 31, a student who was waiting for her boyfriend to propose, said, "I want to feel adored and I feel like if I was doing the proposing, it was kind of like, 'What, I'm not special enough that you're willing to put yourself out there and be vulnerable for me?'" The act of being chosen remained a powerful draw for the women in this study. To be chosen meant to be considered worthy of love and a lifelong commitment. Rather than view a female-initiated proposal as an expression of valid desire and unwillingness to remain passive, women viewed it as embarrassing reflection of their partner's lack of love or their own desperation. When I asked Ashleigh, 29, a stay-at-home mother, if she would have been willing to propose to her husband, she said, "Never. In my mind, that's not my role. Like, I would feel like he didn't really value me if he wasn't going to propose to me," while Alice, 34, a computer programmer, said, "I think I wouldn't do it because I want to make sure the other person loves me as much, if not more."

Yet the majority of the engagements occurred on a mutually agreed-on timetable. Most of the couples discussed marriage extensively before getting engaged, often going over how they envisioned their lives together, as this was considered pragmatic. After the couple decided when they wanted to get engaged, the man was expected to "surprise" the woman with a proposal. . . .

This approach allowed women to preserve the narrative of the male-initiated proposal, cementing their "chosen" status, while protecting their inclusion in the decision-making process.

Only three women said that they "waited it out" until their partner was ready to propose. In fact, a quarter of the women in the study were aggressive in influencing the timing of the engagement, often giving their boyfriends ultimatums and timelines for proposing. Just as with women who pursued men for first dates, these women were more likely to be highly paid professionals than the women who took a more "hands-off" approach, potentially indicating that their careers empowered them to be more assertive. Alice moved out of state when her boyfriend failed to propose on her timetable and agreed to move back only after he expressed a willingness to propose within the year: "I told him, 'If I move back, there better be a ring on my finger.'" He proposed one year later. . . .

Thus, the women in this sample were almost always able to negotiate desired outcome.[1]

However, because of the often repeated sentiment that proposals initiated by women, whether directly or indirectly, were coercive and indicated a lack of interest by the man, women felt conflicted about issuing ultimatums or otherwise influencing the timing of the engagement, again citing the fear of negative reactions for transgressing gender norms. As a result, while women were willing to play a decisive role in the timing of their marriage proposal, they preferred

to keep the illusion of surprise with their peers. Caroline said, "I didn't tell any of my friends what actually happened. I told him to put the ring away so he wouldn't feel like he was backed into a corner. I said he should do it the way he wanted to and that I would say yes. He proposed three weeks later on a boat. That's the story our friends know." In this manner, women's "official" stories of their marriage proposals rarely acknowledged the "backstage work" that took place (Goffman 1959).

The narratives of the women who did not embrace courtship conventions show how support for these norms is rooted in women's desire to secure men's commitment. Only nine women expressed reservations about these conventions and only four uniformly rejected them. These women were not any less likely to express essentialist beliefs about men, but the four who voiced the strongest objections to gendered courtship did not want to get married and have children. Keira, 36, a researcher and recruiter for a tech company, said,

I never fantasized about the wedding the way my friends did in school. . . . I wanted to see what I could do with my life. Getting married and having kids were probably, if they were even on the list, they were like number 99 and 100 on the list of 100. . . . I think the men I was with knew. It would just be ridiculous if they were on a bended knee offering me a ring.

As a result, they didn't need to rely on courtship conventions to ferret out which men were truly interested in commitment, nor did they have to worry about scaring men off by appearing too interested in commitment, because they weren't.

Yet, even though these women disavowed courtship rituals, they often found themselves engaging in them anyway because the men they dated fell back on these patterns and they "just didn't care enough" to challenge them. Rachel, 26, a vice president of business development, said that she let men ask her out because she "wasn't someone who always needed a boyfriend." Keira always brought money to pay her share on dates, but said her partners were "old-fashioned" and insistent on paying. And while her ex-husband did indeed propose to her, she argued that it was because she "didn't want [marriage] enough," not because she saw it as his role: "He definitely felt more strongly about me than I did about him." Thus, this group of women described their courtship behaviors as the result of men's desire for convention and explained their de facto conformity as the result of their disinterest in the assumed relationship goals of women. Still, consistent with the narratives of the women who wanted men to propose, Keira associated the initiation of the marriage proposal with the strength of her partner's love and commitment. His level of interest in her was reflected in his willingness to ask for long-term commitment.

Competing Narratives Reconciled

Although most of the women supported conventional courtship through symbolic gendering, almost all of them also described their ideal relationship as one in which partners shared breadwinning, housework, and child care relatively equally. Consistent with other findings (Damaske 2011), among the 32 women in the sample who wanted or had children, three quarters reported they had not interrupted or would not interrupt their careers. Caroline broke up with the man she dated during business school when it became clear that they had different visions of their life together. While he wanted a wife who would stay home and raise their children, Caroline planned on staying in the workforce and supporting herself financially, arguing, "I don't want to be in a dynamic where anyone is mooching on anybody or anybody feels entitled to other people's stuff." She finally decided to break up with her boyfriend when she saw the way his father treated his stay-at-home wife. . . .

Not only did Caroline enjoy her work, she also recognized that, without a job, she would have less power to negotiate a fair division of housework, a goal shared by 33 of the women in the sample.[2]

As Gerson (2010) found, if an egalitarian relationship seems unlikely, women are more likely to choose self-reliance than a traditional partnership that poses "the dangers of domesticity." Caroline expressed the fear experienced by many that, without financial independence, she would lose power in her relationship and the ability to leave if necessary. Ariana grew up watching her mother suffer physical and emotional abuse by her father and wanted to avoid the same fate, so she attended medical school to become a surgeon: "My mom was a stay-at-home mom and my dad had a lot of financial control over her and she always emphasized be independent, get a good education so you have your own financial independence and so no man can use that to control you. So that's always been embedded in my brain." After observing their parents' relationships or learning of the challenges faced by women without money, many of the women not only wanted access to their own incomes, but also their own bank accounts. Just over two thirds said that it was important for them to have a separate bank account in order to protect their assets and provide them with greater control over their personal finances. While this was aspirational for the unmarried, more than half of the married women had their own bank accounts, including three of the five women with children. When asked why she kept all her money separate from her husband of 18 years, Anna replied, "I needed to have my own money. I don't need [my husband] looking over my shoulder and telling me what to do," echoing the sentiments of many others. This approach provided women not only with income, but with control over it.

Interestingly, the nine women who planned to leave the workforce for more than a year after having children or who planned to take on a greater share of the household labor in their marriages were no more likely to express support for courtship conventions that symbolized men's dominant, breadwinning status than women who desired an egalitarian partnership. Rather, the women in this study differentiated between the symbolic gendering of courtship and gendered behaviors in the home and workplace, most of them denying a relationship between the two. Thus, while the egalitarian narratives expressed by the majority appear to contradict their commitment to courtship norms, they did not perceive that symbolic gendering would undermine these goals. Seeing symbolic gendering as either a personal preference or a mere convention (Hamilton, Geist, and Powell 2011; Swim and Cohen 1997), it appeared inconsequential to interpersonal power relations and any goals for an egalitarian marriage. . . .

Because stereotypical representations can purportedly provide benefits to women, such as "the belief that women should be protected and taken care of by men," there are fewer incentives to challenge symbolic gendering than to address overt sexism or discrimination in the workplace (Becker and Wright 2011, 63). Aashi, 29, a marketing associate, explained:

> I feel like men and women should be treated equally as far as in their career and their political day-to-day lives, things where they should be treated as equals. But when it comes to biology and manners, it's not like a woman can't open the door, it's not like she can't pay for herself, but when a man does it, it's a nice gesture and it's just . . . It's a nice thing.

This interpretation of equality draws on liberal feminist themes, such as women's legal and economic rights, and is consistent with ideologies of American individualism (England 2010). Focused on women's entry into formerly "male" spheres, the women downplayed how difference narratives in personal relationships contribute to inequality. Caroline, who had broken up with the boyfriend who wanted a gendered division of labor, wasn't as opposed to symbolic gendering: "I am okay with the fact that the gestures [my fiancé] makes are not identical to mine . . . sort of in the same way that I know he'll never carry our child for nine months in his belly, but I trust that he'll do other things to be a great father." Thus, even though women and men were expected to engage in distinct behaviors, this was not viewed as inherently unequal.

In addition, because most women were able to support themselves financially, they did not see gestures that grant men symbolic dominance as a risk to their autonomy or power within relationships. Anna was pleased when her now-husband asked her father for permission to propose: "Not that it would really matter because I'm a pretty independent, liberal-thinking woman, but . . . it is what it is." Breanna said,

> I obviously easily could take over. I am, like I mentioned, independent and self-sufficient. So obviously if I wanted to put my foot on the ground and he didn't want to go my way I could walk away—I'm not dependent on him. I don't need him for anything. But I *choose* not to take that position. . . . I do like a dominant man. . . . [I don't want] them to be submissive in any way. Gross. That would totally turn me off that guy. I even came to see where some women were insisting on paying on the dates to establish their independence. I think it's totally wrong. I mean, I think it's good to be strong and independent, but then to, like, you know . . . kind of . . . force it out there, like "I'm letting you know I'm independent." Like, "I don't need you"—that kind of thing. I don't think that's the best. Even if he's not truly dominant, even if you're his equal, I still think you should let him feel like a man, that kind of thing.

Breanna's argument again reflects the essentialist belief that men need to be in charge in their romantic relationships in order to be happy. She frames men's symbolic dominance as a charade that allows men to "do gender" in spite of women's increased economic independence (West and Zimmerman 1987). But she also states that *she* finds this enactment of gender difference attractive, too, revealing the "cathexis" experienced by many of the women that results from this "social patterning of desire" (Connell 1987, 112). By emphasizing this behavior as chosen, however, she denies an association between her behavior and the reproduction of gender inequality.

As Stone (2007) found, "choice rhetoric" is used by high-achieving women to disavow the constraints women continue to face. A narrative of choice is appealing because it draws on "the language of privilege, feminism, and personal agency" and is, therefore, consistent with how they have constructed understandings of themselves (Stone 2007, 125). By emphasizing symbolic gendering as a choice rather than a requirement, and by reaffirming their autonomy, women were able to take comfort in the courtship conventions that felt "safe" and "right," without sacrificing their sense of an independent, empowered self. As McCall (2011) speculates, the educational and professional attainments of privileged women transgress enough gender boundaries in the workplace and the home to allow them to downplay gender inequality as a relevant social problem.

CONCLUSION

This study shows how college-educated women's commitment to courtship norms reinforces narratives of gender difference even as they lay claims to gender equality. New norms about gender equality and women's autonomy now compete with more traditional courtship scripts, creating a cultural contradiction for women as they seek to reconcile discrepant sets of behavioral rules. Women's narratives reveal the interactions between the processes that promote both social change and social persistence. They are encountering men on new terms and creating relationships that challenge the assumptions underlying a gendered division of labor. They express comfort asserting financial independence, personal autonomy, and a desire for an egalitarian partnership. The progress they have made, however, has perhaps led them to believe that they can pick and choose between gendered meanings with no consequences. These findings demonstrate that, to ease the conflict between a desire for equality and a persistence of conventional courtship rituals, women conclude that the symbolic gendering of courtship does not contribute to the perpetuation of gender inequality. They construe men's participation in unequal courtship patterns as natural and inevitable and they explain their own participation as a personal choice that is rooted in their personalities and preferences. In this manner, women are able to reaffirm their autonomy and deny the significance of inequality in courtship,

demonstrating how narratives of empowerment based on ideologies of individualism can be used to conceal the continuation of male privilege in ways that make individuals feel good about their conformity. Unfortunately, this approach not only limits the options for more privileged women, it also reinforces norms for women whose limited resources provide them with fewer opportunities to challenge gender inequality. When solutions are framed as individual rather than structural, the inability to negotiate a preferred arrangement, often the result of a lack of bargaining power, instead becomes framed as a personal failing, discouraging a broader challenge to the norms that structure relationships.

* * *

NOTES

1. This finding is in contrast to Sassler and Miller's (2011) study of working class couples, where women found their efforts to secure desired marriage proposals mostly rebuffed, indicating that well-educated, middle-class women may be better positioned to challenge gender norms successfully.

2. Given space limitations, I do not present findings on how married couples enact gender difference symbolically, although this was discussed by the 17 women who were married or had been married. But activities such as initiating and planning recreation and gifting were more likely to be performed by women, as they took over the bulk of the "relationship work." Household labor remains gendered, as well, and the majority of the married women took their husband's last name.

REFERENCES

Bailey, Beth. 1988. *From front porch to back seat: Courtship in twentieth-century America.* Baltimore: Johns Hopkins University Press.

Becker, Julia, and Stephen Wright. 2011. Yet another dark side of chivalry: Benevolent sexism undermines and hostile sexism motivates collective action for social change. *Journal of Personal and Social Psychology* 101: 62–77.

Bianchi, Suzanne, Melissa Milkie, Liana Sayer, and John Robinson. 2000. Is anyone doing the housework? Trends in the gender division of household labor. *Social Forces* 79: 191–228.

Bianchi, Suzanne, John Robinson, and Melissa Milkie. 2006. *Changing rhythms of American family life.* New York: Russell Sage Foundation.

Bogle, Kathleen. 2008. *Hooking-up: Sex. dating, and relationships on campus.* New York: New York University Press.

Bourdieu, Pierre. 1998. *Masculine domination.* Stanford, CA: Stanford University Press.

Cancian, Francesca. 1987. *Love in America: Gender and self-development.* Cambridge, UK: Cambridge University Press.

Cate, Rodney, and Sally Lloyd. 1992. *Courtship.* Newbury Park, CA: Sage.

Connell, Raewyn. 1987. *Gender and power.* Stanford, CA: Stanford University Press.

Coontz, Stephanie. 2005. *Marriage, a history: How love conquered marriage.* New York: Penguin.

Damaske, Sarah. 2011. *For the family? How class and gender shape women's work.* New York: Oxford University Press.

Eaton, Asia, and Suzanna Rose. 2011. Has dating become more egalitarian? A 35 year review using sex roles. *Sex Roles* 64: 843–62.

England, Paula. 2010. The gender revolution: Uneven and stalled. *Gender & Society* 24: 149–66.

England, Paula, Emily Fitzgibbons Shafer, and Alison Fogarty. 2008. Hooking up and forming romantic relationships on today's college campuses. In *The gendered society reader,* 3rd ed., edited by Michael Kimmel and Amy Aronson. New York: Oxford University Press.

Geller, Jaclyn. 2001. *Here comes the bride: Women, weddings, and the marriage mystique.* New York: Four Walls Eight Windows.

Gerson, Kathleen. 2002. Moral dilemmas, moral strategies, and the transformation of gender: Lessons from two generations of work and family change. *Gender & Society* 16: 8–28.

Gerson, Kathleen. 2010. *The unfinished revolution: How a new generation is reshaping family, work, and gender in America.* New York: Oxford University Press.

Goffman, Erving. 1959. *The presentation of self in everyday life.* New York: Anchor.

Goffman, Erving. 1976. Gender display. *Studies in the Anthropology of Visual Communication* 3: 69–77.

Graf, Nikki, and Christine Schwartz. 2011. The uneven pace of change in heterosexual romantic relationships: Comment on England. *Gender & Society* 25: 101–07.

Hamilton, Laura, and Elizabeth Armstrong. 2009. Gendered sexuality in young adulthood: Double binds and flawed options. *Gender & Society* 23: 589–616.

Hamilton, Laura, Claudia Geist, and Brian Powell. 2011. Marital name change as a window into gender attitudes. *Gender & Society* 25: 145–75.

Humble, Aine, Anisa Zvonkovic, and Alexis Walker. 2008. "The royal we": Gender ideology, display, and assessment in wedding work. *Journal of Family Issues* 29: 3–25.

Laner, Mary Riege, and Nicole Ventrone. 1998. Egalitarian daters/traditionalist dates. *Journal of Family Issues* 19: 468–77.

Laner, Mary Riege, and Nicole Ventrone. 2000. Dating scripts revisited. *Journal of Family Issues* 21: 488–500.

Lareau, Annette. 2003. *Unequal childhoods: Class, race, and family life.* Berkeley: University of California Press.

McCall, Leslie. 2011. Women and men as class and race actors: Comment on England. *Gender and Society* 25: 94–100.

Ridgeway, Cecilia. 2011. *Framed by gender: How gender inequality persists in the modern world.* New York: Oxford University Press.

Rudman, Laurie, and Kimberly Fairchild. 2004. Reactions to counterstereotypic behavior: The role of backlash in cultural stereotype maintenance. *Journal of Personality and Social Psychology* 87: 157–76.

Sassier, Sharon, and Amanda Miller. 2011. Waiting to be asked: Gender, power, and relationship progression among cohabiting couples. *Journal of Family Issues* 32: 482–506.

Stone, Pamela. 2007. *Opting out? Why women really quit careers and head home.* Berkeley: University of California Press.

Swim, Janet, and Laurie Cohen. 1997. Overt, covert, and subtle sexism: A comparison between the attitudes toward women and modern sexism scales. *Psychology of Women Quarterly* 21: 103–18.

Tichenor, Veronica. 2005. *Earning more and getting less: Why successful wives can't buy equality.* New Brunswick, NJ: Rutgers University Press.

Twenge, Jean. 2001. Changes in women's assertiveness in response to status and roles: A cross-temporal meta-analysis. *Journal of Personality and Social Psychology* 81: 133–45.

West, Candace, and Don Zimmerman. 1987. Doing gender. *Gender & Society* 1: 125–51.

Introduction to Reading 38

In this reading, Erin M. Rehel looks at the work/family nexus using a different perspective from that in Chapter 7, looking at the impact of workplace policies on spousal and parenting relationships in the home. She interviewed 50 white-collar fathers along with more than two thirds of their female partners in the United States and Canada. Rehel distinguishes between those men who take "extended" parental leaves of 3 weeks or more and those who take shorter or no parental leaves. She studies these decisions under three different policy frameworks for men who all work for the same organization. The advantage of her research design is that she can look at how fathers make decisions relative to how and for how long they use parental leaves within the same organization but different policy conditions, and she looks at the impact of their decisions on their parenting roles. Although parental leave decisions would seem to be an individual or couple decision, Rehel's research suggests otherwise. This examination of parental leave policies and subsequent attitudes toward such policies within the work organization elaborates on some of the policy and organizational changes Amy S. Wharton, in Chapter 7, suggests are important in changing the institutions of work, family, and gender.

1. What features of these three different policy conditions for family/parental leave seem to be most critical in explaining these men's use of parental leave.

2. How do traditional gender expectations influence decisions even in the face of a policy that allows men to take parental leave upon the birth of their children?

3. What are the consequences of fathers' decisions to take extended parental leaves for parenting and relationships with their spouses and their children across time?

WHEN DAD STAYS HOME TOO

PATERNITY LEAVE, GENDER, AND PARENTING

Erin M. Rehel

The transition to parenthood is a time of dramatic change for a couple. New mothers often exit the workforce, for varying lengths of time, to recover from birth and to adjust to their new role (Fox 2009). In the United States and Canada, maternity leave, whether state or employer sponsored, often provides the context for this temporary exit.[1] Far fewer fathers experience even a temporary absence from the workforce at the transition to parenthood. Instead, new fathers typically maintain, or sometimes strengthen, their employment ties in the post-birth period (Glauber 2008; Sanchez and Thomson 1997). As a result, men and women experience structurally different pathways

From Rehel, Erin M. 2014. "When Dad Stays Home Too: Paternity Leave, Gender, and Parenting." *Gender & Society* 28(1): 110–132.

into parenthood, which can contribute to different understandings and enactments of parenting.

Research on this important life course event consistently demonstrates that the birth of a child results in a gendered division of labor for most heterosexual couples (Cowan and Cowan 1992; Walzer 1998); women take on the bulk of the unpaid labor, particularly child care (Bianchi et al. 2000; Craig and Mullan 2011), even when couples' pre-parenting relationship was relatively egalitarian (Calasanti and Bailey 1991; Shelton 2000). A manager-helper dynamic often develops between new parents: Mothers are primarily responsible for child care and related matters, while fathers serve as helpers when needed and asked (Allen and Hawkins 1999; Coltrane 1996; Ehrensaft 1987; Gerson 1993). Largely overlooked in the literature, however, is what happens when men and women experience the transition to parenthood in structurally *similar* ways. More specifically, do men develop understandings and enactments of parenting that mirror those of women when they, too, exit the workforce temporarily in the immediate post-birth period?

In this article, I argue that when the transition to parenthood is structured for fathers in ways comparable to mothers, fathers come to think about and enact parenting in ways that are similar to mothers. The opportunity to experience the transition to parenthood freed of the demands and constraints of work provides fathers the space to develop a sense of responsibility that is often positioned as a core element of mothering (Fox 2009; Hays 1996; McMahon 1995; Ruddick 1995), while simultaneously gaining mastery of and confidence in parenting tasks. Extended time off for fathers, defined here as greater than three weeks, challenges the popular perception of the naturalness of mothering by highlighting the hands-on, learned nature of parenting (Lamb 2004). By comparing fathers who took extended time off following the birth of a child to fathers who did not, I demonstrate that when fathers do take time off after the birth of a child, they are drawn into the daily realities of responsibility and active parenting much as mothers are.

By sampling fathers employed by the same financial services firm but living in three different policy contexts (the Canadian province of Quebec, Canada, and the United States), several important aspects of a father's employment are held constant across policy context. This research design highlights the importance of state-level policy in facilitating leave-taking experiences for new fathers.

GENDER AND THE TRANSITION TO PARENTHOOD

Research on parenting consistently finds that heterosexual couples respond to parenthood by adopting a gendered division of paid and unpaid labor (Baxter, Hewitt, and Western 2005). This finding endures, even as men continue to increase their levels of involvement in family life (Bianchi, Robinson, and Milkie 2006; Sayer 2005). Time use data from the United States and Canada have shown a steady increase in the number of hours men spend in both domestic labor and child care (Fisher et al. 2007; Hook 2006), but research also illustrates that men's involvement is somewhat selective (Jump and Haas 1987). Men tend to participate more in "fun" aspects of child care, aspects of domestic labor that suit their tastes and interests (Coltrane 1995), and highly visible, or public, fathering activities (Shows and Gerstel 2009); women continue to do the more quotidian, labor-intensive tasks, such as meal preparation and bathing (Offer and Schneider 2011).

Three theoretical approaches have guided much of the research on why this gendering occurs: relative resources, time availability, and gender ideology (Coltrane 2000; Greenstein 2000). The first two approaches, drawing heavily from economics theory (Hank and Jurges 2007), emphasize rationality in the division of paid and unpaid labor, positioning housework as something undesirable that both men and women attempt to avoid. A relative resources explanation posits that the partner who brings the most resources to a relationship, often in terms of income, has the most power, enabling that partner to opt out of unpaid labor (Lundberg and Pollack 1996). Similarly, a time availability explanation suggests that child care and domestic labor should fall to the person who has the most time available (Greenstein 2000); more specifically, that the partner who is engaged in the most hours of paid labor performs less unpaid labor. The gender ideology approach emphasizes how attitudes around who should do what vis-à-vis paid and unpaid labor shape how these forms of labor are distributed within couples (Bianchi et al. 2000; Davis and Greenstein 2009). Beliefs that certain tasks and responsibilities are appropriate for women or for men explain why women are more likely to take on certain tasks, while men are more likely to do others (Bulanda 2004).

Although these theories provide useful frameworks for thinking about the division of domestic labor, some argue that they are less helpful in thinking about child care (Coltrane 2007; Craig and Mullan 2011). Both men and women now spend more time in child care than any previous period since the 1960s (Bianchi, Robinson, and Milkie 2006). Scholars trace this to emerging ideals around intensive parenting (Craig and Mullan 2011; Hays 1996) and concerted cultivation (Lareau 2003). Despite fathers' increased hours spent in child care, models developed specifically to understand father involvement illustrate a persistent lag in the ways fathers are involved with their children.

Lamb and colleagues provide a useful and popular model for understanding father involvement in child care (Lamb 1987, 2004; Lamb et al. 1985). Unlike previous approaches that enumerated specific (and often very gendered) tasks, this typology identifies broad groupings of ways a *parent* might be involved, specifically engagement, accessibility, and responsibility. This model captures various forms of involvement, from reading and playing (engagement), to meal preparation while a child does homework (accessibility), to planning and orchestrating around the child (responsibility). When framing the available data on father involvement using this typology, we see that fathers have significantly increased their levels of engagement and accessibility but have changed little in terms of responsibility. Responsibility for children is consistently understood as one of the most fundamental elements of good mothering (Christopher 2012; Doucet 2009; Fox and Worts 1999; Ruddick 1995) and continues to be a form of labor, often invisible, that adds to women's share of labor in significant ways.

The days, weeks, or months new mothers spend with their newborns following birth, often in the absence of other adults and free of work obligations, is when what is colloquially referred to as maternal instinct develops (Chodorow 1978; Oakley 1979). During this initial period, women develop a sense of responsibility that comes from being the primary care provider, learning cues, needs, and patterns (Bobel 2002; Miller 2007; Walzer 1998). Fathers, more often than not, do not have this time. In important ways, this period establishes parenting patterns that are both difficult to undo and difficult to discern as they become naturalized over time. Moreover, women's childhood socialization and surrogate caretaking experiences (Coltrane 1989; Lamb 2000) provide them with the opportunity to develop some of the necessary skills for and a sense of confidence in parenting, enabling them to adopt the role of primary caretaker more easily. Together, these experiences contribute to the gendered division of labor when partners become parents.

Although a gendered division of labor is most common among parents, and has strong and meaningful roots in social norms and expectations (West and Zimmerman 1987), several studies of couples that intentionally parent equally illustrate that less gendered ways of apportioning paid and unpaid labor are also possible (Deutsch 1999, 2001; Dienhart 1998; Ehrensaft 1987). Much of this research focuses on whether or not men are capable of being active and nurturing co-parents, rather than simply mother's helpers. This research suggests that when parents share parenting tasks from the beginning, men develop greater confidence and skill in their own parenting, leading to greater father involvement (Coltrane 1996; Lamb 2000). My study expands beyond the focus on the choices of individual fathers who have elected to share parenting, found in these studies, to highlight the role played by structure in enabling men to develop as active co-parents.

Lending further support to the idea that men can parent as fully as women do is the small, but growing, body of research on fathers who are primary care providers for their children, specifically stay-at-home dads (Doucet 2006, 2009; Rochlen et al. 2008) and fathers parenting alone (Coles 2010; Hook and Chalasani 2008; Risman 1987; Ziol-Guest 2009). Overall, research on both groups finds that when fathers are required to be primarily *responsible* for all aspects of child care, they are able to do so. By comparing "reluctant fathers," those who find themselves parenting alone not by their own choice, to single mothers and heterosexual co-parents, Risman (1987) finds that fathers who are situated to parent alone do so in ways quite similar to mothers, revealing much about how structure matters in the enactment of parenting. Much of this research demonstrates men's capacity for "mothering" (Doucet 2006, 2009), reinforcing the idea that parenting is most often learned by doing, or, to borrow from Lamb, "on the job" (Lamb 1987, 2000).

In short, the gendered division of labor that occurs when men and women parent together is far from biologically inevitable. We have evidence that men and women can do "parenting" in the same way, but research shows that this occurs less frequently when men and women parent together than when men parent alone. In fact, the research that most clearly and definitively illustrates fathers parenting as completely as mothers is the research on stay-at-home dads and single fathers, fathers who are structurally situated to parent as women most commonly do. All this research led me to suspect that when men experience the transition to parenting in ways that are structurally similar to women, men develop a sense of responsibility that is seen as characteristic of mothers' parenting but far less common in fathers' parenting. Drawing primarily from interview data with fathers, I demonstrate that fathers who are home during the initial transition to parenthood come to develop a sense of responsibility that permits shared parenting, regardless of the policy context in which they live. . . .

DATA AND METHODS

This article draws on data collected as part of a larger, comparative project examining the influence of social policy on father involvement in parenting in the United States, English Canada, and the French-Canadian province of Quebec. I conducted semi-structured interviews with 50 fathers and 35 of their female partners in Chicago, Toronto, and Montreal. These cities were selected to reflect three of the different family-focused social policy contexts that currently exist in North America. An important component of each of these contexts is the family leave policy.

The Family and Medical Leave Act (FMLA), the federal policy of the United States, provides qualified male and female workers 12 weeks of unpaid leave following the birth or adoption of a child. Department of Labor statistics estimate that approximately 60 percent of the U.S. labor force is covered by this policy, leaving many without access to any type of protected family leave. The Canadian federal plan, Employment Insurance Maternity and Parental Leave Benefits (EI), provides new mothers with 15 weeks of maternity leave, paid at a 55 percent wage replacement level up to a maximum amount. An additional 35 weeks of parental leave is available to either parent, again paid at a wage replacement level of 55 percent. Although parents must meet employment criteria in order to qualify, these requirements are significantly less than those of the FMLA, allowing more workers to qualify. Structured in a similar way to the Canadian federal plan, the Quebec Parental Insurance Plan (QPIP) provides 18 weeks of maternity leave and an additional 32 weeks of shared parental leave.

One notable difference from the Canadian plan is the designation of five weeks of nontransferable paternity leave for the father only. Unlike parental leave, this paternity leave is provided on a "use it or lose it" basis: If a father opts not to take it, his female partner cannot add this time to her maternity leave. The Quebec plan also provides a higher average wage replacement level (55–70 percent), higher maximum salary amounts, and lower workforce participation requirements to qualify.

For my study, I recruited fathers from within a single financial services firm with operations in both Canada and the United States. Recruiting within a single firm enabled me to control for some employer-specific structural variation, such as organizational culture around and management support for men's involvement in families, which has been shown to influence father involvement (Russell and Hwang 2004). The firm's interest in providing me access to its employees stems from a strong desire to promote workforce gender equality, a goal consistent with its reputation for workplace diversity initiatives, progressive and generous employee benefits, and corporate social responsibility. With regard to family leave, the firm currently has different policies in Canada and the United States, largely because of significant differences in federal leave policies. Employees in Canada or Quebec who take state-supported leave can have up to six weeks of that leave "topped up" by the firm to 90 percent of an employee's salary, a benefit unavailable to American employees.

* * *

Deciding to Take Leave

To understand the influence of leave-taking on a father's parenting requires first considering the decision to take, or not take, leave. Individual attitudes, structural opportunities or limitations, and maternal desire influence this decision in complicated and nuanced ways. My data suggest that although some men make leave-taking decisions based on personal attitudes about

work, family, and parenting, others' decisions are enabled or constrained by policy.

Personal attitudes certainly inform fathers' decisions around taking leave. This is just as much the case for fathers who do take leave as it is for those who do not. Many fathers who took leave, like 43-year-old Montreal father Tony, expressed a clear desire to be a very involved father, right from the start. For Tony, this included taking the five weeks of paternity leave available to him: "I was just so excited, I was so excited for him. I wanted to be around him 100 percent of the time. I wanted to be his whole world, you know?"[2] Chad, a 39-year-old father of one from Chicago, articulated a similar interest in being involved right from birth: "You know, I just wanted to be there from the beginning with our first child. I wasn't actually sure how much time I wanted to be home, so I wanted to be home as long as I could, really." Tony and Chad captured what most leave-taking fathers described: a sense of excitement about becoming a dad and an enthusiasm for being an involved co-parent. These types of explanations for leave-taking hint at self-selection in terms of who takes leave.

Personal attitudes also played a role in the decision of those men who did not take leave. No less enthusiastic about becoming a dad, fathers who did not take leave either did not see a need to be home or simply did not want to be out of work for an extended period of time. When asked if he would have taken extended (paid) leave were that available, 32-year-old Chicago father Mark said,

> I wouldn't have stayed home for two weeks when [our daughter] was born. Even if it was written in stone and that was common practice, I wouldn't have stayed home for two weeks. I was home for a week, plus the weekend, and they didn't need me, so I don't know if anything more generous, I would take advantage of.

Opting out of leave-taking because of a lack of interest indicates perhaps a more traditional orientation toward gender, parenting, and division of labor. For these leave-takers and non-leave-takers alike, personal beliefs and orientations figured prominently in leave-taking behavior. However, structural factors also influenced fathers' decisions around leave-taking in important ways.

The leave-taking fathers I've described were drawn to paternity leave because of a personal orientation toward shared parenting, but other fathers were more extrinsically motivated to take leave, primarily by policy. Here, the case of Quebec's leave policy is illustrative of how policy matters. In 2005, the year prior to the introduction of the current plan, 32 percent of Quebec fathers took leave (Marshall 2008). In 2011, just six years later, 76 percent took leave (Findlay and Kohen 2012). This dramatic rise in the number of fathers taking leave coincides with the introduction of Quebec's new parental leave plan. A plausible explanation for this rapid change is that the policy itself motivated fathers to take leave. With five weeks of nontransferable paternity leave paid at 70 percent of one's salary, the structure of the Quebec policy makes leave accessible to large numbers of new fathers. A type of threshold effect is detectable: The policy reduces barriers to leave-taking, enabling large numbers of men to take leave. As more men take leave, leave-taking becomes normalized. This suggests that new fathers take leave because that is the norm and not *necessarily* because they share the types of attitudes and beliefs articulated by the fathers described earlier.

Explaining why he took five weeks of leave after the births of both of his daughters, 33-year-old Montreal father Allan aptly captured the idea that, for many fathers in Quebec, the existence of the policy served as a very real motivator:

> Because they gave me five weeks and I was, like, "Yeah!" I mean, really? This is Quebec. I pay, like, 40 percent tax on everything I earn plus 15 percent on everything I buy, plus the extra on gas and alcohol, and anything good in life they tax it twice as much, okay? And then, every once in a while, you get a social program. And this is one of them. So you just look at it and say, "Yeah, I'm taking it."

What this comment, which iterates a commonly expressed sentiment, reveals is that taking leave is not simply a matter of individual attitudes.

Instead, particular types of family leave policies appear to facilitate leave-taking among fathers who might otherwise be disinclined to do so.

Policy also constrained fathers in important ways. Across all three policy contexts, many non-leave-taking fathers described wanting to be home for more time after birth, but pointed to one of three structural limitations that made leave-taking impossible: concerns about reactions from superiors and colleagues; wanting to maximize the weeks of leave available to their partners; and financial limitations.

The most commonly cited reason for not taking more extended time off was a concern for how this would be perceived by supervisors, colleagues, and, sometimes, clients. When asked about the possibility of taking longer than the two weeks he did take, 43-year-old Chicago father Patrick captured a fear expressed by many fathers: "Well, that's kind of a tough question. I probably wouldn't have because of the way it would've been viewed. I mean, honestly—and I've heard executives say this—excuse the language—'I can't fucking believe that guy took a month off after the birth of his baby.' I've heard people say it." Like Patrick, many fathers felt pulled back to work by concerns about how violating the image of the ideal worker would impact their work lives. That this was the only reason given by Quebec fathers who opted not to take paternity leave points to the continued salience of a breadwinner identity among men.

A uniquely Canadian constraint relates to the structure of the federal leave policy. Because the only weeks of leave fathers outside Quebec have access to are the shared weeks of parental leave, a father taking leave reduces the number of weeks a mother can take. Thirty-five-year-old Toronto father Brad, for example, said his wife wanted to be home for the whole year, so he let her take the fifty weeks of combined maternity and parental leave, plus the mandatory two-week waiting period: "I know she loved it and I just would never do that to her. It would've taken weeks off of her year and I just would never have done that."

While fathers like Brad describe not wanting to reduce their partner's leave, others told me that their partners were not open to sharing parental leave, suggesting material gatekeeping when it comes to leave allocation (Allen and Hawkins 1999). When I asked Jack, a 43-year-old Toronto father, why he opted not to take leave, he straightforwardly replied that his wife had said she was taking all the available leave.

Finally, many families felt unable to survive the significant reduction in wages that came with both partners being on leave. Here again we see how much policy can play a role in deciding to take leave: America fathers, who did not have access to any wage replacement, invoked this limitation more than their Canadian counterparts.

There is certainly a degree of selectivity in who does and does not take leave. That some Quebec fathers decide against leave-taking in a policy supportive context, where generous paid leave is available, while American fathers do take leave, despite a lack of significant policy support for this decision, certainly validates the idea that a degree of person preference plays into leave-taking behavior. My data also show, however, that it is not the case that all men who take leave do so because of a predisposition to ideals of co-parenting. Furthermore, it would be inaccurate to assume that all those who do not take leave opt not to because of personal preference or traditional views on gender, parenting, and the division of labor. Whatever the reason for it, leave-taking enables fathers to develop the responsibility necessary for them to actively co-parent along with their partners, as I will now show.

LEAVE-TAKING MEN

Unlike women, who often have some "surrogate" parenting experiences prior to becoming mothers (e.g., babysitting, caring for siblings extended family), men's more limited exposure to infant/child care mean they often find themselves engaged in child care without much direct experience prior to becoming fathers (Lamb 2004). Eric, a 45-year-old father of two from Montreal, described his experience: "Like, in my case I had no exposure. I'm the youngest sibling in my family. No exposure to infants, diapers—I

was walking into a whole new reality." For Eric, taking five weeks of paternity leave was an eye-opening experience, one that he felt really showed him what infant care entails. . . .

The availability of an extended period of parental leave allows fathers the opportunity to gain a sense of the "concerns" of parenting, many of which are invisible and therefore might go unnoticed by a father who is back at work. Forty-three-year-old Toronto father James had taken eight weeks of leave after the birth of his first child and six weeks following the birth of his second child. Like Eric, he found the experience to be invaluable in gaining a deeper understanding of caretaking: "I think, you know, every spouse should do that because it's an experience that will only help you understand in the long run what the heck your wife is going through." While James's comment reflects a continued connection between women and care work, he is also pointing to the way being on leave provides men with a fuller understanding of parenting that might otherwise be inaccessible to them. While paternal skill-building is also important, it is this fuller understanding of parenting that enables fathers to actively engage in parenting in a self-directed way, rather than relying on their partner's guidance. By sharing more than just tasks, partners become more equal co-parents than when one partner manages and delegates child care and related domestic labor.

For Paul, a 27-year-old first-time father from Montreal, five weeks of paternity leave challenged his previous understanding of what it meant to be home with an infant:

> I had this naive thinking that I'm going to be off and I'm going to be able to catch up on all these things. I'm going to have time to myself, to write music and do this stuff. Oh, my gosh, it was such a slap in the face! All my friends at work who were parents didn't say a thing—they just smirked: "Oh yeah, you're going to do all of that, eh? Have fun with that." It did not happen. Those five weeks went by so fast—we were constantly taking care of [our son]. Really made me realize to what extent taking care of a child is more than a full-time job. You don't get your 15-minute breaks, your half-hour breaks when you want. You don't get time off.

You don't have a switch off like you do at work. Really, your attention is always—especially with a newborn—100 percent on him.

Expecting a more leisurely experience while on paternity leave, Paul found his expectations to be at odds with the reality of daily life with an infant. In place of "free time," Paul found his days structured by his new reality as a father. My interview with Paul's wife, Sarah, revealed how this experience continued to inform his parenting after he returned to work, while Sarah was still on maternity leave:

He's never once told me, "You have it easy," you know, he's never, ever said that. He's always respected that this is a job and, I think, the five weeks that they give us paternity leave in the beginning is so fantastic. Because it makes the husband realize what kind of a . . . the responsibility and job, everything that the day entails and I think, you know, Paul experienced that and he's, like, "This is harder than what I do," you know. And he's said that before, because he knows he can take breaks and, you know, he could have his hour lunch and he can just walk away and be hands-free.

Sarah's comment reflects what many mothers whose partners had taken leave said about how leave-taking influenced not only how their partners thought about parenting but also how they enact parenting, even after their leave had ended.

For the men who took advantage of the opportunity to be home for several weeks, this expanded understanding of what it means to care for a child was complemented by the opportunity to develop the skills necessary to share care responsibilities with their partners. Chad, a Chicago father mentioned earlier, pointed to the "24 hours a day" aspect of being on leave as being particularly helpful in learning to parent:

I think I kind of needed that. Because, especially when she was first born, both of us . . . I mean, your mind is going a hundred miles an hour and you really don't know what to expect when you bring the baby home. And what you're supposed to do. And, just in those first few weeks, I think you learn a lot. Being able to spend 24 hours a day, you know, at home with the child, yeah, I think it helped.

Being able to spend "24 hours a day" is key in extended leave-taking. With this kind of presence, freed of workforce obligations, fathers are able to learn to parent in much the same way as mothers, through continuous hands-on participation (Miller 2007), creating the space for shared parenting.

Claudio, a 41-year-old father of one from Montreal who took a total of six weeks of leave, explained why he thought leave-taking is so important:

Because or else it becomes a routine, where the mom does the everyday necessities with the child and the dad comes home at night, spends a little time, plays with him, and that's it. But I find that if you're in there, every day with the child, taking care of him, making his meals in the morning, at lunch, putting him to sleep, like, all the little details, you'll become attached just as much as the mom. Then it no longer seems like just the mom who has the *initiative* to look after all these things. It becomes the dad and the mom together.

Informed by his experience of being on leave, Claudio described parenting as a mutually shared endeavor between partners. He went on to describe a "divide and conquer" strategy of parenting common among leave-taking fathers:

When you have a child, you have to work together. To give an example, say in the evening, depending on who comes home first, we'll eat together, but then I'll go give him his bath and then my partner looks after the kitchen. And the reverse happens: If she goes and does the bath, then I take care of the kitchen and all that.

To use Claudio's language, leave-taking allows fathers to develop "the initiative," which moves a couple beyond a manager-helper style of parenting and toward a co-parenting relationship.

With these parenting skills and newly developed carework capabilities, many fathers who took leave did see themselves as co-parents, capable of all aspects of child care, rather than just helpers. After taking two six-week parental leaves, Jon, a 40-year-old Torontonian father, experienced an internal struggle with having to return to work: "Honestly, I can do everything you can do. Why do I have to go back to work? Then there is the argument, 'Well, I had the kid and I'm the mother.' Yeah, I get that, but I'm a hands-on dad and I can do everything you can do." Jon felt he was capable of all the same dimensions of parenting as his wife; he believed his time off enabled him to gain mastery of the necessary parenting skills and the confidence to parent, two factors that have been shown to enhance father involvement (Lamb 1987; Lamb et al. 1985; Pleck and Masciadrelli 2004).

NON-LEAVE-TAKERS

The experiences of fathers who took more than three weeks of parental leave stand in sharp contrast to those of men who took little leave following the birth of their children. The understandings of parenting articulated by fathers who did not take leave provide further support for the claim that extended leave-taking by fathers has the potential to challenge gendered understandings of parenting in significant ways.

In North America, extended parental leave is uncommon among new fathers. Although concerns about how extended time off would be perceived by co-workers, particularly managers and supervisors, were often cited as reasons for not taking leave, fathers just as frequently said they did not take leave because they did not have a sense of their own utility at home during the first few months following birth. Jack, one of the Toronto fathers whose partner would not let him take any of the available weeks of leave, stated:

> That's kind of the time [the first six weeks] when you're the least helpful around the house, from my perspective. Like, if you told me the last six weeks of the [first] year . . . it would make a lot of sense, right? Because at that point your kid is running around, walking, you know, interactive and a lot of work. But the first six weeks they're just sleeping, pooping, and eating. So, I think that's part of it. It's like, okay, so you take six weeks off. You're really just sitting there most of the time. You're not really helping.

In many ways, this understanding of infant care reflects Paul's views *prior to taking leave*. Jack, who took less than a week of leave following each of his children's births, believed there would have been little for him to do had he taken leave: "You're . . . just sitting there most of the time." Likewise, Paul expected that being home with his new son would involve lots of "free time," but instead experienced quite the opposite. In the absence of this experience, Jack retained an understanding of infant care as undemanding and non-labor intensive. Jack's understanding of parenting focused solely on visible material tasks and physical labor, and responsibility, which is often an invisible form of labor, is completely absent from his viewpoint. Instead, a manager-helper dynamic is evident in how Jack articulates his presence as either helpful or not helpful.

Returning to work after a short time off also serves as an impediment to new fathers gaining the mastery and confidence that would enable them to actively co-parent. Mark, who, earlier in this article, said he wouldn't have taken paid leave were it available, felt that his wife "picked it [parenting] up pretty quickly" and thus saw no reason for him to be home for longer than he was. Later in our interview, however, Mark reflected on the limitations of his parenting:

> I need instructions to feed [our daughter]. I could be more, sort of, in tune with, you know, being able to pick up where Leslie dropped off, you know, right away. Like, I sometimes have to think about, what if, you know, something happened to Leslie and it was just me with Haley? You know, would she be in as good hands? And, I think, she would be eventually because, you know, I would . . . I would learn. But, I guess, I just don't know as much about taking care of [our daughter] as Leslie does now.

In my interview with Mark's wife Leslie, I asked if they had a system for dividing up child care and domestic labor. Leslie was quick to answer: "Oh yes, we have a system. It's called I do everything, and Mark does nothing." She paused and then added, "I take that back; he walks the dog." Taken together, Mark and Leslie's comments clearly illustrate the manager-helper dynamic that commonly develops when fathers quickly return to work: While their wives develop the necessary knowledge and parenting skills, their own parenting capabilities are less autonomous and rely more on the direction of their partners. Right from birth, this structurally different experience of parenting produces a gendered division of labor. Mothers' time at home, engaged completely in parenting, naturalizes and erases the hands-on, learned nature of parenting, while fathers' return to work curbs their growth in this area.

Charles, a 41-year-old Chicago father whose wife was expecting their third child at the time of our interview, planned to take off no more than a week when his son arrived. Echoing the sentiments of other fathers who took about a week off, Charles felt that there was no reason for him, as the dad, to be at home for long: "Well, I mean, I'm the dad, so I don't really need to take that many days off, so I'll probably only take, you know, five days, a week, just to help my wife acclimate." As with the other fathers who were at home briefly, Charles did not see why—as the father—he would need to be off for any extended period of time. Unlike those fathers who took an extended leave, non-leave-taking fathers are not intimately involved in the daily realities of family life beyond this initial period of adjustment. This structural reality very much limits their understanding of parenting, making them less able to respond to new, previously unknown needs or tasks than fathers who do stay home.

CONCLUSION

. . . The findings presented here likely underestimate how paternity leave can help lay the foundation for a co-parenting relationship where mothers and fathers share responsibility. Because all leave-taking fathers in this study took leave concurrently with their partners, they were never solely responsible for their child(ren). Despite this, leave-taking fathers still gained a broader understanding of parenting than fathers

who did not take leave. This suggests that if fathers did have the opportunity to be on leave alone, their understandings and enactments of parenting would have even greater depth. Similarly, the comparatively short leaves taken by fathers, even those defined here as extended, meant that mothers spent significantly longer periods fully immersed in parenting. Again, if fathers spent similarly lengthy periods of time fully engaged in parenting, enhanced parenting skills and sense of responsibility would likely develop.

* * *

NOTES

1.   Within the United States and Canada, access to maternity leave of any kind—paid or unpaid, government sponsored or employer based—is uneven (Hegewisch and Gornick 2011).

2.   All participant names have been changed.

REFERENCES

Allen, Sarah, and Alan Hawkins. 1999. Maternal gatekeeping: Mothers' beliefs and behaviors that inhibit greater father involvement in family work. *Journal of Marriage and Family* 61:199–212.

Baxter, Jennifer, Belinda Hewitt, and Mark Western. 2005. Post-familial families and the domestic division of labor. *Journal of Comparative Family Studies* 36:583–600.

Bianchi, Suzanne, Melissa Milkie, Liana Sayer, and John Robinson. 2000. Is anyone doing the housework? Trends in the gender division of household labor. *Social Forces* 79:191–228.

Bianchi, Suzanne, John Robinson, and Melissa Milkie. 2006. *Changing rhythms of American family life*. New York: Russell Sage Foundation.

Bobel, Chris. 2002. *The paradox of natural mothering*. Philadelphia, PA: Temple University Press.

Bulanda, Ronald. 2004. Paternal involvement with children: The influence of gender ideology. *Journal of Marriage and Family* 66:40–45.

Calasanti, Toni, and Carol Bailey. 1991. Gender inequality and the division of household labor in the United States and Sweden: A socialist-feminist approach. *Social Problems* 38:34–53.

Chodorow, Nancy. 1978. *The reproduction of mothering: Psychoanalysis and the sociology of gender.* Berkeley: University of California Press.

Christopher, Karen. 2012. Extensive mothering: Employed mothers' constructions of the good mother. *Gender & Society* 26:73–96.

Coles, Roberta. 2010. *Best kept secret: Single black fathers.* New York: Rowman & Littlefield.

Coltrane, Scott. 1989. Household labor and the routine production of gender. *Social Problems* 36:473–90.

Coltrane, Scott. 1995. The future of fatherhood: Social, demographic, and economic influences on men's family involvement. In *Fatherhood: Contemporary theory, research, and social policy,* edited by William Marsiglio. Thousand Oaks, CA: Sage.

Coltrane, Scott. 1996. *Family man: Fatherhood, housework, and gender equity.* New York: Oxford University.

Coltrane, Scott. 2000. Research on household labor: Modeling and measuring the social embeddedness of routine family work. *Journal of Marriage and Family* 62:1208–33.

Coltrane, Scott. 2007. Fatherhood, gender and work-family policies. In *Real Utopias,* edited by Erik Olin Wright. Madison, WI: The Havens Center.

Cowan, Carolyn, and Philip Cowan. 1992. *When partners become parents: The big life change for couples.* New York: Basic Books.

Craig, Lyn, and Killian Mullan. 2011. How mothers and fathers share childcare: A cross-national time use comparison. *American Sociological Review* 76:834–61.

Davis, Shannon N., and Theodore N. Greenstein. 2009. Gender ideology: Components, predictors, and consequences. *Annual Review of Sociology* 35:87–105.

Deutsch, Francine. 1999. *Halving it all: How equally shared parenting works.* Cambridge, MA: Harvard University Press.

Deutsch, Francine. 2001. Equally shared parenting. *Current Directions in Psychological Science* 10:25–28.

Dienhart, Anna. 1998. *Reshaping fatherhood: The social construction of shared parenting.* Thousand Oaks, CA: Sage.

Doucet, Andrea. 2006. *Do men mother? Fathering, care and domestic responsibility.* Toronto: University of Toronto Press.

Doucet, Andrea. 2009. Dad and baby in the first year: Gendered responsibilities and embodiment. *Annals of the American Academy of Political and Social Science* 624:78–98.

Ehrensaft, Diane. 1987. *Parenting together: Men and women sharing the care of their children.* New York: Free Press.

Findlay, Leanne C., and Dafna E. Kohen. 2012. Leave practices of parents after the birth or adoption of young children. *Canadian Social Trends.* Statistics Canada Catalogue no. 11–008-X.

Fisher, Kimberly, Muriel Egerton, Jonathan I. Gershuny, and John P. Robinson. 2007. Gender convergence in the American heritage time use study (AHTUS). *Social Indicators Research* 82:1–33.

Fox, Bonnie. 2009. *When couples become parents: The creation of gender in the transition to parenthood.* Toronto: University of Toronto Press.

Fox, Bonnie, and Diana Worts. 1999. Revisiting the critique of medicalized childbirth: A contribution to the sociology of birth. *Gender & Society* 13:326–46.

Gerson, Kathleen. 1993. *No man's land: Men's changing commitment to family and work.* New York: Basic Books.

Glauber, Rebecca. 2008. Gender and race in families and at work: The fatherhood wage premium. *Gender & Society* 22:8–30.

Greenstein, Theodore. 2000. Economic dependence, gender and the division of labor in the home. *Journal of Marriage and Family* 62:322–35.

Hank, Karstan, and Hendrik Jurges. 2007. Gender and the division of household labor in older couples: A European perspective. *Journal of Family Issues* 28:399–421.

Hays, Sharon. 1996. *The cultural contradictions of motherhood.* New Haven, CT: Yale University Press.

Hegewisch, Ariane, and Janet Gornick. 2011. The impact of work-family policies on women's employment: A review of research from OECD countries. *Community, Work & Family* 14:119–38.

Hook, Jennifer. 2006. Care in context: Men's unpaid work in 20 countries, 1965–2003. *American Sociological Review* 71:639–60.

Hook, Jennifer, and Satvika Chalasani. 2008. Gendered expectations? Reconsidering single fathers' child-care time. *Journal of Marriage and Family* 70:978–90.

Jump, Teresa L., and Linda Haas. 1987. Fathers in transition: Dual-career fathers participating in child care. In *Changing men: New directions in research on men and masculinity,* edited by Michael Kimmel. Newbury Park, CA: Sage.

Lamb, Michael. 1987. *The father's role: Cross-cultural perspectives.* Hillsdale, NJ: Lawrence Erlbaum.

Lamb, Michael. 2000. The history of research on father involvement: An overview. *Marriage and Family Review* 29:23–42.

Lamb, Michael, Ed. 2004. *The role of the father in child development,* 4th ed. Hoboken, NJ: Wiley.

Lamb, Michael E., Joseph H. Pleck, Eric Chamov, and James A. Levine. 1985. Paternal behavior in humans. *American Zoologist* 25:883–94.

Lareau, Annette. 2003. *Unequal childhoods: Class, race, and family life.* Berkeley: University of California Press.

Lundberg, Shelly, and Robert A. Pollack. 1996. Bargaining and distribution in marriage. *Journal of Economic Perspectives* 10:139–58.

Marshall, Katherine. 2008. *Fathers' use of paid parental leave.* Statistics Canada, Catalogue no. 75–001-X.

McMahon, Martha. 1995. *Engendering motherhood: Identity and self-transformation in women's lives.* New York: Guilford.

Miller, Tina. 2007. Is this what motherhood is all about? Weaving experiences and discourse through transition to first-time motherhood. *Gender & Society* 21:337–58.

Oakley, Ann. 1979. *Becoming a mother.* Oxford, UK: Oxford University Press.

Offer, Shira, and Barbara Schneider. 2011. Revisiting the gender gap in time-use patterns: Multitasking and well-being among mothers and fathers in dual-earner families. *American Sociological Review* 76:809–33.

Pleck, Joseph, and Brian Masciadrelli. 2004. Paternal involvement by U.S. residential fathers: Levels, sources, and consequences. In *The role of the father in child development,* edited by Michael Lamb. New York: John Wiley.

Risman, Barbara J. 1987. Intimate relationships from a microstructural perspective: Men who mother. *Gender & Society* 1:6–32.

Rochlen, Aaron, Ryan A. McKelley, Marie-Anne Suizzo, and Vanessa Scaringi. 2008. Predictors of relationship satisfaction, psychological well-being, and life satisfaction among stay-at-home fathers. *Psychology of Men and Masculinity* 9:17–28.

Ruddick, Sara. 1995. *Maternal thinking: Towards a politics of peace,* 2nd ed. Boston: Beacon Press.

Russell, Graeme, and Carl Hwang. 2004. The impact of workplace practices on father involvement. In *The role of the father in child development,* 4th ed., edited by Michael Lamb. New York: John Wiley.

Sanchez, Laura, and Elizabeth Thomson. 1997. Becoming mothers and fathers: Parenthood, gender, and the division of labor. *Gender & Society* 11:747–72.

Sayer, Liana. 2005. Gender, time and inequality. *Social Forces* 84:285–303.

Shelton, B. A. 2000. Understanding the distribution of housework between husbands and wives. In *The ties that bind: Perspectives on marriage and cohabitation,* edited by Michelle Hindin, Arland Thornton, Elizabeth Thomson, Christine Bachrach, and Linda Waite. Boston: Aldine de Gruyter.

Shows, Carla, and Naomi Gerstel. 2009. Fathering, class, and gender: A comparison of physicians and emergency medical technicians. *Gender & Society* 23:161–87.

Walzer, Susan. 1998. *Thinking about the baby: Gender and the transitions into parenthood.* Philadelphia, PA: Temple University Press.

West, Candace, and Don Zimmerman. 1987. Doing gender. *Gender & Society* 1:125–51.

Ziol-Guest, Kathleen. 2009. A single father's shopping bag: Purchasing decisions in single-father families. *Journal of Family Issues* 30:605–22.

Introduction to Reading 39

The social construction of gender is embedded in institutions as well as interactions between individuals, as Irene Padavic and Jonniann Butterfield show in this reading. They interviewed 17 women who were nonbiological and nonlegal co-parents of children in lesbian families. These women, from an area near a medium-sized city in Florida, were identified using a snowball sampling method in which individuals interviewed were asked for names of other women in a similar situation. Motherhood and the expectations surrounding it, particularly the expectation that a biological birth was part of the mothering identity, proved to be a major barrier for the nonbiological co-parents they interviewed. These co-parents struggled with "undoing" the social construction of familial expectations, which links gender and biology to mothering, as they attempted to co-parent their children. The obstacles they faced were not just legal but also social, as individuals these women came in contact with during parenting refused to believe that they were their children's "real" mothers who could make daily decisions for their children. Their findings tell us a great deal about how gendered and fixed in heteronormativity the identity of "mother" is.

1. What were the obstacles that stood in the way of co-parenting for these women?

2. What were the differences between lesbian co-parents who identified themselves as "mothers," "fathers," and "mathers," and what factors were involved in their taking on one of these designations?

3. How does the new category some of these women created, "mathers," allow for a less gendered vision of parenting? What stands in the way of a less gendered vision of parenting without a heterosexual, gendered parenting dichotomy?

Mothers, Fathers, and "Mathers"

Negotiating a Lesbian Co-parental Identity

Irene Padavic and Jonniann Butterfield

In a society marked by binary categorizations and an ideological preference for a "one mother–one father" family model, lesbian co-parents muddy the waters. Previous research on the identity struggles of lesbian co-parents has focused on their experiences as mothers, but in doing so scholars themselves may have inadvertently reinscribed the heteronormative relationships that many lesbian families seek to dismantle. The assumption that women engaged in parenting want to be "mothers," with all the behavioral prescriptions the role entails, precludes an understanding of how the existence of lesbian families can help unhinge sex from gender. This article argues that to gain a more complete understanding of lesbian families, we must consider how co-parents negotiate a *parental* identity, rather than presuming that women parents want to *mother*. This article asks how a nonbiological woman parent determines a parental identity in a system constrained by language that offers only two options (mother or father) and in which the dominant motherhood ideology disqualifies her from achieving the status of good mother. Moreover, it asks how these personal and interpersonal dynamics play out in an institutional context that refuses to legally recognize them as parents.

From Padavic, Irene and Jonniann Butterfield. 2011. "Mothers, Fathers, and 'Mathers': Negotiating a Lesbian Co-parental Identity." *Gender & Society* 25(2): 176–196. Published by Sage Publications on behalf of Sociologists for Women in Society.

We employ a social constructionist approach to identity and to gender, which suggests that identities are variable and actively created through interactions (Schwalbe and Mason-Schrock 1996) and that because gender is dynamic, it can be "undone" as well as "done" (Deutsch 2007; West and Zimmerman 1987). As a result of this dynamism, "gender can be openly challenged by non-gendered practices in ordinary interaction, in families, childrearing, language, and organization of space" (Lorber 2000, 88). Lesbian parents have the unique opportunity to experience parenthood and raise children outside the gendered heterosexual context, and by doing so, they can destabilize gendered arrangements (Dalton and Bielby 2000; Weston 1991).

The possibility of undoing gender via such innovative family arrangements is one thing; emotionally creating such "brave new families" (Stacey 1998) is another, and previous research indicates that doing so is not a simple matter, particularly for a nonbiological lesbian parent, who "is denied access to any socially sanctioned parental category" (Gabb 2005, 594). When the state fails to legally recognize the legitimacy of both parents in such families—as is the case in most of the United States (notwithstanding huge civil rights gains in some jurisdictions)—the task of securing a parental identity is especially difficult. Understanding how women parents lacking a legal entitlement to parenthood struggle to forge a parental identity is important because identifying the pitfalls such women face and the successful strategies they devise may provide hope for others seeking to create a society in which gender and sexuality cease to exist as categories that privilege some groups over others.

BARRIERS TO IDENTITY CREATION: THE MOTHERHOOD HIERARCHY, LANGUAGE, AND THE LEGAL SYSTEM

Social expectations present lesbian co-parents with at least three barriers to smoothly constructing a sense of themselves as parents. First, all women become parents in a society that promotes a motherhood ideology validating the identity claims only of mothers who meet certain criteria (Chase and Rogers 2001; Hequembourg and Farrell 1999). Family law, social policies, and cultural representations endorse the married, middle-class, white, heterosexual family as the ideal (Abramovitz 1996; Fineman 1995; Roberts 1997; Thorne 1993), and a "motherhood hierarchy" rewards those who most closely conform to it. The most honored mother is "a heterosexual woman, of legal age, married in a traditional nuclear family, fertile, pregnant by intercourse with her husband, and wants to bear children" (DiLapi 1989, 110). Moreover, much societal and legal reluctance to accept lesbians as good mothers derives from fear that their children will be psychologically harmed or more likely to identify as homosexual (Thompson 2002), despite considerable research evidence to the contrary (Stacey and Biblarz 2001). Media pundits and politicians have also pathologized lesbian parents, portraying them as egocentric and immoral and their relationships as unstable (Hequembourg 2007; Richey 2010). Women who fail to mother in ways congruent with motherhood ideals are subject to "deviance discourses" (Miall and March 2006, 46) and to being labeled as unfit or bad (Arendell 2000). Thus, lesbian parents face a continual struggle to have their parental identity legitimized in a social context that renders it tenuous.

A second barrier is that the language used to identify parents relies on the norm of "one mother–one father," which provides no descriptively accurate label for women who lack a biological or legal tie to the child. Naming is a central—and fraught—component of identity for many lesbian parents. As Gabb (2005, 594) noted, the "materiality of language" is crucial because people come into being only via the power of discourse. Research (Aizley 2006; Sullivan 2004) indicates that co-parents often feel caught in an identity limbo since they neither fit neatly into the "mother" category (because they did not give birth) nor (because they are not men) fit into the only other possibility offered in a binary system, that of "father." While some appreciate this limbo and devise terms such as *lesbian dad, dyke daddy, high-femme dad, mamma II,* and the Hebrew word for mother, *ima* (Aizley 2006), most describe facing difficulty being validated by the outside world and having to continuously justify their family structure, including to people in the gay community (Dunne 2000). Outsiders hold a cultural attachment to the notion that there can be only one mother and that fathers are men, and reactions to the presence of two women parents can run from confusion to discomfort to outright rejection. As one co-parent in Dunne's (2000, 24) study put it, "Well if you're not the biological mother, then what the hell are you?"

The third barrier to creating a parental identity is that co-parents often must surmount a formidable hurdle: The legal system. In many jurisdictions, when lesbian couples create families through artificial insemination, only the birth parent has a legal tie to the child; the other parent has no legally recognized standing. Second-parent adoption is a solution for couples residing in a state permitting it (assuming they have the funds to do this), but 82 percent of states do not explicitly allow this (Human Rights Campaign 2010). [Editor's Note: These legal constraints vary from state to state and may be changing with the recognition of same-sex marriage by the Supreme Court in 2015.]

Our analysis seeks to answer the question of how lesbian co-parents, who cannot conform to societal definitions of good mothering because of both their lesbianism and their nonbiological relationship to their child, contend with the problem of creating a parental—not necessarily a maternal—identity. What factors facilitate and impede their search for a parental identity? How might other lesbian parents and social change agents benefit from an understanding of these factors?

* * *

RESULTS

Co-parents in our study reported that developing a parental identity entailed an emotional struggle made worse by legally sanctioned discrimination

and interpersonal discrimination. For virtually all, grappling with what it means to be a "mother" in a dichotomous "either mother or father" social order was the starting point. Most co-parents engaged in behaviors to align their sense of themselves as parents with the categories available—mother or father—but a third group created a new, hybrid category that stretched the limits of heteronormative categorizations.

Threats to Parental Identity Stemming From Social and From Legal Discrimination

Most of the women we interviewed described how their sense of themselves as legitimate parents was undermined by forays into the public sphere, and virtually all said that this discomfiture was compounded enormously by their lack of legal rights. Of the 17 co-parents, 10 gave examples of interactions in public that required them to field questions about their relationship to their child and the structure of their household. Outsiders, including doctors, teachers, and other parents, challenged co-parents' claims, and thus their identities, by not understanding or accepting them as parents. Ruth explained,

> Other people are really attached to the idea that there can only be one mom. Every Saturday Margaret and I take Cameron to Play Center, and there are lots of other parents there. Even though we know a lot of the parents there now because it's a thing for us to go and so we have explained our situation, I feel like most of them don't take me seriously. Just last week, one of the mothers said that her kid was having a birthday party and Cameron was invited and said she would see if it was okay with Margaret. I said, "You don't need to ask her. Cameron can go. We don't have any other plans." She told me point-blank that she really thought that she should ask Margaret since she was Cam's mother. I had to walk away.

Gretchen said,

> We started seeing a new doctor, who one of my gay friends told me was gay-friendly. I took our daughter for a vaccination and one of the questions on

the form asked what my relationship to the patient was and I put "mather" [a combination of the words *mother* and *father*] and then in parentheses I wrote "parent." When we got in front of the doctor, he asked what a mather was. I told him that I am her parent, but don't consider myself a mother or father. Then he asked me if the child was biologically mine and of course I said no, but I was getting defensive. He refused to give my daughter the vaccination because I was not a legal parent or guardian. He then asked to speak to me alone. He actually told me that in his medical opinion, referring to myself as a mather was harmful to our daughter. This put me into a tailspin about whether I was messing up our daughter.

Stories like these were commonplace. Such troubling interactions are similar to those reported by step-parents, whose lack of biological relationship can also provide grounds for challenge from institutions (Mason et al. 2002). Yet the barely muted hostility in the above excerpts (flatly denying a motherhood claim in the one case and making accusations of bad parenting in the other) raises the possibility of anti-lesbian-family sentiment. Although step-parents facing a question about parental status can usually assume benign intent, lesbian co-parents cannot, which may explain reactions of "having to walk away" and going into a "tailspin."

More destructive to the co-parents' sense of identity, however, was the lack of a legal right to their children. Unlike the public interactions that give rise to social discrimination, which they could choose to ignore, the state's position that women co-parents are not legally allowed to act in the role of parent has more encompassing psychological and social ramifications. Almost all (16 of 17) co-parents indicated they struggled with their parental identities because they were not legally recognized parents, which influenced how they thought about themselves as parents and how they felt others perceived them. For many, legal discrimination was a greater hindrance than the lack of biological relatedness for developing a parental identity. . . .

Karen said,

I knew it would be rough at the beginning to see my partner breastfeed and not have that biological connection, but that can be somewhat compensated by being a legal parent. When you can't establish a legal connection, though, it is really hard to feel like a good parent. Right now, I feel like a nanny or mommy's sidekick.

Thus, the state's lack of acknowledgment undermined their sense of parental identity and compounded any insecurity stemming from the absence of a biological tie. The women felt the lack of a legally recognized status not only in an abstract sense; the feeling was reinforced by institutional structures and policies. The school system was a key site where their lack of rights was brought home to them. Karen continued,

And I think that's how my son's teachers view me. I can't sign any of the official paperwork at school. She has to do the official important stuff. I get delegated to bring in cupcakes or whatever. Apparently, they will allow us non-moms to do that. . . .

The lack of legal rights makes the whole outside world, not just the school system or doctor's office, an arena of potential danger. As their status can always be challenged, many co-parents felt the need to arm themselves with documentation to bolster their claims as legitimate parents. Even so, in a state that allows co-parents no real legal parental status, officials may simply ignore these documents, leaving them vulnerable. . . .

The lack of legal recognition coupled with the lack of institutional acknowledgment, even in matters as trivial as signing report cards, undermined these women's sense of themselves as parents. They found it difficult to feel like parents in the face of the institutional cold shoulder, and they also perceived that their lack of a legal relationship delegitimized their parental status to outsiders. In sum, these women's sense of themselves as parents was undermined by contact with people who distrusted them and a legal system that disenfranchised them.

Parental Identity Construction

A question on the interview guide asked about the word the woman used to describe herself as a parent, but it turned out that naming was a centerpiece of women's stories that required little prompting. One group referred to themselves as mothers, another group rejected that label as not fitting their sense of themselves as masculine and identified as fathers, and a third group collectively coined the term *mather* to denote the amalgam of mother and father characteristics with which they identified.

Mothers. Of the 17 co-parents, 6 were committed to adopting a mother identity despite their lack of biological or legal links to their child. These women said they felt maternal, had longed to be mothers, and wanted to be called mom or mamma, but they encountered many obstacles that undermined their ability to pull this off. One obstacle was that the language they constantly heard was at odds with their identity claims. According to Ruth,

> I'm not the "mother." I'm the "non-legal parent," the "non-birth parent," the "non-adoptive parent." There are so many things I'm *not* in relation to my child that it feels like a battle to be a parent at all. It's exhausting.

Being defined by what they are not loosens the link to motherhood. Seeing a hyphen or hearing an adjective before the mother word, as frequently happened, made clear their tenuous claim to the status and also underlines the power of language in identity construction.

The mothers expressed feelings of futility, being second best, and not succeeding at being a mother, all of which caused them to question their self-worth and sense of themselves as mothers. These negative feelings were brought on by challenges from many quarters. Karen described her feeling of futility stemming from various reminders of her ambiguous status as a mother:

> I have always wanted a baby. I was the quintessential little girl who wanted to be a mom when she grew up. Well, when I realized I was gay I knew it wasn't going to be easy, but I still wanted a baby. Now I have the baby, but I didn't *have* the baby. Before she was born, I kept saying, "It won't

bother me. I know I'm her mother. I don't need a law to say so." Well, I was wrong. I feel like a mother, I do, but not *the* mother. It's like I am always getting slapped in the face. "Oh, you can't breastfeed. Oh, you can't sign this paper. Oh, you have to be related to do that." It's exhausting. . . .

Such reminders, whether intentional or not, police the boundaries of who can be accepted in the motherhood ranks and take an emotional toll.

Samantha considered herself a mother but felt second best because she did not give birth to her child and felt pressured to justify her relationship to him:

> When I was in grad school, I would say something about Evan and people would start with the questions. Like, how do you have a kid? You were never pregnant. Did you adopt? And then I would do this whole explanation thing, like, well, my partner actually birthed him, but he's my kid too. This always made me feel really bad, like I wasn't a real parent you know? One day my [academic] advisor said, "Why don't you just say 'Yes, I'm his mother'? Stop explaining and apologizing." And after that I did. But it took me a long time to get to that place.

As these experiences indicate, the extent of society's commitment to the norm of blood relationships defining the link between parents and children is difficult to overestimate (Katz Rothman 2006; Miall and March 2006). In a study of lesbian families in the United Kingdom, Gabb (2005) also found a pervasive sense of second-class citizenship among nonbiological mothers.

The notion that mothers should be feminine and not masculine is another norm that society readily enforces. A woman who used the mother label despite considering herself masculine faced social pressure to fit into a binary schema of feminine mother and masculine father:

> I look butch. So when my partner and I are together, people assume I must be the "dad" because everyone assumes there is a mom and a dad, even in a lesbian couple. I feel people look us over, like, "Okay, who is the butch here?" Even though I am masculine, I still think of myself as a

mother. A second-class mother, but still a mother. I guess I don't buy that mothers have to be feminine and dads have to be masculine. But, it's hard because everyone else thinks like that. Sometimes I have doubts about myself as a mother, but I know I am *not* a father.

Despite people's reaction to her masculine identity, she insisted on the mother label and was willing to stand up to social pressure urging her to reconsider. Since motherhood and femininity go hand in glove in the popular consciousness (Chodorow 1989; Glenn 1994), her decision forced beholders to question automatic associations between motherhood and femininity, thus raising an alternative to the given order of things. Yet maintaining that stance was an ongoing, lonely, "hard" struggle.

Norms about who may and may not be a mother can also penetrate interactions in the intimate realm, and some co-parents felt expendable even in the privacy of their homes. Yolanda explained,

I think of myself as a mom, but I don't know that anyone else does, even my partner sometimes. I am not identified anywhere as a parent. It goes as far as photographs. I am always the one taking the photograph. So I am not even in very many pictures. It is always "take a picture of us." Like they are the real family.

Taylor similarly felt that her claim of being a mother was contested in the private sphere:

I even feel like my partner doesn't consider me an equal mother. We had been debating whether or not to get a certain vaccination. One day she came home and told me that she decided to get the vaccination done. I was floored. I couldn't believe that she made that kind of executive decision without me. And this was right after she had read me the riot act because I got Shaun a buzz cut without consulting her. I felt so irrelevant.

For the one-third of interviewees who wanted to think of themselves as mothers, the challenge did not lie in knowing the parental term they desired; as one said, "I know in my heart I'm [a] mom." Rather, the challenge lay in surmounting stumbling blocks in the form of marginalization by norms linking femininity and motherhood, by outsiders, by the legal institution, by other children, and even by their partners, which left their mother identity in question. Women in this category struggled to validate their mother identity in the face of social forces that positioned them as inferior, including a language that positioned them as *non*-birth mothers, *second* mothers, *other* mothers, and so on, diminishing their ability to embrace the mother label as strongly as they wanted and creating a void that is not merely social ("What name should I respond to?") but also personal ("Who am I as a parent?"). Despite challenges and personal doubts, these women nevertheless were living evidence of an alternative family form. As they went about their daily public business—a family headed by two mothers—they transgressed the deeply held belief that families contain one and only one mother and by doing so weakened it.

Fathers. About one-third of the women we interviewed also honored the gender binary, but they did so by inverting it; for example, "I don't look like a mother and I don't feel like a mother, so I must be a father." Women in this sample who identified as fathers all described themselves as masculine or "butch." They had strong and clear ideas about how mothers looked and acted and felt they failed to embody these ideas, leading them to reject the mother label and adopt the alternative. According to one,

I am butch. How could I possibly be a mom? It's laughable, really! I would rather ride bikes and play ball with the boys, which is something I think fathers typically do. I do some things moms do, I guess, but I don't feel like a mom. I guess it's more a mental thing. And maybe it's a gender thing. I don't want to be a man, but I guess I kind of feel like a guy.

According to another,

I struggle with it because I know I'm a woman, but I don't look like a mom. I wear work boots and flannels. I drive a truck, not an SUV. And I sure don't act like the moms I knew growing up or the moms I know now. I don't bake cookies. I'm not nurturing in that way. I mean, I am in my own way, but more like a dad, I guess. I don't feel comfortable being called mom, because I don't feel like one. It just doesn't fit me. It makes it difficult, though, because it is really hard for other people to understand that I'm a woman but I feel more like dad. It's confusing.

For these women, a gender identity as masculine precluded using the mother label; indeed, the thought of doing so was "laughable." None tried to keep the mother label and change the meaning of motherhood to include "riding bikes and playing ball" to better fit their personal attributes. Instead, motherhood remained the domain of people like "the moms I knew growing up or the moms I know now." The only other option they saw, and the one they acted on, was to declare themselves fathers.

It was not a perfect fit. A key source of unease was the negative associations many had with heterosexual fathers' behavior, which one described as "not involved with the kid, not affectionate, and a disciplinarian." Mallory had a similar disaffection for the fathering with which she was familiar:

> I chose father, because I am just not a mother. But, it still bugs me. Maybe it's because I am very woman-identified, a lesbian, and I don't like stuff men do, but I don't like how fathers act. I see some at the park when their kid cries, and they do that "toughen up" macho shit. I don't want to be a father like that.

Since their experiences of fathering are based on observations of men, they, as women, had an understandably hard time defining what fathering consists of when done by someone who is not a man. They did not want to practice the fathering style with which they were familiar, nor did they want to be genderless parents (also see Sullivan 2004). As one woman said, "Even though I think of myself as a dad, I am still a woman and a lesbian." Lacking guidance from existing practice about how to father as women,

they tried to invent it. One woman chose a new term for "father" partly to facilitate a new practice of fathering:

> My family is Italian, so Kevin calls me Babbo, which is father in Italian. Calling myself Babbo lets me get a little bit away from the actual dad term, because I don't want to be that 1950s dad. I want to be a lesbian dad, a Babbo. I hope I can figure it out as I go along. I'm not girly at all, but I would like to be a girly father, whatever that means.

She chose a term that allowed her freedom from "acting like the fathers I know," but like the other fathers she struggled with the lack of models. None felt they had a clear sense of how to father in a new way, and variations of her "whatever that means" statement were common.

While most assumed the father label or a close variant on their own volition, this was not the case for all. Some felt pressured by their families and friends to conform to the one mother–one father model. Mallory described how her son pushed her to assume the role of his father:

> I am an androgynous person, and once I picked up Jack at the park and heard him say to his friend, "That's my dad." He had never referred to me as that before; he always called me by my name. Another time he said, "When we go into the store, can you lower your voice?" I think it comes from the social idea that you have a mom and a dad. It made me realize that it was kind of selfish not to be mom or dad for his sake. Jack seemed to think of me as dad, and I sure didn't think of myself as mom—he has one of those—so here I am. A dad.

Krista described the tension with her partner that similarly pushed her to call herself a father:

> To be fair, I am not the mother type, but my partner insisted, very firmly, that I was to take the role of the father. For example, she wants to pick out his clothes because she thinks that's something mothers do. One day I tried to dress him and she freaked out. She felt like I was invading her territory. Oh, another example is our baby shower. She referred to it as *her* baby shower and didn't even want me to come, but I kind of crashed it. One of the

presents was a baby book. She told me that since she was the mother I wouldn't be the one putting stuff in the book, so I went out and bought my own. She flew off the handle. She wants to be the mother and wants me to be a father, so clearly that's what I am. Now I just have to figure out what that means exactly.

Important people in their lives did not permit Mallory and Krista the option of choosing non-alignment with the "father" pole of the gender binary, although for one the pressure was gentle and for the other more coercive. In a final example, Veronica also chose the father label under pressure, although her attempt to adapt to the binary choice was more agonized than for others we interviewed:

People would hold the baby and then pass her back to me and say, "Okay, go back to your Mommy." I think I turned red every time someone said that. The first time I tried to refer to myself as "Mom," I practically had to choke it out. . . . My friends and my girlfriend said, "Just go by 'Daddy.'" But I wasn't down with that either. There is stuff out there like "dyke daddy," but can you imagine the kid calling you that? I can just imagine her telling her teacher, "Yeah, my dyke daddy is picking me up today." Nope. Doesn't work. Poor kid!

She continued,

My friends and girlfriend said things like, "Well you have to come up with *something*. The baby needs to understand who you are." I felt accountable, and I couldn't come up with a way to make it right for everyone.

She ended up referring to herself as a father but having the child use her first name, although she was dissatisfied with this solution. As her story makes clear, having a child was a key moment precipitating an upswing in gender coercion and self-policing. Her close companions pressed her—for the sake of the child—to put aside personal discomfort and choose a label, and an imagined internalized teacher forced her to consider the cost to the child of adopting the gender-radical "dyke daddy" label. As she said, unknowingly echoing West and Zimmerman (1987), when it came to parenting, she felt "accountable" to traditional practices and ideology.

These co-parents identified as fathers because their sense of themselves as masculine precluded using the mother label; for some, pressure from people they were close to also entered into the decision. With no language for the category of "not-mother-and-not-quite-father-either," they used the only other option language afforded: father. Their fit with the label was far from perfect, and all admitted to not knowing how to enact the fatherhood role with their children. Despite these problems, by adopting the father label, these women disrupt the prescription that "fathers are men," and thus their very presence in society as fathers helps deconstruct the edifice of the gender binary.

Mathers. Of 17 co-parents, 6 labeled themselves *mathers.* The term was born of an informal support group that had met for about a year before coining it. The group had begun with gatherings of a few friends meeting biweekly as a lesbian co-parent support group, and in short order acquaintances and friends joined. At the suggestion of one member, they advertised the group at a local LGBT center and on a LGBT Internet forum, and over the course of six months the group grew to about 15 people from across the region.

Interviewees clearly articulated the central problem discussed at these support group meetings: They felt like neither mothers nor fathers and lamented the lack of any other categorization. They sought a label mainly to assuage their pervasive worry about what their children would call them (see also Gabb 2005). Many had experimented with "mother" and "father" and were dissatisfied. Much meeting time was devoted to discussion of the various parental labels popular among lesbian parents, but the consensus was that none fit the bill. They sought a label their children could use publicly and privately and that the co-parents themselves felt good about. After a year of what they described as agonizing discussions, a group member suggested the *mather* term as a gender-bending, gender-blending hybridization of mother and father. . . .

Respondents saw the term as a flexible, dynamic word that captured a larger idea about parenting outside the rigid, gendered mother–father dichotomy, and each co-parent could mold the term as she saw fit.

The common experience seemed to be that once they had established a label, they could now more clearly flesh out their familial roles. Jan explained,

> I don't even know if there is anything a mather does that is really that different from what a mother or father does. Being a mather is more a way of thinking, like a way of dealing with feeling uncertain about what you are. . . . As a mather, I can tell my kid, "Hey, families don't have to have moms and dads. They can be whatever." And I don't have to just do "mom things" or "dad things." We do everything together. We talk, paint, wrestle, whatever. When you think of yourself as mom or dad, there are lots of things that go along with that. Like if you're mom then you do certain things, and dads do certain things. Being a mather, I feel like I can cross those lines without penalties. Like I can play ball with my kid and wear my hat backwards, but I can also let myself be vulnerable.

Jan and others invoked fun (talk, paint, wrestle, play ball, wear backward caps, play, laugh) and conveyed a light heartedness that contrasts starkly to the anxiety pervading the group discussions that preceded the term's invention.

The term had a decidedly serious side as well: women who used it were adamant about deploying the term to promote social change. They wanted their children to call them mather, they introduced themselves as their child's mather, and they considered themselves pioneering agents of social change. . . .

Addison relished how using the term made her feel like a change agent:

> Being a mather feels like activism. I see lots of my gay friends feel like they have to choose. But my options are mom *or* dad, so "Hmm, which do I feel more like?" I get to bust out of those categories. I get to introduce myself to my daughter's teachers and say, "I'm Addison, Jillian's mather." Inevitably, after they get over their shock, they ask me what that means and I get to educate them! I feel like I will make it easier for other parents down the road who don't want to have to be mom or dad. Man, it's about social change.

All the co-parents, not just mathers, promoted social change by bucking strongly held norms, yet it is far easier and more fulfilling to do so with group backing. The contrast is sharp between the angst Lorraine and Addison attribute to their nonmather friends and the sense of empowerment they themselves felt. Some others described how the mather mentality transcended the parental role to affect their sense of self. According to Jan,

> Since I started thinking of myself as a mather, I have changed in lots of ways. I feel more free to express myself without thinking about gender. I stopped thinking about gender when I parent, so I guess it makes sense it would happen in other areas of my life. For example, sometimes now I wear a tie and men's dress shoes to work, which I never would have done before. It's not because I want to be a man; it's because I have always liked the look and now I feel free to do it.

The mathers' stories compared to those of the other groups illustrate the power of language, social support, and a collective identity. The fathers and mothers faced the same challenge as the mathers—feeling like neither a mother nor father—but unlike them lacked a language to redefine themselves and their role. Having a language carved out an ideological space for mathers to redefine their family role, and the realization that they could exist outside the binary reduced their stress significantly. Mathers were the only group that sought validation from significant others outside the privatized home sphere, and by their accounts, the collective act of defiantly creating a new identity and seeking opportunities to educate others about it was empowering. Even so, it was no panacea, as evidenced by the mather sent into a "tailspin" by her doctor's accusation that her choice of label was harming the child. As for effecting social change, like the mothers and fathers, their presence is testimony to the possibility of alternatives to the heteronormative family, and the proliferation of such possibilities increases the likelihood of more appearing.

DISCUSSION AND CONCLUSION

An approach that assumes that because co-parents are women they seek to identify as mothers conceals the complexity of parental identity development for lesbian co-parents. Previous research on the identity struggles of women who parent in the face of a lack of biological ties to their children has focused on their experiences of becoming and being mothers and described such women as members of "dual-mother families," or as "comothers," who negotiate "mothering experiences." This assumption of a link between female sex and mother identity has precluded asking how co-parents negotiate womanhood, intimate relationships, and social expectations to construct a *parental* identity that may be at variance with the mother identity.

These women faced both external and internal assaults on their sense of themselves as parents. The institutions and people they regularly encountered—play groups, schools, doctors, children's friends, and, perhaps most importantly, the law—explicitly challenged their parental identity claims. Most women faced anguished identity struggles because of these external assaults and because they felt like their lesbian parenting fit neither into the biologically inflected "mother" category nor into the father category, the only other possibility the language offers in a binary gender system. Mathers seemed to have had the most successful resolution of the internal dilemma, but they too paid an emotional toll from facing the constant external challenges from people and institutions unwilling to recognize their consciously blended roles and identities.

What do these results imply for the goal of destabilizing gendered arrangements (Lorber 2005)? On one hand, they confirm the continuing

hold on the public and private imagination exerted by the "motherhood institution" (Bernard 1974; Rich 1977). As an institution, motherhood still grants and withholds the material, institutional, and cultural supports that make child rearing easy or difficult (Bernard 1974; Chase and Rogers 2001; Rich 1977). It still shapes what mothers do and how they feel about it, and it privileges women who fit cultural notions about appropriate characteristics of mothers and disfranchises those who do not. As long as rigid prescriptions for gendered behavior are inscribed in the institution—especially when they are backed by law—members of excluded groups will remain in identity limbo. Thus, while planned lesbian families have the potential to help decenter the gender- and power-laden heterosexual nuclear family (e.g., Dalton and Bielby 2000; Weston 1991), this study illustrates that the task is not easy. On the other hand, there is a positive conclusion to be drawn as well. Social change is propelled forward by people, like these lesbian parents, who refuse to live lives consonant with the given order. The mothers were transgressive by embodying a two-mother family, the fathers disrupted the prescription that "fathers are men," and the mathers generated a new family role and included education about it as part of their mission. These women's transgression of the gender binary makes further transgressions more likely and makes a utopian vision of a non-heteronormative family less distant.

The findings point to the necessity of continuing the civil rights struggle, and lesbian parents need not stand alone in the larger struggle to break down parenting ideology and laws. They have common cause with other groups who also suffer from the exclusivity of the good mother category and thus have a stake in degendering the mothering institution. . . .

REFERENCES

Abramovitz, Mimi. 1996. *Regulating the lives of women: Social welfare policy from colonial times to present.* Boston: South End.

Aizley, Harlyn. 2006. *Confessions of the other mother: Non-biological mothers tell all.* Boston: Beacon.

Arendell, Terry. 2000. Conceiving and investigating motherhood: The decade's scholarship. *Journal of Marriage and Family* 62:1192–1207.

Bernard, Jessie. 1974. *The future of motherhood.* New York: Dial Press.

Chase, Susan E., and Mary F. Rogers. 2001. *Mothers and children: Feminist analyses and personal narratives.* New Brunswick, NJ: Rutgers University Press.

Chodorow, Nancy. 1989. *Feminism and psychoanalytic theory.* New Haven, CT: Yale University Press.

Dalton, S., and D. Bielby. 2000. That's our kind of constellation: Lesbian mothers negotiate institutionalized understandings of gender within the family. *Gender & Society* 14:36–61.

Deutsch, Francine M. 2007. Undoing gender. *Gender & Society* 21:106–27.

DiLapi, E. M. 1989. Lesbian mothers and the motherhood hierarchy. *Journal of Homosexuality* 18:101–21.

Dunne, Gillian. 2000. Opting into motherhood: Lesbians blurring the boundaries and transforming the meanings of parenthood and kinship. *Gender & Society* 14:11–35.

Fineman, Martha. 1995. *The neutered mother, the sexual family, and other twentieth century tragedies.* New York: Routledge.

Gabb, Jacqui. 2005. Lesbian motherhood: Strategies of familial-linguistic management in lesbian parent families. *Sociology* 39:385–603.

Glenn, Evelyn N. 1994. Social constructions of mothering: A thematic overview. In *Mothering: Ideology experience, agency,* edited by E. N. Glenn, G. Chang, and L. R. Forcey. New York: Routledge.

Hequembourg, A. 2007. *Lesbian motherhood: Stories of becoming.* Binghamton. NY: Hawthorne Press.

Hequembourg, A., and M. Farrell. 1999. Lesbian motherhood: Negotiating marginal-mainstream identities. *Gender & Society* 13:540–57.

Human Rights Campaign. 2010. Parenting laws: Second-Parent Adoption. http://www.hrc.org/documents/parenting_laws_maps.pdf (accessed 19 December 2010).

Katz Rothman, B. 2006. Adoption and the culture of genetic determinism. In *Adoptive families in a diverse society,* edited by K. Wegar. New Brunswick, NJ: Rutgers University Press.

Lewin, Ellen. 1993. *Lesbian mothers.* Ithaca, NY: Cornell University Press.

Lorber, Judith. 2000. Using gender to undo gender. *Feminist Theory* 1:75–95.

Lorber, Judith. 2005. *Breaking the bowls: Degendering and feminist change.* New York: Norton.

Mason, M. A., S. Hanison-Jay, G. M. Svare, and N. H. Wolfinger. 2002. Stepparents: De-facto parents or legal strangers? *Journal of Family Issues* 23:507–22.

Miall, C. E., and K. March. 2006. Adoption and public opinion: Implications for social policy and practice in adoption. In *Adoptive families in a diverse society,* edited by K. Wegar. New Brunswick, NJ: Rutgers University Press.

Rich, Adrienne. 1977. *Of woman born: Motherhood as experience and institution.* New York: Bantam.

Richey, Warren. 2010. Florida ban on gay adoption unconstitutional, court declares, *Christian Science Monitor,* 23 September. www.csmonitor.com/USA/Justice/2010/0923/Florida-ban-on-gay-adoption-unconstitutional-court-rules (accessed 8 January 2011).

Roberts, Dorothy. 1997. *Killing the Black body: Race, reproduction and the meaning of liberty.* New York: Pantheon.

Schwalbe, Michael L., and Douglas Mason-Schrock. 1996. Identity work as group process. *Advances in Group Processes* 13:113–47.

Stacey, Judith. 1998. *Brave new families: Stories of domestic upheaval in late twentieth century America.* Berkeley: University of California Press.

Stacey, Judith, and Timothy J. Biblarz. 2001. (How) does the sexual orientation of parents matter? *American Sociological Review* 66:159–83.

Sullivan, Maureen. 2004. *The family of woman.* Berkeley: University of California Press.

Thompson, Julie. 2002. *Mommy queerest.* Amherst: University of Massachusetts Press.

Thorne, Barrie. 1993. Feminism and the family: Two decades of thought. In *Rethinking the family: Some feminist questions,* 2nd ed., edited by B. Thorne and M. Yalom. New York: Longman.

West, Candace, and Don H. Zimmerman. 1987. Doing gender. *Gender & Society* 1:121–51.

Weston, Kath. 1991. *Families we choose: Lesbians, gays, kinship.* New York: Columbia University Press.

Introduction to Reading 40

In this reading, Carla Shows and Naomi Gerstel suggest that social contexts and the conditions of work as they are linked to social class can have a powerful impact on the choices men make in parenting. The authors compare the "public fatherhood" of physicians to the more "private fatherhood" of emergency medical technicians (EMTs), examining how work conditions and work culture impact these men's choices for fatherhood. The data they use in this reading are from a larger study (Study of Work Hours and Schedules), which includes surveys, observations at nine work sites, and intensive interviews with 13 physicians and 18 EMTs in the northeastern United States. This research helps explain the results of other studies, which find that working-class fathers are much more involved in their children's lives than professional fathers, and helps us understand how social class shapes gendered relationships in families.

1. What do the authors mean by "public" and "private" fatherhood?

2. What social factors are related to their finding that fathers in working-class homes are more involved parents? How do these factors challenge traditional gendered expectations for men and women and facilitate gender change?

3. What could workplaces do to encourage more involved parenting for all workers?

FATHERING, CLASS, AND GENDER

A COMPARISON OF PHYSICIANS AND EMERGENCY MEDICAL TECHNICIANS

Carla Shows and Naomi Gerstel

A large and growing literature documents recent changes and growing variation in the relationship of gender, paid work, and parenting. Although most of this research focuses on the range of women's experiences, some suggests that most men still emphasize employment as central to their practice of fatherhood (Lamb 1995; Orloff and Monson 2002; Townsend 2002), leaving far more of the parenting and daily caregiving to mothers (Casper and Bianchi 2002; Craig 2006). Few studies, however, focus on the varied experiences of men to examine how employment shapes fatherhood (Astone et al. 2010), fewer explore how parenting shapes men's employment (Lundberg and Rose 2000), and almost none compare fathers in different class positions.

This article examines the relationship between class and fatherhood. We compare two groups of fathers, one in a professional occupation and the

From Shows, Carla and Gerstel, Naomi. "Fathering, Class, and Gender: A Comparison of Physicians and Emergency Medical Technicians." *Gender & Society, 23*(2), pp. 161–187. Copyright © 2009. Published by SAGE Publications on behalf of Sociologists for Women in Society.

other in a nonprofessional occupation; we argue that these map broadly onto two class locations—one upper middle class (physicians) and the other working class (emergency medical technicians, or EMTs). We first compare these men's class-linked practices of fatherhood and, second, argue that their ways of doing fatherhood entail enactments of distinctive masculinities, based in the dynamics of their occupational and familial relations, which have consequences for doing (or undoing) gender.

To address the first issue, we argue that these two groups of men practice different types of fathering—with physicians emphasizing "public fatherhood" and EMTs performing not only public fatherhood but also participating in the daily routines of "private fatherhood." Second, we suggest these different fathering practices can be explained by the contrasting employment conditions of each group and the gendered character of their families, especially their wives' involvement in the labor market and parenting. . . .

FATHERHOOD, MASCULINITY, AND CLASS

Much recent work on the relationship of masculinity to the practice of paid work and domestic life (Coltrane and Adams 2001; Cooper 2000; Townsend 2002) draws on the now classic theoretical formulation of Connell (1992, 1995). Developing the concept of "hegemonic masculinity," she argues that much older literature used a categorical model of gender that treated men as an undifferentiated group, but contemporary research documents a considerable range of masculinities. While prior scholarship tended to conflate sex and gender, Connell offers a counterview; she suggests diverse masculinities can be traced to the "social dynamics generated within gender relations" (1992, 735) and through other structures that vary across social locations. In fact, class is a social location Connell emphasizes, although she criticizes work on masculinity for being "class-bound" (1992, 735). Further, Connell and others (e.g., Brines 1994; Griswold 1993; Kimmel 2000, 2006) suggest

that men's involvement in gender relations at home, especially parenting, provide an important locus of institutionalized inequality and significant site for the (re)construction and expression of various masculinities.

Researchers suggest that the way men combine family and paid work now entails two models of masculinity: (1) the still dominant "neotraditional model of masculinity" (Gerson 2007) in which men put their job prospects (or breadwinning) first but rely on their partners for daily care of children; and (2) an alternate, more egalitarian, model of a "newly constituted masculinity" (Cooper 2002), which entails substantial sharing in the daily care of children in addition to market work (see also Dowd 2000; Townsend 2002).

Some research looks at the relationship of social class to the two models of masculinity. Much quantitative research, especially time-use studies, examines the number of hours men spend with their children; summarizing this literature, Pleck and Masciadrelli (2004, 238) conclude there is "no consistent relationship between paternal involvement and socioeconomic variables." Recent qualitative work on fathering, however, finds some differences by class.

For working-class men, some studies suggest the priority of the breadwinner model, showing that working-class men feel that their masculinity is threatened when they cannot enact the primary breadwinner model of fatherhood (Gerson 1993). Williams (2000), however, indicates that a disjuncture exists between this ideology and the practice of fatherhood, especially for working-class men whose ability to fulfill the primary breadwinner role is waning. Indeed, Pyke (1996) finds that some working-class men emphasize a hypermasculine provider role while sharing in family work. Using longitudinal English data, Sullivan (2006) shows that men assumed more responsibility for family work if they were employed in working-class (manual or clerical) jobs. Deutsch (1999) similarly finds that, among the alternative-shift working-class couples she studied, men did much of the work of parenting even while insisting that their wives were the primary parents.

Research on middle-class fathers finds a contrasting pattern. A number of qualitative studies suggest that such fathers, especially professionals or the "educational elite," espouse some version of egalitarian parenthood (Cooper 2000; Deutsch 1999; LaRossa 1997; Risman 1998). Yet researchers suggest that middle-class fathers do not enact these ideals (Griswold 1993; LaRossa 1997) due to employment constraints as well as the culture of masculinity in which they believe (Coltrane 2004; Cooper 2000; Pyke 1996). Coltrane (2004) argues that whereas managerial and professional couples were the most likely to share family work in the 1970s and 1980s, by the 1990s and 2000s most sharing occurred in the working class.

Not only does the *level* of paternal involvement vary by class, but the *type* of engagement varies as well. Coltrane and Adams (2001) find that if men participate in "enrichment" or leisure activities with children, they are less likely to do daily chores such as cooking and cleaning. Lareau (2002, 749) ties this variation in type of engagement to class. She shows that middle-class parents were much more likely to participate in organized leisure activities with their children than working-class families, who tend to have "more free time and deeper, richer ties with their extended families." As this quotation suggests, one important aspect of Lareau's (2003) work is that she does not simply focus on the nuclear family but widens her lens to include extended kin. Her work suggests that there is class variation in these ties—with working-class parents significantly more likely than those in the middle class to rely on relatives for help with children (for review, see Gerstel and Sarkisian 2008). These ties shape the demands on both fathers and mothers. Although these studies provide important leads for comparing working-class to middle-class fathers, few have made these explicit comparisons.

Work Hours, Schedules, and Families

The total hours of household employment have climbed because of women's increased work hours (Jacobs and Gerson 2004). This is particularly true for parents: Paid working time has increased dramatically for mothers since 1970 (Bluestone and Rose 2000), and the sum of estimated annual hours worked by U.S. mothers and fathers is higher than those of parents in any other country (Bianchi, Robinson, and Milkie 2006). Gender is essential to understanding these hours. On one hand, some research suggests that men do more routine child care when they are employed fewer hours (Coltrane 2000). On the other, while mothers tend to cut back their hours of employment, research suggests that fathers increase their work hours after the birth of a child (e.g., Jacobs and Gerson 2004; for exception, see Astone et al. 2010). Importantly, class influences hours and schedules, with professionals working longer workweeks than other occupational groups (Jacobs and Gerson 2004) and the working class more likely to alternate shifts (Presser 2003). Although longer workweeks decrease fathers' participation in family work, alternative schedules increase it (Barnett and Gareis 2002; Deutsch 1999; Presser 2003). This suggests a bifurcation of job hours and schedules by class.

Gender Within Families: Fathering and Mothering

As Connell (1992, 1995) argues, the organization of gender relations is central to the practice of masculinity. When employed, wives challenge the neotraditional model of masculinity, or as Griswold (1993, 220) puts it, "Women's [paid] work, in short, has destroyed the old assumptions about fatherhood and required new negotiations of gender relations." Research has shown that fathers are likely to be somewhat more involved in parenting when their wives are employed. Moreover, fathers' child care and work time correlates with the employment schedules of mothers (Bianchi, Robinson, and Milkie 2006; Brayfield 1995). Coltrane (2000) argues that the employment schedules of wives and husbands are perhaps the most consistent and important predictors of domestic sharing that researchers have documented. Furthermore, researchers find that when wives have higher relative earnings, or when the gap between husbands' and wives' earnings is lower, the gendered gap in the division of domestic labor is reduced (Cooke 2007).

Although we might expect the influence of mothers on fathers to vary by class, little literature examines this connection. In one important study of equal parenting, Deutsch (1999) finds that mothers influence fathers' participation by either fighting for more equal participation (especially in the middle class) or by using alternate schedules (especially in the working class). Other research shows that among the affluent, wives not only develop an ideology of intensive mothering but also sometimes make the decision to withdraw from the labor force to concentrate on mothering; this frees fathers to focus on breadwinning (e.g., see Blair-Loy 2003). For working-class wives, it is much more difficult to "opt out" (Boushey 2005; Kuperberg and Stone 2008). Indeed, as Stone (2007) argues, opting out is often dependent on the earnings of highly paid husbands. Extending these findings, one of the arguments we make in this article is that wives influence fathers' involvement in parenting but do so in ways that vary dramatically by class.

* * *

PHYSICIANS AND PUBLIC FATHERING: "BEING THERE"

Physicians tended to highlight participation in or presence at their children's public events as the way they were involved in their children's lives. Even with their long hours or hectic schedules, physicians emphasized their concerted attempts to attend those activities. Sometimes this kind of paternal involvement required creativity in scheduling:

> I coached [my son's] soccer, and the way I coached his soccer was I would book two hours in my

afternoon and I would not have patients there, and I would go to [town] and coach his practice and do the work, bring him home and then go back to work, and then work 'til 9:00.

As this father's comment suggests, doctors let their children influence their schedules because they can; when they choose to do so, they exert significant control over their schedules. Physicians engage in other public activities with their children as well. When we were observing in his office, a surgeon showed us—with pride—his phone's screen with a photo of his daughter dressed for Halloween, saying she was going trick-or-treating with him. But during our interview with this physician, he barely mentioned his daughter, suggesting her daily care was his wife's domain.

"Being there" for public events was important to these physicians. Yet even when they were able to leave the office to attend their children's events, work sometimes followed. One physician had a $3,000 car phone installed so that he could return phone calls while watching his children. . . .

Though able to be physically present at the game, his attention was divided between his family and his work. Yet to him, *being* at the game was what mattered. He is demonstrating, possibly to himself, his child, and the community, that he cares as a father. In some sense, the very difficulty of his being there makes this demonstration all the more dramatic.

Through their participation in these activities, the doctors are publicly "doing fatherhood." This performance of gender and fatherhood entails signs of "*paternal* visibility" (Coltrane 1996; West and Zimmerman 1987) to their children and the wider community. Moreover, like the men Townsend (2002) studied, a large part of what it means to them to be a father is to be a provider. Many of these physicians adopted a neotraditional model of masculinity (Gerson 2007)—one suggesting that what it means to be a good father is to be a good breadwinner and provide financially. This is reinforced by the income associated with class position: Participation in public activities often requires a significant financial outlay. How do we explain such public fathering? To answer that question, we first look at the physicians' jobs and then turn to their family lives.

THE DEMANDS OF PHYSICIANS' PAID WORK

In the survey, physicians reported working an average of 50 hours per week. However, these hours are underestimates. As became clear in the intensive interviews, many physicians did not include nondirect patient care or off-hours work in response to survey questions asking how many hours they work. They did not report activities such as checking work-related e-mail, participating in hospital committees, staying current in medical literature (often required for recertification), or being on-call; including these activities often led to estimates of 60 or more hours per week.

While much work entailed direct patient care, paperwork—documenting patients' visits and illnesses, preparing material for insurance companies, making referrals—kept physicians at their desks in the evenings, well after their patients went home. Most said that paperwork could easily take an extra two or three hours per day. We observed a number of them eating lunch on the run, coming in early and staying until 7:00 or 8:00 p.m., even if they finished patient care by 5:00. Sitting at their desks, they completed necessary documentation for patient records, referrals, and "most of all for insurance companies." Several said that since their office had "gone electronic," they would often go to their home computers in the evening to enter patient data they "just had not gotten to during the day." These were hours when their families were likely available or in need of routine care.

Being available to patients was important to many physicians and often meant being on-call. While physicians could sometimes rotate their on-call status with their colleagues, their turn often interrupted their home lives. One hospital physician described being on-call in this way: "I mean, you can't do anything; you're basically . . . it's like a full day of work." Or as another doctor

put it, "You're always aware your beeper is there and could go off at any time; you can't just relax." Importantly, much of this work occurred before or after shifts or during weekends—that is, at key moments when family members are likely to be home.

To explain their long hours, physicians talked about a number of causes. They emphasized the hours and schedules of medical school and residency that helped socialize them to their current long hours. . . . Many years in school, long hours studying and in residency, and hundreds of thousands of dollars for training push physicians toward intense career commitment. As one physician succinctly said, "There was just no time for anything else." . . . [D]octors learn that respect—especially as men physicians—is related to extremely long hours on the job, which means fewer hours at home. Later in the interview, [one doctor] commented that he felt sad that he could not spend more time at home having dinner with his family or putting his children to bed. But his version of fatherhood and masculinity, which he learned in part from the "hazing" in medical school and from the hierarchy in medicine, requires long hours on the job rather than a schedule with fewer hours and more direct family involvement.

Physicians also talked about a sense of obligation to be available to their patients. A private practice physician explained, "I mean, if you take care of people it's really . . . you're at their mercy and not yours. People don't choose when they get sick, and you have to take care of them when they're sick." Although they sometimes tried, physicians found it difficult to "hand off" patients to others—either because of patient insistence and "loyalty" to them or because of a special skill and relationship with that particular patient. . . . In this study, obligations to their patients often resulted in physicians spending more time at work than their EMT counterparts.

Money—to pay back medical school debt, to maintain a particular style of life and consumption—also kept them on the job. Earning income was essential to understanding themselves as physicians, men, and fathers. Indeed, public fatherhood required a significant income.

One physician said, "If I wanted to see less patients I would see less patients. The problem is your income takes a hit. And there's so many things taking a hit on your income anyway." One doctor who worked 60 hours a week reported, "We don't have an extravagant lifestyle by any means, but I am afraid we have gotten used to a particular way of living. I have to work the hours I do to get what we now think we need." At a meeting in which emergency room doctors were arranging shifts for November and December, one doctor said he did not want to work on Christmas. The ER director reminded this younger doctor that he and his wife wanted a new kitchen and, with a smile, indicated it was the young doctor's obligation to provide the domestic accoutrements they desired. The young doctor agreed to come Christmas day. Overall, then, training, paperwork, obligation to patients, the medical hierarchy, desire for respect as men, and the particular style of life that their breadwinning could provide kept these doctors on the job and away from the daily routines of their families.

The Demands of Family: The Role of Physicians' Wives

The ways doctors organized gender relations at home made it possible to work the long hours they did. As the survey showed, physician fathers were likely to have either stay-at-home wives or part-time employed wives (43 percent of physicians had employed wives compared to 86 percent of EMTs; physicians' employed wives also worked far fewer hours: an average of 13 hours compared to 30 for the employed EMT wives). With an occasional exception, the physicians' wives chose jobs that were less demanding or allowed them to work part-time so they could be available for their families; these choices also allowed their husbands to spend long hours on the job. Some doctors said that they sometimes relied on "nannies" or "au pairs" to help with child care and that this allowed their wives to pursue their own careers. Yet even with such paid child care, many physicians relied

primarily on their wives to provide daily and routine parenting. One physician's wife, a physician herself, worked part-time so their children could have a parent who was "more available." Though this father perceives himself to be equally involved, he admitted,

> Quite honestly, on a day-to-day basis, kids need mom more than they need dad, and I honestly think that's true. . . . I don't know whether . . . it's not meant to be a sexist statement or anything like that, but we both share in the house . . . I mean I'll do stuff for the kids just as much as she will, just not as frequently.

This physician's comment entails seemingly contradictory assertions. He views his participation as "just as much" as his wife but "just not as frequent." Thus, the unequal practices entailed in public fathering were sometimes invisible to the physicians. Struggling with an involved father ideology in the context of their demanding work, they often feel unable to reduce job demands to participate in routine daily child care. In doing so, they reinforce the gender order rather than contest it.

Physicians often seemed at a loss when asked whether they took off time to care for their sick children. When asked if he ever stayed home with his kids when they were sick, a doctor explained why his wife typically stayed home with them. . . .

[T]his physician felt very pressed by his obligation to care for his patients, an obligation that took precedence over staying home with his children when they were sick. The structure of his job and family life led him to organize his time so that he took care of patients and his wife took care of their kids.

Leaving most of the care of the children to their wives was not an easy bargain for the physicians. While a minority of EMTs (about one-third) had a family member who wanted them to reduce their hours, more than *half* of the physician fathers reported the same ($\chi^2 = 9.42$; $p < .05$). Occasionally a doctor would emphasize the loss and pain that this sort of parenting entailed. Tears rolled down the cheek of one doctor as he described his need to be in the hospital while his wife was bathing and putting their children to bed.

Even among the doctors, there was some heterogeneity: A very small minority reported reducing hours or shifts in response to their wives' pleas. One doctor who divided his time between patients and research told us he shortened his workday at his wife's insistence: "My wife said I needed to [come home], essentially, and I agreed with her. I didn't have the insight to see the impact of what not being home was having on people." The chief physician at a large medical center said that he tried to come home "by 7:00" at the request of his wife. He told us about their conversations, centering on her telling him to restrict work and "to come home at a certain hour." Gesturing toward the piles of paper on his desk, he remarked that it was often difficult to get home for dinner, especially with the paperwork that piled up by the end of the day. But he tried. Among the male physicians, however, these two were exceptional.

EMTs are very different from physicians. Their fathering routinely emphasized private fathering and more intensive involvement in caregiving. This difference can be explained by the structure of their paid work as well as gendered relations at home.

EMTs and Private Fathering: "Stealing Time"

While the physician fathers were likely to do what they could to attend public events with their children, EMT fathers were much more likely to participate in the daily care of their kids. The EMTs emphasized private fathering in ways that the physicians did not. They talked about routine involvement in the lives of their children—picking them up from day care or school, feeding them dinner, or staying home with them when they got sick. One stated,

> My son's out of school at 2:30 in the afternoon. That means that I have to leave here about 2:15 to make sure I'm at the school to pick him up.

Another remarked,

> Last year I took three out of my five sick days to stay home when one of the smaller ones was sick. So I'll use them more for that than for anything else.

One went further and put it succinctly:

> I will totally refuse the overtime. Family comes first for me.

To explain their fathering, we turn first to their jobs and then to their homes.

The Demands of EMTs' Paid Work

In the survey, EMT fathers reported working an average of 45 hours per week, but EMTs worked closer to 60 hours when including the hours devoted to second jobs. More than two-thirds of the EMT fathers reported having a second job; only 9 percent of the doctors did. In their second jobs, however, many EMTs worked per diem, which allowed them to choose if and when to work. Moreover, when the EMTs went home, they left their jobs behind: They did not have paperwork, nor were they on call. Thus, it is not primarily the number of hours that explains the differences in parenting. Although they resembled the physicians in long, often exhausting hours, the boundaries between work and family were much clearer for EMTs.

Even more than the number of hours, the shifts they work are consequential for their family lives. Many of the EMT fathers in our study work rotating shifts, nights, weekends, and holidays, and in some sense, they had little control over these schedules. At the beginning of each year, management handed them a booklet with their shifts for the next 12 months. Compared to physicians, EMTs were much more likely to report working two or more weekends in the previous 30 days (almost all of the EMT fathers compared to only half of the physicians). But EMTs were able to leave at the conclusion of their shifts, while physicians stayed after their shifts ended. Moreover, unlike physicians who were often unavailable to their families during key hours of their days, EMTs often worked during the hours that their families were sleeping.

In addition to the structure of shifts, relations with coworkers were important in shaping the way these two groups of men organized fatherhood. In contrast to the physicians, EMTs used swaps to create flexibility in their seemingly inflexible, nonstandard schedules. Often with the support of management, EMTs would switch shifts with another EMT or cover for each other for a few hours. Swaps were a useful means of acquiring "off" time without using their limited vacation or sick days. These exchanges were used in response to family needs; the EMTs in some sense "stole" time to be available for family. One EMT often asked someone to cover for him for a few hours at the end or beginning of his shifts so that he could attend his teenage sons' sporting events. Swaps were not just used to attend athletic events. Others would swap when they had to take their kids to medical appointments or pick them up from school. Some of the older or childless EMT men covered for those with younger children. As EMTs highlighted, reciprocity—utilized over the short as well as the long term—was key to swapping, even for a few hours. One EMT had often been on the receiving end of swaps; now that his daughter is older, he happily returns the favor, saying his daughter "is just older and it's nice to have that flexibility to give back to other people that was given to you, to be able to do things like that. I don't mind doing it."

While both occupations offer round-the-clock services, the doctors have to be personally available because one doctor is often not a suitable substitute for another (due to specialized skills or a special relationship with a patient). In contrast, EMTs' skill levels, work requirements, and relationships to patients were more similar to one another; because they were interchangeable, they could practice such "swaps," collectively making possible more daily sharing of fatherhood.

Income played an important role as well, but one that depended on the father's orientation to consumption as well as family demands.

In contrast to physicians, overtime (with time-and-a-half pay) is financially important for EMTs. Due to their small staff, overtime was a significant part of the fire department's ability to function; they relied on a callback system to remain fully staffed at all times. Thus, EMTs were "called back" to the station when the ambulance went out to answer a call. Returning to work could generate a lot of overtime pay for those who answered callbacks, but it was voluntary, and the EMT fathers consciously limited their overtime. The key to this decision was often their sense that they needed to participate in the labor of the home. . . .

While physicians considered the time-money trade-off very carefully, and a few said they would give up some time and reduce their incomes, EMTs—who made considerably less money—routinely turned down overtime in exchange for time with their families. This is not to say that the EMT fathers were always happy to give up the overtime. Many refused it because they were solely responsible for their children at the time they received the call to come in for overtime. In these decisions, EMTs discussed both their worries about pay and their guilt in having to "choose" between spending time with their families and going to work. For one EMT father, the guilt he feels results from wanting or needing to go in for financial reasons but also believing his daughters are "only this age once" and "entitled to their father." . . .

In the interviews, differences between physicians and EMTs in the importance of training also became clear. While the latter were dedicated to patient care, they were not trained in a schema that routinely prioritized work over all other areas of life.

DEMANDS OF FAMILY: THE ROLE OF WIVES AND EXTENDED KIN

Differences in their wives' employment and responses to their husbands' employment were critical to understanding the different styles of fathering. According to the survey data, a large majority (86 percent) of EMT wives were employed, whereas fewer than half of the physicians' wives had jobs. Moreover, EMT wives contributed much more to the family income: The gap between mothers' and fathers' mean income was significantly smaller in the EMT families ($32,000) than in the physicians' families ($177,000) ($t = 4.69$, p $< .00$). EMTs' wives who worked for pay worked substantially more hours than the physicians' wives. Thus, the wives' work hours in concert with explicit demands on their husbands' schedules shaped how much time the men devoted to work and how much they devoted to family.

Like other working-class men, many of the EMT fathers alternated shifts with their wives. But the difference did not simply reside in the structure of jobs. After their children were born, EMTs' wives often insisted that their husbands alternate shifts as well as reduce their paid work hours so they could contribute to daily family care. Their wives had, and used, their power in the relationships. Wives played a key role in callback responses because of their own work schedules and because they wanted (and often insisted) their husbands to be home. An EMT father of two young girls reported that he loves working on the ambulance and would like to answer more callbacks but has learned to accept his wife's signals about accepting overtime. . . .

The wives' influence ranged from subtle signals to outright demands. One EMT kept his pager off and his cell phone on silent at night because his wife told him that callbacks interrupt her sleep and she did not like him going in at night. In another exchange, while eating lunch in the fire station, one EMT responded to the question, "Do your families ever ask you to not come in?" by laughing and saying, "No, they tell you: You're not going in." The other EMTs sitting around joined in the laughter and nodded in agreement.

To be sure, given the demands of two jobs in these families, the EMTs and their wives often had to rely on other people to help take care of their children. Unlike the physicians, however, they often relied on extended family rather than paid child care. One EMT said that he had "definitely roped in" his mother or brother with last-minute child care dilemmas. When another EMT was unable to pick up his son from school on his two daytime shifts, his mother would be there. They relied on kin care because they trusted their relatives and found such help less expensive and more flexible than hired help.

Importantly, EMT fathers did not manipulate their schedules begrudgingly. Like many of the working-class fathers in Francine Deutsch's (1999) study, many of the EMTs seemed happy with their schedules because they allowed the EMTs to participate in child care. While most of the fathers reported being happy with their current schedules (91 percent) on the survey, it was in the interviews that the EMTs discussed their families as a key reason for that happiness. As one remarked, "I love the fact that I can be home with my kids a lot, because it's long hours at times, but honestly, I get four days off in a row with my kids. How many people get that much?" These working-class men exhibit a model of masculinity—based both at home and on the job—that provides valued involvement in their children's daily lives.

CONCLUSION: PUBLIC AND PRIVATE FATHERS

Much has been written about the way gender shapes participation in family and work, but much of that literature focuses on women. In contrast, we focus on men and the ways that their class location shapes gender, family, and work. We argue that class shapes the gendered relations and processes rooted in jobs and the domestic division of labor, which in turn shape the ways men behave as fathers. Illustrating that masculinity is neither unitary nor homogeneous, our findings emphasize the "multiple masculinities—some subordinate, some dominant—which are created by differences in . . . class and occupation" (Cooper 2000, 7). Class locations are major contributors to the construction of masculinities because of their role in shaping fatherhood. Class location sometimes sustains but sometimes refashions the gender order (and the social relations constituting it). Our data accords with the few qualitative pieces that suggest that fathers who are least likely to ideologically endorse gender equality (the working class) are the most likely to engage in equitable actions (e.g., Deutsch 1999; Pyke 1996; Williams 2000). . . .

By comparing these two groups of men, we can specify the particular class-based strategies and conditions found in both jobs and families that contribute to variations in masculinity, the gender order, and fatherhood. Numerous aspects of their jobs were important in shaping the way EMTs practiced fatherhood. While physicians spent long hours on one job, EMTs often worked more than one job and used alternative schedules (a difference found by others in comparisons of the working and middle class; for example, see Presser 2003). In addition, as Acker (2006, 449) suggests in her discussion of class, lower-level jobs tend to have less scheduling flexibility than professionals, but she also notes that these differences are "created and renewed through organizational practices . . . and are also reproduced in everyday interactions." Indeed, in some sense, while the doctors could exert a fair amount of control over their schedules, the EMTs had little control over their rigid schedules, which they received from management a year in advance. But the EMTs could alter these obligations by relying on their relationships with other men at work: These fathers could turn to coworkers for swaps because of the skill similarity and the tight bonds they formed on the job. This helped them create flexibility in their job schedules. Despite the fact that many workplaces tend to be unresponsive to family demands, and though emergency medical services has typically been seen as a hypermasculine culture (Chetkovich 1997), the EMTs in our study managed to create workplaces responsive to the responsibilities associated with working-class fatherhood.

Not just their jobs were important; their gender relations at home—also similar in a number of ways to other working-class men—mattered as well. They did not only rely on extended kin for help in fathering; EMTs were responsive to their wives' and their children's needs when accepting or declining overtime. Some of them turned down promotions or found new jobs in response to their families. They struggled with these decisions and were often strongly influenced by their wives. Their wives' employment—their hours, shifts, pay—typically shaped the involvement of the EMT fathers as they were more likely to swap alternative schedules with their wives. And as Deutsch (1999) reports as characteristic of other working-class men, their wives' agency also affected their fatherhood: EMT wives often insisted their husbands be available. Although subject to the power and control of others both on the job and at home, many of these fathers appreciated their jobs and families because they allowed daily involvement with their children. Most EMT fathers not only related the requirements but also the pleasures of private fathering. We did not hear protests from them about threats to their masculinity. Perhaps this is because they work in highly masculine jobs and do not need to use family relations to shore up their identity as men. Whatever the cause, these working-class men are "undoing gender" in their interactions at home. These analyses respond to Deutsch's (2007, 127) clarion call to examine when and how interactions become less gendered, for, as she writes, "Gendered institutions can be changed, and the social interactions that support them can be undone."

Physicians, on the other hand, participated less in the daily care of their children. Without much resistance from physicians, their organizations continued to practice as "inequality regimes" (Acker 2006), less responsive to the daily needs of these men's families. With gendered subjectivities, most physicians were silent in the face of conflicts between work and parenting. Though they had some control over their hours, the physicians talked of time constraints. They could change an appointment (as they sometimes did to attend a child's game) or trade money for more time with their children (as a few did). But for a variety of reasons ranging from the identities they formed in residency to intense patient demands to consumption patterns, most did not do so. In addition, physicians earn significantly more money than EMTs; this made it easier to pay for the kind of public activities entailed in "concerted cultivation" that Lareau (2003) finds at the center of parenting in middle-class families. But it was not just the characteristics of jobs and organizations that made such inequalities in parenting possible: The physicians' wives rarely insisted that they share more fully in the daily hands-on care of their children. Whether because of their own ideological attachment to the importance of their husbands' career or the pleasure gained in the lifestyle it allowed or for a combination of these and other reasons, the physicians' wives were much less likely to make demands on their husbands' time. Moreover, when the wives had jobs, these families paid for child care. Their bargain entails exchange: relatively high income (and perhaps prestige) garnered by the fathers in exchange for the mothers' (and "her" helpers') family care. Because of the conditions and relations located both in paid work and families, the physicians can perform public fathering.

Public fathering demands less time than private fathering, but it is more visible. Garey (1999) argues that nurses often choose night shifts so that their mothering, which occurs during the day, is visible to the community. In a similar vein, these doctors choose a kind of fathering that gives them visibility and likely garnishes praise from community members (whose support their medical practices are dependent upon; Fowlkes 1980).

There is another implication of this paternal visibility: As Hochschild (1989/2003) argued, when families see other families sharing housework, that may help revise the gendered norms of domestic life. This creates a paradox: At the same time as this type of fathering sustains gender inequality within families, its visibility may contribute to the appearance of norms of gender equality to outsiders who observe them.

We have argued here that for these two groups of men, class shapes fathering. We do not, however, mean to argue that physicians represent all middle-class professionals or that EMTs represent all working-class men. There is too much variation across class to make such an argument. In some sense, the findings we report here are most clearly occupational and organizational differences—important components of class but not the only ones. Given the size and character of our sample, we cannot specify the effects of these particular occupational differences, nor can we generalize to other professional groups (like lawyers or academics) or other working-class groups (like factory workers or janitors). In addition, the limits of our sample restrict our ability to generalize to different types of families that may occur even within each of these two groups. . . .

REFERENCES

Acker, Joan. 2006. Inequality regimes: Gender, class and race in organizations. *Gender & Society* 20:441–64.

Astone, Nan Marie, Jacinda Dariotis, Freya Sonenstein, Joseph Pleck, and Kathryn Hynes. 2010. How do men's work lives change after fatherhood? *Journal of Family and Economic Issues* 31: 3–13.

Barnett, Rosalind Chait, and Karen C. Gareis. 2002. Full time and reduced hours work schedules and marital quality: A study of female physicians with young children. *Work & Occupations* 29:364–79.

Bianchi, Suzanne M., John P. Robinson, and Melissa A. Milkie. 2006. *Changing rhythms of American life.* New York: Russell Sage Foundation.

Blair-Loy, Mary 2003. *Competing devotions.* Cambridge, MA: Harvard University Press.

Bluestone, Barry, and Stephen Rose. 2000. The enigma of working time trends. In *Working time: International trends, theory, and policy perspectives,* edited by L. Golden and D. M. Figart. New York: Routledge.

Boushey, Heather. 2005. Are women opting out? Debunking the myth. Briefing Paper, Center for Economic and Policy Research, Washington DC.

Brayfield, April. 1995. Juggling jobs and kids: The impact of employment schedules on fathers' caring for children. *Journal of Marriage and the Family* 57:321–32.

Brines, Julie. 1994. Economic dependency, gender, and the division of labor at home. *American Journal of Sociology* 100:652–88.

Casper, Lynne, and Suzanne Bianchi. 2002. *Continuity and change in the American family*. Thousand Oaks, CA: Sage.

Chetkovich, Carol A. 1997. *Real heat: Gender and race in the urban fire service*. New Brunswick, NJ: Rutgers University Press.

Coltrane, Scott. 1996. *Family man: Fatherhood, housework and gender equity*. New York: Oxford University Press.

———. 2000. Research on household labor. *Journal of Marriage and the Family* 62:1209–33.

———. 2004. Elite careers and family commitment: It's (still) about gender. *Annals of the American Academy of Political and Social Science* 596:214–20.

Coltrane, Scott, and M. Adams. 2001. Men's family work: Child-centered fathering and the sharing of domestic labor. In *Working families,* edited by Rosanna Hertz and Nancy Marshall. Berkeley: University of California Press.

Connell, R. W. 1992. A very straight guy: Masculinity, homosexual experience, and the dynamics of gender. *American Sociological Review* 57:735–51.

———. 1995. *Masculinities*. Berkeley: University of California Press.

Cooke, Lynn Prince. 2007. Policy pathways to gender power: State-level effects on the US division of housework. *Journal of Social Policy* 36:239–60.

Cooper, Marianne. 2000. Being the "go-to guy": Fatherhood and masculinity and the organization of work in Silicon Valley. *Qualitative Sociology* 23:379–405.

Craig, Lyn. 2006. Does father care mean fathers share? *Gender & Society* 20:259–81.

Deutsch, Francine. 1999. *Halving it all: How equally shared parenting works*. Cambridge, MA: Harvard University Press.

———. 2007. Undoing gender. *Gender & Society* 21:106–27.

Dowd, Nancy E. 2000. *Redefining fatherhood*. New York: New York University Press.

Fowlkes, Martha. 1980. *Behind every successful man: Wives of medicine and academe*. New York: Columbia University Press.

Garey, Anita Ilta. 1999. *Weaving work and motherhood*. Philadelphia: Temple University Press.

Gerson, Kathleen. 1993. *No man's land: Men's changing commitments to family and work*. New York: Basic Books.

———. 2007. What do women and men want? *American Prospect* [online], February 19.

Gerstel, Naomi, and Natalia Sarkisian. 2008. The color of family ties: Race, class, gender, and extended family involvement. In *American families: A multicultural reader,* edited by Stephanie Coontz, Maya Parson, and Gabrielle Rayley. New York: Routledge.

Griswold, Robert E. 1993. *Fatherhood in America: A history*. New York: Basic Books.

Hochschild, Arlie Russell. 1989/2003. *The second shift*. New York: Penguin.

Jacobs, Jerry A., and Kathleen Gerson. 2004. *The time divide: Work, family and gender inequality*. Cambridge, MA: Harvard University Press.

Kimmel, Michael. 2000. *The gendered society*. New York: Oxford University Press.

———. 2006. *Manhood in America*. 2nd ed. New York: Oxford University Press.

Kuperberg, Arielle, and Pamela Stone. 2008. The media depiction of women who opt out. *Gender & Society* 22:497–517.

Lamb, Michael E. 1995. The changing roles of fathers. In *Becoming a father,* edited by J. L. Shapiro, M. J. Diamond, and M. Greenberg. New York: Springer.

Lareau, Annette. 2002. Invisible inequality: Social class and childrearing in Black families and white families. *American Sociological Review* 67:747–76.

———. 2003. *Unequal childhoods*. Berkeley: University of California Press.

LaRossa, Ralph. 1997. *The modernization of fatherhood: A social and political history*. Chicago: University of Chicago Press.

Lundberg, Shelly, and Elaina Rose. 2000. Parenthood and the earnings of married men and women. *Labour Economics* 7:689–710.

Orloff, Ann, and Renne Monson. 2002. Citizens, workers, or fathers? Men in the history of U.S. social policy. In *Making men into fathers: Men masculinities and the social policy of fatherhood,* edited by B. Hobson. New York: Cambridge University Press.

Pleck, J. H., and B. Masciadrelli. 2004. Parental involvement of U.S. residential fathers: Levels, sources, and consequences. In *The role of the father in child development,* 4th ed., edited by M. Lamb. New York: Wiley.

Presser, Harriet. 2003. *Working in a 24/7 economy: Challenges for American families.* New York: Russell Sage Foundation.

Pyke, Karen D. 1996. Class-based masculinities: The interdependence of gender, class, and interpersonal power. *Gender & Society* 10:527–49.

Risman, Barbara. 1998. *Gender vertigo.* New Haven, CT: Yale University Press.

Stone, Pamela. 2007. *Opting out? Why women really quit careers and head home.* Berkeley: University of California Press.

Sullivan, Oriel. 2006. *Changing gender relations, changing families: Tracing the pace of change over time.* Lanham, MD: Rowman & Littlefield.

Townsend, Nicholas. 2002. *The package deal: Marriage, work, and fatherhood in men's lives.* Philadelphia: Temple University Press.

West, Candice, and Don H. Zimmerman. 1987. Doing gender. *Gender & Society* 1:125–51.

Williams, Joan 2000. *Unbending gender: Why family and work conflict and what to do about it.* New York: Oxford University Press.

Introduction to Reading 41

This reading by Christin L. Munsch allows us to look at how power dynamics play out in heterosexual marriages. Using a large, nationally representative survey of more than 2,700 individuals, Munsch applies social exchange theory to explain infidelity in heterosexual couples, a marital outcome that has received relatively little attention. While at first glance it may seem that high-power individuals—meaning those that are economically independent—would be more likely to cheat, that's not what she finds. Rather, people in positions of low power—that is, those who are economically dependent—are more likely to cheat. Yet, men and women respond to economic dependence differently. Munsch uses data from the National Longitudinal Survey of Youth collected by the Bureau of Labor Statistics beginning in 1997, with respondents re-surveyed every year to collect additional data as the individuals aged. The data used in this reading were collected between 2001 and 2011 for respondents between 18 and 32 years old. She limits her sample to heterosexual men and women who were in the same marital relationship for at least 1 year. While the study did not ask people directly if they had an extramarital relationship, as she explains in the conclusion, Munsch was able to measure infidelity using several different questions on the survey, including one that asked how many sexual partners the person had since he or she completed the last survey. Quantitative research uses a much different protocol than many of the qualitative studies you have been reading in this book. Note the careful theoretical development of hypotheses in this research and the use of the data to test those hypotheses in the Results section. This quantitative evidence provides a way to develop and test explanations of why people do what they do in intimate relationships.

1. Which theories make the most sense to you in understanding infidelity—the gender-neutral social exchange theories, equity theories, or the gender-based identity theories?

2. How does this research support the idea that gendered behavior is largely sociostructural rather than based on individual choices?

3. What is the value of quantitative evidence? What are its shortcomings?

HER SUPPORT, HIS SUPPORT

MONEY, MASCULINITY, AND MARITAL INFIDELITY

Christin L. Munsch

It is difficult to think of any other legal behavior of which more people disapprove than infidelity. According to a recent poll, 91 percent of U.S. adults consider extramarital infidelity to be morally wrong, a higher percentage than object to polygamy, an illegal practice (Newport and Himelfarb 2013). The overwhelming majority of married persons expect their spouse to have sex only in marriage and assume their spouse expects the same (Treas and Giesen 2000). Yet, infidelity is relatively common. Due to social desirability and impression management concerns, precise estimates are hard to come by; however, researchers estimate that in the United States, between 20 and 25 percent of married men and between 10 and 15 percent of married women have engaged in extramarital sex (Laumann et al. 1994; Wiederman 1997). The incongruity between our attitudes, expectations, and behaviors suggests there are sociostructural factors that promote infidelity.

Despite evidence that infidelity is relatively widespread, we know rather little about its determinants. Previous research has investigated the link between infidelity and a host of demographic characteristics. For example . . . men, African Americans, and younger adults are more likely to engage in infidelity. But an emphasis on interpersonal dynamics, as opposed to demographics, has become increasingly important to our understanding of the social outcomes related to marriage. In particular, social

scientists are now interested in the effects of heterosexual couples' role specialization and complementarity on marital outcomes. These discussions have become increasingly important as women's labor force participation and men's housework and childcare contributions have increased (Bianchi et al. 2000; Fisher et al. 2007). This has led to debates about the importance of specialization and to scholarly work documenting the effects of various earning and homemaking arrangements on marital outcomes. In this vein, this article examines the relationship between couples' relative income contributions—a measure of household specialization—and infidelity—a martial outcome that has received relatively little attention.

A review of the specialization literature reveals two, somewhat opposing, trends. On the one hand, couples who share responsibility for breadwinning reap a number of benefits. Not only do they bring in more income and experience less financial stress, they also have more to talk about, share common experiences, and are better able to relate to each other's problems (Meers and Strober 2013). They also divide childcare responsibilities more equitably (Raley, Bianchi, and Wang 2012). On the other hand, gender continues to play a central role in organizing marital interactions. Although having both spouses in the workforce provides an opportunity to change the conventional marital script, men and women often collaborate to maintain gender specialization. Men still regard providing as their

From Munsch, Christin L. 2015. "Her Support, His Support: Money, Masculinity, and Marital Infidelity." *American Sociological Review* 80(3): 469–495.

This is a commissioned chapter that draws heavily on the above article in the *American Sociological Review.*

responsibility even if they welcome their partner's contributions (Townsend 2002), couples with similar wages tend to interpret women's earnings as supplemental (Potuchek 1997), and husbands of high-earning women report increasing their work hours to maintain primary-earner status (Deutsch and Saxon 1998). Conversely, breadwinning wives downplay their financial contributions, defer to their husbands in decision making (Meisenbach 2010; Tichenor 2005), and do a disproportionate amount of housework (Bittman et al. 2003; Brines 1994; Evertsson and Nermo 2004; Greenstein 2000; Tichenor 2005). These findings suggest that spouses may be more comfortable with at least some gender specialization in their relationships.

Given these two trends, the relationship between men's and women's relative income contributions and marital stability remains an empirical question. Previous studies generally focus on divorce and yield inconsistent results. Some scholars have found that the higher women's relative earnings are, the higher the probability of divorce (e.g., Jalovaara 2003; Kalmijn, Loeve, and Manting 2007; Manting and Loeve 2004; Moore and Waite 1981; Teachman 2010). Others have found that women's relative earnings have a nonlinear, U-shaped relationship to the risk of marital dissolution. Rogers (2004) found that the odds of divorce are highest when wives contribute between 40 and 50 percent of the total family income, and Heckert, Nowak, and Snyder (1998) found that the odds of divorce are highest when wives contribute between 50 and 75 percent of the total family income. This article contributes to the debate by investigating the link between relative income and a different marital outcome, infidelity. While infidelity is not a proxy for divorce, it is the most often reported reason for divorce, as well as its strongest predictor (Amato and Previti 2003).

Moreover, unlike studies of divorce, studying infidelity allows for the effects of relative earnings on marriage to be gendered. Because it takes only one person to end a marriage, and we typically do not know which spouse initiated a divorce, divorce studies often conceal important gender differences in marital outcomes. A notable exception is the work of Sayer and colleagues (2011), who analyze the effects of employment on divorce and distinguish between cases in which husbands versus wives initiate divorce. They found that, compared to when men are employed, men's unemployment increases the likelihood that both men and women will leave the marriage. By contrast, when wives are employed, women (but not men) are more likely to leave, but only in instances of below-average marital satisfaction. Their research suggests the importance of gendering marital outcome theory by allowing relational dynamics within marriage to predict different outcomes for men and for women. I build on this work by examining relative income, or the contribution of one spouses' income relative to the other, as opposed to employment, because wives' employment has become common. In 2013, couples in which both partners worked outside the home made up close to 50 percent of all married-couple families (Bureau of Labor Statistics 2014); and women's earnings are absolutely and relatively lower than men's. Sayer and colleagues' analysis, however, did not allow for an examination of what happens in marriages where gendered expectations about breadwinning are more seriously challenged, such as when a wife outearns her husband.

The central goal of this article is to determine the effect of relative income contributions within contemporary heterosexual marriages on infidelity. By examining the full range of relative contributions, I am able to consider the effect of economic positions at both ends of the spectrum—spouses who are economically dependent and spouses who are primary breadwinners—and I ask whether these relationships differ for men and for women. . . .

SOCIAL EXCHANGE, DEPENDENCE, AND POWER

According to theories of social exchange (e.g., Blau 1964; Emerson 1962; Homans 1958), relationships are analogous to economic marketplaces where the exchange of goods occurs through interaction. In romantic relationships, actors reciprocally exchange a range of resources, including companionship, love, sex, money, social mobility, housekeeping, and childcare (Becker 1981; Safilios-Rothschild 1976; Sprecher 1998). Rather than bargaining over the division of a finite pool of resources, each actor separately, and without explicit prior agreement, performs acts that bestow benefits upon the other without knowing if, when, or how the acts will be reciprocated.

As suggested by the strong tendency toward homogamy, some resources are exchanged for their equivalent. People tend to marry individuals who are similar in physical appearance, social class, and education (Blossfeld 2009; Kalmijn 1998; Schwartz 2013). Others are exchanged for unlike resources. Historically, for example, women's physical attractiveness was exchanged for men's wealth or social standing (Taylor and Glenn 1976; Udry and Eckland 1984).

From this perspective, resources and power are positively related. According to the principle of least interest (Waller 1937; Waller and Hill 1951), the power of actor A over actor B is a function of B's dependence on A for valued resources (Emerson 1962; McDonald 1981; Thibaut and Kelley 1959). In other words, power is relational. Because resources increase power and decrease dependency, the party receiving fewer benefits has greater bargaining power to improve upon the exchange (Cook and Emerson 1978).

Applying this theory to marital relationships, exchange theory predicts high power and low dependency will increase the odds of an individual leaving a marriage. Empirical tests of this hypothesis generally focus on the relationship between relative income, a quantifiable measure of resource contribution, and divorce.

Thus, the current study empirically tests the social exchange hypothesis—that **persons with greater relative income will be more likely to engage in infidelity (Hypothesis 1)**. . . .

While exchange theory predicts that high relative income will be associated with increased infidelity, the predictions for low relative earners are less clear. On the one hand, as Hatfield and colleagues (1979:325) predict, the "overbenefited partner should have grave reservations about taking such risks." Because **low relative earners are more economically dependent on their partners, they should be less likely to engage in behaviors like infidelity that could damage their lucrative marital arrangements (Hypothesis 2a)**. On the other hand, equity theory, a derivative of exchange theory, states that inequitable relationships cause distress for those who get "too little" *and* those who get "too much" (Adams 1965). Applying equity theory to extramarital relationships, Prins and colleagues (1993) argue that over-benefiting—that is, putting in less than one receives—is a hedonically adverse state, and infidelity may provide over-benefited individuals with the opportunity to escape and prove their desirability. They found that women (but not men) who felt they "contributed less" in general than their partners engaged in more extramarital relationships than women who felt they contributed equally. In an effort to test the application of equity theory to relative earnings and marital infidelity, I empirically test the alternative hypothesis—that is, **economically dependent partners will be more likely to engage in infidelity compared to partners with equivalent earnings (Hypothesis 2b)**.

MASCULINE OVERCOMPENSATION AND DEVIANCE NEUTRALIZATION

Thus far, I have hypothesized about the relationship between relative income and infidelity without putting forth gender-specific predictions. Yet, emerging literature raises questions about the utility of gender-neutral exchange approaches (e.g., Bittman et al. 2003; Brines 1994; Kornrich, Brines, and Leupp 2013). Men and women may respond differently to similar economic positions within the family. Theories of identity provide the theoretical basis for the gender-specific hypotheses. According to these theories, to make sense of the world, humans divide things, including people, into social categories. Categorization leads to a series of distinct social groups, such as men and women. Individuals then self-identify as members of certain social groups and are classified by others as members of social groups. Through this process of categorization, people achieve personally meaningful and socially valuable identities (Burke and Tully 1977; Cialdini et al. 1976; Tajfel and Turner 1979). When individuals receive feedback inconsistent with an identity they value, they sometimes enact extreme behaviors associated with that identity in an effort to restore or confirm group membership (Burke 1991; Burke and Stets 2009; Heise 2007). Similarly, social identity theorists have found that threatened group members often behave in ways that restore the legitimacy of their in-group status by adhering more strongly to group norms (Branscombe et al. 1999; Maass et al. 2003), as well as distancing themselves from, or causing harm to, relevant out-group members (Branscombe et al. 1999; Maass et al. 2003; Quillian 1995; Tajfel 1970, 1982).

For both men and women, gender is one of the most important, salient, and pervasive social identities (Maass et al. 2003). Due to the relational, hierarchical nature of gender, however, men should respond to masculinity threats with extreme demonstrations of masculinity, whereas women should be less affected (Munsch and Willer 2012)—or unaffected (Vandello et al. 2008)—by femininity threats. Simply put, threats to masculinity incur more of a loss of status than do threats to femininity. Schrock and Schwalbe (2009) refer to these reactionary demonstrations as "compensatory manhood acts" (287); Willer and colleagues (2013) dub this process "masculine overcompensation." At its core lies a comparison between hegemonic masculinity (Carrigan, Connell, and Lee 1985; Connell 2005; Connell and Messerschmidt 2005)—or the culturally normative masculine ideal—and men's actual characteristics and behaviors. Men who closely approximate the hegemonic archetype feel secure, whereas men who value their identity as men yet differ from the archetype are likely to engage in behaviors designed to more closely align them with the hegemonic ideal.

Experimental research provides strong evidence in favor of the masculine overcompensation thesis (Maass et al. 2003; Talley and Bettencourt 2008; Willer et al. 2013). For example, by administering a gender identity survey to men and women and then giving randomly determined feedback indicating participants had scored in either the masculine or feminine range relative to past study participants, Willer and colleagues (2013) found that men who had been given feedback suggesting they were feminine expressed more support for the Iraq War, interest in purchasing a sport utility vehicle, and affinity for dominance hierarchies—attitudes culturally associated with masculinity. Women's attitudes were not affected by threats to their femininity.

The strength of this line of research lies in its ability to test the causal impact of threatened masculinity in controlled laboratory settings. Complementing this line of work, survey researchers have also evaluated theories of masculine overcompensation. Because breadwinner status is an important component of contemporary masculinity (Thébaud 2010; Tichenor 2005), researchers have operationalized masculinity threat as earning a low proportion of one's pooled marital income. Specifically, men whose earnings constitute less than half of the total marital income are no longer considered breadwinners and are considered economically dependent and threatened. Research on samples of U.S. men support the masculine overcompensation thesis and find that economic dependency is associated with increased domestic violence (Atkinson, Greenstein, and Lange 2005), decreased housework (Bittman et al. 2003; Brines 1994; Evertsson and Nermo 2004; Greenstein 2000, but see also Gupta 2007), and decreased health (Springer 2010).

In short, substantial empirical evidence shows that direct threats to masculinity, as well as indirect threats to masculinity in the form of economic dependency, increase the likelihood that men will engage in culturally normative male-typed behavior. Accordingly, I hypothesize that **the more economically dependent a married man is on his partner, the greater his likelihood of engaging in infidelity (Hypothesis 3)**. Extramarital sex allows men undergoing a masculinity threat to engage in behavior culturally associated with masculinity. For men—especially young men—the dominant definition of masculinity is scripted in terms of sexual virility and conquest, particularly with respect to multiple sexual partners (Connell 2005; Cornwell and Laumann 2011; Kimmel 1994, 2008; Pascoe 2007). Simultaneously, extramarital sex allows threatened men to distance themselves from, and perhaps punish, a relevant out-group member: their breadwinning spouse. Indeed, threats to gender status have been shown to heighten men's anti-woman reactions (Atkinson et al. 2005; Maass et al. 2003; Munsch and Willer 2012). In this way, engaging in infidelity may be a way of reestablishing threatened masculinity.

While theories of identity, in combination with culturally normative ideas about masculinity, suggest that economic dependency and infidelity will be inversely related, there is little evidence to suggest that economically dependent women will behave similarly. First, the range of acceptable and respected traits associated with masculinity is narrower than the range associated with femininity (Pascoe 2007; Schrock and Schwalbe 2009). Consequently, it is more difficult to threaten femininity. Second, economic dependency is not threatening to women; it is the status quo. Likewise, sexual encounters are a defining feature of masculinity, not femininity. Ample scientific evidence (e.g., England, Shafer, and Fogarty 2008; Hamilton and Armstrong 2009) documents a sexual double standard. Women who have multiple sexual partners, even if they have not engaged in infidelity, are often held accountable for breaking gender norms. Thus, there is little reason to believe threatened women will seek to restore femininity by engaging in extramarital sex.

Women who outearn their husbands, however, do challenge the status quo. Acutely aware of the ways they deviate from the cultural expectation that equates men with breadwinning (Meisenbach 2010), breadwinning women suffer from increased anxiety and insomnia (Pierce, Dahl, and Nielsen 2013). They also engage in deviance neutralization behaviors. For example, breadwinning women often minimize their achievements, defer to their spouses (Tichenor 2005), and increase their housework (Bittman et al. 2003; Brines 1994; Meisenbach 2010). This emotional and physical work is designed to decrease interpersonal conflict and shore up husbands' masculinity. It also helps keep potentially strained relationships intact. This suggests breadwinning women may be particularly hesitant to engage in infidelity. I thus hypothesize that, **for women, greater relative income will be associated with a decrease in infidelity (Hypothesis 4)**.

In summary, the literature mostly promotes the social exchange hypothesis—that is, the greater one's relative income compared to one's spouse, the more likely one will be to engage in infidelity. Traditional theories of social exchange predict that economically dependent partners will be less likely to engage in infidelity; however, equity theory (a derivative of social exchange theory) predicts that economically dependent partners will be more likely to engage in infidelity. These hypotheses are gender-neutral. Yet, emerging literature raises questions about the utility of gender-neutral exchange approaches, particularly in situations that call traditional masculinity and femininity into question. The masculine overcompensation hypothesis and the deviance neutralization hypothesis suggest that men's economic dependence—that is, situations in which women outearn their male partners—will be associated with an increase in male infidelity and a decrease in female infidelity.

* * *

RESULTS

For men, the relationship between economic dependency and infidelity is first negative and then positive, providing initial support for

Hypothesis 1; that is, for men, higher relative income contributions are associated with higher odds of engaging in infidelity. Moreover, these results allow me to distinguish between Hypotheses 2a and 2b. Hypothesis 2a states that the more economically dependent people are on their partner, the *less* likely they are to engage in infidelity, whereas Hypothesis 2b states that the more economically dependent one is, the *more* likely one will be to engage in infidelity. The findings reveal that, for men, lower relative income—that is, economic dependency—is associated with higher odds of engaging in infidelity. I therefore reject Hypothesis 2a and interpret these results as preliminary evidence in favor of Hypothesis 2b. I cannot yet discern between Hypotheses 2b and 3. Whereas Hypothesis 2b states that partners (both men and women) who are economically dependent will be more likely to engage in infidelity, Hypothesis 3 states that economically dependent men (but not women) will be more likely to engage in infidelity. If the relationship between relative income and infidelity differs for women, this will provide further support for Hypothesis 3. I examine this possibility shortly.

The results for women reveal a different pattern. As women's relative income rises—that is, as husbands become more dependent—women report engaging in less infidelity. This provides evidence in favor of the deviance neutralization hypothesis (Hypothesis 4): For women, higher relative income is associated with lower odds of engaging in infidelity.

Figure 8.1 depicts these results and presents the predicted probabilities of infidelity for men and women across the full range of relative income contributions estimated from the statistical models (not shown). All other independent variables such as educational levels and presence of children are controlled. The vertical axis represents the predicted probability of engaging in infidelity. The horizontal axis represents relative income, which was calculated by subtracting the partner's income from the respondent's income and then dividing this number by the pooled marital income (respondent's income plus partner's income). This results in a continuous measure of relative income ranging

from −1 to +1. Values of −1 mean respondents are completely economically dependent on their partner. In these instances, the respondent contributes 0 percent and the partner contributes 100 percent to the pooled marital income. Values of +1 mean the respondent is the sole breadwinner in the marriage: the respondent contributes 100 percent and the partner contributes 0 percent to the pooled marital income. Values of 0 mean both spouses contribute equally.

The figure reveals that, for men, in general, as relative income decreases so does infidelity. For example, men whose wives contribute equally (economic dependency = 0) have a predicted probability of cheating of .034, and men whose wives contribute twice as much to the pooled income (economic dependency = −.50) have a predicted probably of cheating of .058. The highest predicted probabilities correspond with the most economic dependence: Men who are completely dependent on their wives' income have a predicted probability of cheating of .15.

Focusing on men whose wives are economically dependent reveals a different pattern. The point at which the relationship changes direction is equal to .40. Between economic dependency scores of .40 and 1, the figure shows a general weak upward trend in the predicted probability of cheating. In other words, moving from a contribution of 70 percent of the couple's pooled income toward a 100 percent contribution is associated with an increase in infidelity, although the magnitude of this increase is relatively small: The predicted probability of cheating for these individuals falls between .029 and .040. The more prominent trend is the significant increase in the probability that married men will engage in infidelity that occurs as they become more economically dependent.

Figure 8.1 also shows predicted values of infidelity for women. The figure shows that, for women, shifting from a household in which women are completely economically dependent to a household in which women contribute all of the income is associated with a decline in infidelity of approximately .037. Married women who are completely economically dependent on their husbands have a predicted probability of cheating

Figure 8.1   Predicted Probability of Engaging in Infidelity by Relative Income, Married Men and Women

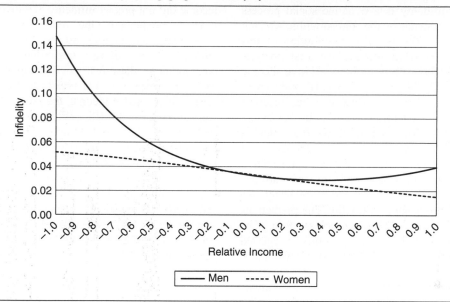

of approximately .052, whereas women who are complete breadwinners—that is, women whose husbands are completely economically dependent—have a predicted probability of cheating of .015. The predicted probability of cheating for women married to equal contributors is .034. For breadwinning women, as noted above, it appears that fidelity may serve to counteract gender atypicality. Conversely, lower relative income is associated with higher infidelity odds. Recall that Hypothesis 2a states that, for both men and women, economic dependency will decrease infidelity, whereas Hypothesis 2b states that economic dependency will increase infidelity. For both men and women, economic dependency is associated with increased infidelity. I interpret this finding as evidence in support of Hypothesis 2b and reject Hypothesis 2a.

At first glance, it appears that Hypothesis 3 should also be rejected. Hypothesis 3 states that economically dependent men, but not women, will be more likely to engage in infidelity, but the results show that economically dependent men and women both cheat more. Yet, it is important to note the substantive size of these effects. While these findings provide some evidence in favor of Hypothesis 2b, recall that the predictions derived from social exchange theory are gender neutral. If low relative income increases infidelity regardless of gender, the effect size should be similar for men and women. According to the results, however, the influence of relative income is much smaller on women's infidelity than on men's infidelity. In other words, while economic dependency increases women's likelihood of engaging in infidelity, there is something about men's economic dependency that increases men's likelihood of engaging in infidelity to a greater extent. This provides evidence in favor of Hypothesis 3, the masculine overcompensation thesis.

* * *

DISCUSSION AND CONCLUSIONS

Sexual decisions are often regarded as extremely private, negotiated by two individuals on the basis of their personal desires. Yet, sociologists can shed light on how situational and structural forces shape these private decisions. As this article suggests, infidelity is a dynamic social process subject to influence by the context within which it is embedded. The primary contribution of this article has been to provide the first analysis considering how each spouse's relative income affects the likelihood of husbands' and wives' infidelity, a marital outcome that has received relatively little attention. I began by reviewing two theories that shed light on the potential relationship between relative earnings and infidelity. The social exchange perspective suggested that the greater one's relative earnings compared to one's spouse, the more likely one would be to engage in infidelity. The predictions for low relative earners were less clear. The traditional social exchange perspective suggested that economically dependent partners would be less likely to engage in infidelity, whereas the equity approach suggested these individuals would be more likely to engage in infidelity. All predictions derived from exchange theory were gender neutral. In contrast, the social identity perspective, in combination with theories of gendered interaction, suggested that in situations that challenge the status quo—namely, when men are economically dependent and women are breadwinners—identity concerns would become salient, threatening men's masculinity. Consequently, men with low relative incomes would be more likely to engage in infidelity, because it would allow them to engage in a compensatory, culturally normative male-typed behavior. I predicted that women with high relative incomes, on the other hand, would be less likely to engage in infidelity. By remaining faithful, breadwinning women would neutralize their gender deviance and avoid further emasculating their husbands, thereby keeping potentially strained relationships intact.

In unconventional earning arrangements, the data supported the social identity perspective. Economic dependency was associated with an increase in men's infidelity, and breadwinning was associated with a decrease in women's infidelity. This is interesting in light of the affairs of high-profile celebrities that regularly make front-page news. According to these accounts, cheating is rampant among well-to-do men. Yet, absolute income did not predict infidelity. Relative income is a better predictor, but the affairs of economically dependent men simply do not garner media attention. In more traditional earnings configurations, these data provide support for the exchange perspective. For breadwinning men, the greater their relative income, the more likely they were to engage in infidelity. While it seems rational that low relative earners might shy away from relationship-damaging behavior like infidelity, for women, as relative earnings decreased, infidelity increased. Equity theory proposes that individuals who perceive themselves as under- or over-rewarded will experience distress, and infidelity may be an attempt to restore relationship equity (Prins et al. 1993). However, such an explanation is not incompatible with the larger increase in economically dependent men's likelihood of engaging in infidelity compared to women. While both men and women likely have an aversion toward economic dependence, men's aversion is potentially greater given the social expectation that links husbands with breadwinning.

An additional contribution of this research was to add theoretical nuance to the emerging sociological literature that focuses on resources and marital stability. *Marital stability* is often defined as the status of a relationship as intact (i.e., married) or not (i.e., divorced or separated), yet infidelity can have a number of deleterious effects on individuals and relationships. A partner's unfaithfulness can breed anger, disappointment, depression, anxiety, and distrust (Buunk 1995; Cano and O'Leary 2000); it is the leading cause of divorce (Amato and Previti 2003; Betzig 1989); and it has been causally linked to domestic violence (Daly and Wilson 1988). Accordingly, infidelity is an important indicator of marital stability. Moreover, unlike divorce, infidelity studies allow researchers to examine the consequences of various economic arrangements for each spouse separately. This is crucial because it allows theories of marital stability to be gendered and to reflect the asymmetric nature of gender change (Sayer et al. 2011). Within marriage, gendered expectations have changed more for women than for men. Women's participation in the paid labor market is now widespread. Yet, men's participation in childcare and housework has not followed suit. Rather, men deemphasize equal responsibility for childcare and regard breadwinning as their primary responsibility. This new understanding, dubbed "modified traditionalism" (Gerson 2002, 2010), has consequences for marital stability. As the findings from this study show, when men are economically dependent, they are more likely to engage in infidelity, a relationship-destabilizing behavior. This does not necessarily mean that as women's wages and relative *earnings* rise, marriages will become less stable. Shifts toward gender equality occur at uneven paces, with heterosexual marriage lagging behind other institutions (England 2010). Among individuals under age 30, about 80 percent of women and 70 percent of men desire an egalitarian marriage in which both partners share breadwinning, housekeeping, and childrearing (Gerson 2010). As the range of acceptable roles and responsibilities continues to expand, men may become more comfortable with economic dependence and no longer seek alternative exchange partners.

For women, men's economic dependency appears to stabilize marriage: Breadwinning women were less likely to cheat. This is especially noteworthy given that breadwinning women may actually have more opportunities to engage in extramarital sex. Conceivably, breadwinning wives have more disposable income to conceal extramarital activity, and they may be more likely than economically dependent wives to work in male-dominated occupations that allow for frequent cross-gender interactions. I did not investigate whether the distribution of men and women by occupation influences infidelity, although Schneider's (2012) recent work on occupations and housework suggests this is a promising area for future research. I interpreted breadwinning women's decreased infidelity as evidence of deviance neutralization. While it is possible that women with economically dependent husbands are simply more satisfied with their relationships than their economically dependent counterparts, and therefore less likely to engage in infidelity,

the relationship between relative income and infidelity was not mediated by relationship satisfaction. Thus, a more plausible interpretation is that women's increased fidelity is the product of women's efforts to counteract their own gender deviance, validate their husbands' masculinity, and safeguard their relationships. These results highlight the asymmetric nature of gender change. The continued importance of breadwinning as central to contemporary definitions of masculinity explains both men's and women's behavior in gender-atypical marriages.

When we compare these findings with previous divorce literature, the findings presented here suggest that the relationship between women's relative earnings and divorce has been misinterpreted. In this study, as women's earnings increased relative to their husbands', they were more likely to engage in relationship-stabilizing behavior: They became more faithful. This suggests that the relationship between women's relative earnings and divorce is not an independence effect but a *dependence* effect. Women who are high relative earners are married to men who are low relative earners. As these data show, it is low relative earning men, not high relative earning women, who engage in relationship-destabilizing behavior.

I acknowledge some limitations of this study. First, due to data limitations, I cannot evaluate arguments about self-reported infidelity. While a more direct assessment of infidelity may appear preferable, infidelity is a potentially sensitive subject. If respondents had been asked directly about infidelity, they may have underreported their activity. Asking about their current relationship status and their number of sexual partners since the date of the last interview reduces social desirability and impression management concerns. Moreover, the sexual activity questions were asked during the computer-assisted, self-administered portion of the survey. Previous research finds that infidelity estimates vary as a function of whether the assessment is based on face-to-face interviews or computer-assisted self-interviews, with larger prevalence rates in self-interviews

(Whisman and Snyder 2007). Thus, the infidelity data used in this analysis are likely more representative than data used in previous research. Second, because infidelity could only be determined in situations in which respondents had the same partner in two consecutive years, individuals whose relationships ended, perhaps as a result of infidelity, are not likely to be in the analyses. By focusing on marital relationships, as opposed to cohabiting or dating relationships that are more easily dissolved, I temper this concern; however, I acknowledge this to be a limitation. Third, these effects were found in a sample of young, heterosexual, married men and women. Researchers should therefore be cautious in assuming that older respondents, gay and lesbian individuals, or cohabiters will behave similarly.

This study provides new insight into the social psychological mechanisms leading to infidelity and, more importantly, it contributes to a broad theoretical account of the relationship between relative earnings and marital stability that acknowledges the asymmetrical change regarding culturally normative expectations for men and women in marriage. Moreover, this article highlights the difficulty of rewriting conventional gender scripts. Marriages in which women outearn men have the potential to undermine old ways of thinking and behaving in contemporary marriages. Yet, this study reveals one way old gender scripts exert influence over new family structures, slowing progression toward more egalitarian marriages. Consequently, one of the most important avenues for future research is the investigation of how spouses come to adopt alternative expectations of themselves and their partners that are no longer based on gender.

REFERENCES

Adams, John S. 1965. "Inequity in Social Exchange." Pp. 267–99 in *Advances in Experimental Social Psychology,* Vol. 2, edited by L. Berkowitz. Chicago, IL: The University of Chicago Press.

Amato, Paul R., and Denise Previti. 2003. "People's Reasons for Divorcing Gender, Social Class, the Life Course, and Adjustment." *Journal of Family Issues* 24(5):602–626.

Atkinson, Maxine P., Theodore N. Greenstein, and Molly M. Lang. 2005. "For Women, Breadwinning Can Be Dangerous: Gendered Resource Theory and Wife Abuse." *Journal of Marriage and Family* 67(5):1137–48.

Becker, Gary S. 1981. *A Treatise on the Family.* Cambridge, MA: Harvard University Press.

Betzig, Laura. 1989. "Causes of Conjugal Dissolution: A Cross-Cultural Study." *Current Anthropology* 30(5):654–76.

Bianchi, Suzanne M., Melissa A. Milkie, Liana C. Sayer, and John P. Robinson. 2000. "Is Anyone Doing the Housework? Trends in the Gender Division of Household Labor." *Social Forces* 79(1):191–228.

Bittman, Michael, Paula England, Liana Sayer, Nancy Folbre, and George Matheson. 2003. "When Does Gender Trump Money? Bargaining and Time in Household Work." *American Journal of Sociology* 109(1):186–214.

Blau, Peter M. 1964. *Exchange and Power in Social Life.* New Brunswick, NJ: Transaction.

Blossfeld, Hans-Peter. 2009. "Educational Assortative Marriage in Comparative Perspective." *Annual Review of Sociology* 35(1):513–30.

Branscombe, Nyla R., Naomi Ellemers, Russell Spears, and Bertjan Doosje. 1999. "The Context and Content of Social Identity Threat." Pp. 35–58 in *Social Identity: Context, Commitment, Content,* edited by R. Spears. Oxford, UK: Blackwell.

Brines, Julie. 1994. "Economic Dependency, Gender, and the Division of Labor at Home." *American Journal of Sociology* 100(3):652–88.

Bureau of Labor Statistics. 2014. "Employment Characteristics of Families—2013." April 25, 2013. Retrieved July 7, 2014 (http://www.bls.gov/news.release/pdf/famee.pdf).

Burke, Peter J. 1991. "Identity Processes and Social Stress." *American Sociological Review* 56(6):836–49.

Burke, Peter J., and Jan E. Stets. 2009. *Identity Theory.* New York: Oxford University Press.

Burke, Peter J., and Judy C. Tully. 1977. "The Measurement of Role Identity." *Social Forces* 55(4):881–97.

Buunk, Bram P. 1995. "Sex, Self-Esteem, Dependency and Extradyadic Sexual Experience as Related to Jealousy Responses." *Journal of Social and Personal Relationships* 12(1):147–53.

Cano, Annmarie, and K. Daniel O'Leary. 2000. "Infidelity and Separations Precipitate Major

Depressive Episodes and Symptoms of Nonspecific Depression and Anxiety." *Journal of Consulting and Clinical Psychology* 68(5):774–81.

Carrigan, Tim, Bob Connell, and John Lee. 1985. "Toward a New Sociology of Masculinity." *Theory and Society* 14(5):551–604.

Cialdini, Robert B., Richard J. Borden, Avril Thorne, Marcus R. Walker, Stephen Freeman, and Lloyd R. Sloan. 1976. "Basking in Reflected Glory: Three (Football) Field Studies." *Journal of Personality and Social Psychology* 34(3):366–75.

Collins, Patricia Hill. 2000. *Black Feminist Thought: Knowledge, Consciousness, and the Politics of Empowerment.* New York: Routledge.

Connell, Robert W. 2005. *Masculinities.* Berkeley, University of California Press.

Connell, Robert W., and James W. Messerschmidt. 2005. "Hegemonic Masculinity: Rethinking the Concept." *Gender & Society* 19(6):829–59.

Cook, Karen S., and Richard M. Emerson. 1978. "Power, Equity and Commitment in Exchange Networks." *American Sociological Review* 43(5):721–39.

Cornwell, Benjamin, and Edward O. Laumann. 2011. "Network Position and Sexual Dysfunction: Implications of Partner Betweenness for Men." *American Journal of Sociology* 117(1):172–208.

Daly, Martin, and Margo Wilson. 1988. *Homicide.* New Brunswick, NJ: Transaction Publishers.

Deutsch, Francine M., and Susan E. Saxon. 1998. "Traditional Ideologies, Nontraditional Lives." *Sex Roles* 38(5–6):331–62.

Emerson, Richard M. 1962. "Power-Dependence Relations." *American Sociological Review* 27(1):31–41.

England, Paula. 2010. "The Gender Revolution: Uneven and Stalled." *Gender & Society* 24(2):149–66.

England, Paula, Emily F. Shafer, and Alison C. Fogarty. 2008. "Hooking Up and Forming Romantic Relationships on Today's College Campuses." Pp. 531–93 in *The Gendered Society Reader,* 3rd ed., edited by M. Kimmel and A. Aronson. New York: Oxford University Press.

Evertsson, Marie, and Magnus Nermo. 2004. "Dependence within Families and the Division of Labor: Comparing Sweden and the United States." *Journal of Marriage and Family* 66(5):1272–86.

Fisher, Kimberly, Muriel Egerton, Jonathan I. Gershuny, and John P. Robinson. 2007. "Gender Convergence in the American Heritage Time Use Study (AHTUS)." *Social Indicators Research* 82(1):1–33.

Gerson, Kathleen. 2002. "Moral Dilemmas, Moral Strategies, and the Transformation of Gender Lessons from Two Generations of Work and Family Change." *Gender & Society* 16(1):8–28.

Gerson, Kathleen. 2010. *The Unfinished Revolution: How a New Generation Is Reshaping Family, Work, and Gender in America.* New York: Oxford University Press.

Greenstein, Theodore N. 2000. "Economic Dependence, Gender, and the Division of Labor in the Home: A Replication and Extension." *Journal of Marriage and Family* 62(2):322–35.

Gupta, Sanjiv. 2007. "Autonomy, Dependence, or Display? The Relationship between Married Women's Earnings and Housework." *Journal of Marriage and Family* 69(2):399–417.

Hamilton, Laura, and Elizabeth A. Armstrong. 2009. "Gendered Sexuality in Young Adulthood: Double Binds and Flawed Options." *Gender & Society* 23(5):589–616.

Hatfield, Elaine, Jane Traupman, and G. William Walster. 1979. "Equity and Extramarital Sex." Pp. 323–34 in *Love and Attraction,* edited by M. Cook and G. Wilson. Oxford, UK: Pergamon Press.

Heckert, D. A., Thomas C. Nowak, and Kay A. Snyder. 1998. "The Impact of Husbands' and Wives' Relative Earnings on Marital Disruption." *Journal of Marriage and the Family* 60(3):690–703.

Heise, David R. 2007. *Expressive Order.* New York: Springer.

Homans, George C. 1958. "Social Behavior as Exchange." *American Journal of Sociology* 63(6):597–606.

Jalovaara, Marika. 2003. "The Joint Effects of Marriage Partners' Socioeconomic Positions on the Risk of Divorce." *Demography* 40(1):67–81.

Kalmijn, Matthijs. 1998. "Intermarriage and Homogamy: Causes, Patterns, Trends." *Annual Review of Sociology* 24(1):395–421.

Kalmijn, Matthijs, Anneke Loeve, and Dorien Manting. 2007. "Income Dynamics in Couples and the Dissolution of Marriage and Cohabitation." *Demography* 44(1):159–79.

Kimmel, Michael S. 1994. "Masculinity as Homophobia: Fear, Shame and Silence in the Construction of Gender Identity." Pp. 119–41 in *Theorizing Masculinities,* edited by H. Broad and M. Kaufman. Thousand Oaks, CA: Sage.

Kimmel, Michael S. 2008. *Guyland: The Perilous World Where Boys Become Men.* New York: Harper.

Kornrich, Sabino, Julie Brines, and Katrina Leupp. 2013. "Egalitarianism, Housework, and Sexual Frequency in Marriage." *American Sociological Review* 78(1):26–50.

Laumann, Edward O., John H. Gagnon, Robert T. Michael, and Stuart Michaels. 1994. *The Social Organization of Sexuality: Sexual Practices in the United States.* Chicago: University of Chicago Press.

Maass, Anne, Mara Cadinu, Gaia Guarnieri, and Annalisa Grasselli. 2003. "Sexual Harassment under Social Identity Threat: The Computer Harassment Paradigm." *Journal of Personality and Social Psychology* 85(5):853–70.

Manting, Dorien, and J. Anneke Loeve. 2004. *Economic Circumstances and Union Dissolution of Couples in the 1990s in the Netherlands.* Statistics Netherlands Voorburg/Heerlen. Retrieved July 7, 2014 (http://www.cbs.nl/NR/rdonlyres/90AE062D-13C5-4EC5-879E-A98FA76A1454/0/discussionpaper04006.pdf).

McDonald, Gerald W. 1981. "Structural Exchange and Marital Interaction." *Journal of Marriage and the Family* 43(4):825–39.

Meers, Sharon, and Joanna Strober. 2013. *Getting to 50/50: How Working Parents Can Have It All.* New York: Cleis Press.

Meisenbach, Rebecca J. 2010. "The Female Breadwinner: Phenomenological Experience and Gendered Identity in Work/Family Spaces." *Sex Roles* 62(1–2):2–19.

Moore, Kristin A., and Linda J. Waite. 1981. "Marital Dissolution, Early Motherhood and Early Marriage." *Social Forces* 60(1):20–40.

Munsch, Christin L., and Robb Willer. 2012. "The Role of Gender Identity Threat in Perceptions of Date Rape and Sexual Coercion." *Violence Against Women* 18(10):1125–46.

Newport, Frank, and Igor Himelfarb. 2013. "In U.S., Record-High Say Gay, Lesbian Relations Morally OK: Americans' Tolerance of a Number of Moral Issues up Since 2001." *Gallup Politics,* May 20, 2013. Retrieved July 7, 2014 (http://www.gallup.com/poll/162689/record-high-say-gay-lesbian-relations-morally.aspx).

Pascoe, C. J. 2007. *Dude, You're a Fag.* Berkeley: University of California Press.

Pierce, Lamar, Michael S. Dahl, and Jimmi Nielsen. 2013. "In Sickness and in Wealth: Psychological and Sexual Costs of Income Comparison in Marriage." *Personality & Social Psychology Bulletin* 39(3):359–74.

Potuchek, Jean L. 1997. *Who Supports the Family? Gender and Breadwinning in Dual-Earner Marriages.* Stanford, CA: Stanford University Press.

Prins, Karin S., Bram P. Buunk, and Nico W. VanYperen. 1993. "Equity, Normative Disapproval and Extramarital Relationships." *Journal of Social and Personal Relationships* 10(1):39–53.

Quillian, Lincoln. 1995. "Prejudice as a Response to Perceived Group Threat: Population Composition and Anti-Immigrant and Racial Prejudice in Europe." *American Sociological Review* 60(4):586–611.

Raley, Sara, Suzanne M. Bianchi, and Wendy Wang. 2012. "When Do Fathers Care? Mothers' Economic Contribution and Fathers' Involvement in Child Care." *American Journal of Sociology* 117(5):1422–59.

Rogers, Stacy J. 2004. "Dollars, Dependency, and Divorce: Four Perspectives on the Role of Wives' Income." *Journal of Marriage and Family* 66(1):59–74.

Ross, Heather L., and Isabel V. Sawhill. 1975. *The Time of Transition: The Growth of Families Headed by Women.* Washington, DC: Urban Institute.

Safilios-Rothschild, Constantina. 1976. "A Macro- and Micro-Examination of Family Power and Love: An Exchange Model." *Journal of Marriage and the Family* 38(2):355–62.

Sayer, Liana C., Paula England, Paul D. Allison, and Nicole Kangas. 2011. "She Left, He Left: How Employment and Satisfaction Affect Men's and Women's Decisions to Leave Marriages." *American Journal of Sociology* 116(6):1982–2018.

Schneider, Daniel. 2012. "Gender Deviance and Household Work: The Role of Occupation." *American Journal of Sociology* 117(4):1029–72.

Schrock, Douglas, and Michael Schwalbe. 2009. "Men, Masculinity, and Manhood Acts." *Annual Review of Sociology* 35(1):277–95.

Schwartz, Christine R. 2013. "Trends and Variation in Assortative Mating: Causes and Consequences." *Annual Review of Sociology* 39(1):451–70.

Sprecher, Susan. 1998. "Social Exchange Theories and Sexuality." *Journal of Sex Research* 35(1):32–43.

Springer, Kristen W. 2010. "Economic Dependence in Marriage and Husbands' Midlife Health: Testing Three Possible Mechanisms." *Gender & Society* 24(3):378–401.

Tajfel, Henri. 1970. "Experiments in Intergroup Discrimination." *Scientific American* 223(5): 96–102.

Tajfel, Henri. 1982. *Social Identity and Intergroup Relations.* Cambridge, UK: Cambridge University Press.

Tajfel, Henri, and John C. Turner. 1979. "An Integrative Theory of Intergroup Conflict." Pp. 33–47 in *The Social Psychology of Intergroup Relations,* edited by W. G. Austin and S. Worchel. Monterey, CA: Brooks.

Talley, Amelia E., and B. Ann Bettencourt. 2008. "Evaluations and Aggression Directed at a Gay Male Target: The Role of Threat and Antigay Prejudice." *Journal of Applied Social Psychology* 38(3):647–83.

Taylor, Patricia A., and Norval D. Glenn. 1976. "The Utility of Education and Attractiveness for Females' Status Attainment through Marriage." *American Sociological Review* 41(3):484–98.

Teachman, Jay. 2010. "Wives' Economic Resources and Risk of Divorce." *Journal of Family Issues* 31(10):1305–1323.

Thébaud, Sarah. 2010. "Masculinity, Bargaining, and Breadwinning: Understanding Men's Housework in the Cultural Context of Paid Work." *Gender & Society* 24(3):330–54.

Thibaut, John W., and Harold H. Kelley. 1959. *The Social Psychology of Groups.* New York: Wiley.

Tichenor, Veronica. 2005. "Maintaining Men's Dominance: Negotiating Identity and Power When She Earns More." *Sex Roles* 53(3–4): 191–205.

Townsend, Nicholas W. 2002. *The Package Deal: Marriage, Work and Fatherhood in Men's Lives.* Philadelphia: Temple University Press.

Treas, Judith, and Deirdre Giesen. 2000. "Sexual Infidelity among Married and Cohabiting Americans." *Journal of Marriage and Family* 62(1):48–60.

Udry, J. Richard, and Bruce K. Eckland. 1984. "Benefits of Being Attractive: Differential Payoffs for Men and Women." *Psychological Reports* 54(1):47–56.

Vandello, Joseph A., Jennifer K. Bosson, Dov Cohen, Rochelle M. Burnaford, and Jonathan R. Weaver. 2008. "Precarious Manhood." *Journal of Personality and Social Psychology* 95(6):1325–39.

Waller, Willard. 1937. "The Rating and Dating Complex." *American Sociological Review* 2(5):727–34.

Waller, Willard, and Reuben Hill. 1951. *The Family: A Dynamic Interpretation.* New York: Dryden.

Whisman, Mark A., and Douglas K. Snyder. 2007. "Sexual Infidelity in a National Survey of American Women: Differences in Prevalence and Correlates as a Function of Method of Assessment." *Journal of Family Psychology* 21(2):147–54.

Wiederman, Michael W. 1997. "Extramarital Sex: Prevalence and Correlates in a National Survey." *Journal of Sex Research* 34(2):167–74.

Willer, Robb, Christabel L. Rogalin, Bridget Conlon, and Michael T. Wojnowicz. 2013. "Overdoing Gender: A Test of the Masculine Overcompensation Thesis." *American Journal of Sociology* 118(4):980–1022.

❦ Topics for Further Examination ❧

- Search the Web for "healthy relationships" and examine the first 20 or so results to see the focus for each website and who is sponsoring it. What does this data collection exercise tell you about how we are to view relationships in our society?
- Check out the most recent research on gender and relationships using an academic database. How does this research differ from that which you found on the Web?
- Examine marriage and engagement announcements in your local paper. What race, gender, and sexuality patterns do you find in these short announcements? Do the same thing with a listing of personal ads from a local paper. What does this tell us about expectations for relationships? How likely is it that women will be dependent or men will be dependent in these relationships?

9

ENFORCING GENDER

JOAN Z. SPADE

Throughout Part II, we have discussed patterns of learning, selling, and doing gender at work and in intimate relationships. In this final chapter of our section on patterns, we look at patterns surrounding the enforcement of gender. Enforcing gender is about more than just *doing* gender; it is about assault, coercion, and restraints on people's behaviors, including subtle and tacit constraints on identities that are used to enforce gender conformity. Enforcing gender involves a range of social control strategies, such as physical abuse and rape, harassment, gossip and name calling, as well as formal and informal laws and rules created by governments, work organizations, and religions to coerce people to conform to gender norms they might not otherwise wish to obey. Many readings throughout this book are about the enforcement of gender, particularly those in Chapter 4. This chapter extends that prior discussion, explicitly focusing on the different forms of social control used to enforce gender.

The enforcement of gender can have profound effects on women's and men's choices, self-esteem, relationships, and abilities to care for themselves. We argue two main points in this chapter. First, doing gender is not something that is innate (i.e., uniquely biological or psychological) or that we freely choose; rather, there are many times that we are forced to do gender, whether we would wish to do it or not. Second, there are many occasions whereby the very acts of maintaining gendered identities hurts ourselves and others, either physically, emotionally, or both.

SOCIAL CONTROL

Enforcing gender is about the physical and emotional control of everyone. Peter L. Berger (1963) describes the processes by which we learn to conform to the norms of society as "a set of concentric rings, each representing a system of social control" (p. 73). At the middle of the concentric rings, Berger places the individual. Social control mechanisms, including family and friends, are in the next ring, and the legal and political systems of a society are in the outer ring. He argues that most social control of behavior occurs in the inner rings, by ourselves and those closest to us, which he described as "broad coercive systems that every individual shares with a vast number of fellow controlees" (p. 75). As such, most gendered behavior is enforced in those center rings, with the forms of social control differing slightly by gender. For example, homophobia is a control mechanism that is often used to enforce gender patterns for men. Friends or peers who call a boy a "fag" or "sissy" can make him uncomfortable and force him to display hegemonic masculinity. Whereas women, such as those in the reading by Laura Hamilton and Elizabeth A. Armstrong in this chapter, risk being called "sluts," reinforcing the expectation that males take the lead in heterosexual encounters. The commodification of gender also enforces emphasized femininity, with young girls comparing themselves to the idealized images of femininity while young boys emulate action figures, as described in Chapter 5. The reading by Scott Melzer in this chapter further reinforces this point as men encourage other men to learn to use violence to enforce masculinity and dominance.

GENDER VIOLENCE

Although most of the enforcement of gender happens as part of normal interaction, as just described, some forms of social control are more coercive, including physical assault, rape, sexual harassment, and even murder. We begin by discussing the harm done when violence is used to enforce gender. We hope you have never experienced physical violence, but many individuals have. The actual incidence of gender violence is not clear. Most intimate partner violence is not reported to the authorities (Centers for Disease Control and Prevention, 2012; Rennison, 2002), making the incidence of intimate partner violence higher than the statistics suggest. In fact, the Bureau of Justice Statistics estimates that 65% of rape and sexual assaults went unreported during the years 2006 through 2010 (Bureau of Justice Statistics, 2012).

Furthermore, gender violence is often normalized, both in relationships and how we define violence. Many young women dismiss acts of sexual violence, using as their explanation the "male sex drive," thus enforcing the idea that men can't help themselves and women have to be passive and just accept what happens (Hlavka, 2014). Male violence in general is expected in Western society, particularly the United States, as described in the reading by Melzer in this chapter. Men are also victims of acts of violence by women, but this violence is likely to be less physically harmful and men may be less likely to talk about it, especially sexual assault (Weiss, 2010), since to claim to be physically harmed by a woman clearly violates gendered expectations.

Women victims of violence often do not report acts of violence because of fear for themselves and their children, based on threats of additional physical violence or the withdrawal of economic support and/or the outcome of emotional abuse, which leads them to believe they "asked for it." Abusers exert "coercive control" over their victims, making victims fearful for their lives and the lives of loved ones. As such, victims, particularly women, often become psychologically battered and emotionally dependent on their perpetrators (Mahoney, Williams, & West, 2001; Sinozich & Langton, 2014). Not only does domestic violence lower the victim's self-esteem, but it also impedes the victim's ability to leave an abusive situation because abusers often control the victim's freedom of movement and finances (even for individuals who work for pay outside the home). Abusers also prevent victims from getting the psychological support they need to leave the abusive situation (Mahoney et al., 2001).

Even given concerns about the accuracy and underreporting of the data, statistics detailing incidences of gender violence should give us pause. The U.S. Department of Justice (Catalano, 2013) reports that in 2010 there were 812,390 cases of intimate partner violence by current or former spouses, boyfriends or girlfriends (terminology used by the Department of Justice), of which 76.4% were female victims. These statistics reflect and reinforce the system of hegemonic masculinity and differential power and control in relationships, as females are more likely than males to be victims of intimate violence.

Homicide and extreme use of force are forms of intimate partner abuse more likely to affect females. According to the U.S. Department of Justice (Catalano, 2013), reports of homicides by intimate partners were much higher for females (1,192) than for males killed by intimate partners (305). And, females are more likely than males to sustain injuries, particularly serious injuries, during intimate partner violence (Catalano, 2013). Violence against women is a global phenomenon, one that the United Nations has targeted in its goal to promote gender equality through a variety of programs around the world (Peacock & Barker, 2014).

Unfortunately, many individuals experience sexual violence, and victimization disproportionately affects young women, which is not surprising given gendered expectations. Based upon a randomly selected national sample of 12,727 interviews in 2011, the Centers for Disease Control and Prevention estimate that 19.3% of women and 1.7% of men have been raped in their lifetimes and 43.9% of women and 23.4% of men have been victims of other sexual violence (Breiding et al., 2014). Studies find that about one in four college women have been raped or were the victims of attempted rape (Association of American Universities, 2015; Bachar & Koss, 2001; Fisher, Cullen, & Turner, 2000). A recent study examined incidence of rape for 483 first-year women at a large northeastern U.S. university (Carey et al., 2015), with respondents completing a sexual experiences survey every four months during their first year. These researchers asked about both attempted and completed rape and differentiated forcible rape or nonconsensual sex using physical force from incapacitated rape that involved the use of drugs or alcohol. Prior to college, 15.4% of respondents reported attempted or completed forcible rape and 17.5% attempted or completed

incapacitated rape. During their first year of college, 9.0% of respondents reported attempted or completed forcible rape and 15.4% attempted or completed incapacitated rape, bringing the lifetime total for these young women who had experienced forcible rape to 21.7% and incapacitated rape to 25.7% (Carey et al., 2015). Taken together, these studies point to a prevalence of sexual assault that is of serious concern.

These estimates of sexual assault of young women, both from the Centers for Disease Control and Prevention and from college campuses, are based on self-reports on surveys; official rates are considerably lower due to victims' unwillingness to report sexual assault. Data from a crime victim's survey found that, while the incidence of sexual assault was similar for women (between the ages of 18 and 24) who were enrolled full time in a postsecondary institution and those who were not, women enrolled in a postsecondary institution were less likely to report sexual assault (20% compared to 32% of the women not enrolled in a postsecondary institution; Sinozich & Langton, 2014). As a result, attention on campuses is focused on how sexual assault is processed by the colleges and universities, as well as how to reduce the incidence of sexual assault.

Unfortunately, this situation of sexual violence and date rape evolves in a culture that encourages and justifies rape and enforces a gender system in which men control women (Boswell & Spade, 1996). The literature provides us with an understanding of the prevalence of rape but has not reduced the likelihood of rape. The reading by Hamilton and Armstrong in this chapter examines changing gender norms and sexual mores for young women in college today, illustrating the complex intersections of gender, sexuality, and social class on women's orientation to relationships. Their findings suggest that changing views of sexuality may alter the role of intimate violence in enforcing gender while continuing to enforce gender (Ronen, 2010).

In fact, researchers have identified a number of rape myths that perpetuate gender differences and maintain a system of male dominance. These myths include the belief that wives cannot be raped by their husbands, that women want to be raped and enjoy rape, that women lie about being raped (Edwards, Turchik, Dardis, Reynolds, & Gidycz, 2011), that rapists are different from other men, and that men cannot stop themselves once they are sexually aroused (Ryan, 2011). Rape myths abound, supported by religious, legal, media, and other institutions (Edwards et al., 2011), and we could even add the one stating that men cannot be raped, particularly by women (Weiss, 2010). This rape myth is substantiated by the fact that rape laws in many states excluded men as victims until the 1980s, and it wasn't until 2012 that the FBI Uniform Crime Code was revised in a way that included males as well as females as victims.

It is important to remember that males are also victims of sexual assault and intimate violence, including being raped by females. Karen G. Weiss's (2010) comparison of men's and women's reports of sexual victimization in the National Crime Victimization Survey found only a small number of differences between men's and women's reports of victimization. Women were more likely to be victims of rape or attempted rape, whereas men reported sexual assaults more often. In addition, while 99% of women reported being victimized by men, 46% of men reported being victimized by women, defying some assumptions about rape and gender. Weiss's findings show that even when men are victimized, their reports of the victimization often enforce gender and masculinity. For example, men are more likely to say that they were too drunk to control the situation or, particularly when victimized by other men, to include descriptions of fighting back. Needless to say, while men as well as women are victimized, gendered expectations influence their experiences.

We argue that the underlying reasons for intimate violence and sexual abuse are complicated and relate to the maintenance of hegemonic masculinity. Hegemonic masculinity depends on the sexual, physical, and emotional degradation of women. Gender is relational. Culturally, males often find that "becoming" a man requires that

one show disdain for women. As Amy M. Denissen and Abigail C. Saguy suggest in their reading in this chapter, many men disrespect women, especially in workplaces where maintaining the projection of masculinity is important. The same patterns and practices we have been discussing throughout this book also explain how men learn to instigate and justify the physical and emotional abuse of women. These patterns also illustrate what encourages men to be violent. Although there have been some changes in the way police and courts handle intimate violence, a long-standing attitude is that the "victims ask for it" (Mahoney et al., 2001)—a pattern that may escalate as women become more sexually active, as described in Hamilton and Armstrong's reading and by others (e.g., Ronen, 2010).

INSTITUTIONALIZED ENFORCEMENT OF GENDER

Although the enforcement of gender mainly occurs in daily activities, as Berger (1963) notes, institutionalized settings also enforce gender. Organizations either participate in or simply ignore more subtle forms of gender enforcement, such as sexual harassment in workplace settings, described in Denissen and Saguy's reading in this chapter. These patterns can be found in schools (e.g., fraternities and school sports teams), the workplace, and men's sports teams (Schact, 1996). Unfortunately, these patterns can even be found in the division of labor among parents who assist with youth sports teams, as Michael A. Messner and Suzel Bozada-Deas describe in their reading in this chapter. In patriarchal societies worldwide, men make the rules (and laws) and write the informal scripts that prescribe behaviors for themselves, other men, and women. These rules, which assume men are the "bosses" and women are the assistants, regardless of individual abilities, become institutionalized in daily patterns of life.

Religion is one institution that often enforces gender difference and inequality. Many religions enforce rules that exclude or segregate women within the practice of that religion. For example, women are excluded from the priesthood in the Catholic Church and marginalized in many other Christian churches (Nesbitt, Baust, & Bailey, 2001). Some Jewish congregations segregate women physically and do not allow women to study the Torah with the same seriousness as men (Rose, 2001). Some Islamic communities also apply rules of gender, such as enforced veiling of women, which women negotiate in a variety of ways (Gerami & Lehnerer, 2001). Religion also defines dichotomous and hierarchical gendered connections in other social institutions, such as the family. Penny Edgell and Danielle Docka (2007) conducted ethnographic studies in three churches, chosen because these churches were serving nontraditional families. They found that churches reinforced a variety of models of families in their programming and preaching, all of which had considerable consequences for the gendered expectations of their parishioners.

In addition, many institutional rules subtly maintain the gendered expectation of the domination of women—including the sexual violation of women by men. Politicians, police, and traffickers construct and maintain the rules supporting human trafficking of women for the sex trade (Kempadoo & Doezema, 1998). These rules allow girls and women to enter countries under dubious documentation and fail to provide the help that trafficked girls and women need to escape lives of prostitution and abuse (Kempadoo & Doezema, 1998). The women sold into virtual sexual slavery, and the men and women who take advantage of vulnerable girls and women, are part of a brutal pattern of gender enforcement. For example, one study of trafficking of women for sex/prostitution estimates that Indonesian women are most likely to go to Japan, Malaysia, and probably Singapore. They are lured to these places by the possibility of jobs in karaoke bars as singers or, in Japan, as cultural ambassadors (American Center for International Labor Solidarity, 2005). Unfortunately, they are forced into and kept in the sex trade by withholding of salary or immigration documents, or by the need to pay off the "debt" they incurred to get to the country. Other women face similar situations as they are forced into domestic labor. The trafficking of women in both contexts helps maintain domination and control of women.

Sexual Harassment

In their reading in this chapter, Denissen and Saguy describe situations that are considered to be sexual harassment. The definition of sexual harassment includes two different types of behaviors (Welsh, 1999). Quid pro quo harassment is that which involves the use of sexual threats or bribery to make employment decisions. Supervisors who threaten to withhold a promotion to someone they supervise unless that person has sex with them engage in quid pro quo harassment. The second form of sexual harassment is termed "hostile environment" harassment, which the U.S. Equal Employment Opportunity Commission defines as consisting of behavior that creates an "intimidating, hostile, or offensive working environment" (Welsh, 1999, p. 170). A hostile environment occurs when a company allows situations that interfere with an individual's job performance.

Unfortunately, we do not know exactly how prevalent sexual harassment is. Reports of the incidence of sexual harassment are not consistent, primarily because of the various ways sexual harassment is measured across studies (Welsh, 1999). Different studies report that anywhere from 16% to 90% of women experience sexual harassment at their workplace (Welsch, 1999). One study summarized 18 different surveys and estimated the prevalence rate of sexual harassment at 44% (Welsh, 1999). Any incidence of sexual harassment, however, creates an uncomfortable workplace for the target and perpetuates gender inequality.

Sexual harassment begins early in school settings, even among young schoolchildren (Hand & Sanchez, 2000; National Coalition for Women and Girls in Education [NCWGE], 2012). Although the experience of harassment is greater for girls, with more than half of the girls and 40% of the boys in a 2010 to 2011 survey reporting being sexually harassed (NCWGE, 2012), girls also endure the more demeaning forms of harassment and at a higher rate than do boys (Hand & Sanchez, 2000). Lesbian, gay, bisexual, and transgender youths also experience high levels of sexual harassment, with 85% of those responding to the 2010 to 2011 survey indicating that they had experienced sexual harassment and 19% indicating physical attack.

Unfortunately, sexual harassment continues long beyond high school, as noted by Denissen and Saguy in this chapter, and helps enforce gender and heterosexuality. Their reading helps us understand how sexual harassment enforces gender for men and women by creating a wall that makes it impossible for co-workers to relate on an equal basis.

Sometimes we see gender enforcement only when we look at someone else's life circumstances, such as the roles of mothers and fathers in supporting youth sports in Messner and Bozada-Deas's article, the reports of men's use of intimidation on the job as in Denissen and Saguy's article, or Melzer's descriptions of men who endorse violence as a way to declare masculinity. Think about your life as you read this chapter and consider the ways conformity to gender is enforced among the people you know and observe, including yourself.

REFERENCES

American Center for International Labor Solidarity. (2005). *When they were sold: Trafficking of women and girls in 15 provinces of Indonesia.* Retrieved from http://www.solidaritycenter.org/publication/when-they-were-sold-trafficking-of-women-and-girls-in-15-provinces-of-indonesia-2006

Bachar, K., & Koss, M. P. (2001). From prevalence to prevention: Closing the gap between what we know about rape and what we do. In C. M. Renzetti, J. L. Edleson, & R. K. Bergen (Eds.), *Sourcebook on violence against women* (pp. 117–142). Thousand Oaks, CA: Sage.

Berger, P. L. (1963). *An invitation to sociology: A humanistic perspective.* Garden City, NY: Anchor Books.

Boswell, A., & Spade, J. Z. (1996). Fraternities and rape culture: Why are some fraternities more dangerous places for women? *Gender & Society, 10*(2), 133–147.

Breiding, M. J., Smith, S. G., Basile, K. C., Walters, M. L., Chen, J., & Merrick, M. T. (2014, September 5). Prevalence and characteristics of sexual violence, stalking, and intimate partner violence victimization—National Intimate Partner and Sexual Violence Survey, United States, 2011: Surveillance summaries. *Morbidity and Mortality Weekly Report (MMWR), 63*(SS08), 1–18. Retrieved from http://www.cdc.gov/mmwr/preview/mmwrhtml/ss6308a1.htm?s_cid=ss6308a1_e

Bureau of Justice Statistics. (2012). *National Crime Victimization Survey: Victimizations not reported to the police, 2006–2010* (NCJ Report No. 238536). Washington, DC: U.S. Department of Justice. Retrieved from http://www.bjs.gov/content/pub/pdf/vnrp0610.pdf

Carey, K. B., Durney, S. E., Shepardson, R. L., & Carey, M. P. (2015). Incapacitated and forcible rape of college women: Prevalence across the first year. *Journal of Adolescent Health, 56*(6), 670–680.

Catalano, Shannan. (2013, November). *Intimate partner violence: Attributes of victimization, 1993–2011* (NCJ Report No. 243300). Washington, DC: U.S. Department of Justice. Retrieved from http://www.bjs.gov/content/pub/pdf/ipvav9311.pdf

Centers for Disease Control and Prevention. (2012). *Understanding intimate partner violence: Fact sheet.* Retrieved from http://www.cdc.gov/violenceprevention/pdf/ipv_factsheet-a.pdf

Edgell, P., & Docka, D. (2007). Beyond the nuclear family: Familialism and gender ideology in diverse religious communities. *Sociological Forum, 22*(1), 25–50.

Edwards, K. M., Turchik, J. A., Dardis, C. M., Reynolds, N., & Gidycz, C. A. (2011). Rape myths: History, individual and institutional-level presence, and implications for change. *Sex Roles, 65,* 761–773.

Fisher, B. S., Cullen, F. T., & Turner, M. G. (2000). *The sexual victimization of college women.* Washington, DC: Bureau of Justice Statistics.

Retrieved from https://www.ncjrs.gov/pdffiles1/nij/182369.pdf

Gerami, S., & Lehnerer, M. (2001). Women's agency and household diplomacy: Negotiating fundamentalism. *Gender & Society, 15*(4), 556–573.

Hand, J. Z., & Sanchez, L. (2000). Badgering or bantering? Gender differences in experience of, and reactions to, sexual harassment among U.S. high school students. *Gender & Society, 14*(6), 718–746.

Hlavka, H. (2014). Normalizing sexual violence: Young women account for harassment and abuse. *Gender & Society, 28*(3), 337–358.

Kempadoo, K., & Doezema, J. (1998). *Global sex workers: Rights, resistance, and redefinition.* New York: Routledge.

Mahoney, P., Williams, L. M., & West, C. M. (2001). Violence against women by intimate relationship partners. In C. M. Renzetti, J. L. Edleson, & R. K. Bergen (Eds.), *Sourcebook on violence against women* (pp. 143–178). Thousand Oaks, CA: Sage.

National Coalition for Women and Girls in Education. (2012). *Title IX at 40: Working to ensure gender equality in education.* Washington, DC: Author.

Nesbitt, P., Baust, J., & Bailey, E. (2001). Women's status in the Christian church. In D. Vannoy (Ed.), *Gender mosaics: Societal perspectives* (pp. 386–396). Los Angeles: Roxbury.

Peacock, D., & Barker, G. (2014). Working with men and boys to prevent gender-based violence: Principles, lessons learned, and ways forward. *Men and Masculinities 17*(5), 578–599.

Rennison, C. M. (2002). *Rape and sexual assault: Reporting to police and medical attention, 1992–2000.* Retrieved from http://bjs.ojp.usdoj.gov/content/pub/pdf/rsarp00.pdf

Ronen, S. (2010). Grinding on the dance floor: Gendered scripts and sexualized dancing at college parties. *Gender & Society, 24*(3), 355–377.

Rose, D. R. (2001). Gender and Judaism. In D. Vannoy (Ed.), *Gender mosaics: Societal perspectives* (pp. 415–424). Los Angeles: Roxbury.

Ryan, K. M. (2011). The relationship between rape myths and sexual scripts: The social construction of rape. *Sex Roles, 65,* 774–782.

Schact, S. P. (1996). Misogyny on and off the "pitch": The gendered world of male rugby players. *Gender & Society, 10*(5), 550–565.

Sinozich, S. & Langton, L. (2014). *Rape and sexual assault victimization among college-age females, 1995–2013* (NCJ Report No. 248471). Washington, DC: U.S. Department of Justice. Retrieved from http://www.bjs.gov/content/pub/pdf/rsavcaf9513.pdf

Weiss, K. G. (2010). Male sexual victimization: Examining men's experiences of rape and sexual assault. *Men and Masculinities, 12*(3), 275–298.

Welsh, S. (1999). Gender and sexual harassment. *Annual Review of Sociology, 25,* 169–190.

Introduction to Reading 42

Norms that define women as essentially sexually passive were challenged as *Sex and the City* and *Fifty Shades of Grey* hit television and movie screens. However, did they actually change the way the expression of sexuality is used to enforce gender inequality? This article would suggest that although things have changed, sexuality is still gendered. In this reading, Laura Hamilton and Elizabeth A. Armstrong report their findings from a 4-year ethnographic and interview study of women at a midwestern university. The study began in 2004, when the authors, along with seven other researchers, "occupied" a room on a dormitory floor in what students identified as a "party dorm." In addition to observing and hanging out with the women, they also conducted interviews with 41 of the 53 women who lived on this floor during the first year. This particular paper summarizes the women's reports about hooking up and relationships and how both changed over the course of their study. Their focus on social interaction is particularly valuable in understanding how gender is understood and enforced within the inner circles of Peter L. Berger's concentric rings of social control, by ourselves and those closest to us, as described in the introduction to this chapter. In addition, the authors provide an intersectional analysis, examining how interaction and meaning of these college relationships vary across social class for the young women they studied. Their findings help us think about how gender continues to influence the expression of sexuality in a world where permanent relationships are delayed and "sex" is the theme for young women as well as men. They also help us understand that gender enforcement, while not consistent, is patterned within intersections of different prisms, such as gender and social class in this piece.

1. How do the women in this study describe "hooking up," and what factors influence their orientation to this expression of sexuality?

2. How did gender influence the expression of sexuality differently for women from different social classes in this study?

3. Do you think heterosexuality will be less important in the future in enforcing gender difference and inequality than it has been in the past? Why or why not?

Gendered Sexuality in Young Adulthood

Double Binds and Flawed Options

Laura Hamilton and Elizabeth A. Armstrong

As traditional dating has declined on college campuses, hookups—casual sexual encounters often initiated at alcohol-fueled, dance-oriented social events—have become a primary form of intimate heterosexual interaction (England, Shafer, and Fogarty 2007; Paul, McManus, and Hayes 2000). Hookups have attracted attention among social scientists and journalists (Bogle 2008; Glenn and Marquardt 2001; Stepp 2007). To date, however, limitations of both data and theory have obscured the implications for women and the gender system. Most studies examine only the quality of hookups at one point during college and rely, if implicitly, on an individualist, gender-only approach. In contrast, we follow a group of women as they move through college—assessing all of their sexual experiences. We use an interactionist approach and attend to how both gender and class shape college sexuality. . . .

GENDER THEORY AND COLLEGE SEXUALITY

Research on Hooking Up

Paul, McManus, and Hayes (2000) and Glenn and Marquardt (2001) were the first to draw attention to the hookup as a distinct social form. As Glenn and Marquardt (2001, 13) explain, most students agree that "a hook up is anything 'ranging from kissing to having sex,' and that it

From Hamilton, Laura and Elizabeth A. Armstrong. 2009. "Gendered sexuality in young adulthood: Double binds and flawed options." *Gender & Society* 23(5): 259–616. Published by Sage Publications on behalf of Sociologists for Women in Society.

takes place outside the context of commitment." Others have similarly found that *hooking up* refers to a broad range of sexual activity and that this ambiguity is part of the appeal of the term (Bogle 2008). Hookups differ from dates in that individuals typically do not plan to do something together prior to sexual activity. Rather, two people hanging out at a party, bar, or place of residence will begin talking, flirting, and/or dancing. Typically, they have been drinking. At some point, they move to a more private location, where sexual activity occurs (England, Shafer, and Fogarty 2007). While strangers sometimes hook up, more often hookups occur among those who know each other at least slightly (Manning, Giordano, and Longmore 2006).

England has surveyed more than 14,000 students from 19 universities and colleges about their hookup, dating, and relationship experiences. Her Online College Social Life Survey (OCSLS) asks students to report on their recent hookups using "whatever definition of a hookup you and your friends use." Seventy-two percent of both men and women participating in the OCSLS reported at least one hookup by their senior year in college. Of these, roughly 40 percent engaged in three or fewer hookups, 40 percent between four and nine hookups, and 20 percent 10 or more hookups. Only about one-third engaged in intercourse in their most recent hookups, although—among the 80 percent of students who had intercourse by the end of college—67 percent had done so outside of a relationship.

Ongoing sexual relationships without commitment were common and were labeled "repeat," "regular," or "continuing" hookups and sometimes "friends with benefits" (Armstrong, England, and Fogarty 2009; Bogle 2008; Glenn and Marquardt 2001). Ongoing hookups sometimes became committed relationships and vice versa; generally, the distinction revolved around the level of exclusivity and a willingness to refer to each other as "girlfriend/boyfriend" (Armstrong, England, and Fogarty 2009). Thus, hooking up does not imply interest in a relationship, but it does not preclude such interest. Relationships are also common among students. By their senior year, 69 percent of heterosexual students had been in a college relationship of at least six months.

To date, however, scholars have paid more attention to women's experiences with hooking up than relationships and focused primarily on ways that hookups may be less enjoyable for women than for men. Glenn and Marquardt (2001, 20) indicate that "hooking up is an activity that women sometimes find rewarding but more often find confusing, hurtful, and awkward." Others similarly suggest that more women than men find hooking up to be a negative experience (Bogle 2008, 173; Owen et al. 2008) and focus on ways that hookups may be harmful to women (Eshbaugh and Gute 2008; Grello, Welsh, and Harper 2006).

This work assumes distinct and durable gender differences at the individual level. Authors draw, if implicitly, from evolutionary psychology, socialization, and psychoanalytic approaches to gender—depicting women as more relationally oriented and men as more sexually adventurous (see Wharton 2005 for a review). For example, despite only asking about hookup experiences, Bogle (2008, 173) describes a "battle of the sexes" in which women want hookups to "evolve into some semblance of a relationship," while men prefer to "hook up with no strings attached" (also see Glenn and Marquardt 2001; Stepp 2007).

The battle of the sexes view implies that if women could simply extract commitment from men rather than participating in hookups, gender inequalities in college sexuality would be alleviated. Yet this research—which often fails to examine relationships—ignores the possibility that women might be the losers in both hookups and relationships. Research suggests that young heterosexual women often suffer the most damage from those with whom they are most intimate: Physical battery, emotional abuse, sexual assault, and stalking occur at high rates in youthful heterosexual relationships (Campbell et al. 2007; Dunn 1999). This suggests that gender inequality in college sexuality is systemic, existing across social forms.

Current research also tends to see hooking up as solely about gender, without fully considering the significance of other dimensions of inequality. Some scholars highlight the importance of the college environment and traditional college students' position in the life course (Bogle 2008; Glenn and Marquardt 2001). However, college is treated primarily as a context for individual sexual behavior rather than as a key location for class reproduction. Analyzing the role of social class in sex and relationships may help to illuminate the appeal of hookups for both college women and men.

Gender Beliefs and Social Interaction

Contemporary gender theory provides us with resources to think about gender inequality in college sexuality differently. Gender scholars have developed and refined the notion of gender as a social structure reproduced at multiple levels of society: Gender is embedded not only in individual selves but also in interaction and organizational arrangements (Connell 1987; Glenn 1999; Risman 2004). This paper focuses on the interactional level, attending to the power of public gender beliefs in organizing college sexual and romantic relations.

Drawing on Sewell's (1992) theory of structure, Ridgeway and Correll (2004, 511) define gender beliefs as the "cultural rules or instructions for enacting the social structure of difference and inequality that we understand to be gender." By believing in gender differences, individuals "see" them in interaction and hold others accountable to this perception. Thus, even if individuals do not internalize gender beliefs, they must still confront them (Ridgeway 2009).

Ridgeway and coauthors (Ridgeway 2000; Ridgeway and Correll 2004) assert that interaction is particularly important to the reproduction of gender inequality because of how frequently men and women interact. They focus on the workplace but suggest that gendered interaction in private life may be intensifying in importance as beliefs about

gender difference in workplace competency diminish (Correll, Benard, and Paik 2007; Ridgeway 2000; Ridgeway and Correll 2004). We extend their insights to sexual interaction, as it is in sexuality and reproduction that men and women are believed to be most different. The significance of gender beliefs in sexual interaction may be magnified earlier in the life course, given the amount of time spent in interaction with peers and the greater malleability of selves (Eder, Evans, and Parker 1995). Consequently, the university provides an ideal site for this investigation.

The notion that men and women have distinct sexual interests and needs generates a powerful set of public gender beliefs about women's sexuality. A belief about what women should not do underlies a *sexual double standard:* While men are expected to desire and pursue sexual opportunities regardless of context, women are expected to avoid casual sex—having sex only when in relationships and in love (Crawford and Popp 2003; Risman and Schwartz 2002). Much research on the sexuality of young men focuses on male endorsement of this belief and its consequences (e.g., Bogle 2008; Kimmel 2008; Martin and Hummer 1989). There is an accompanying and equally powerful belief that normal women should always want love, romance, relationships, and marriage—what we refer to as the *relational imperative* (also see Holland and Eisenhart 1990; Martin 1996; Simon, Eder, and Evans 1992). We argue that these twin beliefs are implicated in the (re)production of gender inequality in college sexuality and are at the heart of women's sexual dilemmas with both hookups and relationships.

An Intersectional Approach

Gender theory has also moved toward an intersectional approach (Collins 1990; Glenn 1999). Most of this work focuses on the lived experiences of marginalized individuals who are situated at the intersection of several systems of oppression (McCall 2005). More recently, scholars have begun to theorize the ways in which systems of inequality are themselves linked (Beisel and Kay 2004; Glenn 1999; McCall 2005). Beisel and Kay

(2004) apply Sewell's (1992) theory of structure to intersectionality, arguing that structures intersect when they share resources or guidelines for action (of which gender beliefs would be one example). Using a similar logic, we argue that gender and class intersect in the sexual arena, as these structures both rely on beliefs about how and with whom individuals should be intimate.

Like gender, class structures beliefs about appropriate sexual and romantic conduct. Privileged young Americans, both men and women, are now expected to defer family formation until the mid-twenties or even early-thirties to focus on education and career investment—what we call the *self-development imperative* (Arnett 2004; Rosenfeld 2007). This imperative makes committed relationships less feasible as the sole contexts for premarital sexuality. Like marriage, relationships can be "greedy," siphoning time and energy away from self-development (Gerstel and Sarkisian 2006; Glenn and Marquardt 2001). In contrast, hookups offer sexual pleasure without derailing investment in human capital and are increasingly viewed as part of life-stage appropriate sexual experimentation. Self-protection—both physical and emotional—is central to this logic, suggesting the rise of a strategic approach to sex and relationships (Brooks 2002; Illouz 2005). This approach is reflected in the development of erotic marketplaces offering short-term sexual partners, particularly on college campuses (Collins 2004).

In this case, gender and class behavioral rules are in conflict. Gender beliefs suggest that young women should avoid nonromantic sex and, if possible, be in a committed relationship. Class beliefs suggest that women should delay relationships while pursuing educational goals. Hookups are often less threatening to self-development projects, offering sexual activity in a way that better meshes with the demands of college. We see this as a case wherein structures intersect, but in a contradictory way (Friedland and Alford 1991; Martin 2004; Sewell 1992). This structural contradiction has experiential consequences: Privileged women find themselves caught between contradictory expectations, while less privileged women confront a foreign sexual culture when they enter college.

* * *

THE POWER OF GENDER BELIEFS . . .

The "Slut" Stigma

Women did not find hookups to be unproblematic. They complained about a pervasive double standard. As one explained, "Guys can have sex with all the girls and *it makes them more of a man,* but if a girl does, then all of a sudden she's a ho, and she's not as quality of a person" ([interview number] 10–1, emphasis added). Another complained, "Guys, they can go around and have sex with a number of girls and they're not called anything" (6–1). Women noted that it was "easy to get a reputation" (11–1) from "hooking up with a bunch of different guys" (8–1) or "being wild and drinking too much" (14–3). Their experiences of being judged were often painful; one woman told us about being called a "slut" two years after the incident because it was so humiliating (42–3).

Fear of stigma constrained women's sexual behavior and perhaps even shaped their preferences. For example, several indicated that they probably would "make out with more guys" but did not because "I don't want to be a slut" (27–2). Others wanted to have intercourse on hookups but instead waited until they had boyfriends. A couple hid their sexual activity until the liaison was "official." One said, "I would not spend the night there [at the fraternity] because that does not look good, but now everyone knows we're boyfriend/girlfriend, so it's like my home now" (15–1). Another woman, who initially seemed to have a deep aversion to hooking up, explained, "I would rather be a virgin for as much as I can than go out and do God knows who." She later revealed a fear of social stigma, noting that when women engage in nonromantic sex, they "get a bad reputation. I know that I wouldn't want that reputation" (11–1). Her comments highlight the feedback between social judgment and internalized preference.

Gender beliefs were also at the root of women's other chief complaint about hookups—the disrespect of women in the hookup scene. The notion that hooking up is okay for men but not for women was embedded in the organization of the Greek system, where most parties occurred: Sorority rules prohibited hosting parties or overnight male visitors, reflecting notions about proper feminine behavior. In contrast, fraternities collected social fees to pay for alcohol and viewed hosting parties as a central activity. This disparity gave fraternity men almost complete control over the most desirable parties on campus—particularly for the underage crowd (Boswell and Spade 1996; Martin and Hummer 1989).

Women reported that fraternity men dictated party transportation, the admittance of guests, party themes such as "CEO and secretary ho," the flow of alcohol, and the movement of guests within the party (Armstrong, Hamilton, and Sweeney 2006). Women often indicated that they engaged in strategies such as "travel[ing] in hordes" (21–1) and not "tak[ing] a drink if I don't know where it came from" (15–1) to feel safer at fraternity parties. Even when open to hooking up, women were not comfortable doing so if they sensed that men were trying to undermine their control of sexual activity (e.g., by pushing them to drink too heavily, barring their exit from private rooms, or refusing them rides home). Women typically opted not to return to party venues they perceived as unsafe. As one noted, "I wouldn't go to [that house] because I heard they do bad things to girls" (14–1). Even those interested in the erotic competition of party scenes tired of it as they realized that the game was rigged.

The sexual double standard also justified the negative treatment of women in the party scene—regardless of whether they chose to hook up. Women explained that men at parties showed a lack of respect for their feelings or interests—treating them solely as "sex objects" (32–1). This disregard extended to hookups. One told us, "The guy gets off and then it's done and that's all he cares about" (12–4). Another complained of

her efforts to get a recent hookup to call: "That wasn't me implying I wanted a relationship—that was me implying I wanted respect" (42–2). In her view, casual sex did not mean forgoing all interactional niceties. A third explained, "If you're talking to a boy, you're either going to get into this huge relationship or you are nothing to them" (24–3). This either-or situation often frustrated women who wanted men to treat them well regardless of the level of commitment.

The Relationship Imperative

Women also encountered problematic gender beliefs about men's and women's different levels of interest in relationships. As one noted, women fight the "dumb girl idea"—the notion "that every girl wants a boy to sweep her off her feet and fall in love" (42–2). The expectation that women should want to be in relationships was so pervasive that many found it necessary to justify their single status to us. For example, when asked if she had a boyfriend, one woman with no shortage of admirers apologetically explained, "I know this sounds really pathetic and you probably think I am lying, but there are so many other things going on right now that it's really not something high up on my list. . . . I know that's such a lame-ass excuse, but it's true" (9–3). Another noted that already having a boyfriend was the only "actual, legitimate excuse" to reject men who expressed interest in a relationship (34–3).

Certainly, many women wanted relationships and sought them out. However, women's interest in relationships varied, and almost all experienced periods during which they wanted to be single. Nonetheless, women reported pressure to be in relationships all the time. We found that women, rather than struggling to get into relationships, had to work to avoid them.

The relational imperative was supported by the belief that women's relational opportunities were scarce and should not be wasted. Women described themselves as "lucky" to find a man willing to commit, as "there's not many guys like that in college" (15–1). This belief persisted despite the fact that most women were in relationships most of the time. As one woman noted, "I don't think anyone really wants to be in a serious relationship, but most, well actually all of us, have boyfriends" (13–1). Belief in the myth of scarcity also led women to stay in relationships when they were no longer happy. A woman who was "sick of" her conflict-ridden relationship explained why she could not end it: "I feel like I have to meet somebody else. . . . I go out and they're all these asshole frat guys. . . . That's what stops me. . . . Boys are not datable right now because . . . all they're looking for is freshman girls to hook up with. . . . [So] I'm just stuck. I need to do something about it, but I don't know what" (30–3). It took her another year to extract herself from this relationship. Despite her fears, when she decided she was ready for another relationship, she quickly found a boyfriend.

Women also confronted the belief that all women are relationally insatiable. They often told stories of men who acted entitled to relationships, expected their relational overtures to be accepted, and became angry when rebuffed— sometimes stalking the rejecting woman. As one explained about a friend, "Abby was having issues with this guy who likes her. He was like, 'You have to like me. . . . I'm not gonna take no for an answer. I'm gonna do whatever it takes to date you'" (24–3). Another noted that "last semester, this guy really wanted to date me, and I did not want to date him at all. He flipped out and was like, 'This is ridiculous, I don't deserve this'" (12–3). A third eventually gave in when a man continually rejected her refusals: "I was like, if I go [out with him] . . . maybe he'll stop. Because he wouldn't stop." She planned to act "extremely conservative" as a way to convince him that he did not want to be with her (39–4).

Gender beliefs may also limit women's control over the terms of interaction within relationships. If women are made to feel lucky to have boyfriends, men are placed in a position of power, as presumably women should be grateful when they commit. Women's reports suggest that men attempted to use this power to regulate their participation in college life. One noted, "When I got here my first semester freshman year, I wanted to go out to the parties . . . and he got pissed off about it. . . . He's like, 'Why do you need to do that? Why can't you just stay with me?'" (4–2). Boyfriends sometimes tried to limit the time women spent with their friends and the activities in which they participated. As a woman explained, "There are times when I feel like Steve can get . . . possessive. He'll be like . . . 'I feel like you're always with your friends over me.' He wanted to go out to lunch after our class, and I was like, 'No, I have to come have this interview.' And he got so upset about it" (42–3). Men's control even extended to women's attire. Another told us about her boyfriend, "He is a very controlling person. . . . He's like, 'What are you wearing tonight?' . . . It's like a joke but serious at the same time" (32–4).

Women also became jealous; however, rather than trying to control their boyfriends, they often tried to change themselves. One noted that she would "do anything to make this relationship work." She elaborated, "I was so nervous being with Dan because I knew he had cheated on his [prior] girlfriend . . . [but] I'm getting over it. When I go [to visit him] now . . . I let him go to the bar, whatever. I stayed in his apartment because there was nothing else to do" (39–3). Other women changed the way they dressed, their friends, and where they went in the attempt to keep boyfriends.

When women attempted to end relationships, they often reported that men's efforts to control them escalated. We heard 10 accounts of men using abuse to keep women in relationships. One woman spent months dealing with a boyfriend who accused her of cheating on him. When she tried to break up, he cut his wrist in her apartment (9–2). Another tried to end a relationship but was forced to flee the state when her car windows were broken and her safety was threatened (6–4). Men often drew on romantic repertoires to coerce interaction after relationships had ended. One woman told us that her ex-boyfriend stalked her for months—even showing up at her workplace, showering her with flowers and gifts, and blocking her entry into work until the police arrived (25–2).

INTERSECTIONALITY: CONTRADICTIONS BETWEEN CLASS AND GENDER

Existing research about college sexuality focuses almost exclusively on its gendered nature. We contend that sexuality is shaped simultaneously by multiple intersecting structures. In this section, we examine the sexual and romantic implications of class beliefs about how ambitious young people should conduct themselves during college. Although all of our participants contended with class beliefs that contradicted those of gender, experiences of this structural intersection varied by class location. More privileged women struggled to meet gender and class guidelines for sexual behavior, introducing a difficult set of double binds. Because these class beliefs reflected a privileged path to adulthood, less privileged women found them foreign to their own sexual and romantic logics.

More Privileged Women and the Experience of Double Binds

The Self-Development Imperative and the Relational Double Bind

The four-year university is a classed structural location. One of the primary reasons to attend college is to preserve or enhance economic position. The university culture is thus characterized by the self-development imperative, or the notion that individual achievement and personal growth are paramount. There are also accompanying rules for sex and relationships: Students are expected to postpone marriage and parenthood until after completing an education and establishing a career.

For more privileged women, personal expectations and those of the university culture meshed. Even those who enjoyed relationships experienced phases in college where they preferred to remain single. Almost all privileged women (94 percent) told us at one point that they did not want a boyfriend. One noted, "All my friends here . . . they're like, 'I don't want to deal with [a boyfriend] right now. I want to be on my own'" (37–1). Another eloquently remarked, "I've always looked at college as the only time in your life when you should be a hundred percent selfish. . . . I have the rest of my life to devote to a husband or kids or my job . . . but right now, it's my time" (21–2).

The notion that independence is critical during college reflected class beliefs about the appropriate role for romance that opposed those of gender. During college, relational commitments were supposed to take a backseat to self-development. As an upper-middle-class woman noted, "College is the only time that you don't have obligations to anyone but yourself. . . . I want to get settled down and figure out what I'm doing with my life before [I] dedicate myself to something or someone else" (14–4). Another emphasized the value of investment in human capital: "I've always been someone who wants to have my own money, have my own career so that, you know, 50 percent of marriages fail. . . . If I want to maintain the lifestyle that I've grown up with . . . I have to work. I just don't see myself being someone who marries young and lives off of some boy's money" (42–4). To become self-supporting, many privileged women indicated they needed to postpone marriage. One told us, "I don't want to think about that [marriage]. I want to get secure in a city and in a job. . . . I'm not in any hurry at all. As long as I'm married by 30, I'm good" (13–4). Even those who wanted to be supported by husbands did not expect to find them in college, instead setting their sights on the more accomplished men they expected to meet in urban centers after college.

More privileged women often found committed relationships to be greedy—demanding of time and energy. As one stated, "When it comes to a serious relationship, it's a lot for me to give into that. [What do you feel like you are giving up?] Like my everything. . . . There's just a lot involved in it" (35–3). These women feared that they would be devoured by relationships and sometimes struggled to keep their self-development projects going when they did get involved. As an upper-class woman told us, "It's hard to have a boyfriend and be really excited about it and still not let it consume you" (42–2). This situation was exacerbated by the gender beliefs discussed earlier, as women experienced pressure to fully devote themselves to relationships.

Privileged women reported that committed relationships detracted from what they saw as the main tasks of college. They complained, for example, that relationships made it difficult to meet people. As an upper-middle-class woman who had just ended a relationship described, "I'm happy that I'm able to go out and meet new people. . . . I feel like I'm doing what a college student should be doing. I don't need to be tied down to my high school boyfriend for two years when this is the time to be meeting people" (14–3). A middle-class woman similarly noted that her relationship with her boyfriend made it impossible to make friends on the floor her first year. She explained, "We were together every day. . . . It was the critical time of making friends and meeting people, [and] I wasn't there" (21–2).

Many also complained that committed relationships competed with schoolwork (also see Holland and Eisenhart 1990). An upper-middle-class woman remarked, "[My boyfriend] doesn't understand why I can't pick up and go see him all the time. But I have school. . . . I just want to be a college kid" (18–3). Another told us that her major was not compatible with the demands of a boyfriend. She said, "I wouldn't mind having a boyfriend again, but it's a lot of work. Right now with [my major] and everything . . . I wouldn't have time even to see him" (30–4). She did not plan to consider a relationship until her workload lessened.

With marriage far in the future, more privileged women often worried about college relationships getting too serious too fast. All planned to marry—ideally to men with greater earnings—but were clear about the importance of temporary independence. Consequently, some worked to slow the progression of relationships. One told us, "I won't let myself think that [I love him]. I definitely don't say that. . . . The person he loves is the person he is going to marry. . . . At the age we are at now, I feel like I don't want anything to be more serious than it has to be until it is" (34–3). Eight privileged women even dated men they deemed unsuitable for marriage to ensure autonomy. One noted, "He fits my needs now because I don't want to get married now. I don't want anyone else to influence what I do after I graduate" (33–3). Others planned to end relationships when boyfriends were not on the same page. An upper-middle-class woman explained, "[He] wants to have two kids by the time he's thirty. I'm like, I guess we're not getting married. . . . I'd rather make money and travel first" (43–3).

For more privileged women, contradictory cultural rules created what we call the *relational double bind*. The relational imperative pushed them to participate in committed relationships; however, relationships did not mesh well with the demands of college, as they inhibited classed self-development strategies. Privileged women struggled to be both "good girls" who limited their sexual activity to relationships and "good students" who did not allow relational commitments to derail their educational and career development.

The Appeal of Hookups and the Sexual Double Bind

In contrast, hookups fit well with the self-development imperative of college. They allowed women to be sexual without the demands of relationships. For example, one upper-class woman described hooking up as "fun and non-threatening." She noted, "So many of us girls, we complain that these guys just want to hook up all the time. I'm going, these guys that I'm attracted to . . . get kind of serious." She saw her last hookup as ideal because "we were physical, and that was it. I never wanted it to go anywhere" (34–2). Many privileged women understood, if implicitly, that hooking up was a delay tactic, allowing sex without participation in serious relationships.

As a sexual solution for the demands of college, hooking up became incorporated into notions of what the college experience should be. When asked which kinds of people hook up the most, one woman noted, "All. . . . The people who came to college to have a good time and party" (14–1). With the help of media, alcohol, and spring break industries, hooking up was so institutionalized that many took it for granted. One upper-middle-class woman said, "It just happens. It's natural" (15–1). They told us that learning about sexuality was something they were supposed to be doing in college. Another described, "I'm glad that I've had my one-night stands and my being in love and having sex. . . . Now I know what it's supposed to feel like when I'm with someone that I want to be with. I feel bad for some of my friends. . . . They're still virgins" (29–1).

High rates of hooking up suggest genuine interest in the activity rather than simply accommodation to men's interests. Particularly early in college, privileged women actively sought hookups. One noted, "You see a lot of people who are like, 'I just want to hook up with someone tonight.' . . . It's always the girls that try to get the guys" (41–1). Data from the OCSLS also suggest that college women like hooking up almost as much as men and are not always searching for something more. Nearly as many women as men (85 percent and 89 percent, respectively) report enjoying the sexual activity of their last hookup "very much" or "somewhat," and less than half of women report interest in a relationship with their most recent hookup.

In private, several privileged women even used the classed logic of hooking up to challenge stereotyped portrayals of gender differences in sexuality. As one noted, "There are girls that want things as much as guys do. There are girls that want things more, and they're like, 'Oh it's

been a while [since I had sex].' The girls are no more innocent than the guys. . . . People think girls are jealous of relationships, but they're like, 'What? I want to be single'" (34–1). When asked about the notion that guys want sex and girls want relationships another responded, "I think that is the absolute epitome of bullshit. I know so many girls who honestly go out on a Friday night and they're like, 'I hope I get some ass tonight.' They don't wanna have a boyfriend! They just wanna hook up with someone. And I know boys who want relationships. I think it goes both ways" (42–2). These women drew on gender-neutral understandings of sexuality characteristic of university culture to contradict the notion of women's sexuality as inevitably and naturally relational.

For more privileged women, enjoyment of hookups was tightly linked to the atmosphere in which they occurred. Most were initiated at college parties where alcohol, music, attractive people, sexy outfits, and flirting combined to generate a collective erotic energy. As one woman enthusiastically noted, "Everyone was so excited. It was a big fun party" (15–1). Privileged women often "loved" it when they had an "excuse to just let loose" and "grind" on the dance floor. They reported turning on their "make-out radar" (18–1), explaining that "it's fun to know that a guy's attracted to you and is willing to kiss you" (16–1). The party scene gave them a chance to play with adult sexualities and interact for purely sexual purposes—an experience that one middle-class woman claimed "empowered" her (17–1).

Hookups enabled more privileged women to conduct themselves in accordance with class expectations, but as we demonstrated earlier, the enforcement of gender beliefs placed them at risk of sanction. This conflict gets to the heart of a *sexual double bind:* While hookups protected privileged women from relationships that could derail their ambitions, the double standard gave men greater control over the terms of hooking up, justified the disrespectful treatment of women, supported sexual stigma, and produced feelings of shame.

Less Privileged Women and the Experience of Foreign Sexual Culture

Women's comfort with delaying commitment and participating in the hookup culture was shaped by class location. College culture reflects the beliefs of the more privileged classes. Less privileged women arrived at college with their own orientation to sex and romance, characterized by a faster transition into adulthood. They often attempted to build both relationships and career at the same time. As a result, a third of the participants from less privileged backgrounds often experienced the hookup culture as foreign in ways that made it difficult to persist at the university.

Less privileged women had less exposure to the notion that the college years should be set aside solely for educational and career development. Many did not see serious relationships as incompatible with college life. Four were married or engaged before graduating—a step that others would not take until later. One reminisced, "I thought I'd get married in college. . . . When I was still in high school, I figured by my senior year, I'd be engaged or married or something. . . . I wanted to have kids before I was 25" (25–4). Another spoke of her plans to marry her high school sweetheart: "I'll be 21 and I know he's the one I want to spend the rest of my life with. . . . Really, I don't want to date anybody else" (6–1).

Plans to move into adult roles relatively quickly made less privileged women outsiders among their more privileged peers. One working-class woman saw her friendships dissolve as she revealed her desire to marry and have children in the near future. As one of her former friends described,

> She would always talk about how she couldn't wait to get married and have babies. . . . It was just like, Whoa. I'm 18. . . . Slow down, you know? Then she just crazy dropped out of school and wouldn't contact any of us. . . . The way I see it is that she's from a really small town, and that's what everyone in her town does . . . get married and have babies. That's all she ever wanted to do maybe? . . . I don't know if she was homesick or didn't fit in. (24–4)

This account glosses over the extent to which the working-class woman was pushed out of the university—ostracized by her peers for not acclimating to the self-development imperative and, as noted below, to the campus sexual climate. In fact, 40 percent of less privileged women left the university, compared to 5 percent of more privileged women. In all cases, mismatch between the sexual culture of women's hometowns and that of college was a factor in the decision to leave.

Most of the less privileged women found the hookup culture to be not only foreign but hostile. As the working-class woman described above told us,

> I tried so hard to fit in with what everybody else was doing here. . . . I think one morning I just woke up and realized that this isn't me at all; I don't like the way I am right now. . . . I didn't feel like I was growing up. I felt like I was actually getting younger the way I was trying to act. Growing up to me isn't going out and getting smashed and sleeping around. . . . That to me is immature. (28–1)

She emphasized the value of "growing up" in college. Without the desire to postpone adulthood, less privileged women often could not understand the appeal of hooking up. As a lower-middle-class woman noted, "Who would be interested in just meeting somebody and then doing something that night? And then never talking to them again? . . . I'm supposed to do this; I'm supposed to get drunk every weekend. I'm supposed to go to parties every weekend . . . and I'm supposed to enjoy it like everyone else. But it just doesn't appeal to me" (5–1). She reveals the extent to which hooking up was a normalized part of college life: For those who were not interested in this, college life could be experienced as mystifying, uncomfortable, and alienating.

The self-development imperative was a resource women could use in resisting the gendered pull of relationships. Less privileged women did not have as much access to this resource and were invested in settling down. Thus, they found it hard to resist the pull back home of local boyfriends, who—unlike the college men they had met—seemed interested in marrying and having children soon. One woman noted after transferring to a branch campus, "I think if I hadn't been connected with [my fiancé], I think I would have been more strongly connected to [the college town], and I think I probably would have stayed" (2–4). Another described her hometown boyfriend: "He'll be like, 'I want to see you. Come home.' . . . The stress he was putting me under and me being here my first year. I could not take it" (7–2). The following year, she moved back home. A third explained about her husband, "He wants me at home. . . . He wants to have control over me and . . . to feel like he's the dominant one in the relationship. . . . The fact that I'm going to school and he knows I'm smart and he knows that I'm capable of doing anything that I want . . . it scares him" (6–4). While she eventually ended this relationship, it cost her an additional semester of school.

Women were also pulled back home by the slut stigma, as people there—perhaps out of frustration or jealousy—judged college women for any association with campus sexual culture. For instance, one woman became distraught when a virulent sexual rumor about her circulated around her hometown, especially when it reached her parents. Going home was a way of putting sexual rumors to rest and reaffirming ties that were strained by leaving.

Thus, less privileged women were often caught between two sexual cultures. Staying at the university meant abandoning a familiar logic and adopting a privileged one—investing in human capital while delaying the transition to adulthood. As one explained, attending college led her to revise her "whole plan": "Now I'm like, I don't even need to be getting married yet [or] have kids. . . . All of [my brother's] friends, 17- to 20-year-old girls, have their . . . babies, and I'm like, Oh my God. . . . Now I'll be able to do something else for a couple years before I settle down . . . before I worry about kids" (25–3). These changes in agendas required them to end relationships with men whose life plans

diverged from theirs. For some, this also meant cutting ties with hometown friends. One resolute woman, whose friends back home had turned on her, noted, "I'm just sick of it. There's nothing there for me anymore. There's absolutely nothing there" (22–4).

Discussion

The Strengths of an Interactional Approach

Public gender beliefs are a key source of gender inequality in college heterosexual interaction. They undergird a sexual double standard and a relational imperative that justify the disrespect of women who hook up and the disempowerment of women in relationships—reinforcing male dominance across social forms. Most of the women we studied cycled back and forth between hookups and relationships, in part because they found both to be problematic. These findings indicate that an individualist, battle of the sexes explanation not only is inadequate but may contribute to gender inequality by naturalizing problematic notions of gender difference.

We are not, however, claiming that gender differences in stated preferences do not exist. Analysis of the OCSLS finds a small but significant difference between men and women in preferences for relationships as compared to hookups: After the most recent hookup, 47 percent of women compared to 37 percent of men expressed some interest in a relationship. These differences in preferences are consistent with a multilevel perspective that views the internalization of gender as an aspect of gender structure (Risman 2004). As we have shown, the pressure to internalize gender-appropriate preferences is considerable, and the line between personal preferences and the desire to avoid social stigma is fuzzy. However, we believe that widely shared beliefs about gender difference contribute more to gender inequality in college heterosexuality than the substantively small differences in actual preferences.

The Strengths of an Intersectional Approach

An intersectional approach sheds light on the ambivalent and contradictory nature of many college women's sexual desires. Class beliefs associated with the appropriate timing of marriage clash with resilient gender beliefs—creating difficult double binds for the more privileged women who strive to meet both. In the case of the relational double bind, relationships fit with gender beliefs but pose problems for the classed self-development imperative. As for the sexual double bind, hookups provide sexual activity with little cost to career development, but a double standard penalizes women for participating. Less privileged women face an even more complex situation: Much of the appeal of hookups derives from their utility as a delay strategy. Women who do not believe that it is desirable to delay marriage may experience the hookup culture as puzzling and immature.

An intersectional approach also suggests that the way young heterosexuals make decisions about sexuality and relationships underlies the reproduction of social class. These choices are part of women's efforts to, as one privileged participant so eloquently put it, "maintain the lifestyle that I've grown up with." Our participants were not well versed in research demonstrating that college-educated women benefit from their own human capital investments, are more likely to marry than less educated women, and are more likely to have a similarly well-credentialed spouse (DiPrete and Buchmann 2006). Nonetheless, most were aware that completing college and delaying marriage until the mid-to-late twenties made economic sense. Nearly all took access to marriage for granted, instead focusing their attention on when and whom they would marry.

The two-pronged strategy of career investment and delay of family formation has so quickly become naturalized that its historical novelty is now invisible. It is based on the consolidation of class, along with heterosexual privilege: Heterosexual men and women attempt to maximize their own earning power and that of their spouse—a pattern that is reflected in increased levels of educational homogamy (Schwatz and Mare 2005; Sweeney 2002). Consolidation of privilege is made possible by women's greater parity with men in education and the workforce. In this new marital marketplace, a woman's educational credentials and earning potential are more relevant than her premarital sexual activity, assuming she avoids having a child before marriage. Relationship commitments that block educational and career investments, particularly if they foreclose future opportunities to meet men with elite credentials, are a threat to a woman's upward mobility.

The gender implications of the consolidation of privilege are most visible when contrasted with gender specialization—a marital strategy once assumed to be universal. Marriage was thought to be a system of complementary interdependence in which the man specialized in the market and the woman in domesticity (Becker 1991). Men maximized earning power while women accessed these benefits by marrying those with greater educational or career credentials. Gender specialization does not logically demand chastity of women; however, historically it has often been offered for trade in the marital marketplace. When this occurs, women's sexual reputation and economic welfare are linked. Although this connection has long been attenuated in the United States, it still exists. For example, the term "classy" refers simultaneously to wealth and sexual modesty.

As marriage in the United States has become less guided by gender specialization and more by the consolidation of privilege, gender inequality—at least within the marriages of the privileged—may have decreased. At the same time, class inequality may have intensified. The consolidation of privilege increases economic gaps between the affluent who are married to each other, the less affluent who are also married to each other, and the poor, who are excluded from marriage altogether (also see Edin and Kefalas 2005; England

2004; Schwartz and Mare 2005; Sweeney 2002). The hookup culture may contribute in a small way to the intensification of class inequality by facilitating the delay necessary for the consolidation of privilege. . . .

REFERENCES

Armstrong, Elizabeth A., Paula England, and Alison C. K. Fogarty. 2009. Orgasm in college hookups and relationships. In *Families as they really are,* edited by B. Risman. New York: Norton.

Armstrong, Elizabeth A., Laura Hamilton, and Brian Sweeney. 2006. Sexual assault on campus: A multilevel, integrative approach to party rape. *Social Problems* 53:483–99.

Arnett, Jeffrey Jensen. 2004. *Emerging adulthood: The winding road from the late teens through the twenties.* New York: Oxford.

Becker, Gary S. 1991. *A treatise on the family.* Cambridge, MA: Harvard University Press.

Beisel, Nicola, and Tamara Kay. 2004. Abortion, race, and gender in nineteenth century America. *American Sociological Review* 69:498–518.

Bogle, Kathleen A. 2008. *Hooking up: Sex, dating, and relationships on campus.* New York: New York University Press.

Boswell, A. Ayres, and Joan Z. Spade. 1996. Fraternities and collegiate rape culture: Why are some fraternities more dangerous places for women? *Gender & Society* 10:133–47.

Brooks, David. 2002. Making it: Love and success at America's finest universities. *The Weekly Standard,* December 23.

Campbell, Jacquelyn C., Nancy Glass, Phyllis W. Sharps, Kathryn Laughon, and Tina Bloom. 2007. Intimate partner homicide. *Trauma, Violence & Abuse* 8:246–69.

Collins, Patricia Hill. 1990. *Black feminist thought: Knowledge, consciousness and the politics of empowerment.* Boston: Unwin Hyman.

Collins, Randall. 2004. *Interaction ritual chains.* Princeton, NJ: Princeton University Press.

Connell, R. W. 1987. *Gender and power: Society, the person, and sexual politics.* Stanford, CA: Stanford University Press.

Correll, Shelley J., Stephen Benard, and In Paik. 2007. Getting a job: Is there a motherhood penalty? *American Journal of Sociology* 112:1297–1338.

Crawford, Mary, and Danielle Popp. 2003. Sexual double standards: A review and methodological critique of two decades of research. *Journal of Sex Research* 40:13–26.

DiPrete, Thomas A., and Claudia Buchmann. 2006. Gender-specific trends in the value of education and the emerging gender gap in college completion. *Demography* 43:1–24.

Dunn, Jennifer L. 1999. What love has to do with it: The cultural construction of emotion and sorority women's responses to forcible interaction. *Social Problems* 46:440–59.

Eder, Donna, Catherine Colleen Evans, and Stephen Parker. 1995. *School talk: Gender and adolescent culture.* New Brunswick, NJ: Rutgers University Press.

Edin, Kathryn, and Maria Kefalas. 2005. *Promises I can keep: Why poor women put motherhood before marriage.* Berkeley: University of California Press.

England, Paula. 2004. More mercenary mate selection? Comment on Sweeney and Cancian (2004) and Press (2004). *Journal of Marriage and the Family* 66:1034–37.

England, Paula, Emily Fitzgibbons Shafer, and Alison C. K. Fogarty. 2007. Hooking up and forming romantic relationships on today's college campuses. In *The gendered society reader,* edited by M. Kimmel. New York: Oxford University Press.

Eshbaugh, Elaine M., and Gary Gute. 2008. Hookups and sexual regret among college women. *Journal of Social Psychology* 148:77–89.

Friedland, Roger, and Robert R. Alford. 1991. Bringing society back in: Symbols. practices, and institutional contradictions. In *The new institutionalism in organizational analysis,* edited by W. W. Powell and P. J. DiMaggio, 232–63. Chicago: University of Chicago Press.

Gerstel, Naomi, and Natalia Sarkisian. 2006. Marriage: The good, the bad, and the greedy. *Contexts* 5:16–21.

Glenn, Evelyn Nakano. 1999. The social construction and institutionalization of gender and race: An integrative framework. In *Revisioning gender,* edited by M. M. Ferree, J. Lorber, and B. B. Hess, 3–43. Thousand Oaks, CA: Sage.

Glenn, Norval, and Elizabeth Marquardt. 2001. *Hooking up, hanging out, and hoping for Mr. Right: College women on mating and dating today.* New York: Institute for American Values.

Grello, Catherine M., Deborah P. Welsh, and Melinda M. Harper. 2006. No strings attached: The nature of casual sex in college students. *Journal of Sex Research* 43:255–67.

Holland, Dorothy C., and Margaret A. Eisenhart. 1990. *Educated in romance: Women, achievement, and college culture.* Chicago: University of Chicago Press.

Illouz, Eva. 2005. *Cold intimacies: The making of emotional capitalism.* Cambridge, UK: Polity.

Kimmel, Michael. 2008. *Guyland: The perilous world where boys become men.* New York: Harper Collins.

Manning, Wendy D., Peggy C. Giordano, and Monica A. Longmore. 2006. Hooking up: The relationship contexts of "nonrelationship" sex. *Journal of Adolescent Research* 21:459–83.

Martin, Karin. 1996. *Puberty, sexuality, and the self: Boys and girls at adolescence.* New York: Routledge.

Martin, Patricia Yancey. 2004. Gender as a social institution. *Social Forces* 82:1249–73.

Martin, Patricia Yancey, and Robert A. Hummer. 1989. Fraternities and rape on campus. *Gender & Society* 3:457–73.

McCall, Leslie. 2005. The complexity of intersectionality. *Signs: Journal of Women in Culture and Society* 30:1771–1800.

Owen, Jesse J., Galena K. Rhoades, Scott M. Stanley, and Frank D. Finchaln 2008. "Hooking up" among college students: Demographic and psychosocial correlates. *Archives of Sexual Behavior,* http://www.springerlink.com/content/44j645v7v38013u4/fulltext.html.

Paul, Elizabeth L., Brian McManus and, Allison Hayes. 2000. "Hookups": Characteristics and correlates of college students' spontaneous and anonymous sexual experiences. *Journal of Sex Research* 37:76–88.

Ridgeway, Cecilia L. 2000. Limiting inequality through interaction: The end(s) of gender. *Contemporary Sociology* 29:110–20.

Ridgeway, Cecilia L. 2009. Framed before we know it: How gender shapes social relations. *Gender & Society* 23:145–60.

Ridgeway, Cecilia L., and Shelley J. Correll. 2004. Unpacking the gender system: A theoretical perspective on gender beliefs and social relations. *Gender & Society* 18:510–31.

Risman, Barbara, and Pepper Schwartz. 2002. After the sexual revolution: Gender politics in teen dating. *Contexts* 1:16–24.

Risman, Barbara J. 2004. Gender as a social structure: Theory wrestling with activism. *Gender & Society* 18:429–50.

Rosenfeld, Michael J. 2007. *The age of independence: Interracial unions, same sex unions and the changing American family.* Cambridge, MA: Harvard University Press.

Schwartz, Christine R., and Robert D. Mare. 2005. Trends in educational assortative marriage from 1940 to 2003. *Demography* 42:621–46.

Sewell, William H. 1992. A theory of structure: Duality, agency, and transformation. *American Journal of Sociology* 98:1–29.

Simon, Robin W., Donna Eder, and Cathy Evans. 1992. The development of feeling norms underlying romantic love among adolescent females. *Social Psychology Quarterly* 55:29–46.

Stepp, Laura Sessions. 2007. *Unhooked: How young women pursue sex, delay love, and lose at both.* New York: Riverhead.

Sweeney, Megan M. 2002. Two decades of family change: The shifting economic foundations of marriage. *American Sociological Review* 67:132–47.

Wharton, Amy S. 2005. *The sociology of gender: An introduction to theory and research.* Malden, MA: Blackwell.

Introduction to Reading 43

Enforcing gender happens everywhere in all sorts of institutions. This reading by Michael A. Messner and Suzel Bozada-Deas about the division of volunteer labor of parents on youth baseball and soccer teams illustrates how all institutions in our daily lives operate to enforce and maintain traditional and unequal gender categories. The first author spent many years participating in and observing these youth sports in his community. Both authors conducted field observations at practices and games, participated in clinics for coaches and referees, and conducted 50 in-depth interviews with both women and men volunteers from the baseball and soccer teams in this community. They present a picture of how gender is seen as natural or essential, despite very clear interactions and expectations that place men and women in roles similar to those in "traditional" families. Unfortunately, the enforcement of gender does not always recognize talents of individual men and women.

1. What do the authors mean by "soft essentialism," and how is it used to enforce a traditional gender division of labor? Find examples of soft essentialism in the reading.

2. What are the ways men and women are sorted into traditional and unequal roles on these teams based on gender?

3. Compare the use of language in this reading to language used in other institutional arenas. We now have "flight attendants" rather than "stewardesses" on airplanes. Can you think of instances where we still use language to enforce gender?

SEPARATING THE MEN FROM THE MOMS

THE MAKING OF ADULT GENDER SEGREGATION IN YOUTH SPORTS

Michael A. Messner and Suzel Bozada-Deas

In volunteer work, just as in many families and workplaces, gender divisions are pervasive and persistent. Women are often expected to do the work of caring for others' emotions and daily needs. Women's volunteer labor is routinely devalued in much the same ways that housework and childcare are devalued in the home and women's clerical and other support work is devalued in the professions (Hook 2004). Similarly, men tend to do the instrumental work of public leadership, just as they do in the family and the workplace, and their informal work is valued accordingly.

This article examines the social construction of adult gender divisions of labor in a community volunteer activity, youth sports. A few scholars have examined women's invisible labor in sports (Boyle & McKay, 1995). In her study of a Little League Baseball league, Grasmuck (2005) estimates that the 111 league administrators, head coaches, and assistant coaches (mostly men) contribute a total of 33,330 hours of volunteer labor in a season—an average of about 300 hours per person. Much of the work women do in youth sports is behind-the-scenes support that is less visible than coaching (Thompson 1999). In a study of Little League Baseball in Texas, Chafetz and Kotarba (1999, 48–49) observed that "team mothers" in this "upper middle class, 'Yuppie' Texas community" do gender in ways that result in "the re-creation and strengthening of the community's collective identity as a place

From Messner, Michael A., and Bozada-Deas, Suzel. "Separating the Men From the Moms: The Making of Adult Gender Segregation in Youth Sports," *Gender & Society, 23*(1), pp. 49–71. Copyright © 2009. Published by SAGE Publications on behalf of Sociologists for Women in Society.

where, among other things, women are primarily mothers to their sons." As yet, no study has focused on how this gender divide among adults in youth sports happens. How do most men become coaches, while most women become "team moms"? How do adult gender divisions of labor in youth sports connect with commonsense notions about divisions between women and men in families and workplaces? This is important: Millions of children play community-based youth sports every year, and these athletic activities are a key part of the daily lives of many families. It is also important for scholars of gender—studying segregation in this context can reveal much about how gender divisions are created and sustained in the course of everyday life.

COACHES AND "TEAM MOMS"

In 1995, when we (the first author, Mike, and his family) arrived at our six-year-old son's first soccer practice, we were delighted to learn that his coach was a woman. Coach Karen, a mother in her mid-30s, had grown up playing lots of sports. She was tall, confident, and athletic, and the kids responded well to her leadership. It seemed to be a new and different world than the one we grew up in. But during the next decade, as our two sons played a few more seasons of soccer, two years of youth basketball, and more than a decade of baseball, they never had another woman head coach. It is not that women were not contributing to the kids' teams. All of the "team parents" (often called "team moms")—parent volunteers who did the behind-the-scenes work of phone-calling, organizing weekly snack schedules and team parties, collecting money for gifts for the coaches, and so on—were women. And occasionally, a team had a woman assistant coach. But women head coaches were few and far between.

In 1999, we started keeping track of the numbers of women and men head coaches in Roseville's[1] annual American Youth Soccer Organization (AYSO) and Little League Baseball/Softball (LLB/S) yearbooks we received at

the end of each season. The yearbooks revealed that from 1999 to 2007, only 13.4 percent of 1,490 AYSO teams had women head coaches. The numbers were even lower for Little League Baseball and Softball; only 5.9 percent of 538 teams were managed by women. In both AYSO and LLB/S, women coaches were clustered in the younger kids' teams (ages five to eight) and in coaching girls. Boys—and especially boys older than age 10—almost never had women coaches. These low numbers are surprising for several reasons. First, unlike during the 1950s and 1960s, when there were almost no opportunities for girls to play sports, today, millions of girls participate in organized soccer, baseball, softball, basketball, and other sports. With this demographic shift in youth sports, we expected that the gender division of labor among parents would have shifted as well. Second, today's mothers in the United States came of age during and after the 1972 institution of Title IX and are part of the generation that ignited the booming growth of female athletic participation. We wondered how it happened that these women did not make a neat transition from their own active sports participation into coaching their own kids. Third, women in Roseville outnumber men significantly in every volunteer activity having to do with kids, such as the Parent and Teacher Association (PTA), Scouts, and school special events. Coaching youth sports is the great exception to this rule. Sport has changed over the past 30 years, from a world set up almost exclusively by and for boys and men to one that is moving substantially (although incompletely) toward gender equity (Messner 2002). Yet, men dominate the very public on-field volunteer leadership positions in community youth sports.

This article is part of a larger study of gender in adult volunteering in two youth sports programs in a small independent suburb of Los Angeles that we call Roseville. Both of the sports leagues are local affiliates of massive national and international organizations. LLB/S and AYSO offer an interesting contrast in youth sports organizations, especially with respect to gender. Little League Baseball began in 1938 and for its first 36 years was an organization set up exclusively for boys. When forced against its will by a court decision in 1974 to include girls, Little League responded by creating a separate softball league into which girls continue to be tracked. Today, LLB/S is an organization that boasts 2.7 million child participants worldwide, 2.1 million of them in the United States. There are 176,786 teams in the program, 153,422 of them in baseball and 23,364 in softball. Little League stays afloat through the labor of approximately 1 million volunteers.

When AYSO started in 1964, it was exclusively for boys, but by 1971, girls' teams had been introduced. Thus, over the years, the vast majority of people who have participated in AYSO have experienced it as an organization set up for boys and girls. AYSO remains today mostly a U.S. organization, with more than 650,000 players on more than 50,000 teams. The national AYSO office employs 50 paid staff members, but like LLB/S, AYSO is an organization largely driven by the labor of volunteers, with roughly 250,000 volunteer coaches, team parents, and referees.

The differently gendered history of these two organizations offers hints as to the origins of the differences we see; there are more women head coaches in soccer than in baseball. Connell (1987) argues that every social institution—including the economy, the military, schools, families, or sport—has a "gender regime," which is defined as the current state of play of gender relations in the institution. We can begin to understand an institution's gender regime by measuring and analyzing the gender divisions of labor and power in the organization (i.e., what kinds of jobs are done by women and men, who has the authority, etc.). The idea that a gender regime is characterized by a "state of play" is a way to get beyond static measurements that result from a quick snapshot of an organizational pyramid and understanding instead that organizations are always being created by people's actions and discourse (Britton 2000). These actions often result in an organizational inertia that reproduces gender divisions and hierarchies; however,

organizations are also subject to gradual—or occasionally even rapid—change.

Institutional gender regimes are connected with other gender regimes. Put another way, people in their daily lives routinely move in, out, and across different gender regimes—families, workplaces, schools, places of worship, and community activities such as youth sports. Their actions within a particular gender regime—for instance, the choice to volunteer to coach a youth soccer team—and the meanings they construct around these actions are constrained and enabled by their positions, responsibilities, and experiences in other institutional contexts. We will show how individual decisions to coach or to serve as team parents occur largely through non-reflexive, patterned interactions that are infused with an ascendant gender ideology that we call "soft essentialism." These interactions occur at the nexus of the three gender regimes of community youth sports, families, and workplaces.

RESEARCH METHODS

The low numbers of women coaches in Roseville AYSO and LLB/S and the fact that nearly all of the team parents are women gave us a statistical picture of persistent gender segregation. But simply trotting out these numbers couldn't tell us *how* this picture is drawn. We wanted to understand the current state of play of the adult gender regime of youth sports, so we developed a study based on the following question: What are the social processes that sustain this gender segregation? And by extension, we wanted to explore another question: What is happening that might serve to destabilize and possibly change this gender segregation? In other words, are there ways to see and understand the internal mechanisms—the face-to-face interactions as well as the meaning-making processes—that constitute the "state of play" of the gender regime of community youth sports?

* * *

THE COACHES' STORIES

When we asked a longtime Little League Softball manager why he thinks most head coaches are men while nearly all team parents are women, he said with a shrug, "They give opportunities to everybody to manage or coach and it just so happens that no women volunteer, you know?" This man's statement was typical of head coaches and league officials who generally offered up explanations grounded in individual choice: Faced with equal opportunities to volunteer, men just *choose* to be coaches, while women *choose* to be team parents.

But our research shows that the gendered division of labor among men and women volunteers in youth coaching results not simply from an accumulation of individual choices; rather, it is produced through a profoundly *social* process. We will first draw from our interviews with head coaches to illustrate how gender divisions of labor among adult volunteers in youth sports are shaped by gendered language and belief systems and are seen by many coaches as natural extensions of gendered divisions of labor in families and workplaces. We next draw observations from our field notes to illustrate how everyday interactions within the gendered organizational context of youth sports shape peoples' choices about men's and women's roles as coaches or team parents. Our main focus here will be on reproductive agency—the patterns of action that reproduce the gender division of labor. But we will also discuss moments of resistance and disruption that create possibilities for change.

Gendered Pipelines

When we asked coaches to describe how they had decided to become coaches, most spoke of having first served as assistant coaches— sometimes for just one season, sometimes for several seasons—before moving into head coaching positions. Drawing from language used by those who study gender in occupations, we can describe the assistant coach position as an essential part of the "pipeline" to the head coach position (England 2006). One of the reasons for this is obvious: Many parents—women and men—believe that as a head coach, they will be under tremendous critical scrutiny by other parents in the community. Without previous youth coaching experience, many lack the confidence that they feel they need to take on such a public leadership task. A year or two of assistant coaching affords one the experience and builds the confidence that can lead to the conclusion that "I can do that" and the decision to take on the responsibility of a head coaching position.

But the pipeline from assistant coaches to head coaches does not operate in a purely individual voluntarist manner. A male longtime Little League manager and a member of the league's governing board gave us a glimpse of how the pipeline works when there is a shortage of volunteers:

> One time we had 10 teams and only like six or seven applicants that wanted to be strictly manager. So you kinda eyeball the yearbook from the year before, maybe a couple of years [before], and see if the same dad is still listed as a[n assistant] coach, and maybe now it's time he wants his own team. So you make a lot of phone calls. You might make 20 phone calls and hopefully you are going to get two or three guys that say, "Yes, I'll be a manager."

. . . To understand how it is that most head coaches are men, we need to understand how the pipeline operates—how it is that, at the entry level, women's and men's choices to become assistant coaches and/or team parents are constrained or enabled by the social context.

Recruiting Dads and Moms to Help

There is a lot of work involved in organizing a successful youth soccer, baseball, or softball season. A head coach needs help from two, three, even four other parents who will serve as assistant coaches during practices and games. Parents also have to take responsibility for numerous support tasks like organizing snacks, making team banners, working in the snack bar during games, collecting donations for year-end gifts for the coaches, and organizing team events and year-end parties. In AYSO, parents also serve as volunteer referees. When we asked head coaches how they determined who would help them with these assistant coaching and other support tasks, a very common storyline developed: the coach would call a beginning-of-the-season team meeting, sometimes preceded by a letter or e-mail to parents, and ask for volunteers. Nearly always, they ended up with dads volunteering to help as assistant coaches and moms volunteering to be team parents. . . .

[T]he assistant coach and team parent positions are sometimes informally set up even before the first team meeting and how a coach's assumption that the team parent will be a "team mom" might make it more likely that women end up in these positions. But even coaches—such as the woman soccer coach quoted below—who try to emphasize that team parent is not necessarily a woman's job find that only women end up volunteering:

> Before the season started, we had a team meeting and I let the parents know that I would need a team parent and I strongly stressed parent, because I don't think it should always be a mother. But we did end up with the mom doing it and she assigns snacks and stuff like that.

None of the head coaches we interviewed said that they currently had a man as the team parent. Four coaches recalled that they had once had a man as a team parent (although one of these four coaches said, "Now that I think about it, that guy actually volunteered his wife do it"). When we asked if they had ever had a team parent who was a man, nearly all of the coaches said never. Many of them laughed at the very thought. A woman soccer coach exclaimed with a chuckle, "I just can't imagine! I wonder if they've *ever* had a 'team mom' who's a dad. I don't know [laughs]." A man soccer coach stammered his way through his response, punctuating his words

with sarcastic laughter: "Ha! In fact, that whole concept—I don't think I've ever *heard* of a team dad [laughs]. Uh—there *is* no team dad, I've never heard of a team dad. But I don't know why that would be." A few coaches, such as the following woman softball coach, resorted to family metaphors to explain why they think there are few if any men volunteering to be team parents: "Oh, it's always a mom [laughs]. 'Team mom.' That's why it's called 'team *mom.*' You know, the coach is a male. And the mom—I mean, that's the *housekeeping*—you know: Assign the snack."

There are gendered assumptions in the language commonly linked to certain professions, so much so that often, when the person holding the position is in the statistical minority, people attach a modifier, such as *male* nurse, *male* secretary, *woman* judge, *woman* doctor. Or *woman* head coach. Over and over, in interviews with coaches, during team meetings, and in interactions during games, practices, and team parties, we noticed this gendered language. Most obvious was the frequent slippage from official term *team parent* to commonly used term "*team mom.*" But we also noticed that a man coach was normally just called a coach, while a woman coach was often gender marked as a woman coach. As feminist linguists have shown, language is a powerful element of social life—it not only reflects social realities such as gender divisions of labor, it also helps to construct our notions of what is normal and what is an aberration (Thorne, Kramarae, and Henley 1983). One statement from a woman soccer coach, "I wonder if they've *ever* had a 'team mom' who's a dad," illustrates how gendered language makes the idea of a man team parent seem incongruous, even laughable. In youth sports, this gendered language supports the notion that a team is structured very much like a "traditional" heterosexual family: The head coach—nearly always a man—is the leader and the public face of the team; the team parent—nearly always a woman—is working behind the scenes, doing support work; assistant coaches—mostly men, but including the occasional woman—help the coach on the field during practices and games.

Teams are even talked about sometimes as "families," and while we never heard a head coach referred to as a team's "dad," we did often and consistently hear the team parent referred to as the "team mom." This gendered language, drawn from family relations, gives us some good initial hints as to how coach and team parent roles remain so gender segregated. In their study of self-managing teams, which was intended to break down gender divisions in workplaces, Ollilainen and Calasanti (2007) show how team members' use of family metaphors serves to maintain the salience of gender, and thus, helps to reproduce a gendered division of labor. Similarly, in youth sports contexts, gendered language structures people's conversations in ways that shape and constrain their actions. Is a man who volunteers to be a team parent now a "team mom"?

Gender Ideology and Work/Family Analogies

When we asked the coaches to consider why it is nearly always women who volunteer to be the team parent, many seemed never to have considered this question before. Some of the men coaches seemed especially befuddled and appeared to assume that women's team-parenting work is a result of an almost "natural" decision on the part of the woman. Some men, such as the following soccer coach, made sense of this volunteer division of labor by referring to the ways that it reflected divisions of labor in men's own families and in their community: "In this area we have a lot of stay-at-home moms, so it seems to kind of fall to them to take over those roles." Similarly, a man baseball coach whose wife served as the team parent explained, "I think it's because they probably do it at home. You know, I mean my wife—even though she can't really commit the time to coach, I don't think she would want to coach—uh, she's very good with that [team parent] stuff." . . .

Another man baseball coach broadened the explanation, drawing connections to divisions of labor in his workplace:

It's kinda like in business. I work in real estate, and most of your deal makers that are out there on the front lines, so to speak, making the deals, doing the shuckin' and jivin,' doing the selling, are men. It's a very Good Ol' Boys network on the real estate brokerage side. There are a ton a females who are on the property management side, because it's *housekeeping,* it's *managing,* it's like running the *household,* it's behind the scenes, it's like cooking in the kitchen—[laughs]—I mean, I hate to say that, but it's that kind of role that's secondary. Coach is out in the front leading the squad, mom sitting behind making sure that the snacks are in order and all that. You know—just the way it is. . . .

When explaining why it is that team parents are almost exclusively women, a small number of women coaches also seemed to see it in essentialist terms—like most of the men coaches saw it.

Many women coaches, however, saw the gendering of the team parent position as a problem and made sense of its persistence, as did many of the men, by referring to the ways that it reflects family- and work-related divisions of labor. But several of the women coaches added an additional dimension to their explanations by focusing on why they think the men don't or won't consider doing team parent work. A woman soccer coach said, "I think it's because the dads want to be involved with the action. And they are not interested in doing paperwork and collecting money for photos or whatever it is. They are not interested in doing that sort of stuff." Another woman soccer coach extended this point: "I think it's probably, well, identity, which is probably why not many men do it. You know, they think that is a woman's job, like secretary or nurse or, you know." In short, many of the women coaches were cognizant of the ways that the team parent job was viewed by men, like all "women's work," as nonmasculine and thus undesirable. A woman Little League coach found it ironically funny that her husband, in fact, does most of the cooking and housework at home but will not take on the role of team parent for his daughter's team. When asked if changing the name to "team dad" might get more men to volunteer, she replied with a sigh,

I don't know. I wish my husband would be a team dad because he's just very much more domesticated than I am [laughs]. You know, "Bring all the snacks, honey, hook us up," you know. I think there's a lot of men out there, but they don't want to be perceived as being domesticated.

This coach's comment illustrates how—even for a man who does a substantial amount of the family labor at home—publicly taking on a job that is defined as "feminine" threatens to saddle him with a "domesticated" public image that would be embarrassing or even humiliating. In sum, most coaches—both women and men—believe that men become coaches and women become team parents largely because these public roles fit with their domestic proclivities and skills. But the women add an important dimension to this explanation: women do the team parent work because it has to be done . . . and because they know that the men will not do it.

FINDING A "TEAM MOM"

The interview data give us a window into how people make sense of decisions that they have made as youth sports volunteers and provide insights into how gendered language and beliefs about men's and women's work and family roles help to shape these decisions. Yet, asking people to explain how (and especially why) things such as gendered divisions of labor persist is not by itself the most reliable basis for building an explanation. Rather, watching *how* things happen gives us a deeper understanding of the social construction of gender (Thorne 1993). Our observations from team meetings and early season practices reveal deeper social processes at work—processes that shaped people's apparently individual decisions to volunteer for assistant coach or team parent positions. . . .

We observed two occasions when a woman who did not volunteer was drafted by the head coach to be the "team mom." In one case, the reluctant volunteer was clearly more oriented toward assistant coaching, as the following composite story from field notes from the

beginning of the season of a seven-year-old boys' baseball team illustrates:

At the first practice, Coach George takes charge, asks for volunteers. I tell him that I am happy to help out at practice and games and that he should just let me know what he'd like me to do. He appoints me Assistant Coach. This happens with another dad, too. We get team hats. Elena, a mother, offers to help out in any way she can. She's appointed "co-team mom" (the coach's wife is the other "team mom"). She shrugs and says okay, fine. Unlike most "team moms," Elena continues to attend all practices. At the fifth practice, Coach George is pitching batting practice to the kids; I'm assigned to first base, the other dad is working with the catcher. Elena (the "team mom") is standing alone on the sidelines, idly tossing a ball up in the air to herself. Coach George's son suddenly has to pee, so as George hustles the boy off to the bathroom, Elena jumps in and starts pitching. She's good, it turns out, and can groove the pitch right where the kids want it. (By contrast, George has recently been plunking the kids with wild pitches.) Things move along well. At one point, when Coach George has returned from the bathroom, with Elena still pitching to the kids, a boy picks up a ball near second base and doesn't know what to do with it. Coach George yells at the kid: "Throw it! Throw it to the 'team mom!'" The kid, confused, says, "Where is she?" I say, "The pitcher, throw it to the pitcher." Coach George says, "Yeah, the 'team mom.'"

A couple of years later, we interviewed Elena and asked her how it was that she became a team parent and continued in that capacity for five straight years. Her response illuminated the informal constraints that channel many women away from coaching and toward being team parents:

The first year, when [my son] was in kindergarten, he was on a T-ball team, and I volunteered to be manager, and of course the league didn't choose me, but they did allow me to be assistant coach. And I was so excited, and [laughs] of course I showed up in heels for the first practice, because it was right after work, and the coach looked at me, and I informed him that "I'm your new assistant." And he looked at me—and I don't know if *distraught* is the correct word, but he seemed slightly *disappointed,* and he went out of his way to ask the parents who were there watching their children if there was anyone who wanted to volunteer, even though I was there. So there was this male who did kind of rise to the occasion, and so that was the end. He demoted me without informing me of his decision [laughs]—I was *really* enthused, because [my son] was in kindergarten, so I *really* wanted to be coach—or assistant coach at least—and it didn't happen. So after that I didn't feel comfortable to volunteer to coach. I just thought, okay, then I can do "team mom."

As this story illustrates, women who have the background, skills, and desire to work as on-field assistant coaches are sometimes assigned by head coaches to be "team moms." Some baseball teams even have a niche for such moms: a "dugout coach" (or "dugout mom") is usually a mom who may help out with on-field instruction during practices, but on game days, she is assigned the "indoors" space of the dugout, where it is her responsibility to keep track of the line-up and to be sure that the boy who is on-deck (next up to bat) is ready with his batting gloves and helmet on. The dugout coach also—especially with younger kids' teams—might be assigned to keep kids focused on the game, to keep equipment orderly, to help with occasional first aid, and to help see that the dugout is cleaned of empty water bottles and snack containers after the game is over. In short, the baseball, softball, and soccer fields on which the children play are gendered spaces (Dworkin 2001; Montez de Oca 2005). The playing field is the public space where the (usually male) coach exerts his authority and command. The dugout is like the home—a place of domestic safety from which one emerges to do one's job. Work happens in the indoor space of the dugout, but it is like family labor, behind-the-scenes, supporting the "real" work of leadership that is done on the field.

CHALLENGES AND RESISTANCE

The head coach's common assumption that fathers will volunteer to be assistant coaches and mothers to be "team moms" creates a context that powerfully channels men and women in these directions. Backed by these commonsense understandings of gendered divisions of labor, most men and women just "go with the flow" of this channeling process. Their choices and actions help to reproduce the existing gendered patterns of the organization. But some do not; some choose to swim against the tide. A mother who had several seasons of experience as a head soccer coach described the first team meeting for her youngest child's team:

> At our first team meeting, the coach announced, "I'm looking for a couple of you to help me out as assistant coaches," and he looked directly at the men, and *only* at the men. None of them volunteered. And it was really amazing because he didn't even *look* at me or at any of the other women. So after the meeting, I went up to him and said, "Hey, I've coached soccer for like 10 seasons; I can help you out, okay?" And he agreed, so I'm the assistant coach for him.

This first team meeting is an example of a normal gendered interaction that, if it had gone unchallenged, would have reproduced the usual gender divisions of labor on the team. It is likely that many women in these situations notice the ways that men are, to adopt Martin's (2001) term, informally (and probably unconsciously) "mobilizing masculinities" in ways that reproduce men's positions of centrality. But this woman's 10 years of coaching experience gave her the confidence and the athletic "capital" that allowed her not only to see and understand but also to challenge the very gendered selection process that was taking place at this meeting. Most mothers do not have this background, and when faced with this sort of moment, they go with the flow.

On another occasion, as the following composite story from field notes describes, Mike observed a highly athletic and coaching-inclined woman assertively use her abilities in a way that initially *seemed* to transcend the gender segregation process, only to be relegated symbolically at season's end to the position of "team mom":

> *A new baseball season, the first team meeting of the year; a slew of dads volunteer to be assistant coaches. Coach George combs the women for a*

"team mom" and gets some resistance; at first, nobody will do it, but then he finds a volunteer. At the first few practices, few assistant coaches actually show up. Isabel, a mom, clearly is into baseball, very knowledgeable and athletic, and takes the field. She pitches to the kids, gives them good advice. On the day when George is passing out forms for assistant coaches to sign, he hands her one too. She accepts it, in a matter-of-fact way. Isabel continues to attend practices, working with the kids on the field.

Though few dads show up for many of the practices, there never seems to be a shortage of dads to serve as assistant coaches at the games. At one game, Coach George invites Isabel to coach third base, but beyond that, she is never included in an on-field coaching role during a game.

End of season, team party. Coach George hands out awards to all the kids. He hands out gift certificates to all the assistant coaches but does not include Isabel. Then he hands out gift certificates to the "team moms," and includes Isabel, even though I don't recall her doing any team parent tasks. She had clearly been acting as an assistant coach all season long.

This story illustrates how, on one hand, a woman volunteer can informally circumvent the sorting process that pushes her toward the "team mom" role by persistently showing up to practices and assertively doing the work of a coach. As Thorne (1993, 133) points out, individual incidences of gender crossing are often handled informally in ways that affirm, rather than challenge, gender boundaries: An individual girl who joins the boys' game gets defined "as a token, a kind of 'fictive boy,' not unlike many women tokens in predominantly men settings, whose presence does little to challenge the existing arrangements." Similarly, Isabel's successful "crossing" led to her becoming accepted as an assistant coach during practices but rarely recognized as a "real" coach during games. She was a kind of "token" or "fictive" coach whose gender transgression was probably unknown to the many adults who never attended practices. So, in the final moment of the season, when adults and children alike were being publicly recognized for their contributions to the team, she was labeled

and rewarded for being a "team mom," reaffirming gender boundaries.

A few coaches whom we interviewed consciously attempted to resist or change this gendered sorting system. Some of the women coaches, especially, saw it as a problem that the team parent job was always done by a woman. A woman softball coach was concerned that the "team mom" amounted to negative role-modeling for kids and fed into the disrespect that women coaches experienced:

> The kids think that the moms should just be "team moms." Which means that they don't take the mothers seriously, and I think that's a bad thing. I mean it's a *bad thing*. I think that's a lack of respect to women, to mothers.

Another woman Little League coach said that most team parents are women because too many people assume

> that's all the women are good for. I think that's what the mentality is. I made it very clear to our parents that it did not have to be a mother, that it could be a father and that I encourage any dad out there that had time to do what team parents are supposed to do, to sign up and do it. But it didn't happen.

Such coaches find that simply degendering the language by calling this role *team parent* and even stressing that this is not a gendered job is unlikely to yield men volunteers. So what some women coaches do is simply refuse to have a team parent. A woman soccer coach said, "I do it all. I don't have a team parent." Another said, "I think in general, compared to the men who coach, I do more of that [team parent work]." This resistance by women coaches is understandable, especially from those who see the phenomenon of "team mom" as contributing to a climate of disrespect for women coaches. However, this form of resistance ends up creating extra work for women coaches—work that most men coaches relegate to a "team mom."

The very few occasions when a father does volunteer—or is recruited by the coach—to be the team parent are moments of gender "cross-ing" that hold the potential to disrupt the normal operation of the gender-category sorting process. But ironically, a team parent who is a man can also reinforce gender stereotypes. One man soccer coach told me that the previous season, a father had volunteered to be the team parent, but that

> he was a disaster [laughs]. He didn't do *anything,* you know, and what little he did it was late; it was ineffective assistance. He didn't come, he didn't make phone calls, I mean he was just like a black hole. And so that—that was an unfortunate disaster. This year it's a woman again.

The idea that a man volunteered—and then failed miserably to do the team parent job—may serve ultimately to reinforce the taken-for-granted assumption that women are naturally better suited to do this kind of work.

The Devaluation of Women's Invisible Labor

The Roseville "team moms" we observed were similar to those studied by Chafetz and Kotarba (1999) in terms of their education, professional-class status, and family structure. The Texasville and Roseville "team moms" are doing the same kinds of activities, simultaneously contributing to the "concerted cultivation" of their own children (Lareau 2003) while helping to enhance the social cohesion of the team, the league, and the community.

Despite the importance of the work team parents are doing, it is not often recognized as equivalent to the work done by coaches. Of course, the team parent typically puts in far fewer hours of labor than does the head coach. However, in some cases, the team parents put in more time than some assistant coaches (dads, for instance, whose work schedules don't allow them to get to many practices but who can be seen on the field during a Saturday game, coaching third base). Yet, the team parent's work

remains largely invisible, and coaches sometimes talk about team parents' contributions as trivial or unimportant. Several coaches, when asked about the team parent job, disparaged it as "not very hard to do," "an easy job." But our interviews suggest that the women team parents are often doing this job as one of many community volunteer jobs, while most of the men who coach are engaged in this and only this volunteer activity. . . .

Sorting and Soft Essentialism

In this article, we have revealed the workings of a gender-category sorting process that reflects the interactional "doing" of gender discussed by West and Zimmerman (1987). Through this sorting process, the vast majority of women volunteers are channeled into a team parent position, and the vast majority of men volunteers become coaches. To say that people are "sorted" is not to deny their active agency in this process. Rather, it is to underline that organizations are characterized by self-perpetuating "inequality regimes" (Acker 2006). What people often think of as "free individual choices" are actually choices that are shaped by social contexts. We have shown how women's choices to become team parents are constrained by the fact that few, if any, men will volunteer to do this less visible and less honored job. Women's choices are enabled by their being actively recruited—"volunteered"—by head coaches or by other parents to become the "team mom." Moreover, men's choices to volunteer as assistant coaches and not as team parents are shaped by the gendered assumptions of head coaches, enacted through active recruiting and informal interactions at the initial team meeting.

This gender-category sorting system is at the heart of the current state of play of the gender regime of adult volunteer work in youth sports in Roseville. There are several ways we can see the sorting system at work. First, our research points to the role of gendered language and meanings in this process. The term *coach* and the term "*team mom*" are saturated with gendered assumptions that are consistent with most people's universe of meanings. These gendered meanings mesh with—and mutually reinforce—the conventional gendered divisions of labor and power in the organization in ways that make decisions to "go with the flow" appear natural. Second, we have shown how having women do the background support work while men do the visible leadership work on the team is also made to appear natural to the extent that it reiterates the gender divisions of labor that many parents experience in their families and in their workplaces. . . .

In the past, sport tended to construct a categorical "hard" essentialism—boys and men, it was believed, were naturally suited to the aggressive, competitive world of sport, while girls and women were not. Today, with girls' and women's massive influx into sport, these kinds of categorical assumptions of natural difference can no longer stand up to even the most cursory examination. Soft essentialism, as an ascendant professional-class gender ideology, frames sport as a realm in which girls are empowered to exercise individual choice (rehearsing choices they will later face in straddling the demands of careers and family labor), while continuing to view boys as naturally "hard wired" to play sports (and ultimately, to have public careers). Girls are viewed as flexibly facing a future of choices; boys as inflexible, facing a linear path toward public careers. Soft essentialism, in short, initiates kids into an adult world that has been only partially transformed by feminism, where many of the burdens of bridging and balancing work and family strains are still primarily on women's shoulders. Men coaches and "team moms" symbolize and exemplify these tensions.

Time after time, we heard leaders of leagues and some women coaches say that the league leadership works hard to recruit more women coaches but just cannot get them to volunteer. The *formal agency* here is to "recruit more women coaches." But what Martin (2001) calls the *informal practicing of gender* (revealed most clearly in our field-note vignettes) amounts to a collective and (mostly) nonreflexive sorting system that, at the entry level, puts most women and men on separate paths. Martin's work has been foundational in showing how gender works in organizations in informal, nonreflexive ways that rely on peoples' "tacit knowledge" about gender. In particular, she points out "how and why well-intentioned, 'good people' practice gender in ways that do harm" (Martin 2006, 255).

Our study shows a similar lack of "bad guys" engaged in overt acts of sexism and discrimination. Instead, we see a systemic reproduction of gender categorization, created nonreflexively by "well intentioned, good people." The mechanisms of this nonreflexive informal practicing of gender are made to seem normal through their congruence with the "tacit knowledge" of soft essentialism that is itself embedded in hegemonic professional-class family and workplace gender divisions of labor. The fact that soft essentialism emerges from the intersections of these different social contexts means that any attempt to move toward greater equality for women and men in youth sports presupposes simultaneous movements toward equality in workplaces and families.

Note

1. Roseville is a pseudonym for the town we studied, and all names of people interviewed or observed for this study are also pseudonyms.

References

Acker, Joan. 2006. Inequality regimes: Gender, class and race in organizations. *Gender & Society* 20:441–64.

Boyle, Maree, and Jim McKay. 1995. You leave your troubles at the gate: A case study of the exploitation of older women's labor and "leisure" in sport. *Gender & Society* 9:556–76.

Britton, Dana. 2000. The epistemology of the gendered organization. *Gender & Society* 14:418–34.

Chafetz, Janet Saltzman, and Joseph A. Kotarba. 1999. Little League mothers and the reproduction of gender. In *Inside sports,* edited by Jay Coakley and Peter Donnelly. London and New York: Routledge.

Connell, R. W. 1987. *Gender and power.* Stanford, CA: Stanford University Press.

Dworkin, Shari L. 2001. Holding back: Negotiating a glass ceiling on women's muscular strength. *Sociological Perspectives* 44:333–50.

England, Paula. 2006. Toward gender equality: Progress and bottlenecks. In *The declining significance of gender?* edited by Francine D. Blau, Mary C. Brinton, and David B. Grusky. New York: Russell Sage.

Grasmuck, Sherri. 2005. *Protecting home: Class, race, and masculinity in boys' baseball.* Piscataway, NJ: Rutgers University Press.

Hook, Jennifer L. 2004. Reconsidering the division of household labor: Incorporating volunteer work and informal support. *Journal of Marriage and Family* 66:101–17.

Lareau, Annette. 2003. *Unequal childhoods: Class, race, and family life.* Berkeley: University of California Press.

Martin, Patricia Yancy. 2001. Mobilizing masculinities: Women's experiences of men at work. *Organization* 8:587–618.

———. 2006. Practicing gender at work: Further thoughts on reflexivity. *Gender, Work and Organization* 13:254–76.

Messner, Michael A. 2002. *Taking the field: Women, men, and sports.* Minneapolis: University of Minnesota Press.

Montez de Oca, Jeffrey. 2005. As our muscles get softer, our missile race becomes harder: Cultural citizenship and the "muscle gap." *Journal of Historical Sociology* 18:145–71.

Ollilainen, Marjukka, and Toni Calasanti. 2007. Metaphors at work: Maintaining the salience of gender in self-managing teams. *Gender & Society* 21:5–27.

Thompson, Shona. 1999. The game begins at home: Women's labor in the service of sport. In *Inside sports,* edited by Jay Coakley and Peter Donnelly. London and New York: Routledge.

Thorne, Barrie. 1993. *Gender play: Girls and boys in school.* New Brunswick, NJ: Rutgers University Press.

Thorne, Barrie, Cheris Kramarae, and Nancy Henley. 1983. *Language, gender and society.* Rowley, MA: Newbury House.

West, Candace, and Don Zimmerman. 1987. Doing gender. *Gender & Society* 1:125–51.

Introduction to Reading 44

Amy M. Denissen and Abigail C. Saguy interviewed women who worked as tradeswomen in the building trades to get a better understanding of how women are treated in a predominantly male workplace. The ability of these women to do their jobs within the building trade was complicated by the enforcement of gender by both the males and the females. While the males enforced masculinity and emphasized the masculine traits that were needed for the job, they also denounced femininity as weak and not belonging on the job sites. However, females also wished to be accepted for their strength and ability to do their jobs. Interestingly, females who were lesbians were more likely to be accepted by the men, while often rejected by other women. Thus, heterosexuality is also used to maintain gendered assumptions on these work sites. These interviews with 35 women, who were located by contacting local unions, apprenticeship training programs, tradeswomen conferences, and through referrals from others interviewed, provide an interesting view of how gender and heteronormativity can be enforced and manipulated on the job.

1. How is both gender and heteronormativity used by the men and the women in this reading, and by doing so, does it maintain male dominance at the workplace?

2. Why do these women distrust each other and fail to work together for change in the workplace?

3. Think about other workplaces you have been in. Was gender reinforced there as well? Imagine how the same dialogues might happen in other male-dominated workplaces, particularly in powerful, upper-level occupations.

GENDERED HOMOPHOBIA AND THE CONTRADICTIONS OF WORKPLACE DISCRIMINATION FOR WOMEN IN THE BUILDING TRADES

Amy M. Denissen and Abigail C. Saguy

The effects of double binds, in which femininity and competence are seen as mutually exclusive, are well documented in male-dominated workplaces (Jamieson 1995; Valian 1998). Previous research shows that women resist double binds in part by "finding a variety of ways to do gender" (Pierce 1995, 13–14) that trouble boundaries of gender difference. Women may directly challenge gender dualities by, for instance, demanding respectful recognition as women while performing masculinity (Denissen 2010b). They may also invoke shared identities based on race, class, occupational hierarchy, or culture to deemphasize gender difference (Denissen 2010b; Janssens, Cappellen, and Zanoni 2006). Women workers thereby participate in "gender maneuvering" (Schippers 2002; see also Finley 2010), or the manipulation of gender rules to redefine the relationship between femininity and masculinity. . . .

Drawing on interviews with a diverse sample of lesbian and straight women in the construction trades, such as electricians and sheet metal workers, of which women comprise less than 2 percent of the workforce nationwide (Bilginsoy 2009), this article extends our understanding of gender maneuvering by exploring how the meaning of race, body size, and seniority impact the constraints tradeswomen face and the cultural resources available to them for resisting gender boundaries. We argue that the presence of women in male-dominated jobs threatens the perception of this work as inherently masculine (Collinson 2010; Epstein 1992; Paap 2006). We further argue that branding all tradeswomen lesbians, and thus—in the popular imagination—as not fully women, can partly be understood as an attempt to neutralize this threat. While the lesbian label (whether or not women personally identify as such) offers some degree of acceptance and freedom from performing emphasized femininity, it can place demands on tradeswomen to perform a subordinate blue-collar masculinity that may include participating in a misogynistic work culture (Connell 1987; West and Zimmerman 1987).

Moreover, the presence of lesbians (and sexually autonomous straight women whose sexuality is not directed toward tradesmen) threatens heteronormativity and men's sexual

From Denissen, Amy M., and Abigail C. Saguy. 2014. Gendered Homophobia and the Contradictions of Workplace Discrimination for Women in the Building Trades. *Gender & Society, 28*(3), 381–403.

subordination of women, or what Ingraham calls "patriarchal heterosexuality" (Ingraham 1994). By sexually objectifying tradeswomen, tradesmen, in effect, attempt to neutralize this threat. While tradeswomen, in turn, are sometimes able to deploy femininity to manage men's conduct and gain some measure of acceptance as women, it often comes at the cost of their perceived professional competence and sexual autonomy and—in the case of lesbians—sexual identity.

Those who refuse to be sexually objectified may subsequently find themselves the target of open hostility. Certain women—including lesbians and those who present as butch, large, or Black—may be less able to access emphasized femininity as a resource and thus more subject to open hostility. We show that tradeswomen navigate among imperfect strategies and engage in complex risk assessments (McDermott 2006). Extending Denissen (2010b), we highlight how tradeswomen reflexively manipulate gender meanings, adding a new emphasis on the intersection between sexuality, gender representation, race, and body size. Ultimately, however, we argue that individual strategies are insufficient and show how tradesmen deploy the stigma of lesbianism to discourage solidarity and collective action among tradeswomen. We consider the implications of these findings within the larger debate about the efficacy of interactional forms of resistance for challenging patriarchy and the dominant gender order.

GENDER AND SEXUALITY IN MALE-DOMINATED OCCUPATIONS

Previous work shows that men working in male-dominated blue-collar occupations accentuate their manliness by distinguishing their work from women's work (Epstein 1992; Schrock and Schwalbe 2009) and how managers manipulate gender ideology to control workers (Collinson 2010; Epstein 1992; Paap 2006). For instance, in a coal miner's protest about being asked to lift too much weight, the foreman asked, "What's the matter? Aren't you man enough?" (Epstein 1992, 243). By encouraging workers to identify with their gender and, also, their race, national, and class identities, employers divide workers and distract them from working conditions in order to enhance labor control (Hossfeld 1990). Generalizing from Ramirez (2010), many "macho" masculinities can be understood as working-class men's "compensatory reactions" to subordination when other sources of masculine identity are blocked (Zinn 1982) or become insecure because of declining wages, job security, union power, and social regard (Paap 2006). When men derive psychic and social rewards and managers derive economic benefits from these identifications, both groups can be expected to resist the entrance of women workers, which undermines the sense that it is, in fact, "men's work" (Epstein 1992).

In addition, tradeswomen are at a structural disadvantage as tokens (Kanter 1977) in "doubly male dominated" workgroups that "create a work culture that is an extension of male culture" and where the "numerical dominance of the workplace by men heightens the visibility of, and hostility toward, women workers" (Gruber 1998, 303). Institutional factors further intensify tradeswomen's visibility and vulnerability. For instance, the decentralization of production in the construction industry means that workers regularly change job sites, entering into new work relationships. As a result, tradeswomen prove themselves without the full benefit of their prior accomplishments. When a tradeswoman's reputation precedes her, it is often a liability, as in the case of tradeswomen managing the "sexual harassment lady" (Denissen 2010a) or "looking for a lawsuit" (Paap 2006) label that is sometimes attached to women who complain.

Moreover, despite the autonomy that construction workers enjoy (Applebaum 1999), tradeswomen's success and safety require good relations with tradesmen because (1) the apprentice model creates dependence on journeymen for training, (2) the work requires the cooperation of various trades to achieve tasks, and (3) workers must rely on each other for their physical safety (Applebaum 1999). While trades-women often emphasize the crucial role that supportive tradesmen play in their careers, their dependence on tradesmen also presents challenges.

Male homosexuality is also widely viewed as a threat to masculinity. It is common, in the male-dominated trades and elsewhere, for men to distance themselves—through homophobic jokes and the use of derogatory terms like "gay" and "faggot"—from homosexuality as a way of affirming their masculinity (Seidman 2010). C.J. Pascoe describes as "gendered homophobia" high school boys' use of the terms "gay" and especially "fag" to police behavior considered insufficiently masculine on the part of other boys (Pascoe 2005). Pascoe argues that fag discourse is targeted specifically at boys, rather than girls, and is as much about policing masculinity as sexuality (Pascoe 2005).

Yet, research suggests that, in male-dominated occupations, both men and women—straight and gay—are targets of sexist and anti-gay harassment (Paap 2006). Men tease other men who exhibit behavior deemed feminine and tell their female coworkers to eschew makeup and to work "like a man" (Denissen 2010b, 1056). In male-dominated contexts, where simply occupying a trade as a woman is associated with other forms of perceived gender inversion, including same-sex desire (Paap 2006), men direct anti-gay harassment at straight women and lesbians alike (Frank 2001). In fact, in this context, the presumption of heterosexuality, or heteronormativity (Ingraham 1994), may be suspended.

Indeed, to the extent to which lesbians are perceived as not fully women, their presence may be less threatening, than that of straight women, to the idea of male-dominated occupations as "men's work" (Paap 2006). Moreover, lesbians are positioned differently than are gay men within the hierarchical gender system that privileges both masculinity and heterosexuality (Schilt and Westbrook 2009). Whereas gay men are devalued both because of their sexuality and because they are perceived as feminine, lesbians (and those perceived as lesbians) may derive benefits in some contexts from their perceived masculinity, while having to negotiate a devalued sexual identity.

This insight helps make sense of studies showing that open lesbians are sometimes more accepted as coworkers in male-dominated work contexts, compared to straight women (Miller, Forest, and Jurik 2003; Myers, Forest, and Miller 2004; Paap 2006). For example, studies find that male police officers better accept lesbian, compared to gay men, coworkers (Miller, Forest, and Jurik 2003, 369), and that lesbians' sexual orientation offers a waiver from social pressures to enact emphasized femininity (Burke 1994). In some cases, heterosexual men's interest in lesbian sexuality may facilitate lesbians' inclusion in workplace banter (Frank 2001).

The experiences of butch, gender-blending women, and transmen further suggest that people may not always be censured for adopting the socially respected traits of masculinity (Devor 1987; Schilt and Westbrook 2009). We use the term "butch/dyke" to refer to performances of masculinity by women, what Halberstam (1998) calls "female masculinities." We use the term "gender-blending" to refer to women who combine interactional strategies that are alternatively coded as feminine or masculine (Devor 1987; Lucal 1999; Moore 2011). Butch and gender-blending women may be lesbian or straight and may sometimes be taken for men, but—unlike transmen—they do not identify as men.

Schilt and Westbrook find that, in nonsexual interactions, transmen are able to establish a male gender identity on the basis of gendered appearance and demeanor, even when they do not possess male genitalia (Schilt and Westbrook 2009). Male coworkers accept transmen—or at least tall, white transmen—as "just one of the guys," based on visible cues of masculinity (e.g., facial hair), even when they know that they were formerly women (Schilt 2011). Yet, transmen who have not had hormonal therapy and therefore do not appear to be men do not receive such social advantages (Schilt 2011).

Women who do "female masculinities" (Halberstam 1998) may similarly receive some forms of patriarchal dividends. For example, Kazyak's (2012) study of rural gays and lesbians shows that female masculinity may be normative in rural settings. However, to the extent that women clearly identify as women, they are unlikely to be granted the full status of "honorary men" (Schilt 2011). Moreover, they may find that inclusion prompts subjection to the rough and demeaning talk that characterizes many male interactions (Denissen 2010b).

If lesbians are perceived as less threatening to notions of "men's work," their visibility threatens the dictates of compulsory heterosexuality (Rich 1993) and, more broadly, the subordination of women's sexuality to men's desire (MacKinnon 1982; Pateman 1988). Men's efforts to sexually objectify women coworkers can be understood as an attempt to restore this gender-sexual order. In response, women skillfully mix performances of femininity and masculinity to resist being depicted as occupationally incompetent or sexually deviant and to assert their sexual autonomy (Denissen 2010b). Yet, resistance to sexual objectification may elicit more overt hostility from male coworkers.

In response to homophobia, lesbian tradeswomen engage in interactional strategies that vary by perceived risk and other contextual factors. These fall along a continuum from "passing" (Goffman 1963) or "playing it straight" (Sullivan 2001), in which they conceal their sexual orientation, and "covering," in which they prevent this identity from "looming large" (Goffman 1963) to fully "coming out" or "telling it like it is" (Sullivan 2001). Most engage in hybrid strategies, such as "speaking half-truths to power" or adopting an "open closet door policy" (Reimann 2001), in which they carefully manage disclosure by selectively revealing their sexual orientation based on specific context. In addition to sexual orientation, we expect that race, gender presentation, and body size inform which interactional strategies are both possible and preferred (Crenshaw 1989; Fikkan and Rothblum 2011; Moore 2011; Saguy 2012).

* * *

NEGOTIATING THREATS TO THE MASCULINE DEFINITION OF THE WORK

Tradeswomen report that homophobic comments, jokes, and graffiti are pervasive and that tradesmen regularly use terms like "gay" and "faggot" to publicly establish heteromasculine identities and to reinforce the masculine definition of the work. For example, Monique says her male coworkers "pick on each other, [saying things] like: 'The electricians are faggots,' 'The carpenters are faggots,' 'Because he walks a certain way, he's gay.'" In this example, tradesmen use homophobic comments to assert dominance over "rival" groups of men (such as men from other trades) and to regulate the gender and sexual behavior of men. Yet, unlike the high school boys studied by Pascoe who claim not to direct fag discourse at boys known to be gay (Pascoe 2005), tradesmen unapologetically use homophobic slurs to repudiate both homosexuality and femininity (in men). This was not lost on the tradeswomen interviewed, who attributed the fact that they did not know any openly gay men to their sense that the trades are dangerous for openly gay men.

Similarly, the presence of women on job sites threatens the definition of the construction trades as "men's work." One way that tradesmen make sense of tradeswomen's presence and neutralize this threat is to label them lesbians or likely lesbians. Lynne, an Asian American lesbian, explains, "People think if you're a tradeswoman, you're a lesbian. You want to do a man's job, so you want to be a man, so you're a lesbian." Stephanie, a straight white woman, says, "People think I'm gay a lot of the time because . . . I don't look real feminine." Holly, another straight white woman, says a fellow apprentice "never discussed her love life at work, and she [then] mentioned having a boyfriend. Everybody looked at her like 'You have a boyfriend?' They thought she was gay." Imagining tradeswomen as lesbians, that is, not fully female, preserves the idea of the trades as "men's work."

This opens up the possibility that straight tradeswomen may be perceived as more of a threat to the masculine definition of the work than lesbian tradeswomen. Indeed, Loretta, a Black lesbian, says that her male coworkers do not "want any women at all," but that "somebody like me is safer for them because they can ignore me like a guy they don't like." . . .

Loretta notes that while some tradesmen resent the presence of all women in the trades, straight or lesbian, that she, as a lesbian, is "not really a chick" and her presence does not limit tradesmen's freedom to perform masculinity as they please. This may be especially true for lesbians like Loretta who present as butch. Indeed, Vicky, a lesbian tradeswoman who describes herself as "a bit girlier" notes that tradesmen are more likely to treat a woman who "doesn't look as feminine on the outside" as "one of the guys," while they are more likely to "watch their potty mouth" around more "girly"-presenting lesbians. We also find some evidence that butch lesbians are somewhat less likely to be targeted by sexual advances.

A few tradeswomen claim that, as lesbians, they are fully accepted as "one of the guys." For example, Toni, a white lesbian, who describes herself as someone who "used to be extremely feminine" but no longer bothers because "it required too much maintenance," describes how she is incorporated into the men's sex talk:

> [My coworker] tells his girlfriend, "She's like one of the guys, you know, I can tell her anything." That's how most of the guys think of me anyways. They just talk about whatever they want to. It's, like, [I'll tell the men,] "You should do this [sexual maneuver] or you should try that [sexual position]." [And, later they'll tell me,] "Oh, that worked! Thanks a lot, Toni." So it's all good.

For Toni, offering advice on women's sexuality is a "good" form of inclusion because it takes place within a supportive working relationship with coworkers.

At the same time, finding acceptance as "one of the guys" can be fraught with danger. Lori, the

Jewish butch lesbian introduced earlier, describes a lunchtime interaction she had as an apprentice, when she was especially vulnerable:

> They're sitting around talking about the Mike Tyson case when he sexually assaulted this woman. For me, rape is no joking matter. So here's nine of 'em, a foreman, journeymen, apprentices, and one shop steward, and I'm the only woman in this discussion. They're all sitting there talking about it and joking about it, and I'm, like, "Whoa. I'm feeling really, really violent." So I said, "The next person who says anything, I'm gonna get really violent." They all shut the fuck up. Then there was another situation where they were talking about wife beating. I got mad, but sometimes it's not worth it 'cause it's, like, "Oh, she's got no sense of humor." So then I just don't eat lunch with them anymore. . . .

While lesbians may be more likely than straight women to be accepted as "one of the guys," and while this can provide some camaraderie and acceptance as a serious worker, they rarely experience full acceptance. Rather, tradeswomen typically emphasize that acceptance as one of the guys is incomplete and conditional. Many tradeswomen say their male coworkers hold them to an exaggerated standard of masculinity, making them carry heavier materials and do dirtier and more dangerous work, in order to prove they can work "like a guy." Further, as we discuss ahead, acceptance as one of the guys in some contexts does not exempt them from the ideals of emphasized femininity in others.

Managing Perceived Threats to the Heterogendered Order

While the presumption that tradeswomen are likely lesbians neutralizes threats to the masculine definition of the work, it threatens heteronormativity and the sexual and economic subordination of women to men. In response, tradesmen sometimes direct gendered homophobic comments at lesbian tradeswomen. In other instances, they sexually objectify (lesbian and straight) tradeswomen. We examine tradeswomen's accounts of this behavior and how they respond to it.

Keeping Them Guessing, Keeping It Private, and Other Responses to Gendered Homophobia. Just as they use fag discourse to police gender noncomformity among men, so tradesmen use the lesbian label to control the gendered conduct of tradeswomen. For example, Elena (a Latina heterosexual) says tradesmen single out lesbian tradeswomen as deviant "freaks": "The guys talk about them really bad, like, she's trying to play a man role, she likes it rough, men can't satisfy her, she must be freaky and have freaky needs." Lauren, a white lesbian who describes herself as tomboyish but not butch, says that she has heard her coworkers make disparaging comments about "hardcore dyke lesbians." She recounts how one tradesman exclaimed, "Damn, I'm working with this guy and next thing I know she turns around and, shit, she's got tits!" When Lauren asked him if she was a good worker, he responded, "I don't know, I couldn't work with her."

Racial minority status and body size can intersect with sexual identity and gender presentation to heighten stigmatization and otherness. Loretta, the Black butch lesbian, is large and has a shaved head. An electrician, a trade that historically has had among the lowest number of minority workers (Bilginsoy 2005), Loretta describes job sites as "bastions of white male supremacy." She notes that, in recent years, an influx of Latino workers has heightened racial tensions and that the prevailing message conveyed to women, "queers," and people of color is "You shouldn't be here." She tells of hearing tradesmen say, "Now they're letting animals in the trade." When asked to whom they were referring, Loretta exclaims, "Me! Or my crew-member who [was] a person of color." Loretta speaks of how she is threatening, not just as a woman, but as a large, Black, butch lesbian woman with an aggressive personality, a composite that "messes with the whole expectation of what your gender, what your behavior's supposed to be."

Loretta says that tradesmen sometimes "picked on" her about her large size, saying things like, "You're fat" or that her size "ain't

cool for chicks." Similarly, Lori, who describes herself as a "big butch dyke" (a "three-part package"), says that her coworkers' negative comments about her size are gendered: "They'll accommodate a big guy where they won't accommodate a big woman."

Sometimes the label "lesbian" is decoupled from women's own sexual identity, as when tradesmen target tradeswomen for gendered homophobia because their appearance or behavior does not conform to tradesmen's gender expectations. For instance, Cheryl, a white heterosexual, explains how one of her coworkers "was mad because I'd showed him up that day," performing better than he in a workplace task. He asked her, "What's the matter with you? Are you one of those lesbian women, you know, and you're not interested in me?" In this example, Cheryl's coworker accuses her of being a lesbian, and thus unfeminine, because she outperforms him. He thereby conflates her occupational competence and sexual orientation, considering both as signs of gender nonconformity.

In response to gendered homophobia, lesbian tradeswomen engage in complex risk assessments and employ a variety of disclosure options. For example, Anna, a Latina lesbian who describes herself as tomboyish and "not real girly but not real butchy," remarks about a coworker, "I've heard him make comments about fags and queers and I didn't want to go there. When he said, 'Are you married?' I said, 'No' and I didn't say I have a partner." Here, Anna speaks a "half-truth to power" (Sullivan 2001). It is true that she is not married, but she conceals the full truth—that she has a same-sex romantic partner—from this coworker because his homophobic comments make that revelation feel unsafe. Further, Anna says that in situations that feel safer, she selectively discloses her sexual identity. . . .

Racial minority status often heightens othering and perceived risk, further limiting tradeswomen's disclosure options. For example, Lori, a self-described Jewish butch lesbian, says she did not disclose her sexual orientation on one job site early in her career because she had heard "a bunch of sexist, racist, and homophobic speech" that made disclosure feel unsafe. While her coworkers were specifically "targeting the Hispanics," their behavior "really frightened" her "because they had swastikas and Nazi and KKK-type talk." Yet, later in her career and on less racist job sites, she developed a strategy of singling out one man with whom she would be more open:

> What I do generally is I'd make allies with one dude who I felt was more open-minded or we have a connection. I would be honest with him about who I was. As long as I had one person I could be myself with, then I felt okay. Now I'm pretty much out. I decided that I'm out in the union as a whole, but I pick and choose how much I say.

Several of the respondents similarly spoke about becoming more open, but still guarded, regarding their sexuality as they gained more occupational seniority.

Sometimes tradeswomen conceal their sexual identity not simply out of fear of retaliation but also to resist the salience of their sexual identity in workplace interactions. We call this strategy "keeping it private." Vanesa, a white lesbian, explains that she brought her best friend, rather than her girlfriend, to union picnics both because she wants to keep her "personal life private" and also because she hopes to "keep away from the stigma" and does not "want a guy not to teach me because of who I am." Anita, a Native American lesbian, similarly evokes a concern with both privacy and homophobia, explaining that she was not initially out because "it's nobody's business, and then going into a man's field I figured it's probably not a good idea to advertise." Yet, she says that "if it came up, I didn't deny it," akin to what others have labeled an "open closet door policy" (Reimann 2001). Similarly, Lauren, a white lesbian, says, "There's some guys that don't know. Maybe that's my way of blending in without any confrontation. I like to get in there, get my job done, and get out. I've had a couple of guys ask me, and if they got the balls to ask me, I'll tell them."

Gina, a large, black, straight, married woman, evokes a "keep them guessing" strategy that entails sending mixed messages about sexual identity as part of an attempt to "break that stereotype":

> I had them so fooled there were people that didn't have any idea what my sexual orientation was. If somebody questioned me, [I'd say,] "I'm gay, leave me alone, I'm a lesbian." Or [I'd say,] "I'm single," or "I have two kids," or "I have a husband." People would be running around, [saying,] "No, she told me she was gay." Or "Gina, you're not gay, I met your husband." So you'd keep them guessing because the point was that your sexual orientation didn't matter.

While keeping the men guessing may function partially as an expression of solidarity with lesbian tradeswomen, a sort of reverse passing intended to challenge stereotypes about lesbians, Gina herself says it is also a way of resisting the salience of women's sexual identities at work.

Similarly, Alex, a white lesbian, talks about mixing displays of subordinated feminine heterosexuality with more stereotypically masculine behavior in order to resist homophobia and sexism. She explains that while she used to be mistaken for a man because she "looked completely androgynous," she has grown her hair since joining the trades because short hair "would be such a red flag" that she is a "dyke" or is "so manly":

> I'd rather act feminine and friendly and cute than get harassed, ignored, or treated worse. But at the same time it's like I have to be careful that I don't act overly feminine because they'll think I can't work. Sometimes I'll say something that will totally throw them for a spin [or] make them raise an eyebrow because I'll say it in a masculine way. I'll say something that's really clear, concise, and to the point, and they don't expect that of me. They think I'm a bubbly person; they stereotype me as a female.

Alex is managing a classic double bind where she is held accountable to conflicting expectations for gendered conduct. She is aware that her coworkers may mark (raised eyebrow) and sanction (harassment, isolation) masculine conduct. Alex says she flirts with men and acts "feminine" in an effort to forestall certain forms of harassment and exclusion, but fears that overdoing it may detract from her perceived competence. She performs an intricate gender maneuvering in trying to strike a balance by varying heterofeminine displays with more assertive (masculine) actions to transgress dualistic sexual and gender boundaries. While white respondents, straight and gay, were more likely to speak of incorporating displays of emphasized femininity into their gender maneuvering, Black, butch, and large tradeswomen were more likely to emphasize their ability to "hold their own" with the heaviest, dirtiest, and most dangerous tasks.

Turning the Tables: Resistance to Compulsory Heterosexuality. Another way that tradesmen neutralize the threat of lesbian/female autonomy is by recasting them as objects of men's sexual desire. Some lesbian tradeswomen say tradesmen embrace them through the heterosexual male fantasy of having 'fancy sex' with multiple women. For instance, when asked if she ever was directly targeted by homophobia, Anna, the Latina lesbian introduced earlier, responds, "No, because I'm a female. Some guys say, 'I don't care about the women. I think that's great! That's fancy for me! I just can't stand the guys.'" Yet, Toni, a white lesbian, suggests that this form of acceptance has its costs: "They'll make innuendos like 'You should hook up with her and then hook up with me later.' They know I'm not interested in them. They just continue to do it because they know it bugs me." In this instance, Toni's coworkers impose heterosexual expectations and meanings onto her and intentionally "bug" her. By redefining lesbian relationships as serving male heterosexual desire, tradesmen neutralize the perceived threat of lesbian desire to heterosexism.

Out lesbian tradeswomen use various strategies to resist their coworkers' efforts to heterosexualize them and, sometimes, to reaffirm their sexual identity as lesbians. Jan, a lesbian of white and Native American descent, who is slim and has long blonde hair, and says she "doesn't go out of her way to be feminine" but "doesn't seem butch to the guys," complains about how she has to tell her coworkers that she is not "free porn." Others speak of resisting traditional gender dynamics by showing a sexually assertive interest in their coworker's women partners. Anna, the Latina lesbian, explains:

> [My coworkers] accept me for who I am. [He'll say,] "That's cool, girl. Can we get some?" [laughs] I'll be, like, "Can I get some of yours? I'll let you talk to my girl if you let me talk to your wife." And he'll be, like, "Fuck you." Guys are cool with me. [They'll say,] "How's your girl? She's pretty hot." I go, "Yeah, thank you. So is your wife." [Laughs.]

While Anna describes her interactions with her coworkers as playful and respectful ("They accept me for who I am"), she also experiences counterresistance from her coworker ("Fuck you"). Indeed, it seems that she gets respect, in large part, because she can give as good as she gets, using masculine displays of dominance to neutralize efforts to sexually dominate her. We call this strategy "turning the tables."

Similarly, Lynne, an Asian American lesbian whom we would describe as gender-blending but who is sometimes mistaken for a man, explains how she responded to a coworker who constantly asked her if he could watch her have sex with another woman:

> I said, "Why don't you talk to your girlfriend about it? Bring me a picture; I want to see what she looks like." He got all defensive: "Who, wait, what'd you mean? I don't have a picture. She ain't going for that shit." He backed off that whole line of conversation after that.

Like Anna, Lynne successfully wards off her coworker's efforts to sexualize her by turning the tables and sexualizing his girlfriend. While this interaction seems to have been successful in curtailing demands to watch Lynne have sex with other women, later in the interview Lynne says this incident led to a strained working relationship with this particular coworker.

Moreover, tradeswomen are not equally able to resist their coworker's efforts to sexualize them. Julia, a Latina lesbian apprentice who described herself as "looking like a little dude," describes an extreme case in which a coworker attempted to sexually force himself on her. . . .

This tradesman disregards Julia's identity as a lesbian, as well as her resistance to his sexual advances, trying to force himself on her. He responds to her defiance with threats to "get her," culminating with a sexual assault on the job site. Fearing for her job, she initially refused to report the incident but ultimately did so, upon the urging of the superintendent and the coworker who witnessed the assault. Julia says she never saw the assailant again.

Other tradeswomen also report being targeted with overt hostility and violence after refusing to engage in sexual banter or feminine displays. Some of the more egregious examples include having electrical wires turned on while they were working on them, having tools dropped on them, or finding feces in their hard hat. These sorts of incidents highlight the risks and limitations of individual-level resistance.

How Gendered Homophobia Limits Collective Resistance. While individual strategies have subversive potential, successful "contestation of gender hierarchy is fundamentally a collective process" (Connell 2009, 109). With typically few allies at work, one might expect tradeswomen to seek each other out for safety and support. Yet many of our respondents say they avoid other women both on and off the construction site. In some cases, this stems from their own homophobia, but it is more often described as an effort to protect themselves from homophobic stigma and sexist stereotypes. Vanesa, a white lesbian, explains, "Women will tell me they don't want to be seen with other women or belonging to a women's group because a lot of the guys say, '[If] you women want to be just like us men so much, then why do you have this little women's group?'" Some tradesmen pressure her and other tradeswomen to avoid associating with other women. Vanesa further describes how tradesmen

reframe women's efforts to support each other as attempts to gain special privileges. For example, her foreman remarked, after seeing her in a tradeswomen's convention T-shirt, "I don't think there should be separate organizations, you guys need to be treated the same."

Loretta, the Black butch lesbian, says that she "would never hang out with the girls" and that "the girls on the crew wouldn't want to hang out with me, because they wouldn't want the other guys to think that they were gay. Because of that guilt by association thing it's, like, 'Well, if we're nice to you, they might think we're like you.'" Loretta's comments speak to how lesbian stigma is attached not only to joining women's associations but also to socializing with other women on the job. Similarly, Lori, a Jewish butch lesbian, says, "I wanted to start a lesbian tradeswomen group but not even the lesbians want to start it with me." Moreover, she says, "Sometimes even other women in the trades are afraid to be seen with me because I'm an out lesbian. Like it'll spill off on them and the guys will see it." At a conference for women in the trades, the women became particularly animated when they heard that tradesmen were referring to the conference as a "big lesbian orgy" in what seemed like an attempt to discredit the conference and keep both straight and lesbian tradeswomen away.

As Lori describes it, tradesmen effectively use the specter of lesbianism to stymie gender solidarity and political activism: "Sometimes there's solidarity, sometimes not, because the lesbians think they have to align themselves with the men for power and that means turning against other women or a more out lesbian. They'll be more closeted or they're afraid to be seen as lesbian whether they're lesbian or not." In distancing themselves from other women in order to protect themselves from the gendered homophobia of their coworkers, both straight and lesbian tradeswomen are made more vulnerable as they become isolated from each other. Yet, there is also evidence of resistance and change. For example, the tradeswomen conference has grown steadily over time from a state to an international event and active tradeswomen's groups have formed online, demonstrating organizational success despite these challenges.

CONCLUSION

Drawing on interviews with a diverse sample of lesbian and straight women in the construction trades, this article examines how the cultural meanings of sexual identity, gender presentation, race, and, more tentatively, body size and seniority, inform how men seek to control tradeswomen and how the latter respond to these efforts. We show that labeling tradeswomen as lesbians, and thus—in the popular imagination— as not fully women, both makes sense of their presence and reaffirms the perception of the trades as "men's work." Some lesbian tradeswomen report being more accepted than their straight women coworkers and claim that the lesbian label offers them some freedom from performing emphasized femininity. This acceptance is limited, however, and can place them in uncomfortable situations where they are expected to perform misogynist versions of masculinity. Moreover, while lesbians may be less threatening to the notion of the trades as men's work, their presence threatens heteronormativity and assumptions about the sexual subordination of women. We explain how tradesmen's efforts to sexually objectify tradeswomen can be understood as attempts to neutralize threats to heteronormativity and male privilege.

We demonstrate that in response to these constraints, tradeswomen use gender maneuvering (Schippers 2002) to combine performances of femininity and masculinity, to gain some measure of acceptance as women, and to maintain their perceived competence as workers. While tradeswomen strategically draw upon multiple strategies, we further show how the meanings attributed to tradeswomen's sexuality, gender presentation, race, body size, and seniority influence their preferred strategies. . . .

While individual tradeswomen are creative and sometimes successful in their efforts to resist men's attempts to marginalize and exclude them,

our study suggests that individual responses may not be enough to produce widespread or lasting change. Tradeswomen's efforts to organize, however, are stymied by insinuations of lesbianism. Thus, gendered homophobia plays a crucial role in isolating and dividing tradeswomen, undermining their efforts to create solidarity, engage in collective resistance, and bring about institutional change. The risks of associating with lesbians and other women may be greatest for women of color and other especially vulnerable populations, a question that merits additional research.

We show how contradictions in the dominant heterogender order constrain tradeswomen, while opening up possibilities for—and even necessitating—more reflexive, varied, and strategic forms of gender and sexual practices (Denissen 2010b). Since gendered expectations of tradeswomen are intrinsically contradictory (e.g., sufficiently masculine to be deemed competent but sufficiently feminine to be socially acceptable), tradeswomen must constantly vary the way they "do gender" (West and Zimmerman 1987). Earlier work shows that exclusion of women in the building trades is reproduced despite women's resistance at the level of interaction and identity construction (Denissen 2010b). This article sheds light on one key mechanism whereby women's strategic agency is limited: the isolation of tradeswomen from other women. Thus, while individual tradeswomen strategically maneuver among gender and sexual meanings in ways that transgress heterogender boundaries and trouble the heterogender order, they face greater counterresistance when they collectively organize. This study expands on previous research that documents how race, class, and gender identities can be used to divide and control workers (Hossfeld 1990) by showing how tradesmen use gendered homophobia as a means of dividing and subordinating women workers.

These findings speak to debates about the extent to which individual-level resistance disrupts patriarchy or, alternatively, unwittingly reinforces the dominant gender order (Devor 1987; Ridgeway and Correll 2004). According to

Finley (2010), transformations in gender relations are more likely in women-controlled than male-dominated spaces. Finley argues that women's networks are crucial for transforming the dominant gender order and that women in male-dominated settings are too isolated from other women to be effective. Our findings regarding women's isolation from each other and limits to collective resistance are consistent with Finley's argument. . . .

REFERENCES

Applebaum, Herbert. 1999. *Construction workers, U.S.A.* Westport, CT: Greenwood.

Bilginsoy, Cihan. 2005. Registered apprentices and apprenticeship programs in the U.S. construction industry between 1989 and 2003: An examination of the AIMS, RAIS, and California Apprenticeship Agency databases. Department of Economics Working Paper Series (Working Paper #2005–09), University of Utah, Salt Lake City.

Bilginsoy, Cihan. 2009. *Wage structure and unionization in the U.S. construction sector.* Salt Lake City, UT: University of Utah, Department of Economics.

Burke, Marc. 1994. Homosexuality as deviance: The case of the gay police officer. *British Journal of Criminology* 34:192–203.

Collinson, David L. 2010. *Managing the shopfloor.* Boston, MA: De Gruyter.

Connell, R. W. 1987. *Gender and power: Society, the person, and sexual politics.* Stanford, CA: Stanford University Press.

Connell, Raewyn. 2009. "Doing gender" in transsexual and political retrospect. *Gender & Society* 23 (1): 94–98.

Crenshaw, Kimberle. 1989. Demarginalizing the intersection of race and sex: A Black feminist critique of antidiscrimination doctrine, feminist theory and antiracist policies. *University of Chicago Legal Forum* 139–67.

Denissen, Amy M. 2010a. Crossing the line: How women in the building trades interpret and respond to sexual conduct at work. *Journal of Contemporary Ethnography* 39:298–327.

Denissen, Amy M. 2010b. The right tools for the job: Constructing gender meanings and identities in the male-dominated building trades. *Human Relations* 63:1051–69.

Devor, Holly. 1987. Gender blending females: Women and sometimes men. *American Behavioral Scientist* 31:12–40.

Epstein, Cynthia Fuchs. 1992. Tinkerbells and pinups. In *Cultivating differences: Symbolic boundaries and the making of inequality,* edited by Michele Lamont and Marcel Foumier. Chicago: University of Chicago Press.

Fikkan, Janna L., and Esther Rothblum. 2011. Is fat a feminist issue? Exploring the gendered nature of weight bias. *Sex Roles* 66:575–92.

Finley, Nancy J. 2010. Skating femininity: Gender maneuvering in women's roller derby. *Journal of Contemporary Ethnography* 39:359–87.

Frank, Miriam. 2001. Hard hats and homophobia: Lesbians in the building trades. *New Labor Forum* 8:25–36.

Goffman, Erving. 1963. *Stigma: Notes on the management of a spoiled identity,* New York: Prentice Hall.

Gruber, James E. 1998. The impact of male work environments and organizational policies on women's experiences of sexual harassment. *Gender & Society* 12:301–20.

Halberstam, Judith. 1998. *Female masculinity.* Durham, NC: Duke University Press.

Hossfeld, Karen J. 1990. "Their logic against them": Contradictions in sex, race, and class in Silicon Valley. In *Women workers and global restructuring,* edited by Kathryn B. Ward. Ithaca, NY: Cornell University Press.

Ingraham, Chrys. 1994. The heterosexual imaginary: Feminist sociology and theories of gender. *Sociological Theory* 12:203–19.

Jamieson, Kathleen H. 1995. *Beyond the double bind: Women and leadership.* New York: Oxford University Press.

Janssens, Maddy, Tineke Cappellen, and Patrizia Zanoni. 2006. Successful female expatriates as agents: Positioning oneself through gender, hierarchy, and culture. *Journal of World Business* 41:133–48.

Kanter, Rosabeth M. 1977. *Men and women of the corporation.* New York: Basic Books.

Kazyak, Emily. 2012. Midwest or lesbian? Gender, rurality, and sexuality. *Gender & Society* 26:825–48.

Lucal, Betsy. 1999. What it means to be gendered me: Life on the boundaries of a dichotomous gender system. *Gender & Society* 13:781–97.

MacKinnon, Catharine. 1982. Feminism, Marxism, method and the state: An agenda for theory. *Signs* 7:533–44.

McDermott, E. 2006. Surviving in dangerous places: Lesbian identity performances in the workplace, social class and psychological health. *Feminism and Psychology* 16:193–211.

Miller, Susan L., Kay B. Forest, and Nancy C. Jurik. 2003. Diversity in blue: Lesbian and gay police officers in a masculine occupation. *Men and Masculinities* 5:355–85.

Moore, Mignon. 2011. *Invisible families: Gay identities, relationships, and motherhood among Black women.* Berkeley: University of California Press.

Myers, Kristen A., Kay B. Forest, and Susan L. Miller. 2004, Officer friendly and the tough cop: Gays and lesbians navigate homophobia and policing. *Journal of Homosexuality* 47:17–37.

Paap, Kris. 2006. *Working construction: Why white working-class men put themselves—and the labor movement—in harm's way.* Ithaca, NY: Cornell University Press.

Pascoe, C. J. 2005. "Dude, you're a fag": Adolescent masculinity and the fag discourse. *Sexualities* 8:329–46.

Pateman, Carol. 1988. *The sexual contract.* Stanford, CA: Stanford University Press.

Pierce, Jennifer L. 1995. *Gender trials: Emotional lives in contemporary law firms.* Berkeley: University of California Press.

Ramirez, Hernan. 2010. Masculinity in the workplace: The case of Mexican immigrant gardeners. *Men and Masculinities* 14:97–116.

Reimann, Renate. 2001. Lesbian mothers at work. In *Queer families, queer politics,* edited by Mary Bernstein and Renate Reimann. New York: Columbia University Press.

Rich, Adrienne. 1993. Compulsory heterosexuality and lesbian existence. In *The lesbian and gay studies reader,* edited by Henry Abelove, Michele Aina Barale, and David Halperin. New York: Routledge.

Ridgeway, Cecilia L., and Shelley J. Correll. 2004. Unpacking the gender system: A theoretical perspective on gender beliefs and social relations. *Gender & Society* 18:510–31.

Saguy, Abigail C. 2012. Why fat is a feminist issue. *Sex Roles* 68:600–7.

Schilt, Kristen. 2011. *Just one of the guys? Transgender men and the persistence of workplace gender inequality.* Chicago: University of Chicago.

Schilt, Kristen, and Laurel Westbrook. 2009. Doing gender, doing heteronormativity: "Gender normals," transgender people, and the social maintenance of heterosexuality. *Gender & Society* 23:440–64.

Schippers, Mimi. 2002. *Rockin' out of the box: Gender maneuvering in alternative hard rock.* New Brunswick: Rutgers University Press.

Schrock, Douglas, and Michael Schwalbe. 2009. Men, masculinity, and manhood acts. *Annual Review of Sociology* 35:277–95.

Seidman, Steven. 2010. *The social construction of sexuality,* 2nd ed. New York: Norton.

Sullivan, Maureen. 2001. Alma mater: Family "outings" and the making of the Modern Other Mother (MOM). In *Queer families, queer politics,* edited by Mary Bernstein and Renate Reimann. New York: Columbia University Press.

Valian, Virginia. 1998. *Why so slow? The advancement of women.* Cambridge: MIT Press.

West, Candace, and Don H. Zimmerman. 1987. Doing gender. *Gender and Society* 1:125–51.

Zinn, Maxine Baca. 1982. Chicano men and masculinity. *Journal of Ethnic Studies* 10:29–44.

Introduction to Reading 45

Gender is enforced in many ways, bullying being one. This reading by Scott Melzer offers a deeper understanding of the systems of controls at the most inner concentric circles of Peter L. Berger's model (discussed in the beginning of this chapter), that is, how we and those closest to us enforce gendered behavior, in this case, masculinity. Melzer's background is in researching gender and masculinities as well as violence. He gives a vivid description of a men's fighting club, providing insights into the way hegemonic masculinity affects how men and young boys feel about themselves. The description of how these men have bought into hegemonic masculinity, including feelings of both dominance and violence in their definitions of themselves and their relationships with others, helps us to understand how men and boys enforce the doing of masculinity in themselves and others. This piece was written for a journal targeted to the general public; therefore, it does not have references but, rather, suggestions for further reading.

1. Why do these men want to fight in a private club?

2. How does childhood bullying continue to influence these men when they are successful adults?

3. Why does Melzer title this piece "ritual violence"?

RITUAL VIOLENCE IN A TWO-CAR GARAGE

Scott Melzer

"Do not cripple your friends. Do not bring them to tears," says the organizer. "If it's your first time at Fight Club," he adds, turning to face me, "you fight first." He hands me a dulled, rounded 9-inch training knife, padded gloves, and a fencing mask. My opponent, Mike, is about the same size as me. He has a knife, too. Unfortunately for me, Mike actually knows how to use his. I have no fight training or experience, and it's about to be painfully evident.

I try not to think about the language in the release form I just signed. "I, the participant, am knowingly risking injury, which typically includes bruises, bumps and scrapes but can include serious injury and death from either fighting or watching." Bruises. Bumps. Scrapes. Death? It's unlikely anybody will come close to dying today—at least not of anything more than humiliation.

Mike and I are fighting under the auspices of The Gentlemen's Fighting Club—a San Francisco Bay Area group formed in the late 1990s. In GFC's history, there have been few serious injuries. This fact, along with the thickly padded gloves and sturdy mask, alleviate most of my concerns. Still, I am tempted to repeat the prefight instructions to Mike: Please do not cripple me or bring me to tears. "Fighters ready?" the timekeeper asks. I tighten my fingers around the handle of the training knife and square off with my opponent. "Fight!"

It's Fight the Professor Day at GFC, a one-time gathering organized at my request. It's a comforting sign of the GFC philosophy that my original title—"Punch the Professor"—was rejected. While typical GFC novices fight in a suburban garage, this event is being held on a concrete patio and grass in a fenced-in backyard. First-timers and longtime members alike fight in a rotation of among five to ten people, usually friends and acquaintances, almost always only men. A few hundred people have fought at GFC, and most fight only a few times. Only a couple dozen were regulars at the club's peak, when they fought biweekly.

Almost all the men have a martial arts or fighting background. None are amateur or

From Melzer, Scott. 2013. Ritual Violence in a Two-Car Garage. *Contexts, 12*(3), 25–31.

professional mixed martial arts (MMA) fighters. Sanctioned, refereed MMA fights are short, violent exchanges that typically end with a knockout or forced submission. GFC provides a more authentic combat experience than martial arts sparring and less risk of injury than MMA, as well as an especially varied and creative array of weapons. In addition to the grappling and hitting that is part of martial arts and MMA, these fighters use brass rods rolled-up into magazines, unopened soda cans or soap bars wrapped in pillowcases, small purses filled with buckshot, folding chairs, cookie sheets, computer keyboards, and even metal chains.

Fighters wear just about any protective gear they choose, or none at all. Bruises, cuts, blood, and pain are routine. Broken fingers happen. The stakes are higher than a schoolyard fight, but only rarely does someone get badly injured. They have to go home to their families and to work the next day, and they want their friends and foes to leave intact, so they can return to fight another day.

Geek Fight Club?

They're crazy! It's fake! A Geek Fight Club!? More like cubicle jockeys desperate to feel something real.

When the media first discovered the Gentlemen's Fight Club, reporters, fighters, martial artists, academics, and others joined in laughter, scorn, and skepticism. What motivated these guys to take up arms and fight? To answer that question, I observed fights, participated in one afternoon of combat, and interviewed 13 GFC fighters on their own and three in a group setting. I found that these men fight to test their skills and toughness, to conquer their fears, and, in some cases, to restore a sense of masculinity and control they lost during experiences of boyhood emasculation.

GFC is a democratic institution. Occupation and social class aren't used as filters for entry. Although members joke about excluding "yuppie punchers" and the "Gentlemen" moniker harkens to upper-class British pugilists, no interested fighter has been turned away. Landscapes, marketers, police officers, community organizers, students, and even a couple self-identified gang members have fought at GFC. Social class and status disappear behind the headgear and weapons.

The media has portrayed the club as primarily for geeks—software engineers and computer programmers—trying to escape their cubicle existence. The high proportion of middle- and upper-middle class tech professionals is primarily due to the Bay Area location, the founders (who came from those fields), and the members' own personal and work networks. More than their profession or economic status, it is a background in martial arts—and some frustration with the limits of their training—that draws men to GFC.

The fighters I chose to interview are a racially and ethnically diverse group in their 20s, 30s and 40s, single or with children, and mostly college-educated. Like most GFC regulars or visitors, they are unlikely to find themselves fighting in a bar or anywhere other than GFC. Of course, each fighter brings a different biography and life experience to the club. But they share a similar cultural upbringing: longtime American attitudes toward men's violence and combat that transcend divisions of class and race.

Boys to Men

American culture simultaneously expects, celebrates, and punishes violence in boys and men. Despite the contradictions, and without a formal rite of passage from boyhood to manhood as found in cultures throughout the world, our society produces the unofficial, nearly universal boyhood ritual of fighting. American educators, parents, and law-enforcement authorities have been trying to discourage fighting, violence, and bullying, now broadly defined to include physical and verbal intimidation.

But real-life fighting continues to be the way most boys prove themselves physically, testing themselves and one another. For some men, GFC is simply an extension of their lifelong fascination with fighting—from vicariously experienced cartoon violence to actual schoolyard clashes and martial arts training. Another inspiration for the GFC was the rise of mixed martial arts, in which fighters use all disciplines; the first Ultimate Fighting Championship was held in 1993.

It's unclear how many fight clubs exist. There are, of course, media stories about teenagers fighting in front of crowds of fellow teenage spectators. These fights may be staged for fun, for gambling, and sometimes to create home-made movies that are sold for profit. They have little in common, though, with the handful of adult fight clubs I discovered during my research. With the exception of GFC, the adult clubs were either no longer active or deeply underground, and they mostly mirror increasingly popular and main-streamed mixed martial arts (MMA) events.

Gentlemen's Fight Club is the only club I located that uses weapons and holds regular fight nights. It is distinct from MMA and other groups in one other significant way: winning and losing is irrelevant. No one scores the fights or keeps track of the number of strikes landed. There's almost a team spirit, despite the one-on-one nature of combat. The fighters have an interest in helping each other build their skills, but they show no interest in ranking each other, playing out anger, or humiliating anyone. The fighters certainly deliver painful blows and cause injuries to opponents, but there's no intent to cause serious harm.

In one of my fights, my stronger opponent skillfully delivered painful strikes using rattan sticks, but he didn't bull-rush or grab me, pin me down, or pummel me. Stronger and more skilled fighters use the weapons to expand their own and their opponent's skills. They gain nothing by overwhelming smaller, less experienced fighters with brute strength. Winning is supplanted by skill development.

A couple of GFC fighters eagerly spoke of physically dominating their opponents, using aggression and overwhelming force. But as sociologist Michael Kimmel argues in his 2006 book *Manhood in America,* being a man isn't really about pursuing domination over others—it's about evoking a fear of being dominated and controlled. For many GFC fighters, it's gratifying just to participate, to put oneself at risk and survive, to experiment with losing and establishing control. All this is to say, asserting masculinity isn't necessarily about inflicting damage. It's about controlling others, and controlling one's own reactions and emotions—especially fear.

LOSING CONTROL

Many men are motivated to fight because they've arrived at adulthood without evidence (at least for themselves) that they've passed the "test." They want to know if their own strength and training would hold up in a real fight, if they have the courage to face an armed attacker. Can they overcome a sometimes paralyzing fear of injury and protect themselves and their families—maybe even kick a little ass if they have to?

One subset of this group wants to exorcise particularly painful memories of fear, humiliation, and defeat that continue to haunt them. Several men I interviewed—including Asher, Sammy, and Freddy—have met many of society's expectations for what men should be and do. Their college degrees, successful careers, and families offset some of the insecurities that arose from their physical shortcomings as boys. They aren't conquering their childhood demons by committing acts of violence in the streets or using alcohol and drugs to escape their memories. Yet they continue to define themselves in part by those boyhood experiences; these scars aren't easy to erase, even for men who measure up in most other areas.

Asher is 34, married, and a father. He has a lucrative career in the technology sector. Like several of the men I met, he was bullied and beaten up as a boy and considers those experiences formative: "I felt like a weakling most of my life." Asher's father enrolled him in martial arts classes, but he quickly quit and has long regretted not being better at "standing up for myself when I was younger."

GFC fighter Sammy, 44, spent years training in martial arts and sparring in dojos, but when he heard about GFC he was still asking himself, "Can I really fight?" He is slight of stature, which, not surprisingly, exposed him to more bullying as a child and teen in the occasionally violent and gang-ridden neighborhoods where he grew up. When threatened by gang members, he said, all of his options felt emasculating: crying for help, submitting by begging for mercy, or suffering the pain and failure of being beaten. He chose submission to avoid the physical pain. "Saying 'Sorry, sorry,' many times definitely hurts your ego," he told me, laughing ruefully. It was "powerful, because I was all cocky when I was young and then, Oh, fuck. A few guys come [at] you and then you're nobody. Definitely, this had something to do with getting me to try to practice [martial arts] and prove my manhood."

Freddy, one of the long-time GFC regulars, says he got into grappling and wrestling to get the feeling that he could control his own body and others.' Once, when he was in elementary school, two older neighbors pinned him down, stripped him of his clothes, and ran away, leaving him to try to sneak back into the house, naked, in front of some older women relatives. He'd not only lost control of his body, but was exposed, literally and figuratively. When he was in college, some "friends" tried to pull a similar stunt, grabbing him and attempting to strip him naked in a dorm hallway. This time, he says, "I kneed the first guy in the balls; I turned around and grabbed the other guy by the throat and threw him down."

Fight Therapy

For these men, Fight Club offers an opportunity to replace the psychological scars of bullying and submission with physical scars they can wear as trophies of manhood. Fighting is therapeutic, and it brings more than understanding. The fighters can confront their feelings of failure directly, as

adults. And they restore a sense of control, paradoxically, by choosing to give it up, placing themselves at risk. Even when they lose, by demonstrating an ability to withstand violence, they are reestablishing their masculinity. A fight is a "situation where you just don't know what's going to happen," says Asher, "but now, I know what I can do and I know that I'm not going to lose my cool." It's not about eliminating fear, he says, "but knowing you're not a coward."

"After I got punched enough times [at Fight Club]," Sammy says, "I understand that I can definitely take a [big] punch and then I'll nail you one." Sammy doesn't expect to be bullied by gang members now that he's an adult, but if he finds himself in that situation, he now has the confidence to deal with it. He expected to reclaim his manhood by beating up his Fight Club opponents. Instead he came to believe that the "true power" was being able to withstand a beating. Getting hit is, in many ways, more important than hitting.

"So, sometimes losing is winning?" I asked him. "Losing is definitely winning," he said. He now invites and even embraces fights with men at GFC who are stronger and may subject him to countless strikes. The same confidence has helped him handle non-violent confrontations at work, he notes.

Freddy's extensive GFC experience has translated to an acute self-awareness and sense of control. "Now I think of myself as a hard target. I don't feel like a mark," he says. "Only *I* kill me." With the skills and confidence he has developed, he believes it's only his own mistakes that lead him to lose a fight.

Ronnie, another experienced martial artist, says he wanted definitive proof that fear could no longer dominate him. "What I get [from fighting at GFC] is the truth. [To know] that I could protect myself and I'm not scared in any situation." He wavers a little. "[Well] you get scared in a lot of different situations. But I feel, well, it gives me a level of confidence."

Social science research reveals that men who fall short on some measure of manhood find other outlets to compensate for their perceived shortcomings. Young men living in poverty and denied access to good jobs may assert themselves through sports, sexual conquests, or risk-taking activities like crime. Adult men who fail as breadwinners are more likely to abuse their wives or girlfriends. Men with physical disabilities may highlight their decision-making skills and authority to offset their inability to live up to men's body ideals.

GFC offers at least one group of men a direct way to repair and bolster their masculine identities. This may help explain why they don't reject cultural expectations of physical toughness and control or embrace a different definition of manhood.

In place of recurrent memories of humiliation, some GFC fighters say they have daily fantasies or daydreams in which they are superheroes or doing heroic things. Some confess to harboring fantasies of violence—such as clearing a bar full of people when forced to defend themselves. Even after proving their courage, toughness, and ability repeatedly at GFC, some fighters return again and again, for months or even years. The ritual binds them.

New fighters may feel as if they are undergoing a controlled hazing ritual, but the regulars help create the best of a fraternal atmosphere—camaraderie and bonding—without fear of being judged by other men. The bond is evident in the post-fight hug, an authentic embrace of appreciation and respect. My afternoon of fighting ended, as they all do, with beer and laughter while watching recordings of the fights. (No copies of the videos are made or distributed.)

GFC may be unique in the way it cultivates the most visceral element of American manhood. Unlike MMA competitors, these garage fighters don't attempt to injure each other to win. And unlike middle school bullies, they don't try to physically humiliate each other. They push and challenge each other, encouraging everyone to grow as fighters—and as people. As one veteran explained as I prepared for my first fight, your fellow fighters are "there to bring you up, not beat you down."

Masculinity is elusive and tenuous, always capable of being undermined by a single failure. GFC gives men a venue where they can prove themselves physically, shielding them from the burden of trying to dominate others—and the fear of being dominated.

RECOMMENDED RESOURCES

Canada, Geoffrey. *Fist Stick Knife Gun: A Personal History of Violence in America* (Beacon Press, 1995). Describes boys' street socialization, unwritten rules about and informal training in fighting, and violence in tough, inner-city neighborhoods, before and after guns were prevalent.

Kimmel, Michael. *Manhood in America: A Cultural History,* 2nd edition (Oxford University Press, 2006). Exhaustively documents and analyzes culturally ascendant and competing versions of American manhood throughout U.S. history.

Messerschmidt, James W. *Nine Lives: Adolescent Masculinities, the Body and Violence* (Westview Press, 1999) Examines young boys who have been physically and sexually abused, and who have attempted to overcome their victimization by committing these acts against peers.

Phillips, Debby. "Punking and Bullying: Strategies in Middle School, High School, and Beyond," *Journal of Interpersonal Violence* (2007), 22(2): 158–178. Explains how boys use verbal and physical abuse to humiliate and shame other boys in an attempt to demonstrate their own masculinity.

ꙮ Topics for Further Examination ꙮ

- Visit http://www.mencanstoprape.org to see what men are doing to stop sexual violence.
- Try to find the latest reports of campus rape for your campus and surrounding campuses. Does this surprise you? What organizations provide support to women who have been sexually abused on your campus?
- Search for "sexual harassment laws" for the federal government and your state. Are they easily accessible? How are they enforced?

PART III

POSSIBILITIES

Chapter 10: Nothing Is Forever

10

NOTHING IS FOREVER

CATHERINE G. VALENTINE

The title of this chapter represents the principle that change is inevitable. Like the ever-evolving patterns of the kaleidoscope, change is inherent in all life's patterns. Anything can be changed and everything does change, from the cells in our bodies to global politics. There is no permanent pattern, no one way of experiencing or doing anything that lasts forever. This fact of life can be scary, but it can also be energizing. The mystery of life, like the wonder of the kaleidoscope, rests in not knowing precisely what will come next.

The readings in this chapter address the changing terrain of gender. If one takes only a snapshot of life, it may appear as though current gender arrangements are relatively fixed. However, an expanded view of gender, over time and across cultures, reveals the well-researched fact that gender meanings and practices are as dynamic as any other aspect of life. Patterns of gender continuously undergo change, and they do so at every level of experience, from the individual to the global. Michael Schwalbe (2001) observes that there is both chance and pattern in the lives of individuals and in the bigger arena of social institutions. He makes the point that no matter how many rules there might be and no matter how much we know about a particular person or situation, "social life remains a swirl of contingencies out of which can emerge events that no one expects" (p. 127). As a result, life, including its gendered dimensions, is full of possibilities.

Social constructionist theory is especially helpful in understanding the inevitability of change in the gender order. Recall that social constructionist research reveals the processes by which people create and maintain the institution of gender. It underscores the fact that gender is a human invention, not a biological absolute. Particular gender patterns keep going only as long as people share the same ideas about gender and keep doing masculinity and femininity in a routine, predictable fashion (Carrera, DePalma, & Lameiras, 2012; Johnson, 1997; Schwalbe, 2001). Given that humans create gender, gender patterns can be altered by people who, individually and collectively, choose to invent and negotiate new ways of thinking about and doing gender.

At the micro level of daily interaction, individuals participate in destabilizing the binary, oppositional sex/gender/sexuality order. They do so by choosing to bend conventional gender rules or changing the rules altogether by undoing or redoing gender (Bobel & Kwan, 2011; Deutsch, 2007;

Lorber, 1994; West & Zimmerman, 2009). For example, women and men are creating new forms of partnership based on shared care work and housework roles. Other individuals purposefully transgress the boundaries of sexual and gender identities by mixing appearance cues via makeup, clothing, hairstyle, and other modes of self-presentation (Bobel & Kwan, 2011; Lorber, 1994). Chris Bobel and Samantha Kwan's (2011) research illustrates a variety of ways people employ their bodies in acts of gender resistance and related forms of resistance such as counter-heteronormativity and counter-homonormativity. For example, within the U.S. gay community, big men or "bears" are masculine-presenting, fat, hairy, gay and bisexual men who, with their admirers ("chasers"), have formed alternative spaces where they can interact in comfort. In addition, they display their bodies with pride and challenge the appearance norms of dominant gay society and the heterosexual world (Pyle & Klein, 2011). Research on embodied resistance, such as bear culture, points to the powerful social fact that "humans can be at once rule-bound and wonderfully inventive agents of social change. We can enact the mandates—trudging along, submitting and rationalizing—but we can also assert ourselves and break away" (Bobel & Kwan, 2011, p. 2). When we do the latter, we engage our potential to alter toxic social patterns such as gender inequality.

TRENDS

At the macro level of the gender order, change comes about through large-scale forces and processes, both planned and unplanned. Trends are unplanned changes in patterns that are sustained over time. For example, Peter Kivisto (2011) states that the Industrial Revolution is a trend, marking the transition from agricultural to industrial economies. This so-called revolution involves complex economic, technological, and related changes, such as urbanization, that have profoundly altered the fabric of social life over time. Consider the impact of industrialization on gender in work and family life in the United States. Prior to industrialization, women's labor was essential to agricultural life. Women, men, and children worked side by side to grow crops, make clothing, raise animals, and otherwise contribute to the family economy (Lorber, 2001). That is, work and family were closely intertwined and the distinction between home and workplace did not exist (Wharton, 2005).

As the Industrial Revolution got under way, productive or waged work moved from the home into factories and other specialist work sites, and work came to be defined as valuable only if it resulted in a paycheck. Although essential work was still done at home, it typically did not produce income. The negative outcome was that household labor was transformed into an invisible and devalued activity. Work and family came to be defined as distinct, firmly gendered domains of life, especially in the White middle class. Women and children were relegated to the home and "good" women were expected to be full-time housewives and mothers, while men were ordained to follow wage work in the capitalist market, embrace the breadwinner role, and participate in the political arena (Godwin & Risman, 2001; Wharton, 2005).

The profound changes in gender relations and the organization of work and family wrought by the Industrial Revolution continue to be a source of conflict for many women and men in the United States today. For example, although most heterosexual married women with children work outside the home, the doctrine of natural separate spheres—unpaid household work for women and paid work for men—continues to operate as an ideal against which "working women" who have children are often negatively evaluated.

Industrialization continues as a force for social change, one that is amplified by processes of globalization. The term *globalization* refers to the increasing interconnectedness of social, political, and economic activities worldwide (Held, McGrew, Goldblatt, & Perraton, 1999). Transnational forces such as geopolitical conflicts, global markets, transnational corporations, transnational media, and the migration of labor now strongly influence what happens in specific countries and locales (Connell, 2000).

For example, the international trading system— dominated by nations such as the United States— encompasses almost every country in the world, while films and television programs, especially those produced in the West, circulate the globe (Barber, 2002).

Offering a valuable perspective on the impact of globalization in her reading in this chapter, R. W. Connell (2000) argues that it has created a worldwide gender order. This world gender order has several interacting dimensions: (1) a gender division of labor in a "global factory" in which poor women and children provide cheap labor for transnational corporations owned by businessmen from the major economic powers, (2) the marginalization of women in international politics, and (3) the dominance of Western gender symbolism in transnational media.

However, despite the order Connell posits, globalization is not monolithic. There are countervailing forces challenging the homogenizing and hegemonic aspects of globalization. For example, indigenous cultures interact with global cultures to produce new cultural forms of art and music. In addition, globalization has spawned transnational social movements such as the reproductive justice movement, environmental justice movement, and domestic workers movement, which address worldwide problems of Western hegemony, global inequality, and human rights. Connell's reading in this chapter includes analysis of the links between local and global social action involving men in gender change. Her discussion of what she calls "the broad cultural shift toward a historical consciousness about gender" provides insight into the complexities of globalization.

Social Movements

Large-scale change may also come about in a planned fashion. Social movements are prime examples of change that people deliberately and purposefully create. They are conscious, organized, collective efforts to work toward cultural and institutional change and share distinctive features, including organization, consciousness, noninstitutionalized strategies (such as boycotts and protest marches), and prolonged duration (Kuumba, 2001). The United States has a long history of people joining together in organizations and movements to bring about justice and equality. The labor union movement; socialist movement; civil rights movement; and gay, lesbian, bisexual, transgender, intersex movement have been among the important vehicles for change that might not otherwise have happened.

One of the most durable and flexible social movements is feminism (Ferree & Mueller, 2004). Consider the fact that the feminist movement has already lasted for more than two centuries. At the opening of the 19th century, feminism emerged in the United States and Europe. By the early 20th century, feminist organizations appeared in urban centers around the world. By the turn of the 21st century, feminism had grown into a transnational movement in which groups work at local and global levels to address militarism, global capitalism, racism, poverty, violence against women, economic autonomy for women, and other issues of justice, human rights, and peace (Shaw & Lee, 2001).

Research on transnational feminism has proliferated and drawn attention to the complex nature of a "highly diversified, globalized social movement" (Hewitt, 2011, p. 65). As discussed earlier, Connell's reading in this chapter offers insight into the issue of men and masculinities in relation to gender equality worldwide and does so by discussing the diversity of men's movements, setting out grounds for optimism as well as pessimism in the struggle to end men's privileges and institute gender equality.

Other readings in this chapter address challenges facing feminist movements today. For example, developing ways to work together across differences and inequalities among women rooted in cultural, national, religious, and other intersectionalities is no easy task (Hewitt, 2011; Ryan, 2001). Simply put, "gender is but one strand of oppression among many," and alliances need to be forged across intramovement differences (Hewitt, 2011; Motta, Flesher Fominaya, Eschie, & Cox, 2011). This problem takes many shapes. Not only is it a matter, for instance, of class-privileged women and poor women or White women and women of color forming working alliances, but it is also a matter of women and men being attuned to pitfalls in thinking and organizing across individual and collective differences and inequalities (Motta et al., 2011).

One response to this problem is suggested by Elora Halim Chowdhury (2009), who calls for the intertwining of U.S. "anti-racist/third world feminisms and third world/transnational feminisms" to build connections across multiple borders, both "intra-national and international" (p. 53). Andrea Smith's reading in this chapter is a good example of feminist analysis that crosses borders. Her indigenous feminist perspective and activist work link Native feminism to women of color feminism more broadly in the United States and to the struggles of colonized peoples globally. She opens up new "social imaginaries" (Carrera et al., 2012, p. 1009) by challenging the nation-state as a viable form of governance and by urging us to think deeply about how to create a new world based on interrelatedness and responsibility. Smith is one of the contributors to the roundtable reading on reproductive justice (Briggs et al. in this chapter), a layered and rich examination of the global and American terrain of reproductive politics. This article highlights the limitations of what is largely a Western, White, middle-class feminism focused on individual choice (choice feminism), and it does so through the lens of the transnational reproductive justice movement. The closing words of Rosalind Petchesky, reproductive justice scholar and activist, underscore the significance of cross-border, cross-boundary feminisms. She calls for feminists to think deeply about systemic change and to build broad coalitions with other social justice and antiracist movements. Two other readings in this chapter examine effective strategies for building bridges across intersectionalities and between feminist organizations. Courtney Martin and Vanessa Valenti assess the critical role of online feminism in the 21st century. They demonstrate how feminist blogs have become a vehicle for consciousness raising and activism that makes a difference. Online feminists and traditional feminist organizations have become allies across boundaries and borders and, together, have successfully altered the genderscape. Martin and Valenti offer clear accounts of the radicalizing force of online feminism. In the reading by the members of the Santa Cruz Feminist of Color Collective, the authors present a model of the creative collective as a supportive and egalitarian space for sharing and honing feminist insight and activism. This collective is linked to a long history of feminist-of-color collectives and to collectives currently at work in the online feminist world and in more traditional settings. Together, these two readings provide tools for creating and sustaining feminist movements in this new century.

The Complexity of Change

Not only is social change pervasive at micro and macro levels of life and a function of both planned and unplanned processes, it is also uneven and complex (Ridgeway, 2009). Change doesn't unfold in a linear, predictable fashion, and it may be dramatically visible or may take us by surprise. Consider the passage of the Nineteenth Amendment to the U.S. Constitution in 1920, which guaranteed women the right to vote. This one historic moment uplifted the public status of women and did so in a visible fashion. But more often, change consists of alterations in the fabric of gender relations that are not immediately visible to us, both in their determinants and their consequences.

For instance, we now know that a complex set of factors facilitated the entry of large numbers of single and married women into the paid workforce and higher education in the second half of the 20th century. Those factors included very broad economic, political, and technological developments that transformed the United States into an urban, industrial capitalist nation (Stone & McKee, 1998). Yet no one predicted the extent of change in gender attitudes and relations that would follow the entry of women into the workforce. It is only "after the fact" that the implications have been identified and assessed.

For example, heterosexual marital relationships in the United States have moved toward greater equity in response to the reality that most married, heterosexual women are not dependent on their husbands' earnings. As married women have increasingly embraced paid work, their spouses have increasingly reconceptualized and rearranged their priorities so they can devote more attention to parenthood (Goldscheider & Rogers, 2001).

PRISMS OF GENDER AND CHANGE

Returning briefly to the metaphor of the kaleidoscope, let us recall that the prism of gender interacts with a complex array of social prisms of difference and inequality, such as race and sexual orientation. The prisms produce ever-changing patterns at micro and macro levels of life. Our metaphor points to yet another important principle of dynamic gender arrangements. We can link gender change to alterations in other structural dimensions of society, such as race, class, and age. For example, as Americans have moved toward greater consciousness and enactment of gender equality, they have also come to greater consciousness about the roles that heterosexism (i.e., the institutionalization of heterosexuality as the only legitimate form of sexual expression) and homophobia (i.e., the fear and hatred of homosexuality) play in reinforcing rigid gender stereotypes and relationships (see Chapter 6). It has become clear to many seeking gender justice that the justice sought after cannot be achieved without eliminating homophobia and the heterosexist framework of social institutions such as family and work.

Additionally, gender transformation in the United States is inextricably tied to movements for racial equality. This is true both historically and today. The first wave of feminism was an outgrowth of the antislavery movement, and the politics of racial justice led to the second wave of feminism (Freedman, 2002). Racism, as well as ageism, classism, and other forms of oppression, had to be addressed by feminists, because the struggle to achieve equal worth for women had

to include all women and men. Anything less would mean failure.

THE INEVITABILITY OF CHANGE

Collectively, the articles in this chapter invite the reader to ask, "Why should I care about or get involved in promoting change in the gender status quo?" That is a good question. After all, why should one go to the trouble of departing from the standard package of gender practices and relationships? Change requires effort and entails risk. On the other hand, the cost of "going with the flow" can be high. There are no safe places to hide from change. Even if we choose "not to rock the boat" by closing ourselves off to inner and outer awareness, change will find us. There are two reasons for this fact of life. First, we cannot live in society without affecting others and in turn being affected by them. Each individual life intertwines with the lives of many other people, and our words and actions have consequences, both helpful and harmful. Every step we take and every choice we make affect the quality of life for a multitude of people. If we choose to wear blinders to our connections with others, we run the risk of inadvertently diminishing their chances, and our own, of living fulfilling lives (Schwalbe, 2001). For example, when a person tells a demeaning joke about women, he or she may intend no harm; however, the (unintended) consequences are harmful. The joke reinforces negative stereotypes, and telling the joke gives other people permission to be disrespectful to women (Schwalbe, 2001).

Second, we can't escape broad, societal changes in gender relations. By definition, institutional- and societal-level change wraps its arms around us all. Think about the widespread impact of laws such as the Equal Pay Act and Title VII, outlawing discrimination against women and people of color, or consider how sexual harassment legislation has redefined and altered relationships in a wide array of organizational settings. Reflect on the enormous impact of the large numbers of women who have entered the workforce since the latter half of the 20th century. The cumulative effect of the sheer numbers of women in the workforce has been revolutionary in its impact on gender relations in family, work, education, law, and other institutions and societal structures.

Given the inevitability of change in gender practices and relationships, it makes good sense to cultivate awareness of who we are and what our responsibilities to one another are. Without awareness, we cannot exercise control over our actions and their impact on others. Social forces shape us, but those forces change. Every transformation in societal patterns reverberates through our lives. Developing the "social literacy" to make sense of the changing links between our personal experience and the dynamics of social patterns can aid us in making informed, responsible choices (O'Brien, 1999; Schwalbe, 2001).

REFERENCES

Barber, B. R. (2002). Jihad vs. McWorld. In G. Ritzer (Ed.), *McDonaldization: The reader* (pp. 191–198). Thousand Oaks, CA: Pine Forge Press.

Bobel, C., & Kwan, S. (2011). Introduction. In C. Bobel & S. Kwan (Eds.), *Embodied resistance: Challenging the norms, breaking the rules* (pp. 1–10). Nashville, TN: Vanderbilt University Press.

Carrera, M. V., DePalma, R., & Lameiras, M. (2012). Sex/gender identity: Moving beyond fixed and 'natural' categories. *Sexualities, 15*(8), 995–1016.

Chowdhury, E. H. (2009). Locating global feminisms elsewhere: Braiding US women of color and transnational feminisms. *Cultural Dynamics, 21*(1), 51–78.

Connell, R. W. (2000). *The men and the boys.* Berkeley: University of California Press.

Deutsch, F. (2007). Undoing gender. *Gender & Society, 21,* 106–127.

Ferree, M., & Mueller, C. (2004). Feminism and the women's movement: A global perspective. In D. Snow, S. Soule, & H. Kriesi (Eds.), *The Blackwell companion to social movements* (pp. 576–607). Malden, MA: Blackwell.

Freedman, E. (2002). *No turning back: The history of feminism and the future of women.* New York: Ballantine Books.

Godwin, F. K., & Risman, B. J. (2001). Twentieth-century changes in economic work and family. In D. Vannoy (Ed.), *Gender mosaics* (pp. 134–144). Los Angeles: Roxbury.

Goldscheider, F. K., & Rogers, M. L. (2001). Gender and demographic reality. In D. Vannoy (Ed.), *Gender mosaics* (pp. 124–133). Los Angeles: Roxbury.

Held, D., McGrew, A., Goldblatt, D., & Perraton, J. (1999). *Global transformations.* Stanford, CA: Stanford University Press.

Hewitt, L. (2011). Framing across differences, building solidarities: Lessons from women's rights activism in transnational spaces. *Interface, 3*(2), 65–99.

Johnson, A. (1997). *The gender knot.* Philadelphia: Temple University Press.

Kivisto, P. (2011). *Key ideas in sociology* (3rd ed.).Thousand Oaks, CA: Sage.

Kuumba, M. B. (2001). *Gender and social movements.* Walnut Creek, CA: AltaMira Press.

Lorber, J. (1994). *Paradoxes of gender.* New Haven, CT: Yale University Press.

Lorber, J. (2001). *Gender inequality: Feminist theories and politics.* Los Angeles: Roxbury.

Motta, S., Flesher Fominaya, C., Eschie, C., & Cox, L. (2011). Feminism, women's movements and women in movements. *Interface, 3*(2), 1–32.

O'Brien, J. (1999). *Social prisms.* Thousand Oaks, CA: Pine Forge Press.

Pyle, N., & Klein, N. L. (2011). Fat. Hairy. Sexy: Contesting standards of beauty and sexuality in the gay community. In C. Bobel & S. Kwan (Eds.), *Embodied resistance: Challenging the norms, breaking the rules* (pp. 78–87). Nashville, TN: Vanderbilt University Press.

Ridgeway, C. (2009). Framed before we know it: How gender shapes social relations. *Gender & Society, 23*(2), 145–160.

Ryan, B. (2001). *Identity politics in the women's movement.* New York: New York University Press.

Schwalbe, M. (2001). *The sociologically examined life.* Mountain View, CA: Mayfield.

Shaw, S. M., & Lee, J. (2001). *Women's voices, feminist visions.* Mountain View, CA: Mayfield.

Stone, L., & McKee, N. P. (1998). *Gender and culture in America.* Upper Saddle River, NJ: Prentice Hall.

West, C., & Zimmerman, D. (2009). Accounting for undoing gender. *Gender & Society, 23*(1), 112–122.

Wharton, A. S. (2005). *The sociology of gender.* Malden, MA: Blackwell.

Introduction to Reading 46

Reproductive justice for all women has been a centerpiece of the feminist movement in the United States since the 1980s. The reproductive justice framework was created by women of color to address the multiple facets of reproductive oppression and to move beyond the limitations of a reproductive choice framework. It is a positive approach that links sexuality, health, and human rights to social justice issues and movements such as immigrants' rights, environmental justice, and population control. Reproductive justice theory asserts that every woman has the human right to decide if and when she will have a baby and the conditions under which she will give birth; decide if she will not have a baby and her options for preventing or ending a pregnancy; parent children in safe, healthy environments. The conversation in this reading is among scholars and activists who have made major contributions to feminist research on reproductive politics and justice. They discuss reproductive justice in light of the legacies of *Roe v. Wade* and related issues and challenges.

1. What is *Roe v. Wade* and, according to the discussants in this reading, what are its negative and positive outcomes?

2. Why have women of color been at the forefront of the reproductive justice movement?

3. What role has racism played in the anti-abortion movement in the United States?

4. How has the United States had significant impact on women's reproductive health issues in other parts of the world?

ROUNDTABLE

REPRODUCTIVE TECHNOLOGIES AND REPRODUCTIVE JUSTICE

Laura Briggs, Faye Ginsburg, Elena R. Gutiérrez, Rosalind Petchesky, Rayna Rapp, Andrea Smith, and Chikako Takeshita

To commemorate the fortieth anniversary of *Roe v. Wade,* and to invite conversation about the broader global and American landscapes of reproductive politics, the *Frontiers'* editors convened a roundtable of scholars and activists who have made major contributions to feminist research in the field. Beginning with a question about the legacies of the *Roe* decision, we also asked our contributors to reflect on other landmarks in the history of struggles for reproductive justice and to share their perspectives on ongoing challenges. . . . The conversation that appears here is based on the contributors' written comments and was put together in this format by Mytheli Sreenivas.

From Briggs, Laura, Faye Ginsburg, Elena R. Gutiérrez, Rosalind Petchesky, Rayna Rapp, Andrea Smith, and Chikako Takeshita. 2013. Roundtable: Reproductive Technologies and Reproductive Justice. *Frontiers, 34*(3).

The year 2013 is the fortieth anniversary of Roe v. Wade. *What do you think are the most important legacies of this Supreme Court decision for contemporary women's reproductive issues, both in the United States and globally?*

SMITH: The legacy of the *Roe v. Wade* decision was to narrow the agenda of reproductive justice to abortion rights. While abortion rights are important, they are only one aspect of a larger reproductive justice agenda. *Roe v. Wade* framed the right to abortion through the right to privacy rather than through the lens of gender equality. This framework easily lent itself to a more libertarian framework around freedom from government intervention. However, this framework was limited in terms of the responsibility of the government to ensure all have equal access to abortion services. Hence, the Hyde Amendment, which prohibits Medicaid funding for abortion except in cases of rape, incest, or if the life of the mother is endangered, was not deemed inconsistent with *Roe v. Wade*. Thus, even today mainstream reproductive rights groups do not address issues like dangerous contraceptives in communities of color, repealing the Hyde Amendment, environmental racism as it impacts the reproductive systems of indigenous women and women of color, poverty as it affects women's ability to access reproductive health services, and so on. Reproductive justice has become equated with the right of some women who can afford it to have abortion.

RAPP AND GINSBURG: *Roe v. Wade* stands as two things: a beacon of the successful U.S. feminist struggle for reproductive rights and an icon of its limitations. As other contributors to this roundtable point out, in the last forty years we have witnessed a shift toward a more encompassing reproductive justice agenda across a broad range of issues linked to women's health. Increasingly, this agenda identifies and struggles against the intersecting and stratified divides through which women experience their reproductive "choices." These include divides that are based on race or ethnicity, class, age, and rural or urban access in the United States and the continued high maternal mortality rates of pregnant women in developing countries, where abortion too often still remains illegal and hence murderously dangerous. Such structural barriers disproportionally affect women from poor and historically discriminated-against communities here as well as abroad. Collectively, feminist activists, advocates, and scholars have taught us to situate our analyses of reproduction in local, national, and global contexts, taking account of the many structural barriers that constrain the real-life choices of women in the actual settings where they live.

GUTIÉRREZ: As when *Roe v. Wade* became law in 1973, the politics of abortion today remain a cornerstone in the health and social disparities that exist for women living in the United States. Forty years after the Supreme Court decided that women have a legal right to have an abortion, most continue to face limited access to pregnancy termination procedures (medical and nonmedical) as well as many other reproductive health care services, including prenatal care, fertility technologies, and pap smears. Although the existence of *Roe v. Wade* has certainly increased the availability of legal abortion services and was responsible for irrevocably bringing reproductive politics into public conversation over the past forty years, the impact of the law has been significantly limited almost since its inception. Most important, the subsequent passage and persistence of the Hyde Amendment in 1977 was essential to establishing a government-regulated reproductive divide for women in the United States that has since only widened. This legislation, in addition to the declining access to services in many states and increasingly restrictive circumstances nationwide, makes it very difficult and often impossible for low-income women to pay for a legal abortion or experience any semblance of actual reproductive choice as it is popularly conceived. In response local abortion funds, which are almost all grassroots, community-based efforts dependent upon private donations, have grown over the United States to assist women who may need financial assistance to pay for pregnancy termination procedures that they cannot afford.

The Guttmacher Institute recently reported that during 2011 and 2012 more abortion restrictions were enacted in U.S. states than in any other previous years. The year 2011 marked a record high, with ninety-two pieces of legislation being passed throughout the country.[1] These types of measures disproportionately impact women who live in poverty, as they are more likely to have to terminate a pregnancy because of an inability to parent another child due to financial constraints. Forty-two percent of women having abortions are poor, and women of color are more likely to live below income than white women. Thus, low-income women of color are those most impacted by dwindling access to abortion services.

Increased attention to these disparate circumstances has developed from and contributed to steadily growing advocacy movements within women-of-color communities that insist that true reproductive "choice" necessitates an intersectional approach to understanding the many factors that impact women's reproductive options and a more comprehensive rubric of reproductive justice. This means that access to all types of reproductive health care, not only abortion services, is a matter not only of gender equity but of racial, class, sexual, and embodied justice.

PETCHESKY: On first glance the most remarkable thing about approaching the fortieth anniversary of *Roe v. Wade* is a landscape of apparent stagnation. Instead of celebrating how far we've come from a moment when the struggle for abortion rights for women and girls seemed blessedly to have been won in the courts, we encounter a never-ending battle over four decades to counter right-wing strategies that make abortion the stand-in for feminism. And feminism here is clearly coded as antifamily, antichildren, pro-sex—especially for young unmarried women. In writing about abortion politics in 1990—in terms that remain depressingly relevant today—I argued "that abortion is the fulcrum of a much broader ideological struggle in which the very meanings of the family, the state, motherhood, and young women's sexuality are contested." And I linked that confluence of meanings directly to an insidious racism that underlies the anti-abortion movement, in which "birth control and abortion services, widely available without age or marital restrictions, have helped to make the young, white woman's sexuality visible, thereby undermining historical race and class stereotypes of 'nice girls' and 'bad girls.'" In a racist society this makes contraception and abortion doubly dangerous.[2]

So today we have national and state funding attacks on Planned Parenthood centers and Title X, plus systematic efforts to keep abortion and contraception out of health care reform plans. (If fire-bombings of clinics have subsided, picketing and harassment of providers and patients have not; and the last murder of an abortion doctor, George Tiller, occurred as recently as 2009.) The assault on contraception has ratcheted up the anti-abortion movement from saving fetuses to sanctifying embryos. In 2012 electoral politics we have the first lady and the aspiring first lady, and a bevy of other politicians, appealing to (white) women voters by proclaiming their allegiance to familialism, momism, and stand-by-your-manism. We have a Republican Party platform that seeks to take us back to a time when abortion was criminal in absolutely every circumstance. And we have a new and more sophisticated twist on the racist themes of the so-called pro-life campaigns through billboards that attempt to convince African Americans that abortion rights are a form of "genocide"—when, in fact, four times as many women of color as white women suffer from unwanted pregnancies due to lack of access to safe, affordable reproductive health care, including contraceptive services and supplies. In turn this lack of access comes largely from the structural racism and class divisions that permeate our society, resulting in exclusions from jobs that provide health insurance with contraceptive coverage; restrictions on Medicaid funding in many states (Texas in the lead) for not only abortion but also contraception, breast exams, and other routine gynecological services; and lives more burdened with sexual violence, single motherhood, and poverty.[3]

Given this bleak landscape, what then can we count as the legacies of *Roe v. Wade* after forty years? On the positive side I still believe the idea of a right to personal ownership over one's body, its sexuality and reproductive capacity, contained in *Roe*'s "privacy" doctrine is powerful and potentially transformative. There's no question that this idea has exploded in thousands of directions and locales, both in the United States (e.g., informing the Supreme Court's 2003 ruling against sodomy statutes in *Lawrence v. Texas*) and among social movements across the globe for freedom of sexual and gender expression. At the same time *Roe*'s very strength was also its weakness: Restricting abortion decisions to the "personal," the "private," also meant severing their deep connection to issues of economic and social justice. Taking "a woman and her doctor" out of the context of all the social and structural reasons why abortion access is one link in a huge chain of conditions necessary for personal well-being made it easier to demonize women seeking abortions as "evil" at worst or hapless victims at best and providers as purveyors of genocide. But the U.S. legal system, with its emphasis on individualism and property rights, doesn't lend itself well to fights for social justice. So here, I think, we might find a lesson from *Roe v. Wade,* a lesson we have to learn again and again: Litigation is only one tool available to movements for social change. It may shift standards in the courts, but it takes a mobilized social movement to change values, images, and power relations.

TAKESHITA: The political right's relentless attempt to undermine the 1973 Supreme Court decision, regrettably, is one of the most significant legacies of *Roe v. Wade.* Forty years after legalization, American women seeking abortion still face harassment from anti-abortion protestors and encounter obstacles set up by state laws. As of October 2013 seventeen states mandate that women be given counseling that includes anxiety-provoking information that is scientifically unsupported, such as the purported link between abortion and breast cancer, the ability of a fetus to feel pain, and long-term mental health consequences for women. Twenty-six states require a woman seeking an abortion to wait twenty-four hours or more between when she receives counseling and the procedure is performed. Thirty-nine states require parental consent or notification in order for a minor to receive abortion.[4] The right wing has been unrelentingly attacking Planned Parenthood, engineering constitutional amendments to overturn *Roe v. Wade,* and is now attempting to challenge President Obama's Affordable Care Act, which requires new health plans to fully cover birth control for women.

While the recent presidential election drew considerable attention to the rights of American women to receive reproductive health care, there is little awareness of the negative impact that the backlash against *Roe v. Wade* has also had on women abroad. After unsuccessfully attempting to challenge *Roe v. Wade* during the 1970s, anti-abortion leaders turned their effort overseas, gradually cutting aid to family planning programs in developing countries from the United States Agency for International Development (USAID). The Reagan administration instituted the Mexico City Policy in 1984, which denied funding from USAID to foreign nongovernmental organizations (NGOs) that provide abortion counseling, referral, and/or services using non-U.S. funds. Known also as the Global Gag Rule because it prevents health care providers from not only performing but also making references to abortion, this executive order has resulted in diminishing much-needed reproductive health care for women in the global South by forcing clinics to close and curtailing contraceptive supplies from USAID in certain areas. The Global Gag Rule also made it difficult for governments fearful of jeopardizing their relationships with USAID to openly discuss abortion-law reforms in their countries. While it had no effect on reducing global abortion rates, the Global Gag Rule most likely drove numerous women to back-alley abortions performed by untrained people. Sadly, unsafe abortions still account for thousands of maternal deaths and injuries worldwide. Although the Global Gag Rule has been rescinded and funding has been restored every time a Democratic president has taken office, overseas programs critical to women's health have perpetually been "held hostage to the ping-pong game of U.S. partisan politics."[5]

The United States has had significant influence on women's reproductive health issues in the global South for decades. Initially American leaders aggressively urged foreign governments to control population growth and prioritized funding family planning programs over providing aid for other development projects. Global population control was a signature imperialist project of the U.S. during the 1960s and 1970s. Over time, however, American aid arguably also helped meet contraceptive needs of women in countries where resources are scarce. Conservative lawmakers' attempts to curb foreign aid for reproductive health care amounts to another form of American tyranny over the reproductive lives of women in the global South. Given this history, we might say that the adversarial legacy of *Roe v. Wade,* namely American antiwomen's rights activists' attempt to restrain abortion, contraception, and women's sexuality in general, has an impact on women beyond the United States.

BRIGGS: As Chikako Takeshita suggests, the transnationalization of the U.S. culture wars is an important legacy of the post-*Roe* decades. Here I will speak only of the United States and Latin America, as that is the context I know best, although the geographic expansion of Evangelical Christian "values" concerns has been crucial to the (significantly condom-free, homophobic) expansion of HIV education in many nations in Africa.[6] As journalist Michelle Goldberg has argued, the "population control" regime of the 1950s, 1960s, and 1970s was replaced with a fight about abortion and women's rights, decisively after the Cairo Conference of 1994, but beginning in the 1980s, with the election of Ronald Reagan and the growing political power of Evangelical Christian actors in the United States

and Latin America. This often occurred in relationship to anticommunism. As Lynn Morgan and Liz Roberts have argued, the same people who so hated the regime of human rights during the anticommunist civil wars in Latin America turned decisively to a regime of reproductive governance that, in their phrase, emphasized the "rights of the unborn" and proliferated a weak notion of rights and responsibilities. Since 1998 abortion has been banned altogether, with no exception even to save the life of the mother, in El Salvador, Nicaragua, the Dominican Republic, and some Mexican states. Costa Rica has banned in vitro fertilization in deference to the Catholic Church.[7]

What additional historical landmarks do you think are important for understanding issues related to reproductive rights, technologies, and justice? For example, how significant has been the policy shift from population control to women's reproductive health, as developed at the UN Conference on Population and Development in Cairo in 1994? What has been the impact of changing reproductive technologies on feminist understandings of reproduction? In other words, if we decenter *Roe v. Wade,* how might our conception of reproductive rights, technologies, and justice change?

PETCHESKY: Thinking historically, let's remember that the campaigns for safe, legal abortion in both the United States and Europe in the early 1970s sparked a profusion of women's health movements—in Latin America and the Caribbean, Asia, Africa, and the Pacific, as well as the "West"—whose aims were far broader than the legalistic and individualistic prism of *Roe v. Wade.* By the mid-1980s the International Women and Health Meetings, which originated in Italy in 1975 and reconvened every three years for over two decades thereafter, were bringing together activists from all these regions and were forging strategies to secure not only safe, legal abortion but also access to safe childbearing; an end to maternal mortality and morbidity; an end to sexual abuse and violence; and effective challenges to racist population policies, poverty, and global economic injustices. Most important, women from the global South not only were building their own context-specific strategies and organizations but also were in the leadership of many of these transnational efforts.[8]

We need to situate the International Conference on Population and Development in Cairo in 1994 and its historic, if still limited, Program of Action in this long trajectory. Cairo was not a beginning but rather a kind of culmination, a (nonbinding) codification at the level of intergovernmental policy making of the visions, aspirations, and energetic campaigns of women's health activists for the previous twenty years. The Program of Action itself was disappointing in terms of its weak resource allocations and its reaffirmation of neoliberal, market-based approaches to "development," to say nothing of its deference to national laws on the matter of abortion and its heteronormative assumptions about sexuality and gender. But it remains to this day a powerful statement of a vision of reproductive health rights that embraces a multitude of intersecting needs. These include (a) a comprehensive definition of reproductive health as a human right encompassing all aspects of obstetric and gynecological care (including prevention and treatment of infertility, HIV, other STDS and gynecological cancers), as well as primary health care; (b) adolescent rights to all these forms of care, as well as full and accurate sexuality education; (c) the legitimacy of "diverse family forms" and the need for government policies that benefit all families; (d) "gender equality, equity and empowerment of women" as not only indispensable to development but also "a highly important end in itself"; and (e) a view of "gender" that includes men (despite regrettable silence on transgender and intersex lives) through demands for "shared male responsibility" around pregnancy, child care, household labor, and sexual health.[9]

With Cairo this expansive definition of reproductive health and its firm link to "internationally recognized human rights" became embedded in the discursive frameworks of UN agencies, donors, health providers, and a wide range of activists and advocates. But for most people in most countries this shift in discourse has still not translated into real-life programs and policies.

SMITH: I would dispute the assumption that Cairo shifted the discourse from population to reproductive health. At Cairo the population paradigm remained. It was simply described in more benevolent language. The impact of Cairo was that people know to use different language, but the assumption that the cause of the world's problems is poor people's ability to reproduce has not fundamentally changed. Dangerous contraceptives are still promoted in third world communities and communities of color in the United States.

I think we not only need to decenter *Roe v. Wade*, but we must decenter the framework of reproductive "choice." This paradigm rests on essentially individualist, consumerist notions of "free" choice that do not take into consideration all the social, economic, and political conditions that frame the so-called choices that women are forced to make. Consequently, pro-choice advocates narrow their advocacy around legislation that affects the one choice of whether or not to have an abortion without addressing all the conditions that give rise to a woman having to make this decision in the first place.

The consequence of the "choice" paradigm is that its advocates often take positions that are oppressive to women from marginalized communities. For instance, this paradigm often makes it difficult to develop nuanced positions on the use of abortion when the fetus is determined to have abnormalities. Focusing solely on the woman's choice to have or not have this child does not address the larger context of able-bodied supremacy that sees children with disabilities as having lives not worth living and provides inadequate resources to women who may otherwise want to have them. Thus, it is important to assess the intersection of expanded reproductive technologies with all structures of domination.

TAKESHITA: However mundane it may seem today, contraceptive development was an important landmark in the history of reproductive rights and justice movements. Since *Roe v. Wade* had not yet passed when oral contraceptives and IUDs became available during the early 1960s, these new technologies of fertility control seemed like a godsend for American women who were desperate to avoid pregnancy. Many suffered health problems, however, from these "scientific" methods, which were initially conceived by their developers as a tool to prevent "global population explosion." In a rush to disseminate contraceptives that can easily be applied to the masses, potential dangers of the Pill and the IUD were overlooked or downplayed. Unaware of the risks, American doctors did not carefully screen contraceptive users for contra-indications, nor did they take very seriously women's complaints of side effects, which sometimes led to severe chronic injuries and life-threatening conditions. The plight of women in the global South and women of color in the United States, who were specifically targeted by long-acting contraceptives such as the IUD, Norplant, and Depo-Provera, was even graver, while underreported. Despite their failings, we cannot deny modern contraceptives have had significant impact on women's ability to manage their reproductive lives. Fortunately, feminist activists' advocacy for women's agency, safer birth-control technologies, and men to share family planning responsibilities has successfully redirected contraceptive research and development away from long-acting "imposable" methods preferred by population control advocates to women-controlled methods such as contraceptive patches, vaginal rings, and gels, as well as to birth control methods for men.[10] In the face of the political right's attack on reproductive rights, contraceptive developers, despite their problematic eugenicist past, have become close allies of pro-choice feminists in supporting women's access to various contraceptive options.

As Rosalind Petchesky points out, the Program of Action of the United Nations Conference on Population and Development in Cairo in 1994 has shifted the language of international population policies and programming that focused on reducing birth rates to one that privileges women-centered reproductive health care and women's empowerment. Together with these

changes, the framing of contraceptive technologies has also shifted. During the 1960s and 1970s contraceptive technologies were openly discussed as population control tools. "Women's unmet need" was later used as a synonym for lack of birth control in regions of high fertility. Recently, with the installation of the women's empowerment discourse, contraceptives are increasingly being framed as something that women in the global South desire. Including "imposable" methods that have problematically targeted underprivileged women of color, contraceptive technologies are becoming politically neutralized as they are cast as "choices" and women are transformed from family-planning service recipients to pseudo-consumers in individualist and neoliberalist terms. As Andrea Smith notes, this kind of universalist framing tends to assume that all women's basic reproductive health care needs are fulfilled and that they are "free" to make decisions, which neglect the realities of the majority of women. Problematizing the politics of contraceptive technologies is one way to decenter *Roe v. Wade* and bring intersectionality to the forefront.

GUTIÉRREZ: Since 1973 activists and scholars have demonstrated and documented how reproductive politics in the United States are shaped by gender and patriarchy but also by white supremacy, heteronormativity, ableism, and classism. Following the publication of Dorothy Roberts's path-breaking treatise *Killing the Black Body: Race, Reproduction and the Meaning of Liberty* (1998), a growing literature has documented and theorized the historical patterns and contemporary dynamics of how stratified reproduction plays out for women in the United States, as well as how women of color have resisted repeated episodes of reproductive coercion upon their communities often in the name of population control. This scholarship includes documentation of the racial politics of reproduction, including the usage of women of color for contraceptive trials (i.e., the IUD, the birth control pill, and foam), as well as the preponderance of controlling images and ideologies that circumscribe the reproductive circumstances women experience (i.e., that African American women are teenage moms, that Mexican immigrant women have too many children, or that Asian women are tiger moms). This body of literature enables a much deeper understanding of how women's relation to reproductive expression is impacted by their social location.

For example, the many episodes of coercive sterilization that have occurred in various communities over the years fundamentally challenge the common assumption that simply because abortion is legally available in the United States, all women here equally experience reproductive "choice." The histories of low-income, African American, Native American, Puerto Rican, and Mexican-origin women's forced sterilization demonstrate that racist and classist rhetoric about overpopulation, care of the irresponsible "poor," economic development, and environmental sustainability are used to justify both official and unofficial policies that limit women's autonomy in their reproductive experience. Members of each of these groups of women faced intentional, strategic, and successful efforts to permanently end their childbearing without their knowledge or consent, some when they were actually in the hospital to deliver a child.

Puerto Rican women were first and perhaps most greatly affected by coercive sterilization, with over one-third of those living on the island being sterilized during the 1940s and 1950s, when the surgery was first being practiced as a means of encouraging women's employment and decreasing "overpopulation" on the island. Although institutionalized programs to sterilize women no longer exist, anthropologist Iris Lopez has demonstrated that these high rates of sterilization continue not only among women who live on the island of Puerto Rico but also for those who live in Puerto Rican communities in New York.

In later years, when the surgery became readily available on the continental United States and the procedure was 90-percent paid for by the availability of federal funds, Native American women were sterilized without their knowledge in Indian Health Service clinics, and low-income women in the South and in urban centers were sterilized without their knowledge at great rates, often at publicly funded hospitals. As I have argued elsewhere, different racial logics were utilized to justify the targeting of various communities of women, although always based in economic difference.[11] Some doctors believed that they were doing women a favor, by limiting the number of children that they could have, or that they were ridding society of a welfare burden. Beyond bringing more attention to the reproductive abuses that have occurred in the United States, documentation of these histories has assisted organized calls for reparative measures and resistance to contemporary ideological discourses that pose the reproduction of women of color and poor women as a threat to the health and well-being of society. Over the past thirty years a parallel effort to mainstream reproductive rights organizing, led primarily by women of color, has evolved into a distinct coalition-based reproductive justice movement that calls for a broad advocacy agenda—one that goes beyond a focus on a woman's "choice" to have an abortion.

RAPP AND GINSBURG: One of the structural barriers that constrains women's real-life reproductive choices but that often goes unexamined is the impact of fetal disability on attitudes and practices surrounding abortion decisions. As the journalist Amy Harmon pointed out in a 2007 *New York Times* article: "Seventy percent of Americans said they believe that women should be able to obtain a legal abortion if there is a strong chance of a serious defect in the baby, according to a 2006 poll conducted by the National Opinion Research Center."[12] What does this portend for a more democratic inclusion of people with disabilities, even as we support the rights of pregnant women to make their own decisions to continue or end any given pregnancy? As many feminist disability activists have pointed out, there is insufficient dialogue between their concerns and those of reproductive justice activists.

Like the women's health movement, the disability rights movement is both national and international; like feminist approaches to reproductive justice it struggles to frame positions that are both ethical and activist. Ranging from philosophical to pragmatist, feminist disability activists and scholars have identified a range of issues that affect both mainstream discrimination against children and adults with disabilities and the rights and possibilities for people with disabilities to express their own sexual and reproductive aspirations. We need an ongoing conversation that takes the disability lens as a framework for thinking about reproductive choices. Why is fetally diagnosed disability so routinely considered cause for abortion? To what extent might the experiences of people living with disabilities provide a more robust social fund of knowledge that could better provide a truly informed reproductive decision as to whether or not to terminate a diagnosed pregnancy?

Some of the context that makes this wider conversation both possible and necessary emerges from recent legal changes catalyzed by disability rights activism. The passage and adjudication of the Americans with Disabilities Act (1990) has changed the cultural milieu in which, for example, the almost automatic sterilization of people with disabilities was considered an unexceptional, even ethical practice. Other aspects of our changed context include the improved health care for infants, children, and young adults with disabilities, from neonatal intensive care units to seizure-controlling medications to increasingly sophisticated prosthetics. All enable fuller social participation—in particular in education—over the life cycle, potentially including reproduction. At the international level a vigorous disability rights movement has brought these issues of survival and inclusion into the UN Convention on the Rights of Persons with Disabilities, which has had the highest number of signatories of any human rights framework to date. . . .

What do you think are important ongoing challenges in struggles for reproductive justice? How do you characterize the relationship between scholarship and activism on reproduction?

RAPP AND GINSBURG: The feminist reproductive health agenda has embraced the inclusion of disability rights in its broad agenda. Yet the actualization of such a commitment is anything but clear. How can feminists justify support for the abortion decisions women make and for a disability-inclusion perspective? The profound segregation and discrimination against disability prevents fully grounded knowledge of what it means to live with an impairment from entering into those deliberations. We want to underscore the significance of continued feminist conversations on this topic across movements and coalitions, which always take place in the context of changing reproductive technologies. As feminist activists we ignore "medical advances" at our peril. . . .

SMITH: The most important scholarly interventions are happening among indigenous and women-of-color reproductive justice organizations. They are decentering *Roe v. Wade* by not assuming that if the decision is overturned, reproductive justice organizations cannot provide reproductive health services themselves. These groups are focusing not simply on influencing law and policy but on building a reproductive justice movement in which people begin to take charge of their reproductive health. Such groups do everything from teaching midwifery to doing community gardening as a way to address the relationship between the environment and reproductive health. These interventions also situate reproductive justice within a broader framework for social justice. Some of these interventions are not necessarily found in books but are circulating through the Web or other social networks in a way that directly influences grassroots organizing.

TAKESHITA: Recently I invited an artist and activist, Heather Ault, for an event that marks the fortieth anniversary of *Roe v. Wade* at the University of California, Riverside (UCR). Her project *4000 Years for Choice* is a series of fifty prints that combine image and text that represent a method of contraception and abortion from the past or a historical figure's comment on birth control.[13] Her intention is to generate new visuals and languages for the pro-choice movement that are more powerful than the iconic wire coat hanger and more inviting than the combative and defensive terms used in its call to action such as *fight, struggle, defend, attack, and threat.* Through her artwork Ault underscores how fundamental birth control has been to the history of humanity and suggests terms such as *cherish, embrace, nourish, trust, and unite* to tell stories of "women's reproductive empowerment, wisdom, and self-care that dates back a millennium."[14] She writes that regardless of an audience's position on reproductive rights, history should serve as testament to "women's deeply ingrained desire to control pregnancies for the good of ourselves, our relationships, and our families."[15]

However disheartened and tired we are of the political and ideological deadlock that "pro-choice" feminists are stuck in, countering the "pro-life" movement still must remain one of our major concerns considering its incessant endeavor to narrow women's access to reproductive health care. While securing legal rights to birth control, as contributors to this roundtable point out, is far from enough to address reproductive justice, we cannot ignore the legal challenges by private employers to mandatory contraceptive health care coverage for employees and conservative lawmakers' constant effort to pass anti-choice legislations. Certainly feminist organizations such as Planned Parenthood and NARAL (the National Abortion and Reproductive Rights Action League) are working tirelessly to "win" this "war on women." But is there anything feminist scholarship can do to intervene in the impasse? I myself have often felt that no dialogue seems possible when both sides believe that their opponents are utterly immoral or irrational and share little in common. Yet there may still be room for feminist scholarship and grassroots movements to disrupt the dichotomous thinking, which is what these opposing positions on abortion have come to be, and foreground the complex gray areas of the debate.

Ault attempts to transcend the reproductive-politics gridlock by proposing alternative visuals

and languages for the pro-choice movement to overcome the stigma of abortion. Using photos of (presumably) aborted fetuses, anti-abortionists have successfully created a visual narrative of pregnancy termination as equivalent to murder and women who choose to have an abortion as evil, selfish, and horrifying. Unfortunately, symbols that have been available to the pro-choice side, namely photographs of women who lost their lives in blotched abortions and a wire coat hanger with a line drawn across it, have not been capable of evoking as strong an emotional response as the opponent's gory images. With this in mind Ault's *4000 Years for Choice* aims to provide alternative beautiful images for the pro-choice movement along with historical evidence for the universality of the desire and action to control birth. Ault's work clearly moved the audience at UCR. Curious students from all walks of campus came through the exhibit throughout the day. Some brought friends and talked to each other while viewing the artwork. Some asked the artist questions. There were as many male students taking photos of the artwork as female students.

Spending most of the day at Ault's art exhibit and talk prompted me to respond to the third question of this roundtable. First, I suggest that it might be constructive for feminist scholars to reexamine what personal stories might accomplish. There may be something to be learned from the open-mike session of the national conference for March of Life, during which women confess their abortions and express sadness, anger, and regret. These intimate and emotional disclosures bond the speaker and audience with empathy and reinforce the group's conviction that abortion must be eradicated. We might think about telling personal stories of women who made the difficult decision to have an abortion that they ultimately do not regret or of women who have decided not to discontinue their unintended pregnancies despite their pro-choice convictions. Real-life stories that represent the "gray" areas of abortion narratives might be instrumental in complicating the "pro-life versus

pro-choice" divide and opening up new dialogues. They might also help establish positive
images of pro-choice women that contradict the
"selfish baby killers" and "angry feminists" as
they have been painted.

Second, echoing the suggestion that Ault
made during the course of the day, I want to
suggest that there be more collaboration among
artists, activists, and scholars. One thing those of
us scholars who have access to college students
and facilities can do would be to bring artists and
activists to campus in order to expose more
young people to the human side of the reproduc-
tive-choice debate that is currently swamped by
political wrestling devoid of discussion that may
move us toward conciliation.

GUTIÉRREZ: A reproductive-justice approach
to abortion demands that all women must have not
only the real choice of terminating a pregnancy
but the opportunity to have the true option to
deliver a child to full term if that is what she
wants, *free from economic constraints*. Thus,
issues such as access to education, health care,
civil rights, and social services all must be considered under the rubric of reproductive choice in
addition to the spectrum of reproductive health
services, and until they are available to all women
who reside in the United States, reproductive justice has not been achieved.

In addition to the fundamental right to have
children, more recent activist developments
increasingly demand that all women have the
right not only to have however many children
they want whenever they want but also to
deliver those children in whatever manner that
they want. This commitment to providing the
kind of childbirth experience that any woman
wants has certainly grown in the past ten to fifteen years; alongside a quickly growing and
diversifying midwifery communities are doula
practitioners who are focused on providing
women with various aspects of practical support
that might be necessary for anyone who may be
having a child. These efforts, which build upon
the work of the women's health movement of
the 1980s, are most often associated with

natural childbirth, but doulas often work with
women who deliver in the hospital and provide
additional support for a woman before, during,
and/or after childbirth, in the form of emotional
and physical assistance.

In recent years the large majority of those in
this practice are birth and postpartum doulas who
are professionally trained in supporting a woman
while she goes through the process of pregnancy.
It is becoming more common for doulas to also
provide support services for pregnancy termination, offering the equivalent emotional and physical support around this experience as during the
birth of a child. Abortion doula services include
emotional support during the procedure, after
care, child care, and practical factors such as
preparation. Although such practices are only
beginning to become more readily available,
they are certainly an important development in
the abortion rights movement given the increasingly deleterious circumstances that most women
must face when they must go through the procedure. . . .

BRIGGS: The deep and intensifying care-
work gap, in the United States and transnationally, would in my mind be a candidate for the
most important reproductive-rights issue in the
present moment. Not only did the Pill and abortion make heterosexual sex possible for those of
us who did not want to be committed to children
and a partner before we were twenty, but they
also have made it possible for educational institutions, corporations, and the labor market in
general to expect many of those in their twenties
to delay childbearing for much of that decade of
our lifespans, too. In the 1970s feminists joked
that they needed a wife so they could work and
still do care work and the reproductive labor of
the household; now companies, universities, and
government demand that we all act like the husbands of that decade—as if we never had a problem because public school is 180 days and the
working year is 260, never had a sick child,
never were made systematically crazy by the
mismatch between school running from 8:30 to
2:30 (when it's not an early-release day) and

work from 8:00 to 5:00 at a minimum. And this is to say nothing of the perfectly normal exceptional circumstances—you can't even get this much coverage from public programs if your child is under six years old or has disabilities or behavior problems that kick them into the "special" programs that run, say, from 8:00 to noon. That problem is multiplied for the growing percentage of women who work more than one job, and the racist right is trying to ensure that immigrant women have no recourse even to the public programs there are, by trying to ban immigrant children from school—and while direct efforts have failed, terror that their children's visible presence will get the family deported has succeeded in places like Alabama and Arizona, at least for some period. While this is a fierce tragedy for children, it is also worth noting that it is a huge added care-work burden for families.

As a growing and important body of scholarship on care work and reproductive labor, particularly in sociology, has noted, in the United States and many comparable postindustrial economies, the care-work gap is increasingly being filled by immigrant nannies and, for the elderly and those with disabilities, home-care workers.[16] As many have noted, the work of immigrants in filling the care gap in one place— for middle-class people in the United States, usually but not necessarily white—merely creates one in another place, as nannies are often mothers themselves, and many leave children behind in home countries as a different kind of transnationalization of care labor. Just as it is cheaper for U.S. families to substitute immigrant labor for their own in caring for children, as declining real wages force middle-class households to have two people working for money, so too is it cheaper for immigrant nannies to "outsource" the raising of their children to family members in the global South, with their wages often making the difference between having funds for school fees and even bare survival or not.[17]

The care-work gap drives a host of other issues—including to some extent infant mortality rates, the rising use of reproductive

technology (contemporary infertility being largely an artifact of the delayed childbearing demanded by women who seek to be in professional sectors of the labor market), surrogacy, and adoption. Adoption, as the transfer of children from the impoverished to those who are middle class, from the global South to the United States, Europe, Canada, and a handful of other places, and from the young to older parents, should trouble us more than it does, as a place where violence, coercion, and power meet (usually single) mothers and their children.[18] The idea of adoption also hovers over the abortion debate in the Americas, as its more desirable other for liberals and conservatives alike; for many conservative commentators it also represents a preferable alternative to single mothers raising their children. Mothers, on the contrary, seem to have voted with their feet that they prefer either alternative to renting out their bodies for nine months, giving rise to sharply declining rates of placing children in adoption in the United States once single mothers can support their children or get an abortion and "unwed mothers' homes" losing their coercive power, except perhaps for some young Evangelical Christian girls and women.[19]

For the most part, though, scholarship on the care-work gap is not brought together with concerns about abortion and adoption, nor do most historians, sociologists, or political scientists who study the dynamics of the abortion debate in the United States think of it as part of a process across the Americas that is linked to anticommunist civil wars. Among scholars there is no field of "reproductive politics," and so the scholarship on abortion or surrogacy is unrelated to work on the medicalization of pregnancy, poverty, or infant mortality, although they are critical to understanding each other. There are reproductive economies just as there are domestic economies, and the globalization of production, finance, and labor did not take place without a concomitant global adjustment of reproduction. I would argue that we need a scholarship and a reproductive-justice movement that are about reproductive politics writ large—from neoliberalism to reproductive governance to welfare reform, from infant mortality and racial and geographic health disparities to reproductive technologies.

PETCHESKY: It's too easy to blame failures to secure reproductive justice for all women on the continued barrage of attacks from the right, who still see "reproductive health and rights" as code for rampant abortion and promiscuous sex; or the retreat of global health providers and policy makers into vertical, single-issue programs that favor HIV treatment or family planning and eschew a comprehensive, rights-based approach to health and sexuality as too complicated and too costly in resource-scarce societies. But responsibility also lies with social, including feminist, movements whose campaigns are still siloed and "issue" oriented rather than foregrounding the deep connections between reproductive and sexual health and rights and social transformations that challenge global capitalist priorities—the structures that keep resources scarce for the many and plentiful for the few. In the United States, I think, the most radical voices of the past decade on reproductive issues have been those of women of color and particularly the work of SisterSong in promoting a concept of *reproductive justice* that insists on the direct links between access to all aspects of reproductive health care, including safe abortion, and addressing poverty, racism, gender-based violence, community development, education, and labor conditions. To make this vision a reality, feminists need to be thinking deeply about systemic change—and building the broad coalitions with Occupy and other social-justice and antiracist movements to make it happen.

NOTES

1. "Laws Affecting Reproductive Health and Rights: 2012 State Policy Review," Guttmacher Institute, http://www.guttmacher.org/statecenter/updates/2012/statetrends42012.html (accessed Mar. 13, 2013).

2. Rosalind P. Petchesky, *Abortion and Woman's Choice: The State, Sexuality, and Reproductive Freedom,* rev. ed. (Lebanon NH: Northeastern University Press, 1990), xi, xviii.

3. See Carole Joffe, "Abortion Patients and the 'Two Americas' of Reproductive Health," chap. 6 of her superb *Dispatches from the Abortion Wars* (Boston: Beacon Press), 2009.

4. For additional information on state abortion laws see "An Overview of Abortion Laws," State Policies in Brief, Guttmacher Institute, http.//www.guttmacher.org/statecenter/spibs/index.html (accessed Jan. 2013).

5. For additional information on the impact of the Global Gag Rule see the website of Population Action International, http//populationaction.org/topics/global-gag-rule/ (accessed Aug. 2012).

6. Sheryl Gay Stolberg, "In Global Battle on AIDS, Bush Creates Legacy," *New York Times,* Jan. 5, 2008, http://www.nytimes.com/2008/01/05/washington.05aids.html.

7. Lynn M. Morgan and Elizabeth F. S. Roberts, "Reproductive Governance in Latin America," *Anthropology and Medicine* 19, no. 2 (Aug. 2012): 241–54; Michelle Goldberg, *The Means of Reproduction: Sex, Power, and the Future of the World* (New York: Penguin Press, 2009).

8. See Rosalind P. Petchesky, *Global Prescriptions: Engendering Health and Human Rights* (London: Zed Books, 2003), chap.1; S. Corrêa, R. Petchesky, and R. Parker, *Sexuality, Health and Human Rights* (London and New York: Routledge, 2008), chaps. 2, 8.

9. Petchesky, *Global Prescriptions, 44–45.*

10. The women-centered methods and male contraceptive methods are a trend I have seen in the research trajectories of the Population Council in New York, an organization that has played a significant role in the development of IUDs and implants, as well as the establishment of family planning programs in the global South. Over the years the organization has expanded its mission to overall reproductive health, including HIV/AIDS. Its current projects on reproductive technology development can be found on its website: http://www.popcouncil.org/topics/reprotech.asp#/Projects (accessed Sept. 2012). Adele Clarke coined the term *impossible* contraceptives to represent methods that last for a long time once administered and are difficult for users to discontinue at will. These include the IUD, implants, and injectables.

11. Elena Gutiérrez, "Policing 'Pregnant Pilgrims': Welfare, Health Care and the Control of Mexican-Origin Women's Fertility," in *Women, Health and Nation: The U.S and Canada since* 1945, ed. Molly Ladd-Taylor, Gina Feldberg, Kathryn McPherson, and Alison Li (Toronto: McGill-Queens University Press, 2003), 379–403; Elena Gutiérrez, *Fertile Matters: The Politics of Mexican-Origin Women's Reproduction* (Austin: University of Texas Press, 2008).

12. Amy Harmon, "Genetic Testing + Abortion = ???" *New York Times,* May 13, 2007, http://www.nytimes.com/2007/05/13/weekinreview/13harm.html?_r=0.

13. Information on Heather Ault and her work is available at www.4000yearsforchoice.com (accessed Feb. 2013).

14. "About *4000 years for choice,*" http://www.4000yearsforchoice.com/pages/about-the-project (accessed Feb. 2013).

15. "About *4000 Years for Choice.*"

16. For different reasons immigrant maids and nannies are also crucial to other kinds of ferociously transnationalized economies like the United Arab Emirates and Singapore.

17. See e.g., Pierrette Hondagneu-Sotelo and Ernestine Avila, "I'm Here, but I'm There: The meanings of Latina Transitional Motherland," *Gender and Society II* no. 5(1997): 548–71; Rhacel Salazar Parreñas, *Children of Global Migration: Transitional Families and Gendered Woes* (Stanford: Stanford University Press, 2005).

18. That at least is the argument I make in *Somebody's Children: The Politics of Transracial and Transnational Adoption* (Durham: Duke University Press, 2012).

19. See Rickie Solinger, *Wake up Little Susie: Single Pregnancy and Race before* Roe v. Wade (New York: Routledge, 1992), and *Beggars and Choosers: How the Politics of Choice Shapes Adoption, Abortion, and Welfare in the United States* (New York: Hill and Wang, 2001). For a first-hand account of the coercive power of Evangelical Christian families and unwed mothers' homes in the present, see Ruth Graham's thoughtful book, with Sara Dormon, *I'm Pregnant . . . Now What?* (Ventura CA: Regal Books, 2004).

Introduction to Reading 47

Courtney E. Martin and Vanessa Valenti discuss the critical role of online feminism in the 21st century. They argue that feminist blogs are the consciousness-raising groups of this era and that online technologies have produced thousands of activists, writers, bloggers, and tweeters around the world who are able to engage one another across boundaries and borders. Online feminists and feminist organizations have become allies in movements for gender equality. Martin and Valenti identify the ways in which online feminism is able to reach beyond traditional feminist institutions (e.g., relationship-building and engaging young people) as well as the challenges facing online feminist organizing (e.g., funding and sustainable infrastructure).

1. Why are feminist blogs defined as "the consciousness-raising groups of the 21st century"?

2. What is culture jamming, and how are online feminists using this tool?

3. How does online feminist activism push media stakeholders to be more accurate and less harmful?

#FemFuture

Online Revolution

Courtney E. Martin and Vanessa Valenti

Part One: A New Landscape

What Is Online Feminism?

Online feminist work has become a new engine for contemporary feminism. No other form of activism in history has empowered one individual to prompt tens of thousands to take action on a singular issue—within minutes. Its influence is colossal and its potential is even greater. Feminists today, young and old, use the Internet to share their stories and analysis, raise awareness and organize collective actions, and discuss difficult issues.

The beginnings of online feminism were primarily in the form of online forums, newsgroups, journals and blogs developed in response to the need for a public platform where young women could voice their opinions about the state of the world around them. Many created websites and online zines early on; Heather Corinna began Scarlet Letters in the late 1990s, the first site online to specifically address and explore women's sexuality, and soon after, Scarleteen.com, an online resource for teen and young adult sex education. Viva La Feminista's Veronica Arreola took the feminist ideas discussed on the listserv of online organization Women Leaders Online to create a website at Geocities.com that discussed sports, pop culture and feminist politics. Later on, she developed the first pro-choice webring. Jennifer Pozner developed Women in Media and News in order to create a space for feminist media analysis and increase women's voices in public debate.[1]

Women were creating powerful spaces for themselves online, helping to build the next frontier of the feminist movement. These forums began as simple websites and developed into communities of hundreds of thousands of people who needed a platform to express themselves. They found it on the Internet.

This is why so many identify feminist blogs as "the consciousness-raising groups of the 21st century." The very functionality of blogs—the self-publishing platforms and commenting community—allow people to connect with each other, creating an intentional space to share personal opinions, experiences of injustice, and ideas, all with a feminist lens. Consciousness-raising groups were said to be the "backbone" of second-wave feminism; now, instead of a living room of 8–10 women, it's an online network of thousands.

As years went by, social technologies began to evolve into a robust diverse field of web-based tools and platforms. YouTube allowed for vlogging, or "video blogging"; Twitter and Tumblr, or "microblogging," allowed for easier and even more immediate sharing capabilities. Today, this evolution of online technologies has produced thousands of activists, writers, bloggers, and tweeters across the globe who live and breathe

From Martin, Courtney E., and Vanessa Valenti. 2012. #FemFuture: Online Revolution. New Feminist Solutions series, vol. 8, Barnard College Center for Research on Women.

this movement, engaging their audience every day in the name of equality.

In a study conducted in 2011, the Pew Research Center's Internet and American Life Project crowned young women between the ages of 18 and 29 years old as "the power users of social networking."[2] Eighty-nine percent of women use social networks and 93 percent of young people between the ages of 18 and 29 are online. Over 584 million people log in to Facebook alone on an average day.

In this rapidly shifting technological age, it shouldn't be a surprise that the next generation of social movement-building in the United States is largely online.

A New Channel for Activism

The typical image of feminist activism has been pretty clear historically: women marching down the street, or protesting at a rally. From suffrage through the second wave, collective chants and painted protest signs had been defining markers of feminist action. And today, offline organizing continues to be a major tactic to galvanize the masses. Waves of protests across South Asia early this year following the death of a 23-year-old gang rape victim in Delhi are just one powerful reminder of the impact that a collective group of people can make on the ground.

The marchers that filled the streets of Delhi, however, weren't just using their feet; they were also using their tweets. #Delhibraveheart—a hashtag, which essentially serves as a filter for a particular theme or meme—was added to millions of impassioned laments for the victim. Government leaders, who initially had an anemic reaction, were compelled to respond to the young people taking up space in the streets, but also those setting the Internet on fire with their rage. This dual approach is just the latest example that demonstrates how feminist activism has expanded to the online sphere.

The rapid innovation and creativity that characterize online activist work are game-changers in the contemporary art of making change. Compared to the weeks or months of prep time it takes to gather thousands of people in one place for a rally or march, online feminists can mobilize thousands within minutes. Whether you're signing an online petition, participating in a Twitter campaign against harmful legislation, or blogging about a news article, technological tools have made it infinitely easier for people invested in social justice to play their part.

Another striking development in online organizing today is the role of citizen-produced media in online activist work. On feminist blogs, for example, writers post commentary about the day's news with a feminist lens, highlighting and amplifying social justice work that is off the mainstream media's radar, and often linking this analysis to action that readers can take. This widespread, collective effort creates the necessary consciousness and a broad range of content that organizations like Hollaback!, Color of Chance, Move On, UltraViolet, and the Applied Research Center draw on as they share articles, connect with others, sign petitions and pledges, and use online tools to mobilize on-the-ground action. Users can then be instantly contacted to request action in the future. Media-making essentially allows activists to become experts in the issues that we care about, and makers—not just advocates—of the change we want to see and be in the world.

As decade-long activists, we have lived and understand the power of boots on the ground. The feminist movement will continue to make strides through lobbying, on-the-ground organizing, and creating meaningful discourse through academia, but online feminism now offers a new entry point for feminist activism.

A Vibrant New Movement

We are currently living in the most hostile legislative environment to reproductive rights in this country in the last forty years. In 2011, we reached a record number of state restrictions on abortion. Contraception coverage is being attacked, access to basic health care services through providers like Planned Parenthood is threatened, and decisions about one's reproductive health are increasingly criminalized. The feminist movement continues to push back against each hurdle thrown at us. The days of proactive work and creating legislation for equality, of securing our rights rather than defending them, has seemed far beyond our capacity when there is so much responsive action to take.

Yet when millions of women and men can tweet their demand for accountability from corporations, governments, and media, we have an opportunity to shift this paradigm. For over a decade, online feminist activists have been working on feminist causes, but it has never been so visible. Now, feminist organizations, media, and corporate stakeholders, and national leaders are beginning to recognize how the power of social media and online organizing is reanimating the feminist movement.

Online Feminism, a Radicalizing Force

For years, online feminists have served as powerful allies for feminist organizations. We liveblog at conferences, tweet calls to action, and translate the sometimes jargon-laden organizational press release into catchy hashtags, nudging people to look twice before they skip to a funny cat video. As we mapped the movement and the role online feminism plays within it at our convening, we were all struck by the hours and hours of labor made visible.

The good news is that most major women's organizations get it. They recognize that online media is a powerful tool to create change, and have begun to leverage online tools in their work. For example, The National Domestic Workers Alliance, an organization that advocates for the rights and support of domestic workers, created a social media campaign, #bethehelp, around the nomination of the Hollywood film *The Help* for an Academy Award. As controversial as the film's portrayal of African American domestic workers was, The National Domestic Workers Alliance recognized that it was a rare moment within mainstream media where domestic workers were in the spotlight, and they didn't shy away from seizing the day for their own

radical purposes. The #bethehelp campaign was helped along by individuals joining in and popularizing the trend.

Traditional feminist organizations and online feminists are becoming more and more symbiotic in this way. Meanwhile, independent online feminists continue to invent new methods of action and catalyze new discussions that are pushing institutional feminism forward. In 2012, when the Susan B. Komen Foundation threatened to withdraw funding from Planned Parenthood because they provide abortions along with many women's and reproductive health services, Planned Parenthood had to respond to the Komen Foundation through formal channels in a professionally appropriate tone. Individual online activists were beholden to no such conventions. Digital strategist Deanna Zandt's Tumblr, Planned Parenthood Saved Me, featured hundreds of women from across the country sharing their stories of how Planned Parenthood's health care has saved their lives. Those stories were a large force behind what compelled Komen to change direction.

Young feminists have been at the helm of online activism for the last several years. "We can't move too quickly over the important cultural (and deeply political) feminist work that younger women are leading, largely online," said Erin Matson, the former Action Vice President of the National Organization for Women, in an intergenerational dialogue at *In These Times*. "All this work is rapidly building into a platform that has the power to force big policy changes, and that's exciting."

Ties between organizations and online feminists have become stronger over the years and have sometimes provided resources for bloggers: organizations may contract bloggers to livetweet at their annual conference, pay for campaign ads on their blogs, or hire online influencers as consultants to assist with communications strategy.

But critical gaps remain between institutional feminism and online feminism. As Jensine Larsen of World Pulse pointed out at the convening, each has expertise that the other can benefit from: nonprofit organizations often have the infrastructure (physical space, resources, womanpower) that online feminists crave, and online feminists often deploy the communications innovations that nonprofit organizations struggle to generate while already stretched thin trying to achieve their larger missions.

Thus far, we've been exchanging our resources in piecemeal, inadequate ways. It's time to come up with a sustainable strategy that serves all of us and strengthens the movement in the process. More meaningful collaborations between two of the most powerful sectors of the feminist movement could create huge impact.

Creating a New Pipeline of Feminist Leadership

. . . Leadership development online can provide a means of resisting the hierarchical, insular, monocultural structure of traditional institutions. There has been a lot of debate about whether the World Wide Web itself can provide new tools for democracy, movement-building and alternative models of leadership. The Internet is not inherently egalitarian; after all, it was first created by the military and can be used in ways that directly reinforce patriarchy and structural violence.

But you don't have to spend years making copies, learning a special language, or knowing people who know people to become a leading voice in online feminism; you just have to have something unique to say and the technological skills needed to amplify that story or idea online. This landscape allows for decentralized movements of multiple voices, communities, and identities.

In fact, many feminist blogs were born out of young women's frustration with entry-level jobs at nonprofits where the mission may have been feminist, but the labor distribution made them feel invisible and, too often, exploited. While more traditional feminist institutions—advocacy organizations, cultural institutions, foundations, etc.—develop initiatives designed to "engage Millennials," they often overlook the young women in their own offices, underutilized and anxious to start flexing their leadership muscles, not to mention the hundreds of thousands of young women and men who are engaging with feminism online every single day. These organizations must stop operating on the "if we build it, they will come" assumption, and start going to meet young people where they are—whether bored and underutilized in their own offices and/ or channeling their energy into active online spaces.

Making the Personal Political

The capacity for storytelling and relationship-building online allows young women—so many of them living in small pockets of conservative middle America—to feel less alone, to feel like they're part of a community. This is one example of the hundreds of emails that feminist blogs receive on a regular basis: *I just wanted to say a quick "thank you." I have been reading this blog for about a year and a half, and it has provided me with strength to live through some situations that I know I would have never gotten from anyone or anything else in my life. You have given me hope that it might get better and I just wanted to let you know.*

This kind of connectivity can be life-saving. So many young women find feminism, not in their classrooms or even controversial novels, but in online blogs like F-Bomb, a site by and for teen girls about women's rights. Marinated in the voices and ideas of young feminists that share their sensibility, they are made to feel a part of something bigger than themselves—even as that connection is forged through the most intimate of stories.

In one of the most popular posts ever at the Crunk Feminist Collective blog, University of Alabama professor and blogger Dr. Robin Turner wrote in "Twenty things I want to say to my twentysomething self":

You are strong (your capacity of strength is so much wider than you think) . . .

but being a strongblackwoman is not a necessity or responsibility in your life. Your frailties and vulnerabilities make you human, not weak.

You are a storyteller and people will need your stories. Don't stop writing them down.

It is these kinds of poetic descriptions that transcend some of the more tangible ways in which online spaces like the Crunk Feminist Collective serve to mobilize young feminists. It's not just about organizing on local issues or taking action on federal policy; it's also about healing, reclamation, solidarity, beauty, and wisdom.

Providing an Entry Point

Decades of stigmatization have resulted in a toxic perception of what a feminist is. But that stigma is beginning to dissipate among young people as they see feminism in action online. Here, feminism is cool again.

At the end of 2011, *New York Magazine* journalist Emily Nussbaum highlighted the ways that feminist blogs use popular culture:

Instead of viewing pop culture as toxic propaganda, bloggers embraced it as a shared language, a complex code to be solved together, and not coincidentally, something fun. In an age of search engines, it was a powerful magnet: Again and again, bloggers described pop culture posts to me as a "gateway drug" for young women—an isolated teenager in rural Mississippi would Google "Beyonce" or "Real Housewives," then get drawn into threads about abortion.

Letting young women know that they can be feminists and care about pop culture gives them social permission to care about equality. Tavi Gevinson is one striking example; she began blogging about fashion and feminism on her blog, Style Rookie, when she was 11-years-old. Five years later, she is the Editor-in-Chief of *Rookie Magazine,* the premiere indie online magazine for teenage girls. In *Rookie,* one piece is about how to create the perfect Fourth of July manicure; the next is a guide to protecting your civil liberties.

Another weapon feminist bloggers and writers use is humor, countering the long-held, wildly inaccurate stereotype that feminists have no funny bones.

Convincing the public that feminism can actually be fun through humorous quips on blog posts has evolved into savvy online campaigns that catch like wildfire. One recent example was the Tumblr blog BWinders Full of Women, created after Mitt Romney's controversial remarks in the 2012 presidential debate about getting binders full of women for possible hires when he was Massachusetts Governor. The Tumblr included snapshots of women dressed up as binders full of women for Halloween screenshots with witty captions, mock campaign ads, etc.

Demonstrating the serious side of cultural entrepreneurship like this, the creator of the Tumblr, Veronica De Souza, wrote in her last post on the site:

Now that the election is over, I think this whole thing is done. I never thought it would get this big, or that anyone would ask me to talk about memes on CNN or that this would help me find a job. I am so thankful for everything.

What De Souza and her peers are doing is essentially "culture jamming"—disrupting mainstream political and cultural narratives using crowd-sourced creativity and playfulness. Latoya Peterson of Racialicious spoke to this in a 2011 interview with *Persephone Magazine:*

In a way, using pop culture to deconstruct oppressive structures in society is culture jamming. We are, in many ways, creating a distortion in the smoothly packaged ideas being sold to us. Pop culture is about selling lifestyles, selling ideas; it normalizes certain elements of our culture and erases others. Why do so many people have the idea that we are all vaguely middle class? Because that's what's represented in our media environment.

"Culture jamming" has historically been used as a tool to shape advertisements and consumer culture into public critiques. Online activists and bloggers use media like memes to transform popular culture into a tool for social change. The result? Young people online are transformed from passive pop-culture consumers to engagers and makers.

Humor, pop culture, fashion, and the punchy, sassy writing, tweeting, and memes that online feminists deploy have become the most effective way to engage young people about the seriousness of injustice, using new Internet culture to speak back to pop culture.

Reclaiming the Frame

Working within a media landscape drenched in reality shows and rape jokes is no easy feat for any feminist. With women comprising only 22%[3] of thought leadership in most mainstream media forums and only 3% of clout positions,[4] it's no surprise that pop culture and legacy news can be such sexist, racist, and homophobic environments. In this context, online feminism continues to constitute an alternative space, where feminist values are suffused in every point and click, *and* to influence legacy media.

The immediacy and viral nature of blogs and Twitter have fundamentally changed how we consume the news. Wherein the past relationship between the media and the public consisted of a top-down flow of information, the Internet has allowed the public to participate in and influence the larger public conversation.

This has resulted in a lateral relationship between the public and news media, to the point where online engagement influences the news of the day. Case in point: when a 31-year-old woman died in an Irish hospital after doctors refused to perform a termination of her pregnancy despite the fact that she was already experiencing a miscarriage, feminist blogs were instrumental in spreading the story. RH Reality Check covered the story on November 13, 2012, and by the next day Jill Filipovic of Feministe wrote about it for the *Guardian,* with a number of other outlets following.

These days, feminist blogs and Twitter accounts can often be a source of both breaking developments and overlooked stories for mainstream media outlets. "Paying attention to feminist media through Twitter is essential," said Jamil Smith, segment and digital producer at MSNBC's *The Melissa Harris-Perry Show.*

> *I originally started using the service as an RSS feed of sorts, and that's how some of the first voices I discovered—Jennifer Pozner, Jessica Valenti, Jill Filipovic, and many more—opened up a new source of political perspective, analysis, and leadership in the media for me. Personally and professionally, I owe them all an enormous debt.*

Melissa Harris-Perry herself rose to prominence in part because of her longtime online presence, including her blog, The Kitchen Table, where she discussed a variety of issues with friend and fellow Princeton Professor Yolanda Pierce.

Online feminism is not only bringing attention to the media gender gap through online activism, but also beginning to fill that space with a new generation of media influencers. Zerlina Maxwell, law student and contributor to Feministing and TheGrio, was, for example, recently featured in *The New York Times* as a political voice on Twitter to follow during election season. She strategically used Twitter to get noticed by mainstream outlets:

> *I picked a handful of folks [on Twitter] I admire that I looked up to and followed everyone they followed. Some of those producers, editors and thought leaders followed me back. Then I started tweeting at media folks if I agreed or disagreed. Figured if they saw my name they wouldn't forget it, and that's exactly what happened . . . Twitter shrinks the world and makes everyone accessible.*

Zerlina is now a blogger for *The New York Daily News,* a columnist for *Ebony Magazine,* and a regular commentator on Fox News & Friends, providing a feminist analysis that was largely absent in these spaces. And her story— one of a law student from New Jersey turned mainstream media commentator—speaks to one of the most remarkable things about online activism: It's bringing feminist analysis and voices into the mainstream. "Mainstreaming the voices of feminist media, particularly at national outlets like MSNBC, is essential given the demands of our news consumers," says Jamil Smith. "As a more technologically sophisticated populace devours its daily news diet from a number of different sources, we not only need to provide spaces for women and men in the feminist movement to contribute to the dialogue and analysis we present on our air—but if we fail to do so, we'll be the ones left behind."

Holding Powerbrokers Accountable

The new lateral relationship between the online public and the media has also created possibilities for a stronger culture of accountability. Sexism, transphobia, and nationalism in mainstream media are far too commonplace, but online responses to these biases are helping to push media stakeholders to be more accurate and less harmful. Online activism has convinced *The New York Times,* for example, to publicly acknowledge victim-blaming content in their articles and reexamine their coverage of transgender people.

Another powerful example: In the summer of 2012, The Applied Research Center and *Colorlines* launched a campaign, "Drop the I-Word," calling on news publications to stop referring to undocumented immigrants as "illegals," "illegal alien" and "illegal immigrant." After a multimedia action strategy, including an online pledge and toolkit, a Twitter campaign and widespread blog coverage, mainstream media picked up the initiative. Announcements followed by those renouncing the usage of the term "illegal immigrant," like *The Miami Herald,* Fox News Latino, ABC News and *The Huffington Post,* as well as those who continue to use it, including *The New York Times.* Today, the Drop the I-Word campaign continues to influence media and individuals in their efforts to create better public representation of undocumented immigrant communities. (And still sends letters to *The New York Times* in response to their continued use of the word.)

Feminists can mobilize online in response to politician and corporate actions as well.

When the news broke that Representative Todd Akin told KTVI-TV that pregnancy from rape is rare because "if it's a legitimate rape, the female body has ways to try to shut that whole thing down," feminists responded immediately. "Todd Akin" quickly became a trending topic on Twitter. Tumblrs, social media campaigns and Internet memes followed suit, calling Akin unelectable. Thousands took to Akin's Facebook page urging him to withdraw from the race. While he didn't take his constituents' and colleagues' advice, social media no doubt played a role in his loss on Election Day.

Akin's story was covered all over the country, but stories of movement toward accountability are happening in different pockets of the online community on a regular basis, demonstrating the need for positive and pro-active communication. In June 2011, Vanessa Valenti wrote a blog post critiquing New York Senator Kirsten Gillibrand for saying that the women's movement was "stalled," because too many women were "not engaged" and "don't want their voices to be heard" on MSNBC's *Morning Joe.* She was on discussing her new initiative, "Off the Sidelines." As a very engaged participant in the women's movement and co-founder of a blog whose success has been built on the hundreds of thousands of voices seeking to be heard, Vanessa felt a responsibility to disagree:

> *I'm not saying there's anything wrong with trying to mobilize women who aren't politically active, because of course there are folks out there who aren't. But how can you say they don't want their voices heard when you're the one speaking for them? Because that is one of the biggest lessons we here at Feministing have learned—young women do want their voices heard, they just need a platform to do it. We're here, we're engaged, and we sure as hell don't have a stalled movement. Our hundreds of thousands of readers every month at this blog alone is proof of that.*

The next morning, the Senator called her personally to discuss her remarks. It was a powerful moment for her, and an honor that Senator Gillibrand had, in fact, heard and valued a young woman's voice. The Senator's staff and Vanessa now speak regularly about issues facing women and various strategies for engaging and empowering them.

Creating Space for Radical Learning

The feminist movement isn't without its complicated history. Combating racism, homophobia, classism, and other forms of oppression within feminist communities is a decades-old struggle that is far from over. But the Internet has allowed for a more open space of accountability and learning, helping to push mainstream feminism to be less monolithic.

Professor and theorist Kimberle Crenshaw coined the term "intersectionality" in 1989 as a recognition of the intersecting and overlapping identities that women hold, contributing to varied experiences of oppression. Intersectionality is today a well-known and often-discussed theory of practice within the online feminist world.

A lot of feminist dialogue online has focused on recognizing the complex ways that privilege shapes our approach to work and community. Andrea Plaid of Racialicious spoke at the convening of the unaccounted for labor of constantly educating people with white privilege about racial justice issues. She said: "What we need is more white allies [to challenge racism online] . . . continue to come get your people, without excuse."

One powerful example of this dialogue is the wave of online conversations among women of color online that emerged from the increased attention to "SlutWalk" marches in the mainstream media. "SlutWalks" began in Toronto following a police officer's statement that women should avoid acting like "sluts" as an act of rape prevention. Women around the world protested the idea that women's safety should be tied to their appearance, but the choice by some to reclaim the word "slut" as a rallying cry was not universally embraced. Many felt that the word held a different valence for women of color than for white women and that the experiences of women of color were not being included or

respected by protest organizers. This was amplified when a picture was shared of an offensive protest sign that a white woman was holding at New York City's SlutWalk, quoting John Lennon and Yoko Ono's song, "Woman is the N—r of the World." The incident sparked emboldened, necessary conversations about racism within the feminist movement, and the women of color who felt that the movement didn't identify with many of their lived experiences. The author of the QueerBlackFeminist blog wrote:

> *I don't think the intent of the organizers of Slutwalk has ever been to trivialize rape, I firmly believe that Nonetheless, intent is of dire importance at this time. Or the ignorance of the real differences and experience of "womanhood," and the intersections of race, class, gender, sex, sexuality and violence that structure the lives of women of color will continue to be a dividing line in feminist movement.*

> *I am hopeful that we will keep these conversations, these critiques, open.*

As people continue to hold one another accountable, as open and honest dialogue persists, as blogs written by diverse voices establish wider and wider audiences, the way we approach feminist activism and leadership is changing.

PART II: CHALLENGES AND OPPORTUNITIES

The Urgency of Now

Nonprofit Organizing in the Margins

Online organizing is a relatively new field of work and as such, we are still struggling to establish sustainable infrastructure. For nonprofits like UltraViolet, Hollaback!, and SPARK Movement, who manage to raise some operating support, funding isn't coming fast enough (or enough, period). "We've had to hustle really hard for every dollar, in part because most foundations just don't have a portfolio that we can fit into," says Hollaback! co-founder and Executive Director Emily May. Although Hollaback! has

250 leaders organizing online and on land across the world, the organization has only two full-time members of staff to support their organizers.

Currently, no women's foundations have initiatives specifically dedicated to online feminist work. There are those who have portfolios committed to funding "nontraditional feminist work," like the incredible FRIDA, a fund that supports young feminists in youth-led organizing. But no major foundation or women's fund has intentionally and explicitly developed a portfolio for online feminist organizations and initiatives. . . .

The Band-Aid Business Structure

Feminist blogs and for-profit online organizations each have our own story of struggle behind why we haven't been able to develop a sustainable infrastructure, but there's one problem that's common: Most of us have what we call "the band-aid business structure"; we operate as LLCs or sole proprietorships relying on third-party advertising or random fundraising drives to pay for server costs and other technical fees. Otherwise, many of us work full-time elsewhere, or rely on social media consulting or speaking engagements as temporary sources of income to supplement our free labor.

Feminist blogs are the least sustained entities within online feminism. Daily website and editorial maintenance generally requires at least one person to be behind a highly active blog every day, as well as general management of media inquiries, organizational partnerships, and advertisements. But ad revenue, even earned by the highest trafficked blogs, can't begin to cover this work. Feministing, which has a readership of over half a million every month, made just $30,000 in 2011, so imagine the number of readers needed to support a movement with this model.

Unfortunately, many of the more lucrative revenue models that organizations have adopted elsewhere online come at a cost and raise difficult ethical questions for feminist blogs. While large sites like Jezebel make money on amassing lucrative page views, the mission of feminist blogs is to send people *away* from our sites to take action, not trap them there. Many of us don't want corporate sponsorship from companies that are antithetical to our mission and don't want to sell our devoted readers' emails to third-party companies. Even one of the biggest success stories of an online social justice organization, Change.org, recently changed its policy to accept right-wing and conservative petitions for the sake of sustaining and expanding the company.

Crowdfunding

Since one of the most powerful things about online feminism is its community, online activists often reach out to their constituencies for funding, whether it be to help pay for their website server costs or a specific project they're trying to jump start. This strategy has been termed "crowdfunding," where money is raised online in a collaborative effort for an organization, individual, or project.

Feminist video blogger Anita Sarkeesian started a campaign on the popular crowdfunding website Kickstarter to raise $6,000 to create videos about depictions of women in video games for her Feminist Frequency series. After being attacked by misogynist trolls who vandalized her Wikipedia page, hacked her website, and sent her death and rape threats, her online fans rallied to support her and her project, ultimately raising nearly $160,000.

Queer Nigerian Afrofeminist writer and media activist Spectra raised over $10,000 for her social media and communications training for African women's and LGBT organizations.[5] Miriam Zoila Pérez raised over $4,000 for her self-authored "The Radical Doula Guide," a booklet inspired by her blog Radical Doula that addresses the political context of supporting people during pregnancy and childbirth. These examples, and so many more, demonstrate that crowdfunding can be an effective way for individuals, collectives, or institutions to raise money while circumventing the need for non-profit status, which many online feminists don't have.

It's far from a systematic or sustainable solution, however. Chances are that none of the activists mentioned above will be going to their communities for support again anytime soon, assuming they've essentially "rapped" their networks.

Crowdfunding is great for discrete projects—a video series, a training, a book—but doesn't lend itself well to creating the infrastructure needed to sustain online organizations. Additionally, the larger a project is, the harder it is to reach the fundraising goal: Only 38% of $10,000 projects on Kickstarter, the most popular crowdfunding site, reach their goal, and that rate drops drastically as the goal gets higher.[6]

Membership and Subscription Model

In counter-point to the foundation and crowdfunding strategies to raise funds, a membership model allows supporters to give funds to online activists that are not project directed. This allows these organizations the freedom to be flexible in their activities with the stability of a constant income stream.

MoveOn, one of the most well-known progressive online nonprofits, follows this membership model; the average donation to MoveOn.org Political Action, according to their site, is less than $20. Women, Action, & the Media (WAM!) is also funded through this system, offering discounts and benefits in exchange for a $45 fee.

A variation on membership is the subscription model common to content producers. A number of media outlets provide enhanced online access for an annual fee, such as *Bitch Magazine*.

But many online platforms balk at the idea of sequestering their content and providing it only to paying customers. And anyone relying on ongoing donations runs a risk that those donations could disappear at any time. Because most membership models are built on a monthly or yearly system, long-term planning can be extremely difficult.

What's at Stake

Online feminism may continue to grow and evolve, but whether it will reach the potential it needs to sustain itself—and make the real, transformative impact the world needs—is yet to be seen. An unfunded online feminist movement isn't merely a threat to the livelihood of these hard-working activists, but a threat to the larger feminist movement itself. Without greater support, the online feminist movement faces a number of risks.

We will remain reactive and myopic.

. . . In spite of the powerful successes of online feminists, our stories of impact have a disappointing common trend: They're almost all reactive and short-term. The lack of infrastructure and sustainability for the online feminist movement makes it nearly impossible to think about more meaningful, long-term strategizing. More than ever, we need to create effective proactive campaigns and policies to prevent sexist encroachments in the first place, rather than being in a perpetual state of pushback.

There will be an incredibly high burnout rate.

In April 2012, one of the largest global feminist blogs online, Gender Across Borders, ceased operating. After three years of collaboration with international organizations and companies, offering over 30,000 readers feminist analysis and global activism opportunities every month, founder Emily Fillingham and the team of editors decided it was just too difficult to maintain. "Unfortunately, none of us could afford to keep it up. We made a lot of progress in just a few years, but it still wasn't enough to earn us any funding," said editor Colleen Hodgetts. And they're not the first; dozens of underpaid, overworked and exhausted online activists have left the movement, their voices lost and the mix—as a result—much less rich.

An unfunded movement further privileges the privileged.

. . . If we don't support this work, the most privileged in the online movement—those who already have the resources and time to blog every day, and do organizing work for free—will have the most amplified voices. Women of color and other groups are already overlooked for adequate media attention and already struggle disproportionately in this culture of scarcity. If feminist movements don't create supportive spaces, the leadership pipeline will grow smaller and more insular, and fewer voices will get promoted.

Anti-feminists will leverage the Internet.

Misogyny, both blatant and covert, is rampant online. Online harassment and threats are a daily experience for online activists, and young women and girls are increasingly bombarded with vitriolic and harmful messaging on the very same forums we use for activism. Radically anti-feminist commentator Ann Coulter has over 300,000 followers on Twitter—four times the number of followers as Planned Parenthood. Pinterest—the social networking site of 17 million visits per day[7]—has become immersed in diet tips and images of Victoria Secret models.[8] Anti-feminist video bloggers outnumber feminists in search results for "feminist" on YouTube. Not only is it up to us to build our influence and challenge the sexism and bigotry that exists online, but also to continue to provide safe spaces for young people to engage with one another in healthy and empowering ways.

We'll repeat the same mistakes.

"If the gender identities were different, it would be a different conversation. How do we combat all of the things in our socialization that teach us that we don't deserve sustainability? We have to embrace the entitlement of saying—'No, I deserve these things, and I need them and I'm not going to wait for someone to hand them to me.'"

—Miriam Zoila Pérez, Radical Doula

The "psychology of deprivation" we speak of is not a new phenomenon for feminist activists. We acknowledge that historically, the feminist movement has not valued its own labor. It has largely depended on unpaid work, slowly evolving into exhaustion and eventual burnout. We believe this is a huge part of what's been holding the movement back from creating the real policy and structural change it needs. We pass this model down to the young women and girls who look up to us: that it's necessary to work for free, and to risk our physical and mental health, and our relationships in order to make change. We convince them that these martyr-like sacrifices are "heroic" and "inspiring," when, in fact, we know they've only been harmful to our well-being and to the movement. We must create a new culture of work, a vibrant and valued feminist economy that could resolve an issue that's existed for waves before us—and create a more hopeful legacy for the generations to come.

What's Needed Now?

To avoid these pitfalls and embrace the opportunities ahead, the online community will have to be strategic and partner with a range of their feminist allies—advocacy and nonprofit organizations, philanthropists and entrepreneurs, corporate leadership with a feminist sensibility, educators, community organizers, artists, and youth—among so many others. It is time to strengthen the connective tissue between those who are most savvy and connected online, and those pushing feminist agendas in our courtrooms, classrooms, boardrooms, and beyond. The results could be profound.

We need to create more spaces and times where strategy and collaboration are prioritized, supported, and expected, and where feminists of all ages—but especially the young and online—have a chance to do the profound work of dreaming together.

Notes

1. Corrected 4/12/13: Based on feedback, this paragraph has been corrected to better reflect the understanding of the work by those mentioned.

2. Madden, Mary and Kathryn Zickuhur, "65% of Online Adults Use Social Networking Sites." Pew Internet and American Life Project, 2011,

http://pewinternet.org/Reports/2011/Social-Networking-Sites.aspx

3. http://in.gov/iew/files/benchmark_wom_leadership.pdf

4. http://annenbergpublicpolicycenter.org/Downloads/Information_And_Society/20010314_Progress_and_Women/200110321_Progress_women_report.pdf

5. Corrected 04/12/13: Spectra was originally incorrectly referred to as an "online activist."

6. Mitroff, Sarah. "4 Keys to a Winning Kickstarter Campaign." *Wired Magazine*, 2012. www.wired.com/business/2012/07/kickstarter/

7. http://mbaonline.com/a-day-in-the-internet/

8. http://buzzfeed.com/arnyodell//how-pinterest-is-killing-feminism

Introduction to Reading 48

The authors of this reading formed a creative collective in which they could share ideas, experiences, and writings on the concept of *women of color*. They collaborated on this article and, in the tradition of collectives such as the Combahee River Collective, the reading represents their shared insights and words. The goals of the article include (1) exploring the complexities of women of color feminisms, (2) discussing three major components of women of color feminisms, and (3) documenting the contribution of creative collectivity in sustaining radical change.

1. What are the three major components of women of color feminisms? Offer examples of each component.

2. How does creative collectivity contribute to struggles for gender justice?

3. Why do the authors believe it is important to remind the next generation that "we were never meant to survive" (Lorde 1978, 31–32)?

Building on "the Edge of Each Other's Battles"

A Feminist of Color Multidimensional Lens

The Santa Cruz Feminist of Color Collective

INTRODUCTION

In a University of California, Santa Cruz seminar, Professor Angela Davis provoked us with these questions: What is the future of women of color feminism? Given the recent emergence of transnational scholarly, artistic, and activist strategies, is "women of color" relevant today?[1] This question marked the beginning of a collective journey of research and reflection that has

From The Santa Cruz Feminist of Color Collective. 2014. Building on "The Edge of Each Other's Battles": A Feminist of Color Multidimensional Lens. *Hypatia, 29*(1).

culminated in these words. We argue that the formation "women of color" resonates in feminist and philosophical debates as a critique of and alternative to oppressive, canonical farms of knowledge that restrict interventions by women, people of color, and queers in the academy and beyond. We came together around the conviction that the formation of "women of color" enables a way of seeing the world through a lens that refracts light in many ways to reveal a world full of possibilities, a world that is constantly shifting and in motion. In this article, we think through this metaphor of a multidimensional lens to articulate the "who, why, and how" of women of color feminisms, identity-formation, political project, and methodology. . . .

To explore the questions Davis raised, we formed a writing group with the intention of collective accountability rooted in community. For the past eight years, our collective has worked to rearticulate women of color feminisms through a multidimensional lens as a way of examining the legacies of women of color scholarship. In this article, we explore the dimensions of women of color feminisms—identity-formation, political project, and methodology. This is the *who,* the *why,* and the *how* of women of color feminist practice, theory, and living. These three aspects are indivisible and create generative openings and conflicts for our work as scholars, artists, advocates, and activists. This multidimensional lens eludes essentialist traps of identity, enunciates the importance of intellectual political projects, and produces creativity and community through methodological practices that embrace contradictions. "Women of color" is an expansive formulation—one that inspires an exploration of and challenge to its limits as a concept, even as we dwell in it to articulate these three co-constitutive dimensions.

This collectively written article illuminates the complicated layers of women of color feminist philosophies. Women of color and decolonial feminist philosophers offer approaches that enable the decolonization of knowledge-production. We build on María Lugones's work; she utilizes women of color feminist thought to critique the universalisin of knowledge-formations and to theorize an intersectional and intersubjective, decolonial analysis (Lugones 2010). . . .

Our Collective

We began writing together in the early years of the new millennium on Ohlone land, where redwood forests meet the Pacific coast. We came together from different disciplines around our commitments to radical transformation and the project of mapping feminist of color trajectories and ancestries of thought. Invested in women of color as a political identity-formation and not simply an identity-marker, we contribute to critical interventions in the production of academic knowledge. We have met around countless kitchen tables, in cyberspace, at the university, and at mobilizations, sharing fears and desires, translating ourselves for one another, and creating coalition despite our conflicts. We experienced our collaborative writing as a form of healing. We opened a space to express the structural violence we were experiencing in the academy and began an intense process of learning one another's histories of migration, colonization, exile, and displacement.[2] Through Jacqui Alexander's textual guidance we built solidarity by sharing our stories with one another and holding a space for our pain and trauma (Alexander 2005). We forged a collective identity as feminists of color, drawing out our interconnections with struggles across the globe without obscuring the privilege associated with our social positioning in the U.S. academy. In what follows, we express both the sentiments guiding our collaborative efforts and simultaneously contribute to the debates and visibility of women of color feminist philosophy (Zack 2000).

As a writing collaborative, working through the tension between individual and collective ways of knowing, we resist binary mappings of race, gender, sexuality, and nationhood onto our bodies—these legacies of colonialism that mark and exploit us. We remind the generation that follows us, as we have been reminded: We live in a world in which "we were never meant to survive" (Lorde 1978, 31–32). We hope this explication of women of color feminisms offers a generative means through which to consider the resonances, tensions, and possibilities nestled within its complications.

IDENTITY-FORMATION

Who are we and with whom do we choose to align? Identity is always forming; it is a historical process that shifts depending on context and community: We are always becoming. Developing a political identity enacts resistance, which Lugones signals as the tension between subjectification and active subjectivity (Lugones 2010, 746). Subjectification is the forming of the subject when acted upon by structural mechanisms of power. Active subjectivity is a "resistant presence . . . of the colonized against the colonial invasion of self in community from the inhabitation of that self" (748). By highlighting the process of identity-formation of resistant presence within the cultural production entitled *Pandora's,* a multimedia theater performance produced and performed by women of color, we show how the broad collaborations within this production elucidate the capaciousness of women of color as an identity-formation and point toward a shared radical political project and methodology.

In "Remembering This Bridge," Alexander reflects on one of the first publications to put forward the formulation "women of color": the anthology *This Bridge Called My Back: Writings by Radical Women of Color.* Here Alexander emphasizes the process of identity-formation for women of color:

We are not born women of color. We become women of color. In order to become women of color, we would need to become fluent in each other's histories, to resist and unlearn an impulse to claim first oppression, most-devastating oppression, one-of-a-kind oppression, defying comparison oppression. We would have to unlearn the impulse that allows mythologies about each other to replace knowing about one another. (Alexander 2005, 269)

"Women of color" is a political identity-formation rooted in histories of resistance to categorizations that have divided and oppressed "people of color." Race is not biological, but rather an ever-shifting, socially constructed demarcation rooted in legacies of colonization, genocide, and slavery that carry contemporary economic and political implications in our everyday global lives (Omi and Winant 1994; Du Bois 2006; Lugones 2010). To understand the process of racialization is not to simply buy into constructed identity categories—"Black" "Arab" "Hispanic" "Muslim" "Mexican" "Native" "Asian" "Middle Eastern." Understanding racialization requires being aware of why these categories exist and how they dynamically adapt to devalue histories, reduce heritages, and keep people apart and disoriented. Women of color feminisms mend frayed connections by tracing the way knowledge shifts depending on historical, social, and political contexts. Although these racialization processes mark all of us, we can work to see ourselves in ways that exceed these fixed categories through the process of building coalitions.

A relational approach to multiple genealogies binds together the identity-formation of women of color formation (Lowe 1997). Shared political commitments to recognizing "common contexts of struggle" nourish this formation (Mohanty, Russo, and Tones 1991). As Chandra Mohanty argues, these are distinct struggles of resistance that make structures of oppression visible (Mohanty et al. 1991, 7). Formations of "women of color" shift from subjectification to active subjectivity, where collectivized and at times paradoxical identities emerge from coalitional strategies across racial, sexual, class, gender, and generational differences. Historically, "of color" has been used to establish solidarity across social, cultural, and geographic communities in the U.S.

The concept "of color" does not so much function to demarcate an inside and an outside, an "us" versus "them," but instead creates the possibility of a larger "we." As a coalitional identity, "of color" rejects the dichotomous colonial logics of separation. Mobilizing "of color" in this identity-formation traces the interconnectedness of racial histories, one that foregrounds complexities rather than reifying the categories themselves.

To illustrate this first dimension, identity-formation, we turn to *Pandora's,* a multimedia theater production, which premiered off Broadway in New York in June 2008 and presented the queer Latina as a coalitional identity. *Pandora's* mixed theater and film, two forms of inherently collaborative media. New York-based Sister Outsider Entertainment, spearheaded by Elisha Miranda, brought together film collective, Womyn Image Makers, and a group of writers and performers to collaborate in the production of *Pandora's*.[3] Every aspect of production intentionally reinforced coalitional practices among those who contributed to the show and demonstrated an active site of expanding women of color feminism. The collaborations that created this production illustrate a resistance to essentialism and commitment to alliance-building. *Pandora's* embodies collaborations that are layered, and not limited to particular sexualized and racialized figures that can be clearly marked as "women," "Latina," or "of color." The show utilizes storytelling to create a dialogue among generations and histories, while holding in tension the differences and relations among the contributors. We argue that *Pandora's* exemplifies the possibility of forging coalitional identity through intergenerational cultural production.

The theater and film production begins in the dark with the voice of elder warrior poet, Audre Lorde.

And when we speak we are afraid

our words will not be heard

nor welcomed

but when we are silent

we are still afraid

So it is better to speak

remembering

we were never meant to survive

As we hear Lorde say "speak" for the second time, her image appears on the screen above the stage, opening the video segment of the production that brings to life the many who live, struggle, and build coalition in the borderlands. *Pandora's* premiere was timed to commemorate the Stonewall riots anniversary, pointing to untold queer of color histories and the contemporary lives of queer women of color. Below the screen, on stage is Pandora's, an imagined nightclub for queer Latinas represented by a bar, some stools and tables, a door, and bathrooms. The show highlights ten monologues and eight short documentaries that chronicle, in the words of Angela Davis, the "crosscutting overlapping and often contradictory relations among race and class and gender and sexuality" in the lives of queer Latinas (Pandora's 2008). . . .

The performances and film shorts show both the challenges and achievements of subjects who are undocumented immigrants, genderqueer, homeless youth, impacted by "Don't Ask, Don't Tell" military policies, struggling with religion and spirituality, and creating new ideas of home and family. The complexities include identifying as Afro-Latinas, passing as straight, as well as Xicana *Indigenas* and Filipinas, who share a Spanish colonial history. All of these identities or subjectivities imply different kinds of relationships to colonial states and multiple communities across borders of race, class, gender, sexuality, and nation. The distinctions embodied within queer Latinas made visible through the monologues and short documentaries speak to the complexities and shifting formation of women of color. We are not the same, we are rooted in particularities, and that is our greatest strength. This is how we identify ourselves to one another. . . .

Pandora's produces an alternative form of knowledge, as do other spaces of cultural representation that, like conferences or anthologies, construct decolonized communal spaces that can hold the productive tensions and possibility of engaging difference. The knowledge surfaces as we translate ourselves to one another and learn one another's struggles and histories (Latina Feminist Group 2001).

"Women of color" is a political identity, a way of acknowledging our interconnections, reflecting upon our common contexts of struggle, and recognizing the different ways that structures impose violence, separation, and war on each of us. From here, a coalitional identity begins to emerge. This is the "who" of how we understand "women of color." Less about how each of us is categorized, this dimension instead emphasizes our commitment to collective well-being for ourselves, each other, and our earth. Who will we stand in solidarity with in this journey? How do we hold ourselves accountable to one another along this journey?

RADICAL POLITICAL PROJECT

"Women of color" as political project enunciates community, shared commitment, and an acknowledgment of the differences among us. As a project, it calls us to recognize our connections and disconnections to the colonized land on which we live in order to be accountable to forms of exploitation enacted by the U.S. (Fregoso 2003; Anzaldúa 2007). Our explication of the radical political project recognizes the expansiveness of mapping transcommunal and intergenerational connections that do not occur in dominant historical narratives, while simultaneously making room for the inherent tensions and contradictions that arise. Along our journey we hold one another accountable to these commitments.

A women of color, feminist, radical, political project excavates and connects histories of violence that are blockaded within different forms of U.S. historiography, including "radical" forms of nationalism (Chicano, Black Power) that

maintain borders of racism, sexism, heterosexism, and classism (Pérez 2003). Women of color have negotiated forms of racism, sexism, and homophobia in women's, gay, and nationalist movements, thus creating a feminist radical space. These movements provoked a social revolution within the U.S., and in many ways also tended to reinscribe the colonial hierarchies implicit in nationalism and U.S. state-formation. In the words of the Combahee River Collective, "It was our experience and disillusionment within these liberation movements, as well as experience on the periphery of the white male left, that led to the need to develop a politics that was antiracist, unlike those of white women, and antisexist, unlike those of Black and white men" (Combahee River Collective 2002, 235). The conflicts within these liberation movements opened the terrain for radical women of color politics.

Instead of feeding nostalgia about past revolutionary struggle, we trace them as transgenerational genealogies to draw lessons for this historical moment (Lorde 1984).[4] Mohanty and Alexander assert that "use of words like 'genealogies' or 'legacies' is not meant to suggest a frozen or embodied inheritance of domination and resistance, but an interested, conscious thinking and rethinking of history and historicity" (Alexander and Mohanty 1997, xvi). Women of color emerged as a political category following the circulation of the identity-formation of "lesbian of color." Davis explains "the term lesbian of color acquired currency before women of color entered into our political vocabulary" (Lowe 1997, 311). Lesbians of color, and women of color, needed ample space for dialogue to work out conflicts as well as to construct and build coalitions.[5]

Political solidarity depends on a careful negotiation of difference. For Lugones, difference stems from colonialism and aligns with the logic of oppression. Understanding the relationship among difference, colonialism, and oppression provides a basis for creative coalition:

The emphasis is on maintaining multiplicity at the point of reduction—not in maintaining a hybrid "product," which hides the colonial difference—in the tense workings of more than one logic, not to be synthesized but transcended. Among the logics at work are the many logics meeting the logic of oppression; many colonial differences, but one logic of oppression. *The responses from the fragmented loci can be creatively in coalition,* a way of thinking of the possibility of coalition that takes up the logic of de-coloniality, and the logic of coalition of feminists of color: the oppositional consciousness of a social erotics (Sandoval 2000) that takes on the differences that make being creative, that permits enactments that are thoroughly defiant of the logic of dichotomies (Lorde 1984). The logic of coalition is defiant of the logic of dichotomies; differences are never seen in dichotomous terms, but the logic has as its opposition the logic of power. The multiplicity is never reduced. (Lugones 2010, 755)

Women of color feminisms reflect a multiplicity of perspectives. These formations grow out of U.S.-based gendered racialization and in solidarity with anticolonial movements in the third world. Maylei Blackwell argues that the category women of color "emerged out of a transnational imaginary of third world liberation struggles" (Blackwell 2003, 3). This broad understanding of linking communities of resistance abroad and in the U.S. underlies the radical political project and offers a clear thread of continuity to the present. Within this, our interconnections also allow us to acknowledge our collective responsibility for global inequalities.

An important example of this emerges during the movement against apartheid in South Africa. Frances Beal, who was instrumental in the formation of the Third World Women's Alliance, and is considered central in theorizing intersecting oppressions or "intersectionality" in the U.S., theorizes the connections of "the system of capitalism" and "its afterbirth—racism" by discussing the distorted views that capitalist ideologies construct of Black women and men (Beal 2005, 109). Beal evokes Sojourner Truth's legendary speech at a "Women's Rights Convention in the nineteenth century" where Truth asks, "Ain't I a woman?" signaling legacies of racism and sexism together with realities of intensive labor in the U.S. under systems of slavery

and capitalism alike, what Lugones calls the colonial/modern gender system or the coloniality of gender (Beal 2005; Lugones 2007; 2010).

Although Beal never uses the term *women of color* directly, she does formulate "Non-White Females"; she argues "exploitative industries" are the reason the "wage scale for non-white women" is the lowest (Beal 2005, 114–15). Critiquing the racist hierarchies in labor unions, Beal questions the decisions of the white male leadership of the International Ladies Garment Workers Union (ILGWU)—whose membership is majority Black and Puerto Rican women— revealing that the "ILGWU has invested heavily in business enterprises in racist, apartheid South Africa—with union funds" (115). Beal makes an important connection here between the exploitation of Black and Puerto Rican women workers in the U.S. and the support of colonialism in South Africa. Beal boldly reveals the bare necessity for Black women and white women to be able to work together, "Any white group that does not have an anti-imperialist and anti-racist ideology has absolutely nothing in common with the Black women's struggle" (120).

Similarly Lugones takes white feminists to task for reducing feminism to a critique of patriarchy, or what she calls the light side of the colonial/modern gender system (Lugones 2007). Particular categorizations of race and gender produced hierarchies with material impacts in the lives of marginalized peoples. Decolonization requires thinking racialization and imposed gender systems together, along with class and sexuality. . . .

Mohanty and Alexander, among others, show the possibility of working within women of color feminist political projects while enacting transnational or global feminist analyses, not for the purpose of theorizing a false "sisterhood" but to map interconnections within unequal power relations (Alexander 1997). Mohanty and Alexander's collaborative anthology unpacks the limitations of women of color feminist formations, through the acknowledgment of various forms of racialization and gender systems that are linked to distinct histories and complex geographies. We are concerned with certain developments in transnational feminist literature that position transnational feminism as distinct from U.S. women of color feminisms (see Soto 2005, 117). Although women of color is not translatable to contexts outside the U.S., denying the analytical connection to forms of subaltern feminism outside of the U.S. sustains an imperialistic feminist gaze.

Gloria Anzaldúa describes borderlands as an alternative epistemological space, a relational, intersubjective epistemology that refuses Eurocentrism's individualism and dichotomous hierarchies. A women of color radical political project calls attention to the spaces of resistance that have been hidden by Eurocentric modernity and its discourses. Thinking through the borderlands bridges dichotomies by seeing from a double- or third-space perspective rooted in local histories. Building on Anzaldúa, Lugones explains, "The emphasis is on maintaining multiplicity at the point of reduction" (Lugones 2010, 755). This calls for coalitional efforts, found in the work of feminists of color, and requires dwelling in resistance with specific attention to the day-to-day interweavings of social relations or the "intimate everyday resistant interactions to the colonial difference" (743). As we dwell in each other's histories, an intersubjective accountability grows in the heart of our women of color feminist political project. This dimension of the lens explains the "why" of women of color feminisms. This political project embodies a commitment to knowledge-production and action based on accountability to communities seeking justice.

METHODOLOGY

The who and why of women of color feminisms inform the how. The legacy of women of color feminisms shows us the way to think and act with a larger vision of the world that exceeds the territorial, political, emotional, economic, and spiritual limits of the nation-state and fixed categories of identity. The methodological dimension of the women of color feminist lens explains how we move together and stand beside one another in tension and through translation.

Intersectionality, the practice of recognizing the intersection of differences, has become the shorthand for the methodological practice of women of color. Long legacies of radical feminist thought and political work gave birth to women of color feminist methodologies. For example, the Combahee River Collective describes their coming together as complicating a simple understanding of race and gender: "a combined antiracist and anti-sexist position drew us together initially, and as we developed politically we addressed ourselves to heterosexism and economic oppression under capitalism" (Combahee River Collective 2002, 236). Inspired by Harriet Tubman and the guerrilla action she led in 1863 that freed 750 slaves in South Carolina, this Collective traces Black women's legacies of resistance through their writing practice. Blackwell refers to the way the Combahee River Collective remembers Harriet Tubman as "retrofitted memory," which she defines as "a practice whereby social actors read the interstices, gaps, and silences of existing historical narratives in order to retrofit, rework, and refashion older narratives to create new historical openings, political possibilities, and genealogies of resistance" (Blackwell 2011, 102). Similarly, we retrofit memory by tracing the intertwined roots of this coalitional approach through our own collaborative writing, different anthologizing practices, and account ability through responsible citational practices.

Collaborating across social positions, identity-formations, national allegiances, and lived experiences gave birth to a method of analysis that is now commonly known as "intersectionality." An academic and activist trend has reduced and dehistoricized this methodological approach to a mainstream mantra: *raceclassgender, raceclassgender.* Davis questions "the current ubiquity of the category intersectionality and the citational practices that tend to disappear the complicated and collaborative processes that helped to produce this category" (Davis 2004). Consider, for example, the remarkably uniform attribution of the term *intersectionality* to Kimberle Williams Crenshaw's 1991 article "Mapping the Margins." Crenshaw's groundbreaking article legitimized (through its publication in the *Stanford Law Review*) a state-based legal approach to address the cases of women of color who are consistently left vulnerable due to legal defenses that rely upon either gender OR race frameworks and cannot hold multiple categories or their intersections (Crenshaw 1991). Although this work of challenging rigid legal frames is absolutely necessary, the citational practices that re-center the concept of intersectionality as the theory of one scholar are problematic. This effectively fixes the concept and deracinates it from the collaborative work feminist of color communities engaged in for decades to strategize resistance and defend their lives (see Zinn et al. 1990).

We situate intersectionality, and the collaborative context in which it emerged, in the rich genealogy of women of color feminist activist scholarship. First, we need to understand why an intersectional analysis is important. Lugones argues that women of color and third world feminists demonstrate how intersectionality serves to critique feminist universalism. *"If woman and black* are terms for homogeneous, atomic, separable categories, then their intersection shows us the absence of black women rather than their presence. So, to see non-white women is to exceed categorical' logic" (Lugones 2010, 742).[6] Then we need to remember how and why intersectional analyses developed. Delinking the method of analysis from its genealogies and context of production contributes to the ongoing erasure of subaltern histories and praxis.

Women of color feminisms analyze systemic violence through the positioning of those historically pushed to social, political, economic, sexual, and racial margins. The knowledge produced at these borders forges connections across struggles, lending the perspectives and tools necessary for expansive projects not limited to the university. Fixating on only one dimension of the indivisible "feminist of color" lens—for

example, identity—conflates women of color bodies with a field of inquiry. This undermines the possibilities of building alliances across national borders. Most notably, third world and transnational feminists argue that "women of color" is a specifically U.S.-based racial identity-formation that cannot be mapped across global contexts. Reading other parts of the world through U.S. race politics, or insisting on a universal sisterhood or biological womanhood, is deeply problematic.[7] U.S. feminists of color can contribute insights from their analysis of power relations, while still recognizing and honoring the specificity of history and geopolitics. This methodological approach demands accountability to our positioning in the belly of the beast. Through political identification we recognize how our "common vantage points" (Smith 2009) intersect with "relations of rule" or systems of oppression like heteropatriarchy, capitalism, racism, and colonialism.[8]

The practice of anthologizing, a significant site of women of color feminist knowledge-production, produces an opening for people concerned with interconnected structures to come together and think, act, and dialogue collectively, weaving what Toni Cade Bambara writes in her foreword to *This Bridge,* "potent networks of all the daughters of the ancient mother cultures" (Bambara 2002). Tracing the circulation of "A Black Feminist Statement" illustrates the network of people with common visions of building solidarity across struggles. Zillah Eisenstein's *Capitalist Patriarchy and the Case for Socialist Feminism* first anthologized the Combahee River Collective's manifesto (Eisenstein 1978). In 1981, it appeared in *This Bridge Called My Back,* followed by a 1982 publication in *All the Women Are White, All the Blacks Are Men, But Some of Us Are Brave,* an anthology that outlines *Black Women's Studies* (Hull et al. 1982). In 1983 it was published in Smith's edited text *Home Girls* (Smith 1983). Many of these women worked together to establish Kitchen Table Press to publish and circulate their writing. Conference organizing commonly functions to catalyze anthologizing practices. The production of an anthology signals years of theorizing collectivity, challenging hierarchical knowledge-formations, and putting forward "theory in flesh" (Moraga and Anzaldúa 2002, 21). Anthologies reflect a conscious method of solidarity across difference that inspires our collaborative writing (Mohanty et al. 1991; Shohat 1998; Hernández and Rehman 2002; INCITE! 2006).

We call for a purposeful relinking of the method of analysis to the embodied histories from which it came, honoring its rich genealogies. This marks our intergenerational connection to the legacy of women of color feminisms through collaborative writing and responsible citational practices. We come to understand our present moment by tracing genealogies of struggle. We work within the productive tension among method of analysis, political project, and identity-formation to maintain both our agility in response to the ever-evolving technologies of oppression and to affirm our space and place in this world for enacting decolonial futures.

OUR CREATIVE PROCESS: AN ARGUMENT FOR EMBODIED SCHOLARSHIP

When we began to gather as a collective, the larger issue of translation was a central point of friction. How could we begin to learn one another and build trust across our differences and familial homelands of Iran, Peru, Colombia, and Mexico? Schutte asserts that "unless exceptional measures are taken to promote a good dialogue" it is extremely difficult to have a nonhierarchical dialogue (Schutte 1998, 56). She continues, "Even so, it is my view that no two cultures or languages can be perfectly transparent to each other. There is always a residue of meaning that will not be reached in cross-cultural endeavors"; Schutte refers to this as "incommensurability" (56). Schutte's analysis is based on the relations between dominant and subaltern people across borders, and although we were all raised in the U.S., in many ways our collective-building was a journey of negotiating positions and languages.

Within the academy, we shared the category of women of color graduate students, yet when we sat down to take stock, we realized our respective histories, visions of the world, ways of relating and speaking, and intellectual formations were distinct from one another. We worked through the doubt, fear, insecurities, and mistrust to arrive at a grounded collaborative dialogue that translates into this writing. . . .

Our vision of solidarity both recognizes and transcends nation-state borders. As activist-scholars we call for critical attention to the "third world," the unrecognized "third world" within the U.S., and displaced Native peoples on whose lands the U.S. is built. This site of feminism argues that we are all responsible for global inequalities because of our interconnections. We fight against white supremacy while resisting the demonization of individuals identified as white (Frankenberg 1993; Harris 1993). Feminists of color recognize the damage that heteropatriarchy and colonialism have done to so many communities in the U.S. and around the world. This lens exemplifies the intersubjective shift that defies binary colonial logics. We are energized by the possibilities of a feminist of color lens, a broader paradigm that rejects gender binaries and other forms of dichotomous thinking, thereby allowing for "unlikely alliances" (Anzaldúa 1990; Lowe 1997; Smith 2008). This feminist of color lens brings into focus decolonial senses of *nos/otras,* our interconnections and the life-sustaining gift that is our earth.[9]

NOTES

1. "Women of Color: Feminist Theories and Practices," History of consciousness graduate writing seminar.

2. The initial collaborative writing group included Elisa Diana Huerta.

3. The phrase "free people of color," used in the 1850s and more recently as "lesbians of color" and "women of color," has been useful for building coalitions along multiple axes of race, gender, class, and sexuality to organize politically. See May 2007.

4. Following Rosa Linda Fregoso's understanding of genealogy, "For Foucault, genealogy is a historical method that gives voice to marginal and submerged people in their resistance to the forces of power and domination. . . . The practice of genealogy alerts us to alternative accounts of the resistances, struggles, and conflicts that in fact constitute history. Genealogy is a method reflected in the scholarly practices of feminist, multicultural, queer, and postcolonial historiographers and researchers" (Fregoso 2003, 105).

5. The Salsa Soul Sisters speak to us, among many others. See Gumbs 2010.

6. Lugones argues that this categorical logic is an exercise in purity with the objectivity of control. Instead, mestizaje and intersectionality are exercised in impurity and follow the logic of curdling: "Mestizaje defies control through simultaneously asserting the impure, curdled multiple state and rejecting fragmentation into pure parts. . . . (T)he mestiza is unclassifiable, unmanageable. She has no pure parts to be 'had,' controlled" (Lugones 1994, 460). For a longer discussion of Lugones's logic of curdling in relation to intersectionality, see Garry 2011.

7. For a critical discussion of Robin Morgan's work, see Mohanty 2003.

8. We borrow "relations of rule" from Lionel Cantú's adaptation of Dorothy Smith's concept (Cantú 2000).

9. Anzaldúa's concept of "*Nos/Otras*" or "nosotras," *roughly* translates into English as "us" but holds "las otras," "the others," too (Keating 2008).

References

Abod-Jennifer, director, writer, producer, 2002. *The edge of each other's battles: The vision of Audre Lorde.* Profile Productions: Videorecording. California.

Alexander, M. Jacqui. 2005. Remembering this bridge, remembering ourselves. In *Pedagogies of crossing: Meditations on feminism, sexual politics, memory, and the sacred.* Durham, N.C.: Duke University Press.

Alexander, M. Jacqui, and Chandra Talpade Mohanty, eds. 1997. *Feminist genealogies, colonial legacies, democratic futures.* New York: Routledge.

Anzaldúa, Gloria, ed. 1990. *Making face, making soul/hacienda caras: Creative and critical perspectives by feminists of color.* San Francisco: Aunt Lute Books.

Anzaldúa, Gloria. 2007. *Borderlands/la frontera: The new mestiza,* 3rd ed. San Francisco: Aunt Lute Books.

Bambara, Toni Cade. 2002. Foreword. In *This bridge called my back: Writings by radical women of color,* ed. Cherríe L. Moraga and Gloria E. Anzaldúa. Berkeley: Third Woman Press.

Beal, Frances. 2005. Double jeopardy: To be black and female. In *The black woman: An anthology,* ed. Toni Cade Bambara. New York: Washington Square Press.

Blackwell, Maylei. 2003. Contested histories: Las hijas de Cuauhtémoc, Chicana feminisms, and print culture in the Chicano movement, 1968–1973. In *Chicana feminisms: A critical reader,* ed. Gabriela Arredondo, Aída Hurtado, Norma Klahn, Olga Nájera-Ramírez and Patricia Zavella. Durham, N.C.: Duke University Press.

———. 2011. *Chicana power! Contested histories of feminism in the Chicano movement.* Austin: University of Texas Press.

Cantú, Lionel. 2000. Entre hombres/between men: Latino masculinities and homosexualities. In *Gay masculinities,* ed. Peter Nardi. Thousand Oaks, Calif.: Sage Publications.

Combahee River Collective. 2002. A black feminist statement. In *This bridge called my back: Writings by radical women of color,* ed. Cherríe L. Moraga and Gloria E. Anzaldúa. Berkeley: Third Woman Press.

Crenshaw, Kimberle. 1991. Mapping the margins: Intersectionality, identity politics, and violence against women of color. *Stanford Law Review* 43 (6): 1241–99.

Davis, Angela Y. 2004. *Legacies of women of color feminism.* Cultural Studies Colloquium: Institute for Humanities Research, University of California, Santa Cruz.

Du Bois, W. E. B. 2006. *Dusk of dawn: An essay toward an autobiography of a race concept.* New Brunswick, N.J.: Transaction Publishers.

Eisenstein, Zillah R., ed. 1978. *Capitalist patriarchy and the case for socialist feminism.* New York: Monthly Review Press.

Frankenberg, Ruth. 1993. *White women, race matters: The social construction of whiteness.* Minneapolis: University of Minnesota Press.

Fregoso, Rosa Linda. 2003. *Mexicana encounters: The making of social identities on the borderlands*. Berkeley: University of California Press.

Gumbs, Alexis Pauline. 2010. Salsa soul audio documentary. http://brokenbeautiful.files.wordpress.com/2010/02/salsa-soul-audio-documentary.mp3 (accessed May 13, 2010).

Harris, Cheryl I. 1993. Whiteness as property. *Harvard Law Review* 106 (8): 1701–91.

Hernández, Daisy, and Bushra Rehman, eds. 2002. *Colonize this! Young women of color on today's feminism*. Emeryville, Calif.: Seal Press.

Hull, Gloria, Patricia Bell-Scott, and Barbara Smith, eds. 1982. *All the women are white, all the blacks are men, but some of us are brave: Black women's studies*. New York: Feminist Press.

INCITE! Women of Color against Violence. 2006. *Color of violence: The INCITE! anthology*. Boston: South End Press.

Keating, AnaLouise. 2008. "I'm a citizen of the universe": Gloria Anzaldúa's spiritual activism as catalyst for social change. *Feminist Studies* 34 (1/2): 53–69.

Latina Feminist Group. 2001. *Telling to live: Latina feminist testimonies*. Durham, N.C.: Duke University Press.

Lorde, Audre. 1978. Litany for survival. In *The Black unicorn: Poems*. New York: Norton.

———. 1984. Age, race, class, and sex; Women redefining difference. In *Sister outsider: Essays and speeches*. Freedom, Calif.: Crossing Press.

Lowe, Lisa. 1997. Interview with Angela Davis: Reflections on race, class, gender in the USA. In *The politics of culture in the shadow of capital*, ed. Lisa Lowe and David Lloyd. Durham, N.C.: Duke University Press.

Lugones, Maria. 1994. Purity, impurity, and separation. *Signs* 19 (2): 458–79.

———. 2007. Heterosexualism and the colonial/modern gender system. *Hypatia* 22 (1): 186–209.

———. 2010. Toward a decolonial feminism. *Hypatia* 25 (4): 742–59.

Mind if I call you sir? 2004. DVD. Rosales, USA.

Mohanty, Chandra Talpade, Ann Russo, and Lourdes Torres, eds. 1991. *Third world women and the politics of feminism*. Bloomington: University of Indiana Press.

Moraga, Cherríe L., and Gloria E. Anzaldúa, eds. 2002. *This bridge called my back: Writings by radical women of color*. Berkeley: Third Woman Press.

Omi, Michael, and Howard Winant. 1994. *Racial formation in the United States: From the 1960s to the 1990s*. New York: Routledge.

Pandora's. 2008. Theater & Video. Directed by Elisha Miranda and produced by Sister Outsider Entertainment, LLC, Theater Row Studios, New York, NY.

Pérez, Emma. 2003. Queering the borderlands: The challenges of excavating the invisible and unheard. *Frontiers* 24 (2 &. 3): 122–31.

Sandoval, Chela. 1990. Feminism and racism: A report on the 1981 national women's studies association conference. *In Making face, making soul/haciendo caras: Creative and critical perspectives by feminists of color*, ed. Gloria Anzaldúa. San Francisco: Aunt Lute Books.

Schutte, Ofelia. 1998. Cultural alterity: Cross-cultural communication and feminist theory in north–south context. *Hypatia* 13 (2): 53–71.

Shohat, Ella, ed. 1998. *Talking visions: Multicultural feminism in transnational age*. Cambridge, Mass.: MIT Press.

Sister Outsider Entertainment, LLC. 2009. http://www.feminishing.com/archives/008070.

———. 2008. *Native Americans and the Christian right. The gendered politics of unlikely alliances*. Durham, N.C.: Duke University Press.

———. 2009. *The color of violence: Angela Davis arid the radicalization of the anti-violence movement*. Paper given at Angela Davis: Legacies in the Making: Building on the Academic, Activist, and Cultural Interventions of a Contemporary Visionary Symposium. Santa Cruz, California.

Smith, Barbara, ed. 1983. *Home girls: A Black feminist anthology*. New Brunswick, N.J.: Rutgers University Press.

Soto, Sandra. 2005. Where in the transnational world are U.S. women of color? In *Women's studies for the future: Foundations, interrogations politics*, ed. Elizabeth Lapovsky Kennedy and Agatha Beins. New Brunswick, N.J.: Rutgers University Press.

Zack, Naomi, ed. 2000. *Women of color and philosophy*. Malden, Mass.: Blackwell Publishers.

Zepeda, Susy, and Sandra Alvarez. 2006. Interview with Womyn Image Makers. *Spectator: The University of Southern California Journal of Film and Television Criticism* 26 (1): 127–34.

Zinn, Maxine Baca, Lynn Weber Cannon, Elizabeth Higginbotham, and Bonnie Thornton Dill. 1990. The costs of exclusionary practices in women's studies. *In Making face, making soul/haciendo caras: Creative and critical perspectives by feminists of color*, ed. Gloria Anzaldúa. San Francisco: Aunt Lute Books.

Introduction to Reading 49

This reading addresses the complex and varied feminist theories developed by Native American women activists, the struggle against sexism within Native communities and society at large, and the importance of developing coalitions with non-Native feminists. In addition, Andrea Smith analyzes current Native feminist sovereignty projects that address both colonialism and sexism through an intersectional framework. Smith, who is Cherokee, is a longtime antiviolence and Native American activist and scholar. She is a leading expert on violence against women of color.

1. Why is gender justice integral to issues of survival for indigenous people?

2. How does the boarding school project reveal connections between interpersonal gender violence and state violence?

3. How does Native feminist theory and activism contribute to feminist politics at large?

NATIVE AMERICAN FEMINISM, SOVEREIGNTY, AND SOCIAL CHANGE

Andrea Smith

When I worked as a rape crisis counselor, every Native client I saw said to me at one point, "I wish I wasn't Indian." My training in the mainstream antiviolence movement did not prepare me to address what I was seeing—that sexual violence in Native communities was inextricably linked to processes of genocide and colonization. Through my involvement in organizations such as Women of All Red Nations (WARN, Chicago), Incite! Women of Color against Violence (www.incite-national.org), and various other projects, I have come to see the importance of developing organizing theories and practices that focus on the intersections of state and colonial violence and gender violence. In my ongoing research projects on Native American critical race feminisms, I focus on documenting and analyzing the theories produced by Native women activists that intervene both in sovereignty and feminist struggles.[1] These analyses serve to complicate the generally simplistic manner in which Native women's activism is often articulated within scholarly and activist circles.

NATIVE WOMEN AND FEMINISM

One of the most prominent writings on Native American women and feminism is Annette

---

Jaimes's (Guerrero) early 1990s article, "American Indian Women: At the Center of Indigenous Resistance in North America." Here, she argues that Native women activists, except those who are "assimilated," do not consider themselves feminists. Feminism, according to Jaimes, is an imperial project that assumes the giveness of U.S. colonial stranglehold on indigenous nations. Thus, to support sovereignty Native women activists reject feminist politics:

> Those who have most openly identified themselves [as feminists] have tended to be among the more assimilated of Indian women activists, generally accepting of the colonialist ideology that indigenous nations are now legitimate sub-parts of the U.S. geopolitical corpus rather than separate nations, that Indian people are now a minority with the overall population rather than the citizenry of their own distinct nations. Such Indian women activists are therefore usually more devoted to "civil rights" than to liberation per se. . . . Native American women who are more genuinely sovereigntist in their outlook have proven themselves far more dubious about the potentials offered by feminist politics and alliances.[2]

According to Jaimes, the message from Native women is the same, as typified by these quotes from one of the founders of WARN, Lorelei DeCora Means:

> We are American Indian women, in that order. We are oppressed, first and foremost, as American Indians, as peoples colonized by the United States of America, not as women. As Indians, we can never forget that. Our survival, the survival of every one of us—man, woman and child—as Indians depends on it. Decolonization is the agenda, the whole agenda, and until it is accomplished, it is the only agenda that counts for American Indians.

The critique and rejection of the label of feminism made by Jaimes is important and shared by many Native women activists. However, it fails to tell the whole story. Consider, for instance, this quote from Madonna Thunder Hawk, who cofounded WARN with Means:

Feminism means to me, putting a word on the women's world. It has to be done because of the modern day. Looking at it again, and I can only talk about the reservation society, because that's where I live and that's the only thing I know. I can't talk about the outside. How I relate to that term feminist, I like the word.

When I first heard, I liked it. I related to it right away. But I'm not the average Indian woman; I'm not the average Indian activist woman, because I refuse to limit my world. I don't like that. . . . How could we limit ourselves? "I don't like that term; it's a white term." Pssshhh. Why limit yourself? But that's me.

My point is not to set Thunder Hawk in opposition to Means: Both talk of the centrality of land and decolonization in Native women's struggle. Although Thunder Hawk supports many of the positions typically regarded as "feminist," such as abortion rights, she contends that Native struggles for land and survival continue to take precedence over these other issues. Rather, my argument is that Native women activists' theories about feminism, about the struggle against sexism both within Native communities and the society at large, and about the importance of working in coalition with non-Native women are complex and varied. These theories are not monolithic and cannot simply be reduced to the dichotomy of feminist versus nonfeminist. Furthermore, there is not necessarily a relationship between the extent to which Native women call themselves feminists, the extent to which they work in coalition with non-Native feminists or value those coalitions, whether they are urban or reservation-based, and the extent to which they are "genuinely sovereigntist." In addition, the very simplified manner in which Native women's activism is theorized straightjackets Native women from articulating political projects that both address sexism and promote indigenous sovereignty simultaneously.

Central to developing a Native feminist politic around sovereignty is a more critical analysis of Native activist responses to feminism and sexism in Native communities. Many narratives of Native women's organizing mirror Jaimes's analysis—that sexism is not a primary factor in Native women's organizing. However, Janet McCloud recounts how the sexism in the Native rights movement contributed to the founding of the Indigenous Women's Network in 1985:

> I was down in Boulder, Colorado and Winona LaDuke and Nilak Butler were there and some others. They were telling me about the different kinds of sexism they were meeting up with in the movement with the men, who were really bad, and a lot of these women were really the backbone of everything, doing a lot of the kind of work that the movement needed. I thought they were getting discouraged and getting ready to pull out and I thought, "wow, we can't lose these women because they have a lot to offer." So, we talked about organizing a women's conference to discuss all the different problems. . . . Marsha Gomez and others decided to formally organize. I agreed to stay with them as a kind of a buffer because the men were saying the "Indignant Women's Organization" and blah, blah, blah. They felt kind of threatened by the women organizing.[3]

My interviews with Native women activists also indicate that sexism in Native communities is a central concern:

> Guys think they've got the big one, man. Like when [name of Native woman in the community] had to go over there and she went to these Indians because they thought they were a bunch of swinging dicks and stuff, and she just let them have it. She just read them out. What else can you do? That's pretty brave. She was nice, she could have laid one of them out. Like you know, [name of Native man in the community], well of course this was more extreme, because I laid him out! He's way bigger than me. He's probably 5'11, I'm five feet tall. When he was younger, and I was younger, I don't even know what he said to me, it was something really awful. I didn't say nothing because he was bigger than me, I just laid him out. Otherwise you could get hurt. So I kicked him right in his little nut, and he fell down on the floor—"I'm going to kill you! You bitch!" But then he said, you're the man! If you be equal on a gut and juice level, on the street, they don't think of you as a woman anymore, and therefore they can be your friend, and they don't hate you. But then they go

telling stuff like "You're the man!" And then what I said back to him was "I've got it swinging!"

And although many Native women do not call themselves feminists for many well-thought-out reasons, including but not limited to the reasons Jaimes outlines, it is important to note that many not only call themselves feminists but also argue that it is important for Native women to call themselves feminists. And many activists argue that feminist, far from being a "white" concept, is actually an indigenous concept white women borrowed from Native women.

(Interviewee 1)

I think one of the reasons why women don't call themselves feminists is because they don't want to make enemies of men, and I just say, go forth and offend without inhibition. That's generally why I see women hold back, who don't want to be seen as strident. I don't want to be seen as a man-hater, but I think if we have enough man-haters, we might actually have the men change for once. . . . I think men, in this particular case, I think men are very, very good at avoiding responsibility and avoiding accountability and avoiding justice. And not calling yourself a feminist, that's one way they do that. Well, feminism, that's for white women. Oh feminists, they're not Indian. They're counter-revolutionary. They're all man-haters. They're all ball-busters. They've gotten out of order. No, first of all that presumes that Native women weren't active in shaping our identity before white women came along. And that abusive male behavior is somehow traditional, and it's absolutely not. So I reject that. That's a claim against sovereignty. I think that's a claim against Native peoples. I think it's an utter act of racism and white supremacy. And I do think it's important that we say we're feminists without apology.

(Interviewee 2)

[On Native women rejecting the term "feminist"] I think that's giving that concept to someone else, which I think is ridiculous. It's something that there has to be more discussion about what that means. I always considered, they took that from us, in a way. That's the way I've seen it. So I can't see it as a bad thing, because I think the origins are from people who had empowered women a long time ago.

This reversal of the typical claim that "feminism" is white then suggests that Native feminist politics is not necessarily similar to the feminist politics of other communities or that Native feminists necessarily see themselves in alliance with white feminists. In addition, the binary between feminist versus nonfeminist politics is false because Native activists have multiple and varied perspectives on this concept. For instance, consider one woman's use of "strategic" feminism with another woman's affirmation of feminist politics coupled with her rejection of the term "feminist." These women are not neatly categorized as feminists versus nonfeminists.

NATIVE FEMINISM AND SOVEREIGNTY

If we successfully decolonize, the argument goes, then we will necessarily eliminate problems of sexism as well. This sentiment can be found in the words of Ward Churchill. He contends that all struggles against sexism are of secondary importance because, traditionally, sexism did not exist in Indian nations. Churchill asks whether sexism exists in Indian country after Native peoples have attained sovereignty. His reply, "Ask Wilma Mankiller," former principal chief of the Cherokee Nation.[4] Well, let's ask Mankiller. She says of her election campaign for deputy chief that she thought people might be bothered by her progressive politics and her activist background. "But I was wrong," she says:

No one challenged me on the issues, not once. Instead, I was challenged mostly because of one fact—I am female. The election became an issue of gender. It was one of the first times I had ever really encountered overt sexism . . . (people) said having a female run our tribe would make the Cherokees the laughing stock of the tribal world.[5]

Regardless of its origins in Native communities, then, sexism operates with full force today and requires strategies that directly address it. Before Native peoples fight for the future of their nations, they must ask themselves, who is included in the nation? It is often the case that gender justice is often articulated as being a separate issue from issues of survival for indigenous peoples. Such an understanding presupposes that we could actually decolonize without addressing sexism, which ignores the fact that it has been precisely through gender violence that we have lost our lands in the first place.[6] In my activist work, I have often heard the sentiment expressed in Indian country: we do not have time to address sexual/domestic violence in our communities because we have to work on "survival" issues first. However, Indian women suffer death rates because of domestic violence twice as high as any other group of women in this country.[7] They are clearly not surviving as long as issues of gender violence go unaddressed. Scholarly analyses of the impact of colonization on Native communities often minimize the histories of oppression of Native women. In fact, many scholars argue that men were disproportionately affected by colonization because the economic systems imposed on Native nations deprived men of their economic roles in the communities more so than women.[8] By narrowing our analyses solely to the explicitly economic realm of society, we fail to account for the multiple ways women have disproportionately suffered under colonization—from sexual violence to forced sterilization. As Paula Gunn Allen argues:

Many people believe that Indian men have suffered more damage to their traditional status than have Indian women, but I think that belief is more a reflection of colonial attitudes toward the primacy of male experience than of historical fact. While women still play the traditional role of housekeeper, childbearer, and nurturer, they no longer enjoy the unquestioned positions of power, respect, and decision making on local and international levels that were not so long ago their accustomed functions.[9]

This tendency to separate the health and well-being of women from the health and well-being of our nations is critiqued in Winona LaDuke's 1994 call to not "cheapen sovereignty." She discusses attempts by men in her community to use the rhetoric of "sovereignty" to avoid paying child support payments.

> What is the point of an Indian Child Welfare Act when there is so much disregard for the rights and well being of the children? Some of these guys from White Earth are saying the state has no jurisdiction to exact child support payments from them. Traditionally, Native men took care of their own. Do they pay their own to these women? I don't think so. I know better. How does that equation better the lives of our children? How is that (real) sovereignty?

> The U.S government is so hypocritical about recognizing sovereignty. And we, the Native community, fall into the same hypocrisy. I would argue the Feds only recognize Indian sovereignty when a first Nation has a casino or a waste dump, not when a tribal government seeks to preserve ground water from pesticide contamination, exercise jurisdiction over air quality, or stop clear-cutting or say no to a nuclear dump. "Sovereignty" has become a politicized term used for some of the most demeaning purposes.[10]

Beatrice Medicine similarly critiques the manner in which women's status is often pitted against sovereignty, as exemplified in the 1978 *Santa Clara Pueblo v. Martinez* case. Julia Martinez sued her tribe for sex discrimination under the Indian Civil Rights Act because the tribe had dictated that children born from female tribal members who married outside the tribe lost tribal status whereas children born from male tribal members who married outside the tribe did not. The Supreme Court ruled that the federal government could not intervene in this situation because the determination of tribal membership was the sovereign right of the tribe. On the one hand, many white feminists criticized the Supreme Court decision without considering how the Court's affirmation of the right of the federal government to determine tribal membership

would constitute a significant attack against tribal sovereignty.[11] On the other hand, as Medicine notes, many tribes take this decision as a signal to institute gender-discriminatory practices under the name of sovereignty.[12] For these difficult issues, it is perhaps helpful to consider how they could be addressed if we put American Indian women at the center of analysis. Is it possible to simultaneously affirm tribal sovereignty and challenge tribes to consider how the impact of colonization and Europeanization may impact the decisions they make and programs they pursue in a manner which may ultimately undermine their sovereignty in the long term? Rather than adopt the strategy of fighting for sovereignty first and then improving Native women's status second, as Jaimes suggests, we must understand that attacks on Native women's status are themselves attacks on Native sovereignty. Lee Maracle illustrates the relationship between colonization and gender violence in Native communities in her groundbreaking work, *I Am Woman* (1988):

If the State won't kill us

we will have to kill ourselves.

It is no longer good etiquette to head hunt savages.

We'll just have to do it ourselves.

It's not polite to violate "squaws"

We'll have to find an Indian to oblige us.

It's poor form to starve an Indian

We'll have to deprive our young ourselves

Blinded by niceties and polite liberality

We can't see our enemy,

so, we'll just have to kill each other.[13]

It has been through sexual violence and through the imposition of European gender relationships on Native communities that Europeans were able to colonize Native peoples in the first place. If we maintain these patriarchal gender systems in place, we are then unable to decolonize and fully assert our sovereignty.

NATIVE FEMINIST SOVEREIGNTY PROJECTS

Despite the political and theoretical straight-jacket in which Native women often find themselves, there are several groundbreaking projects today that address both colonialism and sexism through an intersectional framework. One such attempt to tie indigenous sovereignty with the well-being of Native women is evident in the materials produced by the Sacred Circle, a national American Indian resource center for domestic and sexual violence based in South Dakota. Their brochure Sovereign Women Strengthen Sovereign Nations reads:

Tribal Sovereignty *All Tribal Nations Have an Inherent Right to:*	*Native Women's Sovereignty* *All Native Women Have an Inherent Right to:*
1) A land base: possession and control is unquestioned and honored by other nations. To exist without fear, but with freedom.	1) Their body and path in life: the possession and control is unquestioned and honored by others. To exist without fear, but without freedom.
2) Self-governance: the ability and authority to make decisions regarding all matters concerning the Tribe without the approval or agreement of others. This includes the ways and methods of decision-making in social, political and other areas of life.	2) Self-governance: the ability and authority to make decisions regarding all matters concerning themselves, without others' approval or agreement. This includes the ways and methods of decision-making in social, political and other areas of life.
3) An economic base and resources: the control, use and development of resources, businesses or industries the Tribe chooses. This includes resources that support the Tribal life way, including the practice of spiritual ways.	3) An economic base and resources: the control, use and development of resources, businesses or industries that Native women choose. This includes resources that support individual Native women's chosen life ways, including the practice of spiritual ways.
4) A distinct language and historical and cultural identity: Each tribe defines and describes its history, including the impact of colonization and racism, tribal culture, worldview and traditions.	4) A distinct identity, history and culture: Each Native woman defines and describes her history, including the impact of colonization, racism and sexism, tribal women's culture, worldview and traditions.
***	***
Colonization and violence against Native people means that power and control over Native people's life way and land have been stolen. As Native people, we have the right and responsibility to advocate for ourselves and our relatives in supporting our right to power and control over our tribal life way and land tribal sovereignty.	*Violence against women, and victimization in general, means that power and control over an individual's life and body have been stolen. As relatives of women who have been victimized, it is our right and responsibility to be advocates supporting every woman's right to power and control over her body and life—personal sovereignty.*

Another such project is the Boarding School Healing Project, which seeks to build a movement to demand reparations for U.S. boarding school abuses. This project, founded in 2002, is a coalition of indigenous groups across the United States, such as the American Indian Law Alliance, Incite! Women of Color against Violence, Indigenous Women's Network, and Native Women of Sovereign Nations of the South Dakota Coalition against Domestic Violence and Sexual Assault. In Canada, Native peoples have been able to document the abuses of the residential school system and demand accountability from the Canadian government and churches. The same level of documentation has not taken place in the United States. The Boarding School Healing Project is documenting these abuses to build a movement for reparations and accountability. However, the strategy of this project is not to seek remedies on the individual level, but to demand collective remedy by developing links with other reparations struggles that fundamentally challenge the colonial and capitalist status quo. In addition, the strategy of this project is to organize around boarding schools as a way to address gender violence in Native communities.

That is, one of the harms suffered by Native peoples through state policy was sexual violence perpetrated by boarding school officials. The continuing effect of this human rights violation has been the internalization of sexual and other forms of gender violence within Native American communities. Thus, the question is, how can we form a demand around reparations for these types of continuing effects of human rights violations that are evidenced by violence within communities, but are nonetheless colonial legacies. In addition, this project attempts to organize against interpersonal gender violence and state violence simultaneously by framing gender violence as a continuing effect of human rights violations perpetrated by state policy. Consequently, this project challenges the mainstream anti-domestic/sexual violence movement to conceptualize state-sponsored sexual violence as central to its work. As I have argued elsewhere,

the mainstream antiviolence movement has relied on the apparatus of state violence (in the form of the criminal justice system) to address domestic and sexual violence without considering how the state itself is a primary perpetrator of violence.[14] The issue of boarding schools forces us to see the connections between state violence and interpersonal violence. It is through boarding schools that gender violence in our communities was largely introduced. Before colonization, Native societies were, for the most part, not male dominated. Women served as spiritual, political, and military leaders. Many societies were matrilineal and matrilocal. Violence against women and children was infrequent or unheard of in many tribes.[15] Native peoples did not use corporal punishment against their children. Although there existed a division of labor between women and men, women's and men's labor was accorded similar status.[16] In boarding schools, by contrast, sexual/physical/emotional violence proliferated. Particularly brutalizing to Native children was the manner in which school officials involved children in punishing other children. For instance, in some schools, children were forced to hit other children with the threat that if they did not hit hard enough, they themselves would be severely beaten. Sometimes perpetrators of the violence were held accountable, but generally speaking, even when teachers were charged with abuse, boarding schools refused to investigate. In the case of just one teacher, John Boone at the Hopi school, FBI investigations in 1987 found that he had sexually abused more than 142 boys, but that the principal of that school had not investigated any allegations of abuse.[17] Despite the epidemic of sexual abuse in boarding schools, the Bureau of Indian Affairs did not issue a policy on reporting sexual abuse until 1987 and did not issue a policy to strengthen the background checks of potential teachers until 1989. Although not all Native peoples see their boarding school experiences as negative, it is generally the case that much if not most of the current dysfunctionality in Native communities can be traced to the boarding school era.

The effects of boarding school abuses linger today because these abuses have not been acknowledged by the larger society. As a result, silence continues within Native communities, preventing Native peoples from seeking support and healing as a result of the intergenerational trauma. Because boarding school policies are not acknowledged as human rights violations, Native peoples individualize the trauma they have suffered, thus contributing to increased shame and self-blame. If both boarding school policies and the continuing effects from these policies were recognized as human rights violations, then it might take away the shame from talking about these issues and thus provide an opportunity for communities to begin healing.

Unfortunately, we continue to perpetuate this colonial violence through domestic/sexual violence, child abuse, and homophobia. No amount of reparations will be successful if we do not address the oppressive behaviors we have internalized. Women of color have for too long been presented with the choices of either prioritizing racial justice or gender justice. This dualistic analysis fails to recognize that it is precisely through sexism and gender violence that colonialism and white supremacy have been successful. A question to ask ourselves then is, what would true reparations really look like for women of color who suffer state violence and interpersonal gender violence simultaneously? The Boarding School Healing Project provides an opportunity to organize around the connections between interpersonal gender violence and state violence that could serve as a model for the broader antiviolence movement.

In addition, this project makes important contributions to the struggle for reparations as a whole. That is, a reparations struggle is not necessarily radical if its demands do not call into question the capitalist and colonial status quo. What is at the heart of the issue is that no matter how much financial compensation the United States may give, such compensation does not ultimately end the colonial relationship between the United States and indigenous nations. What is at the heart of the struggle for

native sovereignty is control over land and resources rather than financial compensation for past and continuing wrongs. If we think about reparations less in terms of financial compensation for social oppression and more about a movement to transform the neocolonial economic relationships between the United States and people of color, indigenous peoples, and Third World countries, we see how critical this movement could be to all of us. The articulation of reparations as a movement to cancel the Third World debt, for instance, is instructive in thinking of strategies that could fundamentally alter these relations.

NATIVE FEMINISM AND THE NATION STATE

Native feminist theory and activism make a critical contribution to feminist politics as a whole by questioning the legitimacy of the United States specifically and the nation-state as the appropriate form of governance generally. Progressive activists and scholars, although prepared to make critiques of the U.S. government, are often not prepared to question its legitimacy. A case in point is the strategy of many racial justice organizations in the United States to rally against hate crimes resulting from the attacks of 9/11 under the banner, "We're American too." However, what the analysis of Native women activists suggests is that this implicit allegiance to "America" legitimizes the genocide and colonization of Native peoples, as there could be no "America" without this genocide. Thus by making anticolonial struggle central to feminist politics, Native women make central to their organizing the question of what is the appropriate form of governance for the world in general. Does self-determination for indigenous peoples equal aspirations for a nation-state, or are there other forms of governance we can create that are not based on domination and control?

Questioning the United States, in particular, and questioning the nation-state as the appropriate form of governance for the world, in general, allow us to free our political imagination to begin thinking of how we can begin to build a world we would actually want to live in. Such a political project is particularly important for colonized peoples seeking national liberation because it allows us to differentiate "nation" from "nation-state." Helpful in this project of imagination is the work of Native women activists who have begun articulating notions of nation and sovereignty that are separate from nation-states. Whereas nation-states are governed through domination and coercion, indigenous sovereignty and nationhood are predicated on interrelatedness and responsibility. As Crystal Echohawk states:

> Sovereignty is an active, living process within this knot of human, material and spiritual relationships bound together by mutual responsibilities and obligations. From that knot of relationships is born our histories, our identity, the traditional ways in which we govern ourselves, our beliefs, our relationship to the land, and how we feed, clothe, house and take care of our families, communities and Nations.[18]

It is interesting to me . . . how often non-Indians presume that if Native people regained their landbases, that they would necessarily call for the expulsion of non-Indians from those landbases. Yet, it is striking that a much more inclusive vision of sovereignty is articulated by Native women activists. For instance, this activist describes how indigenous sovereignty is based on freedom for all peoples:

> If it doesn't work for one of us, it doesn't work for any of us. The definition of sovereignty [means that] . . . none of us are free unless all of us are free. We can't, we won't turn anyone away. We've been there. I would hear stories about the Japanese internment camps . . . and I could relate to it because it happened to us. Or with Africans with the violence and rape, we've been there too. So how could we ever leave anyone behind?

This analysis mirrors much of the work currently going on in women of color organizing in the United States and in other countries. Such models rely on this dual strategy of what Sista II

Sista (Brooklyn) describes as "taking power" and "making power."[19] That is, it is necessary to engage in oppositional politics to corporate and state power ("taking power"). However, if we only engage in the politics of taking power, we will have a tendency to replicate the hierarchical structures in our movements. Consequently, it is also important to "make power" by creating those structures within our organizations, movements, and communities that model the world we are trying to create. Many groups in the United States often try to create separatist communities based on egalitarian ideals. However, if we "make power" without also trying to "take power" then we ultimately support the political status quo by failing to dismantle those structures of oppression that will undermine all our attempts to make power. The project of creating a new world governed by an alternative system not based on domination, coercion, and control does not depend on an unrealistic goal of being able to fully describe a utopian society for all at this point in time. From our position of growing up in a patriarchal, colonial, and white supremacist world, we cannot even fully imagine how a world not based on structures of oppression could operate. Nevertheless, we can be part of a collective, creative process that can bring us closer to a society not based on domination. To quote Jean Ziegler from the 2003 World Social Forum held in Porto Alegre, Brazil: "We know what we don't want, but the new world belongs to the liberated freedom of human beings. 'There is no way; you make the way as you walk.' History doesn't fall from heaven; we make history."

NOTES

1. Quotes that are not cited come from interviews conducted in Rapid City, New York City, Santa Cruz, Minneapolis, and Bemidji in 2001. These interviews are derived primarily from women involved in Women of All Red Nations (WARN) and the American Indian Movement (AIM). All are activists today.
2. M. Annette Jaimes and Theresa Halsey, "American Indian Women: At the Center of Indigenous

Resistance in North America," in *State of Native America,* ed. M. Annette Jaimes (Boston: South End Press, 1992), 330–31.

3. Janet McCloud, "The Backbone of Everything," *Indigenous Woman* 1, no. 3 (n.d.): 50.

4. Ward Churchill, *Struggle for the Land* (Monroe, Maine: Common Courage Press, 1993), 419.

5. Wilma Mankiller, *Mankiller* (New York: St. Martin's Press, 1993), 241.

6. Andrea Smith, "Sexual Violence and American Indian Genocide," in *Remembering Conquest: Feminist/Womanist Perspectives on Religion, Colonization, and Sexual Violence,* ed. Nantawan Lewis and Marie Fortune (Binghamton, N.Y.: Haworth Press, 1999), 31–52.

7. Callie Rennison, "Violent Victimization and Race, 1993–1998" (Washington, D.C.: Bureau of Justice Statistics, 2001).

8. Lucy Eldersveld Murphy, "Autonomy and the Economic Roles of Indian Women of the Fox-Wisconsin Riverway Region, 1763–1832," in *Negotiators of Change: Historical Perspectives on Native American Women,* ed. Nancy Shoemaker (New York: Routledge Press, 1995), 72–89; Theda Purdue, "Women, Men, and American Indian Policy: The Cherokee Response to 'Civilization,'" in *Negotiators of Change,* 90–114.

9. Paula Gunn Allen, *The Sacred Hoop* (Boston: Beacon Press, 1986), 202.

10. Winona LaDuke, "Don't Cheapen Sovereignty," *American Eagle* 4 (May 1996): www.alphacdc.com/eagle/op0596.html.

11. Catharine MacKinnon, *Feminism Unmodified* (Cambridge: Harvard University Press, 1987), 63–69.

12. Beatrice Medicine, "North American Indigenous Women and Cultural Domination," *American Indian Culture and Research Journal* 17, no. 3 (1993): 121–30.

13. Lee Maracle, *I Am Woman* (North Vancouver: Write-On Press Publishers, 1988).

14. Smith, "Sexual Violence and American Indian Genocide," 31–52.

15. Paula Gunn Allen, "Violence and the American Indian Woman," *The Speaking Profit Us* (Seattle: Center for the Prevention of Sexual and Domestic Violence, n.d.), 5–7. See also *A Sharing: Traditional Lakota Thought and Philosophy Regarding Domestic Violence* (South Dakota: Sacred Shawl Women's Society, n.d.); and *Sexual Assault Is Not an Indian Tradition* (Minneapolis: Division of Indian Work Sexual Assault Project, n.d.).

16. See Jaimes and Halsey, "American Indian Women," 311–44; and Allen, *The Sacred Hoop.*

17. "Hello New Federalism, Goodbye BIA," *American Eagle* 4, no. 6 (1994): 19.

18. Crystal Echohawk, "Reflections on Sovereignty," *Indigenous Woman* 3, no. 1 (1999): 21–22.

19. Personal conversations with Sista II Sista members, ongoing from 2001–2005.

Introduction to Reading 50

R. W. Connell's article traces the emergence of a worldwide discussion of men and gender-equality reform and assesses the prospects of reform strategies involving men. Connell does so by locating recent policy discussions in the wider context of the cultural problematization of men and boys, the politics of "men's movements," the divided interests of men and boys in gender relations, and the increasing research evidence about the changing and conflict-ridden social construction of masculinities. Connell's analysis ranges from local to global, but the primary concern is with the global nature of debate about the role of men and boys in relation to gender equality.

1. Why is research on diverse social constructions of masculinity critical to worldwide efforts to achieve gender equality?

2. Connell states that men have a lot to lose from pursuing gender equality. But Connell also argues that men's advantages are conditions for the price they pay for their benefits. Discuss.

3. What are the "grounds for optimism" and the "grounds for pessimism" set out in this reading?

Change Among the Gatekeepers

Men, Masculinities, and Gender Equality in the Global Arena

R. W. Connell

Equality between women and men has been a doctrine well recognized in international law since the adoption of the 1948 Universal Declaration of Human Rights (United Nations 1958), and as a principle it enjoys popular support in many countries. The idea of gender equal rights has provided the formal basis for the international discussion of the position of women since the 1975–85 UN Decade for Women, which has been a key element in the story of global feminism (Bulbeck 1988). The idea that men might have a specific role in relation to this principle has emerged only recently.

The issue of gender equality was placed on the policy agenda by women. The reason is obvious: It is women who are disadvantaged by the main patterns of gender inequality and who therefore have the claim for redress. Men are, however, necessarily involved in gender-equality reform. Gender inequalities are embedded in a multidimensional structure of relationships between women and men, which, as the modern sociology of gender shows, operates at every level of human experience, from economic arrangements, culture, and the state to interpersonal relationships and individual emotions (Holter 1997; Walby 1997; Connell 2002). Moving toward a gender-equal society involves profound institutional change as well as change in everyday life and personal conduct. To move far in this direction requires widespread social support, including significant support from men and boys.

Further, the very gender inequalities in economic assets, political power, and cultural authority, as well as the means of coercion, that gender reforms intend to change, currently mean that men

(often specific groups of men) control most of the resources required to implement women's claims for justice. Men and boys are thus in significant ways gatekeepers for gender equality. Whether they are willing to open the gates for major reforms is an important strategic question.

In this article, I will trace the emergence of a worldwide discussion of men and gender-equality reform and will try to assess the prospects of reform strategies involving men. To make such an assessment, it is necessary to set recent policy discussions in the wider context of the cultural problematization of men and boys, the politics of "men's movements," the divided interests of men and boys in gender relations, and the growing research evidence about the changing and conflict-ridden social construction of masculinities.

In an article of this scope, it is not possible to address particular national agendas in detail. I will refer to a number of texts where these stories can be found. Because my primary concern is with the global character of the debate, I will give particular attention to policy discussions in UN forums. These discussions culminated in the 2004 meeting of the UN Commission on the Status of Women, which produced the first world-level policy document on the role of men and boys in relation to gender equality (UN Commission on the Status of Women 2004.)

Men and Masculinities in the World Gender Order

In the last fifteen years, in the "developed" countries of the global metropole, there has been a great deal of popular concern with issues about men and boys. Readers in the United States may recall a volume by the poet Robert Bly, *Iron John: A Book about Men* (1990), which became a huge best seller in the early 1990s, setting off a wave of imitations. This book became popular because it offered, in prophetic language, simple solutions to problems that were increasingly troubling the culture. A therapeutic movement was then developing in the United States, mainly though not exclusively among middle-class men, addressing problems in relationships, sexuality, and identity (Kupers 1993; Schwalbe 1996).

More specific issues about men and boys have also attracted public attention in the developed countries. Men's responses to feminism, and to gender-equality measures taken by government, have long been the subject of debate in Germany and Scandinavia (Metz-Göckel and Müller 1985; Holter 2003). In anglophone countries there has been much discussion of "the new fatherhood" and of supposed changes in men's involvement in families (McMahon 1999). There has been public agonizing about boys' "failure" in school, and in Australia there are many proposals for special programs for boys (Kenway 1997; Lingard 2003). Men's violence toward women has been the subject of practical interventions and extensive debate (Hearn 1998). There has also been increasing debate about men's health and illness from a gender perspective (Hurrelmann and Kolip 2002).

Accompanying these debates has been a remarkable growth of research about men's gender identities and practices, masculinities and the social processes by which they are constructed, cultural and media images of men, and related matters. Academic journals have been founded for specialized research on men and masculinities, there have been many research conferences, and there is a rapidly growing international literature. We now have a far more sophisticated and detailed scientific understanding of issues about men, masculinities, and gender than ever before (Connell 2003a).

This set of concerns, though first articulated in the developed countries, can now be found worldwide (Connell 2000; Pease and Pringle 2001). Debates on violence, patriarchy, and ways of changing men's conduct have occurred in countries as diverse as Germany, Canada, and South Africa (Hagemann-White 1992; Kaufman 1993; Morrell 2001a). Issues about masculine sexuality and fatherhood have been debated and researched in Brazil, Mexico, and many other countries (Arilha, Unbehaum Ridenti, and Medrado 1998; Lerner 1998). A men's center with a reform agenda has been established in Japan, where conferences have been held and media debates about traditional patterns of masculinity and family life continue (Menzu Senta 1997; Roberson and Suzuki 2003). A "traveling seminar" discussing issues about men, masculinities, and gender equality has recently been touring in India (Roy 2003). Debates about boys' education, men's identities, and gender change are active from New Zealand to Denmark (Law, Campbell, and Dolan 1999; Reinicke 2002). Debates about men's sexuality, and changing sexual identities, are also international (Altman 2001).

The research effort is also worldwide. Documentation of the diverse social constructions of masculinity has been undertaken in countries as far apart as Peru (Fuller 2001), Japan (Taga 2001), and Turkey (Sinclair-Webb 2000). The first large-scale comparative study of men and gender relations has recently been completed in ten European countries (Hearn et al. 2002). The first global synthesis, in the form of a world handbook of research on men and masculinities, has now appeared (Kimmel, Hearn, and Connell 2005).

The rapid internationalization of these debates reflects the fact—increasingly recognized in feminist thought (Bulbeck 1998; Marchand and Runyan 2000)—that gender relations themselves have an international dimension. Each of the substructures of gender relations can be shown to have a global dimension, growing out of the history of imperialism and seen in the contemporary process of globalization (Connell 2002). Change in gender relations occurs on a world scale, though not always in the same direction or at the same pace.

The complexity of the patterns follows from the fact that gender change occurs in several different modes. Most dramatic is the direct colonization of the gender order of regions beyond the metropole. There has also been a more gradual recomposition of gender orders, both those of the colonizing society and the colonized, in the process of colonial interaction. The hybrid gender identities and sexualities now much discussed in the context of postcolonial societies are neither unusual nor new. They are a feature of the whole history of imperialism and are visible in many contemporary studies (e.g., Valdés and Olavarría 1998).

Imperialism and globalization change the conditions of existence for gender orders. For instance, the linking of previously separate production systems changes the flow of goods and services in the gendered division of labor, as seen in the impact of industrially produced foods and textiles on household economies. Colonialism itself often confronted local patriarchies with colonizing patriarchies, producing a turbulent and sometimes very violent aftermath, as in southern Africa (Morrell 1998). Pressure from contemporary Western commercial culture has destabilized gender arrangements, and models of masculinity, in Japan (Ito 1992), the Arab world (Ghoussoub 2000), and elsewhere.

Finally, the emergence of new arenas of social relationship on a world scale creates new patterns of gender relations. Transnational corporations, international communications systems, global mass media, and international state structures (from the United Nations to the European Union) are such arenas. These institutions have their own gender regimes and may form the basis for new configurations of masculinity, as has recently been argued for transnational business (Connell 2000) and the international relations system (Hooper 2001). Local gender orders now interact not only with the gender orders of other local societies but also with the gender order of the global arena.

The dynamics of the world gender order affect men as profoundly as they do women, though this fact has been less discussed. The best

contemporary research on men and masculinity, such as Matthew C. Gutmann's (2002) ethnographic work in Mexico, shows in fine detail how the lives of particular groups of men are shaped by globally acting economic and political dynamics.

Different groups of men are positioned very differently in such processes. There is no single formula that accounts for men and globalization. There is, indeed, a growing polarization among men on a world scale. Studies of the "super-rich" (Haseler 2000) show a privileged minority reaching astonishing heights of wealth and power while much larger numbers face poverty, cultural dislocation, disruption of family relationships, and forced renegotiation of the meanings of masculinity.

Masculinities, as socially constructed configurations of gender practice, are also created through a historical process with a global dimension. The old-style ethnographic research that located gender patterns purely in a local context is inadequate to the reality. Historical research, such as Robert Morrell's (2001b) study of the masculinities of the colonizers in South Africa and T. Dunbar Moodie's (1994) study of the colonized, shows how a gendered culture is created and transformed in relation to the international economy and the political system of empire. There is every reason to think this principle holds for contemporary masculinities.

SHIFTING GROUND: MEN AND BOYS IN GENDER-EQUALITY DEBATES

Because of the way they came onto the agenda of public debate, gender issues have been widely regarded as women's business and of little concern to men and boys. In almost all policy discussions, to adopt a gender perspective substantially means to address women's concerns.

In both national and international policy documents concerned with gender equality, women are the subjects of the policy discourse. The agencies or meetings that formulate, implement, or monitor gender policies usually have names referring to women, such as Department for Women, Women's Equity Bureau, Prefectural Women's Centre, or Commission on the Status of Women. Such bodies have a clear mandate to act for women. They do not have an equally clear mandate to act with respect to men. The major policy documents concerned with gender equality, such as the UN Convention on the Elimination of All Forms of Discrimination against Women (United Nations [1979] 1989), often do not name men as a group and rarely discuss men in concrete terms.

However, men are present as background throughout these documents. In every statement about women's disadvantages, there is an implied comparison with men as the advantaged group. In the discussions of violence against women, men are implied, and sometimes named, as the perpetrators. In discussions of gender and HIV/AIDS, men are commonly construed as being "the problem," the agents of infection. In discussions of women's exclusion from power and decision making, men are implicitly present as the power holders.

When men are present only as a background category in a policy discourse about women, it is difficult to raise issues about men's and boys' interests, problems, or differences. This could be done only by falling into a backlash posture and affirming "men's rights" or by moving outside a gender framework altogether.

The structure of gender-equality policy, therefore, created an opportunity for antifeminist politics. Opponents of feminism have now found issues about boys and men to be fertile ground. This is most clearly seen in the United States, where authors such as Warren Farrell (1993) and Christina Hoff Sommers (2000), purporting to speak on behalf of men and boys, bitterly accuse feminism of injustice. Men and boys, they argue, are the truly disadvantaged group and need supportive programs in education and health, in situations of family breakup, and so forth. These ideas have not stimulated a social movement, with the exception of a small-scale (though active and sometimes violent) "father's rights"

movement in relation to divorce. The arguments have, however, strongly appealed to the neoconservative mass media, which have given them international circulation. They now form part of the broad neoconservative repertoire of opposition to "political correctness" and to social justice measures.

Some policy makers have attempted to straddle this divide by restructuring gender-equality policy in the form of parallel policies for women and men. For instance, some recent health policy initiatives in Australia have added a "men's health" document to a "women's health" document (Schofield 2004). Similarly, in some school systems a "boys' education" strategy has been added to a "girls' education" strategy (Lingard 2003).

This approach acknowledges the wider scope of gender issues. But it also risks weakening the equality rationale of the original policy. It forgets the relational character of gender and therefore tends to redefine women and men, or girls and boys, simply as different market segments for some service. Ironically, the result may be to promote more gender segregation, not less. This has certainly happened in education, where some privileged boys' schools have jumped on the "gender equality" bandwagon and now market themselves as experts in catering to the special needs of boys.

On the other hand, bringing men's problems into an existing framework of policies for women may weaken the authority that women have so far gathered in that policy area. In the field of gender and development, for instance, some specialists argue that "bringing men in"—given the larger context in which men still control most of the wealth and institutional authority—may undermine, not help, the drive for gender equality (White 2000).

The role of men and boys in relation to gender equality emerged as an issue in international discussions during the 1990s. This development crystallized at the Fourth World Conference on Women, held in Beijing in 1995. Paragraph 25 of the Beijing Declaration committed participating governments to "encourage men to participate fully in all actions towards equality" (United Nations 2001). The detailed "Platform for Action" that accompanied the declaration prominently restated the principle of shared power and responsibility between men and women and argued that women's concerns could be addressed only "in partnership with men" toward gender equality (2001, pars. 1, 3). The "Platform for Action" went on to specify areas where action involving men and boys was needed and was possible: in education, socialization of children, child care and housework, sexual health, gender-based violence, and the balancing of work and family responsibilities (2001, pars. 40, 72, 83b, 107c, 108e, 120, 179).

Participating member states followed a similar approach in the twenty-third special session of the UN General Assembly in the year 2000, which was intended to review the situation five years after the Beijing conference. The "Political Declaration" of this session made an even stronger statement on men's responsibility: "[Member states of the United Nations] emphasise that men must involve themselves and take joint responsibility with women for the promotion of gender equality" (United Nations 2001, par. 6). It still remained the case, in this and the accompanying "Outcome Document," that men were present on the margins of a policy discourse concerned with women.

The role of men and boys has also been addressed in other recent international meetings. These include the 1995 World Summit on Social Development, its review session in 2000, and the special session of the General Assembly on HIV/AIDS in 2001. In 1997 the UN Educational, Scientific, and Cultural Organization (UNESCO) convened an expert group meeting about "Male Roles and Masculinities in the Perspective of a Culture of Peace," which met in Oslo and produced studies on the links among personal violence, war, and the construction of masculinities (Breines, Connell, and Eide 2000).

International meetings outside the UN system have addressed similar issues. In 1997 the Nordic Council of Ministers adopted the Nordic Action Plan for Men and Gender Equality. In the

same year the Council of Europe conducted a seminar on equality as a common issue for men and women and made the role of men in promoting equality a theme at a ministerial conference. In 1998 the Latin American Federation of Social Science (FLACSO) began a series of conferences about masculinities, boys, and men across Latin America and the Caribbean. The first conference in this series had the specific theme of gender equity (Valdés and Olavarría 1998). The European Commission has recently funded a research network on men and masculinities.

DIVIDED INTERESTS: SUPPORT AND RESISTANCE

There is something surprising about the worldwide problematizing of men and masculinities, because in many ways the position of men has not greatly changed. For instance, men remain a very large majority of corporate executives, top professionals, and holders of public office. Worldwide, men hold nine out of ten cabinet-level posts in national governments, nearly as many of the parliamentary seats, and most top positions in international agencies. Men, collectively, receive approximately twice the income that women receive and also receive the benefits of a great deal of unpaid household labor, not to mention emotional support, from women (Gierycz 1999; Godenzi 2000; Inter-Parliamentary Union 2003).

The UN Development Program (2003) now regularly incorporates a selection of such statistics into its annual report on world human development, combining them into a "gender-related development index" and a "gender empowerment measure." This produces a dramatic outcome, a league table of countries ranked in terms of gender equality, which shows most countries in the world to be far from gender-equal. It is clear that, globally, men have a lot to lose from pursuing gender equality because men, collectively, continue to receive a patriarchal dividend.

But this way of picturing inequality may conceal as much as it reveals. There are multiple dimensions in gender relations, and the patterns of inequality in these dimensions may be qualitatively different. If we look separately at each of the substructures of gender, we find a pattern of advantages for men but also a linked pattern of disadvantages or toxicity (Connell 2003c).

For instance, in relation to the gender division of labor, men collectively receive the bulk of income in the money economy and occupy most of the managerial positions. But men also provide the workforce for the most dangerous occupations, suffer most industrial injuries, pay most of the taxation, and are under heavier social pressure to remain employed. In the domain of power men collectively control the institutions of coercion and the means of violence (e.g., weapons). But men are also the main targets of military violence and criminal assault, and many more men than women are imprisoned or executed. Men's authority receives more social recognition (e.g., in religion), but men and boys are underrepresented in important learning experiences (e.g., in humanistic studies) and important dimensions of human relations (e.g., with young children).

One could draw up a balance sheet of the costs and benefits to men from the current gender order. But this balance sheet would not be like a corporate accounting exercise where there is a bottom line, subtracting costs from income. The disadvantages listed above are, broadly speaking, the conditions of the advantages. For instance, men cannot hold state power without some men becoming the agents of violence. Men cannot be the beneficiaries of women's domestic labor and "emotion work" without many of them losing intimate connections, for instance, with young children.

Equally important, the men who receive most of the benefits and the men who pay most of the costs are not the same individuals. As the old saying puts it, generals die in bed. On a global scale, the men who benefit from corporate wealth, physical security, and expensive health care are a very different group from the men who

provide the workforce of developing countries. Class, race, national, regional, and generational differences cross-cut the category "men," spreading the gains and costs of gender relations very unevenly among men. There are many situations where groups of men may see their interest as more closely aligned with the women in their communities than with other men. It is not surprising that men respond very diversely to gender-equality politics.

There is, in fact, a considerable history of support for gender equality among men. There is certainly a tradition of advocacy by male intellectuals. In Europe, well before modern gender-equality documents were written, the British philosopher John Stuart Mill published "The Subjection of Women" (1912), which established the presumption of equal rights; and the Norwegian dramatist Henrik Ibsen, in plays like *A Doll's House* ([1923] 1995), made gender oppression an important cultural theme. In the following generation, the pioneering Austrian psychoanalyst Alfred Adler established a powerful psychological argument for gender equality (Connell 1995). A similar tradition of men's advocacy exists in the United States (Kimmel and Mosmiller 1992).

Many of the historic gains by women's advocates have been won in alliance with men who held organizational or political authority at the time. For instance, the introduction of equal employment opportunity measures in New South Wales, Australia, occurred with the strong support of the premier and the head of a reform inquiry into the public sector, both men (Eisenstein 1991). Sometimes men's support for gender equality takes the form of campaigning and organizing among men. The most prominent example is the U.S. National Organization of Men Against Sexism (NOMAS), which has existed for more than twenty years (Cohen 1991). Men's groups concerned with reforming masculinity, publications advocating change, and campaigns among men against violence toward women are found widely, for instance, in the United Kingdom, Mexico, and South Africa (Seidler 1991; Zingoni 1998; Peacock 2003).

Men have also been active in creating educational programs for boys and young men intended to support gender reform. Similar strategies have been developed for adult men, sometimes in a religious and sometimes in a health or therapeutic context. There is a strong tradition of such work in Germany, with programs that combine the search for self-knowledge with the learning of antisexist behavior (Brandes and Bullinger 1996). Work of the same kind has developed in Brazil, the United States, and other countries (Denborough 1996; Lyra and Medrado 2001).

These initiatives are widespread, but they are also mostly small-scale. What of the wider state of opinion? European survey research has shown no consensus among men either for or against gender equality. Sometimes a third/third/third pattern appears, with about one-third of men supporting change toward equality, about one-third opposing it, and one-third undecided or intermediate (Holter 1997, 131–34). Nevertheless, examinations of the survey evidence from the United States, Germany, and Japan have shown a long-term trend of growing support for change, that is, a movement away from traditional gender roles, especially among members of the younger generation (Thornton 1989; Zulehner and Volz 1998; Mohwald 2002).

There is, however, also significant evidence of men's and boys' resistance to change in gender relations. The survey research reveals substantial levels of doubt and opposition, especially among older men. Research on workplaces and on corporate management has documented many cases where men maintain an organizational culture that is heavily masculinized and unwelcoming to women. In some cases there is active opposition to gender-equality measures or quiet undermining of them (Cockburn 1991; Collinson and Hearn 1996). Research on schools has also found cases where boys assert control of informal social life and direct hostility against girls and against boys perceived as being different. The status quo can be defended even in the details of classroom life, for instance, when a particular group of boys used misogynist language to resist study of a poem that questioned Australian gender stereotypes (Kenworthy 1994; Holland et al. 1998).

Some men accept change in principle but in practice still act in ways that sustain men's dominance of the public sphere and assign domestic labor and child care to women. In strongly gender segregated societies, it may be difficult for men to recognize alternatives or to understand women's experiences (Kandiyoti 1994; Fuller 2001; Meuser 2003). Another type of opposition to reform, more common among men in business and government, rejects gender-equality measures because it rejects all government action in support of equality, in favor of the unfettered action of the market.

The reasons for men's resistance include the patriarchal dividend discussed above and threats to identity that occur with change. If social definitions of masculinity include being the breadwinner and being "strong," then men may be offended by women's professional progress because it makes men seem less worthy of respect. Resistance may also reflect ideological defense of male supremacy. Research on domestic violence suggests that male batterers often hold very conservative views of women's role in the family (Ptacek 1988). In many parts of the world, there exist ideologies that justify men's supremacy on grounds of religion, biology, cultural tradition, or organizational mission (e.g., in the military). It is a mistake to regard these ideas as simply outmoded. They may be actively modernized and renewed.

GROUNDS FOR OPTIMISM: CAPACITIES FOR EQUALITY AND REASONS FOR CHANGE

The public debates about men and boys have often been inconclusive. But they have gone a long way, together with the research, to shatter one widespread belief that has hindered gender reform. This obstacle is the belief that men cannot change their ways, that "boys will be boys," that rape, war, sexism, domestic violence, aggression, and self-centeredness are natural to men.

We now have many documented examples of the diversity of masculinities and of men's and boys' capacity for equality. For instance, life-history research in Chile has shown that there is no unitary Chilean masculinity, despite the cultural homogeneity of the country. While a hegemonic model is widely diffused across social strata, there are many men who depart from it, and there is significant discontent with traditional roles (Valdés and Olavarría 1998). Though groups of boys in schools often have a dominant or hegemonic pattern of masculinity, there are usually also other patterns present, some of which involve more equal and respectful relations with girls.

Research in Britain, for instance, shows how boys encounter and explore alternative models of masculinity as they grow up (Mac an Ghaill 1994; O'Donnell and Sharpe 2000). Psychological and educational research shows personal flexibility in the face of gender stereotypes. Men and boys can vary, or strategically use, conventional definitions of masculinity. It is even possible to teach boys (and girls) how to do this in school, as experiments in Australian classrooms have shown (Davies 1993; Wetherell and Edley 1999).

Changes have occurred in men's practices within certain families, where there has been a conscious shift toward more equal sharing of housework and child care. The sociologist Barbara J. Risman (1998), who has documented such cases in one region of the United States, calls them "fair families." It is clear from her research that the change has required a challenge to traditional models of masculinity. In the Shanghai region of China, there is an established local tradition of relative gender equality, and men are demonstrably willing to be involved in domestic work. Research by Da Wei Wei (Da 2004) shows this tradition persisting among Shanghai men even after migration to another country.

Perhaps the most extensive social action involving men in gender change has occurred in Scandinavia. This includes provisions for paternity leave that have had high rates of take-up, among the most dramatic of all demonstrations of men's willingness to change gender practices.

Øystein Holter sums up the research and practical experience: "The Nordic 'experiment' has shown that a majority of men can change their practice when circumstances are favorable.... When reforms or support policies are well-designed and targeted towards an ongoing cultural process of change, men's active support for gender-equal status increases" (1997, 126). Many groups of men, it is clear, have a capacity for equality and for gender change. But what reasons for change are men likely to see?

Early statements often assumed that men had the same interest as women in escaping from restrictive sex roles (e.g., Palme 1972). Later experience has not confirmed this view. Yet men and boys often do have substantial reasons to support change, which can readily be listed.

First, men are not isolated individuals. Men and boys live in social relationships, many with women and girls: wives, partners, mothers, aunts, daughters, nieces, friends, classmates, workmates, professional colleagues, neighbors, and so on. The quality of every man's life depends to a large extent on the quality of those relationships. We may therefore speak of men's relational interests in gender equality. For instance, very large numbers of men are fathers, and about half of their children are girls. Some men are sole parents and are then deeply involved in caregiving—an important demonstration of men's capacity for care (Risman 1986). Even in intact partnerships with women, many men have close relationships with their children, and psychological research shows the importance of these relationships (Kindler 2002). In several parts of the world, young men are exploring more engaged patterns of fatherhood (Olavarría 2001). To make sure that daughters grow up in a world that offers young women security, freedom, and opportunities to fulfill their talents is a powerful reason for many men to support gender equality.

Second, men may wish to avoid the toxic effects that the gender order has for them. James Harrison long ago issued a "Warning: The Male Sex Role May Be Dangerous to Your Health" (1978). Since then health research has documented specific problems for men and boys.

Among them are premature death from accident, homicide, and suicide; occupational injury; higher levels of drug abuse, especially of alcohol and tobacco; and in some countries at least, a relative unwillingness by men to seek medical help when it is needed. Attempts to assert a tough and dominant masculinity sustain some of these patterns (Sabo and Gordon 1995; Hurrelmann and Kolip 2002).

Social and economic pressures on men to compete in the workplace, to increase their hours of paid work, and sometimes to take second jobs are among the most powerful constraints on gender reform. Desire for a better balance between work and life is widespread among employed men. On the other hand, where unemployment is high the lack of a paid job can be a damaging pressure on men who have grown up with the expectation of being breadwinners. This is, for instance, an important gender issue in post-Apartheid South Africa. Opening alternative economic paths and moving toward what German discussions have called "multioptional masculinities" may do much to improve men's well-being (Widersprüche 1998; Morrell 2001a).

Third, men may support gender change because they see its relevance to the well-being of the community they live in. In situations of mass poverty and underemployment, for instance in cities in developing countries, flexibility in the gender division of labor may be crucial to a household that requires women's earnings as well as men's. Reducing the rigidity of masculinities may also yield benefits in security. Civil and international violence is strongly associated with dominating patterns of masculinity and with marked gender inequality in the state. Movement away from these patterns makes it easier for men to adopt historically "feminine" styles of nonviolent negotiation and conflict resolution (Zalewski and Parpart 1998; Breines, Connell, and Eide 2000; Cockburn 2003). This may also reduce the toxic effects of policing and incarceration (Sabo, Kupers, and London 2001).

Finally, men may support gender reform because gender equality follows from their political or ethical principles. These may be religious, socialist, or broad democratic beliefs. Mill argued a case based on classical liberal principles a century and a half ago, and the idea of equal human rights still has purchase among large groups of men.

GROUNDS FOR PESSIMISM: THE SHAPE OF MASCULINITY POLITICS

The diversity among men and masculinities is reflected in a diversity of men's movements in the developed countries. A study of the United States found multiple movements, with different agendas for the remaking of masculinity. They operated on the varying terrains of gender equality, men's rights, and ethnic or religious identities (Messner 1997). There is no unified political position for men and no authoritative representative of men's interests.

Men's movements specifically concerned with gender equality exist in a number of countries. A well-known example is the White Ribbon Campaign, dedicated to mobilizing public opinion and educating men and boys for the prevention of men's violence against women. Originating in Canada, in response to the massacre of women in Montreal in 1989, the White Ribbon Campaign achieved very high visibility in that country, with support from political and community leaders and considerable outreach in schools and mass media. More recently, it has spread to other countries. Groups concerned with violence prevention have appeared in other countries, such as Men Against Sexual Assault in Australia and Men Overcoming Violence (MOVE) in the United States. These have not achieved the visibility of the White Ribbon Campaign but have built up a valuable body of knowledge about the successes and difficulties of organizing among men (Lichterman 1989; Pease 1997; Kaufman 1999).

The most extensive experience of any group of men organizing around issues of gender and sexual politics is that of homosexual men, in antidiscrimination campaigns, the gay liberation movement, and community responses to the HIV/AIDS pandemic. Gay men have pioneered in areas such as community care for the sick, community education for responsible sexual practices, representation in the public sector, and overcoming social exclusion, which are important for all groups of men concerned with gender equality (Kippax et al. 1993; Altman 1994).

Explicit backlash movements also exist but have not generally had a great deal of influence. Men mobilizing as men to oppose women tend to be seen as cranks or fanatics. They constantly exaggerate women's power. And by defining men's interests in opposition to women's, they get into cultural difficulties, since they have to violate a main tenet of modern patriarchal ideology—the idea that "opposites attract" and that men's and women's needs, interests, and choices are complementary.

Much more important for the defense of gender inequality are movements in which men's interests are a side effect—nationalist, ethnic, religious, and economic movements. Of these, the most influential on a world scale is contemporary neoliberalism—the political and cultural promotion of free-market principles and individualism and the rejection of state control.

Neoliberalism is in principle gender neutral. The "individual" has no gender, and the market delivers advantage to the smartest entrepreneur, not to men or women as such. But neoliberalism does not pursue social justice in relation to gender. In Eastern Europe, the restoration of capitalism and the arrival of neoliberal politics have been followed by a sharp deterioration in the position of women. In rich Western countries, neoliberalism from the 1980s on has attacked the welfare state, on which far more women than men depend; supported deregulation of labor markets, resulting in increased casualization of women workers; shrunk public sector employment, the sector of the economy where women predominate; lowered rates of personal taxation, the main basis of tax transfers to women; and squeezed public education, the key pathway to labor market advancement for women. However, the same period saw an expansion of the human-rights agenda, which is, on the whole, an asset for gender equality.

The contemporary version of neoliberalism, known as neoconservatism in the United States, also has some gender complexities. George W. Bush was the first U.S. president to place a woman in the very heart of the state security apparatus, as national security adviser to the president. And some of the regime's actions, such as the attack on the Taliban regime in Afghanistan, were defended as a means of emancipating women.

Yet neoconservatism and state power in the United States and its satellites such as Australia remain overwhelmingly the province of men—indeed, men of a particular character: power oriented and ruthless, restrained by little more than calculations of likely opposition. There has been a sharp remasculinization of political rhetoric and a turn to the use of force as a primary instrument in policy. The human rights discourse is muted and sometimes completely abandoned (as in the U.S. prison camp for Muslim captives at Guantanamo Bay and the Australian prison camps for refugees in the central desert and Pacific islands).

Neoliberalism can function as a form of masculinity politics largely because of the powerful role of the state in the gender order. The state constitutes gender relations in multiple ways, and all of its gender policies affect men. Many mainstream policies (e.g., in economic and security affairs) are substantially about men without acknowledging this fact (Nagel 1998; O'Connor, Orloff, and Shaver 1999; Connell 2003b).

This points to a realm of institutional politics where men's and women's interests are very much at stake, without the publicity created by social movements. Public-sector agencies (Jensen 1998; Mackay and Bilton 2000; Schofield, forthcoming), private-sector corporations (Marchand and Runyan 2000; Hearn and Parkin 2001), and unions (Corman et al. 1993; Franzway 2001) are all sites of masculinized power and struggles for gender equality. In each of these sites, some men can be found with a commitment to gender equality, but in each case that is an embattled position. For gender-equality outcomes, it is important to have support from men in the top organizational levels, but this is not often reliably forthcoming.

One reason for the difficulty in expanding men's opposition to sexism is the role of highly conservative men as cultural authorities and managers. Major religious organizations, in Christianity, Islam, and Buddhism, are controlled by men who sometimes completely exclude women, and these organizations have often been used to oppose the emancipation of women. Transnational media organizations such as Rupert Murdoch's conglomerate are equally active in promoting conservative gender ideology.

A specific address to men is found in the growing institutional, media, and business complex of commercial sports. With its overwhelming focus on male athletes; its celebration of force, domination, and competitive success; its valorization of male commentators and executives; and its marginalization and frequent ridicule of women, the sports/business complex has become an increasingly important site for representing and defining gender. This is not traditional patriarchy. It is something new, welding exemplary bodies to entrepreneurial culture. Michael Messner (2002), one of the leading analysts of contemporary sports, formulates the effect well by saying that commercial sports define the renewed centrality of men and of a particular version of masculinity.

On a world scale, explicit backlash movements are of limited importance, but very large numbers of men are nevertheless engaged in preserving gender inequality. Patriarchy is defended diffusely. There is support for change from equally large numbers of men, but it is an uphill battle to articulate that support. That is the political context with which new gender-equality initiatives have to deal.

WAYS FORWARD: TOWARD A GLOBAL FRAMEWORK

Inviting men to end men's privileges, and to remake masculinities to sustain gender equality, strikes many people as a strange or utopian project. Yet this project is already under way. Many men around the world are engaged in gender reforms, for the good reasons discussed above.

The diversity of masculinities complicates the process but is also an important asset. As this diversity becomes better known, men and boys can more easily see a range of possibilities for their own lives, and both men and women are less likely to think of gender inequality as unchangeable. It also becomes possible to identify specific groups of men who might engage in alliances for change.

The international policy documents discussed above rely on the concept of an alliance between men and women for achieving equality. Since the growth of an autonomous women's movement, the main impetus for reform has been located in women's groups. Some groups within the women's movement, especially those concerned with men's violence, are reluctant to work with men or are deeply skeptical of men's willingness to change. Other feminists argue that alliances between women and men are possible, even crucial. In some social movements, for instance, environmentalism, there is a strong ideology of gender equality and a favorable environment for men to support gender change (Connell 1995; Segal 1997).

In local and central government, practical alliances between women and men have been important in achieving equal-opportunity measures and other gender-equality reforms. Even in the field of men's violence against women, there has been cooperation between women's groups and men's groups, for instance, in prevention work. This cooperation can be an inspiration to grassroots workers and a powerful demonstration of women and men's common interest in a peaceful and equal society (Pease 1997; Schofield, forthcoming). The concept of alliance is itself important, in preserving autonomy for women's groups, in preempting a tendency for any one group to speak for others, and in defining a political role for men that has some dignity and might attract widespread support.

Given the spectrum of masculinity politics, we cannot expect worldwide consensus for gender equality. What is possible is that support for gender equality might become hegemonic among men. In that case it would be groups supporting equality that provide the agenda for public discussion about men's lives and patterns of masculinity.

There is already a broad cultural shift toward a historical consciousness about gender, an awareness that gender customs came into existence at specific moments in time and can always be transformed by social action (Connell 1995). What is needed now is a widespread sense of agency among men, a sense that this transformation is something they can actually share in as a practical proposition. This is precisely what was presupposed in the "joint responsibility" of men invoked by the General Assembly declaration of the year 2000.[1]

From this point of view, the recent meeting of the UN Commission on the Status of Women (CSW) is profoundly interesting. The CSW is one of the oldest of UN agencies, dating from the 1940s. Effectively a standing committee of the General Assembly, it meets annually, and its current practice is to consider two main themes at each meeting. For the 2004 meeting, one of the defined themes was "the role of men and boys in achieving gender equality." The section of the UN secretariat that supports the CSW, the Division for the Advancement of Women, undertook background work. The division held, in June–July 2003, a worldwide online seminar on the role of men and boys, and in October 2003 it convened an international expert group meeting in Brasilia on the topic.

At the CSW meetings, several processes occur and (it is to be hoped) interact. There is a presentation of the division's background work, and delegations of the forty-five current member countries, UN agencies, and many of the nongovernmental organizations (NGOs) attending make initial statements. There is a busy schedule of side events, mainly organized by NGOs but some conducted by delegations or UN agencies, ranging from strategy debates to practical workshops. And there is a diplomatic process in which the official delegations negotiate over a draft document in the light of discussions in the CSW and their governments' stances on gender issues.

This is a politicized process, inevitably, and it can break down. In 2003 the CSW discussion on the issue of violence against women reached deadlock. In 2004 it was clear that some participating NGOs were not happy with the focus on men and boys, some holding to a discourse representing men exclusively as perpetrators of violence. Over the two weeks of negotiations, however, the delegations did reach consensus on a statement of "Agreed Conclusions."

Balancing a reaffirmation of commitment to women's equality with a recognition of men's and boys' potential for action, this document makes specific recommendations across a spectrum of policy fields, including education, parenthood, media, the labor market, sexuality, violence, and conflict prevention. These proposals have no force in international law—the document is essentially a set of recommendations to governments and other organizations. Nevertheless, it is the first international agreement of its kind, treating men systematically as agents in gender-equality processes, and it creates a standard for future gender-equality discussions. Most important, the CSW's "Agreed Conclusions" change the logic of the representation of men in gender policy. So far as the international discourse of gender-equality policy is concerned, this document begins the substantive presentation of gender equality as a positive project for men.

Here the UN process connects with the social and cultural possibilities that have emerged from the last three decades of gender politics among men. Gender equality is an undertaking for men that can be creative and joyful. It is a project that realizes high principles of social justice, produces better lives for the women whom men care about, and will produce better lives for the majority of men in the long run. This can and should be a project that generates energy, that finds expression in everyday life and the arts as well as in formal policies, and that can illuminate all aspects of men's lives.

NOTE

1. Twenty-third special session, UN General Assembly, "Political Declaration," para. 6.

REFERENCES

Altman, Dennis. 1994. *Power and Community: Organizational and Cultural Responses to AIDS.* London: Taylor & Francis.
———. 2001. *Global Sex.* Chicago: University of Chicago Press.
Arilha, Margareth, Sandra G. Unbehaum Ridenti, and Benedito Medrado, eds. 1998. *Homens e Masculinidades: Outras Palavras.* Sao Paulo: ECOS/Editora 34.
Bly, Robert. 1990. *Iron John: A Book about Men.* Reading, MA: Addison-Wesley.
Brandes, Holger, and Hermann Bullinger, eds. 1996. *Handbuch Männerarbeit.* Weinheim, Germany: Psychologic Verlags Union.
Breines, Ingeborg, Robert Connell, and Ingrid Eide, eds. 2000. *Male Roles, Masculinities and Violence: A Culture of Peace Perspective.* Paris: UNESCO.
Bulbeck, Chilla. 1988. *One World Women's Movement.* London: Pluto.
———. 1998. *Re-orienting Western Feminisms: Women's Diversity in a Postcolonial World.* Cambridge: Cambridge University Press.
Cockburn, Cynthia. 1991. *In the Way of Women: Men's Resistance to Sex Equality in Organizations.* Ithaca, NY: ILR Press.
———. 2003. *The Line: Women, Partition and the Gender Order in Cyprus.* London: Zed.
Cohen, Jon. 1991. "NOMAS: Challenging Male Supremacy." *Changing Men* (Winter/Spring): 45–46.
Collinson, David L., and Jeff Hearn, eds. 1996. *Men as Managers, Managers as Men: Critical Perspectives on Men, Masculinities and Managements.* London: Sage.
Connell, R. W. 1995. *Masculinities.* Berkeley: University of California Press.
———. 2000. *The Men and the Boys.* Sydney: Allen & Unwin Australia.
———. 2002. *Gender.* Cambridge: Polity.
———. 2003a. "Masculinities, Change and Conflict in Global Society: Thinking about the Future of Men's Studies." *Journal of Men's Studies* 11(3): 249–66.
———. 2003b. "Men, Gender and the State." In *Among Men: Moulding Masculinities,* ed. Søren

Ervø and Thomas Johansson, 15–28. Aldershot: Ashgate.
———. 2003c. "Scrambling in the Ruins of Patriarchy: Neo-liberalism and Men's Divided Interests in Gender Change." In *Gender—from Costs to Benefits,* ed. Ursula Pasero, 58–69. Wiesbaden: Westdeutscher.
Corman, June, Meg Luxton, D. W. Livingstone, and Wally Seccombe. 1993. *Recasting Steel Labour: The Stelco Story.* Halifax: Fernwood.
Da Wei Wei. 2004. "A Regional Tradition of Gender Equity: Shanghai Men in Sydney." *Journal of Men's Studies* 12(2): 133–49.
Davies, Bronwyn. 1993. *Shards of Glass: Children Reading and Writing beyond Gender Identities.* Sydney: Allen & Unwin Australia.
Denborough, David. 1996. "Step by Step: Developing Respectful and Effective Ways of Working with Young Men to Reduce Violence." In *Men's Ways of Being,* ed. Chris McLean, Maggie Carey, and Cheryl White, 91–115. Boulder, CO: Westview.
Eisenstein, Hester. 1991. *Gender Shock: Practising Feminism on Two Continents.* Sydney: Allen & Unwin Australia.
Farrell, Warren. 1993. *The Myth of Male Power: Why Men Are the Disposable Sex.* New York: Simon & Schuster.
Franzway, Suzanne. 2001. *Sexual Politics and Greedy Institutions.* Sydney: Pluto.
Fuller, Norma. 2001. "The Social Constitution of Gender Identity among Peruvian Men." *Men and Masculinities* 3(3): 316–31.
Ghoussoub, Mai. 2000. "Chewing Gum, Insatiable Women and Foreign Enemies: Male Fears and the Arab Media." In *Imagined Masculinities: Male Identity and Culture in the Middle East,* ed. Mai Ghoussoub and Emma Sinclair-Webb, 227–35. London: Saqi.
Gierycz, Dorota. 1999. "Women in Decision-Making: Can We Change the Status Quo?" In *Towards a Women's Agenda for a Culture of Peace,* ed. Ingeborg Breines, Dorota Gierycz, and Betty A. Reardon, 19–30. Paris: UNESCO.
Godenzi, Alberto. 2000. "Determinants of Culture: Men and Economic Power." In *Male Roles, Masculinities and Violence: A Culture of Peace Perspective,* ed. Ingeborg Breines, Robert Connell, and Ingrid Eide, 35–51. Paris: UNESCO.
Gutmann, Matthew C. 2002. *The Romance of Democracy: Compliant Defiance in Contemporary Mexico.* Berkeley: University of California Press.

Hagemann-White, Carol. 1992. *Strategien gegen Gewalt im Geschlechterverhältnis: Bestandsanalyse und Perspektiven*. Pfaffenweiler, Ger.: Centaurus.

Harrison, James. 1978. "Warning: The Male Sex Role May Be Dangerous to Your Health." *Journal of Social Issues* 34(1): 65–86.

Haseler, Stephen. 2000. *The Super-Rich: The Unjust New World of Global Capitalism*. London: Macmillan.

Hearn, Jeff. 1998. *The Violences of Men: How Men Talk about and How Agencies Respond to Men's Violence to Women*. Thousand Oaks, CA: Sage.

Hearn, Jeff, and Wendy Parkin. 2001. *Gender, Sexuality, and Violence in Organizations: The Unspoken of Organization Violations*. Thousand Oaks, CA: Sage.

Hearn, Jeff, Keith Pringle, Ursula Müller, Elzbeieta Oleksy, Emmi Lattu, Janna Chernova, Harry Ferguson, et al. 2002. "Critical Studies on Men in Ten European Countries: (1) The State of Academic Research." *Men and Masculinities* 4(4): 380–408.

Holland, Janet, Caroline Ramazanoglu, Sue Sharpe, and Rachel Thomson. 1998. *The Male in the Head: Young People, Heterosexuality and Power*. London: Tufnell.

Holter, Øystein Gullvåg. 1997. *Gender, Patriarchy and Capitalism: A Social Forms Analysis*. Oslo: Work Research Institute.

———. 2003. *Can Men Do It? Men and Gender Equality—the Nordic Experience*. Copenhagen: Nordic Council of Ministers.

Hooper, Charlotte. 2001. *Manly States: Masculinities, International Relations, and Gender Politics*. New York: Columbia University Press.

Hurrelmann, Klaus, and Petra Kolip, eds. 2002. *Geschlecht, Gesundheit und Krankheit: Männer und Frauen im Vergleich*. Bern: Hans Huber.

Ibsen, Henrik. (1923) 1995. *A Doll's House*. Cambridge: Cambridge University Press.

Inter-Parliamentary Union. 2003. "Women in National Parliaments: Situation at 30 December 2003." Available online at http://www.ipu.org/wmn–e/world.htm.

Ito, Kimio. 1992. "Cultural Change and Gender Identity Trends in the 1970s and 1980s." *International Journal of Japanese Sociology* 1(1): 79–98.

Jensen, Hanne Naxø. 1998. "Gender as the Dynamo: When Public Organizations Have to Change." In *Is There a Nordic Feminism? Nordic Feminist Thought on Culture and Society*, ed. Drude von der Fehr, Bente Rosenberg, and Anna G. Jóasdóttir, 160–75. London: UCL Press.

Kandiyoti, Deniz. 1994. "The Paradoxes of Masculinity: Some Thoughts on Segregated Societies." In *Dislocating Masculinity: Comparative Ethnographies*, ed. Andrea Cornwall and Nancy Lindisfarne, 197–213. London: Routledge.

Kaufman, Michael. 1993. *Cracking the Armour: Power, Pain and the Lives of Men*. Toronto: Viking.

———, ed. 1999. "Men and Violence." Special issue, *International Association for Studies of Men Newsletter* 6, no. 2.

Kenway, Jane, ed. 1997. *Will Boys Be Boys? Boys' Education in the Context of Gender Reform*. Canberra: Australian Curriculum Studies Association.

Kenworthy, Colin. 1994. "'We want to resist your resistant readings': Masculinity and Discourse in the English Classroom." *Interpretations* 27(2): 74–95.

Kimmel, Michael S., Jeff Hearn, and R. W. Connell, eds. 2005. *Handbook of Studies on Men and Masculinities*. Thousand Oaks, CA: Sage.

Kimmel, Michael S., and Thomas E. Mosmiller. 1992. *Against the Tide: Pro-feminist Men in the United States, 1776–1990: A Documentary History*. Boston: Beacon.

Kindler, Heinz. 2002. *Väter und Kinder*. Weinheim, Germany: Juventa.

Kippax, Susan, R. W. Connell, G. W. Dowsett, and June Crawford. 1993. *Sustaining Safe Sex: Gay Communities Respond to AIDS*. London: Falmer.

Kupers, Terry. 1993. *Revisioning Men's Lives: Gender, Intimacy, and Power*. New York: Guilford.

Law, Robin, Hugh Campbell, and John Dolan, eds. 1999. *Masculinities in Aotearo/New Zealand*. Palmerston North, NZ: Dunmore.

Lerner, Susana, ed. 1998. *Varones, sexualidad y reproducción: Diversas perspectivas teórico-metodológicas y hallazgos de investigación*. El Colegio de México, México.

Lichterman, Paul. 1989. "Making a Politics of Masculinity." *Comparative Social Research* 11:185–208.

Lingard, Bob. 2003. "Where to in Gender Policy in Education after Recuperative Masculinity Politics?" *International Journal of Inclusive Education* 7(1): 33–56.

Lyra, Jorge, and Benedito Medrado. 2001. "Constructing an Adolescent Father in Brazil." Paper presented at the Third International Fatherhood Conference, Atlanta, May 28–30.

Mac an Ghaill, Mairtin. 1994. *The Making of Men: Masculinities, Sexualities and Schooling*. Buckingham: Open University Press.

Mackay, Fiona, and Kate Bilton. 2000. *Learning from Experience: Lessons in Mainstreaming Equal Opportunities.* Edinburgh: Governance of Scotland Forum.

Marchand, Marianne H., and Anne Sisson Runyan, eds. 2000. *Gender and Global Restructuring: Sightings, Sites and Resistances.* London: Routledge.

McMahon, Anthony. 1999. *Taking Care of Men: Sexual Politics in the Public Mind.* Cambridge: Cambridge University Press.

Menzu Senta (Men's Center Japan). 1997. *Otokotachi no watashisagashi* (How are men seeking their new selves?). Kyoto: Kamogawa.

Messner, Michael A. 1997. *The Politics of Masculinities: Men in Movements.* Thousand Oaks, CA: Sage.

———. 2002. *Taking the Field: Women, Men and Sports.* Minneapolis: University of Minnesota Press.

Metz-Göckel, Sigrid, and Ursula Müller. 1985. *Der Mann: Die Brigitte Studie.* Hamburg: Boltz.

Meuser, Michael. 2003. "Modernized Masculinities? Continuities, Challenges, and Changes in Men's Lives." In *Among Men: Moulding Masculinities,* vol. 1, ed. Søren Ervø and Thomas Johansson, 127–48. Aldershot: Ashgate.

Mill, John Stuart. 1912. "The Subjection of Women." In *On Liberty; Representative Government; The Subjugation of Women: Three Essays,* 427–548. London: Oxford University Press.

Mohwald, Ulrich. 2002. *Changing Attitudes towards Gender Equality in Japan and Germany.* Munich: Iudicium.

Moodie, T. Dunbar. 1994. *Going for Gold: Men, Mines and Migration.* Johannesburg: Witwatersrand University Press.

Morrell, Robert. 1998. "Of Boys and Men: Masculinity and Gender in Southern African Studies." *Journal of Southern African Studies* 24(4): 605–30.

———, ed. 2001a. *Changing Men in Southern Africa.* Pietermaritzburg, S.A.: University of Natal Press.

———. 2001b. *From Boys to Gentlemen: Settler Masculinity in Colonial Natal, 1880–1920.* Pretoria: University of South Africa Press.

Nagel, Joane. 1998. "Masculinity and Nationalism: Gender and Sexuality in the Making of Nations." *Ethnic and Racial Studies* 21(2): 242–69.

Nordic Council of Ministers. 1997. *Nordic Action Plan for Men and Gender Equality, 1997–2000.* Copenhagen: Nordic Council of Ministers.

O'Connor, Julia S., Ann Shola Orloff, and Sheila Shaver. 1999. *States, Markets, Families: Gender, Liberalism and Social Policy in Australia,* *Canada, Great Britain, and the United States.* Cambridge: Cambridge University Press.

O'Donnell, Mike, and Sue Sharpe. 2000. *Uncertain Masculinities: Youth, Ethnicity and Class in Contemporary Britain.* London: Routledge.

Olavarría, José. 2001. *Y todos querían ser (buenos) padres: Varones de Santiago de Chile en conflicto.* Santiago: FLACSO-Chile.

Palme, Olof. 1972. "The Emancipation of Man." *Journal of Social Issues* 28(2): 237–46.

Peacock, Dean. 2003. "Building on a Legacy of Social Justice Activism: Enlisting Men as Gender Justice Activists in South Africa." *Men and Masculinities* 5(3): 325–28.

Pease, Bob. 1997. *Men and Sexual Politics: Towards a Profeminist Practice.* Adelaide: Dulwich Centre.

Pease, Bob, and Keith Pringle, eds. 2001. *A Man's World? Changing Men's Practices in a Globalized World.* London: Zed.

Ptacek, James. 1988. "Why Do Men Batter Their Wives?" In *Feminist Perspectives on Wife Abuse,* ed. Kersti Yllö and Michele Bograd, 133–57. Newbury Park, CA: Sage.

Reinicke, Kenneth. 2002. *Den Hele Mand: Manderollen i forandring.* Aarhus, Denmark: Schønberg.

Risman, Barbara J. 1986. "Can Men 'Mother'? Life as a Single Father." *Family Relations* 35(1): 95–102.

———. 1998. *Gender Vertigo: American Families in Transition.* New Haven, CT: Yale University Press.

Roberson, James E., and Nobue Suzuki, eds. 2003. *Men and Masculinities in Contemporary Japan: Dislocating the Salaryman Doxa.* London: Routledge.

Roy, Rahul. 2003. "Exploring Masculinities—a Travelling Seminar." Unpublished manuscript.

Sabo, Donald, and David Frederick Gordon, eds. 1995. *Men's Health and Illness: Gender, Power, and the Body.* Thousand Oaks, CA: Sage.

Sabo, Donald, Terry A. Kupers, and Willie London, eds. 2001. *Prison Masculinities.* Philadelphia: Temple University Press.

Schofield, Toni. 2004. *Boutique Health? Gender and Equity in Health Policy.* Sydney: Australian Health Policy Institute.

———. Forthcoming. "Gender Regimes in Public Policy Making." Unpublished manuscript, Faculty of Health Sciences, University of Sydney.

Schwalbe, Michael. 1996. *Unlocking the Iron Cage: The Men's Movement, Gender, Politics, and American Culture.* New York: Oxford University Press.

Segal, Lynne. 1997. *Slow Motion: Changing Masculinities, Changing Men.* 2nd ed. London: Virago.

Seidler, Victor T., ed. 1991. *The Achilles Heel Reader: Men, Sexual Politics and Socialism.* London: Routledge.

Sinclair-Webb, Emma. 2000. "'Our bülent is now a commando': Military Service and Manhood in Turkey." In *Imagined Masculinities: Male Identity and Culture in the Modern Middle East,* ed. Mai Ghoussoub and Emma Sinclair-Webb, 65–92. London: Saqi.

Sommers, Christina Hoff. 2000. *The War against Boys: How Misguided Feminism Is Harming Our Young Men.* New York: Simon & Schuster.

Taga, Futoshi. 2001. *Dansei no Jendâ Keisei: "Otoko-Rashisa" no Yuragi no Naka de* (The gender formation of men: Uncertain masculinity). Tokyo: Tôyôkan Shuppan-sha.

Thornton, Arland. 1989. "Changing Attitudes toward Family Issues in the United States." *Journal of Marriage and the Family 51*(4): 873–93.

United Nations. 1958. *Universal Declaration of Human Rights.* New York: Department of Public Information, United Nations.

———. (1979) 1989. *Convention on the Elimination of All Forms of Discrimination against Women.* New York: Department of Public Information, United Nations.

———. 2001. *Beijing Declaration and Platform for Action, with the Beijing +5 Political Declaration and Outcome Document.* New York: Department of Public Information, United Nations.

United Nations Commission on the Status of Women. 2004. *The Role of Men and Boys in Achieving Gender Equality: Agreed Conclusions.* Available online at http://www.un.org/womenwatch/daw/csw/csw48/ac-men-auv.pdf.

United Nations Development Program (UNDP). 2003. *Human Development Report 2003.* New York: UNDP and Oxford University Press.

Valdés, Teresa, and José Olavarría. 1998. "Ser hombre en Santiago de Chile: A pesar de todo, un mismo modelo." In their *Masculinidades y equidad de género en América Latina,* 12–36. Santiago: FLACSO/UNFPA.

Walby, Sylvia. 1997. *Gender Transformations.* London: Routledge.

Wetherell, Margaret, and Nigel Edley. 1999. "Negotiating Hegemonic Masculinity: Imaginary Positions and Psycho-Discursive Practices." *Feminism and Psychology 9*(3): 335–56.

White, Sara C. 2000. "Did the Earth Move? The Hazards of Bringing Men and Masculinities into Gender and Development." *IDS Bulletin 31*(2): 33–41.

Widersprüche. 1998. "Multioptionale Männlichkeiten?" Special issue, no. 67.

Zalewski, Marysia, and Jane Parpart, eds. 1998. *The "Man" Question in International Relations.* Boulder, CO: Westview.

Zingoni, Eduardo Liendro. 1998. "Masculinidades y violencia desde un programa de accíon en México." In *Masculinidades y equidad de género en América Latina,* ed. Teresa Valdés and José Olavarría, 130–36. Santiago: FLACSO/UNFPA.

Zulehner, Paul M., and Rainer Volz. 1998. *Männer im Aufbruch: Wie Deutschlands Männer sich selbst und wie Frauen sie sehen.* Ostfildern, Ger.: Schwabenverlag.

❧ Topics for Further Examination ❧

- Look up research on men who participated in the first and second waves of feminism in the United States. Find and explore websites devoted to profeminist men's organizations in different countries around the world.
- Browse feminist websites on women's organizations and gender issues such as Institute for Women's Policy Research (http://www.iwpr.org), Feminist Majority Foundation (http://www.feminist.org), Feministing (feministing.com), The F-Word Blog (www.thef-word.org.uk), Crunk Feminist Collective (www.crunkfeministcollective.com), Women Watch (http://www.un.org/womenwatch/), and Women's International League for Peace and Freedom (http://www.wilpf.org).
- Explore the intersection of movements for gender, racial, and sexual equality as they have come together in #BlackLivesMatter. Why did queer women of color emerge as the backbone of #BlackLivesMatter?

EPILOGUE

Possibilities

This book began with the metaphor of the kaleidoscope to aid in understanding the complex and dynamic nature of gender. Viewed kaleidoscopically, gender is not static. Gender patterns are social constructions, reconstructed as they intersect with multiple and changing social prisms such as race, ethnicity, culture, class, and sexuality. In concluding, we want to emphasize the dynamic nature of gender, underscoring the possibilities the future holds. No one can predict the future; therefore, we will illustrate changes in the institution of gender using stories of how changing gender patterns shaped our lives and the lives of many other people.

Reflecting on the course of our lives, we are struck by the depth and breadth of changes that have occurred in American culture, institutions, and social relationships since we were young girls in the 1950s, including changes since we first began working on this book in 2000. Many of these changes have been positive; patterns of oppression were reduced and the opportunity and power to participate meaningfully in America's social institutions were extended to more people. In the past 50 years, we have benefited from, and participated in, bringing about changes in the genderscape.

The cultural climate of the 1950s forged our early lives. Although romanticized in film and TV, that decade was in fact a deeply troubled time of blatant racism, sexism, and other forms of oppression. Civil rights had not yet been extended to people of color, women's rights were negligible, GLBTQI Americans were largely closeted, poverty was ignored, political dissent was strongly discouraged, child abuse went unacknowledged or was hidden, and an atomic war seemed ready to break out at any moment.

We didn't learn about the women's movement then, even though there had been significant organized social movements for gender change in the United States beginning almost 100 years before we were born, culminating in the right to vote in 1920. The second wave of feminism and subsequent women's movements began when we were very young, after World War II, inspired by books such as Simone de Beauvoir's *The Second Sex* (1952), first published in France in 1949, and Betty Friedan's *The Feminine Mystique* (1963). Although not widely recognized, the United Nations Charter of 1945 affirmed the equal rights of men and women and established the U.N. Commission on the Status of Women a few years later (Schneir, 1994). However, in many ways, women were still second-class citizens in the 1950s.

We grew up in families similar to those of many White Americans of the 1950s. Our parents held traditional views of proper roles for women and men. They tried to live up to those roles, and yet, like many, they often failed or fell short. They suffered with their failures in silence, behind the closed doors of the nuclear family of that era. For men and women, marriage and children came with the gender territory. Social sanctions in society maintained this territory. For example, people called women who didn't marry "old maids" pejoratively and looked at (hetero) couples who didn't bear children suspiciously. Also, there were limited reproductive control options, and abortion, although widespread, was illegal. This left most women and many men with few options other than getting married and having children.

Jessie Bernard (1975) described men's and women's roles in White, middle-class families of that time as being destructive to adults and children alike. She spoke of "the work intoxicated father" and the "pathogenic mother" as the end result of the efforts to fulfill the cultural imperative for a traditional family. Bernard observed that middle-class, White family roles at that time were mostly stressful and unsatisfying. Men detached from their families as they struggled to earn enough for the household, while women shouldered the sole responsibility of raising perfect children and keeping a perfect home. Family and gender researchers (e.g., Bernard, 1972; Coontz, 1992, 1997; Rapp, 1982; Schwartz, 1994) found that this arrangement of distinct and separate roles did not foster full and loving relationships between men and women or parents and children. And, of course, by now you can guess that most people could not achieve this "perfect family."

However, television still reflected the image of the happy White family behind the white picket fence, and for decades it stood as an ideal, even for those who failed to meet it. Marriages were supposed to be loving but often were not. Getting out of a conflict-ridden or abusive marriage was very difficult. There were divorces, but the courts granted these only if they decided there were "appropriate violations" of the marriage contract (Weitzman, 1985). As a result, many marriages persisted, even when there was unbearable alienation, violence, and abuse.

Intensifying these struggles further, there was little recognition of domestic violence. Marital rape and rape in general were not taken seriously, legally or socially. For example, the police, when called to a domestic conflict, often ignored pleas of beaten or raped women, and the rules and procedures that guided police work made interventions almost meaningless. There was a great deal of resistance to changes in legislation relative to domestic violence and rape, including marital rape. The words of one U.S. senator captured the general attitude at that time; he said, "If you can't rape your wife, who can you rape" (Russell, 1982). Thus, domestic violence and rape reforms took many years to implement.

As you can imagine, women in our mothers' cohort had few choices and opportunities. The "best" occupations most women could aspire to were limited to clerical or secretarial jobs, teaching, and nursing. Salaries were low, and women had a difficult time living independently, both financially and socially. There was no such legal concept as workplace sexual harassment, and equal pay for equal work was rarely considered. Married women who did work outside the home often had fragmented work lives, defined by their primary responsibility of caring for children and husbands.

The situation for White women was bad, but it was much worse for women of color and immigrant women. For example, most African American women worked outside the home but were mainly confined to the lowest paying and most degrading jobs, such as domestic work. These jobs had even fewer protections against sexual harassment and workplace inequalities. Men of racial minority groups and immigrant men also endured considerable inequalities in the workplace, as well as in other domains of life.

Post–World War II saw a considerable increase in the number of people entering college; however, almost all new students were White men taking advantage of the G.I. Bill.

Considerable gender segregation in higher education persisted throughout the 1950s, with many colleges and universities denying admittance to women and racial minorities. The proportion of women in higher education increased only slightly during the 1950s, from 31.6% in 1950 to 35.9% in 1959 (National Center for Education Statistics, 2005). And some of the most exclusive colleges and universities maintained gender-segregated spaces even after women were admitted. For example, although women were admitted to Harvard Law School in 1950, they were denied access to the only eating space at the law school until 1970 (Deckard, 1979). Harvard Law School even limited the days on which women could ask questions in classes (Deckard, 1979). Money was another resource denied to many women; there were few scholarships for females because administrators and faculty felt "men needed the money more" (Deckard, 1979, p. 130).

The decades of the 1960s and 1970s brought about the awakening of political consciousness and action by Americans from many walks of life. Early in this period, the civil rights movement resulted in the dismantling of many legal barriers to participation in American life for African Americans. In the 1960s, the second wave of feminism picked up steam, spawning several organized political movements around gender and race, ethnicity, nationality, and/or sexuality, as described in Chapter 10. These social movements focused attention on the social disadvantages faced by women and brought about considerable change, including greater legal, economic, political, educational, and familial equality. Other social movements emerged out of this culture of change: GLBTQI rights, antiwar and peace, environmental, and children's rights movements.

We were fortunate to enter early adulthood during this time of positive social change. For example, Title IX (1972) opened up avenues in education previously closed to our mothers; attempts at pay equity made our labor somewhat more valuable than that of our mothers; the naming and litigation of sexual harassment,

marital rape, and other forms of gender violence made our lives somewhat safer than our mothers' lives; and the women's movement empowered us and helped us understand how we could contribute to a more just world. Our lives took us down different pathways, yet many of the same social change forces touched us deeply, and eventually our lives intersected.

Kay joined the ranks of one of the first waves of college-bound baby boomers in the mid-1960s. Her undergraduate years coincided with the civil rights movement, the height of the Vietnam War, the development of a strong political left, and the emergence of countercultural lifestyles. She found her intellectual passion in sociology, a home for her experimental self in the counterculture, and a political focus in the antiwar movement. With BA in hand, Kay entered the work world at the very moment the first of a series of economic recessions set in. She bounced from one unsatisfying, low-paying, "female-type" job to another and quickly found herself at an intellectual and emotional crossroads. Kay then chose a pathway that few women had gone down—graduate school.

In 1971, Kay joined the ranks of a growing number of women graduate students in departments of sociology across the United States. Although dominated by White men, this cohort contained more working-class White women and people of color than earlier generations. They moved through graduate school at the same time the second wave of feminism spawned organized movements for gender equality around the world. With these changes, Kay's consciousness expanded to embrace feminism. She took one of the first gender courses, sex roles, to be offered in any American institution of higher education. Feminism opened up a world of choices never before available to her. Empowered and exhilarated, Kay chose a nontraditional life course, as did many of the women in her graduate school cohort. Women postponed marriage and children. Others chose singlehood or cohabiting relationships. Still others chose child-free marriages. All pursued careers.

Of course, change is never smooth and evenhanded. Although the women's movement was well under way during Kay's graduate school years, women students and professors had regular encounters with sexism both in and out of the classroom. Sexual harassment was built into the everyday educational experiences of women who pursued a PhD. Also, as the women of Kay's cohort entered the professional world of teaching and research, barriers to hiring, tenure, and promotion would prove to be part of their ongoing struggle for respect, security, and equality. The struggle for gender equality has continued in all domains of life in the United States, and although many barriers have been dismantled, sexism has taken on new, subtle, and covert forms that have proven difficult to target and eradicate. These subtle and covert patterns have emerged alongside global gender inequality at the center of contemporary feminist movements.

Joining the first wave of baby boomers, Kay retired from 32 years of college teaching in 2008. She marked that transition by setting off on solo journeys to various parts of the world. Retirement has opened up opportunities for Kay to reconnect with the political left and global feminist movements. It has also allowed Kay to pursue passions such as writing and traveling and to reflect carefully on her principles and practices. Marking these retirement pursuits, she has had the great satisfaction of coediting and contributing to a 2015 Vanderbilt University Press book titled *Letting Go: Feminist and Social Justice Insight and Activism,* a collection of essays calling for the rejection of neoliberalism and its destructive personal and social forms.

But fair warning: Life is no nirvana for aging women in the United States (Calasanti, Slevin, & King, 2006). Kay's transition is also marked by the confluence of sexism and ageism in her life and the lives of similarly situated women. The experience of being "culturally disappeared" while at the same time observing aging men, especially those who are class privileged, experience enhanced status and value is unnerving and a stark reminder that gender equality has not been achieved. For Kay, carving out a life of resistance as she ages is centered on finding pathways that are an alternative to retreating into the limited roles and identities that are culturally approved and reserved for older women.

Meanwhile, unlike Kay, Joan was a "good girl." She went to a secretarial school and pursued a gender-appropriate job as a secretary. She became dissatisfied, though, because she was not receiving raises or being paid as well as others who had 2-year college degrees, so she went to a community college to earn that degree. One course in sociology was all Joan needed to become a student of understanding social processes. She married and had two children but continued on in school, moving from community college to university-level education.

In trying to understand the patterns of daily life, gender became a major explanatory framework for Joan. The isolation of women during child-rearing years and the lack of institutions to support raising children developed into major interests, along with the effects of work patterns on men and women. Despite this lack of support for women who chose to pursue family and profession, Joan pursued and received her PhD while rearing children. Her consciousness raising occurred more informally than Kay's—via books and one-on-one conversations with friends, mostly while caring for children.

Entry into professional sociology, while at first off-putting given the White, male dominance of the field, became a path to connect ideas with action and to form meaningful relationships with an array of women. It was through a relatively new organization, Sociologists for Women in Society, that we met one another and many others who taught and worked to improve the situation for women in society.

Together with another sociologist, Martha Cornwell, we started an upstate New York chapter of Sociologists for Women in Society. We became involved in women's studies on our respective campuses and conducted research on women in the arts, work, family, education, and on women's bodily and emotional experiences.

Joan recently retired. She treasures the extra time, which she spends traveling with her significant other in his RV, visiting new places and their expanded family that includes seven grandchildren. The RVing life gives them the freedom to visit new places and maintain contacts with old friends while making new connections along the way. She continues to write (thanks to modern technologies) and remains involved in professional organizations.

Today, we continue the journey toward a world that is more just and humane, a world in which people can live safe and satisfying lives unimpeded by the social prisms of difference and inequality described in this book.

Although it may seem that most of the work toward gender equality has been accomplished, as individuals and members of a global society, we have more work to do. For example, women still do not have equal pay for equal work; glass ceilings and sticky floors continue to keep women from high-paying jobs while glass escalators move White, mostly upper-middle and upper class men to the top paying jobs; few countries offer gender-equitable parental leaves; most women work a double day, in paid labor and in the home; violence against women remains a serious problem; despite major breakthroughs such as the acceptance and legalization of same-sex marriages, heterosexist and homophobic beliefs and behaviors maintain restrictive gender patterns while oppressing GLBTQI people; racism continues to degrade and diminish the lives of women and men of color; and hegemonic masculinity limits the life experiences of most men.

Although there is still more to be accomplished, the good news is that in a very short period of time—our lifetimes—much positive change has occurred in gender relations. A third wave of feminism has now emerged among young people (as illustrated by readings by Martin and Valenti and The Santa Cruz Feminist of Color Collective in Chapter 10), and many of the new initiatives, including men's and global movements are now actively seeking changes in the genderscape across the globe. Clearly, more change is on the way.

What possibilities for change do *you* see in your gendered future? How might you make a difference and contribute to the eradication of gender dichotomy and inequality?

References

Bernard, J. (1972). *The future of marriage.* New York: World Publishing.

Bernard, J. (1975). *Women, wives, mothers.* Chicago: Aldine.

Calasanti, T., Slevin K., & King, N. (2006). Ageism and feminism: From "et cetera" to center. *NWSA Journal, 18*(1), 13–30.

Coontz, S. (1992). *The way we never were: Americans and the nostalgia trap.* New York: Basic Books.

Coontz, S. (1997). *The way we really are: Coming to terms with America's changing families.* New York: Basic Books.

de Beauvoir, S. (1952). *The second sex.* New York: Knopf.

Deckard, B. S. (1979). *The women's movement: Political, socioeconomic, and psychological issues.* New York: Harper & Row.

Friedan, B. (1963). *The feminine mystique.* New York: W. W. Norton.

National Center for Education Statistics. (2005). Table 170: Total fall enrollment in degree-granting institutions, by attendance status, sex of student, and control of institution: Selected years, 1947 through 2004. In *Digest of education statistics.* Retrieved from http://nces.ed.gov/programs/digest/d05/tables/dt05_170.asp

Rapp, R. (1982). Family and class in contemporary America. In B. Thorne (with M. Yalom) (Ed.), *Rethinking the family: Some feminist questions* (pp. 168–187). New York: Longman.

Russell, D. E. H. (1982). *Rape in marriage.* New York: Macmillan.

Schneir, M. (1994). *Feminism in our time: The essential writings, World War II to the present.* New York: Vintage Books.

Schwartz, P. (1994). *Peer marriage: How love between equals really works.* New York: Free Press.

Weitzman, L. J. (1985). *The divorce revolution: The unexpected social and economic consequences for women and children in America.* New York: Free Press.

About the Editors

Joan Z. Spade is Professor Emerita of sociology at The College at Brockport, State University of New York. She received her PhD from the University at Buffalo, State University of New York, her MA from the University of Rochester; and her BA from the State University of New York at Geneseo. In addition to courses on gender, Joan taught courses on education, family, research methods, and statistics. She published articles on rape culture in college fraternities and on work and family, including women's and men's orientations toward work. She has also coedited two books on education and published articles on education, including research on tracking, and gender and education. Joan is active in Sociologists for Women in Society, Eastern Sociological Society, and the American Sociological Association. In addition to visiting children and grandchildren with her significant other, she enjoys RVing, music and the arts, travel, and being outdoors.

Catherine (Kay) G. Valentine is Professor Emerita of sociology at Nazareth College in Rochester, New York. She received her PhD from Syracuse University and her BA from the State University of New York at Albany. Kay taught a wide range of courses, such as sociology of gender, senior seminar in sociology, sociology of bodies and emotions, sociology of consumerism, and human sexuality. Her publications include articles on teaching sociology, on women's bodies and emotions, on gender and qualitative research, and on the sociology of art museums. Kay is coeditor of *Letting Go: Feminist and Social Justice Insight and Activism* (Vanderbilt University Press, 2015). She is the founding director of women's studies at Nazareth College and a longtime member of Sociologists for Women in Society and the American Sociological Association. She has also served as president of the New York State Sociological Association. Kay and her life partner, Paul J. Burgett, University of Rochester vice president and professor of music, are devotees of the arts and world travel.